THE NORTON ANTHOLOGY OF
WORLD
LITERATURE

FOURTH EDITION

VOLUME C

THE NORTON ANTHOLOGY OF

WORLD LITERATURE

FOURTH EDITION

MARTIN PUCHNER, *General Editor*
HARVARD UNIVERSITY

SUZANNE AKBARI
UNIVERSITY OF TORONTO

WIEBKE DENECKE
BOSTON UNIVERSITY

BARBARA FUCHS
UNIVERSITY OF CALIFORNIA, LOS ANGELES

CAROLINE LEVINE
CORNELL UNIVERSITY

PERICLES LEWIS
YALE UNIVERSITY

EMILY WILSON
UNIVERSITY OF PENNSYLVANIA

VOLUME C

W. W. NORTON & COMPANY | New York · London

W. W. Norton & Company has been independent since its founding in 1923, when William Warder Norton and Mary D. Herter Norton first published lectures delivered at the People's Institute, the adult education division of New York City's Cooper Union. The firm soon expanded its program beyond the Institute, publishing books by celebrated academics from America and abroad. By midcentury, the two major pillars of Norton's publishing program—trade books and college texts—were firmly established. In the 1950s, the Norton family transferred control of the company to its employees, and today—with a staff of four hundred and a comparable number of trade, college, and professional titles published each year—W. W. Norton & Company stands as the largest and oldest publishing house owned wholly by its employees.

Editor: Peter Simon
Associate Editor: Gerra Goff
Project Editor: Kurt Wildermuth
Manuscript Editor: Mike Fleming
Managing Editor, College: Marian Johnson
Managing Editor, College Digital Media: Kim Yi
Production Manager: Sean Mintus
Media Editor: Carly Fraser Doria
Media Project Editor: Cooper Wilhelm
Assistant Media Editor: Ava Bramson
Editorial Assistant, Media: Joshua Bianchi
Marketing Manager, Literature: Kimberly Bowers
Art Direction: Rubina Yeh
Book Design: Jo Anne Metsch
Permissions Manager: Megan Schindel
Permissions Clearer: Margaret Gorenstein
Photo Editor: Catherine Abelman
Composition: Westchester Book Services
Manufacturing: Thomson Reuters

Permission to use copyrighted material is included in the backmatter of this book.

Library of Congress Cataloging-in-Publication Data

Names: Puchner, Martin, 1969- editor. | Akbari, Suzanne Conklin, editor. | Denecke, Wiebke,
    editor. | Fuchs, Barbara, 1970- editor. | Levine, Caroline, 1970- editor. | Lewis, Pericles, editor. |
    Wilson, Emily R., 1971- editor.
Title: The Norton anthology of world literature / Martin Puchner, general editor ; Suzanne
    Akbari, Wiebke Denecke, Barbara Fuchs, Caroline Levine, Pericles Lewis, Emily Wilson.
Description: Fourth edition. | New York : W. W. Norton & Company, [2018] | Includes
    bibliographical references and index.
Identifiers: LCCN 2017060699| ISBN 9780393602814 (pbk. : v. A) | ISBN 9780393602821
    (pbk. : v. B) | ISBN 9780393602838 (pbk. : v. C) | ISBN 9780393602845 (pbk. : v. D) |
    ISBN 9780393602852 (pbk. : v. E) | ISBN 9780393602869 (pbk. : v. F)
Subjects: LCSH: Literature—Collections.
Classification: LCC PN6014 .N66 2018 | DDC 808.8—dc23 LC record available
    at https://lccn.loc.gov/2017060699

ISBN 978-0-393-60283-8 (pbk.)

W. W. Norton & Company, Inc., 500 Fifth Avenue, New York, NY 10110-0017
wwnorton.com
W. W. Norton & Company Ltd., 15 Carlisle Street, London W1D 3BS

3 4 5 6 7 8 9 0

Contents

II. EUROPE AND THE NEW WORLD   109

Preface

They arrive in boats, men exhausted from years of warfare and travel. As they approach the shore, their leader spots signs of habitation: flocks of goats and sheep, smoke rising from dwellings. A natural harbor permits them to anchor their boats so that they will be safe from storms. The leader takes an advance team with him to explore the island. It is rich in soil and vegetation, and natural springs flow with cool, clear water. With luck, they will be able to replenish their provisions and be on their way.

In the world of these men, welcoming travelers is a sacred custom, sanctioned by the gods themselves. It is also good policy among seafaring people. Someday, the roles may very well be reversed: today's host may be tomorrow's guest. Yet the travelers can never be certain whether a particular people will honor this custom. Wondering what to expect, the thirteen men enter one of the caves dotting the coastline.

The owner isn't home, but the men enter anyway, without any compunction. There are pens for sheep and goats, and there is plenty of cheese and milk, so the men begin eating. When the owner returns, they are terrified, but their leader, boldly, asks for gifts. The owner is not pleased. Instead of giving the intruders what they demand, he kills two of them and eats them for dinner. And then two more the next day. All the while, he keeps the men trapped in his cave.

A wily man, the leader devises a scheme to escape. He offers the owner wine, enough to make him drunk and sleepy. Once he dozes off, the men take a staff that they have secretly sharpened and they plunge it into the owner's eye, blinding him. Without sight, he cannot see the men clinging to the undersides of his prized sheep as they stroll, one by one, out of the cave to graze, and cleverly the men cling only to the male sheep, not the females, which get milked.

* * *

This story of hospitality gone wrong comes from *The Odyssey*, one of the best-known works in all of world literature. We learn of this strange encounter of Greek soldiers with the one-eyed Cyclops named Polyphemus from Odysseus, the protagonist of the epic, when he recounts his exploits at the court of another host, the king of the Phaeacians. Unsurprisingly, Polyphemus isn't presented in the best light. Odysseus describes the Cyclopes as a people without a "proper" community, without agriculture, without hospitality. Is Odysseus, who has been wined and dined by his current host, trying to curry favor with the king of the Phaeacians by telling him how terribly he was treated by these non-Greek others? Reading the passage closely, we can see that Polyphemus and the other Cyclopes are adroit makers of cheese, so they can't be all that lazy. When the blinded Polyphemus cries out for help, his associates come to help him as a matter of course, so they don't live quite as isolated from one another as Odysseus claims. Even though Odysseus asserts that Polyphemus is godless, the land is blessed by the gods with fertility, and Polyphemus's divine father comes to his aid when he prays. Odysseus says that the Cyclopes lack laws and custom, yet we are also shown the careful, regular, customary way that Polyphemus takes care of his household. In a touching scene toward the end of his encounter with Odysseus, after he is blinded, Polyphemus speaks gently and respectfully to his favorite ram, so he can't be all that monstrous. The one-eyed giants assist one another, they are shepherds and artisans, and they are capable of kindness. The passage's ambiguities suggest that perhaps it was partly Odysseus's fault that this encounter between cultures went so badly. Were he and his companions simply travelers badly in need of food, or were they looters hoping to enrich themselves? The passage suggests that it's a matter of narrative perspective, from whose point of view the story is told.

Scenes of hospitality (or the lack thereof) are everywhere in world literature, and questions about hospitality, about the courtesies that we owe to strangers and that strangers owe to us (whether we are guests or hosts), are as important today as they were in the ancient world. Although many writers and thinkers today are fond of saying that our era is the first "truly global" one, stories such as this episode from Homer's *Odyssey* remind us that travel, trade, exile, migration, and cultural encounters of all kinds have been features of human experience for thousands of years.

The experience of reading world literature, too, is a form of travel—a mode of cultural encounter that presents us with languages, cultural norms, customs, and ideas that may be unfamiliar to us, even strange. As readers, each time we begin to read a new work, we put ourselves in the role of a traveler in a foreign land, trying to understand its practices and values and hoping to feel, to some degree and in some way, connected to and welcome among the people we meet there. *The Epic of Gilgamesh*, for example, takes its readers on a tour of Uruk, the first large city in human history, in today's Iraq, boasting of its city walls, its buildings and temples with their stairways and foundations, all made of clay bricks. Like a tour guide, the text even lets its readers inspect the city's clay pits, over one square mile large, that provided the material for this miraculous city made from clay. The greatest marvel of them all is of course *The Epic of Gilgamesh* itself, which was inscribed on clay tablets—the first monument of literature.

Foundational Texts

From its beginnings, *The Norton Anthology of World Literature* has been committed to offering students and teachers as many complete or substantially represented texts as possible. This Fourth Edition emphasizes the importance of *foundational* texts as never before by offering new translations of some of the best-known and most-loved works in the history of world literature. *The Epic of Gilgamesh* stands first in line of these foundational texts, which capture the story of an entire people, telling them where they came from and who they are. Some foundational texts become an object of worship and are deemed sacred, while others are revered as the most consequential story of an entire civilization. Because foundational texts inspire countless retellings—as Homer did for the Greek tragedians—these texts are reference points for the entire subsequent history of literature.

Perhaps no text is more foundational than the one with which we opened this preface: Homer's *Odyssey*. In this Fourth Edition, we feature *The Odyssey* in a new translation by our classics editor, Emily Wilson. This version captures the fast pace and rhythmic regularity of the original and offers a fresh perspective on cultural encounters such as the one between Odysseus and Polyphemus that is described above. Astonishingly, Wilson's translation is the first translation of *The Odyssey* into English by a woman. For centuries, commentators have remarked that *The Odyssey* is unusually attuned to the lives of women, especially in its portrait of Odysseus's wife, Penelope, a compelling and powerful character who cunningly holds a rowdy group of suitors at bay. Wilson's translation pays special attention to the poem's characterization of this remarkable woman, who is every bit as intriguing as the "complicated man" who is the eponymous hero of the tale. Other female characters, too, are given a new voice in this translation. For example, Helen, wife of the Greek king Menelaus and (according to legend) possessor of "the face that launched a thousand ships," is revealed through Wilson's translation to speak of herself not as a "whore" for whose sake so many young Greek men fought, suffered, and died (as she does in most other translations) but instead as a perceptive, clever person, onto whom the Greeks, already eager to fight the Trojans, projected their own aggressive impulses: "They made my face the cause that hounded them," she says. The central conflicts of the epic, the very origin of the Trojan War, appear here in a startling new light.

We are also delighted to feature a new translation of the great Indian epic *The Mahabharata* by Carole Satyamurti, whose modern retelling captures the careful, patterned language of the original by rendering it in a fluent blank verse, a form familiar in English literature from Shakespeare to Wordsworth and also used in Wilson's *Odyssey*, a form particularly suitable to narrative. Readers used to older prose versions will find that the quest for honor and fame at the heart of this epic comes across as never before.

These two examples highlight an exciting dimension of our emphasis on new translations. The first several volumes of this anthology have always been dominated by male voices because men enjoyed privileged access to literacy and cultural influence in the centuries prior to modernity. Our focus on new translations has allowed us to introduce into these volumes many female voices—the voices of translators. So, for example, we present Homer's *Iliad* in a new translation by Caroline Alexander, Sophocles' *Antigone* in a recent translation by Ruby Blondell, and Euripides' *Medea* in a new, specially commissioned translation by Sheila H. Murnaghan, and we continue to offer work in the first volumes translated by female translators such as Laura Gibbs (Aesop's *Fables*), Dorothy Gilbert (Marie de France's *Lais*), Sholeh Wolpé (*The Conference of the Birds*), Wendy Belcher (*Kebra Nagast*), Sheila Fisher (Chaucer's *Canterbury Tales*), Rosalind Brown-Grant (Christine de Pizan's *Book of the City of Ladies*), and Pauline Yu (Wang Wei's poetry), among others. This commitment to featuring the work of female translators extends beyond these early centuries as well, for example in the brilliant new translation by Susan Bernofsky of a foundational text of literary modernity—Kafka's *Metamorphosis*. The result throughout the anthology is that these works now speak to today's readers in new and sometimes surprising ways.

Our emphasis in this edition on new translations is based on and amplifies the conviction expressed by the original editors of this anthology over fifty years ago: that world literature gains its power when it travels from its place of origin and speaks to people in different places. While purists sometimes insist on studying literature only in the original language, a dogma that radically shrinks what one can read, world literature not only relies on translation but actually thrives on it. Translation is a necessity; it is what enables a worldwide circulation of literature. It also is an art. One need only think of the way in which translations of the Bible shaped the history of Latin or English or German. Translations are re-creations of works for new readers. This edition pays keen attention to translation, featuring dozens of new translations that make classic texts newly readable and capture the originals in compelling ways. With each choice of translation, we have sought a version that would spark a sense of wonder while still being accessible to a contemporary reader.

Among other foundational texts presented in new translations and selections is the Qur'an, in a verse translation that is the product of a collaboration between M. A. Rafey Habib, a poet, literary scholar, and Muslim, and Bruce Lawrence, a renowned scholar of Islam. Their team effort captures some of the beauty of this extraordinary, and extraordinarily influential, sacred text. Augustine's *Confessions* are newly presented in a version by Peter Constantine, and Dante's *Inferno* is featured in the long-respected and highly readable translation by the American poet John Ciardi.

We have also maintained our commitment to exciting epics that deserve wider recognition such as the Maya *Popol Vuh*, the East African *Kebra Nagast*, and the *Sunjata*, which commemorates the founding of a West African empire in the late Middle Ages. Like *The Odyssey* and *The Mahabharata*, *Sunjata* was transmitted for centuries in purely oral form. But while *The Odyssey* was written down around 800 B.C.E. and *The Mahabharata* several hundred years later, the *Sunjata* was written down only in the twentieth century. We feature it here in a new prose translation by David C. Conrad, who personally recorded this version from a Mande storyteller, Djanka Tassey Condé, in 1994. In this way, *Sunjata* speaks to the continuing importance of oral storytelling, the origin of all foundational epics, from South Asia via Greece and Africa to Central America. Throughout the anthology, we remind readers that writing has coexisted with oral storytelling since the invention of literature and that it will continue to do so in the future.

A Network of Stories

In addition to foundational texts, we include in this edition a great number of story collections. The origins of this form of literature reach deep into the ancient world, as scribes collected oral stories and assembled them in larger works. We've substantially increased our offerings from what is undoubtedly the most famous of these collections, *The Thousand and One Nights*, to give readers a better sense of the intricate structure of this work, with its stories within stories within stories, all neatly framed by the overarching narrative of Shahrazad, who is telling them to her sister and the king to avoid being put to death. What is most notable about these story collections is how interconnected they are. Stories travel with striking ease from one collection to the next, appearing in *The Jataka*, one of the oldest Indian story collections framed by the

Buddha, and the *Pañcatantra*, an Indian collection put together for the education of princes, to *The Thousand and One Nights*, and, in Greece, Aesop's *Fables*. There existed a continent-spanning network of stories that allowed storytellers and scribes to recycle and reframe what they learned in ever new ways; it proved so compelling that later writers, from Marie de France to Chaucer, borrowed from it frequently. To give readers a sense of these connections, we have rethought our selection of stories by including those that appear in different collections, allowing readers to track the changes that occur when a story is told by the Buddha, by Shahrazad, or on a pilgrimage to Canterbury Cathedral.

Expanded Selections

Along with our focus on making foundational texts and story collections fresh and accessible, we have pruned the overall number of authors and were therefore able to increase our offerings from major texts that feature in many world literature courses. *Don Quixote* now includes the compelling "Captive's Tale," in which Cervantes draws on his own experiences as a slave in Algiers, where he spent five years after having been captured by pirates. Sor Juana Inés de la Cruz, whose significance is steadily increasing, is now represented by an additional selection from her mystery play, *The Divine Narcissus*, in Edith Grossman's elegant translation. Other major texts with increased selections include Machiavelli's *Prince* and, in the twentieth century, Lu Xun, who now can be introduced to students as the author not only of *Diary of a Madman* but also of *Ah Q—The Real Story*.

Despite this focus on foundational texts, story collections, and other major works, there are plenty of entirely new texts in this Fourth Edition. The Spanish Renaissance tale *The Abencerraje* tells of a Moorish knight who is taken prisoner by a Christian on his wedding day. Ultimately his captor relents and allows the knight to marry his beloved. This enormously popular tale speaks of the complex relations between Christianity and Islam in the early modern era and is featured here in a new translation by our Renaissance editor, Barbara Fuchs. Equally exciting is our representation of Korean literature. The *Tale of Hong Kiltong*, a story of a Korean Robin Hood endowed with magical powers, is a classic that we paired with excerpts from Lady Hyegyŏng's memoirs, which chronicle with deep psychological insight the horror and violence at the Korean royal court. These older Korean texts are complemented by a modern writer, Park Wansuh, whose work reflects the upheavals of the twentieth century on the Korean peninsula, from Japanese occupation and the Korean War to economic development. One of the first women to achieve critical success in modern Korea, Park offers readers keen insight into Korea's modern struggles.

We are particularly excited to now close the anthology with a story by the Nigerian writer Chimamanda Ngozi Adichie called "The Headstrong Historian," which, since its publication in 2008, has already become a favorite in world literature classrooms. This compact work introduces us to three generations of Nigerians as they navigate a complicated series of personal and cultural displacements. A thought-provoking exploration of the complex results of cultural contact and influence, this probing, searching journey seemed to us the most fitting conclusion to the anthology's survey of 4,000 years of literature.

Cultural Contact

Odysseus's encounter with the Cyclopes speaks not only to hospitality but also to the theme of cultural contact more generally. The earliest civilizations—those that invented writing and hence literature—sprang up where they did because they were located along strategic trading and migration routes. Contact was not just something that happened between fully formed cultures but something that made these cultures possible in the first place.

Committed to presenting the anthology's riches in a way that conveys this central fact of world literature, we have created sections that encompass broad contact zones—areas of intense trade in peoples, goods, art, and ideas where the earliest literatures emerged and intermingled. One of these is the Mediterranean Sea, whose central importance we visualize with four new maps. It was not just a hostile environment that could derail a journey home, as it did for Odysseus, or where nontravelers, like Polyphemus, might encounter violent invaders willing to attack and steal; it was also a connecting tissue, allowing for intense contact around its harbors. Medieval maps of the Mediterranean pay tribute to this fact: so-called portolan charts show a veritable mesh of lines connecting hundreds of ports. For this edition, we have further emphasized these contact zones, the location of intense conflict (including Cervantes's experience as a slave in North Africa) as well as friendly exchange. In a similar manner, the two major traditions of East Asia—China and Japan—are presented in the context of the larger region, including our new emphasis on Korea.

The importance of cultural contact and encounter is expressed not just in the overall organization of the anthology and the selection of material; it is also made visible in clusters of texts on the theme of travel and conquest, giving students access to documents related to travel, contact, trade, and conflict. For not all travel was voluntary. People traveled to escape wars and famine, plagues and environmental disasters. They were abducted, enslaved, and trafficked. Beginning with the early modern era, European empires dominated global politics and economics and accelerated the pace of globalization by laying down worldwide trade routes and communication networks, but old empires, such as China, continued to be influential as well. We added more material to our cluster "At the Crossroads of Empire," including a letter by Machemba, a chief in East Africa under German colonial control, and Mark Twain's trenchant soliloquy of Belgian King Leopold defending his brutal rule in Congo.

To these expanded clusters, we added a new one, "Poetry and Politics," which includes the Polish national poet Adam Mickiewicz and Latin American poet Rubén Darío's *To Roosevelt*, a powerful reminder of the crucial role poetry played in the gaining of national independence across the world. Poets captured the aspirations of nations and often enshrined those aspirations in national anthems, which also led us to include the Puerto Rican national anthem (one poet included in our anthology, Rabindranath Tagore, wrote not one but two national anthems, of both India and Bangladesh).

In the same volume, we also enhanced our cluster "Realism across the Globe," which traces one of the most successful global literary movements, one that found expression in France, Britain, Russia, Brazil, Mexico, and Japan. In keeping with our commitment to frequently taught authors, we increased our selection of Chekhov and present Tolstoy's *Death of Ivan Ilyich* in a new, acclaimed translation by Peter Carson.

The Birth of World Literature

In 1827, a provincial German writer, living in small-town Weimar, recognized that he was in the privileged position of having access not only to European literature but also to literature from much further afield, including Persian poetry, Chinese novels, and Sanskrit drama. The writer was Johann Wolfgang von Goethe, and in 1827, he coined a term to capture this new force of globalization in literature: "world literature." (We now include the "prologue" to Goethe's play *Faust*, which he wrote after encountering a similar prologue in the classical Sanskrit play *Śhakuntalā*, also included in the anthology.)

Since 1827, for less than 200 years, we have been living in an era of world literature. This era has brought many lost masterpieces back to life, including *The Epic of Gilgamesh*, which was rediscovered in the nineteenth century, and the *Popol Vuh*, which languished in a library until well into the twentieth century. Other works of world literature weren't translated and therefore didn't begin to circulate outside their sphere of origin until the last 200 years, including *The Tale of Genji*. With more literature becoming more widely available than ever before, Goethe's vision of world literature has become a reality today.

In presenting world literature from the dawn of writing to the early twenty-first century, and from oral storytelling to literary experiments of the avant-garde, this anthology raises the question not only of what world literature is but also of the nature of literature itself. We call attention to the changing nature of literature with thematic clusters on literature in the early volumes, to give students and teachers access to how early writers from different cultures thought about literature. But the changing role and nature of literature are visible in the anthology as a whole. Greek tragedy and comedy are experienced by modern students as literary genres, encountered in written texts; but for the ancient Athenians, they were primarily dramas, experienced live in an outdoor theater in the context of a religious and civic ritual. Other texts, such as the Qur'an or the Bible, are sacred pieces of writing, central to many people's religious faith, while others appreciate them primarily or exclusively as literature. Some texts, such as those by Laozi or Plato or Kant, belong in philosophy, while others, such as the Declaration of Independence, are primarily political documents. Our modern conception of literature as imaginative literature, as fiction, is very recent, about 200 years old. We have therefore opted for a much-expanded conception of literature that includes creation myths, wisdom literature, religious texts, philosophy, political writing, and fairy tales in addition to poems, plays, and narrative fiction. This answers to an older definition of literature as writing of high quality or of great cultural significance. There are many texts of philosophy or religion or politics that are not remarkable or influential for their literary qualities and that would therefore have no place in an anthology of world literature. But the works presented here do: in addition to or as part of their other functions, they have acquired the status of literature.

This brings us to the last and perhaps most important question: When we study the world, why study it through its literature? Hasn't literature lost some of its luster for us, we who are faced with so many competing media and art forms? Like no other art form or medium, literature offers us a deep history of human thinking. As our illustration program shows, writing was invented not for the composition of literature but for much more mundane purposes, such as the recording of ownership, contracts, or astronomical observations. But literature is writing's most glorious by-product. Literature can be reactivated with each reading. Many of the great architectural monuments of the past are now in ruins. Literature, too, often has to be excavated, as with many classical texts. But once a text has been found or reconstructed it can be experienced as if for the first time by new readers. Even though many of the literary texts collected in this anthology are at first strange, because they originated so very long ago, they still speak to today's readers with great eloquence and freshness. No other art form can capture the human past with the precision and scope of literature because language expresses human consciousness. Language shapes our thinking, and literature, the highest expression of language, plays an important role in that process, pushing the boundaries of what we can think and how we think it. This is especially true with great, complex, and contradictory works that allow us to explore different narrative perspectives, different points of view.

Works of world literature continue to elicit strong emotions and investments. The epic *Rāmāyana*, for example, plays an important role in the politics of India, where it has been used to bolster Hindu nationalism, just as the *Bhagavad-Gītā* continues to be a moral touchstone in the ethical deliberation about war. The so-called religions of the book, Judaism, Christianity, and Islam, make our selections from their scriptures a more than historical exercise as well. China has recently elevated the sayings of Confucius, whose influence on Chinese attitudes about the state had waned in the twentieth century, creating Confucius Institutes all over the world to promote Chinese culture in what is now called New Confucianism. World literature is never neutral. We know its relevance precisely by the controversies it inspires.

There are many ways of studying other cultures and of understanding the place of our own culture in the world. Archaeologists can show us objects and buildings from the past and speculate, through material remains, how people in the past ate, fought, lived, died, and were buried; scientists can date layers of soil. Literature is capable of something much more extraordinary: it allows us a glimpse into the imaginative lives, the thoughts and feelings of humans from thousands of years ago or living halfway around the world. This is the true magic of world literature as captured in this anthology, our shared human inheritance.

About the Fourth Edition

New Selections and Translations

Following is a list of the new translations, selections, and works in the Fourth Edition, in order:

VOLUME A

A new translation of Homer's *The Iliad* by Caroline Alexander • A new translation of Homer's *The Odyssey* by Emily Wilson, complete • Six new Aesop's *Fables*: "The Onager, the Donkey and the Driver," "The Eagle and the Farmer," "The Dung Beetle and the Eagle," "The Fox, the Donkey, and the Lion Skin," "Aesop and His Lamp," and "The Lion, the Fox, and the Deer" • New translations of Sappho's poetry by Philip Freeman, including ten new poems • New translations of *Oedipus the King* by David Grene, *Antigone* by Ruby Blondell, *Medea* by Sheila H. Murnaghan, and *Lysistrata* by Jeffrey Henderson • Benjamin Jowett's translation of *Symposium*, new to this edition • New translations of Catullus's poetry by Charles Martin • A new selection from *The Aeneid* from "The Kingdom of the Dead" • A new translation of *The Mahabharata* by Carole Satyamurti, including new selections from "The Book of Drona" and "Books 17 and 18: The Books of the Final Journey and the Ascent to Heaven" • New selections from *Zhuangzi* from "The Way of Heaven," "Outer Things," and "Of Swords"

VOLUME B

A new translation of Augustine's *Confessions* by Peter Constantine with a new selection from "Book XI [Time]" • A new translation of the Qur'an by M. A. Rafey Habib and Bruce Lawrence with new selections from "Light," "Ya Sin," and "The Sun" • A new translation of Marie de France's *Lais* by Dorothy Gilbert, including the new selection "Bisclavret" • A selection from *Vis and Ramin* translated by Dick Davis • A new translation of *The Conference of the Birds* by Sholeh Wolpé • A new translation and selection of Rumi's poetry, including six new poems: "[The nights I spend with you]," "[Like blood beneath my skin]," "[Profession, profit, trade]," "[A rose is still a rose]," "[How marvelous, that moment]," and "[On death's day]," as well as selections from *The Masnavi* translated by Dick Davis: "[On the Prohibition of Wine]," "[This World as a Dream]," "[On Men's Behavior with Women]," "[Man's Life Compared to That of an Embryo in the Womb]," and "[Moses and the Shepherd]" • John Ciardi's

translation of *The Divine Comedy*, newly included, supplemented by two additional translations from Canto 3 of *Inferno* by Clive James and Mark Musa • A
new translation of *Kebra Nagast* by Wendy Belcher and Michael Kleiner, including a new chapter, "About How King Solomon Swore an Oath to the Queen" •
Seven new tales from *The Thousand and One Nights*: "[The Story of the Porter
and the Three Ladies]," "[The First Dervish's Tale]," "[The Second Dervish's
Tale]," "[The Tale of the Envious and the Envied]," "[The Third Dervish's Tale],"
"[The Tale of the First Lady]," and "[The Tale of the Second Lady]" • "The Nun's
Priest's Tale" from *The Canterbury Tales* • Three new tales from the *Pañcatan-
tra*: "The Bird with Golden Dung" and "The Ass in the Tiger Skin" translated by
Arthur W. Ryder and "The Ass without Ears or a Heart" translated by Patrick
Olivelle • New selections from *The Tale of Genji*: "Sakaki: A Branch of Sacred
Evergreens," "Maboroshi: Spirit Summoner," "Hashihime: The Divine Princess
at Uji Bridge," "Agemaki: A Bowknot Tied in Maiden's Loops," "Yadoriki: Trees
Encoiled in Vines of Ivy," and "Tenarai: Practicing Calligraphy"

VOLUME C

A new prose translation of *Sunjata: A West African Epic of the Mande* by David
C. Conrad • New selections from *The Prince*: "[Liberality and Parsimony],"
"[Love and Fear]," "[Dissimulation]," "[Contempt and Hatred]," "[Princely
Devices; Fortresses]," "[The Excellent Prince]," "[Flatterers]," and "[The Princes
of Italy]" • "The Abencerraje" translated by Barbara Fuchs, Larissa Brewer-
García, and Aaron J. Ilika • A new selection from *Don Quixote*, "[A Story of
Captivity in North Africa, Told to Don Quixote at the Inn]" • A revised *Fuent-
eovejuna* translated by G. J. Racz

VOLUME D

A new translation of "What Is Enlightenment?" by Mary C. Smith • A new
translation of Sor Juana Inés de la Cruz's work translated by Edith Grossman,
including three new sonnets, "[O World, why do you wish to persecute me?]," "[I
adore Lisi but do not pretend]," and "[Because you have died, Laura, let affec-
tions]," as well as *Loa* to the Mystery Play *The Divine Narcissus: An Allegory*
translated by Edith Grossman • Hŏ Kyun's "The Tale of Hong Kiltong" translated by Marshall R. Pihl • A selection from Lady Hyegyŏng's *The Memoirs of
Lady Hyegyŏng* translated by JaHyun Kim Haboush

VOLUME E

A new selection from *Faust*, "Prelude in the Theatre" • Machemba's "Letter to
Major von Wissmann" translated by Robert Sullivan and Sarah Lawall • A
selection from Mark Twain's "King Leopold's Soliloquy" • A new cluster, "Poetry
and Politics," including four new works, Adam Mickiewicz's "The Prisoner's
Return" translated by Jerzy Peterkiewicz and Burns Singer, Speranza's (Lady
Jane Wilde's) "A Lament for the Potato" and "The Exodus," and Lola Rodríguez

de Tió's "The Song of the Borinquen" translated by José Nieto, as well as the new translation of "Guantanamera" by Elinor Randall • A new translation of *The Death of Ivan Ilyich* by Peter Carson • A new translation of "The Cane" by Margaret Jull Costa • José López Portillo y Rojas's "Unclaimed Watch" translated by Roberta H. Kimble • Anton Chekhov's "The Lady with the Dog" translated by Ivy Litvinov

VOLUME F

A new translation of *The Metamorphosis* by Susan Bernofsky • Lu Xun's "Ah Q—The Real Story" translated by William A. Lyell • Eric Bentley's translation, new to this edition, of Pirandello's *Six Characters in Search of an Author* • A new translation of "The Dancing Girl of Izu" by J. Martin Homan • Jorge Luis Borges's "The Library of Babel" translated by James E. Irby • M. D. Herder Norton's translations of Rainer Maria Rilke's poems, newly included • A new translation of "Lament for Ignacio Sánchez Mejías" by Pablo Medina • A new translation of "Matryona's Home" by Michael Glenny • Derek Walcott's "Sea Grapes" • Park Wansuh's "Mother's Hitching Post, Part 2" • Yu Hua's "On the Road at Eighteen" • Chimamanda Ngozi Adichie's "The Headstrong Historian"

Resources for Students and Instructors

Norton is pleased to provide students and instructors with abundant resources to make the teaching and study of world literature an even more interesting and rewarding experience.

We are pleased to launch the new *Norton Anthology of World Literature* website, found at digital.wwnorton.com/worldlit4pre1650 (for volumes A, B, C) and digital.wwnorton.com/worldlit4post1650 (for volumes D, E, F). This searchable and sortable site contains thousands of resources for students and instructors in one centralized place at no additional cost. Following are some highlights:

- A series of eight brand-new video modules are designed to enhance classroom presentation and spark student interest in the anthology's works. These videos, conceived of and narrated by the anthology editors, ask students to consider why it is important for them to read and engage with this literature.
- Hundreds of images—maps, author portraits, literary places, and manuscripts—are available for student browsing or instructor download for in-class presentation.
- Several hours of audio recordings are available, including a 10,000-term audio glossary that helps students pronounce the character and place names in the anthologized works.

The site also provides a wealth of teaching resources that are unlocked with an instructor's log-in:

- "Quick read" summaries, teaching notes, discussion questions, and suggested resources for every work in the anthology, from the much-praised *Teaching with* The Norton Anthology of World Literature: *A Guide for Instructors*
- Downloadable Lecture PowerPoints featuring images, quotations from the texts, and lecture notes in the notes view for in-class presentation

In addition to the wealth of resources in *The Norton Anthology of World Literature* website, Norton offers a downloadable Coursepack that allows instructors to easily add high-quality Norton digital media to online, hybrid, or lecture courses—all at no cost. Norton Coursepacks work within existing learning management systems; there's no new system to learn, and access is free and easy. Content is customizable and includes over seventy reading-comprehension quizzes, short-answer questions, links to the videos, and more.

Acknowledgments

The editors would like to thank the following people, who have provided invaluable assistance by giving us sage advice, important encouragement, and help with the preparation of the manuscript: Sara Akbari, Alannah de Barra, Wendy Belcher, Jodi Bilinkoff, Daniel Boucher, Freya Brackett, Psyche Brackett, Michaela Bronstein, Rachel Carroll, Sookja Cho, Kyeong-Hee Choi, Amanda Claybaugh, Lewis Cook, David Damrosch, Dick Davis, Burghild Denecke, Amanda Detry, Anthony Domestico, Megan Eckerle, Marion Eggert, Merve Emre, Maria Fackler, Guillermina de Ferrari, Alyssa Findley, Karina Galperín, Stanton B. Garner, Kimberly Dara Gordon, Elyse Graham, Stephen Greenblatt, Sara Guyer, Langdon Hammer, Emily Hayman, Iain Higgins, Paulo Lemos Horta, Mohja Kahf, Peter Kornicki, Paul W. Kroll, Peter H. Lee, Sung-il Lee, Lydia Liu, Bala Venkat Mani, Ann Matter, Barry McCrea, Alexandra McCullough-Garcia, Rachel McGuiness, Jon McKenzie, Mary Mullen, Djibril Tamsir Niane, Johann Noh, Felicity Nussbaum, Andy Orchard, John Peters, Michael Pettid, Daniel Taro Poch, Daniel Potts, Megan Quigley, Payton Phillips Quintanilla, Catherine de Rose, Imogen Roth, Katherine Rupp, Ellen Sapega, Jesse Schotter, Stephen Scully, Kyung-ho Sim, Sarah Star, Brian Stock, Tomi Suzuki, Joshua Taft, Sara Torres, J. Keith Vincent, Lisa Voigt, Kristen Wanner, Emily Weissbourd, Karoline Xu, Yoon Sun Yang, and Catherine Vance Yeh.

All the editors would like to thank the wonderful people at Norton, principally our editor Pete Simon, the driving force behind this whole undertaking, as well as Marian Johnson (Managing Editor, College), Christine D'Antonio and Kurt Wildermuth (Project Editors), Michael Fleming (Copyeditor), Gerra Goff (Associate Editor), Megan Jackson (College Permissions Manager), Margaret Gorenstein (Permissions), Catherine Abelman (Photo Editor), Debra Morton Hoyt (Art Director; cover design), Rubina Yeh (Design Director), Jo Anne Metsch (Designer; interior text design), Adrian Kitzinger (cartography), Agnieszka Gasparska (timeline design), Carly Fraser-Doria (Media Editor), Ava Bramson (Assistant Editor, Media), Sean Mintus (Production Manager), and Kim Bowers (Marketing Manager, Literature). We'd also like to thank our Instructor's Guide authors: Colleen Clemens (Kutztown University), Elizabeth Watkins (Loyola University New Orleans), and Janet Zong (Harvard University).

This anthology represents a collaboration not only among the editors and their close advisers but also among the thousands of instructors who teach from the anthology and provide valuable and constructive guidance to the publisher and editors. *The Norton Anthology of World Literature* is as much their book as it is ours, and we are grateful to everyone who has cared enough about this anthology to help make it better. We're especially grateful to the professors of world literature who responded to an online survey in 2014, whom we have listed below. Thank you all.

Michelle Abbott (Georgia Highlands College), Elizabeth Ashworth (Castleton State College), Clinton Atchley (Henderson State University), Amber Barnes (Trinity Valley Community College), Rosemary Baxter (Clarendon College), Khani Begum (Bowling Green State University), Joyce Boss (Wartburg College), Floyd Brigdon (Trinity Valley Community College), James Bryant-Trerise (Clackamas Community College), Barbara Cade (Texas College), Kellie Cannon (Coastal Carolina Community College), Amee Carmines (Hampton University), Farrah Cato (University of Central Florida), Brandon Chitwood (Marquette University), Paul Cohen (Texas State University), Judith Cortelloni (Lincoln College), Randall Crump (Kennesaw State University), Sunni Davis (Cossatot Community College), Michael Demson (Sam Houston State University), Richard Diguette (Georgia Perimeter College, Dunwoody), Daniel Dooghan (University of Tampa), Jeff Doty (West Texas A&M University), Myrto Drizou (Valdosta State University), Ashley Dugas (Copiah-Lincoln Community College), Richmond Eustis (Nicholls State University), David Fell (Carroll Community College), Allison Fetters (Chattanooga State Community College), Francis Fletcher (Folsom Lake College), Kathleen D. Fowler (Surry Community College), Louisa Franklin (Young Harris College), James Gamble (University of Arkansas), Antoinette Gazda (Averett University), Adam Golaski (Central Connecticut State University), Anissa Graham (University of North Alabama), Eric Gray (St. Gregory's University), Jared Griffin (Kodiak College), Marne Griffin (Hilbert College), Frank Gruber (Bergen Community College), Laura Hammons (Hinds Community College), Nancy G. Hancock (Austin Peay State University), C. E. Harding (Western Oregon University), Leslie Harrelson (Dalton State College), Eleanor J. Harrington-Austin (North Carolina Central University), Matthew Hokom (Fairmont State University), Scott Hollifield (University of Nevada, Las Vegas), Catherine Howard (University of Houston, Downtown), Jack Kelnhofer (Ocean County College), Katherine King (University of California, Los Angeles), Pam Kingsbury (University of North Alabama), Sophia Kowalski (Hillsborough Community College), Roger Ladd (University of North Carolina at Pembroke), Jameela Lares (University of Southern Mississippi), Susan Lewis (Delaware Technical Community College), Christina Lovin (Eastern Kentucky University), Richard Mace (Pace University), Nicholas R. Marino (Borough of Manhattan Community College, CUNY), Brandi Martinez (Mountain Empire Community College), Kathy Martinez (Sandhills Community College), Matthew Masucci (State College of Florida), Kelli McBride (Seminole State College), Melissa McCoy (Clarendon College), Geoffrey McNeil (Notre Dame de Namur University), Renee Moore (Mississippi Delta Community College), Anna C. Oldfield (Coastal Carolina University), Keri Overall (Texas Woman's University), Maggie Piccolo (Rutgers University), Oana Popescu-Sandu (University of Southern Indiana), Jonathan Purkiss (Pulaski Technical College), Rocio Quispe-Agnoli (Michigan State University), Evan Radcliffe (Villanova University), Ken Raines (Eastern Arizona College), Jonathan Randle (Mississippi College), Kirk G. Rasmussen (Utah Valley University), Helaine Razovsky (Northwestern State University of Louisiana), Karin Rhodes (Salem State University), Stephanie Roberts (Georgia Military College), Allen Salerno (Auburn University), Shannin Schroeder (Southern Arkansas University), Heather Seratt (University of Houston, Downtown), Conrad Shumaker (University of Central Arkansas), Edward Soloff (St. John's University), Eric Sterling (Auburn University Montgomery), Ron Stormer (Culver-Stockton College), Marianne Szlyk (Montgomery College), Tim Tarkington (Georgia Perimeter College), Allison Tharp (University of Southern Mississippi), Diane Thompson (Northern Virginia Community College), Sevinc Turkkan (College at Brockport, State University of New York), Verne Underwood (Rogue Community College), Patricia Vazquez (College of Southern Nevada), William Wallis (Los Angeles Valley College), Eric Weil (Elizabeth City State University), Denise C. White (Kennesaw State University), Tamora Whitney (Creighton University), Todd Williams (Kutztown University of Pennsylvania), Bertha Wise (Oklahoma City Community College), and Lindsey Zanchettin (Auburn University).

THE NORTON ANTHOLOGY OF

WORLD LITERATURE

FOURTH EDITION

VOLUME C

I

Encounters with Islam

The Prophet Muhammed and the emergence of Islam united disparate Arab tribes over the course of the seventh century, turning them into a potent cultural and political force. Islam initially spread as the religion of a dynamic Arab state that took advantage of the weakness of the Byzantine and Persian Empires in the Middle East, and soon extended its political boundaries even further, to Spain, Central Asia, and Afghanistan. Once conquests slowed down and political boundaries were consolidated, traders carried the religion even further, to West Africa and China, as well as South and Southeast Asia. Arab traders established an increasingly far-flung network of cities and trading posts, facilitating an extraordinary exchange of goods. In Cordoba, the center of Muslim Spain, one had access to goods coming from Delhi, the Sultanate in northern India, and from what is now Bulgaria in eastern Europe to Sudan. Along with commodities, what traveled along these trade routes were armies. Islam became the religion of the ruling classes in the different empires. However, unlike Christianity, Islam did not seek

An illustration of the Ottoman fleet blockading the port of Marseille, from a 16th-century Ottoman manuscript that recounts the military campaigns of Süleyman the Magnificent.

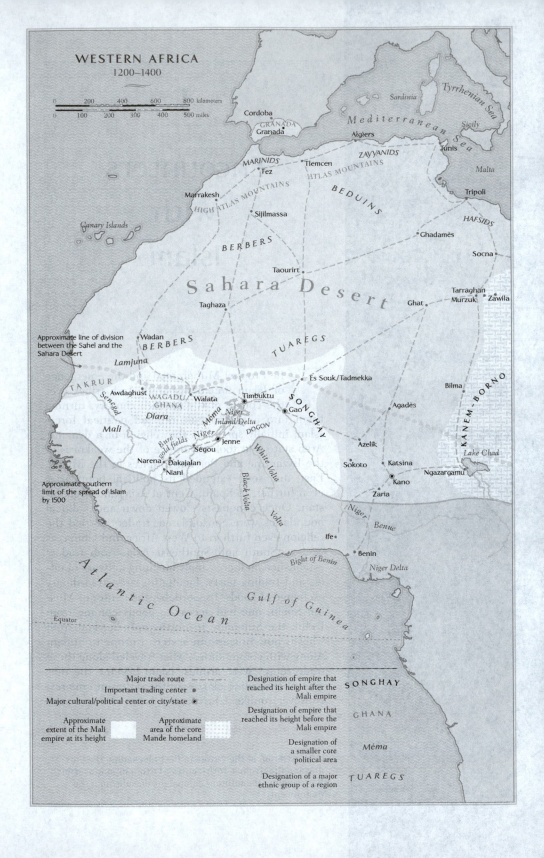

WESTERN AFRICA
1200–1400

0   200   400   600   800 kilometers
0 100 200 300 400 500 miles

Tyrrhenian Sea

Sardinia

Cordoba

GRANADA
Granada

Mediterranean Sea

Sicily

Algiers

Tunis

MARINIDS   Tlemcen   ZAYYANIDS

Fez

ATLAS MOUNTAINS

Malta

Marrakesh

HIGH ATLAS MOUNTAINS

Sijilmassa

BEDUINS

Tripoli

HAFSIDS

Canary Islands

BERBERS

Ghadamès

Socna

Taourirt

Sahara Desert

Ghat

Tarraghan
Murzuk   Zawila

Taghaza

Approximate line of division
between the Sahel and the
Sahara Desert

Wadan

BERBERS

Lamjuna

TAKRUR

Awdaghust

Senegal

WAGADU
GHANA

Walata

Diara

Mali

Méma

Inland Delta

Buré
gold fields

Niger

Ségou

Narena

Dakajalan

Niani

Jenne

TUAREGS

Es Souk/Tadmekka

Timbuktu

Niger

Gao

SONGHAY

DOGON

White Volta

Black Volta

Bilma

Agadès

Azelik

Sokoto

Zaria

Katsina

Kano

Ngazargamu

KANEM–BORNO

Lake Chad

Approximate southern
limit of the spread of Islam
by 1500

Volta

Niger

Benue

Ife

Benin

Bight of Benin

Niger Delta

Atlantic Ocean

Gulf of Guinea

Equator

Major trade route
Important trading center
Major cultural/political center or city/state

Approximate
extent of the Mali
empire at its height

Approximate
area of the core
Mande homeland

Designation of empire that
reached its height after the
Mali empire

Designation of empire that
reached its height before the
Mali empire

Designation of
a smaller core
political area

Designation of a major
ethnic group of a region

SONGHAY

GHANA

Méma

TUAREGS

converts, which meant that it often allowed local religious practices to exist alongside Islam, thus creating multicultural societies in which different religions existed side by side. The Ottoman Empire and the Mughal rule in India, for all the tensions that existed between different groups, set a standard for religious tolerance.

The same pattern held true of culture. Far from seeking to export a homogeneous notion of culture, the various Islamic empires were places of vibrant cultural exchange, in which art and ideas traveled as freely as goods and armies. Writing was especially enriched by the interchange; new literary forms that blended imported styles with existing local ones emerged throughout the Islamic world. Oral literature, such as the ones that fed into the Turkish epic **Dede Korkut** or the Mali epic **Sunjata**, continued to flourish, while incorporating Islamic elements, much as the pre-Christian epic **Beowulf** had received a late Christian layer or veneer to make the traditional story compatible with the new dominant religion. The result was a fascinating encounter of cultures and religions, whose products are presented here.

ISLAM AND PRE-ISLAMIC CULTURE IN NORTH AFRICA

Between 640 and 700 C.E., North Africa was occupied by Arab invaders seeking to expand the growing sphere of influence of an Arab world increasingly united by Islam. One far-reaching result of the Arab conquest was that it led to an economic revolution by combining the faltering economy of late Roman North Africa with the desert and savannah lands of West Africa into a vast commercial network that extended from the Atlantic to East Asia and from the equator throughout northern Europe. By the latter half of the eighth century,

most of the native Berber peoples of the Maghreb (Northwest Africa) had been converted to Islam. Owing to increasingly dynamic market forces to the north of the desert and the spread of camel-herding in the desert itself, Muslim Berber merchants became engaged in the systematic development of trans-Saharan trade.

The ninth-century Arab occupation of southern Morocco gave rise to a string of oasis cities south of the High Atlas Mountains. These included the bustling market town of Sijilmasa, which became the northern counterpart of the commercial centers of Tadmekka and Awdaghust on the southern edge of the Sahara. By the end of the tenth century, the southern trading centers had been colonized by Muslim (mostly Berber) immigrants from the north. They were merchants eager to trade with the markets of desert-edge kingdoms like Ghana, Takrur, and Gao, and especially to extract wealth from parts of the western Sudan described by Arab travelers as "the land of gold."

Thus, Islam arrived in West Africa via Muslim traders, and by 1068 the respected Arab geographer Al-Bakri was writing that there were significant Muslim populations occupying towns of the Mande peoples, which included the Maninka of the Upper Niger region who became founders of the Mali Empire in the thirteenth century.

But Islam was not only an economic force; it also reshaped the cultural landscape. By the thirteenth century Islam had become a common, though not universal, aspect of Mande culture. Far from imposing onto North Africa, including the Mali Empire, its own conception of art, Islam was gradually integrated into Mande culture, with Mande bards (*jeliw*) assimilating elements of Islamic tradition. Some of the stories told by Muslim clerics and by pilgrims returning from Mecca were adapted to local narrative repertoires.

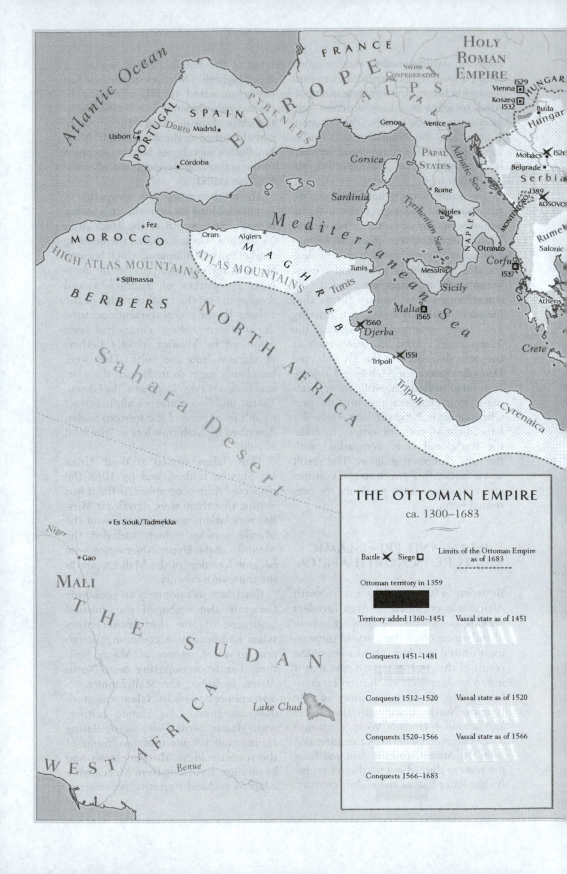

POLAND
LITHUANIA • Kiev

RUSSIAN
EMPIRE

Transylvania
☐ 1660

Podolia

Moldavia

Khanate
of
Crimea ✕

Azov ✕

Aral
Sea

TURKOMANS

Wallachia

1396 • Bucharest
Nicopolis
Sofia •
Bulgaria

Danube

1475 ✕
• Caffa

CENTRAL ASIA
UZBEKS

Black Sea

CAUCASUS MTNS.

(Byzantium)
1453 ✕ Constantinople
(Istanbul)

Bursa ✕
1326

TURKEY

Trebizond •

Caspian
Sea

PERSIA

1402 ✕ Ankara

TAURUS MTNS.

SAFAVID
EMPIRE

1522 ✕
Rhodes

Cyprus

Aleppo ✕
1516

IRAQ

Euphrates

Tabriz •

Tyre •

✕ 1516
Damascus

SYRIA

1534 ✕ Baghdad

Tigris

Alexandria •

• Jerusalem

1517 ✕ • Cairo

Basra •

Egypt

Persian Gulf

Nile

Red Sea

• Medina

Tropic of Cancer

• Mecca

ARABIA

Arabian Sea

• Aden

0   200   400   600   800 kilometers
0 100 200 300 400 500 miles

A contemporary photograph of the Grand Mosque at Djenne, Mali, which was first built in the thirteenth century.

The Prophet Muhammad and various characters from his life and times were borrowed by Mande bards and incorporated into their most important oral traditions, including the epic *Sunjata*, which tells the story of the thirteenth-century hero who is credited with the founding of the Mali Empire.

THE OTTOMAN EMPIRE

The beginnings of the Ottoman Empire can be traced to a small principality established around 1300 C.E. by Turkoman nomads in the little-controlled borderlands of northwestern Asia Minor between the Byzantine Empire and the fragments of the Seljuk Empire. The "Ottoman enterprise," named after Osman Beg (d. probably 1324) was initially one of many similar petty principalities, but it managed, within a century and a half, to eliminate its Islamic competitors in Asia Minor and conquer much of southeastern Europe. The conquest of the city of Constantinople in 1453 finally established it as the inheritor of the eastern Roman Empire. Over time, Ottoman conquests extended further into Europe, including Hungary, and today's Romania. By 1517, the Ottomans also controlled Syria, Egypt, and the Holy Cities of Arabia. Despite this eastern expansion, the Ottoman Empire remained a Mediterranean rather than an Asiatic power.

In this process of empire building, the nomadic origins soon faded away to fond memories preserved in chronicles and heroic epics, such as the *Book of Dede Korkut*, while the remaining nomads were marginalized as a social group and used as a military reserve. The new political and military elite largely consisted of carefully selected and highly educated slaves of the sultan, thus concentrating the administration of the empire in the imperial household. A second pillar of Ottoman power was a feudal army, which never developed into a landed aristocracy (as feudal armies did throughout Europe) that could hold its own against the central power of the sultan. While the Ottoman Dynasty was ethnically Turkish, and the administrative language was Turkish as well, this elite was mostly recruited from Christian subjects, who were converted to Islam and culturally socialized into Ottoman-Turkish elite culture.

This elite culture found its classical expression in art, architecture, and literature between the late fifteenth and the beginning of the seventeenth century. Ottoman literature used a language that is Turkish in principle, but had come to incorporate so many Arabic and Persian words, phrases, and even syntactic constructions that it is sometimes difficult to tell whether a poem is Turkish or Persian. This literary Ottoman Turkish was worlds apart from the Turkish spoken on the street, the reserve of its erudite connoisseurs, who were all expected to be fluent in the "Three Languages"—Arabic, Persian, and Turkish—and their rich literary traditions. Evliya Çelebi's *Book of Travels* is a powerful late homage to these ideals of classical Ottoman culture.

Strictly speaking, the term Ottoman should be used only for the members of the imperial household and everybody else who shared this culturally defined identity, but more generally it has come to include the numerous subcultures that were allowed to thrive alongside it. Within this multilingual and multi-religious empire, place and social status, as well as affiliation with religious and social institutions were more important than ethnic background or language. Lacking a concept of "Ottoman citizenship," the Ottoman state with its small elite had neither an interest nor the means to impose any kind of cultural or religious identity on its subjects, and did not interfere in the internal communal affairs of its populations. This policy has often been praised as Ottoman tolerance, but it is important to realize that tolerance did not mean equality: different religious groups were taxed differently and did

not have the same access to power. Yet the sheer diversity of the Ottoman Empire continues to command respect and elicit fascination.

ISLAM AND HINDUISM IN SOUTH ASIA

Muslim armies from Iraq entered South Asia early in the eighth century, initially conquering what are now the southern and western regions of Pakistan. Over the next three hundred years or so, immigrants from various parts of the Muslim world, together with local converts to Islam, gradually established distinctive settlements for themselves in the western and northwestern parts of the Indian subcontinent, from Sind and Gujarat to Punjab and Kashmir. During the eleventh and twelfth centuries, Muslim armies from Afghanistan and Central Asia (which included Turkish slave-warriors) carried out a succession of raids, or short-lived invasions, on towns and cities in northern India. In 1206, a Turkish slave-warrior proclaimed himself the Sultan of Delhi, laying the foundation for a Muslim empire in northern India that lasted more than three centuries, and was ruled by five different dynasties of Turkish-Afghan descent.

In the early sixteenth century, the Delhi Sultanate, which controlled the greater portion of western, northern, eastern, and central India by then, lost power to the Mughals, a dynasty with origins in today's Uzbekistan. The Mughals ruled most of South Asia from 1526 to 1857, creating a vast empire that, especially in the second half of the sixteenth century and in the seventeenth century, was the richest and most powerful political formation in Asia. Over a period of more than six centuries, the Delhi Sultanate and the Mughal empire, between them, provided a complex framework for the emergence of a

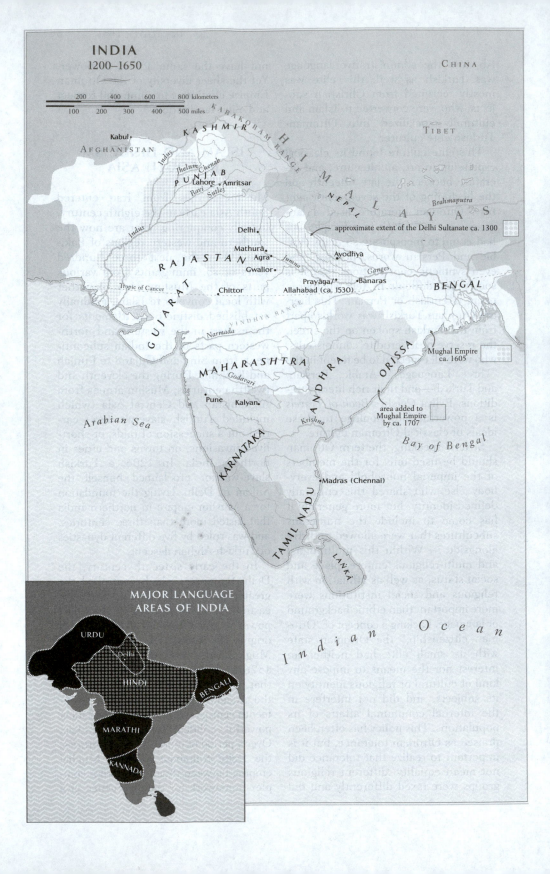

INDIA
1200–1650

CHINA

200   400   600   800 kilometers
100   200   300   400   500 miles

KASHMIR
KARAKORAM RANGE
HIMALAYAS
TIBET

Kabul
AFGHANISTAN
Indus
Jhelum Chenab
PUNJAB
Lahore
Ravi
Sutlej
Amritsar
NEPAL
Brahmaputra

Indus

Delhi
approximate extent of the Delhi Sultanate ca. 1300

RAJASTAN
Mathura
Agra
Jumna
Ayodhya
Gwalior
Ganges
Tropic of Cancer
Chittor
Prayaga
Allahabad (ca. 1530)
Banaras
BENGAL

GUJARAT
VINDHYA RANGE
Narmada
ORISSA

MAHARASHTRA
Godavari
ANDHRA
Mughal Empire
ca. 1605

Pune   Kalyan
Krishna
area added to
Mughal Empire
by ca. 1707

Arabian Sea
KARNATAKA
Bay of Bengal

Madras (Chennai)

TAMIL NADU

Indian   Ocean

LANKA

MAJOR LANGUAGE
AREAS OF INDIA

URDU
Delhi
HINDI
BENGALI
MARATHI
KANNADA

unique Indo-Islamic civilization, which continues to shape the cultural life of South Asia to this day.

Before the arrival of Islam, the Indian subcontinent was predominantly Hindu in religion and culture, with Buddhism and Jainism practiced only by small minorities of the population. For much of the first millennium of the Common Era, Hinduism in its classical form involved polytheism (belief in the existence of many gods), worship in temples officiated by priests (belonging to the Brahmin caste), the worship of idols and the performance of numerous and intricate rituals (in accordance with elaborate scriptures, law books, and codes), and pilgrimages to designated holy places.

When Islam settled into South Asia, it challenged many of these ideas and practices in Hinduism. Islam's uncompromising monotheism (belief in a single, all-powerful God), as well as its attacks on idol-worship, compelled many Hindus to reconsider their polytheism and their worship in temples (which is centered around idols, often representing gods in anthropomorphic forms). Likewise, Islam's emphasis on social equality and a universal fraternity persuaded Hindus to question the caste hierarchy and its practice of discrimination on the basis of birth. Moreover, Sufism—a mystical form of Islam centered on the cultivation of music, dance, poetry, the visual arts, and techniques of ecstasy—offered forms of spiritualism that resonated with some Hindu conceptions of "union with God." The poets collected here, from different regions and religions of South Asia, all work through this productive tension between Islam and Hinduism, testifying to the fact that cross-cultural encounters are sometimes violent, but can also lead to artworks of stunning beauty.

SUNJATA: A WEST AFRICAN EPIC OF THE MANDE PEOPLES

late thirteenth–early fourteenth century

The West African epic named after its central hero, Sunjata, is an essential part of Mande culture. The heartland of Mande territory is located in what is now northeastern Guinea and southern Mali, but the Mande peoples are found throughout a much larger portion of sub-Saharan West Africa, speaking various related languages and dialects. The Mande, also known as "the people of Manden," who include the Bamana of Mali and the Maninka of Guinea, are heirs to a vibrant historical legacy, the high point of which was the Mali Empire that flourished from the mid-thirteenth to the early fifteenth century. The epic narrative of Sunjata and his contemporaries illustrates the Mande peoples' own view of this glorious past both before and after Islam began to influence their culture, and it rightfully credits their ancestors with establishing one of the great empires of the medieval world.

In Mande culture, oral tradition is the domain of bards popularly known as griots, but as *jeliw* or *jelilu* (sing. *jeli*) to their own people. They are the hereditary oral artists responsible for relating the alleged deeds of the early ancestors, keeping them and their exploits alive in the community's memory. For many centuries the *jeliw* have served as genealogists, musicians, praise-singers, spokespersons, and diplomats. As the principal narrators of oral tradition, the bards have been responsible for preserving narratives that express what peoples of the Mande cultural heartland believe to have happened in the distant past. For centuries, stories of the ancestors have passed from one generation of *jeliw* to the next, and the principal Mande clans frame their identities in terms of descent from the ancestors described in epic tradition.

As specialists in maintaining the oral traditions of their culture, *jeliw* are known to their people as guardians of "The Word." In early times they served as the spokespersons of chiefs (*dugu-tigiw*) and kings (*mansaw*), and were thus responsible for their patrons' reputations in the community. Generations of *jeli* families were permanently attached to leading households and ruling dynasties, who supported the bards in exchange for their services in the verbal arts. The *jeliw* encouraged their patrons to strive for ambitious goals by reminding them of the examples set by their heroic ancestors, as described in the epic narratives. They pointed out mistakes through the use of proverbs, and admonished their patrons when they seemed likely to fail in their duties. At the same time, the bards' own security depended on their rulers' political power and social prestige, so the stories they told tended to be biased in favor of their patrons' own ancestors.

In Mande societies, all matters involving family, clan, and ethnic kinship are of supreme importance. People are identified by their *jamu*—the family name or patronymic associated with famous ancestors remembered for important deeds alleged to have occurred around the beginning of the thirteenth century. Thanks to regular exposure to live or locally taped performances by *jeliw* that are played privately or heard regularly on local radio broadcasts, general awareness of the heroes and heroines of ancient times, like those in *Sunjata*, enters the people's consciousness in childhood and grows there throughout their lives. Memories of the ancestors are constantly evoked in praise songs and narrative episodes that are sung or recited by the bards on virtually any occasion that calls for entertainment. When elders meet in village council, the ancestral spirits are felt to be present because, according to tradition, it was they who established the relative status of everyone present, as well as the administrative protocols to be followed and the values underpinning every decision. The ancestors who are described in *kuma koro* or "ancient speech" define the identity of virtually everyone of Mande origin.

The performance of *Sunjata* would often be accompanied by musical instruments: a small lute (*nkoni*), a twenty-one-string calabash harp (*kora*), or a Malian xylophone (*bala*). Even without music, Mande oral poetry incorporates a kind of call-and-response rhythm through the repeated assent of the "*naamu-sayer*" (responding person) to each line sung by the *jeli*. The *naamus* of this secondary performer might be translated as "yes" or "We hear you"; they are preserved here in the original to give a flavor of the repetitive, almost incantatory quality of the response. The variant spellings of *naamu* reflect different pronunciations used for emphasis. Common interjections include *tinye* ("it's true") in the indigenous language, as well as terms borrowed from Arabic and reflecting the influence of Islam, such as *walahi* ("I swear") and *amina* ("amen"). In all cases, the community hears not only the poem but an enthusiastic, repeated approbation of it. The *jeli*'s own language when narrating the stories of the ancestors is also distinct from everyday speech, as he turns to *kuma koro* ("ancient speech") for the

performance. Even the most central names in the story may vary according to the pronunciation of the individual *jeliw* and to regional differences, so that Sunjata, for example, may appear as Son-Jara, So'olon Jara, or Sunjara.

Oral literature that has been passed down from generation to generation is difficult to date. The epic material feeding this version of the *Sunjata* epic was narrated and recorded only in the late twentieth century, although it retells stories that go back centuries. Djanka Tassey Condé, the *jeli* who narrated this version, lived his entire life in the small village of Fadama near the Niandan River in northeastern Guinea. Nominally a Muslim like most people in today's Mande society, Tassey was descended from a lineage of Condé bards who trace their ancestry to forebears who lived before the arrival of Islam in the land of Dò ni Kiri as it is described in the Mande epic. Even among other bardic Manden families, the Condé of Fadama are respected for their vast knowledge of Mande epic tradition. In the 1970s and 1980s, Tassey's brother Mamadi Condé was *belentigi* (chief bard) of Fadama, and one of the best-known Manden orators, distinguished for his depth of knowledge. When Mamadi died in 1994, his brother Tassey became the *belentigi*. Several months later, David C. Conrad, who edited this version of *Sunjata*, began a collaborative relationship with Tassey Condé that lasted until that great bard's death in 1997.

The passages collected here are from the rendering by Tassey Condé of this communal, epic story. The narrative is episodic and often disjunct, full of magic (*dalilu*) and humor, as the *jeli* gives his own version of a story familiar to his listeners. The epic tells of the great expectation surrounding the birth of Sunjata, whose heroism has long been foretold. Foreigners come to

defeat a wild buffalo that has been dec-
imating Mande lands, and their first
achievement is to recognize the buffalo
woman Dò Kamissa as the culprit.
They tame her with kindness, claiming
that she resembles their mother, until
she relents and offers them her wisdom. Urging them to look beyond
appearances, she commends to them
the deformed Sogolon, who will be the
mother of Sunjata. When Sunjata is
finally born, into a world full of sorcery
and treachery, he barely escapes the
many plots against him, and is eventually driven into exile by the jealousy of
his stepbrother. His greatest achievement comes with the defeat of the tyrannous Sumaworo to liberate Manden,
which the text recognizes as a foundational imperial gesture. Sunjata also
emphasizes, however, that the hero's
exalted stature comes at a great cost to
the community: while Sumaworo furiously seeks the man who is fated to
succeed him, we are told, the Mande
people suffer his violent attacks.

Like most epics, Sunjata is a relation
of the hero's many trials, which he sur-
mounts through his courage, tenacity,
and piety. Yet the singular hero is also
deeply ensconced in his community: in
order to lead he must find allies, cultivate friends, and honor his family. Part
of the charm of Sunjata lies in its attention to detail, and its fresh humor as it
relates the interactions of legendary
heroes with the very concrete world
around them. This is a poem about the
power struggles that can lead to war,
certainly, but it is also about people's
relationship to a place and a landscape.
Land takes on a concrete quality beyond
its political significance as Sunjata
pleads for a plot in which to bury his
mother when she dies in exile. In its
vivid re-creation of the hero's experience, Sunjata knits together the mythic
and the everyday, the ancestral and the
contemporary, providing for its Mande
listeners a recognizable, living history,
and for everyone else rich insight into
the culture of a once-glorious empire.

From Sunjata[1]

The Search for a Special Wife

When Maghan Konfara[2] was a *mansa* in Manden, he had power, he had wealth,
he was popular, and he had *dalilu*—but he had no child. Maghan Konfara, Sunjata's father, craved a child. Though his friends had begun to have children, he
still had no child. But then his *dalilu*[3] showed that he would finally have a child.
His *moriw*,[4] his sand diviners, and his pebble diviners[5] all said, "Simbon, you will
sire a child who will be famous." Everybody he consulted said the same thing.
"But try to marry a light-skinned woman," they told him. "If you marry a light-
skinned woman, she will give birth to the child that has been foreseen." Because
Maghan Konfara was powerful, he married nine light-skinned women. But aside

---

1. Translated from the Maninka by David C.
Conrad. All notes were made by the translator
unless otherwise indicated. In an excerpted
section, the narrator, Tassey Condé, introduces
the birth of the seventh king (*mansa*) Sunjata
by recalling the lineage of kings born before
Sunjata. He declares that he will not start from
the very beginning since the listeners and the
Mande people are all Adam's descendants.
2. Maghan Knofara is the father of Sunjata,
also referred to as Simbon (Master Hunter)
and *Mansa* (ruler) [editor's note].

3. Magic, occult, or secret power; in everyday
use, any means used to achieve a goal.
4. Nominal Muslims who, in oral tradition,
often perform divination.
5. Seers and healers who identify the source
of all kinds of problems by spreading a pile of
sand and reading symbols in it, or casting multiple objects such as pebbles or cowrie shells
and reading the configurations in which they
land. Diviners then prescribe appropriate sacrifices to remedy the problem.

from Flaba Naabi, none of them gave him a child. He was perplexed. From the last Wednesday of the month of Jomènè[6] to the same time the following year, Maghan Konfara did not sire a child. (If you want to know about Sunjata, then you have to learn what Sunjata's father and the people of Manden had to endure!)

He sent the *moriw* back into retreat, telling them, "I need a child, so do your best. It's said that if I sire the child that has been foreseen, that child will rule Manden. I must sire this child." The *moriw*, all of whom were present, went back into retreat. When they returned, they told him, "Simbon, marry somebody who is a mulatto." So he married nine mulatto women. But aside from Marabajan Tarawelé, none of those mulatto women gave birth. From that time of the year to the same time the following year, none of those women who were with him in the house bore any male children. Simbon was frustrated. Maghan Konfara sent the *moriw* back into retreat. He said, "Tell me the truth. Ah! If you see that I will not have any children, tell me. A child is something that only God can provide; it cannot be bought in the market." This time the *moriw* told him, "Very well, marry a black woman. Find a black woman who has a white heart." This time he married nine black women. But aside from Nyuma Damba Magasuba, none of them bore any children.

Maghan Konfara was frustrated. His *moriw* told him again, "Very well, man, free one of your slave girls and marry her." (In those days they still practiced slavery.) He liberated and married nine slave girls. But aside from Jonmusoni Manyan, none of the slave girls bore him any children. Frustrated, Simbon gathered the people of Konfara together on the last Wednesday of Jomènè.

When the people of Konfara had gathered, he separated the *moriw*, the sand diviners, and the pebble diviners into groups and sent them all into retreat. He said, "I told you not to hesitate. If you see that I won't have a child, tell me. Go into the house. If you do not tell me the truth, I'll kill all of you and replace you." When the *moriw* came out of retreat, they told him, "Simbon, you will sire a child. Make one of your *jelimusow*[7] happy. Marry her so she will give birth." He made nine *jelimusow* happy, but aside from Tunku Manyan Diawara, none of them ever gave birth.

Now all of Manden was frustrated. (It's hard to give birth to a child who will be famous!) And when all of Manden became frustrated, the diviners were ashamed of themselves. They met and swore an oath: "Any one of us who has broken a taboo should confess it. Maybe this is our fault. If we don't get together and tell this man the truth, the feet of our descendants will not be able to even break an egg in Manden." They went into retreat and came back out, telling Simbon, "Someone will come from the East. He will be coming from the land of the white-skinned people. This much has been revealed to us. Let this man pray to God for a solution to your problem. If you let this man pray to God on the matter of your son, anything he tells you will be God's word. We won't be able to accomplish this ourselves. God has shown us a good man."

While they waited there in Farakoro,[8] Manjan Bereté arrived. Manjan Bereté was the first Muslim leader of Manden; he opened the door[9] to the

---

6. The first month of the year.
7. Female bards (sing. *jelimuso*).
8. Sometimes shortened to "Farako." Evidently the hometown of Sunjata's father, located in the territory (*jamana*) of Konfura [editor's note]. Farakoro appears in the longer

version of Maghan Konfura's name, as he was known to Tassey Condé and his ancestral bards of Fadama: Farako Manko Farakonken.
9. That is, he was instrumental in the introduction of Islam.

Mande people. (He is also the ancestor of the Bereté in Manden. The home of the Bereté people is Farisini Hejaji,[1] a region in the land of Mecca; the Bereté are Suraka.[2]) Bereté packed up some books and came from Farisi to the land of Manden because it was a powerful place. If he found someone in the land of Manden who would join him, who would work with the Koran, then his blessings would be great. Because he could not get used to the food here, Manjan Bereté brought Sansun Bereté, his little sister, with him when he came to meet Simbon. He brought his sister so she could prepare his food until he became better acquainted with the Mande people.

Manjan Bereté came and lived with Simbon. He said, "You need the religion practiced in my homeland. The Prophet has said nobody should take up swords in the religion again, that we should now be gentle with one another. Let us win people over with kindness, so we can awaken their minds and they can join the religion. The blessings will be great for anyone who accomplishes this."

[*In an omitted passage, Konfara suggests that Bereté's sister is his destined wife. Bereté forbids this union, but his fathers and brothers convince him that Konfara can have his sister if he converts to Islam. Bereté's sister gives birth to a son, but it is not the foretold son.*]

Simbon said, "How do I get that son? Pray to God for me to have that son. Will I get that son?"

"Yes, you will get that son."

"Very well, pray to God for that."

Manjan Bereté prayed to God. He said, "Simbon, you will get this child. When I was praying, God revealed to me that there are others like me who will come. They too will come from the land of the white-skins. Those people will not bring any woman with them when they come. But they will tell you the name of the place that is their destination, and if you ask them to, they will bring you a woman from that place. She will bear that child."

[*In an omitted passage, the narrator describes the Moroccan background of two brothers, Abdu Karimi and Abdu Kassimu, who will travel to the land of Dò ni Kiri to hunt a buffalo that is devastating the countryside, and will eventually become known as Danmansa Wulanni and Danmansa Wulanba.*]

Two Hunters Arrive in Manden

Abdu Karimi and Abdu Kassimu came to Manden from Morocco. When they got here they walked all night and all the following day, and were already under the three *nkiliki* trees of Manden by the evening of that second day. When Abdu Karimi and Abdu Kassimu arrived under the trees, they measured out their food, cooked their meal, ate, and slept there.

(People used to rest under those three *nkiliki* trees when traveling to and from Dò ni Kiri, the home of the Condé. Travelers of Manden, from the home of the Mansaré, used to rest there, as did travelers from Negeboriya, the home of

---

1. "Farisi" is from Fars, a region in Persia. "Hejaji" is from Hejaz, a region that was the ancient cradle of Islam, including the Red Sea coast of Arabia and the cities of Mecca, Medina, and others.

2. A Maninka and Bamana term for the local perception of "Arab," which includes "Moors" and North Africans in general.

the Koroma. Travelers from Soso, from the home of the Kanté, also used to rest under those trees. People could get the news of the world there.)

Abdu Karimi and Abdu Kassimu, who were Arab *kamalenw*,[3] were worried, for they did not know where they were headed. They found a place where some traders had left their cooking pots. After eating, the Arab *kamalenw* said, "Let's lie down here and wait for these traders to return. We'll soon learn our next destination."

While Abdu Karimi and Abdu Kassimu were sleeping, some traders who were on their way from Manden arrived. Some traders also arrived from Negeboriya, home of the Koroma. They all greeted one another.

The Arab *kamalenw* asked, "Is everything all right with the people of Manden?"

The traders replied, "There is nothing wrong with them."

"Is everything all right with the Koroma of Negeboriya?"

The traders said, "Nothing is troubling them." They too measured out their food; then they went to sleep.

While the brothers were lying there, some traders who were on their way from Soso arrived. These traders had visited Dò ni Kiri and found it in turmoil. Upon meeting Abdu Karimi and Abdu Kassimu, they asked, "Where are you from?"

The *kamalenw* said, "We are from Morocco."

"Where are you going?"

The *kamalenw* replied, "We were on our way to the land of the Condé, but we don't know the way."

The traders said, "The *mansa* of Dò ni Kiri is Donsamogo Diarra; he is quarreling with his sister."

I just told you about this sister, called Dò Kamissa, the first daughter of Ma'an Solonkan. She and her brother, Donsamogo Diarra, were quarreling over the issue of the legacy left by Ma'an Solonkan, their mother.

Dò Kamissa said, "Donsamogo Diarra, if you refuse to share our mother's legacy with me, I'll take it myself."

The Condé elders said to her, "Go ahead and *try* to take a share for yourself; you are too headstrong."

"You think I can't take it for myself?"

"Yes, that's right." They did not know she had the power to transform herself into different things.

Dò Kamissa left the town and stayed in a farm hamlet near Dò ni Kiri. At that time, the place known as Dò ni Kiri included the twelve towns of Dò, the four towns of Kiri, and the six towns on the other side of the river. At the break of day, Dò Kamissa transformed herself into a buffalo and began to kill the people living in those places.

It became a bad time for Dò ni Kiri.

Donsamogo Diarra said, "This buffalo has killed all of the hunters that I requested from Manden." He sent a message to the Koroma of Negeboriya, but the buffalo killed all of the hunters who came from there. He sent for the hunters of Soso, but when they came the buffalo killed them all, too.

---

3. *Kamalenw*: plural form of *kamalen*, a circumcised youth 15–25 years old.

Donsamogo Diarra was at a loss. He sent out the word from Dò ni Kiri. He said, "People have died because of me. Anyone who kills this buffalo will get to choose a wife from three age sets[4] of Dò ni Kiri's girls." Everybody who visited Dò ni Kiri was told about this. And when the traders returned to the camp under the *nkiliki* tree, they told Abdu Karimi and Abdu Kassimu about the turmoil in Dò ni Kiri.

The traders said, "Things in Dò ni Kiri have become very bad. Donsamogo Diarra's quarrel with his sister has resulted in many deaths. Hunger has come to Kiri because no one can go in or out. The paths to the village and farms have been closed. There is no way for crops to be brought home, for the buffalo is blocking the way. The Condé say that anyone who kills this buffalo will get to choose a wife from three sets of Dò ni Kiri girls."

The Arab *kamalenw* were still camped there. The younger brother, Abdu Karimi, said, "Big brother, do you hear what they are saying?"

Abdu Kassimu replied, "I hear it."

Together they said, "Let us go to Dò ni Kiri."

The elder brother said, "Hey, little brother, what about these things they are talking about? Suppose the buffalo kills us?"

Abdu Karimi replied, "If the buffalo kills us, at least we'll die for the sake of the Condé. They are having a bad time in Dò ni Kiri. I feel bad for them. Remember how our fathers told us the story of the Condé ancestor Samasuna?[5] Before the Prophet could make any progress, God told him to fight at Kaïbara.[6] The Condé ancestor Samasuna took a thousand of his sons to go and help our ancestors fight at the battle of Kaïbara, and there he lost all thousand of his sons. No matter how difficult the fight at Dò ni Kiri will be, it can't be more difficult than the battle at Kaïbara.

"The thousand sons that the Condé ancestor Samasuna gave all died on the battleground of our ancestors' war at Kaïbara. If the two of us should die for the sake of the Condé, will our deaths be equal to the deaths of those thousand men? If it's our time to die, we should die for a good cause. We do not equal a thousand men. But if we should die for the sake of the Condé, we will only be doing what the thousand men did for those ancestors. So let us go to Dò ni Kiri. Knowing what the Condé ancestors suffered for our sake at Kaïbara, we would be bastards if we retreated now, after hearing that the Condé are suffering." Thus Abdu Karimi encouraged his elder brother.

Abdu Kassimu now had the courage to go to Dò ni Kiri. But first the brothers packed their belongings and went straight to Konfara. They bypassed Dò ni Kiri and went straight to Manden.

When the brothers arrived in Manden, Manjan Bereté was sitting in a circle near Maghan Konfara. The two men were playing *wari*.[7] Manjan Bereté was sitting in the circle near Simbon, with prayer beads in his hands, praying to God:

---

4. Children born within the same span of about three years are identified as a single group or age set that grows up together, going through the various initiation rituals into adulthood.
5. Samson (Shamsūn in Arabic) is not mentioned in the Koran, but according to other sources of Muslim tradition (e.g., al-Tha'labi and al-Tabari), he dedicated his life to God and continually fought against idolators.

6. Maninka usage of Khaybar, an oasis ninety-five miles from Medina, Arabia, the site of a famous battle fought by the Prophet Muhammad and his army.
7. A popular game played with two rows of shallow holes, usually in a carved wooden board, with small stones or cowrie shells used as counters.

"May God not let me be embarrassed by my prediction." They remained sitting when they saw Abdu Karimi and Abdu Kassimu approaching. When the two brothers arrived, all of the men met in that same circle, and Manjan Bereté and Maghan Konfara stopped playing *wari*.

Abdu Karimi said, "My respected *karamogo*, we have come to God, we have come to the Mande people, and we have come to Simbon. What makes us walk fast will also make us talk fast."

After greeting the brothers, the Mande people asked them, "Where did you come from?"

The Arab *kamalenw* said, "We come from Morocco."

"What is your family?"

"We are Sharifu."[8]

The Mande people saluted them, "You Haidara,"[9] to which the *kamalenw* replied, "Marahaba."[1]

The Mande people said, "The honor is yours, the honor is Simbon's."

The Arab *kamalenw* said, "We come from Morocco. We are children of Abdu Sharifu. We are descendants of Saïdina Ali."[2]

The *kamalenw* explained, "We have heard that the Condé are suffering, that they are quarreling with their sister who has transformed herself into a buffalo. Every morning the buffalo has killed people in all of the twelve towns of Dò, the four towns of Kiri, and the six towns across the river. That is why we have come. We want to go to Dò ni Kiri, to help the Condé with their trouble. We want you to perform the sand divination for us. If our sand is sweet, we will go to Dò ni Kiri. And if our sand is not sweet, we will still go to Dò ni Kiri."

[*In an omitted passage, the narrator recounts that the sand is indeed sweet and a sacrifice must accompany the divination. Before the hunters leave, Maghan Konfara asks for a wife but the younger brother refuses. The narrator introduces the buffalo's female genie companion, who advises the brothers on how to respond to abusive women they will meet, and how to approach Dò Kamissa, the Buffalo Woman, and avoid being killed by her.*]

Dò Kamissa the Buffalo Woman

After walking for one kilometer, the brothers passed into the land of Konfara, and from there crossed into the land of the Condé. There they met a woman who had borne one child, just as the female genie had told them. The genie had said, "You will not see me again. But if you don't heed the advice I give you, the buffalo will kill you."

When they greeted this woman who had borne one child, she spoke abusively to them. She said, "Eh! Is it the woman who should greet first, or is it the man?

8. Contraction of the longer plural form Sharifulu from the Arabic Shurafa' (sing. Sharīf), a lineage claiming descent from the family of the Prophet Muhammad.
9. A prestigious Muslim family name in Manden, here used in a greeting as the equivalent of Sharifu.
1. Response to a greeting that honors people by saluting their ancestors with the family name

or *jamu* (patronymic, identity). From Arabic *mrehba* ("welcome").
2. 'Alī ibn Abī Tālib, cousin and son-in-law of the Prophet Muhammad, and one of the first converts to Islam; renowned as a warrior during Islam's struggle for survival, he took part in most of the Prophet's expeditions and displayed legendary courage at the battles of Badr and Khaybar.

You do not pass by a beautiful woman without greeting her!" She said every possible bad word to them.

They said, "M'ba.[3] We are children of the road. We do not know anything
about women or men. We have never been to this country. We speak to everyone
we meet, so they can help us."

She replied, "Am I the one who is supposed to help you?"

Huh! They passed on by her without quarreling further.

After they passed that woman, they walked another kilometer and met the
full-breasted girl. When they met this girl they said, "Lady, we greet you, God
is great."

Ah! She abused them. She said every bad word to them.

The younger brother said, "Aaah, you do not understand. A beautiful woman
like you will pass by a man like that? You do not know what is happening." (No
matter how proud a girl is, once you call her "beautiful," she will soften.)

After the hunters passed by the full-breasted girl, she went on her way.
(Humility really comes only with death, but men act humbly until they get
what they want.)

After walking on for another kilometer, they heard the pounding of the mortars and pestles[4] of Dò ni Kiri, and there they met Dò Kamissa herself. She
carried a hoe on her shoulder and a walking staff served as her third leg.

When they said, "Greetings mother." Heeeh! She cursed their father. After
that, she cursed their grandfather. Then she cursed their mother.

"You are calling me mother? Was I the one who gave birth to your father or
your mother?" She said every bad word to them.

Abdu Karimi said, "Big brother, don't you think this lady resembles our mother?"

[*In an omitted passage, the brothers help the buffalo woman feed her chickens
before they arrive in Dò ni Kiri and are given lodging. They set out on their
plan, treating the buffalo woman as they would treat their mother. After three
failed attempts at forming a bond, she finally invites them into her home for a
conversation.*]

Dò Kamissa's Revelations

Dò Kamissa the Buffalo Woman said, "You have outdone me. No one can get the
better of people like you. You are polite. You were brought up well. Eh! Despite
everything you were told, you were not discouraged. You favor me? Now I will
cooperate with you. Were it not for you, I would have wiped out Dò ni Kiri.

"You know that Donsamogo Diarra, with whom I am quarreling, is my brother.
I was the firstborn of my father's children. When I reached puberty, I said, 'My
Lord God, I will give the largest of the two gold earrings that are on my ears to
whoever brings me the news that my father has had a son. My Lord God, I will
also give the beautiful outer one of the two wrappers I am wearing to the person
that brings me such good news.' I was the first to offer a sacrifice for my brother.
So who does he think he is, telling me that women shouldn't have property? Huh!

---

3. Contraction of *marahaba*, a response to a
greeting that honors people by saluting their
ancestors with the family name or jamu (patronymic, identity). From Ar. mrehba ("welcome").

4. The mortar is a large wooden receptacle in
which women pound grain with a heavy,
wooden, dub-shaped pestle that can be as long
as five feet.

"I would have wiped out Donsamogo's entire lineage. But you Sharifu, you have outdone me. I will cooperate with you and give you my life, for I know that if you kill me, you will bury me; you will not let my body go to God as a bad body.

"Before I give myself up to you, though, I will ask you to do three things for me. If you agree to do those three things, then I will cooperate with you. But if you do not agree to those three things, I will keep after you until you do."

The *kamalenw* said, "Ma, tell us the three things you want us to do for you."

She said, "Here's the first: Don't go to town immediately after killing the buffalo; come to this hamlet instead. You'll find me dead. Because I am the only one who knows what I have done,[5] my brother must not see my corpse. When you arrive here, you'll see that I have poured water on the fire. There will be a hoe; there will also be an axe. Take the axe and cut down a *toro* tree. Take the hoe and dig my grave. After you have laid me in it, fire the musket. At no point can my brother, my father's son, see my body; nor can my body be carried to Dò ni Kiri. I have not done any good for them. I have wiped out their children, I have wiped out their wives, I have widowed their husbands; this is all my doing.

"That's the first thing you must do. Now, you know that whoever kills me will be rewarded with the choice of a wife from three sets of Dò ni Kiri's girls. The second thing you must do for me is refuse all of the fine young girls they bring out for you. Do not choose any of those girls as your wife, because they would be forcing my father's last-born to remain in the house. Five sets of girls have gone to their husbands, but she has not married, and if you do not marry her, she will never be married. She holds something special in her breast for whoever marries her. You, Sharifu, must marry her.

"She is very ugly. She's the 'Short Sogolon' you've heard about, the one who is so very ugly. I damaged one of her tear ducts and now her eyes water all the time. Her head is bald, she has a humped back, her feet are twisted, and when she walks, she limps this way and that. I, Dò Kamissa, did all of that to her.

"How could I make her so ugly when I loved her so much? I put my far-seeing mask[6] on her face before she was old enough to wear it, and, in doing so, cut her tear duct, caused her hair to fall out, and put a hump on her back. By putting her on my sorcery horse when she was too young, I twisted her feet, stretched her tendons, and made her knock-kneed. All of this is my fault. I take the blame, and if she does not get married, it will be my curse.

"So, when the men of Dò ni Kiri bring those beautiful Condé women to you, do not accept any of them. Choose my father's last-born. Some call her 'Humpbacked Sogolon.' Some call her 'Ugly Sogolon.' Everybody used to call her whatever they felt like. But the real name of that last-born child is Sogolon Wulen Condé. There will be something special in her breast for you because she'll have all the *dalilu*.[7]

"If you choose her over all the beautiful daughters they offer you and are not satisfied with the way she looks, then cut off the buffalo's tail when you kill it. The tail is heavy with gold and silver, because I took the gold and silver earrings

5. Contrary to what the narrator has previously indicated.
6. A magic object allowing the wearer to see unimaginable distances. The concept might have entered oral tradition when Europeans were observed using telescopes and binoculars,

but there also could have been an indigenous mask imbued with such power.
7. The mother's physical deformities signal her possession of special occult powers that she will pass on to her child.

of every Dò ni Kiri woman I killed and hung them from the hair of my tail. I have a lot of hair on my tail, and it is heavy with the gold and silver ear jewelry of the Dò ni Kiri women. If you exchange some of that gold, you can go and marry a beautiful woman somewhere else, a wife to have along with Sogolon Condé. But do not refuse to take Sogolon! Then there will be no problems. Will you do this, or not?"

The Sharifu said, "We agree to that."

She said, "That is the second thing you must do. Here's the third thing: the dead buffalo's carcass must not be taken to the town."

"Eh, Condé woman! We have agreed to your other demands, but we might not be able to do this. What if we can't convince the people of Dò ni Kiri not to take the carcass back to town? What if they force us? We'll be powerless to fight them off or to take the carcass from them."

"Oh, you will do your best to heed what I have said. If you can do the other things, then forget about that last request. But you must respect my other two wishes."

"Very well."

As the brothers were about to leave, she said to them, "Sit down." Once they were sitting, she said, "The weapons you brought won't do anything to me. The arrows and quivers you brought won't do anything either. I am in control of my own life."

She put her hand in her basket of cleaned cotton, pulled out the spindle, and handed it to them. Then, putting her hand in her storage basket, she took out the distaff that usually holds the thread, and gave it to them, saying, "Put this in your bow and shoot the buffalo with it. It will stop the buffalo. If you do not shoot the buffalo with it—if you shoot a big arrow at the buffalo instead—then the buffalo will kill you."

[*In an omitted passage, Dò Kamissa provides the brothers with various enchanted objects that will help them kill her buffalo wraith.*]

Death of the Buffalo

The brothers left the town and went into the bush, past the lake of Dò ni Kiri and into the forest. They crossed another open space and entered more forest. There, before going any further, they saw the buffalo.

(Before they came to the bush that day, the brothers' name was Sharifu. But afterwards they were called Diabaté or Tarawèlè. They left their Sharifu identity behind in Manden[8] and came to be known as Tarawèlè and Diabaté. We will soon come to the reason for this.)

There was the buffalo. Abdu Karimi, the younger brother, said to Abdu Kassimu, "Big brother! You should be the one to take the magic dart and shoot the buffalo, because the killing of this buffalo will make history. The person who kills this buffalo will be mentioned in all of the future generations' histories, right up until the trumpet is blown on Judgment Day. You are my big brother, so you kill the buffalo."

---

8. Only after the buffalo is mortally wounded does Tassey begin to use the names by which the brothers are usually known, Danmansa Wulanni and Danmansa Wulanba. These prob-ably originated as praise names based on the brothers' exploits, e.g., Danmansa Wulanba can be roughly translated as "Big Lord of the Solitary Forest Buffalo".

Abdu Kassimu said, "Little brother, a job must be left to the experts. Yes, I was the first to be born. But I know what *dalilu* you have—and I know you must be the one to kill the buffalo." He handed the magic dart to his younger brother.

Abdu Karimi told his elder brother to go on ahead. Crawling through the grass, Abdu Karimi came ever closer to the buffalo. He remembered what the old woman had told him: that he should not try to kill the buffalo until he was in its shadow. She'd said, "Do not miss me! If you miss the buffalo, I'll kill you." The younger brother crawled until he reached the buffalo's shadow. He took the distaff and put it on the spindle. He pulled the string of his bow back, back, back, he pulled it still harder, and he could feel that he had something very powerful in his hand. When he'd pulled the bowstring back to his shoulder, he let the spindle go, *pow!* It shot right into the buffalo's chest.

The buffalo was startled when the spindle pierced its chest. It raised its head, saw Abdu Karimi, and bellowed, *hrrr!* And there, while he was still right beside the wounded buffalo, Abdu Karimi told his elder brother, "Run!" for the buffalo had been shot and the struggle between them had begun.

(It's said that greatness will not be acquired without hardship. We've been telling you about the hardship Manden had to endure before the country could know peace. Sunjata would not have been born without this hardship, and without Sunjata, Manden would never have been sweet. And if Manden was never sweet, we Mande people would never have known ourselves!)

Bellowing, the buffalo began to chase the *kamalenw*, it came up behind Abdu Karimi, who was trying to catch up with his elder brother. Abdu Karimi dropped the bamboo stick, which instantly sprouted into a grove of bamboo, and before the buffalo could get through it, the *kamalenw* were far ahead.

Once it was clear of the bamboo, the buffalo started chasing them again. When it came up behind them and bellowed, the brothers dropped the hot charcoal. In those days, the Mande bush had been there a long time and had never been burned. So when the *kamalenw* dropped the hot charcoal, the bush caught on fire, stopping the buffalo and forcing it back while they dashed ahead through the grass.

When the fire died out, the buffalo jumped into the ashes and started chasing them again. But by the time it reached them and bellowed, they were already at the lake of Dò ni Kiri. There Abdu Karimi dropped the egg, which turned the ground into deep mud. The buffalo got stuck in the mud. (This is the mud referred to in the Condé song "Dala Kombo Kamba":

> "Condé drinker of big lake water,
> Those who drank the big lake water,
> They did not stop to clean it.
> Those who clean the big lake,
> They did not drink its big water."

It was Danmansa Wulanba and Danmansa Wulanni[9] who cleaned the water of the big lake.)

By the time the mud started to dry, it was too late for the buffalo: the spindle wounds were letting water into its intestines, and it fell down. When the buffalo fell, Danmansa Wulanni said, "Big brother, look behind you! The buffalo has fallen."

---

9. The elder brother is Wulanba, the younger Wulanni.

A new family lineage was created at the moment the elder brother looked back and saw that the buffalo was dying. Going back, he put his foot on the buffalo's body. He said, "Ah, little brother! You have given me a name. Ah, little brother! You were sired by Abdu Mutulu Budulaye, Abdu Mutulu Babatali. Aba Alibi's own son is Sedina Alia, to whom God gave a sword, and you were sired by Alia. Sedina Alia's son is Hassana Lonsani, and you were sired by him. Hassana Lonsani's son is Sissi; Sissi's son is Kèmo; Kèmo's son is Kèmomo Tènè; Kèmo Tènè's son is Sharifu—and you were sired by Sharifu. Aah, Karimi! You have given us names."

After hearing this praise, the younger brother said, "Eh, big brother! If you were a praise-singer or *jeli*, no one could surpass you (*i jèmba tè*)!"

That was the beginning of the *jeli* family known as Diabaté;[1] that was the origin of the lineage. "Diabaté" was first said in Manden, in the Mande language, when the buffalo was killed in the bush.

Once the buffalo was dead, the brothers saw that its tail was heavy with gold and silver.

In cutting off the buffalo's tail, the brothers were able to take for themselves all of the gold and silver in its hair. The *kamalenw* were also able to use the tail as proof that they really had killed the buffalo. As soon as they showed the tail, people knew that the business was finished, because the tail of Dò Kamissa's buffalo wraith could only be cut off if the buffalo was dead. Ahuh! (And this was the beginning of the custom of removing the tails of dead game.)

[*In an omitted passage, Danmansa Wulanba and Danmansa Wulanni try to respect Dò Kamissa's wish that her wraith be buried in the bush, but the townspeople insist on retrieving the buffalo carcass and dragging it into town to be desecrated.*]

Sogolon Wulen Condé of Dò Ni Kiri

After the buffalo was dead, the people of Dò ni Kiri started beating the ceremonial drum. All of the people living in the twelve towns of Dò, the four towns of Kiri, and the six towns across the river were expected to attend, and they all came. When the twenty-two towns were all present, the people said, "What did we say? We said that we'll bring out three age sets of girls for the hunter that kills this buffalo, and that he can choose any girl from among them to be his wife. Bring your daughters forward." (Huh! If you bring out three age sets of daughters from twenty-two towns, you should bring out the oldest set first, then the next oldest, then the youngest set.)

The villagers brought out the beautiful Condé girls, formed them into three circles, and told the boys to choose. The people said, "Even if you choose ten or twenty girls, they will be your wives. Or if you choose only one girl, she will be your wife. You have delivered us from disaster! And everyone here wants to have their daughters married to you two boys.

1. The singing or chanting of praises is an occupational specialty of *jeliw*. This is a popular etymology explaining how the Diabaté *jeliw* acquired their family name. When the younger brother killed the buffalo and the elder brother praised his courage by reciting their family genealogy, this was the way a *jeli* would do it. When the younger brother said. "no one could surpass you," the phrase *jèmba tè* evolved through repetition into "Diabaté" which, along with "Kouyaté" is one of the two names exclusive to traditional bards.

"You Sharifu, we don't go back on our promises. Take a look at these girls, and take any one that pleases you." The two men followed one another, walking around, around, around the circle. When they had returned to where they started they said, "Where are the rest of the girls?"

The Condé ancestor said, "You young men search every house, so that no one can hide his daughter."

The villagers searched the entire town but found no other girls. Everybody wanted to marry their daughter to the brothers!

When the searchers returned they said, "There is nobody left."

A bystander said, "What about the bad old woman who was just killed? She has her father's last-born still in her house."

Somebody said, "Eeh, man! Heeeye, can we show that one to the strangers?"

Danmansa Wulanni said, "Go and get that woman you're talking about. Has she been married to another man?"

They said, "No."

"Has she been married before?"

"No."

The brothers said, "Well, if she is unmarried, go get her."

The people said, "Out of five age sets of girls that have found husbands, only she has remained unmarried."

The brothers said, "If she is an unmarried girl, go get her."

Ma Dò Kamissa had told them that the door of Sogolon Wulen Condé's father's house was the one facing the town's meeting ground. She'd also told them, "When Sogolon is coming from my father's house to go into the town meeting ground, a little black cat will come from behind her and pass in front of her; the little black cat will go from in front of her and pass behind her. If you see that happening to anyone, then you'll know that she is the girl I am talking about."

They sent for Sogolon, and as she was being brought out of the house—just as she reached the edge of the town meeting ground—a black cat came from behind her and passed in front of her; it went from in front of her and passed behind her.

As soon as the brothers saw Sogolon, they said, "This is the one we've been talking about."

They heard people go, "Wooo!"

They were asked, "Is this really the one you were talking about?"

To which the brothers replied, "Yes, this is the one we have been talking about."

Ancestor Donsamogo Diarra said to them, "You Sharifu, is this the one you want?"

To which they replied, "Yes, this is the one we want."

"Are you *sure* this is the one you want?"

"This is the one we want."

He said, "This one is even more powerful than my sister, whom you killed, and you know how much *dalilu* she had. This one has *really* powerful *dalilu*. But if you say that you want her, I'll give her to you. Go ahead and take her with you. If you're not compatible, just bring her back. I'll return her to where you found her, and I'll give you another wife.

"Now, I don't want to contradict myself, but just take another look at these other girls. We'll give you up to three months. If, after three months, you're not compatible with my sister, come back and I will give you one of these girls. I will put my sister back where she came from."

The brothers said, "Very well."

She was Sogolon, the woman who was given to them, the mother of Simbon. Simbon, whose birth was foretold and who united Manden—this is the child about to be born. We can talk about Turama'an, we can talk about Kankejan, or of Tombonon Sitafa Diawara, of Fakoli, Sumaworo, or of Tabon Wana Faran Kamara; but the one who organized them all, united them into one place and called it Manden, well, the person who did all those things was Sunjata, and this is how his mother was married.

[*In an omitted passage, both brothers try to consummate the marriage but are unsuccessful. They reach Konfara and offer Sogolon to Maghan Konfara. While Simbon prepares for their meeting, the community shows the new bride a mixed welcome. At the threshold of the new couple's home, Sogolon and Konfara test each other with three magical back-and-forth attacks before Sogolon acquiesces to her role as a traditional bride. On their wedding night, she uses sorcery to watch the other women dancing, making them wary of her.*]

Sogolon was still a virgin when she came to Maghan Konfara. After three days, her bloody virgin cloth was taken out. The following month, she became pregnant with Sunjata. That is how Sunjata was conceived.

The co-wives said, "We won't be able to do anything against this woman." She had gone to her husband almost at the end of the lunar month, and for the rest of that month, she did not see the other moon. She had conceived.

When the women of Manden heard this, they went outside the town and held a meeting under a baobab tree. They said, "Getting pregnant is one thing, delivering is another. Make miscarriage medicine, anything that will spoil the belly with a touch. Everyone must prepare her own."

Sogolon Condé also had very powerful *dalilu*. When her belly started to expand, the other wives would visit her, saying, "Younger sister, this is the medicine we use here in Manden for pregnant women. Aah, all of the women here wanted a child, but we have not been able to conceive. You may be the lucky one bearing our husband's child—but the child belongs to all of us. Here, M'ma,[2] dilute this medicine in water and drink it."

Heh, Sogolon, the Condé woman, diluted that medicine in water and drank it. She drank it and drank it, for seven years. And each time she drank it, her belly would shrink away, *jè!*

After seven years of this, Sogolon Condé went outside the town.

She prayed to God. She said, "M'mari! That is enough! Enough of what those Mande people have done to me. I come to you, God. I am only a stranger here, and the men who brought me here cannot help."

[*In an omitted passage, the narrator describes his own family's relationship with characters in the narrative, and with ancestors from Arab tradition.*]

---

2. Affectionate greeting to a woman, equivalent to the masculine "M'ba" [editor's note].

The Childhood of Ma'an Sunjata

God made Ma'an Sunjata into a person, made him into a human fetus and brought him into the world.

When the Mande women heard the news of Ma'an Sunjata's birth, they again gathered together under the Mande baobab tree. They said, "It is one thing to give birth to a son, but another thing for him to survive."

Then what did they do to him? Through sorcery they stretched the tendons of his two feet. They lamed him and forced him to crawl on the ground for one year!

Two years!
Three years!
Four years!
Five years!
Six years!

Then, in Sunjata's seventh year, the co-wives provoked Sogolon to anger. (Because we are walking on a straight path, we cannot wander from one side to the other. We have to take the main road, so we will know how Manden was built.)

One day, in Sunjata's seventh year, Maramajan Tarawèlè was picking some leaves from the same baobab tree that we've already mentioned. As Maramajan Tarawèlè was on her way back to the villiage, Ma Sogolon Wulen Condé, who was sitting under the eaves of the house she shared with Ma'an Sunjata, asked, "Big sister Maramajan Tarawèlè, won't you give me a few of your baobab leaves?"

Maramajan Tarawèlè said, "Ah! Younger sister, you are the only one of us to have a son. Why would you ask us for baobab leaves? Your lame son is sitting right there inside the house. If you want baobab leaves, why don't you tell your son to stand up and go get some?"

Ma Sogolon Wulen Condé said, "Ah, that is not what I meant. I thought I could depend on the help of my sisters. I didn't know you were upset because I had this child."

The two women didn't know Sunjata was listening to them.

Afterwards, when Ma Sogolon Condé walked by, Sunjata said, "Mother! Mother!" She did not answer because she knew he had overheard them.

He said, "Mother, what are they saying?"

"Forget about that talk."

"Ah, how can I ignore that? Mother, I'll walk today. They insult you by saying you have a lame person in your house, and yet you beg them for a baobab leaf? I'll walk today. Go and get my father's *sunsun*[3] staff, and bring it to me. I'll walk today."

Ma Sogolon Condé went and got the *sunsun* staff and brought it to Simbon. When he attempted to stand by thrusting the *sunsun* staff firmly into the ground and holding on to it, the *sunsun* staff broke.

Sunjata said to Sogolon, "Ah, mother. They say you have a lame son in the house, but you gave birth to a real son. Nothing happens before its time. Go and bring my father's iron staff." But when she gave him the iron staff, he broke it, too.

3. An extremely hard wood called "false ebony" or "West African ebony" [editor's note].

He said, "Go and tell my father's blacksmith to forge an iron staff so I can walk." The blacksmith carried one load of iron to the bellows, forged it, and made it into an iron staff. But when Sunjata thrust that iron staff into the ground and tried to stand, the staff bent. (That iron staff, the one they say was bent by Sunjata into a bow, is now in Narena.)

Sunjata broke both of his father's staffs and an iron one that was forged for him. Therefore, when he stood, he did it on his own, first lifting one foot, then the other foot, then the other one, and so on.

His mother said, "Simbon has walked!"

The *jeliw* sang this song:

> "Has walked,
> Jata has walked.
> Has walked,
> Jata has walked."

Thus it was his mother's rivalry with her co-wives, and their humiliation of her, that caused Jata to walk. (That is why I can't believe it when I hear people saying they do not love their mother! Heh! Jelimoril[4] Your father belongs to everyone, but your mother belongs only to you. When you meet people for the first time, they don't ask you about your father; they ask about your mother.)

After that, God gave Sunjata feet. Sunjata went into the house, took his father's bow and quiver, and left town. (Some people say he made the bent iron staff into his bow, but don't repeat that.)

When he reached the baobab tree, he shook it, uprooted it, and put it on his shoulder. He carried it into his mother's yard and said, "Now everyone will come here for baobab leaves."

So it was that when the Mande women next saw Sogolon they said, as they picked the baobab leaves, "Aah, Sogolon Condé! We knew this would happen for you. The prayers and sacrifices we made on your behalf have been answered." (Now, when you are having a hard time, everyone abuses you. But when things are going well for you, people say, "We knew this would happen for you." May God help us persevere!)

Sogolon eventually had three more children. After So'olon Ma'an was born— but before he could walk—his younger brother So'olon Jamori was born. Then, while So'olon Ma'an was still crawling on the ground, Manden Bori was born. Finally after So'olon Ma'an walked, So'olon Kolonkan was born.

[*In an omitted passage, Sunjata's enemies conspire with nine sorceresses to kill him, but one sorceress warns him and reveals that the sorceresses agreed to kill him only because the reward is a dead bull and the sorceresses crave meat. Sunjata suggests that he provide the meat instead and that they spare his life. He upholds his end of the compromise and the sorceresses vow that no female, human or animal or otherwise, will ever hurt him. Dankaran Tuman and his mother conspire to have Sunjata murdered in his sleep. Meanwhile, Sunjata spends a rainy day playing the hunter's harp while he waits for the weather to change so he can go hunting.*]

---

4. During performances, *jeliw* occasionally speak to people in the audience, commenting on something in the narrative.

Mistaken Murder and the Question of Exile

As So'olon Ma'an waited for the rain to stop so he could go hunting, he sat in his hammock with his six-stringed hunter's harp and sang to himself. (His younger brothers Manden Bori and So'olon Jamori were also harp players.) After playing "Kulanjan"[5] for a while, Sunjata changed tunes and played "Sori."[6]

Some youths passing by So'olon Ma'an's door heard him singing in a low, sweet voice and stopped in his door to listen. One of these youths was an apprentice hunter. He said, "I will listen to Sunjata until the rain stops."

While the youth stood at the door, Sunjata put some snuff into his mouth. When the snuff was wet, he stopped playing the harp and went to spit out the door, where he noticed the young man. Sunjata said, "Who's there?"

The youth said, "Brother So'olon Ma'an, it is me."

"Ah, what are you doing here?"

"Your brother sent a message that we should bring him some food and supplies. So that's what I'm doing. But it is raining, and a slave with wet clothes does not enter the house of his betters. I am an apprentice hunter at the farm. I stopped under your eaves when I heard your music. Let me keep listening to you until the rain stops."

(Meanwhile, the musket[7] of conspiracy was being loaded in town.)

So'olon Ma'an said to the youth, "Come into the house."

The young man entered the house and sat on the edge of the bed. Simbon was playing the harp. When he played certain parts, the young man would tap his feet, because the harp music was so sweet. But the youth was also tired, and the warm room felt good to him. He became sleepy and started to nod. Ma'an Sunjata told him, "Lie on the bed." When the young man was asleep on the bed, Simbon stood up and covered the young man with a blanket. When the rain stopped, Sunjata—who forgot about the young man sleeping there—stood up, put on his crocodile-mouth hat, took his hunter's hammock, his quiver, bow, and fly whisk,[8] shut the front door, and went out the back. Taking a deep breath, he went into the bush.

While Simbon was in the bush, Dankaran Tuman came and stood under the eaves of the house, where he heard the young man snoring. He did not know that Ma'an Sunjata had left the house.

Dankaran Tuman went and told the seven young men, "Didn't I tell you that Sunjata sleeps anytime it rains into the evening? He's sleeping now; go get your clubs."

After getting their clubs, the seven young men came to Simbon's door. But they were afraid of him. To each other they said, "Man, don't you know who So'olon Ma'an is? One man can't outdo him, two men can't outdo him, even the

5. One of the oldest melodies in the bards' repertory; often dedicated to hunters, Sumaworo is praised as "Kulanjan."
6. A lesser-known melody dedicated to hunters.
7. Maninka *morifa*. The first firearms did not arrive in West Africa until the 16th century, but the *jeliw* frequently speak of muskets in the time of Sunjata. Linear chronology is not a pressing issue in their views of the distant past,

but what is of interest is the imagery of a formidable weapon and a hero's power to repel any iron projectile.
8. Ideally made from the tail of a dangerous wild animal and possibly symbolizing the one cut from the slain Buffalo of Dò, although elephant tails were highly prized for this essential hunters' device carrying occult protective qualities.

seven of us together can't outdo him. When we go in, listen carefully for the sound of his breathing, and be sure to hit him on the head. If we only hit him on the back, he'll be sure to capture us." They went in and surrounded the young man. When they located the source of his breathing, they raised their clubs and hit him on the head. They beat him until his body went cold.

When the body was cold, they left to tell Dankaran Tuman that they'd finished the work he had given them. Dankaran Tuman told his mother, "Ahah, Mother. The bad thing is now off our backs. He is dead." (No matter how good you think you are, you'll always do something bad to your enemy!)

"Eh! Dankaran Tuman," she said, "has he died?"

"Yes! The son of the Condé woman has died today!"

"Ah, my son! Now I will not be the failure in my husband's home. Now my heart is cool. If you have killed Ma'an Sunjata, *aagba*! Manden Bori and So'olon Jamori can't stand up to you. The only brother I was worried about has been killed."

They did not sleep that night.

Sansun Bereté said, "Heee, just wait until Sogolon Condé knows about this."

When day broke, Dankaran Tuman and his mother went to spy on Sogolon.

"Huh!" they whispered. "Don't say or do anything! When he's slept for a long time, his mother will go and open the door on him."

Sansun Bereté said, "If you don't say anything, no one will guess that you are the one who killed him."

As the soft morning sun rose on them, they saw Sunjata, Danama Yirindi[9]— yes, the son of the Condé woman—walking along, carrying three dead animals; one was hanging over his left shoulder, one was hanging over his right shoulder, and one was on his head.

When they saw him, Sansun Bereté said, "Dankaran Tuman! Didn't you say that Sunjata was dead?"

Dankaran Tuman replied, "Mother, we really killed him."

"Then who is this coming? Who is coming?"

"It is Sunjata who is coming."

When they saw that it really was Sunjata, Dankaran Tuman peed in his pants.

Walking up to them, Sunjata said to Sansun Bereté, "Big mother, here is some wild game for you." Then, laying another animal before his step-brother, he said, "Big brother, here is one for you."

There was nothing they could say.

Sunjata carried the last animal to his mother's place and said, "Mother, here is your animal."

His mother said, "Ah, my son, thank you."

When he returned to his house and pushed the door open, there were flies all over the stinking body—wooooo!

Sunjata shouted, "Mother, Mother! Come here! I'll kill someone today. Ever since I was born, I've never done anything bad like this. My brother did this, and I'll take revenge."

Ma Sogolon Condé came to the door.

Sunjata said, "You see this? I went to the bush and forgot about the young man you see lying here. My brother's men beat him to death with their clubs. I'll kill

---

9. A praise-name for Sunjata that can be translated as "superhero."

for this young man. I know this is Dankaran Tuman's boy, but he died my death. I'll prove to them that I am not the one who died."

Ma Sogolon Condé knew that Konfara would be destroyed by So'olon Ma'an's revenge, because he would kill anyone known to be one of Dankaran Tuman's supporters.

Sunjata dashed out of the house. When he reached for his iron staff, his mother ran and called Jelimusoni Tunku Manyan Diawara.

Sogolon said, "Sunjata is going to kill someone right now if you don't stop him."

Jelimusoni Tunku Manyan Diawara went and took hold of Simbon.

She said, "Simbon, won't you think about your mother? Simbon! Won't you think of me? Won't you leave this to God? Don't you realize that Dankaran Tuman has poked himself in the eye?" Sunjata tried and tried to break away, but she would not let go. Ha! She was able to hold him.

Then Ma Sogolon Condé said, "My son Sunjata, your popularity is your biggest problem. If they have started murdering people because of you, shouldn't we go away?"

This is why they went into exile. (One never sells his father's homeland, but it can be pawned!)

Departure for Exile

[*In an omitted passage, Sunjata repeatedly refuses to flee from his step-brother, but Sogolon argues that neither he nor Dankaran Tuman can understand the special circumstances of her background in Dò ni Kiri and how she was brought to their father because of Sunjata's destiny. She convinces Sunjata that even if they go away, he will eventually take over the leadership of Manden.*]

Ma Sogolon Condé then set out to visit Sansamba Sagado, the Somono[1] ancestor. (This is the Sansamba Sagado you always hear about in the histories of Manden. He was involved with the organization of Manden, and those towns along the bank of the river—Jelibakoro, Sansando, and Baladugu—are populated with his Mande descendants. If you talk about Manden without talking about Sansamba Sagado, you have not covered the subject of Manden.)

Saying, "Sansamba Sagado," Sogolon removed her silver wrist and ankle bracelets and gave them to the Somono ancestor as the price for a future river crossing. This way, he would take her children across the river whenever they needed to cross, at any time of day or night, without anybody in Manden knowing that he'd done so.

The days passed. Then, one day, at three o'clock in the morning, Sogolon woke up her children and said, "The time has come for what we talked about."

They left together. When they came to the riverbank, she took the path to Sansamba Sagado's house. Waking him, she said, "This is the day we talked about."

He was not a man to break his promise. Taking his bamboo pole and his paddle, he left to meet Sogolon and her children in the bushes by the bank of the river. The water was rising; it nearly touched the leaves on the bushes. Sansamba

---

1. Maninka- or Bamana-speaking specialists in fishing, canoeing, boating, and the water-borne transport of people and goods.

Sagado's canoe was attached to a *npeku* tree; he untied it and brought it to them, saying, "Get in!"

Ma Sogolon Condé, her daughter Ma Kolonkan, Manden Bori, and So'olon Jamori got into the canoe. But when they told Sunjata to get in, he refused.

Ma Sogolon Condé said, "Ah, Sunjata! Do you want to make me suffer?"

He said, "Mother, if I told you that I will go with you, then I will go. You take the canoe now; I will join you later."

They crossed the river in the canoe, and before they could reach the other side, they saw Sunjata sitting on the bank. He had brought his *dalilu* with him.

A Visit to Soso

[*In an omitted passage, Sogolon decides to stop in Soso to ask for the help of Sumaworo, a powerful sorcerer who, in his youth, had been her husband's hunting apprentice. Meanwhile, Sumaworo's personal oracle informs him that the man who will eventually take Soso and Manden away from him has not only been born, but has grown up into a hunter and will be identifiable as the one who violates Sumaworo's taboo.*]

They were now in Soso.

Sogolon Condé arrived and said, "Eh, Soso *mansa*. These are the children of your former master. Their relationship with their brother is strained, and murder has been committed as a result. The death of one of two friends[2] does not spoil the friendship; the one who survives continues the friendship. I've come to put Ma'an Sunjata and his younger siblings under your protection. You should train them to be hunters, people who can kill their own game." (Oh! She did not know that Dankaran Tuman had sent a message ahead of them to Soso!)[3]

Sumaworo said, "Condé woman, that pleases me. I agree to care for them and take them under my protection, so long as they do not interfere with my sacred totem."

"God willing, they will never spoil your totem."

"Well, if they do not interfere with my totem, then I agree to protect them."

They spent the day there. That evening Ma Sogolon Condé said that she had brought a small amount of cotton she wanted to spin at night, and asked the children of Soso to collect a pile of dried cow dung she could use to light her lantern of conversation.[4] The children brought her the cow dung she needed. Sumaworo owned all the musical instruments, and he brought all of them—except for the *bala*[5]—out for the first time that night. He brought out the *kèrèlèng-kèngbèng*,[6] the *kòwòro*,[7] the *donso nkoni*,[8] the three-stringed *bolon*,[9] the *soron*,[1]

---

2. Sumaworo and Sunjata's father.
3. Offering a reward to kill Sunjata.
4. When villagers gather after dark to socialize and play music, they do it around a lantern to avoid burning valuable fuel needed for cooking fires.
5. An indigenous xylophone.
6. Named from the sound it makes (i.e., onomatopoeic), this child's instrument consists of a tin can resonator (or a tiny gourd) and a stick for a neck that supports a single string.
7. More commonly known as *dan*, an inverted open calabash instrument with a neck for each

of its six strings; technically known as a pentatonic pluriac.
8. The hunters' harp, a large animal-skin-covered calabash with a single neck and six strings, played to praise hunters.
9. The harp used to praise warriors; larger and deeper toned than the hunters' harp, an animal-skin-covered calabash with a single neck supporting three or four strings.
1. A large, rarely seen harp of northeastern Guinea, similar to the *kora* but with twelve strings.

and the *kora*.[2] (The *kora* was the last of the instruments to be brought out; that is why they call it *ko la*, which means "the last one."[3] Eventually it came to be called *kora*. It is played in Kita and Senegal.)

Taking out his *nkoni*,[4] Sumaworo sat down by the people who were talking. Sunjata and his siblings came and sat down too. Contented, Ma Sogolon Condé said, "Wait. I will sing three songs." They said, "Very well." When anybody sang, Sumaworo would accompany them on the *nkoni*.

For Ma Sogolon Condé's first song, she sang:

"Big ram,
The pen where the rams are kept,
The leopard must not enter,
Big ram.
The pen where the rams are kept,
The leopard must not enter."

Sumaworo's *nkoni* was in harmony with her song.
After that, what else did she sing? She sang:

"Pit water,
Don't compare yourself with clear water flowing over
rocks,
The pure white rocks.
Pit water,
Don't compare yourself with clear water flowing over
rocks,
The pure white rocks."

Again, Sumaworo's *nkoni* was in harmony with her song.
The third song she sang was:

"Big vicious dog,
If you kill your vicious dog,
Somebody else's will bite you,
Vicious dog.
If you kill your vicious dog,
Somebody else's will bite you."

Sumaworo's *nkoni* was still in harmony with her song.
Then the gathering broke up.

[*In omitted passages, Sumaworo performs a ritual to identify his rival for power, learns that it is Sunjata, and resolves to kill him. Sunjata intentionally violates a taboo by sitting in Sumaworo's sacred hammock, confirming that he is the rival described by the oracle. In an episode about Sumaworo's youthful rebelliousness and leadership, he invents different stringed musical instruments at various stages of his youth. The narrator describes Fakoli's birth by his father's second wife, Kosiya Kante, who was also the sister of Sumaworo. During his hunting apprenticeship, Sumaworo encounters a group of genies and their instruments.*

2. With twenty-one strings, the largest of the calabash harps.
3. *Ko la* = literally "later on," another popular etymology.

4. Bamana *ngoni*; a traditional lute consisting of four to five strings attached to a single neck on a wooden, trough-shaped body covered with animal skin.

Sumaworo covets the bala, *but when he hears that the price would be people, four members of his family, he refuses. Kosiya, upon hearing this, decides to sacrifice herself, and Fakoli is raised by his father's first wife, who carries him to the sacred sites of Manden to receive protective devices and become a hunter.*

The scene then shifts back to Soso at the time of Sogolon's visit with her children, when Sumaworo is in power. Sumaworo interprets the meaning of the songs sung earlier by Sogolon. Sunjata violates Sumaworo's sacred taboo, the two men engage in the deadly snuff-taking ritual, and Sunjata is banished from Soso. Continuing the journey into exile, Sunjata violates sacred taboos in each of the places they stop, including Nema, where they remain.]

Sumaworo's Tyranny over Manden

When Sogolon and her children were staying with ancestor Faran Tunkara at Kuntunya in Nema, he sometimes sent Sunjata on journeys out between the edges of the village and the place where the sun sets. Whenever war broke out, the village sent for Sunjata, who would come and join the Kuntunya army, marching along with them. Whenever he captured three prisoners, he kept one for himself. Whenever he captured five prisoners, he kept two. Whenever he captured ten prisoners, he kept four as his share. (The other six captives were given to the Kuntunya *mansa*.) This is how Sunjata collected his own band of men.

Sunjata stayed in Kuntunya for twenty-seven years, and before the end of the twenty-seventh year, well, things turned very bad in Manden. Things were terrible in Manden! Sumaworo, who was looking for Sunjata, had sent his warriors to Manden. Whenever Sumaworo consulted Nènèba, his oracle, it would say, "Your successor has grown."

Before consulting Nènèba, Sumaworo first had to have three age sets of young men pile wood beneath Nènèba's cauldron; this had to be done morning and evening, for the oracle always said, "Fire, fire, fire, fire, fire, fire." Then Sumaworo would bathe in the cauldron's medicines whenever he went to visit Nènèba. And Nènèba would tell Sumaworo what to sacrifice before setting out to war.

Every morning Nènèba told Sumaworo, "Sumaworo, only God knows the day. Your successor has grown up."

Sumaworo asked the Mande people, "Has Ma'an Sunjata returned to Manden?" Meanwhile, he laid waste to Manden nine times. The Mande people struggled and rebuilt their villages nine times during Sumaworo's failed search for Sunjata.

Whenever Sumaworo killed some Mande villagers, he would tell his men to search among the bodies for the Condé woman's son. But his men never found Sunjata; instead, they would return saying, "The Mande people do not know the whereabouts of the Condé woman's son."

Sumaworo then summoned all of the Mande villagers to Kukuba. He killed all of the men who attended this meeting except for the leaders Turama'an and Kankejan, who could disappear in broad daylight, and Fakoli, who could stand and vanish instantly. The people who had that kind of *dalilu* were the only ones he did not kill; he killed all of the other men. The people of Manden mourned and wept. But Ma'an Sunjata and his brothers were not there.

After another month had passed, Sumaworo summoned his men to Bantamba, saying, "I have to finish off the Mande. If I do that, I'll find my successor. If I kill all the human beings, my successor will be among them."

So he called the Mande to a meeting in Bantamba. After looking them over he said to his men, "Kill them all." Only those who had the power to disappear in broad daylight escaped. Again Manden wept.

He summoned the Mande to Nyèmi-Nyèmi, and they wept there, too.

Every time Mande people were summoned by Sumaworo, it ended in mourning. Sumaworo was killing the people of Manden, searching among the bodies for his successor. After every massacre, he would go to his Nènèba. (The Kantés now have that Nènèba in Balandugu, the only town they established. Sumaworo's descendants did not establish any other towns, because he was so ruthless.) The Nènèba would say, "Sumaworo, uh heh. You still haven't found him yet? You've killed so many, yet the one you want is not among them."

Sumaworo asked, "What should I do?" To which the oracle replied, "Keep searching for him. He has reached maturity."

When the Mande people were summoned again, this time to Kambasiga, Fakoli went to see Kani Simbon, the Kulubali ancestor.

He said, "Simbon. Manden is about to be wiped out. We must sit down together and find a solution to this problem in Manden. Manden will be reduced to being Soso's peanut farm, because Sumaworo has said two things. He has said, 'Manden's reputation is better than Manden itself,' and 'The Mande women are better than the Mande men.' By this he meant that Manden has only women because he's killed all the men. He said these things to provoke Sunjata, who he now knows to be his successor, into responding." Having said that, Fakoli then returned to Manden and said, "Let us build a council hall at the edge of town, and let the surviving men of Manden hold meetings there. If we don't get together, Manden is doomed." So the men worked hard and built a council hall. Afterwards, they sat in front of the council hall while Fakoli addressed them.

He said, "We have finished building this council hall, which belongs to all of us—except for the one who wants to destroy Manden. If you are a man of courage, this is your council hall. If you are a man of truth, this is your council hall. If you are a master of sorcery, this is your council hall. If you have love for Manden in your heart, this is your council hall."

The Expedition to Find Sunjata and Return Him to Manden

[*In an omitted passage, the assembled elders decide to summon diviners to learn who will be the liberator of Manden, and where he can be found. After an extended period of divination it is determined that Ma'an Sunjata is the one who was foreseen, and that a special delegation must be sent to find Sogolon and her children. Volunteering for this delegation are the Muslim diviners Manjan Bereté and Siriman Kanda Touré, as well as the female bard Tunku Manyan Diawara and the female slave Jonmusoni Manyan. They plan to visit distant markets with special sauce ingredients that can only be found in Manden, as a way of finding the people they seek.*]

Manjan Bereté laid down his prayer skin[5] as soon as he'd left town, and made two invocations to God: he asked that no one would see the travelers leave, and that they would meet no one on the road. He said, "Siriman Kanda Touré, we

---

5. His Muslim prayer rug, the hide of a goat or sheep.

mustn't be seen on the road. It doesn't matter whether you are a man or a woman: every one of us must use their *dalilu.*" When he'd finished making his two invocations. Manjan Bereté shook hands with his companions, who asked where they would sleep that night.

"Ahhh," said Manjan Bereté, "let us try to reach Soso today. Because tomorrow is Soso's market day."

As a result of his two invocations, each of his companions became invisible when Manjan Bereté shook their hands. When he gave his hand to one of his companions and withdrew it, the person became invisible. Then Manjan Bereté circled his prayer skin and became invisible himself.

They traveled on to the outskirts of Soso, where they spent the night. At daybreak Manjan Bereté said, "Take the things to the market." They set their goods out in the Soso market, but nobody wanted them. They went on to the market of Tabon; but no one wanted what they had. They went to the market of Kirina; no one was interested.

On Thursday they took the road to Kuntunya and slept outside that town to be ready for the market on Friday.

Meanwhile, at a house in that same town, Ma Sogolon Condé was saying to her daughter, "Ma Kolonkan, *aaaoy*! My stomach is hurting me because it's been twenty-seven years since I last had *dado*[6] in Manden. Tomorrow morning, do not wash the dishes, do not scrub the pots; instead, be the first one into the market, my child, and get me some *dado* to eat." (When a *dado* eater goes for a long time without having any, their stomach hurts; this is why Ma Sogolon Condé was complaining all night to Ma Kolonkan. It was a good thing that the Mande people spending the night outside of town had brought *dado*!)

As soon as the sun started to show its face the next morning, Manjan Bereté said, "Take the things into the market." The two women went and sat outside the covered part of the market. They had the *dado* there, along with some *namugu* and some *nèrè* seeds[7] they had on display.

Ma So'olon Wulen Condé said to Ma Kolonkan, "Go early to the market so you can get the *dado* I want." As soon as she'd arrived at the market, Kolonkan saw two women standing there with *dado*. She clapped her hands, saying, "From the time we came from Manden, my mother has not said anything about *dado*, nothing at all. It was only yesterday that she suddenly spoke of *dado*—and here it is! Heh! My mother has *dalilu*." She did not even stop to greet the *dado* seller; she immediately reached for the *dado* and put some in her mouth.

Jelimusoni Tunku Manyan Diawara said, "Eh! You, girl, are impolite! Don't touch our merchandise without greeting us or asking us first."

"Eeeh, I was so surprised! My mother told me to come to the market today to see if I could find *dado*. She said she's gone for so long without eating the old things of Manden that her stomach hurts. We haven't seen *dado* since we arrived here; we haven't even seen anyone who sells it. I just wanted to taste it because it is something we always used to have."

6. Dried hibiscus blossoms and/or leaves, used as a condiment in sauces.
7. *Namugu* is powdered leaves of the baobab tree, used as an ingredient in sauces. *Nèrè*:

Parkia biglobosa; the seeds are pounded into a paste that is fermented and rolled into balls to make a pungent condiment called *sumbala*.

Tunku Manyan Diawara asked, "Who are you? Where do you come from?"
"Ah, mother, we come from Manden."

"Who is with you here?"

"I am here with my mother Sogolon Wulen Condé, my elder brother Ma'an Sunjata, and my elder brother So'olon Jamori."

"Aaah! You are the people we have come for! Our road has been good. Let us go to your house."

[*In omitted passages Kolonkan conducts the Mande delegation to her house for a joyful reunion with Sogolon. Manjan Bereté announces that they have been sent to ask Sogolon to return to Manden because her children are needed there. Sogolon explains that her sons are hunting in the bush and concerns herself with providing the customary hospitality to the guests.*

Kolonkan goes out of town to find meat for the guests from Manden and discovers animals killed by her brothers. Her brother Manden Bori is enraged that she has removed the animals' internal organs, and they fight. Kolonkan's curse on his descendants—they will not be able to decide on a ruler until the final trumpet is blown—still affects them in today's Hamana region of Guinea. Tassey Condé mentions a childhood experience with his famous father, Babu Condé, toward the end of the colonial era and describes how he, Tassey, became the spokesman for the bards of Fadama. Reverting to his story, Tassey describes Sogolon's great happiness at the prospect of her sons' returning to Manden. The next episode describes a momentous family meeting of Sogolon and her children, in which the rarely mentioned brother Jamori plays a conspicuous part.]

Sogolon Bestows the Legacy of Maghan Konfara

Sogolon said to her children, "Let us go outside the town. I want to give you my final words." They left the Mande delegation behind and went out of town. When they arrived there, Ma So'olon Condé said to Manden Bori, "Break off that termite mound."[8]

When Manden Bori broke off the termite mound, Sogolon said, "Pick some leaves." He picked some leaves.

She said, "Lay them on the termite mound."

When they were laid on it, she said, "Ma'an Sunjata, you sit on that."[9]

Then she said, "Go and break off another termite mound." So Manden Bori went and broke another one and put leaves[1] on it.

She said, "So'olon Jamori, you sit on that. Now go and break off another one for you to sit on." Manden Bori broke off another termite mound and brought it over.

The three men sat, but Ma So'olon Condé stood up. Ma Kolonkan stood behind her. Women would usually be seated during a hunter's ceremony,[2] but here they did not sit down.

---

8. As the youngest of three sons, Manden Bori is ordered to perform the menial tasks.
9. Of the many kinds of termite mounds (some well over six feet tall), the type referred to here is approximately one to two feet high, shaped like a hard clay mushroom, and the larger ones could be used as stools.

1. For a soft and clean seat.
2. If present at a hunters' meeting, women would be seated in the background. In this and the following line, the bard explains that mother and daughter remain standing because Sogolon is in charge of this solemn occasion.

While they were standing, Ma So'olon Wulen Condé said, "Manden Bori! What I say to you is also for So'olon Jamori and for Ma'an Sunjata[3] to hear. The people of Manden have come for you; they are calling you to war.

"When your father died, Dankaran Tuman wanted your father's gold and silver; he also wanted your father's *dalilu* but did not know where to find it. That's why he has plotted against you all this time: he thought that when he killed you, he could take your father's legacy, his *dalilu*.

"But my sons, you do not have your father's *dalilu*; Dankaran Tuman does not have it either. I have your father's *dalilu* here. If you are seeing that a man's *dalilu* went to his last wife,[4] it is because my husband trusted me. When my husband was dying, he gave his *dalilu* to me so that I could keep it safe and give it to you when you reached maturity. I have brought you here now to give you your father's *dalilu*, because the Mande people have come to take you to war. But what worries me is that there are three things in your father's *dalilu*, and they cannot be separated. They can only go to one person. Ah! There are three things, but your father had three sons. These three things would not be of any benefit to you if we were to divide them up amongst you.

"The Mande messengers have come for your brother Ma'an Sunjata. You must allow him to be given the three things, because the three things—the sorcery horse, the sorcery bow, and the sorcery mask—all work together: when you sit on the sorcery horse, you must also wear the sorcery mask and take up the sorcery bow. Then you are ready for combat against all comers.

"If you mount the sorcery horse without carrying the sorcery bow, or without wearing the sorcery mask, then somebody will strike you down while the horse is galloping. If you put on the sorcery mask without carrying the sorcery bow and you are not on the horse, you will not be able to kill the enemies you see. If you take up the sorcery bow without wearing the mask and without being on the horse, what good is that? The three things must go to one person: please, allow me to give them to Ma'an Sunjata."

So'olon Jamori said, "Manden Bori, tell our mother that I do not agree to what she is saying. Ah! She herself says there are three things. There are three of us. They are easily divided.

"Have you not heard the Mande saying that if you cannot take your father's legacy on your head, you must at least drag part of it behind you? If I cannot carry it, I will drag it behind me. Let her bring the three things out and divide them between the three of us."

Ma So'olon Condé said, "Eh, So'olon Jamori my son! Eh, So'olon Jamori! I was afraid you'd cause trouble; that is why I wanted to bring you out of the town. Did you not hear me say that there are three things, but they can only solve one problem? Will you not be agreeable?"

---

3. On occasions where oral communication must be precise, it is customary for an important speaker's words to be repeated several times by various people in the presence of the person addressed. When a *jeli* is available the speaker addresses the bard, who repeats and validates what was just heard. At Sogolon's secret meeting, the youngest son serves to repeat and reaffirm her words.

4. The legacy would normally go to the first (senior) wife.

Manden Bori said, "Big brother So'olon Jamori,[5] will you not have pity on our mother, who is so worried about this? Let us agree to give the *dalilu* to brother So'olon Maghan."

Ah! Jamori said if Manden Bori did not shut his mouth, he would slap his ears.

Manden Bori said, "You can't slap my ears. Why should you slap my ears for this? Don't you know our brother can battle Soso with or without our father's legacy?

"And who used up our mother's legacy? You and I did; our brother did not take part in that. Our mother took her gold earring and silver bracelet and gave them to Sansamba Sagado, the Somono ancestor, as a future day's river-crossing fee. And how many of us got into the canoe that day, when we left Manden by crossing the river? The canoe our mother paid for with her legacy? Our mother went in the canoe, our little sister got into the canoe, you got into the canoe, and I got into the canoe. Did our brother get in? Hah! Didn't our brother say he was not getting in? Didn't my mother weep? Didn't he say that we should go ahead and he would follow? And by the time we got to the other side of the river, didn't we see our brother already sitting there?

"The *dalilu* with which our brother crossed the river was our father's legacy, and Sunjata can battle Sumaworo with that. But you say you will slap my ears? Why didn't you slap my ears on the riverbank?"

Ma'an Sunjata said, "Manden Bori, be quiet. Tell my mother that we will not quarrel. If you see somebody taking your friend's share of the sauce, your own sauce cannot satisfy you. Does she think I will quarrel with this foolish person? I will never quarrel with So'olon Jamori over our father's legacy. Even if he were to ask me to give it all to him, I would do it. Tell my mother to bring out the legacy.

"But mother, we will never forget the two things you have done for us. First, we were legitimately born, and it is because of our legitimacy that the Mande people came to find us. Second, my father married fifty women—fifty wives!— and two other women, none of whom gave birth to a child. Sansun Bereté was one of the other two women: she gave birth to Dankaran Tuman and Nana Triban.

"But you! You were the fifty-second wife. Eh! Out of all his wives, why did my father give his legacy to you? Because of your devotion, and it was for us you were so devoted. I trust in God. Even if you do not give me the legacy, I will vanquish Sumaworo because of your devotion. Bring out the legacy."

Ma So'olon Wulen Condé said, "I am pleased with that, now excuse me." She pushed her hand into her abdomen. When she did that, *ho*! The *dalilu* fell out. When the three *dalilu* were piled together, Ma'an Sunjata laughed.

He started to say, "So'olon Jamori," but suddenly his mother began to shake. So'olon Ma'an held his mother until her dizziness passed. When the dizziness left her eyes, Sunjata said, "Manden Bori, tell our mother that she should tell So'olon Jamori he should choose one of the things. Aheh! My little brother and I will not quarrel over my father's legacy."

---

5. In many variants of the epic, Sogolon's son Jamori is not mentioned at all, and the claim here that Manden Bori was the youngest of the three brothers is an especially rare detail.

So'olon Jamori said that he chose the sorcerer's mask. They asked, "Is that your choice?" And he replied, "Uhuh, that is mine." They said, "Very well, take it."

Sunjata said, "Manden Bori, choose one."

Manden Bori said, "I will not take a share in this legacy. I am holding your shirt-tail, and so long as I hold your shirt-tail, nothing will happen to me in the war with Soso. When you die, Sunjata, your legacy will come to me anyway. It was my father's legacy, but you are my father now, and so it belongs to you. Take both my share and your share."

Ma'an Sunjata said, "Is that your word?"

"Uhuh. It is your name, not mine or So'olon Jamori's, that will become attached to the bow and *mansaya*[6] we are quarreling over." (That is why, when people go outside town for a private meeting, they say, "Let us speak with the truth of Manden Bori.")

Manden Bori, the youngest of the brothers, had his oldest brother's blessing. Ma So'olon Wulen Condé spoke. She said, "Manden Bori, is that your word? Come here."

Taking Manden Bori behind a bush, Sogolon said, "Manden Bori, you've honored me, and so now God will honor you. Nobody will ever dishonor you. If you'd acted the way So'olon Jamori acted, then all of the Mande people would know that your father's *dalilu* had been divided—and if your rival knows your secret, he will vanquish you. You preferred to keep all of this secret so I would not be shamed.

"Come and let me give you my legacy. My legacy is something that did not come from here, in Nema, or Manden. It came from Dō ni Kiri, the home of my brothers. I will give this ring to you. So long as you live, it will protect you from genies or enemies that might threaten you; it will also keep you safe in the bush. If you find yourself in trouble, look at this ring and say, 'Ah, mother!' If you do that, God will protect you. If you look at it and say, 'Ah, genie!' God will save you from genies. If you look at it and say, 'Genie and man!' God will spare you from both." (That was the first of the brass rings hunters now wear on their fingers. Some people call such a ring "genie and man.") Sogolon said, "This is your keepsake." Then they all returned to town.

[*In the next scene, Sogolon suddenly dies and Sunjata tells Manden Bori to request a plot of land for her burial.*]

The Burial of Sogolon and Departure from Nema

On the path to town, Manden Bori met with Faran Tunkara, the *mansa* of Nema. He said, "Mansa, my brother says that I should come and tell you that my mother is dead. He'd like you to agree to give him some land he can use for her burial."

Now, Faran Tunkara had been unhappy to see the messengers from Manden arrive in Nema. From the time Sunjata arrived in Nema, he'd helped the Kuntunya people win every single battle they'd faced, and he returned with slaves from every campaign. But Faran Tunkara could not keep Sunjata in Nema, because Sogolon and her family had arrived there by choice. He decided to start a quarrel so he could detain Sunjata.

6. The bow and quiver were symbolic of Mande kingship (*mansaya*).

So Nema Faran Tunkara said, "Manden Bori, go and tell your brother that I, Nema Faran Tunkara, say that I own all the land here. Unless you brought a piece of land with you from Manden to bury your corpse in, you should load her body on your head and carry it back to Manden the same way you brought her. Tell him that if you bury her in my land, I will blast her out of the ground with gunpowder. Go and tell your brother that."

Manden Bori returned on the path and relayed Nema Faran Tunkara's message to Sunjata. When he heard what Manden Bori reported, Manjan Bereté said, "What kind of man is Nema Faran Tunkara? Simbon, let me go and give him a real 'message.'"

"Eee," said Sunjata, "just leave it alone. Don't worry, he'll provide the land. I've spent twenty-seven years here; I'm in his army. And he says I should carry my mother's body back to Manden? He'll soon provide the land."

To Manden Bori, Sunjata said, "Go back and tell Nema Faran Tunkara that I, the son of the Condé woman, say he should give me some land in which I can bury my mother. Tell him it is I who say so."

When Tunkara was told this, he said to Manden Bori, "I do not want ever to see you here again. From the minute you first arrived here, I knew that you're a hotheaded man. Go and tell your brother that I don't go back on what I've said twice. Tell him I have no land for him here."

Manden Bori went and told this to Ma'an Sunjata. Manjan Bereté and Siriman Kanda Touré became angry. They were all brave men; they all had *dalilu*, and they all knew how to fight. But when they started to leave the house to find Nema Faran Tunkara, Ma'an Sunjata said, "Be patient and take your seats. He will soon provide the land."

Sunjata took the path that passed behind the house. Along the way, he picked up a fragment of old clay pot, a piece of old calabash, the feather of a guinea fowl, and a partridge feather. To these things he added a stick of bamboo. He gave all of these things to Manden Bori, and said, "Tell Tunkara that I say he should give me land to bury my mother in. If he's asking a price for his land, well, tell him I'll pay his fees with these things. Tell him he must agree to let me lay my mother in the ground."

As he gave Faran Tunkara these things from Sunjata, Manden Bori said, "My brother says this is payment for your land, and that you should agree to let him bury his mother."

Faran Tunkara said, "Is this what you pay for land in your country? Huh, Manden Bori? I do not ever want to see you here again. Take these things and go away."

But Tunkara's *jeli* man, who was sitting there beside him, said, "He should not take those things away from here. Heh! Sunjata has sent you an important message.

"M'ba, when these people came to Nema, didn't I say you should kill Sunjata? And didn't you reply that Sunjata had come to place himself in your care, and that therefore you must not do anything to him? Ahuh! Well, now he has said something to you; there's a message in these things he sent. Since you do not understand the message, I will tell you what these things mean."

To which Faran Tunkara replied, "All right, tell me what they mean."

The *jeli* said, "This piece of bamboo means that you should give him land so he can bury his mother in it. If you do not give him land, the Mande people will come and take it for themselves. If he should be named king after he finishes fighting that war for Manden, he will bring the Mande army here to Nema, and he will break Nema like this old clay pot or this old calabash. Then the guinea fowls and the partridges will take their dust baths in the ruins of Nema. See? These are the feathers of those guinea fowls and partridges. Nothing will grow in the ruins of Nema but weeds; that's what this piece of bamboo stick means."

Now, Mansa Tunkara was a good debater, and he always won arguments. So he said, "I am right."

The *jeli* said, "How can you be right about this?"

"I am right," said Faran Tunkara, "because these people have been here for twenty-seven years. During the time those three brothers served in my army, I lost no battles. They never cheated me, were never disobedient to me; I never had to discipline them for chasing women. Now their mother has died. Are they going to do the right thing and say the corpse is mine, or are they just going to demand that I give them land?"

Everyone agreed that the three brothers should have observed the custom of saying, "This is your corpse."

Faran Tunkara said, "Ah! This is why I refused. Eh! If they were raised correctly as children, they should have said that God has made this my opportunity, and that this is my corpse. But did they show me the proper respect? Should they be looking for land to lay their mother in?"

Everybody said, "You are right!" Even Manjan Bereté himself came and said, "You are right."

"Very well," said Faran Tunkara. "If I am right, give her to me and I will conduct the funeral."

Even though she was a woman, the people of Nema gave Sogolon a man's funeral. They killed cows, fired their guns, and beat the special drum. (This tradition started with Ma So'olon Wulen Condé's funeral.) Then they took her body to the town of Kuntunya, and on Thursday they buried her.

When they were finished with the burial, Simbon asked for Faran Tunkara's permission to leave Nema. Because all debts had now been settled between the two men, Sunjata was able to say, "I will leave tomorrow."

Faran Tunkara said, "Go with my blessing. I give you the road." But once Sunjata and his brothers had returned to their house, Faran Tunkara summoned his warriors, telling them, "I cannot allow Sunjata to leave with his men, because those men are rightfully mine; Sunjata had no men of his own until he arrived here. Prepare yourselves and go on ahead to cut them off. Go ahead as far as the second village and wait for them there; attack them when they arrive, and try to capture them. If you bring them back, they will never leave Nema again."

Faran Tunkara's warriors left, passing the first village and preparing their attack at the second. And when Sunjata and his companions arrived at the second village, they were attacked. So'olon Jamori did not survive the attack! He died there; he did not live to reach Manden. So the three parts of his father's legacy were combined and given to Simbon. (That is why we say that if a *kamalen* of the Mansaré lineage becomes selfish, do not bother to curse him. He won't live long.)

Sunjata and his men escaped that ambush, and Sunjata added the captives they took from among Faran Tunkara's warriors to his own troops.

[*The narrator explains that despite the ambush that killed So'olon Jamori, Faran Tunkara sent troops to support Manden's campaign against Soso, and Sunjata never attacked Nema. Claiming that he wants to notify Sumaworo of his return so he will not be accused of sneaking back into Manden, Sunjata stops in Soso. Sumaworo issues a series of warnings to Sunjata that he must not attack Soso. They engage in a traditional boasting contest, concluding with Sunjata's vow to return and Sumaworo's reply that he will be waiting.*]

The Return of Sunjata

Sunjata took the road toward home. When they arrived at the edge of town, the townspeople could hear *nege* music[7] played by Jelimusoni Tunku Manyan Diawara.

She sang to Manden:

"The *danama yirindi*[8] that we have been looking for,
He is at the edge of town.
Come, let us go.
For the sake of the Condé woman's son,
Come, let us go.
The person that Manden was busy searching for,
Known as So'olon Ma'an,
Come, let us go."

Sansamba Sagado crossed the river with his canoe that day. He put the canoe into the river without a pole or paddle, and as soon as he untied the canoe, it headed straight for Sunjata and his men—*prrrr*, just as if it had a motor.

Sunjata loaded his men into the canoe and said, "You will now see the power of my *dalilu*." He struck the water, the canoe went *prrrr*, and they landed on the riverbank in Manden, where Simbon stepped out. His fathers, brothers, and all the men of Manden were there to greet and embrace him. (The shade tree under which the people of Manden welcomed Sunjata home is still living today.) When he arrived, Manden was jubilant, Manden celebrated. They named that place Nyani, the town of happiness, the town of rejoicing, *ko anyè nyani so*.[9]

As the people of Manden welcomed Sunjata and his men, they said, "Manjan Bereté, you are welcome; Siriman Kanda Touré, you are welcome; Tunku Manyan Diawara, you are welcome; Jonmusoni Manyan, you are welcome. You have brought a gift for Manden: you have found Simbon! We knew that someday the son of Farako Manko Farakonken and the Condé woman would return. But Manden suffered while he was away; we have suffered so much at Sumaworo's hands. Let Sunjata see for himself how many of those he knew here have been killed by Sumaworo. The only people left here are those with *dalilu*, and Sumaworo has even caused those who have *dalilu* to suffer.

"When we knew Sunjata was returning, we carried out divinations and swore oaths and saw that only he could receive ancestor Mamadi Kani's legacy. And now that he has come, heh! We all—the Kulubali, the Konaté, and the Douno—

---

7. *Nege* = iron; also a synonym for the *nkarin-yan*, a rhythm instrument consisting of a notched iron tube seven to eight inches long, held in one hand and scraped with a thin metal rod.

8. Roughly translated as "superhero."
9. This and the following line comprise a popular etymology.

say that he should accept the legacy and help Manden. Simbon, you have been called to take the legacy." (This saying—"Take your legacy," or *ko ila kè ta*— came to be spoken as "Keita.")

[*In the following brief departure from his narrative, the bard (who is traditionally expected to instruct as well as entertain) reiterates his view of human origins and explains who really built Paris. In the omitted passage, the bard explains the power of the Condé people, their descent from Isiaaka, and the equality of all humans as children of God.*]

Fakoli Reveals His Power

While the Mande men were in a meeting, a message from Sumaworo arrived. He said that he'd been waiting a long time for a message from the Mande. He said it had been a long time since their *mansa* arrived, and that he'd not seen any Mande messengers. Finally, Sumaworo said that since So'olon Ma'an had now returned home, he wanted to see all of the Mande people at Dakajalan on the fourteenth of the new month. The battle had now been set.

As soon as he heard Sumaworo's message, So'olon Ma'an replied by having his people beat the signal drum, calling everyone to the council hall. On his way to the council hall, Fakoli was thinking, "We are going to march against Soso!" But his mother and Sumaworo had suckled at the same breast, and he wondered if it was right for him to join the Mande people in attacking Sumaworo. He decided, "As soon as I get to the council hall, I will ask the Mande people to let me go to Soso. Let Manden come and fight both me and my uncle."

But before Fakoli had the chance to say this to the men gathered in the council hall, Manden Bori laughed at him. Manden Bori always ridiculed Fakoli whenever he entered the council hall. When he heard Manden Bori laughing at him, Fakoli became angry and said, "Turama'an, let me give you a message for Simbon. Tell Simbon to ask his younger brother why he always laughs at me. Of all the people that enter the council hall, it's me that Manden Bori laughs at. Why does he laugh at me? What have I done to him?"

When Ma'an Sunjata was given this message, he said, "Manden Bori, stop laughing at Fakoli. Didn't hear him saying that you are shaming him? Why do you laugh at him?"

Manden Bori replied, "Big brother, the tall men always duck their heads as they enter the council hall. Though Fakoli is only one and a half arm-spans tall, he also ducks his head when he comes in. That is what makes me laugh. Aaah, that Fakoli, heh, heh."

Fakoli said, "Turama'an, tell Simbon that he should tell his younger brother that short Mande people can do things that tall Mande people cannot do. And he'd better believe it."

Manden Bori said, "I won't believe that until I see it. Really, do you believe that? I don't."

Fakoli picked up his goatskin rug and, placing it in the center of the council hall, sat down on it. He waved his hand and grunted. He raised the roof from the house! The sun shone in on everybody. He said, "Well, Manden Bori, what about that?"

Manden Bori said, "You spoke the truth."

(They were fair about crediting one another with the truth, for there was respect among those with *dalilu*.)

The people asked Fakoli to put the roof back where it belonged. They said, "No tall Mande man has ever done such a thing."

Then Fakoli placed his hand in the middle of the council hall floor. He crouched there and wrinkled his face. Wrinkled his face and wrinkled his face! He squeezed everyone against the wall. That was the origin of the song "Nyari Gbasa," which goes:

> "Fakoli, our arms will break,
> Fakoli, our heads will burst,
> Fakoli, our stomachs will rupture."

(That song belongs to the Koroma family.)

The people said, "Fakoli, stop! No tall Mande man has done such a thing."

Fakoli Explains His Dilemma and Takes His Leave from Manden

After performing these feats, Fakoli spoke to the assembled elders. He said, "Turama'an, Simbon, and everyone in the council hall: Sumaworo has sent a message that we should meet at Dakajalan. But my mother and Sumaworo were the children of the three Touré women, and it would be shameful for me to participate in Manden's attack on my uncle. I ask that you give me leave to go to Soso. I should be at my uncle's side when you come to attack him."

Ma'an Sunjata heard what Fakoli said, even though Manden Bori refused to repeat it to him. To Manden Bori, Sunjata said, "Haven't I told you? Fakoli is right. You and I have uncles whose home is Dò ni Kiri. What if we knew that Dò ni Kiri would be attacked? Would we stay here and do nothing?"

Manden Bori said, "Would anyone dare to attack Dò ni Kiri?"

"That's not the point. If Fakoli says he is going to help his mother's kinsman, leave him alone and let him go." Then, turning to Fakoli, Sunjata said, "Fakoli, you have done well by Manden. You helped us during Sumaworo's nine invasions of Manden, and our nine efforts to rebuild our homeland. So if you should say that you are going to help your uncle, very well; we won't stop you. But remember that if we meet on the battlefield there will be no brotherhood, no friendship between us. Don't think us ungrateful. But there's no gratitude when the guns start firing. That is all I have to say."

Fakoli said, "Bisimillahi,"[1] and returned to his house for the night.

The next morning Fakoli bathed in the water of his seven medicine pots. Taking his battle-axe on his shoulder, he brought out his horse and mounted it. His groom, Nyana Jukuduma,[2] was with him. He lifted up his wife, Keleya Konkon, and sat her behind him on his horse; then he took the ends of his scarf and tied them together, saying, "Because I know the kind of man my uncle is, he might wait for me on the road."[3]

While he was preparing to leave, another message from Sumaworo arrived. Sumaworo said that he'd been informed of Fakoli's plan to help him fight against Manden, and that Fakoli must not go to Soso. Sumaworo said he'd learned that if the Mande were successful in defeating him, they planned to replace Sumaworo

---

1. Literally, "in the name of Allah" (Arabic), a traditional Muslim invocation spoken at the outset of an undertaking [editor's note].

2. A slave that cared for his horse.
3. To ambush him.

with Fakoli as ruler of Soso. When the people of Soso heard this, they promised to cut off Fakoli's head, just as the Mande people already wanted to. Thus, one way or another, said Sumaworo, Fakoli's "feet would be bringing his head" if he dared to come to Soso. Fakoli laughed, "I'm not going to die for anyone—not Sunjata, and not Sumaworo." (Even today, that expression is often quoted.)

Fakoli said, "Go and tell my uncle that I'll soon be there. If I were really planning to get myself killed, then I'd let him carry out his threats against me. But since I don't intend to die, I'll go to Soso today. Tell him to get ready."

[*In an omitted passage, Sumaworo deploys soldiers to intercept Fakoli and kill him, but Fakoli makes himself and his companions invisible and arrives unscathed at the gates of Soso.*]

Fakoli Finds Trouble in Soso

When Sumaworo learned that Fakoli was accompanied only by his wife and his slave, he told Bala Fasali,[4] "Take the *bala* and welcome my nephew."

Bala Fasali took up the *bala* and sang the song we now call "Janjon":[5]

"Eh, Fakoli!
You became a son.
If death is inevitable,
A formidable child should be born.
The Mande people said
That if you came, they would wait for you on the road.
The people of Soso said
That if you came, your feet would bring your head.
Knowing that, you still had no fear.
If death is inevitable,
A formidable child should be born."

Sumaworo welcomed Fakoli by standing and raising his elephant tail in salute. Fakoli sat down and explained why he had come to Soso. He said, "Bala Fasali, you take part in this.[6] Let Sumaworo hear what I have to say. I have come because Sumaworo has done many things, and though I was invisible as I traveled, I come in good faith.

"The three Touré women gave birth to my mother and to Sumaworo. I have been thinking about my mother ever since war was declared between Soso and Manden. Had my mother been a man, she would have fought in this war alongside Sumaworo, her brother. That is why I decided to come: to fight in place of my mother. I have come to Sumaworo through the will of God; let us unite and fight the coming war together."

Sumaworo replied, "Bala Fasali, I'll tell you what to say to Fakoli. Tell him that I appreciate his words, and that I am pleased he has come."

---

4. An unusual pronunciation of this famous bard's name, which is usually given as Bala Fasaké, or a variant thereof.
5. One of the oldest and most famous songs of Manden, said to have been originally composed for Fakoli, but in later times played to honor

any distinguished personage.
6. Custom dictated that the dignitary, in this case Fakoli, would speak to the *jeli*, who would then add weight to the message by repeating it to the person addressed.

After this meeting, Fakoli was taken to meet Sumaworo's wives. Sumaworo had three hundred and thirty-three wives. Fakoli had only one wife, Keleya Konkon.

To his three hundred and thirty-three wives, Sumaworo said: "Fakoli has arrived just as I am going to war. The oracle Nènèba says that in order to win this war I must offer three hundred and thirty-three different dishes as sacrifice. I want these dishes to be prepared the day after tomorrow, on Friday. I mention this because Fakoli should know about this sacrifice if we are to be allies."

Fakoli said, "Fine. Since I have come to take the place of my mother, my wife will cook the one bowl of food my mother would have provided."

When the Soso women heard Fakoli say that, they said, "Paki! We'll show that Mande woman how much better a Soso woman's cooking is." This was insulting to Keleya Konkon, who said, "I'm going to build my fire near theirs. Fakoli, go and find a cooking pot for me. Those Soso women want to brag? They'll soon learn that Mande women can also cook. They will realize that Manden has kitchens, too." Fakoli left to find a cooking pot for Keleya Konkon.

Among the three hundred and thirty-three dishes prepared by Sumaworo's wives were beans, rice, fonio, cereal paste, millet wafers, wheat meal, cassava, and porridge: all of these different foods were included in the sacrifice.

Fakoli's wife said to him, "Bring me rice, pounded cassava, and fonio for my pot. God willing, I'm going to cook a meal that the *jelilu* will sing about for years to come."

Keleya Konkon put her one pot on the fire. Whenever she saw the Soso women who were cooking rice put some into their pots, she would put rice in her one pot, then sit down. Whenever she saw the Soso women who were cooking fonio put some into their pots, she would add some fonio in her one pot then sit down.

When the women who were cooking *monie*[7] were rolling their *monie* balls, Keleya Konkon also rolled *monie* balls. When the women put the *monie* balls into their pots, Keleya Konkon would put *monie* balls into her pot too, then take her seat. When the women who were baking *takura*[8] were putting their *takura* balls into their pots, Keleya Konkon also put *takura* balls into her pot, then sat down.

So Keleya Konkon put into her one pot all of the same things the Soso women put into their three hundred and thirty-three pots. Then, when the women started dishing out rice, she took her rice bowl and dished out the rice from her pot. When the women started dishing out the fonio, she took her fonio bowl and dished out her fonio from the same pot.

Sumaworo's wives produced three hundred and thirty-three dishes—but Fakoli's wife also produced three hundred and thirty-three dishes, and all from her one pot! The wives couldn't get the best of her.

Some scandalmongers went to Sumaworo and told him what had happened, adding, "Didn't we tell you that Fakoli came to take your place? You have three hundred and thirty-three wives, who have cooked you three hundred and thirty-three dishes. Your nephew has only one wife, but she has also prepared three

---

7. A millet porridge made with small balls of millet flour flavored with tamarind or lemon.
8. A millet cake made with five balls of soaked millet flour and baked or steamed in a clay pot buried in the ground; one of the preferred foods for sacrifice or alms-giving.

hundred and thirty-three dishes! In fact, Keleya Konkon's servings are bigger than yours! Everything that you have, Fakoli now also has. He came to take your place. If you don't take this Fakoli business seriously, he will take Soso away from you even before you go to war."

Sumaworo said, "Huh? Oho!" And he called his people together. Sumaworo sent the scandalmonger to go and bring Fakoli to the meeting.

Instead of going to find Fakoli, the scandalmonger simply went and stood on the road, then returned to Sumaworo, saying, "I have called him." A lot of time passed; Fakoli did not come to see Sumaworo. When Sumaworo sent for someone, he expected that person to arrive one minute after the messenger returned.

"Ah!" said Sumaworo. "Did you not see my nephew?"

To which the scandalmonger replied, "I saw him."

"Ah, did you not call him?"

"I called him."

"All right, go and tell him I am waiting for him."

The scandalmonger went and stood in the road again. Returning to Sumaworo, he said, "I have called him."

More time passed and still Fakoli did not appear. Now very angry, Sumaworo sent another messenger to get Fakoli. He said, "You go and tell Fakoli that I am waiting for him."

That messenger did find Fakoli. He said, "Fakoli, this is the third time you have been called. Why didn't you come when we called? Who do you think you are?"

Fakoli said, "Me? Was I called three times?"

"Yes, the message came and came again."

"Me? M'ba, I refuse."

That messenger ran back and told Sumaworo, "Your nephew refuses to come."

Sumaworo said, "*Paki!* That's it! Fakoli dares tell me, Sumaworo, 'I refuse'?"

Once Sumaworo's last messenger had gone, Fakoli put on his hat with the three hundred birds' heads. He put his axe on his shoulder and tied his headband around his head, because he knew there was going to be trouble.

When Sumaworo saw Fakoli approaching, he stood up in his royal seat and said, "Fakoli, am I the one to whom you said, 'I refuse'?"

Fakoli replied, "I refuse," for he believed it would be cowardly to explain himself to Sumaworo.

Again, Sumaworo asked, "Am I the one to whom you said, 'I refuse'?"

"I refuse."

"Why?"

"I refuse."

"Ah, very well." Sumaworo said. "What they told me is the truth. You claim that you came to help me. But you have not come to help me. You know what you came for. I have three hundred and thirty-three wives who have prepared three hundred and thirty-three dishes for me. You have only one wife, yet she also produced three hundred and thirty-three dishes for you.

"Did you come to help me? Were you told that your head and my head are equal? I gave you this wife you're so proud of—the one with your mother's name[9]—

9. Fakoli's mother was Kosiya, so his wife Keleya was not exactly her namesake.

and now I am taking her back. You can't brag about what you don't have anymore! This Kosiya Kanté that you have, she is my daughter,[1] so now I am taking her back."

Fakoli said, "Ah! Uncle, have matters between us sunk so low? Has our dispute come to the point of taking back a wife? You can have her! I don't even want her now, at least not until the smoke from our battle with the Mande people at Dakajalan has settled. Until then, I don't want her!"

He brought out his blanket and tore off a strip, *prrrr*! He threw it to Keleya Konkon and told her to use it for a mourning veil, saying, "I will not marry you again until I've defeated your brother[2] in gunsmoke. I am returning to Manden."

Turning his back on Keleya Kondon, he gave the tail of his horse to Nyana Jukuduma,[3] and the two men took the road to Manden, where the diviners were still praying to God.

When Fakoli got back to Manden, he went and stood at the door of the council hall. He said, "Simbon, my uncle and I have quarreled. He has taken my wife from me. I will not take back Keleya Konkon until I do it in gunsmoke."

"Huh," Ma'an Sunjata laughed.

Manjan Bereté and Siriman Kanda Touré also laughed. They said, "Manden is now complete." They said they had put their trust in Turama'an. (This is why you sometimes hear a person say that they put their trust in Turama'an instead of Fakoli.[4] The people gave their trust to Turama'an while Fakoli was off visiting his uncle.)

Still standing on the threshold of the council hall, Fakoli said, "Simbon, I do not want a wife from Manden or Negeboriya. Send a message to your uncles in Dò ni Kiri, and ask them to give you your 'nephew wife.'[5] Then give that wife to me. I want to have that woman before we go to the battle at Dakajalan. Then, regardless of what happens, no one will be able to blame my actions in battle on the fact that I have no wife. If I don't have a wife before going into battle, the people will say I fought well because I was trying to get myself a wife—that I was afraid of staying a bachelor. So let me have your 'nephew wife' before we leave for the war." Ma'an Sunjata sent a message to his uncle (our ancestor!) in Dò ni Kiri, who sent Ma Sira Condé to Sunjata as his nephew wife. Ma'an Sunjata then gave this wife to Fakoli.

At that time, Fakoli was feeling bitter. Having refused to live in Negeboriya, Manden, and Soso, he'd built his own hamlet and remained there until it was time for the battle at Dakajalan. The people all said, "Eeeh, Fakoli is bitter! He

1. Family relationships among Manding peoples are perceived on several levels, or "paths." Keeping in mind that this is the storyteller's viewpoint, this is probably meant in the sense that the wife Sumaworo provided for Fakoli was a classificatory "daughter" of Sumaworo. In Manding societies, the children of one's cousins are considered to be one's own children.
2. In the same way that Keleya Konkon could be a classificatory "daughter" of Sumaworo, she could also be a classificatory "sister." Indeed, on one path a person can be classified as one's sibling, while on another path the same person can be referred to as one's father, uncle, mother, or aunt. This reflects the polygymous practice of

men marrying wives of the same age as their children.
3. The slave would run behind the horse, hanging on to its tail.
4. Turama'an had acquired a leadership position or military command that was formerly held by Fakoli.
5. In Maninka and Bamana society, it is claimed, both jokingly and seriously, that it is the uncle's duty to give his nephew a wife, the so-called nephew wife. The obligation of this uncle–nephew bond is implied in the Bamana proverb: "When your uncle fails to give you a wife, he is no longer your uncle but your mother's brother."

has refused to live with us; he's built his own hamlet." (That hamlet, built in Manden, became Bambugu, and it was there that Sira Condé was brought to Fakoli.)

A Visit to Kamanjan in Sibi

Dressed in his ritual attire, Sunjata said to Fakoli, "Before she died, my mother asked God to help me earn the support of a Mande elder whose *dalilu* is greater than mine, and I believe I must not go to war without having first accomplished this. Now that you're settled, Fakoli, I ask you—just as I'm asking Turama'an, Kankejan, Tombonon Sitafa Diawara, and all the Simbons—please give me sixty men so I can greet Kamanjan, because I esteem him above all other elders."

Kamanjan was much older than Sunjata; Kamanjan and Sunjata's father, Maghan Konfara, were born at the same time. Kamanjan never committed a shameful deed in his entire life, and anyone who commanded an army would seek his advice. This is why Sunjata said, "Let's go to greet Kamanjan."

With sixty men, Sunjata went to salute Kamanjan at the battle site called Kalassa, near Sibi Mountain, where Kamanjan liked to hold torchlit meetings at night. It was a special honor to be asked by Kamanjan to extinguish the torches at the end of such meetings; only those *kamalenw* he knew to be special in their towns would be allowed to put out the flames.

Sunjata arrived as Kamanjan was having one of his nighttime meetings, and all of the torches were lit. With his hand, Sunjata extinguished them all. Then he used a little thing to reignite them, *kan!* Suddenly everything was illuminated again. The people at the meeting said, "As soon as Sunjata put out the torches, he lit his own torch."

(Sunjata's own light was as powerful as the light from a pressure lamp, and the little town where Sunjata extinguished the torches is called Kalassa, which is near Tabon on the Bamako road. The Konaté live there.)

After relighting the torches, Sunjata saluted Kamanjan and explained the purpose of his visit, saying, "I left here with my mother; now I have returned."

Kamanjan said, "Simbon! Have you come?"

"Yes, I have come."

"Ah, are you the one that Manden will send against Sumaworo?"

"Uhuh. That is why I have come to greet you, father Kamanjan. The last person to be told you're leaving on a trip must be the first person you greet upon your return."

"Sunjata, what *dalilu* did you bring with you? Hm? Sumaworo is a bad one. Haven't you heard people sing his praises? They sing:

'Transforms in the air,
Sumaworo,
Transforms on the ground,
Sumaworo.
Manden pi-pa-pi,
Whirlwind of Manden,
Kukuba and Bantamba,
Nyemi-Nyemi and Kambasiga,
Sege and Babi'?"

Sunjata said, "Yes, Father Kamanjan, I've heard that."

"Then what kind of *dalilu* did you bring to use against him?"

"Ah, father Kamanjan, that is why I have come to greet you and tell you my thoughts."

"Well, I've become old since we last met here. I can't go to war again, nor can I ask anyone else to do that. All those who attacked Sumaworo have been defeated, and this is Manden's fault; it was Manden that made it possible for Sumaworo to become what he is. It was a mistake for us to give him the four *jamanaw*.[6] Not satisfied with that, he now wants to add Manden to Soso. That is what we must fight to avoid."

Kamanjan and Sunjata were talking beneath the tree that is called *balansan*[7] in Manden, and when Kamanjan said, "Ah!" the *balansan* flipped upside down onto its top branches.

When Sunjata also said, "Ah!" the *balansan* flipped back over onto its roots. (It's true, *binani tinima*!)

Kamanjan said, "Ah!" a second time, and the *balansan* flipped back over onto its top branches.

Before Sunjata could say, "Ah," again, his sister whispered in his ear, "Big brother, this is not what my mother told you to do. Let Kamanjan do this. Our mother prayed that you would be blessed by an elder with *dalilu* stronger than yours. Kamanjan is trying to demonstrate to you how strong his *dalilu* is. If you beat him with your own *dalilu*, he will not give you anything. Let him do this, and he will flip the tree back once he's satisfied. If you add his *dalilu* to what you already have, maybe you will win the war against Sumaworo. You should act like you do not know anything, so Kamanjan will give you his *dalilu*."

A Strategic Alliance: Kolonkan's Marriage

The battle that followed Sunjata's meeting with Kamanjan did not go well for Manden, and the town was filled with sorrow. But Kamanjan didn't let Sunjata leave him empty-handed. Kamanjan said, "Simbon, I see that your sister has matured since we last met. Yes, she has matured, and you should give her to me so I can marry her. Though your sister spent twenty-seven years at Nema, your mother—who was of the best stock—said she would never be given to a man there. You yourself agreed that your sister would only be married here in Manden. So give her to me."

Ma'an Sunjata said, "Eh! Father Kamanjan, that won't be possible. If I give you my younger sister, I would be embarrassed to discuss certain subjects with you. There are things I could discuss with you so long as there's no marriage between us. Now that my mother and father are both dead, I'm depending on your counsel on such matters. But a marriage between us would make it embarrassing for me to do so.[8] Besides that, you are a battle commander. If we do something to displease you, if you become offended, we might quarrel."

---

6. The four main provinces of Soso that commonly appear in praise-lines to Sumaworo (though rarely identified in the same way): Kukuba, Bantamba, Nyemi-Nyemi, and Kambasiga. This comment, which the bard attributes to a contemporary of Sunjata's father, appears to imply a failed policy of appeasement toward Sumaworo.

7. *Acacia albida*; in Mande lore, one of the many trees, including the baobab and the dubalen, that carry strong associations with the spirit world.

8. In this case of *buranya* ("having an older in-law"), Sunjata would have to practice great restraint and lack of familiarity toward his sister's husband, and would no longer be able to appeal to him for help or advice.

Kamanjan said, "Ah, give her to me."

"Well, I'll give her to you if you will command the Kamara people to show respect for the Mansaré people. Tell the Kamara people to show respect for my people and for me. The Kamara should respect us, *Kamaralu yé dan a na.*" (The Dannalu, who take their name from that saying, live between Balia and Wulada. Now, because of Ma Kolonkan's marriage to Kamanjan, the Dannalu must be mentioned whenever the Kamara are discussed.) Ma Kolonkan was given to Kamanjan Kamara as soon as he made this promise to Sunjata. Kamanjan entered her, and she eventually gave birth to his son Fadibali.

The Battle of Negeboriya

Kamanjan said, "Simbon, I respect you, and believe you'll be successful in the war against Sumaworo. But listen: don't go to Dakajalan yet. Go to Negeboriya first and pay your respects to Fakoli's relatives. Though Fakoli is from Negeboriya, not Manden, he has done much for us. Besides, haven't you ever heard the saying, 'Negeboriya Maghan, Kayafaya Maghan'?[9] The Negeboriyans are our in-laws.

"Fakoli has said, 'The Mande people are wrong if they think I am helping them only because I want to win the *mansaya* for myself,' and we believe him. After all, none of the Koroma living in our Mansaré towns have ever tried to take the *mansaya* for themselves.

"Fakoli has also said, 'I am only helping Manden because of Ma Tenenba Condé; it was she who raised and blessed me. Tenenba Condé's sister is So'olon Wulen Condé, and So'olon Wulen Condé's son is Ma'an Sunjata. So I am not helping you because of personal ambition. If you listen to the Mande people's gossip about me now, you'll be ashamed to face me later.'

"Turama'an and Kankejan have said the same sorts of things. So go and pay your respects to the people of Negeboriya."

Taking their leave from Tabon, Ma'an Sunjata and his companions mounted their horses and rode straight to Negeboriya. But Sumaworo had built a wall around that town by the time they arrived. In fact, Sumaworo had built walls around many towns of Manden and was occupying them with his troops.

When Sumaworo's men heard that So'olon Ma'an and his troops were coming to pay their respects to the people of Negeboriya, they lined their musket barrels along the top of the wall and waited. When Sunjata and his men arrived, the muskets fired and fired and fired at them!

Forced to retreat, Sunjata returned to find Manden in mourning over his defeat at the Battle of Negeboriya. But Sunjata's powerful army was not destroyed, and Sumaworo had lost his sacred drum Dunun Mutukuru during the battle. (That drum, the Dunun Mutukuru, was never found; only the *bala* was saved.)

[*In omitted passages, back in Manden two rams that are named for Sunjata and Sumaworo, respectively, fight one another in a symbolic preview of the battle to come. Preparing for the Battle of Dakajalan, Sunjata calls for volunteers. The army of Manden is divided into companies of men who possess occult powers, companies of those who have no magic, and one unit made up of famous ancestral figures with the power to become invisible. In a secret meeting with Manjan*

9. Kayafaya is said to have been a *jamana*, or province, attached to Negeboriya under the Koroma ruling lineage.

Bereté, Sunjata learns the elaborate strategy he must adopt to defeat Sumaworo. He exchanges his sorcery horse for the sorcery mare of the jelimuso Tunku Man-yan Diawara. He also sends a messenger to his sister, Nana Triban, who is in Soso, to retrieve from her the dibilan medicine that she steals from the tail of Sumaworo's horse]

Trading Insults and Swearing Oaths

Manden mourned after each of their battles against Sumaworo. He made many women widows. He made shirts and pants from the skins of Mande and Soso people. He sewed a hat of human skin. He even made shoes of human skin and then ordered the surviving Mande people to come and name them. If one of the people tried to name the shoes "Finfirinya Shoes," Sumaworo would say, "That is not the name." If someone tried "Dulubiri shoes," he would say, "That is not the name." Finally, the people asked him, "All right, Sumaworo, what are your shoes called?" He said, "My human-skin shoes are called 'Take the Air, take the Ground from the Chief.' I wear your skins because the Mande people will always be around me, Sumaworo. You will always be in my power."

After both sides had made their preparations, the war began. Briefly, here's what happened:

The three Mande divisions—including those men who could become invisible in the daytime and the five *mori* diviners—arrived at the first battle. Simbon was placed in the middle of his men, with Manjan Bereté directly in front of him. The men were packed so tightly that the head of one man's horse touched the tail of the horse in front of him. Sanbari Mara Cissé and Siriman Kanda Touré were there, as were Kòn Mara and Djané, Manden Bori, Tombonon Sitafa Diawara, Turama'an, Kankejan, and Fakoli. Sunjata ordered them to maintain their positions on the battlefield, so they marched back and forth in a line, like an army of ants. Simbon was in the middle!

When they arrived at the battlefield, Ma'an Sunjata said, "Men of Manden, wait here," and crossed the field with his masked flag bearers, headed for Suma-woro's camp. Sumaworo's troops were also there, waiting in position. Sumaworo sat astride his horse, surrounded by his corps of personal guards.

As he approached Sumaworo, Sunjata said, "Father Sumaworo, good morn-ing." (True bravery is revealed by the mouth!)

Sumaworo said, "Marahaba, good morning. Where are the Mande troops?"

"Ah, Father Sumaworo, they are over on the Mande side."

"Ah, is that how you usually arrange your troops?"

Sunjata said, "Well, I am new at this. This is our first encounter in battle. If I brought my men over here, they'd mingle with your troops, and we'd be unable to tell whose men are whose.[1] You can see them standing over there on the Mande side."

"Ah, So'olon Ma'an, this is not the usual procedure."

Feeling bold, Sunjata said, "Well, you killed all of the other leaders; there was nobody left to lead the Mande troops."

Sumaworo said, "I say to you, Bala Fasali, tell Simbon that I am doing him a favor by inviting him to meet here on the battlefield. I understand that the Mande

---

1. The problem of distinguishing between ally and enemy in the heat of battle was a serious concern. In an episode not included in this book, the narrator describes how Kamanjan Kamara introduced facial scarification for that purpose.

people sent for Sunjata so he could be their commander in battle. But apparently they did not tell him about anything that happened while he was away.

"This is why I have invited him to come and meet in the field: so that I can tell him what I have to say, and he can tell me what is on his mind. Then I will do to him what I planned to do—or he can try to do to me what he wants to."

Simbon said, "I appreciate the invitation. Ah! You are my respected elder. The person who has helped one's father is also one's father. But let me tell you something, father Sumaworo: people may refuse peanuts, but not the ones that have been placed right in front of them."

Sumaworo said, "M'ba, give me some snuff from Manden."[2]

"Ah! Father Sumaworo, it is more appropriate for the master to give snuff to his apprentice, rather than for the apprentice to give snuff to his master. Give me some snuff from Soso, so that I will know I have met my master."

Sumaworo took out his snuffbox and handed it to Sunjata. Simbon put some snuff in his palm, took a pinch and snorted it, took another pinch and snorted it, and put some in his mouth. He closed the snuffbox and gave it back to Sumaworo. The snuff did not even make Sunjata's tongue quiver.

Sumaworo was surprised. Anybody who took that snuff would immediately fall over. It was poison! But So'olon Ma'an sucked on the snuff and didn't even cough. He spit the snuff on the ground.

Then Sumaworo said, "Give me some Mande snuff." Simbon reached in his pocket, took out his snuffbox, and handed it to Sumaworo, who put some in his palm. He took a pinch of snuff and snorted it, took some more and snorted it, and put the rest in his mouth. That was specially prepared snuff, too, but it did not do anything to him.

Sumaworo said to him, "I asked you to meet with me because the Mande people seem to think you are their *mansa*, and it's true that you would not be here if you didn't have some *dalilu*. But your *dalilu* will do no good against me. I told you before, when you passed through Soso, that if the Mande people tried to send you to fight me, you should refuse. As you now know, I have become hot ashes surrounding Manden and Soso; any toddler who tries to cross me will be burned up to his thighs. And yet here you are."

"Ah, father Sumaworo, as I told you, this is my father's home, not yours. You are not from here: your grandfather came from Folonengbe; your father was a latecomer to Manden. You are only the second generation of your people in Manden. But we have been here for eight generations: our ancestor Mamadi Kani first came here from Hejaji. After him came Mamadi Kani's son, Kani Simbon, Kani Nyogo Simbon, Kabala Simbon, Big Simbon Mamadi Tanyagati, Balinene, Bele, and Belebakòn, and Farako Manko Farakonken. Now I am Farako Manko Farakonken's son, the eighth generation. My people have been here all along; you only arrived yesterday, your dawn is just breaking today.

"Huh!" continued Sunjata. "And you say that I have just arrived? M'ba, huh! You are my respected elder, so I will not be the first to make a move. You invited me here to tell me that I'm a disrespectful child? You just go ahead and show what you've got."

Sumaworo said, "Bisimillahi."

2. This request commences a standard ritual called *sigifili*, conducted between opposing commanders before a battle; it involved boast- ing about one's powers and swearing oaths while taking a poisonous snuff that would kill a liar.

The Battle of Dakajalan and Fakoli's Revenge

When something is filled to the brim, it will overflow.

When Sumaworo took his sword and struck at Sunjata, his blade flexed like a whip. Sunjata also struck with his sword; the blade of his sword also bent. Sumaworo raised his musket and fired, but nothing touched So'olon Ma'an. So'olon Ma'an then fired his musket at Sumaworo but failed to wound him.

With that, the *dalilu* was finished, and the two men just stood there. Sumaworo reached into his saddlebag and took his whip. As he raised his hand like this, So'olon Ma'an seized his reins like this—*Clap!*—and dashed away.

The two armies were waiting, Soso on one side, Manden on the other. Everybody was watching the commanders on the battlefield. Fakoli stood off to one side of Sunjata; Turama'an was on his other side. Sumaworo was also flanked by his men.

Blu, blu! Sunjata, Sumaworo, and their men dashed across the field and up the hill. Near the top of the hill, they faded from sight; even their dust disappeared. Soon they reached the edge of a very deep ravine. Gathering all her strength, Sunjata's sorcery mare (Tunku Manyan Diawara's horse) jumped the ravine and landed on the other side. When Sumaworo's horse tried to jump the ravine, it tumbled to the bottom.[3] Fakoli and Turama'an—whose horses safely jumped the ravine—turned and, with Sunjata, went to look down at Sumaworo who was trapped at the bottom of the ravine.

Sunjata called down, "Sumaworo, what is the matter?"

"So'olon Ma'an, kill me here; do not carry me to the town. Do not bring such shame to me. God controls all time. Please do not take me back."

Sumaworo removed his *dalilu* and dropped his horse-whip. He stripped completely, taking off his human-skin shirt and trousers.

Sunjata said, "I am not going to finish you off. No one can climb out of that ravine; you're stuck. I do not want your shirt of human skin, because it is the skin of my father's relatives. I will not take it." Turning to his companions he said, "Come, let's go home."

They had gone some distance when Fakoli made a decision, turned, and went back to the ravine. When he arrived there, he said to Sumaworo, "What did I tell you? When you took back your sister,[4] what did I say?" Taking his axe from his shoulder, Fakoli struck Sumaworo on the head, *poh!* He said, "This will be mentioned in Ma'an Sunjata's praise song." (And he was right! Though we sing, "Head-breaking Mari Jata," it was Fakoli who broke Sumaworo's head.)[5]

Fakoli started to leave. But he was still angry, so he went back to the ravine again and struck Sumaworo on the leg, *gbao!* Fakoli broke Sumaworo's leg,

---

3. Though not usually seen in versions of the Sunjata epic, the incident of the horse tumbling into a ravine is a popular motif in *jeli* storytelling, a favorite way of disposing of the hero's enemy.

4. Fakoli's wife, Keleya Konkon.

5. It is unusual for a *jeli* to describe the death of Sumaworo, as Tassey Condé does here. In many versions, Sumaworo flees to the mountain at Koulikoro where he disappears. The Kouyaté and Diabaté *jeliw*, among others, are usually careful not to say that Sumaworo was slain by Sunjata, Fakoli, or anybody else. Such things arc taken seriously in modern times, because Maninka and Bamana identify with the ancestors whose names they carry. The version translated here was recorded in a private performance in the narrator's own house, but in a public performance, giving details of a humiliating defeat (even one alleged to have occurred more than seven centuries ago) risks embarrassing any people in the audience who regard themselves as descendants of the defeated ancestor.

saying, "This will also be mentioned in Ma'an Sunjata's praise song." (That is why we sing, "Leg-Breaking Mari Jata.")

With his axe, Fakoli returned to the ravine a third time and broke Sumaworo's arm, saying, "This, too, will be mentioned in Ma'an Sunjata's praise song." (And so we sing, "Arm-Breaking Mari Jata." Aheh! It was not Jata who broke it! It was Fakoli who broke it.)

Finally Sunjata and his men went home. Laughter returned to Manden, and eventually Soso joined in.

[*In omitted passages, the narrator describes how, following the defeat of Sumaworo, the people of Soso dispersed and eventually settled in various communities along the Atlantic coast. Meanwhile, Sunjata begins to initiate reforms and organize the newly unified Mali Empire.*]

The Campaign against Jolofin Mansa

After the war was over, Ma'an Sunjata said, "My fathers and my brothers: now that the war has ended and the *mansaya* has come to us, the Mansaré, let's send our horse-buyers to Senu to replace the many Mande horses killed by Sumaworo. We should buy enough horses for each of our elders and warriors to have one."

So the horse-buyers went to Senu and bought hundreds of horses. On the way back to Manden, the horse-buyers stopped at the *jamana* of Jolofin Mansa, and there Jolofin Mansa robbed the buyers of their horses; he then took the horse-buyers captive and beheaded all but two. Jolofin Mansa sent the two survivors to tell Ma'an Sunjata that even though Ma'an Sunjata had taken over the power—that Sunjata had recently received the Mande *mansaya*—he knew the Mande walked on all fours like dogs, and that they should leave horse-riding to others.

The two horse-buyers arrived in Manden and gave the message to Ma'an Sunjata, who said, "Jolofin Mansa has extended an invitation to me. I myself will lead the campaign against Jolofin Mansa."

His younger brother Manden Bori said, "Elder brother, are you going to lead us in that campaign? Give me the command, and I will do the fighting."

"I am not giving you command of the army."

Fakoli said, "Simbon, give me the army! We will not stay here while you lead the army. Give the army to me, Fakoli, so I can go after Jolofin Mansa."

Simbon said, "I will not give you the army. I will go myself."

Meanwhile, Turama'an was digging his own grave. He cut some *tòrò* branches, laid them on his grave, and had his shroud sewn. Then he said to Ma'an Sunjata, "Simbon, I'll kill myself if you do not give me the army. Would you really leave us behind while you lead the army to go after Jolofin Mansa? Give me the army. If you don't, if you go after Jolofin Mansa yourself, you will lose me, for I'll kill myself."

"Ah," said Simbon. "I did not know you felt so strongly, Turama'an. Your *dalilu* and my *dalilu* are tied together: my mother was given to your fathers, who killed the buffalo of Dò ni Kiri. If your father and my mother had gotten along, my mother would have stayed with your father. Because my mother did not get along with your fathers, your fathers brought my mother to my father, and I was born out of that marriage, as were my younger brothers Manden Bori and So'olon Jamori.

"My father took my younger siblings Nana Triban and Tenenbajan, and gave them to Danmansa Wulanni and Danmansa Wulanba, your fathers. You, Turama'an, are the son of Danmansa Wulanni. Considering what you have said, you and I are equal in this war, and I will let you take the army."

So Sunjata gave Turama'an command of the army, and Turama'an prepared the army for war. With the campaign underway, they marched to Jolofin Mansa's land.

(You know Jolofin Mansa, he was one of the Mansaré. The son of Latali Kalabi, the Mansaré ancestor, was Danmatali Kalabi; Danmatali Kalabi then also named his son Latali Kalabi. This second Latali sired Kalabi Doman and Kalabi Bomba, and Kalabi Doman sired Mamadi Kani. Mamadi Kani sired Kani Simbon, Kani Nyogo Simbon, Kabala Simbon, Big Simbon Madi Tanyagati, and M'balinene; M'balinene sired Bele, Bele sired Belebakon, Belebakon sired Maghan Konfara, and this Farako Manko Farakonken was Ma'an Sunjata's father.

So Jolofin *Mansa* and Ma'an Sunjata both descended from the same person. And Jolofin's people—the *Jolofin na mò'òlu*—became known as the Wolofo.[6] Have you heard people calling the Wolofo "little Mande people"? That's because they all came from Manden.)

Turama'an marched the army of Manden to Jolofin Mansa's land and there destroyed Jolofin Mansa's place like it was an old clay pot; Turama'an broke it like an old calabash. He also captured those who were supposed to be captured, killed those who were supposed to be killed.

Though his soldiers had been defeated, Jolofin Mansa had not been captured, so he fled with Turama'an in pursuit. Jolofin Mansa headed for the big river.[7]

At that time, no one knew that Jolofin Mansa could transform himself into a crocodile, living on land or under water. When he came to the big river, Jolofin Mansa plunged in and swam into a cave; there he transformed himself into a crocodile and lay down to wait.

Standing above the cave, Turama'an and his men said, "Jolofin Mansa went in here." The Mande men were good warriors, but they were not used to water fighting. All of the battle commanders standing there were dressed for fighting on land; they were all wearing hunting clothes and carried quivers and bows. Until they stood at the entrance to that cave, the Mande people did not know that they had a warrior who could fight under water.

Turama'an said, "Jolofin Mansa has changed himself into a crocodile and gone into that cave. We can't leave him there, for if we destroy the war *mansa*'s home without killing the war *mansa* himself, we have not won the battle. But who will go after him?"

Everybody kept quiet, *lele!*

Again Turama'an asked, "Who will go after him?" Nobody spoke up, so Turama'an asked a third time, "Who will follow this man?"

The Diawara chief, whose name was Tombonon Sitafa Diawara, stepped out from among the soldiers. He said, "Turama'an, tell the Mande people that if they agree, I, Sitafa Diawara, will go after Jolofin Mansa. But also tell them that I am

6. Maninka pronunciation attaches an extra vowel. The Wolof, who call their country Jolof (see previous sentence), arc mainly in Senegal (the narrator's "Senu"), and they speak a lan- guage that is not interintelligible with Mand- ing languages.
7. The Senegal River.

not doing this to prove my manhood. I'm doing it because we can't return home to Simbon having only destroyed Jolofin Mansa's home. If we return home without also having killed Jolofin Mansa himself, Simbon will wonder why we told him to stay home."

(That is why, if you are a real man, you should stay low to the ground when you are among the *kamalenw*. You should only reveal the kind of man you are when somebody challenges your group.)

Meanwhile, Jolofin Mansa's crocodile wraith was lying in the cave, its mouth open wide. The upper jaw reached to the top of the entrance, the lower jaw reached to the bottom. Anybody who went after the crocodile would end up in its stomach, and the crocodle would just close his mouth. Eh! There would be no need to chew.

Sitafa Diawara said, "I'll give you two signs when I get down to where the crocodile is. If, while the water is bubbling and churning and turning the color of blood, you see a pelican flying from where the sun sets to where it rises, Manden should weep, for you'll know that Jolofin Mansa has defeated me. But if, while the water is bubbling and churning and turning the color of blood, the pelican flies from where the sun rises to where it sets, you Mande people should be happy, for it will mean I have honored you and God. Those are the signs I've given you."

Diawara put on his medicine clothes and gathered all his *dalilu*. He had a small knife fastened to his chest, and a short Bozo[8] fish-spear hung from his waist.

To the other warriors Diawara said, "Excuse me. We may meet in this world or we may meet in God's kingdom. If I'm successful, we'll meet in this world; I'll come back and find you here. But if I'm overcome by the crocodile, we'll meet in God's kingdom." Then he dove into the water and swam into the cave, unaware that he was actually swimming straight into the crocodile's stomach. The crocodile closed its mouth on him.

As the crocodile closed its mouth on him, Diawara the hunter demonstrated his *dalilu*. Though he was trapped inside the crocodile, he was still alive, as comfortable as if he were in his own house. Taking his spear from his side, he stabbed the crocodile here, *pu!*; he stabbed it there, *pu!* The crocodile went *kututu*. Diawara speared the crocodile over and over again.

The water bubbled, and blood came to the surface. As the water around him turned bloody, Diawara reached for the knife on his chest. He sliced a hole in the crocodile's belly and swam out of it. Then, still under the water, he twisted the crocodile's front legs and tied them together.

As Diawara swam to the surface with the crocodile, a pelican flew by, squawking, from east to west. Manden laughed. As they hauled the crocodile wraith up onto the riverbank, Jolofin Mansa himself appeared. He was captured, tied up, and taken to Sunjata, the *mansa*.

Turama'an, who was the commander at that battle, brought Jolofin Mansa's treasure to Ma'an Sunjata. Manden was at last free, and the war was over.

---

8. An ethnic group of the Middle Niger, specializing in fishing and boating occupations, mainly located between Sansanding and Lake Debo in Mali.

THE BOOK OF DEDE KORKUT
fifteenth century

The anonymous *Book of Dede Korkut* is the oldest example from the rich oral epic tradition of the Turkic peoples, which include, besides the Turks of Turkey, the Kazakhs, Kyrghyz, Uzbeks, Karakalpaks, Tatars, and many other nations in Central and northern Asia. Preserved almost by chance in manuscript, it gives us insight into the life and literary imagination of Asia Minor even as it invites comparison with other national epics. Combining the many cultures that shaped Asia Minor, *The Book of Dede Korkut* is a multilayered text that confronts individual heroism with a devout belief in an omnipotent god, and high literary style with moments of satire. Like other examples of oral literature, it preserves the unique atmosphere of a story being told to a live audience.

In the ninth and tenth centuries, the Oghuz federation of Turkic nomadic tribes, migrating westward from the area of today's Mongolia, converted to Islam in the region between the Syr Darya and Amu Darya rivers—where modern-day Kazakhstan and Uzbekistan meet. Their migration over subsequent centuries into the larger Middle East marked the beginning of Turkish domination of the region, which would last until World War I, when the Ottoman Empire collapsed. The Seljuq and later the Ottoman dynasties, who ruled over far-flung empires, both traced their genealogy back to the Oghuz nomads.

As the Ottomans refashioned themselves as heirs to a Byzantine imperial tradition, the Turkic nomadic tribes were increasingly marginalized politically, and as the Ottoman elite developed distinctly urban tastes, they were alienated from nomadic culture. Yet nomads continued to be an important part of the social fabric of Asia Minor. There, Oghuz bards continued to compose heroic tales populated with the leaders (khans) and heroes of a mythical, idealized past. These tales preserved and transmitted the fundamental values of the tribe and a code of conduct for their aristocracy, including the ideals of courage, generosity, chivalry, and compassion. Just as the *Iliad* did for the ancient Greeks, or the *Song of Roland* did for medieval France, so the heroic tales collected in *The Book of Dede Korkut* told its Oghuz audiences who they were and to what they should aspire.

The Book of Dede Korkut was written down around the second half of the fifteenth century, making it the oldest Turkic epic known today. While elements may go back to pre-Islamic Central Asia, its current form reflects the politics and geography of eastern Asia Minor at that time, centered on the Turkmen Empire of the "White Sheep" (Aqqoyunlu), which flourished in the fourteenth and fifteenth centuries, before it succumbed to the Ottomans.

Although preserved as a written text, *The Book of Dede Korkut* displays many hallmarks of oral literature. Among the Turks, oral epics were performed on special occasions, like festivities, banquets, weddings, at contests, or during meetings among several tribes. The khan, the supreme leader of a tribe or tribal confederation, himself invited the singer to present his tales, and the singer would frequently address the khan directly during the performance. In *The Book of Dede Korkut*, occasional interjections of the phrase, "Oh, my Khan," replicate this aspect of oral performance.

Unlike western epics such as the *Iliad* or *Odyssey*, Turkic epics are not entirely rendered in verse. The language of *The Book of Dede Korkut* is mostly a simple, colorful prose in which parallel sentence structures and the unique properties of Turkic languages aid scansion and create a strong effect of rhythm. Cyclical narrative patterns and symmetries, as well as other devices that are typical of oral narratives, such as the association of certain topical phrases with certain characters, aided the memory of the singer. The prose narrative is interspersed with lyrical passages in verse that not only heighten the sense of drama, but also provided the singer with a space for adaptation and improvisation.

In its present form, *Dede Korkut* consists of a lengthy prologue and twelve tales, which, however, are not unified into a coherent cycle. Ten of these tales focus on conflicts either among the tribes or between the Oghuz and their enemies. Its cast of characters consists of the khan of the tribe of Oghuz, his family, and his courtiers, all of them noble and brave, and a varied cast of villains, demons, monsters, and infidels as their adversaries. The most important figure is Dede (Grandfather) Korkut, the wise man and advisor to the khan. Dede Korkut is the spiritual authority who gives names to children, an important rite of passage among the ancient Turks. He is also the source of wisdom, often consulted for his sage advice; a set of his aphorisms constitutes a separate chapter of the book. Most significantly, he is the narrator of the tales, and thus plays the dual role of singer and shaman, a magician of word and spirit.

Bayindir Khan is the paramount chief in *The Book of Dede Korkut*, but he is not the hero of these tales. That role is played by his son-in-law and commander-in-chief, Salur Kazan, an exemplary hero who leads and inspires the other warriors. Four of the tales are devoted to his adventures and those of other members of his family, and his presence is felt in the other stories as well.

The episode we've chosen, "The Story of How Basat Killed Goggle-Eye," has another hero at its center: Basat, son of Uruz Koja, one of the inner circle of Oghuz noblemen. The story is a marvelous and surprising parallel to the story in Homer's *Odyssey* of the man-eating, one-eyed giant Polyphemus. The monstrous Goggle-Eye is born from a *peri*, a female spirit or fairy who had been raped by a man of the Oghuz. The character of Basat, who spends his childhood raised by lions after having been lost as a baby during a hasty Oghuz escape from an approaching enemy, also calls to mind the character Enkidu from *The Epic of Gilgamesh*, another "wild man" who must be taught the ways of humans after spending his early life "consort[ing] with wild beasts." How, exactly, these elements of the tale traveled from Greece and Mesopotamia to the Oghuz is impossible to say; no one has ever proposed a plausible scenario of transmission. And yet, the parallels are undeniable.

An important cultural ingredient of the tale, and of *The Book of Dede Korkut* generally, is Islam. In one episode, not reprinted here, a father, convinced by a blood-stained shirt that his son has been killed, loses his sight grieving over the loss, and is healed as his son returns. This echo of the biblical story of Joseph, an important touchstone for Muslims (as well as Jews and Christians), is just one of many moments in *Dede Korkut* where the traditional, pre-Islamic oral tales of the Oghuz were adapted to incorporate elements of Islamic theology and culture. Sometimes, the melding of the two has unusual effects. In our selected episode, for example, the hero escapes Goggle-

Eye not by using his own wit and strength, but by means of a miracle reminiscent of popular Islamic hagiographies, a motif that seems at odds with the heroic ideal. Another narrative complication, and another bit of evidence of the hybrid status of *Dede Korkut*, is the presence of satirical passages, scattered here and there, that seem to undermine the serious intent of the epic. The existence of numerous layers in *The Book of Dede Korkut*, despite its early date, speaks to the degree of adaptation possible within oral narratives.

Turkish oral epic narratives were a living part of the aristocratic society of the nomadic tribes, and for this reason they were likely to lose their meaning and be forgotten once that society changed. Such a process seems to have been under way in Asia Minor in the second half of the fifteenth century. And yet, at that point somebody decided to write down *The Book of Dede Korkut*, preserving it for a reading (and probably urban) audience. No one knows who made that decision, or why. At first, the work did not find a place in the genres of written Ottoman literature. Interest in *The Book of Dede Korkut* was only rekindled in the twentieth century, when Kemal Atatürk, the founder and long-time president of modern-day Turkey, sought to emphasize a non-Muslim Turkish national heritage in contradistinction to the Ottoman Islamic tradition. Centuries after having been written down and forgotten, *The Book of Dede Korkut* acquired an important role in fashioning cultural identity once more.

The Story of How Basat Killed Goggle-Eye[1]

It is related, my Khan, that once while the Oghuz were sitting in their encampment the enemy fell upon them. In the darkness of night they broke and scattered. As they fled, the baby son of Uruz Koja fell. A lioness found him, carried him off and nursed him. Time passed, and the Oghuz came back and settled in their old home. One day the horse-drover of Oghuz Khan brought him news. 'My Khan, there is a lion comes out of the thicket roaring, but he walks with a swagger, like a man. He attacks the horses and sucks their blood.' Said Uruz, 'My Khan, maybe it is my little son who fell that time when we scattered.' The nobles mounted their horses and came to the lair of the lioness. They drove her off and seized the boy. Uruz took him to his tent. They held a celebration, there was eating and drinking. But for all that they had brought the boy home he would not stay; back he went to the lion's lair. Again they seized him and brought him back. Dede Korkut came and said, 'My boy, you are a human being; do not consort with wild beasts. Come, ride fine horses, amble and trot in company with fine young men. Your elder brother's name is Kiyan Seljuk, your name shall be Basat. I have given you your name; may God give you long life.'[2]

One day the Oghuz migrated to their summer pasture. Now Uruz had a shepherd whom they called Konur Koja Saru Choban. Whenever the Oghuz migrated this man always went first. There was a spring called Uzun Pinar, which had become a haunt of the peris.[3] Suddenly something startled the sheep. The shepherd was angry with the goat which led the flock, and he went forward, to see that the peri maidens had spread their wings and were flying.

1. Translated from the Turkish by Geoffrey Lewis.
2. Among the Oghuz, naming was a rite of passage into manhood. The young man's name, Basat, means "who attacks horses."
3. Fairies or female demons.

He threw his cloak over them and caught one. He desired her and straightway violated her. The flock began to scatter; he ran to head them off, and the peri beat her wings and flew away, saying, 'Shepherd, you have left something in trust with me. When a year has passed, come and take it. But you have brought ruination on the Oghuz.' Fear fell on the shepherd's heart and his face turned pale with anxiety at the peri's words.

Time passed, and again the Oghuz migrated to that summer pasture. Again the shepherd came to that spring. Again something startled the sheep and again the shepherd went forward. He saw a brightly glittering shape lying on the ground. The peri appeared and said, 'Come, shepherd, take back your property. But you have brought ruination on the Oghuz.' Seeing this shape, the shepherd was seized with dread. He turned round and began to rain stones on it from his sling. As each stone struck it, it grew bigger. The shepherd abandoned the shape and fled, and the sheep followed him. Now it happened that at that time Bayindir Khan and the nobles had gone out riding, and they chanced on this spring. They saw a monstrous thing lying there, its head indistinguishable from its arse. They surrounded it, and one warrior dismounted and kicked it. At every kick it grew in size. Several other warriors dismounted and kicked it, and still it grew at every kick. Uruz Koja also dismounted and kicked it. His spur drove into it and the shape split down the middle, and out came a child. Its body was that of a man, but it had one eye at the top of its head. Uruz took this child, wrapped it in the skirt of his garment and said, 'My Khan, give this to me and I shall rear it together with my son Basat.' 'Take it,' said Bayindir Khan, 'it's yours.'

Uruz took Goggle-Eye and brought him to his house. He ordered a wet-nurse to come, and she put her nipple into the child's mouth. He gave one suck and took all her milk; a second suck, and he took her blood; a third, and took her life. Several other wet-nurses were brought and he destroyed them. Seeing that this was impossible, they decided to feed him on milk, but a cauldronful a day was not enough. They fed him and he grew; he began to walk, he began to play with the little boys. He started to eat the nose of one, the ear of another. The upshot was that the whole camp was greatly upset at him, but there was nothing they could do. They complained and wept in chorus before Uruz. Uruz beat Goggle-Eye, he abused him, he ordered him to stop it, but he paid no attention. Finally he drove him from his house.

Goggle-Eye's peri mother came and put a ring on her son's finger, saying, 'My son, this is so that no arrow will pierce you or sword cut you.' Goggle-Eye left the Oghuz land and came to a high mountain. He infested the roads, he seized men, he became a notorious outlaw. Many men were sent against him; they shot arrows, which did not pierce him; they struck at him with swords, which did not cut him; they thrust at him with lances, which did not penetrate him. No shepherd, no herd-boy was left; he ate them all. Then he began to eat people from the Oghuz. The Oghuz assembled and marched against him. Seeing them, Goggle-Eye was angered; he uprooted a tree, threw it, and destroyed fifty or sixty men. He dealt a blow at the prince of heroes, Kazan, and the world became too narrow for his head. Kara Göne, Kazan's brother, became helpless in Goggle-Eye's hand. Alp Rüstem son of Düzen was killed. So valiant a man as the son of Ushun Koja died by his hand. His two pure-souled brothers perished at his hand. So too did Bügdüz Emen of the bloody moustaches. White-headed Uruz Koja he made vomit blood, and his son Kiyan Seljuk's gall-bladder split with terror. The Oghuz could do nothing against Goggle-Eye, they broke and fled. Goggle-Eye hemmed them in and barred their way, he would not let them go, he brought them back to where they were. In all, the Oghuz broke seven times, and seven times he barred their way and brought them back. The Oghuz were totally helpless in Goggle-Eye's hand.

They went and called Dede Korkut, they consulted with him and said, 'Come, let us make terms.' They sent Dede Korkut to Goggle-Eye. He came and greeted him, then he said, 'Goggle-Eye, my son, the Oghuz are helpless in your hand, they are overwhelmed. They have sent me to the dust of your feet; they wish to come to terms with you.' Goggle-Eye said, 'Give me sixty men a day to eat.' Dede Korkut replied, 'This way you won't have any men left; you'll exhaust the supply. Let us give you two men and five hundred sheep a day.' 'Very well,' replied Goggle-Eye, 'so be it, I agree. And give me two men to prepare my food for me to eat.' Dede Korkut returned to the Oghuz and told them, 'Give Goggle-Eye Yünlü Koja and Yapaghilu Koja to cook his food. He also asks for two men and five hundred sheep a day.' They agreed. Whoever had four sons gave one of them, leaving three. Whoever had three gave one of them, leaving two. Whoever had two gave one, leaving one. There was a man called Kapak Kan, who had two sons. One he gave and one was left. His turn came round again. The mother screamed and cried and lamented.

Now it seems, my Khan, that Basat son of Uruz, who had gone on an expedition into the lands of the infidel, returned at this point. The poor woman said to herself, 'Basat has just come back from raiding. I'll go and perhaps he might give me a prisoner so that I can ransom my son.' Basat had pitched his gold-adorned pavilion and was sitting in it, when he saw a lady approaching. She came in, greeted Basat and wept, saying,

'Son of Uruz, my lord Basat,
Renowned among the Inner Oghuz and the Outer Oghuz.
With your flighted arrows that do not stay in your hand,
With your strong bow of the horn of the he-goat,
Help me!'

Said Basat, 'What is it you desire?' The poor woman replied, 'On the face of this treacherous world there has erupted a man who has not let the Oghuz rest in their domain. Those who wield the pure black steel swords have not cut a hair of his that might be cut; those who brandish the bamboo lances have not been able to make them penetrate; those who shoot the hornbeam arrows have achieved nothing. He dealt a blow at Kazan, prince of heroes; Kazan's brother Kara Göne and Bügdüz Emen of the bloody moustaches became powerless in his hand. Your white-bearded father Uruz he made vomit blood; your brother Kiyan Seljuk's gall-bladder burst on the field of battle and he gave up his soul. Of the other nobles of the teeming Oghuz, some he overpowered and some he killed. Seven times he drove the Oghuz from their place. Then he agreed to make terms; he demanded two men and five hundred sheep a day. They gave him Yünlü Koja and Yapaghilu Koja to serve him. Whoever had four sons gave one of them, whoever had three sons gave one of them, whoever had two sons gave one of them. I had two dear sons and gave one, and one remained. Now the turn has come round to me again and they are asking for him too. Help me, my lord!' Basat's dark eyes filled with tears. He declaimed for his brother; let us see, my Khan, what he declaimed.

'Your tents, pitched in a place apart,
Can that pitiless one have overthrown, brother?
Your swift-running horses from their stalls
Can that pitiless one have stolen, brother?
Your sturdy young camels from their file
Can that pitiless one have taken, brother?
The sheep you would slaughter at your feasting
Can that pitiless one have slaughtered, brother?
Your dear bride I proudly saw you bring home
Can that pitiless one have parted from you, brother?
You have made my white-bearded father mourn his son;
Can this be, O my brother?
You have made my white-skinned mother weep;
Can this be, O my brother?
Brother, pinnacle of my black mountain yonder!
Brother, flood of my lovely eddying river!
Brother, strength of my strong back!
Brother, light of my dark eyes!
I have lost my brother.'

So saying, he wept and lamented greatly. Then he gave that lady a captive and said, 'Go, ransom your son.' The lady took the captive and came and gave him in place of her son. Moreover she brought Uruz the good news that his son had come home.

Uruz rejoiced, and came with the nobles of the teeming Oghuz to meet Basat. Basat kissed his father's hand and they cried and wept together. He came to his mother's house. His mother came to meet him and pressed her dear son to her heart. Basat kissed his mother's hand, they embraced and wept together. The Oghuz nobles assembled and there was eating and drinking. Basat said, 'Princes, I shall meet Goggle-Eye for my brother's sake; what do you say?' Thereupon Kazan Bey declaimed; let us see, my Khan, what he declaimed.

'Goggle-Eye burst forth, a black dragon!
I chased him round the face of the sky but could not catch him, Basat.
Goggle-Eye burst forth, a black tiger!
I chased him round the darkling mountains but could not catch him, Basat.
Goggle-Eye burst forth, a raging lion!
I chased him round the dense forests but could not catch him, Basat.
Though you be a man, though you be a prince,
You will not be like me, Kazan.
Do not make your white-bearded father cry!
Do not make your white-haired mother weep!'

'I shall surely go,' said Basat, and Kazan replied, 'You know best.' Then Uruz wept and said, 'Son, do not leave my hearth desolate. I beg you, don't go.' Basat answered, 'No, my white-bearded honoured father, I shall go,' and he would not listen. He took from his quiver a fistful of arrows and stuck them in his belt, he girded on his sword, he grasped his bow, he rolled up his skirts, he kissed his parents' hands, he made his peace with all, he said 'Good-bye!'

He came to the crag of Salakhana, where Goggle-Eye was. He saw Goggle-Eye lying with his back to the sun. He took an arrow from his belt and shot it at Goggle-Eye's back. The arrow did not penetrate, it broke. He shot another, which also broke. Goggle-Eye said to the cooks, 'The flies here are a bit of a nuisance.' Basat shot another arrow, and that broke too. One piece fell in front of Goggle-Eye, who leaped up and looked around. When he saw Basat, he clapped his hands and bellowed with laughter. He said to the cooks, 'Another spring lamb from the Oghuz!' He clutched Basat and held him, he dangled him by the throat, he brought him into his den, he pushed him into the leg of his boot and said, 'Cooks! This afternoon you will put this one on the spit for me and I'll eat him.' Then he fell asleep again. Now Basat had a dagger, and he cut the boot and slipped out. 'Tell me, men,' said he, 'how can this creature be killed?' 'We do not know,' they answered, 'but there is no flesh anywhere except his eye.' Basat advanced right up to Goggle-Eye's head, raised his eyelid and saw that his eye was indeed flesh. 'Come on, men,' he said, 'put the spit in the fire and get it red-hot.' They did so. Then Basat took it in his hand, invoked blessings on Muhammad of beautiful name, and drove the spit into Goggle-Eye's eye, which was destroyed. So loud did he scream and bellow that the mountains and rocks echoed.

Basat bounded into the midst of the sheep, down into the cave. Goggle-Eye knew Basat was in the cave. He set himself at the entrance, put a foot on each side of it and said, 'Ho billy-goats, leaders of the flock, come one by one and pass through.' They did so, and he patted each one's head. 'My dear yearlings, and you my good fortune, my white-blazed ram, come and pass through.' A ram rose up and stretched itself. At once Basat leaped at it, cut its throat and flayed it. He left the head and tail attached to the skin, and got inside it. Basat came in front of Goggle-Eye. Now Goggle-Eye guessed that Basat was inside the skin, and said, 'White-blazed ram, you knew through what part I might be destroyed. I shall dash you against the cave-wall so that your tail greases the cave.' Basat gave the ram's head into Goggle-Eye's hand, and Goggle-Eye grasped it tightly by the muzzle. He lifted it and held the muzzle with the skin hanging. Basat slipped between Goggle-Eye's legs and away. Goggle-Eye raised the muzzle, dashed it against the ground and said, 'Boy, have you escaped?' Basat replied, 'My God has saved me.' Said Goggle-Eye, 'Boy, take this ring which is on my finger and put it on your own finger, and arrow and sword will have no effect on you.' Basat took the ring and put it on his finger. 'Boy,' said Goggle-Eye, 'have you taken the ring and put it on?' 'I have,' said Basat. Goggle-Eye rushed at Basat, flailing and cutting with a dagger. He leaped away and stood on open ground. He saw that the ring was now lying under Goggle-Eye's foot. 'Have you escaped?' asked Goggle-Eye. Basat replied, 'My God has saved me.' Said Goggle-Eye, 'Boy, do you see that vault?' 'I see it,' he replied. Goggle-Eye said, 'I have a treasure; go and seal it so that the cooks don't take it.' Basat entered the vault and saw mounds of gold and silver. Looking at it, he forgot himself. Goggle-Eye shut the door of the vault and said, 'Are you inside there?' 'I am,' replied Basat. Goggle-Eye said, 'I shall shake it so that you and the vault are dashed to pieces.' There came to Basat's tongue the words 'There is no god but God; Muhammad is the Messenger of God.' Straightway the vault split and doors were opened in seven places, through one of which he came out. Goggle-Eye put his hand against the vault and pushed so hard that the vault crumbled to bits. Said Goggle-Eye, 'Boy, have you escaped?' Basat replied, 'My God has saved me.' Said Goggle-Eye, 'It seems you can't be killed. Do you see that cave?' 'I see it,' said Basat. 'There are two swords in it,' said Goggle-Eye, 'one with a scabbard and one without. The one without a scabbard will cut off my head. Go fetch it and cut off my head.' Basat went up to the opening of the cave. He saw a sword without a scabbard, ceaselessly moving up and down. 'I shan't get hold of this,' said he, 'without a bit of trouble.' He drew his own sword and held it out, and the moving sword split it in two. He went and fetched a tree and held it against the sword, which split it in two also. Then he took his bow in his hand, and with an arrow he struck the chain by which the sword was suspended. The sword fell and buried itself in the ground. He put it into his own scabbard and held it firmly by the hilt. He came out and said, 'Hey Goggle-Eye! How are you?' Goggle-Eye answered, 'Hey boy! Aren't you dead yet?' 'My God has saved me,' replied Basat. 'It seems you can't be killed,' said Goggle-Eye. Then crying loudly he declaimed; let us see, my Khan, what he declaimed.

'My eye, my eye, my only eye!
With you, my only eye,
I once routed the Oghuz.
Man, you have robbed me of my chestnut eye;
May the Almighty rob you of your sweet life!
Such pain I suffer in my eye,
May God Almighty give no man pain in the eye.'

Then again he spoke:

'What is the place where you dwell, man, and whence you migrate in
    the summer?
If you lose your way in the dark night, what is your watchword?
Who is your Khan who carries the great standard?
Who is your hero who leads on the day of battle?
What is the name of your white-bearded father?
For a valiant warrior to conceal his name from another is shameful;
What is your name, man? Tell me.'

Basat declaimed to Goggle-Eye; let us see, my Khan, what he declaimed.

'My place where I dwell, whence I migrate in the summer, is the
    southland.
If I lose my way in the dark night, my watchword is God.
Our Khan who carries the great standard is Bayindir Khan.
Our hero who leads on the day of battle is Salur Kazan.
If you ask my father's name, it is Mighty Tree.
If you ask my mother's name, it is Raging Lioness.
If you ask my name, it is Basat son of Uruz.'

'Then we are brothers!' said Goggle-Eye, 'Spare me!' Basat replied,

'You filthy scoundrel, you have made my white-bearded father weep,
You have made my old white-haired mother cry,
You have killed my brother Kiyan,
You have widowed my white-skinned sister-in-law,
You have orphaned her chestnut-eyed babes;
Shall I let you be?
Till I have wielded my pure black steel sword,
Till I have cut off your pointed-capped head,
Till I have spilled your red blood on the ground,

Till I have avenged my brother Kiyan,
I shall not let you be.'

Thereupon Goggle-Eye declaimed once more:

'I meant to rise up from my place,
To break my pact with the nobles of the teeming Oghuz,
To kill their newborn young,
To have once more my fill of man-meat.
I meant, when the nobles of the teeming Oghuz massed against me,
To flee and shelter at the crag of Salakhana,
To cast rocks from a mighty catapult,
To go down, let the rocks fall on my head, and die.
Man, you have robbed me of my chestnut eye;
May the Almighty rob you of your sweet life!'

Yet again Goggle-Eye declaimed:

'I have made the white-bearded old men weep much;
Their white beards' curse must have smitten you, O my eye!
I have made the white-haired old women weep much;
Their tears must have smitten you, O my eye!
Many the dark-moustached youths I have eaten;
Their manhood must have smitten you, O my eye!
Many the maidens I have eaten, their little hands dyed with henna;
Their small curses must have smitten you, O my eye!
Such pain I suffer in my eye,
May God Almighty give no man pain in the eye.
My eye, my eye, O my eye, my only eye!'

Basat, enraged, rose up and forced him down on his knees like a camel, and
with Goggle-Eye's own sword he cut off Goggle-Eye's head. He made a hole in
it, tied his bowstring to it and dragged it and dragged it until he reached the
door of the cave. He sent Yünlü Koja and Yapaghilu Koja to take the good news
to the Oghuz. They mounted grey-white horses and galloped away.

The news came to the lands of the teeming Oghuz. Horse-mouthed Uruz Koja
galloped to his tent and gave Basat's mother glad tidings. 'Good news!' he said,
'Your son has killed Goggle-Eye!' The nobles of the teeming Oghuz arrived, they
came to the crag of Salakhana and brought out the head of Goggle-Eye for all to
see. Dede Korkut came and played joyful music. He related the adventures of the
valiant fighters for the Faith, and he invoked blessings on Basat:

'When you reach the black mountain may He make a way,
May He give you passage across the blood-red water.'

And he said,

'Manfully have you avenged your brother's blood,
You have saved the nobles of the teeming Oghuz from a heavy burden;
May Almighty God give you honour and glory, Basat!'

When the hour of death comes may it not part you from the pure Faith, and
may He forgive your sins for the sake of Muhammad the Chosen of beautiful
name, O my Khan!

EVLIYA ÇELEBI

1611–ca. 1683

Evliya Çelebi's detailed descriptions of the far-flung corners of the Ottoman Empire, collected in his ten-volume *Book of Travels*, represent a high-water mark of travel literature. *The Book of Travels'* sheer scale and sweep, spanning more than forty years and the entire expanse of the empire, from Sudan to Vienna, the literary quality of its abundant anecdotes and other narratives, and the intertwining of observation and imagination make it an indispensable and immensely compelling window onto lost times, places, and people.

LIFE

Evliya's father was a goldsmith who worked for the Ottoman sultans. His mother was related to Grand Vizier Melek Ahmed Pasha, later Evliya's most important patron. His title "çelebi" marks him as educated and sets him apart from the career lines in Ottoman officialdom and in the military. Evliya distinguished himself early on by his beautiful voice, acting as müezzin (the caller to prayer) and reciter of the Qur'an. His seemingly effortless eloquence and wit, coupled with his impressive erudition (the product of a vast traditional education), made him an ideal boon companion first for Sultan Murad IV, then for Melek Ahmed Pasha and other members of the elite. Evliya accompanied these dignitaries to posts in every corner of the empire, serving them in a number of occasional tasks, like envoy, inspector, and müezzin. Remunerations and profits from such

tasks, together with a modest fortune from his family, allowed him to live an independent life, and no marriage hindered his mobility. In 1671 he went on the pilgrimage to Mecca, and then settled in Cairo. Throughout his travels, Evliya gathered impressions and material; the anecdotal style and rich language of his narrative suggests that he may have told much of it orally first, during evening conversations in the social gatherings of his patrons and other members of the Ottoman elite. What sets him apart from many other entertaining travelers in a highly mobile elite was that, late in life, he wrote his impressions down in ten large volumes. Although complete, the book is missing the final touches, which suggests that he worked on it until his death. The date of his death, however, is a matter of speculation, because outside of his *Book of Travels*, there is barely any record of Evliya.

THE BOOK OF TRAVELS

Widely acclaimed today as the single most important work of Ottoman literature, *The Book of Travels* languished in obscurity for a long time after Evliya's death. Very few manuscript copies were made, and the scarce references by later authors dismiss Evliya as a storyteller and a liar. In the nineteenth century western orientalists began to draw attention to *The Book of Travels*, which was printed for the first time in the twentieth century, but only in the last few decades has appreciation of this text as a literary monument truly begun.

Bracketed by descriptions of the two most important Ottoman cities, Istanbul, where Evliya was born, and Cairo, where he spent his later years writing, *The Book of Travels* is many things. It is a factual account, perceived with the eye of an administrator, of provinces, cities, villages, fiefs and other sources of revenue, roads, and waystations. It is also a repository for innumerable factoids and narratives—legends, histories, local lore, personal adventures, and tall tales—that the passionate storyteller inserted in order to make his work as entertaining as it was informative. Taken altogether, *The Book of Travels* is a carefully crafted, monumental mirror that Evliya presents to his Ottoman audience to show them who they are or ought to be.

Evliya wrote in a sophisticated and often playful style, afforded by Ottoman Turkish with its rich vocabulary of Persian and Arabic, that moved through every register between crude colloquialism and artistic rhymed prose. As the American Turcologist Robert Dankoff has observed, two discourses alternate, often unpredictably, in *The Book of Travels*: "one of persuasion, in which it was important that [Evliya's] listeners give credence to what he was saying; and one of diversion, in which it was more important to arouse their wonder and delight." Evliya measured cities and listed tax revenues, he recorded ancient legends of kings and saints, and he provided samples of all the languages he encountered, often in amazing accuracy. But he also noted the sensational and fantastical, such as the case of the girl who gave birth to a baby elephant, and the seemingly mundane, such as the typical names of the male and female slaves of Diyarbakir, a town in southeastern Turkey. His own adventures feature prominently, sometimes casting him in a heroic light, as when he faced down a notorious bandit in the Balkans, but they can also be farcical, as when an infidel fighter surprised him relieving himself not far from the battlefield. Everything goes, as long as it yields a good story, and it does not have to be true: Evliya's readers will certainly have known that the prophet Kaffah, whom he narrates in much detail, never existed, and might have recognized that some stories are patterned on ancient lore.

Serious or joking, however, Evliya remained a true Ottoman, committed to its elite ideals of cosmopolitan, multilingual erudition. His attention to the sacred spaces of mosques, dervish lodges, and tombs of saints betray a profound Islamic piety, lightened by the awareness of human fallibility and the wisdom which characterize the mystical form of Islam, Sufism. His rhetoric abounds with references to holy warfare (*ghaza*) and the ideal of Ottoman world domination, yet, in his work it is tinged with a kind of romantic nostalgia for an ideal of the past. Instead of religious fanaticism, his account is imbued with a deep spirit of humanism, which allowed him to acknowledge and overcome difference.

These various ingredients are especially visible in one of the rare instances of Evliya's travel leading beyond Ottoman boundaries—his visit to Vienna in 1665 (which is represented in the excerpt below). Evliya came to Vienna with the delegation of Kara Mehmed Pasha to negotiate a peace agreement after an Ottoman campaign had been halted at St. Gotthard in western Hungary. His description makes the Habsburg capital another part of the mirror, in which the Ottoman audience recognized itself, in positive or negative terms. Although not an official representative, Evliya writes with a keen awareness of Ottoman state interests, as he observes the symbolic jousting of the two diplomatic delegations in their encounter at the border. He explores every corner of Vienna with a natural curiosity, and is not shy to socialize with the locals, without losing his cultural superiority. As he mocks the Catholic ritual, he implicitly extols the somber practices of Islam; as he praises Austrian achievements in the arts, sciences, and technology, he criticizes his fellow countrymen for neglecting them. His truly Ottoman appreciation of beauty and the good life extends to the pretty youth and the lush gardens of infidel Austria.

Most importantly, however, Vienna for Evliya was a place charged with history and meaning. Vienna was identified with the "Golden Apple" of the old Turkish myth that promised eternal conquest to the Ottomans and that also held a prominent place in Ottoman political ritual. The memory of the first Ottoman siege of Vienna in 1529 under Süleyman I (1520–66), the idealized sultan of a "Golden Age," remained with Evliya throughout his visit. In Ottoman legendary lore on which Evliya draws, Süleyman's *ghazis* (warriors of faith) left numerous tokens throughout the city, such as the golden sphere on the bell tower of St. Stephen, that promised, even as they were retreating, future conquest of the city. Yet at the time of his writing, Evliya had probably heard the news of the disastrous defeat that the Ottomans had suffered at the gates of Vienna in 1683, a defeat that forever tipped the balance of power in southeastern Europe toward the West.

The mixing of the factual and the legendary in Evliya's account of Vienna has puzzled readers to the point that historians long doubted that he was even there. Only the discovery in the 1970s of Evliya's name on a roster of the Ottoman delegation in the Austrian archives has ended these doubts. As a traveler records his impressions of foreign places and peoples, he gives them meaning in dialogue with his domestic audience and according to their cultural horizon. Evliya Çelebi's *Book of Travels* is a particularly rich and complex product of this process.

From The Book of Travels[1]

[*In 1665, Evliya Çelebi accompanied a diplomatic delegation under Kara Mehmed Pasha to Vienna to exchange the ratification of the peace treaty. In our first excerpt, delegations from the Habsburgs and the Ottomans have arrived at the border between the two empires to conclude the peace arrangement previously negotiated. Evliya describes the complicated ritual of the encounter at the border posts as a symbolic tournament of the two states, of course taking sides with his patron, the Ottoman ambassador.*]

The description of the border posts

These things they call border posts: when the deceased Sultan Süleyman took Esztergom and Székesfehérvár from the hands of the German Emperor he had

---

1. These sections have been translated from the Turkish by Gottfried Hagan with guidance of the German translation by Richard Kreutel and Erich Prokosch: *Im Reiche des Goldenen Apfels. Des türkischen Weltenbummlers Evliyâ* *Çelebi denkwürdige Reise in das Giaurenland und in die Stadt und Festung Wien anno 1665*, Osmanische Geschichtsschreiber. Graz, Wien, Köln: Verlag Styria, 1985.

a hillock thrown up about twelve hours from both of these cities, on the Danube river near Komárom.[2] On top there is plenty of space, enough to form a circle. The hillock is round and extends from east to west; on our side as well as on the side of the infidels a wooden pole is erected, more than five times the height of a man. Exactly in the middle between the two poles there is a third, which demarcates the border. This is what they call border post.

* * *

The two ambassadors climbed the border mound erected by Sultan Süleyman, and from both sides the dragomans started to go back and forth, but the ambassadors themselves stood near their respective poles, each surrounded by fifty elders and experienced advisors. Our pasha, too, halted with his neat swordbearers and footmen with their tassels and embroidered quivers and belts and sashes, and his lackeys in full armor, and his flask-bearers and his neatly dressed attendants, and was only talking to Hacı Mustafa Pasha of Székesfehérvár and İskender Pasha of Esztergom, and some elders and dragomans.[3] Occasionally, stewards and dragomans went to and fro, working to bring the two ambassadors to the middle pole so that they should shake hands and conclude the peace. The distance from one ambassador to the other was one hundred steps, and they were both fifty steps away from the middle pole.

* * *

Now the ambassador of the infidels got up from the foot of the pole on their side, and in the most circumspect way came towards our Pasha, dragging his feet all the while. When our ambassador saw this, he also got up from his stool, and very slowly walked towards their ambassador and drew nearer until the soldiers were only separated by the poles; the ambassadors were moving at a snail's pace.[4] In those situations ambassadors need to have the most considerate, circumspect, reasonable men around them, because according to the truthful hadith, "he who makes peace between two parties deserves the same reward as the martyr," one needs men who can improve the relations between the two emperors, so that the peace is not violated, because previously here there had been two months of fighting instead of peace.[5]

* * *

Finally, the infidel ambassador walked with hundred thousand pauses, so slowly as if he did not want to step on a single ant, and ours also came, until they joined hands at the middle pole, and greeted each other with greatest respect. They sat down at the middle pole on stools, and after a thousand

---

2. Sultan Süleyman (r. 1520–66) conquered Hungary for the Ottoman Empire and led a campaign against Vienna in 1529, the farthest point of Ottoman expansion into Europe. His reign is idealized by Evliya as the Golden Age of the Ottoman Empire.
3. Translators in the Ottoman service. "Pasha": title for the governors and military leaders, here of the border provinces next to the Habsburg dominions. Other denominations of ranks here refer to the personal service of Kara Mehmed Pasha, the ambassador.
4. To arrive at the border post *before* the other ambassador would have been interpreted as a sign of weakness.
5. The reward for the martyr, who dies for the sake of Islam, is paradise.

excuses he accepted all the peace agreements, consisting of twenty-two articles from either party, for twenty-two years, according to the felicitous decree of our felicitous sultan.

Description of Schwechat (Peşpihil)

[Shortly before arriving in Vienna, the Ottoman delegation passes through the town of Schwechat, where they observe local customs, and also mingle with the locals.]

These were the ignoble Ayanta holidays of the infidels.[6] Ten thousand monks and seventy or eighty thousand faithless infidels came to this large monastery with their crucifixes and flags and banners and organs and trumpets to conduct their worthless rituals. Afterward, they indulged in such wickedness and debauchery, jollity and drinking in the gardens of Schwechat that it is beyond description. Several thousand infidels and priests, burning incense and aloe and amber in gold and silver censers, paraded through the streets playing the trumpets, and returned to their monasteries.

The domes of every monastery are idolatrous temples covered with tin, tinfoil, yellow brass, and lead. In each of them are idols and chandeliers each worth the annual tribute of Egypt,[7] and on every dome and tower are golden crosses as tall as a man, which are sparkling all across the city. Their clock towers, too, are covered with tinned sheet metal, and the sound of the bells carries as far as one day's travel.

The river * * * passes through the middle of the town. It is just a little creek but [as sweet as] the water of life. It comes from the Little German [Mountains], flows through hamlets, villages, and small towns, waters the vineyards and gardens of this city, and then empties into the Danube below it. On both sides of the city there are innumerable vineyards and gardens with fruit trees and roses, and in paradisiac gardens like the garden of Aspuzu,[8] with tall castles, and enclosures decorated with water basins and fountains, remarkable pleasure grounds according to the taste of the Franks. In each garden a perfect master has erected an artful castle like the castle of Khavarnaq,[9] and in each there are colorful paintings by Frank painters like Mani with his Erjeng,[1] done in such remarkable, indeed magic art that anybody who understands painting puts the finger of astonishment to his lips full of admiration.[2]

All the notable and noble infidels from Vienna enjoy themselves for weeks and months in this city and its gardens, and their young boys and pretty girls swim in the river which runs through it, and, embracing each other in the heat

---

6. The delegation stayed in Schwechat during the holiday of Corpus Christi. How Evliya came up with the word Ayanta is not clear.

7. Egypt being the wealthiest Ottoman province, this is Evliya's hyperbolic way of saying "a lot of money."

8. The urbanites of Malatya in southeastern Anatolia used to have their summer residences in Aspuzu, which was famous for its orchards and vineyards.

9. The pre-Islamic palace of Khavarnaq in

Iraq was frequently cited by the ancient Arabian poets as one of the wonders of the world.

1. In the Islamic world Mani (c. 216–276 c.e.), the founder of Manicheism, is remembered as the most accomplished painter of all times; Erjeng is the book in which his paintings were collected.

2. Putting one index finger to the lip was a common gesture of admiration, frequently seen in Islamic miniature paintings.

of the joy of wine and liquor, amuse themselves in a quiet corner. Due to the mild climate [the beauty of] their boys and girls is famous far and wide.

Their men and women do not avoid each other; even when their wives sat together with us Ottomans in jollity and drinking, the husbands did not say anything. They go out freely, which is not sinful, because in this entire land of the infidels it is the women who rule, which is their evil custom since the days of Virgin Mary.

Evliya's strange adventure in Vienna

About a most marvelous and bewildering spectacle: One day when I, your humble servant full of faults, strolled through the inner city, I came to the market of doctors which has about one hundred shops. In front of some of the shops I saw captives from the nation of Muhammad[3] sitting on stools, with white turbans, and Bosnian fur hats, and felt caps from Tekke and Hamid,[4] or with Tatar features and in Tatar garb, hands and feet of all of them in iron chains, some of them black negroes, and others young heroes, and others white-bearded feeble old men. Their necks bowed in grief, they sat on their stools grinding nutmeg, cinnamon, pepper, cardamom, ginger, and other spices in huge bronze mortars, working hard as if someone was holding a sword to their necks, in order to make them work faster. But the old ones worked agonizingly slow, their eyes rolling right and left with exhaustion.

I your humble servant felt my vein of compassion swelling, and reached for my wallet to give these old men a few silver coins. But my companion, fiefholder Boshnaq 'Ali from Esztergom prevented my good deed, saying: Hold on for now, give it to them when we come along again towards the evening. Now the owners of these captives are around, and would just take away what you give them. I your humble servant found this reasonable and put my wallet back into my pocket. We continued to stroll through markets, business streets, residential neighborhoods and other monuments we had not seen before, and around nightfall returned to the place of the captives. As we stood and watched they started to close the shops, and some infidels came and loosened the Muslim captives' belts, and took off their turbans and fur hats and felt caps, and took all their clothes. Then they stuck a key like one for a clock mechanism in the armpit of each of them and turned it around, and immediately these Muslim captives' hands and heads and eyes and eyebrows stopped moving. Now as their turbans had been taken off their heads and their clothes from their bodies I realized that these were all clock mechanisms made of bronze in the shape of humans, and moved like clock mechanisms if wound up. I was flabbergasted, and my companion 'Ali Agha mocked to me: For God's sake, Evliya Çelebi, give those poor captives a few silver coins. This was a marvelous and wonderful adventure indeed!

[*Evliya visits St. Stephen's Cathedral in Vienna, marveling at the various paintings and frescoes, and admiring the sound of the organ and the boys' choir. He also discovers a magnificent library*]

3. I.e., Islam.
4. Two Ottoman provinces in Asia Minor.

In the walls there are niches for the Gospels, the Thora, the Psalms, and the Quran, and their walls are all plastered with raw ambergris.[5] As many nations of different languages as there are, of all their authors and writers in their languages there are many times a hundred thousand books here, and specially employed priests look after them. It is a magnificent library well worth seeing.

Such a collection of precious books does not exist in any other country. There are God knows how many books in the mosques of Sultan Barqūq and Sultan Faraj[6] in Cairo, and in the mosques of [Sultan Meḥmed] The Conqueror and Sultan Süleymān and Sultan Bāyezīd and the New Mosque,[7] but in this St. Stephen's Monastery in Vienna there are even more, since there are, in the scripts of every language of the infidels, so many illustrated books, theological commentaries, the Atlas and the Atlas Minor, geography books, astronomy books called Mappa mundi; we do not have any of those because images are forbidden. This is why this monastery in Vienna has so many books. I, your humble servant, entered this library with the permission of the chief priest, and was stunned when I walked through it while the scents of musk and ambergris wafted through my brains.

Thus, my friend, the result and outcome of what I am saying is this: Despite all their infidelity these infidels, considering that they are God's own word, have all these books dusted off once a week, and have seventy or eighty servants for that purpose. Whereas we do in fact have the [mosque called] Jami' al-'Attarin in Alexandria which has so many shops and hostels and baths and stores and works of beneficence [to generate income for its maintenance], and yet is wrecked and in ruins, and in its library because of the rain of mercy several thousand volumes containing the precious word of glory written by the noble hands of Yāqūt al-Musta'simī and 'Abdallah al-Qirīmī and Shamsaddīn Ghumrawī and Sheykh Jūshī are rotting in the rain.[8] All the Muslims who come to the Friday prayer to this mosque once a week can hear the noises of the moths and worms and mice eating away at these books, but none of this nation of Muhammad ever thinks of saying: There are so many books of God perishing here, let us do something about it. [That is] because they do not love God's scripture as much as the infidels do. If only they could reconstruct that mosque like this church, and if only its servants and scholars would look at that poor mosque with the eye of mercy.

Description of the golden sphere on the steeple of St. Stephen

A strange adventure: In the city of Vienna there are 360 cathedrals and churches, each has one or two clock towers, with a total of 470. At noon first that big clock at St. Stephen's strikes once, and then, before its harmony has fully developed, all the other clock towers in the fortress of Vienna strike at one

5. All these texts are considered valid revelations in Islam.
6. "Barqūq": Mamluk sultan of Egypt (r. 1382–99); "Faraj": Barqūq's son and successor, (r. 1399–1412).
7. The mosque of Aḥmed I (r. 1603–17), today known as the Blue Mosque. Meḥmed II

(r. 1451–81), Bāyezīd II (r. 1481–1512), Süleyman I (r. 1520–66), Ottoman sultans, all of whom erected mosques in Istanbul.
8. Four famous calligraphers, the most important being Yāqūt al-Musta'simī (1221–1298).

time. They have found a marvelous way of synchronizing those clocks. If a fellow in Rum has two clocks, one will definitively be one degree and two minutes ahead or behind the other, but the clocks of Vienna all strike at the same moment—so skillfully are their clocks made. That steeple of St. Stephen's cathedral is higher than all the others, and its stair has 770 stone steps, and it has 360 large and small cells for the monks. On its highest tip there is a golden sphere, made from 150 oqqa of pure gold, big enough to hold ten shinik[9] of wheat. When Sultan Süleyman besieged Vienna in the year 936 [1529 C.E.] he could not bring himself to fire his cannons at this steeple, thinking that ultimately this would be a minaret for the call to Muslim prayer at a Muslim temple. [He thought to himself:] So this steeple should carry my sign. Thus he had that golden sphere made out there and sent it into the fortress to the king, and that erring king put the sphere up on the highest tip of that steeple in the very same night. That is why the fortress of Vienna is called the Golden Apple of Germany and Hungary because of this golden sphere. When Sultan Süleyman lifted the siege without victory and left, King Ferdinand[1] put a golden crescent and a silver sun on top of Süleyman Khan's sphere. When Sultan Süleyman heard that the infidels had dared to put some stuff on top of his own sphere, he warned them: Watch out, I am going to wage war against you. He went on his German campaign, conquered 176 fortresses within one year, and laid his country and provinces to waste. Finally King Ferdinand took the crescent and sun down from Sultan Süleyman's sphere and made peace with him. In the course of time Sultan Murad [IV] conquered Baghdad, the paradisical city, in 1048 [1638 C.E.], but after his return to Constantinople he took to drinking, and died soon thereafter. When Sultan Ibrahim succeeded him on the throne, the German emperor and evildoing king * * * violated the peace of Sultan Süleyman with the foolish act of putting a sort of fork shaped like a golden cross on top of the sphere. When he was asked: Why did you put this cross-shaped thing on Sultan Süleyman's Golden Apple?, he responded: We put this weather vane in the form of a cross up there so that no bird should perch up there. And indeed, it is a kind of weather vane in the shape of a cross on which no bird can perch when it whirls around in the wind like a top. Surely there will be a powerful sultan like Süleyman one day who takes this down from the sphere!

* * *

May God Almighty make it a minaret and grant that the call for the Muhammadan prayer is sounded from it—peace upon you.

9. A unit of volume, used for grain, about a quarter of a bushel. "Oqqa": a unit of weight, standardized at 1,283 gr (45.26 oz.).
1. Ferdinand I of Habsburg, King of Bohemia and Hungary since 1526, Holy Roman Emperor (r. 1558–64). In fact, the steeple had carried a crescent and star (a universal symbol that had nothing to do with Islam) in the 16th century.

INDIAN POETRY AFTER ISLAM
twelfth–seventeenth centuries

The mutual engagement of Islam and Hinduism in South Asia began as a "clash of civilizations" in the eighth century, and has continued to generate fresh political, economic, social, and ideological conflicts ever since. As faiths and as ways of life, they are each other's contraries, mainly because Islam is a religion of the Book whereas Hinduism (like Buddhism and Jainism) is not. Nevertheless, especially in literature, art, and modern popular culture, they have converged in unexpected ways in India to create a cultural synthesis that is rare in world history.

One prominent example of the encounter of Islam and Hinduism was the *bhakti* movement, which began on a smaller scale in southern India before the end of the first millennium C.E. *Bhakti* ("devotion"), which emphasized intense commitment and service to one chosen god out of many in the Hindu pantheon, was as much a theological, social, and political phenomenon as it was a literary and artistic one. It started as a movement to reform classical Hinduism and the caste system, rejecting temples, pollution, endogamy, hierarchy, and ritual. After the arrival of Islam, *bhakti* increasingly engaged with monotheism, iconoclasm, and abstract divinity (as contrasted to idols), as well as egalitarianism and community. In this apparent synthesis, however, *bhakti*

did not completely overturn the central concepts of Hinduism. It retained the logic of karma and *mokṣa*, so that union with God and liberation from reincarnation remained principal goals; it preserved the classical mythologies of Śiva and Viṣṇu; and it continued with earlier Hindu pantheism, in which godhead ("the God beyond God") pervades the universe, and hence can be found everywhere.

This cluster offers selections of poetry by five major figures in the *bhakti* movement from across the subcontinent. Among them, **Basavaṇṇā** and **Mahādevīyakkā** (a woman poet) belong to the Kannada-speaking region of southern India in the twelfth century, and represent the movement's social, political, and religious upheaval shortly before Islam's impact. **Kabir** comes from the Hindi heartland in northern India in the fifteenth century, and articulates an early synthesis of Hindu and Muslim ideas, focusing on "the God beyond God" and seeking to mediate the conflicts between the two religions. **Mīrabāī** (also a woman), from the western edge of the Hindi-speaking region in the sixteenth century, embodies a subsequent blend of Hindu and Sufi traditions of erotic mysticism, but also a reaction to Islam. **Tukaram**, who belongs to the Marathi-speaking region along the western edge of the Indian peninsula in the seventeenth century, represents a late phase in which *bhakti* responds to Islam's dominance in the public realm by revitalizing its own roots in Hinduism within local communities. Between them, these five poets help us

A gathering of holy figures from different faiths, including the poet Kabir, on the left, depicted by the South Asian painter Mir Kalan Khan (active c. 1730–1775).

map out about half a millennium in the literary history of India, a period in which, despite violent conflicts, Islam and Hinduism interacted with each other in remarkably creative ways, creating a unique amalgam of cultures.

BASAVAṆṆĀ

Basavaṇṇā (1106–1167), or Basava for short, was born a *brāhmaṇa* (in Karnataka state, southern India) but orphaned at an early age. Raised by a Sanskrit scholar, he received an orthodox Hindu education but, by his late teens, he developed a strong aversion to caste and ritual. He gave up his *brāhmaṇa* status and left home, settling at Kūḍalasangama, literally a place "where two rivers meet"; there he learned the worship of Śiva from an unorthodox guru (master), and had a series of mystical experiences. In his *vacana*s ("sayings" or poems) composed in Kannada, he referred to Śiva as "the lord of the meeting rivers"—a phrase that became his characteristic signature line.

Thinking of himself as Śiva's servant, Basava resolved to create a community of devotees. He went to the northern Karnataka city of Kalyāṇa, where an uncle was the king's minister; establishing himself as a courtier, Basava married the king's foster-sister, and subsequently became the kingdom's treasurer. As a powerful and famous official, he began to attract other devotees to Kalyāṇa, which thus became the nucleus of a new community of Vīraśaivas ("Śiva's warriors").

The group, however, was egalitarian to an extreme: it welcomed any devotee of Śiva, regardless of caste, class, and gender; it openly challenged social conventions; and it rejected classical Hindu rituals. Its unconventionality quickly triggered a backlash. When the Vīraśaivas blessed the wedding of an untouchable man and a woman of *brāhmaṇa* birth among their members, the king ordered the execution of the couple's fathers. Some Vīraśaivas protested violently, and the king was assassinated during a riot; persecuted thereafter, the community scattered across the Kannada-speaking region, never to be reunited. Despondent at his failure to curb the extremism and violence, Basava retired to Kūḍalasangama and died shortly afterward.

Nearly one thousand short poems have been preserved in Basava's name. About half of them deal with various phases of the poet's spiritual progress, while the rest focus on the difficulties and conflicts of worldly life, especially its corruptions and temptations. In our selection, poems such as "The master of the house, is he at home, or isn't he" and "Don't you take on" represent the former half of the canon, whereas "Look, the world, in a swell" and "Cripple me, father" represent the latter. "The rich" unites the themes of worldliness and transcendence: if a human being is truly committed to God, then even the lowliest devotee can achieve the ultimate goal, because "things standing"—such as worldly palaces and temples—"shall fall," but "the moving"—intangible human and divine Love—"ever shall stay."

8[1]

Look, the world, in a swell
of waves, is beating upon my face.[2]

Why should it rise to my heart,
tell me.
O tell me, why is it   5
rising now to my throat?
Lord,
how can I tell you anything
when it is risen high
over my head   10
lord lord
listen to my cries
O lord of the meeting rivers[3]
listen.

21

Father, in my ignorance you brought me
through mothers' wombs,[4]
through unlikely worlds.

Was it wrong just to be born,
O lord?   5

Have mercy on me for being born
once before.
I give you my word,
lord of the meeting rivers,
never to be born again.   10

59

Cripple me, father,
that I may not go here and there.
Blind me, father,
that I may not look at this and that.

1. This and the following poems by Basavaṇṇā
were translated by A. K. Ramanujan.
2. Basava uses a traditional Indian metaphor
for the world as a "raging sea."
3. This is Basava's signature phrase, which
commemorates his mystical experience of
Śiva, which occurred at Kūḍalasangama, "the
place where two rivers meet," shortly after his
initiation by a spiritual master (guru) there.
4. Basava takes it for granted that action in
the world inevitably leads to the self or soul's
net accumulation of "bad karma" in a lifetime,
and hence to its repeated rebirth or reincarnation. The self can change this trajectory only if
it determines to perform an excess of good
deeds in this life, and hence to attain liberation from the cycle and be reunited with God
or godhead. Hence this poem's line of reasoning, addressed directly to Śiva simultaneously
as a confession, a prayer, and a vow.

Deafen me, father,
that I may not hear anything else.   5

Keep me
at your men's feet[5]
looking for nothing else,
O lord of the meeting rivers.   10

97

The master of the house,[6] is he at home, or isn't he?
   Grass on the threshold,
   dirt in the house:
the master of the house, is he at home, or isn't he?

   Lies in the body,   5
   lust in the heart:
no, the master of the house is not at home,
  our lord of the meeting rivers.

111

I went to fornicate,[7]
but all I got was counterfeit.

I went behind a ruined wall,
but scorpions stung me.

The watchman who heard my screams   5
just peeled off my clothes.

I went home in shame,
my husband raised weals on my back.

---

5. "Your men" refers to the community of Śiva's devotees (*bhakta*s); being at their "feet" represents spiritual humility and openness to education in the complex ways of *bhakti* (devotion, in this case uncompromisingly to Śiva alone). In Basava's religious practice, the individual is subsumed by the community, and hence cannot be spiritually autonomous; this was a founding principle of the Vīraśaiva community that he established and led.
6. This phrase is a metaphor for the true self or soul, whose "home" in the current lifetime is this person and personality. The poem's repeated question, and the negative answer to it in the second verse, are designed to remind us that, unless the true self is "in charge" of our daily lives, no spiritual progress is possible.
7. This poem is a dramatic monologue; its speaker is a married woman, who metaphorically represents the individual self or soul trapped in worldliness. The poem's sequence of vignettes therefore adds up to the moral that the world "dupes" the individual self at every level of experience, from that of private desire to that of politics. One implication is that the only way to overcome "bad karma" is to extricate oneself from—to renounce—worldly engagement altogether.

All the rest, O lord of the meeting rivers,
the king took for his fines.   10

212

Don't you take on
this thing called bhakti:

> like a saw
> it cuts when it goes
>
> and it cuts again   5
> when it comes.

If you risk your hand

with a cobra in a pitcher[8]
will it let you
pass?   10

494

I don't know anything like time-beats and metre
nor the arithmetic of strings and drums;
I don't know the count of iamb and dactyl.[9]

> My lord of the meeting rivers,
> as nothing will hurt you   5
> I'll sing as I love.

563

> The pot is a god. The winnowing
> fan is a god. The stone in the
> street is a god. The comb is a
> god. The bowstring is also a
> god. The bushel is a god and the   5
> spouted cup is a god.[1]

8. An ancient Indian ordeal, used to test a person's loyalty, purity, or honesty.
9. Metaphors to contrast what is measured and regulated with what is spontaneous.
1. Here Basava satirizes and attacks Hinduism's older polytheism; his claim at the end of the poem that Śiva is the only one true god articulates the "monotheistic" tendency in the bhakti movement, which may be a trace of Islam's influence on Indian religious thought from about the 12th century onward.

Gods, gods, there are so many
there's no place left
for a foot.

    There is only   10
one god. He is our lord
of the meeting rivers.

703

Look here, dear fellow:
I wear these men's clothes
only for you.[2]

Sometimes I am man,
sometimes I am woman.   5

O lord of the meeting rivers
I'll make wars for you
but I'll be your devotees' bride.

820

The rich[3]
will make temples for Śiva.
What shall I,
a poor man,
do?   5

My legs are pillars,
the body the shrine,
the head a cupola[4]
of gold.

Listen, O lord of the meeting rivers,   10
things standing shall fall,
but the moving ever shall stay.[5]

2. The *bhakta* often portrays himself or herself as transgendered, as being above the arbitrariness of human gender roles. Basava ends this poem provocatively by suggesting that he is willing to "feminize" himself for God's cause.

3. *Bhakti* poetry often subversively points to the unequal distribution of wealth in human society as evidence of injustice and immorality.

4. Architecturally, the topmost "pinnacle" of a Hindu temple, often metaphorically called its "head."

5. The poem's last two lines highlight a paradox central to human history: things that are assumed to last forever often prove perishable, whereas what seems to be merely transitory endures. Here Basava appropriates this paradox to the advantage of *bhakti*.

MAHĀDEVĪYAKKĀ

Mahādevī (twelfth century) probably died in her early twenties, but left behind some 350 short poems remarkable for their consistent voice, imagery, and content. She is one of the earliest women poets in Indian and world literature for whom we have a sizable and aesthetically complete body of work. Her bold and unique expression of her feelings and desires gives us an exceptional opportunity to understand women's lives, experiences, and imaginations before modernity.

A younger contemporary of Basavaṇṇā, Mahādevī came from a village near Shimoga, now in Karnataka state in southern India. At ten, she was initiated as a devotee of Śiva, and fell in love with the form in which the god was represented in her village temple— as Mallikārjuna, "the lord white as jasmine." This phrase became Mahādevī's signature line: she was apparently so enamored that she symbolically betrothed herself to Śiva at that age. Her experience of marriage in the real world was short-lived and unpleasant; compelled as a teenager to wed a local chieftain, she left him when he forced himself upon her. Homeless, she became a wandering mystic who discarded all clothing and covered her body with only her long tresses. She walked from central Karnataka to Kalyāṇa in the north, where Basavaṇṇā had established his unorthodox and egalitarian Vīraśaiva community; she was admitted after passing a difficult spiritual test, and died soon afterward, but came to be prized as the community's most gifted poet.

Mahādevī uses three main categories for her erotic longing for Śiva and her desire for mystical ecstasy: love forbidden by society and morality, as in "He bartered my heart"; love tested by intolerable separation from the beloved, as in "Four parts of the day"; and love that finally overcomes obstacles and celebrates union, as in "Look at." She also projects her longing onto the cyclical processes in the natural world created by God; in "Like a silkworm weaving," for example, she compares her desire for the "lord white as jasmine" to the desire embodied in the silkworm who spins silk out of its own body's substance. At the same time, as in "You are the forest," she draws on an older Hindu pantheism to find God potentially everywhere in nature. But the relationship with Śiva can never be merely erotic or mundane; as the final poem, "Look at," suggests, for the human self God is (and can only be) the ultimate soulmate.

17[1]

Like a silkworm weaving[2]
her house with love
from her marrow,
      and dying
in her body's threads   5
winding tight, round
and round,
      I burn
desiring what the heart desires.

Cut through, O lord,   10
my heart's greed,
and show me
your way out,

O lord white as jasmine.[3]

60

Not seeing you
in the hill, in the forest,
from tree to tree[4]
I roamed,
      searching, gasping: 5
lord, my lord, come
      show me your kindness!
till I met your men
and found you.
      You hide   10
lest I seek and find.
Give me a clue,
O lord
white as jasmine,
      to your hiding places.   15

---

1. This and the following poems by Mahādevī-yakkā were translated by A. K. Ramanujan.
2. Silk culture has been a vital part of the handloom weaving industry in southern India since early in the Common Era. Here Mahādevī uses a local image with memorable originality, contrasting it with the ancient Hindu figure of the spider weaving its web out of its own bodily substance.
3. This is Mahādevī's signature phrase, which captures her childhood experience of an idol of Śiva (in a temple in her hometown of Shimoga) as Mallikārjuna, "white as jasmine."
4. Among *bhakti* poets, Mahādevī is the closest to being a "nature poet," as these images indicate.

75

You are the forest[5]

you are all the great trees
in the forest

you are bird and beast
playing in and out
of all the trees

O lord white as jasmine
filling and filled by all

why don't you
show me your face?

79

Four parts of the day[6]
I grieve for you.
Four parts of the night
I'm mad for you.

I lie lost
sick for you, night and day,
O lord white as jasmine.

Since your love
was planted,
I've forgotten hunger,
thirst, and sleep.

88

He bartered my heart,
looted my flesh,
claimed as tribute
my pleasure,

5. This and the next few lines are a poetic expression of pantheism, the belief that God or godhead is manifest throughout the created universe. The poem centers on the paradox that seems to undermine pantheism: that, even though God is supposed to be present everywhere, he is nowhere to be found "face to face."

6. The conventional Indian unit of time that Mahādevī uses here is about three hours, so "the day" is about twelve hours long, and is divided into quarters accordingly.

took over
all of me.   5

I'm the woman of love[7]
for my lord, white as jasmine.

199

For hunger,
    there is the town's rice in the begging bowl.

For thirst,
    there are tanks, streams, wells.

For sleep,   5
    there are the ruins of temples.[8]

For soul's company
    I have you, O lord
white as jasmine.

336

Look at
love's marvellous
ways:

    if you shoot an arrow
    plant it   5
    till no feather shows;

    if you hug
    a body, bones
    must crunch and crumble;

weld,   10
    the welding must vanish.

Love is then
our lord's love.

---

7. Here Mahādevī projects herself as Śiva's mistress or sexual plaything, a metaphor that profoundly disturbs the strict normal separation of the divine from the profane. Her intention is to shock us into understanding the erotic underpinnings of divine love, which can be grasped only mystically.

8. All the images in this poem echo the key position in *bhakti* that the devotee must renounce privilege and pleasure, voluntarily adopt poverty, and throw himself or herself at "God's mercy." Mahādevī reinforces this last idea with her reference to sleeping in ruined temples.

KABIR

Kabir (ca. 1398–1448), whose name is of Arabic origin, was probably born a Muslim; he is said to have lived most of his life in Banaras (Varanasi) in northern India, the oldest and holiest city of Hinduism, and was a handloom weaver by occupation. Though poor and illiterate, he became a poet in the oral tradition, composing songs (*padas*) as well as proverb-like couplets (*dohās*), besides witty and stringent satires (classified as *sākhīs*, "poems of witness"). He is likely to have been persecuted equally by orthodox Hindus, conservative Muslims, and political authorities for his outspoken criticism of society and organized religion.

Kabir probably acquired an extensive reputation in his own lifetime; in the centuries following his death, a large and varied body of poetry was recorded in his name. More than 500 poems bearing his signature line were included in the *Ādi Grantha* (1604), the original scripture of Sikhism composed in Punjab, in which he is classified as the principal *bhagat* (a variant of *bhakta*, devotee of God) who preceded the Gurus, the canonized teachers of the new faith. Between the sixteenth and early nineteenth centuries, two other major repositories of Kabir's verse emerged in Rajasthan and Banaras, defining a legacy of nearly 6,000 short poems preserved in a mixture of scripts, languages, and dialects. A large number of songs, satires, and aphorisms ascribed to Kabir also circulated in oral and musical forms during this period, making him the best-known and most frequently quoted poet across northern India in the past half a millennium.

In the *bhakti* tradition, in Sikhism, among Hindus and Muslims, and among modern secular audiences, Kabir is celebrated mainly for his belief in "the God beyond God," or godhead in its absolute, undifferentiated form. In our selection, this theological position is expressed in "The Final State," where both godhead and the union of the self or soul with it prove to be indescribable in human terms. In a parable such as "Ant," the God beyond God hides like grains of sugar amid grains of sand, so that only someone as industrious and adept as an ant (in contrast to a clumsy elephant) can find Him or It.

In keeping with this view, Kabir's poems also criticize organized religion for promoting anthropomorphic representations of God, which falsify the nature of divinity; and for instituting pointless rituals that distract human worshipers from the true goal of life, which is union with godhead. "Mosque with Ten Doors" and "Purity" therefore satirize some of the ritual practices of Islam and Hinduism, respectively; whereas "The Simple State" attacks superstition and hypocrisy among various kinds of self-aggrandizing men of religion who exploit only the business potential of piety. Offering alternatives to such practices, "Don't Stay" points toward stoical forbearance in the face of the world's transitoriness and of the pain and suffering that afflict human life.

The Final State[1]

The ineffable tale
of that final simple state:

it's utterly different.

It can't be weighed on a scale,
can't be whittled down.   5
It doesn't feel heavy
and doesn't feel light.

It has no rain, no sea,
no sun or shade.
It doesn't contain   10
creation or destruction.

No life, no death exist in it,
no grief, no joy.
Both solitude and blissful union
are absent from it.   15

It has no up or down,
no high or low.
It doesn't contain
either night or day.

There's no water, no air,   20
no fire that flares again and again.
The True Master permeates
everything there.

The Eternal One remains
unmoving, imperceptible, unknowable.   25
You can attain Him
with the Guru's grace.[2]

Kabir says, sacrifice yourself
to the Guru,

1. This and the following poems by Kabir were translated by Vinay Dharwadker. This poem seeks to describe "the final state" into which the enduring human self or soul must enter when it "reunites" with godhead. It is a "simple" state because it is elemental or primordial; and, as the poem's successive verses argue, it lacks any physical or "normal" attributes. In fact, it is indescribable in human terms; and it is identical to the "state" of godhead itself. In older Hindu terms, "the final state" is the state of the soul's *mokṣa*, liberation from karma and rebirth.

2. The words and phrases "It," "the True Master," "the Eternal One," "Him," and "Guru" all refer to godhead, "the God beyond God." So the human soul can find or attain godhead or *mokṣa* only by "God's grace."

and remain ensconced 30
    in the true community.

Ant

Beware of the world,
    brothers,
    be alert—
you're being robbed
    while wide awake. 5
Beware of the Vedas,[3]
    brothers,
    be vigilant—
Death will carry you away
while the guard 10
    looks on.

The neem tree[4]
becomes the mango tree,
    the mango tree becomes
    the neem. 15
The banana plant
spreads into a bush—
    the fruit on the coconut palm
ripens into a berry
right under your noses, 20
    you dumb and foolish
    rustics!

Hari[5] becomes sugar
    and scatters Himself
    in the sand. 25
No elephant can sift
the crystals from the grains.
    Kabir says, renounce
    all family, caste, and clan.
Turn into an ant 30
    instead—
pick the sugar from the sand
    and eat.

3. Here the Vedas represent institutional Hinduism, which is organized by human beings;
hence, in Kabir's radically subversive perspective, Hindu scripture is not divine revelation
but a manmade text.

4. The margosa tree, very common across
South Asia.
5. An ancient Hindu epithet for God, most
often used for Viṣṇu; here a name for God in
his most transcendent form.

Mosque with Ten Doors

Broadcast, O mullāh,[6]
your merciful call to prayer—
    you yourself are a mosque
with ten doors.[7]

Make your mind your Mecca,   5
your body, the Ka'aba[8]—
    your Self itself
is the Supreme Master.

In the name of Allāh,[9] sacrifice
your anger, error, impurity—   10
    chew up your senses,
become a patient man.

The lord of the Hindus and Turks[1]
is one and the same—
    why become a mullāh,   15
why become a sheikh?[2]

Kabir says, brother,
I've gone crazy—
    quietly, quietly, like a thief,
my mind has slipped into the simple state.   20

Purity

Tell me, O pandit,[3]
    what place is pure—
where I can sit
    and eat my meal?

---

6. A priest and theologian in Sunni Islam.
7. Kabir here imagines the Muslim priest's body as the "true mosque" of his religion, as contrasted with the physical mosque built with stone. "Ten doors" refers figuratively to the natural orifices of the human body.
8. Mecca is Islam's holiest city. The Ka'aba is the large black cubical structure in the Masjid al-Haram in Mecca; it marks Islam's most sacred site. At prayer-time anywhere in the world, a Muslim must face in the direction of the Ka'aba from his or her location.
9. God's principal name in the Qur'an, the scripture of Islam.
1. Since the early 13th century, Indians have commonly referred to Muslims as "Turks," mainly because armies made up of Turkish

slaves were the successful conquerors of northern India, and the first to establish Muslim rule on the subcontinent.
2. Alludes to the title usually given to Sufi masters.
3. Common title of a learned priest of the *brāhmaṇa* caste group, which dominates the Hindu caste system. This poem attacks the system's insistence on ritual purity (which is very different from hygiene or cleanliness), and its discrimination against pollution; the higher castes maintain their superiority by claiming that they are "purer" than the "polluted" low castes. Kabir's strategy is to show that many supposedly pure things are manifestly impure; and that the supposed purity or impurity of many things leads to logical contradictions.

Mother was impure,   5
   father was impure—
the fruits they bore
   were also impure.
They arrived impure,
   they left impure—   10
unlucky folks,
   they died impure.

My tongue's impure,
   my words are impure,
my ears, my eyes,   15
   they're all impure—
you brahmins,
   you've stolen the fire,
but you can't burn off
   the impurity of the senses!   20

The fire, too, is impure,
   the water's impure—
so even the kitchen's
   nothing but impure.
The ladle's impure   25
   that serves a meal,
and they're impure
   who sit and eat their fill.

Cowdung's impure,
   the bathing-square's impure—   30
its very curbs
   are nothing but impure.
Kabir says,
   only they are pure
who've completely cleansed   35
   their thinking.

Debate

If you love your followers, Rāma,
   settle this quarrel, once and for all.[4]

Is Brahmā greater, or where He came from?
   Is the Veda greater, or its origin?

4. The quarrel Kabir asks God to settle is over a series of intellectual puzzles, which take two basic forms with enormous consequences for religious belief. When we have a cause and an effect (or a source and an outcome), which of the two is greater? And when we have a knower and an object of knowledge, which is greater? The poem's tantalizing suggestion is that an effect can be greater than its cause, and that a person who knows may logically be greater than what he knows.

Is this mind greater, or what it believes in?   5
    Is Rāma greater, or the one who knows Him?

Kabir says, I'm in despair. Which is greater?
    The pilgrim-station, or Hari's devoted slave?

Moth

Joy is brief.
Sorrow and grief are endless.
The mind's an elephant,
    mad, amnesiac.

Air and flame burn as one,   5
just as when the moth, its eye enchanted by light,
flies straight into the lamp,
    and wing and fire flare together.[5]

Who hasn't found
restful peace in a moment of pleasure?   10
So you brush aside the truth,
    and chase the lies you hold so dear.

At the end of your days
you feel the temptation, you covet joy,
even though old age and death   15
    are close at hand.

The world's embroiled in illusion, error:
this is the process always in motion.
Man attains a human birth:
    why does he waste and destroy it?   20

The Simple State

Listen,
you saints—
I see that the world
is crazy.

When I tell the truth,   5
people run
to beat me up—
when I tell lies,
they believe me.

---

5. This poem centers on a popular image in Sufism (a mystical branch of Islam): the moth is so attracted to the flame of an oil lamp that it flies straight to its death in the flame.

I've seen　　　　　　　　　　　　　　　　　　　10
the pious ones,
the ritual-mongers—
they bathe at dawn.[6]

They kill the true Self
and worship rocks[7]—　　　　　　　　　　　15
they know nothing.

I've seen
many masters and teachers—
they read their Book,
their Qur'ān.　　　　　　　　　　　　　　20

They teach many students
their business tricks—
that's all they know.

They sit at home
in pretentious poses—　　　　　　　　　　25
their minds are full
of vanity.

They begin to worship
brass and stone—
they're so proud　　　　　　　　　　　　30
of their pilgrimages,
they forget the real thing.

They wear caps and beads,
they paint their brows
with the cosmetics　　　　　　　　　　　35
of holiness.[8]

They forget the true words
and the songs of witness
the moment they've sung them—
they haven't heard　　　　　　　　　　　40
the news of the Self.

The Hindu says
Rāma's dear to him,
the Muslim says it's Rahīm.

They go to war　　　　　　　　　　　　　45
and kill each other—

6. This verse refers to Hindu *brāhmaṇas*, who bathe to ritually cleanse themselves of all "pollution."
7. Idols made of stone.
8. Practitioners of many faiths in India wear "signs" of their religious identity or status; these include various types of caps or headgear, beads (like rosaries), and distinctive cosmetic marks painted on the body.

no one knows
the secret of things.

They do their rounds
from door to door,   50
selling their magical formulas—
they're vain
about their reputations.

All the students
will drown with their teachers—   55
at the last moment
they'll repent.

Kabir says,
listen,
you saintly men,   60
forget all this vanity.

I've said it so many times
but nobody listens—
you must merge into
the simple state[9]   65
simply.

Don't Stay

Don't stay—
    the land's a wilderness.

This world's a paltry paper packet—
    a spot of rain
    will wash it away.   5

This world's a garden of thorns—
    snarled and snared,
    we'll perish in pain.

This world's all tree and tinder—
    kindled, it will roast us   10
    like sacrificial victims.

Kabir says, listen, my good men,
    the True Master's name[1]
    is our lasting abode—

    our station, our destination.   15

---

9. The self or soul's union with the godhead; the same as "the final state" described in the first poem in this selection.
1. God's "name," which mystics in Kabir's tra- dition are supposed to repeat constantly as a magical formula (*mantra*) for liberation from karma and rebirth.

Aphorisms

3

Don't be vain, Kabir:
   you're just a wrapping of skin on bone.

Even those who ride on horses, under parasols,
   are buried quickly in the mud.

9

Kabir, sow such a seed
   that its tree will flourish perennially:

cool shade, abundant fruit,
   foliage full of birds at play.

12

Even if you were to transform
   the seven oceans into ink,

the world's trees into pens, the whole earth into paper,
   you couldn't write down the list of God's excellences.

20

The man with a truthful heart is best:
   there's no happiness without the truth,

no matter how many millions of times
   one tries to find it by other means.

31

Knowledge ahead, knowledge behind,
   knowledge to the left and right.

The knowledge that knows what knowledge is:
   that's the knowledge that's mine.

32

The one who stays within the limits assigned to him is a man.
   The one who roams beyond those limits is a saint.

To reject both limits and their absence:
   that's a thought with immeasurable depths.

37

Accomplish one thing and you accomplish all.
　　Seek to do all and you lose the one vital thing.

When you water the root of a plant,
　　it flowers and bears fruit to satisfaction.

46

The poem of witness is the eye of knowledge:
　　to understand it, gaze into your heart and mind.

Without the song of testimony,
　　the quarrels of this world don't end.

MĪRABĀĪ

We know nothing for certain about Mīrabāī (sixteenth century), except that she was from Rajasthan, northern India's westernmost state. Legends claim that she was a princess from a Rajput clan (an ethnic group of the warrior caste); as a young married woman, she developed an interest in *bhakti*, and probably broke many social codes to keep company with itinerant ascetics, yogis, Sufis, and other "dubious" spiritual practitioners. Her husband, father, or father-in-law perhaps tried to poison her for nonconformity, and she gave up her life of privilege to become a homeless wanderer searching for union with God.

For Mīra (as she is commonly known), the god of choice was Kṛṣṇa, an avatar of Viṣṇu, part of the story of whose incarnation on earth is narrated in the ancient Sanskrit epic, the *Mahābhārata*. But she devoted herself to the aspect of Kṛṣṇa in which he is a young erotic god, in whom women of all ages and from every social class are said to find the fulfillment of their desires and destinies. The poetry attributed to Mīra—preserved in several varieties of Hindi—is a candid, ongoing, lyrical conversation with and about God as a divine lover.

Though few, if any, of Mīra's compositions have survived verifiably in their original forms, the several hundred *pada*s (short songs in metrical, rhymed couplets) preserved in her name represent Kṛṣṇa as "the dark one" and as "the cowherd" who moves, carries, or lifts "mountains"—phrases that evoke the erotic god's classical mythology, physical attractions, superhuman strength, and miracles. As our selection indicates, most of Mīra's poems represent the devotee in a state of painful separation from her divine beloved; she is lonely and wretched, anxious and desperate, full of emotional longing and physical desire. In "My sleep's rotten, my friend," she is like a "stranded fish thrashing for water," whereas in "Darling, come visit me," she is lovesick, with "No hunger by day, no sleep by night." She is also alienated from normal human society, being constantly persecuted: in "The cowherd who carries mountains," the chieftain sends her a cup of poison, and she leaves her relatives and companions and loses her "honor in the world."

The only woman poet in the *bhakti* movement in northern India between the fourteenth and eighteenth centuries, Mīra has been promoted in modern times by Mahatma Gandhi and others as a historical ideal of Indian womanhood: sensitive, bold, determined, rebellious, and spiritually self-reliant. This image has found wide appeal in India's popular culture today, from music, dance, and visual art to film, television, and other mass media.

[My sleep's rotten, my friend][1]

My sleep's rotten, my friend,
   my sleep's rotten.

I've spent my nights staring at the path
   my lover will take
when he comes to me.[2]   5

My friends, concerned,
   decided to intervene—
but my heart accepted nothing they said.

If I don't see him, there's no tomorrow—
   but I'm determined   10
not to be sore with him.

My body's lean with anxious waiting—
   My love, my love,
the only words locked upon my lips.

This separation, an agony inside me—   15
   no one else
can understand this pain.

Just like the thirsty bird
   obsessed with rain-clouds—
just like the stranded fish thrashing for water.   20

Being a woman
   wracked by separation,
Mīra has lost her wits.

1. This and the following poems by Mīrabāī were translated by Vinay Dharwadker.
2. Mīra's poetry of devotion to God is explicitly erotic. She consistently projects God—in his anthropomorphic forms as Viṣṇu, and as Viṣṇu's avatar, Kṛṣṇa—as her lover or husband. As a woman in the human world, she lives in a state of separation from her divine paramour, who exists "beyond" this world; as his metaphorical wife, she perpetually waits for him to come to her.

[The cowherd who carries mountains]

The cowherd who carries mountains[3]
    is the one for me—
I want no one else.

I've looked and looked
    all over the world—
I have no other savior.   5

I've left my brothers,
    left my bondsmen,
left my blood relations.

I've been hanging out   10
    with the likes of roaming holy men—
I've lost my honor in the world.[4]

I'm delighted to see
    my fellow devotees,
but I weep and weep when I see the world.   15

I've sown love's vine—
    I water it
with my flowing tears.

I've garnered the butter
    from the curds,
and thrown away the whey.[5]   20

The chieftain sent me a poison cup[6]—
    lost in love,
I gulped it down, straight.

---

3. This phrase, considered as one of Mīra's poetic signatures, refers to one part of the composite mythology of Kṛṣṇa, in which he is born as a cowherd in the Braj region of northern India (around Mathura, between modern Delhi and Agra). In this part of his human life, Kṛṣṇa is a young erotic god, with whom all the women of the region—young and old, married and unmarried—seek union; the women's longing for him is a "personification" of the soul's desire for union with God, for permanent liberation from earthly existence. In one episode, Kṛṣṇa saves the people of Braj from a deluge by uprooting and lifting an entire mountain, and holding it up with his superhuman strength like an enormous parasol or cover against the rain. He is thus their "ultimate savior."

4. In the settled society of Indian householders, wandering holy men are often regarded with distrust and suspicion; and it is especially dishonorable for women, whether unmarried or married (as Mīra is said to have been), to keep their company.

5. For at least 3,500 years, yogurt has been an essential part of Indian cuisine. When yogurt is churned to make buttermilk, the creamy portion of the suspension rises to the surface, and can be skimmed off to make butter. The solids that remain in the buttermilk can then be separated as "curds" from the liquid, which is called "whey." The butter is considered the most—and the whey, the least—nutritious and valuable portion of the suspension.

6. The most popular legend associated with Mīra says that she was a princess in a Rajput clan in Rajasthan (now a western Indian state), and that she married a chieftain or into a chieftain's family in the region. When she became a devoted worshipper (bhakta) of Kṛṣṇa, either her husband or father or father-in-law tried to poison her; the legend claims that she swallowed the poison, but her love of God was so great that she remained unharmed.

Mīra, you've found   25
  your true attachments[7]—
whatever happens now,

O let it happen as it will.

[I'm steeped]

I'm steeped,
  steeped
in the dark one's color.[8]

I dressed up in my finery,
  put on my dancing anklets,   5
abandoned all shame, and danced in public.[9]

Gave up reason, went crazy,
  kept the company of holy men,
found the true form of a devotee.

Sang and sang the praises
  of Hari's virtues,[1] night and day—   10
so saved myself from the serpent of mortality.[2]

Without my lord, the whole world's brackish—
  merely a mouthful of salt.
Apart from him, everything's disposable.   15

Mīra asks her lord who lifts mountains[3]
  to give her the kind of devotion
that seeps with sweetness—that's luscious, flavorful.[4]

[Darling, come visit me]

Darling, come visit me,
  give me a vision of yourself—
I can't live without you.

7. In contrast to her "false" attachments to
her fellow human beings and to worldly things,
her attachments to Kṛṣṇa and his divine love
are "true."
8. In Hindu mythology, Viṣṇu in his anthropomorphic form is dark-complexioned, and so
is his avatar Kṛṣṇa. Here Mīra suggests that
she is "steeped" in Kṛṣṇa's dark skin color.
9. In conservative 16th-century Hindu society—
probable historical context of Mīra's life—
women did not dance in public.
1. Hari is one of Viṣṇu's, and hence also

Kṛṣṇa's, most common alternative names; "virtues" here refers to Kṛṣṇa's divine qualities.
2. In *bhakti* poetry, the serpent usually represents the poisonous nature either of the world
or of mortal human life.
3. An allusion to the episode in Kṛṣṇa's
mythology, in which he lifted up a mountain
to save people from a deluge.
4. The sweetness and flavor of devotion
invoke the idea that *bhakti* has its own special
rasa or poetic emotion; here *rasa* explicitly
refers to classical Indian aesthetics.

A lotus without water, a night without the moon.
　　That's what you look like
without your beloved—me.

Distressed, distraught,
　　I wander night and day,
our separation gnawing at my heart.

No hunger by day, no sleep by night—
　　and, when I speak,
no words from my mouth.

What shall I say? What's said is no use.
　　Come visit me—
quench my body heat.[5]

You pervade my self, control my moods—
　　why torment me with yearning?
Have mercy, my master—come visit me.

Your lifelong slave, in life after life,[6]
　　Mīra
falls at your feet.

5

10

15

20

[My lord who lifts mountains]

My lord who lifts mountains—
　　I'm off to his home.

He's my one true love.
　　The moment I see his form,
I'm entranced.

When night falls, I get up and go to him—
　　when day breaks,
I get up and return.[7]

Night and day, I play with him.
　　I keep him happy
any which way I can.

5

10

5. Here Mīra boldly invites her divine lover to a physical encounter with her in human sexual terms.
6. In this verse, Mīra claims that she has voluntarily enslaved herself to God in all her reincarnations.
7. The extended metaphor in this verse suggests that Mīra spends her days in the human world but her nights in Kṛṣṇa's divine realm.

I wear whatever he asks me to wear—
 I eat whatever
he gives me to eat.

Our love's an ancient love.   15
 I can't survive
a single moment without him.

I sit wherever he tells me to sit—
 if he were ever to sell me,
I'd be willing to be sold.[8]   20

Mīra's master is the lord
 who lifts mountains—
again and again, she sacrifices herself to him.

8. Her voluntary obedience of and enslavement to God is so complete that even if he were to choose to "sell" her in the marketplace (like a callous slaveowner), she would accept his decision.

TUKARAM

Tukaram (1608–1649) is associated with Dehu, a village near the city of Pune in Maharashtra state, India. He was a peasant by birth and hence a *śūdra* by caste; he probably earned a meager living as a grocer. He was married twice early, first to an invalid and then to a shrewish woman; his parents died when he was seventeen, which made him the head of an impoverished household that included several siblings. During a severe drought and famine across western India in 1629–31, he turned to poetry as a means of spiritual survival; for the rest of his life, he was a devoted worshiper of the god Viṭṭhala, popularly believed to be a local manifestation of Viṣṇu.

Over two decades or more, Tukaram composed a large number of short poems in Marathi in the *abhanga* form (a lyric in metrical quatrains); the canon of his poetry contains about 4,600 *abhanga*s. The poems are designed to be sung, and hence are set to music and performed with a one-string drone, castanets, and a drum. Since the mid-seventeenth century, they have been sung in temples in Dehu and around Maharashtra, and during large pilgrimages; they are prominent in the folk as well as classical musical traditions of western India. Tukaram's poetry has been disseminated widely in oral, musical, written, and printed forms, and is a vital presence in both literary and popular culture in Marathi. The majority of Maharashtrians regard him as their community's most important poetic and spiritual "voice."

As our selection shows, Tukaram plays this role because, beyond his particular religious affiliation, he is a poet of the general human condition. He often speaks directly and without intrusive artifice as an ordinary man engaged in everyday domestic and community life; he refers to his personal feelings and circumstances humbly and honestly, without embarrassment. He is therefore able to explore moods, states of mind, and psychological and existential crises—from inadequacy and failure to guilt and despair—in remarkably modern and even secular ways. "The Prisoner" and "Begging for God's Compassion," for example, are both frankly confessional poems: the poet is inextricably trapped by his own deeds and feels "completely powerless." Nevertheless, Tukaram is also a fearless social poet and critic; "The Rich Farmer" attacks the wealthy for their selfishness, greed, and moral double-standards, whereas "The Harvest" celebrates the unstinting labor and essential goodness of the common farmer. His prayers, such as "Viṭṭhala," are addressed to a Hindu god, but they contain universal expressions of frailty and desire in a hostile world, which resonate with people of many faiths in different times and places.

The Rich Farmer[1]

He has vowed undying devotion
to a god of stone,
but he won't let his wife go
listen to a holy recitation.

He has built a crematorium   5
with his hoarded wealth,
but he thinks it wrong to grow
holy basil at his door.

Thieves plunder his home
and bring him much grief,   10
but he won't give a coin
to a poor brahman.

He treats his son-in-law
like a guest of honor,
but he turns his back upon   15
his real guests.

Tukā says, curse him,
may he burn.
He's only a burden
and drains the earth.   20

1. This and the following poems by Tukaram were translated by Vinay Dharwadker. Like other *bhakti* poems, this *abhanga* by Tukaram adopts the persona of a poor man—in a country village, in this case—to forthrightly criticize the wealthy for their hypocritical piety, greed, stinginess, incivility, and lack of compassion.

The Harvest[2]

The field has ripened:
watch its four corners.
The grain is ready for harvest,
but you mustn't stop working.

Guard it, guard it!   5
Don't fall asleep,
don't take it easy:
the crop's still standing on the ground.

Put a stone in your sling:
the force of your shot,   10
your shouting and shooing
will scatter all the flocks of birds.

Light a fire, keep awake,
keep changing places:
when your head rolls,   15
you won't have your strength, your wits.

Give generously from the threshing floor,
make the world happy.
When the grain's piled up,
pay your taxes, give everyone his share.   20

Tukā says that's the moment
when there's nothing left to be done.
What's ours is in our hands,
and the chaff and husks have been thrown away.

The Waterwheel

How long must you endure
the whirlwind of death, of time?
It's at your back
all the while.

Free yourself   5
from your eighty-four hundred thousand births.[3]

2. A parable about the spiritual worth of labor on the land, this poem treats the various activities involved in farming as "good karma" that results in salvation. Incessant, selfless, and vigilant labor is thus its own reward, because it yields a harvest that embodies justice and happiness for all.
3. The traditional number of successive lifetimes for which a human self or soul is reborn in the world due to the consequences of karma.

enter the shelter
of Pāṇḍuranga.[4]

The seed that sprouts to life
brings death with it,   10
and when it dies
it's quickly born again.

Tukā says one's lives
are strung like pots on a waterwheel:
a pot frees itself   15
only when the cord is broken.[5]

The Prisoner[6]

I find ways and means
to set myself free:
but, look, they only
entangle my feet.

I'm caught like a prisoner   5
under this sorrow's warrant:
I've lost my strength,
my wits.

All my past deeds
and present actions,   10
gathered in one place,
come dragging after me.

I'm trapped in the snare
of do's and don'ts:
I cut them one by one   15
but they can't be sorted out,

I collect them, but they grow back
like each other's limbs.

---

4. Pāṇḍuranga ("the one who is white in color") is one of the forms or aspects of Viṭṭhala, an autochthonous god of the Maharashtra region, now a state in western peninsular India. Viṭṭhala is identified with—but is not an avatar of—Viṣṇu, the god of preservation in classical Hinduism. Viṭṭhala-Pāṇḍuranga is the god that Tukaram, as a *bhakta*, chooses to worship.
5. The waterwheel is a multifaceted metaphor for the cycle of rebirth under the effects of karma; the breaking of the cord on which the pots on the wheel are strung signifies the breaking of the bondage of karma, and hence the attainment of *mokṣa* or final liberation from earthly existence.
6. This *abhanga* succinctly expresses the whole logic of karma and reincarnation, and the role of God's grace in ending the karmic cycle for an individual soul.

In desire's company
I've found unhappiness.   20

Tukā says, Lord,
now you must set me free:
I've become
completely powerless.

Begging for God's Compassion

The world has bothered me no end.
I've lain in the womb in my mother's belly.
I've become the beggar who begs at the doors
of eighty-four hundred thousand yonis.[7]

I live like a slave in someone else's hands.   5
I'm caught and whirled in the powerful snare
of all my deeds, done now and in earlier births,
whose fruits stick to me, to ripen now and later.

My belly's empty and there's no rest.
No destination, no resting place, no home town.   10
Lord, don't spin me like this, I've lost my strength.
My soul sputters in torment, like a rice grain on a hot griddle.

So many times have gone by like this,
and I don't know how many more lie ahead of me.
They come around again and again without a break.   15
Maybe the string will snap only when the world ends.

Who will take away such anguish from me?
On whom can I press my burden?
Your name ferries us across the world's ocean,
but you hide in a hole, waiting in ambush.   20

Strike me now, run me over, O Nārāyaṇa.[8]
Do this for me, impoverished wretch that I am.
Don't ask a man without goodness for good things.
Tukā begs for your compassion.

---

7. The number of rebirths that an individual
self undergoes, if it cannot break the chain of
action and its consequences; and hence also the
number of mothers' "wombs" or *yonis* through
which it must "pass" before being liberated.
8. Like Hari, one of the ancient Indian names
of God in his most general form; often used
for Viṣṇu in his universal aspect.

Viṭṭhala[9]

His name is good, his form lovely.
They cool my eye and drive away my fever.
Viṭṭhala, Viṭṭhala is my rosary.
So short and sweet, so easy, and always there.

This name is a weapon, the arrow of nirvāṇa,[1]   5
a means for the moment when death is near.
What's the use of preparing for a funeral?
Nārāyaṇa[2] breaks up your pain if you fix your sights on him.

This is the very best of all that's known.
Because it frees you from the world, and frees you forever,   10
you must go and seek out the Lord's protection.
It's all you need to do, and it's enough.

That's why I'm angry with the world,
this gleaming, poisonous serpent.[3]
It keeps us apart, me and you, my giver,   15
with its sharp and hostile stratagems.

It has made me taste the fruit of this world,
it has fixed the wrong verses in my mind.
I've grown fat and heavy with my many sojourns.
I've grown bald with the mockery heaped on me.   20

I've had the punishment for what I've done.
I've eaten what's eaten in many castes and births.
I must break it up now, put an end to it.
Lord, Tūka lays himself down at your feet.

---

9. A local god associated with the region of Maharashtra in western India, who is identified with Viṣṇu.
1. Buddhist term for liberation from karma and rebirth by means of "extinguishing" the self, but used in many Hindu and *bhakti* texts as a broad synonym for *mokṣa*, liberation from

karma when the self reunites with God or godhead.
2. A name for Viṣṇu in his universal aspect, here used as an epithet for Viṭṭhala, Tukaram's chosen local god.
3. A personification of the world's deceptiveness and viciousness.

II

Europe and the New World

"All the world's a stage, / And all the men and women merely players." **Shakespeare**'s famous comparison of human beings to actors playing their various roles in the great theater of the world conjures up the exhilarating liberty and mobility we associate with the memorable characters of Renaissance literature. Because "merely" meant, in Shakespeare's day, "wholly" and "entirely," the line evokes a lively sense of the men and women of that world performing their roles with the gusto of actors. Their social roles as princes, clowns, thieves, or housewives appear, from one angle, as exciting opportunities for the characters to explore. Yet such roles are also clearly confining: Renaissance men and women were born into societies that strictly regulated their actions and even their clothing—only actors had the right to vary their garb and dress above their station. Whether Renaissance subjects relished the pleasures of playing or resented the constraints of their social roles is a subject often taken up in the literature of the day.

The most memorable characters of Renaissance literature enjoy greater autonomy and more fully realized personalities, and are much more prone to introspection than their medieval predecessors. Characters like **Cervantes**' idealistic but mad Don

A detail from Hans Holbein's 1533 painting, commonly called *The Ambassadors*.

Quixote; Shakespeare's hesitant Hamlet; and **Milton**'s "domestic" Adam and "adventurous" Eve are frequently presented in acts of thought, fantasy, planning, doubt, and internal debate. Deliberating with others and themselves about what to do seems at least as important to these characters as putting their plans into action.

One reason for this shift toward internal, mental, and psychological portraiture is that Renaissance authors, like the characters they invent, inhabited a world of such widespread revolutionary change that they could not passively receive the traditional wisdom of previous ages. The stage on which they played was transformed and expanded by both the scientific and the geographical advances of the age. When Nicolaus Copernicus (1473–1543) discovered that the earth moves around the sun and when Galileo Galilei (1564–1642) turned his telescope up to the heavens, the nature of the universe and creation had to be reconceived. When **Christopher Columbus** (1451–1506) sailed to what he thought were the Indies, he introduced a New World to Europe, which began for the first time to think of itself as the Old World. Around the time that Columbus was sailing to America, humanist thinkers in Italy began to use new scholarly methods that gave them fuller access to the cultural legacy of ancient Greece and Rome as well as a new sense of their own place in history. On scientific, geographical, and scholarly fronts, the world of Renaissance Europe was undergoing revolutionary change.

After Johannes Gutenberg's invention of the printing press in 1439, the new ideas and controversies of the age reached a broader audience than ever before. Texts of all sorts were printed widely, and the spread of the printing press across Europe meant that writers could often avoid local censorship by having texts printed elsewhere, as occurred with Protestant bibles in local languages that circulated widely despite Catholic prohibitions, or works like the biting satire *Lazarillo de Tormes*, which the Inquisition banned in Spain but which were printed and reprinted in the Netherlands or Italy. Despite censorship, the average person's access to information increased dramatically.

The new discoveries, rapidly circulating, were avidly resisted in some quarters, as when the Inquisition forced Galileo to repudiate the Copernican theory that the earth rotates around the sun. At the same time, they led to an unprecedented sense of possibility. In his dialogue *The City of the Sun* (1602) Galileo's friend and supporter Tommasso Campanella (1568–1639) optimistically asserted that the three great inventions of his day—the compass, the printing press, and the gun—were "signs of the union of the entire world."

As the two great powers of the age, Habsburg Spain and the Ottoman Empire, grew ever more dominant, this "union of the world" could also seem threatening. With the defeat of the Muslim stronghold of Granada in 1492, and the expulsion of the Jews in the same year, Spain emerged as a centralized, militantly Christian state. Spain's modernized army effectively replaced older chivalric forms of combat with new troops armed with guns and cannons, making great inroads into Italy and France. Charles, King of Spain, was crowned Holy Roman Emperor in 1519, consolidating many of the great dynastic houses of Europe. Soon the Habsburg domains extended across the globe, from Europe to the New World in the west to Asia, in an empire without precedent.

ENCOUNTERING THE NEW WORLD

As emperor, Charles V took for his emblem the pillars of Hercules, which for the ancients had signaled the end of the known world at the Straits of Gibraltar. But Charles reversed the motto that accompanied the emblem, from the forbidding "Ne Plus Ultra" (*no further*, [Latin]) to the endlessly ambitious "Plus Ultra," which encouraged going *ever further*. So the Spanish did across the globe, all while battling the Ottomans' own expansion into the Mediterranean and North Africa.

The new discoveries challenged European centrality in the world and in creation. Contact with New World peoples forced Europeans to consider as never before what counted as culture, civilization, and even humanity, casting into doubt the authority of the classics that scholars had recently embraced with a new fervor. In an ironic exchange on Prospero's island in Shakespeare's *The Tempest*, Miranda exclaims, "Oh brave new world, that has such people in it," only to suffer her father's devastating correction: "Tis new to thee." Although Columbus considered the New World a *tabula rasa*—a clean slate ready to be imprinted with Christianity and European ways—by the time the conquerors **Hernán Cortés** (1485–1547) and Francisco Pizarro (1478–1541) encountered the great civilizations of the Aztecs and the Incas in the 1520s and 1530s, Europe was forced to grapple with other versions of what culture could mean.

As the explorers contemplated complex societies that had been completely unknown to the Old World, the arbitrariness of European social arrangements became visible to many thoughtful observers. **Thomas More** (1478–1535) was inspired by reports of new social arrangements to imagine his own island of *Utopia*, a wry fantasy nonetheless full of hope for reform. In one of his skeptical, probing *essais* (called "On Cannibals") **Michel de Montaigne** (1533–1592) elaborated on **Jean de Léry's** detailed and even-handed ethnography of the Tupinamba Indians in Brazil, to ask larger questions about European society, whose peculiarities proved as unintelligible to the "cannibals" as Tupinamba society was to Europeans.

Europeans assumed that the New World existed for their profit and delectation—an idea expressed everywhere from the famous engraving by Jan van der Straet that depicted America as a seductive woman welcoming the explorer Amerigo Vespucci with open arms, to **John Donne's** poem "To his mistress going to bed," in which he exclaims as he finally manages to peel off her clothes, "Oh, my America, my new found land." Yet these assumptions were quickly challenged in the New World, both by an impregnable landscape and by the continued resistance of the native population. New World authors both indigenous and *mestizo* (born of the union of a European and an Indian), such as **Inca Garcilaso de la Vega** or **Guaman Poma**, demonstrated that America had its own history, far predating the encounter, and decried the abuses of the conquest as they argued for their own role in governing their societies. Spanish reformers such as **Bartolomé de las Casas** (1484–1566) also took up the cause of the Indians, promoting legal protections that ultimately failed to stop abuses that occurred far from the metropole. As the New World yielded untold mineral wealth, Spain set up an elaborate political structure to control it, while other European nations mounted their own expeditions or turned to piracy in efforts to rival Spanish successes. Meanwhile, the tremendous influx of wealth from the New World had a destabilizing effect across Europe, leading to persistent inflation and new possibilities of social mobility.

CONFLICTS IN EUROPE

If the New World proved difficult to control from across the ocean, Europe was no less riven by conflict. Not even

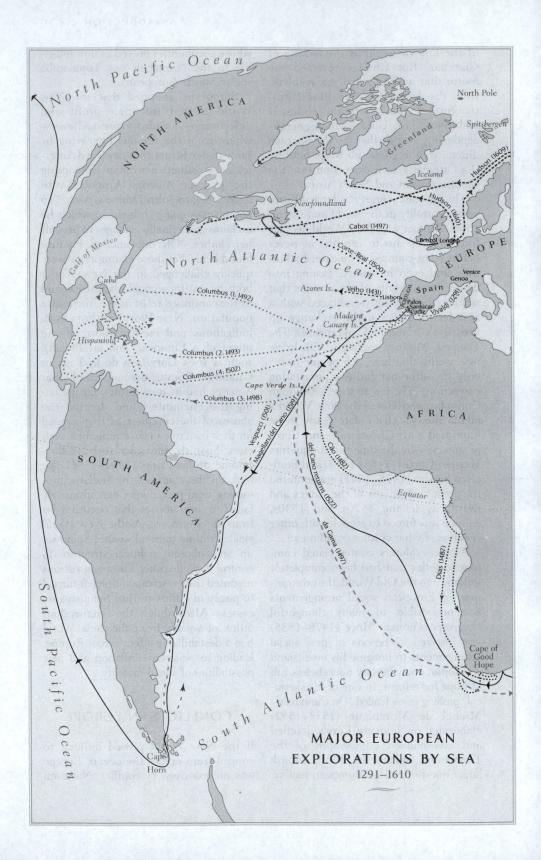

North Pacific Ocean

North Pole

NORTH AMERICA

NORTH AMERICA

Spitsbergen

Greenland

Hudson (1609)

Iceland

Hudson (1610)

Newfoundland

Cabot (1497)

EUROPE

Bristol London

Gulf of Mexico

North Atlantic Ocean

Corte-Real (1500)

Venice
Genoa

Azores Is. • Velho (1431)

Columbus (1: 1492)

Lisbon

Spain

Cuba

Palos
Sanlúcar
Cádiz

Madeira
Canary Is.

Vivaldi (1291)

Hispaniola

Columbus (2: 1493)

Columbus (4: 1502)

Cape Verde Is.1

AFRICA

Columbus (3: 1498)

Vespucci (1501)

Magellan (del Cano (1519)

Cão (1482)

SOUTH AMERICA

del Cano returns (1522)

Equator

Dias (1487)

da Gama (1497)

South Pacific Ocean

Cape of
Good
Hope

South Atlantic Ocean

Cape
Horn

MAJOR EUROPEAN
EXPLORATIONS BY SEA
1291–1610

From Jan van der Straet, *Vespucci Discovering America*, 1589. The fertility of the New World is represented as a sexualized female body.

the threat of "the Turk," as the Europeans referred to the Ottoman expansion, could paper over the serious rifts that divided the continent. The Protestant Reformation, which initially targeted the abuses and corruption of the Catholic Church, quickly became a political as well as a religious crisis. Movements originally intended to reform the Church—such as those led by **Martin Luther** (1483–1546) and John Calvin (1509–1564)—were rapidly adopted by Renaissance princes bridling under papal authority. The reformers' attacks on the Pope, who wielded enormous political and military as well as spiritual power, provided an opportunity for rulers across Europe to increase their own sway. Henry VIII of England famously broke with the Catholic Church and declared himself head of the Church of England, and the pattern of contesting or breaking with papal authority was repeated throughout Europe. By nationalizing religious authority, monarchs claimed for themselves more and more rights that traditionally had belonged to the Pope or that had been shared by parliaments. Securing these rights from these other institutions brought monarchs closer to the absolutist rule that they craved. And yet, the Protestant Reformation had so emboldened subjects to challenge religious and political authority that the advantage enjoyed by European monarchs in the later sixteenth century would occasionally give way to a violent overthrow, as it did during the English Civil War (1642–51), when Charles I, a king reviled for his dismissal of Parliament and for failure to grant religious liberties to the more extreme Protestants among his subjects, was beheaded and the monarchy temporarily abolished.

Given the political force of the Catholic Church and the Protestant Reformation, it is no wonder that the Renaissance often appears to be more preoccupied with earthly princes and empires than

EUROPE
ca. 1590

MOSTLY ROMAN CATHOLIC

MOSTLY PROTESTANT
(Lutheran, Calvinist, Anglican, Presbyterian)

MOSTLY EASTERN ORTHODOX

MOSTLY MUSLIM

Areas of mixed
religious populations

SCOTLAND

ENGLAND

IRELAND

Wales

Stratford-upon-Avon

Thames

London
Canterbury

North Sea

DENMARK

Hamburg

Rotterdam

NETHERLANDS

Brussels

Münster

Cologne

Holy Roman

Mainz

Worms

Rouen

Seine

Paris

FRANCE

Strasbourg

Rhine

Augsburg

Munich

Nantes

Orléans

Loire

Basel

Zurich

SWITZERLAND

Poitiers

La Rochelle

Geneva

Trent

Bordeaux

AQUITAINE/
GUIENNE

Lyon

PIEDMONT

Milan

Veron

Pavia

Po

NAVARRE

Rhône

Genoa

Ferrara

Bologna

Avignon

Marseille

ALPS

PYRENEES

Florence

Tuscany

Atlantic Ocean

Ebro

Corsica

Douro

Valladolid

Salamanca

Spain

ARAGON

Avila

Madrid

Tagus

Toledo

PORTUGAL

CASTILE

Valencia

Sardinia

Lisbon

Córdoba

Seville

Granada

Mediterranean

Cadiz

Gibraltar

Algiers

BARBARY

COAST

Tunis

AFRICA

Rabat

Fez

STOCKHOLM

Novgorod

SWEDEN

Baltic Sea

Courland

RUSSIA

Copenhagen

K

TEUTONIC ORDER

Vistula

Warsaw

Prut

Berlin

KINGDOM OF POLAND

Wittenberg

Silesia

Oder

Kiev

Empire

Bohemia

Prague

Cracow

Moravia

Dneiper

Danube

Elbe

Bavaria

Austria

Vienna

ROYAL HUNGARY

Buda

Dneister

Sava

CARPATHIAN MOUNTAINS

Venice

Belgrade

Danube

Black Sea

Adriatic Sea

Rome

Italy

Tiber

O T T O M A N   E M P I R E

Naples

Tyrrhenian Sea

Constantinople

Palermo

ASIA MINOR

Sicily

Chios

Thebes

Aegean Sea

Smyrna (Izmir)

Athens

S e a

Morea

Malta

Crete

Rhodes

Cyprus

0   200   400   600   800 kilometers

0   100   200   300   400   500 miles

Approximate line
of division between
Roman Catholics and
Eastern Orthodox
Christians

with the heavenly King. In this new world of politics, the role of the Renaissance prince and his courtiers was instrumental. **Niccolò Machiavelli's** revolutionary treatise *The Prince* underscored the importance of the strong ruler—or at least a ruler who always appeared strong—as the head of his state. Dispelling with all pieties in favor of practical advice and placing ruthless effectiveness over morality, Machiavelli broke with a long tradition of advisors who preached moral behavior to their rulers, recognizing instead the exigencies of his time and the importance of projecting strength and authority. In his *Book of the Courtier*, Baldassare Castiglione (1478–1529) explained how to comport oneself with courtly grace, suggesting in the process that nobility could be learned. In an uncertain and rapidly changing world, performance and self-improvement were intertwined.

HUMANISM

The new Renaissance consciousness of how individuals could fashion themselves through their actions was in part due to the influence of the classics. Humanism, the intellectual movement that championed the return to the culture of Greece and Rome as a way to renew Europe, sought civic and moral guidance as well as aesthetic inspiration in the ancient texts. As the modern European rulers took on cadres of secretaries, ambassadors, and advisors, humanist pedagogy made education a road to power and privilege as never before.

The literal meaning of the word *renaissance*—"rebirth"—casts the great intellectual and artistic achievements of the period as a reprise of ancient culture. The artists and intellectuals of the Renaissance imagined the world of antiquity "reborn" through their work, in a vigorous renewal comparable to the thrilling discoveries of their own age. The degree to which European intellectuals of the period engaged with the writings of the ancient world is difficult for the average modern reader to realize. For these writers, references to classical mythology, philosophy, and literature are not ornaments or affectations. Along with references to the Scriptures, they are a major part of their mental equipment and way of thinking. Every cultivated person wrote and spoke Latin, with the result that a Western community of intellectuals could exist, a spiritual "republic of letters" above individual nations.

The archetypal humanist is often said to be the poet and scholar **Francis Petrarch** (1304–1374), who anticipated certain ideals of the high Renaissance: a lofty conception of the literary art, a taste for the good life, and a strong sense of the memories and glories of antiquity. In this last respect, what should be emphasized is the imaginative quality, the visionary impulse with which the writers of the period looked at those memories—the same vision and imagination with which they regarded such contemporary heroes as the great navigators and astronomers.

The vision of an ancient age of glorious intellectual achievement that is "now" brought to life again implies, of course, however roughly, the idea of an intervening "middle" age, by comparison ignorant and dark. The hackneyed, vastly inaccurate notion that the "light" of the Renaissance broke through a long "night" of the Middle Ages was not devised by subsequent centuries; it was held by the humanist scholars of the Renaissance themselves. Petrarch imagined himself living in "sad times": "It were better to be born either earlier or much later, for there was once and perhaps will be again a happier age. In the middle, you see, in our time, squalor and baseness have flowed together." Addressing his book, Petrarch expresses his longing for a new age: "But if you, as is my wish and ardent hope, shall live on after me, a more propitious age will come again: this Lethean stupor surely can't endure forever. Our posterity, perchance, when the shadows have lifted, may enjoy once more the radiance the ancients knew." The combination of self-deprecation, aspiration, and arrogance aptly characterizes the period's sense of its own superiority over not only the New World but also the recent past.

Despite the fractured political and religious landscape of Europe, especially in the sixteenth century, the great intellectual innovations of the Renaissance expanded across all boundaries. The movement had its inception in Italy with Petrarch, and developed most remarkably in the visual arts, made its way across Europe to Spain, France, and England, where its main achievements were in literature, particularly the drama. The intellectual fervor of humanism, like the poetic conventions of Petrarchism, gradually expanded into multiple languages and national traditions. Their dissemination led to new genres and to playful recombinations of older ones, inaugurating a period of great innovation in all forms of literature.

Definitions of the Renaissance must take account of the period's preoccupation with this life rather than with the life beyond. Though an oversimplification, one might say that an ideal medieval man or woman, whose mode of action is basically oriented toward the thought of the afterlife (and who therefore conceives of life on earth as transient and preparatory) contrasts with an ideal Renaissance man or woman, whose enthusiasm for earthly interests is actually enhanced by the knowledge that one's time on earth is fleeting. Once again, Petrarch provides the best example: the **Rime Sparse** (Scattered Rhymes), the extensive sequence of love poems for which he is best known, are full of renunciation, as the poet searches in vain for religious consolation for the travails of earthly desire. Yet in the process of charting the futility of earthly love, the poems paint an incredibly detailed portrait of the poet-lover in all his earthly variations, rendering his interior life both immediate and engrossing.

THE WELL-LIVED LIFE

The emphasis on the immediate and tangible is reflected in the earthly, amoral, and aesthetic character of what we may call the Renaissance code of behavior. Human action is judged not in terms of right and wrong, of good and evil (as it is judged when life is viewed as a moral "test," with reward or punishment in the afterlife), but in terms of its present concrete validity and effectiveness, of the delight it affords, of its memorability and its beauty. Much of what is typical of the Renaissance, then, from architecture to poetry, from sculpture to rhetoric, may be related to a taste for the harmonious and the memorable, for the spectacular effect, for the successful striking of a pose. Individual human action, seeking in itself its own reward, finds justification in its formal appropriateness; in its being a well-rounded achievement, perfect of its kind; in the zest and gusto with which it is, here and now, performed; and, finally, in its proving worthy of remaining as a testimony to the performer's power on earth. In this sense, the purpose of life is the unrestrained and self-sufficient practice of one's "virtue," the competent and delighted exercise of one's skill.

The leaders of the period saw in a work of art the clearest instance of beautiful, harmonious, and self-justified performance. To create such a work became the valuable occupation par excellence, the most satisfactory display of virtue. The Renaissance view of antiquity exemplifies this attitude. The artists and intellectuals of the period not only drew on antiquity for certain practices and forms but also found there a recognition of the place of the arts among outstanding modes of human action. In this way, the concepts of "fame" and "glory" became particularly associated with the art of poetry because the Renaissance drew from antiquity the idea of the poet as celebrator of high deeds, the "dispenser of glory."

At the same time, there is no reason to forget that such virtues and skills are God's gift. Renaissance intellectuals, artists, aristocrats, and princes did not lack in abiding religious faith or fervor. Machiavelli, **Rabelais**, and Cervantes take for granted the presence of God in their own and in their heroes' lives. For many, the Protestant Reformation and the growth of mysticism within the Catholic Church led to a more intimate and individualized relationship with the divine. Much about the religious temper of the age is expressed in its art, particularly in Italian painting, where Renaissance Madonnas celebrate earthly beauty even as they inspire thoughts of the divine.

Madonna and Child, c. 1465, by Fra Filippo Lippi. The object of the painting's devotions is somewhat unclear: is our eye focused on the baby Jesus, or on the beauty of Mary's face?

SKEPTICISM AND MELANCHOLY

Especially where there is a close association between the practical and the intellectual—as in the exercise of political power, the act of scientific discovery, the creation of works of art—the Renaissance assumption is that there are things here on earth that are highly worth doing, and that by doing them, humanity proves its privileged position in creation and therefore incidentally follows God's intent. The often-cited phrase "the dignity of man" describes this positive, strongly affirmed awareness of the intellectual and physical "virtues" of the human being, and of the individual's place in creation. And yet, alongside the delight of earthly achievement, there lurked in many Renaissance minds nagging doubts: What is the purpose or ultimate worth of all this activity? What meaningful relation does it bear to any all-inclusive, cosmic pattern? The Renaissance coincided with, and perhaps to some extent occasioned, a loss of firm belief in the final unity and the final intelligibility of the universe. In the wake of the geographic and scientific discoveries, thinkers such as Montaigne and Descartes became skeptics, doubting and questioning received knowledge.

For some Renaissance writers and artists, the sense of uncertainty became so strong as to paralyze their aspiration to power or thirst for knowledge or delight in beauty. The resulting attitude we may call Renaissance melancholy. It was sometimes openly expressed (as by some characters in Elizabethan drama) and other times

Young Man Holding a Skull, 1519, by Lucas van Leyden. This young nobleman, a paragon of Renaissance fashion, points to a skull that he cradles in his left arm, reminding the viewer of the inevitable fate that even the best-dressed courtier will face.

merely provided an undercurrent of sadness or wise resignation to a work (as in More's *Utopia* or Montaigne's *Essays*). Thus while on one, and perhaps the better-known, side of the picture, human intellect in Renaissance literature enthusiastically illuminates the realms of knowledge and unveils the mysteries of the universe, on the other it is beset by puzzling doubts and a profound mistrust of its own powers.

Doubts about the value of human action within the scheme of eternity did not, however, diminish the outpouring of ideas about the ideal ordering of this world. Renaissance poets and intellectuals tested ideas about the ideal prince, courtier, councilor, and humble subject as well as the ideal court and society. More's *Utopia* imagines a perfectly ordered society, as improbable as it is optimistic, while Machiavelli proposes his amoral ideas about the effective (rather than ideal) prince. Shakespeare's *Hamlet* gives us a prince far from ideal, confronting the effects of private violations on the public realm. Other writers shift the focus from the court to the entire commonwealth, as when **Lope de Vega** transforms the historical case of a peasant uprising against an abusive overlord into a play, *Fuenteovejuna*, that makes an ethical and political case for resistance. In all these works, Renaissance writers can be seen tirelessly examining the nature of their own world, the problem of power, and the vexed relations between the absolute authority of the prince and the rights and liberties of the people. Its zeal for defining the social contract partly explains why the Renaissance is often viewed as the "early modern" period; the "rebirth" and flourishing of antiquity also heralded ideas that we associate with the modern political world.

The joining of philosophical and imaginative thinking in literary expression is characteristic of the Renaissance, which cultivated the idea of "serious play." Throughout the literature of the period, we see the creative and restless mind of the Renaissance intellectual "freely ranging," as Sir Philip Sidney put it, "only in the zodiac of his own wit," creating fictional characters and worlds that might, if the poet is sufficiently persuasive, be put into practice and change the nature of the real world.

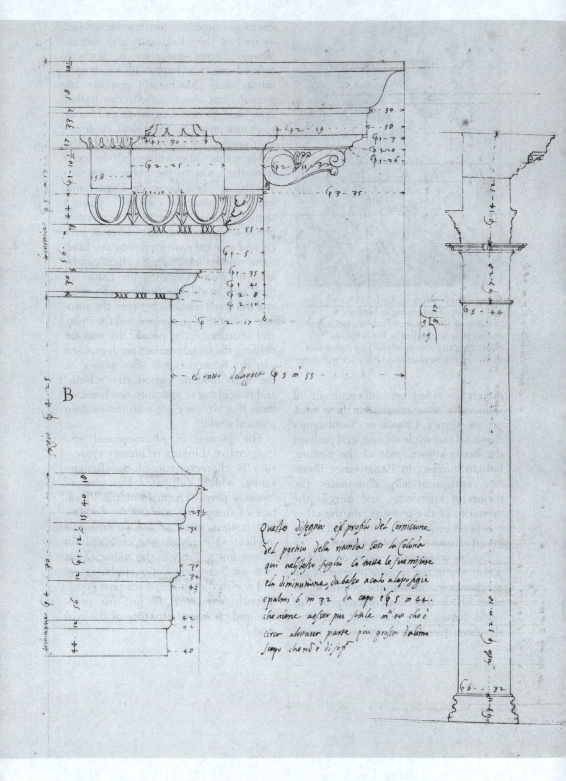

B

Questo disegnio è il profilo del Cornicione
del portio della ritonda Cosi la Colonia
qui nel isesso foglio Co tutte le sue misure
e la diminutione, da basso a Como a lapo sigie
e palmi 6 m 32 da capo e 6 5 m 44.
che viene a esser piu sottile m' 00 che è
circo aletant parte piu grosso dalimo
sapo che n de è di sopt

HUMANISM AND THE REDISCOVERY OF THE CLASSICAL PAST

"**A**d fontes!" ("To the sources!") With this rousing cry thinkers and writers urged early modern Europeans to connect to the Greco-Roman tradition and find in it the inspiration for their own societies. Starting at about the middle of the fourteenth century, this turn to the classics as a source of insight gave birth to the movement we know as humanism. Although humanists did not reject the Christian tradition, they turned their focus to this world and to the living potential of humankind as opposed to its ultimate destiny in a heavenly realm. Intellectually, humanists often positioned themselves against the medieval tradition of scholasticism, which privileged generations of commentators and latter-day authorities over the original texts. Humanists, by contrast, sought a close intellectual communion with the ancients, even as they also took care to make their texts available again. **Francis Petrarch** (1304–1374), arguably the first humanist, followed his discovery of Cicero's personal correspondence with his own letters to the ancients, in an imaginative conversation that collapsed all distance. Similarly, the political theorist **Niccolò Machiavelli** (1469–1527), who was intimately involved in the power struggles of his native Florence and whose revolutionary *The Prince* is included in

this volume, found comfort and inspiration in the classics: "entering the ancient courts of ancient men," he wrote to his friend Francesco Vettori, "I feel no boredom and forget every worry; I do not fear poverty, and death does not terrify me."

Humanism was an intellectual and aesthetic movement, to be sure, yet it was particularly important in the civic realm: its proponents hoped to form citizens who would be able to participate in political life, to speak and write with eloquence and to inspire others to virtuous action. This was to be accomplished through the study of grammar, rhetoric, history, poetry, and moral philosophy—subjects that today we call the humanities. The growth of literacy and the advent of the newly invented printing press, combined with the new humanist pedagogy, offered new opportunities for educating future citizens of the commonwealth.

The humanist conviction that education trumped authority, and the close association between humanism and the incipient religious reform movements, made some humanists controversial and even persecuted figures. A key example is the French scholar **François Rabelais** (1495–1553), who had once been a priest but, dispirited by the antihumanist oppression of the religious establishment, gave up his monk's habit to pursue a career as a physician. Perhaps the most irreverent of all humanists, Rabelais crafted a flamboyant fantasy, ***Gargantua and Pantagruel*** (1541), in which he brings together classical learning and folk

A sixteenth-century architectural study by Giovanni Antonio Dosio of the Pantheon in Rome.

humor—the giant Gargantua, whom Rabelais grants a son, Pantagruel—in a masterful satire. Rabelais pokes fun at everything from the imperial ambitions of early modern rulers to the repressiveness of the Sorbonne, the University of Paris's school of theology. In the sections reproduced here, his hopes for humanist renewal shine through the humor. In the utopian and highly unconventional Abbey of Thélème, endowed by the humanist Gargantua, educated, wellborn men and women come together for a life of pleasure (*Thélème* means desire) and virtue. Rabelais stresses the importance of an informed and trained free will over authority, in a radically humanist gesture of trust in human perfectibility. The Great Gate of Thélème staves off those who are not welcome—"Hypocrites, bigots, stay away! Old humbugs, puffed-up liars, playful / Religious frauds"—but once in the Abbey, the rule is "DO WHAT YOU WILL." In a second excerpt, Gargantua lays out for his son Pantagruel his prescription for a humanist education, including the study of Greek, Latin, Hebrew, Chaldean, and Arabic, so that all important texts— and, crucially, the Bible—will be accessible in the original. Yet although Pantagruel acquires "incomparable learning," the last excerpt presents a hilarious display of wits over antiquated knowledge, as his sidekick Panurge steps in to show up the limitations of the scholastic Thaumaste.

Although no actual Abbey of Thélème ever existed, humanists across Europe participated in a "republic of letters" that transcended individual nations, and that found a shared language in Latin. While they traveled widely as emissaries or ambassadors for their rulers, in the new age of print their texts traveled even farther, reaching across vast distances to readers who shared their interests and education. Humanists formed a new lettered class of (almost exclusively) men whose talents propelled them within their polities, as they helped to staff the bureaucracies of the new nation-states, and who also created important intellectual networks beyond them. Figures such as the Flemish Desiderius Erasmus (ca. 1466–1536) and the English **Thomas More** (1478–1535) transcended their place of origin to become famous across Europe. Yet their tight intellectual circles meant that texts such as Erasmus's *Praise of Folly* or More's *Utopia* were often read as inside jokes, both deadly serious in their satirical thrust and yet dependent on a savvy, learned audience. Beyond their specific targets, these texts question the very possibility of received wisdom, arguing instead for tireless inquiry, all while merrily recalling the folly of human behavior.

On occasion, humanism could also take on a much more melancholy tinge, given the enormous temporal and cultural distance that writers had to traverse in order to engage with the classical world. By the mid-sixteenth century, the optimism of the earliest Italian humanists had been replaced by a more cautious and skeptical stance. In the sonnets of the French poet **Joachim Du Bellay** (1522–1560) included here, looking to Rome is a complicated gesture, far from the cozy confabulations with the ancients of Petrarch or Machiavelli. Hardly celebratory, Du Bellay's poems on Rome confront in the sixteenth-century city the decadence of what was once a great empire. Yet while the ruins are no more than a lifeless portrait, a sepulchral shade of Rome's ancient glory (as Sonnet 5 puts it), its writings "keep her specter wandering around the world." The spectral Rome haunts the Renaissance writer, whose works must, paradoxically, measure up to the glories of a past that is no more.

One version of the tension between antiquity and modernity, so neatly expressed in Du Bellay's sonnets, is the development of literary humanism in the vernacular, or modern, languages. Petrarch, Rabelais, and du Bellay are all known for their writings in their everyday spoken languages, as opposed to Latin. For while humanists revered the classical tradition and pursued the study of ancient languages, they also embarked on an ambitious program to dignify their own languages and to give them an equal standing to Latin.

Du Bellay argued in his "Defense and Illustration of the French Language" (1549) that though French might seem rough in comparison to Latin, proper cultivation would help equate it with the classical languages. Similar movements to defend and promote the vernaculars were spearheaded by humanists across Europe, leading to an unprecedented period of literary innovation that drew equally from the rediscovered classics and the newly confident vernaculars. Even as they looked to the Greco-Roman tradition for inspiration, humanists and their students innovated and transformed the languages of the Renaissance.

NICCOLÒ MACHIAVELLI

B orn in Florence to a family that was well connected but hardly wealthy, Machiavelli (1469–1527) was introduced to the scholarly circles around the ruler Lorenzo de Medici. Machiavelli's adult life was closely bound up with Florence's political fortunes, in an Italy constantly overrun by the armies of France, Spain, and the Holy Roman Empire. He built a distinguished career of public service in the Florentine Republic, a city-state whose government was the most widely representative of its time. As a student of politics and an acute observer of historical events, Machiavelli offered in his most famous work, *The Prince* (1513), prescriptions for effective rule that paid

little heed to conventional morality. With the end of the Republic and the return of the Medici, Machiavelli was unjustly accused of conspiracy, and eventually retreated from the city to his family's farm. There, he imagined himself in conversation with the classical writers he most admired, as he writes in his "Letter to Francesco Vettori" below. During his prolonged exile he also wrote works of history and even a popular comedy, *The Mandrake*. Although he again served Florence under the Medici in the 1520s, developing its military fortifications, he never regained his early prominence. He died in 1527, after being passed over for public office by a new republican government.

Letter to Francesco Vettori[1]

["That Food Which Alone Is Mine"]

I am living on my farm, and since my last troubles[2] I have not been in Florence twenty days, putting them all together. Up to now I have been setting snares for thrushes with my own hands; I get up before daylight, prepare my birdlime, and go out with a bundle of cages on my back, so that I look like Geta when he came back from the harbor with the books of Amphitryo,[3] and catch at the least two thrushes and at the most six. So I did all of September; then this trifling diversion, despicable and strange as it is, to my regret failed. What my life is now I shall tell you.

In the morning I get up with the sun and go out into a grove that I am having cut; there I remain a couple of hours to look over the work of the past day and kill some time with the woodmen, who always have on hand some dispute either among themselves or among their neighbors. . . .

When I leave the grove, I go to a spring, and from there into my aviary. I have a book in my pocket, either Dante or Petrarch or one of the minor poets, as Tibullus,[4] Ovid, and the like. I read about their tender passions and their loves, remember mine, and take pleasure for a while in thinking about them. Then I go along the road to the inn, talk with those who pass by, ask the news of their villages, learn various things, and note the varied tastes and different fancies of men. It gets to be dinner time, and with my troop I eat what food my poor farm and my little property permit. After dinner, I return to the inn; there I usually find the host, a butcher, a miller, and two furnace-tenders. With these fellows I sink into vulgarity for the rest of the day, playing at *cricca* and *tricche-trach*;[5] from these games come a thousand quarrels and numberless offensive and insulting words; we often dispute over a penny, and all the same are heard shouting as far as San Casciano.[6] So, involved in these trifles, I keep my brain from getting mouldy, and express the perversity of Fate, for I am willing to have her drive me along this path, to see if she will be ashamed of it.

In the evening, I return to my house, and go into my study. At the door I take off the clothes I have worn all day, mud spotted and dirty, and put on regal and courtly garments. Thus appropriately clothed, I enter into the ancient courts of ancient men,[7] where, being lovingly received, I feed on that

---

1. Translated by Allan H. Gilbert. From a letter dated December 10, 1513, to Vettori, ambassador in Rome.
2. Machiavelli had been suspected of participation in a conspiracy led by two young friends of his and had been imprisoned and subjected to torture before his innocence was recognized.
3. Allusion to a popular tale in which Amphitryo, returning to Thebes after having studied at Athens, sends forward from the harbor his servant Geta to announce his arrival to

his wife, Alemene, and loads him with his books.
4. Albius Tibullus (1st century B.C.E.), Roman elegiac poet.
5. Two popular games, the first played with cards, the second with dice thrown to regulate the movements of pawns on a chessboard.
6. Nearby village, in the region around Florence.
7. Machiavelli here refers figuratively to his study of ancient history.

food which alone is mine, and which I was born for; I am not ashamed to speak with them and to ask the reasons for their actions, and they courteously answer me. For four hours I feel no boredom and forget every worry; I do not fear poverty, and death does not terrify me. I give myself completely over to the ancients. And because Dante says that there is no knowledge unless one retains what one has read,[8] I have written down the profit I have gained from their conversation, and composed a little book *De principatibus*,[9] in which I go as deep as I can into reflections on this subject, debating what a principate is, what the species are, how they are gained, how they are kept, and why they are lost. If ever any of my trifles can please you, this one should not displease you; and to a prince, and especially a new prince, it ought to be welcome.

8. *Paradiso* 5.41–42: "For knowledge none can vaunt / Who retains not, although he have understood."

9. Of princedoms.

FRANÇOIS RABELAIS

Rabelais (1495–1553) created a distinctive blend of broad, lusty humor so influential that it took his name: to this day, we call that blend of high and low, elegant and grotesque, erudite and physical, *Rabelaisian*. A learned humanist, Rabelais was also a most serious critic of the intellectual foibles of his time. Trained initially as a Franciscan monk and priest, Rabelais quickly came up against the conservative, antihumanist forces of the Sorbonne—the theologians of the University of Paris—who banned the study of Greek and confiscated his books. Around 1527 he decided to give up his monk's habit and pursue a career in medicine, and by 1532 he was a suc- cessful physician practising in Lyon. Under the pseudonym Alcofribas Nasier (an anagram of his name), Rabelais published a book about Pantagruel, the son he invented for Gargantua, a gigantic folk hero of French tradition. Rabelais's witty invention was both timely and sensitive: he satirized the Church by contrasting its fossilized learning with the excellence of a humanist education, which Gargantua insists on for his son. Rabelais's subversive book coincided with heightened unrest by Protestants in Paris and their subsequent persecution, leading Rabelais first into temporary hiding and finally, in fear of execution, to his renunciation of Protestantism.

From Gargantua and Pantagruel

[The Abbey of Thélème][1]

BOOK I, CHAPTER 52

How Gargantua Built the Abbey of Desire (Thélème) for Brother John

The only one still left to be provided for was the monk.[2] Gargantua wanted to make him abbot of Seuilly, but the monk refused. Gargantua also offered him the abbey of Bourgueil or that of Saint-Florent, whichever best pleased him— and said he could have both those rich, old Benedictine cloisters, if he preferred that.[3] But the monk answered him in no uncertain terms: he wanted neither to govern nor to be in charge of other monks:

"And how," he asked, "should I govern others, when I don't know how to govern myself? If you really think I've done something for you, and I might in the future do something to please you, grant me this: establish an abbey according to my plan."

The request pleased Gargantua, so he offered him the whole land of Thélème, alongside the river Loire, two leagues from the great forest of Port-Huault. And the monk then asked Gargantua to establish this abbey's rules and regulations completely differently from all the others.

"Obviously," said Gargantua, "it won't be necessary to build walls all around it, because all the other abbeys are brutally closed in."

"Indeed," said the monk, "and for good reason. Whenever you've got a whole load of stones in front and a whole load of stones in back, you've got a whole lot of grumbling and complaining, and jealousy, and all kinds of conspiracies."

Moreover, since some of the cloisters already built in this world are in the habit, whenever any woman enters them (I speak only of modest, virtuous women), of washing the ground where she walked, it was decreed that if either a monk or a nun happened to enter the abbey of Thélème, they would scrub the blazes out of the places where they'd been. And since everything is completely regulated, in all the other cloistered houses, tied in and bound down, hour by hour, according to a fierce schedule, it was decreed that in Thélème there would not be a single clock, or even a sundial, and that work would be distributed strictly according to what was needed and who was available to do it—because (said Gargantua) the worst waste of time he knew of was counting the hours—what good could possibly come of it?—and the biggest, fattest nonsense in the whole world was to be ruled by the tolling of a bell rather than by the dictates of common sense and understanding.

Item: because in these times of ours women don't go into convents unless they're blind in one eye, lame, humpbacked, ugly, misshapen, crazy, stupid, deformed, or pox-ridden, and men only if they're tubercular, low born, blessed with an ugly nose, simpletons, or a burden on their parents . . .

---

1. Translated by Burton Raffel.
2. Brother John of the Funnels, the muscular and highly unconventional monk who has had a major part in helping the party of Gargantua's father win the mock-heroic war against the arrogant Picrochole.
3. A satiric allusion to the custom of accumulating church livings.

("Oh yes," said the monk, "speaking of which: if a woman isn't pretty and she isn't good, what sort of path can she cut for herself?"

"Straight into a convent," said Gargantua.

"To be sure," said the monk, "especially with a scissors and a needle.")

. . . it was decreed that, in Thélème, women would be allowed only if they were beautiful, well formed, and cheerful, and men only if they were handsome, well formed, and cheerful.

Item: since men were not allowed in convents, unless they sneaked in under cover of darkness, it was decreed that in Thélème there would never be any women unless there were men, nor any men unless there were women.

Item: because both men and women, after they'd entered a cloister and served their probationary year, were obliged to spend the entire rest of their lives there, it was decided that men and women who came to Thélème could leave whenever they wanted to, freely and without restriction.

Item: because monks and nuns usually took three vows—chastity, poverty, and obedience—it was decided that in Thélème one could perfectly honorably be married, that anyone could be rich, and that they could all live wherever they wanted to.

As an age limitation, women should be allowed in at any time from ten to fifteen, and men from twelve to eighteen.

BOOK I, CHAPTER 53
How the Abbey of Desire (Thélème) Was Built and Endowed

In order to build and equip the abbey, Gargantua gave two million seven hundred thousand eight hundred and thirty-one gold pieces. Further, until everything had been completed, he assigned the yearly sum of one million six hundred and sixty thousand gold pieces, from the tolls on the river Dive, payable in funds of an unimaginable astrological purity. To endow and perpetually maintain the abbey he gave two million three hundred thousand and sixty-nine English pounds in property rentals, tax-free, fully secured, and payable yearly at the abbey gate, to which effect he had written out all the appropriate deeds and grants.

The building was hexagonal, constructed so that at each angle there was a great round tower sixty feet in diameter, and each of the towers was exactly like all the others. The river Loire was on the north side. One of the towers, called Artice (meaning "Arctic," or "Northern"), ran down almost to the riverbank; another, called Calaer (meaning "Lovely Air"), was just to the east. Then came Anatole (meaning "Oriental," or "Eastern"), and Mesembriné (meaning "Southern"), and then Hesperia (meaning "Occidental," or "Western"), and finally Cryere (meaning "Glacial"). The distance between each of the towers was three hundred and twelve feet. The building had six floors, counting the subterranean cellars as the first. The second or ground floor had a high vault, shaped like a basket handle. The other floors were stuccoed in a circular pattern, the way they do such things in Flanders; the roof was of fine slate, the coping being lead-decorated with small figurines and animals, handsomely colored and gilded; and there were rainspouts jutting out from the walls, between the casement windows, painted all the way to the ground with blue and gold stripes and ending in great pipes which led down to the river, below the building.

This was all a hundred times more magnificent than the grand chateau at Bonnivet, or that at Chambord, or that at Chantilly,[4] because it had nine thousand three hundred and thirty-two suites, each furnished with an antechamber, a private reading room, a dressing room, and a small personal chapel, and also because each and every room adjoined its own huge hall. Between each tower, in the middle of the main building, was a spiral staircase, its stairs made of crystal porphyry and red Numidian marble and green marble struck through with red and white, all exactly twenty-two feet wide and three fingers thick, there being twelve stairs between each landing. Further: each landing had a beautiful double arch, in Greek style, thus allowing light to flood through and also framing an entryway into overhanging private rooms, each of them just as broad as the stairway itself. The stair wound all the way to the roof, ending there in a pavilion. Off the stair, on each side, one could come to a great hall; the stair also led the way to the private suites and rooms.

Between the tower called Artice and that called Cryere were great beautiful reading rooms, well stocked with books in Greek, Latin, Hebrew, French, Italian, and Spanish, carefully divided according to the languages in which they had been written.

In the center of the main building, entered through an arch thirty-six yards across, stood a marvelous circular ramp. It was fashioned so harmoniously, and built so large, that six men-at-arms, their lances at the ready, could ride clear up to the top of the building, side by side.

Between the tower called Anatole and that called Mesembriné were beautiful galleries, large and open, painted with scenes of ancient heroism, episodes drawn from history, and strange and fascinating plants and animals. Here, too, just as on the side facing the river, were a ramp and a gate. And on this gate was written, in large antique letters, the poem which follows:

BOOK I, CHAPTER 54

[*The Inscription on the Great Gate of Thélème*]

Hypocrites, bigots, stay away!
Old humbugs, puffed-up liars, playful
Religious frauds, worse than Goths
Or Ostrogoths (or other sloths):
No hairshirts, here, no sexy monks,   5
No healthy beggars, no preaching skunks,
No cynics, bombasts ripe with abuse:
Go peddle them elsewhere, your filthy views.

    Your wicked talk
    Would clutter our walks   10
    Like clustering flies:
    But flies or lies,

---

4. Châteaux built in the early and middle years of the 16th century. Rabelais is again mixing realism with fantasy.

We've no room for your cries,
Your wicked talk.

Hungry lawyers, stay away!   15
People eaters, who grab while praying,
Scribes and assessors, and gouty judges
Who beat good men with the law's thick cudgels
And tie old pots to their tails, like dogs,
We'll hop you up and down like frogs,   20
We'll hang you high from the nearest tree:
We're decent men, not legal fleas.

    Summons and complaints
    Don't strike us as quaint,
    And we haven't got time   25
    For your legal whine
    As you hang from the line
    Of your summons and complaints.

Money suckers, stay away!
Greedy gougers, spending your days   30
Gobbling up men, stuffing your guts
With gold, you black-faced crows, busting
Your butts for another load of change,
Though your cellar's bursting with rotten exchange.
O lazy scum, you'll pile up more,   35
Till smiling death knocks at your door.

    Inhuman faces
    With ghastly spaces
    That no heart can see,
    Find other places: 40
    Here you can't be,
    You inhuman faces.

Slobbering old dogs, stay away!
Old bitter faces, old sour ways,
We want you elsewhere—the jealous, the traitors,   45
The slime who live as danger creators,
Wherever you come from, you're worse than wolves:
Shove it, you mangy, scabby oafs!
None of your stinking, ugly sores:
We've seen enough, we want no more.   50

    Honor and praise
    Fill all our days:
    We sing delight
    All day, all night:
    These are our ways: 55
    Honor and praise.

But you, you, you can always come,
Noble knights and gentlemen,

For this is where you belong: there's money
Enough, and pleasure enough: honey 60
And milk for all, and all as one:
Come be my friends, come join our fun,
O gallants, sportsmen, lovers, friends,
Or better still: come, gentlemen.

   Gentle, noble, 65
   Serene and subtle,
   Eternally calm;
   Civility's balm
   To live without trouble,
   Gentle, noble. 70

And welcome, you who know the Word
And preach it wherever the Word should be heard:
Make this place your holy castle
Against the false religious rascals
Who poison the world with filthy lies: 75
Welcome, you with your eyes on the skies
And faith in your hearts: we can fight to the death
For truth, fight with our every breath.

   For the holy Word
   Can still be heard, 80
   That Word is not dead:
   It rings in our heads,
   And we rise from our beds
   For that holy Word.

And welcome, ladies of noble birth, 85
Live freely here, like nowhere on earth!
Flowers of loveliness, with heaven in your faces,
Who walk like angels, the wisdom of ages
In your hearts: welcome, live here in honor,
As the lord who made this refuge wanted: 90
He built it for you, he gave it gold
To keep it free: Enter, be bold!

   Money's a gift
   To give, to lift
   The souls of others: 95
   It makes men brothers
   In eternal bliss:
   For money's a gift.

BOOK I, CHAPTER 55

How They Lived at Thélème

In the middle of the inner court was a magnificent fountain of beautiful alabaster.
Above it stood the three Graces, holding the symbolic horns of abundance: water
gushed from their breasts, mouths, ears, eyes, and every other body opening.

The building which rose above this fountain stood on giant pillars of translucent quartz and porphyry, joined by archways of sweeping classical proportions. And inside there were handsome galleries, long and large, decorated with paintings and hung with antlers and the horns of the unicorn, rhinoceros, hippopotamus, as well as elephant teeth and tusks and other spectacular objects.

The women's quarters ran from the tower called Artice all the way to the gates of the tower called Mesembriné. The rest was for men. Right in front of the women's quarters was a kind of playing field, an arena-like space set just between the two first towers, on the outer side. Here too were the horse-riding circle, a theater, and the swimming pools, with attached baths at three different levels, all provided with everything one could need, as well as with an endless supply of myrtle water.

Next to the river was a beautiful pleasure garden, and in the middle of it stood a handsome labyrinth. Between the other two towers were fields for playing palm ball and tennis. Alongside the tower called Cryere were the orchards, full of fruit trees of every description, carefully arranged in groups of five, staggered by rows of three. At the end was a great stretch of pastures and forest, well stocked with all kinds of wild animals.

Between the third pair of towers were the target ranges for muskets, bows, and crossbows. The offices were in a separate building, only one story high, which stood just beside the tower called Hesperia, and the stables were just beyond there. The falcon house was situated in front of the offices, staffed with thoroughly expert falconers and hawk trainers: every year supplies of every sort of bird imaginable, all perfect specimens of their breed, were sent by the Cretans, the Venetians, and the Sarmatian-Poles: eagles, great falcons, goshawks, herons and cranes and wild geese, partridge, gyrfalcons, sparrow hawks, tiny but fierce merlins, and others, so well trained and domesticated that, when they left the chateau to fly about in the fields, they would catch everything they found and bring everything to their handlers. The kennels were a bit farther away, in the direction of the woods and pastures.

All the rooms in all the suites, as well as all the smaller private rooms, were hung with a wide variety of tapestries, which were regularly changed to suit the changing seasons. The floors were covered with green cloth, the beds with embroidery. Every dressing room had a mirror of Venetian crystal, framed in fine gold, decorated around with pearls, and so exceedingly large that one could in truth see oneself in it, complete and entire. Just outside the doorways, in the ladies' quarters, were perfumers and hairdressers, who also attended to the men who visited. Every morning, too, they brought rose-water to each of the ladies' rooms, and also orange and myrtle water—and brought each lady a stick of precious incense, saturated with all manner of aromatic balms.

BOOK I, CHAPTER 56

How the Men and Women Who Dwelled at Thélème Were Dressed

In the beginning, the ladies dressed themselves as they pleased. Later, of their own free will, they changed and styled themselves all as one, in the following way:

They wore scarlet or yellow stockings, bordered with pretty embroidery and fretwork, which reached exactly three fingers above the knee. Their garters were colored like their bracelets (gold, enameled with black, green, red, and white), fastened both above and below the knee. Their shoes, dancing pumps, and slippers were red or purple velvet, with edges jagged like lobsters' claws.

Over the chemise they wore a handsome corset, woven of rich silk shot through with goat hair. Over this they wore taffeta petticoats, in white, red, tan, gray, and so on, and on top of this petticoat a tunic of silver taffeta embroidered with gold thread, sewn in tight spirals—or if they were in the mood and the weather was right, their tunics might be of satin, or damask, or orange-colored velvet, or perhaps tan, green, mustard gray, blue, clear yellow, red, scarlet, white, gold, or silvered linen, with bordered spirals, or embroidery, according to what holiday was being celebrated.

Their dresses, again according to the season, were of golden linen waved with silver, or red satin decorated with gold thread, or taffeta in white, blue, black, or tan, or silk serge, or that same rich silk shot through with goat hair, or velvet slashed with silver, or silvered linen, or golden, or else velvet or satin laced with gold in a variety of patterns.

Sometimes, in the summer, they wore shorter gowns, more like cloaks, ornamented in the ways I have described, or else full-length capes in the Moorish style, of purple velvet waved with gold and embroidered with thin spirals of silver, or else with heavier gold thread, decorated at the seams with small pearls from India. They were never without beautiful feathers in their hair, colored to match the sleeves of their gowns and always spangled in gold. In the winter they wore taffeta dresses, colored as I have described, lined with lynx fur, or black skunk, or Calabrian marten, or sable, or some other precious pelt.

Their prayer beads, rings, neck chains, and collar pieces were made of fine gems—red garnets, rubies, orange-red spinels, diamonds, sapphires, emeralds, turquoises, garnets, agates, green beryls, pearls, and fat onion pearls of a rare excellence.

They covered their heads, once again, as the season demanded: in winter, in the French style, with a velvet hood hanging down in the back like a pigtail; in spring, in the Spanish style, with a lace veil; in summer, in the Italian mode, with bare ringed hair studded with jewels, except on Sundays and holidays, when they used the French fashion, which seemed to them both more appropriate and more modest.

And the men wore their fashions, too: their stockings were of light linen or serge, colored scarlet, yellow, white, or black; their breeches were velvet, in the same colors (or very nearly), embroidered and patterned however they pleased. Their jackets were of gold or silver cloth, in velvet, satin, damask, taffeta, once again in the same colors, impeccably patterned and decorated and worn. Their shoes were laced to the breeches with silken thread, colored as before, each lace closed with an enameled gold tip. Their undervests and cloaks were of golden cloth or linen, or silver cloth, or velvet embroidered however they liked. Their gowns were as costly and beautiful as the women's, with silk belts, colored to match their breeches. Each of them wore a handsome sword, with a decorated hilt, the scabbard of velvet (the color matching their stockings), its endpiece of gold and heavily worked jewelry—and their daggers were exactly the same. Their hats were of black velvet, thickly garnished with golden berries and buttons, and the feathered plumes were white, delicately spangled in gold rows and fringed with rubies, emeralds, and the like.

But there was such a close fellowship between the men and the women that they were dressed almost exactly alike, day after day. And to make sure that this happened, certain gentlemen were delegated to inform the others, each and every morning, what sort of clothing the women had chosen to wear that day—because of course the real decisions, in this matter, were made by the women.

Although they wore such well-chosen and rich clothing, don't think these women wasted a great deal of time on their gowns and cloaks and jewelry. There were wardrobe men who, each day, had everything prepared in advance, and their ladies' maids were so perfectly trained that everyone could be dressed from head to toe, and beautifully, in the twinkling of an eye. And to make sure that all of this was perpetually in good order, the wood of Thélème was surrounded by a vast block of houses, perhaps half a league long, good bright buildings well stocked and supplied, and here lived goldsmiths, jewelers, embroiderers, tailors, specialists in hammering and filamenting gold and silver, velvet makers, tapestry weavers, and upholsterers, and they all worked at their trades right there alongside Thélème, and only for the men and women who dwelled in that abbey. All their supplies, metals and minerals and cloths, came to them courtesy My Lord Shipmaster (Nausiclète, in Greek), who each year brought in seven boats from the Little Antilles, the Pearl and Cannibal islands, loaded down with gold ingots, raw silk, pearls, and all sorts of gemstones. And any of the fat pearls which began to lose their sparkle and their natural whiteness were restored by feeding them to handsome roosters (as Avicenna recommends), just as we give laxatives to hawks and falcons.

BOOK I, CHAPTER 57

How the Men and Women of Thélème Governed Their Lives

Their lives were not ordered and governed by laws and statutes and rules, but according to their own free will. They rose from their beds when it seemed to them the right time, drank, ate, worked, and slept when they felt like it. No one woke them or obliged them to drink, or to eat, or to do anything whatever. This was exactly how Gargantua had ordained it. The constitution of this abbey had only a single clause:

DO WHAT YOU WILL

—because free men and women, wellborn, well taught, finding themselves joined with other respectable people, are instinctively impelled to do virtuous things and avoid vice. They draw this instinct from nature itself, and they name it "honor." Such people, if they are subjected to vile constraints, brought down to a lower moral level, oppressed and enslaved and turned away from that noble passion toward which virtue pulls them, find themselves led by that same passion to throw off and break any such bondage, just as we always seek out forbidden things and long for whatever is denied us.

And their complete freedom set them nobly in competition, all of them seeking to do whatever they saw pleased any one among them. If he or she said,

"Let's drink," everyone drank. If he or she said, "Let's play," they all played. If he or she said, "Let's go and have fun in the meadows," there they all went. If they were engaged in falconry or hunting, the women joined in, mounted on their good tame horses, light but proud, delicately sporting heavy leather gloves, a sparrow hawk perched on their wrists, or a small falcon, or a tiny but fierce merlin. (The other birds were carried by men.)

All of them had been so well educated that there wasn't one among them who could not read, write, sing, play on harmonious instruments, speak five or six languages, and write easy poetry and clear prose in any and all of them. There were never knights so courageous, so gallant, so light on their feet, and so easy on their horses, knights more vigorous, agile, or better able to handle any kind of weapon. There were never ladies so well bred, so delicate, less irritable, or better trained with their hands, sewing and doing anything that any free and worthy woman might be asked to do.

And for this reason, when the time came for anyone to leave the abbey, whether because his parents had summoned him or on any other account, he took one of the ladies with him, she having accepted him, and then they were married. And whatever devotion and friendship they had shown one another, when they lived at Thélème, they continued and even exceeded in their marriage, loving each other to the end of their days just as much as they did on the first day after their wedding. . . .

[Pantagruel: Birth and Education]

BOOK II, CHAPTER 2

The Birth of the Very Formidable Pantagruel

When he was four hundred and ninety-four, plus four more, Gargantua begat his son Pantagruel on his wife, the daughter of the king of the Amaurotes, in Utopia. Her name was Bigmouth, or Babedec,[1] as we say in the provinces, and she died giving birth to the baby: he was so immensely big, and weighed so incredibly much, that it was impossible for him to see the light without snuffing out his mother.

Now, to truly understand how he got his name, which was bestowed on him at the baptismal font, you must be aware that in the year of his birth there had been such a fearful drought, all across the continent of Africa, that it had not rained for more than thirty-six months, three weeks, four days, thirteen hours, and a little bit over, and the sun had been so hot, and so fierce, that the whole earth had dried up. It wasn't any hotter even in the days of the prophet Elijah than in that year, for not a tree on earth had a leaf or a bud. Grass never turned green, rivers dried up, fountains went dry; the poor fish, deprived of their proper element, flopped about on the ground, crying horribly; since there was no dew to make the air dense enough, the

---

1. Names taken from Sir Thomas More's *Utopia*. Literally, "no place," the word *utopia* has become synonymous with "ideal country."

birds could not fly; dead animals lay all over the fields and meadows, their mouths gaping wide—wolves, foxes, stags, wild boars, fallow does, hares, rabbits, weasels, martens, badgers, and many, many others. And it was no better for human beings, whose lives became pitiful things. You could see them with their tongues hanging out, like hares that have been running for six solid hours. Some of them threw themselves down into wells; others crawled into a cow's belly, to stay in the shade (Homer calls them *Alibantes*, desiccated people[2]). Everything everywhere stood still, like a ship at anchor. It was painful to see how hard men worked to protect themselves from this ghastly change in nature: it wasn't easy to keep even the holy water in churches from being used up, though the pope and the College of Cardinals expressly ordered that no one should dare to dip from these blessed basins more than once. All the same, when a priest entered his church you'd see dozens and dozens of these poor parched people come crowding around behind him, and if he blessed anyone the mouths would all gape open to snatch up every single drop, letting nothing fall wasted to the ground—just like the tormented rich man in Luke, who begged for the relief of cool water.[3] Oh, the fortunate ones, in that burning year, whose vaults were cool and well stocked!

The Philosopher tells us, asking why seawater is salty, that once, when Phoebus Apollo let his son Phaeton drive his gleaming chariot,[4] the boy had no idea how to manage it, nor any notion how to follow the sun's proper orbit from tropic to tropic, and drove off the right road and came so close to the earth that he dried up all the countries over which he passed, and burned a great swath through heaven, called by the philosophers *Via Lactea*, the Milky Way, but known to drunkards and lazy louts as Saint John's Road. But the fancy-pants poets say it's really where Juno's milk fell, when she suckled Hercules. Then the earth got so hot that it developed an enormous sweat, which proceeded to sweat away the entire ocean, which thus became salty, because sweat is always salty. And you can see for yourself that this is perfectly true, because all you have to do is taste it—or the sweat of pox-ridden people when they're put in steam baths and work up a great sweat. Try whichever you like: it doesn't matter to me.

It was almost exactly like that, in this year of which I write. One Friday, when everyone was saying prayers and making a beautiful procession, and litanies were being said, and psalms chanted, and they were begging omnipotent God to look mercifully down on them in their desolation, they could suddenly see great drops of water coming out of the earth, exactly as if someone were sweating profusely. And the poor people began to rejoice, as if this were something truly useful, some of them saying that since there wasn't a drop of liquid in the air from which one could have expected rain, the very ground itself was making up for what they lacked. Others, more scholarly,

---

2. The allusion to Homer is apparently mistaken, but *Alibantes*—possibly derived from Alibas, a dry river in hell—is used by other ancient writers with reference to the dead or the very old.
3. Luke 16.24: "And he cried and said, Father

Abraham, have mercy on me, and send Lazarus, that he may dip the tip of his finger in water, and cool my tongue; for I am tormented in this flame."
4. The chariot of the sun.

said that this was rain from the opposite side of the earth, as Seneca explains in the fourth book of *Questionum naturalium*, in which he speaks of the source and origin of the river Nile. But they were deceived: once the procession was over, and they went back to collect this precious dew and drink down a full glass, they found that it was just pickle brine, even worse to drink, and even saltier, than seawater.

And it was precisely because Pantagruel was born that very day that his father named him as he did: *Panta* in Greek means "all," and *Gruel* in Arabic means "thirsty," thus indicating that at the hour of his birth the whole world was thirsty—and he saw, prophetically, that someday his son would be lord of the thirsty, for this was shown to him at that same time and by a sign even more obvious. For when the child's mother was in labor, and all the midwives were waiting to receive him, the first thing that came out of her womb was sixty-eight mule drivers, each one leading a pack mule loaded with salt by its halter, after which came nine one-humped camels loaded with hams and smoked beef tongue, and then seven two-humped camels loaded with pickled eels, followed by twenty-five carts all loaded with onions, garlic, leeks, and spring onions. The midwives were frightened out of their wits. But some of them said to the others:

"Here's God's plenty. It signifies that we shouldn't either hold back, when we drink, or, on the other hand, pour it down the way the Swiss do. It's a good sign: these are truly wining signs."

And while they were gabbling and cackling about such trivialities, out popped Pantagruel, as hairy as a bear, at which one of them pronounced prophetically:

"He's been born all covered with fur, so he'll do wonderful things, and if he lives he'll live to an immense age."

[Father's Letter from Home]

BOOK II, CHAPTER 8

How Pantagruel, at Paris, Received a Letter from His Father, Gargantua, with a Copy of That Letter

Pantagruel studied hard, of course, and learned a great deal, because his brain was twice normal size and his memory was as capacious as a dozen kegs of olive oil. While he was thus occupied in Paris,[5] one day he received a letter from his father, which read as follows:

"My very dear son,
    "Among the gifts, the graces and the prerogatives with which from the very beginning our sovereign Creator and God has blessed and endowed human nature, that which seems to me uniquely wonderful is the power

---

5. Like his father before him, Pantagruel has been sent to Paris to study. The letter, patterned after Ciceronian models of eloquence, summarizes Rabelais's view of an ideal education, and generally illustrates the attitude of the Renaissance intellectual elite toward culture.

to acquire a kind of immortality while still in this our mortal state—that is, while passing through this transitory life a man may perpetuate both his name and his race, and this we accomplish through the legitimate issue of holy wedlock. And by that means we partially reestablish that which we lost through the sin of our first parents, Adam and Eve, to whom it was declared that, because they had not obeyed the commands of God their Creator, they would know death and in dying would utterly destroy the magnificent form in which mankind had been shaped.

"But this seminal propagation permits what the parents lose to live on in their children, and what dies in the children to live on in the grand-children, and so it will continue until the hour of the Last Judgment, when Jesus Christ will return to the hands of God the Father His purified and peaceful kingdom, now utterly beyond any possibility or danger of being soiled by sin. And then all the generations and all the corruptions will come to an end, and all the elements will be taken from their endless cycle of transformations, for the peace so devoutly desired will be achieved, and will be perfect, and all things will be brought to their fit and proper ending.

"So I have very fair and just cause to be thankful to God, my preserver, for having permitted me to see my hoary old age blossoming once again in your youth. Whenever, at His pleasure, He who rules and governs all things, my soul leaves this human dwelling place, I will not consider myself entirely dead, but simply transported from one place to another, for in you, and by you, my visible image lives in this world, wholly alive, able to see and speak to all honorable men, and all my friends, just as I myself was able to do. I confess that my life on this earth, though I have had divine help and divine grace to show me the way, has not been sin-less (for indeed we are all sinners and continually beg God to wash away our sins), and yet it has been beyond reproach.

"Just as the image of my flesh lives on in you, so too shine on the ways of my soul, or else no one would think you the true keeper and treasure of our immortal name, and I would take little pleasure in seeing that, because in that case the least part of me, my body, would live on, and the best part, my soul, in which our name lives and is blessed among men, would be decayed and debased. Nor do I say this because I have any doubt about your virtue, which I have long since tested and approved, but simply to encourage you to proceed from good to still better. And the reason I write to you now is not so much to ensure that you follow the pathways of virtue, but rather that you rejoice in thus living and having lived, and find new joys and fresh courage for the future.

"To consummate and perfect that task, it should be enough for you to remember that I have held back nothing, but have given help and assis-tance as if I had no other treasure in the world but to someday see you, while I still lived, accomplished and established in virtue, integrity, and wisdom, perfected in all noble and honorable learning, and to be able to thus leave you, after my death, as a mirror representing me, your father—perhaps in actual practice not so perfect an image as I might have wished, but certainly exactly that in both intention and desire.

"But though my late father of worthy memory, Grandgousier, devoted all his energy to those things of which I might take the fullest advantage, and from which I might acquire the most sensible knowledge, and though my own effort matched his—or even surpassed it—still, as you know very well, it was neither so fit nor so right a time for learning as exists today, nor was there an abundance of such teachers as you have had. It was still a murky, dark time, oppressed by the misery, unhappiness, and disasters of the Goths, who destroyed all worthwhile literature of every sort. But divine goodness has let me live to see light and dignity returned to humanistic studies, and to see such an improvement, indeed, that it would be hard for me to qualify for the very first class of little schoolboys—I who, in my prime, had the reputation (and not in error) of the most learned man of my day. Nor do I say this as an empty boast, though indeed I could honorably do so in writing to you—for which you have the authority of Cicero in his book *On Old Age*, and also the judgment of Plutarch, in his book *How a Man May Praise Himself without Fear of Reproach*. No, I say these things to make you wish to surpass me.

"For now all courses of study have been restored, and the acquisition of languages has become supremely honorable: Greek, without which it is shameful for any man to be called a scholar; Hebrew; Chaldean; Latin.[6] And in my time we have learned how to produce wonderfully elegant and accurate printed books,[7] just as, on the other hand, we have also learned (by diabolic suggestion) how to make cannon and other such fearful weapons. The world is full of scholars, of learned teachers, of well-stocked libraries, so that in my opinion study has never been easier, not in Plato's time, or Cicero's, or Papinian's.[8] From this day forward no one will dare to appear anywhere, or in any company, who has not been well and properly taught in the wisdom of Minerva. Thieves and highwaymen, hangmen and executioners, common foot soldiers, grooms and stableboys, are now more learned than the scholars and preachers of my day. What should I say? Even women and girls have come to aspire to this marvelous, this heavenly manna of solid learning. Old as I am, I have felt obliged to learn Greek, though I had not despised it, as Cato[9] did: I simply had no leisure for it, when I was young. And how exceedingly glad I am, as I await the hour when it may please God, my Creator, to call me to leave this earth, to read Plutarch's *Morals*, Plato's beautiful *Dialogues*, Pausanias's *Monuments*, and Athenaeus's *Antiquities*.[1]

"Which is why, my son, I strongly advise you not to waste your youth, but to make full use of it for the acquisition of knowledge and virtue. You are in Paris, you have your tutor, Epistemon: you can learn from them, by listening and speaking, by all the noble examples held up in front of your eyes.

6. The languages that are the instruments of classical learning are listed along with those useful for the study of the Old Testament of the Bible.
7. Printing from movable type was invented in Europe about the middle of the 15th century.
8. Jurisconsult of the time of Emperor Septimius Severus (reigned 193–211 C.E.).
9. Plutarch's life of Cato is the source of the notion that he despised Greek.
1. The works of Pausanias and Athenaeus were standard sources of information on ancient geography, art, and everyday life.

"It is my clear desire that you learn languages perfectly, first Greek, as Quintilian decreed, and then Latin.[2] And after that Hebrew, for the Holy Bible, and similarly Chaldean and Arabic. I wish you to form your literary style both on the Greek, following Plato, and on the Latin, following Cicero. Let there be nothing in all of history that is not clear and vivid in your mind, a task in which geographical texts will be of much assistance.

"I gave you some awareness of the liberal arts—geometry, arithmetic, and music—when you were still a child of five and six. Follow them further, and learn all the rules of astronomy. Ignore astrology and its prophecies, and all the hunt for the philosopher's stone which occupied Raymond Lully[3]—leave all those errors and vanities alone.

"As for the civil law, I wish you to know by heart all the worthy texts: deal with them and philosophy side by side.

"I wish you to carefully devote yourself to the natural world. Let there be no sea, river, or brook whose fish you do not know. Nothing should be unknown to you—all the birds of the air, each and every tree and bush and shrub in the forests, every plant that grows from the earth, all the metals hidden deep in the abyss, all the gems of the Orient and the Middle East—nothing.

"Then carefully reread all the books of the Greek physicians, and the Arabs and Romans, without turning your back on the talmudic scholars or those who have written on the Cabala. Make free use of anatomical dissection and acquire a perfect knowledge of that other world which is man himself. Spend several hours each day considering the holy Gospels, first the New Testament and the Apostles' letters, in Greek, and then the Old Testament, in Hebrew.

"In short, plumb all knowledge to the very depths, because when you are a grown man you will be obliged to leave the peace and tranquillity of learning, and acquire the arts of chivalry and warfare, in order to defend my house and lands and come to the aid of our friends if in any way they are attacked by evildoers.

"And soon I shall ask you to demonstrate just how much you have learned, which you can do in no better way than by publicly defending, in front of the entire world and against all who may come to question you, a thesis of your own devising. And continue, as you have been doing, to frequent the company of those learned men who are so numerous in Paris.

"But since, as the wise Solomon says, wisdom can find no way into a malicious heart, and knowledge without self-awareness is nothing but the soul's ruin, you should serve, and love, and fear God. Put all your thought in Him, and all your hopes, and by faith which has been shaped by love unite yourself with Him so firmly that sin will never separate you away. Be ever watchful of the world's wicked ways. Never put your heart in vanity, for ours is a transitory existence and the Word of God lives forever. Help your neighbors and love them as you love yourself. Honor your teachers. Avoid the company of those you do not desire to imitate;

---

2. In his *Institutio oratoria* 1.1.12 Quintilian recommends studying Greek before Latin.

3. Raymond Lully (13th century), Spanish philosopher who dabbled in magic.

do not take in vain the blessings God has given you. And when, finally, you know that you have learned all that Paris can teach you, return to me, so that I may look on you and, before I die, give you my blessing.

"My son, may the peace and grace of our Lord be with you. *Amen.*

"Written from Utopia, this seventeenth day of the month of March.

Your father,
GARGANTUA"

After receiving and reading this letter, Pantagruel was filled with new zeal, positively on fire to learn more than ever before—so much so that, had you seen him at his studies, and observed how much he learned, you would have declared that he was to his books like a fire in dry grass, burning with such an intense and consuming flame.

[Disputation with Thaumaste]

BOOK II, CHAPTER 18

How a Great English Scholar Wanted to Dispute with Pantagruel, But Was Beaten by Panurge

At about the same time, a scholar named Thaumaste (in Greek, "Wonderful"), hearing all the fuss over Pantagruel's incomparable learning, and seeing how famous he'd become, came from England with the sole intention of meeting Pantagruel and finding out if his knowledge matched his reputation. Arriving in Paris, he immediately went to Pantagruel's lodgings, which were at the abbey of Saint Denis.[4] At that moment, Pantagruel was in the garden with Panurge, walking up and down and philosophizing after the fashion of the ancient Peripatetics.[5] Thaumaste quivered with fear, seeing how huge Pantagruel was, but then he greeted him in customary style and said, with great courtesy:

"How true it is, as Plato, prince of philosophers, says, that if the image of wisdom and learning is a physical matter, visible to human eyes, it excites the whole world with admiration. The very word of such accomplishments, spread through the air and received by the ears of those who study and love philosophy, prevents them from taking any further rest, stirring them, urging them to hurry to where they may find and see the person in whom knowledge has erected its temple and given forth its oracles. Which was clearly demonstrated for us by the queen of Sheba, who traveled from the farthest reaches of the Orient and the Persian Sea to visit the house of the wise Solomon and hear his sage words;[6]

"and by Anacharsis,[7] who came from Scythia only to see Solon;

"and by Pythagoras, who journeyed to the prophets of Memphis;[8]

---

4. A college for Benedictines.
5. Followers of the Greek philosopher Aristotle, who wandered about in the Lyceum of ancient Athens while lecturing.
6. 2 Chronicles 9.1–12; the Queen of Sheba came from southern Arabia to test Solomon's

legendary wisdom.
7. Scythian prince, renowned for his travels and wisdom (6th century B.C.E.).
8. Capital of ancient Egypt. "Pythagoras": Greek philosopher of the 6th century B.C.E.

"and by Plato, who visited the Egyptian magi, and also Archytas of Tarentum;[9]

"and by Apollonius of Tyana,[1] who went to the Caucasian mountains, who journeyed among the Scythians, the Massagetae, and the Indians, who sailed down the great river Physon, all the way to the land of the Brahmans, to see Hiarchos, and who traveled in Babylonia, Chaldea, the land of the Medes, Assyria, Parthia, Syria, Phoenicia, Arabia, Palestine, and Alexandria, and in Ethiopia, too, to see the Gymnosophists.[2]

"We have another example in Livy,[3] to see and hear whom certain studious folk came to Rome from the farthest boundaries of France and Spain.

"I am not so presumptuous as to include myself among the ranks of such illustrious men. But I deeply desire to be thought of as a student and lover not only of humanistic learning but also of men of such learning.

"And, in fact, hearing of your priceless learning, I have left my country, my parents, and my home and come here, indifferent to the weariness of the journey, the anxiety of a voyage by sea, the strangeness of different lands, solely for the purpose of seeing and conferring with you about certain passages of philosophy, and geometrical divination, and also of cabalistic knowledge,[4] passages of which I am myself unsure and, about which I cannot rest content. If you can resolve these difficulties for me, I will be your servant from this day forth, and not only me but all my posterity, for I command no other gifts sufficient to repay you.

"I will put all of this in writing, and tomorrow I shall notify all the learned men of this city, so that we can discuss these matters publicly and in their presence.

"But I intend that our discussions, and any disputes in which we may engage, shall be conducted as follows. I do not wish to argue any bare-bones *for* and *against*, as do the besotted sophistical minds[5] of this and other cities. Nor do I wish to dispute after the fashion of academics, by declamation, or by the use of numbers, as Pythagoras did and as Picodella Mirandola,[6] at Rome, wished to do. I wish to dispute simply by signs, without a word being spoken, for these are matters so intricate and difficult that, as far as I am concerned, mere human speech will not be adequate to deal with them.

"May it please Your Magnificence to accept my invitation and join me, at seven in the morning, in the great hall of the College of Navarre."

When he had finished, Pantagruel said to him, courteously:

"My dear sir, how could I deny anyone the right to share in whatever blessings God has given me? All good things come from Him, and surely He wishes us to spread the celestial manna we have from Him among men both worthy and capable of receiving true learning—among whose number in our time, as I know very well, you belong in the very first rank. Let me say to you, therefore, that you will find me ready at any time to accede to any of your requests, to the extent that my poor powers may enable me, and well aware as I am that it is I

---

9. Said to be the founder of mathematics (4th century B.C.E.).
1. An ascetic wandering teacher of the early Christian period.
2. Ancient sect of Hindu ascetics.
3. Titus Livius (59 B.C.E.–17 C.E. or 64 B.C.E.–12 C.E.), Roman historian.
4. Lore from an occult system of mystical speculation of rabbinical origin.
5. Sophists, for Thaumaste, are specious, overly subtle rhetoricians.
6. Pico della Mirandola (1463–1494), Italian humanist scholar. Pythagoras (6th century B.C.E.) discovered the mathematical basis of the musical intervals.

who should be learning from you. And so, as you have declared, we will discuss these doubts of yours together, and hunt as hard as we can for their resolution, diving even as far as the bottom of that bottomless well in which, according to Heraclitus,[7] the truth is said to be hidden.

"And I highly commend the style of argument you have proposed, that is to say, by using signs, without any words, for thus you and I will truly understand one another, free from the sort of hand clapping and applause produced during their discussions by these puerile sophists, whenever one party has the better of the argument.

"So, then, tomorrow I shall appear without fail at the time and place you have requested. I ask of you only that, as between us, there may be no contentiousness and fuss, and that we seek neither honor nor men's applause, but only the truth."

To which Thaumaste replied:

"Sir, may God keep you in His grace. I thank Your High Magnificence for being so willing to condescend to my humble talents. Until tomorrow, I leave you in His hands."

"Farewell," said Pantagruel.

Gentlemen, you who may read this book, please don't imagine that anyone was ever more exalted, more transported, that whole night long, than Thaumaste and Pantagruel. Thaumaste told the concierge at his lodgings, in the abbey of Cluny, that in his entire life he had never been so incredibly thirsty:

"It feels to me," he said, "as if Pantagruel has me by the throat. Order me wine, if you please, and make sure that there's enough fresh water so I can lubricate the roof of my mouth."

And for his part, Pantagruel felt himself carried away, so that all that night he did nothing but tear through:

> The Venerable Bede's *De numeris et signis*, Numbers and Signs;
> Plotinus's *De inenarrabilibus*, Inexpressible Things;
> Proclus's *De sacrificio et magia*, Sacrifices and Magic;
> Artemidorus's *Per onirocriticon*, On the Interpretation of Dreams;
> Anaxagoras's *Peri semion*, On Signs;
> Dinarius's *Peri aphaton*, Unknowable Things;
> Philistion's books;
> Hipponax's *Peri anecphoneton*, Things Better Left Undiscussed;

And many, many others, so that finally Panurge said to him:

"My lord, stop all this intellectual groping and go to bed, for I can see you're far too agitated—indeed, such an extravagance of thinking and straining may well make you feverish. But first, have twenty-five or thirty good drinks, then go to bed and sleep comfortably—for tomorrow I will answer our English friend, I will argue with him, and if I don't get him *ad metam non loqui*,[8] to the point where he can't say a word, well, then you can say anything you like about me."

"All right," said Pantagruel, "but Panurge, my good friend, he's a deeply learned man. How will you deal with him?"

7. Greek philosopher of the 6th century B.C.E.
8. Translated in the next phrase, "to the point where he can't say a word."

"Very easily," said Panurge. "Please: don't even speak about it. Just leave the whole thing to me. Do you know any man as learned as the devils in hell?"

"Not really," said Pantagruel, "unless blessed by some special divine grace."

"You see?" said Panurge. "I've had many arguments with devils, and I've made them look like idiots, I've knocked them on their asses. So tomorrow you can be sure I'll make this glorious Englishman shit vinegar, right out in public."

Then Panurge spent the night boozing with the servants and playing games, at which he lost all the roses and ribbons from his breeches. And then, when the agreed-upon hour came, he conducted his master Pantagruel to the assigned meeting place, where as you can easily understand everyone in Paris, from the most important to the least, had assembled, all of them thinking:

"This devil of a Pantagruel, he's beaten all our clever fellows, and all those naive theologians and philosophers. But now he'll get what's coming to him, because this Englishman is a regular devil. We'll see who beats whom today."

Everyone was assembled; Thaumaste was waiting for them. And when Pantagruel and Panurge arrived in the hall, all the students—elementary, high school, and college—began to applaud, in their usual ridiculous way. But Pantagruel shouted at them, his voice as loud as the sound of a double cannon:

"Quiet! In the name of the devil, quiet! By God, you rascals, bother me and I'll cut the heads off every last one of you!"

Which announcement struck them as dumb as ducks: they were afraid even to cough, no matter if they'd swallowed fifteen pounds of feathers. And the very sound of his voice left them so parched and dry that their tongues hung half a foot out of their mouths, as if Pantagruel had roasted their throats.

Then Panurge began to speak, saying to the Englishman:

"Sir, have you come here seeking a debate, a contest, about these propositions which you have posted, or are you here to learn, to honestly understand the truth?"

To which Thaumaste answered:

"Sir, the only thing which has brought me here is my deep desire to understand that which I have struggled all my life to understand, and which neither books nor men have ever been able to resolve for me. As far as disputing and arguing is concerned, I have no interest whatever in that. That is a vulgar affair, and I leave it to villainous sophists, who never truly seek for truth when they argue, but only contradict each other and emptily debate."

"And so," said Panurge, "if I, who am no more than a minor disciple of my master Pantagruel, am able to satisfy you in all these matters, it would be an indignity and an imposition to trouble my master. Accordingly, it would be better if for now he simply presided over this discussion, judging what we say— and I need hardly say that he will himself satisfy you, should I be unable to fully quench your scholarly thirst."

"Indeed," said Thaumaste, "that's perfectly true."

"Then let us begin."

But note, please, that Panurge had hung a handsome tassel of red, white, green, and blue silk at the end of his long codpiece,[9] and inside it he had stuffed a fat, juicy orange.

---

9. Ornamental pouch at the crotch of tightly fitting breeches, worn by men in the 15th and 16th centuries.

BOOK II, CHAPTER 19

How Panurge Made the Englishman Who Argued by Signs Look Like an Idiot

Then, with everyone watching and listening in absolute silence, the Englishman raised his hands high in the air, first one and then the other, holding his fingertips in the shape called, in Chinon, the hen's asshole. He struck the nails of one hand against the nails of the other four times in a row, then opened his hands and slapped his palms together with a sharp crack. Joining his hands once again, as he had done at the start, he clapped them twice, then opened them out and clapped them four times more. Then he clasped them and extended one right over the other, as if praying devoutly to God.

Suddenly Panurge raised his right hand and stuck his thumb into his nose, keeping the other four fingers extended in a row straight out from the tip of his nose. He closed his left eye and winked the right one, making a deep hollow between eyebrow and eyelid. Then he lifted his left hand, the four fingers held rigidly extended, the thumb raised, and lined it up precisely with his right hand, keeping it perhaps half again the width of his nose distant. Then he lowered both hands, keeping them just as they were, and ended by raising them halfway and holding them there, as if aiming at the Englishman's nose.

"And yet if Mercury[1]—" the Englishman began.

But Panurge interrupted him:

"You have spoken. Be silent."

Then the Englishman made the following sign: With palm open, he raised his left hand high in the air, then closed its four fingers in a tight fist, with the thumb lying across the bridge of his nose. And then, suddenly, he raised his right hand, palm out, and lowered it again, placing the thumb against the little finger of his left hand, the four fingers of which he moved slowly up and down. Then, in reverse, he repeated with his right hand what he had just done with his left and with his left hand what he had done with his right.

Not a bit surprised, Panurge lifted his immense codpiece with his left hand, and with his right pulled from it a piece of white ox rib and two bits of wood in the same shape, one of black ebony, the other of rose-colored brazilwood. Arranging these objects symmetrically, in the fingers of his right hand, he clapped them together, making a sound exactly like that produced by the lepers in Brittany, to warn people off—but a sound infinitely more resonant and harmonious. And then, pulling his tongue slowly back into his mouth, he stood there, humming happily, staring at the Englishman.

The theologians, physicians, and surgeons thought this sign meant that the Englishman was a leper.

The counselors, jurists, and canon lawyers, however, thought his meaning was that being a leper brought with it a certain sort of happiness, as once our Lord had declared.

Not at all frightened, the Englishman raised both hands, holding them with the three largest fingers balled into a fist, then placed both thumbs between the

---

1. Thaumaste may be referring to the messenger god or to quicksilver, used in alchemy. Panurge reminds him of the rule of silent, gestural communication.

index and middle fingers, with the little fingers sticking straight out. He presented his hands to Panurge, then rearranged them so that the right thumb touched the left one, and his little fingers, too, were pressed against each other.

At this, without a word, Panurge raised his hands and made the following sign: he put the nail of his right index finger against the thumbnail, shaping a loop. He bent all the fingers of his right hand into a fist, except for the index finger, which he jabbed in and out of the space framed by his other hand. Then he extended both the index and the middle fingers of his right hand, separating them as widely as he possibly could and pointing them at Thaumaste. Then placing his left thumb in the corner of his left eye, he extended his entire hand like a bird's wing or a fish's backbone, and waved it very delicately up and down. Then he did the same thing with his right hand and his right eye.

Thaumaste began to turn pale and tremble, then made the following sign: he struck the middle finger of his right hand against the muscle of his palm, just below the thumb, then inserted the index finger of his right hand into a loop shaped exactly like that Panurge had made, except that Thaumaste inserted it from below, not from above.

Accordingly, Panurge clapped his hands together and breathed into his palms. Then, once again, he shaped a loop with his left hand and, over and over, inserted into it the index finger of his right hand. Then he thrust his chin forward and stood staring at Thaumaste.

And though no one there understood what these signs meant, they understood perfectly well that he was asking Thaumaste, without a word being spoken:

"Hey, what do you make of that, eh?"

And indeed Thaumaste began to sweat heavily, looking like a man swept away by high contemplation. Then he stared back at Panurge and put the nails of his left hand against those of his right, opening all the fingers into semicircles, then raised his hands as high as he could, exhibiting this sign.

At which Panurge suddenly put his right thumb under his jaw, and stuck the little finger into the loop fashioned by his left hand, and proceeded to vigorously snap his jaw, making his teeth crash harmoniously together.

In great anguish, Thaumaste stood up, but as he rose let fly a fat baker's fart, with the dung right after it. He pissed a good dose of vinegar, and stank like the devils in hell. All those in the hall began to hold their noses, because, clearly, it was anxiety that was obliging him to beshit himself. Then he raised his right hand, the ends of all the fingers clutched together, and spread out his left hand, flat against his chest.

At which Panurge pulled out his long codpiece with its waving tassel, stretching it a good foot and a half or more, holding it in the air with his left hand and with his right, taking the ripe orange, he threw it in the air seven times, the eighth time catching it in his right fist and then holding it quietly, calmly high in the air. Then he began to shake his handsome codpiece, as if displaying it to Thaumaste.

After this, Thaumaste began to puff out his cheeks like a bagpipe musician, blowing as hard as if he were inflating a pig's bladder.

At which Panurge stuck one finger of his left hand right up his ass, sucking in air with his mouth, as if eating oysters in the shell or inhaling soup. Then he opened his mouth a bit and slapped himself with the palm of his right hand, making an immensely loud sound which seemed to work its way up from the very depths of his diaphragm all along the trachial artery. And he did this sixteen times.

But all Thaumaste could do was snuffle like a goose.

So Panurge next stuck his right index finger into his mouth, clamping down hard on it. Then he pulled it out and, as he did so, made a loud noise, like little boys firing turnips from an elderwood cannon. And he did this nine times.

And Thaumaste cried:

"Ah ha, gentlemen! The great secret! He's got his hand in there up to the elbow."

And he pulled out a dagger, holding it with the point facing down.

At which Panurge grabbed his great codpiece and shook it against his breeches as hard as he could. Then he joined his hands like a comb and put them on top of his head, sticking out his tongue as far as he could and rolling his eyes like a dying goat.

"Ah ha, I understand," said Thaumaste. "But what?" And he set the handle of his dagger against his chest, and put his palm over the point, letting his fingertips turn lightly against it.

At which Panurge bent his head to the left and put his middle finger in his left ear, raising his thumb. Then he crossed his arms on his chest, coughed five times, and the fifth time banged his right foot on the ground. Then he raised his left arm and, tightening his fingers into a fist, held the thumb against his forehead, and with his right hand clapped himself six times on the chest.

But Thaumaste, as though still unsatisfied, put his left thumb to the end of his nose and closed the rest of that hand.

So Panurge put his forefingers on each side of his mouth, pulling back as hard as he could and showing all his teeth. His thumbs drew his lower eyelids as far down as they would go, making an exceedingly ugly face, or so it seemed to everyone watching.

BOOK II, CHAPTER 20

What Thaumaste Said about Panurge's Virtues and His Learning

Then Thaumaste stood up and, removing his hat, thanked Panurge graciously, then turned to the audience and said in a loud voice:

"Gentlemen, now I can truly speak the biblical words: *Et ecce plus quam Solomon hic*, And here is one who is greater than Solomon.[2] You see in front of you an incomparable treasure: and that is Monsieur Pantagruel, whose fame drew me from the farthest reaches of England in order to discuss with him certain insoluble problems, involving not only magic, academy, cabalistic learning, geometrical divination, and astrology but philosophy as well, which had long been troubling me. But now his fame bothers me, because it seems to be afflicted with jealousy—certainly, it hasn't granted him a thousandth part of what he deserves.

"You have seen for yourselves how his only disciple has satisfied my questions—has even told me more than I'd asked. Moreover, he has first shown and then solved for me other problems of inexpressible difficulty and importance, and in

2. Matthew 12.42 and Luke 11.31.

so doing he has opened for me, I can assure you, the deepest, purest well of encyclopedic learning, and in a fashion, indeed, that I had never thought any man could accomplish—not even begin to accomplish. I refer to our disputation by signs alone, without a word being spoken. But in due time I will record everything he has said and shown me, so no one will think that this has been more tomfoolery in which we have been engaged, and I will have that record put into print so others can learn from it as I have. Then you will be able to judge how little the master is truly esteemed, when the mere disciple can demonstrate such ability, for as it is written, *Non est discipulus super magistrum*, The disciple is not superior to his master.[3]

"And now let praise be given to God, and let me humbly thank you all for the honor you have shown us. May the good Lord repay you through all the eternity."

Pantagruel said similarly courteous things to all who were gathered there, and as he left took Thaumaste with him, to dine—and you will believe they drank until they had to open their breeches to let their bellies breathe. (In those days men buttoned up their bellies, the way they buttoned up their collars today.) They drank, indeed, until all they could say was, "Where do *you* come from?"

Holy Mother of God, how they guzzled, and how many bottles of wine they put away:

"Over here!"

"More, more!"

"Waiter, wine!"

"Pour it, in the name of the devil, pour it!"

No one drank fewer than twenty-five or thirty jugs, and do you know how? *Sicut terra sine aqua*, Like a dry land with no water—for it was warm weather and, besides, they were good and thirsty.

But as for Thaumaste's explanation of the signs they used, in their disputation, well, I'd be glad to explain them all myself, but I'm told that Thaumaste in fact wrote a huge book, printed in London, in which he sets out everything, omitting not a single item. In consideration of which, for now at least I'll just leave the subject.

---

3. Matthew 10.24.

JOACHIM DU BELLAY

Du Bellay (1522–1560) was born to a noble family in the west of France and orphaned very young. He studied law at Poitiers, where he joined a circle of humanist poets and thinkers. A fateful meeting with his contemporary, the poet Pierre de Ronsard, led to the formation of the hugely influential literary circle known as the Pléiade, whose manifesto was written by Du Bellay. In the "Defense and Illustration of the French Language," Du Bellay argued for cultivating French as a poetic language, although he continued to write in both French and Latin. In 1550 Du Bellay traveled to Rome as secretary to his cousin, Cardinal Du Bellay and there produced the *Antiquities of Rome*, a collection of sonnets from which the poems below are taken.

From The Antiquities of Rome[1]

3

Newcomer, you who seek Rome in Rome and find nothing of Rome in Rome, these old palaces, these old arches that you see, and these old walls, this is what they call Rome.

See what pride, what ruin, and how she who brought the world under her laws, in vanquishing all, at last vanquished herself and became the prey of time, which devours all.

Rome is the only monument to Rome, and only Rome conquered Rome. Only the Tiber,[2] which flees toward the sea,

Remains of Rome. O worldly inconstancy! Whatever stands firm is destroyed by time. And whatever flees resists time.

5

Whoever wishes to see all that nature, art, and heaven have been able to do, let him come see you, Rome—if, that is, he can imagine your greatness from what is only your lifeless portrait.

Rome is no more, and if her ruins still show us some shade of Rome, it is like a body raised by magic powers from its sepulchre at night.

The body of Rome has returned to ashes, and her soul has gone to rejoin the great soul of the material universe.

---

1. Translated by Richard Helgerson.
2. Rome's main watercourse; the city was founded on the eastern banks of the river.

But her writings, which in spite of time wrest her fairest praise from the grave, keep her specter wandering throughout the world.

13

Neither the fury of raging flame, nor the sharp edge of victorious steel, nor the destruction of the furious soldier, which have so often pillaged you, Rome,

Nor vicissitudes of your changing fortune, nor the destruction of envious time, nor the spite of men and gods, nor your own power turned against yourself,

Nor the shock of impetuous winds, nor the overflowing of that twisting god who has so often flooded you with his waters[3]

Have so lowered your pride that the greatness of the nothing they have left you does not still amaze the world.

15

Pale Spirits and you ashen shades, who, while you enjoyed the light of day, brought forth this proud city, whose dusty remains we see,

Tell me, Spirits (and may the dark banks of the Styx,[4] which forbid all return, binding you with a three times triple turn, not confine your shadowy forms),

Tell me then (for one of you may still be hidden here below), do you not feel your pain increase

When you see on these Roman hills the work of your hands reduced to nothing but a dusty plain?

3. I.e., the river Tiber.
4. The river that separates Earth from the underworld in Greek mythology; it also circles the underworld nine times.

PETRARCH AND THE
LOVE LYRIC

Although **Petrarch**, a contemporary of **Dante** and **Boccaccio**, lived and died in the Middle Ages, he did everything in his power to distinguish himself and his scholarship from the period he dismissed as the "Dark Ages." Petrarch dedicated himself to the recovery of classical learning in a spirit commonly associated with a later period, in which humanist scholars zealously pursued the rebirth of antiquity. Yet Petrarch's status as a precursor of the Renaissance is primarily due to an aspect of his work that neither he nor his contemporaries regarded as a lasting contribution: his 366 lyric poems in the vernacular, mostly dedicated to his frustrated desire for an elusive woman named Laura. Petrarch's experience of love and sense of his own fragmented and fluid self set the standard for the lyric expression of subjective and erotic experience in the Renaissance. His efforts to scrutinize himself intently and at times unflatteringly and to capture his own elusive inner workings in verse inspired a poetic tradition that has influenced lyric sequences from **Shakespeare**'s sonnets to Walt Whitman's *Leaves of Grass* to contemporary pop lyrics.

Francis Petrarch was born in Arezzo on July 20, 1304, three years after his father and Dante Alighieri were exiled

An early 16th-century Venetian portrait of Petrach and Laura de Noves, the real-life Laura. She holds a laurel branch like that which crowns the poet. The double portrait, now in the Ashmolean Museum at Oxford, is based on a 15th-century manuscript that depicts the two subjects separately.

from Florence. In 1314, Petrarch's father moved his family to Avignon, the new seat of the papacy (1309–77), where he became prosperous in the legal profession. Petrarch himself initially trained as a law student, but chose instead to pursue the study of classical culture and literature. He soon came to the attention of the powerful Colonna family, whose patronage launched his career as a diplomat-scholar and allowed him to travel widely and move in the intimate circles of European princes and scholars. He refused the offices of bishop and papal secretary, preferring instead to ground his growing prestige in his humanistic scholarship. Imaginative conversation with the ancients, like imitation of their poetry, brought him into contact with the past: his research into classical history and arts profoundly influenced his sense of himself and his own cultural moment. He died in 1374 near Padua, his head resting on a volume of his beloved **Virgil**.

Petrarch's most famous work, the *Rime Sparse* (Scattered Rhymes) or *Rerum Fragmenta Vulgarium* (Fragments in the Vernacular), is a collection of 366 songs and sonnets (based on the calendar year associated with the liturgy) of extraordinary technical virtuosity and variety. Written in Italian and woven into a highly introspective narrative, the lyric collection takes the poet himself as its object of study. The poems painstakingly record how his thoughts and identity are scattered and transformed by the experience of love for a beautiful, unattainable woman named Laura. Even some of his friends suspected that Laura was merely the theme and emblem of his lyric poetry and not a historical woman; she appears to have been both. On the flyleaf of his magnificent copy of Virgil, Petrarch inscribed a note on her life:

Laura, illustrious through her own virtues, and long famed through my verses, first appeared to my eyes in my youth, in the year of our Lord 1327, on the sixth day of April, in the church of St. Clare in Avignon, at matins; and in the same city, also on the sixth day of April, at the same first hour, but in the year 1348, the light of her life was withdrawn from the light of day, while I, as it chanced, was in Verona, unaware of my fate. * * * Her chaste and lovely form was laid to rest at vesper time, on the same day on which she died in the burial place of the Brothers Minor. I am persuaded that her soul returned to the heaven from which it came, as Seneca says of Africanus. I have thought to write this, in bitter memory, yet with a certain bitter sweetness, here in this place that is often before my eyes, so that I may be admonished, by the sight of these words and by the consideration of the swift flight of time, that there is nothing in this life in which I should find pleasure; and that it is time, now that the strongest tie is broken, to flee from Babylon; and this, by the prevenient grace of God, should be easy for me, if I meditate deeply and manfully on the futile cares, the empty hopes, and the unforeseen events of my past years.

(Translated by E. H. Wilkins)

Petrarch's note illuminates the powerful role that Laura plays in his personal struggles between spiritual aspirations and earthly attachments. Thoughts of Laura return him to the problem of his own will, torn between spiritual and sensual desires, always delaying worldly renunciation. Even when he expresses disgust with earthly rewards and pleasures, it is conditional: he will choose the right course of action, Petrarch writes, *if* he meditates "deeply and manfully" on the disappointments and failures of his past and denies memory's seductively bittersweet pleasures.

In the *Rime Sparse*, Laura's ambiguous position between divine guide and earthly temptress contrasts sharply with the role that Beatrice played in Dante's spiritual pilgrimage, the *Divine Comedy*. Whereas Dante's love finally leads him to paradise, it is never clear to Petrarch whether he is pursuing heavenly or earthly delights and whether he will safely reach any destination or "port" (in the nautical image of sonnet 189). When Dante looks into Beatrice's eyes on Mount Purgatory, he sees a reflection of the heavens; when Petrarch gazes into Laura's eyes, he sees himself. Not even his use of the liturgical year (especially the anniversaries of Christ's death and resurrection) to structure his account of their relationship guarantees that a spiritual conversion will follow Petrarch's self-analysis or "confession" of his life. In a contrary and skeptical mood at the end of one of his most philosophical poems (song 264), Petrarch asserts, "I see the better, but choose the worse."

The lyric collection's first sonnet, in which Petrarch solicits compassion as well as pardon from his readers, establishes the *Rime Sparse*'s close relationship to confessional narrative. Its themes of conversion, memory, and forgetfulness (of God and oneself) evoke the model of **St. Augustine** and raise the question of whether Petrarch will follow suit: will he ultimately transcend his attachment to a woman's physical beauty, his love of language and poetic figures, and his narcissistic preoccupation with himself? In dramatic opposition to the transcendent model of Augustine is **Ovid** of the *Metamorphoses*, the classical counterepic that artfully uses fragmentation, fluid change, and scattering to describe the effects of power—divine, political, or erotic—on bodies and on minds. Petrarch refers to a variety of Ovidian figures in the *Rime Sparse*, including Narcissus and Echo, Actaeon and Diana, Medusa, and Pygmalion. His chief Ovidian model, however, is the story of Apollo, the god who "invents" the genre of lyric during his amorous chase of the nymph Daphne. While running, Apollo describes her various beauties—eyes, figure, and hair—and imaginatively embellishes what he sees. When Daphne eludes him through her transformation into the laurel, Apollo claims her as his tree, if not his lover, and declares that the laurel will be the sign of triumph in letters and warfare. The prominence of this tale in the *Rime Sparse* suggests that if Laura had not lived, Petrarch would have had to invent her. Her name interweaves key attributes of Petrarch's poetic imagination: *lauro* and *alloro* ("laurel"), *oro* ("gold," for her tresses and value), *l'aura* ("breeze" and "inspiration," which etymologically relates to "breath"), *laus* or *lauda* ("praise"). Such wordplay suggests the selective, even obsessive character of Petrarch's poetic style. Like Apollo, Petrarch also "translates" his beloved's elusive body into the more tangible figures of rhetoric.

Petrarch's great legacy to Renaissance European literature is the *Rime Sparse*'s language of self-description, which starts from the conventional hyperbole, antithesis, and oxymoron (rhetorical exaggeration and opposition) that characterized troubadour songs, provençal lyric, and classical love elegy: *I freeze and burn, love is bitter and sweet, my sighs are tempests and my tears are floods, I am in ecstasy and agony, I am possessed by memories of her and I am in exile from myself*. Petrarch transformed such rhetorical figures or tropes of love into a powerful language of introspection and self-fashioning that swept through European literature. Although it soon became so popular that writers

endlessly repeated and even trivialized it, Petrarchism had serious dimensions that helped articulate growing questions about the self: is it determined by God or flexible and in the shaping hands of humankind? Do culture, history, and force of will compose and transform it?

Petrarchism offered rich formal possibilities as well: although Petrarch often wrote in other meters, the *sonnet* became in his hands an extraordinarily supple metrical form. A *Petrarchan sonnet*, as the form is now known, is a fourteen-line poem with a break after line eight. The *octet* is usually broken into two stanzas of four lines each, with a rhyme scheme of *a-b-b-a*, and the *sestet* is made up of two three-line stanzas, rhyming *c-d-c*. The sonnet proved remarkably flexible, allowing poets to express themselves in a compact and striking manner. The sestet and the octet may contrast formally or semantically, as may the stanzas within a section of the sonnet, while its rhyme can reinforce or contradict meaning. The possibilities are virtually endless, as Petrarch's many imitators were to demonstrate.

Across sixteenth- and seventeenth-century Europe, writers such as **Garcilaso** in Spain, **Du Bellay** in France, and Sidney, Spenser, and Shakespeare in England all turned to Petrarch as a beacon of Italian humanism who offered a powerful intellectual and formal toolkit for introspection. Through their own poems, they made Petrarchism into an international language, adapting it to various national traditions and rehearsing it in countless iterations. Garcilaso's "When I stand and contemplate my state" (sonnet 1) evokes Dante as well as Petrarch to give us an anguished self who both longs for and rues the end of erotic longing that will come with death. Garcilaso elaborates on nostalgia as a central theme of Petrarchism: memory brings joy and pain ("O sweet mementoes to my sorrow found," sonnet 10), while the poet urges the beloved to seize the day (*carpe diem*, in the Latin phrase) before it, too, is past ("For as long as the lily and the rose," sonnet 23).

The poetic sequence was itself a much-imitated model, allowing the poet to chart the minute transformations of the desiring self over time. The beloved does not fare as well: the eloquent expression of the male poet-lover's complex *interior* life in these sequences depends, as Petrarchan successors noticed, on a correspondingly detailed description of the beloved's *exterior*. In the Petrarchan inventory of the beloved's adorable parts, from eyes to hair, cheeks, and hand, the poet converts her living body to ornaments, metal, and minerals, such as gold, topaz, and pearls. Although any one of her beauties is capable of scattering the poet's thoughts, the beloved herself has little independent coherence: as one critic puts it, "some of Laura's parts are greater than her whole person." While male Renaissance writers turned to Petrarch to investigate their own interiority, groundbreaking female poets such as **Louise Labé** and **Veronica Franco** chose instead to give voice to the object of male longing, whether by challenging the Petrarchan "scattering" of the female presence, or by voicing an urgent female desire. Labé's poems, especially "Kiss Me Again" (sonnet 18), are striking for their immediacy, as though in response to the infinite deferment of Petrarchan introspection. The poet insists on the here and now with a force that dispels Petrarch's doubts and hesitations, yet her lyric "I" speaks a Petrarchan language in a Petrarchan form. Beyond the expression of desire, the defiant lyric personae that these female poets assume affords them a poetic voice, arguing for their very right to be heard as artists. In Labé's sonnet 10, love and poetic admiration are intertwined, as the poet expresses her desire for a beloved who is himself crowned with laurel. Franco's "A Challenge to a Lover Who Has Offended Her" dares the lover to a fight here and now, in a "love match" that makes the Petrarchan oxymoron of love as war urgent and concrete. Yet the poem is Franco's first blow, reminding the reader that the contest is not only physical but poetic.

By Shakespeare's time, the Petrarchan idiom had become a trite convention ripe for parody ("My mistress' eyes are nothing like the sun," sonnet 130), yet it remained the most powerful language available for describing desire, the ephemeral nature of love, and the fragility of the self when confronted with an impossible object. Shakespeare explicitly harnesses the conventionality of the form to create a highly skeptical poetic voice, which recognizes the tradition and yet questions it. He reflects on the limits of poetic invention, noting the paradox in always finding a novel way to describe fidelity: "O know, sweet love, I always write of you" ("Why is my verse so barren of new pride," sonnet 76). Thematically, Shakespeare occupies an oblique position in relation to Petrarchism, for his sequence includes *two* distinct love objects, one homoerotic: the beautiful, often inattentive aristocratic youth of sonnets 1–126, and the "dark lady" of 127–52. Sonnet 135, "Whoever hath her wish, thou hast thy Will" reveals a love triangle in which the poet must share his beloved's affection. Yet the brilliant saturation of the poem with puns on "will"— the poet's name, but also wishes, desire, the future, a testament—signals the power of the poetic voice to transcend the immediacy of the betrayal. We can recognize the symptoms in everything from a Renaissance sonnet to a twentieth-century Motown lyric ("Tracks of My Tears," Smokey Robinson and the Miracles): the lover who dies and is reborn a thousand times a day, who is mentally scattered and physically immobile, and who is never more alone than in a crowd, suffers from Petrarchan love. Petrarch did not invent the idea of a divided, tormented lover, but his authoritative self-portrait defined an infinitely rich poetic tradition of erotic longing.

FRANCIS PETRARCH
1304–1374

SONNETS

1[1]

You who hear in scattered rhymes the sound of those sighs with
which I nourished my heart during my first youthful error,[2] when
I was in part another man from what I am now:

for the varied style in which I weep and speak between vain
hopes and vain sorrow, where there is anyone who understands   5
love through experience, I hope to find pity, not only pardon.

But now I see well how for a long time I was the talk of the
crowd, for which often I am ashamed of myself within;[3]

and of my raving, shame is the fruit, and repentance, and the
clear knowledge that whatever pleases in the world is a brief   10
dream.

3[4]

It was the day when the sun's rays turned pale with grief for his
Maker[5] when I was taken, and I did not defend myself against it,
for your lovely eyes, Lady, bound me.

It did not seem to me a time for being on guard against Love's
blows; therefore I went confident and without fear, and so my   5
misfortunes began in the midst of the universal woe.[6]

Love found me altogether disarmed, and the way open through
my eyes to my heart, my eyes which are now the portal and
passageway of tears.

Therefore, as it seems to me, it got him no honor to strike me   10
with an arrow in that state,[7] and not even to show his bow to
you, who were armed.

---

1. Translated by Robert M. Durling.
2. Mental and physical "wandering" as well as a
moral "mistake." "Scattered rhymes": reference
to the sonnet collection's title, *Rime Sparse*.
3. The Italian, *di me medesmo meco mi ver-
gogno*, suggests intense self-consciousness.
4. Translated by Robert M. Durling.

5. The anniversary of Christ's crucifixion.
Elsewhere (sonnet 211 and a note in Petrarch's
copy of Virgil) given as April 6, 1327.
6. The communal Christian grief that contrasts with Petrarch's private woes.
7. State of grief over the crucifixion.

34[8]

Apollo, if the sweet desire is still alive that inflamed you beside
the Thessalian waves,[9] and if you have not forgotten, with the
turning of the years, those beloved blond locks;

against the slow frost and the harsh and cruel time that lasts as
long as your face is hidden, now defend the honored and holy   5
leaves where you first and then I were limed;

and by the power of the amorous hope that sustained you in
your bitter life, disencumber the air of these impressions.[1]

Thus we shall then together see a marvel[2]—our lady sitting on the
grass and with her arms making a shade for herself.   10

62[3]

Father in heaven, after each lost day,
Each night spent raving with that fierce desire
Which in my heart has kindled into fire
Seeing your acts adorned for my dismay;

Grant henceforth that I turn, within your light[4]   5
To another life and deeds more truly fair,
So having spread to no avail the snare
My bitter foe[5] might hold it in despite.

The eleventh year,[6] my Lord, has now come round
Since I was yoked beneath the heavy trace   10
That on the meekest weighs most cruelly.

Pity the abject plight where I am found;
Return my straying thoughts to a nobler place;
Show them this day you were on Calvary.

8. Translated by Robert M. Durling.
9. Petrarch links his love of Laura to the love
of Apollo for Daphne in Ovid's *Metamorphoses*. Daphne, daughter of the god of the Peneus
River in Thessaly, was pursued by Apollo, the
god of poetry. She begged her father to change
her form, which had "given too much pleasure," and was transformed into the laurel
tree. Apollo, whom Petrarch associates with

the sun god, claimed the laurel as his personal
emblem.
1. Grief, cloudy weather, and aging.
2. Supernatural and highly meaningful
spectacle.
3. Translated by Bernard Bergonzi.
4. Of grace.
5. Satan.
6. I.e., 1338.

126[7]

Clear, fresh, sweet waters,[8] where she who alone seems lady
to me rested her lovely body,
  gentle branch where it pleased her (with sighing I remember)
to make a column for her lovely side,
    grass and flowers that her rich garment covered along with   5
her angelic breast, sacred bright air where Love opened my heart
with her lovely eyes: listen all together to my sorrowful dying
words.

If it is indeed my destiny and Heaven exerts itself that Love
close these eyes while they are still weeping,   10
  let some grace bury my poor body among you and let my soul
return naked to this its own dwelling;
    death will be less harsh if I bear this hope to the fearful pass,
for my weary spirit could never in a more restful port or a more
tranquil grave flee my laboring flesh and my bones.   15

There will come a time perhaps when to her accustomed
sojourn the lovely, gentle wild one will return
  and, seeking me, turn her desirous and happy eyes toward
where she saw me on that blessed day,
    and oh the pity! seeing me already dust amid the stones,   20
Love will inspire her to sigh so sweetly that she will win mercy
for me and force Heaven, drying her eyes with her lovely veil.

From the lovely branches was descending (sweet in
memory) a rain of flowers over her bosom,
  and she was sitting humble in such a glory,[9] already covered   25
with the loving cloud;
    this flower was falling on her skirt, this one on her blond
braids, which were burnished gold and pearls to see that day;
this one was coming to rest on the ground, this one on the water,
this one, with a lovely wandering, turning about seemed to say: 30
"Here reigns Love."[1]

How many times did I say to myself then, full of awe: "She was
surely born in Paradise!"
  Her divine bearing and her face and her words and her sweet
smile had so laden me with forgetfulness   35
    and so divided me from the true image, that I was sighing:
"How did I come here and when?" thinking I was in Heaven, not
there where I was. From then on this grass has pleased me so that
elsewhere I have no peace.

If you had as many beauties as you have desire, you could   40
boldly leave the wood and go among people.[2]

---

7. Translated by Robert M. Durling.
8. Of the river Sorgue.
9. An image associated with the Virgin Mary.
1. Amor (Cupid) or Christ. The floral and
bejeweled images associate Laura's body with

the bride of the Song of Songs, whose erotic
chastity is celebrated as an "enclosed garden"
and "fountain sealed."
2. The last two lines are addressed to the
poem.

189[3]

My ship laden with forgetfulness passes through a harsh sea, at
midnight, in winter, between Scylla and Charybdis, and at the
tiller sits my lord, rather my enemy;[4]

each oar is manned by a ready, cruel thought that seems to scorn
the tempest and the end; a wet, changeless wind of sighs, hopes,   5
and desires breaks the sail;

a rain of weeping, a mist of disdain wet and loosen the already
weary ropes, made of error twisted up with ignorance.

My two usual sweet stars[5] are hidden; dead among the waves are
reason and skill; so that I begin to despair of the port.   10

333[6]

Go, grieving rimes of mine, to that hard stone
Whereunder lies my darling, lies my dear,
And cry to her to speak from heaven's sphere.
Her mortal part with grass is overgrown.

Tell her, I'm sick of living; that I'm blown   5
By winds of grief from the course I ought to steer,
That praise of her is all my purpose here
And all my business; that of her alone

Do I go telling, that how she lived and died
And lives again in immortality,   10
All men may know, and love my Laura's grace.

Oh, may she deign to stand at my bedside
When I come to die; and may she call to me
And draw me to her in the blessèd place!

---

3. Translated by Robert M. Durling.
4. Love. Scylla and Charybdis are the twinned
oceanic dangers through which Odysseus, in
Homer's *Odyssey*, and Aeneas, in Virgil's *Aeneid*, must chart a middle course. Forgetfulness

of oneself and of God is sinful in Augustinian
terms. The ship, captained by Reason, is a traditional figure for the embodied soul.
5. Laura's eyes.
6. Translated by Morris Bishop.

GARCILASO DE LA VEGA

Born to a noble family in Toledo, Spain, the courtier and soldier Garcilaso (ca. 1501–1536) traveled to Italy with the armies of Emperor Charles V. He was deeply influenced by the poetry he encountered there and, with his friend Joan Boscán, adopted Petrarchism for Iberia. Using the sonnet form and the Italianate hendecasyllable (the eleven-syllable line), Garcilaso developed an extraordinarily nuanced voice to describe a subject set both geographically and emotionally adrift. Though he died an early death of battle wounds, his slim but elegant corpus, collected by Boscán, proved foundational for Spanish Renaissance lyric.

SONNETS[1]

1

When I stand and contemplate my state,
and look back at the path that brought me here,
I find, in light of how I lost my way,
I might have met a much more bitter fate;
   if I ignore my steps along that road,   5
then I know not just how I came to grief;
I know my life is over, and I rue
the passing of my sorrow when I die.
   I shall meet my end, for I gave my heart
to one who could destroy and ruin me   10
if she should wish, and she could learn to wish;
   for if my will can bring about my death,
hers, less partial to my cause, will kill me
if it can, and why should it refrain?

10

O sweet mementoes, to my sorrow found,
so dear and joyous when it was God's will!
Joined forever in memory and mind,
together you conspire to see my death.
   No one could have told me in times long past,   5
when you and you alone brought so much joy,

---

1. Translated by Edith Grossman.

that on a bitter day you'd come back to me
in the bleak company of so much grief.
    Since in one hour you have taken from me
the joys doled out a little at a time,   10
take from me too the sorrow left behind;
    if you do not, I cannot but believe
you brought me joy only because you wished
to see me die of memories filled with grief.

23

For as long as the lily and the rose
give their color and hue to your fair face,
and the look in your eyes, ardent and chaste,
inflames my heart and yet restrains it too;
    and for as long as your hair, taken from veins   5
of purest gold, shimmers around your throat
—so beautiful, so slender, and so white—
blown in disarray by the gentle breeze:
    oh gather, in the joy of this your spring
the sweetest fruit before a sullen time   10
covers that gleaming mountaintop with snow.
    The icy wind will wither the fair rose,
fleet-footed age will change and transform all
but never alter its own ancient ways.

LOUISE LABÉ

Writing in a tradition marked by male desire, the French poet Louise Labé (ca. 1520–1566) adds a new dimension to Petrarchism by giving voice to a female lover who longs for her male beloved. Born to a rich ropemaker in the city of Lyons, Labé, known as La Belle Cordière (the beautiful ropemaker), was educated in Italian and in music, possibly at a convent school. One of the most important women writers of the Renaissance, Labé moved in humanist circles and was part of a lively community of poets, many of whom dedicated their own poems to her. Her own *Works* were published in 1555. In the early 1540s Labé had married Ennemond Perrin, who was a ropemaker like her parents. Although there has been much speculation about the identity of the beloved in her poems, unlike Petrarch's Laura, he is never named.

SONNETS[1]

1

Not even Ulysses,[2] or someone as wise as he,
would guess that a face like yours—so full of grace
and honor and respect—such a divine face—
could bring suffering like the pain you're causing me.
Yes, Love, your eyes in all their piercing beauty   5
have stabbed my innocent breast in the same place
once nourished and kept warm in your embrace;
and still, you are my only remedy.
Hard destiny makes me act like one who's been
stung by a scorpion but still hopes to heal,   10
taking an antidote of the same poison.
I am wounded. I ask you only to kill the pain,
but not to extinguish the burning I crave to feel,
this desire whose broken life would break my own.

10

When I see your blond head in its laurel crown
and hear your melancholy lute strings sing
with a sound that would seduce almost anything,
even rocks or trees;[3] when I hear of your renown,
all the ten thousand ornaments that surround   5
your virtue, endowing you more than a king
so the highest praise grows dim with your sparkling—
then my heart cries, in a secret passion of her own:
since all your graces are well-loved and known—
since everyone's esteem for you has grown   10
so strong—shouldn't these graces help you start
to love? To all the virtues that make you great
adding knowledge of my own pitiable state,
so that my love can softly inflame your heart?

18

Kiss me again, rekiss me, and then kiss
me again, with your richest, most succulent
kiss; then adore me with another kiss, meant
to steam out fourfold the very hottest hiss

---

1. Translated by Annie Finch.
2. The Roman name for Odysseus, the Greek hero, who was famous for his intelligence and his trickery in the Trojan War. His long voyage home to Ithaca and his wife, Penel-

ope, is related in the *Odyssey*.
3. The beloved is compared to Orpheus, the famed musician in Greek mythology whose playing could move inanimate objects.

from my love-hot coals. Do I hear you moaning? This   5
is my plan to soothe you: ten more kisses, sent
just for your pleasure. Then, both sweetly bent
on love, we'll enter joy through doubleness,
and we'll each have two loving lives to tend:
one in our single self, one in our friend.   10
I'll tell you something honest now, my love:
it's very bad for me to live apart.
There's no way I can have a happy heart
without some place outside myself to move.

VERONICA FRANCO

1546–1591

The writer and courtesan Veronica Franco (1546–1591) was a brilliant literary voice who wrote and published works in many different genres. Her collection of elegant and erudite verse in *terza rima*—the poetic form used by **Dante**—is characterized by a frank eroticism that is wholly unique. Similarly, Franco's familiar letters take Cicero as a model, but position the courtesan-writer as the moral center of the work to consider with keen insight the plight of women who must depend upon men for their survival. Deeply engaged with Venice's literary life and its salons, Franco also encountered great hostility. She was the target of vicious poetic attacks and was also accused of practicing witchcraft, which led to her trial by the Inquisition. Though Franco was acquitted, she never regained the stature and success she had once enjoyed.

Capitolo 13[1]

A Challenge to a Lover Who Has Offended Her

No more words! To deeds, to the battlefield, to arms![2]
For, resolved to die, I want to free myself
from such merciless mistreatment.
   Should I call this a challenge? I do not know,
since I am responding to a provocation;   5
but why should we duel over words?
   If you like, I will say that you've challenged me;
if not, I challenge you; I'll take any route,
and any opportunity suits me equally well.

---

1. Translated by Ann Rosalind Jones and Margaret F. Rosenthal.
2. The metaphor of the duel, with the atten-
dant choice of place, weapons, and seconds, is developed throughout the poem.

Yours be the choice of place or of arms,   10
and I will make whatever choice remains;
rather, let both be your decision.
    At once, I am sure, you will realize
how ungrateful and faithless you have been
and how wrongfully you have betrayed me.   15
    And unless my rage yields to overwhelming love,
with these very hands I will, in all boldness,
tear your living heart from your very breast.
    The deceiving tongue that lies to do me harm
I will tear out by its root, after it's been bitten   20
against the palate with repentant teeth;
    and if this brings no relief to my life,
abandoning all hope, I will rejoice
at having turned to bloodshed for my revenge.
    Then, with the same knife, my own breast,   25
satisfied and appeased by slaying you,
I may cut open, regretting my deed.
    Now, while I'm intent on pursuing revenge,
enter the arena, cruel, rebellious lover,
and present at once whatever arms you wish.   30
    Do you wish, for the field, the secret inn
that, hardhearted and deceptive, once watched
over so many of my now bitter delights?
    Here before me now stands the bed
where I took you in my arms, and which still   35
preserves the imprint of our bodies, breast to breast.
    In it I find now neither joy nor sleep,
but only weeping, by night and by day,
which transforms me into a river of tears.
    But this very place, which once was   40
the cherished shelter of my joys,
where I now live alone, in torment and grief,
    choose this as a battleground, so that the news
of your betrayal will reach no other place
but die here with you, cruel, faithless man.   45
    Come here, and, full of most wicked desire,
braced stiff for your sinister task,
bring with daring hand a piercing blade.
    Whatever weapon you hand over to me,
I will gladly take, especially if it is sharp   50
and sturdy and also quick to wound.
    Let all armor be stripped from your naked breast,
so that, unshielded and exposed to blows,
it may reveal the valor it harbors within.
    Let no one else intervene in this match,   55
let it be limited to the two of us alone,
behind closed doors, with all seconds sent away.
    This is the custom of noble knights,
who, without clamor, strive to clear their names
when they consider their honor to be stained: 60

either they reach an agreement on their own,
or, if they can find no road to peace,
they may sate their thirst for each other's blood.
    This is the style in which I like to fight,
and this manner fulfills and satisfies   65
my desire for bitter revenge.
    Although I hope, without any doubt, to spill
a river of your blood—indeed, I am certain
I can, without shedding a drop of my own—
    what if you were to offer me peace?   70
What if, all weapons laid aside, you took
the path opened to a love match in bed?
    Must I continue to battle against you,
since whoever refuses pardon when asked
wends his erring way reputed a coward?   75
    When you finally came to this point
with me, I'd not, perhaps, depart
from what is decent and proper to do.
    Perhaps I would even follow you to bed,
and, stretched out there in skirmishes with you,   80
I would yield to you in no way at all.
    To take revenge for your unfair attack,
I'd fall upon you, and in daring combat,
as you too caught fire defending yourself,
    I would die[3] with you, felled by the same blow.   85
Oh, empty hopes, over which cruel fate
forces me to weep forever!
    But hold firm, my strong, undaunted heart,
and with that felon's final destruction,
avenge your thousand deaths with his one.   90
    Then end your agony with the same blade.

3. Reach sexual climax.

WILLIAM SHAKESPEARE

Shakespeare's sonnets are as celebrated as his plays. The poems have
been read and debated as records of his
own loves, even though poets often used
the Petrarchan idiom to create poetic
fictions far removed from actual erotic
entanglements. Born to a middle-class
family in Stratford-upon-Avon, Shakespeare (1564–1616) married young and
quickly moved to London, leaving his
wife, Anne Hathaway, behind as he
made his career as an actor and dramatist. Editors have long speculated on
the "beloveds" in the sonnet sequence:
most of the poems refer to a noble
young man, often addressed directly,

who toys with his devoted "Will" (Shakespeare makes abundant use of the puns on his own name, which become as rich here as the puns on Laura for **Petrarch**), while a smaller subset concern a "dark lady." The poems circulated privately for many years; Shakespeare finally published them in 1609. Although Shakespeare himself makes fun of the Petrarchan tradition, in the mocking "My mistress' eyes are nothing like the sun" (sonnet 130 below), his sonnet sequence demonstrates Petrarchism's enduring appeal and endless flexibility.

SONNETS

76

Why is my verse so barren of new pride,
So far from variation or quick change?
Why with the time do I not glance aside
To new-found methods and to compounds strange?
Why write I still[1] all one, ever the same,   5
And keep invention in a noted weed,[2]
That[3] every word doth almost tell my name,
Showing their birth and where they did proceed?
O, know, sweet love, I always write of you,
And you and love are still my argument;[4]   10
So all my best is dressing old words new,
Spending again what is already spent:
   For as the sun is daily new and old,
   So is my love still telling[5] what is told.

116

Let me not to the marriage of true minds
Admit impediments.[6] Love is not love
Which alters when it alteration finds,
Or bends with the remover to remove:
O no! it is an ever-fixèd mark   5
That looks on tempests and is never shaken;
It is the star to every wandering bark,[7]

---

1. Always.
2. Keep my subject matter in a familiar garb.
3. So that.
4. Theme.
5. Telling—i.e., counting—continues the play on money and poetry of line 12.

6. The marriage service in the Elizabethan Book of Common Prayer requires those being wed to speak up if they know of any impediment to the union.
7. Boat. "Star": guiding star.

Whose worth's unknown, although his height be taken.[8]
Love's not Time's fool, though rosy lips and cheeks
Within his bending sickle's compass come: 10
Love alters not with his brief hours and weeks,
But bears it out even to the edge of doom.
    If this be error and upon me proved,
    I never writ, nor no man ever loved.

129

Th' expense of spirit in a waste of shame
Is lust in action,[9] and, till action, lust
Is perjured, murderous, bloody,[1] full of blame,
Savage, extreme, rude, cruel, not to trust,
Enjoyed no sooner but despisèd straight,   5
Past reason hunted, and no sooner had
Past reason hated, as a swallowed bait
On purpose laid to make the taker mad;
Mad in pursuit and in possession so;
Had, having, and in quest to have, extreme;   10
A bliss in proof, and proved, a very woe;[2]
Before, a joy proposed, behind, a dream.
    All this the world well knows, yet none knows well
    To shun the heaven that leads men to this hell.[3]

130

My mistress' eyes are nothing like the sun;
Coral is far more red than her lips' red;
If snow be white, why then her breasts are dun;
If hairs be wires, black wires grow on her head.
I have seen roses damasked, red and white,[4]   5
But no such roses see I in her cheeks;
And in some perfumes is there more delight
Than in the breath that from my mistress reeks.
I love to hear her speak, yet well I know
That music hath a far more pleasing sound.   10
I grant I never saw a goddess go;
My mistress, when she walks, treads on the ground:
    And yet, by heaven, I think my love as rare
    As any she belied with false compare.

---

8. Altitude be measured. Sailors calculated latitude by measuring the height of the pole star over the horizon.
9. The end of lust is the shameful squandering of energy. "Spirit": may mean semen.
1. Violent. "Perjured": false.

2. A delight while experienced, a source of misery after.
3. The hell of guilt, also a colloquial term for the vagina.
4. Damask roses mingle the colors red and white.

135

Whoever hath her wish, thou hast thy Will,[5]
And Will to boot,[6] and Will in overplus;
More than enough am I that vex thee still,
To thy sweet will making addition thus.
Wilt thou, whose will is large and spacious,   5
Not once vouchsafe to hide my will in thine?
Shall will in others seem right gracious,
And in my will no fair acceptance shine?
The sea, all water, yet receives rain still
And in abundance addeth to his store;   10
So thou, being rich in Will, add to thy Will
One will of mine, to make thy large Will more.
    Let no unkind no fair beseechers kill;[7]
    Think all but one, and me in that one Will.

---

5. The poem plays on the multiple meanings of *will*: (a) what you want; (b) sexual desire; (c) the poet's first name; (d) sexual organs, male or female; (e) shall.

6. In addition.

7. Let no ungenerous refusal kill any attractive suitor.

NICCOLÒ MACHIAVELLI
1469–1527

Widely vilified and secretly admired, Niccolò Machiavelli attempted to teach the rulers of his time how to get power and hold on to it. With his mix of clear-eyed, pragmatic observation and humanist idealism, Machiavelli transformed our conception of political power. Sharply contrasting traditional morality to the pragmatic necessities of ruling, Machiavelli tried to address the painful fragmentation and constant warfare of the many states that then made up what is today Italy. His solution—a strong, effective prince unconstrained by moral pieties—struck his contemporaries as a terrifying prescription for the use of force and deception, even though Machiavelli always stressed the ruler's need for popular support. Seeking to discuss the conduct of political affairs from a new rational basis, Machiavelli has been credited with having turned politics into a science.

LIFE AND TIMES

The son of a lawyer, Machiavelli was born to a well-connected but not wealthy family in the city-state of Florence, ruled by the beloved Lorenzo di Medici. He received a modest education, and was introduced to the scholarly circles around the ruler. Machiavelli's adult life was closely bound up with the political fortunes of his city-state. Renaissance

Italy was a fractured collection of polities, constantly overrun by the armies of France, Spain, and the Holy Roman Empire, all of which took advantage of Italian fragmentation to expand their territorial claims. When Machiavelli was a young man, Florence experienced its own profound political upheavals: after Lorenzo's death in 1492, the Medici were expelled from power and Florence was ruled by the Dominican preacher Savonarola. When Savonarola's regime collapsed, the city returned to republican government, and Machiavelli embarked on a distinguished career of public service, serving a city-state whose government was the most widely representative of its time. From 1498 to 1512, Machiavelli was secretary to the Second Chancery, charged with internal and war affairs. He also served as a diplomatic envoy (his low rank meant he could not be an ambassador), and, during the conflict between Florence and Pisa, he dealt with military problems firsthand. His many missions to some of the most powerful rulers of his time—King Louis XII of France, Cesare Borgia, Pope Julius II, the Emperor Maximilian—allowed him to observe up close their methods for gaining and maintaining political power; this led to two books—*Portraits*—of the affairs of their territories, written in 1508 and 1510. Machiavelli noted what made for effective conquest and rule, and contrasted the ruthlessness of a figure like Borgia to the slow deliberations of the consensus-based government in his own city. The constant threats and emergencies faced by Florence and other Italian states made Machiavelli's ideal leader— the hardheaded, strong prince—seem an appealing figure as a possible savior against foreign invasions.

As a student of politics and an acute observer of historical events, Machiavelli tried to apply his experience of other states to strengthening his own. He noted that one weakness of the Italian city-states was their reliance on mercenary soldiers, who were ever ready to change sides for higher pay. Instead, following Cesare Borgia's example, he set out in 1505 to establish an army of Florentine citizens, animated by their love for their country, which achieved some surprising victories. Yet the republican forces were not enough to fend off all attackers, and, in 1512, in a moment of military weakness, the Medici faction regained power. With the end of the republic, Machiavelli lost his post. The Medici accused him unjustly of conspiracy and had him imprisoned and tortured. Once released, he retreated from the city to his family's farm, with his wife, Marietta Corsini, and their five children. There, in a study where he imagined himself in conversation with the classical writers he most admired (as detailed in the "Letter to Francesco Vettori," also included in this anthology), Machiavelli produced his major works: a study of republican government, the *Discourses on the First Ten Books of Livy* (1513–21), and one on statecraft, *The Prince*, written in 1513 with the hope that the Medici would ultimately grant him a public office. As his exile grew longer, he also wrote a number of literary works, including the much-applauded comedy *La mandragola* (The Mandrake), first performed in 1520. That same year Machiavelli was commissioned to write a history of Florence, which he presented in 1525 to Pope Clement VII (Giulio de' Medici).

After a reconciliation of sorts with the ruling Medicis, Machiavelli was entrusted with the upkeep of military fortifications in Florence. Here, too, he served the city well, presenting a strong enough defense that when the Holy Roman Empire invaded Italy in 1527, Florence avoided being attacked. Instead, the imperial forces sacked Rome with incredible violence. For Florence, which had long benefited from the strength of a series of Medici popes in Rome, the result was the collapse of Medici domination and, once more, the return of republican government. Despite Machiavelli's long history of service to the republic, however, he was now regarded as a Medici sympathizer and passed over for public office. This last disappointment may have accelerated his demise. He died on June 22, 1527, and was buried in the church of Santa Croce.

THE PRINCE

Although he wrote widely across many genres, Machiavelli's reputation—and his notoriety—is based on *The Prince*. This "handbook" on how to obtain and keep political power consists of twenty-six chapters. The first eleven deal with different types of dominions and how they are acquired and preserved—the early title of the whole book, in Latin, was *De principatibus* (Of Princedoms)— while the twelfth through fourteenth chapters focus on problems of military power. The book's astounding fame, however, is based on the final part (from chapter fifteen to the end), which deals primarily with the attributes and "virtues" of the prince himself.

Traditional manuals for rulers—a genre often referred to as the "mirror of princes"—couched their advice in the language of Christian morality. Their point was to remind the ruler to remain virtuous as they educated him and gave him advice. Erasmus's roughly contemporary *The Education of a Christian Prince* (1516), for example, which he presented to the future Charles V of Spain and also to Henry VII of England, held that what the prince most needed was "the best possible understanding of Christ." Machiavelli's point, by stark contrast, is to make the ruler effective by giving him advice on how to stay in power. For Machiavelli, the end of political stability justifies the means, even if those means include deception and violent force.

The view of humanity in Machiavelli is not cheerful. Indeed, the pessimistic notion that humanity is evil is not so much Machiavelli's conclusion about human nature as his premise, the point of departure for the course a ruler should follow: "A prudent ruler . . . cannot and should not observe faith when such observance is to his disadvantage and the causes that made him give his promise have vanished. If men were all good, this advice would not be good, but since men are wicked and do not keep their promises to you, you likewise do not have to keep yours to them." The idealism of Christian morality is checked by realism, by the facts on the ground. Machiavelli sees humanity as it is, not as it should be, and indicates the rules of the game as his experience shows it must, under the circumstances, be played. This kind of bald assessment did not sit well with European Christians invested in moral absolutes and in the idea that it was God who bestowed power to rulers.

Yet despite his emphasis on ruthlessly preserving power, Machiavelli stresses over and over again the importance for a ruler of preserving the goodwill of his subjects. In Machiavelli's view, a ruthless leader such as Cesare Borgia would at least avoid the weakness of lords who "plundered their subjects rather than governed them" and allowed "thefts, brawls, and every sort of excess." It is better for a prince to be thought stingy, he explains, than for him to grow poor through lavishness and then be forced to rob his subjects.

Machiavelli's pragmatism, his emphasis on fact, on how the real world works rather than on lofty ideals, contrasts with his own idealization of the strong ruler. His picture of the perfectly efficient ruler shows the Renaissance tendency toward "perfected" form. In this, he is closer than one might suspect to that more obvious treatise of political idealism, **Thomas More**'s *Utopia* (1516), in which the desires and venality of humankind are curbed by a strong ruler and the rules he bequeaths to society. Most clearly at the end of the book, Machiavelli abandons complex reality in favor of an ideal vision and he offers the conclusion to his many lessons: the ideal ruler, now technically equipped by Machiavelli's lessons, is to undertake a mission—the liberation of Italy. The realistic method described throughout now appears directed toward an ideal task. Instead of technical political considerations (choice of the opportune moment, evaluation of military power), Machiavelli invokes religious and ancient precedents, calling for a new Moses to lead Italy out of bondage: "Everything is now fully disposed for the work . . . if only your House adopts the methods of those I have set forth as examples. Moreover, we have before our eyes extraordinary and unexampled means prepared by God. The sea has been divided. A cloud has guided you on your way. The rock has given forth water. Manna has fallen."

Although *The Prince* did not succeed in winning Machiavelli the favor of the Medici, or, for that matter, in achieving the unification of Italy, it was hugely influential throughout Europe. The work circulated widely in manuscript before being published in 1532, and the response to it was unmitigated outrage. Whatever truths readers recognized in Machiavelli's little book, it was tempting to accuse him of provoking the amorality (or immorality) that in some cases he simply described. "Machiavellian" became an insult denoting amorality in the service of *Realpolitik*, and the intricacies of Machiavelli's study of political power were overlooked. A careful reading of *The Prince* offers a very different impression, however, as the acute realism of the political observer gives way to the humanist dreaming of ancient glories.

FROM THE PRINCE[1]

[New Princedoms Gained with Other Men's Forces and through Fortune]

From CHAPTER 7

* * *

[Cesare Borgia][2]

Cesare Borgia, called by the people Duke Valentino, gained his position through his father's Fortune and through her lost it, notwithstanding that he made use of every means and action possible to a prudent and vigorous man for putting down his roots in those states that another man's arms and Fortune bestowed on him. As I say above, he who does not lay his foundations beforehand can perhaps through great wisdom and energy lay them afterward, though he does so with trouble for the architect and danger to the building. So on

---

1. Translated by Allan H. Gilbert.
2. Son of Pope Alexander VI and duke of Valentinois and Romagna. His skillful and merciless

subjugation of the local lords of Romagna occurred between 1499 and 1502.

examining all the steps taken by the Duke, we see that he himself laid mighty foundations for future power. To discuss these steps is not superfluous; indeed I for my part do not see what better precepts I can give a new prince than the example of Duke Valentino's actions. If his arrangements did not bring him success, the fault was not his, because his failure resulted from an unusual and utterly malicious stroke of Fortune.[3]

[Pope Alexander VI Attempts to Make Cesare a Prince]

Alexander VI,[4] in his attempt to give high position to the Duke his son, had before him many difficulties, present and future. First, he saw no way in which he could make him lord of any state that was not a state of the Church, yet if the Pope tried to take such a state from the Church, he knew that the Duke of Milan and the Venetians[5] would not allow it because both Faenza and Rimini were already under Venetian protection. He saw, besides, that the weapons of Italy, especially those of which he could make use, were in the hands of men who had reason to fear the Pope's greatness; therefore he could not rely on them, since they were all among the Orsini and the Colonnesi[6] and their allies. He therefore was under the necessity of disturbing the situation and embroiling the states of Italy so that he could safely master part of them. This he found easy since, luckily for him, the Venetians, influenced by other reasons, had set out to get the French to come again into Italy. He did not merely oppose their coming; he made it easier by dissolving the early marriage of King Louis.[7] The King then marched into Italy with the Venetians' aid and Alexander's consent; and he was no sooner in Milan than the Pope got soldiers from him for an attempt on Romagna; these the King granted for the sake of his own reputation.[8]

[Borgia Determines to Depend on Himself]

Having taken Romagna, then, and suppressed the Colonnesi, the Duke, in attempting to keep the province and to go further, was hindered by two things: one, his own forces, which he thought disloyal; the other, France's intention. That is, he feared that the Orsini forces which he had been using would fail him and not merely would hinder his gaining but would take from him what he had gained, and that the King would treat him in the same way. With the Orsini, he had experience of this when after the capture of Faenza he attacked Bologna, for he saw that they turned cold over that attack. And as to the King's purpose, the Duke learned it when, after taking the dukedom of Urbino, he invaded Tuscany—an expedition that the King made him abandon. As a result, he determined not to depend further on another man's armies and Fortune.

---

3. Ill health.
4. Rodrigo Borgia (c. 1431–1503), pope (1492–1503), father of Cesare and Lucrezia Borgia.
5. The Venetian Republic opposed the expansion of the papal states. "Duke of Milan": Ludovico Il Moro, the flamboyant duke of the

Sforza family.
6. Powerful Roman families.
7. Louis XII, king of France (d. 1515).
8. According to his agreement with Pope Alexander VI.

[*The Duke Destroys His Disloyal Generals*]

The Duke's first act to that end was to weaken the Orsini and Colonnesi parties in Rome by winning over to himself all their adherents who were men of rank, making them his own men of rank and giving them large subsidies; and he honored them, according to their stations, with military and civil offices, so that within a few months their hearts were emptied of all affection for the Roman parties, and it was wholly transferred to the Duke. After this, he waited for a good chance to wipe out the Orsini leaders, having scattered those of the Colonna family; such a chance came to him well and he used it better. When the Orsini found out, though late, that the Duke's and the Church's greatness was their ruin, they held a meeting at Magione, in Perugian territory. From that resulted the rebellion of Urbino, the insurrections in Romagna, and countless dangers for the Duke, all of which he overcame with the aid of the French. Thus having got back his reputation, but not trusting France or other outside forces, in order not to have to put them to a test, he turned to trickery. And he knew so well how to falsify his purpose that the Orsini themselves, by means of Lord Paulo,[9] were reconciled with him (as to Paulo the Duke did not omit any sort of gracious act to assure him, giving him money, clothing and horses) so completely that their folly took them to Sinigaglia into his hands. Having wiped out these leaders, then, and changed their partisans into his friends, the Duke had laid very good foundations for his power, holding all the Romagna along with the dukedom of Urbino, especially since he believed he had made the Romagna his friend and gained the support of all those people, through their getting a taste of well-being.

[*Peace in Romagna; Remirro de Orco*]

Because this matter is worthy of notice and of being copied by others, I shall not omit it. After the Duke had seized the Romagna and found it controlled by weak lords who had plundered their subjects rather than governed them, and had given them reason for disunion, not for union, so that the whole province was full of thefts, brawls, and every sort of excess, he judged that if he intended to make it peaceful and obedient to the ruler's arm, he must of necessity give it good government. Hence he put in charge there Messer[1] Remirro de Orco, a man cruel and ready, to whom he gave the most complete authority. This man in a short time rendered the province peaceful and united, gaining enormous prestige. Then the Duke decided there was no further need for such boundless power, because he feared it would become a cause for hatred; so he set up a civil court in the midst of the province, with a distinguished presiding judge, where every city had its lawyer. And because he knew that past severities had made some men hate him, he determined to purge such men's minds and win them over entirely by showing that any cruelty which had gone on did not originate with himself but with the harsh nature of his agent. So getting an opportunity for it, one morning at Cesena he had Messer Remirro laid in two pieces in the public square with a block of wood and a bloody sword near him. The ferocity of this spectacle left those people at the same time gratified and awe-struck.

---

9. Member of the Orsini.   1. My lord (from the French *monsieur*).

[Princely Virtues]

From CHAPTER 15

On the Things for Which Men, and Especially Princes, Are Praised or Censured

* * * Because I know that many have written on this topic, I fear that when I too write I shall be thought presumptuous, because, in discussing it, I break away completely from the principles laid down by my predecessors. But since it is my purpose to write something useful to an attentive reader, I think it more effective to go back to the practical truth of the subject than to depend on my fancies about it. And many have imagined republics and principalities that never have been seen or known to exist in reality. For there is such a difference between the way men live and the way they ought to live, that anybody who abandons what is for what ought to be will learn something that will ruin rather than preserve him, because anyone who determines to act in all circumstances the part of a good man must come to ruin among so many who are not good. Hence, if a prince wishes to maintain himself, he must learn how to be not good, and to use that ability or not as is required.

Leaving out of account, then, things about an imaginary prince, and considering things that are true, I say that all men, when they are spoken of, and especially princes, because they are set higher, are marked with some of the qualities that bring them either blame or praise. To wit, one man is thought liberal, another stingy (using a Tuscan word, because *avaricious* in our language is still applied to one who desires to get things through violence, but *stingy* we apply to him who refrains too much from using his own property); one is thought open-handed, another grasping; one cruel, the other compassionate; one is a breaker of faith, the other reliable; one is effeminate and cowardly, the other vigorous and spirited; one is philanthropic, the other egotistic; one is lascivious, the other chaste; one is straightforward, the other crafty; one hard, the other easy to deal with; one is firm, the other unsettled; one is religious, the other unbelieving; and so on.

And I know that everybody will admit that it would be very praiseworthy for a prince to possess all of the above-mentioned qualities that are considered good. But since he is not able to have them or to observe them completely, because human conditions do not allow him to, it is necessary that he be prudent enough to understand how to avoid getting a bad name because he is given to those vices that will deprive him of his position. He should also, if he can, guard himself from those vices that will not take his place away from him, but if he cannot do it, he can with less anxiety let them go. Moreover, he should not be troubled if he gets a bad name because of vices without which it will be difficult for him to preserve his position. I say this because, if everything is considered, it will be seen that some things seem to be virtuous, but if they are put into practice will be ruinous to him; other things seem to be vices, yet if put into practice will bring the prince security and well-being.

CHAPTER 16

On Liberality and Parsimony

Beginning, then, with the first of the above-mentioned qualities, I assert that it is good to be thought liberal. Yet liberality, practiced in such a way that you get a reputation for it, is damaging to you, for the following reasons: If you use it wisely and as it ought to be used, it will not become known, and you will not escape being censured for the opposite vice. Hence, if you wish to have men call you liberal, it is necessary not to omit any sort of lavishness. A prince who does this will always be obliged to use up all his property in lavish actions; he will then, if he wishes to keep the name of liberal, be forced to lay heavy taxes on his people and exact money from them, and do everything he can to raise money. This will begin to make his subjects hate him, and as he grows poor he will be little esteemed by anybody. So it comes about that because of this liberality of his, with which he has damaged a large number and been of advantage to but a few, he is affected by every petty annoyance and is in peril from every slight danger. If he recognizes this and wishes to draw back, he quickly gets a bad name for stinginess.

Since, then, a prince cannot without harming himself practice this virtue of liberality to such an extent that it will be recognized, he will, if he is prudent, not care about being called stingy. As time goes on he will be thought more and more liberal, for the people will see that because of his economy his income is enough for him, that he can defend himself from those who make war against him, and that he can enter upon undertakings without burdening his people. Such a prince is in the end liberal to all those from whom he takes nothing, and they are numerous; he is stingy to those to whom he does not give, and they are few. In our times we have seen big things done only by those who have been looked on as stingy; the others have utterly failed. Pope Julius II,[2] though he made use of a reputation for liberality to attain the papacy, did not then try to maintain it, because he wished to be able to make war. The present King of France[3] has carried on great wars without laying unusually heavy taxes on his people, merely because his long economy has made provision for heavy expenditures. The present King of Spain,[4] if he had continued liberal, would not have carried on or completed so many undertakings.

Therefore a prince ought to care little about getting called stingy, if as a result he does not have to rob his subjects, is able to defend himself, does not become poor and contemptible, and is not obliged to become grasping. For this vice of stinginess is one of those that enables him to rule. Somebody may say: Caesar, by means of his liberality, became emperor, and many others have come to high positions because they have been liberal and have been thought so. I answer: Either you are already prince, or you are on the way to become one. In the first case liberality is dangerous; in the second it is very necessary to be thought liberal. Caesar was one of those who wished to attain dominion over Rome. But if, when he had attained it, he had lived for a long time and had not moderated his expenses, he would have

2. Pope Julius II (r. 1503–13) was known as the "Warrior Pope" and led efforts to drive French forces from Italy.
3. Louis XII (r. 1498–1515), mocked for his economy.
4. Ferdinand the Catholic (1452–1516), king of Aragon, whose marriage to Isabel of Castile unified Spain.

destroyed his authority. Somebody may answer: Many who have been thought very liberal have been princes and done great things with their armies. I answer: The prince spends either his own property and that of his subjects or that of others. In the first case he ought to be frugal; in the second he ought to abstain from no sort of liberality. When he marches with his army and lives on plunder, loot, and ransom, a prince controls the property of others. To him liberality is essential, for without it his soldiers would not follow him. You can be a free giver of what does not belong to you or your subjects, as were Cyrus, Caesar, and Alexander,[5] because to spend the money of others does not decrease your reputation but adds to it. It is only the spending of your own money that hurts you.

There is nothing that eats itself up as fast as does liberality, for when you practice it you lose the power to practice it, and become poor and contemptible, or else to escape poverty you become rapacious and therefore are hated. And of all the things against which a prince must guard himself, the first is being an object of contempt and hatred. Liberality leads you to both of these. Hence there is more wisdom in keeping a name for stinginess, which produces a bad reputation without hatred, than in striving for the name of liberal, only to be forced to get the name of rapacious, which brings forth both bad reputation and hatred.

From CHAPTER 17

On Cruelty and Pity, and Whether It Is Better to Be Loved or to Be Feared, and Vice Versa

Coming then to the other qualities already mentioned, I say that every prince should wish to be thought compassionate and not cruel; still, he should be careful not to make a bad use of the pity he feels. Cesare Borgia was considered cruel, yet this cruelty of his pacified the Romagna, united it, and changed its condition to that of peace and loyalty. If the matter is well considered, it will be seen that Cesare was much more compassionate than the people of Florence, for in order to escape the name of cruel they allowed Pistoia to be destroyed.[6] Hence a prince ought not to be troubled by the stigma of cruelty, acquired in keeping his subjects united and faithful. By giving a very few examples of cruelty he can be more truly compassionate than those who through too much compassion allow disturbances to continue, from which arise murders or acts of plunder. Lawless acts are injurious to a large group, but the executions ordered by the prince injure a single person. The new prince, above all other princes, cannot possibly avoid the name of cruel, because new states are full of perils. Dido in Virgil puts it thus: "Hard circumstances and the newness of my realm force me to do such things, and to keep watch and ward over all my lands."[7]

5. Great conquerors and imperial leaders of the classical world: Cyrus the Great, founder of the Achaemenid (Persian) Empire; Julius Caesar, Roman general and statesman; and Alexander the Great, king of Macedonia.

6. Pistoia was a city under Florentine rule, riven by quarrels among its aristocratic families, which Cesare Borgia attempted to conquer. Machiavelli was Florence's envoy to Pistoia on several occasions in 1501–2, and wrote a memorandum on its problems. Here, he condemns what he considers Florence's insufficiently decisive actions against the leaders of the rival factions in Pistoia.

7. Virgil, *Aeneid* 1.563–4. Dido, queen of Carthage, is building her city as Aeneas arrives on her shores.

All the same, he should be slow in believing and acting, and should make no one afraid of him, his procedure should be so tempered with prudence and humanity that too much confidence does not make him incautious, and too much suspicion does not make him unbearable.

All this gives rise to a question for debate: Is it better to be loved than to be feared, or the reverse? I answer that a prince should wish for both. But because it is difficult to reconcile them, I hold that it is much more secure to be feared than to be loved, if one of them must be given up. The reason for my answer is that one must say of men generally that they are ungrateful, mutable, pretenders and dissemblers, prone to avoid danger, thirsty for gain. So long as you benefit them they are all yours; as I said above, they offer you their blood, their property, their lives, their children, when the need for such things is remote. But when need comes upon you, they turn around. So if a prince has relied wholly on their words, and is lacking in other preparations, he falls. For friendships that are gained with money, and not with greatness and nobility of spirit, are deserved but not possessed and in the nick of time one cannot avail himself of them. Men hesitate less to injure a man who makes himself loved than to injure one who makes himself feared, for their love is held by a chain of obligation, which, because of men's wickedness, is broken on every occasion for the sake of selfish profit; but their fear is secured by a dread of punishment which never fails you.

Nevertheless the prince should make himself feared in such a way that, if he does not win love, he escapes hatred. This is possible, for to be feared and not to be hated can easily coexist. In fact it is always possible, if the ruler abstains from the property of his citizens and subjects, and from their women. And if, as sometimes happens, he finds that he must inflict the penalty of death, he should do it when he has proper justification and evident reason. But above all he must refrain from taking property, for men forget the death of a father more quickly than the loss of their patrimony. Further, causes for taking property are never lacking, and he who begins to live on plunder is always finding cause to seize what belongs to others. But on the contrary, reasons for taking life are rarer and fail sooner.

But when a prince is with his army and has a great number of soldiers under his command, then above all he must pay no heed to being called cruel, because if he does not have that name he cannot keep his army united or ready for duty. It should be numbered among the wonderful feats of Hannibal[8] that he led to war in foreign lands a large army, made up of countless types of men, yet never suffered from dissension, either among the soldiers or against the general, in either bad or good fortune. His success resulted from nothing else than his inhuman cruelty, which, when added to his numerous other strong qualities, made him respected and terrible in the sight of his soldiers. Yet without his cruelty his other qualities would not have been adequate. So it seems that those writers have not thought very deeply who on one side admire his accomplishment and on the other condemn the chief cause for it.

* * *

8. Carthaginian leader who fought against Rome in the Second Punic War (218–201 B.C.E.). He famously marched his army, including war elephants, across the Alps into Italy.

Returning, then, to the debate on being loved and feared, I conclude that since men love as they please and fear as the prince pleases, a wise prince will evidently rely on what is in his own power and not on what is in the power of another. As I have said, he need only take pains to avoid hatred.

CHAPTER 18
In What Way Faith Should Be Kept by Princes

Everybody knows how laudable it is in a prince to keep his faith and to be an honest man and not a trickster. Nevertheless, the experience of our times shows that the princes who have done great things are the ones who have taken little account of their promises and who have known how to addle the brains of men with craft. In the end they have conquered those who have put their reliance on good faith.

You must realize, then, that there are two ways to fight. In one kind the laws are used, in the other, force. The first is suitable to man, the second to animals. But because the first often falls short, one has to turn to the second. Hence a prince must know perfectly how to act like a beast and like a man. This truth was covertly taught to princes by ancient authors, who write that Achilles and many other ancient princes were turned over for their upbringing to Chiron[9] the centaur, that he might keep them under his tuition. To have as teacher one who is half beast and half man means nothing else than that a prince needs to know how to use the qualities of both creatures. The one without the other will not last long.

Since, then, it is necessary for a prince to understand how to make good use of the conduct of the animals, he should select among them the fox and the lion, because the lion cannot protect himself from traps, and the fox cannot protect himself from the wolves. So the prince needs to be a fox that he may know how to deal with traps, and a lion that he may frighten the wolves. Those who act like the lion alone do not understand their business. A prudent ruler, therefore, cannot and should not observe faith when such observance is to his disadvantage and the causes that made him give his promise have vanished. If men were all good, this advice would not be good, but since men are wicked and do not keep their promises to you, you likewise do not have to keep yours to them. Lawful reasons to excuse his failure to keep them will never be lacking to a prince. It would be possible to give innumerable modern examples of this and to show many treaties and promises that have been made null and void by the faithlessness of princes. And the prince who has best known how to act as a fox has come out best. But one who has this capacity must understand how to keep it covered, and be a skilful pretender and dissembler. Men are so simple and so subject to present needs that he who deceives in this way will always find those who will let themselves be deceived.

I do not wish to keep still about one of the recent instances. Alexander VI[1] did nothing else than deceive men, and had no other intention; yet he always

9. In Greek myth, Chiron was the wisest of the centaurs (half men, half horses). He was renowned as the teacher of gods and heroes, including the great warrior Achilles, the Greek champion in the Trojan War.
1. Pope Rodrigo Borgia (r. 1492–1503), father of Cesare Borgia, was widely considered worldly and corrupt.

found a subject to work on. There never was a man more effective in swearing that things were true, and the greater the oaths with which he made a promise, the less he observed it. Nonetheless his deceptions always succeeded to his wish, because he thoroughly understood this aspect of the world.

It is not necessary, then, for a prince really to have all the virtues mentioned above, but it is very necessary to seem to have them. I will even venture to say that they damage a prince who possesses them and always observes them, but if he seems to have them they are useful. I mean that he should seem compassionate, trustworthy, humane, honest, and religious, and actually be so; but yet he should have his mind so trained that, when it is necessary not to practice these virtues, he can change to the opposite, and do it skilfully. It is to be understood that a prince, especially a new prince, cannot observe all the things because of which men are considered good, because he is often obliged, if he wishes to maintain his government, to act contrary to faith, contrary to charity, contrary to humanity, contrary to religion. It is therefore necessary that he have a mind capable of turning in whatever direction the winds of Fortune and the variations of affairs require, and, as I said above, that he should not depart from what is morally right, if he can observe it, but should know how to adopt what is bad, when he is obliged to.

A prince, then, should be very careful that there does not issue from his mouth anything that is not full of the above-mentioned five qualities. To those who see and hear him he should seem all compassion, all faith, all honesty, all humanity, all religion. There is nothing more necessary to make a show of possessing than this last quality. For men in general judge more by their eyes than by their hands; everybody is fitted to see, few to understand. Everybody sees what you appear to be; few make out what you really are. And these few do not dare to oppose the opinion of the many, who have the majesty of the state to confirm their view. In the actions of all men, and especially those of princes, where there is no court to which to appeal, people think of the outcome. A prince needs only to conquer and to maintain his position. The means he has used will always be judged honorable and will be praised by everybody, because the crowd is always caught by appearance and by the outcome of events, and the crowd is all there is in the world; there is no place for the few when the many have room enough. A certain prince of the present day,[2] whom it is not good to name, preaches nothing else than peace and faith, and is wholly opposed to both of them, and both of them, if he had observed them, would many times have taken from him either his reputation or his throne.

From CHAPTER 19

On Avoiding Contempt and Hatred

But because I have spoken of the more important of the qualities above, I wish to cover the others briefly with this generality. To wit, the prince should give his attention, as is in part explained above, to avoiding the things that make him hateful and contemptible. As long as he escapes them, he will have done his duty, and will find no danger in other injuries to his reputation. Hatred, as I have said, comes upon him chiefly from being rapacious and seizing the prop-

2. Ferdinand the Catholic, king of Spain.

erty and women of his subjects. He ought to abstain from both of these, for the majority of men live in contentment when they are not deprived of property or honor. Hence the prince has to struggle only with the ambition of the few which can be restrained in many ways and with ease. Contempt is his portion if he is held to be variable, volatile, effeminate, cowardly, or irresolute. From these a prince should guard himself as from a rock in the sea. He should strive in all his actions to give evident signs of greatness, spirit, gravity, and fortitude. Also in the private affairs of his subjects he should make it understood that his opinion is irrevocable. In short he should keep up such a reputation that nobody thinks of trying to deceive him or outwit him.

The prince who makes people hold that opinion has prestige enough. And if a prince has a high reputation, men hesitate to conspire against him and hesitate to attack him, simply because he is supposed to be of high ability and respected by his subjects. For a prince must needs have two kinds of fear: one within his state, because of his subjects; the other without, because of foreign rulers. From these dangers he defends himself with good weapons and good friends. And if his weapons are good, he will always have good friends. Conditions within the state, too, will always remain settled when those without are settled, if they have not already been unsettled by some conspiracy. And when things without are in movement, if he has ruled and lived as I have said, and does not fail himself, he will surely repel every attack, as I said Nabis the Spartan did.[3]

But with respect to his subjects, when there is no movement without, he has to fear that they will make a secret conspiracy. From this the prince protects himself adequately if he avoids being hated and despised and keeps the people satisfied with him. The latter necessarily follows the former, as was explained above at length. Indeed one of the most potent remedies the prince can have against conspiracies is not to be hated by the majority of his subjects. The reason for this is that a man who conspires always thinks he will please the people by killing the prince; but when he thinks he will offend them by it, he does not pluck up courage to adopt such a plan, because the difficulties that fall to the portion of conspirators are numerous. Experience shows that there have been many conspiracies and that few have come out well. They fail because the conspirator cannot be alone, and he can get companions only from those who, he thinks, are discontented. But as soon as you have revealed your purpose to a malcontent, you have given him an opportunity to become contented, because he evidently can hope to gain every advantage from his knowledge. Such is his position that, seeing on the one hand certain gain, and on the other gain that is uncertain and full of danger, he must needs be a rare friend, or, at any rate, an obstinate enemy of the prince, if he keeps faith with you. To put the thing briefly, I say that on the part of those who conspire there is nothing but fear, jealousy, and the expectation of punishment, which terrifies them. But on the part of the prince are the majesty of his high office, the laws, the power of his friends and his party that protects him. Evidently when the popular goodwill is joined to all these things, it is impossible that anybody can be so foolhardy as to conspire against him. Ordinarily the conspirator must be afraid before the execution of

3. Last ruler (d. 192 B.C.E.) of independent Sparta, a Greek city-state. A controversial figure, he was known for ably maintaining his power in a time of war, but was also reviled in classical sources for his use of mercenaries and abuse of power.

his evil deed, but in this case he also has reason to fear after his transgression, because he will have the people against him and therefore cannot hope for any escape.

* * *

I conclude, therefore, that a prince need not pay much attention to conspiracies when the people are well disposed to him. But when they are unfriendly and hate him, he must fear everything and everybody. Further, well-organized governments and wise princes have striven with all diligence not to make the upper classes feel desperate, and to satisfy the populace and keep them contented. In fact this is one of the most important matters a prince has to deal with.

Among the kingdoms well organized and well governed in our times is France. In this country there are numerous good institutions on which depend the liberty and security of the king. The first of these is the parliament and its authority. He who organized this kingdom set up the parliament because he knew the ambition of the nobles and their arrogance, and judged it necessary that the nobility should have a bit in its mouth to restrain it. On the other hand, he knew the hatred, founded on fear, of the generality of men for the nobles, and intended to secure the position of the latter. Yet he did not wish this to be the special concern of the king, because he wished to relieve the king from the hatred he would arouse among the great if he favored the people, and among the people if he favored the nobles. Therefore he set up a third party as judge, to be the one who, without bringing hatred on the king, should restrain the nobles and favor the people. This institution could not be better or more prudent, nor could there be a stronger cause for the security of the king and the realm. From this can be deduced another important idea: to wit, princes should have things that will bring them hatred done by their agents, but should do in person those that will give pleasure. Once more I conclude that a prince should esteem the nobles but should not make himself hated by the populace.

* * *

It should here be observed that hate is gained through good deeds as well as bad ones. Therefore, as I said above, if a prince wishes to keep his position, he is often obliged not to be good. For if that large body, whether made up of people or soldiers or grandees, whose support you believe you need to maintain yourself, is corrupt, you must feed its humor in order to satisfy it. In such conditions, good deeds are enemies to you. But let us come to Alexander. He was of such goodness that among the other matters for which he is praised is this, that, in the fourteen years during which he held the empire, no one was ever put to death by him without trial. All the same, since he was thought to be under the influence of women, and a man who allowed his mother to govern him, he came to be despised. Then the army plotted against him and killed him.

* * *

I say that the princes of our times are less troubled than the emperors were by the necessity of making their conduct satisfy the soldiers above all others. It is true that they do have to give their troops some consideration, yet it is quickly settled, because none of these princes have armies already formed that have grown old along with the governments and administrations of the provinces, as did the armies of the Roman Empire. If, therefore, it was then necessary to satisfy the soldiers rather than the people, it was because the soldiers were more powerful than the people. Now it is more necessary to princes, except the Turk and the Soldan,[4] to satisfy the people rather than the soldiers, for the people are the more powerful. I make an exception of the Turk, who always keeps about him twelve thousand infantry and fifteen thousand cavalry, on whom depend his security and the strength of his kingdom. So it is necessary that, giving second place to any other consideration, that lord should keep the friendship of his soldiers. Since the kingly authority of the Soldan is likewise entirely in the hands of the soldiers, it is needful for him to have them as his friends, without regard for the people. You should observe that this government of the Soldan is unlike all other principates; it is like the Christian papacy, which can be called neither a hereditary principality nor a new one. The sons of the old prince are not heirs and do not carry on a line of princes, but the successor is he who is chosen to that rank by those who have the right to do so. And yet, since this method of government has long been used, it cannot be called a new principality, because it encounters none of the difficulties of new ones. Even if the ruler is new, the institutions of the state are old and arranged to receive him as though he were their hereditary lord.

[The Best Defense]

From CHAPTER 20

Whether Fortresses and Other Things That Princes Employ Every Day Are Useful or Useless

Some princes, in order to hold their positions securely, have disarmed their subjects. Others have kept their subject territories divided. Some have nourished enmities against themselves. Yet others, by a change in policy, have tried to gain to their side those they suspected at the beginnings of their reigns. Some have built fortresses. Some have dismantled and destroyed them. From all these things it is not possible to educe a final decision, without coming to the particulars of those states where matters like these must be decided. Hence I shall speak in the general manner that the material in itself justifies.

It has never been true, then, that a new prince has disarmed his subjects. On the contrary, when he has found them disarmed, he has always armed them, because, when you arm them, their arms become your own; those whom you have suspected become faithful; those who were faithful are kept so, and instead of your subjects they become your partisans. It is impossible to arm all your subjects, yet if you benefit those you arm, you can deal much more securely with those who are left unarmed. The very diversity of procedure which the favored ones see applied to them, binds them to you. The others excuse you, holding it necessary that those should have more favor who undergo the most danger and have the greatest obligation. But when you disarm new subjects you get their ill

---

4. Turk: ruler of the Ottoman Empire, supported by a corps of Janissaries (elite infantry troops); Soldan: sultan of Egypt, supported by a corps of Mamluks (slave soldiers).

will; for you show that you distrust them either for their worthlessness or their lack of fidelity. Either one of these beliefs rouses hatred against you. And because you are not able to remain unarmed, you are obliged to turn to mercenary soldiers * * *. Even if mercenaries were good, they could not be sufficient to defend you from hostile rulers and untrustworthy subjects. Hence, as I have said, a new prince, in a new principate, has always organized armies there. Histories are full of examples of this.

But when a prince acquires a new state that he joins as a member to his old one, then it is necessary to disarm the new state, except for those who have been your partisans in gaining it. And even these it is necessary to render soft and effeminate as time and opportunity permit; and you must arrange things in such a way that the arms of your whole state are in the hands of your own soldiers, who live in your old state close to you.

* * *

There is no doubt that princes become great when they overcome difficulties and opposition. Therefore Fortune avails herself of this, especially when she wishes to bestow greatness on a new prince, who has more need to acquire reputation than a hereditary one. For she causes enemies to rise up against him, and makes him undertake campaigns against them, that he may have an opportunity to conquer them, and rise high by ascending the ladder provided by his enemies. Hence many think that a wise prince, whenever he has opportunity for it, should craftily nourish some hatreds against himself, in order that by overthrowing them he may increase his greatness.

Princes, and especially new ones, sometimes find more fidelity and helpfulness in those whom they have distrusted at the beginning of their rule, than in those who at first were attached to them. Pandolfo Petrucci,[5] prince of Siena, ruled his state more with those he distrusted than with the others. But of this thing it is not possible to speak in general because it varies according to the individual case. I shall say only this. Those men who are unfriendly in the early days of a reign, and are of such a kind that they have need of support if they are to maintain themselves, are always to be gained by the prince with the greatest ease, and they are obliged to serve him faithfully, in proportion as they know it is needful for them to cancel with their deeds the unfavorable opinion he had of them. Hence the prince always derives more profit from them than from those who feel too secure in his service, and as a result neglect his affairs.

And because the subject demands it, I do not wish to omit a reminder to princes who have secured a brand-new state by means of the favor of persons within it. They should consider well what cause moved those who favored the change to do so. If it is not natural affection for the new ruler, but merely discontent with the government as it was, a prince will succeed in keeping them as his friends only with effort and great difficulty, because it is impossible for him to satisfy them. And if he will examine the cause of this, with the aid of examples derived from ancient and modern affairs, he will see that it is much easier to gain the friendship of the men who had been contented with the ear-

5. Ruler of the Italian Republic of Siena (1452–1512).

lier government, and therefore were his enemies, than to gain that of those who became his friends and favored his occupation merely because they were not contented.

In order to hold their positions more securely, princes have been in the habit of building fortresses, which serve as bridle and bit for those who plan to act against them; princes also wish to have secure places of refuge from sudden assaults. I praise this method, because it has been used from ancient times. Nonetheless, Messer Niccolò Vitelli,[6] in our times, has been seen dismantling two fortresses in Città di Castello, in order to keep that state. Guido Ubaldo,[7] duke of Urbino, when he returned into his dominions after Cesare Borgia had been driven out of them, completely ruined all the fortresses of that province, and believed that without them it would be more difficult for him to lose that territory again. The Bentivogli,[8] when they returned to Bologna, employed similar methods.

Fortresses, then, are useful or not according to the times. If they benefit you in some circumstances, they will damage you in others. This matter can be considered as follows: a prince who has more fear of the people than of foreigners ought to build fortresses; but he who has more fear of foreigners than of his people should leave them out of his plans. The castle of Milan, which Francesco Sforza[9] built there, has done and will do more damage to the house of Sforza than any other cause of trouble in that state. Therefore not to be hated by the people is the best fortress there is. Even if you have fortresses, and the people hate you, you will not be safe, because, when the people have taken arms, foreigners who will assist them are never lacking. * * * Considering all these things, then, I praise him who builds fortresses and him who does not build them. I blame any prince who, trusting in his castles, thinks it of little importance that his people hate him.

[Ferdinand of Spain, Exemplary Prince]

CHAPTER 21

What Is Necessary to a Prince That He May Be Considered Excellent

Nothing gives a prince so much respect as great undertakings and unusual examples of his own ability. In our day we have Ferdinand of Spain. He can be called, as it were, a new king, because, though at the beginning he was weak, he has become the first king of the Christians in fame and glory. If you will consider his actions, you will find them all great and some of them extraordinary. In the beginning of his reign he attacked Granada,[1] and that undertaking was the foun-

6. Military ruler of the Italian city-state of Città di Castello (1414–1486).
7. Ruler of the Italian city-state of Urbino (1472–1508).
8. Ruling family of the Italian city-state of Bologna during the Renaissance.
9. Duke of Milan (1401–1466), founder of

the Sforza dynasty that ruled the city-state of Milan from 1450–1535.
1. City in southern Spain that was the seat of Nasrid rule in Spain for centuries before it was conquered by Ferdinand and Isabella of Spain in 1492.

dation of his power. In the first place, he carried it on when he was without other occupation and had no fear of being impeded; he used it to occupy the minds of the barons of Castile, who, when they were thinking about that war, did not think of rebelling. By this means he gained reputation and control over them without their realizing it. He was able to support armies with the money of the Church and the people, and, by means of that long war, to lay a foundation for his army, which later did him honor. Besides this, in order to undertake greater enterprises, he availed himself of religion and turned to a pious cruelty, hunting down the Moors and driving them out of his kingdom. Nothing can be more wretched or more unusual than this example of his ability. Cloaked with this same mantle, he attacked Africa; he undertook his enterprise in Italy; and finally he assailed France. And so he has always kept the minds of his subjects in suspense and wonder, and concerned with the outcome of his deeds. And his actions have begun in such a way, one coming from another, that between any two of them, he has never given men time enough to enable them to work quietly against him.

It is also to the profit of a prince to give unusual examples of his ability in internal affairs, like those that are related of Messer Bernabò of Milan.[2] I mean when he has an opportunity because someone does something extraordinary, either good or bad, in ordinary life, and the prince takes a method of rewarding or punishing him that will be widely talked of. And above all, a prince should endeavor in all his actions to show that he deserves fame as a great man and one of high mental capacity.

A prince is also esteemed when he is a true friend or a true enemy; that is, when without any reservation he shows himself favorable to one ruler and against another. This procedure is always more profitable than to remain neutral, because if two potentates, your neighbors, come to grips, they are such that when one of them conquers, you either will have to be afraid of the conqueror, or you will not. In either of these two cases, it will be better for you to make your policy plain and put up a good fight. In the first of them, if you do not adopt an open policy, you will always be the prey of the conqueror, to the pleasure and satisfaction of him who is conquered. You can give no reason why anybody should protect you and receive you, and will find nobody to do it. The one who conquers does not wish friends whom he suspects and who will not aid him in adversity, and the loser will not receive you because you have not been willing to share his fortunes with arms in your hands.

When Antiochus[3] led his army into Greece, summoned there by the Aetolians to drive out the Romans, he sent ambassadors to the Achaeans, who were friends of the Romans, to advise them to remain neutral. On the other side, the Romans tried to persuade them to take arms with them. This matter came up for decision in the council of the Achaeans, where the agent of Antiochus advised them to remain neutral. The Roman legate answered: "As to what the

---

2. Bernabò Visconti, ruler of Milan from 1354 to 1385.
3. Antiochus III "the Great" (c. 241–187

B.C.E.), ruler of the Seleucid Empire in Asia Minor.

others say about not getting yourselves into the war, nothing is less advantageous to you; without thanks, without dignity, you will be the reward of the victor."

It will always come about that he who is not your friend will ask you to be neutral, and he who is friendly to you will ask you to come out clearly with arms. Princes of irresolute character, in order to escape the perils of the moment, generally take the way of neutrality, and generally go to smash. But when a prince comes out vigorously in favor of one side, if the one you have joined wins, even though he is powerful and you are at his discretion, he is under obligation to you, and has formed a friendship for you. Moreover, men are never so dishonorable that they will give so great an example of ingratitude as to oppress you. And then victories are never so decided that the victor is not subject to qualifications, and especially with regard to justice. But if the one to whom you adhere loses, you are received by him, he aids you as long as he can, and you are the companion of a fortune that may rise again.

In the second case, when those who fight are of such a sort that you do not need to fear whichever one conquers, it is so much the more prudent for you to join your friend, because you go to the ruin of one neighbor with the aid of another who, if he were wise, would protect him. If your ally is victorious he is at your discretion, and it is impossible that with your aid he will not win.

Here it may be observed that a prince should be careful not to join company with one more powerful than himself, in order to attack someone, except when necessity constrains him, in the way mentioned above. If your powerful ally conquers, you remain his prisoner. And princes should avoid, as much as they can, being at the discretion of others. The Venetians joined the King of France against the Duke of Milan, when they were able to avoid making that alliance, and it resulted in their ruin. But when such an alliance cannot be avoided (as happened to the Florentines when the Pope and the King of Spain went with their armies to attack Lombardy), then a prince should join in for the reasons I have given. No state should believe it can always make plans certain of success; it should rather expect to make only doubtful ones. For the course of human events teaches that man never attempts to avoid one disadvantage without running into another. Prudence, therefore, consists in the power to recognize the nature of disadvantages and to take the less disagreeable as good.

A prince should also show himself a lover of excellence by giving preferment to gifted men and honoring those who excel in some art. Besides, he should encourage his citizens by giving them a chance to exercise their functions quietly, in trade and agriculture and every other occupation of man. A citizen should not hesitate to increase his property for fear it will be taken away from him, or to open a new business for fear of taxes. On the contrary the prince should offer rewards to those who undertake to do these things, and to anybody who thinks of improving in any way his city or his dominion. Besides this, at suitable times of the year he should engage the attention of the people with festivals and shows. And because every city is divided into gilds or wards, he should take account of these bodies, meet with them sometimes, and give in person an example of humanity and generosity. At the same time he should always preserve the dignity befitting his rank, for this ought never to be lacking in any circumstances.

[Good Counsel vs. Flattery]

From CHAPTER 23

In What Way Flatterers Are to Be Avoided

I do not wish to omit an important subject and an error from which princes with difficulty protect themselves, if they are not unusually prudent, or if they are not able to choose well. I refer to flatterers, of whom courts are full. Men are generally so well pleased with their own abilities and so greatly deceived about them that they protect themselves with difficulty from this plague, and when they do endeavor to protect themselves, they run the risk of becoming contemptible, for the reason that there is no way of protecting yourself from flattery except to have men understand that they do not offend you by speaking the truth to you; but when anyone can speak the truth to you, you do not receive proper respect. Hence a prudent prince must adopt a third method. He should choose wise men in his state, and to them alone he should give full power to speak the truth freely, but only on the matters he asks about, and on nothing else. Yet he should ask them about everything, and heed their opinions. Then he should make up his mind in private, at his leisure. With these pieces of advice, and with every one of them, he should conduct himself in such a way that each adviser may know that he will be so much the more in favor in proportion as he speaks more freely. But the prince should not consent to listen to anyone except these advisers, should carry out what he decides on, and should be firm in his decisions. He who does otherwise is either ruined by flatterers, or changes often, because of the varied opinions he listens to. As a result, he receives little respect.

* * *

A prince, therefore, should always take advice, but he should do it when he pleases and not when someone else pleases. On the contrary he should not let anyone dare to advise him when he does not ask for advice. But he should be a big asker, and a patient listener to the truth about the things asked. Still further, he should be angry if for any reason anybody should not tell him the truth. Many think that if a prince gives the impression of being prudent, he should be thought so not because of his own natural gifts but because of the good advice he has at hand; but without question they are wrong. For this is a general rule that never fails: a prince who is not wise himself cannot be well advised, unless by chance he gives himself over to one man who entirely directs him, and that man is exceedingly prudent. In this instance the prince surely would be, but such a condition would not last long, because in a short time that tutor of his would take away his throne. As a matter of fact, an unwise prince who asks counsel from more than one man will never receive unified advice, nor will he be able to unify it unaided. Each of the advisers will think about what concerns himself, and the prince will not be able to control them or to understand them. It cannot be otherwise; men are always wicked at bottom, unless they are made good by some compulsion. Hence I conclude that good counsels, whatever their source, necessarily result from the prudence of the ruler, and not the prudence of the ruler from good counsels.

[Why Princes Fail]

CHAPTER 24

Why the Princes of Italy Have Lost Their Authority

The things written above, if they are prudently carried into effect, will make a new prince seem to be an old one, and will immediately make him safer and firmer in his realm than if he had grown old in it. For the actions of a new prince are more closely watched than those of a hereditary one; and when they are seen to show great ability they influence men more and attach them to the prince more closely than ancient blood can, for men are much more impressed with present things than with past ones, and when in the present they find something good, they enjoy it and seek for nothing further. In fact, they will take every means of defending such a prince, if only he does not fail himself in other things. And thus he will secure a double glory: that of having begun a new princedom, and of having enriched and strengthened it with good laws, good arms, and good examples. On the contrary, he is doubly disgraced who, though born a prince, loses his dominion because he is not prudent.

And if those lords are examined who have lost their positions in Italy in our times, such as the King of Naples, the Duke of Milan, and others, they will exhibit first a common defect in their armies, for the reasons that have been discussed at length above. Further, it will be seen that some of them either had the people as enemies, or they had the friendship of the people, but had not been able to secure themselves against the upper classes. For realms without these defects are not lost if the prince has strength enough to keep an army in the field. Philip of Macedon,[4] not the father of Alexander but the one who was conquered by Titus Quintus, did not have a large realm, in comparison with the greatness of the Romans and the Greeks who attacked him. Nevertheless, because he was a warrior, and knew how to deal with his people and to secure himself against the upper classes, he kept up the war for several years. Even though at the end he lost control of some cities, he nevertheless retained his royal authority.

Therefore these princes of ours who have been many years in their positions should blame for the loss of them not Fortune, but their own worthlessness. In good weather they never thought of change (it is a common defect of men not to reckon on a storm when the sea is calm). Hence when times of adversity came, they thought about running away and not about defending themselves; and they hoped that the people, disgusted by the insolence of the conquerors, would call them back. This plan, when there are no others, is good, but it is a bad thing to abandon other resources for this one. A prince should not be willing to fall, just because he believes he will find somebody to set him up again; that may not come about, or if it does, it cannot bring you security, because such an expedient for defence is base and does not depend on yourself. Only those means of security are good, are certain, are lasting, that depend on yourself and your own vigor.

---

4. Philip V: (238–179 B.C.E.), king of Macedonia, defeated in 197 B.C.E. by a Roman army led by Titus Quintus Flaminius.

["Fortune is a woman"]

From CHAPTER 25

The Power of Fortune in Human Affairs, and to What Extent She Should Be Relied On

It is not unknown to me that many have been and still are of the opinion that the affairs of this world are so under the direction of Fortune and of God that man's prudence cannot control them; in fact, that man has no resource against them. For this reason many think there is no use in sweating much over such matters, but that one might as well let Chance take control. This opinion has been the more accepted in our times, because of the great changes in the state of the world that have been and now are seen every day, beyond all human surmise. And I myself, when thinking on these things, have now and then in some measure inclined to their view. Nevertheless, because the freedom of the will should not be wholly annulled, I think it may be true that Fortune is arbiter of half of our actions, but that she still leaves the control of the other half, or about that, to us.

I liken her to one of those raging streams that, when they go mad, flood the plains, ruin the trees and the buildings, and take away the fields from one bank and put them down on the other. Everybody flees before them; everybody yields to their onrush without being able to resist anywhere. And though this is their nature, it does not cease to be true that, in calm weather, men can make some provisions against them with walls and dykes, so that, when the streams swell, their waters will go off through a canal, or their currents will not be so wild and do so much damage. The same is true of Fortune. She shows her power where there is no wise preparation for resisting her, and turns her fury where she knows that no walls and dykes have been made to hold her in. And if you consider Italy—the place where these variations occur and the cause that has set them in motion—you will see that she is a country without dykes and without any wall of defence. If, like Germany, Spain, and France, she had had a sufficient bulwark of military vigor, this flood would not have made the great changes it has, or would not have come at all.

And this, I think, is all I need to say on opposing oneself to Fortune, in general. But limiting myself more to particulars, I say that a prince may be seen prospering today and falling in ruin tomorrow, though it does not appear that he has changed in his nature or any of his qualities. I believe this comes, in the first place, from the causes that have been discussed at length in preceding chapters. That is, if a prince bases himself entirely on Fortune, he will fall when she varies. I also believe that a ruler will be successful who adapts his mode of procedure to the quality of the times, and likewise that he will be unsuccessful if the times are out of accord with his procedure. Because it may be seen that in things leading to the end each has before him, namely glory and riches, men proceed differently. One acts with caution, another rashly; one with violence, another with skill; one with patience, another with its opposite; yet with these different methods each one attains his end. Still further, two cautious men will be seen, of whom one comes to his goal, the other does not. Likewise you will see two who succeed with two different methods, one of them being cautious and the other rash. These results are caused by nothing else than the nature of the times, which is or is not in harmony with the procedure of men. It also accounts for what I have mentioned, namely, that two persons, working differently, chance to arrive at the same result; and that of two who work in the same way, one attains his end, but the other does not.

On the nature of the times also depends the variability of the best method. If a man conducts himself with caution and patience, times and affairs may come around in such a way that his procedure is good, and he goes on successfully. But if times and circumstances change, he is ruined, because he does not change his method of action. There is no man so prudent as to understand how to fit himself to this condition, either because he is unable to deviate from the course to which nature inclines him, or because, having always prospered by walking in one path, he cannot persuade himself to leave it. So the cautious man, when the time comes to go at a reckless pace, does not know how to do it. Hence he comes to ruin. Yet if he could change his nature with the times and with circumstances, his fortune would not be altered.

Pope Julius II proceeded rashly in all his actions, and found the times and circumstances so harmonious with his mode of procedure that he was always so lucky as to succeed. Consider the first enterprise he engaged in, that of Bologna, while Messer Giovanni Bentivogli[5] was still alive. The Venetians were not pleased with it; the King of Spain felt the same way; the Pope was debating such an enterprise with the King of France. Nevertheless, in his courage and rashness Julius personally undertook that expedition. This movement made the King of Spain and the Venetians stand irresolute and motionless, the latter for fear, and the King because of his wish to recover the entire kingdom of Naples. On the other side, the King of France was dragged behind Julius, because the King, seeing that the Pope had moved and wishing to make him a friend in order to put down the Venetians, judged he could not refuse him soldiers without doing him open injury. Julius, then, with his rash movement, attained what no other pontiff, with the utmost human prudence, would have attained. If he had waited to leave Rome until the agreements were fixed and everything arranged, as any other pontiff would have done, he would never have succeeded, for the King of France would have had a thousand excuses, and the others would have raised a thousand fears. I wish to omit his other acts, which are all of the same sort, and all succeeded perfectly. The brevity of his life did not allow him to know anything different. Yet if times had come in which it was necessary to act with caution, they would have ruined him, for he would never have deviated from the methods to which nature inclined him.

I conclude, then, that since Fortune is variable and men are set in their ways, they are successful when they are in harmony with Fortune and unsuccessful when they disagree with her. Yet I am of the opinion that it is better to be rash than over-cautious, because Fortune is a woman and, if you wish to keep her down, you must beat her and pound her. It is evident that she allows herself to be overcome by men who treat her in that way rather than by those who proceed coldly. For that reason, like a woman, she is always the friend of young men, because they are less cautious, and more courageous, and command her with more boldness.

5. Of the ruling family Bentivogli. The pope undertook to dislodge him from Bologna in 1506.

[The Roman Dream]

From CHAPTER 26

An Exhortation to Take Hold of Italy and Restore Her to Liberty from the Barbarians

Having considered all the things discussed above, I have been turning over in my own mind whether at present in Italy the time is ripe for a new prince to win prestige, and whether conditions there give a wise and vigorous ruler occasion to introduce methods that will do him honor, and bring good to the mass of the people of the land. It appears to me that so many things unite for the advantage of a new prince, that I do not know of any time that has ever been more suited for this. And, as I said, if it was necessary to make clear the ability of Moses that the people of Israel should be enslaved in Egypt, and to reveal Cyrus's greatness of mind that the Persians should be oppressed by the Medes, and to demonstrate the excellence of Theseus that the Athenians should be scattered, so at the present time, in order to make known the greatness of an Italian soul, Italy had to be brought down to her present position, to be more a slave than the Hebrews, more a servant than the Persians, more scattered than the Athenians; without head, without government; defeated, plundered, torn asunder, overrun; subject to every sort of disaster.

And though before this, certain persons[6] have showed signs from which it could be inferred that they were chosen by God for the redemption of Italy, nevertheless it has afterwards been seen that in the full current of action they have been cast off by Fortune. So Italy remains without life and awaits the man, whoever he may be, who is to heal her wounds, put an end to the plundering of Lombardy and the tribute laid on Tuscany and the kingdom of Naples, and cure her of those sores that have long been suppurating. She may be seen praying God to send some one to redeem her from these cruel and barbarous insults. She is evidently ready and willing to follow a banner, if only some one will raise it. Nor is there at present anyone to be seen in whom she can put more hope than in your illustrious House, because its fortune and vigor, and the favor of God and of the Church, which it now governs,[7] enable it to be the leader in such a redemption. This will not be very difficult, as you will see if you will bring to mind the actions and lives of those I have named above. And though these men were striking exceptions, yet they were men, and each of them had less opportunity than the present gives; their enterprises were not more just than this, nor easier, nor was God their friend more than he is yours. Here justice is complete. "A way is just to those to whom it is necessary, and arms are holy to him who has no hope save in arms."[8] Everything is now fully disposed for the work, and when that is true an undertaking cannot be difficult, if only your House adopts the methods of those I have set forth as examples. Moreover, we have before our eyes extraordinary and unexampled means prepared by God. The sea has been divided. A cloud has guided you on your

6. Possibly Cesare Borgia and Francesco Sforza, who were discussed earlier in the book.

7. Pope Leo X (1475–1521) was a Medici (Giovanni de' Medici). "House": of Medici.

The Prince was first meant for Giuliano de' Medici. After Giuliano's death it was dedicated to his nephew Lorenzo, later duke of Urbino.

8. Livy's *History* 9.1, para. 10.

way. The rock has given forth water. Manna has fallen.[9] Everything has united to make you great. The rest is for you to do. God does not intend to do everything, lest he deprive us of our free will and the share of glory that belongs to us.

It is no wonder if no one of the above-named Italians[1] has been able to do what we hope your illustrious House can. Nor is it strange if in the many revolutions and military enterprises of Italy, the martial vigor of the land always appears to be exhausted. This is because the old military customs were not good, and there has been nobody able to find new ones. Yet nothing brings so much honor to a man who rises to new power, as the new laws and new methods he discovers. These things, when they are well founded and have greatness in them, make him revered and worthy of admiration. And in Italy matter is not lacking on which to impress forms of every sort. There is great vigor in the limbs if only it is not lacking in the heads. You may see that in duels and combats between small numbers, the Italians have been much superior in force, skill, and intelligence. But when it is a matter of armies, Italians cannot be compared with foreigners. All this comes from the weakness of the heads, because those who know are not obeyed, and each man thinks he knows. Nor up to this time has there been a man able to raise himself so high, through both ability and fortune, that the others would yield to him. The result is that for the past twenty years, in all the wars that have been fought when there has been an army entirely Italian, it has always made a bad showing. Proof of this was given first at the Taro, and then at Alessandria, Capua, Genoa, Vailà, Bologna, and Mestri.[2]

If your illustrious House, then, wishes to imitate those excellent men who redeemed their countries, it is necessary, before everything else, to furnish yourself with your own army, as the true foundation of every enterprise. You cannot have more faithful, nor truer, nor better soldiers. And though every individual of these may be good, they become better as a body when they see that they are commanded by their prince, and honored and trusted by him. It is necessary, therefore, that your House should be prepared with such forces, in order that it may be able to defend itself against the foreigners with Italian courage.

And though the Swiss and the Spanish infantry are properly estimated as terribly effective, yet both have defects. Hence a third type would be able not merely to oppose them but to feel sure of overcoming them. The fact is that the Spaniards are not able to resist cavalry, and the Swiss have reason to fear infantry, when they meet any as determined in battle as themselves. For this reason it has been seen and will be seen in experience that the Spaniards are unable to resist the French cavalry, and the Swiss are overthrown by Spanish infantry. And though of this last a clear instance has not been observed, yet an approach to it appeared in the battle of Ravenna,[3] when the Spanish infantry met the German battalions, who use the same methods as the Swiss. There the Spanish, through their ability and the assistance given by their shields, got

---

9. Another allusion to Moses.
1. Perhaps another reference to Borgia and Sforza.

2. Sites of battles occurring between the end of the 15th century and 1513.
3. Between Spain and France in April 1512.

within the points of the spears from below, and slew their enemies in security, while the Germans could find no means of resistance. If the cavalry had not charged the Spanish, they would have annihilated the Germans. It is possible, then, for one who realizes the defects of these two types, to equip infantry in a new manner, so that it can resist cavalry and not be afraid of foot-soldiers; but to gain this end they must have weapons of the right sorts, and adopt varied methods of combat. These are some of the things which, when they are put into service as novelties, give reputation and greatness to a new ruler.[4]

This opportunity, then, should not be allowed to pass, in order that after so long a time Italy may see her redeemer. I am unable to express with what love he would be received in all the provinces that have suffered from these foreign deluges; with what thirst for vengeance, what firm faith, what piety, what tears! What gates would be shut against him? what peoples would deny him obedience? what envy would oppose itself to him? what Italian would refuse to follow him? This barbarian rule stinks in every nostril. May your illustrious House, then, undertake this charge with the spirit and the hope with which all just enterprises are taken up, in order that, beneath its ensign, our native land may be ennobled, and, under its auspices, that saying of Petrarch may come true: "Manhood[5] will take arms against fury, and the combat will be short, because in Italian hearts the ancient valor is not yet dead."

---

4. Machiavelli was subsequently the author of the treatise *Art of War* (1521).
5. An etymological translation of the original

virtù (from the Latin *vir*, "man"). The quotation is from the canzone "My Italy."

LUDOVICO ARIOSTO
1474–1533

The *Orlando Furioso* (Orlando Gone Crazy) is as witty and playful in tone as it is philosophically and politically serious. The poem follows the hero Orlando as he chases the elusive princess Angelica, against the backdrop of Charlemagne's battles against the Saracens. The most important achievement of Renaissance Italy's greatest poet, it is also a study in contrasts, at once brilliantly original and a comical imitation of the epic and romance traditions.

LIFE

Born into a large family of the lower nobility in the city-state of Ferrara, Ariosto could not afford the life of cultured leisure enjoyed by the upper nobility there. In 1503 he entered the service of Ippolito d'Este, the warlike and profligate cardinal. Ippolito could be demanding and stingy, but he understood Ariosto's importance as a poet well enough to finance the publication of the first edition of *Orlando Furioso* in 1516. When Ariosto refused to join him on a mission to Hungary in 1517, however, he fired the poet on the spot, and Ariosto transferred his services to the more cultured Duke Alfonso, whose sister Isabella was the poet's most avid reader. Alfonso was himself strapped for cash in his constant negotiations with the Venetian Republic, King Francis I of France, and Emperor Charles V to keep the pope from seizing Ferrara. His solution to Ariosto's financial woes was to make him governor of the bandit-infested region of Ganfagnana in 1522. In 1525, after begging for release from this unwelcome charge, Ariosto finally returned to Ferrara, to his family, and to his poetic labors. He died in 1533 after seeing the final edition of the *Furioso* through publication in 1532.

ORLANDO FURIOSO

Orlando Furioso reprises the works of **Homer, Virgil, Ovid, St. Augustine, Dante, Boccaccio,** and **Petrarch** as well as **the Song of Roland,** from which Ariosto's title hero ultimately derives. The *Furioso* is, in turn, itself a source of inspiration to such writers of the later Renaissance as Rabelais, Cervantes, Shakespeare, and Milton. In his title, which recalls the popular romance epic *Orlando in Love*, Ariosto announces his plan to outdo other poets in the romance epic tradition: he will show how Orlando, under the influence of desire, crosses the line from love to lunatic frenzy. Much of Ariosto's humor in fact comes from placing heroes of the past in new and unexpected situations. The mood of the poem moves up and down the scale of genres, from epic fury to romance dalliance to pastoral repose, from tragedy to comedy, from praise to satire, and from the sublime to the grotesque. Range also characterizes the *Furioso*'s geography, which stretches from France, Italy, Spain, Holland, England, Scotland, India, Tunisia, Libya, Syria, and Nubia to Byzantium and beyond (including a voyage to the Moon). From these diverse countries come Christian and pagan knights who mingle and clash as they try to make names for themselves.

The breadth of *Orlando Furioso*'s geographic survey is matched by the depth of its scrutiny of human psychology. Wrath and desire are the passions Ariosto explores in greatest depth, and no character experiences them more violently than Orlando. For twenty-three cantos of the poem, neglecting his obligations to his king, Charlemagne, he pursues his obsessive love for the beautiful Chinese princess, Angelica, who constantly flees the attentions of her many suitors. At the poem's exact center, Orlando enters into a frenzy of epic proportions when he discovers that Angelica loves the young Saracen soldier Medor and that the pair have consummated their mutual passion. Although Angelica had not promised her love to him, Orlando experiences her loss as an immeasurable betrayal, and in his fury becomes more bestial than human. In a typical ironic gesture, Ariosto's narrator inserts himself into the story, expressing his sympathy for Orlando at his most outrageous and his own anger at the "nasty tribe" of women, then immediately apologizing for introducing a "discordant note."

Orlando's story is not the sole, or even the most important, of Ariosto's tales; the poet weaves into a single tapestry an extraordinary range of story lines. The other story represented here is also of forbidden love. Narrated by Richardet, the twin brother of Ariosto's famous woman warrior, Bradamante, the tale recounts the passionate love that the Spanish princess Fiordispina conceived for Bradamante, whom Fiordispina had mistaken for a man. Full of confused identities and impersonation, the episode explores the artificiality of gender roles and the capricious nature of desire. The tale has all the characteristics for which Ariosto is celebrated as a poet and raconteur: charm, wit, and humor blend with searching and serious questions about human nature (especially in love) and its relationship to civic norms.

From Orlando Furioso[1]

FROM CANTOS 23 AND 24

[Orlando's Great Madness]

* * *

He came to a stream which looked like crystal; a pleasant meadow bloomed on its banks, picked out with lovely pure colors and adorned with many beautiful trees.[2] / A welcome breeze tempered the noontide for the rugged flock and naked shepherd, and Orlando felt no discomfort, for all that he was wearing breastplate, helmet, and shield. Here he stopped, then, to rest—but his welcome proved to be harsh and painful, indeed quite unspeakably cruel, on this unhappy, ill-starred day. / Looking about him, he saw inscriptions on many of the trees by the shady bank; he had only to look closely at the letters to be sure that they were formed by the hand of his goddess. This was one of the spots described earlier, to which the beautiful damsel, Queen of Cathay, often resorted with Medor, from the shepherd's house close by. / He saw "Angelica" and "Medor" in a hundred places, united by a hundred love-knots. The letters were so many nails with which Love pierced and wounded his heart. He searched in his mind for any number of excuses to reject what he could not help believing; he tried to persuade himself that it was some other Angelica who had written her name on the bark. / "But I recognize these characters," he told himself; "I've seen and read so many just like them. Can she perhaps be inventing this Medor? Perhaps by this name she means me." Thus deceiving himself with far-fetched notions, disconsolate Orlando clung to hopes which he knew he was stretching out to grasp. / But the more he tried to smother his dark suspicions the more they flared up with new vigor: he was like an unwary bird caught in a web or in bird-lime—the more he beats his wings and tries to free himself, the worse ensnared he becomes.

Orlando came to where a bow-shaped curve in the hillside made a cave overlooking the clear spring. / Twisting on their stems, ivy and rambling vines adorned the entrance. Here during the heat of the day the two happy lovers used to lie in each other's arms. Their names figured here more than elsewhere; they were inscribed within and without, sometimes in charcoal, sometimes in chalk, or scratched with the point of a knife. / The dejected count approached on foot. At the entrance he saw many words which Medor had written in his own hand; they seem to have been freshly inscribed. The inscription was written in verse and spoke of the great pleasure he had enjoyed in this cave. I believe it was written in his native tongue; in ours this is how it reads: /

1. Translated by Guido Waldman.   2. The scene resembles Orlando's dream.

"Happy plants, verdant grass, limpid waters, dark, shadowy cave, pleasant and cool, where fair Angelica, born of Galafron, and loved in vain by many, often lay naked in my arms. I, poor Medor, cannot repay you for your indulgence otherwise than by ever praising you, / and by entreating every lover, knight, or maiden, every person, native or alien, who happens upon this spot by accident or by design, to say to the grass, the shadows, the cave, stream, and plants: 'May sun and moon be kind to you, and the chorus of the nymphs, and may they see that shepherds never lead their flocks to you.'" / It was written in Arabic, which the count knew as well as he knew Latin. He knew many and many a tongue, but Arabic is one with which he was most familiar: his grasp of it had saved him on more than one occasion from injury and insult when he was among the Saracens. But he was not to boast if formerly his knowledge had helped him—the pain it now brought him quite discounted every former advantage. /

Five and six times the unfortunate man re-read the inscription, trying in vain to wish it away, but it was more plain and clear each time he read it. And each time, he felt a cold hand clutch his heart in his afflicted breast. Finally he fell to gazing fixedly at the stone—stonelike himself. / He was ready to go out of his mind, so complete was his surrender to grief. Believe one who has experienced it—this is a sorrow to surpass all others. His chin had dropped onto his chest, his head was bowed, his brow had lost its boldness. So possessed was he by sorrow that he had no voice for laments, no moisture for tears. / His impetuous grief, set upon erupting all too quickly, remained within. A broad-bellied, narrow-necked vase full of water has the same effect, as can be observed: when the vase is inverted, the liquid so surges to the neck that it blocks its own egress, and can scarcely do more than come out drop by drop. / Returning to himself a little, he considered how he might yet be mistaken about it: he hoped against hope that it might simply be someone trying to besmirch his lady's name this way, or to charge him with a burden of jealousy so unendurable that he would die of it; and that whoever it was who had done this had copied her hand most skilfully. / With such meager, such puny hopes he roused his spirits and found a little courage.

He mounted Brigliador, now that the sun was giving place to his sister in the sky. Before he had gone far he saw smoke issuing from the housetops, and heard dogs barking and cows lowing; he came to a farmhouse and found lodging. / Listlessly he dismounted, and left Brigliador to the care of a discreet stable-boy. Others there were to help him off with his armor and his golden spurs, and to refurbish them. This was the house where Medor lay wounded, and met with his great good fortune. Orlando did not ask for supper but for a bed: he was replete with sadness, not with other fare. / The harder he sought for rest, the worse the misery and affliction he procured himself—every wall, every door, every window was covered with the hateful inscriptions. He wanted to make enquiries there, but chose to keep his lips sealed: he was afraid to establish too clearly the very question he wanted to cloud with mist so as to dull the pain. / Little good did it do him to deceive himself; somebody there was to speak of the matter unasked. The herdsman, who saw him so downcast and sad and wanted to cheer him up, embarked, without asking leave, upon the story of those two lovers: he knew it well, and often repeated it to those who would listen. There were many who enjoyed hearing it. / He told how at the prayer of beautiful Angelica he had brought Medor back to his house. Medor was gravely wounded, and she tended his wound, and in a few days had healed it—but Love inflicted upon her heart a wound far worse than his, and from a small spark kindled so blazing a fire that she was all aflame and quite beside herself, / and, forgetting that she was daughter of the greatest monarch of the East, driven by excessive passion, she chose to become wife to a poor simple soldier. The herdsman ended his story by having the bracelet brought in—the one Angelica had given him on her departure as a token of thanks for his hospitality. /

This evidence shown in conclusion proved to be the axe which took his head off his shoulders at one stroke, now that Love, that tormentor, was tired of raining blows upon him. Orlando tried to conceal his grief, but it so pressed him, he could not succeed: willy nilly the sighs and tears had to find a vent through his eyes and lips. / When he was free to give rein to his sorrow, once he was alone without others to consider, tears began to stream from his eyes and furrow his cheeks, running down onto his breast. He sighed and moaned, and made great circular sweeps of the bed with his arms: it felt harder than rock; it stung worse than a bed of nettles. / Amid such bitter anguish the thought occurred to him that on this very bed in which he was lying the thankless damsel must have lain down many a time with her lover. The downy bed sent a shudder through him and he leapt off it with all the alacrity of a yokel who has lain down in the grass for a nap and spies a snake close by. /

The bed, the house, the herdsman filled him on a sudden with such revulsion that, without waiting for moonrise, or for the first light preceding the new day, he fetched his arms and his steed and went out into the darkest, most tangled depths of the wood; when he felt he was quite alone, he gave vent to his grief with cries and howls. / There was no checking his cries and tears; night and day he allowed himself no respite. Towns and villages he avoided, and lay out in the open on the hard forest-floor. He wondered that his head could hold such an unquenchable source of water, and that he could sigh so much. Frequently as he wept he said to himself: / "These are no longer tears that drop from my eyes so copiously. The tears were not enough for my grief: they came to an end before my grief was half expressed. Urged by fire, my vital spirit is now escaping by the ducts which lead to the eyes: this is what is now spilling out, and with it my sorrow and my life will flow out at its last hour. / These sighs, which are a token of my anguish, are not truly sighs: sighs are not like this—now and then they will cease, but never do I feel a relaxing of my pain as my breast exhales it. Love, which burns my heart, makes this wind, beating his wings about the flames. By what miracle, Love, do you keep my heart ever burning but never consumed by fire? / I am not who my face proclaims me; the man who was Orlando is dead and buried, slain by his most thankless lady who assailed him by her betrayal. I am his spirit sundered from him, and wandering tormented in its own hell, so that his shade, all that remains of him, should serve as an example to any who place hope in Love." /

All night the count wandered in the wood; at sunrise, Fate brought him back to the spring where Medor had carved his inscription. To see his calamity written there in the hillside so inflamed him that he was drained of every drop that was not pure hate, fury, wrath, and violence. On impulse he drew his sword, / and slashed at the words and the rock-face, sending tiny splinters shooting skywards. Alas for the cave, and for every trunk on which the names of Medor and Angelica were written! They were left, that day, in such a state that never more would they afford cool shade to shepherd or flock. The spring, too, which had been so clear and pure, was scarcely safer from wrath such as his; / branches, stumps and boughs, stones and clods he kept hurling into the lovely waters until he so clouded them from surface to bottom that they were clear and pure never again. In the end, exhausted and sweat-soaked, his stamina given out and no longer answering to his deep, bitter hate, his burning wrath, he dropped onto the grass and sighed up at the heavens. / Weary and heart-stricken, he dropped onto the grass and gazed mutely up at the sky. Thus he remained, without food or sleep while the sun three times rose and set. His bitter agony grew and grew until it drove him out of his mind.

On the fourth day, worked into a great frenzy, he stripped off his armor and chain-mail. / The helmet landed here, the shield there, more pieces of armor further off, the breastplate further still: arms and armor all found their resting-place here and there about the wood. Then he tore off his clothes and exposed his hairy belly and all his chest and back.

Now began the great madness, so horrifying that none will ever know a worse instance. / He fell into a frenzy so violent that his every sense was darkened. He did not think to draw his sword, with which I expect he would have performed marvels. But in view of his colossal strength he had no need of it, nor of any hatchet or battle-axe. He now performed some truly astonishing feats: at one jerk he rooted up a tall pine, / after which he tore up several more as though they were so many celery-stalks. He did the same to oaks and ancient elms, to beech and ash-trees, to ilexes and firs. What a birdcatcher does when clearing the ground before he lays nets—rooting up rushes, brushwood, and nettles—Orlando did to oaks and other age-old timber. / The shepherds who heard the din left their flocks scattered through the woodland and hastened from all parts to this spot to see what was happening. But I have reached a point which I must not overstep for fear of boring you with my story; I should rather postpone it than annoy you by making it too long.

* * *

If you have put your foot in the birdlime spread by Cupid, try to pull it out, and take care not to catch your wing in it too: love, in the universal opinion of wise men, is nothing but madness. Though not everyone goes raving mad like Orlando, Love's folly shows itself in other ways; what clearer sign of lunacy than to lose your own self through pining for another? / The effects vary, but the madness which promotes them is always the same. It is like a great forest into which those who venture must perforce lose their way: one here, another there, one and all go off the track. Let me tell you this, to conclude: whoever grows old in love ought, in addition to Cupid's torments, to be chained and fettered. / "You, my friend, are preaching to others," someone will tell me, "but you overlook your own failing." The answer is that now, in an interval of lucidity, I understand a great deal. And I am taking pains (with imminent success, I hope) to find peace and withdraw from the dance— though I cannot do so as quickly as I should wish, for the disease has eaten me to the bone. /

In the last canto I was telling you, my Lord, how Orlando, crazed and demented, had torn off arms and armor and scattered them everywhere, ripped his clothes, tossed away his sword, rooted up trees, and made the hollow caves and deep woods re-echo. And some shepherds were attracted to the noise, whether by their stars, or for some wicked misdeed of theirs. / When they had a closer sight of the madman's incredible feats and his prodigious strength, they turned to flee, but without direction, as people do when suddenly scared. The madman was after them at once; he grabbed one and took off his head with all the ease of a person plucking an apple from a tree or a dainty bloom from a briar. / He picked up the heavy carcass by one leg and used it to club the rest; he laid out two, leaving them in a sleep from which perhaps they would awake on Judgment Day. The others cleared off at once: they were quickfooted and had their wits about them. The madman would not have been slow to pursue them, but he had now turned upon their flocks. /

In the fields the laborers, wise from the shepherds' example, left their ploughs, hoes, and sickles and scrambled onto the housetops or onto the church roofs— there being no safety up elm or willow tree. From here they contemplated the fearsome frenzy unleashed upon horse and oxen: they were shattered, battered, and destroyed by dint of punches, thumps, and bites, kicks and scratches. It was a fast mover who could escape him. / Now you could have heard the neighboring farms resound with shouts, the shrill of horns, and rustic trumpets and, most persistently, the peal of clarions; you could have seen a thousand men streaming down from the hills, armed with pikes and bows, spears, and slings; as many more came up from the plain, ready to wage a peasant war against the madman. / Imagine waves, driven by the South Wind which earlier had been playful, breaking on the shore; the second wave is higher than the first, the third follows with greater force; and, each time, the water builds up more and seethes more widely across the beach. Thus did the pitiless mob increase, coming down from the hills and out of the valleys against Orlando. / Out of that disorderly throng ten he killed who came within his reach, and then another ten. This experiment made it clear that it was far safer to stand well away. No one was able to draw blood from his body; steel was powerless to strike and wound it—the King of Heaven had given him this endowment so as to make him guardian of His holy faith. / Had he been capable of dying, his life would have been in danger; he might have learned what it was to throw aside his sword and, unarmed, to overreach himself.[3]

Now having seen their every blow prove ineffective, the throng began to ebb. With no one left to confront him, Orlando made off and came to a hamlet. / Here he found not a soul, man or child, for everyone had abandoned the place in terror. There was plenty of food set out, humble fare of which shepherds partake. Spurred by hunger and frenzy, he made no distinction between bread and acorns but set to with his hands and teeth and devoured whatever came first within reach, whether raw or cooked. / After this he roamed about the countryside, preying upon men and wild beasts. He would range through the woods catching fleet-footed goats and nimble fawns. Often he would fight with bears and boars, wrestling them to the ground bare-handed; often he filled his

---

3. Orlando's frenzy resembles that of Hercules, the strongest man in classical mythology.

ravenous belly with their meat, carcass and all. / He roamed across the length and breadth of France, until one day he came to a bridge. Beneath it a broad, full river flowed between steep, craggy banks. Beside it there stood a tower commanding a sweeping view in all directions. What he did here you shall learn later on.

FROM CANTO 25

[Fiordispina's Love for Bradamant]

Oh what conflict there can be in a young man's mind between a thirst for glory and the impulses of Love! There is no telling which of the two motives is the stronger when now one, now the other predominates. * * * / He had not traveled a mile beyond the well before he saw a messenger approaching at a gallop; he was one of those sent by Agramant to the warriors from whom he was expecting help. He learnt that the Saracens were in such danger from Charlemagne's blockade that, short of immediate assistance, degradation or even death would be their lot. / Ruggiero was perplexed by many thoughts which all assailed him at once; but this was not the time or the place to decide on his best course. He let the messenger go, then turned his steed to follow the damsel who was guiding him; he kept urging her to hasten, as there was no time to lose. / They continued along their way until, as the sun was setting, they came to a stronghold of Marsilius in the middle of France, one which he had seized from Charlemagne in the course of the war. They did not stop at the drawbridge nor at the gate—nobody blocked or obstructed their entry, even though the palisade and fosse were thronged with armed men. / As the damsel accompanying him was recognized by the bystanders, they were allowed through unhindered without even being asked from where they had come. They reached the square which they found aglow with flames and teeming with a malicious throng.

In the middle he saw the young man condemned to death. His face was white; / it was tearful and downcast, and when Ruggiero looked up at it he imagined he was looking at Bradamant, so closely did the youth resemble her. The more he gazed at his face and figure the more the likeness struck him. "Either this is Bradamant," he told himself, "or else I'm no longer Ruggiero. / Perhaps she was over-hasty in taking up the condemned boy's defence: her intervention must have miscarried and she has been captured, as I see. Oh why such haste, why could I not have been with her on this venture? But I have arrived, thank God, and there's still time for me to save her." / And without further delay he grasped his sword—he had broken his lance at Pinabello's castle—and drove his steed into the unarmed throng, assailing them in the chest, sides, and belly. He whirled his sword, catching one man on the brow, the next at the throat, another on the cheek. The rabble fled screaming: the entire throng was left maimed, if not with cracked skulls. / Imagine a flock of birds by a lake, flitting about confidently as they grub for food, when suddenly a hawk plummets down upon them from the sky and strikes or snatches one of their number; the rest scatter, each deserting his companion to attend to his own escape. Thus you would have seen the crowd behave the moment Ruggiero drove into them. / Some half dozen who were slow in leaving had their heads lopped off clean; as many more he split down to the chest, while a count-less number were cleft down to the eyes or the jaw.

I'll grant you that they were not wearing helmets, but merely head-pieces of shining metal; had they been properly helmeted, though, he would have slashed them with almost as much ease. / No knight of the present day could match him for sheer strength—nor could any bear or lion or more ferocious beast, whether native or foreign to our shores. An earthquake might have equaled him, or the mighty Devil: not the one in hell—it's my Lord's Devil[4] I mean, the one which spits fire and forces its way everywhere, by land, sea, and air. / At every stroke at least one man fell, and more often two; he killed four and even five at a stroke, which soon brought the total to a hundred. The sword he had unsheathed could cut through steel as though it were soft whey. Falerina the sorceress[5] had made this cruel sword in the garden of Orgagna, for the purpose of slaying Orlando; / much did she regret having made it when she saw it used to destroy her garden. Imagine, then, the havoc and devastation wrought by it in the hands of a cham-pion such as Ruggiero! If ever he manifested his rage, his strength, his supreme valor it was here and now as he strove to rescue his lady. /

The mob stood up to him as well as hare to unleashed hounds. A good num-ber were killed; those who fled were legion. Meanwhile the damsel guiding Ruggiero had released the youth from the bonds tying his wrists, and procured him arms as best she could, a sword for his hand, a shield to sling from his neck. / He now did his utmost to avenge himself on these folk who had done him grievous wrong; he laid about him to such effect that he left a reputation for prowess and valor. The sun had dipped his golden rays into the Western sea when victorious Ruggiero and the young man set out from the castle. /

When the youth was outside the gates with Ruggiero, he thanked him profusely and most gracefully: his benefactor had, after all, risked his life to save him with-out knowing who he was. He asked Ruggiero to divulge his name, as he wanted to know who it was to whom he owed such a debt of gratitude. / "I am looking at the comely face and beautiful figure of my Bradamant," Ruggiero mused, "but I do not hear the dulcet tones of her voice. And her words are not appropriate to thanking a faithful lover. If she really is Bradamant, how is it that she has so soon forgotten my name?" / To establish who it was, Ruggiero employed subtlety. "I have seen you somewhere before," he remarked, "but though I have pondered and racked my brains I cannot remember where it was. Will you remind me, then, if you can recollect? And do me the pleasure of telling me your name, so that I may know who it was whom I saved today from the pyre." /

"It could be that you have seen me before," replied the other, "but I cannot say where or when. I too wander about the world seeking high adventure. Perhaps it was a sister of mine you saw, one who wears armor and carries a sword at her side; we are twins from birth and look so alike that even our family cannot tell us apart. / You are not the first, nor the second, nor even the fourth to have mis-taken us; neither our father, nor our brothers, nor even our mother who bore us at one birth is able to tell us apart. True, our hair used to mark a sharp difference between us when I wore my hair short and loose in the male fashion, while she wore hers long and coiled in a plait. / But one day she was wounded in the head

4. Duke Alfonso's great cannon.
5. Boiardo's sorceress, who created the sword Balisardo to kill Orlando.

(it would take too long to tell the story) and to heal her a servant of God cut her hair till it only half covered her ears. After that there was nothing to distinguish us beyond our sex and name: mine is Richardet, hers is Bradamant; we are brother and sister to Rinaldo. / And if it would not bore you to listen, I would tell you a story to amuse you—something that happened to me on account of my resemblance to her: at first it was rapture, but it ended in agony." Ruggiero, in whose ears no song was sweeter, no story dearer than one in which his lady featured, begged him to tell his story. /

"My sister had been wounded by a party of Saracens who had come upon her without a helmet, so she had been obliged to cut her long tresses if her dangerous head-wound was to heal. Now recently she happened to be traveling through these woods, her head shorn as I have said. / On her way she came to a shady spring and, being weary and dejected, she dismounted, took off her helmet and fell asleep in the tender grass. (I don't believe there can be a story more beautiful than this one.) Who should come upon her but the Spanish Princess Fiordispina, who had come into the woods to hunt. / When she saw my sister clad in armor all except for her face, and with a sword in place of a distaff, she imagined she was looking at a knight. After gazing awhile at her face and her manly build she felt her heart stolen. So she invited my sister to join the hunt, and ended by eluding her retinue and disappearing with her among the shady boughs. /

"Once she had brought her into a solitary place where she felt unlikely to be disturbed, little by little, by words and gestures she revealed that she was love-struck. With burning looks and fiery sighs she showed how consumed she was with desire. She paled and blushed and, summoning her courage, gave her a kiss. / It was clear to my sister that the damsel had illusions about her; my sister could never have satisfied her need and was quite perplexed as to what to do. 'My best course is to undeceive her,' she decided, 'and to reveal myself as a member of the gentle sex rather than to have myself reckoned an ignoble man.' / And she was right. It would have been a sheer disgrace, the conduct of a man made of plaster, if he had kept up a conversation with a damsel as fair as Fiordispina, sweet as nectar, who had set her cap at him, while like a cuckoo, he just trailed his wings. So Bradamant tactfully had her know that she was a maiden. / She was in quest of glory at arms, like Hippolyta and Camilla[6] of old. Born in Africa, in the seaside city of Arzilla, she was accustomed from childhood to the use of lance and shield. These revelations did not abate love-struck Fiordispina's passion one jot; Cupid had thrust in his dart to make so deep a gash that this remedy was now too late. / To Fiordispina my sister's face seemed no less beautiful for this, her eyes, her movements no less graceful; she did not on this account retrieve mastery over her heart, which had gone out to Bradamant to bask in her adorable eyes. Seeing her accoutred as a man, she had imagined that there would be no need for her passion to remain unassuaged; but now the thought that her beloved was also a woman made her sigh and weep and betray boundless sorrow. /

"Anyone who heard her tears and grieving that day would have wept with her. 'Never was any torment so cruel,' she lamented, 'but mine is crueler. Were it a question of any other love, evil or virtuous, I could hope to see it consummated, and I should know how to cull the rose from the briar. My desire alone can have no fulfilment. / If you wanted to torment me, Love, because my happy

6. Virgil's Amazon warrior. "Hippolyta": queen of the Amazons.

state offended you, why could you not rest content with those torments which other lovers experience? Neither among humans nor among beasts have I ever come across a woman loving a woman; to a woman another woman does not seem beautiful, nor does a hind to a hind, a ewe to a ewe. / By land, sea, and air I alone suffer thus cruelly at your hands—you have done this to make an example of my aberration, the ultimate one in your power. King Ninus's wife was evil and profane in her love for her son; so was Myrrha, in love with her father, and Pasiphae with the bull. But my love is greater folly than any of theirs. / These females made designs upon the males and achieved the desired consummation, so I am told. Pasiphae went inside the wooden cow, the others achieved their end by other means. But even if Daedalus came flying to me with every artifice at his command, he would be unable to untie the knot made by that all-too-diligent Maker, Nature, who is all-powerful.[7] /

"Thus the fair damsel grieved and fretted and would not be assuaged. She struck her face and tore her hair and sought to vent her feelings against her own person. My sister wept for pity and felt embarrassed[8] as she listened to her grieving. She tried to deflect her from this insane and profitless craving, but her words were in vain and to no effect. / It was help, not consolation, that she required and her grief only continued to increase. The day was now drawing to a close and the sun was reddening in the West; rather than spending the night in the woods it was time now to withdraw to some lodging. So the damsel invited Bradamant to this castle of hers not far away. / My sister was unable to refuse, so they came to the very spot where the wicked mob would have burned me to death had you not appeared. Here Fiordispina made much of my sister; she dressed her once more in feminine attire and made it plain to one and all that her guest was a woman. / Realizing how little benefit she derived from Bradamant's apparent masculinity, Fiordispina did not want any blame to attach to herself on her guest's account. In addition, she nurtured the hope that the sickness already implanted in her as a result of Bradamant's male aspect might be dispelled by a dose of femininity to show how matters really stood. /

"That night they shared a bed but they did not rest equally well. The one slept, the other wept and moaned, her desire ever mounting. And if sleep did occasionally press upon her eyelids, it was but a brief sleep charged with dreams in which it seemed to her that Heaven had allotted to her a Bradamant transformed into a preferable sex. / If a thirst-tormented invalid goes to sleep craving for water, in his turbid, fitful rest he calls to mind every drop of water he ever saw. Likewise her dreaming mind threw up images to requite her desires. Then she would wake and reach out, only to find that what she had seen was but an empty dream. / How many prayers and vows did she not offer that night to Mahomet and all the gods, asking them to change Bradamant's sex for the better by a clear and self-evident miracle! But she saw that all her prayers were vain; perhaps Heaven even mocked her. The night ended and Phoe-

---

7. The entire speech is based on the soliloquy of Ovid's Myrrha, who loved her father (*Metamorphoses* 10). "King Ninus's wife": Semiramis, Syrian queen who married her son. "Pasiphae": wife of King Minos, who loved a bull. "Daedalus": created the labyrinth in which Minos kept the Minotaur, the monstrous offspring of Pasiphae.

8. The Italian verb for Bradamant's emotional response, *è costretta*, indicates that she feels obliged or compelled to help Fiordispina rather than "embarrassed," as the translator puts it.

bus lifted his fair head out of the sea and gave light to the world. / With the new day they left their bed, and Fiordispina's pain was aggravated when Bradamant, anxious to be clear of her predicament, mentioned that she was leaving. As a parting gift, Fiordispina presented her with an excellent jennet, caparisoned in gold; also with a costly surcoat woven by her own hand. / Fiordispina accompanied her a step of the way then returned, weeping, to her castle, while my sister pressed on so hastily that she reached Montauban the same day. Our poor mother and we, her brothers, crowded round her, rejoicing—for lack of news of her, we had been gravely anxious for fear she were dead. /

"When she removed her helmet we all stared at her cropped hair which previously had fallen about her neck; and the new surcoat she was wearing also caught our attention. And she told us all that had befallen her, from start to finish just as I've told you: how after she was wounded in the wood she cut off her fair tresses in order to be healed; / and how the beautiful huntress came upon her as she was by the spring; and how she took to her deceptive appearance and segregated her from her party. She did not pass in silence over Fiordispina's grief, and we were all filled with pity at it. She described how she lodged with her, and all she did until her return to our castle. /

"Now I had heard a great deal about Fiordispina, whom I had seen in Saragossa and in France. I had been much allured by her lovely eyes and smooth cheeks, but had not let my thoughts dwell upon her; to love without hope is idle dreaming. But, brought again so fully to the fore, she reawakened my passion at once. / Out of this hope, Love prepared bonds for me, having no other cord with which to capture me. He showed me how to set about obtaining what I wanted of this damsel. A little deception would procure an easy success: the similarity between my sister and myself had often deceived others, so perhaps it would deceive her too. / Shall I, shan't I? My conclusion was that it is always good to go in pursuit of one's pleasure. I did not divulge my thought to a soul, nor seek anyone's advice on the matter. When it was night, I went to where my sister had left her armor; I put it on and away I went on her horse without waiting for dawn to break. / I set off by night, with Cupid for guide, to be with lovely Fiordispina, and I arrived before the Sun had hidden his radiance in the sea. Happy the man who outstripped his fellows in bringing the news to the princess: as bearer of good tidings he could expect thanks and a reward from her. /

"They all of them took me for Bradamant—just as you did—the more so in that I had both the attire and the horse with which she had left the previous day. Fiordispina lost no time in coming out to meet me; she was so jubilant and affectionate, she could not possibly have shown greater pleasure and joy. / Throwing her graceful arms around my neck, she softly hugged me and kissed me on the lips. You can imagine after this how Love guided his dart to pierce me at the heart of my heart! She took me by the hand and quickly led me into her bedroom; here she would suffer none but herself to undo my armor, from helmet to spurs; no one else was to take a hand. / Next she sent for a dress of hers, richly ornate, which she herself spread out and put on me as though I were a woman; and she caught my hair in a golden net. I studied modesty in my glances, and none of my gestures betrayed my not being a woman. My voice might have betrayed me, but I controlled it so well that it aroused no suspicions. / Then we went into a hall crowded with knights and ladies who received us with the sort of honor paid to queens and great ladies. Here several times I was amused when certain men, unaware that my skirts concealed something sturdy and robust, kept making eyes at me. / When the evening was further advanced and the meal had been over for some while—the fare had been an excellent choice of what was then in season—Fiordispina did not wait for me to ask the favor which was the object of my visit, but invited me hospitably to share her bed for the night. /

"When the waiting-women and maidens, the pages, and attendants had withdrawn, and we were both changed and in bed, while the flaming sconces left the room bright as day, I said to her: 'Do not be surprised, my lady, at my returning to you so soon—perhaps you thought that you would not see me again for God knows how long. / First I shall tell you why I left, then why I have returned. Had I been able to abate your ardor by staying, I should have wanted to live and die in your service, and never for an hour be without you. But seeing how much pain my presence occasioned you, as I could do you no better service, I chose to leave. / Fate drew me off my path into the thick of a tangled wood, where I heard a cry sound close by, as of a damsel calling for help. I came running and found myself at the edge of a crystal lake where a faun had hooked a naked maiden in the water and was cruelly preparing to eat her raw. / I went over, sword in hand— only this way could I help her—and slew the boorish fisherman. Straight away she dived into the water and said: "It is not for nothing that you have saved me. You shall be richly rewarded and given as much as you ask for: I am a nymph and I live in this limpid lake. / I have the power to perform miracles, to coerce nature and the elements. Ask to the limits of my capabilities, then just leave it to me: at my singing the moon comes down from the sky, fire turns to ice, the air turns brittle, and with mere words I have moved the earth and stopped the sun." /

"'I did not ask her for a hoard of treasure, or for power over nations, or for greater valor or might, or for honorable victory in every war. My only request was that she would show me some way I could fulfil your desire; I did not ask to achieve this in one way or in another, but left the method up to her own discretion. / Scarcely had I disclosed my wish than I saw her dive a second time, and for all reply to my request she splashed the enchanted water at me. The moment it touched my face I was quite transformed, I know not how. I could see, I could feel—though I could scarcely believe my senses—that I was changing from woman to man.[9] / You would never believe me, except that now, right away, you shall be able to see for yourself. In my new sex as in my old, my desire is to give you ready service. Command my faculties, then, and you shall find them now and ever more alert and bestirred for you.' Thus I spoke to her, and I guided her hand to test the truth for herself. /

"Imagine the case of a person who has given up hope of having something for which he craves; the more he bemoans his deprivation, the more he works himself into a state of despair; and if later he acquires it, he is so vexed over the time wasted sowing seed in the sand, and despair has so eroded him that he is dumbfounded and cannot believe his luck. / So it was with Fiordispina: she

---

9. Richardet invents a fictional metamorphosis, which he bases generally on Ovid's tales, with specific allusions to the famous tales of Actaeon (who sees the goddess Diana naked and is metamorphosed into a stag when she sprinkles him with water) and Salmacis and Hermaphroditus (who together become the hermaphrodite).

saw and touched the object she had so craved for, but she could not believe her eyes or her fingers or herself, and kept wondering whether she were awake or asleep. She needed solid proof to convince her that she was actually feeling what she thought she felt. 'O God, if this is a dream,' she cried, 'keep me asleep for good, and never wake me again!' /

"There was no roll of drums, no peal of trumpets to herald the amorous assault: but caresses like those of billing doves gave the signal to advance or to stand firm. We used arms other than arrows and slingstones; and I, without a ladder, leapt onto the battlements and planted my standard there at one jab, and thrust my enemy beneath me. / If on the previous night that bed had been laden with heavy sighs and laments, this night made up for it with as much laughter and merriment, pleasure and gentle playfulness. Never did twisting acanthus entwine pillars and beams with more knots than those which bound us together, our necks and sides, our arms, legs, and breasts in a close embrace. / It remained a secret between us, so our pleasure continued for a few months. But eventually someone found us out, so the matter became known to the king—to my undoing. You, who rescued me from his people who had lit the pyre in the square, you can understand the rest: but God knows what an ache I am left with." /

THOMAS MORE
1478–1535

Somewhere between a learned joke and a visionary dream of social reform, Thomas More's *Utopia* is the first modern example of the genre now known as "utopian literature." With its vision of an elusive and remote ideal society, *Utopia* offers readers the tantalizing possibility of an alternative to their own world. From the Renaissance and into our own time, More's humanist inquiry into the proper organization of society has inspired other writers to imagine their own alternatives to the way we live.

LIFE AND TIMES

As a scholar and statesman, Thomas More was one of the most influential English thinkers of the early sixteenth century. Humanism had created a new professional class of secretaries, ambassadors, and counselors to kings, and More's career in law and government was a shining example of what education could achieve in Tudor England. Born not of noble, but of honest stock, as he wrote in his own epitaph, More came from families with a tradition of civic service to London and to the crown. As a young boy, he served as a page in the household of the famed prelate and statesman Cardinal Morton, who appears in Book One of *Utopia*. At London's finest grammar school, at Oxford University, and at the Inns of Court, he received a first-rate education in the classics and law. He befriended the famous humanist Erasmus of Rotterdam and his circle, and had close connections to a London religious order. More was married twice and oversaw a pious, industrious household, in which, unusually, his daughters as well as his son were educated. He led a life of intense spirituality, his interest in living piously but without renouncing worldly power matching his study of classical virtue. Early in his career, More wrote a history of Richard III (ca. 1513) in which he grappled with the complexities of power and virtue, themes also explored in *Utopia* (1516).

More was to experience the vicissitudes of royal power firsthand, as he held increasingly important offices, from Member of Parliament to ambassador to, finally, Lord Chancellor of England (one of the highest positions in the government, advisor to the king, Henry VIII, and head of the judiciary). Yet the tumultuous events of the early 1530s cut short his brilliant ascent. Henry VIII became increasingly frustrated as the Pope refused to grant him a divorce from Catherine of Aragon, which Henry needed in order to marry Anne Boleyn. In a bold move to bolster his own authority, Henry formally broke with the Church of Rome, and, in the 1534 "Act of Supremacy," proclaimed himself the "only and supreme head" of his realm. England was convulsed by the unprecedented break, and by the political and religious firestorms that ensued. Although Henry did not seek Protestant reforms, his actions encouraged those who did.

As a loyal Catholic and high official, More had vigorously persecuted Protestant heretics, written tracts against Protestantism, and strived to keep the new reform movements out of England, a land far less tolerant than the *Utopia* he had imagined, where "no man's religion, as such, shall be held against him." Given his position, More could not condone Henry's claim to lead the English church. In 1532, just three years after being named Chancellor, More resigned and defended his stance in print. Staunchly refusing to take an oath to acknowledge Henry's supremacy, More was imprisoned in the Tower of London, where he wrote his last works, on the spiritual benefits of tribulation. He was finally executed as a traitor in 1535. Considered a Catholic martyr, he was canonized in 1935.

UTOPIA

More's *Utopia* is a serious text full of inside jokes, paradoxes, and contradictions, a slippery satire of More's world that simultaneously proposed a provocative alternative. *Utopia* is actually two very different books: the first, sometimes referred to as "The Dialogue of Counsel," introduces More and his humanist friends as characters. On an embassy for Henry VIII to Flanders, More meets a worldly, wise, and entirely fictional traveler, Raphael Hythloday, who had sailed with Amerigo Vespucci. When More suggests that Hythloday should put his knowledge to use in public service, the traveler replies with a strong indictment of European monarchies for their greed and ambition. The dialogue turns to social inequality in England, exacerbated in More's time by the enclosure of agricultural common land for private sheep-pastures. Hythloday insists that private property makes social justice impossible, and offers the distant commonwealth of Utopia as a counterexample.

The second book, modeled closely on travel narratives of the New World, describes the island Utopia, from its geography to its society to its moral philosophy. By framing *Utopia* as a travel narrative, More contrasts the supposed certainties of the classics and of established knowledge with the earth-shattering novelty of the New World.

Utopia is itself both new and old: new to Europeans, certainly, but the beneficiary of a wealth of trans-ferred knowledge from the Old World, including Christianity, which Hythlo-day's expedition has recently brought to them.

Based on the ideal commonwealth of **Plato**'s *Republic*, on **St. Augustine**'s *City of God*, and on monastic commu-nal living, *Utopia* looks back as much as it looks forward. The island that Hythlo-day describes is ruled by a set of hyper-rational, simplified laws that treat (almost) everyone equally and attempt to quiet the desires, such as greed or lust, that can wreak havoc with such arrangements. More's own career had made him acutely aware of the distance between ideals and political realities, and his island commonwealth satirizes human folly as well as offering possible solutions.

Uniquely slippery and as difficult to fix as the island is to find, *Utopia* beck-ons for its political engagement and its literary richness. Written in Latin for an audience of European humanists, *Uto-pia* assumes a learned reader who can understand puns in Greek and Latin, the cutting-edge disciplines of More's time. The most important of these puns is the name of the island: Utopia means "no place" (from the Greek *u-topos*), but also sounds like "good place" (*eu-topos*). The puns undercut the seeming solid-ity of Raphael Hythloday's account—named after an archangel, his last name means "peddler of nonsense," while a river is named Anyder, or "waterless." More presents us with a mirage, an island both elusive and exemplary, desir-able and impossible.

Despite the geographical remove of the island it describes, *Utopia* hews very close to More's world, from its dis-cussion of the privatization of public lands to its preoccupation with social justice to the many echoes of England in that other, fictional island. Yet the force of *Utopia* lies in its relevance beyond the English case. Extraordi-narily influential for writers such as **Rabelais**, **Montaigne**, and **Shake-speare**, the text also spawned a whole archipelago of ideal commonwealths and their dystopian counterparts, such as Francis Bacon's *The New Atlantis* (1627) and George Orwell's *1984* (1949). *Utopia* also inspired actual communities in the New World, where European colonists tried to rule indig-enous peoples by the principles of More's playfully imagined society, as well as later European and American experiments in socialism.

CONCERNING THE BEST STATE OF A COMMONWEALTH AND THE NEW ISLAND OF UTOPIA[1]

A Truly Golden Handbook
No Less Beneficial Than Entertaining
by the Most Distinguished and Eloquent Author
THOMAS MORE
Citizen and Undersheriff[2] of the Famous City of London

Book I

The most invincible king of England, Henry, the eighth of that name, a prince adorned with the royal virtues beyond any other, had recently some differences of no slight import with Charles, the most serene prince of Castille,[3] and sent me into Flanders as his spokesman to discuss and settle them. I was companion and associate to that incomparable man Cuthbert Tunstall, whom the king has recently created master of the rolls,[4] to everyone's great satisfaction. I will say nothing in praise of this man, not because I fear the judgment of a friend might be questioned, but because his integrity and learning are greater than I can describe and too well known everywhere to need my commendation—unless I would, according to the proverb, "light up the sun with a lantern."

Those appointed by the prince to deal with us, all excellent men, met us at Bruges by prearrangement. Their head and leader was the mayor of Bruges,[5] a most distinguished person. But their main speaker and guiding spirit was Georgius de Theimseke,[6] the provost of Cassel, a man eloquent by nature as well as by training, very learned in the law, and most skillful in diplomatic affairs through his ability and long practice. After we had met several times, certain points remained on which we could not come to agreement; so they adjourned the meetings and went to Brussels for some days to learn their prince's pleasure.

Meanwhile, since my business required it, I went to Antwerp. Of those who visited me while I was there, no one was more welcome than Peter Giles.[7] He was a native of Antwerp, a man of high reputation, already appointed to a good position and worthy of the very best: I hardly know whether the young man is

---

1. Translated by Robert M. Adams and George M. Logan.
2. More was appointed Undersheriff of London in 1510. Sheriffs were legal officials charged with keeping the peace and enforcing royal justice.
3. Future Holy Roman Emperor Charles V (Charles I of Spain). The dispute was over Dutch import duties.
4. Scholar and cleric appointed ambassador to Brussels in 1515. The Master of the Rolls was responsible for keeping legal records but also held judicial functions.
5. Bruges was an important manufacturing center for English wool in the Low Countries.
6. Chief magistrate of a small town in what is today northeastern France.
7. A pupil of Erasmus, the humanist Peter Giles (c. 1486–1533) was town clerk of Antwerp, as well as a poet and Latin editor. "Antwerp": an important international trading center in the Low Countries.

more distinguished in learning or in character. Apart from being cultured, virtuous, and courteous to all, with his intimates he is so open-hearted, affectionate, loyal, and sincere that you would be hard-pressed to find anywhere a man comparable to him in all the points of friendship. No one is more modest or more frank; none better combines simplicity with wisdom. His conversation is so pleasant, and so witty without malice, that the ardent desire I felt to see again my native country, my wife, and my children (from whom I had been separated more than four months) was much eased by his agreeable company and delightful talk.

One day after I had heard mass at Nôtre Dame, the most beautiful and most popular church in Antwerp, I was about to return to my quarters when I happened to see him talking with a stranger, a man of quite advanced years. The stranger had a sunburned face, a long beard, and a cloak hanging loosely from his shoulders; from his appearance and dress, I took him to be a ship's captain. When Peter saw me, he approached and greeted me. As I was about to return his greeting, he drew me aside, and, indicating the stranger, said, "Do you see that fellow? I was just on the point of bringing him to you."

"He would have been very welcome on your behalf," I answered.

"And on his own too, if you knew him," said Peter, "for there is no mortal alive today can tell you so much about unknown peoples and lands; and I know that you're always greedy for such information."

"In that case," said I, "my guess wasn't a bad one, for at first glance I supposed he was a skipper."

"Then you're far off the mark," he replied, "for his sailing has not been like that of Palinurus,[8] but more that of Ulysses, or rather of Plato. This man, who is named Raphael—his family name is Hythloday[9]—knows a good deal of Latin, and is particularly learned in Greek. He studied Greek more than Latin because his main interest is philosophy, and in that field he found that the Romans have left us nothing very valuable except certain works of Seneca and Cicero.[1] Being eager to see the world, he left to his brothers the patrimony to which he was entitled at home (he is a native of Portugal) and took service with Amerigo Vespucci.[2] He was Vespucci's constant companion on the last three of his four voyages, accounts of which are now common reading everywhere; but on the last voyage, he did not return home with the commander. After much persuasion and expostulation he got Amerigo's permission to be one of the twenty-four men who were left in a fort at the farthest point of the last voyage.[3] Being marooned in this way was altogether agreeable to him, as he was more anxious to pursue his travels than afraid of death. He would often say, 'The man who has no grave is covered by the sky,' and 'The road to heaven is the

8. In the *Aeneid*, the pilot who fell asleep at the ship's wheel and drowned. In contrast, the hero Ulysses (Odysseus) represents the man who learns from traveling, while the philosopher Plato travels to learn.
9. From the Greek *huthlos*, "nonsense" and *daien*, "to distribute," Hythloday means roughly "peddler of nonsense." "Raphael": the most sociable of the biblical archangels.

1. Cicero (106–43 B.C.E.): statesman and philosopher. Seneca (3 B.C.E.–65 C.E.): Stoic philosopher, statesman, and dramatist.
2. Amerigo Vespucci (1454–1512): Italian explorer and cartographer after whom the Americas are named. His last two voyages were made for the King of Portugal.
3. In Cape Frio, north of Rio de Janeiro in Brazil.

same length from all places.' Yet this frame of mind would have cost him dear, if God had not been gracious to him. After Vespucci's departure, he traveled through many countries with five companions from the garrison. At last, by strange good fortune, he got, via Ceylon, to Calicut,[4] where he opportunely found some Portuguese ships; and so, beyond anyone's expectation, he returned to his own country."

When Peter had told me this, I thanked him for his great kindness in wishing to introduce me to a man whose conversation he hoped I would enjoy, and then I turned to Raphael. After we had greeted each other and exchanged the usual civilities of strangers upon their first meeting, we all went off to my house. There in the garden we sat down on a bench covered with turf, to talk together.

He told us that when Vespucci sailed away, he and his companions who had stayed behind in the fort often met with the people of the countryside, and by ingratiating speeches gradually won their friendship. Before long they came to dwell with them safely and even affectionately. The prince (I have forgotten his name and that of his country) also gave them his favor, furnishing Raphael and his five companions not only with ample provisions but with means for traveling—rafts when they went by water, wagons when they went by land. In addition, he sent with them a most trusty guide, who was to conduct them to other princes to whom he heartily recommended them. After many days' journey, he said, they came to towns and cities, and to commonwealths that were both very populous and not badly governed.

To be sure, under the equator and as far on both sides of the line as the sun moves, there lie vast empty deserts, scorched with perpetual heat. The whole region is desolate and squalid, grim and uncultivated, inhabited by wild beasts, serpents, and also by men no less wild and dangerous than the beasts themselves. But as you go on, conditions gradually grow milder. The sun is less fierce, the earth greener, the creatures less savage. At last you reach people, cities, and towns which not only trade among themselves and with their neighbors but even carry on commerce by sea and land with remote countries. After that, he said, they were able to visit different lands in every direction, for he and his companions were welcome as passengers aboard any ship about to make a journey.

The first vessels they saw were flat-bottomed, he said, with sails made of stitched papyrus-reeds or wicker, or elsewhere of leather. Farther on, they found ships with pointed keels and canvas sails, in every respect like our own. The seamen were not unskilled in managing wind and water; but they were most grateful to him, Raphael said, for showing them the use of the compass, of which they had been ignorant. For that reason, they had formerly sailed with great timidity, and only in summer. Now they have such trust in the compass that they no longer fear winter at all, and tend to be overconfident rather than cautious. There is some danger that through their imprudence this device, which they thought would be so advantageous to them, may become the cause of much mischief.

4. Ceylon (Sri Lanka) and Calicut, in southern India, were both major trading posts for spices, reached by Portuguese explorers at the turn of the 16th century. Roughly fifteen thousand miles separate them from Brazil.

It would take too long to repeat all that Raphael told us he had observed in each place, nor would it make altogether for our present purpose. Perhaps on another occasion we shall tell more about the things that are most profitable, especially the wise and sensible institutions that he observed among the civilized nations. We asked him many eager questions about such things, and he answered us willingly enough. We made no inquiries, however, about monsters, for nothing is less new or strange than they are. Scyllas, ravenous Celaenos, man-eating Lestrygonians,[5] and that sort of monstrosity you can hardly avoid, but well and wisely trained citizens you will hardly find anywhere. While he told us of many ill-considered usages in these new-found nations, he also described quite a few other customs from which our own cities, nations, races, and kingdoms might take example in order to correct their errors. These I shall discuss in another place, as I said. Now I intend to relate only what he told us about the customs and institutions of the Utopians, first recounting the conversation that led him to speak of that commonwealth. Raphael had been talking very sagely about the faulty arrangements and also the wise institutions found in that hemisphere and this (many of both sorts in each), speaking as shrewdly about the manners and governments of each place he had visited as though he had lived there all his life. Peter was amazed.

"My dear Raphael," he said, "I'm surprised that you don't enter some king's service; for I don't know of a single prince who wouldn't be eager to employ you. Your learning and your knowledge of various countries and peoples would entertain him, while your advice and your supply of examples would be very helpful in the council chamber. Thus you might advance your own interests and be useful at the same time to all your relatives and friends."

"I am not much concerned about my relatives and friends," he replied, "because I consider that I have already done my duty by them. While still young and healthy, I distributed among my relatives and friends the possessions that most men do not part with till they are old and sick (and then only reluctantly, because they can no longer keep them). I think they should be content with this gift of mine, and not expect that for their sake I should enslave myself to any king whatever."

"Well said," Peter replied; "but I do not mean that you should be in servitude to any king, only in his service."

"The difference is only a matter of one syllable," said Raphael.

"All right," said Peter, "but whatever you call it, I do not see any other way in which you can be so useful to your friends or to the general public, in addition to making yourself happier."

"Happier indeed!" exclaimed Raphael. "Would a way of life so absolutely repellent to my spirit make my life happier? As it is now, I live as I please, and I fancy very few courtiers, however splendid, can say that. As a matter of fact, there are so many men soliciting favors from the powerful that it will be no great loss if they have to do without me and a couple of others like me."

Then I said, "It is clear, my dear Raphael, that you seek neither wealth nor power, and indeed I value and revere a man of such a disposition as much as I do the mightiest persons in the world. Yet I think if you would devote your time

---

5. Monsters from classical mythology. Scylla and the Lestrygonians appear in *The Odyssey* (books 12 and 10, respectively), while Celaeno tortures Aeneas and his men in *Aeneid* 3.

and energy to public affairs, you would do a thing worthy of a generous and philosophical nature, even if you did not much like it. You could best perform such a service by joining the council of some great prince and inciting him to just and noble actions (as I'm sure you would): for a people's welfare or misery flows in a stream from their prince, as from a never-failing spring. Your learning is so full, even if it weren't combined with experience, and your experience is so great, even apart from your learning, that you would be an extraordinary counselor to any king in the world."

"You are twice mistaken, my dear More," he replied, "first in me and then in the situation itself. I don't have the capacity you ascribe to me, and if I had it in the highest degree, the public would still not be any better off if I exchanged my contemplative leisure for this kind of action. In the first place, most princes apply themselves to the arts of war, in which I have neither ability nor interest, instead of to the good arts of peace. They are generally more set on acquiring new kingdoms by hook or by crook than on governing well those they already have. Moreover, the counselors of kings are all so wise already that they need no advice from anyone else (or at least that's the way they see it). At the same time, they approve and even flatter the most absurd statements of favorites through whose influence they seek to stand well with the prince. It is only natural, of course, that each man should think his own opinions best: the crow loves his fledgling, and the ape his cub.

"Now in a court composed of people who envy everyone else and admire only themselves, if a man should suggest something he had read of in other ages or seen in practice elsewhere, the other counselors would think their reputation for wisdom was endangered and they would look like simpletons, unless they could find fault with his proposal. If all else failed, they would take refuge in some remark like this: 'The way we're doing it was good enough for our ancestors, and I only hope we're as wise as they were.' And with this deep thought they would take their seats, as though they had said the last word on the subject—implying, of course, that it would be a very dangerous matter if anyone were found to be wiser in any point than his ancestors were. As a matter of fact, we have no misgivings about neglecting the best examples they have left us; but if something better is proposed, we eagerly seize upon the excuse of reverence for times past and cling to it desperately. Such proud, obstinate, ridiculous judgments I have encountered many times, and once even in England."

"What!" I said. "Were you ever in my country?"

"Yes," he answered, "I spent several months there. It was not long after the revolt of the Cornishmen against the king had been put down, with the miserable slaughter of the rebels.[6] During my stay I was deeply beholden to the reverend father John Cardinal Morton,[7] archbishop of Canterbury, and in addition at that time lord chancellor of England. He was a man, my dear Peter (for More knows about him, and can tell what I'm going to say), as much respected for his wisdom and virtue as for his authority. He was of medium height, not bent over despite his years; his looks inspired respect rather than fear. In conversation, he

---

6. 1497 Cornish revolt against taxation, violently suppressed.
7. A distinguished cleric and statesman. As a

child More had served as a page in his household, as part of his education.

was not forbidding, though serious and grave. When suitors came to him on business, he liked to test their spirit and presence of mind by speaking to them sharply, though not rudely. He liked to uncover these qualities, which were those of his own nature, as long as they were not carried to the point of effrontery; and he thought such men were best qualified to carry on business. His speech was polished and pointed; his knowledge of the law was great; he had an incomparable understanding and a prodigious memory, for he had improved extraordinary natural abilities by study and practice. At the time when I was in England, the king relied heavily on his advice, and he seemed the chief support of the nation as a whole. He had been taken from school to court when scarcely more than a boy, had devoted all his life to important business, and had acquired from weathering violent changes of fortune and many great perils a supply of practical wisdom, which is not soon lost when so purchased.

"One day when I was dining with him, there was present a layman, learned in the laws of your country, who for some reason took occasion to praise the rigid execution of justice then being practiced upon thieves. They were being executed everywhere, he said, with as many as twenty at a time being hanged on a single gallows. And then he declared that he could not understand how so many thieves sprang up everywhere, when so few of them escaped hanging. I ventured to speak freely before the cardinal, and said, 'There is no need to wonder: this way of punishing thieves goes beyond the call of justice, and is not, in any case, for the public good. The penalty is too harsh in itself, yet it isn't an effective deterrent. Simple theft is not so great a crime that it ought to cost a man his life, yet no punishment however severe can withhold those from robbery who have no other way to eat. In this matter not only you in England but a good part of the world seem to imitate bad schoolmasters, who would rather whip their pupils than teach them. Severe and terrible punishments are enacted against theft, when it would be much better to enable every man to earn his own living, instead of being driven to the awful necessity of stealing and then dying for it.'

"'Oh, we've taken care of that,' said the fellow. 'There are the trades and there is farming, by which men may make a living unless they choose deliberately to be rogues.'

"'Oh no you don't,' I said, 'you won't get out of it that way. We may disregard for the moment the cripples who come home from foreign and civil wars, as lately from the Cornish battle and before that from your wars with France. These men, who have lost limbs in the service of king and country, are too badly crippled to follow their old trades, and too old to learn new ones. But since wars occur only from time to time, let us, I say, disregard these men, and consider what happens every day. There are a great many noblemen who live idly like drones off the labor of others, their tenants whom they bleed white by constantly raising their rents. (This is the only instance of their tightfistedness, because they are prodigal in everything else, ready to spend their way to the poorhouse.) These noblemen drag around with them a great train of idle servants, who have never learned any trade by which they could earn a living. As soon as their master dies, or they themselves fall ill, they are promptly turned out of doors, for lords would rather support idlers than invalids, and the son is often unable to maintain as big a household as his father had, at least at first. Those who are turned off soon set about starving, unless they set about stealing. What else can they do? Then when a wandering life has left their health impaired and their clothes threadbare, when their faces look pinched and their garments tattered, men of rank will not care to engage them. And country people dare not do so, for they don't have to be told that one who has been raised softly to idle pleasures, who has been used to swaggering about with sword and buckler, is likely to look down on the whole neighborhood and despise everybody else as beneath him. Such a man can't be put to work with spade and mattock; he will not serve a poor man faithfully for scant wages and sparse diet.'

"'But we ought to encourage these men in particular,' said the lawyer. 'In case of war the strength and power of our army depend on them, because they have a bolder and nobler spirit than workmen and farmers have.'

"'You may as well say that thieves should be encouraged for the sake of wars,' I answered, 'since you will never lack for thieves as long as you have men like these. In fact thieves don't make bad soldiers, and soldiers turn out to be pretty good robbers—so nearly are these two ways of life related. But the custom of keeping too many retainers is not peculiar to this nation; it is common to almost all of them. France suffers from an even more grievous plague. Even in peacetime—if you can call it peace—the whole country is crowded with foreign mercenaries, imported on the same principle that you've given for your noblemen keeping idle servants. Wise fools think that the public safety depends on having ready a strong army, preferably of veteran soldiers. They think inexperienced men are not reliable, and they sometimes hunt out pretexts for war, just so they may have trained soldiers and experienced cutthroats—or, as Sallust neatly puts it, that "hand and spirit may not grow dull through lack of practice." But France has learned to her cost how pernicious it is to feed such beasts. The examples of the Romans, the Carthaginians, the Syrians, and many other peoples show the same thing; for not only their governments but their fields and even their cities were ruined more than once by their own standing armies. Besides, this preparedness is unnecessary: not even the French soldiers, practiced in arms from their cradles, can boast of having often got the best of your raw recruits. I shall say no more on this point, lest I seem to flatter present company. At any rate, neither your town workmen nor your rough farm laborers—except for those whose physiques aren't suited for strength or boldness, or whose spirits have been cowed by inability to feed their families—seem to be much afraid of fighting the idle attendants of noblemen. So you need not fear that retainers, once strong and vigorous (for that's the only sort noblemen deign to corrupt), but now soft and flabby because of their idle, effeminate life, would be weakened if they were taught practical crafts to earn their living, and trained to manly labor. Anyway, I cannot think it's in the public interest to maintain for the emergency of war such a vast multitude of people who trouble and disturb the peace. You never have war unless you choose it, and peace is always more to be considered than war. Yet this is not the only circumstance that makes thieving necessary. There is another one, which, I believe, applies more especially to you Englishmen.'

"'What is that?' asked the cardinal.

"'Your sheep,' I replied, 'that used to be so meek and eat so little. Now they have become so greedy and fierce that they devour human beings themselves, as I hear. They devastate and depopulate fields, houses, and towns.[8] For in

8. As the English wool trade prospered, public lands on which peasants had farmed and lived were gradually enclosed (i.e., privatized) and dedicated to sheep-rearing.

whatever parts of the land the sheep yield the softest and most expensive wool, there the nobility and gentry, yes, and even some abbots—holy men—are not content with the old rents that the land yielded to their predecessors. Living in idleness and luxury, without doing any good to society, no longer satisfies them; they have to do positive harm. For they leave no land free for the plow: they enclose every acre for pasture; they destroy houses and abolish towns, keeping only the churches, and those for sheepbarns. And as if enough of your land were not already wasted on woods and game-preserves, these worthy men turn all human habitations and cultivated fields back to wilderness. Thus one greedy, insatiable glutton, a frightful plague to his native country, may enclose many thousand acres of land within a single hedge. The tenants are dismissed; some are stripped of their belongings by trickery or brute force, or, wearied by constant harassment, are driven to sell them. By hook or by crook these miserable people—men, women, husbands, wives, orphans, widows, parents with little children, whole families (poor but numerous, since farming requires many hands)—are forced to move out. They leave the only homes familiar to them, and they can find no place to go. Since they cannot afford to wait for a buyer, they sell for a pittance all their household goods, which would not bring much in any case. When that little money is gone (and it's soon spent in wandering from place to place), what remains for them but to steal, and so be hanged—justly, you'd say!—or to wander and beg? And yet if they go tramping, they are jailed as idle vagrants. They would be glad to work, but they can find no one who will hire them. There is no need for farm labor, in which they have been trained, when there is no land left to be planted. One herdsman or shepherd can look after a flock of beasts large enough to stock an area that would require many hands if it were plowed and harvested.

"'This enclosing has had the effect of raising the price of food in many places. In addition, the price of raw wool has risen so much that poor people who used to make cloth are no longer able to buy it, and so great numbers are forced from work to idleness. One reason is that after the enlarging of the pasture-land, a murrain killed a great number of sheep—as though God were punishing greed by sending a plague upon the animals, which in justice should have fallen on the owners! But even if the number of sheep should increase greatly, their price will not fall a penny. The reason is that the wool trade, though it can't be called a monopoly, because it isn't in the hands of one single person, is concentrated in few hands (an oligopoly, you might say), and these so rich that the owners are never pressed to sell until they have a mind to, and that is only when they can get their price.

"'For the same reason other kinds of livestock also are priced exorbitantly, the more so because with so many farmhouses being pulled down, and farming in a state of decay, there are not enough people to look after the breeding of animals. These rich men will not breed other animals as they do lambs, but buy them lean and cheap, fatten them in their own pastures, and then sell them at a high price. I don't think the full impact of this bad system has yet been felt. We know these dealers raise prices where the fattened animals are sold. But when, over a period of time, they keep buying beasts from other localities faster than they can be bred, then as the supply gradually diminishes where they are purchased, a severe shortage is bound to ensue. So your island, which seemed especially fortunate in this matter, will be ruined by the crass avarice of a few.

For the high food prices cause everyone to dismiss as many retainers as he can from his household; and what, I ask, can these men do, but rob or beg? And a man of courage is more likely to steal than to cringe.

"'To make this hideous poverty and scarcity worse, they exist side by side with wanton luxury. Not only the servants of noblemen, but tradespeople, even some farmers, and people of every social rank are given to ostentatious dress and gluttonous greed. Look at the eating houses, the bawdy houses, and those other places just as bad, the wine bars and alehouses. Look at all the crooked games of chance, dice, cards, backgammon, tennis, bowling, and quoits, in which money slips away so fast. Don't all these lead their habitués straight to robbery? Banish these blights, make those who have ruined farmhouses and villages restore them, or hand them over to someone who will rebuild. Restrict the right of the rich to buy up anything and everything, and then to exercise a kind of monopoly. Let fewer people be brought up in idleness. Let agriculture be restored and the wool manufacture revived as an honest trade, so there will be useful work for the whole crowd of those now idle—whether those whom poverty has already made into thieves, or those whom vagabondage and habits of lazy service are converting, just as surely, into the robbers of the future.

"'If you do not find a cure for these evils, it is futile to boast of your justice in punishing theft. Your policy may look superficially like justice, but in reality it is neither just nor practical. If you allow young folk to be abominably brought up and their characters corrupted, little by little, from childhood; and if then you punish them as grownups for committing crimes to which their early training has inclined them, what else is this, I ask, but first making them thieves and then punishing them for it?'

"As I was speaking thus, the lawyer had made ready his answer, choosing the usual style of disputants who are better at summing up than at replying, and who like to show off their memory. So he said to me, 'You have talked very well for a stranger, but you have heard about more things than you have been able to understand correctly. I will make the matter clear to you in a few words. First, I will summarize what you have said; then I will show how you have been misled by ignorance of our customs; finally, I will demolish all your arguments and reduce them to rubble. And so to begin where I promised, on four points you seemed to me—'

"'Hold your tongue,' said the cardinal, 'for you won't be finished in a few words, if this is the way you start. We will spare you the trouble of answering now, and reserve the pleasure of your reply till our next meeting, which will be tomorrow, if your affairs and Raphael's permit it. Meanwhile, my dear Raphael, I am eager to hear why you think theft should not be punished with death, or what other punishment you think would be more in the public interest. For I'm sure even you don't think it should go unpunished entirely. Even as it is, the fear of death does not restrain evildoers; once they were sure of their lives, as you propose, what force or fear could restrain them? They would look on a lighter penalty as an open invitation to commit more crimes—it would be like offering them a reward.'

"'It seems to me, most kind and reverend father,' I said, 'that it's altogether unjust to take someone's life for taking money. Nothing in the world that fortune can bestow is equal in value to a human life. If they say the thief suffers not for the money, but for violation of justice and transgression of laws, then this extreme justice should really be called extreme injury. We ought not to approve of these fierce Manlian edicts[9] that invoke the sword for the smallest violations. Neither should we accept the Stoic view that considers all crimes equal, as if there were no difference between killing a man and taking a coin from him. If equity means anything, there is no proportion or relation at all between these two crimes. God has said, "Thou shalt not kill"; shall we kill so readily for the theft of a bit of small change? Perhaps it will be argued that God's commandment against killing does not apply where human law allows it. But then what prevents men from making other laws in the same way—perhaps even laws legalizing rape, adultery, and perjury? God has taken from each person the right not only to kill another, but even to kill himself. If mutual consent to human laws on manslaughter entitles men freely to exempt their agents from divine law and allows them to kill those condemned by human decrees where God has given no precedent, what is this but preferring the law of man to the law of God? The result will be that in every situation men will decide for themselves how far it suits them to observe the laws of God. The law of Moses was harsh and severe, as for an enslaved and stubborn people, but it punished theft with a fine, not death.[1] Let us not think that in his new law of mercy, where he rules us with the tenderness of a father, God has given us greater license to be cruel to one another.

"'These are the reasons why I think it is wrong to put thieves to death. But surely everybody knows how absurd and even harmful to the public welfare it is to punish theft and murder alike. If theft carries the same penalty as murder, the thief will be encouraged to kill the victim whom otherwise he would only have robbed. When the punishment is the same, murder is safer, since one conceals both crimes by killing the witness. Thus while we try to terrify thieves with extreme cruelty, we really invite them to kill the innocent.

"'As for the usual question of what more suitable punishment can be found, in my judgment it would be much easier to find a better one than a worse. Why should we question the value of the punishments long used by the Romans, who were most expert in the arts of government? They condemned those convicted of heinous crimes to work, shackled, for life, in stone quarries and mines. But of all the alternatives, I prefer the method which I observed in my Persian travels, among the people commonly called the Polylerites.[2] They are a sizable nation, not badly governed, free and subject only to their own laws, except that they pay annual tribute to the Persian king. Living far from the sea, they are nearly surrounded by mountains. Being contented with the products of their own land, which is by no means unfruitful, they do not visit other nations, nor are they much visited. According to their ancient customs, they do not try to enlarge their boundaries, and easily protect themselves behind their mountains by paying tribute to their overlord. Thus they have no wars and live in a comfortable rather than a showy manner, more contented than renowned or glorious. Indeed, I think they are hardly known by name to anyone but their next-door neighbors.

9. The Roman consul Manlius (4th century B.C.E.) was proverbial for his strictness.
1. Exodus 22 in the Old Testament gives various penalties for theft, but never death. England

was supposedly operating under the gentler "new law" of Christ.
2. From the Greek polus and leiros, "much nonsense."

"'In their land, whoever is found guilty of theft must make restitution to the owner, not (as elsewhere) to the prince; they think the prince has no more right to the stolen goods than the thief. If the stolen property has disappeared, its value is repaid from the thief's possessions. Whatever remains of those is handed over to his wife and children, while the thief himself is sentenced to hard labor.

"'Unless their crimes were compounded with atrocities, thieves are neither imprisoned nor shackled, but go freely and unconstrained about their work on public projects. If they shirk and do their jobs slackly, they are not chained, but they are whipped. If they work hard, they are treated without any indignities, except that at night after roll call they are locked up in their dormitories. Apart from constant work, they undergo no discomfort in living. As they work for the public good, they are decently fed out of the public stores, though arrangements vary from place to place. In some districts they are supported by alms. Unreliable as this support may seem, the Polylerites are so compassionate that no way is found more rewarding. In other places, public revenues are set aside for their support, or a special tax is levied on every individual for their use; and sometimes they do not do public work, but anyone in need of workmen can go to the market and hire some of them by the day at a set rate, a little less than that for free men. If they are lazy, it is lawful to whip them. Thus they never lack for work, and each one of them brings a little profit into the public treasury beyond the cost of his keep.

"'They are all dressed in clothes of the same distinctive color. Their hair is not shaved but trimmed close about the ears, and the tip of one ear is cut off. Their friends are allowed to give them food, drink, or clothing, as long as it is of the proper color; but to give them money is death, both to the giver and to the taker. It is just as serious a crime for any free man to take money from them for any reason whatever; and it is also a capital crime for any of these slaves (as the condemned are called) to carry weapons. In each district of the country they are required to wear a special badge. It is a capital crime to throw away the badge, to go beyond one's own district, or to talk with a slave of another district. Plotting escape is no more secure than escape itself: it is death for any other slave to know of a plot to escape, and slavery for a free man. On the other hand, there are rewards for informers—money for a free man, freedom for a slave, and for both of them pardon and amnesty. Thus it can never be safer for them to persist in an illicit scheme than to renounce it.

"'Such are their laws and policies in this matter. It is clear how mild and practical they are, for the aim of the punishment is to destroy vices and save men. The criminals are treated so that they become good of necessity, and for the rest of their lives they atone for the wrong they have done before. There is so little danger of relapse that travelers going from one part of the country to another think slaves the most reliable guides, changing them at the boundary of each district. The slaves have no means of committing robbery, since they are unarmed, and any money in their possession is evidence of a crime. If caught, they would be punished, and there is no hope of escape anywhere. Since every bit of a slave's clothing is unlike the usual clothing of the country, how could a slave escape, unless he fled naked? Even then his cropped ear would give him away. Might not the slaves form a conspiracy against the government? Perhaps. But the slaves of one district could hardly expect to succeed unless they first involved in their plot the slave-gangs of many other districts.

And that is impossible, since they are not allowed to meet or talk together or even to greet one another. No one would risk a plot when they all know joining is so dangerous to the participant and betrayal so profitable to the informer. Besides, no one is quite without hope of gaining his freedom eventually if he accepts his punishment in the spirit of obedience and patience, and gives promise of future good conduct. Indeed, every year some are pardoned as a reward for their submissive behavior.'

"When I had finished this account, I added that I saw no reason why this system could not be adopted even in England, and with much greater advantage than the 'justice' which my legal antagonist had praised so highly. But the lawyer replied that such a system could never be established in England without putting the commonwealth in serious peril. And so saying, he shook his head, made a wry face, and fell silent. And all the company sided with him.

"Then the cardinal remarked, 'It is not easy to guess whether this scheme would work well or not, since nobody has yet tried it out. But perhaps when the death sentence has been passed on a thief, the king might reprieve him for a time without right of sanctuary,[3] and thus see how the plan worked. If it turned out well, then he might establish it by law; if not, he could execute immediate punishment on the man formerly condemned. This would be neither less nor more unjust than if the condemned man had been put to death at once, and the experiment would involve no risk. I think vagabonds too might be treated this way, for though we have passed many laws against them, they have had no real effect as yet.'

"When the cardinal had concluded, they all began praising enthusiastically ideas which they had received with contempt when I suggested them; and they particularly liked the idea about vagabonds, because it was the cardinal's addition.

"I don't know whether it is worthwhile telling what followed, because it was silly, but I'll tell it anyhow, for there's no harm in it, and it bears on our subject. There was a hanger-on standing around, who was so good at playing the fool that you could hardly tell him from the real thing. He was constantly making jokes, but so awkwardly that we laughed more at him than at them; yet sometimes a rather clever thing came out, confirming the old proverb that a man who throws the dice often will sooner or later make a lucky cast. One of the company happened to say that in my speech I had taken care of the thieves, and the cardinal had taken care of the vagabonds, so now all that was left to do was to take care of the poor whom sickness or old age had reduced to poverty and kept from earning a living.

"'Leave that to me,' said the fool, 'and I'll set it right at once. These are people I'm eager to get out of my sight, having been so often vexed with them and their woeful complaints. No matter how pitifully they beg for money, they've never whined a single penny out of my pocket. They can't win with me: either I don't want to give them anything, or I haven't anything to give them. Now they're getting wise; they know me so well, they don't waste their breath, but let me pass without a word or a hope—no more, by heaven, than if I were a priest. But I would make a law sending all these beggars to Benedictine monasteries,[4] where the men could become lay brothers, as they're called, and the women could be nuns.'

3. In certain cases, criminals could seek refuge from the law in a church.
4. Benedictines were a very strict monastic order.

"The cardinal smiled and passed it off as a joke; the rest took it seriously. But a certain friar, a theologian, took such pleasure in this jest at the expense of priests and monks that he too began to make merry, though generally he was grave to the point of sourness. 'Even so, you will not get rid of the beggars,' he began, 'unless you take care of us friars too.'

"'You have been taken care of already,' retorted the fool. 'The cardinal provided for you splendidly when he said vagabonds should be arrested and put to work, for you friars are the greatest vagabonds of all.'[5]

"When the company, watching the cardinal closely, saw that he admitted this jest like the other, they all took it up with vigor—except for the friar. He, as you can easily imagine, was stung by the vinegar, and flew into such a rage that he could not keep from abusing the fool. He called him a knave, a slanderer, a sneak, and a 'son of perdition,' quoting the meanwhile terrible denunciations from Holy Scripture. Now the joker began to jest in earnest, for he was clearly on his own ground.

"'Don't get angry, good friar,' he said, 'for it is written, "In your patience possess ye your souls."'[6]

"In reply, the friar said, and I quote his very words, 'I am not angry, you gallowsbird, or at least I do not sin, for the psalmist says, "Be ye angry, and sin not."'[7]

"At this point the cardinal gently cautioned the friar to calm down, but he answered: 'No, my lord, I speak only from righteous zeal, as I ought to. For holy men have had great zeal. That is why Scripture says, "the zeal of thine house hath eaten me up," and we sing in church, "those who mocked Elisha as he went up to the house of God, felt the zeal of the baldhead,"[8] just as this mocker, this rascal, this guttersnipe may very well feel it.'

"'Perhaps you mean well,' said the cardinal, 'but you would act in a holier, and certainly in a wiser way, if you didn't set your wit against a fool's wit and try to spar with a buffoon.'

"'No, my lord,' he replied, 'I would not act more wisely. For Solomon himself, the wisest of men, said, "Answer a fool according to his folly,"[9] and that's what I'm doing now. I am showing him the pit into which he will fall if he does not take care. For if the many mockers of Elisha, who was only one bald man, felt the effects of his zeal, how much more effect shall be felt by a single mocker of many friars, who include a great many baldheads! And besides, we have a papal bull, by which all who mock us are excommunicated.'

"When the cardinal saw there was no end to the matter, he nodded to the fool to leave, and turned the conversation to another subject. Soon after, he rose from table, and, going to hear petitioners, dismissed us.

"Look, my dear More, what a long story I have inflicted on you. I would be quite ashamed, if you had not yourself asked for it, and seemed to listen as if you did not want any part to be left out. Though I ought to have related this conversation more concisely, I did feel bound to recount it, so you might see how those who rejected what I said at first approved of it immediately afterward, when they saw the cardinal did not disapprove. In fact they went so far

---

5. Friars, unlike monks, did not live in a cloister.
6. Luke 21.19.
7. Psalms 4.4.

8. Psalms 69.9. In Kings 2.23, the children who mock the prophet Elijah are eaten by bears.
9. Proverbs 26.5.

in their flattery that they indulged and almost took seriously ideas that he tolerated only as the jesting of a fool. From this episode you can see how little courtiers would value me or my advice."

To this I answered, "You have given me great pleasure, my dear Raphael, for everything you've said has been both wise and witty. As you spoke, I seemed to be a child and in my own native land once more, through the pleasant recollection of that cardinal in whose court I was brought up as a lad. Dear as you are to me on other accounts, you cannot imagine how much dearer you are because you honor his memory so highly. Still, my friend Raphael, I don't give up my former opinion: I think if you could overcome your aversion to court life, your advice to a prince would be of the greatest advantage to the public welfare. This, after all, is the chief duty of every good man, including you. Your friend Plato thinks that commonwealths will become happy only when philosophers become kings or kings become philosophers.[1] No wonder we are so far from happiness, when philosophers do not condescend even to assist kings with their counsels."

"They are not so ungracious," Raphael replied, "but that they would gladly do it; in fact, they have already done it in a great many published books, if the rulers would only read their good advice. But doubtless Plato was right in foreseeing that unless kings became philosophical themselves, they would never take the advice of real philosophers, drenched as they are and infected with false values from boyhood on. Plato certainly had this experience with Dionysius of Syracuse.[2] If I proposed wise laws to some king, and tried to root out of his soul the seeds of evil and corruption, don't you suppose I would be either banished forthwith, or treated with scorn?

"Imagine, if you will, that I am at the court of the king of France. Suppose I were sitting in his royal council, meeting in secret session with the king himself presiding, and all the cleverest councillors were hard at work devising a set of crafty machinations by which the king might keep hold of Milan, recover Naples, which has proved so slippery; then overthrow the Venetians and subdue all Italy;[3] next add Flanders, Brabant, and the whole of Burgundy to his realm, besides some other nations he has in mind to invade. One man urges him to make an alliance with the Venetians for just as long as the king finds it convenient—perhaps to develop a common strategy with them, and even allow them some of the loot, which can be recovered later when things work out according to plan. While one recommends hiring German mercenaries, his neighbor proposes paying the Swiss to stay neutral. A fourth voice suggests soothing the offended divinity of the emperor with an offering of gold. Still another, who is of a different mind, thinks a settlement should be made with the king of Aragon, and that, to cement the peace, he should be allowed to take Navarre from its proper ruler.[4] Meanwhile, someone suggests snaring the prince of Castille into a marriage alliance—a first step would be to buy up some nobles of his court with secret pensions.

"The hardest problem of all is what to do about England. They all agree that peace should be made, and that the alliance, which is weak at best, should be

1. Plato's *Republic*, like *Utopia*, imagines an ideal commonwealth.
2. Plato tried in vain to tutor the young ruler.
3. In this period, France, like Spain, attempted to gain control of Italy.
4. The mountain kingdom of Navarre had long been fought over by Spain and France.

strengthened as much as possible; but while the English are being treated as friends, they should also be suspected as enemies. And so the Scots must be kept in constant readiness, poised to attack the English in case they stir ever so little. Also a banished nobleman with some pretensions to the English throne must be secretly encouraged (there are treaties against doing it openly), and in this way pressure can be brought to bear on the English king, and a ruler kept in check who can't really be trusted.

"Now in a meeting like this one, where so much is at stake, where so many brilliant men are competing to think up intricate strategies of war, what if an insignificant fellow like me were to get up and advise going on another tack entirely? Suppose I said the king should leave Italy alone and stay at home, because the single kingdom of France all by itself is almost too much for one man to govern well, and the king should not dream of adding others to it? Then imagine I told about the decrees of the Achorians,[5] who live off the island of Utopia toward the southeast. Long ago, these people went to war to gain another realm for their king, who had inherited an ancient claim to it through marriage. When they had conquered it, they soon saw that keeping it was going to be as hard as getting it had been. The seeds of war were constantly sprouting, their new subjects were continually rebelling or being attacked by foreign invaders, the Achorians had to be constantly at war for them or against them, and they saw no hope of ever being able to disband their army. In the meantime, they were being heavily taxed, money flowed out of their kingdom, their blood was being shed for the advantage of others, and peace was no closer than it had ever been. The war corrupted their own citizens by encouraging lust for robbery and murder; and the laws fell into contempt because their king, distracted with the cares of two kingdoms, could give neither one his proper attention.

"When they saw that the list of these evils was endless, the Achorians took counsel together and very courteously offered their king his choice of keeping whichever of the two kingdoms he preferred, because he couldn't rule them both. They were too numerous a people, they said, to be ruled by half a king; and they added that a man would not even hire a muledriver, if he had to divide his services with somebody else. The worthy king was thus obliged to be content with his own realm and give his new one to a friend, who before long was driven out.

"Finally, suppose I told the French king's council that all this warmongering, by which so many different nations were kept in turmoil as a result of one man's connivings, would exhaust his treasury and demoralize his people, and yet in the end come to nothing, through some mishap or other. And therefore he should look after his ancestral kingdom, improve it as much as he could, cultivate it in every conceivable way. He should love his people and be loved by them; he should live among them, govern them kindly, and let other kingdoms alone, since his own is big enough, if not too big, for him. How do you think, my dear More, the other councillors would take this speech of mine?"

"Not very well, I'm sure," said I.

"Well, let's go on," he said. "Suppose the councillors of some other king are discussing various schemes for raising money to fill his treasury. One man

5. From the Greek, *a* ("without") and *chora* ("place"): "people from nowhere."

recommends increasing the value of money when the king pays his debts and devaluing it when he collects his revenues. Thus he can discharge a huge debt with a small payment, and collect a large sum when only a small one is due him. Another suggests a make-believe war, so that money can be raised under pretext of carrying it on; then, when the money is in, he can conclude a ceremonious peace treaty—which the deluded common people will attribute to the piety of their prince and his careful compassion for the lives of his subjects. Another councillor calls to mind some old motheaten laws, antiquated by long disuse, which no one remembers being made and consequently everyone has transgressed. By imposing fines for breaking these laws, the king will get great sums of money, as well as credit for upholding law and order, since the whole procedure can be made to look like justice. Another recommendation is that he forbid under particularly heavy fines a lot of practices that are contrary to the public interest; afterward, he can dispense with his own rules for large sums of money. Thus he pleases the people and makes a double profit, one from the heavy fines imposed on lawbreakers, and the other from selling dispensations. Meanwhile he seems careful of his people's welfare, since it is plain he will not allow private citizens to do anything contrary to the public interest, except for a huge price.

"Another councillor proposes that he work on the judges so that they will decide every case in favor of the king. They should be summoned to court often, and invited to debate his affairs in the royal presence. However unjust his claims, one or another of the judges, whether from love of contradiction, or desire to seem original, or simply to serve his own interest, will be bound to find some way of twisting the law in the king's favor. If the judges can be brought to differ, then the clearest matter in the world will be obscured, and the truth itself brought into question. The king is given leverage to interpret the law as he will, and everyone else will acquiesce from shame or fear. The judges will have no hesitation about supporting the royal interest, for there are always plenty of pretexts for giving judgment in favor of the king. Either equity is on his side, or the letter of the law happens to make for him, or the words of the law can be twisted into obscurity—or, if all else fails, he can appeal above the law to the royal prerogative, which is a never-failing argument with judges who know their 'duty.'

"Then all the councillors agree with the famous maxim of Crassus:[6] a king can never have too much gold, because he must maintain an army. Further, that a king, even if he wants to, can do no wrong, for all property belongs to the king, and so do his subjects themselves; a man owns nothing but what the king, in his goodness, sees fit to leave him. The king should in fact leave his subjects as little as possible, because his own safety depends on keeping them from growing insolent with wealth and freedom. For riches and liberty make people less patient to endure harsh and unjust commands, whereas meager poverty blunts their spirits, makes them docile, and grinds out of the oppressed the lofty spirit of rebellion.

"Now at this point, suppose I were to get up again and declare that all these counsels are both dishonorable and ruinous to the king? Suppose I said his

6. A rich Roman general and statesman.

honor and his safety alike rest on the people's resources rather than his own? Suppose I said that the people choose a king for their own sake, not for his, so that by his efforts and troubles they may live in comfort and safety? This is why, I would say, it is the king's duty to take more care of his people's welfare than of his own, just as it is the duty of a shepherd who cares about his job to feed his sheep rather than himself.

"They are absolutely wrong when they say that the people's poverty safeguards public peace—experience shows the contrary. Where will you find more squabbling than among beggars? Who is more eager for revolution than the man who is most discontented with his present position? Who is more reckless about creating disorder than the man who knows he has nothing to lose and thinks he may have something to gain? If a king is so hated or despised by his subjects that he can rule them only by mistreatment, plundering, confiscation, and pauperization of his people, then he'd do much better to abdicate his throne—for under these circumstances, though he keeps the name of authority, he loses all the majesty of a king. A king has no dignity when he exercises authority over beggars, only when he rules over prosperous and happy subjects. This was certainly what that noble and lofty spirit Fabricius meant when he said he would rather be a ruler of rich men than be rich himself.

"A solitary ruler who enjoys a life of pleasure and self-indulgence while all about him are grieving and groaning is acting like a jailer, not a king. Just as an incompetent doctor can cure his patient of one disease only by throwing him into another, so it's an incompetent king who can rule his people only by depriving them of all life's pleasures. Such a king openly confesses that he does not know how to rule free men.

"A king of this stamp should correct his own sloth or arrogance, because these are the vices that cause people to hate or despise him. Let him live on his own income without wronging others, and limit his spending to his income. Let him curb crime, and by wise training of his subjects keep them from misbehavior, instead of letting it breed and then punishing it. Let him not suddenly revive antiquated laws, especially if they have been long forgotten and never missed. And let him never take money as a fine when a judge would regard an ordinary subject as a low fraud for claiming it.

"Suppose I should then describe for them the law of the Macarians,[7] a people who also live not far from Utopia? On the day that their king first assumes office, he must take an oath confirmed by solemn ceremonies that he will never have in his treasury at any one time more than a thousand pounds in gold, or its equivalent in silver. They say this law was made by an excellent king, who cared more for his country's prosperity than for his own wealth; he established it as a barrier against any king heaping up so much money as to impoverish his people. He thought this sum would enable the king to put down rebellions or repel hostile invasions, but would not tempt him into aggressive adventures. His law was aimed chiefly at keeping the king in check, but he also wanted to ensure an ample supply of money for the daily business transactions of the citizens. Besides, a king who has to distribute all his excess money to the people will not be much disposed to seek out opportunities for extortion. Such a king will be both a terror to evildoers and beloved by the good.—Now, don't

7. From the Greek *makarios*, "fortunate."

you suppose if I set such ideas before men strongly inclined to the contrary, they would turn deaf ears to me?"

"Stone deaf, indeed, there's no doubt about it," I said, "and no wonder! To tell you the truth, I don't think you should offer advice or thrust on people ideas of this sort, that you know will not be listened to. What good can it do? When your listeners are already prepossessed against you and firmly convinced of opposite opinions, how can you win over their minds with such out-of-the-way speeches? This academic philosophy is quite agreeable in the private conversation of close friends, but in the councils of kings, where grave matters are being authoritatively decided, there is no place for it."

"That is just what I was saying," Raphael replied. "There is no place for philosophy in the councils of kings."

"Yes, there is," I said, "but not for this school philosophy which supposes that every topic is suitable for every occasion. There is another philosophy that is better suited for political action, that takes its cue, adapts itself to the drama in hand, and acts its part neatly and appropriately. This is the philosophy for you to use. Otherwise, when a comedy of Plautus is being played, and the household slaves are cracking trivial jokes together, you propose to come on stage in the garb of a philosopher and repeat Seneca's speech to Nero from the *Octavia*.[8] Wouldn't it be better to take a silent role than to say something wholly inappropriate, and thus turn the play into a tragicomedy? You pervert and ruin a play when you add irrelevant speeches, even if they are better than the original. So go through with the drama in hand as best you can, and don't spoil it all simply because you happen to think of a play by someone else that would be better.

"That's how things go in the commonwealth, and in the councils of princes. If you cannot pluck up bad ideas by the root, if you cannot cure long-standing evils as completely as you would like, you must not therefore abandon the commonwealth. Don't give up the ship in a storm because you cannot hold back the winds. And don't force strange ideas on people who you know have set their minds on a different course from yours. You must strive to influence policy indirectly, handle the situation tactfully, and thus what you cannot turn to good, you may at least make as little bad as possible. For it is impossible to make everything good unless you make all men good, and that I don't expect to see for a long time to come."

"The only result of this," he answered, "will be that while I try to cure others of madness, I'll be raving along with them myself. If I am to speak the truth, I will simply have to talk in the way I have described. For all I know, it may be the business of a philosopher to tell lies, but it certainly isn't mine. Though my advice may be repugnant and irksome to the king's councillors, I don't see why they should consider it eccentric to the point of folly. What if I told them the kind of thing that Plato advocates in his republic, or that the Utopians actually practice in theirs? However superior those institutions might be (and as a matter of fact they are), yet here they would seem inappropriate, because private property is the rule here, and there all things are held in common.

---

8. The Roman playwright Plautus wrote comedies, while the tragedian and philosopher Seneca is associated with high seriousness.

"People who have made up their minds to rush headlong down the opposite road are never pleased with someone who calls them back and tells them they are on the wrong course. But, apart from that, what did I say that could not and should not be said anywhere and everywhere? If we dismiss as out of the question and absurd everything which the perverse customs of men have made to seem alien to us, we shall have to set aside most of the commandments of Christ, even in a community of Christians. Yet he forbade us to dissemble them, and even ordered that what he had whispered to his disciples should be preached openly from the housetops. Most of his teachings differ more radically from the common customs of mankind than my discourse did. But preachers, like the crafty fellows they are, have found that people would rather not change their lives to conform to Christ's rule, and so, just as you suggest, they have accommodated his teaching to the way people live, as if it were a leaden yardstick.[9] At least in that manner they can get the two things to correspond in some way or other. The only real thing they accomplish that I can see is to make people feel more secure about doing evil.

"And this is all that I could accomplish in the councils of princes. For either I would have different ideas from the others, and that would come to the same thing as having no ideas at all, or else I would agree with them, and that, as Mitio says in Terence, would merely confirm them in their madness.[1] When you say I should 'influence policy indirectly,' I simply don't know what you mean; remember, you said I should try hard to handle the situation tactfully, and what can't be made good I should try to make as little bad as possible. In a council, there is no way to dissemble, no way to shut your eyes to things. You must openly approve the worst proposals, and consent to the most vicious policies. A man who went along only halfheartedly even with the worst decisions would immediately get himself a name as a spy and perhaps a traitor. How can one individual do any good when he is surrounded by colleagues who would more readily corrupt the best of men than do any reforming of themselves? Either they will seduce you by their evil ways or, if you keep yourself honest and innocent, you will be made a screen for the knavery and folly of others. Influencing policy indirectly! You wouldn't have a chance.

"This is why Plato in a very fine comparison declares that wise men are right in keeping clear of public business. They see the people swarming through the streets and getting soaked with rain, and they cannot persuade them to go indoors and get out of the wet. They know if they go out themselves, they can do no good but only get drenched with the rest. So they stay indoors and are content to keep at least themselves dry, since they cannot remedy the folly of others.

"But as a matter of fact, my dear More, to tell you what I really think, as long as you have private property, and as long as money is the measure of all things, it is scarcely ever possible for a commonwealth to be just or happy. For justice cannot exist where all the best things in life are held by the worst people; nor can anyone be happy where property is limited to a few, since even those few are always uneasy, and the many are utterly wretched.

---

9. A flexible yardstick in ancient building, often used as a metaphor for flexible moral standards.

1. In a play by the Roman writer Terence, the slave Mitio claims that listening to his mad master will make him equally crazy.

"So I reflect on the wonderfully wise and sacred institutions of the Utopians, who are so well governed with so few laws. Among them virtue has its reward, yet everything is shared equally, and everyone lives in plenty. I contrast them with the many other nations, which are constantly passing new ordinances and yet can never order their affairs satisfactorily. In these other nations, whatever a man can get he calls his own private property; but all the mass of laws old and new don't enable him to secure his own, or defend it, or even distinguish it from someone else's property—as is shown by innumerable and interminable lawsuits, fresh ones every day. When I consider all these things, I become more sympathetic to Plato and do not wonder that he declined to make laws for any people who refused to share their goods equally.[2] Wisest of men, he saw easily that the one and only road to the welfare of all lies through the absolute equality of goods. I doubt whether such equality can ever be achieved where property belongs to individuals. However abundant goods may be, when everyone tries to get as much as he can for his own exclusive use, a handful of men end up sharing the whole pile, and the rest are left in poverty. The result generally is two sorts of people whose fortunes ought to be interchanged: the rich are rapacious, wicked, and useless, while the poor are unassuming, modest men who work hard, more for the benefit of the public than of themselves.

"Thus I am wholly convinced that unless private property is entirely done away with, there can be no fair or just distribution of goods, nor can the business of mortals be happily conducted. As long as private property remains, by far the largest and the best part of the human race will be oppressed by a heavy and inescapable burden of cares and anxieties. This load, I admit, may be lightened to some extent, but I maintain it cannot be entirely removed. Laws might be made that no one should own more than a certain amount of land or receive more than a certain income. Or laws might be passed to prevent the prince from becoming too powerful and the populace too unruly. It might be made unlawful for public offices to be solicited, or put up for sale, or made burdensome for the officeholder by great expense. Otherwise, officials are tempted to get their money back by fraud or extortion, and only rich men can afford to accept positions which ought to be held by the wise. Laws of this sort, I agree, may have as much effect as poultices continually applied to sick bodies that are past cure. The social evils I mentioned may be alleviated and their effects mitigated for a while, but so long as private property remains, there is no hope at all of effecting a cure and restoring society to good health. While you try to cure one part, you aggravate the disease in other parts. Suppressing one symptom causes another to break out, since you cannot give something to one person without taking it away from someone else."

"But I don't see it that way," I replied. "It seems to me that people cannot possibly live well where all things are in common. How can there be plenty of commodities where every man stops working? The hope of gain will not spur him on; he will rely on others, and become lazy. If men are driven by need, and yet cannot legally protect what they have gained, what can follow but continual bloodshed and turmoil, especially when respect for magistrates and their

2. Asked to legislate for a new city, Plato refused to do so unless property would be held in common.

authority has been lost? I for one cannot conceive of authority existing among men who are equal to one another in every respect."[3]

"I'm not surprised," said Raphael, "that you think of it this way, since you have no idea, or only a false idea, of such a commonwealth. But you should have been with me in Utopia, and seen with your own eyes their manners and customs as I did—for I lived there more than five years, and would never have left, if it had not been to make that new world known to others. If you had seen them, you would frankly confess that you had never seen a people well governed anywhere but there."

"You will have a hard time persuading me," said Peter Giles, "that people in that new land are better governed than in the world we know. Our minds are not inferior to theirs, and our governments, I believe, are older. Long experience has helped us develop many conveniences of life, and by good luck we have discovered many other things which human ingenuity could never have hit upon."

"As for the relative ages of the governments," Raphael replied, "you might judge more accurately if you had read their histories. If we believe these records, they had cities before there were even people here. What ingenuity has discovered or chance hit upon could have turned up just as well in one place as the other. For the rest, I believe that even if we surpass them in natural intelligence, they leave us far behind in their diligence and zeal to learn.

"According to their chronicles, they had heard nothing of ultraequatorials (that's their name for us) until we arrived, except that once, some twelve hundred years ago, a ship which a storm had blown toward Utopia was wrecked on their island. Some Romans and Egyptians were cast ashore, and never departed. Now note how the Utopians profited, through their diligence, from this one chance event. They learned every single useful art of the Roman empire either directly from their guests or indirectly from hints and surmises on which they based their own investigations. What benefits from the mere fact that on a single occasion some Europeans landed there! If a similar accident has hitherto brought anyone here from their land, the incident has been completely forgotten, as it will perhaps be forgotten in time to come that I was ever in their country. From one such accident they made themselves masters of all our useful inventions, but I suspect it will be a long time before we accept any of their institutions which are better than ours. This willingness to learn is, I think, the really important reason for their being better governed and living more happily than we do, though we are not inferior to them in brains or resources."

"Then let me implore you, my dear Raphael," said I, "to describe that island to us. Do not try to be brief, but explain in order everything relating to their land, their rivers, towns, people, manners, institutions, laws—everything, in short, that you think we would like to know. And you can take it for granted that we want to know everything that we don't know yet."

"There's nothing I'd rather do," he replied, "for these things are fresh in my mind. But it will take quite some time."

"In that case," I said, "let's first go to lunch. Afterward, we shall have all the time we want."

---

3. These objections are adapted from Aristotle's *Politics*, in which Aristotle challenges Plato's claims that common property solves social problems.

"Agreed," he said. So we went in and had lunch. Then we came back to the same spot, and sat down on the bench. I ordered my servants to take care that no one should interrupt us. Peter Giles and I urged Raphael to keep his promise. When he saw that we were attentive and eager to hear him, he sat silent and thoughtful a moment, and then began as follows.

Book II

[The Geography of Utopia]

The island of the Utopians is two hundred miles across in the middle part, where it is widest, and is nowhere much narrower than this except toward the two ends, where it gradually tapers. These ends, drawn toward one another as if in a five-hundred-mile circle, make the island crescent-shaped, like a new moon. Between the horns of the crescent, which are about eleven miles apart, the sea enters and spreads into a broad bay. Being sheltered from the wind by the surrounding land, the bay is never rough, but quiet and smooth instead, like a big lake. Thus nearly the whole inner coast is one great harbor, across which ships pass in every direction, to the great advantage of the people. What with shallows on one side and rocks on the other, the entrance into the bay is perilous. Near the middle of the channel, there is one rock that rises above the water, and so presents no danger in itself; on top of it a tower has been built, and there a garrison is kept. Since the other rocks lie underwater, they are very dangerous to navigation. The channels are known only to the Utopians, so hardly any strangers enter the bay without one of their pilots; and even they themselves could not enter safely if they did not direct their course by some landmarks on the coast. If these landmarks were shifted about, the Utopians could easily lure to destruction an enemy fleet coming against them, however big it was.

On the outer side of the island there are likewise occasional harbors; but the coast is rugged by nature, and so well fortified that a few defenders could beat off the attack of a strong force. They say (and the appearance of the place confirms this) that their land was not always an island. But Utopus, who conquered the country and gave it his name (it had previously been called Abraxa),[1] and who brought its rude and uncouth inhabitants to such a high level of culture and humanity that they now excel in that regard almost every other people, also changed its geography. After winning the victory at his first landing, he cut a channel fifteen miles wide where their land joined the continent, and caused the sea to flow around the country. He put not only the natives to work at this task, but all his own soldiers too, so that the vanquished would not think the labor a disgrace. With the work divided among so many hands, the project was finished quickly, and the neighboring peoples, who at first had laughed at his folly, were struck with wonder and terror at his success.

There are fifty-four cities on the island, all spacious and magnificent, identical in language, customs, institutions, and laws. So far as the location permits,

1. A mysterious name from Gnostic cosmology.

all of them are built on the same plan and have the same appearance. The nearest are twenty-four miles apart, and the farthest are not so remote that a person cannot go on foot from one to the other in a day.

Once a year each city sends three of its old and experienced citizens to Amaurot[2] to consider affairs of common interest to the island. Amaurot lies at the navel of the land, so to speak, and is convenient to every other district, so it acts as a capital. Every city has enough ground assigned to it so that at least twelve miles of farm land are available in every direction, though where the cities are farther apart, they have much more land. No city wants to enlarge its boundaries, for the inhabitants consider themselves good tenants rather than landlords. At proper intervals all over the countryside they have built houses and furnished them with farm equipment. These houses are inhabited by citizens who come to the country by turns. No rural household has fewer than forty men and women in it, besides two slaves bound to the land. A master and mistress, serious and mature persons, are in charge of each household. Over every thirty households is placed a single phylarch.[3] Each year twenty persons from each household move back to the city, after completing a two-year stint in the country. In their place, twenty others are sent out from town, to learn farm work from those who have already been in the country for a year and are therefore better skilled in farming. They, in turn, will teach those who come the following year. If all were equally unskilled in farm work, and new to it, they might harm the crops out of ignorance. This custom of alternating farm workers is the usual procedure, so that no one will have to do such hard work unwillingly for more than two years; but many of them, who take a natural pleasure in farm life, are allowed to stay longer.

The farm workers till the soil, feed the animals, hew wood, and take it to the city by land or by water, as is more convenient. They breed an enormous number of chickens by a marvelous method. The farmers, not hens, hatch the eggs, by keeping them in a warm place at an even temperature. As soon as they come out of the shell, the chicks recognize the humans, follow them around, and are devoted to them instead of to their mothers.

They raise very few horses, and those full of mettle, which they keep only to exercise the young people in the art of horsemanship. For all the work of plowing and hauling they use oxen, which they agree are inferior to horses over the short haul, but which can hold out longer under heavy burdens, are less subject to disease (as they suppose), and can be kept with less cost and trouble. Moreover, when oxen are too old for work, they can be used for meat.

Grain they use only to make bread. They drink wine, apple or pear cider, or simple water, which they sometimes boil with honey or licorice, of which they have an abundance. Although they know very well, down to the last detail, how much food each city and its surrounding district will consume, they produce much more grain and cattle than they need for themselves, and share the surplus with their neighbors. Whatever goods the folk in the country need which cannot be produced there, they request of the town magistrates, and since there is nothing to be paid or exchanged, they get what they want without any trouble. They generally go to town once a month in any case, for the feast day.

---

2. Dark city (Greek).   3. Head of a tribe (Greek).

When harvest time approaches, the phylarchs in the country notify the town magistrates how many hands will be needed. Crews of harvesters come just when they're wanted, and in one day of good weather they can usually get in the whole crop.

Their Cities, Especially Amaurot

If you know one of their cities, you know them all, for they're exactly alike, except where geography itself makes a difference. So I'll describe one of them, and no matter which. But what one rather than Amaurot, the most worthy of all?—since its eminence is acknowledged by the other cities, which send representatives to the annual meeting there; besides which, I know it best, because I lived there for five full years.

Well, then, Amaurot lies up against a gently sloping hill; the town is almost square in shape. From a little below the crest of the hill, it runs down about two miles to the river Anyder,[4] and then spreads out along the river bank for a somewhat greater distance. The Anyder rises from a small spring about eighty miles above Amaurot, but other streams flow into it, two of them being pretty big, so that, as it runs past Amaurot, the river has grown to a width of five hundred yards. It continues to grow even larger until at last, sixty miles farther along, it is lost in the ocean. In all this stretch between the sea and the city, and also for some miles above the city, the river is tidal, ebbing and flowing every six hours with a swift current. When the tide comes in, it fills the whole Anyder with salt water for about thirty miles, driving the fresh water back. Even above that, for several miles farther, the water is brackish; but a little higher up, as it runs past the city, the water is always fresh, and when the tide ebbs, the river runs clean and sweet all the way to the sea.

The two banks of the river at Amaurot are linked by a bridge, built not on wooden piles but on remarkable stone arches. It is placed at the upper end of the city, farthest removed from the sea, so that ships can sail along the entire length of the city quays without obstruction. There is also another stream, not particularly large, but very gentle and pleasant, which gushes from the hill on which the city is situated, flows down through the center of town, and into the Anyder. The inhabitants have walled around the source of this river, which takes its rise a little outside the town, and joined it to the town proper so that if they should be attacked, the enemy would not be able to cut off the stream or divert or poison it. Water from the stream is carried by tile piping into various sections of the lower town. Where the terrain makes this impractical, they collect rain water in cisterns, which serve just as well.

The town is surrounded by a thick, high wall, with many towers and bastions. On three sides it is also surrounded by a dry ditch, broad and deep and filled with thorn hedges; on its fourth side the river itself serves as a moat. The streets are conveniently laid out for use by vehicles and for protection from the wind. Their buildings are by no means shabby; unbroken rows of houses face each other across the streets along the whole block. The streets are twenty feet

4. Waterless (Greek).

wide. Behind each row of houses—at the center of every block and extending the full length of the street—there are large gardens.

Every house has a door to the street and another to the garden. The doors, which are made with two leaves, open easily and swing shut automatically, letting anyone enter who wants to—so there is nothing private anywhere. Every ten years, they change houses by lot. The Utopians are very fond of these gardens of theirs. They raise vines, fruits, herbs, and flowers, so well cared for and flourishing that I have never seen any gardens more productive or elegant than theirs. They keep interested in gardening, partly because they delight in it, and also because of the competition between different blocks, which challenge one another to produce the best gardens. Certainly you will not easily find anything else in the whole city more useful or more pleasant to the citizens. And this gives reason to think that the founder of the city paid particular attention to the siting of these gardens.

They say that in the beginning the whole city was planned by Utopus himself, but that he left to posterity matters of adornment and improvement such as could not be perfected in one man's lifetime. Their records began 1,760 years ago with the conquest of the island, have been diligently compiled, and are carefully preserved. From these it appears that the first houses were low, like cabins or peasant huts, built out of any sort of timber, with mud-plastered walls and pointed roofs thatched with straw. But now their houses are all three stories high and handsomely constructed; the fronts are faced with fieldstone, quarried rock, or brick, over rubble construction. The roofs are flat, and are covered with a kind of plaster that is cheap but fireproof, and more weather-resistant even than lead. Glass (which is plentiful there) is used in windows to keep out the weather; and they also use thin linen cloth treated with oil or gum so that it lets in more light and keeps out more wind.

Their Officials

Once a year, every group of thirty households elects an official, formerly called the syphogrant, but now called the phylarch. Over every group of ten syphogrants with their households there is another official, once called the tranibor[5] but now known as the head phylarch. All the syphogrants, two hundred in number, elect the governor. They take an oath to choose the man they think best qualified; and then by secret ballot they elect the governor from among four men nominated by the people of the four sections of the city. The governor holds office for life, unless he is suspected of aiming at a tyranny. Though the tranibors are elected annually, they are not changed for light or casual reasons. All their other officials hold office for a single year only.

The tranibors meet to consult with the governor every other day, and more often if necessary: they discuss affairs of state, and settle any disputes between private parties (there are very few), acting as quickly as possible. The tranibors always invite two syphogrants to the senate chamber, different ones every day. There is a rule that no decision can be made on a matter of public business unless it has been discussed in the senate on three separate days. It is a capital offense to make plans about public business outside of the senate or the popular

---

5. Neither *syphogrant* nor *tranibor* have any clear meaning or etymology.

assembly.[6] The purpose of these rules, they say, is to prevent the governor and the tranibors from conspiring together to alter the government and enslave the people. Therefore all matters which are considered important are first laid before the assembly of the syphogrants. They talk the matter over with the households they represent, debate it with one another, then report their recommendation to the senate. Sometimes a question is brought before the general council of the whole island.

The senate also has a standing rule never to discuss a matter on the day when it is first introduced; all new business is deferred to the next meeting. They do this so that a man will not blurt out the first thought that occurs to him, and then devote all his energies to defending those foolish impulses, instead of considering impartially the public good. They know that some men would rather jeopardize the general welfare than admit to having been heedless and shortsighted—so perverse and preposterous is their sense of pride. They should have had enough foresight at the beginning to speak with prudence rather than haste.

Their Occupations

Agriculture is the one occupation at which everyone works, men and women alike, with no exceptions. They are trained in it from childhood, partly in the schools, where they learn theory, and partly through field trips to nearby farms, which make something like a game of practical instruction. On these trips they not only watch the work being done, but frequently pitch in and get a workout by doing the jobs themselves.

Besides farm work (which, as I said, everybody performs), each person is taught a particular trade of his own, such as wool-working, linen-making, masonry, metal-work, or carpentry. There is no other craft that is practiced by any considerable number of them. Throughout the island people wear, and throughout their lives always wear, the same style of clothing, except for the distinction between the sexes, and between married and unmarried persons. Their clothing is attractive, does not hamper bodily movement, and serves for warm as well as cold weather; what is more, each household makes its own.

Every person (and this includes women as well as men) learns a second trade, besides agriculture. As the weaker sex, women practice the lighter crafts, such as working in wool or linen; the heavier jobs are assigned to the men. As a rule, the son is trained to his father's craft, for which most feel a natural inclination. But if anyone is attracted to another occupation, he is transferred by adoption into a family practicing the trade he prefers. Both his father and the authorities make sure that he is assigned to a grave and responsible householder. After someone has learned one trade, if he wants to learn another he gets the same permission. When he has learned both, he pursues whichever he likes better, unless the city needs one more than the other.

The chief and almost the only business of the syphogrants is to manage matters so that no one sits around in idleness, and assure that everyone works hard at his trade. But no one has to exhaust himself with endless toil from early morning to late at night, as if he were a beast of burden. Such wretchedness,

6. The fear of conspiracy may explain the severity of the prohibition.

really worse than slavery, is the common lot of workmen almost everywhere except Utopia. Of the day's twenty-four hours, the Utopians devote only six to work. They work three hours before noon, when they go to lunch. After lunch they rest for a couple of hours, then go to work for another three hours. Then they have supper, and at eight o'clock (counting the first hour after noon as one) they go to bed, and sleep eight hours.

The other hours of the day, when they are not working, eating, or sleeping, are left to each person's individual discretion, provided that free time is not wasted in roistering or sloth but used properly in some chosen occupation. Generally these periods are devoted to intellectual activity. For they have an established custom of giving daily public lectures before dawn;[7] attendance at these lectures is required only of those who have been specially chosen to devote themselves to learning, but a great many other people, both men and women, choose voluntarily to attend. Depending on their interests, some go to one lecture, some to another. But if anyone would rather devote his spare time to his trade, as many do who don't care for the intellectual life, this is not discouraged; in fact, such persons are commended as especially useful to the commonwealth.

After supper, they devote an hour to recreation, in their gardens in summer, or during winter in the common halls where they have their meals. There they either play music or amuse themselves with conversation. They know nothing about gambling with dice, or other such foolish and ruinous games. They do play two games not unlike chess. One is a battle of numbers, in which one number captures another. The other is a game in which the vices fight a battle against the virtues. The game is ingeniously set up to show how the vices oppose one another, yet combine against the virtues; then, what vices oppose what virtues, how they try to assault them openly or undermine them insidiously; how the defenses of the virtues can break the strength of the vices or skillfully elude their plots; and finally, by what means one side or the other gains the victory.

But in all this, you may get a wrong impression, if we don't go back and consider one point more carefully. Because they allot only six hours to work, you might think the necessities of life would be in scant supply. This is far from the case. Their working hours are ample to provide not only enough but more than enough of the necessities and even the conveniences of life. You will easily appreciate this if you consider how large a part of the population in other countries exists without doing any work at all. In the first place, hardly any of the women, who are a full half of the population, work; or, if they do, then as a rule their husbands lie snoring in bed. Then there is a great lazy gang of priests and so-called religious. Add to them all the rich, especially the landlords, who are commonly called gentlemen and nobles. Include with them their retainers, that mob of swaggering bullies. Finally, reckon in with these the sturdy and lusty beggars who go about feigning some disease as an excuse for their idleness. You will certainly find that the things which satisfy our needs are produced by far fewer hands than you had supposed.

And now consider how few of those who do work are doing really essential things. For where money is the standard of everything, many vain, superfluous

---

7. Renaissance universities held lectures at dawn, or even earlier.

trades are bound to be carried on simply to satisfy luxury and licentiousness. Suppose the multitude of those who now work were limited to a few trades, and set to producing just those commodities that nature really requires. They would be bound to produce so much that prices would drop and the workmen would be unable to gain a living. But suppose again that all the workers in useless trades were put to useful ones, and that all the idlers (who now guzzle twice as much as the workingmen who make what they consume) were assigned to productive tasks—well, you can easily see how little time would be enough and more than enough to produce all the goods that human needs and conveniences require— yes, and human pleasure too, as long as it's true and natural pleasure.

The experience of Utopia makes this perfectly apparent. In each city and its surrounding countryside barely five hundred of those men and women whose age and strength make them fit for work are exempted from it. Among these are the syphogrants, who by law are free not to work; yet they don't take advantage of the privilege, preferring to set a good example to their fellow citizens. Some others are permanently exempted from work so that they may devote themselves to study, but only on the recommendation of the priests and through a secret vote of the syphogrants. If any of these scholars disappoints their hopes, he becomes a workman again. On the other hand, it happens from time to time that a craftsman devotes his leisure so earnestly to study, and makes such progress as a result, that he is relieved of manual labor and promoted to the class of learned men. From this class of scholars are chosen ambassadors, priests, tranibors, and the governor himself, who used to be called Barzanes, but in their modern tongue is known as Ademus.[8] Since almost all the rest of the population is neither idle nor occupied in useless trades, it is easy to see why they produce so much in so short a working day.

Apart from all this, in several of the necessary crafts their way of life requires less total labor than does that of people elsewhere. In other countries, building and repairing houses requires the constant work of many men, because what a father has built, his thriftless heir lets fall into ruin; and then his successor has to repair, at great expense, what could easily have been maintained at a very small charge. Further, when a man has built a splendid house at vast cost, someone else may think he has finer taste, let the first house fall to ruin, and then build another one somewhere else for just as much money. But among the Utopians, where everything has been well ordered and the commonwealth properly established, building a brand-new home on a new site is a rare event. They are not only quick to repair damage, but foresighted in preventing it. The result is that their buildings last for a very long time with minimal repairs; and the carpenters and masons sometimes have so little to do that they are set to hewing timber and cutting stone in case some future need for it should arise.

Consider, too, how little labor their clothing requires. Their work clothes are unpretentious garments made of leather, which last seven years. When they go out in public, they cover these rough working-clothes with a cloak. Throughout the entire island, these cloaks are of the same color, which is that of natural wool. As a result, they not only need less wool than people in other countries, but what they do need is less expensive. Even so, they use linen cloth most,

8. Without people (Greek). "Barzanes": the name of a Persian governor in the age of Alexander the Great (4th century B.C.E.).

because it requires least labor. They like linen cloth to be white and wool cloth to be clean; but they put no price on fineness of texture. Elsewhere a man may not be satisfied with four or five woolen cloaks of different colors and as many silk shirts; or if he's a clotheshorse, even ten are not enough. But there everyone is content with a single cloak, and generally wears it for two years. There is no reason at all why he should want any others, for if he had them, he would not be better protected against the cold, nor would he appear in any way better dressed.

Since there is an abundance of everything, as a result of everyone working at useful trades and the trades requiring less work, they sometimes assemble great numbers of people to work on the roads, if any of them need repairing. And when there is no need even for this sort of work, then the officials very often proclaim a shorter workday, since they never force their citizens to perform useless labor. The chief aim of their constitution is that, whenever public needs permit, all citizens should be free to withdraw as much time as possible from the service of the body and devote themselves to the freedom and culture of the mind. For in that, they think, is the real happiness of life.

Social Relations

Now I must explain how the citizens behave toward one another, the nature of their social relations, and how they distribute their goods within the society.

Each city, then, consists of households, the households consisting generally of blood-relations. When the women grow up and are married, they move into their husbands' households. On the other hand, male children and after them grandchildren remain in the family, and are subject to the oldest member, unless his mind has started to fail, in which case the next oldest takes his place. To keep the cities from becoming too large or too small, they take care that there should be no more than six thousand households in each (exclusive of the surrounding countryside), each family containing between ten and sixteen adults. They do not, of course, try to regulate the number of minor children in a family. The limit on adults is easily observed by transferring individuals from a household with too many into a household with not enough. Likewise if a city has too many people, the extra persons serve to make up a shortage of population in other cities. And if the population throughout the entire island exceeds the quota, they enroll citizens out of every city and plant a colony under their own laws on the mainland near them, wherever the natives have plenty of unoccupied and uncultivated land. Those natives who want to live with the Utopian settlers are taken in. When such a merger occurs, the two peoples gradually and easily blend together, sharing the same way of life and customs, much to the advantage of both. For by their policies the Utopians make the land yield an abundance for all, though previously it had seemed too poor and barren even to support the natives. But if the natives will not join in living under their laws, the Utopians drive them out of the land they claim for themselves, and if they resist make war on them. They think it is perfectly justifiable to make war on people who leave their land idle and waste, yet forbid the use of it to others who, by the law of nature, ought to be supported from it.[9]

9. The doctrine of *res nullius* ("that which belongs to nobody," Latin) was frequently invoked by English colonizers in Ireland and in North America to claim lands used by nomadic peoples.

If for any reason one of their cities shrinks so sharply in population that it cannot be made up from other cities without bringing them too under proper strength, the numbers are restored by bringing people back from the colonies. This has happened only twice, they say, in their whole history, both times as a result of a frightful plague. They would rather that their colonies disappeared than that any of the cities on their island should get too small.

But to return to their manner of living. The oldest of every household, as I said, is the ruler. Wives are subject to their husbands, children to their parents, and generally the younger to their elders. Every city is divided into four equal districts, and in the middle of each district is a market for all kinds of commodities. Whatever each household produces is brought here and stored in warehouses, each kind of goods in its own place. Here the head of each household looks for what he or his family needs, and carries off what he wants without any sort of payment or compensation. Why should anything be refused him? There is plenty of everything, and no reason to fear that anyone will claim more than he needs. Why would anyone be suspected of asking for more than is needed, when everyone knows there will never be any shortage? Fear of want, no doubt, makes every living creature greedy and rapacious—and, in addition, man develops these qualities out of sheer pride, pride which glories in getting ahead of others by a superfluous display of possessions. But this kind of vice has no place whatever in the Utopian way of life.

Next to the marketplace of which I just spoke are the food markets, where people bring all sorts of vegetables, fruit, and bread. Fish, meat, and poultry are also brought there from designated places outside the city, where running water can carry away all the blood and refuse. Bondsmen do the slaughtering and cleaning in these places: citizens are not allowed to do such work. The Utopians feel that slaughtering our fellow creatures gradually destroys the sense of compassion, which is the finest sentiment of which our human nature is capable. Besides, they don't allow anything dirty or filthy to be brought into the city, lest the air become tainted by putrefaction and thus infectious.

Each block has its own spacious halls, equally distant from one another, and each known by a special name. In these halls live the syphogrants. Thirty families are assigned to each hall, to take their meals in common—fifteen live on one side of the hall, fifteen on the other. The stewards of all the halls meet at a fixed time in the market and get food according to the number of persons for whom each is responsible.

But first consideration goes to the sick, who are cared for in public hospitals. Every city has four of these, built at the city limits, slightly outside the walls, and spacious enough to appear like little towns. The hospitals are large for two reasons: so that the sick, however numerous they may be, will not be packed closely and uncomfortably together, and also so that those who have a contagious disease, such as might pass from one to the other, may be isolated. The hospitals are well ordered and supplied with everything needed to cure the patients, who are nursed with tender and watchful care. Highly skilled physicians are in constant attendance. Consequently, though nobody is sent there against his will, there is hardly anyone in the city who would not rather be treated for an illness at the hospital than at home.

When the hospital steward has received the food prescribed for the sick by their doctors, the best of the remainder is fairly divided among the halls according to the number in each, except that special regard is paid to the governor, the high priest, and the tranibors, as well as to ambassadors and foreigners, if there are any. In fact, foreigners are very few; but when they do come, they have certain furnished houses assigned to them.

At the hours of lunch and supper, a brazen trumpet summons the entire syphogranty to assemble in their hall, except for those who are bedridden in the hospitals or at home. After the halls have been served with their quotas of food, nothing prevents an individual from taking food home from the marketplace. They realize that no one would do this without good reason. For while it is not forbidden to eat at home, no one does it willingly, because it is not thought proper; and besides, it would be stupid to take the trouble of preparing a worse meal at home when there is an elegant and sumptuous one near at hand in the hall.

In this hall, slaves do all the particularly dirty and heavy work. But planning the meal, as well as preparing and cooking the food, is carried out by the women alone, with each family taking its turn. Depending on their number, they sit down at three or more tables. The men sit with their backs to the wall, the women on the outside, so that if a woman has a sudden qualm or pain, such as occasionally happens during pregnancy, she may get up without disturbing the others and go off to the nurses.

A separate dining room is assigned to the nurses and infants, with a plentiful supply of cradles, clean water, and a warm fire. Thus the nurses may lay the infants down, or remove their swaddling clothes and let them refresh themselves by playing freely before the fire. Each child is nursed by its own mother, unless death or illness prevents. When that happens, the wives of the syphogrants quickly find a nurse. The problem is not difficult. Any woman who can, gladly volunteers for the job, since everyone applauds her kindness and the child itself regards its nurse as its natural mother.

Children under the age of five sit together in the nursery. All other minors, both boys and girls up to the age of marriage, either wait on table or, if not old and strong enough for that, stand by in absolute silence. Both groups eat whatever is handed to them by those sitting at the table, and have no other set time for their meals.

The syphogrant with his wife sits at the middle of the first table, in the highest part of the dining hall. This is the place of greatest honor, and from this table, which is placed crosswise to the others, the whole gathering can be seen. Two of the eldest sit with them, for they always sit in groups of four; if there is a church in the district, the priest and his wife sit with the syphogrant, so as to preside. On both sides of them sit younger people, next to them older people again, and so through the hall: those of about the same age sit together, yet are mingled with others of a different age. The reason for this, as they explain it, is that the dignity of the aged, and the respect due them, may restrain the younger people from improper freedom of words and gestures, since nothing said or done at table can pass unnoticed by the old, who are present on every side.

Dishes of food are not served down the tables in order from top to bottom, but all the old persons, who are seated in conspicuous places, are served with the best food; and then equal shares are given to the rest. The old people, as they feel inclined, give their neighbors a share of those delicacies which are not plentiful enough to be served to everyone. Thus due respect is paid to seniority, yet everyone enjoys some of the benefits.

They begin every lunch and supper with some reading on a moral topic, but keep it brief lest it become a bore. Taking that as an occasion, the elders introduce proper topics of conversation, which they try not to make gloomy or dull. They never monopolize the conversation with long monologues, but are eager to hear what the young people say. In fact, they deliberately draw them out, in order to discover the natural temper and quality of each one's mind, as revealed in the freedom of mealtime talk.

Their lunches are light, their suppers rather more elaborate, because lunch is followed by work, supper by rest and a night's sleep, which they think particularly helpful to good digestion. No evening meal passes without music, and the dessert course is never scanted; during the meal, they burn incense and scatter perfume, omitting nothing which will make the occasion festive. For they are somewhat inclined to think that no kind of pleasure is forbidden, provided harm does not come of it.

This is the pattern of life in the city; but in the country, where they are farther removed from neighbors, they all eat in their own homes. No family lacks for food, since, after all, whatever the city-dwellers eat comes originally from those in the country.

The Travels [and Trade] of the Utopians

Anyone who wants to visit friends in another city, or simply to see the place itself, can easily obtain permission from his syphogrant and tranibor, unless for some special reason he is needed at home. They travel together in groups, taking a letter from the governor granting leave to travel and fixing a day of return. They are given a wagon and a public slave to drive the oxen and look after them, but unless women are in the company they dispense with the wagon as an unnecessary bother. Wherever they go, though they take nothing with them, they never lack for anything, because they are at home everywhere. If they stay more than a day in one place, each one practices his trade there, and is kindly received by his fellow artisans.

Anyone who takes upon himself to leave his district without permission, and is caught without the governor's letter, is treated with contempt, brought back as a runaway, and severely punished. If he is bold enough to try it a second time, he is made a slave. Anyone who wants to stroll about and explore the extent of his own district is not prevented, provided he first obtains his father's permission and his wife's consent. But wherever he goes in the countryside, he gets no food until he has completed either a morning's or an afternoon's stint of work. On these terms, he may go where he pleases within his own district, yet be just as useful to the city as if he were at home.

So you see there is no chance to loaf or any pretext for evading work; there are no wine bars or alehouses or brothels, no chances for corruption, no hiding places, no spots for secret meetings. Because they live in the full view of all, they are bound to be either working at their usual trades or enjoying their leisure in a respectable way. Such customs must necessarily result in plenty of life's good things, and since they share everything equally, it follows that no one can ever be reduced to poverty or forced to beg.

In the senate at Amaurot (to which, as I said before, three representatives come every year from each city), they survey the island to find out where there are shortages and surpluses, and promptly satisfy one district's shortage with another's surplus. These are outright gifts; those who give receive nothing in return from those to whom they give. Though they give freely to one city, asking nothing in return, they get freely from another to which they gave nothing; and thus the whole island is like a single family.

After they have accumulated enough for themselves—and this they consider to be a full two-year's store, because next year's crop is always uncertain—then they export their surpluses to other countries: great quantities of grain, honey, wool, flax, timber, scarlet and purple dyestuffs, hides, wax, tallow, and leather, as well as livestock. One-seventh of their cargo they give freely to the poor of the importing country, and the rest they sell at moderate prices. In exchange they receive not only such goods as they lack at home (in fact, about the only important thing they lack is iron) but immense quantities of silver and gold. They have been carrying on trade for a long time now, and have accumulated a greater supply of the precious metals than you would believe possible. As a result, they now care very little whether they sell for cash or on credit, and most payments to them actually take the form of promissory notes. However, in all such transactions, they never trust individuals but insist that the foreign city become officially responsible. When the day of payment comes, the city collects the money due from private debtors, puts it into the treasury, and enjoys the use of it till the Utopians claim payment. Most of it, in fact, is never claimed. The Utopians think it hardly right to take what they don't need away from people who do need it. But if they need to lend some part of the money to another nation, then they call it in—as they do also when they must wage war. This is the only reason that they keep such an immense treasure at home, as a protection against extreme peril or sudden emergency. They use it above all to hire, at extravagant rates of pay, foreign mercenaries, whom they would much rather risk in battle than their own citizens. They know very well that for large enough sums of money many of the enemy's soldiers can themselves be bought off or set at odds with one another, either secretly or openly.

[Their Attitude to Gold and Silver]

For this reason, therefore, they have accumulated a vast treasure; but they do not keep it like a treasure. I'm really quite ashamed to tell you how they do keep it, because you probably won't believe me. I would not have believed it myself if someone had just told me about it; but I was there, and saw it with my own eyes. It is a general rule that the more different anything is from what people are used to, the harder it is to accept. But, considering that all their other customs are so unlike ours, a sensible judge will perhaps not be surprised that they treat gold and silver quite differently from the way we do. After all, they never do use money among themselves, but keep it only for a contingency which may or may not actually arise. So in the meanwhile they take care that no one shall overvalue gold and silver, of which money is made, beyond what the metals themselves deserve. Anyone can see, for example, that iron is far superior to either; men could not live without iron, by heaven, any more than without fire or water. But Nature granted to gold and silver no function with which we cannot easily dispense. Human folly has made them precious because they are rare. In contrast, Nature, like a most indulgent mother, has placed the best things out in the open, like air, water, and the earth itself; but vain and unprofitable things she has hidden away in remote places.

If in Utopia gold and silver were kept locked up in some tower, foolish heads among the common people might concoct a story that the governor and senate were out to cheat ordinary folk and get some advantage for themselves. They might indeed put the gold and silver into plate-ware and such handiwork, but then in case of necessity the people would not want to give up such articles, on which they had begun to fix their hearts, only to melt them down for soldiers' pay. To avoid all these inconveniences, they thought of a plan which conforms with their institutions as clearly as it contrasts with our own. Unless one has actually seen it working, their plan may seem incredible, because we prize gold so highly and are so careful about protecting it. While they eat from pottery dishes and drink from glass cups, well made but inexpensive, their chamber pots and all their humblest vessels, for use in the common halls and even in private homes, are made of gold and silver. The chains and heavy fetters of slaves are also made of these metals. Finally, criminals who are to bear the mark of some disgraceful act are forced to wear golden rings in their ears and on their fingers, golden chains around their necks, and even golden headbands. Thus they hold gold and silver up to scorn in every conceivable way. As a result, if they had to part with their entire supply of these metals, which other nations give up with as much agony as if they were being disemboweled, the Utopians would feel it no more than the loss of a penny.

They pick up pearls by the seashore, and diamonds and garnets from certain cliffs, but never go out of set purpose to look for them. If they happen to find some, they polish them and give them to the children, who, when they are small, feel proud and pleased with such gaudy decorations. But after, when they grow a bit older, and notice that only babies like such toys, they lay them aside. Their parents don't have to say anything; the children simply put these trifles away out of shame, just as our children when they grow up put away their marbles, baubles, and dolls.

These customs so different from those of other people produce quite different attitudes: this never became clearer to me than it did in the case of the Anemo-lian[1] ambassadors, who came to Amaurot while I was there. Because they came to discuss important business, the national council had assembled ahead of time, three citizens from each city. The ambassadors from nearby nations, who had visited Utopia before and knew something of their customs, understood that fine clothing was not respected in that land, silk was despised, and gold a badge of contempt; therefore they always came in the very plainest of their clothes. But the Anemolians, who lived farther off and had had fewer dealings with the Uto-pians, had heard only that they all dressed alike and very simply; so they took for granted that their hosts had nothing to wear that they didn't put on. Being them-selves rather more proud than wise, they decided to dress as resplendently as the very gods, and dazzle the eyes of the poor Utopians by the glitter of their garb.

Consequently the three ambassadors made a grand entry with a suite of a hundred attendants, all in clothing of many colors, and most in silk. Being

1. Windy people (Greek).

noblemen at home, the ambassadors were arrayed in cloth of gold, with heavy gold chains on their necks, gold earrings, gold rings on their fingers, and sparkling strings of pearls and gems on their caps. In fact, they were decked out in all the articles which in Utopia are used to punish slaves, shame wrongdoers, or entertain infants. It was a sight to see how they strutted when they compared their finery with the dress of the Utopians, who had poured out into the streets to see them pass. But it was just as funny to see how wide they fell of the mark, and how far they were from getting the consideration they wanted and expected. Except for a very few Utopians who for some special reason had visited foreign countries, all the onlookers considered this pomp and splendor a mark of disgrace. They therefore bowed to the humblest of the party as lords, and took the ambassadors, because of their golden chains, to be slaves, passing them by without any reverence at all. You might have seen children, who had themselves thrown away their pearls and gems, nudge their mothers when they saw the ambassadors' jeweled caps, and say:

"Look at that big lummox, mother, who's still wearing pearls and jewels as if he were a little boy!"

But the mother, in all seriousness, would answer:

"Hush, son, I think he is one of the ambassadors' fools."

Others found fault with the golden chains as useless, because they were so flimsy any slave could break them, and so loose that he could easily shake them off and run away whenever he wanted, footloose and fancy-free. But after the ambassadors had spent a couple of days among the Utopians, they saw the immense amounts of gold which were as thoroughly despised there as they were prized at home. They saw too that more gold and silver went into making the chains and fetters of a single runaway slave than into costuming all three of them. Somewhat ashamed and crestfallen, they put away all the finery in which they had strutted so arrogantly, especially after they had talked with the Utopians enough to learn their customs and opinions.

[Their Philosophy]

The Utopians marvel that any mortal can take pleasure in the dubious sparkle of a little jewel or bright gemstone, when he has a star, or the sun itself, to look at. They are amazed at the foolishness of any man who considers himself a nobler fellow because he wears clothing of specially fine wool. No matter how delicate the thread, they say, a sheep wore it once, and still was nothing but a sheep. They are surprised that gold, a useless commodity in itself, is everywhere valued so highly that man himself, who for his own purposes conferred this value on it, is considered far less valuable than the gold. They do not understand why a dunderhead with no more brains than a post, and who is as depraved as he is foolish, should command a great many wise and good men simply because he happens to have a great pile of gold. Yet if this master should lose his money to the lowest rascal in his household (as can happen by chance, or through some legal trick—for the law can produce reversals as violent as Fortune herself), he would promptly become the servant of his servant, as if he were personally attached to the coins, and a mere appendage to them. Even more than this, the Utopians are appalled at those people who practically worship a rich man, though they neither owe him anything nor are obligated to him in any way. What impresses them is simply that the man is rich. Yet all the while they know he is so mean and grasping that as long as he lives not a single penny out of that great mound of money will ever come their way.

These and the like attitudes the Utopians have picked up partly from their upbringing, since the institutions of their commonwealth are completely opposed to such folly, and partly from instruction and their reading of good books. For though not many people in each city are excused from labor and assigned to scholarship full-time (these are persons who from childhood have given evidence of excellent character, unusual intelligence, and devotion to learning), every child gets an introduction to good literature, and throughout their lives a large part of the people, men and women alike, spend their leisure time in reading.

They study all the branches of learning in their native tongue, which is not deficient in terminology or unpleasant in sound, and adapts itself as well as any to the expression of thought. Just about the same language is spoken throughout that entire area of the world, though elsewhere it is corrupted to various degrees.

Before we came there, the Utopians had never so much as heard about a single one of those philosophers whose names are so celebrated in our part of the world. Yet in music, dialectic, arithmetic, and geometry they have found out just about the same things as our great men of the past. But while they equal the ancients in almost all subjects, they are far from matching the inventions of our modern logicians.[2] In fact they have not discovered even one of those elaborate rules about restrictions, amplifications, and suppositions which our own young men study in the *Litle Logicbook*.[3] They are so far from being able to speculate on "second intentions" that not one of them was able to see "man-in-general," though I pointed straight at him with my finger, and he is, as you well know, bigger than any giant, maybe even a colossus. On the other hand, they have learned to plot expertly the courses of the stars and the movements of the heavenly bodies. They have devised a number of different instruments by which they compute with the greatest exactness the course and position of the sun, the moon, and the other stars that are visible in their area of the sky. As for the conjunctions and oppositions of the planets, and that whole deceitful business of divination by the stars, they have never so much as dreamed of it. From long experience in observation, they are able to forecast rains, winds, and other changes in the weather. But as to the causes of the weather, of the tides in the sea and its saltiness, and the origins and nature of the heavens and the earth, they have various opinions. They agree with our ancient philosophers on some matters, but on others, just as the ancients disagreed with one another, so the Utopians differ from all the ancients and yet reach no consensus among themselves.

In matters of moral philosophy, they carry on the same arguments as we do. They inquire into the nature of the good, distinguishing goods of the body from goods of the mind and external goods. They ask whether the name of "good" may be applied to all three, or applies only to goods of the mind. They discuss virtue and pleasure, but their chief concern is what to think of human

---

2. As a humanist, More mocks scholasticism's formalism and abstraction.   3. A scholastic textbook.

happiness, and whether it consists of one thing or of more. On this point, they seem overly inclined to the view of those who think that all or most human happiness consists of pleasure. And what is more surprising, they seek support for this comfortable opinion from their religion, which is serious and strict, indeed almost stern and forbidding. For they never discuss happiness without joining to their philosophic rationalism certain principles drawn from religion. Without these religious principles, they think that reason by itself is weak and defective in its efforts to investigate true happiness.

Their religious principles are of this nature: that the soul of man is immortal, and by God's goodness born for happiness; that after this life, rewards are appointed for our virtues and good deeds, punishments for our sins. Though these are indeed religious beliefs, they think that reason leads us to believe and accept them. And they add unhesitatingly that if these beliefs were rejected, no one would be so stupid as not to feel that he should seek pleasure, regardless of right and wrong. His only care would be to keep a lesser pleasure from standing in the way of a greater one, and to avoid pleasures that are inevitably followed by pain. They think you would have to be actually crazy to pursue harsh and painful virtue, give up the pleasures of life, and suffer pain from which you can expect no advantage. For if there is no reward after death, you have no compensation for having passed your entire existence without pleasure, that is, miserably.

To be sure, they believe happiness is found, not in every kind of pleasure, but only in good and honest pleasure.[4] Virtue itself, they say, draws our nature to this kind of pleasure, as to the supreme good. There is an opposed school which declares that virtue is itself happiness.

They define virtue as living according to nature; and God, they say, created us to that end. When an individual obeys the dictates of reason in choosing one thing and avoiding another, he is following nature. Now the first rule of reason is to love and venerate the Divine Majesty to whom we owe our existence and our capacity for happiness. The second rule of nature is to lead a life as free of anxiety and as full of joy as possible, and to help all one's fellow men toward that end. The most hard-faced eulogist of virtue and the grimmest enemy of pleasure, while they invite us to toil and sleepless nights and self-laceration, still admonish us to relieve the poverty and misfortune of others as best we can. It is especially praiseworthy, they tell us, when we provide for our fellow creatures' comfort and welfare. Nothing is more humane (and humanity is the virtue most proper to human beings) than to relieve the misery of others and, by removing all sadness from their lives, restore them to enjoyment, that is, pleasure. Well, if this is the case, why doesn't nature equally invite us to do the same thing for ourselves? Either a joyful life (that is, one of pleasure) is a good thing, or it isn't. If it isn't, then you should not help anyone to it—indeed, you ought to take it away from everyone you can, as being harmful and deadly to them. But if such a life is good, and if we are supposed, indeed obliged, to help others to it, why shouldn't we first of all seek it for ourselves, to whom we owe no less charity than to anyone else? When nature prompts you to be kind to your neighbors, she does not mean that you should be cruel and merciless to

---

4. The Utopians owe much to Epicureanism, which advocated seeking simple pleasures and limiting one's desires to live in a state of tranquility.

yourself. Thus they say that nature herself prescribes for us a joyous life, in other words, pleasure, as the goal of our actions; and living according to her prescriptions is to be defined as virtue. But as nature bids mortals to make one another's lives merrier, to the extent that they can, so she warns us constantly not to seek our own advantage in ways that cause misfortune to our fellows. And the reason for this is an excellent one; for no one is placed so far above the rest that he is nature's sole concern: she cherishes alike all those living beings to whom she has granted the same form.

Consequently, the Utopians maintain that one should not only abide by private agreements but also obey all those public laws which control the distribution of vital goods, such as are the very substance of pleasure. Any such laws, provided they have been properly promulgated by a good king, or ratified by a people free of force and fraud, should be observed; and as long as they are observed, to pursue your own interests is prudent; to pursue the public interest as well is pious; but to pursue your own pleasure by depriving others of theirs is unjust. On the other hand, deliberately to decrease one's own pleasure in order to augment that of others is a work of humanity and benevolence which never fails to reward the doer over and above his sacrifice. You may be repaid for your kindness; and in any case you are conscious of having done a good deed. Your mind draws more joy from recalling the affection and good will of those whom you have benefited than your body would have drawn pleasure from the things you gave up. Finally, they believe (as religion easily persuades a well-disposed mind to believe) that God will recompense us, for surrendering a brief and transitory pleasure here, with immense and neverending joy in heaven. And so they conclude, after carefully considering and weighing the matter, that all our actions and the virtues exercised within them look toward pleasure and happiness as their ultimate end.

By pleasure they understand every state or movement of body or mind in which we find delight in accordance with the behests of nature. They are right in adding that the desire must accord with nature. By simply following our senses and right reason we may discover what is pleasant by nature: it is a delight that does not injure others, that does not preclude a greater pleasure, and that is not followed by pain. But a pleasure which is against nature, and which men call "delightful" only by the emptiest of fictions (as if one could change the real nature of things just by changing their names), does not, they hold, really make for happiness; in fact, they say it often precludes happiness. And the reason is that men whose minds are filled with false ideas of pleasure have no room left for true and genuine delight. As a matter of fact, there are a great many things which have no genuine sweetness in them but are for the most part actually bitter, yet which, through the perverse enticements of evil desires, are considered very great pleasures, and even included among the supreme goals of life.

Among the devotees of this false pleasure, they include those whom I mentioned before, the people who think themselves finer fellows because they wear finer clothes. These people are twice mistaken: first in thinking their clothes better than anyone else's, and then in thinking themselves better because of their clothes. As far as a garment's usefulness goes, what does it matter if it was woven of fine thread or coarse? Yet they act as if they were set apart by nature herself, rather than their own fantasies; they strut about, and put on airs. Because they have a fancy suit, they think themselves entitled to honors they would never have expected if they were dressed in homespun, and they grow indignant if someone passes them by without showing special respect.

It is the same kind of absurdity to be pleased by empty, ceremonial honors. What true and natural pleasure can you get from someone's bent knee or bared head? Will the creaks in your own knees be eased thereby, or the madness in your head? The phantom of false pleasure is illustrated by others who run mad with delight over their own blue blood, plume themselves on their nobility, and applaud themselves for all their rich ancestors (the only ancestors that count nowadays), and especially for all their ancient family estates. Even if they don't have the shred of an estate themselves, or if they've squandered every penny of their inheritance, they don't consider themselves a bit less noble.

In the same class the Utopians put those people I described before who are mad for jewelry and gems, and think themselves divinely happy if they find a good specimen, especially of the sort that happens to be fashionable in their country at the time—for stones vary in value from one market to another. The collector will not make an offer for a stone till it's taken out of its gold setting, and even then he will not buy unless the dealer guarantees and gives security that it is a true and genuine stone. What he fears is that his eyes will be deceived by a counterfeit. But if you consider the matter, why should a counterfeit give any less pleasure, when your eyes cannot distinguish it from a real gem? Both should be of equal value to you—as they would be, in fact, to a blind man.

What about those who pile up money not because they want to do anything with the heap, but so they can sit and look at it? Is that true pleasure they experience, or aren't they simply cheated by a show of pleasure? Or what of those with the opposite vice, who hide away gold they will never use and perhaps never even see again? In their anxiety to hold onto it, they actually lose it. For what else happens when you deprive yourself, and perhaps other people too, of a chance to use your gold, by burying it in the ground? And yet when you've hidden your treasure away, you exult over it as if your mind were now free to rejoice. Suppose someone stole it, and you died ten years later, knowing nothing of the theft. During all those ten years, what did it matter whether the money was stolen or not? In either case, it was equally useless to you.

To these false and foolish pleasures they add gambling, which they have heard about, though they've never tried it, as well as hunting and hawking. What pleasure can there be, they wonder, in throwing dice on a table? If there were any pleasure in the action, wouldn't doing it over and over again quickly make one tired of it? What pleasure can there be in listening to the barking and yelping of dogs—isn't that rather a disgusting noise? Is there any more pleasure felt when a dog chases a hare than when a dog chases a dog? If what you like is fast running, there's plenty of that in both cases; they're just about the same. But if what you really want is slaughter, if you want to see a living creature torn apart under your eyes—you ought to feel nothing but pity when you see the little hare fleeing from the hound, the weak creature tormented by the stronger, the fearful and timid beast brutalized by the savage one, the harmless hare killed by the cruel dog. The Utopians, who regard this whole activity of hunting as unworthy of free men, have assigned it, accordingly, to their butchers, who, as I said before, are all slaves. In their eyes, hunting is the lowest thing even butchers can do. In the slaughterhouse, their work is more useful and honest, since there they kill animals only from necessity; but the hunter seeks merely his own pleasure from the killing and mutilating of some poor little creature. Even in beasts, taking such relish in the sight of death reveals, in the Utopians' opinion, a cruel disposition, or else one that has become so through the constant practice of such brutal pleasures.

Common opinion considers these activities, and countless others like them, to be pleasures; but the Utopians say flatly they have nothing at all to do with real pleasure, since there's nothing naturally pleasant about them. They often please the senses, and in this they are like pleasure, but that does not alter their basic nature. The enjoyment doesn't arise from the experience itself, but only from the perverse habits of the mob, as a result of which they mistake the bitter for the sweet, just as pregnant women, whose taste has been turned awry, sometimes think pitch and tallow taste sweeter than honey. A person's taste may be similarly depraved by disease or by custom, but that does not change the nature of pleasure, or of anything else.

They distinguish several different classes of true pleasure, some being pleasures of the mind and others pleasures of the body. Those of the mind are knowledge and the delight which rises from contemplating the truth, also the gratification of looking back on a well-spent life and the unquestioning hope of happiness to come.

Pleasures of the body they also divide into two classes. The first is that which fills the senses with immediate delight. Sometimes this happens when bodily organs that have been weakened by natural heat are restored with food and drink; sometimes it happens when we eliminate some excess in the body, as when we move our bowels, generate children, or relieve an itch somewhere by rubbing or scratching it. Now and then pleasure arises, not from restoring a deficiency or discharging an excess, but from something that excites our senses with a hidden but unmistakable force, and attracts them to itself. Such is the power of music.

The second kind of bodily pleasure they describe as nothing but the calm and harmonious state of the body, its state of health when undisturbed by any disorder. Health itself, when not oppressed by pain, gives pleasure, without any external excitement at all. Even though it appeals less directly to the senses than the gross gratifications of eating and drinking, many consider this to be the greatest pleasure of all. Most of the Utopians regard it as the foundation and basis of all the pleasures, since by itself alone it can make life peaceful and desirable, whereas without it there is no possibility of any other pleasure. Mere absence of pain, without positive health, they regard as insensibility, not pleasure.

Some have maintained that a stable and tranquil state of health is not really a pleasure, on the grounds that the presence of health cannot be felt except through some external stimulus. The Utopians (who have considered the matter thoroughly) long ago rejected this opinion. On the contrary, they nearly all agree that health is crucial to pleasure. Since pain is inherent in disease, they argue, and pain is the bitter enemy of pleasure, just as disease is the enemy of health, then pleasure must be inherent in quiet good health. You may say pain is not the disease itself, simply an accompanying effect; but they argue that that makes no difference, since the effect is the same either way. For whether health is itself a pleasure or is merely the cause of pleasure (as fire is the cause of heat), the fact remains that those who have stable health must also have pleasure.

When we eat, they say, what happens is that health, which was starting to fade, takes food as its ally in the fight against hunger. While our health gains strength, the simple process of returning vigor gives us pleasure and refreshment. If our health feels delight in the struggle, will it not rejoice when the victory has been won? When at last it is restored to its original strength, which was its aim all through the conflict, will it at once become insensible, and fail to recognize and embrace its own good? The idea that health cannot be felt they consider completely wrong. Every man who's awake, they say, feels that he's in good health—unless he isn't. Is anyone so torpid and dull that he won't admit health is delightfully agreeable to him? And what is delight except pleasure under another name?

Of all the different pleasures, they seek primarily those of the mind, and prize them most highly. The foremost mental pleasure, they believe, arises from the practice of the virtues and the consciousness of a good life. Among the pleasures of the body, they give the first place to health. As for eating and drinking and other delights of that sort, they consider them desirable, but only for the sake of health. They are not pleasant in themselves, but only as ways to withstand the insidious attacks of sickness. A wise man would rather escape sickness altogether than have a good cure for it; he would rather prevent pain than find a palliative for it. And so it would be better not to need this kind of pleasure at all than to be assuaged by it.

Anyone who thinks happiness consists of this sort of pleasure must confess that his ideal life would be one spent in an endless round of hunger, thirst, and itching, followed by eating, drinking, scratching, and rubbing. Who can fail to see that such an existence is not only disgusting but miserable? These pleasures are certainly the lowest of all, as they are the most adulterate—for they never occur except in connection with the pains that are their contraries. Hunger, for example, is linked to the pleasure of eating, and far from equally, since the pain is sharper and lasts longer; it precedes the pleasure, and ends only when the pleasure ends with it. So the Utopians think pleasures of this sort should not be much valued, except insofar as they are necessary to life. Yet they enjoy these pleasures too, and acknowledge gratefully the kindness of Mother Nature, who coaxes her children with allurements and cajolery to do what in any case they must do from necessity. How wretched life would be if the daily diseases of hunger and thirst had to be overcome by bitter potions and drugs, like some other diseases that afflict us less often!

Beauty, strength, and agility, as special and pleasant gifts of nature, they joyfully accept. The pleasures of sound, sight, and smell they also pursue as the special seasonings of life, recognizing that nature intended these delights to be the particular province of man. No other kind of animal admires the shape and loveliness of the universe, or enjoys odors, except in the way of searching for food, or distinguishes harmonious from dissonant sounds. But in all their pleasures, the Utopians observe this rule, that the lesser pleasure must not interfere with the greater, and that no pleasure shall carry pain with it as a consequence. If a pleasure is dishonorable, they think it will inevitably lead to pain.

Moreover, they think it is crazy for a man to despise beauty of form, to impair his own strength, to grind his energy down to lethargy, to exhaust his body with fasts, to ruin his health, and to scorn all other natural delights, unless by so doing he can better serve the welfare of others or the public good. Then indeed he may expect a greater reward from God. But otherwise for a man to inflict pain on himself does no one any good. He gains, perhaps, the empty and shadowy reputation of virtue; and no doubt he hardens himself against fantastic adversities which may never occur. But such a person the Utopians consider absolutely crazy—cruel to himself, as well as most ungrateful to nature—as if, to avoid being in her debt, he rejects all her gifts.

This is the way they think about virtue and pleasure. Human reason, they believe, can attain to no surer conclusions than these, unless a revelation from heaven should inspire men with holier notions. In all this, I have no time now to consider whether they are right or wrong, and don't feel obliged to do so. I have undertaken only to describe their principles, not to defend them. But of this I am sure, that whatever you think of their ideas, there is not a more excellent people or a happier commonwealth anywhere in the whole world.

In body they are nimble and lively, and stronger than you would expect from their stature, though they're by no means tiny. Their soil is not very fertile, nor their climate of the best, but they protect themselves against the weather by temperate living, and improve their soil by industry, so that nowhere do grain and cattle flourish more plentifully, nowhere are people more vigorous, and liable to fewer diseases. There you can see not only that they do all the things farmers usually do to improve poor soil by hard work and technical knowledge, but you can see a forest which they uprooted with their own hands and moved to another site. They did this not so much for the sake of better growth but to make transport easier, by having wood closer to the sea, the rivers, or the cities themselves. For grain is easier than wood to carry by land over a long distance.

[Their Delight in Learning]

The people in general are easygoing, cheerful, clever, and like their leisure. When they must, they can stand heavy labor, but otherwise they are not very fond of it. In intellectual pursuits, they are tireless. When they heard from us about the literature and learning of the Greeks (for we thought there was nothing in Latin, except the historians and poets, that they would value), it was wonderful to behold how eagerly they sought to be instructed in Greek. We therefore began to study a little of it with them, at first more to avoid seeming lazy than out of any expectation that they would profit by it. But after a short trial, their diligence convinced us that our efforts would not be wasted. They picked up the forms of the letters so easily, pronounced the language so aptly, memorized it so quickly, and began to recite so accurately that it seemed like a miracle. Most of our pupils were established scholars, of course, picked for their unusual ability and mature minds; and they studied with us, not just of their own free will, but at the command of the senate. Thus in less than three years they had perfect control of the language and could read the best authors fluently, unless the text was corrupt. I have a feeling they picked up Greek more easily because it was somewhat related to their own tongue. Though their language resembles Persian in most respects, I suspect their race descends from the Greeks, because their language retains some vestiges of Greek in the names of cities and in official titles.

Before leaving on the fourth voyage, I placed on board, instead of merchandise, a good-sized packet of books; for I had resolved not to return at all rather than come home soon. Thus they received from me most of Plato's works and more of Aristotle's, as well as Theophrastus's book *On Plants*,[5] though the latter, I'm sorry to say, was somewhat mutilated. During the voyage I carelessly left it lying around, a monkey got hold of it, and from sheer mischief ripped out a few pages here and there and tore them up. Of the grammarians they have only Lascaris, for I did not take Theodorus with me, nor any dictionary except that of Hesychius; and they have Dioscorides.[6] They are very fond of Plutarch's writings, and delighted with the witty persiflage of Lucian.[7] Among the poets they have Aristophanes, Homer, and Euripides, together with Sophocles in the small typeface of the Aldine edition.[8] Of the historians they possess Thucydides and Herodotus, as well as Herodian.[9]

As for medical books, a comrade of mine named Tricius Apinatus[1] brought with him some small treatises by Hippocrates, and the *Microtechne* of Galen.[2] They were delighted to have these books. Even though there's hardly a country in the world that needs doctors less, medicine is nowhere held in greater honor: they consider it one of the finest and most useful parts of philosophy. They think that when, with the help of philosophy, they explore the secrets of nature they are gratifying not only themselves but the author and maker of nature. They suppose that, like other artists, he created this beautiful mechanism of the world to be admired—and by whom, if not by man, who is alone in being able to appreciate so great a thing? Therefore he is bound to prefer a careful observer and sensitive admirer of his work before one who, like a brute beast, looks on the grand spectacle with a stupid and blockish mind.

Once stimulated by learning, the minds of the Utopians are wonderfully quick to seek out those various arts which make life more agreeable. Two inventions, to be sure, they owe to us: the art of printing and the manufacture of paper. At least they owe these arts partly to us, though partly to their own ingenuity. While we were showing them the Aldine editions of various works, we talked about papermaking and how letters are printed, though without going into detail, for none of us had had any practical experience of either skill. But with great sharpness of mind they immediately grasped the basic principles. While previously they had written only on vellum, bark, and papyrus, they

5. Hythloday's traveling library is a compendium of Renaissance knowledge. Humanists revered Plato and Aristotle as the basis of Greek thought. Theophrastus was a student of Aristotle's whose botanical works influenced medieval science.

6. Dioscorides (1st century C.E.) wrote on drugs and herbs; Lascaris and Theodorus wrote Renaissance dictionaries of Greek. Hesychius (5th century C.E.) wrote on Greek dialects.

7. Lucian (c. 125–180 C.E.): Assyrian satirist who wrote in Greek. Plutarch (46–120 C.E.): Greek historian and moralist.

8. Aldus Manutius's press, founded in Venice in the late 15th century, first printed Greek texts in Greek and was admired for its book design.

9. A canon of the classics rediscovered by the Renaissance, many newly edited and published in More's time.

1. Trica and Apina were tiny Roman towns, symbolizing insignificance; thus "Tricius Apinatus": Mr. Nobody.

2. Hippocrates (5th century B.C.E.) and Galen (2nd century C.E.): medical authorities of the classical world.

now undertook to make paper and to print with type. Their first attempts were not altogether successful, but with practice they soon mastered both arts. They became so proficient that, if they had texts of the Greek authors, they would soon have no lack of volumes; but as they have no more than those I mentioned, they have contented themselves with reprinting each in thousands of copies.

Any sightseer coming to their land who has some special intellectual gift, or who has traveled widely and seen many countries, is sure of a warm welcome, for they love to hear what is happening throughout the world. This is why we were received so kindly. Few merchants, however, go there to trade. What could they import except iron—or else gold and silver, which everyone would rather bring home than send abroad? As for the export trade, the Utopians prefer to do their own transportation, rather than invite strangers to do it. By carrying their own cargos they are able to learn more about foreign countries on all sides, and keep up their skill in navigation.

Slaves

The only prisoners of war the Utopians enslave are those captured in wars they fight themselves. The children of slaves are not automatically enslaved, nor are slaves obtained from foreign countries. Their slaves are either their own citizens, enslaved for some heinous offense, or else foreigners who were condemned to death in their own land. Most are of the latter sort. Sometimes the Utopians buy them at a very modest rate, more often they ask for them, get them for nothing, and bring them home in considerable numbers. Both kinds of slaves are kept constantly at work, and are always fettered. But the Utopians deal with their own people more harshly than with the others, feeling that their crimes are worse and deserve stricter punishment because they had an excellent education and the best of moral training, yet still couldn't be restrained from wrongdoing. A third class of slaves consists of hardworking penniless drudges from other nations who voluntarily choose to become slaves in Utopia. Such people are treated well, almost as well as citizens, except that they are given a little extra work, on the score that they're used to it. If one of them wants to leave, which seldom happens, no obstacles are put in his way, nor is he sent off emptyhanded.

[Suicide and Euthanasia]

As I said before, the sick are carefully tended, and nothing is neglected in the way of medicine or diet which might cure them. Everything possible is done to mitigate the pain of those who are suffering from incurable diseases; and visitors do their best to console them by sitting and talking with them. But if the disease is not only incurable but excruciatingly and constantly painful, then the priests and public officials come and urge the invalid not to endure such agony any longer. They remind him that he is now unfit for any of life's duties, a burden to himself and to others; he has really outlived his own death. They tell him he should not let the disease prey on him any longer, but now that life is simply torture, he should not hesitate to die but should rely on hope for something better. Since life has become a mere prison cell, where he is bitterly tormented, he should free himself, or let others free him, from the rack of living. This would be a wise act, they say, since for him death would put an end not to pleasure but to agony. In addition, he would be obeying the advice of the priests, who are the interpreters of God's will; which ensures that it would be a holy and pious act.

Those who have been persuaded by these arguments either starve themselves to death or, having been put to sleep, are freed from life without any sensation of dying. But they never force this step on a man against his will; nor, if he decides against it, do they lessen their care of him. Under these circumstances, when death is advised by the authorities, they consider self-destruction honorable. But the suicide, who takes his own life without the approval of priests and senate, they consider unworthy either of earth or fire, and throw his body, unburied and disgraced, into a bog.

[Marriage and Divorce]

Women do not marry till they are eighteen, nor men till they are twenty-two. Premarital intercourse, if discovered and proved, brings severe punishment on both man and woman, and the guilty parties are forbidden to marry during their whole lives, unless the governor by his pardon remits the sentence. In addition both the father and mother of the household where the offense occurred suffer public disgrace for having been remiss in their duty. The reason they punish this offense so severely is that they suppose few people would join in married love—with confinement to a single partner, and all the petty annoyances that married life involves—unless they were strictly restrained from a life of promiscuity.

In choosing marriage partners, they solemnly and seriously follow a custom which seemed to us foolish and absurd in the extreme. Whether she is a widow or a virgin, the woman is shown naked to the suitor by a responsible and respectable matron; and similarly, some respectable man presents the suitor naked to the woman. We laughed at this custom and called it absurd; but they were just as amazed at the folly of all other peoples. When men go to buy a colt,[3] where they are risking only a little money, they are so suspicious that, though the beast is almost bare, they won't close the deal until the saddle and blanket have been taken off, lest there be a hidden sore underneath. Yet in the choice of a mate, which may cause either delight or disgust for the rest of their lives, people are completely careless. They leave all the rest of her body covered up with clothes and estimate the attractiveness of a woman from a mere handsbreadth of her person, the face, which is all they can see. And so they marry, running great risk of bitter discord, if something in either's person should offend the other. Not all people are so wise as to concern themselves solely with character; and even the wise appreciate physical beauty, as a supplement to the virtues of the mind. There's no question but that deformity may lurk under clothing, serious enough to make a man hate his wife when it's too late to be separated from her. If some disfiguring accident occurs after marriage, each person must bear his own fate; but beforehand everyone should be legally protected from deception.

3. The maiden name of More's first wife was Jane Colt.

There is extra reason for them to be careful, because in that part of the world they are the only people who practice monogamy. Their marriages are seldom terminated except by death, though they do allow divorce for adultery or for intolerably offensive behavior. A husband or wife who is the aggrieved party in such a divorce is granted permission by the senate to remarry, but the guilty party is considered disreputable and is permanently forbidden to take another mate. They absolutely forbid a husband to put away his wife against her will and without any fault on her part, just because of some bodily misfortune; they think it cruel that a person should be abandoned when most in need of comfort; and they add that old age, since it not only entails disease but is actually a disease itself, needs more than a precarious fidelity.

It happens occasionally that a married couple cannot get along, and have both found other persons with whom they hope to live more harmoniously. After getting the approval of the senate, they may then separate by mutual consent and contract new marriages. But such divorces are allowed only after the senators and their wives have carefully investigated the case. They allow divorce only very reluctantly, because they know that husbands and wives will find it hard to settle down together if each has in mind that a new marriage is easily available.

They punish adulterers with the strictest form of slavery. If both parties were married, they are both divorced, and the injured parties may marry one another, if they want, or someone else. But if one of the injured parties continues to love such an undeserving spouse, the marriage may go on, providing the innocent person chooses to share in the labor to which the slave is condemned. And sometimes it happens that the repentance of the guilty and the devotion of the innocent party move the governor to pity, so that he restores both to freedom. But a second conviction of adultery is punished by death.

[Punishments and Rewards; Customs and Laws]

No other crimes carry fixed penalties; the senate sets specific penalties for each particular misdeed, as it is considered atrocious or venial.[4] Husbands chastise their wives, and parents their children, unless the offense is so serious that public punishment is called for. Generally, the gravest crimes are punished by slavery, for they think this deters offenders just as much as getting rid of them by immediate capital punishment, and is more beneficial to the commonwealth. In addition, slaves contribute more by their labor than by their death, and they are permanent and visible reminders that crime does not pay. If the slaves rebel against their condition, then, like savage beasts which neither bars nor chains can tame, they are finally put to death. But if they are patient, they are not left altogether without hope. When subdued by long hardships, if they show by their behavior that they regret the crime more than the punishment, their slavery is lightened or remitted altogether, sometimes by the governor's pardon, sometimes by popular vote.

---

4. A marked contrast with the English system of common law, in which More was trained, and which is determined by precedents.

Attempted seduction is subject to the same penalty as seduction itself. They think that a crime clearly and deliberately attempted is as bad as one committed, and that failure should not confer advantages on a criminal who did all he could to succeed.

They are very fond of fools, and think it contemptible to insult them. There is no prohibition against enjoying their foolishness, and they even regard this as beneficial to the fools. If anyone is so serious and solemn that the foolish behavior and comic patter of a clown do not amuse him, they don't entrust him with the care of such a person, for fear that a man who gets not only no use from a fool but not even any amusement—a fool's only gift—will not treat him kindly.

To mock a person for being deformed or crippled is considered ugly and disfiguring, not to the victim but to the mocker, who stupidly reproaches the cripple for something he cannot help.

They think it a sign of a weak and sluggish character to neglect one's natural beauty, but they consider cosmetics a detestable affectation. From experience they have learned that no physical beauty recommends a wife to her husband so effectually as goodness and respect. Though some men are captured by beauty alone, none are held except by virtue and compliance.

As they deter people from crime by penalties, so they incite them to virtue by public honors. They set up in the marketplace statues of distinguished men who have served their country well, thinking thereby to preserve the memory of their good deeds and to spur on the citizens to emulate the glory of their ancestors.

Any man who campaigns for a public office is disqualified for all of them. They live together harmoniously, and the public officials are never arrogant or unapproachable. Instead, they are called "fathers," and that is the way they behave. Because the officials never extort respect from the people against their will, the people respect them spontaneously, as they should. Not even the governor is distinguished from his fellow citizens by a robe or crown; he is known only by a sheaf of grain he carries, just as the high priest is distinguished by a wax candle borne before him.

They have very few laws, and their training is such that they need no more. The chief fault they find with other nations is that, even with infinite volumes of laws and interpretations, they cannot manage their affairs properly. They think it completely unjust to bind people by a set of laws that are too many to be read and too obscure for anyone to understand. As for lawyers, a class of men whose trade it is to manipulate cases and multiply quibbles, they exclude them entirely. They think it is better for each man to plead his own case, and say the same thing to the judge that he would tell his lawyer. This makes for less ambiguity, and readier access to the truth. A man speaks his mind without tricky instructions from a lawyer, and the judge examines each point carefully, taking pains to protect simple folk against the false accusations of the crafty. It is hard to find this kind of plain dealing in other countries, where they have such a multitude of incomprehensibly intricate laws. But in Utopia everyone is a legal expert. For the laws are very few, as I said, and they consider the most obvious interpretation of any law to be the fairest. As they see things, all laws are promulgated for the single purpose of teaching every man his duty. Subtle interpretations teach very few, since hardly anybody is able to understand them, whereas the more simple and apparent sense of the law is open to everyone. If laws are not clear, they are useless; for simpleminded men (and most men are of this sort, and need to be told where their duty lies), there might as well be no laws at all as laws which can be interpreted only by devious minds after endless disputes. The dull common man cannot understand this legal chicanery, and couldn't even if he studied it his whole life, since he has to earn a living in the meantime.

[Foreign Relations]

Some of the Utopians' free and independent neighbors (many of whom were previously liberated by them from tyranny), having learned to admire Utopian virtues, have made a practice of asking the Utopians to supply magistrates for them. Some of these magistrates serve one year, others five. When their service is over, they bring them home with honor and praise, and take back new ones to their country. These peoples seem to have settled on an excellent scheme to safeguard the commonwealth. Since the welfare or ruin of a commonwealth depends on the character of its officials, where could they make a more prudent choice than among Utopians, who cannot be tempted by money? For money is useless to them when they go home, as they soon must, and they can have no partisan or factional feelings, since they are strangers in the city over which they rule. Wherever they take root in men's minds, these two evils, greed and faction, are the destruction of all justice—and justice is the strongest bond of any society. The Utopians call these people who have borrowed magistrates from them their *allies*; others whom they have benefited they call simply *friends*.

While other nations are constantly making treaties, breaking them, and renewing them, the Utopians never make any treaties at all. If nature, they say, doesn't bind man adequately to his fellow man, will an alliance do so? If a man scorns nature herself, is there any reason to think he will care about mere words? They are confirmed in this view by the fact that in that part of the world, treaties and alliances between kings are not generally observed with much good faith.

In Europe, of course, the dignity of treaties is everywhere kept sacred and inviolable, especially in those regions where the Christian religion prevails. This is partly because the kings are all so just and virtuous, partly also because of the reverence and fear that everyone feels toward the popes. Just as the popes themselves never promise anything which they do not most conscientiously perform, so they command all other princes to abide by their promises in every way. If someone declines to do so, they compel him to obey by means of pastoral censure and sharp reproof. The popes rightly declare that it would be particularly disgraceful if people who are specifically called "the faithful" acted in bad faith.[5]

But in that new world, which is as distant from ours in customs and way of life as in the distance the equator puts between us, nobody trusts treaties. The greater the formalities, the more numerous and solemn the oaths, the sooner the treaty will be broken. The rulers will easily find some defect in the wording

5. The irony here is compounded by the fact that Renaissance popes, much like other rulers of the time, routinely violated treaties.

of it, which often enough they deliberately inserted themselves. No treaty can be made so strong and explicit that a government will not be able to worm out of it, breaking in the process both the treaty and its own word. If such craft, deceit, and fraud were practiced in private contracts, the politicians would raise a great outcry against both parties, calling them sacrilegious and worthy of the gallows. Yet the very same politicians think themselves clever fellows when they give this sort of advice to kings. As a consequence, people are apt to think that justice is a humble, plebeian virtue, far beneath the majesty of kings. Or else they conclude that there are two kinds of justice, one which is only for the common herd, a lowly justice that creeps along the ground, hedged in everywhere and encumbered with chains; and the other, which is the justice of princes, much more free and majestic, so that it can do anything it wants and nothing it doesn't want.

This royal practice of keeping treaties badly there is, I suppose, the reason the Utopians don't make any; doubtless if they lived here in Europe they would change their minds. However, they think it a bad idea to make treaties at all, even if they are faithfully observed. A treaty implies that people who are separated by some natural obstacle as slight as a hill or a brook are joined by no bond of nature; it assumes that they are born rivals and enemies, and are right in aiming to destroy one another except insofar as a treaty restrains them. Moreover, they see that treaties do not really promote friendship; for both parties still retain the right to prey upon one another to whatever extent incautious drafting has left the treaty without sufficient provisions against it. The Utopians think, on the other hand, that no one should be considered an enemy who has done you no harm, that the fellowship of nature is as good as a treaty, and that men are united more firmly by good will than by pacts, by their hearts than by their words.

Military Practices

They despise war as an activity fit only for beasts, yet practiced more by man than by any other creature. Unlike almost every other people in the world, they think nothing so inglorious as the glory won in battle. Yet on certain fixed days, men and women alike carry on vigorous military training, so they will be fit to fight should the need arise. But they go to war only for good reasons: to protect their own land, to protect their friends from an invading army, or to liberate an oppressed people from tyranny and servitude. Out of human sympathy, they not only protect their friends from present danger but sometimes avenge previous injuries; they do this, however, only if they themselves have previously been consulted, have approved the cause, and have demanded restitution in vain. Then and only then they think themselves free to declare war. They take this final step not only when their friends have been plundered but also, and even more fiercely, when their friends' merchants have been subjected to extortion in another country, either on the pretext of laws unjust in themselves or through the perversion of good laws.

This and no other was the cause of the war which the Utopians waged a little before our time on behalf of the Nephelogetes against the Alaopolitans.[6] Under

6. "People born of the clouds" vs. "People of a country without people."

pretext of right, a wrong (as they saw it) had been inflicted on some Nephelo-
gete traders residing among the Alaopolitans. Whatever the rights and wrongs
of the quarrel, it developed into a fierce war, into which, apart from the hostile
forces of the two parties themselves, the neighboring nations poured their
efforts and resources. Some prosperous nations were ruined completely, others
badly shaken. One trouble led to another, and in the end the Alaopolitans were
crushed and reduced to slavery (since the Utopians weren't involved on their
own account) by the Nephelogetes—a people who, before the war, had not
been remotely comparable in power to their rivals.

So severely do the Utopians punish wrong done to their friends, even in matters of mere money; but they are not so strict in enforcing their own rights.
When they are cheated out of their goods, so long as no bodily harm is done,
their anger goes no further than cutting off trade relations with that nation till
restitution is made. The reason is not that they care more for their allies' citizens than for their own, but simply this: when the merchants of their friends
are cheated, it is their own property that is lost, but when the Utopians lose
something, it comes from the common stock, and is bound to be in plentiful
supply at home; otherwise they wouldn't have been exporting it. Hence no one
individual even notices the loss. So small an injury, which affects neither the
life nor the livelihood of any of their own people, they consider it cruel to
avenge by the deaths of many soldiers. On the other hand, if one of their own
is maimed or killed anywhere, whether by a government or by a private citizen,
they first send envoys to look into the circumstances; then they demand that
the guilty persons be surrendered; and if that demand is refused, they are not to
be put off, but at once declare war. If the guilty persons are surrendered, their
punishment is death or slavery.

The Utopians are not only troubled but ashamed when their forces gain a
bloody victory, thinking it folly to pay too high a price even for the best goods.
But if they overcome the enemy by skill and cunning, they exult mightily, celebrate a public triumph, and raise a monument as for a hard-won victory. They
think they have really acted with manly virtue when they have won a victory
such as no animal except man could have won—a victory achieved by strength
of understanding. Bears, lions, boars, wolves, dogs, and other wild beasts fight
with their bodies, they say; and most of them are superior to us in strength and
ferocity; but we outdo them all in shrewdness and rationality.

The only thing they aim at, in going to war, is to secure what would have
prevented the declaration of war, if the enemy had conceded it beforehand. Or
if they cannot get that, they try to take such bitter revenge on those who have
provoked them that they will be afraid ever to do it again. These are their chief
aims, which they try to achieve quickly, yet in such a way as to avoid danger
rather than to win fame and glory.

As soon as war is declared, therefore, they have their secret agents simultaneously post many placards, each marked with their official seal, in the most
conspicuous places throughout the enemy territory. In these proclamations
they promise immense rewards to anyone who will kill the enemy's king. They
offer smaller but still very substantial sums for killing any of a list of other
individuals whom they name. These are the persons whom they regard as most
responsible, after the king, for plotting aggression against them. The reward
for an assassin is doubled for anyone who succeeds in bringing in one of the

proscribed men alive. The same reward, plus a guarantee of personal safety, is offered to any one of the proscribed men who turns against his comrades. As a result, the enemies of the Utopians quickly come to suspect everyone, particularly one another; and the many perils of their situation lead to panic. They know perfectly well that many of them, including their princes, have been betrayed by those in whom they placed complete trust—so effective are bribes as an incitement to crime. Knowing this, the Utopians are lavish in their promises of bounty. Being well aware of the risks their agents must run, they make sure that the payments are in proportion to the peril; thus they not only offer, but actually deliver, enormous sums of gold, as well as large landed estates in very secure locations on the territory of their friends.

Everywhere else in the world, this process of bidding for and buying the life of an enemy is condemned as the cruel villainy of a degenerate mind; but the Utopians consider it good policy, both wise and merciful. In the first place, it enables them to win tremendous wars without fighting any actual battles; and in the second place it enables them, by the sacrifice of a few guilty men, to spare the lives of many innocent persons who would have died in battle, some on their side, some on the enemy's. They pity the mass of the enemy's soldiers almost as much as their own citizens, for they know common people do not go to war of their own accord, but are driven to it by the madness of princes.

If assassination does not work, they sow the seeds of dissension in enemy ranks by inciting the prince's brother or some other member of the nobility to scheme for the crown. If internal discord dies down, they try to rouse up neighboring peoples against the enemy by reviving forgotten claims to dominion, of which kings always have an ample supply.

When they promise their resources to help in a war, they send money very freely, but commit their own citizens only sparingly. They hold their own people dear, and value them so highly that they would not willingly exchange one of their citizens for an enemy's prince. Since they keep their gold and silver for the purpose of war alone, they spend it without hesitation; after all, they will continue to live just as well even if they expend the whole sum. Besides the wealth they have at home, they have a vast treasure abroad, since, as I said before, many nations owe them money. So they hire mercenary soldiers from all sides, especially the Zapoletes.[7]

These people live five hundred miles to the east of Utopia, and are rude, rough, and fierce. The forests and mountains where they are bred are the kind of country they like: tough and rugged. They are a hard race, capable of standing heat, cold, and drudgery, unacquainted with any luxuries, careless of what houses they live in or what they wear; they don't till the fields but raise cattle instead. Most of them survive by hunting and stealing. These people are born for battle and are always eager for a fight; they seek one out at every opportunity. Leaving their own country in great numbers, they offer themselves for cheap hire to anyone in need of warriors. The only art they know for earning a living is the art of taking life.

They fight with great courage and incorruptible loyalty for the people who pay them, but they will not bind themselves to serve for any fixed period of time. If someone, even the enemy, offers them more money tomorrow, they will take his

---

7. "Busy sellers." The best-known mercenaries of the time were the Swiss.

side; and day after tomorrow, if a trifle more is offered to bring them back, they'll return to their first employers. Hardly a war is fought in which a good number of them are not engaged on both sides. It happens every day that men who are united by ties of blood and have served together in friendship, but who are now separated into opposing armies, meet in battle. Forgetful of kinship and comradeship alike, they furiously run one another through, driven to mutual destruction for no other reason than that they were hired for paltry pay by opposing princes. They care so much about money that they can easily be induced to change sides for an increase of only a penny a day. They have picked up the habit of avarice, but none of the profit; for what they earn by shedding blood, they quickly squander on debauchery of the most squalid sort.

Because the Utopians give higher pay than anyone else, these people are ready to serve them against any enemy whatever. And the Utopians, who seek out the best possible men for proper uses, hire these, the worst possible men, for improper uses. When the situation requires, they thrust the Zapoletes into the positions of greatest danger by offering them immense rewards. Most of them never come back to collect their pay, but the Utopians faithfully pay off those who do survive, to encourage them to try it again. As for how many Zapoletes get killed, the Utopians never worry about that, for they think they would deserve very well of all mankind if they could exterminate from the face of the earth that entire disgusting and vicious race.

Besides the Zapoletes, they employ as auxiliaries the soldiers of the people for whom they have taken up arms, and then squadrons of their other friends. Last, they add their own citizens, including some man of known bravery to command the entire army. In addition, they appoint two substitutes for him, who hold no rank as long as he is safe. But if the commander is captured or killed, the first of these two substitutes becomes his successor, and in case of a mishap to him, the other. Thus, though the accidents of war cannot be foreseen, they make sure that the whole army will not be disorganized through the loss of their leader.

In each city, soldiers are chosen from those who have volunteered. No one is forced to fight abroad against his will, because they think a man who is naturally fearful will act weakly at best, and may even spread panic among his comrades. But if their own country is invaded, they call everyone to arms, posting the fearful (as long as they are physically fit) on shipboard among braver men, or here and there along fortifications, where there is no place to run away. Thus shame at failing their countrymen, desperation at the immediate presence of the enemy, and the impossibility of flight often combine to overcome their fear, and they make a virtue out of sheer necessity.

Just as no man is forced into a foreign war against his will, so women are allowed to accompany their men on military service if they want to—not only not forbidden, but encouraged and praised for doing so. Each goes with her husband to the front, and stands shoulder to shoulder with him in the line of battle; in addition, they place around a man his children and blood- or marriage-relations, so that those who by nature have most reason to help one another may be closest at hand for mutual aid. It is a matter of great reproach for either partner to come home without the other, or for a son to return after losing a parent. The result is that if the enemy stands his ground, the hand-to-hand fighting is apt to be long and bitter, ending only when everyone is dead.

As I observed, they take every precaution to avoid having to fight in person, so long as they can bring the war to an end with mercenaries. But when they are forced to take part in battle, they are as bold in the struggle as they were prudent in avoiding it while they could. In the first charge they are not fierce, but gradually as the fighting goes on they grow more determined, putting up a steady, stubborn resistance. Their spirit is so strong that they will die rather than yield ground. They are certain that everyone at home will be provided for, and they have no worries about the future of their families (and that sort of worry often daunts the boldest courage); so their spirit is exalted and unconquerable. Their skill in the arts of war gives them extra confidence; also from childhood they have been trained in sound principles of conduct (which their education and the good institutions of their commonwealth reinforce); and that too adds to their courage. They don't hold life so cheap that they throw it away recklessly, nor so dear as to grasp it avidly at the price of shame, when duty bids them give it up.

At the height of the battle, a band of the bravest young men, who have taken a special oath, devote themselves to seeking out the opposing general. They attack him directly, they lay secret traps for him, they hit at him from near and far. A long and continuous supply of fresh men keep up the assault as the exhausted drop out. In the end, they rarely fail to kill or capture him, unless he takes to flight.

When they win a battle, it never ends in a massacre, for they would much rather take prisoners than cut throats. They never pursue fugitives without keeping one line of their army drawn up under the colors. They are so careful of this that if they win the victory with this last reserve force (supposing the rest of their army has been beaten), they would rather let the enemy army escape than pursue fugitives with their own ranks in disorder. They remember what has happened more than once to themselves: that when the enemy seemed to have the best of the day, had routed the main Utopian force and, exulting in their victory, had scattered to pursue the fugitives, a few Utopians held in reserve and watching their opportunity have suddenly attacked the dispersed and scattered enemy at the very moment when he felt safe and had lowered his guard. Thereby they changed the fortune of the day, snatched certain victory out of the enemy's hands, and, though conquered themselves, conquered their conquerors.

It is not easy to say whether they are more crafty in laying ambushes or more cautious in avoiding those laid for them. Sometimes they seem to be on the point of breaking and running when that is the last thing they have in mind; but when they really are ready to retreat, you would never guess it. If they are outnumbered, or if the terrain is unsuitable, they shift their ground silently by night or slip away from the enemy by some stratagem. Or if they have to withdraw by day, they do so gradually, and in such good order that they are as dangerous to attack then as if they were advancing. They fortify their camps very carefully with a deep, broad ditch all around them, the earth being thrown inward to make a wall; the work is done not by workmen but by the soldiers themselves with their own hands. The whole army pitches in, except for an armed guard posted around the rampart to prevent a surprise attack. With so many hands at work, they complete great fortifications, enclosing wide areas with unbelievable speed.

The armor they wear is strong enough to protect them from blows, but does not prevent easy movement of the body; in fact, it doesn't interfere even with their swimming, and part of their military training consists of swimming in armor. For long-range fighting they use arrows, which they fire with great force and accuracy, and from horseback as well as on foot. At close quarters they use not swords but battle-axes, which because of their sharp edge and great weight are lethal weapons, whether used in slashing or thrusting. They are very skillful in inventing machines of war, but conceal them with the greatest care, since if they were made known before they were needed, they might be more ridiculous than useful. Their first consideration in designing them is to make them easy to move and aim.

When the Utopians make a truce with the enemy, they observe it religiously, and will not break it even if provoked. They do not ravage the enemy's territory or burn his crops; indeed, so far as possible, they avoid any trampling of the fields by men or horses, thinking they may need the grain themselves later on. Unless he is a spy, they injure no unarmed man. When cities are surrendered to them, they keep them intact; even when they have stormed a place, they do not plunder it, but put to death the men who prevented surrender, enslave the other defenders, and do no harm to the civilians. If they find any inhabitants who recommended surrender, they give them a share in the property of the condemned, and present their auxiliaries with the rest; for the Utopians themselves never take any booty.

After a war is ended, they collect the cost of it, not from the allies for whose sake they undertook it, but from the conquered. They take as indemnity not only money, which they set aside to finance future wars, but also landed estates, from which they may enjoy forever a substantial annual income. They now have revenues of this sort in many different countries, acquired little by little in various ways, till it now amounts to over seven hundred thousand ducats a year.[8] As managers of these estates, they send abroad some of their own citizens to serve as collectors of revenue. Though they live on the properties in grand style and conduct themselves like great lords, plenty of income is still left over to be put in the public treasury, unless they choose to give the conquered nation credit. They often do the latter, until they happen to need the money, and even then it's rare for them to call in the entire debt. Some of the estates are given, as I've already described, to those who have risked great dangers on their behalf.

If any prince takes up arms and prepares to invade their land, they immediately attack him in full force outside their own borders. They are most reluctant to wage war on their own soil, and no necessity could ever compel them to admit foreign auxiliaries onto their island.

The Religions of the Utopians

There are different forms of religion throughout the island, and even in individual cities. Some worship as a god the sun, others the moon, and still others one of the planets. There are some who worship a man of past ages who was conspicuous either for virtue or glory; they consider him not only a god but the supreme god. The vast majority, however, and these by far the wisest, believe nothing of the sort: they believe in a single power, unknown, eternal, infinite, inexplicable, beyond the grasp of the human mind, and diffused throughout the universe, not physically, but in influence. Him they call their parent, and to him alone they attribute the origin, increase, progress, changes, and ends of all things; they do not offer divine honors to any other.

8. Venetian ducats became an international currency in the 16th century. Although difficult to measure precisely, this is an enormous sum of money.

Though the other sects of the Utopians differ from this main group in various particular doctrines, they agree with them in this single head, that there is one supreme power, the maker and ruler of the universe, whom they all call in their native language Mithra.[9] Different people define him differently, and each supposes the object of his worship is that one and only nature to whose divine majesty, by the consensus of all nations, the creation of all things is attributed. But gradually they are coming to forsake this mixture of superstitions, and to unite in that one religion which seems more reasonable than any of the others. And there is no doubt that the other religions would have disappeared long ago, had not various unlucky accidents that befell certain Utopians who were thinking about changing their religion been interpreted, out of fear, as signs of divine anger, not chance, as if the deity who was being abandoned were avenging an insult against himself.

But after they had heard from us the name of Christ, and learned of his teachings, his life, his miracles, and the no less marvelous constancy of the many martyrs whose blood, freely shed, has drawn many nations far and near into the Christian fellowship, you would not believe how eagerly they assented to it, either through the mysterious inspiration of God, or because Christianity seemed very like the religion already prevailing among them. But I think they were also much influenced by the fact that Christ approved a communal way of life for his disciples, and that among the truest communities of Christians the practice still prevails.[1] Whatever the reason, no small number of them chose to join our communion, and received the holy water of baptism. By that time, two of our group had died, and among us four survivors there was, I am sorry to say, no priest; so, though they received the other sacraments, they still lack those which in our religion can be administered only by priests. They do, however, understand what these are, and earnestly desire them. In fact, they dispute vigorously whether a man chosen from among themselves could legitimately assume the functions of a priest without the dispatch of a Christian bishop. Though they seemed on the point of selecting such a person, they had not yet done so when I left.

Those who have not accepted Christianity make no effort to restrain others from it, nor do they criticize new converts to it. While I was there, only one of the Christians was interfered with. As soon as he was baptized, he took upon himself to preach the Christian religion publicly, with more zeal than discretion. We warned him not to do so, but he soon worked himself up to a pitch where he not only set our religion above the rest but condemned all others as profane in themselves, leading their impious and sacrilegious followers to the hell-flames they richly deserved. After he had been going on in this style for a long time, they arrested him. He was tried on a charge, not of despising their religion, but of creating a public disorder, convicted, and sentenced to exile. For it is one of their oldest rules that no man's religion, as such, shall be held against him.

Utopus had heard that before his arrival the inhabitants were continually quarreling over religious matters. In fact, he found it was easy to conquer the country because the different sects were too busy fighting one another to oppose him. As soon as he had gained the victory, therefore, he decreed that everyone could cultivate the religion of his choice, and strenuously proselytize for it too, provided he did so quietly, modestly, rationally, and without bitterness toward

---

9. The spirit of light and truth in ancient Zoroastrian cosmology, in what is today Iran.

1. This practice is described in Acts 2.44–45 and 4.32–35, and echoed in many monastic orders.

others. If persuasion failed, no one was allowed to resort to abuse or violence. Anyone who fights wantonly about religion is punished by exile or enslavement.

Utopus laid down these rules not simply for the sake of peace, which he saw was in danger of being destroyed by constant quarrels and implacable hatreds, but also for the sake of religion itself. In matters of religion, he was not at all quick to dogmatize, because he suspected that God perhaps likes diverse and manifold forms of worship and has therefore deliberately inspired different people with different views. On the other hand, he was quite sure that it was arrogant folly for anyone to enforce conformity with his own beliefs on everyone else by means of threats or violence. He supposed that if one religion is really true and the rest false, the true one will sooner or later emerge and prevail by its own natural strength, provided only that men consider the matter reasonably and moderately. But if they try to decide these matters by fighting and rioting, since the worst men are always the most headstrong, the best and holiest religion in the world will be crowded out by blind superstitions, like grain choked out of a field by thorns and briars. So he left the whole matter open, allowing each individual to choose what he would believe. The only exception he made was a solemn and strict law against any person who should sink so far below the dignity of human nature as to think that the soul perishes with the body, or that the universe is ruled by mere chance rather than divine providence.[2]

Thus the Utopians all believe that after this life vices are to be punished and virtue rewarded; and they consider that anyone who denies this proposition is not even one of the human race, since he has degraded the sublimity of his own soul to the base level of a beast's wretched body. Still less will they count him as one of their citizens, since he would openly despise all the laws and customs of society, if not prevented by fear. Who can doubt that a man who has nothing to fear but the law, and no hope of life beyond the grave, will do anything he can to evade his country's laws by craft or break them by violence, in order to gratify his own private greed? Therefore a person who holds such views is offered no honors, entrusted with no offices, and given no public responsibility; he is universally regarded as low and torpid. Yet they do not afflict him with punishments, because they are persuaded that no one can choose to believe by a mere act of the will. They do not compel him by threats to dissemble his views, nor do they tolerate in the matter any deceit or lying, which they detest as next door to deliberate malice. The man may not argue with the common people in behalf of his opinion; but in the presence of the priests and other important persons, in private, they not only permit but encourage it. For they are confident that in the end his madness will yield to reason.

There are some others, in fact no small number of them, who err in the opposite direction, in supposing that animals too have immortal souls,[3] though not comparable to ours in excellence, nor destined to equal felicity. These people are not thought to be evil, their opinion is not thought to be wholly unreasonable, and so they are not interfered with.

Almost all the Utopians are absolutely convinced that human bliss after death will be enormous; thus they lament every individual's sickness, but mourn over

---

2. These views, which even the tolerant Utopians seem unable to contemplate, appear in the Epicurean philosopher Lucretius's (99–55 B.C.E.) *On the Nature of Things.*

3. In ancient Greece, followers of Pythagoras believed in the transmigration of souls into other animals.

a death only if the person was torn from life anxiously and unwillingly. Such behavior they take to be a very bad sign, as if the soul, despairing and conscious of guilt, dreaded death through a secret premonition of punishments to come. Besides, they suppose God can hardly be well pleased with the coming of one who, when he is summoned, does not come gladly but is dragged off reluctantly and against his will. Such a death fills the onlookers with horror, and they carry the corpse out to burial in melancholy silence. There, after begging God to have mercy on his spirit and to pardon his infirmities, they commit his body to the earth. But when someone dies blithely and full of good hope, they do not mourn for him but carry the body cheerfully away, singing and commending the dead man's soul to God. They cremate him in a spirit more of reverence than of grief, and erect a column on which the dead man's honors are inscribed. After they have returned home, they talk of his character and deeds, and no part of his life is mentioned more frequently or more gladly than his joyful death.

They think that recollecting the dead person's goodness helps the living to behave virtuously and is also the most acceptable form of honor to the dead. For they think that dead people are actually present among us, and hear what we say about them, though through the dullness of human sight they are invisible to our eyes. Given their state of bliss, the dead must be able to travel freely where they please, and it would be unkind of them to cast off every desire of revisiting their friends, to whom they had been bound by mutual affection and charity during their lives. Like all other good things, they think that after death charity is increased rather than decreased in good men; and thus they believe the dead come frequently among the living, to observe their words and actions. Hence they go about their business the more confidently because of their trust in such protectors; and the belief that their forefathers are physically present keeps them from any secret dishonorable deed.

Fortune-telling and other vain forms of superstitious divination, such as other peoples take very seriously, they have no part of and consider ridiculous. But they venerate miracles which occur without the help of nature, considering them direct and visible manifestations of the divine power. Indeed, they report that miracles have frequently occurred in their country. Sometimes in great and dangerous crises they pray publicly for a miracle, which they then anticipate with great confidence, and obtain.

They think that the contemplation of nature, and the sense of reverence arising from it, are acts of worship to God. There are some people, however, and not just a few of them, who from religious motives reject learning and pursue no studies; but none of them is the least bit idle. Constant dedication to the offices of charity, these people think, will increase their chances of happiness after death; and so they are always busy in the service of others. Some tend the sick; others repair roads, clean ditches, rebuild bridges, dig turf, sand, or stones; still others fell trees and cut them up, and transport wood, grain, or other commodities into the cities by wagon. They work for private citizens as well as for the public, and work even harder than slaves. They undertake with cheery good will any task that is so rough, hard, and dirty that most people refuse to tackle it because of the toil, boredom, and frustration involved. While constantly engaged in heavy labor themselves, they secure leisure for others, and yet they claim no credit for it. They do not criticize the way other people live, nor do they boast of their own doings. The more they put themselves in the position of slaves, the more highly they are honored by everyone.

These people are of two sects. The first are celibates who abstain not only from sex but also from eating meat, and some of them from any sort of animal food whatever. They reject all the pleasures of this life as harmful, and look forward only to the joys of the life to come, which they hope to deserve by hard labor and all-night vigils. As they hope to attain it soon, they are cheerful and active in the here and now. The other kind are just as fond of hard work, but prefer to marry. They don't despise the comforts of marriage, but think that, as their duty to nature requires work, so their duty to their country requires them to beget children. They avoid no pleasures unless it interferes with their labor, and gladly eat meat, precisely because they think it makes them stronger for any sort of heavy work. The Utopians regard the second sort as more sensible, but the first sort as holier. If they claimed to prefer celibacy to marriage, and a hard life to a comfortable one, on grounds of reason alone, the Utopians would think them absurd. But since these men claim to be motivated by religion, the Utopians respect and revere them. There is no subject on which they are warier of jumping to conclusions than in this matter of religion. These then are the men whom in their own language they call Buthrescas, a term which may be translated as "the especially religious."

Their priests are of great holiness, and therefore very few. In each city, there are no more than thirteen, one for each church. In case of war, seven of them go out with the army, and seven substitutes are appointed to fill their places for the time being. When the regular priests come back, the substitutes return to their former posts—that is, they serve as assistants to the high priest, until one of the regular thirteen dies, and then one of them succeeds to his position. The high priest is, of course, in authority over all the others. Priests are elected, just like all other officials, by secret popular vote, in order to avoid partisan feeling. After election they are ordained by the college of priests.

They preside over divine worship, attend to religious matters, and act as censors of public morality. For a man to be summoned before them and scolded for not living an honorable life is considered a great disgrace. As the duty of the priests is simply to counsel and advise, so correcting and punishing offenders is the duty of the governor and the other officials, though the priests do exclude from divine service persons whom they find to be extraordinarily wicked. Hardly any punishment is more dreaded than this; the excommunicate incurs great disgrace, and is tortured by the fear of damnation. Not even his body is safe for long, for unless he quickly convinces the priests of his repentance he will be seized and punished by the senate for impiety.

The priests are entrusted with teaching the children and young people. Instruction in morality and virtue is considered just as important as the accumulation of learning. From the very first they try to instill in the pupils' minds, while they are still young and tender, principles which will be useful to preserve the commonwealth. What is planted in the minds of children lives on in the minds of adults, and is of great value in strengthening the commonwealth: the decline of society can always be traced to vices which arise from wrong attitudes.

Women are not debarred from the priesthood, but only a widow of advanced years is ever chosen, and it doesn't happen often. The wives of the male priests are the very finest women in the whole country.

No official in Utopia is more honored than the priest. Even if one of them commits a crime, he is not brought into a court of law, but left to God and his own conscience. They think it is wrong to lay human hands on a man, however guilty, who has been specially consecrated to God as a holy offering, so to speak. This custom is the easier for them to observe because their priests are very few and very carefully chosen. Besides, it rarely happens that a man selected for his goodness and raised to high dignities wholly because of his moral character will fall into corruption and vice. And even if such a thing should happen, human nature being as changeable as it is, no great harm is to be feared, because the priests are so few and have no power beyond that which derives from their good reputation. In fact, the reason for having so few priests is to prevent the order, which the Utopians now esteem so highly, from being cheapened by numbers. Besides, they think it would be hard to find many men qualified for a dignity for which merely ordinary virtues are not sufficient.

Their priests are esteemed no less highly abroad than at home, which can be seen from the following fact: Whenever their armies join in battle, the Utopian priests are to be found, a little removed from the fray but not far, wearing their sacred vestments and down on their knees. With hands raised to heaven, they pray first of all for peace, and then for victory to their own side, but without much bloodshed on either hand. Should their side be victorious, they rush among the combatants and restrain the rage of their own men against the enemy. If any of the enemy see these priests and call to them, it is enough to save their lives; to touch the flowing robes of a priest will save all their property from confiscation. This custom has brought them such veneration among all peoples, and given them such genuine authority, that they have saved the Utopians from the rage of the enemy as often as they have protected the enemy from Utopians. Instances of this are well known. Sometimes when the Utopian line has buckled, when the field was lost, and the enemy was rushing in to kill and plunder, the priests have intervened to stop the carnage and separate the armies, and an equitable peace has been concluded. There was never anywhere a tribe so fierce, cruel, and barbarous as not to hold their persons sacrosanct and inviolable.

The Utopians celebrate the first and last days of every month, and likewise of each year, as feast days. They divide the year into months which they measure by the orbit of the moon, just as they measure the year itself by the course of the sun. In their language, the first days are known as the Cynemerns and the last days as the Trapemerns,[4] which is to say "First-feasts" and "Last-feasts." Their churches are beautifully constructed, finely adorned, and large enough to hold a great many people. This is a necessity, since churches are so few. Their interiors are all rather dark, not from architectural ignorance but from deliberate policy; for the priests think that in bright light the congregation's thoughts will go wandering, whereas a dim light tends to concentrate the mind and encourage devotion.

Though there are various religions in Utopia, all of them, even the most diverse, agree in the main point, which is worship of the divine nature; they are like travelers going to one destination by different roads. So nothing is seen or heard in the churches that does not square with all the creeds. If any sect has a special rite of its own, that is celebrated in a private house; the public service is ordered by a ritual which in no way derogates from any of the private services. Therefore in the churches no image of the gods is to be seen, so that each person may be free to form his own image of God according to his own religion, in any shape he pleases. They do not invoke God by any name except Mithra. Whatever the nature of the divine majesty may be, they all agree to refer to it by that single word, and their prayers are so phrased as to accommodate the beliefs of all the different sects.

---

4. Turning day (Greek). "Cynemern": dog-day (Greek).

On the evening of the "Last-feast" they meet in their churches, and while still fasting they thank God for their prosperity during that month or year which is just ending. Next day, which is "First-feast," they all flock to the churches in the morning, to pray for prosperity and happiness in the month or year which is just beginning. On the day of "Last-feast," in the home before they go to church, wives kneel before their husbands and children before their parents, to confess their various sins of commission or of negligence and beg forgiveness for their offenses. Thus if any cloud of anger or resentment has arisen in the family, it is dispersed, and they can attend divine services with clear and untroubled minds—for they consider it sacrilege to worship with a rankling conscience. If they are conscious of hatred or anger toward anyone, they do not take part in divine services till they have been reconciled and have cleansed their hearts, for fear of some swift and terrible punishment.

As they enter the church, they separate, men going to the right side and women to the left. Then they take their seats so that the males of each household are placed in front of the head of that household, while the womenfolk are directly in front of the mother of the family. In this way they ensure that everyone's behavior in public is supervised by the same person whose authority and discipline direct him at home. They take great care that the young are everywhere placed in the company of their elders. For if children were trusted to the care of other children, they might spend in childish foolery the time they should devote to developing a religious fear of the gods, which is the greatest and almost the only incitement to virtue.

They do not slaughter animals in their sacrifices, and do not think that a merciful God, who gave life to all creatures precisely so that they might live, will be gratified with the shedding of blood. They burn incense, scatter perfumes, and display a great number of candles—not that they think these practices profit the divine nature in any way, any more than human prayers do; but they like this harmless kind of worship. They feel that sweet smells, lights, and other such rituals elevate the mind and lift it with a livelier devotion toward the adoration of God.

When they go to church, the people all wear white. The priest wears robes of various colors, wonderful for their workmanship and decoration, though not of materials as costly as one would suppose. The robes have no gold embroidery nor any precious stones, but are decorated with the feathers of different birds so skillfully woven together that the value of the handiwork far exceeds the cost of the most precious materials. Also, certain symbolic mysteries are hidden in the patterning of the feathers on the robes, the meaning of which is carefully handed down among the priests. These messages serve to remind them of God's benefits toward them, and consequently of the devotion they owe to God, as well as of their duty to one another.

As the priest in his robes appears from the vestibule, the people all fall to the ground in reverence. The stillness is so complete that the scene strikes one with awe, as if a divinity were actually present. After remaining in this posture for some time, they rise at a signal from the priest. Then they sing hymns to the accompaniment of musical instruments, most of them quite different in shape from those in our part of the world. Many of them produce sweeter tones than ours, but others are not even comparable. In one respect, however, they are beyond doubt far ahead of us, because all their music, both vocal and instrumental, renders and expresses natural feelings and perfectly matches the sound to the subject. Whether the words of the hymn are supplicatory, cheerful, troubled, mournful, or angry, the music represents the meaning through the contour of the melody so admirably that it penetrates and inspires the minds of the ardent hearers. Finally, the priest and the people together recite certain fixed forms of prayer, so composed that what they all repeat in unison each individual can apply to himself.

In these prayers, the worshipers acknowledge God to be the creator and ruler of the universe and the author of all good things. They thank God for benefits received, and particularly for the divine favor which placed them in the happiest of commonwealths and inspired them with religious ideas which they hope are the truest. If they are wrong in this, and if there is some sort of society or religion more acceptable to God, they pray that he will, in his goodness, reveal it to them, for they are ready to follow wherever he leads. But if their form of society is the best and their religion the truest, then they pray that God will keep them steadfast, and bring other mortals to the same way of life and the same religious faith—unless, indeed, there is something in this variety of religions which delights his inscrutable will.

Then they pray that after an easy death God will receive each of them to himself, how soon or how late it is not for them to say. But if God's divine majesty so please, they ask to be brought to him soon, even by the hardest possible death, rather than be kept away from him longer, even by the most fortunate of earthly lives. When this prayer has been said, they prostrate themselves on the ground again; then after a little while they rise and go to lunch. The rest of the day they pass in games and military training.

Now I have described to you as accurately as I could the structure of that commonwealth which I consider not only the best but indeed the only one that can rightfully claim that name. In other places men talk very liberally of the commonwealth, but what they mean is simply their own wealth; in Utopia, where there is no private business, everyone zealously pursues the public business. And in both places people are right to act as they do. For among us, even though the commonwealth may flourish, there are very few who do not know that unless they make separate provision for themselves, they may perfectly well die of hunger. Bitter necessity, then, forces them to think that they must look out for themselves rather than for others, that is, for the people. But in Utopia, where everything belongs to everybody, no one need fear that, so long as the public warehouses are filled, anyone will ever lack for anything he needs. For the distribution of goods is not niggardly; in Utopia no one is poor, there are no beggars, and though no one owns anything, everyone is rich.

For what can be greater riches than to live joyfully and peacefully, free from all anxieties, and without worries about making a living? No man is bothered by his wife's querulous entreaties about money, no man fears poverty for his son, or struggles to scrape up a dowry for his daughter. Everyone can feel secure of his own livelihood and happiness, and of his whole family's as well: wife, sons, grandsons, great-grandsons, great-great-grandsons, and that whole long line of descendants that gentlefolk are so fond of contemplating. Indeed, even those who once worked but can no longer do so are cared for just as well as those who are still working.

Now here I'd like to see anyone try to compare this equity of the Utopians with the so-called justice that prevails among other peoples—among whom let me perish if I can discover the slightest scrap of justice or fairness. What kind of justice is it when a nobleman or a goldsmith or a moneylender, or someone else who makes his living by doing either nothing at all or something completely useless to the commonwealth, gets to live a life of luxury and grandeur, while in the meantime a laborer, a carter, a carpenter, or a farmer works so hard and so constantly that even a beast of burden could scarcely endure it? Although this work of theirs is so necessary that no commonwealth could survive a year without it, they earn so meager a living and lead such miserable lives that beasts of burden would really seem to be better off. Beasts do not have to work every minute, and their food is not much worse; in fact they like it better. And besides, they do not have to worry about their future. But workingmen not only have to sweat and suffer without present reward, but agonize over the prospect of a penniless old age. Their daily wage is inadequate even for their present needs, so there is no possible chance of their saving toward the future.

Now isn't this an unjust and ungrateful commonwealth? It lavishes rich rewards on so-called gentry, goldsmiths, and the rest of that crew, who don't work at all or are mere parasites, purveyors of empty pleasures. And yet it makes no provision whatever for the welfare of farmers and colliers, laborers, carters, and carpenters, without whom the commonwealth would simply cease to exist. After society has taken the labor of their best years, when they are worn out by age and sickness and utter destitution, then the thankless commonwealth, forgetting all their sleepless nights and great services, throws them out to die a miserable death. What is worse, the rich constantly try to grind out of the poor part of their meager wages, not only by private swindling but by public laws. Before, it appeared to be unjust that people who deserve most from the commonwealth should receive least; but now, by promulgating law, they have palmed injustice off as "legal." When I run over in my mind the various commonwealths flourishing today, so help me God, I can see in them nothing but a conspiracy of the rich, who are fattening up their own interests under the name and title of the commonwealth. They invent ways and means to hang onto whatever they have acquired by sharp practice, and then they scheme to oppress the poor by buying up their toil and labor as cheaply as possible. These devices become law as soon as the rich, speaking for the commonwealth—which, of course, includes the poor as well—say they must be observed.

And yet, when these insatiably greedy and evil men have divided among themselves all the goods which would have sufficed for the entire people, how far they remain from the happiness of the Utopian republic, which has abolished not only money but with it greed! What a mass of trouble was cut away by that one step! What a multitude of crimes was pulled up by the roots! Everyone knows that if money were abolished, fraud, theft, robbery, quarrels, brawls, altercations, seditions, murders, treasons, poisonings, and a whole set of crimes which are avenged but not prevented by the hangman would at once die out. If money disappeared, so would fear, anxiety, worry, toil, and sleepless nights. Even poverty, the one condition which seems more than anything else to need money for its relief, would die away if money were entirely abolished.

Consider, if you will, this example. Take a barren year of failed harvests, when many thousands of people have been carried off by famine. If at the end of the scarcity the barns of the rich were searched, I dare say positively that enough grain would be found in them to have kept all those who died of starvation and disease from even realizing that a shortage ever existed—if only it had been divided among them. So easily might people get the necessities of life if that cursed money, that marvelous invention which is supposed to provide access to them, were not in fact the only barrier to our getting what we need to live. Even the rich, I'm sure, understand this. They must know that it's better to have enough of what we really need than an abundance of superfluities, much better to escape from our many present troubles than to be burdened with great masses of wealth. And in fact I have no doubt that every man's perception of where his true interest lies, along with the authority of Christ our Savior (whose wisdom could not fail to recognize the best, and whose goodness would not fail to counsel it), would long ago have brought the whole world to adopt Utopian laws, if it were not for one single monster, the prime plague and begetter of all others—I mean Pride.

Pride measures her advantages not by what she has but by what others lack. Pride would not condescend even to be made a goddess, if there were no wretches for her to sneer at and domineer over. Her good fortune is dazzling only by contrast with the miseries of others, her riches are valuable only as they torment and tantalize the poverty of others. Pride is a serpent from hell that twines itself around the hearts of men; and it acts like a suckfish⁵ in holding them back from choosing a better way of life.

Pride is too deeply fixed in human nature to be easily plucked out. So I am glad that the Utopians at least have been lucky enough to achieve this commonwealth, which I wish all mankind would imitate. The institutions they have adopted have made their community most happy, and, as far as anyone can tell, capable of lasting forever. Now that they have rooted up the seeds of ambition and faction at home, along with most other vices, they are in no danger from internal strife, which alone has been the ruin of many cities that seemed secure. As long as they preserve harmony at home, and keep their institutions healthy, the Utopians can never be overcome or even shaken by all the envious princes of neighboring countries, who have often attempted their ruin, but always in vain.

When Raphael had finished his story, I was left thinking that not a few of the customs and laws he had described as existing among the Utopians were quite absurd. These included their methods of waging war, their religious practices, as well as other customs of theirs, but my chief objection was to the basis of their whole system, that is, their communal living and their moneyless economy. This one thing alone takes away all the nobility, magnificence, splendor, and majesty which (in the popular view) are the true ornaments and glory of any commonwealth. But I saw Raphael was tired with talking, and I was not sure he could take contradiction in these matters, particularly when I remembered what he had said about certain people who were afraid they might not appear wise unless they found out something to criticize in the ideas of others. So with praise for the Utopian way of life and his account of it, I took him by the hand and led him in to supper. But first I said that we would find some other time for thinking of these matters more deeply, and for talking them over in more detail. And I still hope such an opportunity will present itself someday.

Meanwhile, though he is a man of unquestionable learning, and highly experienced in the ways of the world, I cannot agree with everything he said. Yet I freely confess there are very many things in the Utopian commonwealth that in our own societies I would wish rather than expect to see.

---

5. A small fish that attaches itself to the underbelly of larger fish or the hulls of ships.

MARGUERITE DE NAVARRE
1492–1549

The French "discovered" Italy in the latter part of the fifteenth century, both through travel and, starting in 1494, through military invasions. Eager to imitate more sophisticated Italian city-states, French rulers and aristocrats adapted Italian artistic, literary, and social values to their own culture. Marguerite de Navarre, one of the most influential members of French courtly society, played a significant part in bringing about this transformation. As a writer and a patron of artists, she also responded seriously to the spiritual and intellectual challenge to Christian faith brought about by the Reformation. Her lively collection of stories modeled on **Boccaccio**, the *Heptameron*, gives voice to characters whose different positions afford them starkly different views of the world.

LIFE AND TIMES

Marguerite was born in 1492 into the French royal family. Her brother, the future King Francis I, was born two years later. From her earliest years, Marguerite received an exceptionally good education, including instruction in Latin, Italian, Spanish, and German; later in life she also studied Greek and Hebrew. At seventeen she was married to Charles, duke of Alençon, a feudal lord who was intellectually not her match. When her brother succeeded Louis XII to the French throne in 1515, Marguerite became one of the most influential women at the royal court, where she advised the king and received dignitaries and ambassadors as well as eminent men of letters. Under Francis I, the French court flourished culturally, hiring Ital-

ian artists as famous as Leonardo da Vinci (1452–1519) and Benvenuto Cellini (1500–1571).

Francis I continued the Italian wars, the complicated conflicts fought on Italian soil between his forces and those of the Holy Roman Emperor, Charles V. His defeat in the crucial battle of Pavia in 1525 was a double blow for Marguerite: her brother was taken to Madrid as a prisoner and her husband died of battle wounds. Marguerite went to Madrid to assist her sick brother and helped negotiate with Charles V for his release.

The year following her husband's death, Marguerite became "queen of Navarre" when she married Henri d'Albret, the king of Navarre in title only, since most of that domain had been annexed by Spain in 1516. Eleven years younger than Marguerite, Henri d'Albret was a dashing, flighty, and intellectually disappointing husband—and is thought to be the prototype for the philandering and misogynistic character of Hircan in the *Heptameron*. Their only daughter, Jeanne, born in 1527, was the mother of the future King Henry IV of France.

Marguerite continued to be involved in her royal brother's activities, participating in diplomacy and peace talks. Her interest, however, was increasingly focused on intellectual and literary pursuits and on religious meditation and debate. Erasmus, John Calvin, and Pope Paul III were among her numerous correspondents. Throughout her life she was a protector of writers and thinkers accused or suspected of Protestant leanings, including **Rabelais**, who dedicated the third book of *Gargantua and Pantagruel* to her. Her first published work, *The Mirror of the Sinful Soul* (1531), was found by the theologians of the Sorbonne to contain elements of Protestant "heresy"; the edition of 1533, containing an additional "Dialogue in the Form of a Night Vision" on the theological problem of salvation, was condemned. The king had to intervene on behalf of his sister and her chaplain. Later it became more difficult for Francis I to manage the rivalry between Catholics and Protestants, which was a political and military matter as much as it was a religious dispute. Protestants and their sympathizers were persecuted, and several prominent intellectuals went into prudent exile or were burned at the stake. Marguerite, who had an intellectual and mystical faith, appears never to have abandoned Catholicism but to have hoped for internal reform.

After the death of her brother in 1547, she published her *Marguerite de la Marguerite des Princesses* (with a play on the word *marguerite*, which in French means both "pearl" and "daisy"), a collection including long devotional poems and theatrical pieces ranging from allegory to farce. In 1549 she retired to Navarre and died in the castle of Odos on December 21.

THE *HEPTAMERON*

Marguerite's greatest literary achievement is the *Heptameron*, which was not published until 1559, a decade after her death. A collection of seventy stories told over seven days, it is framed by a larger narrative that reveals the storytellers' characters and relationships with each other. We do not know the exact circumstances of its production, and there are doubts that Marguerite herself authored all of its parts. Some scholars have concluded that Marguerite collected or commissioned tales for the narrative, and perhaps composed only the frame narrative—in many ways the work's most

compelling feature. In the prologue, five men and five women, all nobles, are brought together in the Pyrenees when natural and criminal forces—including a flood, bandits, a bear, and murderers—prevent them from returning home. They arrive independently at an abbey, where, at the suggestion of Parlamente, thought to represent Marguerite herself, they agree to tell stories each day until they are able to return home. The stories deal above all with the antagonism between the sexes, particularly concerning issues of marital fidelity and the status of women. The *Heptameron* pays considerable attention to ideas of masculinity and to ideals and stereotypes about women. Class tensions are somewhat more muted, although the stories often pit powerful lords and husbands against those whose only weapon is their cleverness. The courtly men and women who narrate and hear the stories are, to say the least, unafraid to disagree with each other about the tales' significances, both in the frame and through their stories, which implicitly debate such issues as the just desserts for the philandering husband or the clever wife. For example, Ennasuite, the female narrator of story 10, celebrates a high-spirited, intelligent princess who physically resists and humiliates a gentleman who assaults her in her bedchamber. Yet the aggressive Hircan retorts that Ennasuite's gentleman should have raped the princess rather than suffer humiliation, and uses his own tale to present manly dominance—which other characters have been disparaging—in an attractive and romantic light.

The *Heptameron* belongs to a tradition of framed storytelling that includes the **Arabian Nights**, Chaucer's **Canterbury Tales**, and Boccaccio's **Decameron**. In the prologue, Parlamente overtly ties the storytelling game to the *Decameron* and a recent translation into French (commissioned by Marguerite) that drew, she says, the admiration of the French court. In writing a French *Decameron*, however, the group proposed, "they should not write any story that was not truthful." The relationship between language and truth therefore becomes a dominant theme. Unable to devote themselves entirely to religious pursuits, the characters choose "truthful" stories as a worthwhile pastime.

By truthfulness, Marguerite means stories that are honest about social tensions. When the characters comment— in the frame and in their own stories—on each others' tales, they reveal how social factors influence their view of the world. Divine "truth" gives way to individual and social perspective: age, gender, social standing, education, marital status, and religious disposition form the grounds for rivalry and dispute among the group members.

The two stories reproduced here show strong female characters managing male desire. The social differences among the characters are key to understanding their positions. In story 8, a wise wife protects her chambermaid and foils her philandering husband at the same time, exposing the blindness of his sexual infatuation. In the more complex story 10, the heroic Amador can only worship his beloved Florida from a distance, as she is "of far higher birth than he." As an old-fashioned knight of romance, Amador ("he who loves") seems content to stick to this kind of service, but when he is called to aid his king, he seeks to force an immediate union with his beloved, who bravely resists him. In this tale of dutiful devotion gone awry, a modernizing monarchy and the increasing irrelevance of older aristocratic forms lead to the demise of courtly love.

The "amusing and virtuous" pastime of a privileged group of storytellers forced into reclusion becomes in these pages a lively debate on gender roles, true virtue, and the force of society's disapproval. Balanced between the court and broader social concerns, between older certainties and new challenges, the *Heptameron* presents a lively and complex portrait of Marguerite de Navarre's changing world. At the same time, it offers an enduring account of the gendered division of experience, exploring how men and women manage and mismanage their desires.

From The Heptameron[1]

From *Prologue*

* * *

Parlamente, the wife of Hircan,[2] was not one to let herself become idle or melancholy, and having asked her husband for permission, she spoke to the old Lady Oisille.[3]

1. Translated by P. A. Chilton.
2. Hircan is variously described, in the book itself and by its commentators, as brilliant, flighty, sensual, capable of sarcasm and grossness. The name is related to Hircania, an imaginary and proverbially wild region in classical literature; the root is that of *hircus*, Latin for "goat" (cf. English *hircine*: libidinous). Parlamente probably represents Marguerite, whose name can be construed as *perle amante*, "loving pearl," or as *parlementer*, which refers to eloquent speaking.
3. The oldest, most authoritative, and most evangelical of the storytellers; she seems to be named for Louise—either Louise of Savoy, Marguerite's mother, or her lady-in-waiting, Louise de Daillon.

"Madame," she said. "you have had much experience of life, and you now occupy the position of mother in regard to the rest of us women, and it surprises me that you do not consider some pastime to alleviate the boredom and distress that we shall have to bear during our long stay here. Unless we have some amusing and virtuous way of occupying ourselves, we run the risk of [falling][4] sick."

Longarine,[5] the young widow, added, "What is worse, we'll all become miserable and disagreeable—and that's an incurable disease. There isn't a man or woman amongst us who hasn't every cause to sink into despair, if we consider all that we have lost."

Ennasuite[6] laughed and rejoined, "Not everyone's lost a husband, like you, you know. And as for losing servants, no need to despair about that—there are plenty of men ready to do service! All the same, I do agree that we ought to have something to amuse us, so that we can pass the time as pleasantly as we can."

Her companion Nomerfide[7] said that this was a very good idea, and that if she had to spend a single day without some entertainment, she would be sure to die the next.

All the men supported this, and asked the Lady Oisille if she would kindly organize what they should do.

"My children," replied Oisille, "when you ask me to show you a pastime that is capable of delivering you from your boredom and your sorrow, you are asking me to do something that I find very difficult. All my life I have searched for a remedy, and I have found only one—the reading of holy Scripture, in which one may find true and perfect spiritual joy, from which proceed health and bodily repose. And if you ask what the prescription is that keeps me happy and healthy in my old age, I will tell you. As soon as I rise in the morning I take the Scriptures and read them. I see and contemplate the goodness of God, who for our sakes has sent His son to earth to declare the holy word and the good news by which He grants remission of all our sins, and payment of all our debts, through His gift to us of His love, His passion and His merits. And my contemplations give me such joy, that I take my psalter, and with the utmost humility, sing the beautiful psalms and hymns that the Holy Spirit has composed in the heart of David and the other authors. The contentment this affords me fills me with such well-being that whatever the evils of the day, they are to me so many blessings, for in my heart I have by faith Him who has borne these evils for me. Likewise, before supper, I withdraw to nourish my soul with readings and meditations. In the evening I ponder in my mind everything I have done during the day, so that I may ask God forgiveness of my sins, and give thanks to Him for His mercies. And so I lay myself to rest in His love, fear and peace, assured against all evils. And this,

4. Brackets indicate translator's interpolations.
5. A young and wisely talkative widow, often identified with one of Marguerite's ladies-inwaiting, who among her titles had that of lady of Langrai (hence her name, which is also interpreted as a play on *langue orine*, meaning "tongue of gold").
6. *Enna* may stand for "Anne," and *suite*

means "retinue"; so the character is identifiable with Anne de Vivonne, one of the ladies in Marguerite's entourage who collaborated on the *Heptameron* project at court. Her attitude toward men can be bitter and sharply ironic.
7. The youngest member of the group, who generally views life with joyful optimism.

my children, is the pastime that long ago I adopted. All other ways have I tried, but none has given me spiritual contentment. I believe that if, each morning, you give one hour to reading, and then, during mass, say your prayers devoutly, you will find even in this wilderness all the beauty a city could afford. For, a person who knows God will find all things beautiful in Him, and without Him all things will seem ugly. So I say to you, if you would live in happiness, heed my advice."

Then Hircan spoke: "Madame, anyone who has read the holy Scriptures—as indeed I think we all have here—will readily agree that what you have said is true. However, you must bear in mind that we have not yet become so mortified in the flesh that we are not in need of some sort of amusement and physical exercise in order to pass the time. After all, when we're at home, we've got our hunting and hawking to distract us from the thousand and one foolish thoughts that pass through one's mind. The ladies have their housework and their needlework. They have their dances, too, which provide a respectable way for them to get some exercise. All this leads me to suggest, on behalf of the men here, that you, Madame, since you are the oldest among us, should read to us every morning about the life of our Lord Jesus Christ, and the great and wonderful things He has done for us. Between dinner and vespers I think we should choose some pastime, which, while not being prejudicial to the soul, will be agreeable to the body. In that way we shall spend a very pleasant day."

Lady Oisille replied that she herself found it so difficult to put behind her the vanities of life, that she was afraid the pastime suggested by Hircan might not be a good choice. However, the question should, she thought, be judged after an open discussion, and she asked Hircan to put his point of view first.

"Well, my point of view wouldn't take long to give," he began, "if I thought that the pastime I would really like were as agreeable to a certain lady among us as it would be to me. So I'll keep quiet for now, and abide by what the others say."

Thinking he was intending this for her, his wife, Parlamente, began to blush. "It may be, Hircan," she said, half angrily and half laughing, "that the lady you think ought to be the most annoyed at what you say would have ways and means of getting her own back, if she so desired. But let's leave on one side all pastimes that require only two participants, and concentrate on those which everybody can join in."

Hircan turned to the ladies. "Since my wife has managed to put the right interpretation on my words," he said, "and since private pastimes don't appeal to her, I think she's in a better position than anyone to know which pastime all of us will be able to enjoy. Let me say right now that I accept her opinion as if it were my own."

They all concurred in this, and Parlamente, seeing that it had fallen to her to make the choice, addressed them all as follows.

"If I felt myself to be as capable as the ancients, by whom the arts were discovered, then I would invent some pastime myself that would meet the requirements you have laid down for me. However, I know what lies within the scope of my own knowledge and ability—I can hardly even remember the clever things other people have invented, let alone invent new things myself.

So I shall be quite content to follow closely in the footsteps of other people who have already provided for your needs. For example, I don't think there's one of us who hasn't read the hundred tales by Boccaccio,[8] which have recently been translated from Italian into French, and which are so highly thought of by the [most Christian] King Francis I, by Monseigneur the Dauphin, Madame the Dauphine[9] and Madame Marguerite. If Boccaccio could have heard how highly these illustrious people praised him, it would have been enough to raise him from the grave. As a matter of fact, the two ladies I've mentioned, along with other people at the court, made up their minds to do the same as Boccaccio. There was to be one difference—that they should not write any story that was not truthful. Together with Monseigneur the Dauphin the ladies promised to produce ten stories each, and to get together a party of ten people who were qualified to contribute something, excluding those who studied and were men of letters. Monseigneur the Dauphin didn't want their art brought in, and he was afraid that rhetorical ornament would in part falsify the truth of the account. A number of things led to the project being completely forgotten—the major affairs of state that subsequently overtook the King, the peace treaty between him and the King of England, the confinement of Madame the Dauphine and several other events of sufficient importance to keep the court otherwise occupied. However, it can now be completed in the ten days of leisure we have before us, while we wait for our bridge to be finished. If you so wished, we could go each afternoon between midday and four o'clock to the lovely meadow that borders the Gave de Pau, where the leaves on the trees are so thick that the hot sun cannot penetrate the shade and the cool beneath. There we can sit and rest, and each of us will tell a story which he has either witnessed himself, or which he has heard from somebody worthy of belief. At the end of our ten days we will have completed the whole hundred. And if, God willing, the lords and ladies I've mentioned find our endeavors worthy of their attention, we shall make them a present of them when we get back, instead of the usual statuettes and beads. I'm sure they would find that preferable. In spite of all this, if any of you is able to think of something more agreeable, I shall gladly bow to his or her opinion."

But every one of them replied that it would be impossible to think of anything better, and that they could hardly wait for the morrow. So the day came happily to a close with reminiscences of things they had all experienced in their time.

As soon as morning came they all went into Madame Oisille's room, where she was already at her prayers. When they had listened for a good hour to the lesson she had to read them, and then devoutly heard mass, they went, at ten o'clock, to dine, after which they retired to their separate rooms to attend to what they had to do. At midday they all went back as arranged to the meadow, which was looking so beautiful and fair that it would take a Boccaccio to describe it as it really was. Enough for us to say that a more beautiful meadow there never was seen. When they were all seated on the grass, so green and soft

8. The *Decameron*.
9. The future queen Catherine de Médici.

"Monseigneur the Dauphin": the future Henry II, nephew of Marguerite.

that there was no need for carpets or cushions, Simontaut[1] said: "Which of us shall be [the one in charge]?"

*　*　*

Story 8

In the county of Alès there was once a man by the name of Bornet, who had married a very decent and respectable woman. He held her honor and reputation very dear, as I am sure all husbands here hold the honor and reputation of *their* wives dear. He wanted her to be faithful to him, but was not so keen on having the rule applied to them both equally. He had become enamored of his chambermaid, though the only benefit he got from transferring his affections in this way was the sort of pleasure one gets from varying one's diet. He had a neighbor called Sendras, who was of similar station and temperament to himself—he was a tailor and a drummer. These two were such close friends that, with the exception of the wife, there was nothing that they did not share between them. Naturally he told him that he had designs on the chambermaid.

Not only did his friend wholeheartedly approve of this, but did his best to help him, in the hope that he too might get a share in the spoils.

The chambermaid herself refused to have anything to do with him, although he was constantly pestering her and in the end she went to tell her mistress about it. She told her that she could not stand being badgered by him any longer, and asked permission to go home to her parents. Now the good lady of the house, who was really very much in love with her husband, had often had occasion to suspect him, and was therefore rather pleased to be one up on him, and to be able to show him that she had found out what he was up to. So she said to her maid: "Be nice to him dear, encourage him a little bit, and then make a date to go to bed with him in my dressing-room. Don't forget to tell me which night he's supposed to be coming, and make sure you don't tell anyone else."

The maid did exactly as her mistress had instructed. As for her master, he was so pleased with himself that he went off to tell his friend about his stroke of luck, whereupon the friend insisted on taking his share afterwards, since he had been in on the business from the beginning. When the appointed time came, off went the master, as had been agreed, to get into bed, as he thought, with his little chambermaid. But his wife, having abandoned her position of authority in order to serve in a more pleasurable one, had taken her maid's place in the bed. When he got in with her, she did not act like a wife, but like a bashful young girl, and he was not in the slightest suspicious. It would be impossible to say which of them enjoyed themselves more—the wife deceiving

1. Identified with François de Bourdeille, the husband of Anne of Vivonne. He is the long-standing *serviteur* to Parlamente: "According to the *serviteur*'s practice, as the *Heptameron* presents it, a married aristocratic woman has the right to maintain several devoted knights in her service.... Since it is supposed to be chaste, the *serviteur*'s relationship, this remnant of courtly and chivalrous love, can coexist with faithful marriage.... Nevertheless, there is evidently considerable anxiety about the institution as such" [From the translator's introduction]. His name punningly alludes to masculinity (*monte haut*: rises high).

her husband, or the husband who thought he was deceiving his wife. He stayed in bed with her for some time, not as long as he might have wished (many years of marriage were beginning to tell on him), but as long as he could manage. Then he went out to rejoin his accomplice, and tell him what a good time he had had. The lustiest piece of goods he had ever come across, he declared. His friend, who was younger and more active than he was, said: "Remember what you promised?"

"Hurry up, then," replied the master, "in case she gets up, or my wife wants her for something."

Off he went and climbed into bed with the supposed chambermaid his friend had just failed to recognize as his wife. *She* thought it was her husband again, and did not refuse anything he asked for (I say "asked," but "took" would be nearer the mark, because he did not dare open his mouth). He made a much longer business of it than the husband, to the surprise of the wife, who was not used to these long nights of pleasure. However, she did not complain, and looked forward to what she was planning to say to him in the morning, and the fun she would have teasing him. When dawn came, the man got up, and fondling her as he got out of bed, pulled off a ring she wore on her finger, a ring that her husband had given her at their marriage. Now the women in this part of the world are very superstitious about such things. They have great respect for women who hang on to their wedding rings till the day they die, and if a woman loses her ring, she is dishonored, and is looked upon as having given her faith to another man. But she did not mind him taking it, because she thought it would be sure evidence against her husband of the way she had hoodwinked him.

The husband was waiting outside for his friend, and asked him how he had got on. The man said he shared the husband's opinion, and added that he would have stayed longer, had he not been afraid of getting caught by the daylight. The pair of them then went off to get as much sleep as they could. When morning came, and they were getting dressed together, the husband noticed that his friend had on his finger a ring that was identical to the one he had given his wife on their wedding day. He asked him where he had got it, and when he was told it had come from the chambermaid the night before, he was aghast. He began banging his head against the wall, and shouted: "Oh my God! Have I gone and made myself a cuckold without my wife even knowing about it?"

His friend tried to calm him down. "Perhaps your wife had given the ring to the girl to look after before going to bed?" he suggested. The husband made no reply, but marched straight out and went back to his house.

There he found his wife looking unusually gay and attractive. Had she not saved her chambermaid from staining her conscience, and had she not put her husband to the ultimate test, without any more cost to herself than a night's sleep? Seeing her in such good spirits, the husband thought to himself: "She wouldn't be greeting me so cheerfully if she knew what I'd been up to."

As they chatted, he took hold of her hand and saw that the ring, which normally never left her finger, had disappeared. Horrified, he stammered: "What have you done with your ring?"

She was pleased that he was giving her the opportunity to say what she had to say.

"Oh! You're the most dreadful man I ever met! Who do you think you got it from? You think you got it from the chambermaid, don't you? You think you got it from that girl you're so much in love with, the girl who gets more out of you than I've ever had! The first time you got into bed you were so passionate that I thought you must be about as madly in love with her as it was possible for any man to be! But when you came back the *second* time, after getting up, you were an absolute devil! Completely uncontrolled you were, didn't know when to stop! You miserable man! You must have been blinded by desire to pay such tribute to my body—after all you've had me long enough without showing much appreciation for my figure. So it wasn't because that young girl is so pretty and so shapely that you were enjoying yourself so much. Oh no! You enjoyed it so much because you were seething with some depraved pent-up lust—in short the sin of concupiscence was raging within you, and your senses were dulled as a result. In fact you'd worked yourself up into such a state that I think any old nanny-goat would have done for you, pretty or otherwise! Well, my dear, it's time you mended your ways. It's high time you were content with me for what I am—your own wife and an honest woman, and it's high time that you found *that* just as satisfying as when you thought I was a poor little erring chambermaid. I did what I did in order to save you from your wicked ways, so that when you get old, we can live happily and peacefully together without anything on our consciences. Because if you go on in the way you have been, I'd rather leave you altogether than see you destroying your soul day by day, and at the same time destroying your physical health and squandering everything you have before my very eyes! But if you will acknowledge that you've been in the wrong, and make up your mind to live according to the ways of God and His commandments, then I'll overlook all your past misbehavior, even as I hope God will forgive me *my* ingratitude to Him, and failure to love Him as I ought."

If there was ever a man who was dumbfounded and despairing, it was this poor husband. There was his wife, looking so pretty, and yet so sensible and so chaste, and he had gone and left her for a girl who did not love him. What was worse, he had had the misfortune to have gone and made her do something wicked without her even realizing what was happening. He had gone and let another man share pleasures which, rightly, were his alone to enjoy. He had gone and given himself cuckold's horns and made himself look ridiculous for evermore. But he could see she was already angry enough about the chambermaid, and he did not dare tell her about the other dirty trick he had played. So he promised that he would leave his wicked ways behind him, asked her to forgive him and gave her the ring back. He told his friend not to breathe a word to anybody, but secrets of this sort nearly always end up being proclaimed from the [roof-tops], and it was not long before the facts became public knowledge. The husband was branded as a cuckold without his wife having done a single thing to disgrace herself.

"Ladies, it strikes me that if all the men who offend their wives like that got a punishment like that, then Hircan and Saffredent ought to be feeling a bit nervous."

"Come now, Longarine," said Saffredent, "Hircan and I aren't the only married men here, you know."

"True," she replied, "but you're the only two who'd play a trick like that."

"And just when have you heard of us chasing our wives' maids?" he retorted.

"If the ladies in question were to tell us the facts," Longarine said, "then you'd soon find plenty of maids who'd been dismissed before their pay-day!"

"Really," intervened Geburon, "a fine one you are! You promise to make us all laugh, and you end up making these two gentlemen annoyed."

"It comes to the same thing," said Longarine. "As long as they don't get their swords out, their getting angry makes it all the more amusing."

"But the fact remains," said Hircan, "that if our wives were to listen to what this lady here has to say, she'd make trouble for every married couple here!"

"I know what I'm saying, and who I'm saying it to," Longarine replied. "Your wives are so good, and they love you so much, that even if you gave them horns like a stag's, they'd still convince themselves, and everybody else, that they were garlands of roses!"

Everyone found this remark highly amusing, even the people it was aimed at, and the subject was brought to a close. Dagoucin,[2] however, who had not yet said a word, could not resist saying: "When a man already has everything he needs in order to be contented, it is very unreasonable of him to go off and seek satisfaction elsewhere. It has often struck me that when people are not satisfied with what they already have, and think they can find something better, then they only make themselves worse off. And they do not get any sympathy, because inconstancy is one thing that is universally condemned."

"But what about people who have not yet found their other half?" asked Simontaut. "Would you still say it was inconstancy if they seek her wherever she may be found?"

"No man can know," replied Dagoucin, "where his other half is to be found, this other half with whom he may find a union so equal that between [the parts] there is no difference; which being so, a man must hold fast where Love constrains him and, whatever may befall him, he must remain steadfast in heart and will. For if she whom you love is your true likeness, if she is of the same will, then it will be your own self that you love, and not her alone."

"Dagoucin, I think you're adopting a position that is completely wrong," said Hircan. "You make it sound as if we ought to love women without being loved in return!"

"What I mean, Hircan, is this. If love is based on a woman's beauty, charm and favors, and if our aim is merely pleasure, ambition, or profit, then such love can never last. For if the whole foundation on which our love is based should collapse, then love will fly from us and there will be no love left in us. But I am utterly convinced that if a man loves with no other aim, no other desire, than to love truly, he will abandon his soul in death rather than allow his love to abandon his heart."

"Quite honestly, Dagoucin, I don't think you've ever really been in love," said Simontaut, "because if you had felt the fire of passion, as the rest of us have, you wouldn't have been doing what you've just been doing—describing Plato's republic, which sounds all very fine in writing, but is hardly true to experience."

2. The most philosophical member of the group, described elsewhere (story 11) as "so wise that he would rather die than say something foolish." He is also the saintliest; our translator indicates that his name is "a fairly obvious pun: de goûts saints (of saintly tastes)."

"If I have loved," he replied, "I love still, and shall love till the day I die. But my love is a perfect love, and I fear lest showing it openly should betray it. So greatly do I fear this, that I shrink to make it known to the lady whose love and friendship I cannot but desire to be equal to my own. I scarcely dare think my own thoughts, lest something should be revealed in my eyes, for the longer I conceal the fire of my love, the stronger grows the pleasure in knowing that it is indeed a perfect love."

"Ah, but all the same," said Geburon, "I don't think you'd be sorry if she did return your love!"

"I do not deny it. But even if I were loved as deeply as I myself love, my love could not possibly increase, just as it could not possibly decrease if I were loved less deeply than I love."

At this point, Parlamente, who was suspicious of these flights of fancy, said: "Watch your step, Dagoucin. I've seen plenty of men who've died rather than speak what's in their minds."

"Such men as those," he replied, "I would count happy indeed."

"Indeed," said Saffredent, "and worthy to be placed among the ranks of the Innocents—of whom the Church chants 'Non loquendo, sed moriendo confessi sunt'![3] I've heard a lot of talk about these languishing lovers, but I've never seen a single one actually die. I've suffered enough from such torture, but I got over it in the end, and that's why I've always assumed that nobody else ever really dies from it either."

"Ah! Saffredent, the trouble is that you desire your love to be returned," Dagoucin replied, "and men of your opinions never die for love. But I know of many who *have* died, and died for no other cause than that they have loved, and loved perfectly."

Story 10

In Aragon, in the province of Aranda, there once lived a lady. She was the widow of the Count of Aranda, who had died while she was still very young, and left her with a son and a daughter, who was called Florida.[4] As was right and proper for the children of a noble lord, they were brought up by her according to the strictest codes of virtue and honor. So carefully did she school them that her house was known far and wide as the most honorable in the whole of Spain. She would often go to Toledo, which was then the seat of the King of Spain,[5] and when she visited Saragossa, which was not far from the family home, she would spend her time at the Queen's court, where she was as highly esteemed as any lady could be.

One day, when the King was in residence at his castle in Saragossa, the Castillo de la Aljaferia, the Countess, on her way to pay her respects as was her wont, was passing through a little village that belonged to the Viceroy of Catalonia.[6] Normally the Viceroy never moved from the border at Perpignan, where he

---

3. "Not by speaking but by dying they confessed," a line recited during the Feast of the Holy Innocents.

4. "In bloom."
5. Ferdinand V of Spain (1452–1516).
6. Don Enrique of Aragon.

was in command during the war between France and Spain, but peace[7] had just been declared, and he returned with his officers in order to do homage to his King. He knew that the Countess would be passing through his lands, and went to meet her, not only to do her the honor that was her due as the King's kinswoman, but also because of the goodwill that he had long borne her. Now in the Viceroy's entourage there were not a few noblemen of outstanding valor, courageous men, who, after long service in the wars had earned such heroic reputations that there was no one in the land who was not anxious to meet them and be seen in their company. Amongst these men there was one by the name of Amador.[8] Although he was only eighteen or nineteen years of age, he had such confidence, and such sound judgment, that you could not have failed to regard him as one of those rare men fit to govern any state. Not only was he a man of sound judgment, he was also endowed with an appearance so handsome, so open and natural, that he was a delight for all to behold. This was not all, for his handsome looks were equally matched by the fairness of his speech. Poise, good looks, eloquence—it was impossible to say with which gift he was more richly blessed. But what gained him even higher esteem was his fearlessness, which, despite his youth, was famed throughout all lands. For he had already in many different places given evidence of his great abilities. Not only throughout the kingdoms of Spain, but also in France and Italy people looked upon him with admiration. Not once during the recent wars had he shrunk from battle, and when his country had been at peace, he had gone to seek action in foreign parts, and there too had been loved and admired by friend and foe alike.

This young nobleman had devotedly followed his commander back home, to meet the Countess of Aranda. He could not fail to notice her daughter, Florida, who was then but twelve years of age. Never, he thought to himself, as he contemplated her grace and beauty, had he beheld so fair and noble a creature. If only she might look with favor upon him, that alone would give him more happiness than anything any other woman in the world could ever give him. For a long while he gazed at her. His mind was made up. He would love her. The promptings of reason were in vain. He would love her even though she was of far higher birth than he. He would love her, even though she was not yet of an age to hear and understand the words of love. But his misgivings were as nothing against the firm hope that grew within him, as he promised himself that time and patient waiting would in the end bring his toils to a happy conclusion. Noble Love, through the power that is its own, and for no other cause, had entered Amador's breast and now held out to him the promise of a happy end, and the means of attaining it.

The greatest obstacle was the distance that separated his own homeland from that of Florida, and the lack of opportunity to see her. To [overcome] this problem he decided, contrary to his previous intentions, to marry some lady from Barcelona or Perpignan. His reputation stood so high there that there was little or nothing anyone would refuse him. Moreover, he had spent so long on the frontier during the wars, that although he came from the region of Toledo, he was more like a Catalan than a Castilian.[9] His family was rich and

---

7. Treaty of Blois (1505).
8. "He who loves."
9. Although a native of Castile, Amador has

lived with, and fought alongside of, the Catalans and Aragonese—i.e., although a foreigner, he looks like a native.

distinguished, but he was the youngest son, and possessed little in the way of inheritance. But Love and Fortune, seeing him ill-provided for by his parents, and resolving to make him their paragon, bestowed upon him through the gift of virtue and valor that which the laws of the land denied him. He was experienced in matters of war, and much sought after by noble lords and princes. He did not have to go out of his way to ask for rewards. More often than not he had to refuse them.

The Countess meanwhile continued on her way, and arrived at Saragossa, where she was well received by the King and the whole court. The Viceroy of Catalonia visited her frequently, and Amador took the opportunity of accompanying him. In this way he might at least have the chance of looking at Florida, for there was no way in which he might be able to speak to her. In order to introduce himself into the society of the Countess, he approached the daughter of an old knight, who came from his home town. Her name was Avanturada,[1] and she [had been brought up alongside] Florida, so that she knew the innermost secrets of her heart. Since she was a good, respectable girl, and expected to receive three thousand ducats a year by way of dowry, Amador made up his mind to address himself to her as a suitor, and seek her hand in marriage. She was only too willing to listen. But her father was a rich man, and she felt that he would never consent to her marriage with a man as poor as Amador unless she enlisted the aid of the Countess. So she first approached Florida.

"My lady, you have seen the Castilian gentleman, who often talks to me," she said. "I believe that it is his intention to ask my hand in marriage. But you know what my father is like. You know that he will never consent, unless the Countess and yourself persuade him."

Florida, who loved the young lady dearly, assured her that she would do everything she could for her, just as if her own interests were at stake. Then Avanturada presented Amador to Florida. As he kissed her hand, he almost fainted in rapture. He, the most eloquent man in Spain, was speechless as he stood before her. This somewhat surprised Florida, for, although she was only twelve years of age, she knew well enough that there was not a man in Spain who could express his mind more eloquently than Amador. He stood there in silence, so she said to him:

"Señor Amador, your reputation has spread through all the kingdoms of Spain, and it would be surprising indeed if you were not known to us also. All of us who have heard about you are anxious to find some way in which we can be of service. So if there is anything I can do, I hope you will not be afraid to ask."

Amador stood gazing at his lady's beauty. He was transported with joy, and was only just able to utter a few words of grateful thanks. Florida was astonished to see that he was still incapable of making any kind of reply, but she attributed it to some momentary whim, completely failing to see that the true cause of his behavior lay in the violence of his love. She ignored his silence, and said no more.

Amador, for his part, had perceived what great virtue was beginning to appear in Florida, young as she was, and later he said to the lady he was planning to marry:

"Avanturada, do not be surprised that I couldn't speak a word in front of Lady Florida. She is so young, yet she speaks so well and so wisely, and behind

---

1. "Aventurada" (Spanish), daring or uncertain.

her tender years there clearly lie hidden such virtues, that I was overcome with admiration and didn't know what to say to her. Tell me, Avanturada, since you are her friend and must know her closest secrets, how is it possible that she hasn't stolen the heart of every single man at court? Any man who has met her, and hasn't fallen in love with her, must be a dumb beast or made of stone!"

Avanturada, who by now was much in love with Amador, could keep nothing from him. She told him that the Lady Florida was indeed greatly loved by everyone, but that very few people actually spoke with her, that being the custom in that part of the land. There were only two men who seemed to show any inclination—Don Alfonso, son of Henry of Aragon, otherwise known as the Infante of Fortune,[2] and the young Duke of Cardona.

"Tell me," said Amador, "which of the two do you think she likes the best?"

"She is so good and wise," replied Avanturada, "that she would never confess to anything that was not in accordance with the wishes of her mother. But, as far as we can judge, she prefers the son of the Infante of Fortune to the Duke of Cardona, although it is the Duke of Cardona her mother prefers, because with him she would stay closer to home. But you are a man of perception and sound judgment, so perhaps you would help us decide what the truth of the matter is. It's like this. The son of the Infante of Fortune was brought up at this court, and he is one of the most handsome and most accomplished young princes in Christendom. What I and the other girls think is that he is the one she should marry—they'd make the loveliest couple in the whole of Spain. And I ought to tell you as well that although they're both very young—she's only twelve and he's fifteen—they've been in love for three years already. If you want to get in her good books you ought to make a friend of him and enter into his service."

Amador was relieved to hear that his lady was capable of love at all. One day, he hoped, he might win the right to become her true and devoted servant, even though he might never become her husband. Of her virtue he was not afraid. His sole anxiety had been that she might reject love completely. From this conversation onward, Amador made friends with the son of the Infante of Fortune. He had little difficulty in gaining his goodwill, for he was versed in all the sports and diversions that the young prince enjoyed, being an excellent horseman, skilled in the use of arms and indeed good at everything that a young man ought to be able to do.

War broke out again in Languedoc, and Amador was obliged to return with the governor. His sorrow was great, the more so as he had no means of ensuring that he would return to a post where he would still be able to see his Florida. So before his departure, he spoke to a brother of his, who was major-domo[3] in the household of the Queen. He told him what an excellent match he had found in the Lady Avanturada while in the Countess's household, and asked him to do everything in his power during his absence to bring the marriage about, by drawing on the influence of the Queen, the King and all his other friends. The brother, who was very fond of Amador, not only because of their common blood, but because he admired his prowess, promised to do as he was bidden. He was as good as his word. The Countess of Aranda, the young

---

2. A son of the Spanish king other than the heir-apparent. 3. Head steward in the royal household.

Count, who was growing to appreciate virtue and valor, and above all the beautiful Florida, joined in singing the praises of Amador. The result was that Avanturada's miserly old father put aside his grasping habits for once and was brought to recognize Amador's excellent qualities. The marriage was duly agreed upon by the parents of the couple, and, during the truce that had been declared by the two warring kings, Amador was summoned home by his brother.

It was at that time that the King of Spain withdrew to Madrid, where he was safe from the unhealthy air that was affecting a number of places throughout the country. Acting on the advice of his Council, but also at the request of the Countess, he had arranged a marriage between her son, the little Count, and a rich heiress, the Duchess of Medinaceli, in order to bring the two families together in an advantageous union and to please the Countess herself, whose interests were very dear to his heart. In accordance with his wishes the marriage was celebrated in the King's palace at Madrid. Amador was present, and was able to pursue his own matrimonial plans so successfully that he too was married—to Avanturada, in whom he inspired a good deal more love than he returned. His marriage was no more than a cover, no more than a convenient excuse to enable him to visit her on whom his mind constantly dwelled.

After his marriage he made himself so familiar in the Countess's household that no one took any more notice of him than if he had been a woman. He was only twenty-two at this time, but had such good sense that the Countess used to keep him informed of all her business affairs. She even instructed her son and her daughter to listen carefully to his conversation, and heed any advice he might give. Having reached these heights in the Countess's esteem, he behaved in such a sensible, such a restrained manner, that even the lady whom he loved so dearly failed to perceive his feelings. In fact, being so fond of Amador's wife, she hid nothing from Amador himself, not even her most intimate thoughts, [and went so far as] to tell him about her love for the son of the Infante of Fortune. Amador's sole concern was to win her completely, and he talked to her constantly about the Infante's son. Provided he was able to converse with her, he did not care what was the topic of their conversation. However, he had been there hardly a month after his marriage when he was obliged to go back to the wars. Not once, during the two years that followed, did he return to see his wife, who waited for him, living as she always had done in the household of the Countess. Throughout this time Amador would write to his wife, but his letters consisted principally of messages for Florida. She for her part would reply, and even insert something amusing in her own hand in Avanturada's letters—which alone was enough to make Amador very conscientious in writing to his wife. But throughout all this Florida was aware of nothing, except perhaps that she was as fond of Amador as if he had been her own brother.

Several times Amador came and went, but for five whole years he never saw Florida for two months together. Yet in spite of these long absences, and the long distances that separated them, his love grew. At last he was able to travel to see his wife. He found the Countess far from the court, for the King had gone into Andalusia, taking with him the young Count of Aranda, who had already started to bear arms. The Countess had moved to a country house she owned on the borders of Aragon and Navarre. She was delighted to see Amador, who had been away now for three years, and commanded that he was to be treated like a son. There was nobody who did not make him welcome. During his stay, the Countess told him all her domestic business, and asked his advice on almost every aspect of it. The family's regard for him was unbounded. Wherever he went, there was always an open door. He was looked upon as a man of such integrity that he was trusted in everything. Had he been a saint or an angel, he could hardly have been trusted more. Florida, fond as she was of Avanturada, went straight to Amador whenever she saw him. Having not the slightest suspicion as to his true intentions, she was quite unreserved in her behavior toward him. There was not a trace of passion in her heart, unless it was a feeling of contentment at being by his side. Nothing else occurred to her. But there are people who can guess from the expression in a man's eyes whether that man is in love or not, and Amador was constantly anxious lest he be thus found out. When Florida came to speak to him alone, in complete innocence, the fire that burned in his breast would flare up so violently that, do what he might, the color would mount to his cheeks and the flames of passion would gleam in his eyes.

In order that no one should guess from his intimacy with Florida that he was in love with her, he began to make approaches to an extremely attractive lady called Paulina, whose charms were highly celebrated in her day, and from whose snares few men managed to escape. She had heard how Amador had been successful with the ladies in Barcelona and Perpignan, and how he had won the hearts of the most beautiful and most noble ladies in the land; in particular she had heard how a certain Countess of Palamos, who was regarded as the most beautiful woman in Spain, had lost her heart to him. So she told him how deeply she pitied him for having married such an ugly wife, after all his past good fortunes in love. Amador realized from what she said that she was ready to provide him with any consolation he might require, and replied with as encouraging words as he was able, thinking that it would be possible to cover up the truth of his real feelings by making her believe a lie. But she was shrewd, experienced in the ways of love, and not a woman to make do with mere words. She sensed that his heart was not entirely taken up with love for her, and suspected that he wanted to use her as a cover. She watched him so closely that not a single glance escaped her. Amador's eyes were well-practiced in the art of dissembling, however, and Paulina could get no further than her vague suspicions. But it was only with extreme difficulty that he was able to hide his feelings, especially when Florida, who had not the slightest idea of the game he was playing, talked to him with her customary intimacy in front of Paulina herself. It was only by making the most painful effort that on such occasions he was able to control the expression in his eyes, and prevent them reflecting the feelings in his heart. So to forestall any unfortunate consequences in the future, he said to her one day as he leaned against the window where they had been chatting: "Tell me, [my Lady], is it better to speak or to die?"

"I would always advise my friends to speak," she replied quickly, "because there are very few words that can't be remedied, but once you've lost your life, there's no way of getting it back."

"So will you promise that you will not only not be angry at what I am going to say, but also, if you are shocked, that you will not say anything until I have finished?"

"Say whatever you please," she said, "because if *you* shock me, then there's no one in the world who could reassure me."

So he began.

"My Lady, there are two reasons why I have not yet told you of the feelings I have for you. One reason is that I hoped to give you proof of my love through long and devoted service. The other is that I feared that you would consider it [overweening presumption] that I, an ordinary nobleman, should dare to aspire to the love of a lady of birth so high. Even if I were, like you, my Lady, of princely estate, a heart so true and loyal as your own would not suffer such talk of love from anyone but the son of the Infante of Fortune, who has taken possession of your heart. Yet, my Lady, just as in the hardships of war one may be compelled to destroy one's own land, to lay waste one's rising crops, in order to prevent the enemy taking advantage of them, even so do I now seek to anticipate the fruit that I had hoped to reap only in the fullness of time, in order to prevent our enemies from taking advantage of it to your loss. I must tell you, my Lady, that from the time I first saw you, when you were still so young, I have wholly consecrated myself to your service. I have never ceased to seek the means to obtain your good grace, and it was for this reason alone that I married the very lady who is your own dearest friend. Knowing, too, that you loved the son of the Infante, I did my utmost to serve him, to become his friend. In short, I have striven to do everything that I thought would give you pleasure. You have seen how the Countess, your mother, has looked favorably upon me, as has the Count your brother, and all those of whom you are fond, with the result that I am treated in this house, not as a man serving his superiors, but as a son. All the efforts that I made five years ago were for no other end than to live my whole life by you. But you must believe me, my Lady, when I tell you that I am not one of those men who would exploit this advantage. I desire no favor, nor pleasure, from you, except what is in accordance with the dictates of virtue. I know that I cannot marry you. And even if I could, I should not seek to do so, for your love is given to another, and it is he whom I long to see your husband. Nor is my love a base love. I am not one of those men who hope that if they serve their lady long enough they will be rewarded with her dishonor. Such intentions could not be further from my heart, for I would rather see you dead, than have to admit that my own gratification had sullied your virtue, had, in a word, made you less worthy to be loved. I ask but one thing in recompense of my devotion and my service. I ask only that you might be my true and faithful Lady, so true, so faithful, that you will never cast me from your good grace, that you will allow me to continue in my present estate, and that you will place your trust in me above all others. And if your honor, or any cause close to your heart, should demand that a noble gentleman lay down his life, then mine will I gladly lay down for your sake. On this you may depend. Know, too, that whatsoever deeds of mine may be counted noble, good or brave, these deeds will be performed for love of you alone. Yes, and if for ladies less exalted my deeds have met acclaim, then be you assured that for a lady such as you I shall perform such deeds of greatness, that acts which once I deemed impossible I shall now perform with ease. But if you will not accept me as wholly yours, my Lady, then I shall make up my mind to abandon my career at arms. I shall renounce the valor and the virtue that were mine, for they will have availed me nought. Wherefore, my Lady, I do humbly beseech that my just demand might be granted, since your honor and your conscience cannot refuse it."

The young Lady Florida changed color at this speech, the like of which she had never heard before. Then she lowered her gaze, like a mature woman, her modesty shocked. Then, with all the virtue and good sense that was hers, she said:

"If, as seems to be the case, Amador, you're only asking me for something that you already have, then why do you insist on making such a long, high-flown speech about it? I am rather afraid that there is some evil intent hidden away underneath all these fine words, and that you're trying to beguile me because I'm young and innocent. It makes me very uncertain as to how I should reply to you. If I were to reject the noble love that you offer me, I would only be contradicting the way I've behaved toward you up till now, because in you I've placed more trust than in any other man in the world. Neither my honor nor my conscience stand in the way of your request. Nor does the love I bear the son of the Infante of Fortune, for my love for him is founded on marriage, to which you lay no claim. In fact I can think of no reason why I should not grant your wishes, except perhaps for one anxiety that troubles my mind. You have no reason to address me in the way you do. If you already have what you desire, what can it be that now makes you tell me about it in such an emotional manner?"

Amador was ready with his reply.

"My Lady, you speak most prudently," he said, "and do me great honor to place in me such trust as you declare. If I were not happy to receive this blessing from you, I should be unworthy indeed to receive any other. But let me explain, my Lady, that the man who desires to build an edifice that will endure throughout eternity should take the utmost care to lay a safe and sure foundation. So it is that I, who desire most earnestly to serve you through all eternity, should take the greatest care that I have the means to ensure not only that I shall remain always by you, but that I shall be able to prevent all others from knowing of the great love I bear you. For, though my love is pure and noble enough to be announced to the whole world, yet there are people who will never understand a lover's soul, and whose pronouncements will always belie the truth. The rumors that result are none the less unpleasant for being untrue. The reason why I have made so bold as to say all this to you, is that Paulina has become very suspicious. She senses in her heart that I am unable to give her my love, and she is constantly on the watch for me to give myself away. And when you come to talk to me alone in your affectionate way, I am so nervous lest she discern something in my expression to confirm her suspicions that I find myself in just the awkward situation that I am most anxious to avoid. So I made up my mind to beg you not to take me unawares when Paulina is present, or anyone else whom you know to have an equally malicious disposition. For I would die rather than let any living creature know of my feelings. Were it not that your honor is so dear to me, I should never have entertained the idea of speaking to you in the way I have spoken. For I feel myself so content in the love that you have for me, that there is nothing further that I desire, unless it be that you should continue in the same for ever."

At these words Florida was filled with delight beyond bounds. Deep within her heart she began to feel stirrings that she had never felt before. And as she could see that the arguments he brought forth were honorable and good, she was able to grant his request, saying that virtue and honor answered for her. Amador was transported with joy, as anyone who has ever truly loved will understand.

However, Florida took his advice too seriously. She became nervous, not only in the presence of Paulina, but in other circumstances too, until she began not to seek Amador's company at all in the way she had in the past. Moreover, she took it badly that he spent so much time with Paulina, who seemed so attractive that she felt it impossible for Amador not to be in love with her. To relieve her distress she would talk at great length with Avanturada, who was herself beginning to be jealous of her husband and Paulina, and often bemoaned her lot to her friend. Florida, suffering from the same affliction, would offer what consolation she was able. It was not long before Amador noticed Florida's strange behavior, and concluded that she was keeping away from him, not just as a result of his advice, but because she was displeased with him. One day, as they were returning from vespers at a monastery, he said to her: "My Lady, why do you treat me the way you do?"

"Because that is the way I thought you wanted it," she replied.

Then, suspecting the truth of the matter, and wishing to know whether he was right, Amador said: "My Lady, because of the time I have spent with her, Paulina no longer suspects you."

"Then you couldn't have done better, either for yourself or for me," she answered, "for in giving yourself a little pleasure, you are acting in the interests of my honor."

Amador understood from these words that she thought he derived pleasure from talking with Paulina. So hurt was he that he could not restrain his anger:

"Ah! My Lady, so you're starting already to torment your servant, by hurling abuse at him for [acting in your interests]! There's nothing more irksome and distressing than being obliged to spend one's time with a woman one isn't even in love with! Since you take exception to tasks I undertake solely in your service, I'll never speak to her again. And let the consequences take care of themselves! To cover up my anger, just as in the past I've hidden my joy, I shall go away to a place not far from here, and wait until your mood has passed. But I hope that when I get there I shall receive orders from my commanding officer to return to the wars, where I shall stay long enough to prove to you that nothing keeps me here but you, my Lady."

So saying, he went, without even waiting for her reply. Florida was left utterly dejected and downcast. Love, having been thwarted, was aroused now, and began to demonstrate its power. She acknowledged that she had wronged Amador, and wrote to him over and over again, beseeching him to come back to her—as indeed he did several days later, once his anger had subsided. I could not begin to tell you in detail what they said to one another to resolve their jealousies. To cut a long story short, he won the day. She promised that she would never again suspect him of being in love with Paulina. More than that, she swore she was and would remain convinced that it was for Amador almost unbearable to have to speak with Paulina or any other woman, nay that it was a martyrdom suffered for no other reason than to render service to his lady.

No sooner had Love overcome these first suspicions and jealousies, no sooner had the two lovers begun to take more pleasure than ever from talking together, than word came that the King of Spain was sending the entire army to Salces. Amador, who was accustomed to be the first to join the royal standards, was as eager as ever to follow the path of honor and glory. Yet this time it was with particular regret, a regret deeper than that which he had experienced before, for not only was he relinquishing the one pleasure of his life, but he now feared that Florida might change during his absence. She had already reached the age of fifteen or sixteen, and was wooed by lords and princes from far and wide. He feared that she might be married while he was away, and that he might never see her again. He had one safeguard, however—that the Countess should make his wife the special companion to Florida. Accordingly, he employed his influence to obtain promises both from the Countess and from Florida herself that wherever she should go after her marriage Avanturada should go with her. And so, in spite of the fact that the talk at that time was of a marriage in Portugal, Amador was certain in his mind that she would never abandon him. With this assurance, yet none the less filled with sorrow beyond words, he departed for the wars, leaving his wife with the Countess.

After her faithful servant had left, Florida found herself quite alone. She set herself to perform all manner of good and virtuous deeds, hoping thereby to acquire the reputation of being the most perfect lady in the land, and worthy to have a man such as Amador devoted to her service. As for Amador himself, when he arrived at Barcelona, he was, as he had been in the past, greeted with delight by all the ladies. But they found him a changed man. They would never have thought that marriage had such a hold over a man, for he now seemed to have nothing but distaste for all the things that before he had pursued. Even the Countess of Palamos, of whom he had once been so enamored, could no longer find a way of luring him even as far as the door of her residence. Anxious to be away to the scene of battle [where glory was to be won], Amador spent as little time as possible in Barcelona. No sooner had he arrived at Salces, than war did indeed break out between the two kings.[4] It was a great and merciless war. I have no intention of relating the course of events in detail, or even of recounting the many heroic deeds accomplished by Amador, for to tell you all this I should need a whole day. Suffice it to say that Amador won renown above all his comrades in arms. The Duke of Nájera arrived at Perpignan in charge of two thousand men, and invited Amador to be his second-in-command. He answered the call of duty, and led his men with such success that in every skirmish the air rang with shouts of "Nájera! Nájera!"

Now it came to the ears of the King of Tunis that the kings of Spain and France were waging war on the border between Perpignan and Narbonne. He had long been at war himself with the King of Spain, and he now saw that he could not wish for a better opportunity to harass him more. So he sent a large fleet of galleys and other vessels to pillage and lay waste every inch of unguarded territory that he could find along the Spanish coasts. When the inhabitants of Barcelona saw the vast number of sailing ships looming on the horizon, they immediately sent word to their Viceroy at Salces, who reacted by sending the Duke of Nájera to Palamos without delay. The Moors[5] arrived to find the coasts

4. When the Treaty of Blois failed, the wars between Spain and France resumed at the   border of the two countries (Perpignan).
5. Muslims from North Africa.

well garrisoned and acted as if they were sailing on. But toward midnight they returned, and put large numbers of men ashore. The Duke was taken completely by surprise, and was in fact taken prisoner. Amador, vigilant as ever, had heard the noise, marshaled as many of his men as he could and defended himself so effectively that it was a long time before the stronger forces of the enemy were able to make any inroads. In the end, however, realizing that the Duke of Nájera had been captured, and that the Turks were determined to set fire to the whole of Palamos, and destroy the building which he had defended against them, he thought it better to surrender than to be the cause of the annihilation of his valiant comrades. It was also in his mind that if he were held to ransom, there would be some hope of seeing Florida again. Without more ado, he gave himself up to the Turkish chief-in-command, a man called Dorlin, who took Amador before the King of Tunis himself. He was received respectfully and treated well. He was guarded well, too, for the Turkish King was aware that the man he had in his hands was the veritable Achilles of Spain.

For two years Amador remained the prisoner of the King of Tunis. When the news reached Spain, the family of the Duke of Nájera was stricken with grief, but people who held the honor of their country dear judged the capture of Amador an even greater loss. It was broken to the Countess of Aranda and her household at a time when the poor Avanturada lay seriously ill. The Countess (who had guessed how Amador felt about her daughter, and had kept quiet, raising no objections, because she appreciated the young man's qualities) called Florida to one side to tell her the distressing news. But Florida knew how to hide her true feelings, and merely said that it was a great loss for all the family, and that she felt especially sorry for Amador's poor wife lying sick in bed. But seeing her mother weeping bitterly, she shed a few tears with her, lest her secret be discovered by being too well disguised. From this time on the Countess often spoke to Florida about Amador, but never once was she able to draw from her any reaction that would confirm her thoughts. I shall leave aside for now the pilgrimages, the prayers, the devotions, the fasts, which Florida began regularly to offer for Amador's salvation. As for Amador himself, as soon as he reached Tunis, he lost no time in sending messengers to his friends. To Florida he naturally sent the most trustworthy man he could find, to let her know that he was well and living in the hope of seeing her again. This was all she had to sustain her in her distress, but you may be sure that since she was allowed to write to him, she assiduously performed this task, and Amador did not go without the consolation of her letters.

The Countess of Aranda was summoned to Saragossa, where the King had taken up residence. There she found the young Duke of Cardona, who had been actively seeking the support of the King and Queen in his suit for the hand of Florida. Pressed by the King to agree to the marriage, the Countess, as a loyal subject, could not refuse his request. She was sure that her daughter, still so young in years, could have no other will than that of her mother, and, once the agreement was concluded, she took her on one side to explain how she had chosen for her the match which was most fitting. Florida knew that the matter was already settled and that further deliberation was useless. "May the Lord be praised in everything," was all she could bring herself to say, for her mother looked so stern, and she judged it preferable to obey rather than indulge in self-pity. To crown all her sorrows, she then heard that the son of the Infante of Fortune had fallen sick and was close to death. But never once in the presence of her mother, or of anyone else, did she show any sign of how she felt. So hard indeed did she repress her feelings that her tears, having been held back in her heart by force, caused violent bleeding from the nose which threatened her life. And all the cure she got was marriage to a man she would gladly have exchanged for death. After the marriage was over she went to the Duchy of Cardona. With her went Avanturada, to whom she was able to unburden herself, bemoaning the harsh treatment she had received from her mother and the sorrow she nursed in her heart at the loss of the son of the Infante. But never once did she mention the fact that she missed Amador, except by way of consoling Avanturada herself. In short, the young Lady Florida resolved to have God and honor constantly before her eyes, and she so carefully hid her troubles, that no one had the slightest suspicion that her husband gave her no pleasure.

For a long time Florida lived this life, a life that seemed to her little better than death. She wrote of her woe to her servant Amador, who, knowing how great and noble was his lady's heart, and how deep was her love for the son of the Infante, could only think her end was nigh. This new anguish heightened his affliction, and he grieved bitterly, for Florida's plight seemed already worse than death. Yet he knew what torment his beloved must be suffering, and his own paled into insignificance. Gladly would he have stayed a slave to the end of his days, if only that might have ensured Florida the husband of her desires. One day he learned from a friend he had made at the court of Tunis that the King, who would have liked to keep Amador in his service, provided he could make a good Turk of him, was planning to threaten him with impalement if he did not renounce his faith. To forestall this move, therefore, he prevailed upon the man who had captured him and had become his master to let him go on parole, without informing the King. The ransom was set so high that the Turk reckoned no one as poor as Amador could ever possibly find the money to pay it.

So, having been allowed to depart, he went to the court of the King of Spain, from where, as soon as he was able, he set off again to seek his ransom among his friends. He went straight to Barcelona, where the young Duke of Cardona, his mother and Florida were staying on account of some family business. As soon as Amador's wife, Avanturada, heard the news, she told Florida, who, as if for Avanturada's sake, expressed her joy. But she was afraid lest the joy she felt at seeing him again should show in her face, and lest people who did not know her well should put a bad interpretation on it. So instead of going to meet him, she stood at a window to watch his arrival from afar. Immediately he came into sight she went down by way of a staircase, which was dark enough to prevent anybody seeing whether her cheeks changed color. She embraced Amador, took him to her room, and then to meet her husband's mother, who had not yet made his acquaintance. Needless to say, he had not been there two days before he had endeared himself to the whole household, exactly as he had in the house of the Countess of Aranda. I shall leave you to imagine the words that passed between him and Florida, and how Florida sorrowfully told of all that she had been through during his absence. She wept bitterly at having had to marry against her inclinations, and at having lost the man whom she loved so dearly, without hope of ever seeing him again. Then she made up her mind to take consolation in her love for Amador and the sense of security it afforded her, though she never once dared declare to him her intent. Amador guessed, however, and never lost an opportunity to make known to her how great was his love for her.

Florida was almost won. She was almost at the point where she was ready not merely to accept Amador as a devoted servant, but to admit him as a sure and perfect lover. But it was then that a most unhappy accident occurred. Amador had received word from the King to go to him immediately on urgent business. Avanturada was very upset at the news, and fainted. Unfortunately she happened to be standing at the top of a flight of stairs. She fell, and injured herself so badly that she never recovered. Florida was deeply affected by Avanturada's death. There could be no consolation for her now. It was as if she felt herself bereft of all relatives and friends. She went into deep mourning for her loss. To Amador the blow was even more overwhelming, for not only had he lost one of the most virtuous wives who ever lived, but he had also lost all hope now of continuing to be near Florida. He sank into a state of such dejection, that he thought he himself had not long to live. The old Duchess of Cardona visited him at frequent intervals, and quoted the sayings of the philosophers, in the hope of inducing him to bear the death of his wife with fortitude. But to no avail. The specter of death tormented him from one side. From the other, his martyrdom was made more painful by the force of his love. His wife was dead and buried. His sovereign lord had called him. What further reason could he have for staying where he was? In his heart was such despair that he thought he would lose his reason. Florida sought to give consolation, but desolation was all she brought him. One whole afternoon she spent in an attempt to console him with gentle words, doing all she would to lessen the pain of his grief, and assuring him that she would find a way of seeing him far more often than he supposed. Since he was due to depart the following morning, and since he was so weak that he was unable to move from his bed, he begged her to come and visit him again that same evening, when everyone else had gone. This she promised to do, not realizing that such extremity of love as Amador's knew no rational bounds. He had served her long and well, without any reward other than what I have described in my story. Now he despaired of ever being able to return to see her again, and, racked by a love that had been hidden away within him, he made up his mind to make one last desperate gamble—to risk losing all, or to gain everything and treat himself to one short hour of the bliss that he considered he had earned. He had his bed hung with heavy curtains, so that it was impossible for anyone in the room to see in, and when his visitors came he moaned even more than before, so that people thought that he must surely die before another day passed.

In the evening, when all the visitors had gone, Florida came, with the full approval of her husband, who had encouraged her to tend the sick man. She hoped to give him consolation by declaring her feelings and her desire to love him within the limits permitted by honor. She sat down on a chair at the head of his bed, and began, as she thought, to comfort him, by joining her tears to his. Seeing her so overcome with sorrow and regret, Amador judged that it was now, while she was in this state of torment, that his intentions would most easily be accomplished. He rose from his bed. Florida, thinking he was too weak for such exertions, tried to stop him. But he fell on his knees in front of her, saying, "Must I lose you for ever from my sight?" Whereupon he collapsed into her arms, as if all his strength had suddenly drained from him. The poor Florida put her arms around him and supported him for a while, doing her utmost to console him. He said not a word, and pretending still that he was at the brink of death, began to pursue the path that leads to the forbidden goal of a lady's honor. When Florida realized that his intentions were not pure, she found it beyond belief. Had not his conversation in the past always been pure and good? She asked him what he was trying to do. Amador still said nothing. He did not want to receive a reply that could not but be virtuous and chaste. He struggled with all the strength in his body to have his way. Florida, terrified, thought he must be out of his mind. Rather that, than have to admit he had desired to stain her honor. She called out to a gentleman who she knew would be in the room. Amador, now utterly despairing, threw himself back on the bed with such violence that the other man thought he had breathed his last. Florida, who had now got up from her chair, said: "Quick, go and fetch some fresh vinegar!"

While the gentleman was doing as he had been bidden, she turned to Amador.

"What kind of madness is this, Amador? Are you beginning to lose your mind? What did you think you were trying to do?"

"What cruelty!" exclaimed Amador, now bereft of all reason through the violence of love. "Is this the only reward I deserve after serving you so long?"

"And what," she replied, "has become of the honor you preached about so often?"

"Ah! my Lady," he said, "no one in the world could possibly hold your honor as dear as I do! Before you were married I was able to overcome the desires of my heart so successfully that you knew nothing at all of my feelings. But now you are a married woman. You have a cover and your honor is safe. So what wrong can I possibly be doing you in asking for what is truly mine? It is I who have really won you, through the power of my love. The man who first won your heart so irresolutely pursued your body that he well deserved to lose both. As for the man who now possesses your body—he's not worthy of the smallest corner in your heart. So you do not really belong to him, even in body. But consider, my Lady, what trials and tribulations I have gone through in the last five or six years for your sake. Surely you cannot fail to realize that it is to me alone that you belong, body and heart, for is it not for you that I have refused to give thought to my own body and my own heart? And if you are thinking that you can justify yourself on grounds of conscience, bear in mind that no sin may be imputed when the heart and the body are constrained by the power of love. When men kill themselves in a violent fit of madness, in no way do they commit a sin. For passion leaves no room for reason. And if it is the case that the passion of love is the most difficult to bear of all, if it is—as indeed it is—the passion that most completely blinds the senses, then what sin can you impute to a man who merely lets himself be swept along by an insuperable force? Now I must depart. All hope of seeing you again is gone. Had I but the guarantee that my great love deserves, I would have all the strength I need to endure in patience what will surely be a long and painful absence. If, however, you do not deign to grant me my request, then ere long you shall hear that your severity has brought me to a cruel and unhappy end!"

Florida was as distressed as she was taken aback to hear a speech like this from a man of whom she would never have expected anything of the kind, and her tears flowed.

"Alas! Amador," she began, "what has happened to all the virtuous things you used to say to me when I was young? Is this the honor, is this the conscience, for which you so often told me to die, rather than lose my soul? Have you forgotten all the lessons you taught me from examples of virtuous ladies who resisted senseless and wicked passion? Have you forgotten how you have always spoken with scorn of women who succumb to it? It is hard, Amador, to believe that you have left your former self so far behind that all regard for God, for your conscience, and for my honor is completely dead. But if it really is as you seem to say, then I thank God that in His goodness He has forewarned me of the disaster that was about to befall me. By the words you have uttered God has revealed to me what your heart is really like. How could I have remained ignorant for so long? I lost the son of the Infante of Fortune, not just because I was obliged to marry somebody else, but because I knew that he really loved another woman. Now I am married to a man whom I cannot love and cherish however hard I try. That is why I had made up my mind to give you all the love that is in me, to love you with my whole heart. And the foundation of this love was to have been virtue, that virtue which holds honor and conscience dearer than life itself, that virtue which I first found in you, and which, through you, I think I have now attained. Thus it was that I came to you, Amador, firmly resolved to build upon this rock of honor. But in this short space of time you have clearly demonstrated to me that I would have been building not upon the solid rock of purity, but upon the shifting sands, nay, upon a treacherous bog of vice. I had begun to build a dwelling in which I could live for evermore, but with a single blow you have razed it to the ground. So now you must abandon hope. You must be resolved never again, wherever it may be, to seek to speak to me or look into my eyes. Nor may you hope that one day I could change my mind, even should I so desire. My heart brims with sorrow for what might have been. But had it come to pass that I had sworn myself to you in the bond of perfect love, my poor heart would have been wounded unto death by what has transpired. To think that I have been so deceived! If it does not bring me to an early grave, I shall surely suffer for the rest of my days. This is my final word to you. Adieu. For ever more adieu!"

I shall not try to describe Amador's feelings as he listened to these words. It would be impossible to set such anguish down in writing. It is difficult even for anyone to imagine such anguish, unless they have experienced the same kind of suffering themselves. What a cruel end! Realizing that she was going to leave him on this note, and that he would lose her for ever if he did not clear his name, he seized her by the arm.

"My Lady," he said, putting on the most convincing expression he could manage, "for as long as I can remember I have longed to love a good and honorable woman. But I have found few who are truly virtuous, and that is why I wanted to test you out—to see if you were as worthy to be admired for your virtue, as you are to be loved for your other attributes. And now I know for certain that you are. For this I praise God, and give Him thanks that He has brought my heart to love such consummate perfection! So I beseech you, forgive this whim, pardon my rash behavior. For as you can see, all has turned out for the best. Your honor is vindicated, and I am happy indeed that this should be so!"

But Florida was beginning to understand the evil ways of men. If she had before found it hard to believe that Amador's intentions were bad, she now found it even harder to believe him when he said that in reality they were good.

"Would to God that you were speaking the truth!" she said. "But I am a married woman, and I am not so ignorant that I do not clearly realize that it was violent passion that drove you to do what you did. If God had not stood by me, and my hold on the reins had slackened, I am not at all convinced that you would have been the one to tighten the bridle. Those who truly seek virtue do not take the route that you took. But enough has been said. I was too ready to believe you were a good man. It is time that I recognized the truth, for it is by truth that now I am delivered from your clutches."

With these words, Florida left the room. The whole night long she wept. This sudden change caused her such pain that her heart was hard pressed to withstand the assaults of bitter regret which love hurled against it. For, while in accordance with reason she was determined to love him no more, the heart, over which none of us has control, would never yield. Thus, unable to love him less than before, she resolved to propitiate love, since love it was that was the cause. She resolved, in short, to go on loving Amador with all her heart, but, in order to obey the dictates of honor, never to let it be known, either to him or to anyone.

The next morning Amador departed in a state of mind which I leave to your imagination. But no one in the world had a more valiant heart than he, and, instead of sinking into despair, he began to seek new ways of seeing Florida again, and winning her. So, being due to present himself to the King of Spain, who at that time was in residence at Toledo, he went by way of the County of Aranda. He arrived late one night at the castle of the Countess, and found her ailing, and pining for her daughter. When she saw Amador she put her arms around him and kissed him, as if he were her own son, for she loved him dearly, and had guessed that he was in love with Florida. She pressed him for news, and he told her as much as he could without telling the whole truth. Then he told her what her daughter had always concealed, and confessed their love, begging the Countess to help him have news of Florida, and to bring her soon to live with her.

The next morning he left, and continued on his journey. When his business with the King had been dispatched, he went off to join the army on active service. He was downcast and so changed in every respect that the ladies and officers whose company he had always kept no longer recognized him. He continually dressed himself in clothes of coarse black cloth, much more austere than was called for by the death of his wife. But the death of his wife served merely as a cover for a much deeper grief. Three or four years went by, and Amador never once returned to court. The Countess meanwhile had word that such a change had come over her daughter that she was piteous to behold. She summoned Florida to her, in the hope that she might want to come back and live with her permanently. But Florida would not hear of it. When she heard that Amador had told her mother about their love, and that her mother, good and wise as she was, had confided in Amador and told him she approved, her consternation was great indeed. On the one hand, she could see that her mother had considerable admiration for Amador, and that if she had the truth told to her, it might bring him harm. That was the last thing she wanted, and in any case, she felt quite well able to punish him for his outrageous behavior without help from her family. On the other hand, she could see that if she concealed the bad things she knew about him, she would be obliged by her mother and all her friends to talk with him and receive him favorably. That, she feared, could only strengthen him in his base intentions. However, he was in distant parts, so she made little fuss, and wrote him letters whenever the Countess asked her to do so. But when she did write, she made sure that he would realize that they were written out of obedience, and not from any inclination of her own. There had once been a time when her letters had brought him transports of joy. Now he felt nothing but sorrow as he read them.

Three years went by, during which time Amador performed so many glorious deeds that no writer could ever hope to set them all down, even if he had all the paper in Spain. It was now that he devised his grand scheme—not a scheme to win back Florida's heart, for he deemed her lost for ever, but a scheme to score a victory over her as his mortal enemy, for that was how she now appeared. Throwing all reason to the winds, and setting aside all fear of death, he took the greatest risk of his life. His mind was made up. He was not to be deterred from his aim. Since his credit stood high with the governor, he was able to get himself appointed to a mission to the King for the purpose of discussing some secret campaign directed against the town of Leucate. He also managed to get himself issued with orders to inform the Countess of Aranda of the plan, and to take her advice before meeting the King. Knowing that Florida was there, he went post-haste into Aranda, and on his arrival sent a friend in secrecy to tell the Countess that he wished to see her, and that they must meet only at dead of night, without anyone else knowing about it. Overjoyed to hear that Amador was in the neighborhood, the Countess told Florida, and sent her to undress in her husband's room, so that she should be ready to be called once everyone had retired. Florida made no objection. But she had not yet recovered from her earlier terrifying experience, and, instead of doing as she was bidden, went straight to an oratory to commend herself to our Lord, and to pray to Him that He might preserve her heart from all base affections. Remembering that Amador had often praised her beauty, which in spite of long sickness had in no way diminished, she could not bear the thought that this beauty of hers should kindle so base a fire in the heart of a man who was so worthy and so good. Rather than that she would disfigure herself, impair her beauty. She seized a stone that lay on the chapel floor, and struck herself in the face with great force, severely injuring her mouth, nose and eyes. Then, so that no one would suspect her when she was summoned, she deliberately threw herself against a [large piece of stone] as she left the chapel. She lay with her face to the ground, screaming, and was found in this appalling state by the Countess, who immediately had her wounds dressed and her face swathed in bandages.

Once she had been made comfortable, the Countess took her into her chamber and told her that she wanted her to go and talk to Amador in her private room till she had dismissed her attendants. Thinking that Amador would not be unaccompanied, Florida obeyed, but, once the door closed behind her, she was horrified to find herself completely alone with him. Amador, for his part, was not at all displeased, for now, he thought, he would by fair means or foul surely get what he had so long desired. A few words were sufficient to tell him that her attitude was the same as when he had last seen her, and that she would die rather than change her mind. In a state of utter desperation he said:

"Almighty God, Florida, I'm not going to have the just desserts of all my efforts frustrated by your scruples! Seeing that all my love, all my patient waiting, all my begging and praying are useless, I shall use every ounce of strength in my body to get the one thing that will make life worth living! Without it I shall die!"

His whole expression, his face, his eyes, had changed as he spoke. The fair complexion was flushed with fiery red. The kind, gentle face was contorted with a terrifying violence, as if there was some raging inferno belching fire in his heart and behind his eyes. One powerful fist roughly seized hold of her two weak and delicate hands. Her feet were held in a vice-like grip. There was nothing she could do to save herself. She could neither fight back, nor could she fight free. She had no other recourse than to see if there might not yet be some trace of his former love, for the sake of which he might relent and have mercy.

"Amador," she gasped, "even if you think I'm your enemy now, I beg you, in the name of that pure love which I used to think you felt for me in your heart, please listen to me, before you torture me!"

Seeing that he was prepared to hear her out, she continued: "Alas, Amador! What is it that drives you to seek that which can give you no satisfaction, and to cause me the greatest sorrow anyone could ever cause me? You came to know my feelings so well in the days when I was young, when my beauty was at its most fresh, and when your passion might have had some excuse, that I marvel now that at the age I am, ugly as I am, ravaged by deepest sorrow as I am, you should seek that which you know you cannot find. I am certain that you can have no doubt but that my feelings remain as they have always been, and that [only by use of force therefore can you obtain that which you ask]. If you will look at the way my face is now adorned, you will lose all memory of the delights that once you found there, you will lose all your desire to approach it nearer! If there is the slightest trace in you of the love you used to bear me, you must surely have pity on me and overcome this violent madness. In the name of all the [pity and noble virtue] that I have known in you in the past, I plead with you, and beg you for mercy. Just let me live in peace! Let me live the life of honor and virtue to which, as you yourself once urged me, I have committed myself. And if your former love for me really has turned to hatred, and if, more out of a desire for revenge than some form of love, your intention is to make me the most wretched woman on earth, then I tell you plainly that you will not have your way. I shall be forced, against all my previous intentions, to make known your vicious designs to the very lady, who hitherto has held you in the highest esteem. You will realize that if I take this action, you will be in danger of your life . . ."

"If I am to die anyway," Amador broke in, "then the agony will be over all the sooner! Nor am I going to be deterred because you've disfigured your face! I'm quite sure you did it yourself, of your own volition. No! If all I could get were your bare bones, still I should want to hold them close!"

Florida could see that neither tears, nor entreaties, nor reasoning were to any avail. She could see that he was going to act out his evil desires, unmoved and merciless. Exhausted and unable to struggle any more, there was only one thing left she could do to save herself, the one thing that she had shrunk from as from death itself. With a heart-rending cry, she shouted out to her mother with all the strength that was in her. There was something in Florida's voice that made the Countess go cold with horror. Suspecting what had happened, she flew to the room with all possible haste. Amador, not quite so ready to die as he had just declared, had had enough time to gather himself together. When the Countess entered, there he was standing by the door, with Florida at a distance.

"Amador, what's the matter?" she demanded. "Tell me the truth!"

Amador was never at loss when it came to finding his way out of a difficult situation. Looking shocked and pale, he gave his answer.

"Alas! Madame, what has come over Florida? I've never been so astonished as I am at this moment. I used to think, as you know, that I had some share in her goodwill. But now I see that I have none at all. I do not think that she was any less modest, any less virtuous in the days when she was living in your household than she is now, but she used not to have such scruples about seeing men and talking to them. I only have to look at her now, and she can't bear it! I thought it was a dream or a trance, when I saw her acting like that, and I asked her if I could kiss her hand, which after all is quite normal in this part of the world, but she completely refused! I am prepared to admit that I was in the wrong over one thing, Madame, and for this I do ask your forgiveness: I'm afraid I did hold her hand as you might say by force, and kissed it. But that was the only thing I asked of her. But she seems to be so determined that I should die, that she called out to you, as you must have heard. I can't understand why she did it, unless she was afraid that I had other intentions. Anyway, whatever the reason, Madame, I take the blame for it. She really ought to show affection for all your loyal servants. But such is fate! I happen to be the one who's in love, and yet I'm the only one who loses favor! Of course, I'll always feel the same way about you, Madame, and about your daughter, as I have in the past, and I hope and pray that I shan't lose your good opinion, even if, through no fault of my own, I have lost hers."

The Countess, who half believed, half doubted these words, turned to Florida. "Why did you call out for me like that?" she asked.

Florida replied that she had been afraid, and, in spite of her mother's insistent and repeated questions, she refused ever to give more details. It was enough for her that she had been delivered from the hands of her enemy, and as far as she was concerned Amador had been quite sufficiently punished by being thwarted in his attempt. The Countess had a long talk with Amador, and then let him speak again to Florida, though she stayed in the room while he did so, in order to observe from a distance how he would comport himself. He had little to say, though he did thank Florida for not telling her mother the whole truth, and he did ask her that since he was banished from her heart for ever, she would at least not admit a successor.

"If I had had any other way of protecting myself," came her reply, "I would not have shouted out, and no one would have heard anything about what happened. Provided that you don't drive me to it, that is the worst you will have from me. And you need have no fear that I shall give my love to some other man. For since I have not found that which I desired in the heart which I regarded as the most virtuous in the world, I shall never believe it is to be found in any man. Thanks to what has happened I shall be free for ever more from the passions that can arise from love."

So saying, she bade Amador farewell. The Countess had been watching closely, but she could come to no conclusion, except that her daughter plainly no longer felt any affection for Amador. She was convinced that Florida was just being perverse, and had taken it into her head to dislike anyone that her mother was fond of. From that time on, the Countess became so hostile toward her daughter, that for seven whole years she did not speak to her except in anger—and all this for the sake of Amador.

Up till this time Florida had had a horror of being with her husband, but during this period her attitude changed, and, in order to [escape] the harshness of her mother, she refused to move from his side. But this did not help her in her plight, so she conceived a plan which involved deceiving Amador. Dropping for a day or two her hostile air, she advised Amador to make amorous overtures to a certain woman, who, she said, had spoken of their love. The woman in question was a lady by the name of Loretta, who was attached to the household of the Queen. Amador believed Florida, and in the hope of eventually regaining her favor, he made advances to Loretta, who was only too pleased to have such an eminently desirable servant. Indeed she made it so obvious by her simperings, that the whole court soon got to hear of it. The Countess herself was at court at this time, and when she heard the rumors, she began to be less severe than she had been with her daughter. One day, however, it came to Florida's ears that Loretta's husband, who was a high-ranking officer in the army, and one of the King of Spain's highest governors, had become so jealous, that he had sworn to stop at nothing to kill Amador. Now Florida was incapable of wishing harm on Amador, however harsh a mask she might wear, and she informed him immediately of the danger he was in. Amador, anxious to return to her, replied that he would never again speak a word to Loretta, provided that Florida would agree to see him for three hours each day. To that she could not give her consent.

"Then why," said Amador to her, "if you do not wish to give me life, do you wish to save me from death? There can only be one reason—that you want to keep me alive in order to torture me, and hope thereby to cause me greater pain than a thousand deaths could ever do. Death may shun me, yet I shall seek it out, and I shall find it, for only in death shall I have repose!"

Even as they spoke, news arrived that the King of Granada had declared war on the King of Spain, and had attacked so fiercely that the King had had to send his son, the Prince, to the front, together with two old and experienced lords, the Constable of Castile and the Duke of Alba. The Duke of Cardona, too, and the Count of Aranda, were anxious to join the campaign, and petitioned the King for a commission. His majesty granted their requests, appointing each to the command appropriate to his birth. Amador was appointed to lead them. His exploits during that campaign were so extraordinary that they had more the appearance of acts of desperation than acts of bravery. Indeed, to bring my story to its conclusion, this bravery, going beyond all bounds, was demonstrated at the last in death.

The Moors had indicated that they were about to join battle. Then, seeing the size of the Christian forces, they had staged a sham retreat. The Spaniards had been about to follow in hot pursuit. But the old Constable and the Duke of Alba, realizing that it was a trap, had managed to restrain the Prince from crossing the river. The Count of Aranda and the Duke of Cardona, however, had defied orders. The Moors, seeing their pursuers were reduced in number, had wheeled round. Cardona had been killed, cut down by thrusts from Moorish scimitars. Aranda had been left gravely wounded, and as good as dead. In the midst of the carnage Amador arrived, riding furiously, and forcing his way like a madman through the thick of the battle. He had the two bodies transported back to the Prince's encampment. The Prince was as overcome as if they had been his own brothers. When the wounds were examined, however, it was found that the Count of Aranda was still alive, so he was carried back in a litter[6] to the family home, where he lay ill for a very long time. The Duke's corpse was sent back to Cardona. Amador, having rescued the two bodies, was so heedless of his own safety that he found himself surrounded by vast numbers of Moors. He made up his mind what he should do. His enemies would not enjoy the glory either of capturing him alive or of slaying him. Even as he had failed to take his lady, so now his enemies would be frustrated in taking him. His faith to her he had broken. His faith to God he would not break. He knew, too, that if he was taken before the King of Granada, he would have to abjure Christianity, or die a horrible death. Commending body and soul to God, he kissed the cross of his sword, and plunged it with such force into his body that he killed himself in one fell blow.

Thus died poor Amador, his loss bemoaned as his virtue and prowess deserved. The news of his death spread throughout Spain, and eventually reached Florida, who was at Barcelona, where her husband had expressed his wish to be buried. She conducted the obsequies with due honor. Then, saying not a word either to her own mother or to the mother of her dead husband, she entered the Convent of Jesus. Thus she took Him as lover and as spouse who had delivered her from the violent love of Amador and from the misery of her life with her earthly husband. All her affections henceforth were bent on the perfect love of God. As a nun she lived for many long years, until at last she commended her soul to God with the joy of the bride who goes to meet her bridegroom.

"I'm afraid, Ladies, that this story has been rather long, and that some of you might have found it somewhat tedious—but it would have been even longer if I'd done justice to the person who originally told it to me. I hope you will take Florida's example to heart, but at the same time I would beg you to be less harsh, and not to have so much faith in men that you end up being disappointed when you learn the truth, drive them to a horrible death and give yourselves a miserable life."

Parlamente had had a patient and attentive audience. She now turned to Hircan, and said: "Don't you think that this woman was tried to the limits of her endurance, and that she put up a virtuous resistance in the face of it all?"

6. A stretcher.

"No," replied Hircan, "for screaming is the least resistance a woman can offer. If she'd been somewhere where nobody could have heard her, I don't know what she'd have done. And as for Amador, if he'd been more of a lover and less of a coward, he wouldn't have been quite so easily put off. The example of Florida is not going to make me change my opinion on this matter. I still maintain that no man who loved perfectly, or who was loved by a lady, could fail in his designs, provided he went about things in a proper manner. All the same, I must applaud Amador for at least partly fulfilling his duty."

"What duty?" demanded Oisille. "Do you call it duty when a man who devotes himself to a lady's service tries to take her by force, when what he owes to her is obedience and reverence?"

"Madame," replied Saffredent, "when our ladies are holding court and sit in state like judges, then we men bend our knees before them, we timidly invite them to dance, we serve them so devotedly that we anticipate their every wish. Indeed, we have the appearance of being so terrified of offending them, so anxious to serve their every whim, that anybody else observing us would think we must be either out of our minds, or struck dumb, so idiotic is our animal-like devotion. Then all the credit goes to the ladies, because they put on such haughty expressions and adopt such refined ways of speaking, that people who see nothing but their external appearance go in awe of them, and feel obliged to admire and love them. However, in private it is quite another matter. Then Love is the only judge of the way we behave, and we soon find out that they are just women, and we are just men. The title 'lady' is soon exchanged for 'mistress,' and her 'devoted servant' soon becomes her 'lover.' Hence the well-known proverb: 'loyal service makes the servant master.'"

"They have honor, just as men, who can give it to them or take it away, have honor; and they see the things we patiently endure; but it is therefore only right that our long-suffering should be rewarded when honor cannot be injured."

"But you are not talking about true honor," intervened Longarine, "true honor which alone gives true contentment in this world. Suppose that everybody said I was a decent woman, while I knew that the opposite was true—then their praise would only increase my dishonor and make me feel inwardly ashamed. Equally, if everybody criticized me, while I knew that I was completely innocent, I would only derive contentment from their criticism. For no one is truly contented, unless he is contented within himself."

"Well, whatever you all might say," said Geburon, "in my opinion Amador was the most noble and valiant knight that ever lived. I think I recognize him beneath his fictitious name, but since Parlamente has preferred not to disclose the identities of her characters, I shall not disclose them either. Suffice it to say that if it's the man I think it is, then he's a man who never experienced fear in his life, a man whose heart was never devoid of love or the desire for courageous action."

Then Oisille turned to them all and said: "I think it has been a delightful day, and if the remaining days are equally enjoyable, then we shall have seen how swiftly the time can be made to pass in refined conversation. See how low the sun is already. And listen to the Abbey bell calling us to vespers! It started ringing a while ago, but I didn't draw your attention to it because your desire to hear the end of the story was more devout than your desire to hear vespers!"

Upon these words they all got up and made their way to the Abbey, where they found the monks had been waiting for them for a good hour. After hearing vespers, they had their supper, and spent the evening discussing the stories they had heard that day and racking their brains for new stories to make the next day as enjoyable as the first. Then, after playing not a few games in the meadow, they retired to bed, thus bringing the first day to a happy and contented close.

THE ABENCERRAJE

sixteenth century

Although it announces itself as a love story (its full title is *The History of the Abencerraje and the Lovely Jarifa*), the primary focus of *The Abencerraje* is the unlikely friendship between two knights: a gallant lovelorn Moor and his Christian captor. Offering an idealized version of life on the Andalusian Christian/Muslim frontier in what is today southern Spain, the book also takes long-familiar traditions of the sixteenth century—ideas about chivalry and courtly love that were already well known and well worn—and puts them to new and surprising uses.

The Abencerraje was published anonymously, as were several of the most influential and popular early-modern Spanish works that tackled sensitive topics. Several versions of the novella, with minor differences, appeared in quick succession in the 1560s: in an anonymous history of the conquest of the city of Antequera; as an interpolated story in the wildly popular pastoral romance *Diana*; and as one item in a humanist anthology of miscellaneous texts.

Although *The Abencerraje* was read far beyond its time and place, it was written in a very specific political context, when not only Islam but most cultural forms recognized as deriving from Al-Andalus, the formerly Muslim part of the Iberian peninsula, were forbidden in Spain. In contrast, *The Abencerraje* celebrates that cultural inheritance, advocates sympathy toward Muslims and their Christian-converted descendants, and expresses a humanist belief in the power of chivalry to overcome religious differences.

By the late fifteenth century, when the story is set, Christians had gained control of all of modern-day Spain except the Nasrid kingdom of Granada. Much of the warfare on the frontier was carried out through raids, skirmishes, and the taking of captives for ransom. In 1492—the same year in which they decreed the expulsion of Spain's Jews and in which Columbus first reached the New World on their behalf—King Ferdinand II of Aragon and Queen Isabella I of Castile, known as Spain's "Catholic Monarchs," conquered Granada.

Soon after their victory, Ferdinand and Isabella reneged on the guarantees of religious freedom that they had offered, and instead set out to align Spain exclusively with the Roman Catholic Church. The Muslims of Castile and Aragon, like the Jews before them, were offered the choice of conversion or forced exile. A few noble families managed to assimilate by converting and marrying into the Christian nobility and thereafter known dismissively as New Christians, or Moriscos. The "Moors" of mid-sixteenth-century Spain, when *The Abencerraje* first appeared, were thus a persecuted and ostracized minority. In this context, the idealized representation of a sympathetic, noble Moor and his beloved participates in an urgent debate about the nature of the newly unified Spanish nation and how it would manage the large numbers of converted "Moors" that remained in Spain. How to reconcile the idealized figures of the text with the realities of its context? How should we remember our history, and what role does it serve? From the wry question at the start, concerning whether Spain could ever pay due homage to its many heroes, to Rodrigo de Narváez's claim at the end that, of all his feats, he would most like to commemorate his friendship with Abindarráez, *The Abencerraje* foregrounds the stakes of the stories we choose to tell ourselves about the past.

The Abencerraje works within genres that were extremely popular at the time, such as the chivalric and the sentimental romance, to present the relationship between a Moor and his Christian foe. It makes literal the metaphors of Petrarchan love—the idea of love as a form of captivity, the state of seeming enmity between lover and beloved—to explore what kinds of ties bind knights of different faiths. The novella tells of a Moorish knight, Abindarráez, of the unfortunate Abencerraje clan, who is brought up in exile, away from Granada. He is raised with a supposed sister, Jarifa, with whom he falls in love. Once they discover they are not related, they decide to marry in secret. As Abindarráez is on his way to meet Jarifa to consummate their union, his journey is interrupted. Rodrigo de Narváez—a historical figure of the Andalusian wars,

and governor of the frontier town of Álora—and his Christian knights attack him in a skirmish, and Abindarráez, despite his valor, is taken captive. Abindarráez tells Rodrigo the tragic story of his lineage, falsely accused of treason and driven from Granada—a lament that some critics have read as an oblique reference to the persecution of Jews and Muslims by the Spanish Crown.

Moved by Abindarráez's story, and relying on his chivalry, Narváez frees him temporarily so that he can pursue his interrupted nuptials, while Abindarráez gives his solemn word as a knight that he will return. The novella is much more invested in chivalry and nobility than in religious differences; in fact, religion is only ever mentioned to make the point that it does not impede the friendship between the two knights. Yet for all its idealization of the friendship between Moor and Christian, *The Abencerraje* also questions the costs and contradictions of that ideal, just as Jarifa also appears as a skeptical observer of the relations between men, repeatedly voicing her surprise at the choices they make and drawing our attention to how little agency they grant even the women they profess to adore.

The Abencerraje was a tremendously influential work for its sympathetic depiction of an idealized Moor in love. It inaugurated a genre of idealizing Moorish tales in Spain and beyond. In the huge late-sixteenth-century vogue for ballads on Moorish themes, the story of Abindarráez and Jarifa was repeated across Spain. So popular was the figure of the Moorish knight that when Don Quijote (1605) lies wounded after his first sortie, he imagines himself as Abindarráez. Translated widely across Europe in the early modern period, and read as part of the best-selling *Diana* (1562), the *Abencerraje* anchored a tradition of idealized, orientalist storytelling that would continue well into the nineteenth century.

The Abencerraje[1]

Prologue

This is a living portrait of virtue, generosity, valor, nobility, and loyalty, composed of Rodrigo de Narváez[2] and the Abencerraje and Jarifa,[3] as well as her father and the king of Granada. Although the two make up the body of this work, the others adorn the canvas and have left their own marks on it. And just as a precious diamond, whether set in gold or silver or lead, retains its fair value according to its carats and its luster, so too virtue shines and shows its qualities in any flawed subject, just like the seed that grows when it falls on fertile soil and in the barren soil is lost.[4]

The Abencerraje

The story goes that in the time of Prince Ferdinand, who conquered Antequera, there was a knight named Rodrigo de Narváez, famous for his virtue and feats of arms. He fought the Moors with great valor, and especially in the campaign and the battle for Antequera he performed deeds worthy of eternal memory, were it not that our Spain takes such skill for granted. For it is so natural to Spain and so common here that anything one does seems too little; unlike for the Greeks and Romans, who in their writings turned men who once risked death into immortals and set them among the stars. This knight, then, did so much in the service of his king and his faith that after the town was conquered he was named governor, so that having played such a great role in taking it, he would now do the same in defending it. He was also made governor of Álora, and so commanded both garrisons, dividing his time between the two and always attending to the greater need. He was usually to be found in Álora, where he had fifty noble squires in the king's service for the defense and safety of the town. And none was ever found lacking, for, like the immortal knights of King Darius,[5] whenever one died, they set another in his place. They all had such great faith in their captain's virtue and took such strength from it that nothing was ever difficult for them: they never ceased to attack their enemies and defend themselves against them. They triumphed every time they skirmished, winning honor and profit, which enriched them always.

One night when the weather was very mild, the governor spoke these words to his squires after supper:

---

1. Translated by Barbara Fuchs, Larissa Brewer-García, and Aaron J. Ilika.
2. Rodrigo de Narváez was the name of a historical person who participated in the Christian conquest of Antequera in 1410 and was named its governor by Prince Ferdinand of Aragon.
3. In Arabic, Abindarráez (the first name of the Abencerraje) means "captain's son," and Jarifa means "noble, precious, or beautiful one." The Abencerraje family was a noble clan in Al-Andalus.

4. In the biblical parable (Matthew 13.3–23; Mark 4.3–20; Luke 8.5–8), Christ compares spreading his word to the sowing of seeds: just as soils may be fertile or barren, some people will be more receptive to the spreading of the Word than others.
5. Darius the Great (550–486 B.C.E.) ruled the Persian Empire at its peak. The "Immortals," so called by the ancient Greek historian Herodotus, were an elite corps in the Persian army, whose number was maintained constant by replacing dead, wounded, or sick soldiers.

"It seems to me, noblemen, my brothers and lords, that nothing so rouses the hearts of men as the continual exercise of arms, through which we gain experience with our own weapons and lose fear of the enemy's. There is no need for me to invoke distant examples of this, as you yourselves are the best proof. I mention this because it has been many a day since we have done anything to increase our renown, and I would not be doing my duty to my office and my person if I let the time go to waste with such virtuous men and valiant troops at my command. It seems to me, if you are all in agreement, that with this clear and safe night beckoning to us, we should let our enemies know that the guardians of Álora do not sleep. That is my wish; do what you will."

They answered that he should lead and all would follow him. He chose nine of them and had them armed. Once ready, they left through a hidden door so that they would not be noticed and the fortress would remain safe. Setting out on their way, they came to a fork in the road, where the governor addressed them:

"If we all take one path, our prey might escape on the other. You five take this one, and I will take the other with these four. If by chance any of you find enemies that you cannot defeat, blow your horn, and the sound of it will call the others to your aid."

The five squires set out on their path, speaking of various things, when one of them said, "Hold on, friends, for unless I am mistaken, there is someone coming."

They hid in a thicket by the road and heard noises. Taking a closer look, they saw a gallant Moor coming toward them on a roan horse. He was of powerful build and had a beautiful face, and he looked very fine in the saddle. He wore a crimson cloak and a damask burnoose of the same color, all embroidered in gold and silver. His right sleeve was turned back, with a beautiful lady embroidered on it, and he held a fine and sturdy lance with two points. He carried a shield and a scimitar, and wore a Tunisian head wrap with many folds that served to both adorn and protect him.[6] So dressed, the Moor advanced with a noble air, singing a song he had composed in fond memory of his love, and which went like this: "Born in Granada, raised in Cártama, I fell in love in Coín, bordering Álora."

Although the music lacked artistry, the Moor did not lack for happiness, and his heart, which was full of love, gave charm to his every word. The squires, transported by the sight of him, almost let him through before they set upon him. Finding himself ambushed, he bravely came to his senses and waited to see what they would do.

Four of the five squires rode off to the side while one attacked him. But since the Moor was more skilled in those matters, with a stroke of his lance he forced the squire and his horse to the ground. Seeing this, three of the four remaining attacked him at the same time, for he seemed to them very strong. Now there were three Christians, any one of whom could take on ten Moors, against this one Moor, and yet all of them together could not defeat him. Soon the Moor found himself in great danger, as his lance broke and the squires pressed him hard. Feigning flight, he spurred his horse on with his legs and rushed toward the squire he had unhorsed. Like a bird he swooped from his saddle and grabbed the man's lance, and with it he turned upon the enemies who chased him as he pretended to flee. He fought so skillfully that in a short time he had two of the three on the

6. Fine "Moorish" garments such as those worn here by Abindarráez would have been admired and worn not only by Muslims but also by Christians of the aristocratic classes.

ground. The last one, seeing his companions' dire need, sounded his horn as he rode to help them. Now the skirmish became very fierce, for they were affronted to have one knight last so long against them, while he fought for his life and more. Then one of the squires struck him on the thigh with his lance, in a blow so hard that, had it not landed askew, it would have gone right through him. Furious at finding himself wounded, the Moor turned and struck him with the lance, throwing both horse and rider to the ground, badly wounded.

Rodrigo de Narváez drew near, sensing that his companions needed help. As he rode the best horse, he took the lead. When he witnessed the Moor's bravery, he was astonished: the Moor had four of the five squires on the ground and the fifth one on the way.

"Moor, ride against me," he said, "and if you defeat me, I will vouch for the others." They joined in a bitter fight, but since the governor was fresh and the Moor and his horse were injured, Narváez pressed him so that he could not keep up. Yet seeing that his life and happiness hung on this one battle, the Moor threw such a blow at Narváez that it would no doubt have killed him, had he not stopped it with his shield. Parrying the blow, Narváez charged against him and wounded him on his right arm. Closing in, he grappled with him and threw him from his saddle to the ground. Then, leaning over him, he said, "Sir, concede defeat, or I shall kill you."

"You may well kill me," said the Moor, "for I am in your hands, but I cannot be vanquished except by the one who once vanquished me."

The governor did not remark on the mystery of these words; with his usual decency, he helped the Moor to his feet, for the wound that the squire had given him on his thigh and the other one on his arm (though not severe), coupled with his great exhaustion and the fall from his horse, had quite drained him. With supplies he took from the squires, Rodrigo bound up the Moor's wounds. Then he helped him onto one of the squires' horses, for his own was wounded, and they took the road back to Álora. While they all rode along, discussing the Moor's good bearing and bravery, he let out a great deep sigh and spoke a few words in Arabic that none of them could make out.[7] Observing the Moor's fine build and bearing, and recalling what he had seen him do, Rodrigo de Narváez suspected that such great sadness in such a brave heart could hardly come from what had just occurred.

To learn more, he said to him, "Sir, consider that the prisoner who loses all hope forfeits his right to liberty. Consider, too, that in war knights must both win and lose, for the better part of their battles are subject to fortune. For one who has just shown such valor, it seems like weakness to show so little now. If you sigh from the pain of your wounds, know that you are on your way to a place where you will soon be cured. If you lament your imprisonment, know that these are the ways of war, to which all who wage it are subject. And if you suffer some other secret torment, confide in me, for I promise you on my honor as a knight to do all in my power to remedy it."

The Moor, lifting his gaze from the ground, said, "What is your name, knight, you who show such understanding of my plight?"

---

7. The original uses *entendió* (understood) instead of *entendía* (could understand) here: the squires may well have known Arabic but could not make out what Abindarráez mumbled. Christians on the frontier in Al-Andalus would have been likely to know Arabic.

He responded, "They call me Rodrigo de Narváez; I am the governor of Ante-quera and Álora."

The Moor, whose face brightened a bit at this, said, "Truly now some of my sorrow lifts, since though fortune was against me, it has left me in your hands. For although I have never seen you before, I have heard of your virtue and experienced your strength. So that you will not think that the pain from my wounds is what makes me sigh, and since it seems to me that you could keep any secret, send off your squires so that I may have two words with you."

The governor had them fall back. When they were alone, the Moor said to him with a great sigh:

"Rodrigo de Narváez, renowned governor of Álora, listen to what I shall tell you now, and you shall see whether my misfortunes are enough to break the heart of a captive man. They call me Abindarráez the Younger, to distinguish me from an uncle of mine, my father's brother, of the same name. I come from the line of the Abencerrajes of Granada, of whom you must have often heard—although my present grief is quite enough, without recalling sorrows past, I want to tell you that story.

"In Granada there lived a line of noblemen called the Abencerrajes who were the finest in the kingdom: in their elegance, good grace, disposition, and bravery they excelled all others. They were favored by the king and all the nobles and well loved by the common people. They emerged as victors from any combat they entered and distinguished themselves in all tournaments; they devised all the finery and costumes. So one could truly say that in times of peace as in war they were a model and example for the entire kingdom. It is said that there was never an Abencerraje who was miserly or cowardly or ill disposed. A man was not considered an Abencerraje if he did not serve a lady, nor was a woman considered a lady if she had no Abencerraje as a suitor.

"Yet fortune, their great enemy, decreed that they should fall from this excellence, as you will now hear. The King of Granada, led on by false information he had received against them, did a great wrong to two of these noblemen, the bravest of them all. And it was said, though I don't believe it, that these two and ten others at their request conspired to kill the King and divide the kingdom among themselves, avenging their insult. This conspiracy, whether true or false, was discovered, and so as not to scandalize the kingdom that loved them so, the King had them all beheaded in one night, for had he delayed his injustice, he would not have been able to carry it out. The King was offered huge ransoms for their lives, but he would not even hear of it. When the people saw that there was no hope for their lives, they began to lament anew. The fathers who had sired them wept, as did the mothers who had given birth to them; the ladies whom they served wept, as did the knights who were their companions. The common people raised such a great and lasting outcry it was as though enemies had invaded the city. If their lives could have been bought with tears, the Abencerrajes would not have died so miserably.

"Behold what became of such a distinguished lineage and its famous knights! Consider how long it takes for Fortune to raise a man and how quickly she cuts him down; how long it takes for a tree to grow and how quickly it goes to the fire; how difficult it is to build a house and how rapidly it burns! How many could learn from those wretched men, who blamelessly suffered their public disgrace! Even though they were so numerous and so important and had enjoyed the favor of the King himself, their houses were destroyed, their estates given to others, and their name proclaimed treasonous throughout the kingdom. Because of this unfortunate episode, no Abencerraje was allowed to live in Granada, except for my father and uncle, who were found innocent of this crime, on the condition that any sons born to them be raised outside the city, never to return, and any daughters married outside the kingdom."

Rodrigo de Narváez, who observed the suffering with which the Abencerraje related his misfortunes, said to him:

"Yours is certainly a strange story, sir, and a great injustice was done to the Abencerrajes, for it is hard to believe that men such as they could have committed treason."

"It is just as I have told you," answered the Abencerraje, "Wait and you shall hear how, from that time on, all the Abencerrajes were unfortunate. When I came into the world from my mother's womb, my father sent me to the governor of Cártama, his close friend, in order to fulfill the king's decree. The governor had a daughter about my age, whom he loved more than himself, for not only was she his only child and most beautiful, but she had cost him his wife, who had died giving birth to her. She and I were as brother and sister in our childhood because that is what we heard people call us. I cannot recall a moment when we were not together. We were raised together, walked together, ate and drank together. From this closeness came a natural affection that increased with age. I remember that one afternoon when I walked into the place they call the Garden of Jasmine, I found her seated by the fountain, arranging her lovely hair. I gazed at her, vanquished by her beauty, and she seemed to me like Salmacis.[8] I said to myself, 'O to be Hermaphroditus and appear before this beautiful goddess!' How I regretted that she was my sister! Yet I rushed to her, and when she saw me, she hurried to meet me with arms outstretched. Seating me by her side, she said to me,

"'Brother, why did you leave me alone for so long?'

"'My lady,' I replied, 'I have been searching for you for a long time, and no one could say where you were, until my heart told me. But tell me now, how certain are you that we are brother and sister?'

"'I only know it from the great love I have for you, and from the fact that everyone calls us that,' she said.

"'And if we were not,' said I, 'would you love me as much?'

"'Can you not see,' she said, 'that if we were not, my father would never let us spend so much time alone together?'

"'Well, if it would mean the loss of that good fortune,' I said, 'I would rather have my present sorrow.'

"Then she began to blush, and said, 'What do you lose from our being brother and sister?'

"'I lose myself and you,' I said.

"'I don't understand you,' she said. 'In fact, it seems to me that simply being brother and sister naturally compels us to love one another.'

"'Only your beauty compels me. The kinship actually seems to discourage me sometimes.'

8. In the Greek myth retold by Ovid in book four of the *Metamorphoses*, Salmacis falls in love with Hermaphroditus (son of Hermes and Aphrodite) when he is bathing by a fountain. When he rejects her, she asks the gods to combine their bodies into one.

"Lowering my eyes in embarrassment at what I had said, I saw her exact likeness in the waters of the fountain. Wherever I turned my head, I saw her image, and most of all in my heart. I said to myself (for I would not have wanted anyone to hear me), 'If I were to drown myself in the fountain where I see my lady, I would have a better excuse than Narcissus![9] If she loved me as I love her, how happy I would be! And if fortune allowed us to live together always, what a life I could lead!'

"Saying this, I stood up and gathered some of the jasmine that surrounded the fountain, threading it with myrtle to make a beautiful garland. Placing it on my head, I turned to her, both crowned and vanquished. She looked at me, more sweetly it seemed than usual, took the garland from me and placed it on her head. At that moment she seemed to me more beautiful than Venus when she was judged for the apple.[1] Turning to me, she asked, 'How do I look now, Abindarráez?'

"'As though you have just vanquished the world and they are crowning you its queen and lady,' I answered. She stood up and took me by the hand, saying, 'If that were the case, brother, you would lose nothing by it.' I did not answer and instead followed her out of the garden. We led this life of dissimulation for a long time, until Love took revenge on us and exposed the ruse, for as we grew older, we both learned that we were not siblings. I know not what she felt when she first found out, but nothing has ever made me happier, although I have paid dearly for it since. No sooner were we certain of this, but the pure and healthy love we had for each other began to spoil, turning into a raging malady that will last until our deaths. Here there were no first causes to excuse because our love came from a pleasure and delight that was nothing but good. Yet the harm did not come at first, but suddenly and all at once: I now found all my joy in her, and my soul followed the measure of her soul. What I did not see in her seemed to me ugly, unnecessary, and of no use in the world; all my thoughts were with her. By this point, our pastimes had changed: I now looked at her in fear of being found out and was jealous of the very sun that touched her. Her presence wounded me, and her absence broke my heart. And yet for all this, she did not owe me anything because she paid me in the same coin. Then Fortune, jealous of our sweet life, decided to snatch away our happiness, as you shall hear.

"The king of Granada, wishing to promote the governor of Cártama, ordered him to leave his garrison for Coín, which is that town near yours, and to leave me in Cártama under the new governor. Imagine, if you have ever been in love, how my lady and I felt when we learned this disastrous news. We met in a secret place to weep at our parting. I called out to her, 'My lady, my soul, my only happiness,' and other names love had taught me. 'When your beauty is far away from me, will you ever remember this captive of yours?' Here my tears and sighs cut short my words. Forcing myself to continue, I half muttered some confused notions that I cannot even remember because my lady took my memory with her. Who could relate how she lamented, although it still seemed too little to me! She said a thousand sweet words to me that I can hear even now. Finally, so that no

9. In the myth retold in book three of Ovid's *Metamorphoses*, the beautiful Narcissus falls in love with his image reflected in a stream, falls in while gazing at himself, and drowns.

1. When Venus, Juno, and Minerva competed for a golden apple promised to the fairest goddess, Paris of Troy awarded Venus the prize.

one would hear us, we said good-bye with many tears and sobs, and with a sigh wrenched from our souls, we gave each other an embrace as a pledge of our love.

"Then, because she saw me in such straits, looking as though I would die, she said, 'Abindarráez, leaving you is breaking my heart, and since I know you feel the same, I want to be yours until death. My heart is yours, my life is yours, my honor and wealth. As proof of this, as soon as I find a way to meet you while my father is indisposed or away, which I eagerly await, I will send word to you from Coín, where I now go with him. Come to me wherever I am, and there I shall give you, as my husband, that which I carry with me, for neither your loyalty nor my nature would allow it otherwise, and everything else has been yours for many years.'

"With this promise my heart calmed down somewhat, and I kissed her hands for the favor she promised me. They left the next day, and I was left as one who, walking through steep and rugged mountains, loses sight of the sun. I began to feel her absence sharply and sought false cures for it. I gazed at the windows where she used to sit, the waters where she bathed, the room where she slept, the garden where she rested. I visited all her stations,[2] and in all of them I found an image of my suffering. The hope she had given me that she would summon me sustained me, and so I fooled my cares somewhat. Sometimes the delay caused me even greater pain, so that I would have preferred for her to leave me in despair, which causes pain only until it is believed certain, while hope troubles us until desire is fulfilled.

"My good fortune had it so that this morning my lady fulfilled her promise to me and sent one of her trusted servants to summon me. Her father had left for Granada, called for by the King to return immediately. Revived by this good news, I readied myself. I waited for nightfall so as to leave in secret, and put on the garments in which you found me to show my lady the joy in my heart. I would not have thought that a hundred knights at once would have been enough to stop me since I carried my lady on my sleeve. If you defeated me, it was not by force, which is not possible, but rather because my bad luck or heaven's will snatched away my good fortune. So consider now, at the end of my story, the good I have lost and the misfortune that weighs on me. I was traveling from Cártama to Coín—a short trip, although desire made it longer—the proudest Abencerraje ever: I went at the behest of my lady, to see my lady, to love my lady, and to marry my lady. Now I find myself wounded, captive and defeated, and the worst part is that the short space of my good fortune ends this evening. Allow me to find consolation in my sighs, Christian, and consider them not weakness, for it would take even greater fortune to be able to suffer such desperate straits."

Rodrigo de Narváez was amazed and touched by the Moor's strange affair, and since it seemed to him that nothing could harm his purpose more than delay, said to him:

"Abindarráez, I want to show you that my virtue is stronger than your ill fortune. If you give me your word as a knight to return as my captive in three days' time, I will set you free to go on your way, since I would be sorry to prevent such an affair."

The Moor was so happy when he heard this that he tried to throw himself at Narváez's feet, saying, "Rodrigo de Narváez, if you do this, you will have done

---

2. Abindarráez visits the places where Jarifa used to be with the reverence of a worshipper viewing representations of Christ at the stations of the cross.

the greatest kindness that man ever did, and you would give me new life. As for what you ask of me, take whatever assurance you will, for I shall fulfill it."

The governor called his squires and said, "My lords, entrust this prisoner to me, for I will guarantee his ransom." They told him to command as he pleased. Taking the Moor's right hand between his own, he said, "Do you swear to me as a knight to return to my castle in Álora to be my prisoner within three days?"

He said, "I swear."

"Then good luck, and if you should need me or anything else for your enterprise, it shall be done as well."

Abindarráez thanked him and set off in haste for Coín. Rodrigo de Narváez and his squires returned to Álora, discussing the bravery and fine bearing of the Moor.

In his hurry, Abindarráez pressed on and did not take long to reach Coín, heading straight for the castle. He did not stop until he found a door, as he had been instructed. Pausing there, he began his reconnaissance to see if there was any need to defend himself. Seeing that all was well, he knocked on the door with the back of his lance, for this was the signal that the lady-in-waiting had given him. She quickly opened the door herself and said to him, "What has taken you so long, my lord? Your delay had us greatly worried. My lady has long awaited you; dismount, and you shall go to her."

He dismounted and placed his horse in a well-hidden spot nearby. He left his lance with his shield and scimitar, and then the lady-in-waiting led him by the hand as quietly as possible so that the people of the castle would not hear him. They climbed a staircase and reached the bedchamber of the lovely Jarifa, for this was the lady's name. She had already heard him and came out to welcome him with outstretched arms. In their great joy, they embraced without a word.

Then the lady said, "What has taken you so long, my lord? Your delay has caused me great sadness and alarm."

"My lady," he said, "you know full well it could not have been my negligence, but things do not always turn out the way we wish."

She took him by the hand and led him to a secret chamber. Sitting on a bed that was there, she said, "Abindarráez, I long to show you how the captives of love keep their promises, for from the day I gave you my heart as a token, I have been trying to win it back. I ordered you to come to this castle to be my prisoner, as I am yours, and, as my husband, to make you the owner of my person and of my father's estate, even though I suspect that shall go against his wishes. He does not know your bravery, nor has he experienced your virtue as I have, and he would like to give me a richer husband. But I take your person and my happiness to be the greatest treasure in the world."

And saying this, she hung her head, ashamed to have revealed so much. The Moor took her in his arms, kissing her hands many times for the favor she granted him, and said, "My lady, in exchange for all the good you have offered me, I have nothing to offer you that is not yours already, save this token as a sign that I take you as my lady and wife."

After summoning the lady-in-waiting, they spoke their marriage vows. Now, being married, they lay in their bed, where the new experience stoked the fire in their hearts. In this conquest, many loving words and actions were exchanged, which are better imagined than written.

Afterward, the Moor became lost in thought and, distracted, let out a great sigh. The lady, unable to suffer such a slight to her beauty and devotion, lovingly brought him back to his senses and asked, "What is this, Abindarráez? It seems that my happiness brings you sorrow. I hear you sigh and twist and turn all around. If I am your all and your happiness as you told me, for whom do you sigh? And if I am not, why did you deceive me? If you have found some fault with my body, look upon my devotion, which should be enough to outweigh many faults. If you serve another lady, tell me who she is so that I may serve her too. If you have another secret sorrow that will not offend me, tell me, for I will either free you from it or die in the attempt."

The Abencerraje, embarrassed by what he had done and believing that if he did not confess he would provoke great suspicion, told her with an impassioned sigh, "My lady, if I did not love you more than myself, I would not have complained. I suffered my grief bravely when it was just my own, but now that it forces me to leave you, I have no strength to bear it. Know that my sighs come from too much fidelity rather than the lack of it. I want to tell you what has happened, so you will not wonder."

Then he told her everything that had occurred and at the end said, "So, my lady, your captive is also the governor of Álora's. I do not fear the sorrow of imprisonment for you taught my heart to endure, but living without you would be death itself."

The lady smiled and told him, "Do not worry, Abindarráez. I shall take care of your ransom for it is my duty. I hold that any knight who gives his word to return to prison keeps it as long as he sends whatever ransom is asked of him. And so name the sum you see fit, for I have the keys to my father's treasure and will give them to you so that you can send of it what you will. Rodrigo de Narváez is a praiseworthy knight. He gave you your liberty once when you entrusted this matter to him, and this now obliges him to be even more virtuous. I think he will be satisfied, since if he had you in his power, he would only ask for the same."

The Abencerraje replied, "My lady, your great love for me prevents you from counseling me wisely; I shall certainly not commit such a great fault. If I was obliged to keep my word when I came on my own behalf to see you, now that I am yours, my obligation has redoubled. I shall return to Álora and place myself in the governor's hands; after I do what I must, let him do as he pleases."

"May God never allow you to go into captivity while I go free, for I would not be so," Jarifa said. "I wish to accompany you on this journey, for neither my love for you nor my fear of my father, having offended him, will allow me any choice in the matter."

The Moor, weeping tears of happiness, embraced her and said, "My lady, you are always granting favors upon favors; do as you please for that is what I want."

Having come to this agreement, they gathered provisions and set out the next morning. The lady covered her face so as not to be recognized.

As they were on their way, discussing various things, they came across an old man. The lady asked him where he was going, and he answered, "I'm going to Álora for I have some business with the governor, who is the most virtuous and honorable knight I have ever known."

Jarifa was pleased to hear this, for it seemed to her that if everyone found so much virtue in this knight, they, who were in so much need of it, would find it also. Turning to the traveler, she said, "Tell me, brother, do you know of any memorable deed this knight has done?"

"I know many," he said, "but I can tell you one that will stand in for all the rest. This knight was first the governor of Antequera, where for a long time he was in love with a beautiful lady. He performed a thousand courtesies in her service, too many to relate. Yet even though she knew the worth of this knight, she paid him little attention because she loved her husband so much.

"It happened that one summer day, having finished dinner, she and her husband went down to an orchard in their estate. He carried a sparrowhawk on his hand and slipped it at some birds, which fled and hid in the brambles. The wise hawk, holding its body back, reached in with its talons and killed many of them. The knight fed it and, turning to the lady, said, 'What do you think, my lady, of how cleverly the hawk trapped the birds and then killed them? I'll have you know that when the governor of Antequera skirmishes with Moors, he pursues them and kills them like that.' She asked who the governor was, pretending not to know him. 'He's the bravest and most virtuous knight I've ever seen.' He began to speak of him very highly, so that the lady felt a certain regret and said to herself, 'Well! Men are in love with this knight, and I am not, though he is in love with me? Surely I shall be forgiven for whatever I do for him, since my own husband has told me how deserving he is.'

"The next day it happened that the husband was away from the city and the lady could resist no longer, so she had a servant send for the knight. Narváez was nearly beside himself with joy, although he could hardly believe it, recalling the harshness she had always shown him. Yet he still went discreetly to see her at the appointed time. She waited for him in a hidden place, and there she realized the great wrong she had committed and the shame in seeking one who had sought her for so long. Her thoughts turned to Fame, who reveals all things; she feared the fickleness of men and the offense to her husband. All these obstacles served only to vanquish her even further, as is usually the case. Ignoring them all, she received him sweetly and ushered him into her bedchamber, where they exchanged many kind words. At last she said, 'Lord Rodrigo de Narváez, I am yours from this day forward, as is everything in my power. Do not thank me, for all your passions and entreaties, whether true or false, had no effect on me. Rather, thank my husband, who told me such things about you that they have put me in this state.' Then she told him about the conversation with her husband and concluded, 'In fact, my lord, you owe more to my husband than he owes you.'

"These words struck Narváez, causing him worry and remorse for the wrong he was committing against one who had so praised him. He stepped away, and said, 'In truth, my lady, I love you full well and shall love you always, but God forbid that I should commit such a cruel offense against one who has spoken of me so highly. Instead, from this day forward, I shall safeguard your husband's honor as though it were my own, for that is the best way to repay him for the good things he has said of me.' And without further ado, he left the way he came. The lady must have felt duped, yet the knight no doubt acted with great virtue and bravery, my lords, for he overcame his own desire."

The Abencerraje and his lady were amazed at the story. He praised Narváez greatly, saying that he had never seen greater virtue in a man. She replied, "By God, my lord, I would not wish for such a virtuous servant. He must not have been too much in love since he left so quickly and the husband's honor moved him more than the lady's beauty." And she said a few other clever things about the matter.

Just then they arrived at the fortress. They knocked at the gate, and it was opened by guards who already knew what had happened. One man ran to summon the governor, saying, "My lord, the Moor you defeated is here in the castle, and he has brought a noble lady with him."

The governor suspected who it was and came downstairs. The Abencerraje, taking his bride by the hand, approached him and said:

"Rodrigo de Narváez, see whether I have kept my word, for I promised one prisoner and I bring you two, one of whom would suffice to vanquish many others. Behold my lady; consider if I have suffered rightly. Take us as your own, for I trust you with my lady and my honor."

Narváez was delighted to see them and said to the lady, "I know not which of you owes more to the other, but I am in great debt to you both. Come in, and take your ease in this your house; consider it as such from now on, for its owner is your servant."

With that they went to the rooms that had been prepared for them, and soon after they ate something, for they were weary from their journey. "How are your wounds, sir?" the governor asked Abindarráez.

"It seems that with the journey they are inflamed and somewhat sore, sir."

The lovely Jarifa became upset: "What is this, my lord? You have wounds of which I know nothing?"

"My lady, whoever survives the wounds that you give thinks little of any others. It is true that the skirmish the other night left me with a few scrapes, and the journey and not tending to them must have done me some harm."

"It would be best," the governor said, "for you to lie down, and a surgeon from the castle will attend you."

Immediately the lovely Jarifa began to undress him in great dismay. When the doctor came and examined him, he said it was nothing and applied an ointment to relieve the pain. In three days' time, he was cured.

One day after dinner, the Abencerraje spoke these words: "Rodrigo de Narváez, since you are so wise, you may well surmise our situation from the manner in which we arrived. My hope is that you will be able to solve this unfortunate business. This lady is the beautiful Jarifa, of whom I spoke to you, my lady and my wife. She did not wish to remain in Coín for fear of having offended her father—she fears this even now. I know full well that the king loves you for your virtue, even though you are a Christian—I beg you to ask her father to pardon us for having done this without his knowledge, since Fortune brought it about in this way."

The governor said to them, "Take heart, for I promise you I shall do everything in my power." And taking ink and paper he wrote a letter to the King, which read thus:

Letter from Rodrigo de Narváez, Governor of Álora,
to the King of Granada

Most noble and powerful King of Granada:

Rodrigo de Narváez, Governor of Álora, your servant, kisses your royal hands and says: the Abencerraje Abindarráez the Younger, who was born in Granada and raised in Cártama under the authority of its Governor, fell in love with the beautiful Jarifa, his daughter. Later, you favored the Governor by transferring him to Coín. The lovers were secretly betrothed to confirm their love. When Abindarráez was summoned to the fortress due to the absence of Jarifa's father, whom you have with you, I happened across him on his way. After a skirmish I fought with him, in which he proved himself to be very valiant, I took him prisoner. When he told me his situation, I took pity on him and freed him for two days; he went to see his wife, so that on his journey he lost his freedom but won the lady. When she learned that the Abencerraje was returning to my captivity, she came with him and thus both of them are now in my power. I beg you not to let the name Abencerraje offend you, for I know that both this one and his father were not to blame in the conspiracy perpetrated against your royal person; they live as evidence of that. I entreat your Royal Highness to join me in assisting these unfortunate ones. I will pardon their ransom and will graciously release them, but only you can make her father pardon them and receive them in his good graces. And with this you will prove true to your greatness, proceeding as I would always expect of you.

When he had written the letter, he dispatched it with a squire, who gave it to the King as soon as he reached him. The King, knowing whose letter it was, was very pleased, for he loved this one Christian for his merits and good deeds. When he read it, he turned to the Governor of Coín, who was with him, and calling him aside, said:

"Read this letter from the Governor of Álora." When Jarifa's father read it he became very upset. The King said, "Do not be angry, even though you have good cause; know that there is nothing the Governor of Álora can ask me that I will not grant. And so I command that you go straight to Álora now to see him and to pardon your children and take them home. In return for this service, I will always favor them and you."

The Moor resented it in his heart, but seeing that he could not avoid the King's commandment, he put a good face on things and said he would do as his highness commanded.

He immediately left for Álora, where already they had heard from the squire what had happened and where everyone received him with great happiness and rejoicing. The Abencerraje and Jarifa came before him with great contrition and kissed his hands. He received them graciously and said:

"Let us not dwell on the past. I forgive you for having married without my consent, and as for the rest, my daughter, you chose a better husband than I could ever have given you."

Narváez held feasts in their honor for many days, and one night, after dining in a garden, he said, "I am so proud to have played a part in bringing this matter to a good end that nothing could make me happier. The only ransom I require, therefore, is the honor of having had you as my prisoners. From this day forth, lord Abindarráez, I free you to do as you wish."

They kissed his hands for the favor and kindness he had shown them, and the next morning they left the fortress with the Governor accompanying them partway.

Once they had arrived in Coín and were enjoying the good fortune they had so longed for, their father said to them, "My children, now that by my wish you control my estate, it would be right to show Rodrigo de Narváez the gratitude you owe him for the good deed he did you. He should not lose your ransom just because he was so generous; instead, he deserves a much larger one. I shall give you six thousand Zahene gold coins;[3] send them to him and keep him henceforth as a friend, even though we are of different faiths."

Abindarráez kissed his hands and received the doubloons. He sent them to the Governor of Álora, along with four beautiful horses and four lances with golden hilts and points, as well as four shields, and wrote him this letter:

Letter from the Abencerraje Abindarráez to the Governor of Álora

If you think, Rodrigo de Narváez, that by freeing me in your castle so that I could return to mine you set me free, you deceive yourself, for when you freed my body, you captured my soul. Good works make prisoners of noble hearts. Where you are in the habit of doing good to those you could destroy so as to gain honor and fame, I am obliged to thank you and serve you so as to follow my forebears and not sully the noble bloodline of the Abencerrajes but instead gather and distill in my veins all their blood that was shed. This small gift comes with the great love of the one who sends it, and that of Jarifa, which is so pure and loyal that it pleases me.

The Governor admired the worth and uniqueness of the gift, and accepting the horses, lances, and shields, he wrote this to Jarifa:

Letter from the Governor of Álora to the Fair Jarifa

Fair Jarifa: Abindarráez has not allowed me to enjoy the real triumph of his captivity, which consists in forgiving and doing good. Since never was a mission offered me in this land so noble or worthy of a Spanish captain, I would like to enjoy it fully and to craft a statue of it for my postcrity and descendants. I accept the horses and weapons to defend him from his enemies. And if by sending the coins, he proved himself a generous knight, by accepting them I would seem a greedy merchant. I grant them to you in payment for the favor you showed me by making use of me in my castle. Besides, my lady, I am not accustomed to robbing ladies, but rather to serving them and honoring them.

And with that he sent the doubloons back to them. Jarifa received them and said, "Whoever thinks to surpass Rodrigo de Narváez in combat or courtesy should think again." And so they remained very satisfied and pleased with each other, and linked by bonds of friendship so tight that they lasted a lifetime.

---

3. The *zahén* was a valuable gold coin still used by Moors in the time of the Catholic Monarchs. In the late sixteenth century, 6,000 Zahene gold pieces (approximately 2,550,000 *maravedís*) amounted to what an average laborer (who made approximately 85 *maravedís* a day) could only have made after 30,000 days of work.

MICHEL DE MONTAIGNE

1533–1592

The probing, skeptical essays of Michel Eyquem de Montaigne show a Renaissance mind exploring its own workings. The first writer to ask "Who am I?" and pursue the question with extraordinary honesty and rigor, Montaigne at times appears surprisingly modern in his outlook. He pays unflinching attention to the embarrassing realities of his own body and mind, even as he considers the most abstract questions. His radical break with traditional forms of writing and thinking is particularly striking in that Montaigne was an avid student of the classical even as he also paved the way for the modern form of the essay.

LIFE AND TIMES

Montaigne was born on February 28, 1533, in the castle of Montaigne, to a Catholic father and a Protestant mother of Spanish-Jewish descent. His father, Pierre Eyquem, was for two terms mayor of Bordeaux and had fought in Italy under Francis I. Though no man of learning, Pierre had unconventional ideas of upbringing: Michel was awakened in the morning by the sound of music and was taught Latin as his mother tongue. At six Michel went to the famous Collège de Guienne at Bordeaux; later he studied law; and in 1557 he became a member of the Bordeaux parliament. In 1565 he married Françoise de la Chassaigne, daughter of a man who, as one of Montaigne's colleagues in the Bordeaux parliament, was a member of the new legal nobility.

Perhaps because of disappointed political ambitions, Montaigne retired from politics in 1570 at the age of thirty-eight: he sold his post as magistrate and retreated to his castle of Montaigne, which he had inherited two years earlier. There he devoted himself to meditation and writing. Although Montaigne spent, as he put it, "most of his days, and most hours of the day" in his library on the third floor of a round tower, the demands of his health and France's tumultuous politics often drew him out of retirement. For the sake of his health (he suffered from gallstones), in 1580 he took a journey through Switzerland, Germany, and Italy. While in Italy he received news that he had been appointed mayor of Bordeaux, an office that he held for two terms (1581–85).

His greatest political distractions, however, concerned the Catholic and Protestant factions that violently divided the court and France itself. French politics profoundly influenced the attitudes toward warfare, political resistance, and mercy expressed in Montaigne's *Essays*. When Henry II died in a jousting accident in 1559 and left the fifteen-year-old Francis II to succeed him, the Huguenots (French Reformers in the tradition of John Calvin), recognized the opportunity to influence the weakened royal government. Catherine de Médicis, the queen mother, seized power when Francis II died in 1560 (his successor, Charles IX, was only ten years old). Her policy of limited religious toleration satisfied neither the Catholic nor the Huguenot factions, and from 1562 to 1598 France repeatedly fell into civil war. In the infamous St. Bartholomew's Day Massacre of August 24, 1572, noblemen, municipal authorities, and the Parisian mobs indiscriminately slaughtered the Protestants in Paris.

The slaughter was imitated in other French cities, and the civil wars once again broke out.

Throughout his country's political struggles, Montaigne sympathized with the unfanatical Henry of Navarre, leader of the Protestants, but his attitude was neutral and conservative. He expressed his joy when Henry of Navarre became King Henry IV and turned Catholic to do so: "Paris," Henry memorably observed, "is well worth a Mass." Montaigne, who died on September 13, 1592, did not live to see Henry's triumphal entrance into Paris.

ESSAYS

Montaigne's *Essays*, which began as a collection of interesting quotations, observations, and recordings of remarkable events, slowly developed into its final form of three large books. The essays are at once highly personal and outward looking; they present a curious mind investigating history, the complex and changing sociopolitical world, and the mind's own slightly mysterious workings. To *essay*—from the French *essayer*, meaning to attempt or try out—is Montaigne's characteristic intellectual operation, as he carefully examines his topics from a variety of possible angles. The literary result of that operation is the *essay*, the common noun that, in the wake of Montaigne, describes a short piece of highly personal and exploratory writing.

Though fascinated by the complexities of self-understanding, Montaigne explores far more than his own circumstances or thoughts. "I am a man," he says, quoting the Roman playwright Terence, and "I consider nothing human to be alien to me." As an ethnographer and historian, Montaigne studies geographically and historically distant cultures, insisting that cultural norms are relative and should be free from judgment by sixteenth-century European standards. As a psychologist, he is drawn to the stranger thoughts and experiences of himself and his countrymen. His method is not didactic or moralizing, and his criticism, which he reserves for fellow Europeans, emerges largely through subtle ironies that he leaves readers to detect.

When Montaigne looks inward, he does not aggrandize or justify himself but tries to understand how the mind works. Far from prizing his capacity for reason and judgment, for example, he neutrally observes, "My judgment floats, it wanders." Montaigne is, in fact, disarmingly modest: "Reader, I am myself the subject of my book; it is not reasonable to expect you to waste your leisure on a matter so frivolous and empty." Although massively learned, he emphasizes not what he knows but rather, like his revered model, Plato's Socrates, the ways that knowledge reveals how little he truly knows.

Although he refuses certainty and mocks vanity, Montaigne's stance is skeptical, not cynical. Thus when he "essays" or probes the human capacity to act purposefully and coherently—as he does in "Of the Inconsistency of Our Actions"—he does not aim to prove that action is futile. Instead, he resists granting the mind a coherence it does not possess; to Montaigne, the Stoic ideal of the "constant man," unmoved by emotion or circumstance, is an impoverished version of humankind. Instead, he emphasizes the strangeness and instability of the self: "There is as much difference between us and ourselves as between us and others." This idea became highly influential in Renaissance thinking and shaped such haunting insights as **John Donne**'s observation that "ourselves are what we know not." For Renaissance thinkers who embraced Montaigne's doubt, the difficult philosophical imperative of Socrates, "know thyself," seemed unattainable.

Montaigne charts the elusive "self" through a wide range of anecdotes, both contemporary and classical. A slippery or indefinable historical character intrigues him far more than a monolithic or single-minded one. The legendary warrior Alexander the Great is rendered frighteningly transparent by his obsession with power and conquest: he wants nothing less than to be a god. Emperor Augustus, on the other hand, rewards study precisely because his character has "escaped" the willful reductions of historians bent on "fashioning a consistent and solid fabric" of his character.

Why was Montaigne so unusually able to suspend the self-interest and bias he considered ingrained in human nature in order to analyze himself, and his culture? As his life in politics indicates, the violent instability of French history taught him tolerance, skepticism about human self-interest, and hatred of dogmatic positions: "It demands a great deal of self-love and presumption, to take one's own opinions so seriously as to disrupt the peace in order to establish them, introducing so many inevitable evils, and so terrible a corruption of manners as civil wars and political revolutions with them." His hatred of political radicalism influenced much of what he saw in ancient history and in contemporary accounts of New World discovery and conquest. Alienated from his own political context, Montaigne developed a rich double perspective, both ethnographic (outward-looking and impartial) and self-critical (introspective and moral). As he reflects on the ancient and new worlds, he pays special attention to how human beings respond to adversity, oppression, and physical torture.

In the best known of the selections included here, "Of Cannibals" (which influenced **Shakespeare**'s reflections in *The Tempest* on the ideal commonwealth, colonialism, and the nature of savages), Montaigne compares the behavioral codes of Brazilian cannibals and those of "ourselves" (Europeans) and concludes that "each man calls barbarism whatever is not his own practice." Once he has asserted the relativity of customs, Montaigne is able to praise elements of the savages' culture that he regards as superior to Europe's. He admires the savages' courage, for instance, in which "the honor of valor consists in combating, not in beating." Moreover, he finds in the positive example of the Brazilian cannibals an implicit criticism of violence by Europeans both at home and in the New World.

As an ethnographer, Montaigne is able to grapple with a distinct and alien culture without passing judgment; but when he reflects on France, he becomes a moralist. Central to "Of Cannibals" is the invocation of the Catholics' torture and burning of fellow citizens. Montaigne juxtaposes two kinds of savagery: that which appears foreign (cannibalism) and that which has grown too familiar (religious persecution). His own country's civil strife enables him to transcend smug cultural bias, making him a powerful critic of European culture and allowing him to imagine communities other than his own. Like the world of antiquity, which also riveted his imagination, the idea of America allowed Montaigne to explore alternate worlds for their own sake and for their illumination of his own.

The genre that Montaigne inaugurated quickly made its way into the English tradition, with the *Essays* of Francis Bacon (1597). Yet its larger influence reached much further: with the advent of the Enlightenment and the rise of periodicals, the essay enabled the intellectual exchange of carefully considered, highly personal opinions in the public realm and thus shapes our own thinking and writing to this day.

FROM ESSAYS[1]

To the Reader

This book was written in good faith, reader. It warns you from the outset that in it I have set myself no goal but a domestic and private one. I have had no thought of serving either you or my own glory. My powers are inadequate for such a purpose. I have dedicated it to the private convenience of my relatives and friends, so that when they have lost me (as soon they must), they may recover here some features of my habits and temperament, and by this means keep the knowledge they have had of me more complete and alive.

If I had written to seek the world's favor, I should have bedecked myself better, and should present myself in a studied posture. I want to be seen here in my simple, natural, ordinary fashion, without straining or artifice; for it is myself that I portray. My defects will here be read to the life, and also my natural form, as far as respect for the public has allowed. Had I been placed among those nations which are said to live still in the sweet freedom of nature's first laws, I assure you I should very gladly have portrayed myself here entire and wholly naked.

Thus, reader, I am myself the matter of my book; you would be unreasonable to spend your leisure on so frivolous and vain a subject.

So farewell. Montaigne, this first day of March, fifteen hundred and eighty.

Of the Power of the Imagination

A strong imagination creates the event, say the scholars. I am one of those who are very much influenced by the imagination. Everyone feels its impact, but some are overthrown by it. Its impression on me is piercing. And my art is to escape it, not to resist it. I would live solely in the presence of gay, healthy people. The sight of other people's anguish causes very real anguish to me, and my feelings have often usurped the feelings of others. A continual cougher irritates my lungs and throat. I visit less willingly the sick toward whom duty directs me than those toward whom I am less attentive and concerned. I catch the disease that I study, and lodge it in me. I do not find it strange that imagination brings fevers and death to those who give it a free hand and encourage it.

Simon Thomas was a great doctor in his time. I remember that one day, when he met me at the house of a rich old consumptive with whom he was discussing ways to cure his illness, he told him that one of these would be to give me occasion to enjoy his company; and that by fixing his eyes on the freshness of my face and his thoughts on the blitheness and overflowing vigor of my youth, and filling all his senses with my flourishing condition, he might improve his constitution. But he forgot to say that mine might get worse at the same time.

Gallus Vibius[2] strained his mind so hard to understand the essence and impulses of insanity that he dragged his judgment off its seat and never could

---

1. Translated by Donald Frame.
2. Roman orator. Montaigne illustrates his points with many examples from both antiquity and contemporary Europe: it is less important to know who these historical persons were than to follow Montaigne's presentation of telling moments of their lives.

get it back again; and he could boast of having become mad through wisdom. There are some who through fear anticipate the hand of the executioner. And one man who was being unbound to have his pardon read him dropped stone dead on the scaffold, struck down by his mere imagination. We drip with sweat, we tremble, we turn pale and turn red at the blows of our imagination; reclining in our feather beds we feel our bodies agitated by their impact, sometimes to the point of expiring. And boiling youth, fast asleep, grows so hot in the harness that in dreams it satisfies its amorous desires:

> So that as though it were an actual affair,
> They pour out mighty streams, and stain the clothes they wear.
> LUCRETIUS[3]

And although it is nothing new to see horns grow overnight on someone who did not have them when he went to bed, nevertheless what happened to Cippus,[4] king of Italy, is memorable; having been in the daytime a very excited spectator at a bullfight and having all night in his dreams had horns on his head, he grew actual horns on his forehead by the power of his imagination. Passion gave the son of Croesus the voice that nature had refused him. And Antiochus took fever from the beauty of Stratonice too vividly imprinted in his soul. Pliny says he saw Lucius Cossitius changed from a woman into a man on his wedding day. Pontanus[5] and others report similar metamorphoses as having happened in Italy in these later ages. And through his and his mother's vehement desire,

> Iphis the man fulfilled vows made when he was a girl.
> OVID[6]

Passing through Vitry-le-François, I might have seen a man whom the bishop of Soissons had named Germain at confirmation, but whom all the inhabitants of that place had seen and known as a girl named Marie until the age of twenty-two. He was now heavily bearded, and old, and not married. Straining himself in some way in jumping, he says, his masculine organs came forth; and among the girls there a song is still current by which they warn each other not to take big strides for fear of becoming boys, like Marie Germain. It is not so great a marvel that this sort of accident is frequently met with. For if the imagination has power in such things, it is so continually and vigorously fixed on this subject that in order not to have to relapse so often into the same thought and sharpness of desire, it is better off if once and for all it incorporates this masculine member in girls.

Some attribute to the power of imagination the scars of King Dagobert and of Saint Francis. It is said that thereby bodies are sometimes removed from their places. And Celsus tells of a priest who used to fly with his soul into such ecstasy that his body would remain a long time without breath and without sensation. Saint Augustine[7] names another who whenever he heard lamentable

3. Titus Lucretius Caro (94–55 B.C.E.), Roman poet and Epicurean philosopher: *On the Nature of Things* 4.1035–36.
4. The story of Cippus is told by Pliny (23/24–79 C.E.).
5. Johannes Pontanus (1426–1503), Renaissance scholar and philosopher. Croesus, last

king of Lydia (c. 560–546 B.C.E.). Antiochus 1 (324–261 B.C.E.), who ruled the eastern Seleucid territories from 293/2 B.C.E., took Seleucus's wife, Stratonice.
6. *Metamorphoses* 9.793.
7. Early Christian Church father (354–430 C.E.).

and plaintive cries would suddenly go into a trance and get so carried away that it was no use to shake him and shout at him, to pinch him and burn him, until he had come to; then he would say that he had heard voices, but as if coming from afar, and he would notice his burns and bruises. And that this was no feigned resistance to his senses was shown by the fact that while in this state he had neither pulse nor breath.

It is probable that the principal credit of miracles, visions, enchantments, and such extraordinary occurrences comes from the power of imagination, acting principally upon the minds of the common people, which are softer. Their belief has been so strongly seized that they think they see what they do not see.

I am still of this opinion, that those comical inhibitions by which our society is so fettered that people talk of nothing else are for the most part the effects of apprehension and fear. For I know by experience that one man,[8] whom I can answer for as for myself, on whom there could fall no suspicion whatever of impotence and just as little of being enchanted, having heard a friend of his tell the story of an extraordinary impotence into which he had fallen at the moment when he needed it least, and finding himself in a similar situation, was all at once so struck in his imagination by the horror of this story that he incurred the same fate. And from then on he was subject to relapse, for the ugly memory of his mishap checked him and tyrannized him. He found some remedy for this fancy by another fancy: which was that by admitting this weakness and speaking about it in advance, he relieved the tension of his soul, for when the trouble had been presented as one to be expected, his sense of responsibility diminished and weighed upon him less. When he had a chance of his own choosing, with his mind unembroiled and relaxed and his body in good shape, to have his bodily powers first tested, then seized and taken by surprise, with the other party's full knowledge of his problem, he was completely cured in this respect. A man is never after incapable, unless from genuine impotence, with a woman with whom he has once been capable.

This mishap is to be feared only in enterprises where our soul is immoderately tense with desire and respect, and especially if the opportunity is unexpected and pressing; there is no way of recovering from this trouble. I know one man who found it helpful to bring to it a body that had already begun to be sated elsewhere, so as to lull his frenzied ardor, and who with age finds himself less impotent through being less potent. And I know another who was helped when a friend assured him that he was supplied with a counter-battery of enchantments that were certain to save him. I had better tell how this happened.

A count, a member of a very distinguished family, with whom I was quite intimate, upon getting married to a beautiful lady who had been courted by a man who was present at the wedding feast, had his friends very worried and especially an old lady, a relative of his, who was presiding at the wedding and holding it at her house. She was fearful of these sorceries, and gave me to understand this. I asked her to rely on me. I had by chance in my coffers a certain little flat piece of gold on which were engraved some celestial figures, to protect against sunstroke and take away a headache by placing it precisely on the suture of the skull; and, to keep it there, it was sewed to a ribbon intended to be tied under the chin: a kindred fancy to the one we are speaking of. Jacques

8. Possibly Montaigne himself.

Peletier[9] had given me this singular present. I thought of making some use of it, and said to the count that he might incur the same fate as others, there being men present who would like to bring this about; but that he should boldly go to bed and I would do him a friendly turn and would not, if he needed it, spare a miracle which was in my power, provided that he promised me on his honor to keep it most faithfully secret; he was only to make a given signal to me, when they came to bring him the midnight meal, if things had gone badly with him. He had had his soul and his ears so battered that he did find himself fettered by the trouble of his imagination, and gave me his signal. I told him then that he should get up on the pretext of chasing us out, and playfully take the bathrobe that I had on (we were very close in height) and put it on him until he had carried out my prescription, which was this: when we had left, he should withdraw to pass water, say certain prayers three times and go through certain motions; each of these three times he should tie the ribbon I was putting in his hand around him and very carefully lay the medal that was attached to it on his kidneys, with the figure in such and such a position; this done, having tied this ribbon firmly so that it could neither come untied nor slip from its place, he should return to his business with complete assurance and not forget to spread my robe over his bed so that it should cover them both. These monkey tricks are the main part of the business, our mind being unable to get free of the idea that such strange means must come from some abstruse science. Their inanity gives them weight and reverence. All in all, it is certain that the characters on my medal proved themselves more venereal than solar, more useful for action than for prevention. It was a sudden and curious whim that led me to do such a thing, which was alien to my nature. I am an enemy of subtle and dissimulated acts and hate trickery in myself, not only for sport but also for someone's profit. If the action is not vicious, the road to it is.

Amasis,[1] king of Egypt, married Laodice, a very beautiful Greek girl; and he, who showed himself a gay companion everywhere else, fell short when it came to enjoying her, and threatened to kill her, thinking it was some sort of sorcery. As is usual in matters of fancy, she referred him to religion; and having made his vows and promises to Venus, he found himself divinely restored from the first night after his oblations and sacrifices.

Now women are wrong to greet us with those threatening, quarrelsome, and coy countenances, which put out our fires even as they light them. The daughter-in-law of Pythagoras used to say that the woman who goes to bed with a man should put off her modesty with her skirt and put it on again with her petticoat. The soul of the assailant, when troubled with many various alarms, is easily discouraged; and when imagination has once made a man suffer this shame—and it does so only at the first encounters, inasmuch as these are more boiling and violent, and also because in this first intimacy a man is much more afraid of failing—having begun badly, he gets from this accident a feverishness and vexation which lasts into subsequent occasions.

Married people, whose time is all their own, should neither press their undertaking nor even attempt it if they are not ready; it is better to fail unbecomingly to handsel the nuptial couch,[2] which is full of agitation and feverishness, and

9. Renaissance mathematician (1517–1582).   2. To consummate the marriage on one's
1. Pharaoh c. 569 B.C.E., known for his great   wedding night.
public works and unconventional life.

wait for some other more private and less tense opportunity, than to fall into perpetual misery for having been stunned and made desperate by a first refusal. Before taking possession, the patient should try himself out and offer himself, lightly, by sallies at different times, without priding himself and obstinately insisting on convincing himself definitively. Those who know that their members are naturally obedient, let them take care only to counteract the tricks of their fancies.

People are right to notice the unruly liberty of this member, obtruding so importunately when we have no use for it, and failing so importunately when we have the most use for it, and struggling for mastery so imperiously with our will, refusing with so much pride and obstinacy our solicitations, both mental and manual.

If, however, in the matter of his rebellion being blamed and used as proof to condemn him, he had paid me to plead his cause, I should perhaps place our other members, his fellows, under suspicion of having framed this trumped-up charge out of sheer envy of the importance and pleasure of the use of him, and of having armed everyone against him by a conspiracy, malignantly charging him alone with their common fault. For I ask you to think whether there is a single one of the parts of our body that does not often refuse its function to our will and exercise it against our will. They each have passions of their own which rouse them and put them to sleep without our leave. How many times do the forced movements of our face bear witness to the thoughts that we were holding secret, and betray us to those present. The same cause that animates this member also animates, without our knowledge, the heart, the lungs, and the pulse; the sight of a pleasing object spreading in us imperceptibly the flame of a feverish emotion. Are there only these muscles and these veins that stand up and lie down without the consent, not only of our will, but even of our thoughts? We do not command our hair to stand on end or our skin to shiver with desire or fear. The hand often moves itself to where we do not send it. The tongue is paralyzed, and the voice congealed, at their own time. Even when, having nothing to put in to fry, we should like to forbid it, the appetite for eating and drinking does not fail to stir the parts that are subject to it, no more nor less than that other appetite; and it likewise abandons us inopportunely when it sees fit. The organs that serve to discharge the stomach have their own dilatations and compressions, beyond and against our plans, just like those that are destined to discharge the kidneys. To vindicate the omnipotence of our will, Saint Augustine alleges that he knew a man who commanded his behind to produce as many farts as he wanted, and his commentator Vives[3] goes him one better with another example of his own time, of farts arranged to suit the tone of verses pronounced to their accompaniment; but all this does not really argue any pure obedience in this organ; for is there any that is ordinarily more indiscreet or tumultuous? Besides, I know one so turbulent and unruly, that for forty years it has kept its master farting with a constant and unremitting wind and compulsion, and is thus taking him to his death.

But as for our will, on behalf of whose rights we set forth this complaint, how much more plausibly may we charge it with rebellion and sedition for its disorderliness and disobedience! Does it always will what we would will it to

---

3. Juan Luis Vives (1492–1540), Renaissance philosopher and scholar.

will? Doesn't it often will what we forbid it to will, and that to our evident disadvantage? Is it any more amenable than our other parts to the decisions of our reason?

To conclude, I would say this in defense of the honorable member whom I represent: May it please the court to take into consideration that in this matter, although my client's case is inseparably and indistinguishably linked with that of an accessory, nevertheless he alone has been brought to trial; and that the arguments and charges against him are such as cannot—in view of the status of the parties—be in any manner pertinent or relevant to the aforesaid accessory. Whereby is revealed his accusers' manifest animosity and disrespect for law. However that may be, Nature will meanwhile go her way, protesting that the lawyers and judges quarrel and pass sentence in vain. Indeed, she would have done no more than is right if she had endowed with some particular privilege this member, author of the sole immortal work of mortals. Wherefore to Socrates generation is a divine act; and love, a desire for immortality and itself an immortal daemon.[4]

Perhaps it is by this effect of the imagination that one man here gets rid of the scrofula which his companion carries back to Spain.[5] This effect is the reason why, in such matters, it is customary to demand that the mind be prepared. Why do the doctors work on the credulity of their patient beforehand with so many false promises of a cure, if not so that the effect of the imagination may make up for the imposture of their decoction? They know that one of the masters of the trade left them this in writing, that there have been men for whom the mere sight of medicine did the job.

And this whole caprice[6] has just come to hand apropos of the story that an apothecary, a servant of my late father, used to tell me, a simple man and Swiss, of a nation little addicted to vanity and lying. He had long known a merchant at Toulouse,[7] sickly and subject to the stone, who often needed enemas, and ordered various kinds from his doctors according to the circumstances of his illness. Once they were brought to him, nothing was omitted of the accustomed formalities; often he tested them by hand to make sure they were not too hot. There he was, lying on his stomach, and all the motions were gone through—except that no injection was made. After this ceremony, the apothecary having retired and the patient being accommodated as if he had really taken the enema, he felt the same effect from it as those who do take them. And if the doctor did not find its operation sufficient, he would give him two or three more, of the same sort. My witness swears that when to save the expense (for he paid for them as if he had taken them) this sick man's wife sometimes tried to have just warm water used, the effect revealed the fraud; and having found that kind useless, they were obliged to return to the first method.

A woman, thinking she had swallowed a pin with her bread, was screaming in agony as though she had an unbearable pain in her throat, where she thought she felt it stuck; but because externally there was neither swelling nor alteration, a smart man, judging that it was only a fancy and notion derived

4. Socrates (c. 470–399 B.C.E.) describes love as a *daemon* in Plato's *Symposium*.
5. Scrofula, or king's evil, was supposed to be curable by the touch of the kings of France. In Montaigne's time great numbers of Spaniards

came to France for this purpose [Translator's note].
6. Montaigne's "cure" for his impotent friend.
7. City of southwestern France.

from some bit of bread that had scratched her as it went down, made her vomit, and, on the sly, tossed a crooked pin into what she threw up. The woman, thinking she had thrown it up, felt herself suddenly relieved of her pain. I know that one gentleman, having entertained a goodly company at his house, three or four days later boasted, as a sort of joke (for there was nothing in it), that he had made them eat cat in a pie; at which one lady in the party was so horrified that she fell into a violent stomach disorder and fever, and it was impossible to save her. Even animals are subject like ourselves to the power of imagination. Witness dogs, who let themselves die out of grief for the loss of their masters. We also see them yap and twitch in their dreams, and horses whinny and writhe.

But all this may be attributed to the narrow seam between the soul and body, through which the experience of the one is communicated to the other. Sometimes, however, one's imagination acts not only against one's own body, but against someone else's. And just as a body passes on its sickness to its neighbor, as is seen in the plague, the pox, and soreness of the eyes, which are transmitted from one body to the other—

> By looking at sore eyes, eyes become sore:
> From body into body ills pass o'er
>
> OVID[8]

—likewise the imagination, when vehemently stirred, launches darts that can injure an external object. The ancients maintained that certain women of Scythia,[9] when animated and enraged against anyone, would kill him with their mere glance. Tortoises and ostriches hatch their eggs just by looking at them, a sign that their sight has some ejaculative virtue. And as for sorcerers, they are said to have baleful and harmful eyes:

> some evil eye bewitched my tender lambs.
>
> VIRGIL[1]

To me, magicians are poor authorities. Nevertheless, we know by experience that women transmit marks of their fancies to the bodies of the children they carry in their womb; witness the one who gave birth to the Moor.[2] And there was presented to Charles, king of Bohemia and Emperor, a girl from near Pisa, all hairy and bristly, who her mother said had been thus conceived because of a picture of Saint John the Baptist hanging by her bed.

With animals it is the same: witness Jacob's sheep,[3] and the partridges and hares that the snow turns white in the mountains. Recently at my house a cat was seen watching a bird on a treetop, and, after they had locked gazes for some time, the bird let itself fall as if dead between the cat's paws, either intoxicated by its own imagination or drawn by some attracting power of the

---

8. *The Cure for Love*, lines 615–16.
9. Scythians, the Greek name for Asian tribes who lived in what are now parts of Iran and Turkey, were legendary in the Renaissance for their "barbarity."
1. *Eclogue* 3.103.
2. Saint Jerome tells of a woman who, accused of adultery for giving birth to a black child, was

absolved when Hippocrates explained that she had a picture of a dark man hanging in her room by her bed [translator's note].
3. Genesis 30.37–42. After Laban agreed to give Jacob the striped sheep from his flocks, Jacob bred the sheep in front of rods (the visual stimulation was thought to cause the females to produce striped offspring).

cat. Those who like falconry have heard the story of the falconer who, setting his gaze obstinately upon a kite in the air, wagered that by the sole power of his gaze he would bring it down, and did. At least, so they say—for I refer the stories that I borrow to the conscience of those from whom I take them. The reflections are my own, and depend on the proofs of reason, not of experience; everyone can add his own examples to them; and he who has none, let him not fail to believe that there are plenty, in view of the number and variety of occurrences. If I do not apply them well, let another apply them for me.

So in the study that I am making of our behavior and motives, fabulous testimonies, provided they are possible, serve like true ones. Whether they have happened or no, in Paris or Rome, to John or Peter, they exemplify, at all events, some human potentiality, and thus their telling imparts useful information to me. I see it and profit from it just as well in shadow as in substance. And of the different readings that histories often give, I take for my use the one that is most rare and memorable. There are authors whose end is to tell what has happened. Mine, if I could attain it, would be to talk about what can happen. The schools are justly permitted to suppose similitudes when they have none at hand. I do not do so, however, and in that respect I surpass all historical fidelity, being scrupulous to the point of superstition. In the examples that I bring in here of what I have heard, done, or said, I have forbidden myself to dare to alter even the slightest and most inconsequential circumstances. My conscience does not falsify one iota; my knowledge, I don't know.

In this connection, I sometimes fall to thinking whether it befits a theologian, a philosopher, and such people of exquisite and exact conscience and prudence, to write history. How can they stake their fidelity on the fidelity of an ordinary person? How can they be responsible for the thoughts of persons unknown and give their conjectures as coin of the realm? Of complicated actions that happen in their presence they would refuse to give testimony if placed under oath by a judge; and they know no man so intimately that they would undertake to answer fully for his intentions. I consider it less hazardous to write of things past than present, inasmuch as the writer has only to give an account of a borrowed truth.

Some urge me to write the events of my time, believing that I see them with a view less distorted by passion than another man's, and from closer, because of the access that fortune has given me to the heads of different parties.[4] What they forget is that even for all the glory of Sallust,[5] I would not take the trouble, being a sworn enemy of obligation, assiduity, perseverance; and that there is nothing so contrary to my style as an extended narration. I cut myself off so often for lack of breath; I have neither composition nor development that is worth anything; I am more ignorant than a child of the phrases and terms that serve for the commonest things. And so I have chosen to say what I know how to say, accommodating the matter to my power. If I took a subject that would lead me along, I might not be able to measure up to it; and with my freedom being so very free, I might publish judgments which, even according to my own opinion and to reason, would be illegitimate and punishable. Plutarch[6] might

---

4. A centrist, Montaigne knew leaders of the rivaling factions in France.

5. Roman historian (probably 86–35 B.C.E.).

6. Philosopher and biographer (c. 50–120 C.E.).

well say to us, concerning his accomplishments in this line, that the credit belongs to others if his examples are wholly and everywhere true; but that their being useful to posterity, and presented with a luster which lights our way to virtue, that is his work. There is no danger—as there is in a medicinal drug—in an old story being this way or that.

Of Cannibals

When King Pyrrhus[7] passed over into Italy, after he had reconnoitered the formation of the army that the Romans were sending to meet him, he said: "I do not know what barbarians these are" (for so the Greeks called all foreign nations), "but the formation of this army that I see is not at all barbarous." The Greeks said as much of the army that Flaminius brought into their country, and so did Philip, seeing from a knoll the order and distribution of the Roman camp, in his kingdom, under Publius Sulpicius Galba.[8] Thus we should beware of clinging to vulgar opinions, and judge things by reason's way, not by popular say.

I had with me for a long time a man who had lived for ten or twelve years in that other world which has been discovered in our century, in the place where Villegaignon landed, and which he called Antarctic France.[9] This discovery of a boundless country seems worthy of consideration. I don't know if I can guarantee that some other such discovery will not be made in the future, so many personages greater than ourselves having been mistaken about this one. I am afraid we have eyes bigger than our stomachs, and more curiosity than capacity. We embrace everything, but we clasp only wind.

Plato brings in Solon,[1] telling how he had learned from the priests of the city of Saïs in Egypt that in days of old, before the Flood, there was a great island named Atlantis, right at the mouth of the Strait of Gibraltar, which contained more land than Africa and Asia put together, and that the kings of that country, who not only possessed that island but had stretched out so far on the mainland that they held the breadth of Africa as far as Egypt, and the length of Europe as far as Tuscany, undertook to step over into Asia and subjugate all the nations that border on the Mediterranean, as far as the Black Sea; and for this purpose crossed the Spains, Gaul, Italy, as far as Greece, where the Athenians checked them; but that some time after, both the Athenians and themselves and their island were swallowed up by the Flood.

It is quite likely that that extreme devastation of waters made amazing changes in the habitations of the earth, as people maintain that the sea cut off Sicily from Italy—

> 'Tis said an earthquake once asunder tore
> These lands with dreadful havoc, which before
> Formed but one land, one coast
>
> VIRGIL[2]

7. King of Epirus (in Greece) who fought the Romans in Italy in 280 B.C.E.
8. Both Titus Quinctius Flaminius and Publius Sulpicius Galba were Roman statesmen and generals who fought Philip V of Macedon in the early years of the 2nd century B.C.E.
9. In Brazil. Villegaignon landed there in 1557.
1. In his *Timaeus*.
2. *Aeneid* 3.414–15.

—Cyprus from Syria, the island of Euboea from the mainland of Boeotia; and elsewhere joined lands that were divided, filling the channels between them with sand and mud:

> A sterile marsh, long fit for rowing, now
> Feeds neighbor towns, and feels the heavy plow.
> HORACE[3]

But there is no great likelihood that that island was the new world which we have just discovered; for it almost touched Spain, and it would be an incredible result of a flood to have forced it away as far as it is, more than twelve hundred leagues; besides, the travels of the moderns have already almost revealed that it is not an island, but a mainland connected with the East Indies on one side, and elsewhere with the lands under the two poles; or, if it is separated from them, it is by so narrow a strait and interval that it does not deserve to be called an island on that account.

It seems that there are movements, some natural, others feverish, in these great bodies, just as in our own. When I consider the inroads that my river, the Dordogne, is making in my lifetime into the right bank in its descent, and that in twenty years it has gained so much ground and stolen away the foundations of several buildings, I clearly see that this is an extraordinary disturbance; for if it had always gone at this rate, or was to do so in the future, the face of the world would be turned topsy-turvy. But rivers are subject to changes: now they overflow in one direction, now in another, now they keep to their course. I am not speaking of the sudden inundations whose causes are manifest. In Médoc, along the seashore, my brother, the sieur d'Arsac, can see an estate of his buried under the sands that the sea spews forth; the tops of some buildings are still visible; his farms and domains have changed into very thin pasturage. The inhabitants say that for some time the sea has been pushing toward them so hard that they have lost four leagues of land. These sands are its harbingers; and we see great dunes of moving sand that march half a league ahead of it and keep conquering land.

The other testimony of antiquity with which some would connect this discovery is in Aristotle, at least if that little book *Of Unheard-of Wonders* is by him. He there relates that certain Carthaginians, after setting out upon the Atlantic Ocean from the Strait of Gibraltar and sailing a long time, at last discovered a great fertile island, all clothed in woods and watered by great deep rivers, far remote from any mainland; and that they, and others since, attracted by the goodness and fertility of the soil, went there with their wives and children, and began to settle there. The lords of Carthage, seeing that their country was gradually becoming depopulated, expressly forbade anyone to go there any more, on pain of death, and drove out these new inhabitants, fearing, it is said, that in course of time they might come to multiply so greatly as to supplant their former masters and ruin their state. This story of Aristotle does not fit our new lands any better than the other.

This man I had was a simple, crude fellow—a character fit to bear true witness; for clever people observe more things and more curiously, but they interpret them; and to lend weight and conviction to their interpretation, they

---

3. Horatius Flaccus (65–8 B.C.E.), great poet of Augustan Rome; *Art of Poetry*, lines 65–66.

cannot help altering history a little. They never show you things as they are, but bend and disguise them according to the way they have seen them; and to give credence to their judgment and attract you to it, they are prone to add something to their matter, to stretch it out and amplify it. We need a man either very honest, or so simple that he has not the stuff to build up false inventions and give them plausibility; and wedded to no theory. Such was my man; and besides this, he at various times brought sailors and merchants, whom he had known on that trip, to see me. So I content myself with his information, without inquiring what the cosmographers say about it.

We ought to have topographers who would give us an exact account of the places where they have been. But because they have over us the advantage of having seen Palestine, they want to enjoy the privilege of telling us news about all the rest of the world. I would like everyone to write what he knows, and as much as he knows, not only in this, but in all other subjects; for a man may have some special knowledge and experience of the nature of a river or a fountain, who in other matters knows only what everybody knows. However, to circulate this little scrap of knowledge, he will undertake to write the whole of physics. From this vice spring many great abuses.

Now, to return to my subject, I think there is nothing barbarous and savage in that nation, from what I have been told, except that each man calls barbarism whatever is not his own practice; for indeed it seems we have no other test of truth and reason than the example and pattern of the opinions and customs of the country we live in. *There* is always the perfect religion, the perfect government, the perfect and accomplished manners in all things. Those people are wild, just as we call wild the fruits that Nature has produced by herself and in her normal course; whereas really it is those that we have changed artificially and led astray from the common order, that we should rather call wild. The former retain alive and vigorous their genuine, their most useful and natural, virtues and properties, which we have debased in the latter in adapting them to gratify our corrupted taste. And yet for all that, the savor and delicacy of some uncultivated fruits of those countries is quite as excellent, even to our taste, as that of our own. It is not reasonable that art should win the place of honor over our great and powerful mother Nature. We have so overloaded the beauty and richness of her works by our inventions that we have quite smothered her. Yet wherever her purity shines forth, she wonderfully puts to shame our vain and frivolous attempts:

> Ivy comes readier without our care;
> In lonely caves the arbutus grows more fair;
> No art with artless bird song can compare.
> PROPERTIUS[4]

All our efforts cannot even succeed in reproducing the nest of the tiniest little bird, its contexture, its beauty and convenience; or even the web of the puny spider. All things, says Plato,[5] are produced by nature, by fortune, or by art; the greatest and most beautiful by one or the other of the first two, the least and most imperfect by the last.

---

4. *Elegies* 1.2.10–12.   5. See his *Laws*.

These nations, then, seem to me barbarous in this sense, that they have been fashioned very little by the human mind, and are still very close to their original naturalness. The laws of nature still rule them, very little corrupted by ours; and they are in such a state of purity that I am sometimes vexed that they were unknown earlier, in the days when there were men able to judge them better than we. I am sorry that Lycurgus[6] and Plato did not know of them; for it seems to me that what we actually see in these nations surpasses not only all the pictures in which poets have idealized the golden age and all their inventions in imagining a happy state of man, but also the conceptions and the very desire of philosophy. They could not imagine a naturalness so pure and simple as we see by experience; nor could they believe that our society could be maintained with so little artifice and human solder. This is a nation, I should say to Plato, in which there is no sort of traffic, no knowledge of letters, no science of numbers, no name for a magistrate or for political superiority, no custom of servitude, no riches or poverty, no contracts, no successions, no partitions, no occupations but leisure ones, no care for any but common kinship, no clothes, no agriculture, no metal, no use of wine or wheat.[7] The very words that signify lying, treachery, dissimulation, avarice, envy, belittling, pardon—unheard of. How far from this perfection would he find the republic that he imagined: *Men fresh sprung from the gods* [Seneca].[8]

> These manners nature first ordained.
>
> VIRGIL[9]

For the rest, they live in a country with a very pleasant and temperate climate, so that according to my witnesses it is rare to see a sick man there; and they have assured me that they never saw one palsied, bleary-eyed, toothless, or bent with age. They are settled along the sea and shut in on the land side by great high mountains, with a stretch about a hundred leagues wide in between. They have a great abundance of fish and flesh which bear no resemblance to ours, and they eat them with no other artifice than cooking. The first man who rode a horse there, though he had had dealings with them on several other trips, so horrified them in this posture that they shot him dead with arrows before they could recognize him.

Their buildings are very long, with a capacity of two or three hundred souls; they are covered with the bark of great trees, the strips reaching to the ground at one end and supporting and leaning on one another at the top, in the manner of some of our barns, whose covering hangs down to the ground and acts as a side. They have wood so hard that they cut with it and make of it their swords and grills to cook their food. Their beds are of a cotton weave, hung from the roof like those in our ships, each man having his own; for the wives sleep apart from their husbands.

They get up with the sun, and eat immediately upon rising, to last them through the day; for they take no other meal than that one. Like some other

---

6. The half-legendary Spartan lawgiver (9th century B.C.E.).
7. This passage is always compared with Shakespeare's *The Tempest* 2.1.147 ff.

8. Roman tragedian (c. 4 B.C.E.–65 C.E.), philosopher, and political leader, *Epistles* 90.
9. *Georgics* 2.20.

Eastern peoples, of whom Suidas[1] tells us, who drank apart from meals, they do not drink then; but they drink several times a day, and to capacity. Their drink is made of some root, and is of the color of our claret wines. They drink it only lukewarm. This beverage keeps only two or three days; it has a slightly sharp taste, is not at all heady, is good for the stomach, and has a laxative effect upon those who are not used to it; it is a very pleasant drink for anyone who is accustomed to it. In place of bread they use a certain white substance like preserved coriander. I have tried it; it tastes sweet and a little flat.

The whole day is spent in dancing. The younger men go to hunt animals with bows. Some of the women busy themselves meanwhile with warming their drink, which is their chief duty. Some one of the old men, in the morning before they begin to eat, preaches to the whole barnful in common, walking from one end to the other, and repeating one single sentence several times until he has completed the circuit (for the buildings are fully a hundred paces long). He recommends to them only two things: valor against the enemy and love for their wives. And they never fail to point out this obligation, as their refrain, that it is their wives who keep their drink warm and seasoned.

There may be seen in several places, including my own house, specimens of their beds, of their ropes, of their wooden swords and the bracelets with which they cover their wrists in combats, and of the big canes, open at one end, by whose sound they keep time in their dances. They are close shaven all over, and shave themselves much more cleanly than we, with nothing but a wooden or stone razor. They believe that souls are immortal, and that those who have deserved well of the gods are lodged in that part of heaven where the sun rises, and the damned in the west.

They have some sort of priests and prophets, but they rarely appear before the people, having their home in the mountains. On their arrival there is a great feast and solemn assembly of several villages—each barn, as I have described it, makes up a village, and they are about one French league[2] from each other. The prophet speaks to them in public, exhorting them to virtue and their duty; but their whole ethical science contains only these two articles: resoluteness in war and affection for their wives. He prophesies to them things to come and the results they are to expect from their undertakings, and urges them to war or holds them back from it; but this is on the condition that when he fails to prophesy correctly, and if things turn out otherwise than he has predicted, he is cut into a thousand pieces if they catch him, and condemned as a false prophet. For this reason, the prophet who has once been mistaken is never seen again.

Divination is a gift of God; that is why its abuse should be punished as imposture. Among the Scythians, when the soothsayers failed to hit the mark, they were laid, chained hand and foot, on carts full of heather and drawn by oxen, on which they were burned. Those who handle matters subject to the control of human capacity are excusable if they do the best they can. But these others who come and trick us with assurances of an extraordinary faculty that is beyond our ken, should they not be punished for not making good their promise, and for the temerity of their imposture?

1. A Byzantine lexicographer.   2. About 2.49 miles.

They have their wars with the nations beyond the mountains, further inland, to which they go quite naked, with no other arms than bows or wooden swords ending in a sharp point, in the manner of the tongues of our boar spears. It is astonishing what firmness they show in their combats, which never end but in slaughter and bloodshed; for as to routs and terror, they know nothing of either.

Each man brings back his trophy the head of the enemy he has killed, and sets it up at the entrance to his dwelling. After they have treated their prisoners well for a long time with all the hospitality they can think of, each man who has a prisoner calls a great assembly of his acquaintances. He ties a rope to one of the prisoner's arms, by the end of which he holds him, a few steps away, for fear of being hurt, and gives his dearest friend the other arm to hold in the same way; and these two, in the presence of the whole assembly, kill him with their swords. This done, they roast him and eat him in common and send some pieces to their absent friends. This is not, as people think, for nourishment, as of old the Scythians used to do; it is to betoken an extreme revenge. And the proof of this came when they saw the Portuguese, who had joined forces with their adversaries, inflict a different kind of death on them when they took them prisoner, which was to bury them up to the waist, shoot the rest of their body full of arrows, and afterward hang them. They thought that these people from the other world, being men who had sown the knowledge of many vices among their neighbors and were much greater masters than themselves in every sort of wickedness, did not adopt this sort of vengeance without some reason, and that it must be more painful than their own; so they began to give up their old method and to follow this one.

I am not sorry that we notice the barbarous horror of such acts, but I am heartily sorry that, judging their faults rightly, we should be so blind to our own. I think there is more barbarity in eating a man alive than in eating him dead; and in tearing by tortures and the rack a body still full of feeling, in roasting a man bit by bit, in having him bitten and mangled by dogs and swine (as we have not only read but seen within fresh memory, not among ancient enemies, but among neighbors and fellow citizens, and what is worse, on the pretext of piety and religion),[3] than in roasting and eating him after he is dead.

Indeed, Chrysippus and Zeno, heads of the Stoic sect, thought there was nothing wrong in using our carcasses for any purpose in case of need, and getting nourishment from them; just as our ancestors,[4] when besieged by Caesar in the city of Alesia, resolved to relieve their famine by eating old men, women, and other people useless for fighting.

> The Gascons once, 'tis said, their life renewed
> By eating of such food.
>
> JUVENAL[5]

And physicians do not fear to use human flesh in all sorts of ways for our health, applying it either inwardly or outwardly. But there never was any opinion so

---

3. The allusion is to the spectacles of religious warfare that Montaigne himself had witnessed in his time and country.
4. The Gauls.

5. Decimus Junius Juvenal (fl. early 2nd century C.E.), last great Roman satirist; *Satires* 15.93–94.

disordered as to excuse treachery, disloyalty, tyranny, and cruelty, which are our ordinary vices.

So we may well call these people barbarians, in respect to the rules of reason, but not in respect to ourselves, who surpass them in every kind of barbarity.

Their warfare is wholly noble and generous, and as excusable and beautiful as this human disease can be; its only basis among them is their rivalry in valor. They are not fighting for the conquest of new lands, for they still enjoy that natural abundance that provides them without toil and trouble with all necessary things in such profusion that they have no wish to enlarge their boundaries. They are still in that happy state of desiring only as much as their natural needs demand; anything beyond that is superfluous to them.

They generally call those of the same age, brothers; those who are younger, children; and the old men are fathers to all the others. These leave to their heirs in common the full possession of their property, without division or any other title at all than just the one that Nature gives to her creatures in bringing them into the world.

If their neighbors cross the mountains to attack them and win a victory, the gain of the victor is glory, and the advantage of having proved the master in valor and virtue; for apart from this they have no use for the goods of the vanquished, and they return to their own country, where they lack neither anything necessary nor that great thing, the knowledge of how to enjoy their condition happily and be content with it. These men of ours do the same in their turn. They demand of their prisoners no other ransom than that they confess and acknowledge their defeat. But there is not one in a whole century who does not choose to die rather than to relax a single bit, by word or look, from the grandeur of an invincible courage; not one who would not rather be killed and eaten than so much as ask not to be. They treat them very freely, so that life may be all the dearer to them, and usually entertain them with threats of their coming death, of the torments they will have to suffer, the preparations that are being made for the purpose, the cutting up of their limbs, and the feast that will be made at their expense. All this is done for the sole purpose of extorting from their lips some weak or base word, or making them want to flee, so as to gain the advantage of having terrified them and broken down their firmness. For indeed, if you take it the right way, it is in this point alone that true victory lies:

> It is no victory
> Unless the vanquished foe admits your mastery.
> CLAUDIAN[6]

The Hungarians, very bellicose fighters, did not in olden times pursue their advantage beyond putting the enemy at their mercy. For having wrung a confession from him to this effect, they let him go unharmed and unransomed, except, at most, for exacting his promise never again to take up arms against them.

We win enough advantages over our enemies that are borrowed advantages, not really our own. It is the quality of a porter, not of valor, to have sturdier arms and legs; agility is a dead and corporeal quality; it is a stroke of luck to

---

6. *Of the Sixth Consulate of Honorius*, lines 248–49.

make our enemy stumble, or dazzle his eyes by the sunlight; it is a trick of art and technique, which may be found in a worthless coward, to be an able fencer. The worth and value of a man is in his heart and his will; there lies his real honor. Valor is the strength, not of legs and arms, but of heart and soul; it consists not in the worth of our horse or our weapons, but in our own. He who falls obstinate in his courage, *if he has fallen, he fights on his knees* [Seneca].[7] He who relaxes none of his assurance, no matter how great the danger of imminent death; who, giving up his soul, still looks firmly and scornfully at his enemy—he is beaten not by us, but by fortune; he is killed, not conquered.

The most valiant are sometimes the most unfortunate. Thus there are triumphant defeats that rival victories. Nor did those four sister victories, the fairest that the sun ever set eyes on—Salamis, Plataea, Mycale, and Sicily[8]—ever dare match all their combined glory against the glory of the annihilation of King Leonidas and his men at the pass of Thermopylae.[9]

Who ever hastened with more glorious and ambitious desire to win a battle than Captain Ischolas to lose one? Who ever secured his safety more ingeniously and painstakingly than he did his destruction? He was charged to defend a certain pass in the Peloponnesus against the Arcadians. Finding himself wholly incapable of doing this, in view of the nature of the place and the inequality of the forces, he made up his mind that all who confronted the enemy would necessarily have to remain on the field. On the other hand, deeming it unworthy both of his own virtue and magnanimity and of the Lacedaemonian name to fail in his charge, he took a middle course between these two extremes, in this way. The youngest and fittest of his band he preserved for the defense and service of their country, and sent them home; and with those whose loss was less important, he determined to hold this pass, and by their death to make the enemy buy their entry as dearly as he could. And so it turned out. For he was presently surrounded on all sides by the Arcadians, and after slaughtering a large number of them, he and his men were all put to the sword. Is there a trophy dedicated to victors that would not be more due to these vanquished? The role of true victory is in fighting, not in coming off safely; and the honor of valor consists in combating, not in beating.

To return to our story. These prisoners are so far from giving in, in spite of all that is done to them, that on the contrary, during the two or three months that they are kept, they wear a gay expression; they urge their captors to hurry and put them to the test; they defy them, insult them, reproach them with their cowardice and the number of battles they have lost to the prisoners' own people.

I have a song composed by a prisoner which contains this challenge, that they should all come boldly and gather to dine off him, for they will be eating at the same time their own fathers and grandfathers, who have served to feed and nourish his body. "These muscles," he says, "this flesh and these veins are your own, poor fools that you are. You do not recognize that the substance of your ancestors' limbs is still contained in them. Savor them well; you will find in them the taste of your own flesh." An idea that certainly does not smack of

7. *Of Providence* 2.
8. References to the famous Greek victories against the Persians and (at Himera, Sicily) against the Carthaginians in or about 480 B.C.E.

9. The Spartan king Leonidas's defense here also took place in 480 B.C.E., during the war against the Persians.

barbarity. Those that paint these people dying, and who show the execution, portray the prisoner spitting in the face of his slayers and scowling at them. Indeed, to the last gasp they never stop braving and defying their enemies by word and look. Truly here are real savages by our standards; for either they must be thoroughly so, or we must be; there is an amazing distance between their character and ours.

The men there have several wives, and the higher their reputation for valor the more wives they have. It is a remarkably beautiful thing about their marriages that the same jealousy our wives have to keep us from the affection and kindness of other women, theirs have to win this for them. Being more concerned for their husbands' honor than for anything else, they strive and scheme to have as many companions as they can, since that is a sign of their husbands' valor.

Our wives will cry "Miracle!" but it is no miracle. It is a properly matrimonial virtue, but one of the highest order. In the Bible, Leah, Rachel, Sarah, and Jacob's wives gave their beautiful handmaids to their husbands; and Livia seconded the appetites of Augustus to her own disadvantage; and Stratonice, the wife of King Deiotarus,[1] not only lent her husband for his use a very beautiful young chambermaid in her service, but carefully brought up her children, and backed them up to succeed to their father's estates.

And lest it be thought that all this is done through a simple and servile bondage to usage and through the pressure of the authority of their ancient customs, without reasoning or judgment, and because their minds are so stupid that they cannot take any other course, I must cite some examples of their capacity. Besides the warlike song I have just quoted, I have another, a love song, which begins in this vein: "Adder, stay; stay, adder, that from the pattern of your coloring my sister may draw the fashion and the workmanship of a rich girdle that I may give to my love; so may your beauty and your pattern be forever preferred to all other serpents." This first couplet is the refrain of the song. Now I am familiar enough with poetry to be a judge of this: not only is there nothing barbarous in this fancy, but it is altogether Anacreontic.[2] Their language, moreover, is a soft language, with an agreeable sound, somewhat like Greek in its endings.

Three of these men, ignorant of the price they will pay some day, in loss of repose and happiness, for gaining knowledge of the corruptions of this side of the ocean; ignorant also of the fact that of this intercourse will come their ruin (which I suppose is already well advanced: poor wretches, to let themselves be tricked by the desire for new things, and to have left the serenity of their own sky to come and see ours!)—three of these men were at Rouen, at the time the late King Charles IX was there. The king talked to them for a long time; they were shown our ways, our splendor, the aspect of a fine city. After that, someone asked their opinion, and wanted to know what they had found most amazing. They mentioned three things, of which I have forgotten the third, and I am very sorry for it; but I still remember two of them. They said that in the first place they thought it very strange that so many grown men, bearded, strong, and armed, who were around the king (it is likely that they were talking about the Swiss of his guard) should submit to obey a child, and that one of them was

1. Tetrarch of Galatia, in Asia Minor.
2. Worthy of Anacreon (572?–488? B.C.E.), major Greek writer of amatory lyrics.

not chosen to command instead. Second (they have a way in their language of speaking of men as halves of one another), they had noticed that there were among us men full and gorged with all sorts of good things, and that their other halves were beggars at their doors, emaciated with hunger and poverty; and they thought it strange that these needy halves could endure such an injustice, and did not take the others by the throat, or set fire to their houses.

I had a very long talk with one of them; but I had an interpreter who followed my meaning so badly, and who was so hindered by his stupidity in taking in my ideas, that I could get hardly any satisfaction from the man. When I asked him what profit he gained from his superior position among his people (for he was a captain, and our sailors called him king), he told me that it was to march foremost in war. How many men followed him? He pointed to a piece of ground, to signify as many as such a space could hold; it might have been four or five thousand men. Did all this authority expire with the war? He said that this much remained, that when he visited the villages dependent on him, they made paths for him through the underbrush by which he might pass quite comfortably.

All this is not too bad—but what's the use? They don't wear breeches.

Of the Inconsistency of Our Actions

Those who make a practice of comparing human actions are never so perplexed as when they try to see them as a whole and in the same light; for they commonly contradict each other so strangely that it seems impossible that they have come from the same shop. One moment young Marius is a son of Mars, another moment a son of Venus.[3] Pope Boniface VIII, they say, entered office like a fox, behaved in it like a lion, and died like a dog. And who would believe that it was Nero, that living image of cruelty, who said, when they brought him in customary fashion the sentence of a condemned criminal to sign: "Would to God I had never learned to write!" So much his heart was wrung at condemning a man to death!

Everything is so full of such examples—each man, in fact, can supply himself with so many—that I find it strange to see intelligent men sometimes going to great pains to match these pieces; seeing that irresolution seems to me the most common and apparent defect of our nature, as witness that famous line of Publilius, the farce writer:

> Bad is the plan that never can be changed.
> PUBLILIUS SYRUS[4]

There is some justification for basing a judgment of a man on the most ordinary acts of his life; but in view of the natural instability of our conduct and

---

3. Goddess of love. "Marius": the nephew of the older and better-known Marius. Montaigne's source is Plutarch's *Life of Marius*.

"Mars": the god of war.
4. *Apothegms* (*Sententiae*), line 362.

opinions, it has often seemed to me that even good authors are wrong to insist on fashioning a consistent and solid fabric out of us. They choose one general characteristic, and go and arrange and interpret all a man's actions to fit their picture; and if they cannot twist them enough, they go and set them down to dissimulation. Augustus has escaped them; for there is in this man throughout the course of his life such an obvious, abrupt, and continual variety of actions that even the boldest judges have had to let him go, intact and unsolved. Nothing is harder for me than to believe in men's consistency, nothing easier than to believe in their inconsistency. He who would judge them in detail and distinctly, bit by bit, would more often hit upon the truth.

In all antiquity it is hard to pick out a dozen men who set their lives to a certain and constant course, which is the principal goal of wisdom. For, to comprise all wisdom in a word, says an ancient [Seneca], and to embrace all the rules of our life in one, it is "always to will the same things, and always to oppose the same things."[5] I would not deign, he says, to add "provided the will is just"; for if it is not just, it cannot always be whole.

In truth, I once learned that vice is only unruliness and lack of moderation, and that consequently consistency cannot be attributed to it. It is a maxim of Demosthenes, they say, that the beginning of all virtue is consultation and deliberation; and the end and perfection, consistency. If it were by reasoning that we settled on a particular course of action, we would choose the fairest course—but no one has thought of that:

> He spurns the thing he sought, and seeks anew
> What he just spurned; he seethes, his life's askew.
> HORACE[6]

Our ordinary practice is to follow the inclinations of our appetite, to the left, to the right, uphill and down, as the wind of circumstance carries us. We think of what we want only at the moment we want it, and we change like that animal which takes the color of the place you set it on. What we have just now planned, we presently change, and presently again we retrace our steps: nothing but oscillation and inconsistency:

> Like puppets we are moved by outside strings.
> HORACE[7]

We do not go; we are carried away, like floating objects, now gently, now violently, according as the water is angry or calm:

> Do we not see all humans unaware
> Of what they want, and always searching everywhere,
> And changing place, as if to drop the load they bear?
> LUCRETIUS[8]

---

5. *Epistles* 20.
6. *Epistles* 1.1.98–99.
7. *Satires* 2.7.82.
8. *On the Nature of Things* 3.1057–59.

Every day a new fancy, and our humors shift with the shifts in the weather:

> Such are the minds of men, as is the fertile light
> That Father Jove himself sends down to make earth bright.
>   HOMER[9]

We float between different states of mind; we wish nothing freely, nothing absolutely, nothing constantly. If any man could prescribe and establish definite laws and a definite organization in his head, we should see shining throughout his life an evenness of habits, an order, and an infallible relation between his principles and his practice.

Empedocles noticed this inconsistency in the Agrigentines, that they abandoned themselves to pleasures as if they were to die on the morrow, and built as if they were never to die.[1]

This man would be easy to understand, as is shown by the example of the younger Cato:[2] he who has touched one chord of him has touched all; he is a harmony of perfectly concordant sounds, which cannot conflict. With us, it is the opposite: for so many actions, we need so many individual judgments. The surest thing, in my opinion, would be to trace our actions to the neighboring circumstances, without getting into any further research and without drawing from them any other conclusions.

During the disorders of our poor country,[3] I was told that a girl, living near where I then was, had thrown herself out of a high window to avoid the violence of a knavish soldier quartered in her house. Not killed by the fall, she reasserted her purpose by trying to cut her throat with a knife. From this she was prevented, but only after wounding herself gravely. She herself confessed that the soldier had as yet pressed her only with requests, solicitations, and gifts; but she had been afraid, she said, that he would finally resort to force. And all this with such words, such expressions, not to mention the blood that testified to her virtue, as would have become another Lucrece.[4] Now, I learned that as a matter of fact, both before and since, she was a wench not so hard to come to terms with. As the story[5] says: Handsome and gentlemanly as you may be, when you have had no luck, do not promptly conclude that your mistress is inviolably chaste; for all you know, the mule driver may get his will with her.

Antigonus,[6] having taken a liking to one of his soldiers for his virtue and valor, ordered his physicians to treat the man for a persistent internal malady that had long tormented him. After his cure, his master noticed that he was going about his business much less warmly, and asked him what had changed him so and made him such a coward. "You yourself, Sire," he answered, "by delivering me from the ills that made my life indifferent to me." A soldier of Lucullus[7] who had been robbed of everything by the enemy made a bold attack on them to get revenge. When he had retrieved his loss, Lucullus, having

---

9. *Odyssey* 18.135–36, 152–53 in the Fitzgerald translation.
1. From Diogenes Laertius's life of the Greek philosopher Empedocles (5th century).
2. Cato Uticensis (1st century B.C.E.), a philosopher. He is traditionally considered the epitome of moral and intellectual integrity.

3. See p. 334, n. 3.
4. The legendary virtuous Roman who stabbed herself after being raped by King Tarquinius Superbus's son.
5. A common folktale.
6. Macedonian king (382–301 B.C.E.).
7. Roman general (1st century B.C.E.).

formed a good opinion of him, urged him to some dangerous exploit with all the fine expostulations he could think of,

> With words that might have stirred a coward's heart.
> HORACE[8]

"Urge some poor soldier who has been robbed to do it," he replied;

> Though but a rustic lout,
> "That man will go who's lost his money," he called out;
> HORACE[9]

and resolutely refused to go.

We read that Sultan Mohammed outrageously berated Hassan, leader of his Janissaries, because he saw his troops giving way to the Hungarians and Hassan himself behaving like a coward in the fight. Hassan's only reply was to go and hurl himself furiously—alone, just as he was, arms in hand—into the first body of enemies that he met, by whom he was promptly swallowed up; this was perhaps not so much self-justification as a change of mood, nor so much his natural valor as fresh spite.

That man whom you saw so adventurous yesterday, do not think it strange to find him just as cowardly today: either anger, or necessity, or company, or wine, or the sound of a trumpet, had put his heart in his belly. His was a courage formed not by reason, but by one of these circumstances; it is no wonder if he has now been made different by other, contrary circumstances.

These supple variations and contradictions that are seen in us have made some imagine that we have two souls, and others that two powers accompany us and drive us, each in its own way, one toward good, the other toward evil; for such sudden diversity cannot well be reconciled with a simple subject.

Not only does the wind of accident move me at will, but, besides, I am moved and disturbed as a result merely of my own unstable posture; and anyone who observes carefully can hardly find himself twice in the same state. I give my soul now one face, now another, according to which direction I turn it. If I speak of myself in different ways, that is because I look at myself in different ways. All contradictions may be found in me by some twist and in some fashion. Bashful, insolent; chaste, lascivious; talkative, taciturn; tough, delicate; clever, stupid; surly, affable; lying, truthful; learned, ignorant; liberal, miserly, and prodigal: all this I see in myself to some extent according to how I turn; and whoever studies himself really attentively finds in himself, yes, even in his judgment, this gyration and discord. I have nothing to say about myself absolutely, simply, and solidly, without confusion and without mixture, or in one word. *Distinguo*[1] is the most universal member of my logic.

Although I am always minded to say good of what is good, and inclined to interpret favorably anything that can be so interpreted, still it is true that the strangeness of our condition makes it happen that we are often driven to do good by vice itself—were it not that doing good is judged by intention alone.

---

8. *Epistles* 2.2.36.
9. *Epistles* 2.2.39–40.

1. I distinguish (Latin)—that is, I separate into its components.

Therefore one courageous deed must not be taken to prove a man valiant; a man who was really valiant would be so always and on all occasions. If valor were a habit of virtue, and not a sally, it would make a man equally resolute in any contingency, the same alone as in company, the same in single combat as in battle; for, whatever they say, there is not one valor for the pavement and another for the camp. As bravely would he bear an illness in his bed as a wound in camp, and he would fear death no more in his home than in an assault. We would not see the same man charging into the breach with brave assurance, and later tormenting himself, like a woman, over the loss of a lawsuit or a son. When, though a coward against infamy, he is firm against poverty; when, though weak against the surgeons' knives, he is steadfast against the enemy's swords, the action is praiseworthy, not the man.

Many Greeks, says Cicero, cannot look at the enemy, and are brave in sickness; the Cimbrians and Celtiberians, just the opposite; *for nothing can be uniform that does not spring from a firm principle* [Cicero].[2]

There is no more extreme valor of its kind than Alexander's; but it is only of one kind, and not complete and universal enough. Incomparable though it is, it still has its blemishes; which is why we see him worry so frantically when he conceives the slightest suspicion that his men are plotting against his life, and why he behaves in such matters with such violent and indiscriminate injustice and with a fear that subverts his natural reason. Also superstition, with which he was so strongly tainted, bears some stamp of pusillanimity. And the excessiveness of the penance he did for the murder of Clytus[3] is also evidence of the unevenness of his temper.

Our actions are nothing but a patchwork—*they despise pleasure, but are too cowardly in pain; they are indifferent to glory, but infamy breaks their spirit* [Cicero][4]—and we want to gain honor under false colors. Virtue will not be followed except for her own sake; and if we sometimes borrow her mask for some other purpose, she promptly snatches it from our face. It is a strong and vivid dye, once the soul is steeped in it, and will not go without taking the fabric with it. That is why, to judge a man, we must follow his traces long and carefully. If he does not maintain consistency for its own sake, *with a way of life that has been well considered and preconcerted* [Cicero];[5] if changing circumstances makes him change his pace (I mean his path, for his pace may be hastened or slowed), let him go: that man goes before the wind, as the motto of our Talbot[6] says.

It is no wonder, says an ancient [Seneca], that chance has so much power over us, since we live by chance.[7] A man who has not directed his life as a whole toward a definite goal cannot possibly set his particular actions in order. A man who does not have a picture of the whole in his head cannot possibly arrange the pieces. What good does it do a man to lay in a supply of paints if he does not know what he is to paint? No one makes a definite plan of his life; we think about it only piecemeal. The archer must first know what he is aiming at,

2. Marcus Tullius Cicero (106–43 B.C.E.), Roman orator; *Tusculan Disputations* 2.27.
3. A commander in Alexander's army who was killed by him during an argument, an act Alexander immediately and bitterly regretted, as related by Plutarch in his *Life of Alexander*,

chaps. 50–52.
4. *On Duties (De officiis)* 1.21.
5. *Paradoxes* 5.
6. An English captain who fought in France and died there in 1453.
7. *Epistles* 71.

and then set his hand, his bow, his string, his arrow, and his movements for that goal. Our plans go astray because they have no direction and no aim. No wind works for the man who has no port of destination.

I do not agree with the judgment given in favor of Sophocles, on the strength of seeing one of his tragedies, that it proved him competent to manage his domestic affairs, against the accusation of his son. Nor do I think that the conjecture of the Parians sent to reform the Milesians was sufficient ground for the conclusion they drew. Visiting the island, they noticed the best-cultivated lands and the best-run country houses, and noted down the names of their owners. Then they assembled the citizens in the town and appointed these owners the new governors and magistrates, judging that they, who were careful of their private affairs, would be careful of those of the public.

We are all patchwork, and so shapeless and diverse in composition that each bit, each moment, plays its own game. And there is as much difference between us and ourselves as between us and others. *Consider it a great thing to play the part of one single man* [Seneca].[8] Ambition can teach men valor, and temperance, and liberality, and even justice. Greed can implant in the heart of a shop apprentice, brought up in obscurity and idleness, the confidence to cast himself far from hearth and home, in a frail boat at the mercy of the waves and angry Neptune; it also teaches discretion and wisdom. Venus herself supplies resolution and boldness to boys still subject to discipline and the rod, and arms the tender hearts of virgins who are still in their mothers' laps:

> Furtively passing sleeping guards, with Love as guide,
> Alone by night the girl comes to the young man's side.
> TIBULLUS[9]

In view of this, a sound intellect will refuse to judge men simply by their outward actions; we must probe the inside and discover what springs set men in motion. But since this is an arduous and hazardous undertaking, I wish fewer people would meddle with it.

Of Coaches

It is very easy to demonstrate that great authors, when they write about causes, adduce not only those they think are true but also those they do not believe in, provided they have some originality and beauty. They speak truly and usefully enough if they speak ingeniously. We cannot make sure of the master cause; we pile up several of them, to see if by chance it will be found among them.

> For one cause will not do;
> We must state many, one of which is true.
> LUCRETIUS[1]

8. *Epistles* 120.
9. *Elegies* 2.1.75–76.

1. *On the Nature of Things* 6.704–705.

Do you ask me whence comes this custom of blessing those who sneeze? We produce three sorts of wind. That which issues from below is too foul; that which issues from the mouth carries some reproach of gluttony; the third is sneezing. And because it comes from the head and is blameless, we give it this civil reception. Do not laugh at this piece of subtlety; it is, they say, from Aristotle.

It seems to me I have read in Plutarch (who, of all the authors I know, is the one who best combined art with nature and judgment with knowledge) that he gives the reason for the heaving of the stomach that afflicts those who travel by sea, as fear, having found some reason by which he proves that fear can produce such an effect. I, who am very subject to seasickness, know very well that this cause does not affect me, and I know it, not by reasoning, but by necessary experience. Not to mention what I have been told, that the same thing often happens to animals, and especially to pigs, without any apprehension of danger; and what an acquaintance of mine has told me about himself, that though he was very subject to it, the desire to vomit had left him two or three times when he found himself oppressed with fright in a big storm. And hear this ancient: *I was too sick to think about the danger* [Seneca].[2] I was never afraid on the water, nor indeed anywhere else (and I have often enough had just occasions, if death is one), at least not to the point of being confused or bewildered.

Fear sometimes arises from want of judgment as well as from want of courage. All the dangers I have seen, I have seen with open eyes, with my sight free, sound, and entire; besides, it takes courage to be afraid. It once served me in good stead, compared with others, so to conduct my flight and keep it orderly, that it was carried out, if not without fear, at all events without terror and without dismay; it was excited, but not dazed or distracted.

Great souls go much further yet and offer us examples of flights not merely composed and healthy, but proud. Let us tell of the one that Alcibiades reports of Socrates, his comrade in arms:[3] "I found him," he says, "after the rout of our army, him and Laches, among the last of the fugitives; and I observed him at my leisure and in safety, for I was on a good horse and he on foot, and we had fought that way. I noticed first how much presence of mind and resolution he showed compared with Laches; and then the boldness of his walk, no different from his ordinary one, his firm and steady gaze, considering and judging what was going on around him, looking now at one side, now the other, friends and enemies, in a way that encouraged the former and signified to the latter that he was a man to sell his blood and his life very dear to anyone who should try to take them away. And thus they made their escape; for people are not inclined to attack such men; they run after the frightened ones." That is the testimony of that great captain, which teaches us what we experience every day, that there is nothing that throws us so much into dangers as an unthinking eagerness to get clear of them. *Where there is less fear, there is generally less danger* [Livy].[4]

Our common people are wrong to say that such-and-such a man fears death, when they mean to say that he thinks about it and foresees it. Foresight is equally suitable in whatever concerns us, whether for good or ill. To consider and judge the danger is in a way the opposite of being stunned by it.

2. *Moral Epistles* 53.3.
3. Plato, *Symposium*.
4. Titus Livius (59 B.C.E.–17 C.E. or 64

B.C.E.–12 C.E.), Roman historian; *On the Founding of Rome* 22.5.

I do not feel myself strong enough to sustain the impact and impetuosity of this passion of fear, or of any other vehement passion. If I were once conquered and thrown by it, I would never get up again quite intact. If anything made my soul lose its footing, it would never set it back upright in its place; it probes and searches itself too keenly and deeply, and therefore would never let the wound that had pierced it close up and heal. It has been well for me that no illness has yet laid it low. Each attack made on me I meet and fight off in my full armor; thus the first one that swept me off my feet would leave me without resources. I have no secondary defense: no matter where the torrent should break my dike, I would be helpless and be drowned for good.

Epicurus[5] says that the wise man can never pass into a contrary state. I have an opinion about the converse of this saying: that anyone who has once been very foolish will never at any other time be very wise.

God tempers the cold according to the cloak, and gives me passions according to my means of withstanding them. Nature, having uncovered me on one side, has covered me up on the other; having disarmed me of strength, she has armed me with insensibility and a controlled, or dull, apprehensiveness.

Now I cannot long endure (and I could endure them less easily in my youth) either coach, or litter, or boat; and I hate any other transportation than horseback, both in town and in the country. But I can endure a litter less than a coach, and for the same reason I can more easily bear a rough tossing on the water, whereby fear is produced, than the movement felt in calm weather. By that slight jolt given by the oars, stealing the vessel from under us, I somehow feel my head and stomach troubled, as I cannot bear a shaky seat under me. When the sail or the current carries us along evenly or when we are towed, this uniform movement does not bother me at all. It is an interrupted motion that annoys me, and most of all when it is languid. I cannot otherwise describe its nature. The doctors have ordered me to bind and swathe my abdomen with a towel to remedy this trouble; which I have not tried, being accustomed to wrestle with the weaknesses that are in me and overcome them by myself.

If my memory were sufficiently stored with them, I should not begrudge my time to tell here the infinite variety of examples that histories offer us of the use of coaches in the service of war, varying according to the nations and according to the age; of great effect, it seems to me, and very necessary, so that it is a wonder that we have lost all knowledge of them. I will say only this, that quite recently, in our fathers' time, the Hungarians put coaches very usefully to work against the Turks, there being in each one a targeteer and a musketeer and a number of harquebuses lined up, loaded and ready, the whole thing covered with a wall of shields, like a galiot. They formed their battlefront of three thousand such coaches, and after the cannon had played, had them advance and made the enemy swallow this salvo before tasting the rest; which was no slight advantage. Or they launched them into the enemy squadrons to break them and open them up; not to mention the advantage they could derive from them by flanking enemy troops on their march through open country where they were vulnerable, or by covering a camp in haste and fortifying it.

In my time a gentleman on one of our frontiers, who was unwieldy of person and found no horse capable of bearing his weight, having a feud on his hands,

5. Greek moral and natural philosopher (341–270 B.C.E.)

went about the country in a coach of this very description, and made out very well. But let us leave these war coaches. The kings of our first dynasty went about the country in a chariot drawn by four oxen.

Mark Antony[6] was the first who had himself drawn in Rome—and a minstrel girl beside him—by lions harnessed to a chariot. Heliogabalus did as much later, calling himself Cybele, the mother of the gods; and also by tigers, imitating the god Bacchus; he also sometimes harnessed two stags to his coach, and another time four dogs, and yet again four naked wenches, having himself, stark naked too, drawn by them in pomp. The Emperor Firmus had his chariot drawn by ostriches of marvelous size, so that it seemed rather to fly than to roll.

The strangeness of these inventions puts into my head this other notion: that it is a sort of pusillanimity in monarchs, and evidence of not sufficiently feeling what they are, to labor at showing off and making a display by excessive expense. It would be excusable in a foreign country; but among his own subjects, where he is all-powerful, he derives from his dignity the highest degree of honor he can attain. Just as, it seems to me, for a gentleman it is superfluous to dress with studied care at home: his house, his retinue, his cuisine, answer for him sufficiently.

The advice that Isocrates[7] gives his king seems to me not without reason: that he be splendid in furniture and plate, since that is a lasting investment which passes on to his successors; and that he avoid all magnificences that flow away immediately out of use and memory.

I liked to adorn myself when I was a youth, for lack of other adornments, and it was becoming to me; there are those on whom fine clothes weep. We have marvelous stories of the frugality of our kings about their own persons and in their gifts—kings great in prestige, in valor, and in fortune. Demosthenes[8] fights tooth and nail against the law of his city that allotted public monies to lavish games and feasts; he wants the greatness of the city to be manifest in its quantity of well-equipped ships and of good, well-supplied armies.

And Theophrastus[9] is rightly blamed for setting forth a contrary opinion in his book on riches, and maintaining that lavish expenditure was the true fruit of opulence. These are pleasures, says Aristotle, that touch only the lowest of the people, that vanish from memory as soon as people are sated with them, and that no judicious and serious man can esteem. The outlay would seem to me much more royal as well as more useful, just, and durable, if it were spent on ports, harbors, fortifications, and walls, on sumptuous buildings, churches, hospitals, colleges, and the improvement of streets and roads, for which Pope Gregory XIII is gratefully remembered in my time, and in which our Queen Catherine[1] would leave evidence for many years of her natural liberality and munificence, if her means were equal to her wish. Fortune has given me great displeasure by interrupting the construction of the handsome new bridge[2] of our great city, and depriving me of the hope of seeing it in full use before I die.

---

6. Marcus Antonius (83–31 B.C.E.), Roman general, libertine, and triumvir, whose associations with Eastern luxury and religious cults are invoked here.
7. Athenian orator (436–338 B.C.E.).
8. Greatest Athenian orator (384–322 B.C.E.).
9. Greek philosopher and botanist, follower of Aristotle (c. 370–288 B.C.E.).
1. Catherine de Médici (1519–1589).
2. The Pont Neuf, as it is still called, was completed in 1604 [translator's note].

Besides, it seems to the subjects, spectators of these triumphs, that they are given a display of their own riches, and entertained at their own expense. For peoples are apt to assume about kings, as we do about our servants, that they should take care to prepare for us in abundance all we need, but that they should not touch it at all for their own part. And therefore the Emperor Galba,[3] having taken pleasure in a musician's playing during his supper, sent for his money box and gave into his hand a handful of crowns that he fished out of it, with these words: "This is not the public money, this is my own." At all events, it most often happens that the people are right, and that their eyes are feasted with what should go to feed their bellies.

Liberality itself is not in its proper light in the hands of a sovereign; private people have more right to exercise it. For, to be precise about it, a king has nothing that is properly his own; he owes his very self to others.

The authority to judge is not given for the sake of the judge, but for the sake of the person judged. A superior is never appointed for his own benefit, but for the benefit of the inferior, and a doctor for the sick, not for himself. All authority, like all art, has its end outside of itself: *no art is directed to itself* [Cicero].[4]

Wherefore the tutors of young princes who make it a point to impress on them this virtue of liberality and preach to them not to know how to refuse anything, and to think nothing so well spent as what they give away (a lesson that I have seen in great favor in my time), either look more to their own profit than to their master's, or do not well understand to whom they speak. It is all too easy to impress liberality on a man who has the means to practice it all he wants at the expense of others. And since its value is reckoned not by the measure of the gift, but by the measure of the giver's means, it amounts to nothing in such powerful hands. They find themselves prodigal before they are liberal. Therefore liberality is little to be commended compared with other royal virtues, and it is the only one, as the tyrant Dionysius said, that goes with tyranny itself. I would rather teach him this verse of the ancient farmer: that whoever wants to reap a good crop must sow with the hand, not pour out of the sack; he must scatter the seed, not spill it; and that since he has to give, or, to put it better, pay and restore to so many people according to their deserts, he should be a fair and wise distributor. If the liberality of a prince is without discretion and without measure, I would rather he were a miser.

Royal virtue seems to consist most of all in justice; and of all the parts of justice, that one best marks kings which accompanies liberality; for they have particularly reserved it as their function, whereas they are prone to exercise all other justice through the intermediary of others. Immoderate largesse is a feeble means for them to acquire good will; for it alienates more people than it wins over: *The more you have already practiced it on, the fewer you will be able to practice it on. What is more foolish than to take pains so that you can no longer do what you enjoy doing?* [Cicero.][5] And if it is exercised without regard to merit, it puts to shame him who receives it, and is received ungraciously. Tyrants have been sacrificed to the hatred of the people by the hands of the very ones whom they have unjustly advanced; for such men think to assure their possession of undeserved goods by showing contempt and hatred for the

---

3. Roman emperor (c. 3 B.C.E.–69 C.E.) after Nero.

4. *De finibus* 5.6.16.

5. *On Duties* 2.15.52–54.

man from whom they received them, and rallying to the judgment and opinion of the people in that respect.

The subjects of a prince who is excessive in gifts become excessive in requests; they adjust themselves not to reason but to example. Surely we often have reason to blush for our impudence; we are overpaid according to justice when the recompense equals our service; for do we owe no service to our prince by natural obligation? If he bears our expenses, he does too much; it is enough that he helps out. The surplus is called benefit, and it cannot be exacted, for the very name of liberality rings of liberty. By our method, it is never done; the receipts are no longer taken into account; people love only the future liberality. Wherefore the more a prince exhausts himself in giving, the poorer he makes himself in friends. How could he assuage desires that grow the more they are fulfilled? He who has his mind on taking, no longer has it on what he has taken. Covetousness has nothing so characteristic about it as ingratitude.

The example of Cyrus[6] will not be amiss here to serve the kings of our time as a touchstone for ascertaining whether their gifts are well or ill bestowed, and to make them see how much more happily that emperor dealt them out than they do. Whereby they are reduced to doing their borrowing from unknown subjects, and rather from those they have wronged than from those they have benefited; and from them they receive no aid that is gratuitous in anything but the name.

Croesus reproached Cyrus for his extravagance and calculated how much his treasure would amount to if he had been more close-fisted. Cyrus, wanting to justify his liberality, sent dispatches in all directions to the grandees of his state whose career he had particularly advanced, and asked each one to help him out with as much money as he could for an urgent need of his, and to send him a declaration of the amount. When all these statements were brought to him, since each of his friends, thinking it was not enough to offer him merely as much as he had received from his munificence, added much that was more properly his own, it turned out that the total amounted to much more than the savings estimated by Croesus. Whereupon Cyrus said to him: "I am no less in love with riches than other princes, and am rather a more careful manager of them. You see at how small a cost I have acquired the inestimable treasure of so many friends, and how much more faithful treasurers they are to me than mercenary men without obligation, without affection, would be; and how much better my wealth is lodged than in coffers, where it would call down upon me the hatred, envy, and contempt of other princes."

The emperors derived an excuse for the superfluity of their public games and spectacles from the fact that their authority depended somewhat (at least in appearance) on the will of the Roman people, who from time immemorial had been accustomed to being flattered by that sort of spectacle and extravagance. But it was private citizens who had nourished this custom of gratifying their fellow citizens and companions, chiefly out of their own purse, by such profusion and magnificence; this had an altogether different flavor when it was the masters who came to imitate it. *The transfer of money from its rightful owners to strangers should not be regarded as liberality* [Cicero].[7]

---

6. Ideal prince of Xenophon's *Education of Cyrus.*

7. *On Duties* 1.14.43.

Philip, because his son was trying to win the good will of the Macedonians by presents, scolded him for it in a letter in this manner: "What, do you want your subjects to regard you as their purser, not as their king? Do you want to win them over? Win them over with the benefits of your virtue, not the benefits of your coffers."[8]

It was, however, a fine thing to bring and plant in the amphitheater a great quantity of big trees, all branching and green, representing a great shady forest, arranged in beautiful symmetry, and on the first day to cast into it a thousand ostriches, a thousand stags, a thousand wild boars, and a thousand fallow deer, leaving them to be hunted down by the people; on the next day to have a hundred big lions, a hundred leopards, and three hundred bears slaughtered in their presence; and for the third day, to have three hundred pairs of gladiators fight it out to the death, as the Emperor Probus[9] did.

It was also a fine thing to see those great amphitheaters faced with marble on the outside, wrought with ornaments and statues, the inside sparkling with many rare enrichments—

> Here is the diamond circle, the golden portico
> CALPURNIUS[1]

—all the sides of this vast space filled and surrounded from top to bottom with three or four score tiers of seats, also of marble, covered with cushions—

> "Let him begone," he says,
> "And leave the cushioned seats of knights, seeing he pays
> None of the lawful tax"
> JUVENAL[2]

—where a hundred thousand men could sit at their ease. Also, first of all, to have the place at the bottom, where the games were played, open artificially and split into crevasses representing caverns that vomited forth the beasts destined for the spectacle; and then, second, to flood it with a deep sea, full of sea monsters and laden with armed vessels to represent a naval battle; and third, to level it and dry it off again for the combat of the gladiators; and for the fourth show to strew it with vermilion and storax instead of sand, in order to set up a stately banquet there for all that huge number of people—the final act of a single day:

> How often have we seen
> Part of the sandy floor sink down, wild beasts emerge
> Out of the open chasm, and from its depths upsurge
> Forests of golden growing trees with yellow bark.
> Not only forest monsters were for us to mark,
> But I saw sea-calves mingled in with fighting bears,

---

8. *On Duties* 2.15.53–54; Philip of Macedon was the father of Alexander the Great.
9. Marcus Aurelius Probus (232–282 C.E.), a stern disciplinarian, eventually killed by his own troops.
1. Calpurnius Siculus (1st century C.E.), pastoral poet; *Bucolics* 7.47.
2. *Satires* 3.153–55.

And hippopotami, the shapeless herd that wears
The name of river-horse.
                                        CALPURNIUS[3]

Sometimes they created a high mountain there, full of fruit trees and other trees in leaf, spouting a stream of water from its top as from the mouth of a living spring. Sometimes they brought in a great ship which opened and came apart of itself and, after having spewed forth from its belly four or five hundred fighting beasts, closed up again and vanished without assistance. At other times, from the floor of the place, they made spouts and jets of water spring forth which shot upward to an infinite height, then sprinkled and perfumed that infinite multitude. To protect themselves against damage from the weather, they had that immense space hung with awnings, sometimes made of purple worked with the needle, sometimes of silk of one color or another, and they drew them forward or back in a moment, as they had a mind to:

The awnings, though the sun scorches the skin,
Are, when Hermogenes appears, drawn in.
                                        MARTIAL[4]

The nets, too, which they put in front of the people to protect them from the violence of the loosened beasts, were woven of gold:

                Even the woven nets
    Glitter with gold.
                                        CALPURNIUS[5]

If there is anything excusable in such extravagances, it is when the inventiveness and the novelty of them, not the expense, provide amazement.

Even in these vanities we discover how fertile those ages were in minds different from ours. It is with this sort of fertility as with all other productions of Nature. This is not to say that she then put forth her utmost effort. We do not go in a straight line; we rather ramble, and turn this way and that. We retrace our steps. I fear that our knowledge is weak in every direction; we do not see very far ahead or very far behind. It embraces little and has a short life, short in both extent of time and extent of matter:

    Ere Agamemnon, heroes were the same;
    Many there were, but no one knows their name;
        They all are hurried on unwept
        Into unending night.
                                        HORACE

    Before the Trojan War, before Troy fell,
    Were other bards with other tales to tell.
                                        LUCRETIUS[6]

3. *Bucolics* 7.64–75.
4. Marcus Valerius Martial (c. 40–ca. 104 C.E.), famous for his witty epigrams; *Epigrams* 12.29.15–16.
5. *Bucolics* 7.53–54.
6. *On the Nature of Things* 5.327–28. Above, *Odes* 4.9.25–28.

And Solon's story of what he had heard from the priests of Egypt about the long life of their state, and their manner of learning and preserving the histories of other countries, does not seem to me a testimony to be rejected in this consideration. *If we could view that expanse of countries and ages, boundless in every direction, into which the mind, plunging and spreading itself, travels so far and wide that it can find no limit where it can stop, there would appear in that immensity an infinite capacity to produce innumerable forms* [adapted from Cicero].[7]

Even if all that has come down to us by report from the past should be true and known by someone, it would be less than nothing compared with what is unknown. And of this very image of the world which glides along while we live on it, how puny and limited is the knowledge of even the most curious! Not only of particular events which fortune often renders exemplary and weighty, but of the state of great governments and nations, there escapes us a hundred times more than comes to our knowledge. We exclaim at the miracle of the invention of our artillery, of our printing; other men in another corner of the world, in China, enjoyed these a thousand years earlier. If we saw as much of the world as we do not see, we would perceive, it is likely, a perpetual multiplication and vicissitude of forms.

There is nothing unique and rare as regards nature, but there certainly is as regards our knowledge, which is a miserable foundation for our rules and which is apt to represent to us a very false picture of things. As vainly as we today infer the decline and decrepitude of the world from the arguments we draw from our own weakness and decay—

This age is broken down, and broken down the earth

LUCRETIUS[8]

—so vainly did this poet infer the world's birth and youth from the vigor he saw in the minds of his time, abounding in novelties and inventions in various arts:

The universe, I think, is very new,
The world is young, its birth not far behind;
Hence certain arts grow more and more refined
Even today; the naval art is one.

LUCRETIUS[9]

Our world has just discovered another world (and who will guarantee us that it is the last of its brothers, since the daemons, the Sibyls,[1] and we ourselves have up to now been ignorant of this one?) no less great, full, and well-limbed than itself, yet so new and so infantile that it is still being taught its A B C; not fifty years ago it knew neither letters, nor weights and measures, nor clothes, nor wheat, nor vines. It was still quite naked at the breast, and lived only on what its nursing mother provided. If we are right to infer the end of our world, and that poet is right about the youth of his own age, this other world will only be coming into the light when ours is leaving it. The universe will fall into paralysis; one member will be crippled, the other in full vigor.

7. *On the Nature of the Gods* 1.20.54. Solon (c. 200 C.E.), geographer.
8. *On the Nature of Things* 2.1136.

9. *On the Nature of Things* 5.331–35.
1. Female prophets.

I am much afraid that we shall have very greatly hastened the decline and ruin of this new world by our contagion, and that we will have sold it our opinions and our arts very dear. It was an infant world; yet we have not whipped it and subjected it to our discipline by the advantage of our natural valor and strength, nor won it over by our justice and goodness, nor subjugated it by our magnanimity. Most of the responses of these people and most of our dealings with them show that they were not at all behind us in natural brightness of mind and pertinence.

The awesome magnificence of the cities of Cuzco[2] and Mexico (and, among many similar things, the garden of that king in which all the trees, the fruits, and all the herbs were excellently fashioned in gold, and of such size and so arranged as they might be in an ordinary garden; and in his curio room were gold replicas of all the living creatures native to his country and its waters), and the beauty of their workmanship in jewelry, feathers, cotton, and painting, show that they were not behind us in industry either. But as for devoutness, observance of the laws, goodness, liberality, loyalty, and frankness, it served us well not to have as much as they: by their advantage in this they lost, sold, and betrayed themselves.

As for boldness and courage, as for firmness, constancy, resoluteness against pains and hunger and death, I would not fear to oppose the examples I could find among them to the most famous ancient examples that we have in the memories of our world on this side of the ocean. For as regards the men who subjugated them, take away the ruses and tricks that they used to deceive them, and the people's natural astonishment at seeing the unexpected arrival of bearded men, different in language, religion, shape, and countenance, from a part of the world so remote, where they had never imagined there was any sort of human habitation, mounted on great unknown monsters, opposed to men who had never seen not only a horse, but any sort of animal trained to carry and endure a man or any other burden; men equipped with a hard and shiny skin and a sharp and glittering weapon, against men who, for the miracle of a mirror or a knife, would exchange a great treasure in gold and pearls, and who had neither the knowledge nor the material by which, even in full leisure, they could pierce our steel; add to this the lightning and thunder of our cannon and harquebuses—capable of disturbing Caesar[3] himself, if he had been surprised by them with as little experience and in his time—against people who were naked (except in some regions where the invention of some cotton fabric had reached them), without other arms at the most than bows, stones, sticks, and wooden bucklers; people taken by surprise, under color of friendship and good faith, by curiosity to see strange and unknown things: eliminate this disparity, I say, and you take from the conquerors the whole basis of so many victories.

When I consider that indomitable ardor with which so many thousands of men, women, and children came forth and hurled themselves so many times into inevitable dangers for the defense of their gods and of their liberty, and that noble, stubborn readiness to suffer all extremities and hardships, even death, rather than submit to the domination of those by whom they had been so shamefully deceived (for some of them when captured chose rather to let

2. Former capital of the Inca Empire in southeastern Peru.

3. Julius Caesar (100–44 B.C.E.), the great Roman general and conqueror.

themselves perish of hunger and fasting than to accept food from the hands of such basely victorious enemies), I conclude that if anyone had attacked them on equal terms, with equal arms, experience, and numbers, it would have been just as dangerous for him as in any other war we know of, and more so.

Why did not such a noble conquest fall to Alexander or to those ancient Greeks and Romans? Why did not such a great change and alteration of so many empires and peoples fall into hands that would have gently polished and cleared away whatever was barbarous in them, and would have strengthened and fostered the good seeds that nature had produced in them, not only adding to the cultivation of the earth and the adornment of cities the arts of our side of the ocean, in so far as they would have been necessary, but also adding the Greek and Roman virtues to those originally in that region? What an improvement that would have been, and what an amelioration for the entire globe, if the first examples of our conduct that were offered over there had called those peoples to the admiration and imitation of virtue and had set up between them and us a brotherly fellowship and understanding! How easy it would have been to make good use of souls so fresh, so famished to learn, and having, for the most part, such fine natural beginnings! On the contrary, we took advantage of their ignorance and inexperience to incline them the more easily toward treachery, lewdness, avarice, and every sort of inhumanity and cruelty, after the example and pattern of our ways. Who ever set the utility of commerce and trading at such a price? So many cities razed, so many nations exterminated, so many millions of people put to the sword, and the richest and most beautiful part of the world turned upside down, for the traffic in pearls and pepper! Base and mechanical victories! Never did ambition, never did public enmities, drive men against one another to such horrible hostilities and such miserable calamities.

Coasting the sea in quest of their mines, certain Spaniards landed in a fertile, pleasant, well-populated country, and made their usual declarations to its people: that they were peaceable men, coming from distant voyages, sent on behalf of the king of Castile, the greatest prince of the habitable world, to whom the Pope, representing God on earth, had given the principality of all the Indies; that if these people would be tributaries to him, they would be very kindly treated. They demanded of them food to eat and gold to be used in a certain medicine, and expounded to them the belief in one single God and the truth of our religion, which they advised them to accept, adding a few threats.

The answer was this: As for being peaceable, they did not look like it, if they were. As for their king, since he was begging, he must be indigent and needy; and he who had awarded their country to him must be a man fond of dissension, to go and give another person something that was not his and thus set him at strife with its ancient possessors. As for food, they would supply them. Gold they had little of, and it was a thing they held in no esteem, since it was useless to the service of their life, their sole concern being with passing life happily and pleasantly; however, they might boldly take any they could find, except what was employed in the service of their gods. As for one single God, the account had pleased them, but they did not want to change their religion, having followed it so advantageously for so long, and they were not accustomed to take counsel except of their friends and acquaintances. As for the threats, it was a sign of lack of judgment to threaten people whose nature and means were unknown to them. Thus they should promptly hurry up and vacate their land, for they were not accustomed to take in good part the civilities and declarations of armed strangers; otherwise they would do to them as they had done to these others—showing them the heads of some executed men around their city.

There we have an example of the babbling of this infancy. But at all events, neither in that place nor in several others where the Spaniards did not find the merchandise they were looking for, did they make any stay or any attack, whatever other advantages there might be; witness my Cannibals.[4]

Of the two most powerful monarchs of that world, and perhaps of this as well, kings of so many kings, the last two that they drove out, one, the king of Peru, was taken in a battle and put to so excessive a ransom that it surpasses all belief; and when this had been faithfully paid, and the king in his dealings had given signs of a frank, liberal, and steadfast spirit and a clear and well-ordered understanding, the conquerors, after having extracted from him one million three hundred and twenty-five thousand five hundred ounces of gold, besides silver and other things that amounted to no less, so that their horses thenceforth went shod with solid gold, were seized with the desire to see also, at the price of whatever treachery, what could be the remainder of this king's treasures, and to enjoy freely what he had reserved. They trumped up against him a false accusation and false evidence that he was planning to rouse his provinces in order to regain his freedom. Whereupon, in a beautiful sentence pronounced by those very men who had set afoot this treachery against him, he was condemned to be publicly hanged and strangled, after being permitted to buy his way out of the torment of being burned alive by submitting to baptism at the moment of the execution. A horrible and unheard-of calamity, which nevertheless he bore without belying himself either by look or word, with a truly royal bearing and gravity. And then, to lull the people, stunned and dazed by such a strange thing, they counterfeited great mourning over his death and ordered a sumptuous funeral for him.

The other one, the king of Mexico, had long defended his besieged city and shown in this siege all that endurance and perseverance can do, if ever prince and people did so, when his bad fortune put him in his enemies' hands alive, on their promise that they would treat him as a king; nor did he in his captivity show anything unworthy of this title. After this victory, his enemies, not finding all the gold they had promised themselves, first ransacked and searched everything, and then set about seeking information by inflicting the cruelest tortures they could think up on the prisoners they held. But having gained nothing by this, and finding their prisoners' courage stronger than their torments, they finally flew into such a rage that, against their word and against all law of nations, they condemned the king himself and one of the principal lords of his court to the torture in each other's presence. This lord, finding himself overcome with the pain, surrounded with burning braziers, in the end turned his gaze piteously toward his master, as if to ask his pardon because he could hold out no longer. The king, fixing his eyes proudly and severely on him in reproach for his cowardice and pusillanimity, said to him only these words, in a stern, firm voice: "And I, am I in a bath? Am I more comfortable than you?" The other immediately after succumbed to the pain and died on the spot. The king, half roasted, was carried away from there, not so much out of pity (for

4. "Of Cannibals."

what pity ever touched souls who, for dubious information about some gold vase to pillage, had a man grilled before their eyes, and what is more, a king so great in fortune and merit?), but because his fortitude made their cruelty more and more shameful. They hanged him later for having courageously attempted to deliver himself by arms from such a long captivity and subjection, and he made an end worthy of a great-souled prince.

Another time they burned alive, all at once and in the same fire, four hundred and sixty men, the four hundred being of the common people, the sixty from among the chief lords of a province, all merely prisoners of war.

We have these narrations from themselves, for they not only admit them but boast of them and preach them. Would it be as a testimonial to their justice or their zeal for religion? Truly, those are ways too contrary and hostile to so holy an end. If they had proposed to extend our faith, they would have reflected that faith is not spread by possession of territory but by possession of men, and they would have been more than satisfied with the murders brought about by the necessity of war, without adding to these an indiscriminate butchery, as of wild animals, as universal as fire and sword could make it, after purposely sparing only as many as they wanted to make into miserable slaves for the working and service of their mines: with the result that many of the leaders were punished with death by order of the kings of Castile, who were justly shocked by the horror of their conduct; and almost all were disesteemed and loathed. God deservedly allowed this great plunder to be swallowed up by the sea in transit, or by the intestine wars in which they devoured one another; and most of them were buried on the spot without any profit from their victory.

As for the fact that the revenue from this, even in the hands of a thrifty and prudent prince,[5] corresponds so little to the expectation of it given to his predecessors and to the abundance of riches that was first encountered in these new lands (for although much is being gotten out, we see that it is nothing compared with what was to be expected), the reason is that the use of money was entirely unknown, and that consequently their gold was found all collected together, being of no other use than for show and parade, like a chattel preserved from father to son by many powerful kings who were constantly exhausting their mines to make that great heap of vases and statues for the adornment of their palaces and their temples; whereas our gold is all in circulation and in trade. We cut it up small and change it into a thousand forms; we scatter and disperse it. Imagine it if our kings thus accumulated all the gold they could find for many centuries and kept it idle.

The people of the kingdom of Mexico were somewhat more civilized and skilled in the arts than the other nations over there. Thus they judged, as we do, that the universe was near its end, and they took as a sign of this the desolation that we brought upon them. They believed that the existence of the world was divided into five ages and into the life of five successive suns, of which four had already run their time, and that the one which gave them light was the fifth. The first perished with all other creatures by a universal flood of water. The second, by the heavens falling on us, which suffocated every living thing; to which age they assign the giants, and they showed the Spaniards some of their bones, judging by the size of which these men must have stood

5. Philip II of Spain (1527–1598).

twenty hands high. The third, by fire, which burned and consumed everything. The fourth, by a turbulence of air and wind which beat down even many mountains; the men did not die, but they were changed into baboons (to what notions will the laxness of human credulity not submit!). After the death of this fourth sun, the world was twenty-five years in perpetual darkness, in the fifteenth of which a man and a woman were created who remade the human race; ten years later, on a certain day of their calendar, the sun appeared newly created, and since then they reckon their years from that day. The third day after its creation the old gods died; the new ones have been born since little by little. What they think about the manner in which this last sun will perish, my author[6] did not learn. But their calculation of this fourth change coincides with that great conjunction of stars which produced, some eight hundred years ago, according to the reckoning of the astrologers, many great alterations and innovations in the world.

As for pomp and magnificence, whereby I entered upon this subject, neither Greece nor Rome nor Egypt can compare any of its works, whether in utility or difficulty or nobility, with the road which is seen in Peru, laid out by the kings of the country, from the city of Quito as far as Cuzco (a distance of three hundred leagues), straight, even, twenty-five paces wide, paved, lined on both sides with fine high walls, and along these, on the inside, two ever-flowing streams, bordered by beautiful trees, which they call *molly*. Wherever they encountered mountains and rocks, they cut through and leveled them, and filled the hollows with stone and lime. At the end of each day's journey there are fine palaces furnished with provisions, clothes, and arms, for travelers as well as for the armies that have to pass that way.

In my estimate of this work I have counted the difficulty, which is particularly considerable in that place. They did not build with any stones less than ten feet square; they had no other means of carrying than by strength of arm, dragging their load along; and they had not even the art of scaffolding, knowing no other device than to raise an equal height of earth against their building as it rose, and remove it afterward.

Let us fall back to our coaches. Instead of these or any other form of transport, they had themselves carried by men, and on their shoulders. That last king of Peru, the day that he was taken, was thus carried on shafts of gold, seated in a chair of gold, in the midst of his army. As many of these carriers as they killed to make him fall—for they wanted to take him alive—so many others vied to take the place of the dead ones, so that they never could bring him down, however great a slaughter they made of those people, until a horseman seized him around the body and pulled him to the ground.

---

6. López de Gómara (1511–1564), a Spanish contemporary of Montaigne; Montaigne read his histories of Cortez and the West Indies in translation [translator's note].

MIGUEL DE CERVANTES

1547–1616

Often described as the first novel, Miguel de Cervantes' *Don Quixote* uses the conventions of fiction to question the accepted truths of his own society. What happens when readers take books at their word, or try to live out ideal versions of the world around them, as does the would-be knight Don Quixote? How does life in early modern Spain fall short of the wishful fictional version? In *Don Quixote*, the narrative breaks off and leaves the reader hanging, characters reflect on what it means to exist in print, and a complicated cast of antagonistic narrators all quarrel over the *real* truth, as Cervantes ironically surveys his world while examining the nature of fiction.

LIFE

The author of Don Quixote's extravagant adventures himself had a most unusual and adventurous life. As a student, soldier, captive, and tax collector, he witnessed his contemporaries at their best and at their worst. His skeptical, ironic perspective on both the literary and political pieties of his day is combined in his works with a profound sympathy for human striving. The son of an apothecary, Miguel de Cervantes Saavedra was born in Alcalá de Henares, a university town near Madrid. Almost nothing is known of his childhood and early education. Only in 1569 is he mentioned as a favorite pupil by a Madrid humanist, Juan López. Records indicate that by the end of that year he had left Spain and was living in Rome, for a time in the service of a future cardinal. He enlisted in the Spanish fleet under the command of Don John of Austria and took part in the struggle of the allied forces of Christendom against the Ottomans. He was at the crucial Battle of Lepanto (1571), where in spite of fever he fought valiantly and received three gunshot wounds, one of which permanently impaired the use of his left hand, "for the greater glory of the right." After further military action at Palermo and Naples, he and his brother Rodrigo, bearing testimonials from Don John and from the viceroy of Sicily, began the journey back to Spain, where Miguel hoped to obtain a captaincy. In September 1575 their ship was captured near Marseille by Barbary pirates, and the two brothers were taken as prisoners to Algiers. Cervantes' captors, considering him a person of some consequence because of the letters he carried, held him as a slave for a high ransom. His daring and fortitude as he attempted repeatedly to escape excited the admiration of Hassan Pasha, the viceroy of Algiers, who bought him for five hundred crowns after five years of captivity.

Cervantes was finally ransomed on September 15, 1580, and reached Madrid in December of that year, though his experience of coptivity would remain with him throughout his literary career. That career began rather inauspiciously; he wrote some ten to twenty plays, with middling success, and in 1585 published *Galatea*, a pastoral romance that anticipates the formal experimentation of *Don Quixote* but ends inconclusively. None of these established his reputation or, more important, allowed him to live from his writing. At about this time he had a daughter with Ana Franca de Rojas, and during the same period married Catalina de Salazar, who was eighteen years his junior. Seeking nonliterary employment, he obtained a position in the navy, requisitioning and collecting supplies for the "Invincible Armada." Irregularities in his administration, for which he was held responsible if not directly guilty, caused him to spend more time in prison. In 1590 he was denied colonial employment in the New World. Later he served as tax collector in the province of Granada but was dismissed from government service in 1597.

The following years of Cervantes' life are the most obscure; there is a legend that *Don Quixote* was first conceived and planned while its author was in prison in Seville. In 1604 he was in Valladolid, then the temporary capital of Spain, living in sordid surroundings with the numerous women of his family (his wife, daughter, niece, and two sisters). It was in Valladolid, in late 1604, that he obtained the official license for the publication of *Don Quixote* (Part I). The book appeared in 1605 and was a popular success. Cervantes followed the Spanish court when it returned to Madrid, where he continued to live poorly in spite of a popularity with readers that quickly made proverbial figures of his heroes. A false sequel to his book appeared, prompting him to write his own continuation, *Don Quixote*, Part II, published in 1615. His *Exemplary Novellas* had appeared in 1613. He died on April 23, 1616. *Persiles and Sigismunda*, his last novel, was published posthumously in 1617.

TIMES

Cervantes' Spain was a great empire, with huge possessions in the New World, in Italy, and in Flanders, sustained by an equally enormous army of disciplined soldiers organized in infantry battalions—the famous *tercios españoles*. It was ruled by Philip II, the devout Habsburg monarch who became known as "the prudent king" for his careful administration. In 1580, Philip annexed the Portuguese crown and its commercial empire in Asia, Africa, and the New World, rendering Spain a truly global power. At the same time, the enormous influx of gold from the Americas led to inflation and widespread poverty, and to the general perception that everything and everyone could be bought. As the vivacious gypsy Preciosa jokes to an impoverished official in one of Cervantes' novellas, if he only took bribes as everyone expects him to do, he would not be so poor. Both as a tax collector and as a convict, Cervantes had ample experience of a down-and-out, picaresque Spain that held the law in small regard, a world depicted in colorful detail in the earthier episodes of *Don Quixote*.

Overburdened with military expenses and foreign debt, the Crown experienced repeated bankruptcies despite the heavy taxes it imposed on its subjects. In 1588, it suffered the added indignity of the Armada's defeat by the English navy, and Spain entered a long period of decline and disillusion. Philip's death in 1598 signaled the end of an era. Cervantes marked the occasion with a devastating sonnet on the king's funerary monument. Its greatness, the poem suggests, is but an illusion: as soon as the admiring glances of the impressionable viewers wander, king, reign, and monument are reduced to nothingness.

Meanwhile, the Counter-Reformation led to an increased emphasis on religious orthodoxy, and heightened suspicions of the humanist reform traditions that had shaped Cervantes' thought. Increasingly, his society scrutinized not only people's religious practices but also their roots, stigmatizing them for Jewish or Muslim forebears and holding all *conversos* and *Moriscos* (converts from Judaism and Islam, respectively) suspect. Cervantes' own fortunes may have been complicated by his origins: we cannot be sure whether he came from a line of *conversos*, but his family connections to the medical profession, the denial of his request for New World employment, and the refusal of the authorities to reward his heroic military service and captivity with any real preferment all suggest a striking disregard for his services. If he was in fact descended from Jews, Cervantes would have been barred from many honors and privileges in his time, however sincere his own Christian faith. Cervantes mocked the Inquisitorial and popular anxiety about origins in his dramatic interlude *The Miracle Show*. In this satire of Spanish obsessions with honor, legitimacy, and "blood purity," rascally entertainers trick village notables by convincing them that only those who are legitimate and free of the Jewish "taint" can actually see their marvelous show. In his version of "The Emperor's New Clothes," Cervantes holds up a sly theatrical mirror to his own society's prejudices.

During Cervantes' life, Spain faced challenges to both its political power and its religious orthodoxy. Protestants across Europe and humanist reformers within the Catholic Church constantly defied the strictures of the Counter-Reformation. The Ottoman Empire, which encroached on Italy, the Mediterranean, and North Africa, represented the greatest geopolitical threat to Spain, and also the religious threat of Islam as a competing faith. In its own territories, Spain struggled to incorporate the descendants of its Muslim subjects. Though this population had been forcibly converted to Christianity, their place and that of their descendants within a belligerently Christian nation were increasingly threatened. Their customs and language were forbidden by law, in an attempt to enforce acculturation. Beginning in 1609, the Moriscos, though Christians, were forcibly expelled from Spain, prompting widespread condemnation by Church authorities across Europe. Cervantes comments directly on the situation of the Moriscos in *Don Quixote*. In "The Captive's Tale" of Part I, he considers how Spanish society might receive a hugely sympathetic young woman, a fresh convert from Islam, who had saved a Spanish captive much like the author himself. In Part II, published after the expulsions, in a section not included in this anthology, Sancho Panza, Don Quixote's earthy sidekick, runs into his Morisco former neighbor, Ricote, now back in Spain disguised as a German pilgrim. They proceed to share a communal meal, with plenty of wine to go around. Thus Cervantes turns again and again to his own experience of captivity and to the Morisco problem within Spain, to explore how a newly unified and forcibly homogenized nation might include those it had led to Christianity.

DON QUIXOTE

The Ingenious Gentleman Don Quixote de la Mancha was a popular success from the time Part I was published in 1605, although it was only later recognized as an important work of literature. This delay was due partly to the fact that in a period of established and well-defined literary genres such as the epic, the tragedy, and the pastoral romance (Cervantes himself had tried his hand at some of these forms), the unconventional combination of elements in *Don Quixote* resulted in a work of considerable novelty, with the serious aspects hidden under a mocking surface.

The proclaimed purpose of the book was to satirize the romances of chivalry. In those long yarns—based on the Carolingian and Arthurian legends, and full of supernatural deeds of valor, implausible and complicated adventures, duels, and enchantments—the literature that had expressed the medieval spirit of chivalry and romance had become conventional and formulaic (much as, in our day, certain literary conventions have become "pulp" fiction and film melodrama). Up to a point, then, what Cervantes set out to do was to produce a parody, a caricature of a hugely popular literary type. But he did not limit himself to such a relatively simple and direct undertaking. To expose the silliness of the romances of chivalry, he showed to what extraordinary consequences they would lead a man insanely infatuated with them, once this man set out to live "now" according to their patterns of action and belief. While the anachronism of Don Quixote makes him a figure of fun, it also allows Cervantes to examine the realities of his own time: an impoverished Spain full of underemployed noblemen; an overextended empire burdened by too many modern, impersonal wars; widespread anxiety about religious and political conformity, as well as genealogical "purity."

So what we have is not mere parody or caricature, for there is a great deal of difference between presenting a remote and more or less imaginary world and presenting an individual deciding to live by the standards of that world in a modern and realistic context. The first consequence is a mingling of genres. Don Quixote sees the world through the lens of medieval chivalry as its authors had portrayed it, and often the narrator echoes his vision, albeit in an ironic mode. The chivalric world is continuously jostled by elements of contemporary life evoked by the narrator—the realities of landscape and speech, peasants and nobles, inns and highways. The hero attempting to recreate the world of the romances is not, as we know, a cavalier; he is an impoverished country gentleman who embraces that code in the "modern"

world. His squire, the peasant Sancho Panza, is only too happy to point out Don Quixote's delusions. Nevertheless, he too becomes invested in the quest, in search of material wealth and aggrandizement. The exchanges between Don Quixote and Sancho pit a gentleman against a peasant, yet more often than not the two find common ground in their conviction that they can improve their lot through their own actions.

Don Quixote soon finds that he is not the only one modeling his life after books. Other characters follow their own idealizing genres, such as the pastoral romance to which Don Quixote and his friends will turn at the end. All must make their peace with the reality of the world that surrounds them. That debased world, in turn, produces its own stories, such as the picaresque "life" that the rascally Ginés de Pasamonte has written in prison (Part I, chapter 22), and the mix of recent history and romance that is the "Captive's Tale," related by its protogonist at the inn.

Along the way, Cervantes casts doubt on the possibility of reconstructing history from written sources. The facts about Don Quixote are never fully available to the primary narrator, who confesses to the many gaps in his knowledge and keeps losing track of the story. While the prologue describes the text as the author's "child," the narrator is not even certain of his protagonist's name. More spectacularly, the first part of the novel breaks off entirely at the end of chapter 8, leaving both characters and readers in suspense. The problem of finding more text then leads to one of Cervantes' most interesting narrative games: a second author, Cid Hamete Benengeli, who just happens to be an "Arabic historian," and whose disheveled account must be translated from a forbidden language by a "Spanish-speaking Moor"—a

Morisco. The entire story from this point forth is thus supposedly written by a Moor, the traditional enemy of a Spanish knight, and translated by a marginalized contemporary Morisco. Don Quixote and his narrator both worry about the implications of such authorship for the story on which they are embarked: will the Moorish author distort Don Quixote's adventures, or diminish his greatness? Part I also moves away from Don Quixote and Sancho to present a number of other stories that play with generic conventions—of lovelorn shepherds and the shepherdesses who puncture their illusions, young lovers who fall prey to ignoble lords, friendships undone by sexual jealousy, and captives redeemed by mysterious ladies. The narrative games are fully fleshed out in Part II, when Don Quixote and Sancho, now famous from Part I, must confront their own celebrity and grapple with the selves that the printing press has given them, while the authorial voice of Cide Hamete intervenes more and more frequently to make sure that the reader gets the "right" story.

Generally speaking, the encounters between the ordinary world and Don Quixote confront reality with illusion, and reason with imagination. Among the first adventures are some that have most contributed to the popularity of the Don Quixote legend: he sees windmills and decides they are giants, country inns become castles, and flocks of sheep become armies. Though the conclusions of such episodes often have the ludicrousness of slapstick comedy, there is a powerfully imposing quality about Don Quixote's insanity; his madness always has method, a commanding persistence and coherence. And there is perhaps an inevitable sense of moral grandeur in the spectacle of anyone remaining so unflinchingly faithful to his or her own vision. The world of "reason" may win in point of fact, but we come to wonder whether from a moral point of view Quixote is not the victor.

Yet at the same time the novel explores the deterioration of the chivalric ideals that inspire its protagonist— for instance, the notion of love as devoted "service." Don Quixote loves a purely fantastic lady, Dulcinea, so remote and unattainable that she does not even exist. Other plots interwoven through the text, and not included in our selection, show lovers struggling with problems of class and religious difference, and pervasive sexual jealousy. *Don Quixote* also examines the anachronism of individual heroics: new forms of warfare had rendered knights passé in more than the literary sense— battles are now fought with artillery and squadrons of infantry. The episode of the lions (Part II, chapter 17) features the knight, crowned with cottage cheese, seeking a challenge at all costs. That challenge comes in the ironic form of a caged animal being sent to the king, and who has no intention of engaging in battle. Unwilling to confront the futility of the knight in an age of gunpowder, Don Quixote will take what he can get in the form of challenges. The ridiculousness of the situation is counterbalanced by the basic seriousness of Quixote's motives; his notion of courage for its own sake appears, and is recognized, as singularly noble, a sort of generous display of integrity in a world usually ruled by lower standards. Thus the distinction between reason and madness, truth and illusion, becomes, to say the least, ambiguous. The hero's delusions are indeed exposed when they come up against hard facts, but the authority of such facts is seen to be morally questionable. A similar ambiguity colors a later episode where he frees a group of thuggish galley slaves (Part I, chapter 22). Don Quixote, comically anachronistic, ignores the existence of a centralized state with its own justice system, which has tried the men and found them guilty. Yet his intervention and his determination to hear out the prisoners raises more basic questions of social justice, and insists on the imagination, however anachronistic, as a basic tool for rethinking the status quo.

Don Quixote has been intensely read and reread, since its first publication, for its broad humor and its slippery ironies alike. Both parts of the novel were immediately translated across Europe, giving rise to such rewritings and imitations as the Jacobean comedy The Knight of the Burning Pestle (1607), the early feminist novel The Female Quixote (1752), and, more recently, the Broadway musical Man of la Mancha (1964). In Spain, Don Quixote has long been embraced as the symbol of a kind of national idealism; the philosopher Miguel de Unamuno in his Life of Don Quixote and Sancho (1905) argued that the novel was the true "Spanish Bible," a degree of respect that might well have amused the more irreverent Cervantes.

From DON QUIXOTE[1]

From Part I

[Prologue]

Idling reader, you may believe me when I tell you that I should have liked this book, which is the child of my brain, to be the fairest, the sprightliest, and the cleverest that could be imagined; but I have not been able to contravene the law of nature which would have it that like begets like. And so, what was to be expected of a sterile and uncultivated wit such as that which I possess if not an offspring that was dried up, shriveled, and eccentric: a story filled with thoughts that never occurred to anyone else, of a sort that might be engendered in a prison where every annoyance has its home and every mournful sound its habitation?[2] Peace and tranquillity, the pleasures of the countryside, the serenity of the heavens, the murmur of fountains, and ease of mind can do much toward causing the most unproductive of muses to become fecund and bring forth progeny that will be the marvel and delight of mankind.

It sometimes happens that a father has an ugly son with no redeeming grace whatever, yet love will draw a veil over the parental eyes which then behold only cleverness and beauty in place of defects, and in speaking to his friends he will make those defects out to be the signs of comeliness and intellect. I, however, who am but Don Quixote's stepfather, have no desire to go with the current of custom, nor would I, dearest reader, beseech you with tears in my eyes as others do to pardon or overlook the faults you discover in this book; you are neither relative nor friend but may call your soul your own and exercise your free judgment. You are in your own house where you are master as the king is of his taxes, for you are familiar with the saying, "Under my cloak I kill the king."[3] All

---

1. Translated by Samuel Putnam.
2. Cervantes was imprisoned in Seville in 1597 and 1602.
3. I.e., the king does not own your body.

of which exempts and frees you from any kind of respect or obligation; you may say of this story whatever you choose without fear of being slandered for an ill opinion any more than you will be rewarded for a good one.

I should like to bring you the tale unadulterated and unadorned, stripped of the usual prologue and the endless string of sonnets, epigrams, and eulogies such as are commonly found at the beginning of books. For I may tell you that, although I expended no little labor upon the work itself, I have found no task more difficult than the composition of this preface which you are now reading. Many times I took up my pen and many times I laid it down again, not knowing what to write. On one occasion when I was thus in suspense, paper before me, pen over my ear, elbow on the table, and chin in hand, a very clever friend of mine came in. Seeing me lost in thought, he inquired as to the reason, and I made no effort to conceal from him the fact that my mind was on the preface which I had to write for the story of Don Quixote, and that it was giving me so much trouble that I had about decided not to write any at all and to abandon entirely the idea of publishing the exploits of so noble a knight.

"How," I said to him, "can you expect me not to be concerned over what that venerable legislator, the Public, will say when it sees me, at my age, after all these years of silent slumber, coming out with a tale that is as dried as a rush, a stranger to invention, paltry in style, impoverished in content, and wholly lacking in learning and wisdom, without marginal citations or notes at the end of the book when other works of this sort, even though they be fabulous and profane, are so packed with maxims from Aristotle and Plato and the whole crowd of philosophers as to fill the reader with admiration and lead him to regard the author as a well read, learned, and eloquent individual? Not to speak of the citations from Holy Writ! You would think they were at the very least so many St. Thomases[4] and other doctors of the Church; for they are so adroit at maintaining a solemn face that, having portrayed in one line a distracted lover, in the next they will give you a nice little Christian sermon that is a joy and a privilege to hear and read.

"All this my book will lack, for I have no citations for the margins, no notes for the end. To tell the truth, I do not even know who the authors are to whom I am indebted, and so am unable to follow the example of all the others by listing them alphabetically at the beginning, starting with Aristotle and closing with Xenophon, or, perhaps, with Zoilus or Zeuxis, notwithstanding the fact that the former was a snarling critic, the latter a painter. This work will also be found lacking in prefatory sonnets by dukes, marquises, counts, bishops, ladies, and poets of great renown; although if I were to ask two or three colleagues of mine, they would supply the deficiency by furnishing me with productions that could not be equaled by the authors of most repute in all Spain.

"In short, my friend," I went on, "I am resolved that Señor Don Quixote shall remain buried in the archives of La Mancha until Heaven shall provide him with someone to deck him out with all the ornaments that he lacks; for I find myself incapable of remedying the situation, being possessed of little learning or aptitude, and I am, moreover, extremely lazy when it comes to hunting up authors who will say for me what I am unable to say for myself. And if I am in

---

4. Thomas Aquinas (1225–1274), Italian philosopher and theologian, venerated by Roman Catholics as a "Doctor of the Church."

a state of suspense and my thoughts are woolgathering, you will find a sufficient explanation in what I have just told you."

Hearing this, my friend struck his forehead with the palm of his hand and burst into a loud laugh.

"In the name of God, brother," he said, "you have just deprived me of an illusion. I have known you for a long time, and I have always taken you to be clever and prudent in all your actions; but I now perceive that you are as far from all that as Heaven from the earth. How is it that things of so little moment and so easily remedied can worry and perplex a mind as mature as yours and ordinarily so well adapted to break down and trample underfoot far greater obstacles? I give you my word, this does not come from any lack of cleverness on your part, but rather from excessive indolence and a lack of experience. Do you ask for proof of what I say? Then pay attention closely and in the blink of an eye you shall see how I am going to solve all your difficulties and supply all those things the want of which, so you tell me, is keeping you in suspense, as a result of which you hesitate to publish the history of that famous Don Quixote of yours, the light and mirror of all knight-errantry."

"Tell me, then," I replied, "how you propose to go about curing my diffidence and bringing clarity out of the chaos and confusion of my mind?"

"Take that first matter," he continued, "of the sonnets, epigrams, or eulogies, which should bear the names of grave and titled personages: you can remedy that by taking a little trouble and composing the pieces yourself, and afterward you can baptize them with any name you see fit, fathering them on Prester John of the Indies or the Emperor of Trebizond, for I have heard tell that they were famous poets; and supposing they were not and that a few pedants and bachelors of arts should go around muttering behind your back that it is not so, you should not give so much as a pair of maravedis[5] for all their carping, since even though they make you out to be a liar, they are not going to cut off the hand that put these things on paper.

"As for marginal citations and authors in whom you may find maxims and sayings that you may put in your story, you have but to make use of those scraps of Latin that you know by heart or can look up without too much bother. Thus, when you come to treat of liberty and slavery, jot down:

Non bene pro toto libertas venditur auro.[6]

And then in the margin you will cite Horace or whoever it was that said it. If the subject is death, come up with:

Pallida mors aequo pulsat pede pauperum tabernas
Regumque turres.[7]

If it is friendship or the love that God commands us to show our enemies, then is the time to fall back on the Scriptures, which you can do by putting yourself out very little; you have but to quote the words of God himself:

---

5. Coin worth a thirty-fourth of a *real*; that is, even two *maravedíes* were worth very little. "Prester John": in medieval and early modern European folklore, the priest-monarch of a lost Christian kingdom in Asia or Africa. "Trebizond": successor state to the Byzantine Empire in modern-day Turkey; it flourished from the 13th to the 15th century.
6. Freedom is not bought by gold (Latin); from the anonymous *Aesopian Fables* 3.14.
7. Pale death knocks at the cottages of the poor and the palaces of kings with equal foot (Latin); from Horace, *Odes* 1.4.13–14.

Ego autem dico vobis: diligite inimicos vestros.[8]

If it is evil thoughts, lose no time in turning to the Gospels:

De corde exeunt cogitationes malae.[9]

If it is the instability of friends, here is Cato for you with a distich:

Donec eris felix multos numerabis amicos;
Tempora si fuerint nubila, solus eris.[1]

With these odds and ends of Latin and others of the same sort, you can cause yourself to be taken for a grammarian, although I must say that is no great honor or advantage these days.

"So far as notes at the end of the book are concerned, you may safely go about it in this manner: let us suppose that you mention some giant, Goliath let us say; with this one allusion which costs you little or nothing, you have a fine note which you may set down as follows: *The giant Golias or Goliath. This was a Philistine whom the shepherd David slew with a mighty cast from his slingshot in the valley of Terebinth, according to what we read in the Book of Kings,* chapter so-and-so where you find it written.[2]

"In addition to this, by way of showing that you are a learned humanist and a cosmographer, contrive to bring into your story the name of the River Tagus, and there you are with another great little note: *The River Tagus was so called after a king of Spain; it rises in such and such a place and empties into the ocean, washing the walls of the famous city of Lisbon; it is supposed to have golden sands,* etc. If it is robbers, I will let you have the story of Cacus,[3] which I know by heart. If it is loose women, there is the Bishop of Mondoñedo,[4] who will lend you Lamia, Laïs, and Flora, an allusion that will do you great credit. If the subject is cruelty, Ovid will supply you with Medea; or if it is enchantresses and witches, Homer has Calypso and Vergil Circe. If it is valorous captains, Julius Caesar will lend you himself, in his *Commentaries,* and Plutarch will furnish a thousand Alexanders. If it is loves, with the ounce or two of Tuscan that you know you may make the acquaintance of Leon the Hebrew,[5] who will satisfy you to your heart's content. And in case you do not care to go abroad, here in your own house you have Fonseca's *Of the Love of God,*[6] where you will encounter in condensed form all that the most imaginative person could wish upon this subject. The short of the matter is, you have but to allude to these names or touch upon those stories that I have mentioned and leave to me the business of the notes and citations; I will guarantee you enough to fill the margins and four whole sheets at the back.

"And now we come to the list of authors cited, such as other works contain but in which your own is lacking. Here again the remedy is an easy one; you

---

8. But I say unto you, love your enemies (Latin); Matthew 5.44.
9. For out of the heart proceed evil thoughts (Latin); Matthew 15.19.
1. As long as you are happy, you will count many friends, but if times become clouded, you will be alone (Latin); not from Cato but instead Ovid, *Sorrows* 1.9.5–6.
2. 1 Samuel 17.48–49.

3. Gigantic thief defeated by Hercules in Virgil's *Aeneid* 8.
4. Father Antonio de Guevara (c. 1481–1545).
5. Judah Leon Abravanel, known as León Hebreo (c. 1465–c. 1523), Neoplatonic author of the *Dialogues of Love* (1535).
6. Cristóbal de Fonseca, *Treatise of the Love of God* (1592).

have but to look up some book that has them all, from A to Z as you were saying, and transfer the entire list as it stands. What if the imposition is plain for all to see? You have little need to refer to them, and so it does not matter; and some may be so simple-minded as to believe that you have drawn upon them all in your simple unpretentious little story. If it serves no other purpose, this imposing list of authors will at least give your book an unlooked-for air of authority. What is more, no one is going to put himself to the trouble of verifying your references to see whether or not you have followed all these authors, since it will not be worth his pains to do so.

"This is especially true in view of the fact that your book stands in no need of all these things whose absence you lament; for the entire work is an attack upon the books of chivalry of which Aristotle never dreamed, of which St. Basil has nothing to say, and of which Cicero had no knowledge; nor do the fine points of truth or the observations of astrology have anything to do with its fanciful absurdities; geometrical measurements, likewise, and rhetorical argumentations serve for nothing here; you have no sermon to preach to anyone by mingling the human with the divine, a kind of motley in which no Christian intellect should be willing to clothe itself.

"All that you have to do is to make proper use of imitation in what you write, and the more perfect the imitation the better will your writing be. Inasmuch as you have no other object in view than that of overthrowing the authority and prestige which books of chivalry enjoy in the world at large and among the vulgar, there is no reason why you should go begging maxims of the philosophers, counsels of Holy Writ, fables of the poets, orations of the rhetoricians, or miracles of the saints; see to it, rather, that your style flows along smoothly, pleasingly, and sonorously, and that your words are the proper ones, meaningful and well placed, expressive of your intention in setting them down and of what you wish to say, without any intricacy or obscurity.

"Let it be your aim that, by reading your story, the melancholy may be moved to laughter and the cheerful man made merrier still; let the simple not be bored, but may the clever admire your originality; let the grave ones not despise you, but let the prudent praise you. And keep in mind, above all, your purpose, which is that of undermining the ill-founded edifice that is constituted by those books of chivalry, so abhorred by many but admired by many more; if you succeed in attaining it, you will have accomplished no little."

Listening in profound silence to what my friend had to say, I was so impressed by his reasoning that, with no thought of questioning them, I decided to make use of his arguments in composing this prologue. Here, gentle reader, you will perceive my friend's cleverness, my own good fortune in coming upon such a counselor at a time when I needed him so badly, and the profit which you yourselves are to have in finding so sincere and straightforward an account of the famous Don Quixote de la Mancha, who is held by the inhabitants of the Campo de Montiel region to have been the most chaste lover and the most valiant knight that had been seen in those parts for many a year. I have no desire to enlarge upon the service I am rendering you in bringing you the story of so notable and honored a gentleman; I merely would have you thank me for having made you acquainted with the famous Sancho Panza, his squire, in whom, to my mind, is to be found an epitome of all the squires and their drolleries scattered here and there throughout the pages of those vain and empty books of chivalry. And with this, may God give you health, and may He be not unmindful of me as well. VALE.[7]

["I Know Who I Am, and Who I May Be, If I Choose"]

CHAPTER I

Which treats of the station in life and the pursuits of the famous gentleman, Don Quixote de la Mancha.

In a village of La Mancha[1] the name of which I have no desire to recall, there lived not so long ago one of those gentlemen who always have a lance in the rack, an ancient buckler, a skinny nag, and a greyhound for the chase. A stew with more beef than mutton in it, chopped meat for his evening meal, scraps for a Saturday, lentils on Friday, and a young pigeon as a special delicacy for Sunday, went to account for three-quarters of his income. The rest of it he laid out on a broadcloth greatcoat and velvet stockings for feast days, with slippers to match, while the other days of the week he cut a figure in a suit of the finest homespun. Living with him were a housekeeper in her forties, a niece who was not yet twenty, and a lad of the field and marketplace who saddled his horse for him and wielded the pruning knife.

This gentleman of ours was close on to fifty, of a robust constitution but with little flesh on his bones and a face that was lean and gaunt. He was noted for his early rising, being very fond of the hunt. They will try to tell you that his surname was Quijada or Quesada—there is some difference of opinion among those who have written on the subject—but according to the most likely conjectures we are to understand that it was really Quejana. But all this means very little so far as our story is concerned, providing that in the telling of it we do not depart one iota from the truth.

You may know, then, that the aforesaid gentleman, on those occasions when he was at leisure, which was most of the year around, was in the habit of reading books of chivalry with such pleasure and devotion as to lead him almost wholly to forget the life of a hunter and even the administration of his estate. So great was his curiosity and infatuation in this regard that he even sold many acres of tillable land in order to be able to buy and read the books that he loved, and he would carry home with him as many of them as he could obtain.

Of all those that he thus devoured none pleased him so well as the ones that had been composed by the famous Feliciano de Silva,[2] whose lucid prose style and involved conceits were as precious to him as pearls; especially when he came to read those tales of love and amorous challenges that are to be met with in many places, such a passage as the following, for example: "The reason of the unreason that afflicts my reason, in such a manner weakens my reason that I with reason lament me of your comeliness." And he was similarly affected when his eyes fell upon such lines as these: ". . . the high Heaven of your divin-

---

7. Farewell (Latin).
1. Efforts at identifying the village have proved inconclusive. La Mancha is a region of central Spain south of the capital, Madrid.

2. Author of romances (16th century); the lines that follow are from his *Don Florisel de Niguea*.

ity divinely fortifies you with the stars and renders you deserving of that desert your greatness doth deserve."

The poor fellow used to lie awake nights in an effort to disentangle the meaning and make sense out of passages such as these, although Aristotle himself would not have been able to understand them, even if he had been resurrected for that sole purpose. He was not at ease in his mind over those wounds that Don Belianís[3] gave and received; for no matter how great the surgeons who treated him, the poor fellow must have been left with his face and his entire body covered with marks and scars. Nevertheless, he was grateful to the author for closing the book with the promise of an interminable adventure to come; many a time he was tempted to take up his pen and literally finish the tale as had been promised, and he undoubtedly would have done so, and would have succeeded at it very well, if his thoughts had not been constantly occupied with other things of greater moment.

He often talked it over with the village curate, who was a learned man, a graduate of Sigüenza,[4] and they would hold long discussions as to who had been the better knight, Palmerin of England or Amadis of Gaul; but Master Nicholas, the barber of the same village, was in the habit of saying that no one could come up to the Knight of Phoebus,[5] and that if anyone *could* compare with him it was Don Galaor, brother of Amadis of Gaul, for Galaor was ready for anything—he was none of your finical knights, who went around whimpering as his brother did, and in point of valor he did not lag behind him.

In short, our gentleman became so immersed in his reading that he spent whole nights from sundown to sunup and his days from dawn to dusk in poring over his books, until, finally, from so little sleeping and so much reading, his brain dried up and he went completely out of his mind. He had filled his imagination with everything that he had read, with enchantments, knightly encounters, battles, challenges, wounds, with tales of love and its torments, and all sorts of impossible things, and as a result had come to believe that all these fictitious happenings were true; they were more real to him than anything else in the world. He would remark that the Cid Ruy Díaz had been a very good knight, but there was no comparison between him and the Knight of the Flaming Sword, who with a single backward stroke had cut in half two fierce and monstrous giants. He preferred Bernardo del Carpio, who at Roncesvalles had slain Roland despite the charm the latter bore, availing himself of the stratagem which Hercules employed when he strangled Antaeus,[6] the son of Earth, in his arms.

He had much good to say for Morgante[7] who, though he belonged to the haughty, overbearing race of giants, was of an affable disposition and well brought up. But, above all, he cherished an admiration for Rinaldo of Montalbán,[8] espe-

---

3. The allusion is to a romance by Jerónimo Fernández.
4. Ironic, for Sigüenza was the seat of a minor and discredited university.
5. Or Knight of the Sun. Heroes of romances customarily adopted emblematic names and also changed them according to circumstances. "Palmerin . . . Amadis": each a hero of a very famous chivalric romance, as are those mentioned in the following paragraphs.
6. The mythological Antaeus was invulnerable as long as he maintained contact with his mother, Earth. Hercules killed him while hold-

ing him raised in his arms. "Charm": the magic gift of invulnerability.
7. In Pulci's *Morgante Maggiore* (1483), a comic-epic poem of the Italian Renaissance.
8. Roland's cousin in Boiardo's *Roland in Love* (*Orlando Innamorato*) and Ariosto's *Roland Mad* (*Orlando Furioso*), romantic and comic-epic poems of the Italian Renaissance. Roland (or Orlando) was a military leader under the Frankish king Charlemagne in the 8th century; in legend he became the hero of many popular romances.

cially as he beheld him sallying forth from his castle to rob all those that crossed his path, or when he thought of him overseas stealing the image of Mohammed which, so the story has it, was all of gold. And he would have liked very well to have had his fill of kicking that traitor Galalón,[9] a privilege for which he would have given his housekeeper with his niece thrown into the bargain.

At last, when his wits were gone beyond repair, he came to conceive the strangest idea that ever occurred to any madman in this world. It now appeared to him fitting and necessary, in order to win a greater amount of honor for himself and serve his country at the same time, to become a knight-errant and roam the world on horseback, in a suit of armor; he would go in quest of adventures, by way of putting into practice all that he had read in his books; he would right every manner of wrong, placing himself in situations of the great-est peril such as would redound to the eternal glory of his name. As a reward for his valor and the might of his arm, the poor fellow could already see himself crowned Emperor of Trebizond at the very least; and so, carried away by the strange pleasure that he found in such thoughts as these, he at once set about putting his plan into effect.

The first thing he did was to burnish up some old pieces of armor, left him by his great-grandfather, which for ages had lain in a corner, moldering and for-gotten. He polished and adjusted them as best he could, and then he noticed that one very important thing was lacking: there was no closed helmet, but only a morion, or visorless headpiece, with turned-up brim of the kind foot soldiers wore. His ingenuity, however, enabled him to remedy this, and he pro-ceeded to fashion out of cardboard a kind of half-helmet, which, when attached to the morion, gave the appearance of a whole one. True, when he went to see if it was strong enough to withstand a good slashing blow, he was somewhat disappointed; for when he drew his sword and gave it a couple of thrusts, he succeeded only in undoing a whole week's labor. The ease with which he had hewed it to bits disturbed him no little, and he decided to make it over. This time he placed a few strips of iron on the inside, and then, convinced that it was strong enough, refrained from putting it to any further test; instead, he adopted it then and there as the finest helmet ever made.

After this, he went out to have a look at his nag; and although the animal had more *cuartos*, or cracks, in its hoof than there are quarters in a real,[1] and more blemishes than Gonela's steed which *tantum pellis et ossa fuit*,[2] it nonetheless looked to its master like a far better horse than Alexander's Bucephalus or the Babieca of the Cid.[3] He spent all of four days in trying to think up a name for his mount; for—so he told himself—seeing that it belonged to so famous and worthy a knight, there was no reason why it should not have a name of equal renown. The kind of name he wanted was one that would at once indicate what the nag had been before it came to belong to a knight-errant and what its present status was; for it stood to reason that, when the master's worldly condition changed, his

---

9. Ganelón, the villain in the Charlemagne legend who betrayed the French at Ronces-valles.

1. A silver coin worth about $16 in today's US currency. "Cuarto": copper coin worth four *maravedíes*.

2. Was so much skin and bones (Latin, from Plautus, *Andalucia* 3.6). "Gonela": legendary fool in the 15th-century court of Ferrara.

3. The Chief (Spanish)—that is, Ruy Díaz, celebrated hero of *Poema del Cid* (12th century). "Bucephalus": the horse of Alexan-der the Great.

horse also ought to have a famous, high-sounding appellation, one suited to the new order of things and the new profession that it was to follow.

After he in his memory and imagination had made up, struck out, and discarded many names, now adding to and now subtracting from the list, he finally hit upon "Rocinante," a name that impressed him as being sonorous and at the same time indicative of what the steed had been when it was but a hack,[4] whereas now it was nothing other than the first and foremost of all the hacks in the world.

Having found a name for his horse that pleased his fancy, he then desired to do as much for himself, and this required another week, and by the end of that period he had made up his mind that he was henceforth to be known as Don Quixote, which, as has been stated, has led the authors of this veracious history to assume that his real name must undoubtedly have been Quijada, and not Quesada as others would have it. But remembering that the valiant Amadis was not content to call himself that and nothing more, but added the name of his kingdom and fatherland that he might make it famous also, and thus came to take the name Amadis of Gaul, so our good knight chose to add his place of origin and become "Don Quixote de la Mancha"; for by this means, as he saw it, he was making very plain his lineage and was conferring honor upon his country by taking its name as his own.

And so, having polished up his armor and made the morion over into a closed helmet, and having given himself and his horse a name, he naturally found but one thing lacking still: he must seek out a lady of whom he could become enamored; for a knight-errant without a ladylove was like a tree without leaves or fruit, a body without a soul.

"If," he said to himself, "as a punishment for my sins or by a stroke of fortune I should come upon some giant hereabouts, a thing that very commonly happens to knights-errant, and if I should slay him in a hand-to-hand encounter or perhaps cut him in two, or, finally, if I should vanquish and subdue him, would it not be well to have someone to whom I may send him as a present, in order that he, if he is living, may come in, fall upon his knees in front of my sweet lady, and say in a humble and submissive tone of voice, 'I, lady, am the giant Caraculiambro, lord of the island Malindrania, who has been overcome in single combat by that knight who never can be praised enough, Don Quixote de la Mancha, the same who sent me to present myself before your Grace that your Highness may dispose of me as you see fit'?"

Oh, how our good knight reveled in this speech, and more than ever when he came to think of the name that he should give his lady! As the story goes, there was a very good-looking farm girl who lived near by, with whom he had once been smitten, although it is generally believed that she never knew or suspected it. Her name was Aldonza Lorenzo, and it seemed to him that she was the one upon whom he should bestow the title of mistress of his thoughts. For her he wished a name that should not be incongruous with his own and that would convey the suggestion of a princess or a great lady; and, accordingly, he resolved to call her "Dulcinea del Toboso," she being a native of that place. A musical name to his ears, out of the ordinary and significant, like the others he had chosen for himself and his appurtenances.

---

4. In Spanish, *rocín*. The suffix *"ante"* is comically taken for *"antes"* (Spanish, before).

CHAPTER II

Which treats of the first sally that the ingenious Don Quixote made from his native heath.

Having, then, made all these preparations, he did not wish to lose any time in putting his plan into effect, for he could not but blame himself for what the world was losing by his delay, so many were the wrongs that were to be righted, the grievances to be redressed, the abuses to be done away with, and the duties to be performed. Accordingly, without informing anyone of his intention and without letting anyone see him, he set out one morning before daybreak on one of those very hot days in July. Donning all his armor, mounting Rocinante, adjusting his ill-contrived helmet, bracing his shield on his arm, and taking up his lance, he sallied forth by the back gate of his stable yard into the open countryside. It was with great contentment and joy that he saw how easily he had made a beginning toward the fulfillment of his desire.

No sooner was he out on the plain, however, than a terrible thought assailed him, one that all but caused him to abandon the enterprise he had undertaken. This occurred when he suddenly remembered that he had never formally been dubbed a knight, and so, in accordance with the law of knighthood, was not permitted to bear arms against one who had a right to that title. And even if he had been, as a novice knight he would have had to wear white armor, without any device on his shield, until he should have earned one by his exploits. These thoughts led him to waver in his purpose, but, madness prevailing over reason, he resolved to have himself knighted by the first person he met, as many others had done if what he had read in those books that he had at home was true. And so far as white armor was concerned, he would scour his own the first chance that offered until it shone whiter than any ermine. With this he became more tranquil and continued on his way, letting his horse take whatever path it chose, for he believed that therein lay the very essence of adventures.

And so we find our newly fledged adventurer jogging along and talking to himself. "Undoubtedly," he is saying, "in the days to come, when the true history of my famous deeds is published, the learned chronicler who records them, when he comes to describe my first sally so early in the morning, will put down something like this: 'No sooner had the rubicund Apollo spread over the face of the broad and spacious earth the gilded filaments of his beauteous locks, and no sooner had the little singing birds of painted plumage greeted with their sweet and mellifluous harmony the coming of the Dawn, who, leaving the soft couch of her jealous spouse, now showed herself to mortals at all the doors and balconies of the horizon that bounds La Mancha—no sooner had this happened than the famous knight, Don Quixote de la Mancha, forsaking his own downy bed and mounting his famous steed, Rocinante, fared forth and began riding over the ancient and famous Campo de Montiel.'"[5]

And this was the truth, for he was indeed riding over that stretch of plain.

"O happy age and happy century," he went on, "in which my famous exploits shall be published, exploits worthy of being engraved in bronze, sculptured in marble, and depicted in paintings for the benefit of posterity. O wise magician,

---

5. The scene of a battle in 1369.

whoever you be, to whom shall fall the task of chronicling this extraordinary history of mine! I beg of you not to forget my good Rocinante, eternal companion of my wayfarings and my wanderings."

Then, as though he really had been in love: "O Princess Dulcinea, lady of this captive heart! Much wrong have you done me in thus sending me forth with your reproaches and sternly commanding me not to appear in your beauteous presence. O lady, deign to be mindful of this your subject who endures so many woes for the love of you."

And so he went on, stringing together absurdities, all of a kind that his books had taught him, imitating insofar as he was able the language of their authors. He rode slowly, and the sun came up so swiftly and with so much heat that it would have been sufficient to melt his brains if he had had any. He had been on the road almost the entire day without anything happening that is worthy of being set down here; and he was on the verge of despair, for he wished to meet someone at once with whom he might try the valor of his good right arm. Certain authors say that his first adventure was that of Puerto Lápice, while others state that it was that of the windmills; but in this particular instance I am in a position to affirm what I have read in the annals of La Mancha; and that is to the effect that he went all that day until nightfall, when he and his hack found themselves tired to death and famished. Gazing all around him to see if he could discover some castle or shepherd's hut where he might take shelter and attend to his pressing needs, he caught sight of an inn not far off the road along which they were traveling, and this to him was like a star guiding him not merely to the gates, but rather, let us say, to the palace of redemption. Quickening his pace, he came up to it just as night was falling.

By chance there stood in the doorway two lasses of the sort known as "of the district"; they were on their way to Seville in the company of some mule drivers who were spending the night in the inn. Now, everything that this adventurer of ours thought, saw, or imagined seemed to him to be directly out of one of the storybooks he had read, and so, when he caught sight of the inn, it at once became a castle with its four turrets and its pinnacles of gleaming silver, not to speak of the drawbridge and moat and all the other things that are commonly supposed to go with a castle. As he rode up to it, he accordingly reined in Rocinante and sat there waiting for a dwarf to appear upon the battlements and blow his trumpet by way of announcing the arrival of a knight. The dwarf, however, was slow in coming, and as Rocinante was anxious to reach the stable, Don Quixote drew up to the door of the hostelry and surveyed the two merry maidens, who to him were a pair of beauteous damsels or gracious ladies taking their ease at the castle gate.

And then a swineherd came along, engaged in rounding up his drove of hogs—for, without any apology, that is what they were. He gave a blast on his horn to bring them together, and this at once became for Don Quixote just what he wished it to be: some dwarf who was heralding his coming; and so it was with a vast deal of satisfaction that he presented himself before the ladies in question, who, upon beholding a man in full armor like this, with lance and buckler, were filled with fright and made as if to flee indoors. Realizing that they were afraid, Don Quixote raised his pasteboard visor and revealed his withered, dust-covered face.

"Do not flee, your Ladyships," he said to them in a courteous manner and gentle voice. "You need not fear that any wrong will be done you, for it is not in accordance with the order of knighthood which I profess to wrong anyone, much less such highborn damsels as your appearance shows you to be."

The girls looked at him, endeavoring to scan his face, which was half hidden by his ill-made visor. Never having heard women of their profession called damsels before, they were unable to restrain their laughter, at which Don Quixote took offense.

"Modesty," he observed, "well becomes those with the dower of beauty, and, moreover, laughter that has not good cause is a very foolish thing. But I do not say this to be discourteous or to hurt your feelings; my only desire is to serve you."

The ladies did not understand what he was talking about, but felt more than ever like laughing at our knight's unprepossessing figure. This increased his annoyance, and there is no telling what would have happened if at that moment the innkeeper had not come out. He was very fat and very peaceably inclined; but upon sighting this grotesque personage clad in bits of armor that were quite as oddly matched as were his bridle, lance, buckler, and corselet, mine host was not at all indisposed to join the lasses in their merriment. He was suspicious, however, of all this paraphernalia and decided that it would be better to keep a civil tongue in his head.

"If, Sir Knight," he said, "your Grace desires a lodging, aside from a bed—for there is none to be had in this inn—you will find all else that you may want in great abundance."

When Don Quixote saw how humble the governor of the castle was—for he took the innkeeper and his inn to be no less than that—he replied, "For me, Sir Castellan,[6] anything will do, since

> *Arms are my only ornament,*
> *My only rest the fight,* etc."

The landlord thought that the knight had called him a castellan because he took him for one of those worthies of Castile, whereas the truth was, he was an Andalusian from the beach of Sanlúcar, no less a thief than Cacus[7] himself, and as full of tricks as a student or a page boy.

"In that case," he said,

> *"Your bed will be the solid rock,*
> *Your sleep: to watch all night.*

This being so, you may be assured of finding beneath this roof enough to keep you awake for a whole year, to say nothing of a single night."

With this, he went up to hold the stirrup for Don Quixote, who encountered much difficulty in dismounting, not having broken his fast all day long. The knight then directed his host to take good care of the steed, as it was the best piece of horseflesh in all the world. The innkeeper looked it over, and it did not impress him as being half as good as Don Quixote had said it was. Having stabled the animal, he came back to see what his guest would have and found the latter being relieved of his armor by the damsels, who by now had made their peace

---

6. The Spanish *castellano* means both "castellan" and "Castilian" (i.e., a native of Castile, or, more generally, of Spain).

7. In Roman mythology, Cacus stole some of Hercules' cattle, concealing the theft by having them walk backward into his cave; he was finally discovered and slain.

with the new arrival. They had already removed his breastplate and backpiece but had no idea how they were going to open his gorget or get his improvised helmet off. That piece of armor had been tied on with green ribbons which it would be necessary to cut, since the knots could not be undone, but he would not hear of this, and so spent all the rest of that night with his headpiece in place, which gave him the weirdest, most laughable appearance that could be imagined.

Don Quixote fancied that these wenches who were assisting him must surely be the chatelaine and other ladies of the castle, and so proceeded to address them very gracefully and with much wit:

> "Never was knight so served
> By any noble dame
> As was Don Quixote
> When from his village he came,
> With damsels to wait on his every need
> While princesses cared for his hack . . .

"By hack," he explained, "is meant my steed Rocinante, for that is his name, and mine is Don Quixote de la Mancha. I had no intention of revealing my identity until my exploits done in your service should have made me known to you; but the necessity of adapting to present circumstances that old ballad of Lancelot has led to your becoming acquainted with it prematurely. However, the time will come when your Ladyships shall command and I will obey and with the valor of my good right arm show you how eager I am to serve you."

The young women were not used to listening to speeches like this and had not a word to say, but merely asked him if he desired to eat anything.

"I could eat a bite of something, yes," replied Don Quixote. "Indeed, I feel that a little food would go very nicely just now."

He thereupon learned that, since it was Friday, there was nothing to be had in all the inn except a few portions of codfish, which in Castile is called *abadejo*, in Andalusia *bacalao*, in some places *curadillo*, and elsewhere *truchuella* or small trout. Would his Grace, then, have some small trout, seeing that was all there was that they could offer him?

"If there are enough of them," said Don Quixote, "they will take the place of a trout, for it is all one to me whether I am given in change eight reales or one piece of eight. What is more, those small trout may be like veal, which is better than beef, or like kid, which is better than goat. But however that may be, bring them on at once, for the weight and burden of arms is not to be borne without inner sustenance."

Placing the table at the door of the hostelry, in the open air, they brought the guest a portion of badly soaked and worse cooked codfish and a piece of bread as black and moldy as the suit of armor that he wore. It was a mirth-provoking sight to see him eat, for he still had his helmet on with his visor fastened, which made it impossible for him to put anything into his mouth with his hands, and so it was necessary for one of the girls to feed him. As for giving him anything to drink, that would have been out of the question if the inn-keeper had not hollowed out a reed, placing one end in Don Quixote's mouth while through the other end he poured the wine. All this the knight bore very patiently rather than have them cut the ribbons of his helmet.

At this point a gelder of pigs approached the inn, announcing his arrival with four or five blasts on his horn, all of which confirmed Don Quixote in the belief that this was indeed a famous castle, for what was this if not music that they were playing for him? The fish was trout, the bread was of the finest, the wenches were ladies, and the innkeeper was the castellan. He was convinced that he had been right in his resolve to sally forth and roam the world at large, but there was one thing that still distressed him greatly, and that was the fact that he had not as yet been dubbed a knight; as he saw it, he could not legitimately engage in any adventure until he had received the order of knighthood.

CHAPTER III

Of the amusing manner in which Don Quixote had himself dubbed a knight.

Wearied of his thoughts, Don Quixote lost no time over the scanty repast which the inn afforded him. When he had finished, he summoned the landlord and, taking him out to the stable, closed the doors and fell on his knees in front of him.

"Never, valiant knight," he said, "shall I arise from here until you have courteously granted me the boon I seek, one which will redound to your praise and to the good of the human race."

Seeing his guest at his feet and hearing him utter such words as these, the innkeeper could only stare at him in bewilderment, not knowing what to say or do. It was in vain that he entreated him to rise, for Don Quixote refused to do so until his request had been granted.

"I expected nothing less of your great magnificence, my lord," the latter then continued, "and so I may tell you that the boon I asked and which you have so generously conceded me is that tomorrow morning you dub me a knight. Until that time, in the chapel of this your castle, I will watch over my armor, and when morning comes, as I have said, that which I so desire shall then be done, in order that I may lawfully go to the four corners of the earth in quest of adventures and to succor the needy, which is the chivalrous duty of all knights-errant such as I who long to engage in deeds of high emprise."

The innkeeper, as we have said, was a sharp fellow. He already had a suspicion that his guest was not quite right in the head, and he was now convinced of it as he listened to such remarks as these. However, just for the sport of it, he determined to humor him; and so he went on to assure Don Quixote that he was fully justified in his request and that such a desire and purpose was only natural on the part of so distinguished a knight as his gallant bearing plainly showed him to be.

He himself, the landlord added, when he was a young man, had followed the same honorable calling. He had gone through various parts of the world seeking adventures, among the places he had visited being the Percheles of Málaga, the Isles of Riarán, the District of Seville, the Little Market Place of Segovia, the Olivera of Valencia, the Rondilla of Granada, the beach of Sanlúcar, the Horse Fountain of Cordova, the Small Taverns of Toledo,[8] and numerous other

---

8. All reputed to be haunts of robbers and rogues.

localities where his nimble feet and light fingers had found much exercise. He had done many wrongs, cheated many widows, ruined many maidens, and swindled not a few minors until he had finally come to be known in almost all the courts and tribunals that are to be found in the whole of Spain.

At last he had retired to his castle here, where he lived upon his own income and the property of others; and here it was that he received all knights-errant of whatever quality and condition, simply out of the great affection that he bore them and that they might share with him their possessions in payment of his good will. Unfortunately, in this castle there was no chapel where Don Quixote might keep watch over his arms, for the old chapel had been torn down to make way for a new one; but in case of necessity, he felt quite sure that such a vigil could be maintained anywhere, and for the present occasion the courtyard of the castle would do; and then in the morning, please God, the requisite ceremony could be performed and his guest be duly dubbed a knight, as much a knight as anyone ever was.

He then inquired if Don Quixote had any money on his person, and the latter replied that he had not a cent, for in all the storybooks he had never read of knights-errant carrying any. But the innkeeper told him he was mistaken on this point: supposing the authors of those stories had not set down the fact in black and white, that was because they did not deem it necessary to speak of things as indispensable as money and a clean shirt, and one was not to assume for that reason that those knights-errant of whom the books were so full did not have any. He looked upon it as an absolute certainty that they all had well-stuffed purses, that they might be prepared for any emergency; and they also carried shirts and a little box of ointment for healing the wounds that they received.

For when they had been wounded in combat on the plains and in desert places, there was not always someone at hand to treat them, unless they had some skilled enchanter for a friend who then would succor them, bringing to them through the air, upon a cloud, some damsel or dwarf bearing a vial of water of such virtue that one had but to taste a drop of it and at once his wounds were healed and he was as sound as if he had never received any.

But even if this was not the case, knights in times past saw to it that their squires were well provided with money and other necessities, such as lint and ointment for healing purposes; and if they had no squires—which happened very rarely—they themselves carried these objects in a pair of saddlebags very cleverly attached to their horses' croups in such a manner as to be scarcely noticeable, as if they held something of greater importance than that, for among the knights-errant saddlebags as a rule were not favored. Accordingly, he would advise the novice before him, and inasmuch as the latter was soon to be his godson, he might even command him, that henceforth he should not go without money and a supply of those things that have been mentioned, as he would find that they came in useful at a time when he least expected it.

Don Quixote promised to follow his host's advice punctiliously; and so it was arranged that he should watch his armor in a large barnyard at one side of the inn. He gathered up all the pieces, placed them in a horse trough that stood near the well, and, bracing his shield on his arm, took up his lance and with stately demeanor began pacing up and down in front of the trough even as night was closing in.

The innkeeper informed his other guests of what was going on, of Don Quixote's vigil and his expectation of being dubbed a knight; and, marveling greatly at so extraordinary a variety of madness, they all went out to see for themselves and stood there watching from a distance. For a while the knight-to-be, with tranquil mien, would merely walk up and down; then, leaning on his lance, he would pause to survey his armor, gazing fixedly at it for a considerable length of time. As has been said, it was night now, but the brightness of the moon, which well might rival that of Him who lent it, was such that everything the novice knight did was plainly visible to all.

At this point one of the mule drivers who were stopping at the inn came out to water his drove, and in order to do this it was necessary to remove the armor from the trough.

As he saw the man approaching, Don Quixote cried out to him, "O bold knight, whoever you may be, who thus would dare to lay hands upon the accouterments of the most valiant man of arms that ever girded on a sword, look well what you do and desist if you do not wish to pay with your life for your insolence!"

The muleteer gave no heed to these words—it would have been better for his own sake had he done so—but, taking it up by the straps, tossed the armor some distance from him. When he beheld this, Don Quixote rolled his eyes heavenward and with his thoughts apparently upon his Dulcinea exclaimed, "Succor, O lady mine, this vassal heart in this my first encounter; let not your favor and protection fail me in the peril in which for the first time I now find myself."

With these and other similar words, he loosed his buckler, grasped his lance in both his hands, and let the mule driver have such a blow on the head that the man fell to the ground stunned; and had it been followed by another one, he would have had no need of a surgeon to treat him. Having done this, Don Quixote gathered up his armor and resumed his pacing up and down with the same calm manner as before. Not long afterward, without knowing what had happened—for the first muleteer was still lying there unconscious—another came out with the same intention of watering his mules, and he too was about to remove the armor from the trough when the knight, without saying a word or asking favor of anyone, once more adjusted his buckler and raised his lance, and if he did not break the second mule driver's head to bits, he made more than three pieces of it by dividing it into quarters. At the sound of the fracas everybody in the inn came running out, among them the innkeeper; whereupon Don Quixote again lifted his buckler and laid his hand on his sword.

"O lady of beauty," he said, "strength and vigor of this fainting heart of mine! Now is the time to turn the eyes of your greatness upon this captive knight of yours who must face so formidable an adventure."

By this time he had worked himself up to such a pitch of anger that if all the mule drivers in the world had attacked him he would not have taken one step backward. The comrades of the wounded men, seeing the plight those two were in, now began showering stones on Don Quixote, who shielded himself as best he could with his buckler, although he did not dare stir from the trough for fear of leaving his armor unprotected. The landlord, meanwhile, kept calling to them to stop, for he had told them that this was a madman who would be sure to go free even though he killed them all. The knight was shouting louder than ever, calling them knaves and traitors. As for the lord of the castle, who allowed knights-errant to be treated in this fashion, he was a lowborn villain, and if he,

Don Quixote, had but received the order of knighthood, he would make him pay for his treachery.

"As for you others, vile and filthy rabble, I take no account of you; you may stone me or come forward and attack me all you like; you shall see what the reward of your folly and insolence will be."

He spoke so vigorously and was so undaunted in bearing as to strike terror in those who would assail him; and for this reason, and owing also to the persuasions of the innkeeper, they ceased stoning him. He then permitted them to carry away the wounded, and went back to watching his armor with the same tranquil, unconcerned air that he had previously displayed.

The landlord was none too well pleased with these mad pranks on the part of his guest and determined to confer upon him that accursed order of knighthood before something else happened. Going up to him, he begged Don Quixote's pardon for the insolence which, without his knowledge, had been shown the knight by those of low degree. They, however, had been well punished for their impudence. As he had said, there was no chapel in this castle, but for that which remained to be done there was no need of any. According to what he had read of the ceremonial of the order, there was nothing to this business of being dubbed a knight except a slap on the neck and one across the shoulder, and that could be performed in the middle of a field as well as anywhere else. All that was required was for the knight-to-be to keep watch over his armor for a couple of hours, and Don Quixote had been at it more than four. The latter believed all this and announced that he was ready to obey and get the matter over with as speedily as possible. Once dubbed a knight, if he were attacked one more time, he did not think that he would leave a single person in the castle alive, save such as he might command be spared, at the bidding of his host and out of respect to him.

Thus warned, and fearful that it might occur, the castellan brought out the book in which he had jotted down the hay and barley for which the mule drivers owed him, and, accompanied by a lad bearing the butt of a candle and the two aforesaid damsels, he came up to where Don Quixote stood and commanded him to kneel. Reading from the account book—as if he had been saying a prayer—he raised his hand and, with the knight's own sword, gave him a good thwack upon the neck and another lusty one upon the shoulder, muttering all the while between his teeth. He then directed one of the ladies to gird on Don Quixote's sword, which she did with much gravity and composure; for it was all they could do to keep from laughing at every point of the ceremony, but the thought of the knight's prowess which they had already witnessed was sufficient to restrain their mirth.

"May God give your Grace much good fortune," said the worthy lady as she attached the blade, "and prosper you in battle."

Don Quixote thereupon inquired her name, for he desired to know to whom it was he was indebted for the favor he had just received, that he might share with her some of the honor which his strong right arm was sure to bring him. She replied very humbly that her name was Tolosa and that she was the daughter of a shoemaker, a native of Toledo who lived in the stalls of Sancho Bienaya.[9] To this the knight replied that she would do him a very great favor if

9. An old square in Toledo.

from then on she would call herself Doña Tolosa, and she promised to do so. The other girl then helped him on with his spurs, and practically the same conversation was repeated. When asked her name, she stated that it was La Molinera and added that she was the daughter of a respectable miller of Antequera. Don Quixote likewise requested her to assume the "don" and become Doña Molinera and offered to render her further services and favors.

These unheard-of ceremonies having been dispatched in great haste, Don Quixote could scarcely wait to be astride his horse and sally forth on his quest for adventures. Saddling and mounting Rocinante, he embraced his host, thanking him for the favor of having dubbed him a knight and saying such strange things that it would be quite impossible to record them here. The innkeeper, who was only too glad to be rid of him, answered with a speech that was no less flowery, though somewhat shorter, and he did not so much as ask him for the price of a lodging, so glad was he to see him go.

CHAPTER IV

Of what happened to our knight when he sallied forth from the inn.

Day was dawning when Don Quixote left the inn, so well satisfied with himself, so gay, so exhilarated, that the very girths of his steed all but burst with joy. But remembering the advice which his host had given him concerning the stock of necessary provisions that he should carry with him, especially money and shirts, he decided to turn back home and supply himself with whatever he needed, and with a squire as well; he had in mind a farmer who was a neighbor of his, a poor man and the father of a family but very well suited to fulfill the duties of squire to a man of arms. With this thought in mind he guided Rocinante toward the village once more, and that animal, realizing that he was homeward bound, began stepping out at so lively a gait that it seemed as if his feet barely touched the ground.

The knight had not gone far when from a hedge on his right hand he heard the sound of faint moans as of someone in distress.

"Thanks be to Heaven," he at once exclaimed, "for the favor it has shown me by providing me so soon with an opportunity to fulfill the obligations that I owe to my profession, a chance to pluck the fruit of my worthy desires. Those, undoubtedly, are the cries of someone in distress, who stands in need of my favor and assistance."

Turning Rocinante's head, he rode back to the place from which the cries appeared to be coming. Entering the wood, he had gone but a few paces when he saw a mare attached to an oak, while bound to another tree was a lad of fifteen or thereabouts, naked from the waist up. It was he who was uttering the cries, and not without reason, for there in front of him was a lusty farmer with a girdle who was giving him many lashes, each one accompanied by a reproof and a command, "Hold your tongue and keep your eyes open"; and the lad was saying, "I won't do it again, sir; by God's Passion, I won't do it again. I promise you that after this I'll take better care of the flock."

When he saw what was going on, Don Quixote was very angry. "Discourteous knight," he said, "it ill becomes you to strike one who is powerless to defend himself. Mount your steed and take your lance in hand"—for there was a lance leaning against the oak to which the mare was tied—"and I will show you what a coward you are."

The farmer, seeing before him this figure all clad in armor and brandishing a lance, decided that he was as good as done for. "Sir Knight," he said, speaking very mildly, "this lad that I am punishing here is my servant; he tends a flock of sheep which I have in these parts and he is so careless that every day one of them shows up missing. And when I punish him for his carelessness or his roguery, he says it is just because I am a miser and do not want to pay him the wages that I owe him, but I swear to God and upon my soul that he lies."

"It is you who lie, base lout," said Don Quixote, "and in my presence; and by the sun that gives us light, I am minded to run you through with this lance. Pay him and say no more about it, or else, by the God who rules us, I will make an end of you and annihilate you here and now. Release him at once."

The farmer hung his head and without a word untied his servant. Don Quixote then asked the boy how much his master owed him. For nine months' work, the lad told him, at seven reales the month. The knight did a little reckoning and found that this came to sixty-three reales; whereupon he ordered the farmer to pay over the money immediately, as he valued his life. The cowardly bumpkin replied that, facing death as he was and by the oath that he had sworn—he had not sworn any oath as yet—it did not amount to as much as that; for there were three pairs of shoes which he had given the lad that were to be deducted and taken into account, and a real for two blood-lettings when his servant was ill.

"That," said Don Quixote, "is all very well; but let the shoes and the blood-lettings go for the undeserved lashes which you have given him; if he has worn out the leather of the shoes that you paid for, you have taken the hide off his body, and if the barber let a little blood for him when he was sick,[1] you have done the same when he was well; and so far as that goes, he owes you nothing."

"But the trouble is, Sir Knight, that I have no money with me. Come along home with me, Andrés, and I will pay you real for real."

"I go home with him!" cried the lad. "Never in the world! No, sir, I would not even think of it; for once he has me alone he'll flay me like a St. Bartholomew."

"He will do nothing of the sort," said Don Quixote. "It is sufficient for me to command, and he out of respect will obey. Since he has sworn to me by the order of knighthood which he has received, I shall let him go free and I will guarantee that you will be paid."

"But look, your Grace," the lad remonstrated, "my master is no knight; he has never received any order of knighthood whatsoever. He is Juan Haldudo, a rich man and a resident of Quintanar."

"That makes little difference," declared Don Quixote, "for there may well be knights among the Haldudos, all the more so in view of the fact that every man is the son of his works."

"That is true enough," said Andrés, "but this master of mine—of what works is he the son, seeing that he refuses me the pay for my sweat and labor?"

"I do not refuse you, brother Andrés," said the farmer. "Do me the favor of coming with me, and I swear to you by all the orders of knighthood that there are in this world to pay you, as I have said, real for real, and perfumed at that."

---

1. Barbers were also surgeons.

"You can dispense with the perfume," said Don Quixote; "just give him the reales and I shall be satisfied. And see to it that you keep your oath, or by the one that I myself have sworn I shall return to seek you out and chastise you, and I shall find you though you be as well hidden as a lizard. In case you would like to know who it is that is giving you this command in order that you may feel the more obliged to comply with it, I may tell you that I am the valorous Don Quixote de la Mancha, righter of wrongs and injustices; and so, God be with you, and do not fail to do as you have promised, under that penalty that I have pronounced."

As he said this, he put spurs to Rocinante and was off. The farmer watched him go, and when he saw that Don Quixote was out of the wood and out of sight, he turned to his servant, Andrés.

"Come here, my son," he said. "I want to pay you what I owe you as that righter of wrongs has commanded me."

"Take my word for it," replied Andrés, "your Grace would do well to observe the command of that good knight—may he live a thousand years; for as he is valorous and a righteous judge, if you don't pay me then, by Roque,[2] he will come back and do just what he said!"

"And I will give you my word as well," said the farmer; "but seeing that I am so fond of you, I wish to increase the debt, that I may owe you all the more." And with this he seized the lad's arm and bound him to the tree again and flogged him within an inch of his life. "There, Master Andrés, you may call on that righter of wrongs if you like and you will see whether or not he rights this one. I do not think I have quite finished with you yet, for I have a good mind to flay you alive as you feared."

Finally, however, he unbound him and told him he might go look for that judge of his to carry out the sentence that had been pronounced. Andrés left, rather down in the mouth, swearing that he would indeed go look for the brave Don Quixote de la Mancha; he would relate to him everything that had happened, point by point, and the farmer would have to pay for it seven times over. But for all that, he went away weeping, and his master stood laughing at him.

Such was the manner in which the valorous knight righted this particular wrong. Don Quixote was quite content with the way everything had turned out; it seemed to him that he had made a very fortunate and noble beginning with his deeds of chivalry, and he was very well satisfied with himself as he jogged along in the direction of his native village, talking to himself in a low voice all the while.

"Well may'st thou call thyself fortunate today, above all other women on earth, O fairest of the fair, Dulcinea del Toboso! Seeing that it has fallen to thy lot to hold subject and submissive to thine every wish and pleasure so valiant and renowned a knight as Don Quixote de la Mancha is and shall be, who, as everyone knows, yesterday received the order of knighthood and this day has righted the greatest wrong and grievance that injustice ever conceived or cruelty ever perpetrated, by snatching the lash from the hand of the merciless foeman who was so unreasonably flogging that tender child."

At this point he came to a road that forked off in four directions, and at once he thought of those crossroads where knights-errant would pause to consider which path they should take. By way of imitating them, he halted there for a while; and when he had given the subject much thought, he slackened Rocinante's rein and

2. The origin of this oath is unknown.

let the hack follow its inclination. The animal's first impulse was to make straight for its own stable. After they had gone a couple of miles or so Don Quixote caught sight of what appeared to be a great throng of people, who, as was afterward learned, were certain merchants of Toledo on their way to purchase silk at Murcia. There were six of them altogether with their sunshades, accompanied by four attendants on horseback and three mule drivers on foot.

No sooner had he sighted them than Don Quixote imagined that he was on the brink of some fresh adventure. He was eager to imitate those passages at arms of which he had read in his books, and here, so it seemed to him, was one made to order. And so, with bold and knightly bearing, he settled himself firmly in the stirrups, couched his lance, covered himself with his shield, and took up a position in the middle of the road, where he paused to wait for those other knights-errant (for such he took them to be) to come up to him. When they were near enough to see and hear plainly, Don Quixote raised his voice and made a haughty gesture.

"Let everyone," he cried, "stand where he is, unless everyone will confess that there is not in all the world a more beauteous damsel than the Empress of La Mancha, the peerless Dulcinea del Toboso."

Upon hearing these words and beholding the weird figure who uttered them, the merchants stopped short. From the knight's appearance and his speech they knew at once that they had to deal with a madman; but they were curious to know what was meant by that confession that was demanded of them, and one of their number who was somewhat of a jester and a very clever fellow raised his voice.

"Sir Knight," he said, "we do not know who this beauteous lady is of whom you speak. Show her to us, and if she is as beautiful as you say, then we will right willingly and without any compulsion confess the truth as you have asked of us."

"If I were to show her to you," replied Don Quixote, "what merit would there be in your confessing a truth so self-evident? The important thing is for you, without seeing her, to believe, confess, affirm, swear, and defend that truth. Otherwise, monstrous and arrogant creatures that you are, you shall do battle with me. Come on, then, one by one, as the order of knighthood prescribes; or all of you together, if you will have it so, as is the sorry custom with those of your breed. Come on, and I will await you here, for I am confident that my cause is just."

"Sir Knight," responded the merchant, "I beg your Grace, in the name of all the princes here present, in order that we may not have upon our consciences the burden of confessing a thing which we have never seen nor heard, and one, moreover, so prejudicial to the empresses and queens of Alcarria and Estremadura,[3] that your Grace will show us some portrait of this lady, even though it be no larger than a grain of wheat, for by the thread one comes to the ball of yarn; and with this we shall remain satisfied and assured, and your Grace will likewise be content and satisfied. The truth is, I believe that we are already so much of your way of thinking that though it should show her to be blind of one eye and distilling vermilion and brimstone from the other, nevertheless, to please your Grace, we would say in her behalf all that you desire."

"She distills nothing of the sort, infamous rabble!" shouted Don Quixote, for his wrath was kindling now. "I tell you, she does not distill what you say at all,

---

3. Ironic, because both were known as particularly backward regions.

but amber and civet[4] wrapped in cotton; and she is neither one-eyed nor hunch-backed but straighter than a spindle that comes from Guadarrama. You shall pay for the great blasphemy which you have uttered against such a beauty as is my lady!"

Saying this, he came on with lowered lance against the one who had spoken, charging with such wrath and fury that if fortune had not caused Rocinante to stumble and fall in mid-career, things would have gone badly with the merchant and he would have paid for his insolent gibe. As it was, Don Quixote went rolling over the plain for some little distance, and when he tried to get to his feet, found that he was unable to do so, being too encumbered with his lance, shield, spurs, helmet, and the weight of that ancient suit of armor.

"Do not flee, cowardly ones," he cried even as he struggled to rise. "Stay, cravens, for it is not my fault but that of my steed that I am stretched out here."

One of the muleteers, who must have been an ill-natured lad, upon hearing the poor fallen knight speak so arrogantly, could not refrain from giving him an answer in the ribs. Going up to him, he took the knight's lance and broke it into bits, and then with a companion proceeded to belabor him so mercilessly that in spite of his armor they milled him like a hopper[5] of wheat. The merchants called to them not to lay on so hard, saying that was enough and they should desist, but the mule driver by this time had warmed up to the sport and would not stop until he had vented his wrath, and, snatching up the broken pieces of the lance, he began hurling them at the wretched victim as he lay there on the ground. And through all this tempest of sticks that rained upon him Don Quixote never once closed his mouth nor ceased threatening Heaven and earth and these ruffians, for such he took them to be, who were thus mishandling him.

Finally the lad grew tired, and the merchants went their way with a good story to tell about the poor fellow who had had such a cudgeling. Finding himself alone, the knight endeavored to see if he could rise; but if this was a feat that he could not accomplish when he was sound and whole, how was he to achieve it when he had been thrashed and pounded to a pulp? Yet nonetheless he considered himself fortunate; for as he saw it, misfortunes such as this were common to knights-errant, and he put all the blame upon his horse; and if he was unable to rise, that was because his body was so bruised and battered all over.

CHAPTER V

In which is continued the narrative of the misfortune that befell our knight.

Seeing, then, that he was indeed unable to stir, he decided to fall back upon a favorite remedy of his, which was to think of some passage or other in his books; and as it happened, the one that he in his madness now recalled was the story of Baldwin and the Marquis of Mantua, when Carloto left the former wounded upon the mountainside,[6] a tale that is known to children, not unknown to young men, celebrated and believed in by the old, and, for all of that, not any truer than the miracles of Mohammed. Moreover, it impressed

---

4. A musky substance used in perfume, imported from Africa in cotton packings.
5. Funnel-shaped container for grain.

6. The allusion is to an old ballad about Charlemagne's son Charlot (Carloto) wounding Baldwin, nephew of the Marquis of Mantua.

him as being especially suited to the straits in which he found himself; and, accordingly, with a great show of feeling, he began rolling and tossing on the ground as he feebly gasped out the lines which the wounded knight of the wood is supposed to have uttered:

> *"Where art thou, lady mine,*
> *That thou dost not grieve for my woe?*
> *Either thou art disloyal,*
> *Or my grief thou dost not know."*

He went on reciting the old ballad until he came to the following verses:

> *"O noble Marquis of Mantua,*
> *My uncle and liege lord true!"*

He had reached this point when down the road came a farmer of the same village, a neighbor of his, who had been to the mill with a load of wheat. Seeing a man lying there stretched out like that, he went up to him and inquired who he was and what was the trouble that caused him to utter such mournful complaints. Thinking that this must undoubtedly be his uncle, the Marquis of Mantua, Don Quixote did not answer but went on with his recitation of the ballad, giving an account of the Marquis' misfortunes and the amours of his wife and the emperor's son, exactly as the ballad has it.

The farmer was astounded at hearing all these absurdities, and after removing the knight's visor which had been battered to pieces by the blows it had received, the good man bathed the victim's face, only to discover, once the dust was off, that he knew him very well.

"Señor Quijana," he said (for such must have been Don Quixote's real name when he was in his right senses and before he had given up the life of a quiet country gentleman to become a knight-errant), "who is responsible for your Grace's being in such a plight as this?"

But the knight merely went on with his ballad in response to all the questions asked of him. Perceiving that it was impossible to obtain any information from him, the farmer as best he could relieved him of his breastplate and backpiece to see if he had any wounds, but there was no blood and no mark of any sort. He then tried to lift him from the ground, and with a great deal of effort finally managed to get him astride the ass, which appeared to be the easier mount for him. Gathering up the armor, including even the splinters from the lance, he made a bundle and tied it on Rocinante's back, and, taking the horse by the reins and the ass by the halter, he started out for the village. He was worried in his mind at hearing all the foolish things that Don Quixote said, and that individual himself was far from being at ease. Unable by reason of his bruises and his soreness to sit upright on the donkey, our knight-errant kept sighing to Heaven, which led the farmer to ask him once more what it was that ailed him.

It must have been the devil himself who caused him to remember those tales that seemed to fit his own case; for at this point he forgot all about Baldwin and recalled Abindarráez, and how the governor of Antequera, Rodrigo de Narváez, had taken him prisoner and carried him off captive to his castle. Accordingly, when the countryman turned to inquire how he was and what was troubling him, Don Quixote replied with the very same words and phrases that the captive Abindarráez used in answering Rodrigo, just as he had read in the story *Diana* of Jorge de Montemayor,[7] where it is all written down, applying them very aptly to the present circumstances as the farmer went along cursing his luck for having to listen to such a lot of nonsense. Realizing that his neighbor was quite mad, he made haste to reach the village that he might not have to be annoyed any longer by Don Quixote's tiresome harangue.

"Señor Don Rodrigo de Narváez," the knight was saying, "I may inform your Grace that this beautiful Jarifa of whom I speak is not the lovely Dulcinea del Toboso, in whose behalf I have done, am doing, and shall do the most famous deeds of chivalry that ever have been or will be seen in all the world."

"But, sir," replied the farmer, "sinner that I am, cannot your Grace see that I am not Don Rodrigo de Narváez nor the Marquis of Mantua, but Pedro Alonso, your neighbor? And your Grace is neither Baldwin nor Abindarráez but a respectable gentleman by the name of Señor Quijana."

"I know who I am," said Don Quixote, "and who I may be, if I choose: not only those I have mentioned but all the Twelve Peers of France and the Nine Worthies[8] as well; for the exploits of all of them together, or separately, cannot compare with mine."

With such talk as this they reached their destination just as night was falling; but the farmer decided to wait until it was a little darker in order that the badly battered gentleman might not be seen arriving in such a condition and mounted on an ass. When he thought the proper time had come, they entered the village and proceeded to Don Quixote's house, where they found everything in confusion. The curate and the barber were there, for they were great friends of the knight, and the housekeeper was speaking to them.

"Señor Licentiate Pero Pérez," she was saying, for that was the manner in which she addressed the curate, "what does your Grace think could have happened to my master? Three days now, and not a word of him, nor the hack, nor the buckler, nor the lance, nor the suit of armor. Ah, poor me! I am as certain as I am that I was born to die that it is those cursed books of chivalry he is always reading that have turned his head; for now that I recall, I have often heard him muttering to himself that he must become a knight-errant and go through the world in search of adventures. May such books as those be consigned to Satan and Barabbas,[9] for they have sent to perdition the finest mind in all La Mancha."

The niece was of the same opinion. "I may tell you, Señor Master Nicholas," she said, for that was the barber's name, "that many times my uncle would sit reading those impious tales of misadventure for two whole days and nights at a stretch; and when he was through, he would toss the book aside, lay his hand on his sword, and begin slashing at the walls. When he was completely exhausted, he would tell us that he had just killed four giants as big as castle towers, while the sweat that poured off him was blood from the wounds that he

7. The reference is to **The Abencerraje**, the tale of the love of Abindarráez, a captive Moor, for the beautiful Jarifa. See pp. 303–17.
8. In a tradition originating in France, the Nine Worthies consisted of three biblical, three classical, and three Christian figures (David, Hector, Alexander, Charlemagne, and so on). In French medieval epics, the Twelve Peers (Roland, Oliver, and so on) were warriors all equal in rank, forming a kind of guard of honor around Charlemagne.
9. The thief whose release, rather than that of Jesus, the crowd requested when Pilate, conforming to Passover custom, was ready to have one prisoner set free.

had received in battle. He would then drink a big jug of cold water, after which he would be very calm and peaceful, saying that the water was the most precious liquid which the wise Esquife, a great magician and his friend, had brought to him. But I blame myself for everything. I should have advised your Worships of my uncle's nonsensical actions so that you could have done something about it by burning those damnable books of his before things came to such a pass; for he has many that ought to be burned as if they were heretics."

"I agree with you," said the curate, "and before tomorrow's sun has set there shall be a public *auto de fe*',[1] and those works shall be condemned to the flames that they may not lead some other who reads them to follow the example of my good friend."

Don Quixote and the farmer overheard all this, and it was then that the latter came to understand the nature of his neighbor's affliction.

"Open the door, your Worships," the good man cried. "Open for Sir Baldwin and the Marquis of Mantua, who comes badly wounded, and for Señor Abindarráez the Moor whom the valiant Rodrigo de Narváez, governor of Antequera, brings captive."

At the sound of his voice they all ran out, recognizing at once friend, master, and uncle, who as yet was unable to get down off the donkey's back. They all ran up to embrace him.

"Wait, all of you," said Don Quixote, "for I am sorely wounded through fault of my steed. Bear me to my couch and summon, if it be possible, the wise Urganda to treat and care for my wounds."

"There!" exclaimed the housekeeper. "Plague take it! Did not my heart tell me right as to which foot my master limped on? To bed with your Grace at once, and we will take care of you without sending for that Urganda of yours. A curse, I say, and a hundred other curses, on those books of chivalry that have brought your Grace to this."

And so they carried him off to bed, but when they went to look for his wounds, they found none at all. He told them it was all the result of a great fall he had taken with Rocinante, his horse, while engaged in combating ten giants, the hugest and most insolent that were ever heard of in all the world.

"Tut, tut," said the curate. "So there are giants in the dance now, are there? Then, by the sign of the cross, I'll have them burned before nightfall tomorrow."

They had a thousand questions to put to Don Quixote, but his only answer was that they should give him something to eat and let him sleep, for that was the most important thing of all; so they humored him in this. The curate then interrogated the farmer at great length concerning the conversation he had had with his neighbor. The peasant told him everything, all the absurd things their friend had said when he found him lying there and afterward on the way home, all of which made the licentiate more anxious than ever to do what he did the following day,[2] when he summoned Master Nicholas and went with him to Don Quixote's house.

1. Literally, "act of faith" (Portuguese); the act of publicly burning a heretic at the stake by the Spanish Inquisition.

2. He and the barber burned most of Don Quixote's library.

[*Fighting the Windmills and a Choleric Biscayan*]

From CHAPTER VII

Of the second sally of our good knight,
Don Quixote de la Mancha.

* * *

After that he remained at home very tranquilly for a couple of weeks, without giving sign of any desire to repeat his former madness. During that time he had the most pleasant conversations with his two old friends, the curate and the barber, on the point he had raised to the effect that what the world needed most was knights-errant and a revival of chivalry. The curate would occasionally contradict him and again would give in, for it was only by means of this artifice that he could carry on a conversation with him at all.

In the meanwhile Don Quixote was bringing his powers of persuasion to bear upon a farmer who lived near by, a good man—if this title may be applied to one who is poor—but with very few wits in his head. The short of it is, by pleas and promises, he got the hapless rustic to agree to ride forth with him and serve him as his squire. Among other things, Don Quixote told him that he ought to be more than willing to go, because no telling what adventure might occur which would win them an island, and then he (the farmer) would be left to be the governor of it. As a result of these and other similar assurances, Sancho Panza forsook his wife and children and consented to take upon himself the duties of squire to his neighbor.

Next, Don Quixote set out to raise some money, and by selling this thing and pawning that and getting the worst of the bargain always, he finally scraped together a reasonable amount. He also asked a friend of his for the loan of a buckler and patched up his broken helmet as well as he could. He advised his squire, Sancho, of the day and hour when they were to take the road and told him to see to laying in a supply of those things that were most necessary, and, above all, not to forget the saddlebags. Sancho replied that he would see to all this and added that he was also thinking of taking along with him a very good ass that he had, as he was not much used to going on foot.

With regard to the ass, Don Quixote had to do a little thinking, trying to recall if any knight-errant had ever had a squire thus asininely mounted. He could not think of any, but nevertheless he decided to take Sancho with the intention of providing him with a nobler steed as soon as occasion offered; he had but to appropriate the horse of the first discourteous knight he met. Having furnished himself with shirts and all the other things that the innkeeper had recommended, he and Panza rode forth one night unseen by anyone and without taking leave of wife and children, housekeeper or niece. They went so far that by the time morning came they were safe from discovery had a hunt been started for them.

Mounted on his ass, Sancho Panza rode along like a patriarch, with saddlebags and flask, his mind set upon becoming governor of that island that his master had promised him. Don Quixote determined to take the same route and road over the Campo de Montiel that he had followed on his first journey; but he was not so uncomfortable this time, for it was early morning and the sun's rays fell upon them slantingly and accordingly did not tire them too much.

"Look, Sir Knight-errant," said Sancho, "your Grace should not forget that island you promised me; for no matter how big it is, I'll be able to govern it right enough."

"I would have you know, friend Sancho Panza," replied Don Quixote, "that among the knights-errant of old it was a very common custom to make their squires governors of the islands or the kingdoms that they won, and I am resolved that in my case so pleasing a usage shall not fall into desuetude. I even mean to go them one better; for they very often, perhaps most of the time, waited until their squires were old men who had had their fill of serving their masters during bad days and worse nights, whereupon they would give them the tide of count, or marquis at most, of some valley or province more or less. But if you live and I live, it well may be that within a week I shall win some kingdom with others dependent upon it, and it will be the easiest thing in the world to crown you king of one of them. You need not marvel at this, for all sorts of unforeseen things happen to knights like me, and I may readily be able to give you even more than I have promised."

"In that case," said Sancho Panza, "if by one of those miracles of which your Grace was speaking I should become king, I would certainly send for Juana Gutiérrez, my old lady, to come and be my queen, and the young ones could be infantes."

"There is no doubt about it," Don Quixote assured him.

"Well, I doubt it," said Sancho, "for I think that even if God were to rain kingdoms upon the earth, no crown would sit well on the head of Mari Gutiérrez,[3] for I am telling you, sir, as a queen she is not worth two maravedis. She would do better as a countess, God help her."

"Leave everything to God, Sancho," said Don Quixote, "and he will give you whatever is most fitting; but I trust you will not be so pusillanimous as to be content with anything less than the title of viceroy."

"That I will not," said Sancho Panza, "especially seeing that I have in your Grace so illustrious a master who can give me all that is suitable to me and all that I can manage."

CHAPTER VIII

Of the good fortune which the valorous Don Quixote had in the terrifying and never-before-imagined adventure of the windmills, along with other events that deserve to be suitably recorded.

At this point they caught sight of thirty or forty windmills which were standing on the plain there, and no sooner had Don Quixote laid eyes upon them than he turned to his squire and said, "Fortune is guiding our affairs better than we could have wished; for you see there before you, friend Sancho Panza, some thirty or more lawless giants with whom I mean to do battle. I shall deprive them of their lives, and with the spoils from this encounter we shall begin to enrich ourselves; for this is righteous warfare, and it is a great service to God to remove so accursed a breed from the face of the earth."

"What giants?" said Sancho Panza.

"Those that you see there," replied his master, "those with the long arms some of which are as much as two leagues in length."

3. Sancho's wife, Juana Gutiérrez.

"But look, your Grace, those are not giants but windmills, and what appear to be arms are their wings which, when whirled in the breeze, cause the mill-stone to go."

"It is plain to be seen," said Don Quixote, "that you have had little experience in this matter of adventures. If you are afraid, go off to one side and say your prayers while I am engaging them in fierce, unequal combat."

Saying this, he gave spurs to his steed Rocinante, without paying any heed to Sancho's warning that these were truly windmills and not giants that he was riding forth to attack. Nor even when he was close upon them did he perceive what they really were, but shouted at the top of his lungs, "Do not seek to flee, cowards and vile creatures that you are, for it is but a single knight with whom you have to deal!"

At that moment a little wind came up and the big wings began turning.

"Though you flourish as many arms as did the giant Briareus,"[4] said Don Quixote when he perceived this, "you still shall have to answer to me."

He thereupon commended himself with all his heart to his lady Dulcinea, beseeching her to succor him in this peril; and, being well covered with his shield and with his lance at rest, he bore down upon them at a full gallop and fell upon the first mill that stood in his way, giving a thrust at the wing, which was whirling at such a speed that his lance was broken into bits and both horse and horseman went rolling over the plain, very much battered indeed. Sancho upon his donkey came hurrying to his master's assistance as fast as he could, but when he reached the spot, the knight was unable to move, so great was the shock with which he and Rocinante had hit the ground.

"God help us!" exclaimed Sancho, "did I not tell your Grace to look well, that those were nothing but windmills, a fact which no one could fail to see unless he had other mills of the same sort in his head?"

"Be quiet, friend Sancho," said Don Quixote. "Such are the fortunes of war, which more than any other are subject to constant change. What is more, when I come to think of it, I am sure that this must be the work of that magi-cian Frestón, the one who robbed me of my study and my books,[5] and who has thus changed the giants into windmills in order to deprive me of the glory of overcoming them, so great is the enmity that he bears me; but in the end his evil arts shall not prevail against this trusty sword of mine."

"May God's will be done," was Sancho Panza's response. And with the aid of his squire the knight was once more mounted on Rocinante, who stood there with one shoulder half out of joint. And so, speaking of the adventure that had just befallen them, they continued along the Puerto Lápice highway; for there, Don Quixote said, they could not fail to find many and varied adventures, this being a much traveled thoroughfare. The only thing was, the knight was exceed-ingly downcast over the loss of his lance.

"I remember," he said to his squire, "having read of a Spanish knight by the name of Diego Pérez de Vargas, who, having broken his sword in battle, tore from an oak a heavy bough or branch and with it did such feats of valor that day, and pounded so many Moors, that he came to be known as Machuca,[6] and he and his descendants from that day forth have been called Vargas y Machuca. I tell you this because I too intend to provide myself with just such a bough as

---

4. In Greek mythology, a giant with a hun-dred arms.
5. Don Quixote had promptly attributed the ruin of his library to magical intervention (see p. 386, n. 2).
6. "The Crusher," the hero of a folk ballad.

the one he wielded, and with it I propose to do such exploits that you shall deem yourself fortunate to have been found worthy to come with me and behold and witness things that are almost beyond belief."

"God's will be done," said Sancho. "I believe everything that your Grace says; but straighten yourself up in the saddle a little, for you seem to be slipping down on one side, owing, no doubt, to the shaking-up that you received in your fall."

"Ah, that is the truth," replied Don Quixote, "and if I do not speak of my sufferings, it is for the reason that it is not permitted knights-errant to complain of any wound whatsoever, even though their bowels may be dropping out."

"If that is the way it is," said Sancho, "I have nothing more to say; but, God knows, it would suit me better if your Grace did complain when something hurts him. I can assure you that I mean to do so, over the least little thing that ails me—that is, unless the same rule applies to squires as well."

Don Quixote laughed long and heartily over Sancho's simplicity, telling him that he might complain as much as he liked and where and when he liked, whether he had good cause or not; for he had read nothing to the contrary in the ordinances of chivalry. Sancho then called his master's attention to the fact that it was time to eat. The knight replied that he himself had no need of food at the moment, but his squire might eat whenever he chose. Having been granted this permission, Sancho seated himself as best he could upon his beast, and, taking out from his saddlebags the provisions that he had stored there, he rode along leisurely behind his master, munching his victuals and taking a good, hearty swig now and then at the leather flask in a manner that might well have caused the biggest-bellied tavernkeeper of Málaga to envy him. Between draughts he gave not so much as a thought to any promise that his master might have made him, nor did he look upon it as any hardship, but rather as good sport, to go in quest of adventures however hazardous they might be.

The short of the matter is, they spent the night under some trees, from one of which Don Quixote tore off a withered bough to serve him as a lance, placing it in the lance head from which he had removed the broken one. He did not sleep all night long for thinking of his lady Dulcinea; for this was in accordance with what he had read in his books, of men of arms in the forest or desert places who kept a wakeful vigil, sustained by the memory of their ladies fair. Not so with Sancho, whose stomach was full, and not with chicory water. He fell into a dreamless slumber, and had not his master called him, he would not have been awakened either by the rays of the sun in his face or by the many birds who greeted the coming of the new day with their merry song.

Upon arising, he had another go at the flask, finding it somewhat more flaccid than it had been the night before, a circumstance which grieved his heart, for he could not see that they were on the way to remedying the deficiency within any very short space of time. Don Quixote did not wish any breakfast; for, as has been said, he was in the habit of nourishing himself on savorous memories. They then set out once more along the road to Puerto Lápice, and around three in the afternoon they came in sight of the pass that bears that name.

"There," said Don Quixote as his eyes fell upon it, "we may plunge our arms up to the elbow in what are known as adventures. But I must warn you that even though you see me in the greatest peril in the world, you are not to lay hand upon your sword to defend me, unless it be that those who attack me are rabble and men of low degree, in which case you may very well come to my aid; but if they be gentlemen, it is in no wise permitted by the laws of chivalry that you should assist me until you yourself shall have been dubbed a knight."

"Most certainly, sir," replied Sancho, "your Grace shall be very well obeyed in this; all the more so for the reason that I myself am of a peaceful disposition and not fond of meddling in the quarrels and feuds of others. However, when it comes to protecting my own person, I shall not take account of those laws of which you speak, seeing that all laws, human and divine, permit each one to defend himself whenever he is attacked."

"I am willing to grant you that," assented Don Quixote, "but in this matter of defending me against gentlemen you must restrain your natural impulses."

"I promise you I shall do so," said Sancho. "I will observe this precept as I would the Sabbath day."

As they were conversing in this manner, there appeared in the road in front of them two friars of the Order of St. Benedict, mounted upon dromedaries—for the she-mules they rode were certainly no smaller than that. The friars wore travelers' spectacles and carried sunshades, and behind them came a coach accompanied by four or five men on horseback and a couple of mule-teers on foot. In the coach, as was afterwards learned, was a lady of Biscay,[7] on her way to Seville to bid farewell to her husband, who had been appointed to some high post in the Indies. The religious were not of her company although they were going by the same road.

The instant Don Quixote laid eyes upon them he turned to his squire. "Either I am mistaken or this is going to be the most famous adventure that ever was seen; for those black-clad figures that you behold must be, and without any doubt are, certain enchanters who are bearing with them a captive princess in that coach, and I must do all I can to right this wrong."

"It will be worse than the windmills," declared Sancho. "Look you, sir, those are Benedictine friars and the coach must be that of some travelers. Mark well what I say and what you do, lest the devil lead you astray."

"I have already told you, Sancho," replied Don Quixote, "that you know little where the subject of adventures is concerned. What I am saying to you is the truth, as you shall now see."

With this, he rode forward and took up a position in the middle of the road along which the friars were coming, and as soon as they appeared to be within earshot he cried out to them in a loud voice, "O devilish and monstrous beings, set free at once the highborn princesses whom you bear captive in that coach, or else prepare at once to meet your death as the just punishment of your evil deeds."

The friars drew rein and sat there in astonishment, marveling as much at Don Quixote's appearance as at the words he spoke. "Sir Knight," they answered him, "we are neither devilish nor monstrous but religious of the Order of St. Benedict who are merely going our way. We know nothing of those who are in that coach, nor of any captive princesses either."

"Soft words," said Don Quixote, "have no effect on me. I know you for what you are, lying rabble!" And without waiting for any further parley he gave spur to Rocinante and, with lowered lance, bore down upon the first friar with such

7. The Basque region in northern Spain and southwestern France.

fury and intrepidity that, had not the fellow tumbled from his mule of his own accord, he would have been hurled to the ground and either killed or badly wounded. The second religious, seeing how his companion had been treated, dug his legs into his she-mule's flanks and scurried away over the countryside faster than the wind.

Seeing the friar upon the ground, Sancho Panza slipped lightly from his mount and, falling upon him, began stripping him of his habit. The two mule drivers accompanying the religious thereupon came running up and asked Sancho why he was doing this. The latter replied that the friar's garments belonged to him as legitimate spoils of the battle that his master Don Quixote had just won. The muleteers, however, were lads with no sense of humor, nor did they know what all this talk of spoils and battles was about; but, perceiving that Don Quixote had ridden off to one side to converse with those inside the coach, they pounced upon Sancho, threw him to the ground, and proceeded to pull out the hair of his beard and kick him to a pulp, after which they went off and left him stretched out there, bereft at once of breath and sense.

Without losing any time, they then assisted the friar to remount. The good brother was trembling all over from fright, and there was not a speck of color in his face, but when he found himself in the saddle once more, he quickly spurred his beast to where his companion, at some little distance, sat watching and waiting to see what the result of the encounter would be. Having no curiosity as to the final outcome of the fray, the two of them now resumed their journey, making more signs of the cross than the devil would be able to carry upon his back.

Meanwhile Don Quixote, as we have said, was speaking to the lady in the coach.

"Your beauty, my lady, may now dispose of your person as best may please you, for the arrogance of your abductors lies upon the ground, overthrown by this good arm of mine; and in order that you may not pine to know the name of your liberator, I may inform you that I am Don Quixote de la Mancha, knight-errant and adventurer and captive of the peerless and beauteous Doña Dulcinea del Toboso. In payment of the favor which you have received from me, I ask nothing other than that you return to El Toboso and on my behalf pay your respects to this lady, telling her that it was I who set you free."

One of the squires accompanying those in the coach, a Biscayan, was listening to Don Quixote's words, and when he saw that the knight did not propose to let the coach proceed upon its way but was bent upon having it turn back to El Toboso, he promptly went up to him, seized his lance, and said to him in bad Castilian and worse Biscayan,[8] "Go, *caballero*, and bad luck go with you; for by the God that created me, if you do not let this coach pass, me kill you or me no Biscayan."

Don Quixote heard him attentively enough and answered him very mildly, "If you were a *caballero*,[9] which you are not, I should already have chastised you, wretched creature, for your foolhardiness and your impudence."

"Me no *caballero*?" cried the Biscayan. "Me swear to God, you lie like a Christian. If you will but lay aside your lance and unsheath your sword, you will soon

8. Castilian is the language of Castile; Biscayan is the Basque language.   9. Knight, gentleman (Spanish).

see that you are carrying water to the cat![1] Biscayan on land, gentleman at sea, but a gentleman in spite of the devil, and you lie if you say otherwise."

"'"You shall see as to that presently," said Agrajes,'"[2] Don Quixote quoted. He cast his lance to the earth, drew his sword, and, taking his buckler on his arm, attacked the Biscayan with intent to slay him. The latter, when he saw his adversary approaching, would have liked to dismount from his mule, for she was one of the worthless sort that are let for hire and he had no confidence in her; but there was no time for this, and so he had no choice but to draw his own sword in turn and make the best of it. However, he was near enough to the coach to be able to snatch a cushion from it to serve him as a shield; and then they fell upon each other as though they were mortal enemies. The rest of those present sought to make peace between them but did not succeed, for the Biscayan with his disjointed phrases kept muttering that if they did not let him finish the battle then he himself would have to kill his mistress and anyone else who tried to stop him.

The lady inside the carriage, amazed by it all and trembling at what she saw, directed her coachman to drive on a little way; and there from a distance she watched the deadly combat, in the course of which the Biscayan came down with a great blow on Don Quixote's shoulder, over the top of the latter's shield, and had not the knight been clad in armor, it would have split him to the waist.

Feeling the weight of this blow, Don Quixote cried out, "O lady of my soul, Dulcinea, flower of beauty, succor this your champion who out of gratitude for your many favors finds himself in so perilous a plight!" To utter these words, lay hold of his sword, cover himself with his buckler, and attack the Biscayan was but the work of a moment; for he was now resolved to risk everything upon a single stroke.

As he saw Don Quixote approaching with so dauntless a bearing, the Biscayan was well aware of his adversary's courage and forthwith determined to imitate the example thus set him. He kept himself protected with his cushion, but he was unable to get his she-mule to budge to one side or the other, for the beast, out of sheer exhaustion and being, moreover, unused to such childish play, was incapable of taking a single step. And so, then, as has been stated, Don Quixote was approaching the wary Biscayan, his sword raised on high and with the firm resolve of cleaving his enemy in two; and the Biscayan was awaiting the knight in the same posture, cushion in front of him and with uplifted sword. All the bystanders were trembling with suspense at what would happen as a result of the terrible blows that were threatened, and the lady in the coach and her maids were making a thousand vows and offerings to all the images and shrines in Spain, praying that God would save them all and the lady's squire from this great peril that confronted them.

But the unfortunate part of the matter is that at this very point the author of the history breaks off and leaves the battle pending, excusing himself upon the ground that he has been unable to find anything else in writing concerning the exploits of Don Quixote beyond those already set forth.[3] It is true, on the other hand, that the second author of this work could not bring himself to believe

---

1. An inversion of a proverbial phrase: "carrying the cat to the water."
2. A violent character in the romance *Amadís de Gaula*. His challenging phrase is the conventional opener of a fight.

3. "The author" is Cervantes himself, adopting here—with tongue in cheek—a device used in the romances of chivalry to create suspense.

that so unusual a chronicle would have been consigned to oblivion, nor that the learned ones of La Mancha were possessed of so little curiosity as not to be able to discover in their archives or registry offices certain papers that have to do with this famous knight. Being convinced of this, he did not despair of coming upon the end of this pleasing story and Heaven favoring him, he did find it, as shall be related in the second part.

CHAPTER IX

In which is concluded and brought to an end the stupendous battle between the gallant Biscayan and the valiant Knight of La Mancha.

In the first part of this history we left the valorous Biscayan and the famous Don Quixote with swords unsheathed and raised aloft, about to let fall furious slashing blows which, had they been delivered fairly and squarely, would at the very least have split them in two and laid them wide open from top to bottom like a pomegranate; and it was at this doubtful point that the pleasing chronicle came to a halt and broke off, without the author's informing us as to where the rest of it might be found.

I was deeply grieved by such a circumstance, and the pleasure I had had in reading so slight a portion was turned into annoyance as I thought of how difficult it would be to come upon the greater part which it seemed to me must still be missing. It appeared impossible and contrary to all good precedent that so worthy a knight should not have had some scribe to take upon himself the task of writing an account of these unheard-of exploits; for that was something that had happened to none of the knights-errant who, as the saying has it, had gone forth in quest of adventures, seeing that each of them had one or two chroniclers, as if ready at hand, who not only had set down their deeds, but had depicted their most trivial thoughts and amiable weaknesses, however well concealed they might be. The good knight of La Mancha surely could not have been so unfortunate as to have lacked what Platir and others like him had in abundance. And so I could not bring myself to believe that this gallant history could have remained thus lopped off and mutilated, and I could not but lay the blame upon the malignity of time, that devourer and consumer of all things, which must either have consumed it or kept it hidden.

On the other hand, I reflected that inasmuch as among the knight's books had been found such modern works as *The Disenchantments of Jealousy* and *The Nymphs and Shepherds of Henares*, his story likewise must be modern, and that even though it might not have been written down, it must remain in the memory of the good folk of his village and the surrounding ones. This thought left me somewhat confused and more than ever desirous of knowing the real and true story, the whole story, of the life and wondrous deeds of our famous Spaniard, Don Quixote, light and mirror of the chivalry of La Mancha, the first in our age and in these calamitous times to devote himself to the hardships and exercises of knight-errantry and to go about righting wrongs, succoring widows, and protecting damsels—damsels such as those who, mounted upon their palfreys and with riding-whip in hand, in full possession of their virginity, were in the habit of going from mountain to mountain and from valley to valley; for unless there were some villain, some rustic with an ax and hood, or some monstrous giant to force them, there were in times past maiden ladies who at the end of eighty years, during all which time they had not slept for a single day beneath a roof, would go to their graves as virginal as when their mothers had borne them.

If I speak of these things, it is for the reason that in this and in all other respects our gallant Quixote is deserving of constant memory and praise, and even I am not to be denied my share of it for my diligence and the labor to which I put myself in searching out the conclusion of this agreeable narrative; although if heaven, luck, and circumstance had not aided me, the world would have had to do without the pleasure and the pastime which anyone may enjoy who will read this work attentively for an hour or two. The manner in which it came about was as follows:

I was standing one day in the Alcaná, or market place, of Toledo when a lad came up to sell some old notebooks and other papers to a silk weaver who was there. As I am extremely fond of reading anything, even though it be but the scraps of paper in the streets, I followed my natural inclination and took one of the books, whereupon I at once perceived that it was written in characters which I recognized as Arabic. I recognized them, but reading them was another thing; and so I began looking around to see if there was any Spanish-speaking Moor near by who would be able to read them for me. It was not very hard to find such an interpreter, nor would it have been even if the tongue in question had been an older and a better one.[4] To make a long story short, chance brought a fellow my way; and when I told him what it was I wished and placed the book in his hands, he opened it in the middle and began reading and at once fell to laughing. When I asked him what the cause of his laughter was, he replied that it was a note which had been written in the margin.

I besought him to tell me the content of the note, and he, laughing still, went on, "As I told you, it is something in the margin here: 'This Dulcinea del Toboso, so often referred to, is said to have been the best hand at salting pigs of any woman in all La Mancha.'"

No sooner had I heard the name Dulcinea del Toboso than I was astonished and held in suspense, for at once the thought occurred to me that those notebooks must contain the history of Don Quixote. With this in mind I urged him to read me the title, and he proceeded to do so, turning the Arabic into Castilian upon the spot: *History of Don Quixote de la Mancha, Written by Cid Hamete Benengeli,*[5] *Arabic Historian.* It was all I could do to conceal my satisfaction and, snatching them from the silk weaver, I bought from the lad all the papers and notebooks that he had for half a real; but if he had known or suspected how very much I wanted them, he might well have had more than six reales for them.

The Moor and I then betook ourselves to the cathedral cloister, where I requested him to translate for me into the Castilian tongue all the books that had to do with Don Quixote, adding nothing and subtracting nothing; and I offered him whatever payment he desired. He was content with two arrobas of raisins and two fanegas[6] of wheat and promised to translate them well and faithfully and

---

4. I.e., Hebrew.

5. Citing some ancient chronicle as the author's source and authority is very much in the tradition of the romances. "*Benengeli*": eggplant

(Arabic).

6. About fifty pounds. "Two arrobas": three bushels.

with all dispatch. However, in order to facilitate matters, and also because I did not wish to let such a find as this out of my hands, I took the fellow home with me, where in a little more than a month and a half he translated the whole of the work just as you will find it set down here.

In the first of the books there was a very lifelike picture of the battle between Don Quixote and the Biscayan, the two being in precisely the same posture as described in the history, their swords upraised, the one covered by his buckler, the other with his cushion. As for the Biscayan's mule, you could see at the distance of a crossbow shot that it was one for hire. Beneath the Biscayan there was a rubric which read: "Don Sancho de Azpeitia," which must undoubtedly have been his name; while beneath the feet of Rocinante was another inscription: "Don Quixote." Rocinante was marvelously portrayed: so long and lank, so lean and flabby, so extremely consumptive-looking that one could well understand the justness and propriety with which the name of "hack" had been bestowed upon him.

Alongside Rocinante stood Sancho Panza, holding the halter of his ass, and below was the legend: "Sancho Zancas." The picture showed him with a big belly, a short body, and long shanks, and that must have been where he got the names of Panza y Zancas[7] by which he is a number of times called in the course of the history. There are other small details that might be mentioned, but they are of little importance and have nothing to do with the truth of the story—and no story is bad so long as it is true.

If there is any objection to be raised against the veracity of the present one, it can be only that the author was an Arab, and that nation is known for its lying propensities; but even though they be our enemies, it may readily be understood that they would more likely have detracted from, rather than added to, the chronicle. So it seems to me, at any rate; for whenever he might and should deploy the resources of his pen in praise of so worthy a knight, the author appears to take pains to pass over the matter in silence; all of which in my opinion is ill done and ill conceived, for it should be the duty of historians to be exact, truthful, and dispassionate, and neither interest nor fear nor rancor nor affection should swerve them from the path of truth, whose mother is history, rival of time, depository of deeds, witness of the past, exemplar and adviser to the present, and the future's counselor. In this work, I am sure, will be found all that could be desired in the way of pleasant reading; and if it is lacking in any way, I maintain that this is the fault of that hound of an author rather than of the subject.

But to come to the point, the second part, according to the translation, began as follows:

As the two valorous and enraged combatants stood there, swords upraised and poised on high, it seemed from their bold mien as if they must surely be threatening heaven, earth, and hell itself. The first to let fall a blow was the choleric Biscayan, and he came down with such force and fury that, had not his sword been deflected in mid-air, that single stroke would have sufficed to put an end to this fearful combat and to all our knight's adventures at the same time; but fortune, which was reserving him for greater things, turned aside his adversary's blade in such a manner that, even though it fell upon his left shoulder, it did him no other damage than to strip him completely of his armor on that side,

---

7. Paunch and Shanks (Spanish).

carrying with it a good part of his helmet along with half an ear, the headpiece clattering to the ground with a dreadful din, leaving its wearer in a sorry state.

Heaven help me! Who could properly describe the rage that now entered the heart of our hero of La Mancha as he saw himself treated in this fashion? It may merely be said that he once more reared himself in the stirrups, laid hold of his sword with both hands, and dealt the Biscayan such a blow, over the cushion and upon the head, that, even so good a defense proving useless, it was as if a mountain had fallen upon his enemy. The latter now began bleeding through the mouth, nose, and ears; he seemed about to fall from his mule, and would have fallen, no doubt, if he had not grasped the beast about the neck, but at that moment his feet slipped from the stirrups and his arms let go, and the mule, frightened by the terrible blow, began running across the plain, hurling its rider to the earth with a few quick plunges.

Don Quixote stood watching all this very calmly. When he saw his enemy fall, he leaped from his horse, ran over very nimbly, and thrust the point of his sword into the Biscayan's eyes, calling upon him at the same time to surrender or otherwise he would cut off his head. The Biscayan was so bewildered that he was unable to utter a single word in reply, and things would have gone badly with him, so blind was Don Quixote in his rage, if the ladies of the coach, who up to then had watched the struggle in dismay, had not come up to him at this point and begged him with many blandishments to do them the very great favor of sparing their squire's life.

To which Don Quixote replied with much haughtiness and dignity, "Most certainly, lovely ladies, I shall be very happy to do that which you ask of me, but upon one condition and understanding, and that is that this knight promise me that he will go to El Toboso and present himself in my behalf before Doña Dulcinea, in order that she may do with him as she may see fit."

Trembling and disconsolate, the ladies did not pause to discuss Don Quixote's request, but without so much as inquiring who Dulcinea might be they promised him that the squire would fulfill that which was commanded of him.

"Very well, then, trusting in your word, I will do him no further harm, even though he has well deserved it."

CHAPTER X

Of the pleasing conversation that took place between
Don Quixote and Sancho Panza, his squire.

By this time Sancho Panza had got to his feet, somewhat the worse for wear as the result of the treatment he had received from the friars' lads. He had been watching the battle attentively and praying God in his heart to give the victory to his master, Don Quixote, in order that he, Sancho, might gain some island where he could go to be governor as had been promised him. Seeing now that the combat was over and the knight was returning to mount Rocinante once more, he went up to hold the stirrup for him; but first he fell on his knees in front of him and, taking his hand, kissed it and said, "May your Grace be pleased, Señor Don Quixote, to grant me the governorship of that island which you have won in this deadly affray; for however large it may be, I feel that I am indeed capable of governing it as well as any man in this world has ever done."

To which Don Quixote replied, "Be advised, brother Sancho, that this adventure and other similar ones have nothing to do with islands; they are affairs of the crossroads in which one gains nothing more than a broken head or an ear the less. Be patient, for there will be others which will not only make you a governor, but more than that."

Sancho thanked him very much and, kissing his hand again and the skirt of his cuirass, he assisted him up on Rocinante's back, after which the squire bestraddled his own mount and started jogging along behind his master, who was now going at a good clip. Without pausing for any further converse with those in the coach, the knight made for a nearby wood, with Sancho following as fast as his beast could trot; but Rocinante was making such speed that the ass and its rider were left behind, and it was necessary to call out to Don Quixote to pull up and wait for them. He did so, reining in Rocinante until the weary Sancho had drawn abreast of him.

"It strikes me, sir," said the squire as he reached his master's side, "that it would be better for us to take refuge in some church; for in view of the way you have treated that one with whom you were fighting, it would be small wonder if they did not lay the matter before the Holy Brotherhood[8] and have us arrested; and faith, if they do that, we shall have to sweat a-plenty before we come out of jail."

"Be quiet," said Don Quixote. "And where have you ever seen, or read of, a knight being brought to justice no matter how many homicides he might have committed?"

"I know nothing about omecils,"[9] replied Sancho, "nor ever in my life did I bear one to anybody; all I know is that the Holy Brotherhood has something to say about those who go around fighting on the highway, and I want nothing of it."

"Do not let it worry you," said Don Quixote, "for I will rescue you from the hands of the Chaldeans, not to speak of the Brotherhood. But answer me upon your life: have you ever seen a more valorous knight than I on all the known face of the earth? Have you ever read in the histories of any other who had more mettle in the attack, more perseverance in sustaining it, more dexterity in wounding his enemy, or more skill in overthrowing him?"

"The truth is," said Sancho, "I have never read any history whatsoever, for I do not know how to read or write; but what I would wager is that in all the days of my life I have never served a more courageous master than your Grace; I only hope your courage is not paid for in the place that I have mentioned. What I would suggest is that your Grace allow me to do something for that ear, for there is much blood coming from it, and I have here in my saddlebags some lint and a little white ointment."

"We could well dispense with all that," said Don Quixote, "if only I had remembered to bring along a vial of Fierabrás's[1] balm, a single drop of which saves time and medicines."

"What vial and what balm is that?" inquired Sancho Panza.

"It is a balm the recipe for which I know by heart; with it one need have no fear of death nor think of dying from any wound. I shall make some of it and

---

8. A tribunal instituted by Ferdinand and Isabella at the end of the 15th century to punish highway robbers.
9. In Spanish, a wordplay on *homocidios* (homicides) / *omecillos* (grudges). In English,

omecils appears only in this passage of *Don Quixote*.
1. A giant Saracen healer in the medieval epics of the Twelve Peers (see p. 385, n. 7).

give it to you; and thereafter, whenever in any battle you see my body cut in two—as very often happens—all that is necessary is for you to take the part that lies on the ground, before the blood has congealed, and fit it very neatly and with great nicety upon the other part that remains in the saddle, taking care to adjust it evenly and exactly. Then you will give me but a couple of swallows of the balm of which I have told you, and you will see me sounder than an apple in no time at all."

"If that is so," said Panza, "I herewith renounce the governorship of the island you promised me and ask nothing other in payment of my many and faithful services than that your Grace give me the recipe for this wonderful potion, for I am sure that it would be worth more than two reales the ounce anywhere, and that is all I need for a life of ease and honor. But may I be so bold as to ask how much it costs to make it?"

"For less than three reales you can make something like six quarts," Don Quixote told him.

"Sinner that I am!" exclaimed Sancho. "Then why does your Grace not make some at once and teach me also?"

"Hush, my friend," said the knight, "I mean to teach you greater secrets than that and do you greater favors; but, for the present, let us look after this ear of mine, for it is hurting me more than I like."

Sancho thereupon took the lint and the ointment from his saddlebags; but when Don Quixote caught a glimpse of his helmet, he almost went out of his mind and, laying his hand upon his sword and lifting his eyes heavenward, he cried, "I make a vow to the Creator of all things and to the four holy Gospels in all their fullness of meaning that I will lead from now on the life that the great Marquis of Mantua did after he had sworn to avenge the death of his nephew Baldwin: not to eat bread off a tablecloth, not to embrace his wife, and other things which, although I am unable to recall them, we will look upon as understood—all this until I shall have wreaked an utter vengeance upon the one who has perpetrated such an outrage upon me."

"But let me remind your Grace," said Sancho when he heard these words, "that if the knight fulfills that which was commanded of him, by going to present himself before my lady Dulcinea del Toboso, then he will have paid his debt to you and merits no further punishment at your hands, unless it be for some fresh offense."

"You have spoken very well and to the point," said Don Quixote, "and so I annul the vow I have just made insofar as it has to do with any further vengeance, but I make it and confirm it anew so far as leading the life of which I have spoken is concerned, until such time as I shall have obtained by force of arms from some other knight another headpiece as good as this. And do not think, Sancho, that I am making smoke out of straw; there is one whom I well may imitate in this matter, for the same thing happened in all literalness in the case of Mambrino's helmet[2] which cost Sacripante so dear."

"I wish," said Sancho, "that your Grace would send all such oaths to the devil, for they are very bad for the health and harmful for the conscience as well. Tell me, please: supposing that for many days to come we meet no man

2. The enchanted helmet of Mambrino, a Moorish king, is stolen by Dardinel (not Sacripante, as Don Quixote mistakenly recalls) in Boiardo's *Roland in Love*.

wearing a helmet, then what are we to do? Must you still keep your vow in spite of all the inconveniences and discomforts, such as sleeping with your clothes on, not sleeping in any town, and a thousand other penances contained in the oath of that old madman of a Marquis of Mantua, an oath which you would now revive? Mark you, sir, along all these roads you meet no men of arms but only muleteers and carters, who not only do not wear helmets but quite likely have never heard tell of them in all their livelong days."

"In that you are wrong," said Don Quixote, "for we shall not be at these crossroads for the space of two hours before we shall see more men of arms than came to Albraca to win the fair Angélica."[3]

"Very well, then," said Sancho, "so be it, and pray God that all turns out for the best so that I may at last win that island that is costing me so dearly, and then let me die."

"I have already told you, Sancho, that you are to give no thought to that; should the island fail, there is the kingdom of Denmark or that of Sobradisa, which would fit you like a ring on your finger, and you ought, moreover, to be happy to be on *terra firma*.[4] But let us leave all this for some other time, while you look and see if you have something in those saddlebags for us to eat, after which we will go in search of some castle where we may lodge for the night and prepare that balm of which I was telling you, for I swear to God that my ear is paining me greatly."

"I have here an onion, a little cheese, and a few crusts of bread," said Sancho, "but they are not victuals fit for a valiant knight like your Grace."

"How little you know about it!" replied Don Quixote. "I would inform you, Sancho, that it is a point of honor with knights-errant to go for a month at a time without eating, and when they do eat, it is whatever may be at hand. You would certainly know that if you had read the histories as I have. There are many of them, and in none have I found any mention of knights eating unless it was by chance or at some sumptuous banquet that was tendered them; on other days they fasted. And even though it is well understood that, being men like us, they could not go without food entirely, any more than they could fail to satisfy the other necessities of nature, nevertheless, since they spent the greater part of their lives in forests and desert places without any cook to prepare their meals, their diet ordinarily consisted of rustic viands such as those that you now offer me. And so, Sancho my friend, do not be grieved at that which pleases me, nor seek to make the world over, nor to unhinge the institution of knight-errantry."

"Pardon me, your Grace," said Sancho, "but seeing that, as I have told you, I do not know how to read or write, I am consequently not familiar with the rules of the knightly calling. Hereafter, I will stuff my saddlebags with all manner of dried fruit for your Grace, but inasmuch as I am not a knight, I shall lay in for myself a stock of fowls and other more substantial fare."

"I am not saying, Sancho, that it is incumbent upon knights-errant to eat only those fruits of which you speak; what I am saying is that their ordinary sustenance should consist of fruit and a few herbs such as are to be found in the fields and with which they are well acquainted, as am I myself."

3. Another allusion to *Roland in Love*.
4. Solid earth (Latin, literal trans.), here referring to Firm Island, a legendary final destination for the squires of knights-errant. "Sobradisa": an imaginary realm.

"It is a good thing," said Sancho, "to know those herbs, for, so far as I can see, we are going to have need of that knowledge one of these days."

With this, he brought out the articles he had mentioned, and the two of them ate in peace, and most companionably. Being desirous, however, of seeking a lodging for the night, they did not tarry long over their humble and unsavory repast. They then mounted and made what haste they could that they might arrive at a shelter before nightfall; but the sun failed them, and with it went the hope of attaining their wish. As the day ended they found themselves beside some goatherds' huts, and they accordingly decided to spend the night there. Sancho was as much disappointed at their not having reached a town as his master was content with sleeping under the open sky; for it seemed to Don Quixote that every time this happened it merely provided him with yet another opportunity to establish his claim to the title of knight-errant.

[Of Goatherds, Roaming Shepherdesses, and Unrequited Loves]

CHAPTER XI

Of what happened to Don Quixote in the company of certain goatherds.

He was received by the herders with good grace, and Sancho having looked after Rocinante and the ass to the best of his ability, the knight, drawn by the aroma, went up to where some pieces of goat's meat were simmering in a pot over the fire. He would have liked then and there to see if they were done well enough to be transferred from pot to stomach, but he refrained in view of the fact that his hosts were already taking them off the fire. Spreading a few sheepskins on the ground, they hastily laid their rustic board and invited the strangers to share what there was of it. There were six of them altogether who belonged to that fold, and after they had urged Don Quixote, with rude politeness, to seat himself upon a small trough which they had turned upside down for the purpose, they took their own places upon the sheep hides round about. While his master sat there, Sancho remained standing to serve him the cup, which was made of horn. When the knight perceived this, he addressed his squire as follows:

"In order, Sancho, that you may see the good that there is in knight-errantry and how speedily those who follow the profession, no matter what the nature of their service may be, come to be honored and esteemed in the eyes of the world, I would have you here in the company of these good folk seat yourself at my side, that you may be even as I who am your master and natural lord, and eat from my plate and drink from where I drink; for of knight-errantry one may say the same as of love: that it makes all things equal."

"Many thanks!" said Sancho, "but if it is all the same to your Grace, providing there is enough to go around, I can eat just as well, or better, standing up and alone as I can seated beside an emperor. And if the truth must be told, I enjoy much more that which I eat in my own corner without any bowings and scrapings, even though it be only bread and onions, than I do a meal of roast turkey where I have to chew slowly, drink little, be always wiping my mouth, and can neither sneeze nor cough if I feel like it, nor do any of those other things that you can when you are free and alone.

"And so, my master," he went on, "these honors that your Grace would confer upon me as your servant and a follower of knight-errantry—which I am, being your Grace's squire—I would have you convert, if you will, into other things that will be of more profit and advantage to me; for though I hereby acknowledge them as duly received, I renounce them from this time forth to the end of the world."

"But for all that," said Don Quixote, "you must sit down; for whosoever humbleth himself, him God will exalt."[5] And, laying hold of his squire's arm, he compelled him to take a seat beside him.

The goatherds did not understand all this jargon about squires and knights-errant; they did nothing but eat, keep silent, and study their guests, who very dexterously and with much appetite were stowing away chunks of meat as big as your fist. When the meat course was finished, they laid out upon the sheep-skins a great quantity of dried acorns and half a cheese, which was harder than if it had been made of mortar. The drinking horn all this while was not idle but went the rounds so often—now full, now empty, like the bucket of a water wheel—that they soon drained one of the two wine bags that were on hand. After Don Quixote had well satisfied his stomach, he took up a handful of acorns and, gazing at them attentively, fell into a soliloquy.

"Happy the age and happy those centuries to which the ancients gave the name of golden, and not because gold, which is so esteemed in this iron age of ours, was then to be had without toil, but because those who lived in that time did not know the meaning of the words 'thine' and 'mine.' In that blessed era all things were held in common, and to gain his daily sustenance no labor was required of any man save to reach forth his hand and take it from the sturdy oaks that stood liberally inviting him with their sweet and seasoned fruit. The clear-running fountains and rivers in magnificent abundance offered him palatable and transparent water for his thirst; while in the clefts of the rocks and the hollows of the trees the wise and busy honey-makers set up their republic so that any hand whatever might avail itself, fully and freely, of the fertile harvest which their fragrant toil had produced. The vigorous cork trees of their own free will and grace, without the asking, shed their broad, light bark with which men began to cover their dwellings, erected upon rude stakes merely as a protection against the inclemency of the heavens.

"All then was peace, all was concord and friendship; the crooked plowshare had not as yet grievously laid open and pried into the merciful bowels of our first mother, who without any forcing on man's part yielded her spacious fertile bosom on every hand for the satisfaction, sustenance, and delight of her first sons. Then it was that lovely and unspoiled young shepherdesses, with locks that were sometimes braided, sometimes flowing, went roaming from valley to valley and hillock to hillock with no more garments than were needed to cover decently that which modesty requires and always has required should remain covered. Nor were their adornments such as those in use today—of Tyrian purple and silk worked up in tortured patterns; a few green leaves of burdock or of ivy, and they were as splendidly and as becomingly clad as our ladies of the court with all the rare and exotic tricks of fashion that idle curiosity has taught them.

"Thoughts of love, also, in those days were set forth as simply as the simple hearts that conceived them, without any roundabout and artificial play of words

5. Matthew 23.12.

by way of ornament. Fraud, deceit, and malice had not yet come to mingle with truth and plain-speaking. Justice kept its own domain, where favor and self-interest dared not trespass, dared not impair her rights, becloud, and persecute her as they now do. There was no such thing then as arbitrary judgments, for the reason that there was no one to judge or be judged. Maidens in all their modesty, as I have said, went where they would and unattended; whereas in this hateful age of ours none is safe, even though she go to hide and shut herself up in some new labyrinth like that of Crete; for in spite of all her seclusion, through chinks and crevices or borne upon the air, the amorous plague with all its cursed importunities will find her out and lead her to her ruin.

"It was for the safety of such as these, as time went on and depravity increased, that the order of knights-errant was instituted, for the protection of damsels, the aid of widows and orphans, and the succoring of the needy. It is to this order that I belong, my brothers, and I thank you for the welcome and the kindly treatment that you have accorded to me and my squire. By natural law, all living men are obliged to show favor to knights-errant, yet without being aware of this you have received and entertained me; and so it is with all possible good will that I acknowledge your own good will to me."

This long harangue on the part of our knight—it might very well have been dispensed with—was all due to the acorns they had given him, which had brought back to memory the age of gold; whereupon the whim had seized him to indulge in this futile harangue with the goatherds as his auditors. They listened in open-mouthed wonderment, saying not a word, and Sancho himself kept quiet and went on munching acorns, taking occasion very frequently to pay a visit to the second wine bag, which they had suspended from a cork tree to keep it cool.

It took Don Quixote much longer to finish his speech than it did to put away his supper; and when he was through, one of the goatherds addressed him.

"In order that your Grace may say with more truth that we have received you with readiness and good will, we desire to give you solace and contentment by having one of our comrades, who will be here soon, sing for you. He is a very bright young fellow and deeply in love, and what is more, you could not ask for anything better than to hear him play the three-stringed lute."

Scarcely had he done saying this when the sound of a rebec[6] was heard, and shortly afterward the one who played it appeared. He was a good-looking youth, around twenty-two years of age. His companions asked him if he had had his supper, and when he replied that he had, the one who had spoken to Don Quixote said to him, "Well, then, Antonio, you can give us the pleasure of hearing you sing, in order that this gentleman whom we have as our guest may see that we of the woods and mountains also know something about music. We have been telling him how clever you are, and now we want you to show him that we were speaking the truth. And so I beg you by all means to sit down and sing us that love-song of yours that your uncle the prebendary composed for you and which the villagers liked so well.

"With great pleasure," the lad replied, and without any urging he seated himself on the stump of an oak that had been felled and, tuning up his rebec, soon began singing, very prettily, the following ballad:

6. Three-stringed instrument played with a bow.

THE BALLAD THAT ANTONIO SANG

I know well that thou dost love me,
My Olalla, even though
Eyes of thine have never spoken—
Love's mute tongues—to tell me so.

Since I know thou knowest my passion,
Of thy love I am more sure;
No love ever was unhappy
When it was both frank and pure.

True it is, Olalla, sometimes
Thou a heart of bronze hast shown,
And it seemed to me that bosom,
White and fair, was made of stone.

Yet in spite of all repulses
And a chastity so cold,
It appeared that I Hope's garment
By the hem did clutch and hold.

For my faith I ever cherished;
It would rise to meet the bait;
Spurned, it never did diminish;
Favored, it preferred to wait.

Love, they say, hath gentle manners:
Thus it is it shows its face;
Then may I take hope, Olalla,
Trust to win a longed-for grace.

If devotion hath the power
Hearts to move and make them kind,
Let the loyalty I've shown thee
Plead my cause, be kept in mind.

For if thou didst note my costume,
More than once thou must have seen,
Worn upon a simple Monday
Sunday's garb so bright and clean.

Love and brightness go together.
Dost thou ask the reason why
I thus deck myself on Monday?
It is but to catch thine eye.

I say nothing of the dances
I have danced for thy sweet sake;
Nor the serenades I've sung thee
Till the first cock did awake.

Nor will I repeat my praises
Of that beauty all can see;
True my words but oft unwelcome—
Certain lasses bated me.

One girl there is, I well remember—
She's Teresa on the hill—
Said, "You think you love an angel,
But she is a monkey still.

"Thanks to all her many trinkets
And her artificial hair

> *And her many aids to beauty,*
> *Love's own self she would ensnare."*
>   *She was lying, I was angry,*
> *And her cousin, very bold,*
> *Challenged me upon my honor;*
> *What ensued need not be told.*
>   *Highflown words do not become me;*
> *I'm a plain and simple man.*
> *Pure the love that I would offer,*
> *Serving thee as best I can.*
>   *Silken are the bonds of marriage,*
> *When two hearts do intertwine;*
> *Mother Church the yoke will fasten;*
> *Bow your neck and I'll bow mine.*
>   *Or if not, my word I'll give thee,*
> *From these mountains I'll come down—*
> *Saint most holy be my witness—*
> *Wearing a Capuchin[7] gown.*

With this the goatherd brought his song to a close, and although Don Quixote begged him to sing some more, Sancho Panza would not hear to this as he was too sleepy for any more ballads.

"Your Grace," he said to his master, "would do well to find out at once where his bed is to be, for the labor that these good men have to perform all day long does not permit them to stay up all night singing."

"I understand, Sancho," replied Don Quixote. "I perceive that those visits to the wine bag call for sleep rather than music as a recompense."

"It tastes well enough to all of us, God be praised," said Sancho.

"I am not denying that," said his master; "but go ahead and settle yourself down wherever you like. As for men of my profession, they prefer to keep vigil. But all the same, Sancho, perhaps you had better look after this ear, for it is paining me more than I like."

Sancho started to do as he was commanded, but one of the goatherds, when he saw the wound, told him not to bother, that he would place a remedy upon it that would heal it in no time. Taking a few leaves of rosemary, of which there was a great deal growing thereabouts, he mashed them in his mouth and, mixing them with a little salt, laid them on the ear, with the assurance that no other medicine was needed; and this proved to be the truth.

CHAPTER XII

Of the story that one of the goatherds told to
Don Quixote and the others.

Just then, another lad came up, one of those who brought the goatherds their provisions from the village.

"Do you know what's happening down there, my friends?" he said.

"How should we know?" one of the men answered him.

---

7. An austere order of Franciscan friars.

"In that case," the lad went on, "I must tell you that the famous student and shepherd known as Grisóstomo died this morning, muttering that the cause of his death was the love he had for that bewitched lass of a Marcela, daughter of the wealthy Guillermo—you know, the one who's been going around in these parts dressed like a shepherdess."

"For love of Marcela, you say?" one of the herders spoke up.

"That is what I'm telling you," replied the other lad. "And the best part of it is that he left directions in his will that he was to be buried in the field, as if he were a Moor, and that his grave was to be at the foot of the cliff where the Cork Tree Spring is; for, according to report, and he is supposed to have said so himself, that is the place where he saw her for the first time. There were other provisions, which the clergy of the village say cannot be carried out, nor would it be proper to fulfill them, seeing that they savor of heathen practices. But Grisóstomo's good friend, the student Ambrosio, who also dresses like a shepherd, insists that everything must be done to the letter, and as a result there is great excitement in the village.

"Nevertheless, from all I can hear, they will end by doing as Ambrosio and Grisóstomo's other friends desire, and tomorrow they will bury him with great ceremony in the place that I have mentioned. I believe it is going to be something worth seeing; at any rate, I mean to see it, even though it is too far for me to be able to return to the village before nightfall."

"We will all do the same," said the other goatherds. "We will cast lots to see who stays to watch the goats."

"That is right, Pedro," said one of their number, "but it will not be necessary to go to the trouble of casting lots. I will take care of the flocks for all of us; and do not think that I am being generous or that I am not as curious as the rest of you; it is simply that I cannot walk on account of the splinter I picked up in this foot the other day."

"Well, we thank you just the same," said Pedro.

Don Quixote then asked Pedro to tell him more about the dead man and the shepherd lass; to which the latter replied that all he knew was that Grisóstomo was a rich gentleman who had lived in a near-by village. He had been a student for many years at Salamanca[8] and then had returned to his birthplace with the reputation of being very learned and well read; he was especially noted for his knowledge of the science of the stars and what the sun and moon were doing up there in the heavens, "for he would promptly tell us when their clips was to come."

"*Eclipse*, my friend, not *clips*," said Don Quixote, "is the name applied to the darkening-over of those major luminaries."

But Pedro, not pausing for any trifles, went on with his story. "He could also tell when the year was going to be plentiful or estil—"

"*Sterile*, you mean to say, friend—"

"*Sterile* or *estil*," said Pedro, "it all comes out the same in the end. But I can tell you one thing, that his father and his friends, who believed in him, did just as he advised them and they became rich; for he would say to them, 'This year, sow barley and not wheat'; and again, 'Sow chickpeas and not barley'; or, 'This season there will be a good crop of oil,[9] but the three following ones you will not get a drop.'"

---

8. Town west of Madrid that is home to Spain's oldest university, founded in 1134.

9. I.e., olive oil.

"That science," Don Quixote explained, "is known as astrology."

"I don't know what it's called," said Pedro, "but he knew all this and more yet. Finally, not many months after he returned from Salamanca, he appeared one day dressed like a shepherd with crook and sheepskin jacket; for he had resolved to lay aside the long gown that he wore as a scholar, and in this he was joined by Ambrosio, a dear friend of his and the companion of his studies. I forgot to tell you that Grisóstomo was a great one for composing verses; he even wrote the carols for Christmas Eve and the plays that were performed at Corpus Christi by the lads of our village, and everyone said that they were the best ever.

"When the villagers saw the two scholars coming out dressed like shepherds, they were amazed and could not imagine what was the reason for such strange conduct on their part. It was about that time that Grisóstomo's father died and left him the heir to a large fortune, consisting of land and chattels, no small quantity of cattle, and a considerable sum of money, of all of which the young man was absolute master; and, to tell the truth, he deserved it, for he was very sociable and charitably inclined, a friend to all worthy folk, and he had a face that was like a benediction. Afterward it was learned that if he had changed his garments like this, it was only that he might be able to wander over the wastelands on the trail of that shepherdess Marcela of whom our friend was speaking, for the poor fellow had fallen in love with her. And now I should like to tell you, for it is well that you should know, just who this lass is; for it may be— indeed, there is no maybe about it—you will never hear the like in all the days of your life, though you live to be older than Sarna."

"You should say *Sarah*," Don Quixote corrected him; for he could not bear hearing the goatherd using the wrong words all the time.[1]

"The itch," said Pedro, "lives long enough; and if, sir, you go on interrupting me at every word, we'll never be through in a year."

"Pardon me, friend," said Don Quixote, "it was only because there is so great a difference between Sarna and Sarah that I pointed it out to you; but you have given me a very good answer, for the itch does live longer than Sarah; and so go on with your story, and I will not contradict you anymore."

"I was about to say, then, my dear sir," the goatherd went on, "that in our village there was a farmer who was richer still than Grisóstomo's father. His name was Guillermo, and, over and above his great wealth, God gave him a daughter whose mother, the most highly respected woman in these parts, died in bearing her. It seems to me I can see the good lady now, with that face that rivaled the sun and moon; and I remember, above all, what a friend she was to the poor, for which reason I believe that her soul at this very moment must be enjoying God's presence in the other world.

"Grieving for the loss of so excellent a wife, Guillermo himself died, leaving his daughter Marcela, now a rich young woman, in the custody of one of her uncles, a priest who holds a benefice in our village. The girl grew up with such beauty as to remind us of her mother, beautiful as that lady had been. By the time she was fourteen or fifteen no one looked at her without giving thanks to God who had created such comeliness, and almost all were hopelessly in love

---

1. Actually in this case the goatherd is not really wrong, for *sarna* means "itch" and "older than the itch" was a proverbial expression. ("Sarah" is a reference to the wife of Abraham in the Old Testament.)

with her. Her uncle kept her very closely shut up, but, for all of that, word of her great beauty spread to such an extent that by reason of it, as much as on account of the girl's wealth, her uncle found himself besought and importuned not only by the young men of our village, but by those for leagues around who desired to have her for a wife.

"But he, an upright Christian, although he wished to marry her off as soon as she was of age, had no desire to do so without her consent, not that he had any eye to the gain and profit which the custody of his niece's property brought him while her marriage was deferred. Indeed, this much was said in praise of the good priest in more than one circle of the village; for I would have you know, Sir Knight, that in these little places everything is discussed and becomes a subject of gossip; and you may rest assured, as I am for my part, that a priest must be more than ordinarily good if his parishioners feel bound to speak well of him, especially in the small towns."

"That is true," said Don Quixote, "but go on. I like your story very much, and you, good Pedro, tell it with very good grace."

"May the Lord's grace never fail me, for that is what counts. But to go on: Although the uncle set forth to his niece the qualities of each one in particular of the many who sought her hand, begging her to choose and marry whichever one she pleased, she never gave him any answer other than this: that she did not wish to marry at all, since being but a young girl she did not feel that she was equal to bearing the burdens of matrimony. As her reasons appeared to be proper and just, the uncle did not insist but thought he would wait until she was a little older, when she would be capable of selecting someone to her taste. For, he said, and quite right he was, parents ought not to impose a way of life upon their children against the latters' will. And then, one fine day, lo and behold, there was the finical Marcela turned shepherdess; and without paying any attention to her uncle or all those of the village who advised against it, she set out to wander through the fields with the other lasses, guarding flocks as they did.

"Well, the moment she appeared in public and her beauty was uncovered for all to see, I really cannot tell you how many rich young bachelors, gentlemen, and farmers proceeded to don a shepherd's garb and go to make love to her in the meadows. One of her suitors, as I have told you, was our deceased friend, and it is said that he did not love but adored her. But you must not think that because Marcela chose so free and easy a life, and one that offers little or no privacy, that she was thereby giving the faintest semblance of encouragement to those who would disparage her modesty and prudence; rather, so great was the vigilance with which she looked after her honor that of all those who waited upon her and solicited her favors, none could truly say that she had given him the slightest hope of attaining his desire.

"For although she does not flee nor shun the company and conversation of the shepherds, treating them in courteous and friendly fashion, the moment she discovers any intentions on their part, even though it be the just and holy one of matrimony, she hurls them from her like a catapult. As a result, she is doing more damage in this land than if a plague had fallen upon it; for her beauty and graciousness win the hearts of all who would serve her, but her disdain and the disillusionment it brings lead them in the end to despair, and then they can only call her cruel and ungrateful, along with other similar epithets that reveal all too plainly the state of mind that prompts them. If you were to stay here some time, sir, you would hear these uplands and valleys echo with the laments of those who have followed her only to be deceived.

"Not far from here is a place where there are a couple of dozen tall beeches, and there is not a one of them on whose smooth bark Marcela's name has not been engraved; and above some of these inscriptions you will find a crown, as if by this her lover meant to indicate that she deserved to wear the garland of beauty above all the women on the earth. Here a shepherd sighs and there another voices his lament. Now are to be heard amorous ballads, and again despairing ditties. One will spend all the hours of the night seated at the foot of some oak or rock without once closing his tearful eyes, and the morning sun will find him there, stupefied and lost in thought. Another, without giving truce or respite to his sighs, will lie stretched upon the burning sands in the full heat of the most exhausting summer noontide, sending up his complaint to merciful Heaven.

"And, meanwhile, over this one and that one, over one and all, the beauteous Marcela triumphs and goes her own way, free and unconcerned. All those of us who know her are waiting to see how far her pride will carry her, and who will be the fortunate man who will succeed in taming this terrible creature and thus come into possession of a beauty so matchless as hers. Knowing all this that I have told you to be undoubtedly true, I can readily believe this lad's story about the cause of Grisóstomo's death. And so I advise you, sir, not to fail to be present tomorrow at his burial; it will be well worth seeing, for he has many friends, and the place is not half a league from here."

"I will make a point of it," said Don Quixote, "and I thank you for the pleasure you have given me by telling me so delightful a tale."

"Oh," said the goatherd, "I do not know the half of the things that have happened to Marcela's lovers; but it is possible that tomorrow we may meet along the way some shepherd who will tell us more. And now it would be well for you to go and sleep under cover, for the night air may not be good for your wound, though with the remedy that has been put on it there is not much to fear."

Sancho Panza, who had been sending the goatherd to the devil for talking so much, now put in a word with his master, urging him to come and sleep in Pedro's hut. Don Quixote did so; and all the rest of the night was spent by him in thinking of his lady Dulcinea, in imitation of Marcela's lovers. As for Sancho, he made himself comfortable between Rocinante and the ass and at once dropped off to sleep, not like a lovelorn swain but, rather, like a man who has had a sound kicking that day.

CHAPTER XIII

In which is brought to a close the story of the shepherdess Marcela, along with other events.

Day had barely begun to appear upon the balconies of the east when five or six goatherds arose and went to awaken Don Quixote and tell him that if he was still of a mind to go see Grisóstomo's famous burial they would keep him company. The knight, desiring nothing better, ordered Sancho to saddle at once, which was done with much dispatch, and then they all set out forthwith.

They had not gone more than a quarter of a league when, upon crossing a footpath, they saw coming toward them six shepherds clad in black sheepskins and with garlands of cypress and bitter rosebay on their heads. Each of them carried a thick staff made of the wood of the holly, and with them came two gentlemen on horseback in handsome traveling attire, accompanied by three lads on foot. As the two parties met they greeted each other courteously, each inquiring as to the other's destination, whereupon they learned that they were all going to the burial, and so continued to ride along together.

Speaking to his companion, one of them said, "I think, Señor Vivaldo, that we are going to be well repaid for the delay it will cost us to see this famous funeral; for famous it must surely be, judging by the strange things that these shepherds have told us of the dead man and the homicidal shepherdess."

"I think so too," agreed Vivaldo. "I should be willing to delay our journey not one day, but four, for the sake of seeing it."

Don Quixote then asked them what it was they had heard of Marcela and Grisóstomo. The traveler replied that on that very morning they had fallen in with those shepherds and, seeing them so mournfully trigged out, had asked them what the occasion for it was. One of the fellows had then told them of the beauty and strange demeanor of a shepherdess by the name of Marcela, her many suitors, and the death of this Grisóstomo, to whose funeral they were bound. He related, in short, the entire story as Don Quixote had heard it from Pedro.

Changing the subject, the gentleman called Vivaldo inquired of Don Quixote what it was that led him to go armed in that manner in a land that was so peaceful.

"The calling that I profess," replied Don Quixote, "does not permit me to do otherwise. An easy pace, pleasure, and repose—those things were invented for delicate courtiers; but toil, anxiety, and arms—they are for those whom the world knows as knights-errant, of whom I, though unworthy, am the very least."

No sooner had they heard this than all of them immediately took him for a madman. By way of assuring himself further and seeing what kind of madness it was of which Don Quixote was possessed, Vivaldo now asked him what was meant by the term knights-errant.

"Have not your Worships read the annals and the histories of England that treat of the famous exploits of King Arthur, who in our Castilian balladry is always called King Artús? According to a very old tradition that is common throughout the entire realm of Great Britain, this king did not die, but by an act of enchantment was changed into a raven; and in due course of time he is to return and reign once more, recovering his kingdom and his scepter; for which reason, from that day to this, no Englishman is known to have killed one of those birds. It was, moreover, in the time of that good king that the famous order of the Knights of the Round Table was instituted; and as for the love of Sir Lancelot of the Lake and Queen Guinevere, everything took place exactly as the story has it, their confidante and go-between being the honored matron Quintañona; whence comes that charming ballad that is such a favorite with us Spaniards:

> Never was there a knight
> So served by maid and dame
> As the one they call Sir Lancelot
> When from Britain be came—

to carry on the gentle, pleasing course of his loves and noble deeds.

"From that time forth, the order of chivalry was passed on and propagated from one individual to another until it had spread through many and various parts of the world. Among those famed for their exploits was the valiant Amadis of Gaul, with all his sons and grandsons to the fifth generation; and there was also the brave Felixmarte of Hircania, and the never sufficiently praised Tirant lo Blanch; and in view of the fact that he lived in our own day, almost, we came near to seeing, hearing, and conversing with that other courageous knight, Don Belianís of Greece.[2]

"And that, gentlemen, is what it means to be a knight-errant, and what I have been telling you of is the order of chivalry which such a knight professes, an order to which, as I have already informed you, I, although a sinner, have the honor of belonging; for I have made the same profession as have those other knights. That is why it is you find me in these wild and lonely places, riding in quest of adventure, being resolved to offer my arm and my person in the most dangerous undertaking fate may have in store for me, that I may be of aid to the weak and needy."

Listening to this speech, the travelers had some while since come to the conclusion that Don Quixote was out of his mind, and were likewise able to perceive the peculiar nature of his madness, and they wondered at it quite as much as did all those who encountered it for the first time. Being endowed with a ready wit and a merry disposition and thinking to pass the time until they reached the end of the short journey which, so he was told, awaited them before they should arrive at the mountain where the burial was to take place, Vivaldo decided to give him a further opportunity of displaying his absurdities.

"It strikes me, Sir Knight-errant," he said, "that your Grace has espoused one of the most austere professions to be found anywhere on earth—even more austere, if I am not mistaken, than that of the Carthusian monks."

"Theirs may be as austere as ours," Don Quixote replied, "but that it is as necessary I am very much inclined to doubt. For if the truth be told, the soldier who carries out his captain's order does no less than the captain who gives the order. By that I mean to say that the religious, in all peace and tranquility, pray to Heaven for earth's good, but we soldiers and knights put their prayers into execution by defending with the might of our good right arms and at the edge of the sword those things for which they pray; and we do this not under cover of a roof but under the open sky, beneath the insufferable rays of the summer sun and the biting cold of winter. Thus we become the ministers of God on earth, and our arms the means by which He executes His decrees. And just as war and all the things that have to do with it are impossible without toil, sweat, and anxiety, it follows that those who have taken upon themselves such a profession must unquestionably labor harder than do those who in peace and tranquility and at their ease pray God to favor the ones who can do little in their own behalf.

"I do not mean to say—I should not think of saying—that the state of knight-errant is as holy as that of the cloistered monk; I merely would imply, from what I myself endure, that ours is beyond a doubt the more laborious and arduous calling, more beset by hunger and thirst, more wretched, ragged, and ridden with lice. It is an absolute certainty that the knights-errant of old

---

2. Each of the knights praised here is the fictitious hero of a romance popular in Cervantes' time.

experienced much misfortune in the course of their lives; and if some by their might and valor came to be emperors, you may take my word for it, it cost them dearly in blood and sweat, and if those who rose to such a rank had lacked enchanters and magicians to aid them, they surely would have been cheated of their desires, deceived in their hopes and expectations."

"I agree with you on that," said the traveler, "but there is one thing among others that gives me a very bad impression of the knights-errant, and that is the fact that when they are about to enter upon some great and perilous adventure in which they are in danger of losing their lives, they never at that moment think of commending themselves to God as every good Christian is obliged to do under similar circumstances, but, rather, commend themselves to their ladies with as much fervor and devotion as if their mistresses were God himself; all of which to me smacks somewhat of paganism."

"Sir," Don Quixote answered him, "it could not by any means be otherwise; the knight-errant who did not do so would fall into disgrace, for it is the usage and custom of chivalry that the knight, before engaging in some great feat of arms, shall behold his lady in front of him and shall turn his eyes toward her, gently and lovingly, as if beseeching her favor and protection in the hazardous encounter that awaits him, and even though no one hears him, he is obliged to utter certain words between his teeth, commending himself to her with all his heart; and of this we have numerous examples in the histories. Nor is it to be assumed that he does not commend himself to God also, but the time and place for that is in the course of the undertaking."

"All the same," said the traveler, "I am not wholly clear in this matter; for I have often read of two knights-errant exchanging words until, one word leading to another, their wrath is kindled; whereupon, turning their steeds and taking a good run up the field, they whirl about and bear down upon each other at full speed, commending themselves to their ladies in the midst of it all. What commonly happens then is that one of the two topples from his horse's flanks and is run through and through with the other's lance; and his adversary would also fall to the ground if he did not cling to his horse's mane. What I do not understand is how the dead man would have had time to commend himself to God in the course of this accelerated combat. It would be better if the words he wasted in calling upon his lady as he ran toward the other knight had been spent in paying the debt that he owed as a Christian. Moreover, it is my personal opinion that not all knights-errant have ladies to whom to commend themselves, for not all of them are in love."

"That," said Don Quixote, "is impossible. I assert there can be no knight-errant without a lady; for it is as natural and proper for them to be in love as it is for the heavens to have stars, and I am quite sure that no one ever read a story in which a loveless man of arms was to be met with, for the simple reason that such a one would not be looked upon as a legitimate knight but as a bastard one who had entered the fortress of chivalry not by the main gate, but over the walls, like a robber and a thief."

"Nevertheless," said the traveler, "if my memory serves me right, I have read that Don Galaor, brother of the valorous Amadis of Gaul, never had a special lady to whom he prayed, yet he was not held in any the less esteem for that but was a very brave and famous knight."

Once again, our Don Quixote had an answer. "Sir, one swallow does not make a summer. And in any event, I happen to know that this knight was secretly very much in love. As for his habit of paying court to all the ladies that caught his fancy, that was a natural propensity on his part and one that he was unable to resist. There was, however, one particular lady whom he had made the mistress of his will and to whom he did commend himself very frequently and privately; for he prided himself upon being a reticent knight."

"Well, then," said the traveler, "if it is essential that every knight-errant be in love, it is to be presumed that your Grace is also, since you are of the profession. And unless it be that you pride yourself upon your reticence as much as did Don Galaor, then I truly, on my own behalf and in the name of all this company, beseech your Grace to tell us your lady's name, the name of the country where she resides, what her rank is, and something of the beauty of her person, that she may esteem herself fortunate in having all the world know that she is loved and served by such a knight as your Grace appears to me to be."

At this, Don Quixote heaved a deep sigh. "I cannot say," he began, "as to whether or not my sweet enemy would be pleased that all the world should know I serve her. I can only tell you, in response to the question which you have so politely put to me, that her name is Dulcinea, her place of residence El Toboso, a village of La Mancha. As to her rank, she should be at the very least a princess, seeing that she is my lady and my queen. Her beauty is superhuman, for in it are realized all the impossible and chimerical attributes that poets are accustomed to give their fair ones. Her locks are golden, her brow the Elysian Fields, her eyebrows rainbows, her eyes suns, her cheeks roses, her lips coral, her teeth pearls, her neck alabaster, her bosom marble, her hands ivory, her complexion snow-white. As for those parts which modesty keeps covered from the human sight, it is my opinion that, discreetly considered, they are only to be extolled and not compared to any other."

"We should like," said Vivaldo, "to know something as well of her lineage, her race and ancestry."

"She is not," said Don Quixote, "of the ancient Roman Curtii, Caii, or Scipios, nor of the modern Colonnas and Orsini, nor of the Moncadas and Requesenses of Catalonia, nor is she of the Rebellas and Villanovas of Valencia, or the Palafoxes, Nuzas, Rocabertis, Corellas, Lunas, Alagones, Urreas, or Gurreas of Aragon, the Cerdas, Manriques, Mendozas, or Guzmanes of Castile, the Alencastros, Pallas, or Menezes of Portugal; but she is of the Tobosos of La Mancha, and although the line is a modern one, it well may give rise to the most illustrious families of the centuries to come. And let none dispute this with me, unless it be under the conditions which Zerbino has set forth in the inscription beneath Orlando's arms:

> These let none move
> Who dares not with Orlando his valor prove."[3]

"Although my own line," replied the traveler, "is that of the Gachupins of Laredo, I should not venture to compare it with the Tobosos of La Mancha, in view of the fact that, to tell you the truth, I have never heard the name before."

3. From Ludovico Ariosto's *Orlando Furioso*, 24.57.

"How does it come that you have never heard it!" exclaimed Don Quixote.

The others were listening most attentively to the conversation of these two, and even the goatherds and shepherds were by now aware that our knight of La Mancha was more than a little insane. Sancho Panza alone thought that all his master said was the truth, for he was well acquainted with him, having known him since birth. The only doubt in his mind had to do with the beauteous Dulcinea del Toboso, for he knew of no such princess and the name was strange to his ears, although he lived not far from that place.

They were continuing on their way, conversing in this manner, when they caught sight of some twenty shepherds coming through the gap between two high mountains, all of them clad in black woolen garments and with wreaths on their heads, some of the garlands, as was afterward learned, being of cypress, others of yew. Six of them were carrying a bier covered with a great variety of flowers and boughs.

"There they come with Grisóstomo's body," said one of the goatherds, "and the foot of the mountain yonder is where he wished to be buried."

They accordingly quickened their pace and arrived just as those carrying the bier had set it down on the ground. Four of the shepherds with sharpened picks were engaged in digging a grave alongside the barren rock. After a courteous exchange of greetings, Don Quixote and his companions turned to look at the bier. Upon it lay a corpse covered with flowers, the body of a man dressed like a shepherd and around thirty years of age. Even in death it could be seen that he had had a handsome face and had been of a jovial disposition. Round about him upon the bier were a number of books and many papers, open and folded.

Meanwhile, those who stood gazing at the dead man and those who were digging the grave—everyone present, in fact—preserved an awed silence, until one of the pallbearers said to another, "Look well, Ambrosio, and make sure that this is the place that Grisóstomo had in mind, since you are bent upon carrying out to the letter the provisions of his will."

"This is it," replied Ambrosio; "for many times my unfortunate friend told me the story of his misadventure. He told me that it was here that he first laid eyes upon that mortal enemy of the human race, and it was here, also, that he first revealed to her his passion, for he was as honorable as he was lovelorn; and it was here, finally, at their last meeting, that she shattered his illusions and showed him her disdain, thus bringing to an end the tragedy of his wretched life. And here, in memory of his great misfortune, he wished to be laid in the bowels of eternal oblivion."

Then, turning to Don Quixote and the travelers, he went on, "This body, gentlemen, on which you now look with pitying eyes was the depository of a soul which heaven had endowed with a vast share of its riches. This is the body of Grisóstomo, who was unrivaled in wit, unequaled in courtesy, supreme in gentleness of bearing, a model of friendship, generous without stint, grave without conceit, merry without being vulgar—in short, first in all that is good and second to none in the matter of misfortunes. He loved well and was hated, he adored and was disdained; he wooed a wild beast, importuned a piece of marble, ran after the wind, cried out to loneliness, waited upon ingratitude, and his reward was to be the spoils of death midway in his life's course—a life that was brought to an end by a shepherdess whom he sought to immortalize that she might live on in the memory of mankind, as those papers that you see there would very plainly show if he had not commanded me to consign them to the flames even as his body is given to the earth."

"You," said Vivaldo, "would treat them with greater harshness and cruelty than their owner himself, for it is neither just nor fitting to carry out the will of one who commands what is contrary to all reason. It would not have been a good thing for Augustus Caesar to consent to have them execute the behests of the divine Mantuan in his last testament.[4] And so, Señor Ambrosio, while you may give the body of your friend to the earth, you ought not to give his writings to oblivion. If out of bitterness he left such an order, that does not mean that you are to obey it without using your own discretion. Rather, by granting life to these papers, you permit Marcela's cruelheartedness to live forever and serve as an example to the others in the days that are to come in order that they may flee and avoid such pitfalls as these.

"I and those that have come with me know the story of this lovesick and despairing friend of yours; we know the affection that was between you, and what the occasion of his death was, and the things that he commanded be done as his life drew to a close. And from this lamentable tale anyone may see how great was Marcela's cruelty; they may behold Grisóstomo's love, the loyalty that lay in your friendship, and the end that awaits those who run headlong, with unbridled passion, down the path that doting love opens before their gaze. Last night we heard of your friend's death and learned that he was to be buried here, and out of pity and curiosity we turned aside from our journey and resolved to come see with our own eyes that which had aroused so much compassion when it was told to us. And in requital of that compassion, and the desire that has been born in us to prevent if we can a recurrence of such tragic circumstances, we beg you, O prudent Ambrosio!—or, at least, I for my part implore you—to give up your intention of burning these papers and let me carry some of them away with me."

Without waiting for the shepherd to reply he put out his hand and took a few of those that were nearest him.

"Out of courtesy, sir," said Ambrosio when he saw this, "I will consent for you to keep those that you have taken; but it is vain to think that I will refrain from burning the others."

Vivaldo, who was anxious to find out what was in the papers, opened one of them and perceived that it bore the title "Song of Despair."

Hearing this, Ambrosio said, "That is the last thing the poor fellow wrote; and in order, sir, that you may see the end to which his misfortunes brought him, read it aloud if you will, for we shall have time for it while they are digging the grave."

"That I will very willingly do," said Vivaldo.

And since all the bystanders had the same desire, they gathered around as he in a loud clear voice read the following poem.

---

4. Virgil (born near Mantua in 70 B.C.E.) had left instructions that his Roman epic, the *Aeneid*, should be burned.

CHAPTER XIV

*In which are set down the despairing verses of the deceased
shepherd, with other unlooked-for happenings.*

Grisóstomo's Song

Since thou desirest that thy cruelty
Be spread from tongue to tongue and land to land,
The unrelenting sternness of thy heart
Shall turn my bosom's hell to minstrelsy
That all men everywhere may understand
The nature of my grief and what thou art.
And as I seek my sorrows to import,
Telling of all the things that thou hast done,
My very entrails shall speak out to brand
Thy heartlessness, thy soul to reprimand,
Where no compassion ever have I won.
Then listen well, lend an attentive ear;
This ballad that thou art about to hear
Is not contrived by art; 'tis a simple song
Such as shepherds sing each day throughout the year—
Surcease of pain for me, for thee a prong.
    Then let the roar of lion, fierce wolf's cry,
The horrid hissing of the scaly snake,
The terrifying sound of monsters strange,
Ill-omened call of crow against the sky,
The howling of the wind as it doth shake
The tossing sea where all is constant change,
Bellow of vanquished bull that cannot range
As it was wont to do, the piteous sob
Of the widowed dove as if its heart would break,
Hoot of the envied owl,[5] ever awake,
From hell's own choir the deep and mournful throb—
Let all these sounds come forth and mingle now.
For if I'm to tell my woes, why then, I vow,
I must new measures find, new modes invent,
With sound confusing sense, I may somehow
Portray the inferno where my days are spent.
    The mournful echoes of my murmurous plaint
Father Tagus shall not hear as he rolls his sand,
Nor olive-bordered Betis;[6] my lament shall be
To the tall and barren rock as I acquaint
The caves with my sorrow; the far and lonely strand
No human foot has trod shall hear from me
The story of thine inhumanity
As told with lifeless tongue but living word.
I'll tell it to the valleys near at hand
Where never shines the sun upon the land;

---

5. Envied by other birds as the only one that
witnessed the Crucifixion.

6. The river Guadalquivir. "Father Tagus": the
river Tagus, the Iberian Peninsula's longest river.

By venomous serpents shall my tale be heard
On the low-lying, marshy river plain.
And yet, the telling will not be in vain;
For the reverberations of my plight,
Thy matchless austerity and this my pain,
Through the wide world shall go, thee to indict.

    Disdain may kill; suspicion false or true
May slay all patience; deadliest of all
Is jealousy; while absence renders life
Worse than a void; Hope lends no roseate hue
Against forgetfulness or the dread call
Of death inevitable, the end of strife.
Yet—unheard miracle!—with sorrows rife,
My own existence somehow still goes on;
The flame of life with me doth rise and fall.
Jealous I am, disdained; I know the gall
Of those suspicions that will not be gone,
Which leave me not the shadow of a hope,
And, desperate, I will not even grope
But rather will endure until the end,
And with despair eternally I'll cope,
Knowing that things for me will never mend.

    Can one both hope and fear at the same season?
Would it be well to do so in any case,
Seeing that fear, by far, hath the better excuse?
Confronting jealousy, is there any reason
For me to close my eyes to its stern face,
Pretend to see it not? What is the use,
When its dread presence I can still deduce
From countless gaping wounds deep in my heart?
When suspicion—bitter change!—to truth gives place,
And truth itself, losing its virgin grace,
Becomes a lie, is it not wisdom's part
To open wide the door to frank mistrust?
When disdain's unveiled, to doubt is only just.
O ye fierce tyrants of Love's empery!
Shackle these hands with stout cord, if ye must.
My pain shall drown your triumph—woe is me!

    I die, in short, and since nor life nor death
Yields any hope, to my fancy will I cling.
That man is freest who is Love's bond slave:
I'll say this with my living-dying breath,
And the ancient tyrant's praises I will sing.
Love is the greatest blessing Heaven e'er gave.
What greater beauty could a lover crave
Than that which my fair enemy doth show
In soul and body and in everything?
E'en her forgetfulness of me doth spring
From my own lack of grace, that I well know.
In spite of all the wrongs that he has wrought,
Love rules his empire justly as he ought.

Throw all to the winds and speed life's wretched span
By feeding on his self-deluding thought.
No blessing holds the future that I scan.
   Thou whose unreasonableness reason doth give
For putting an end to this tired life of mine,
From the deep heart wounds which thou mayest plainly see,
Judge if the better course be to die or live.
Gladly did I surrender my will to thine,
Gladly I suffered all thou didst to me;
And now that I'm dying, should it seem to thee
My death is worth a tear from thy bright eyes,
Pray hold it back, fair one, do not repine,
For I would have from thee no faintest sign
Of penitence, e'en though my soul thy prize.
Rather, I'd have thee laugh, be very gay,
And let my funeral be a festive day—
But I am very simple! knowing full well
That thou art bound to go thy blithesome way,
And my untimely end thy fame shall swell.
   Come, thirsting Tantalus from out Hell's pit;
Come, Sisyphus with the terrifying weight
Of that stone thou rollest; Tityus, bring
Thy vulture and thine anguish infinite;
Ixion[7] with thy wheel, be thou not late;
Come, too, ye sisters ever laboring;[8]
Come all, your griefs into my bosom fling,
And then, with lowered voices, intone a dirge,
If dirge be fitting for one so desperate,
A body without a shroud, unhappy fate!
And Hell's three-headed gateman,[9] do thou emerge
With a myriad other phantoms, monstrous swarm,
Beings infernal of fantastic form,
Raising their voices for the uncomforted
In a counterpoint of grief, harmonious storm.
What better burial for a lover dead?
   Despairing song of mine, do not complain,
Nor let our parting cause thee any pain,
For my misfortune is not wholly bad,
Seeing her fortune's bettered by my demise.
Then, even in the grave, be thou not sad.

Those who had listened to Grisóstomo's poem liked it well enough, but the one who read it remarked that it did not appear to him to conform to what had been told him of Marcela's modesty and virtue, seeing that in it the author

---

7. In Greek myth, all four are proverbial images of mortals punished by the Gods with different forms of torture: Tantalus, craving water and fruit which he always fails to reach; Sisyphus, forever vainly trying to roll a stone upward to the top of a hill; Tityus, having his liver devoured by a vulture; and Ixion, being bound to a revolving wheel.
8. In classical mythology, the three Fates (*Moerae* to the Greeks, *Parcae* to the Romans), spinners of man's destiny.
9. Cerberus, a doglike three-headed monster, the mythological guardian of Hell.

A detail from the Codex Féjerváry-Mayer, a pre-Hispanic Aztec manuscript on deerskin parchment, believed to have originated in Veracruz. Pictured is an Aztec origin myth: the Nahuatl god Tezcatlipoca uses his foot as bait to lure the Earth Monster to the surface. After she swallows his foot, she is unable to sink back to her lair, and thus the surface of the earth is created by her immobilized body.

Wonbeheyligung des sibenden tags

Als nw die werlt durch das gepew götlicher weißheit der sechs tag: volendē vn himel vn erdē beschaffē
geordnet gezieret vn zu letst volbracht wordē sind. do hat der glou wirdig got sein werck erfüllet vn am
sybendē tag von den werckē seiner hendt geruet. nach dē er die ganzē werlt vnd alle ding die dar in sind beschaf
fen het do hat er auffgehört. nit als zewurckē muede. sunder zemachen ein newe creatur d materi oder gleichnus
nit vergangē wer dan er hort nit auff zewurckē das werck der geperungen. vnd der herr hat den selbē tag gebe
nedeyet vn geheiligt vnd ine geheissē sabathū. das nach hebreyscher zūge ein rūe bedeutet darūmb das er an dē
selben tag ruet vō allem werck das er gemacht het. do vō auch die iuden an dem tag vō aigner arbait zefeiren er
kant werde. Dē selbē tag habē auch ettlich haidenische völker vor dem gesetz feirlich gehaltē. vnd also sein wir
zu end der göttlichen werck kome. darumb so söllen wir dē in den alle sichtliche vnd vnsichtliche ding sind för
chten. liebhaben vnd eren. vnd von dem herren des himels. von dem herren aller gütter. dem gewalt gegebe ist
in himel vnd erden. die gegenwürtigen gütter. sofer die gut sind. vnd auch die waren seligkait des ewigen lebes
suchen.

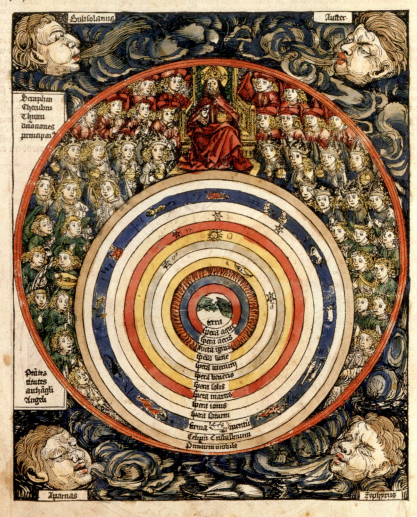

Hartmann Schedel's 1493 book, *World Chronicle* (in German, *Weltchronik*), an
illustrated world history, was one of the first printed books to bring maps and illustrations
to a wide readership. This page depicts the universe as it was understood at the time:
with the earth at the center and other celestial bodies surrounding it. Fifty years later,
the Renaissance astronomer Nicolaus Copernicus (1473–1543) overturned this model,
placing the sun at the center.

Dedicatory page from Antoine du Four's *The Lives of Famous Women* (c. 1505). The author, on bended knee, offers the book to Queen Anne of Brittany (1477–1514), who commissioned the work and for whom du Four served as confessor. The book chronicles

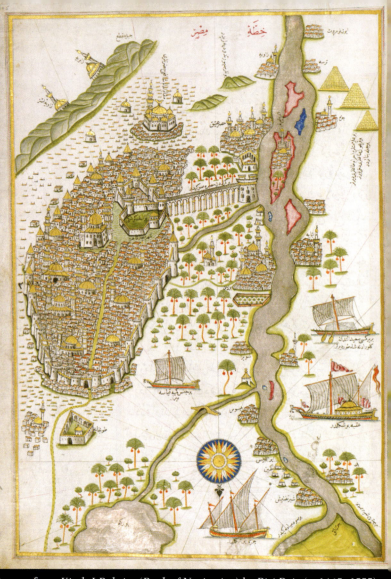

A page from *Kitab-I Bahriye* (*Book of Navigation*) by Piri Reis (c. 1465–1555), an Ottoman military commander, geographer, and cartographer. Published in 1521, the *Kitab-I Bahriye* is one of the most famous books of navigation from early modernity. It provided a comprehensive and detailed overview of the known world of the time, including the recently explored shorelines of the African and American continents. Pictured here is a map of Egypt, with different settlements along the Nile, including the large city of Cairo.

The Reader. A Persian miniature from an unidentified manuscript, c. sixteenth century.

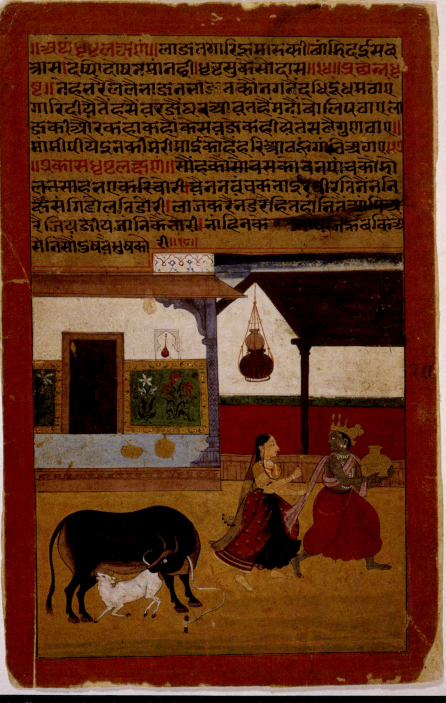

An illustration from the north Indian poetry anthology *Rasik Priya* (1591), by the Sanskrit scholar and Hindi poet Keśavdās (1555–1617). This manuscript dates from the early 17th century, after Keśavdās's death.

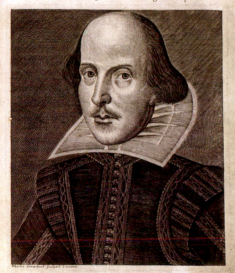

To the Reader.

This Figure, that thou here seest put,
　It was for gentle Shakespeare cut;
Wherein the Grauer had a strife
　with Nature, to out-doo the life :
O, could he but haue drawne his wit
　As well in brasse, as he hath hit
His face ; the Print would then surpasse
　All, that vvas euer vvrit in brasse.
But, since he cannot, Reader, looke
　Not on his Picture, but his Booke.

B. I.

Mr. WILLIAM
SHAKESPEARES
COMEDIES,
HISTORIES, &
TRAGEDIES.

Published according to the True Originall Copies.

LONDON
Printed by Isaac Iaggard, and Ed. Blount. 1623.

Frontispiece and title page of one of the most famous books of the Renaissance: the 1623 "First Folio" of the plays of William Shakespeare. The portrait by Martin Droeshout was not made from life, and yet it has fixed the public's sense of Shakespeare's appearance. The poem on the facing page, by Ben Jonson, urges readers to "looke / Not on his Picture, but his Booke."

This 1645 portrait of the court jester Don Diego de Acedo is by the Spanish master Diego Velázquez (1599–1660). Intending to convey de Acedo's status and his intelligence (while also acknowledging his deformity), Velázquez poses him with a book (a traditional signal in court portraiture of gentlemanly status), notebook, stylus, and inkwell.

complains of jealousy, suspicion, and absence, all to the prejudice of her good name. To this Ambrosio, as one who had known his friend's most deeply hidden thoughts, replied as follows:

"By way of satisfying, sir, the doubt that you entertain, it is well for you to know that when the unfortunate man wrote that poem, he was by his own volition absent from Marcela, to see if this would work a cure; but when the enamored one is away from his love, there is nothing that does not inspire in him fear and torment, and such was the case with Grisóstomo, for whom jealous imaginings, fears, and suspicions became a seeming reality. And so, in this respect, Marcela's reputation for virtue remains unimpaired; beyond being cruel and somewhat arrogant, and exceedingly disdainful, she could not be accused by the most envious of any other fault."

"Yes, that is so," said Vivaldo.

He was about to read another of the papers he had saved from the fire when he was stopped by a marvelous vision—for such it appeared—that suddenly met his sight; for there atop the rock beside which the grave was being hollowed out stood the shepherdess Marcela herself, more beautiful even than she was reputed to be. Those who up to then had never seen her looked on in silent admiration, while those who were accustomed to beholding her were held in as great a suspense as the ones who were gazing upon her for the first time.

No sooner had Ambrosio glimpsed her than, with a show of indignation, he called out to her, "So, fierce basilisk[1] of these mountains, have you perchance come to see if in your presence blood will flow from the wounds of this poor wretch whom you by your cruelty have deprived of life?[2] Have you come to gloat over your inhuman exploits, or would you from that height look down like another pitiless Nero upon your Rome in flames and ashes?[3] Or perhaps you would arrogantly tread under foot this poor corpse, as an ungrateful daughter did that of her father Tarquinius?[4] Tell us quickly why you have come and what it is that you want most; for I know that Grisóstomo's thoughts never failed to obey you in life, and though he is dead now, I will see that all those who call themselves his friends obey you likewise."

"I do not come, O Ambrosio, for any of the reasons that you have mentioned," replied Marcela. "I come to defend myself and to demonstrate how unreasonable all those persons are who blame me for their sufferings and for Grisóstomo's death. I therefore ask all present to hear me attentively. It will not take long and I shall not have to spend many words in persuading those of you who are sensible that I speak the truth.

"Heaven made me beautiful, you say, so beautiful that you are compelled to love me whether you will or no; and in return for the love that you show me, you would have it that I am obliged to love you in return. I know, with that natural understanding that God has given me, that everything beautiful is lov-

1. A mythical lizardlike creature whose gaze and breath were supposed to be lethal.
2. According to folklore, the corpse of a murdered person was supposed to bleed in the presence of the murderer.
3. In tale and proverb, the Roman emperor Nero is supposed to have been singing while from a tower he observed the burning of Rome

in 64 C.E.
4. The inaccurate allusion is to Tullia, actually the wife of the last of the legendary kings of early Rome, Tarquinius; she let the wheel of her carriage trample over the body of her father—the previous king, Servius Tullius—whom her husband Tarquinius had liquidated.

able; but I cannot see that it follows that the object that is loved for its beauty must love the one who loves it. Let us suppose that the lover of the beautiful were ugly and, being ugly, deserved to be shunned; it would then be highly absurd for him to say, 'I love you because you are beautiful; you must love me because I am ugly.'

"But assuming that two individuals are equally beautiful, it does not mean that their desires are the same; for not all beauty inspires love, but may sometimes merely delight the eye and leave the will intact. If it were otherwise, no one would know what he wanted, but all would wander vaguely and aimlessly with nothing upon which to settle their affections; for the number of beautiful objects being infinite, desires similarly would be boundless. I have heard it said that true love knows no division and must be voluntary and not forced. This being so, as I believe it is, then why would you compel me to surrender my will for no other reason than that you say you love me? But tell me: supposing that Heaven which made me beautiful had made me ugly instead, should I have any right to complain because you did not love me? You must remember, moreover, that I did not choose this beauty that is mine; such as it is, Heaven gave it to me of its grace, without any choice or asking on my part. As the viper is not to be blamed for the deadly poison that it bears, since that is a gift of nature, so I do not deserve to be reprehended for my comeliness of form.

"Beauty in a modest woman is like a distant fire or a sharp-edged sword: the one does not burn, the other does not cut, those who do not come near it. Honor and virtue are the adornments of the soul, without which the body is not beautiful though it may appear to be. If modesty is one of the virtues that most adorn and beautify body and soul, why should she who is loved for her beauty part with that virtue merely to satisfy the whim of one who solely for his own pleasure strives with all his force and energy to cause her to lose it? I was born a free being, and in order to live freely I chose the solitude of the fields; these mountain trees are my company, the clear-running waters in these brooks are my mirror, and to the trees and waters I communicate my thoughts and lend them of my beauty.

"In short, I am that distant fire, that sharp-edged sword, that does not burn or cut. Those who have been enamored by the sight of me I have disillusioned with my words; and if desire is sustained by hope, I gave none to Grisóstomo or any other, and of none of them can it be said that I killed them with my cruelty, for it was rather their own obstinacy that was to blame. And if you reproach me with the fact that his intentions were honorable and that I ought for that reason to have complied with them, I will tell you that when, on this very spot where his grave is now being dug, he revealed them to me, I replied that it was my own intention to live in perpetual solitude and that only the earth should enjoy the fruit of my retirement and the spoils of my beauty; and if he with all this plain-speaking was still stubbornly bent upon hoping against hope and sailing against the wind, is it to be wondered at if he drowned in the gulf of his own folly?

"Had I led him on, it would have been falsely; had I gratified his passion, it would have been against my own best judgment and intentions; but, though I had disillusioned him, he persisted, and though I did not hate him, he was driven to despair. Ask yourselves, then, if it is reasonable to blame me for his woes! Let him who has been truly deceived complain; let him despair who has been cheated of his promised hopes; if I have enticed any, let him speak up; if I have accepted the attentions of any, let him boast of it; but let not him to whom I have promised nothing, whom I have neither enticed nor accepted, apply to me such terms as cruel and homicidal. It has not as yet been Heaven's will to destine me to love any man, and there is no use expecting me to love of my own free choice.

"Let what I am saying now apply to each and every one of those who would have me for their own, and let it be understood from now on that if any die on account of me, he is not to be regarded as an unfortunate victim of jealousy, since she that cares for none can give to none the occasion for being jealous; nor is my plain-speaking to be taken as disdain. He who calls me a wild beast and a basilisk, let him leave me alone as something that is evil and harmful; let him who calls me ungrateful cease to wait upon me; let him who finds me strange shun my acquaintance; if I am cruel, do not run after me; in which case this wild beast, this basilisk, this strange, cruel, ungrateful creature will not run after them, seek them out, wait upon them, nor endeavor to know them in any way.

"The thing that killed Grisóstomo was his impatience and the impetuosity of his desire; so why blame my modest conduct and retiring life? If I choose to preserve my purity here in the company of the trees, how can he complain of my unwillingness to lose it who would have me keep it with other men? I, as you know, have a worldly fortune of my own and do not covet that of others. My life is a free one, and I do not wish to be subject to another in any way. I neither love nor hate anyone; I do not repel this one and allure that one; I do not play fast and loose with any. The modest conversation of these village lasses and the care of my goats is sufficient to occupy me. Those mountains there represent the bounds of my desire, and should my wishes go beyond them, it is but to contemplate the beauty of the heavens, that pathway by which the soul travels to its first dwelling place."

Saying this and without waiting for any reply, she turned her back and entered the thickest part of a nearby wood, leaving all present lost in admiration of her wit as well as her beauty. A few—those who had felt the powerful dart of her glances and bore the wounds inflicted by her lovely eyes—were of a mind to follow her, taking no heed of the plainly worded warning they had just had from her lips; whereupon Don Quixote, seeing this and thinking to himself that here was an opportunity to display his chivalry by succoring a damsel in distress, laid his hand upon the hilt of his sword and cried out, loudly and distinctly, "Let no person of whatever state or condition he may be dare to follow the beauteous Marcela under pain of incurring my furious wrath. She has shown with clear and sufficient reasons that little or no blame for Grisóstomo's death is to be attached to her; she has likewise shown how far she is from acceding to the desires of any of her suitors, and it is accordingly only just that in place of being hounded and persecuted she should be honored and esteemed by all good people in this world as the only woman in it who lives with such modesty and good intentions."

Whether it was due to Don Quixote's threats or because Ambrosio now told them that they should finish doing the things which his good friend had desired should be done, no one stirred from the spot until the burial was over and Grisóstomo's papers had been burned. As the body was laid in the grave, many tears were shed by the bystanders. Then they placed a heavy stone upon it until the slab which Ambrosio was thinking of having made should be ready, with an epitaph that was to read:

> *Here lies a shepherd by love betrayed,*
> *His body cold in death,*
> *Who with his last and faltering breath*
> *Spoke of a faithless maid.*
> *He died by the cruel, heartless hand*
> *Of a coy and lovely lass,*
> *Who by bringing men to so sorry a pass*
> *Love's tyranny doth expand.*

They then scattered many flowers and boughs over the top of the grave, and, expressing their condolences to the dead man's friend, Ambrosio, they all took their leave, including Vivaldo and his companions. Don Quixote now said good-bye to the travelers as well, although they urged him to come with them to Seville, assuring him that he would find in every street and at every corner of that city more adventures than are to be met with anywhere else. He thanked them for the invitation and the courtesy they had shown him in offering it, but added that for the present he had no desire to visit Seville, not until he should have rid these mountains of the robbers and bandits of which they were said to be full.

Seeing that his mind was made up, the travelers did not urge him further but, bidding him another farewell, left him and continued on their way; and the reader may be sure that in the course of their journey they did not fail to discuss the story of Marcela and Grisóstomo as well as Don Quixote's madness. As for the good knight himself, he was resolved to go seek the shepherdess and offer her any service that lay in his power; but things did not turn out the way he expected.* * *

[Fighting the Sheep]

From CHAPTER XVIII

In which is set forth the conversation that Sancho
Panza had with his master, Don Quixote, along with
other adventures deserving of record.

* * *

Don Quixote caught sight down the road of a large cloud of dust that was drawing nearer.

"This, O Sancho," he said, turning to his squire, "is the day when you shall see the boon that fate has in store for me; this, I repeat, is the day when, as well as on any other, shall be displayed the valor of my good right arm. On this day I shall perform deeds that will be written down in the book of fame for all centuries to come. Do you see that dust cloud rising there, Sancho? That is the dust stirred up by a vast army marching in this direction and composed of many nations."

"At that rate," said Sancho, "there must be two of them, for there is another one just like it on the other side."

Don Quixote turned to look and saw that this was so. He was overjoyed by the thought that these were indeed two armies about to meet and clash in the middle of the broad plain; for at every hour and every moment his imagination was filled with battles, enchantments, nonsensical adventures, tales of love, amorous challenges, and the like, such as he had read of in the books of chivalry, and every word he uttered, every thought that crossed his mind, every act he performed, had to do with such things as these. The dust clouds he had sighted were raised by two large droves of sheep coming along the road in opposite directions, which by reason of the dust were not visible until they were close at hand, but Don Quixote insisted so earnestly that they were armies that Sancho came to believe it.

"Sir," he said, "what are we to do?"

"What are we to do?" echoed his master. "Favor and aid the weak and needy. I would inform you, Sancho, that the one coming toward us is led and commanded by the great emperor Alifanfarón, lord of the great isle of Trapobana. This other one at my back is that of his enemy, the king of the Garamantas, Pentapolín of the Rolled-up Sleeve, for he always goes into battle with his right arm bare."

"But why are they such enemies?" Sancho asked.

"Because," said Don Quixote, "this Alifanfarón is a terrible pagan and in love with Pentapolín's daughter, who is a very beautiful and gracious lady and a Christian, for which reason her father does not wish to give her to the pagan king unless the latter first abjures the law of the false prophet, Mohammed, and adopts the faith that is Pentapolín's own."

"Then, by my beard," said Sancho, "if Pentapolín isn't right, and I am going to aid him all I can."

"In that," said Don Quixote, "you will only be doing your duty; for to engage in battles of this sort you need not have been dubbed a knight."

"I can understand that," said Sancho, "but where are we going to put this ass so that we will be certain of finding him after the fray is over? As for going into battle on such a mount, I do not think that has been done up to now."

"That is true enough," said Don Quixote. "What you had best do with him is to turn him loose and run the risk of losing him; for after we emerge the victors we shall have so many horses that even Rocinante will be in danger of being exchanged for another. But listen closely to what I am about to tell you, for I wish to give you an account of the principal knights that are accompanying these two armies; and in order that you may be the better able to see and take note of them, let us retire to that hillock over there which will afford us a very good view."

They then stationed themselves upon a slight elevation from which they would have been able to see very well the two droves of sheep that Don Quixote took to be armies if it had not been for the blinding clouds of dust. In spite of this, however, the worthy gentleman contrived to behold in his imagination what he did not see and what did not exist in reality.

Raising his voice, he went on to explain, "That knight in the gilded armor that you see there, bearing upon his shield a crowned lion crouched at the feet of a damsel, is the valiant Laurcalco, lord of the Silver Bridge; the other with the golden flowers on his armor, and on his shield three crowns argent on an azure field, is the dread Micocolembo, grand duke of Quirocia. And that one on Micocolembo's right hand, with the limbs of a giant, is the ever undaunted Brandabarbarán de Boliche, lord of the three Arabias. He goes armored in a serpent's skin and has for shield a door which, so report has it, is one of those from the temple that Samson pulled down, that time when he avenged himself on his enemies with his own death.

"But turn your eyes in this direction, and you will behold at the head of the other army the ever victorious, never vanquished Timonel de Carcajona, prince of New Biscay, who comes with quartered arms—azure, vert, argent, and or[5]—and who has upon his shield a cat or on a field tawny, with the inscription *Miau*, which is the beginning of his lady's name; for she, so it is said, is the peerless Miulina, daughter of Alfeñiquén, duke of Algarve. And that one over there, who weights down and presses the loins of that powerful charger, in a suit of snow-white armor with a white shield that bears no device whatever—he is a novice knight of the French nation, called Pierres Papin, lord of the baronies of Utrique. As for him you see digging his iron spurs into the flanks of that fleet-footed zebra courser and whose arms are vairs azure, he is the mighty duke of Nervia, Espartafilardo of the Wood, who has for device upon his shield an asparagus plant with a motto in Castilian that says '*Rastrea mi suerte.*'"[6]

In this manner he went on naming any number of imaginary knights on either side, describing on the spur of the moment their arms, colors, devices, and mottoes; for he was completely carried away by his imagination and by this unheard-of madness that had laid hold of him.

Without pausing, he went on, "This squadron in front of us is composed of men of various nations. There are those who drink the sweet waters of the famous Xanthus; woodsmen who tread the Massilian plain; those that sift the fine gold nuggets of Arabia Felix; those that are so fortunate as to dwell on the banks of the clear-running Thermodon, famed for their coolness; those who in many and diverse ways drain the golden Pactolus; Numidians, whose word is never to be trusted; Persians, with their famous bows and arrows; Medes and Parthians, who fight as they flee; Scythians, as cruel as they are fair of skin; Ethiopians, with their pierced lips; and an infinite number of other nationalities whose visages I see and recognize although I cannot recall their names.

"In this other squadron come those that drink from the crystal currents of the olive-bearing Betis; those that smooth and polish their faces with the liquid of the ever rich and gilded Tagus; those that enjoy the beneficial waters of the divine Genil; those that roam the Tartessian plains with their abundant pasturage; those that disport themselves in the Elysian meadows of Jerez; the men of La Mancha, rich and crowned with golden ears of corn; others clad in iron garments, ancient relics of the Gothic race; those that bathe in the Pisuerga, noted for the mildness of its current; those that feed their herds in the wide-spreading pasture lands along the banks of the winding Guadiana, celebrated for its underground course;[7] those that shiver from the cold of the wooded Pyrenees or dwell amid the white peaks of the lofty Apennines—in short, all those whom Europe holds within its girth."

So help me God! How many provinces, how many nations did he not mention by name, giving to each one with marvelous readiness its proper attributes; for he was wholly absorbed and filled to the brim with what he had read in those lying books of his! Sancho Panza hung on his words, saying nothing, merely turning his head from time to time to have a look at those knights and

---

5. Heraldic terms for, respectively, blue, green, silver, and gold.
6. Probably a pun on *rastrear* (Spanish for "to track" or "to drag"). The meaning of the motto may be either "On Fortune's track" or "My

Fortune creeps." "Arms": i.e. coat of arms, heraldic device.
7. The Guadiana does run underground part of the way through La Mancha.

giants that his master was pointing out to him; but he was unable to discover any of them.

"Sir," he said, "may I go to the devil if I see a single man, giant, or knight of all those that your Grace is talking about. Who knows? Maybe it is another spell, like last night."[8]

"How can you say that?" replied Don Quixote. "Can you not hear the neighing of the horses, the sound of trumpets, the roll of drums?"

"I hear nothing," said Sancho, "except the bleating of sheep."

And this, of course, was the truth; for the flocks were drawing near.

"The trouble is, Sancho," said Don Quixote, "you are so afraid that you cannot see or hear properly; for one of the effects of fear is to disturb the senses and cause things to appear other than what they are. If you are so craven as all that, go off to one side and leave me alone, and I without your help will assure the victory to that side to which I lend my aid."

Saying this, he put spurs to Rocinante and, with his lance at rest, darted down the hillside like a flash of lightning.

As he did so, Sancho called after him, "Come back, your Grace, Señor Don Quixote; I vow to God those are sheep that you are charging. Come back! O wretched father that bore me! What madness is this? Look you, there are no giants, nor knights, nor cats, nor shields either quartered or whole, nor vairs azure or bedeviled. What is this you are doing, O sinner that I am in God's sight?"

But all this did not cause Don Quixote to turn back. Instead, he rode on, crying out at the top of his voice, "Ho, knights, those of you who follow and fight under the banners of the valiant Pentapolín of the Rolled-up Sleeve; follow me, all of you, and you shall see how easily I give you revenge on your enemy, Alifanfarón of Trapobana."

With these words he charged into the middle of the flock of sheep and began spearing at them with as much courage and boldness as if they had been his mortal enemies. The shepherds and herdsmen who were with the animals called to him to stop; but seeing it was no use, they unloosed their slings and saluted his ears with stones as big as your fist.

Don Quixote paid no attention to the missiles and, dashing about here and there, kept crying, "Where are you, haughty Alifanfarón? Come out to me; for here is a solitary knight who desires in single combat to test your strength and deprive you of your life, as a punishment for that which you have done to the valorous Pentapolín Garamanta."

At that instant a pebble from the brook struck him in the side and buried a couple of ribs in his body. Believing himself dead or badly wounded, and remembering his potion, he took out his vial, placed it to his mouth, and began to swallow the balm; but before he had had what he thought was enough, there came another almond, which struck him in the hand, crushing the tin vial and carrying away with it a couple of grinders from his mouth, as well as badly mashing two of his fingers. As a result of these blows the poor knight tumbled from his horse. Believing that they had killed him, the shepherds hastily collected their flock and, picking up the dead beasts, of which there were more than seven, they went off down the road without more ado.

8. The inn where they had spent the previous night had been pronounced by Don Quixote to be an enchanted castle.

Sancho all this time was standing on the slope observing the insane things that his master was doing; and as he plucked savagely at his beard he cursed the hour and minute when luck had brought them together. But when he saw him lying there on the ground and perceived that the shepherds were gone, he went down the hill and came up to him, finding him in very bad shape though not unconscious.

"Didn't I tell you, Señor Don Quixote," he said, "that you should come back, that those were not armies you were charging but flocks of sheep?"

"This," said Don Quixote, "is the work of that thieving magician, my enemy, who thus counterfeits things and causes them to disappear. You must know, Sancho, that it is very easy for them to make us assume any appearance that they choose; and so it is that malign one who persecutes me, envious of the glory he saw me about to achieve in this battle, changed the squadrons of the foe into flocks of sheep. If you do not believe me, I beseech you on my life to do one thing for me, that you may be undeceived and discover for yourself that what I say is true. Mount your ass and follow them quietly, and when you have gone a short way from here, you will see them become their former selves once more; they will no longer be sheep but men exactly as I described them to you in the first place. But do not go now, for I need your kind assistance; come over here and have a look and tell me how many grinders are missing, for it feels as if I did not have a single one left."

* * * *

["To Right Wrongs and Come to the Aid of the Wretched"]

CHAPTER XXII

Of how Don Quixote freed many unfortunate ones who, much against their will, were being taken where they did not wish to go.

Cid Hamete Benengeli, the Arabic and Manchegan[9] author, in the course of this most grave, high-sounding, minute, delightful, and imaginative history, informs us that, following the remarks that were exchanged between Don Quixote de la Mancha and Sancho Panza, his squire, as related at the end of Chapter xxi, the knight looked up and saw coming toward them down the road which they were following a dozen or so men on foot, strung together by their necks like beads on an iron chain and all of them wearing handcuffs. They were accompanied by two men on horseback and two on foot, the former carrying wheel-lock muskets while the other two were armed with swords and javelins.

"That," said Sancho as soon as he saw them, "is a chain of galley slaves, people on their way to the galleys where by order of the king they are forced to labor."

"What do you mean by 'forced'?" asked Don Quixote. "Is it possible that the king uses force on anyone?"

"I did not say that," replied Sancho. "What I did say was that these are folks who have been condemned for their crimes to forced labor in the galleys for his Majesty the King."

9. Of La Mancha.

"The short of it is," said the knight, "whichever way you put it, these people are being taken there by force and not of their own free will."

"That is the way it is," said Sancho.

"Well, in that case," said his master, "now is the time for me to fulfill the duties of my calling, which is to right wrongs and come to the aid of the wretched."

"But take note, your Grace," said Sancho, "that justice, that is to say, the king himself, is not using any force upon, or doing any wrong to, people like these, but is merely punishing them for the crimes they have committed."

The chain of galley slaves had come up to them by this time, whereupon Don Quixote very courteously requested the guards to inform him of the reason or reasons why they were conducting these people in such a manner as this. One of the men on horseback then replied that the men were prisoners who had been condemned by his Majesty to serve in the galleys, whither they were bound, and that was all there was to be said about it and all that he, Don Quixote, need know.

"Nevertheless," said the latter, "I should like to inquire of each one of them, individually, the cause of his misfortune." And he went on speaking so very politely in an effort to persuade them to tell him what he wanted to know that the other mounted guard finally said, "Although we have here the record and certificate of sentence of each one of these wretches, we have not the time to get them out and read them to you; and so your Grace may come over and ask the prisoners themselves, and they will tell you if they choose, and you may be sure that they will, for these fellows take a delight in their knavish exploits and in boasting of them afterward."

With this permission, even though he would have done so if it had not been granted him, Don Quixote went up to the chain of prisoners and asked the first whom he encountered what sins had brought him to so sorry a plight. The man replied that it was for being a lover that he found himself in that line.

"For that and nothing more?" said Don Quixote. "And do they, then, send lovers to the galleys? If so, I should have been rowing there long ago."

"But it was not the kind of love that your Grace has in mind," the prisoner went on. "I loved a wash basket full of white linen so well and hugged it so tightly that, if they had not taken it away from me by force, I would never of my own choice have let go of it to this very minute. I was caught in the act, there was no need to torture me, the case was soon disposed of, and they supplied me with a hundred lashes across the shoulders and, in addition, a three-year stretch in the *gurapas*, and that's all there is to tell."

"What are *gurapas*?" asked Don Quixote.

"*Gurapas* are the galleys," replied the prisoner. He was a lad of around twenty-four and stated that he was a native of Piedrahita.

The knight then put the same question to a second man, who appeared to be very downcast and melancholy and did not have a word to say. The first man answered for him.

"This one, sir," he said, "is going as a canary—I mean, as a musician and singer."

"How is that?" Don Quixote wanted to know. "Do musicians and singers go to the galleys too?"

"Yes, sir; and there is nothing worse than singing when you're in trouble."

"On the contrary," said Don Quixote, "I have heard it said that he who sings frightens away his sorrows."

"It is just the opposite," said the prisoner; "for he who sings once weeps all his life long."

"I do not understand," said the knight.

One of the guards then explained. "Sir Knight, with this *non sancta*[1] tribe, to sing when you're in trouble means to confess under torture. This sinner was put to the torture and confessed his crime, which was that of being a *cuatrero*, or cattle thief, and as a result of his confession he was condemned to six years in the galleys in addition to two hundred lashes which he took on his shoulders; and so it is he is always downcast and moody, for the other thieves, those back where he came from and the ones here, mistreat, snub, ridicule, and despise him for having confessed and for not having had the courage to deny his guilt. They are in the habit of saying that the word *no* has the same number of letters as the word *sí*, and that a culprit is in luck when his life or death depends on his own tongue and not that of witnesses or upon evidence; and, in my opinion, they are not very far wrong."

"And I," said Don Quixote, "feel the same way about it." He then went on to a third prisoner and repeated his question.

The fellow answered at once, quite unconcernedly. "I'm going to my ladies, the *gurapas*, for five years, for the lack of five ducats."[2]

"I would gladly give twenty," said Don Quixote, "to get you out of this."

"That," said the prisoner, "reminds me of the man in the middle of the ocean who has money and is dying of hunger because there is no place to buy what he needs. I say this for the reason that if I had had, at the right time, those twenty ducats your Grace is now offering me, I'd have greased the notary's quill and freshened up the attorney's wit with them, and I'd now be living in the middle of Zocodover Square in Toledo instead of being here on this highway coupled like a greyhound. But God is great; patience, and that's enough of it."

Don Quixote went on to a fourth prisoner, a venerable-looking old fellow with a white beard that fell over his bosom. When asked how he came to be there, this one began weeping and made no reply, but a fifth comrade spoke up in his behalf.

"This worthy man," he said, "is on his way to the galleys after having made the usual rounds clad in a robe of state and on horseback."[3]

"That means, I take it," said Sancho, "that he has been put to shame in public."

"That is it," said the prisoner, "and the offense for which he is being punished is that of having been an ear broker, or, better, a body broker. By that I mean to say, in short, that the gentleman is a pimp, and besides, he has his points as a sorcerer."

"If that point had not been thrown in," said Don Quixote, "he would not deserve, for merely being a pimp, to have to row in the galleys, but rather should be the general and give orders there. For the office of pimp is not an indifferent one; it is a function to be performed by persons of discretion and is most necessary in a well-ordered state; it is a profession that should be followed only by the wellborn, and there should, moreover, be a supervisor or examiner as in the case of other offices, and the number of practitioners should be fixed by law as is done

---

1. Unholy (Latin).
2. Gold or silver coins minted in Spain and elsewhere in Europe to facilitate trade.

3. I.e., after having been flogged in public, with all the ceremony that accompanied that punishment.

with brokers on the exchange. In that way many evils would be averted that arise when this office is filled and this calling practiced by stupid folk and those with little sense, such as silly women and pages or mountebanks with few years and less experience to their credit, who, on the most pressing occasions, when it is necessary to use one's wits, let the crumbs freeze between their hand and their mouth and do not know which is their right hand and which is the left.

"I would go on and give reasons why it is fitting to choose carefully those who are to fulfill so necessary a state function, but this is not the place for it. One of these days I will speak of the matter to someone who is able to do something about it. I will say here only that the pain I felt at seeing those white hairs and this venerable countenance in such a plight, and all for his having been a pimp, has been offset for me by the additional information you have given me, to the effect that he is a sorcerer as well; for I am convinced that there are no sorcerers in the world who can move and compel the will, as some simple-minded persons think, but that our will is free and no herb or charm can force it.[4] All that certain foolish women and cunning tricksters do is to compound a few mixtures and poisons with which they deprive men of their senses while pretending that they have the power to make them loved, although, as I have just said, one cannot affect another's will in that manner."

"That is so," said the worthy old man; "but the truth is, sir, I am not guilty on the sorcery charge. As for being a pimp, that is something I cannot deny. I never thought there was any harm in it, however, my only desire being that everyone should enjoy himself and live in peace and quiet, without any quarrels or troubles. But these good intentions on my part cannot prevent me from going where I do not want to go, to a place from which I do not expect to return; for my years are heavy upon me and an affection of the urine that I have will not give me a moment's rest."

With this, he began weeping once more, and Sancho was so touched by it that he took a four-real piece from his bosom and gave it to him as an act of charity.

Don Quixote then went on and asked another what his offense was. The fellow answered him, not with less, but with much more, briskness than the preceding one had shown.

"I am here," he said, "for the reason that I carried a joke too far with a couple of cousins-german[5] of mine and a couple of others who were not mine, and I ended by jesting with all of them to such an extent that the devil himself would never be able to straighten out the relationship. They proved everything on me, there was no one to show me favor, I had no money, I came near swinging for it, they sentenced me to the galleys for six years, and I accepted the sentence as the punishment that was due me. I am young yet, and if I live long enough, everything will come out all right. If, Sir Knight, your Grace has anything with which to aid these poor creatures that you see before you, God will reward you in Heaven, and we here on earth will make it a point to ask God in our prayers to grant you long life and good health, as long and as good as your amiable presence deserves."

---

4. Here Don Quixote despises charms and love potions, although often elsewhere, in his own vision of himself as a knight-errant, he accepts enchantments and spells as part of his world of fantasy.

5. First cousins.

This man was dressed as a student, and one of the guards told Don Quixote that he was a great talker and a very fine Latinist.

Back of these came a man around thirty years of age and of very good appearance, except that when he looked at you his eyes were seen to be a little crossed. He was shackled in a different manner from the others, for he dragged behind him a chain so huge that it was wrapped all around his body, with two rings at the throat, one of which was attached to the chain while the other was fastened to what is known as a keep-friend or friend's foot, from which two irons hung down to his waist, ending in handcuffs secured by a heavy padlock in such a manner that he could neither raise his hands to his mouth nor lower his head to reach his hands.

When Don Quixote asked why this man was so much more heavily chained than the others, the guard replied that it was because he had more crimes against him than all the others put together, and he was so bold and cunning that, even though they had him chained like this, they were by no means sure of him but feared that he might escape from them.

"What crimes could he have committed," asked the knight, "if he has merited a punishment no greater than that of being sent to the galleys?"

"He is being sent there for ten years," replied the guard, "and that is equivalent to civil death. I need tell you no more than that this good man is the famous Ginés de Pasamonte, otherwise known as Ginesillo de Parapilla."

"Señor Commissary," spoke up the prisoner at this point, "go easy there and let us not be so free with names and surnames. My just name is Ginés and not Ginesillo; and Pasamonte, not Parapilla as you make it out to be, is my family name. Let each one mind his own affairs and he will have his hands full."

"Speak a little more respectfully, you big thief, you," said the commissary, "unless you want me to make you be quiet in a way you won't like."

"Man goes as God pleases, that is plain to be seen," replied the galley slave, "but someday someone will know whether my name is Ginesillo de Parapilla or not."

"But, you liar, isn't that what they call you?"

"Yes," said Ginés, "they do call me that; but I'll put a stop to it, or else I'll skin their you-know-what. And you, sir, if you have anything to give us, give it and may God go with you, for I am tired of all this prying into other people's lives. If you want to know anything about my life, know that I am Ginés de Pasamonte whose life story has been written down by these fingers that you see here."

"He speaks the truth," said the commissary, "for he has himself written his story, as big as you please, and has left the book in the prison, having pawned it for two hundred reales."

"And I mean to redeem it," said Ginés, "even if it costs me two hundred ducats."

"Is it as good as that?" inquired Don Quixote.

"It is so good," replied Ginés, "that it will cast into the shade *Lazarillo de Tormes*[6] and all others of that sort that have been or will be written. What I

6. A picaresque or rogue novel, published anonymously about the middle of the 16th century.

would tell you is that it deals with facts, and facts so interesting and amusing that no lies could equal them."

"And what is the title of the book?" asked Don Quixote.

"The Life of Ginés de Pasamonte."

"Is it finished?"

"How could it be finished," said Ginés, "when my life is not finished as yet? What I have written thus far is an account of what happened to me from the time I was born up to the last time that they sent me to the galleys."

"Then you have been there before?"

"In the service of God and the king I was there four years, and I know what the biscuit and the cowhide are like. I don't mind going very much, for there I will have a chance to finish my book. I still have many things to say, and in the Spanish galleys I shall have all the leisure that I need, though I don't need much, since I know by heart what it is I want to write."

"You seem to be a clever fellow," said Don Quixote.

"And an unfortunate one," said Ginés; "for misfortunes always pursue men of genius."

"They pursue rogues," said the commissary.

"I have told you to go easy, Señor Commissary," said Pasamonte, "for their Lordships did not give you that staff in order that you might mistreat us poor devils with it, but they intended that you should guide and conduct us in accordance with his Majesty's command. Otherwise, by the life of—But enough. It may be that someday the stains made in the inn will come out in the wash. Meanwhile, let everyone hold his tongue, behave well, and speak better, and let us be on our way. We've had enough of this foolishness."

At this point the commissary raised his staff as if to let Pasamonte have it in answer to his threats, but Don Quixote placed himself between them and begged the officer not to abuse the man; for it was not to be wondered at if one who had his hands so bound should be a trifle free with his tongue. With this, he turned and addressed them all.

"From all that you have told me, my dearest brothers," he said, "one thing stands out clearly for me, and that is the fact that, even though it is a punishment for offenses which you have committed, the penalty you are about to pay is not greatly to your liking and you are going to the galleys very much against your own will and desire. It may be that the lack of spirit which one of you displayed under torture, the lack of money on the part of another, the lack of influential friends, or, finally, warped judgment on the part of the magistrate, was the thing that led to your downfall; and, as a result, justice was not done you. All of which presents itself to my mind in such a fashion that I am at this moment engaged in trying to persuade and even force myself to show you what the purpose was for which Heaven sent me into this world, why it was it led me to adopt the calling of knighthood which I profess and take the knightly vow to favor the needy and aid those who are oppressed by the powerful.

"However, knowing as I do that it is not the part of prudence to do by foul means what can be accomplished by fair ones, I propose to ask these gentlemen, your guards, and the commissary to be so good as to unshackle you and permit you to go in peace. There will be no dearth of others to serve his Majesty under more propitious circumstances; and it does not appear to me to be just to make slaves of those whom God created as free men. What is more, gentlemen of the guard, these poor fellows have committed no offense against you. Up there, each of us will have to answer for his own sins; for God in Heaven will not fail to punish the evil and reward the good; and it is not good for self-respecting men to be executioners of their fellow-men in something that does not concern them. And so, I ask this of you, gently and quietly, in order that, if you comply with my request, I shall have reason to thank you; and if you do not do so of your own accord, then this lance and this sword and the valor of my arm shall compel you to do it by force."

"A fine lot of foolishness!" exclaimed the commissary. "So he comes out at last with this nonsense! He would have us let the prisoners of the king go free, as if we had any authority to do so or he any right to command it! Be on your way, sir, at once; straighten that basin that you have on your head, and do not go looking for three feet on a cat."[7]

"You," replied Don Quixote, "are the cat and the rat and the rascal!" And, saying this, he charged the commissary so quickly that the latter had no chance to defend himself but fell to the ground badly wounded by the lance blow. The other guards were astounded by this unexpected occurrence; but, recovering their self-possession, those on horseback drew their swords, those on foot leveled their javelins, and all bore down on Don Quixote, who stood waiting for them very calmly. Things undoubtedly would have gone badly for him if the galley slaves, seeing an opportunity to gain their freedom, had not succeeded in breaking the chain that linked them together. Such was the confusion that the guards, now running to fall upon the prisoners and now attacking Don Quixote, who in turn was attacking them, accomplished nothing that was of any use.

Sancho for his part aided Ginés de Pasamonte to free himself, and that individual was the first to drop his chains and leap out onto the field, where, attacking the fallen commissary, he took away that officer's sword and musket; and as he stood there, aiming first at one and then at another, though without firing, the plain was soon cleared of guards, for they had taken to their heels, fleeing at once Pasamonte's weapon and the stones which the galley slaves, freed now, were hurling at them. Sancho, meanwhile, was very much disturbed over this unfortunate event, as he felt sure that the fugitives would report the matter to the Holy Brotherhood, which, to the ringing of the alarm bell, would come out to search for the guilty parties. He said as much to his master, telling him that they should leave at once and go into hiding in the nearby mountains.

"That is all very well," said Don Quixote, "but I know what had best be done now." He then summoned all the prisoners, who, running riot, had by this time despoiled the commissary of everything that he had, down to his skin, and as they gathered around to hear what he had to say, he addressed them as follows:

"It is fitting that those who are wellborn should give thanks for the benefits they have received, and one of the sins with which God is most offended is that of ingratitude. I say this, gentlemen, for the reason that you have seen and had manifest proof of what you owe to me; and now that you are free of the yoke which I have removed from about your necks, it is my will and desire that you should set out and proceed to the city of El Toboso and there present yourselves before the lady Dulcinea del Toboso and say to her that her champion,

7. I.e., looking for the impossible ("five feet" is the more usual form of the proverb).

the Knight of the Mournful Countenance, has sent you; and then you will relate to her, point by point, the whole of this famous adventure which has won you your longed-for freedom. Having done that, you may go where you like, and may good luck go with you."

To this Ginés de Pasamonte replied in behalf of all of them, "It is absolutely impossible, your Grace, our liberator, for us to do what you have commanded. We cannot go down the highway all together but must separate and go singly, each in his own direction, endeavoring to hide ourselves in the bowels of the earth in order not to be found by the Holy Brotherhood, which undoubtedly will come out to search for us. What your Grace can do, and it is right that you should do so, is to change this service and toll that you require of us in connection with the lady Dulcinea del Toboso into a certain number of Credos and Hail Marys which we will say for your Grace's intention, as this is something that can be accomplished by day or night, fleeing or resting, in peace or in war. To imagine, on the other hand, that we are going to return to the fleshpots of Egypt, by which I mean, take up our chains again by setting out along the highway for El Toboso, is to believe that it is night now instead of ten o'clock in the morning and is to ask of us something that is the same as asking pears of the elm tree."

"Then by all that's holy!" exclaimed Don Quixote, whose wrath was now aroused, "you, Don Son of a Whore, Don Ginesillo de Parapilla, or whatever your name is, you shall go alone, your tail between your legs and the whole chain on your back."

Pasamonte, who was by no means a long-suffering individual, was by this time convinced that Don Quixote was not quite right in the head, seeing that he had been guilty of such a folly as that of desiring to free them; and so, when he heard himself insulted in this manner, he merely gave the wink to his companions and, going off to one side, began raining so many stones upon the knight that the latter was wholly unable to protect himself with his buckler, while poor Rocinante paid no more attention to the spur than if he had been made of brass. As for Sancho, he took refuge behind his donkey as a protection against the cloud and shower of rocks that was falling on both of them, but Don Quixote was not able to shield himself so well, and there is no telling how many struck his body, with such force as to unhorse and bring him to the ground.

No sooner had he fallen than the student was upon him. Seizing the basin from the knight's head, he struck him three or four blows with it across the shoulders and banged it against the ground an equal number of times until it was fairly shattered to bits. They then stripped Don Quixote of the doublet which he wore over his armor, and would have taken his hose as well, if his greaves had not prevented them from doing so, and made off with Sancho's greatcoat, leaving him naked; after which, dividing the rest of the battle spoils amongst themselves, each of them went his own way, being a good deal more concerned with eluding the dreaded Holy Brotherhood than they were with burdening themselves with a chain or going to present themselves before the lady Dulcinea del Toboso.

They were left alone now—the ass and Rocinante, Sancho and Don Quixote: the ass, crestfallen and pensive, wagging its ears now and then, being under the impression that the hurricane of stones that had raged about them was not yet over; Rocinante, stretched alongside his master, for the hack also had been felled by a stone; Sancho, naked and fearful of the Holy Brotherhood; and Don

Quixote, making wry faces at seeing himself so mishandled by those to whom he had done so much good.

[A Story of Captivity in North Africa, Told to Don Quixote at the Inn]

From CHAPTER XXXIX

In which the captive narrates the events of his life.[8]

"It was in a village in the mountains of León[9] that the line of which I come had its beginnings, a family more favored by nature than by fortune, although amid the poverty that prevailed in that region my father had the reputation of being a rich man and indeed might have been one, had he displayed the same skill in conserving his property that he did in squandering it. His inclination to liberal spending came from his having been a soldier in his youth, for that is a school in which the miser becomes generous and the generous becomes prodigal; if there are some soldiers that are parsimonious, they may be said to be freaks such as are rarely to be met with.

"My father went beyond the bounds of liberality and came close to prodigality, which is not a profitable thing for a married man with children to bring up who are to succeed him and carry on his name. He had three of them, all of them males and of an age to decide upon their calling in life. Accordingly, when he saw that, as he put it, there was no use in his trying to overcome his natural propensity, he made up his mind to rid himself of the instrument and cause of his lavish spending; in other words, he would get rid of his property, for without his fortune Alexander himself would have appeared in straitened circumstances. And so, calling the three of us together one day and closing himself alone with us, he proceeded to address us somewhat in the following manner:

"'My sons, there is no need of my telling you that I have your welfare at heart; it is enough to know and state that you are my sons. On the other hand, the fact that I am unable to control myself when it comes to preserving your estate may well give you a contrary impression. For this reason, in order that you may be assured from now on that I love you as a father should and have no desire to ruin you as a stepfather might, I have decided to do for you something that I have long had in mind and to which I have given the most mature consideration. You are of an age to enter upon your professions in life, or at least to choose the ones which, when you are older, will bring you profit and honor.

"'What I have thought of doing is to divide my estate into four parts, three of which I will turn over to you so that each has that which is his by right, while the fourth part I will retain for my own livelihood and support for the rest of

---

8. Chapters 39–41 show Don Quixote once again listening to other characters' interpolated stories, in this case, that of a former captive who had arrived at the inn with a mysterious veiled woman. Cervantes himself spent five years as a captive in North Africa, and the captive's marvelous narrative is full of precise details about piracy in the Mediterranean, life in captivity, and the complicated connections across the Christian–Muslim divide.
9. A region in northern Spain, associated with Christian resistance to the Muslim invasion of the peninsula.

the time that Heaven shall be pleased to grant me. But after each of you has had his due share of the property, I would have you follow one of the courses that I shall indicate. We have here in Spain a proverb which to my mind is a very true one, as indeed they all are, being wise maxims drawn from long experience. This one runs, "The Church, the sea, or the Royal Household," which in plainer language is equivalent to saying, "He who would make the most of himself and become a rich man, let him become a churchman, or go to sea and be a merchant, or enter the service of kings in their palaces." For there is another saying, "Better a king's crumb than a lord's favor."

"'I tell you this because it is my wish that one of you follow the profession of letters, that another go into trade, and that the third serve his king as a soldier, seeing that it is a difficult thing to obtain service in his household; for if the military life does not bring much wealth, it does confer fame and high esteem. Within a week, I will give you your shares in money, without defrauding you of a single penny, as you shall see in due course. Tell me, then, if you feel inclined to follow my advice and precepts in relation to what I have suggested.'

"He then called upon me as the eldest to answer; and after having told him that he ought not to rid himself of his property in that manner but should spend as much of it as he wished, since we were young and able to make our own way, I ended by assuring him that I would do as he desired, my own choice being to follow the profession of arms and thus serve God and my king. My second brother, having made a similar declaration, announced his intention of going to the Indies and investing his share in commerce. The youngest one, and in my opinion the wisest, said that he preferred to enter the Church or to go to Salamanca[1] to complete the course of study that he had already begun.

"When we had made our choice of callings, my father embraced us all, and within the brief space of time mentioned he carried out his promise by giving each of us his share, which as I remember amounted to three thousand ducats in currency; for an uncle of ours had purchased the estate and paid for it in cash in order to keep it in the family. On that same day the three of us took leave of our goodhearted father; but inasmuch as it seemed to me an inhuman thing for him to be left with so little money in his old age, I prevailed upon him to take two of my three thousand ducats, since the remainder would be sufficient to meet my wants as a soldier. Moved by my example, my two brothers each gave him a thousand, so that he had in all four thousand, plus the three thousand which, as it appeared, his share of the estate was worth; for he did not care to dispose of his portion but preferred to keep it in land.

"And so, then, as I was saying, we took our leave of him and of our uncle, not without much feeling and many tears on the part of all. They charged us to let them know, whenever it was possible for us to do so, as to how we were faring and whether we were meeting with prosperity or adversity, and we promised them that we would. When he had embraced us and given us his benediction, we all departed, one setting out for Salamanca, another for Seville,[2] while I made for Alicante, where I had heard there was a Genoese craft taking on a cargo of wool for that city.

1. Site of the oldest and most prestigious university in Spain.
2. Seville was the port city for trade and travel to the New World; Alicante was a port for Mediterranean trade.

"It is now twenty-two years since I left my father's house, and although in the course of that time I have written a number of letters, I have had no word either of him or of my brothers. As to my own experiences during those years, I shall relate them for you briefly. Embarking at Alicante, I had a fair voyage to Genoa, and from there I went on to Milan, where I fitted myself out with arms and a few accessories. For it was my intention to take service in the Piedmont, and I was already on my way to Alessandria dell Paglia when I heard that the great Duke of Alva was starting for Flanders. I then changed my plan and, joining his army, served with him in the three campaigns that he waged. I was present at the deaths of the Counts of Egmont and Hoorne and rose to the rank of ensign under a famous captain of Guadalajara, Diego de Urbina by name. After I had been in Flanders for some while, news came of the league which his Holiness, Pope Pius V of blessed memory, had formed with Venice and Spain against the common enemy, the Turk, who about that time had taken, with his fleet, the famous island of Cyprus, which was then under the rule of the Venetians.[3] This was a serious loss and one truly to be deplored.

"It was known for a fact that the commanding general of this league was to be his Most Serene Highness, John of Austria, brother of our good King Philip, and there was much talk of the great and warlike preparations that he was making. I was deeply stirred by all this and felt a desire to take part in the coming campaign; and although I had prospects and almost certain promises of being promoted to captain where I then served, on the first occasion that offered, I chose to leave all this and return to Italy. And as it happened, John of Austria had just arrived in Genoa on his way to Naples to join the Venetian fleet, as he afterward did at Messina.

"In short, I may tell you that I was soon taking part in that most fortunate campaign,[4] having already been made a captain of infantry, an honor that I owed to my good fortune rather than to my merits. And on that day that was so happy a one for all Christendom, since it revealed to all the nations of the world the error under which they had been laboring in believing that the Turks were invincible at sea—on that day, I repeat, in which the haughty Ottoman pride was shattered, among all the happy ones that were there (and those Christians that died were even happier than those that remained alive and victorious), I alone was wretched; for in place of a naval crown[5] such as I might have hoped for had it been in Roman times, I found myself on the night that followed that famous day with chains on my feet and manacles on my hands.

"The way in which it came about was this: El Uchali,[6] King of Algiers, a bold and successful corsair, had attacked and captured the flagship of Malta, on which only three knights were left alive and those three badly wounded; where-

---

3. All the figures mentioned here are historical. The Captive fights for Habsburg Spain on various fronts: in Flanders, where the Spanish general Fernando Alvarez de Toledo, Duke of Alba (1507–1582) was charged with putting down the revolt of the Northern Provinces, and in the Mediterranean, where Spain joined in a "Holy League" with the papacy and Venice to combat the Ottoman Empire ("the Turk"). "Counts of Egmont and Hoorne": Belgian nobles executed for their rebellion in 1568. "Diego de Urbina":

Cervantes served under this captain at the naval battle of Lepanto, where the Ottomans were defeated.
4. I.e., the Battle of Lepanto, fought in the Ionian Sea near Corinth, Greece.
5. Awarded to the first man to board the enemy ship during battle.
6. Uluch Ali (1519–1587), viceroy of Algiers (an Ottoman protectorate) and commander of the Ottoman fleet, defeated the Maltese flagship at Lepanto.

upon the ship of Giovanni Andrea[7] on which I and my company were stationed, came to its assistance. Doing what was customary under the circumstances, I leaped aboard the enemy galley, which, by veering off from the attacking vessel, prevented my men from following me. Thus I was alone among the enemy, who so greatly outnumbered me that any hope of resistance was vain; and the short of it is, after I had been badly wounded, they captured me. As you know, gentlemen, El Uchali and all his fleet made their escape, so that I was left a prisoner in his hands; and that is the reason why it was that only I was miserable among so many who were happy, and a captive among so many who were free. For there were fifteen thousand Christians slaving at the oars in the Turkish fleet who that day obtained their liberty.[8]

"They took me to Constantinople, where the Grand Turk Selim[9] made my master commander at sea for having done his duty in battle so well and displayed his bravery by carrying off the standard of the Order of Malta.[1] The following year, which was '72, I was in Navarino, rowing in the flagship with the three lanterns, and there I saw and noted how the opportunity was lost for capturing the entire Turkish fleet in the harbor; for all the sailors and Janizaries[2] were convinced that they would be attacked while in port and had their clothing and their *passamaques*, or shoes, in readiness in order that they might be able to flee overland without waiting to give combat, so great was the fear that our fleet inspired in them. But Heaven ordained otherwise, not because of any fault or carelessness on the part of our commander, but as a punishment for the sins of Christendom, since it is God's will that we should have with us always the agents of his wrath.

"The upshot of it was, El Uchali withdrew to Modon, which is an island near Navarino, and there, disembarking his men, he proceeded to fortify the mouth of the harbor, after which he waited quietly until John retired. On this voyage one of the galleys, called the *Prize*, whose captain was a son of the famous corsair Barbarossa, was captured by the Neapolitan craft known as the *She-Wolf*, commanded by that thunderbolt of war, that father to his men, the fortunate and never-vanquished captain, Don Alvaro de Bazán, Marquis of Santa Cruz.

"I must not omit telling you what took place in connection with this capture. Barbarossa's son was so cruel and treated his captives so badly that the moment the rowers saw the *She-Wolf* bearing down and gaining upon them, they all at one and the same time dropped their oars and seized the captain, who was standing upon the gangway platform, urging them to row faster. Laying hold of him, they passed him on from bench to bench and from poop to prow, and so bit and chewed him that before he had gone much farther than the ship's mast his soul had already gone to Hell. Such, as I have said, was the cruelty with which he treated them and the hatred that they had for him.

"We then returned to Constantinople, and the next year, which was '73, we learned how John had captured Tunis, driven the Turks out of that kingdom,

---

7. The Genoese admiral Giovanni Andrea Doria (1539–1606), who led the forces of the Holy League at Lepanto.
8. Captives on either side of the Habsburg-Ottoman conflict were primarily put to work as oarsmen in Mediterranean galleys.
9. Selim II (1524–1574, r. 1566–74), sultan

of the Ottoman Empire.
1. I.e., the flag of the militant Christian religious order based on the island of Malta, in the Mediterranean, from where they attacked North African ships.
2. Ottoman soldiers; originally an elite corps made up of captured Christian boys.

and placed Muley Hamet on the throne, thus cutting short the hopes that Muley Hamida,[3] bravest and crudest Moor in all the world, had of returning to rule there. The Great Turk felt this loss very keenly and, having resort to the cunning which all those of his line possess, he made peace with the Venetians, who desired it much more than he did; and the following year, in '74, he attacked the Goleta[4] and the Fort near Tunis which John had left in a state of semi-completion.

"During all this time I was at the oar, with no hope whatever of gaining my freedom. At least I had no hope of ransom, for I was determined not to write the news of my misfortune to my father. Both the Goleta and the Fort finally fell, for in front of them were massed seventy-five thousand Turkish regulars, while the number of Moors and Arabs from all over Africa was in excess of four hundred thousand; and this enormous force was equipped with so many munitions and engines of war and accompanied by so many sappers that the latter might readily have buried both their objectives under handfuls of earth.

"The Goleta, which had previously been looked upon as inexpugnable, was the first to succumb; and if it was lost, this was not the fault of its defenders, who did all that they should and could have done. It was rather due to the fact that, as experience showed, it was easy to throw up entrenchments in the desert sand; for water was commonly found there at a depth of two palms, but the Turks went down for a depth of two *varas*[5] without striking any, and as a result, piling their sandbags one on top of another, they were able to raise ramparts so high that they could command the walls of the fort and fire upon them as from a bastion, so that it was impossible to make a stand or put up a defense.

* * *

From CHAPTER XL

In which the captive's story is continued.

* * *

"Well, then, the Goleta and the Fort having fallen, the Turks ordered the former stronghold dismantled, there being nothing left of the Fort to raze; and in order to accomplish the task more speedily and with less labor, they mined three-quarters of it, but by no device could they succeed in blowing up what appeared to be the weakest part, namely the old walls. On the other hand, all that remained of the new fortifications that the Little Friar[6] had built was brought to the ground with the greatest of ease.

"Finally, the victorious fleet returned in triumph to Constantinople, and a few months afterward my master, El Uchali, died, the one who was known as 'Uchali Fartax,' which in the Turkish tongue means 'scurvy renegade'; for that is what he was, and it is the custom of the Turks to bestow names that signify some fault or virtue. This is for the reason that they have only four surnames

---

3. Muley Hamet (Muley Mohammed) became ruler of Tunis in 1573, but was captured by the Ottomans the following year. His brother Muley Hamida (Ahmed Sultan) had joined the attack on Tunis by John of Austria.

4. Fortress at the mouth of Tunis's harbor.
5. One *vara* is a measure equivalent to about 2.8 feet.
6. Nickname for the Italian architect Giacome Paleazzo, who served Philip II.

altogether, which apply to those descended from the Ottoman line, the others, as I started to say, take their names and surnames from bodily defects or moral characteristics. And this Scurvy One, being a slave of the Grand Seignior's, had slaved at the oar for fourteen years, being then more than thirty-four years of age when he turned renegade. The way it came about was this: as he was rowing one day a Turk had dealt him a blow, and in order to be revenged on the fellow he renounced his faith. After that, his valor proved to be so outstanding that he did not have to resort to the usual underhanded ways and means by which the Great Turk's favorites rise at court, but was made king of Algiers and later commander at sea, which is the office that is third in rank in that seigniory.

"El Uchali was a Calabrian by birth and a man of moral principle who treated his captives with great humanity. He came to have three thousand of them, and after his death they were divided in accordance with the provisions of his will between the Grand Seignior (who is heir to all who die and who shares with the offspring left by the deceased) and his renegades. I fell to a Venetian renegade who, as a cabin boy aboard a ship, had been captured by Uchali. His master grew so fond of him that the youth became his prime favorite, and he also came to be the cruelest one of his kind that was ever seen. His name was Hassan Aga,[7] and, amassing great wealth, he rose to be king of Algiers. I accompanied him there from Constantinople and was somewhat pleased at being so near to Spain. Not that I intended to write to anyone there concerning my misfortunes; but I wished to see if fortune would be more favorable to me here than it had been in Turkey, where I had unsuccessfully essayed a thousand different means of escape. In Algiers I thought to find other ways of attaining what I desired; for never once did the hope leave me of achieving my freedom; and when my plottings and schemings did not come up to expectations and my attempts were unsuccessful, I did not at once abandon myself to despair but began to look for or invent some fresh hope to sustain me, however faint and weak it might be.

"In this way I managed to keep myself alive, shut up in a prison or house which the Turks call a bagnio, in which they confine their Christian captives, both those of the king and those belonging to certain private individuals, and also those that are referred to as being *del Almacen*, that is to say, captives that belong to the Council and serve the city in public works and other employment. It is very difficult for these last to obtain their freedom, for inasmuch as they are held in common and have no individual for a master, there is no one with whom to treat regarding their ransom even where they have the means for purchasing their liberation. In these bagnios, as I have said, they are accustomed to place captives belonging to certain private citizens of the town, chiefly the ones that are to be ransomed, since there they may keep them in safety and leisure. For the king's captives do not go out to labor with the rest of the galley crew, unless their ransom be late in coming, in which case, by way of inducing them to write for it more urgently, they put them to work and send them to gather wood with the others, which is no small task.

"I, then, was one of this group; for when they discovered that I was a captain, although I told them that I had no fortune and few prospects, they neverthe-

---

7. Hasan Aga, or Hasan the Venetian, was captured at a young age and converted to Islam. A protegé of Uluch Ali, he ruled Algiers from 1577 to 1578.

less insisted upon placing me among those gentlemen and others who were waiting for ransom. They put a chain upon me, but more as a mark of my status than
in order to keep me from escaping; and thus I spent my days in that bagnio along
with many important personages who had been designated and were being held
for the purpose I have mentioned. And although we were at times harassed by
hunger and the want of clothing, nothing distressed us so much as what we
almost constantly saw and heard of the cruelties, such as never before were
heard of or seen, which my master practiced upon the Christians. Each day
he hanged his man, impaled one, cut off the ear of another; and all this with so
little excuse, or with none at all, that the Turks had to admit he did it simply to
be doing it, inasmuch as their natural bent toward the entire human race is a
homicidal one.

"The only person who made out well with him was a Spanish soldier by the
name of Saavedra,[8] for although this man had done things which will remain in
the memory of that people for years to come, and all by way of obtaining his
liberty, yet the Moor never dealt him a blow nor ordered him flogged; as a
matter of fact, he never even gave him so much as a harsh word. And for the
least of the many things that Saavedra did, we were all afraid that he would be
impaled, and he himself feared it more than once. If time permitted, which
unfortunately it does not, I could tell you here and now something of that soldier's exploits which would interest and amaze you much more than my own
story.

"To continue: Overlooking the courtyard of our prison were the windows of a
wealthy Moor of high rank. These, as is usually the case, more nearly resembled
peepholes and were, moreover, covered with very thick and tightly drawn blinds.
It happened, then, that one day I and three companions were on the prison terrace, amusing ourselves by seeing how far we could leap with our chains on; and,
since we were alone, all the rest of the Christians having gone out to labor, I
chanced to raise my eyes, when through one of those closed windows I saw a
reed appear with a piece of linen cloth attached to the end of it, and it was moving and waving as if signaling for us to come and take it. As we stood gazing up
at it, one of those who was with me went over and placed himself directly beneath
the reed to see if it would be released or what would happen; but the moment he
did so, it was raised and moved from side to side as if someone were saying no by
shaking the head. The Christian then came back, and at once it was lowered
again and the person above began making exactly the same motions with it as
before. Another of my companions repeated the performance, and the same
thing happened with him. And a third man had a similar experience.

"Seeing this, I could not resist the temptation to try my luck, and as soon as
I was beneath the reed, it was dropped. It fell at my feet there in the bagnio,
and I immediately hastened to untie the linen cloth, whereupon I found knotted in it ten cianis, which are gold coins of base alloy in use among the Moors,
each being worth ten reales in our money. I need not tell you how happy I was
over this windfall, and my happiness was equaled by my wonder as to how it
had come to us, and to me in particular, since the unwillingness of the donor
to release the reed to anyone other than me showed clearly that I was the one
for whom the favor was intended. Taking the welcome money, I broke the reed

8. Cervantes refers to himself here; his full name was Miguel de Cervantes Saavedra.

and went back to the terrace, where I once more gazed up at the window. Then it was I saw a very white hand emerge, which opened and closed very quickly; and by this we understood or were led to imagine that it was some woman who lived in that house who had shown us this act of kindness. By way of thanking her, we salaamed after the fashion of the Moors, which is done by bowing the head, bending the body at the waist, and crossing the arms upon the bosom.

"Shortly afterward, through the same window, there came a little cross made of reeds, only to be at once withdrawn. This strengthened us in the belief that some Christian woman must be a captive in that house, and that it was she who had done us the favor; but the whiteness of the hand and the Moorish bracelets of which we had caught a glimpse inclined us to think otherwise, although we fancied that it might be some fair renegade, for such women are commonly taken as lawful wives by their masters, who are glad to do this, since they esteem them more highly than those of their own race.

"In all our discussions about the matter, however, we were very far from the truth; but from that time forth we were solely concerned with looking up at that window from which the reed had appeared, as if it had been our north star. Two weeks went by in which we had no further sight of it, nor of the hand, nor any signal whatsoever. And although during that time we did our best to find out who lived in the house and if there was any renegade Christian woman in it, we found no one who could tell us any more about the matter than that the house belonged to a rich and prominent Moor by the name of Hadji Morato, a former alcaide of La Pata, which is a very important office with them.[9]

"But just as we had given up hope of a second rain of cianis, we unexpectedly saw the reed appear again with another knotted cloth on the end of it, a thicker one this time. This happened at an hour when the bagnio was all but deserted, as it had been on the previous occasion, and we made the same test, each of the others in turn going to stand beneath the window before I did, but it was only when I came up that the reed was released and dropped. I undid the knot and found forty Spanish gold crowns and a message written in Arabic with the sign of the cross beneath it. I kissed the cross, took the crowns, and returned to the terrace, where we all again salaamed. Then the hand appeared once more, and I made signs that we would read the message, after which the window was closed. We were at once pleased and bewildered by what had occurred, and as none of us understood Arabic, great was our curiosity to know what the message contained, and greater still our difficulty in finding someone who could read it for us.

"Finally, I decided to take a certain renegade into my confidence. He was a native of Murcia who professed to be a good friend of mine and who had promised to keep any secret that I might entrust to him; for it is the custom of some renegades, when they intend to return to Christian territory, to carry about with them testimonials of one sort or another from important captives to the effect that So-and-So is a good man, has always shown kindness to Christians, and is anxious to flee at the first opportunity that offers. There are those who procure these certificates with a proper object in mind, and there are others who cunningly misemploy them in case of need. The latter, when they go to commit depredations on Christian soil, if perchance they are lost or captured, will pro-

---

9. Hajji Murad, a Slavonian who converted to Islam and became a powerful official in Algiers. "Alcaide": commander of a fortress or garrison, in this case the city of al-Batha.

duce their affidavits as evidence of the purpose for which they came: namely, that of remaining in a Christian land; and they will assert that it was for this reason they joined the Turks. In such a manner they escape the immediate consequences of their act and are reconciled with the Church before it can punish them; and then, as soon as they are able to do so, they return to Barbary to become what they were before. But, as has been said, there are others who make honest use of these certificates and actually do remain with their coreligionists.

"It was one of these renegades who was my friend. He had testimonials from all of us in which we expressed our confidence in him as forcefully as we could, and if the Moors had found him with these papers on his person, they would have burned him alive. He was known to be well versed in Arabic, being able not only to speak it but to write it as well. And so, before I unbosomed myself to him, I asked him to read the message for me, telling him that I had accidentally come upon it in a hole in my cell. He opened it and studied it for some little time, muttering to himself all the while. I asked him if he understood it, and he assured me that he did, very well, and that if I wished him to give it to me word for word, I should provide him with pen and ink, as he could do it better that way. We gave him what he asked for, and he translated the message little by little. When he had finished he said, 'You will find set down here in Spanish absolutely everything that is written on this paper; and you are to remember that where it says Lela Marien, that means Our Lady the Virgin Mary.'

"Following is the message as he had transcribed it:

"When I was young, my father had a slave girl who taught me the Christian *zala*[1] in my language, and she also told me many things about Lela Marien. The Christian woman died, and I know that she did not go to the fire but is with Allah, for twice afterward I saw her and she told me to make my way to the land of the Christians to see Lela Marien, who loved me a great deal. I do not know how to do so. I have seen many Christians from this window, and only you have seemed to me to be a gentleman. I am very young and beautiful and have much money to take with me. See if you can arrange for us to go, and there you may be my husband if you wish. If you do not wish it so, it will not matter to me, for Lela Marien will provide someone to marry me. I myself have written this; have a care as to whom you give it to read; do not trust any Moor, for they are all treacherous. I am deeply concerned lest you show this to someone, for if my father knew of it, he would cast me into a well and cover me with stones. On the reed I shall put a thread. Attach your reply to it, and in case you have no one who can write Arabic for you, tell me by means of signs and Lela Marien will make me understand. May She and Allah and this cross protect you. The cross I kiss many times, as the Christian slave woman bade me.

"You can imagine, gentle folk, how astonished and pleased we were by the contents of this message. Indeed, we showed our feelings so openly that the renegade realized it was not by chance that this paper had been found but that it was in reality addressed to one of our number. He accordingly now asked us if his suspicions were true, telling us that we should confide everything to him, as he would be willing to risk his life for our freedom. Saying this, he brought forth from his bosom a metal crucifix and with many tears swore by the God

1. Salaam, here with the sense of prayer or ceremony.

whom that image represented and in whom he, though a wicked sinner, still fully and faithfully believed, that he would loyally guard all the secrets we might see fit to reveal to him; for he felt—indeed, he was almost certain—that through the one who had written that message he and all of us would be able to gain our freedom and it would be possible for him to fulfill his dearest wish, that of returning to the bosom of Holy Mother Church, from which like a rotten limb he had been severed and separated through ignorance and sin.

"So many tears did the renegade shed, and so many signs of repentance did he show, that we all of us unanimously consented and agreed to tell him the truth of the matter; and so we proceeded to give him an account of everything, keeping nothing hidden. We pointed out to him the little window through which the reed had appeared, and he then and there made note of the house and announced his intention of taking special pains to find out who lived in it. We also decided that it would be well to reply to the Moorish damsel's note, and, seeing that we had someone there who was capable of doing this, the renegade at once wrote out the words that I dictated to him, which were exactly as I shall give them to you; for nothing of any importance that happened to me in the course of this adventure has slipped my memory, nor shall it escape me as long as I live. This was the reply that we sent to the Moorish lady:

"May the true Allah protect you, my lady, and that blessed Mary who is the true Mother of God and who has put it in your heart to go to the land of the Christians, because she loves you well. Pray to her to show you how you may carry out her command, for she is well disposed and will assuredly do so. Do not fail to write and advise me of your plans, and I will always let you have an answer. The great Allah has given us a Christian captive who knows how to read and write your language, as you can plainly see from this message. Thus, with nothing to fear, we shall be able to know your wishes. You say that if you go to the land of the Christians, you will be my wife, and I as a good Christian promise you that you shall be, and you know that Christians keep their promises better than Moors. May Allah and Mary His Mother watch over you, my lady.

"Having written and sealed this message, I waited two days until the bagnio was deserted as usual, and then I went out to my accustomed place on the terrace to see if the reed would appear, which it did very shortly. As soon as I caught sight of it, although I could not see who was letting it down, I held up the paper as a sign the person above should attach the thread. This had already been done, however, and I now fastened the paper to it, and shortly thereafter our star once more made its appearance with the white banner of peace in the form of a little bundle. It fell at my feet, and, upon picking it up, I found in the cloth all sorts of gold and silver coins, more than fifty crowns, which more than fifty times doubled our happiness and strengthened our hope of obtaining our liberty.

"That same night our renegade came back and told us what he had learned. The one who lived in that house was the same Moor whose name, Hadji Morato, had been mentioned to us. He was enormously rich and had one daughter, the only heir to all his wealth; and it was the general opinion in the city that she was the most beautiful woman in Barbary. Many of the viceroys who came there had sought her hand in marriage, but she had been unwilling to wed; and it was also known that she had had a female slave who was a Christian and who was now dead. All of which bore out what was said in the note. We then took counsel with the renegade as to what we should do in order to rescue the Moorish damsel and make our escape to the land of Christians, and it was finally agreed that we should wait until we had further word from Zoraida, which was the name of the one who now wishes to be known as Maria.[2] For we saw plainly enough that she and no other would be able to provide a way out of all these difficulties. When we had reached this decision, the renegade told us not to worry, that he would set us at liberty or lose his life in the attempt.

"For four days the bagnio was full of people, and as a result the reed did not appear, but at the end of that period, when the place was once more empty, the bundle was again let down, so pregnant-looking as to promise a very happy birth. The reed and the cloth descended to me, and I found in the latter a message and a hundred gold crowns, with no other money whatsoever. The renegade being present, we gave him the note to read inside our cell, and he translated it for us as follows:

"Sir, I do not know how to arrange for us to go to Spain, nor has Lela Marien told me, although I have asked it of her. The thing that can be done is for me to give you for this venture much money in gold. Ransom yourself and your friends with it, and let one of you go ahead to the land of the Christians, purchase a boat there, and return for the others. He will find me in my father's garden, which is at the Babazón gate[3] near the seashore. I expect to be there all this summer with my father and my servants. You will be able to take me away from there by night and carry me to the boat with nothing to fear. And remember that you are to be my husband, or I shall ask Mary to punish you. If you can trust no one to go for the boat, ransom yourself and go; for I know that you are more trustworthy than any other, being a gentleman and a Christian. Make it a point to become familiar with the garden; and, meanwhile, when I see you out for a stroll, I shall know that the bagnio is empty and will give you much money. Allah protect you, my lord.

"Such were the contents of the second note; and when all had heard it read, each offered to be the ransomed one, promising to go and return with all haste; and I myself made the same offer. But the renegade opposed all this, saying he would by no means consent for anyone to go free until we all went together; for experience had taught him that men when freed were lax about keeping the word they had given in captivity. He added that many times certain important captives had had recourse to this expedient and had ransomed one of their number to go to Valencia or Majorca, providing him with sufficient money to fit out a boat and return for them, but he had never come back. For, the renegade observed, liberty recovered and the dread of losing it again would erase from their memories all the obligations that there are. By way of showing us the truth of this statement, he briefly related for us what had recently happened to some Christian gentlemen, one of the strangest cases that had ever been heard of in those parts where the most astonishing and terrifying things are all the time occurring.

"In short, he told us that what we could and should do was to give him the ransom money intended for one of us Christians, and he would buy a boat

---

2. Zoraida is based on a historical figure. Hajji Murad had a daughter named Zahara, who married first Abd al-Malik, future sultan of Morocco, and then, after his death, Hasan Pasha, with whom she moved to Constantinople.
3. Bab Azoun, gate to the city of Algiers.

there in Algiers under pretext of turning merchant and trading with Tetuan and along the coast in that region. Being a ship's master, it would be easy for him to hit upon a way of rescuing us from the bagnio and putting us all aboard, especially if the Moorish lady, as she said, was to provide the money for ransoming the entire lot of us. As free men, it would be the easiest thing in the world to embark, even at midday. The greatest obstacle lay in the fact that the Moors would not permit any renegade to buy or own a boat, unless it was a vessel to go on pillaging expeditions; for they feared that if he purchased a small one, especially if he was a Spaniard, he merely wanted it for the purpose of escaping to Christian territory. He, our friend, could readily overcome this difficulty, however, by taking a Tagarin Moor[4] into partnership with him in the purchase of the boat and the profits to be derived from it, and under cover of this arrangement he could become master of the craft; and with that he regarded the rest of it as something already accomplished.

"Although it seemed to me and to my comrades that it would have been better to send to Majorca for the boat as the Moorish lady had suggested, we did not dare oppose him, being fearful that if we did not do as he said he would reveal our plans and put us in danger of losing our lives when our dealings with Zoraida were discovered, for whose life we would all have given our own. We accordingly determined to leave the matter in the hands of God and in those of the renegade, and we therewith replied to Zoraida that we would do all that she had counseled us, since the advice she had given us was as good as if it had come from Lela Marien herself, adding that it remained for her to decide as to whether the project was to be postponed or put into execution at once. I also, once more, made an offer to marry her. And so it came about that the next day, when there was no one in the bagnio, she on various occasions by means of the reed and the cloth conveyed to us two thousand gold crowns and a message in which she informed us that on the next *Jumá*, that is to say, Friday, she was leaving for her father's summer place and that before she left she would give us more money. In case this was not enough, we were to let her know and we might have anything we asked for; for her father had so much that he would never miss it, and, what was more, she held the keys to everything.

"We at once gave the renegade fifteen hundred crowns with which to buy the boat, while I took eight hundred to procure my own ransom, giving the money to a merchant of Valencia who was in Algiers at the time and who had the king release me on the promise that, when the next boat arrived from home, he would pay the ransom fee; for if he were to pay it at once, the king might suspect that the funds had been in Algiers for some time and that the merchant for his own profit had kept the matter secret. Moreover, my master was so captious that I on no account dared pay him immediately. And so, on the Thursday before the Friday that the beauteous Zoraida had fixed as the day for going to her father's summer place, she gave us another thousand crowns, at the same time advising us of her departure and requesting me, in case I was ransomed, to make myself acquainted with the site or, in any event, to seek to procure an opportunity for going there to see her. I replied in a few words that

4. Term used in North Africa for a Muslim who had lived among Christians, particularly in the kingdom of Aragon.

I would do this, urging her to be sure and commend us to Lela Marien by making use of all those prayers that the slave woman had taught her.

"When this had been done, it was arranged that my three companions likewise should be ransomed, so that they would be able to leave the bagnio; since if they saw me set at liberty while they remained behind, despite the fact that there was sufficient money to ransom them, they might create a disturbance and the devil might put it into their heads to do something that would injure Zoraida. It was true that, in view of their rank, I could feel reasonably safe in this regard, but, nevertheless, I did not wish to imperil the undertaking, and so I had them released at the same time as myself, paying over all the money to the merchant in order that he might with confidence and security pledge his word, although we never once divulged to him our secret plan, as there would have been too much danger in doing so."

CHAPTER XLI

In which the captive's story is still further continued.

"A fortnight had not gone by before our renegade had bought a boat capable of carrying more than thirty persons; and by way of rendering the project safer and allaying suspicion, he made a voyage, as he had suggested, to a place called Shershel which is thirty leagues from Algiers in the direction of Oran and which does a large trade in dried figs. Two or three times he did this in the company of the Tagarin Moor I have mentioned; for *Tagarinos* is the name given in Barbary to the Moors of Aragon, while those of Granada are called *Mudéjares*; but in the kingdom of Fez the *Mudéjares* are termed *Elches*, and they are the ones whom that king chiefly employs in war.

"To go on with my story, then: Each time that he passed with his boat he anchored in a cove that was not two crossbow shots from the house where Zoraida was waiting, and there, with the two little Moors that served him as oarsmen, he would deliberately station himself, either to say his prayers or by way of acting out the part he was later to perform in earnest. Thus, he would go to Zoraida's garden and beg fruit, and her father would give it to him without recognizing him. As he told me afterward, he would have liked to have a word with Zoraida herself so he could tell her he was there on my orders to bear her off to the land of the Christians and at the same time urge her to feel safe and happy.

"This, however, was impossible, for Moorish ladies do not permit themselves to be seen by any of their own race or by any Turk unless their husband or father so commands them. With Christian captives, on the other hand, they are allowed to converse and have dealings to a rather surprising extent. For my part, I was just as glad that he had not spoken to her, for she might have been disturbed to find her plan being discussed by renegades.

"But God in any case had ordained otherwise, and our renegade did not have an opportunity of gratifying his laudable desire. Seeing how safely he was able to go to Shershel and return and anchor where he chose, and perceiving that the Tagarin, his companion, was wholly compliant with his wishes and that all that was needed now was a few Christians to man the oars, he told me to look about for some that I might take with me in addition to those that were being ransomed and to engage them for the following Friday, which was the date he had set for our departure. I accordingly spoke to a dozen Spaniards, all of them powerful rowers. They were chosen from among those that were best in a position to leave the city, and it was no small task finding so many of them at that particular moment, since there were then twenty ships at sea and they had taken all the available oarsmen.

"I should not have been able to find them if it had not been that their master that summer was not going on a cruise but was occupied with completing the construction of a galiot which he had on the stocks. All that I told these men was that the next Friday afternoon they should steal out one by one and wait for me in the vicinity of Hadji Morato's garden. I gave these directions to each one separately, instructing them that if they saw any other Christians in the neighborhood, all they were to say to them was that I had ordered them to stay there until I came.

"Having attended to this, I had something else to do that was still more important, and that was to let Zoraida know how far our plans had progressed in order that she might be forewarned and not be caught off guard if we suddenly decided to abduct her before, as she would think, the Christian's boat would have had time to return. I therefore resolved to go to the garden and see if I could speak with her; so on a day before my departure I went there under pretense of gathering a few herbs, and the first person I encountered was her father, who addressed me in the language that throughout Barbary and even in Constantinople is in use between captives and Moors, and which is neither Moorish nor Castilian nor the tongue of any other nation, but a mixture of all of them by means of which we manage to understand one another. It was in this language that he asked me who I was and what I was doing in his garden. I replied that I was Arnaut Mami's[5] slave—because I knew for a certainty that Arnaut Mami was a very great friend of his—and that I was looking for herbs to make him a salad. He then inquired as to whether I was a ransomed man or not and what price my master wanted for me.

"As I was thus engaged in answering his questionings, the lovely Zoraida came out of the garden house. She had caught sight of me some while before; and since Moorish women, as I have said, are not at all prudish about showing themselves to Christians and do not avoid their company, she thought nothing of coming up to where her father stood conversing with me. In fact, when her father saw her slowly approaching, he called to her to come. It would be too much for me to undertake to describe for you now the great beauty, the air of gentle breeding, the rich and elegant attire with which my beloved Zoraida presented herself to my gaze. I shall merely tell you that more pearls hung from her comely throat, her ears, her hair than she has hairs on her head. On her feet, which, as is the custom, were bare, she wore two *carcajes*—for that is what they call bracelets for the ankles in the Moorish tongue—made of purest gold and set with many diamonds whose value, as she told me afterward, her father estimated at ten thousand doblas,[6] while those upon her wrist were worth fully as much as the others.

"The pearls also were numerous, for the way that Moorish women have of displaying their magnificence is by decking themselves out in this manner. And

5. The corsair captain who captured Cervantes himself in 1575.

6. Gold coin worth six reales.

so it is you find more pearls of one kind or another among the Moors than all the other nations combined have to show, and Zoraida's father was reputed to have an abundance of them and the best that there were in Algiers. In addition, he had more than two hundred thousand Spanish crowns, and the fair one I now call mine was mistress of all this wealth.

"If you would form an idea of how beautiful she was in her prosperous days and when so adorned, you have but to observe how much of beauty is left her now after all that she has suffered. For it is a well-known fact that the beauty of some women has its day and season and is diminished or heightened by accidental causes. It is, moreover, a natural thing that the passions of the mind should add to or detract from it, and most often they destroy it utterly. What I am trying to say is that, as she came toward me that day, she impressed me as being, both in herself and in her adornments, the most dazzling creature that I had ever seen, and when I thought of all that I owed to her, it seemed to me that I had before me a goddess from Heaven who had come to earth for my delight and comfort.

"As she came up, her father told her in their language that I was the captive of his friend, Arnaut Mami, and that I had come to look for a salad. She gave me her hand and, in that admixture of tongues that I have described, asked me if I was a gentleman and why it was I had not been ransomed. I replied that I already had been, and that from the price paid she could see the esteem in which my master held me, for the sum of one thousand five hundred soltanis[7] had been put up for me. To which she answered, 'In truth, had you been my father's slave, I would not have permitted him to let you go for twice as much, for you Christians always lie in everything you say and make yourselves out to be poor in order to cheat the Moors.'

"'That may be, lady,' I said, 'but I dealt truthfully with my master, as I do and shall do with everybody in this world.'

"'And when are you going?' Zoraida asked.

"'Tomorrow, I expect; for there is a vessel here from France that sets sail then and I intend to go on it.'

"'Would it not be better,' said Zoraida, 'to wait for one from Spain, seeing that the French are not your friends?'

"'No,' I told her, 'although if I were certain that a ship from Spain was on the way, I would wait for it. It is more likely, however, that I shall go tomorrow, for the desire I have to see my native land and my loved ones is such that I cannot bear to wait for another opportunity, even though a better one, if it be late in coming.'

"'You no doubt have a wife in your own country,' she said, 'and I suppose you are anxious to see her.'

"'No,' I assured her, 'I am not married, but I have promised to wed as soon as I return.'

"'And is the lady to whom you have given this promise beautiful?'

"'She is so beautiful,' I replied, 'that by way of praising her and telling the simple truth, I will say that she very much resembles you.'

"Her father laughed heartily at this. 'In Allah's name, Christian,' he said, 'she must be beautiful indeed if she is like my daughter, who is the most beautiful in all this realm. If you do not believe me, look at her well and tell me if I do not speak the truth.'

7. Ottoman coin worth seventeen reales.

"Throughout the greater part of this conversation, Zoraida's father acted as our interpreter, being the more adept at languages; for while she spoke the bastard tongue that, as I have said, is in use there, she expressed her meaning by signs rather than by words.

"As we were discussing these and other subjects, a Moor came running up, crying in a loud voice that four Turks had leaped the garden railing or wall and were picking the fruit although it was not yet ripe. Both the old man and Zoraida were alarmed at this; for the fear that the Moors have of the Turks is a common and, so to speak, an instinctive thing. They are especially afraid of Turkish soldiers, who treat their Moorish subjects more haughtily, insolently, and cruelly than if the latter were their slaves.

"Zoraida's father then said to her, 'Daughter, retire to the house and shut yourself in while I speak to these dogs. As for you, Christian, gather your herbs and go in peace, and may Allah bring you safely to your own country.'

"I bowed, and he went away to look for the Turks, leaving me alone with Zoraida, who made as if to go back into the house as her father had commanded her. He had no sooner disappeared among the garden trees, however, than she, her eyes brimming with tears, turned to me and said, '*Tamejí*, Christian, *tamejí*?' Which means, 'Are you going, Christian, are you going?'

"And I answered her, 'Yes, lady, but under no condition without you. Wait for me next *Jumá*, and do not be frightened when you see us, for we are surely going to the land of the Christians.'

"I said this in such a way that she understood everything very well; and, throwing her arm about my neck, she began with faltering step to walk toward the house. But as luck would have it—and it would have been very unlucky indeed for us if Heaven had not ordered it otherwise—as we were going along in this manner, her father, who was coming back from his encounter with the Turks, caught sight of us, and we knew that he had seen us and had seen her arm about me. But Zoraida, cleverly on her guard, did not remove her arm; instead, she clung to me more than ever and laid her head upon my bosom, swaying at the knees a little and giving every evidence of having fainted, while I pretended to be supporting her against my will. The old man ran up to us and, seeing his daughter in this condition, asked her what the matter was.

"'Undoubtedly,' he said, when he received no reply, 'it was those dogs coming into the garden that did this to her.' And, taking her off my bosom, he pressed her to his own, as she, her eyes not yet dry from her tears, sighed deeply and said, '*Amejí*, Christian, *amejí*!'[8]

"'It is not necessary, my daughter, for the Christian to go,' her father said. 'He has done you no harm, and the Turks have left. There is no cause for you to be frightened, for nothing is going to hurt you, since the Turks at my request have gone back to where they belong.'

"'It is true, sir, as you have said,' I told him, 'that they have given her a fright; but since she says for me to go, I would not cause her any annoyance; and so, peace be with you, and with your permission I will return to this garden for herbs, if I find it necessary, for my master says there are no better ones for salad than those that grow here.'

8. "Go, Christian, go."

"'Come back for all that you need,' replied Hadji Morato. 'My daughter does not say this because you or any of the other Christians annoy her. She either meant that the Turks should go, not you, or else that it was time you were looking for your herbs.'

"With this, I at once took my leave of both of them, and Zoraida, who appeared to be suffering deeply, went away with her father, while I, under pretense of gathering my salad, was able to roam the garden at will. I carefully noted the entrances and exits, the means they used to secure the house, and everything that might facilitate our plan; after which, I went to give an account of what had happened to the renegade and my companions. In the meanwhile, I looked forward to the time when I should be able to enjoy undisturbed the boon which fate had bestowed upon me in the person of the beauteous and charming Zoraida.

"Time went by, and at length the day came that meant so much to us. With all of us following the plan which, after many long discussions and the most careful consideration, we had decided upon, we met with the success that we longed for. On the next Friday after the day on which I had spoken to Zoraida in the garden, our renegade at nightfall anchored his boat almost directly opposite the house where she was, the Christians who were to man the oars having been notified in advance that they might hide themselves in various places round about. As they waited for me, they were all of them anxious and elated, eager to board the vessel on which their gaze was fixed; for they were unaware of the arrangement with the renegade and thought that they would have to gain their freedom by force of arms, through slaying the Moors who were on the boat.

"Accordingly, as soon as I and my companions showed ourselves, those who were in hiding sighted us and came up. This was at an hour when the gates of the city were closed, and in the whole of the countryside not a soul was to be seen. When we were all together, we discussed the question as to whether it would be better to go first for Zoraida or to make prisoners of the Moorish oarsmen. Before we had reached a decision, our renegade arrived and asked us what was the cause of our delay, for it was now time, all the Moors being off guard and most of them asleep. I told him why we were hesitating, and he replied that the most important thing was to capture the vessel first of all, which could be done very easily and with no danger whatever, and after that we could go for Zoraida. We all agreed with him, and so, without waiting any longer and with him as our guide, we went to the vessel, where he was the first to leap aboard. Laying a hand on his cutlass, he cried in the Moorish tongue, 'None of you stir from here or it will cost you your lives!'

"By this time nearly all the Christians were aboard; and the Moors, who were possessed of little courage, upon hearing their captain address them in this manner, were thoroughly terrified. None of them dared reach for his weapons, and for that matter, they had few if any; and so, without saying a word, they let themselves be shackled by the Christians, who accomplished this very quickly, threatening them that if they raised any kind of outcry they would all die by the knife.

"When this had been achieved, with half our number remaining behind to guard the prisoners, the rest of us, again with the renegade as our guide, made our way to Hadji Morato's garden; and it was our good fortune that, as we went to try the gate, it swung open as readily as if it had not been locked. We then, very quietly and saying nothing, went on to the house without our presence being discovered by anyone. Zoraida, fairest of the fair, was waiting for us at a window, and as soon as she heard the sound of people below, she asked in a low voice if we were *Nizarani*, that is to say, Christians. I answered in the affirmative, saying that she should come down. Recognizing me, she did not hesitate for a moment, but without a word she came down instantly and, opening the door, appeared there in the sight of all, so beautiful and so richly clad that I cannot possibly tell you how she looked.

"As soon as I saw her, I took one of her hands and began kissing it, and the renegade and my two comrades did the same, while the others, being unacquainted with the circumstances, followed our example, since it seemed to them that we were merely recognizing and thanking her as the lady who was responsible for our going free. The renegade asked in Moorish if her father was in the house, and she replied that he was sleeping.

"'Then it will be necessary to wake him,' he said, 'for we must take him with us and everything of value that there is in this beautiful summer place.'

"'No,' she answered, 'you must by no means lay hands on my father. In this house there is nothing for you save that which I bring with me, and it is enough to make you all rich and happy. Wait a moment and you will see.'

"She then went back into the house, saying she would return at once and bidding us meanwhile not to make any noise. I took this opportunity of asking the renegade what had passed between them, and when he told me, I made it clear to him that under no condition was he to go beyond Zoraida's wishes. She now reappeared with a small trunk filled with gold crowns, so heavy that she could hardly carry it. At that instant, unfortunately, her father awoke and, hearing a noise in the garden, came to the window and looked out. Recognizing us all as Christians, he began bawling at the top of his lungs in Arabic, 'Christians! Christians! Thieves! Thieves!' This frightened us very much and threw us into confusion; but the renegade, perceiving the danger we were in and how important it was to go through with our undertaking before being detected, ran up as fast as he could to where Hadji Morato was, being accompanied by some of the rest of us. As for myself I did not dare leave Zoraida unprotected, for she, half fainting, had fallen in my arms.

"In brief, those who went up handled the matter so expeditiously that in a moment they were back, bringing with them Hadji Morato, his hands bound and with a napkin over his mouth so that he could not speak a word—and they threatened him that if he tried to speak it would cost him his life. When his daughter saw him, she put her hands over her eyes, and her father in turn was horrified at sight of her, not knowing that she had placed herself in our hands of her own free will. But it was essential now for us to be on our way, and so we hastily but with due care boarded the ship, where those that we had left behind were waiting for us, fearful that some untoward accident had befallen us.

"It was a little after two in the morning by the time we were all on the vessel. They then untied Hadji Morato's hands and removed the napkin from his mouth, but the renegade again warned him not to say anything or they would kill him. As the old man looked at his daughter, he began sighing mournfully, especially when he saw her held tightly in my embrace, and when he observed that she did not struggle, protest, or attempt to escape me; but he nonetheless remained silent lest they carry out the renegade's threat.

"Finding herself on the boat now and perceiving that we were about to row away while her father and the other Moors remained bound, Zoraida spoke to the renegade, requesting him to do her the favor of releasing the prisoners, particularly her father, as she would rather cast herself into the sea than have a parent who loved her so dearly carried away captive in front of her eyes and through her fault. The renegade repeated to me what she had said, and, for my part, I was quite willing. He, however, replied that this was not the wise thing to do, for the reason that, if they were left behind, they would alarm the entire city and countryside, whereupon some fast-sailing craft would put out in pursuit of us and so comb the sea and land that there would be no possibility of our escaping. What we might do, he added, was to give them their freedom as soon as we set foot on Christian soil. We all agreed to this, and when the matter was explained to Zoraida, along with the reasons why we could not comply with her wishes, she also was satisfied. And then, gladly and silently, cheerfully and with alacrity, each one of our powerful rowers took up his oar, as, commending ourselves with all our hearts to God, we set out on our voyage to the island of Majorca, which is the nearest Christian territory.

"However, inasmuch as the tramontane wind[9] was blowing a little and the sea was a bit rough, it was impossible for us to follow the route to Majorca, and we were compelled to hug the coast in the direction of Oran. This worried us considerably, for we feared that we would be discovered from the town of Shershel, which is about seventy miles from Algiers. And we also were afraid that we might encounter in those waters one of the galiots that commonly ply the coast with merchandise of Tetuán, although each of us secretly felt that if we did meet with a merchant vessel of that sort, providing it was not a cruiser, we not only should not be captured but, rather, should be able to come into possession of a craft in which we could more safely complete our voyage. In the meantime, as we were sailing along, Zoraida buried her face in my hands in order not to see her father, and I could hear her calling on Lela Marien to come to our aid.

"We must have gone a good thirty miles when dawn came, and we found ourselves at a distance of something like three musket shots off land. The shore was deserted, and we saw no one who might descry us, but, nevertheless, by rowing as hard as we could we put out a little more to the open sea, which was now somewhat calmer. When we were about two leagues from the coast, the order was given to row by turns so that we could have a bite to eat, the ship being well stocked with food; but those at the oars said it was not yet time for them to take a rest—the others might eat, but they themselves did not wish on any account to relax their efforts. We were starting to do as they had suggested when a strong wind came up, which obliged us to leave off rowing and set sail at once for Oran, that being the only course left us. All this was done very quickly, and with the sail we made more than eight miles an hour, with no fear other than that of falling in with a vessel that was out cruising.

"We gave the Moorish rowers some food, and the renegade consoled them by telling them they were not captives but would be given their freedom at the first opportunity. He said the same to Zoraida's father, who replied, 'If you promised me anything else, O Christian, I might believe it and hope for it by reason of the generous treatment you have accorded me, but when it comes to setting me free, do not think that I am so simple-minded as to put any credence in that; for you would never have incurred the risk of depriving me of my liberty only to restore

9. I.e., wind from beyond the mountains (in this case the Alps), hence north wind.

it to me so freely, especially since you know who I am and the profit you may derive from releasing me. Indeed, if you wish to name the sum, I hereby offer you whatever you ask for me and for this unfortunate daughter of mine, or for her alone, for she is the greater and better part of my soul.'

"As he said this, he began weeping so bitterly that we were all moved to compassion, and Zoraida could not resist stealing a glance at him. When she saw him weeping, she was so touched that she rose from my feet and went over to embrace him, and as she laid her cheek against his the two of them shed so many tears that a number of us could not but join them in their weeping. But when her father perceived that she was in festive attire and decked out in all her jewels, he spoke to her in their own language.

"'How does it come, my daughter,' he said, 'that last night, at dusk, before this terrible thing happened to us, I saw you clad in ordinary household garb; and now, without your having had time to dress, and without my having brought you any good news to celebrate by thus adorning and bedecking your person, I nonetheless behold you wearing the best garments with which I was able to provide you when fortune smiled upon us? Answer me this, for I am even more astonished and bewildered by it than I am by this misfortune that has come to us.'

"The renegade informed us of all that the Moor had said to his daughter, who did not utter a word in reply. And when the old man saw, over at one side of the boat, the small trunk in which she was in the habit of keeping her jewels, he was more bewildered than ever; for he knew very well that he had not brought it to the summer place but had left it in Algiers. He thereupon asked her how the trunk had come into our hands and what was inside it; and then the renegade, without giving Zoraida time to answer, spoke up.

"'You need not trouble, sir, to ask your daughter Zoraida so many questions, for I can give you one answer that will serve for all. I would have you know that she is a Christian, and that it is she who has filed our chains for us and set us free from our captivity. She goes of her own free will and, I fancy, is as happy about it as one who emerges from darkness into light, from death into life, or from the pains of hell into glory everlasting.'

"'Is it true, my daughter, what this man says?' asked the Moor.

"'It is,' said Zoraida.

"'So you are a Christian,' said the old man, 'and it is you who have placed your father in the hands of his enemies?'

"'As to my being a Christian,' she told him, 'that is true enough, but it is not true that I am responsible for your being in this situation; for I never had any desire to leave you or to do you harm, but only to do good to myself.'

"'And what good have you done yourself, daughter?'

"'Put that question,' she said, 'to Lela Marien, for she can tell you better than I.'

"No sooner had he heard this than the Moor, with an incredibly swift movement, hurled himself head foremost into the sea; and he would undoubtedly have drowned if the long and cumbersome robe that he wore had not tended to bear him up. Zoraida screamed for someone to rescue him, whereupon we all ran forward and, seizing him by his robe, hauled him in, half drowned and unconscious, at which his daughter was so distressed that she wept over him as bitterly and mournfully as if he were already dead. We turned him face downward and he disgorged much water, and after a couple of hours he was himself once more.

"Meanwhile, the wind had changed and we had to make for land, exerting all our strength at the oars in order not to be driven ashore. Luck was with us, and we were able to put into a cove alongside a promontory or cape which the Moors call *Cava Rumia*, signifying in our language 'the wicked Christian woman'; for it is a tradition among them that La Cava, through whom Spain was lost, is buried in that spot, '*cava*' in their tongue meaning 'bad woman,' while '*rumia*' is 'Christian.'[1] They regard it as bad luck to be compelled to drop anchor there, and they never do so unless it is absolutely necessary. But for us it was not the 'bad woman's' shelter; rather, it was a haven in distress, as the sea was now raging.

"Stationing our sentinels on land and never once relinquishing the oars, we ate what the renegade had provided and prayed to God and Our Lady with all our hearts that they would favor and aid us in order that we might bring to a happy conclusion an undertaking that had begun so propitiously. Upon Zoraida's request, the order was given to set her father and all the other Moors ashore, for her tender heart could not bear to see her father thus bound and her fellow countrymen held prisoners in front of her very eyes. We promised her that this should be done as soon as it came time for us to depart; for we ran no risk by leaving them in this deserted place. Our prayers were not in vain; for, Heaven favoring us, the wind changed and the sea grew calm, inviting us to resume with cheerful hearts the voyage that we had begun.

"We then unbound the Moors and, one by one, set them on land, at which they were greatly astonished; but when it came to disembarking Zoraida's father, who had by now completely recovered his senses, he gave us a piece of his mind.

"'Why do you think, Christians,' he said, 'that this wicked female is happy at your giving me my liberty? Do you imagine that it is out of filial affection? Assuredly not. It is only because my presence is an impediment to the carrying out of her base designs. And do not think that what has led her to change her religion is a belief that yours is better than ours; it is because she knows that in your country immodesty is more freely practiced than in ours.'

"As her father spoke, another Christian and I held Zoraida's arms that she might not be tempted to some foolish act. The old man now turned upon her.

"'O infamous and ill-advised maiden! Where do you think you are going, so blindly and foolishly, with these dogs, our natural enemies? Cursed be the hour in which I begot you, and cursed all the luxury in which I have reared you!'

"Seeing that he was likely to go on in this way for some while, I hastened to put him ashore; and from there he kept on shouting at us, pursuing us with his curses and lamentations as he implored Mohammed to pray to Allah that we be destroyed, confounded, and brought to an end. And when, having set sail, we could no longer hear his words, we could still see his gestures, could see him plucking out his beard, tearing his hair, and rolling on the ground. At one point he raised his voice to such a pitch that we could make out what he said.

"'Return, my beloved daughter, return to land, and I will forgive you everything. Give those men the money that is yours and come back to comfort your

---

1. Legend had it that Rodrigo, the last Visigothic king of Iberia, seduced Florinda ("La Cava"), the daughter of Count Julián. Her father took revenge on Rodrigo by betraying Spain to the invading Moors in 711.

brokenhearted father, who, if you leave him now, will leave his bones on these deserted sands.'

"Zoraida heard all this and was deeply grieved by it. Weeping, she could only say to him in reply, 'O my father, may it please Allah that Lela Marien, who has been the cause of my turning Christian, console you in your sorrow! Allah well knows that I could have done nothing other than what I did. These Christians are in no wise to blame, for even had I not wished to come with them, even had I chosen to remain at home, it would have been impossible, so eagerly did my soul urge me to do that which to me seems as good, my dear father, as it seems evil to you.'

"When she said this, her father could no longer hear her, for we had lost him from view; and so, while I comforted Zoraida, we all of us turned our attention to the voyage, as we now had a wind so favorable that we firmly expected to be off the coast of Spain by dawn the next day.

"Blessings, however, are almost never unmixed with some evil that, without our having foreseen it, comes to disturb them. It may have been simply our misfortune, or it may have been those curses that the Moor had heaped upon his daughter (for a curse of that kind is always to be dreaded, whatever the father may be like), but, in any event, our luck now changed. We were on the high seas, and the night was a little more than three hours gone. We were proceeding at full sail with the oars lashed, since the wind had relieved us of the necessity of using them, when by the light of the moon, which was shining brightly, we sighted alongside us a square-rigged vessel with all sails set that was luffing a little and standing across our course. It was so close upon us that we had to strike sail in order not to run foul of her, while they swung their prow about to give us room to pass.

"They now came to the ship's rail to ask us who we were, from where we came, and where we were going. When these questions were put to us in French, our renegade said, 'Let no one answer, for they are undoubtedly French pirates who plunder everything in sight.' As a result of this warning, no one said a word in reply. We were a little ahead, and the other vessel was lying to leeward, when suddenly they fired two pieces of artillery, both of them, as it seemed, loaded with chain-shot; for with one they cut our mast in half and brought both mast and sail down into the sea, while the other cannon, discharged at the same moment, sent a shot into the middle of our craft, laying it wide open but doing no further damage to it. As we saw ourselves sinking, we began crying out for help, imploring those on the other ship to come to our aid as we were filling with water. They then struck their own sails, and, lowering a skiff or boat, as many as a dozen Frenchmen, all well armed, with matchlocks and matches lighted, came alongside us. When they saw how few we were and how our craft was going down, they took us in, telling us that this had come about through our discourtesy in not answering them.

"Our renegade, then, without anyone's seeing what he did, took the trunk containing Zoraida's wealth and dumped it into the sea. To make a long story short, we all went aboard with the Frenchmen, who, after they had learned everything they wished to know about us, proceeded to despoil us of all that we possessed as if we had been their deadly enemies. They even took Zoraida's anklets, but this did not grieve me as much as it did her. What I feared more was that, having deprived her of her exceedingly rich and precious gems, they would go on to steal that jewel that was worth more than all the others and which she most esteemed. Their desires, however, did not go beyond money, in which regard they were insatiable in their covetousness. They would even have taken the garments their captives wore if these had been of any use to them. Some of them were for wrapping us all in a sail and tossing us into the sea; for it was their intention, by passing themselves off as Bretons, to put in at certain Spanish ports, and if they brought us in alive they would be punished when the theft was discovered.

"But the captain, who was the one who had despoiled my beloved Zoraida, said that he was content with the prize that he had and did not wish to stop at any port in Spain. Instead, he preferred to slip through the Strait of Gibraltar at night, or any way he could, and go on to La Rochelle, the port from which he had put out. Accordingly, they agreed to let us take their small boat and all that we needed for the brief voyage that remained for us. This they did the next day, within sight of the Spanish coast, a sight that caused us wholly to forget all our sufferings and hardships, which were as if they had never been, so great is the joy that comes from recovering one's lost freedom.

"It may have been around midday when they put us in the boat, giving us two kegs of water and some biscuit. And as the lovely Zoraida went to embark, the captain, moved by some sympathetic impulse or other, gave her as many as twenty gold crowns and would not permit his men to take from her those same garments that she is now wearing. As we entered the small boat, we thanked them for their kindness, our manner being one of gratitude rather than indignation, and they then put out to sea, making for the Strait, while we, needing no other compass than the land that lay ahead of us, bent to the oars so lustily that by sundown we were, as we thought, near enough to be able to reach it before the night was far gone.

"But as there was no moon and the sky was darkened over and we were ignorant of our exact whereabouts, it did not seem wise to attempt a landing, although many of us thought that we should do so, saying that it would be better to run ashore even if it were on some rocks, far from any inhabited place, since in that way we would assure ourselves against the very likely danger of Tetuán corsairs, who at night are in Barbary and by morning off the coast of Spain, where they commonly take some prize and then return to sleep in their own houses. There were a number of conflicting suggestions, but the one that was finally adopted was that we should gradually draw near the shore and, if the sea was calm enough to permit it, land wherever we were able.

"This was the plan followed, and shortly before midnight we came to the foot of an enormous and very high mountain that was not so near the sea but that it afforded a convenient space for a landing. We ran up on the sand and leaped ashore, kissing the ground on which we stood and shedding many joyful tears as we gave thanks to God, Our Lord, for the incomparable blessing that He had conferred upon us. Removing the provisions from the boat, we drew it ashore and then went a long way up the mountain; for even here we could not feel in our hearts or bring ourselves to believe that the land beneath our feet was Christian soil. The sun, it seemed to me, came up more slowly than we could have wished, and in the meanwhile we had climbed the entire mountainside in an effort to see if we could discover any village or even a few shepherds' huts; but however much we strained our eyes, we were able to descry no village, no human being, no path, no road.

"Nevertheless, we determined to keep on and go farther inland, since surely we could not fail to come upon someone who could give us our bearings. What distressed me more than anything else was seeing Zoraida go on foot over this rough country; for though I once tried carrying her on my shoulders, my weariness wearied her more than she was rested by her repose, and so she would not again consent to my making the exertion but went along very cheerfully and patiently, her hand in mine. We had gone, I imagine, a little less than a quarter of a league when there reached our ears the sound of a little bell, which showed plainly that we must be near some flock or herd, and as we all gazed about us attentively to see if we could discern any, we saw at the foot of a cork tree a young shepherd who very calmly and unconcernedly was engaged in whittling a stick with his knife.

"We called to him, and he, raising his head, got to his feet very nimbly. As we afterward learned, the first persons that he caught sight of among us were the renegade and Zoraida, and seeing them in Moorish costume, he thought that all Barbary must have descended upon him. Dashing with amazing swiftness into a nearby wood, he began raising a terrible din as he shouted, 'Moors! Moors! The Moors have landed! Moors! Moors! To arms! To arms!'

"We were quite perplexed by all this, not knowing what to do; but, reflecting that the shepherd's cries would arouse the countryside and that the mounted coast guard would soon be along to find out what the trouble was, we decided that the renegade should take off his Turkish clothes and put on a captive's jacket, which one of us now gave him though he himself was left with only his shirt. And then, commending ourselves to God, we proceeded along the same path that the shepherd had taken, expecting that the guard would be upon us at any moment. In this we were not wrong, for two hours had not gone by when, as we were coming out of a thicket onto a plain, we caught sight of all of fifty horsemen coming toward us at top speed.

"As soon as we saw them, we stopped and watched them, and they, when they came up and found, in place of the Moors they were seeking, a handful of poor Christians, were very much surprised. One of them asked if it was we who had caused the shepherd to sound the call to arms. 'Yes,' I replied, and was about to go on and tell him our story, who we were and from whence we came, when one of our number happened to recognize the horseman who had put the question and, without giving me a chance to reply, spoke up and said, 'Thanks be to God, sirs, for having brought us into such good hands; for unless I am mistaken, this region where we now are is in the neighborhood of Vélez Málaga—unless all the years of my captivity have so deprived me of my memory that I cannot recall that you, sir, who have just asked us our names, are Pedro de Bustamente, my uncle.'

"The Christian captive had no sooner said this than the horseman dismounted and came up to embrace the young fellow. 'My dearest nephew!' he cried. 'I recognize you now. I and my sister—your mother—and all your relatives who are still alive have wept for you as dead, and now it appears that God has been pleased to prolong their lives that they might have the pleasure of seeing you again. We had heard that you were in Algiers, but from the look of your garments and those of all this company I realize that you have been miraculously liberated.'

"'That,' replied the young man, 'is the truth, and there will be time to tell you all about it.'

"As soon as the guardsmen realized that we were Christian captives, they dismounted, and each then offered us his own horse to carry us to the city of Vélez Málaga, which was a league and a half from there. We told them where we had left the boat, and some of them went back to get it and take it to the town. Others mounted behind us on the cruppers, Zoraida going with the young man's uncle.

"The entire town came out to receive us, for someone had ridden ahead and told them of our coming. They were not the kind of folk to be astonished at seeing captives free or Moors held prisoner, being quite accustomed to such a sight. What they rather marveled at was Zoraida's beauty. Despite the fact that she was weary from the journey, she looked her loveliest at that moment, so joyful was she at finding herself on Christian soil with nothing to fear any longer. Happiness had put so much color into her face that—unless it can be that my love for her deceived me—I shall venture to say that there never was a more beautiful creature in all this world, none that I have ever seen, at any rate.

"We went directly to the church to thank God for his mercy; and as soon as Zoraida entered the portals, she remarked that there were faces there that resembled that of Lela Marien. We informed her that these were images of the Virgin, and the renegade to the best of his ability then went on to explain what their meaning was and how she might worship them as if each were the same Lela Marien who had spoken to her. Being possessed of a good, clear mind, she understood all this very readily. After that, they took us to various houses in the town, and the Christian who had come with us brought the renegade, Zoraida, and me to the home of his parents, who were people in moderately comfortable circumstances and who entertained us with as great a show of affection as they did their own son.

"We were in Vélez for six days, at the end of which time the renegade, having ascertained what he had to do, departed for Granada in order that, through the mediation of the Holy Inquisition, he might be restored to the sacred bosom of the Church. Each of the other liberated Christians went his own way, Zoraida and I being left with no other means than the crowns which the French captain had courteously given her. With them I purchased the beast on which she now rides; and with me serving her up to now as father and squire, not as husband, we are at present on our way to see if my own father is still alive or if one of my brothers has prospered to a greater extent than I.

"Seeing that Heaven has seen fit to give her to me as my companion, I can imagine no other fortune, however good, that might come to me which I should hold to be of greater worth. The patience with which she endures the hardships that poverty brings with it, and her desire to become a Christian, are such as to fill me with admiration and induce me to serve her all my life long. My happiness, however, at knowing that I am hers and she is mine is marred by the fact that I am at a loss where to find a nook in my own country in which to shelter her. For it may be that time and death have wrought such changes in the life and fortunes of my father and my brothers that, if they should not be there, I shall hardly find anyone who is acquainted with me.

"Gentle folk, that is all there is to my story. As to whether it be a pleasing and a curious one, that is for you in your good judgment to decide. For my own part, I may say that I should like to have told it more briefly, although, as it is, the fear of tiring you has led me to omit a number of incidents."

["Set Free at Once That Lovely Lady"]

CHAPTER LII

*Of the quarrel that Don Quixote had with the goatherd, together with
the rare adventure of the penitents, which the knight by the sweat of
his brow brought to a happy conclusion.*[2]

* * *

The goatherd stared at Don Quixote, observing in some astonishment the
knight's unprepossessing appearance.

"Sir, he said, turning to the barber who sat beside him, "who is this man who
looks so strange and talks in this way?"

"Who should it be," the barber replied, "if not the famous Don Quixote de la
Mancha, righter of wrongs, avenger of injustices, protector of damsels, terror
of giants, and champion of battles?"

"That," said the goatherd, "sounds to me like the sort of thing you read of in
books of chivalry, where they do all those things that your Grace has mentioned
in connection with this man. But if you ask me, either your Grace is joking or
this worthy gentleman must have a number of rooms to let inside his head."

"You are the greatest villain that ever was!" cried Don Quixote when he heard
this. "It is you who are the empty one; I am fuller than the bitch that bore you ever
was." Saying this, he snatched up a loaf of bread that was lying beside him and
hurled it straight in the goatherd's face with such force as to flatten the man's
nose. Upon finding himself thus mistreated in earnest, Eugenio, who did not
understand this kind of joke, forgot all about the carpet, the tablecloth, and the
other diners and leaped upon Don Quixote. Seizing him by the throat with both
hands, he would no doubt have strangled him if Sancho Panza, who now came
running up, had not grasped him by the shoulders and flung him backward over
the table, smashing plates and cups and spilling and scattering all the food and
drink that was there. Thus freed of his assailant, Don Quixote then threw himself
upon the shepherd, who, with bleeding face and very much battered by Sancho's
feet, was creeping about on his hands and knees in search of a table knife with
which to exact a sanguinary vengeance, a purpose which the canon and the curate
prevented him from carrying out. The barber, however, so contrived it that the
goatherd came down on top of his opponent, upon whom he now showered so
many blows that the poor knight's countenance was soon as bloody as his own.

As all this went on, the canon and the curate were laughing fit to burst, the
troopers[3] were dancing with glee, and they all hissed on the pair as men do at
a dog fight. Sancho Panza alone was in despair, being unable to free himself of
one of the canon's servants who held him back from going to his master's aid.
And then, just as they were all enjoying themselves hugely, with the exception

2. Last chapter of Part I. Through various
devices, including the use of Don Quixote's own
belief in enchantments and spells, the curate
and the barber have persuaded the knight to let
himself be taken home in an oxcart.
3. A canon from Toledo who has joined Don
Quixote and his guardians on the way; conversing about chivalry with the knight, he has had

cause to be "astonished at Don Quixote's well-
reasoned nonsense." Eugenio, a very literate
goatherd they have met on the way, has just
told them the story of his unhappy love for
Leandra. The girl, instead of choosing one of
her local suitors, had eloped with a flashy and
crooked soldier; robbed and abandoned by him,
she had been put by her father in a convent.

of the two who were mauling each other, the note of a trumpet fell upon their ears, a sound so mournful that it caused them all to turn their heads in the direction from which it came. The one who was most excited by it was Don Quixote; who, very much against his will and more than a little bruised, was lying pinned beneath the goatherd.

"Brother Demon," he now said to the shepherd, "for you could not possibly be anything but a demon, seeing that you have shown a strength and valor greater than mine, I request you to call a truce for no more than an hour; for the doleful sound of that trumpet that we hear seems to me to be some new adventure that is calling me."

Tired of mauling and being mauled, the goatherd let him up at once. As he rose to his feet and turned his head in the direction of the sound, Don Quixote then saw, coming down the slope of a hill, a large number of persons clad in white after the fashion of penitents; for, as it happened, the clouds that year had denied their moisture to the earth, and in all the villages of that district processions for prayer and penance were being organized with the purpose of beseeching God to have mercy and send rain. With this object in view, the good folk from a nearby town were making a pilgrimage to a devout hermit who dwelt on these slopes. Upon beholding the strange costumes that the penitents wore, without pausing to think how many times he had seen them before, Don Quixote imagined that this must be some adventure or other, and that it was for him alone as a knight-errant to undertake it. He was strengthened in this belief by the sight of a covered image that they bore, as it seemed to him this must be some highborn lady whom these scoundrelly and discourteous brigands were forcibly carrying off; and no sooner did this idea occur to him than he made for Rocinante, who was grazing not far away.

Taking the bridle and his buckler from off the saddletree, he had the bridle adjusted in no time, and then, asking Sancho for his sword, he climbed into the saddle, braced his shield upon his arm, and cried out to those present, "And now, valorous company, you shall see how important it is to have in the world those who follow the profession of knight-errantry. You have but to watch how I shall set at liberty that worthy lady who there goes captive, and then you may tell me whether or not such knights are to be esteemed."

As he said this, he dug his legs into Rocinante's flanks, since he had no spurs, and at a fast trot (for nowhere in this veracious history are we ever told that the hack ran full speed) he bore down on the penitents in spite of all that the canon, the curate, and the barber could do to restrain him—their efforts were as vain as were the pleadings of his squire.

"Where are you bound for, Señor Don Quixote?" Sancho called after him. "What evil spirits in your bosom spur you on to go against our Catholic faith? Plague take me, can't you see that's a procession of penitents and that lady they're carrying on the litter is the most blessed image of the Immaculate Virgin? Look well what you're doing, my master, for this time it may be said that you really do not know."

His exertions were in vain, however, for his master was so bent upon having it out with the sheeted figures and freeing the lady clad in mourning that he did not hear a word, nor would he have turned back if he had, though the king himself might have commanded it. Having reached the procession, he reined in Rocinante, who by this time was wanting a little rest, and in a hoarse, excited voice he shouted, "You who go there with your faces covered, out of shame, it may be, listen well to what I have to say to you."

The first to come to a halt were those who carried the image; and then one of the four clerics who were intoning the litanies, upon beholding Don Quixote's weird figure, his bony nag, and other amusing appurtenances, spoke up in reply.

"Brother, if you have something to say to us, say it quickly, for these brethren are engaged in macerating their flesh, and we cannot stop to hear anything, nor is it fitting that we should, unless it is capable of being said in a couple of words."

"I will say it to you in one word," Don Quixote answered, "and that word is the following: 'Set free at once that lovely lady whose tears and mournful countenance show plainly that you are carrying her away against her will and that you have done her some shameful wrong. I will not consent to your going one step farther until you shall have given her the freedom that should be hers.'"

Hearing these words, they all thought that Don Quixote must be some madman or other and began laughing heartily; but their laughter proved to be gunpowder to his wrath, and without saying another word he drew his sword and fell upon the litter. One of those who bore the image, leaving his share of the burden to his companions, then sallied forth to meet the knight, flourishing a forked stick that he used to support the Virgin while he was resting; and upon this stick he now received a mighty slash that Don Quixote dealt him, one that shattered it in two, but with the piece about a third long that remained in his hand he came down on the shoulder of his opponent's sword arm, left unprotected by the buckler, with so much force that the poor fellow sank to the ground sorely battered and bruised.

Sancho Panza, who was puffing along close behind his master, upon seeing him fall cried out to the attacker not to deal another blow, as this was an unfortunate knight who was under a magic spell but who had never in all the days of his life done any harm to anyone. But the thing that stopped the rustic was not Sancho's words; it was, rather, the sight of Don Quixote lying there without moving hand or foot. And so, thinking that he had killed him, he hastily girded up his tunic and took to his heels across the countryside like a deer.

By this time all of Don Quixote's companions had come running up to where he lay; and the penitents, when they observed this, and especially when they caught sight of the officers of the Brotherhood with their crossbows, at once rallied around the image, where they raised their hoods and grasped their whips as the priests raised their tapers aloft in expectation of an assault; for they were resolved to defend themselves and even, if possible, to take the offensive against their assailants, but, as luck would have it, things turned out better than they had hoped. Sancho, meanwhile, believing Don Quixote to be dead, had flung himself across his master's body and was weeping and wailing in the most lugubrious and, at the same time, the most laughable fashion that could be imagined; and the curate had discovered among those who marched in the procession another curate whom he knew, their recognition of each other serving to allay the fears of all parties concerned. The first curate then gave the second a very brief account of who Don Quixote was, whereupon all the penitents came up to see if the poor knight was dead. And as they did so, they heard Sancho Panza speaking with tears in his eyes.

"O flower of chivalry,"[4] he was saying, "the course of whose well-spent years has been brought to an end by a single blow of a club! O honor of your line,

---

4. Note how Sancho has absorbed some of his master's speech mannerisms.

honor and glory of all La Mancha and of all the world, which, with you absent from it, will be full of evildoers who will not fear being punished for their deeds! O master more generous than all the Alexanders, who after only eight months of service presented me with the best island that the sea washes and surrounds! Humble with the proud, haughty with the humble, brave in facing dangers, long-suffering under outrages, in love without reason, imitator of the good, scourge of the wicked, enemy of the mean—in a word, a knight-errant, which is all there is to say."

At the sound of Sancho's cries and moans, Don Quixote revived, and the first thing he said was, "He who lives apart from thee, O fairest Dulcinea, is subject to greater woes than those I now endure. Friend Sancho, help me onto that enchanted cart, as I am in no condition to sit in Rocinante's saddle with this shoulder of mine knocked to pieces the way it is."

"That I will gladly do, my master," replied Sancho, "and we will go back to my village in the company of these gentlemen who are concerned for your welfare, and there we will arrange for another sally and one, let us hope, that will bring us more profit and fame than this one has."

"Well spoken, Sancho," said Don Quixote, "for it will be an act of great prudence to wait until the present evil influence of the stars has passed."

The canon, the curate, and the barber all assured him that he would be wise in doing this; and so, much amused by Sancho Panza's simplicity, they placed Don Quixote upon the cart as before, while the procession of penitents reformed and continued on its way. The goatherd took leave of all of them, and the curate paid the troopers what was coming to them, since they did not wish to go any farther. The canon requested the priest to inform him of the outcome of Don Quixote's madness, as to whether it yielded to treatment or not; and with this he begged permission to resume his journey. In short, the party broke up and separated, leaving only the curate and the barber, Don Quixote and Panza, and the good Rocinante, who looked upon everything that he had seen with the same resignation as his master. Yoking his oxen, the carter made the knight comfortable upon a bale of hay, and then at his customary slow pace proceeded to follow the road that the curate directed him to take. At the end of six days they reached Don Quixote's village, making their entrance at noon of a Sunday, when the square was filled with a crowd of people through which the cart had to pass.

They all came running to see who it was, and when they recognized their townsman, they were vastly astonished. One lad sped to bring the news to the knight's housekeeper and his niece, telling them that their master had returned lean and jaundiced and lying stretched out upon a bale of hay on an oxcart. It was pitiful to hear the good ladies' screams, to behold the way in which they beat their breasts, and to listen to the curses which they once more heaped upon those damnable books of chivalry, and this demonstration increased as they saw Don Quixote coming through the doorway.

At news of the knight's return, Sancho Panza's wife had hurried to the scene, for she had some while since learned that her husband had accompanied him as his squire; and now, as soon as she laid eyes upon her man, the first question she asked was if all was well with the ass, to which Sancho replied that the beast was better off than his master.

"Thank God," she exclaimed, "for all his blessings! But tell me now, my dear, what have you brought me from all your squirings? A new cloak to wear? Or shoes for the young ones?"

"I've brought you nothing of the sort, good wife," said Sancho, "but other things of greater value and importance."

"I'm glad to hear that," she replied. "Show me those things of greater value and importance, my dear. I'd like a sight of them just to cheer this heart of mine which has been so sad and unhappy all the centuries that you've been gone."

"I will show them to you at home, wife," said Sancho. "For the present, be satisfied that if, God willing, we set out on another journey in search of adventures, you will see me in no time a count or the governor of an island, and not one of those around here, but the best that is to be had."

"I hope to Heaven it's true, my husband, for we certainly need it. But tell me, what is all this about islands? I don't understand."

"Honey," replied Sancho, "is not for the mouth of an ass. You will find out in good time, woman; and you're going to be surprised to hear yourself called 'my Ladyship' by all your vassals."

"What's this you are saying, Sancho, about ladyships, islands, and vassals?" Juana Panza insisted on knowing—for such was the name of Sancho's wife, although they were not blood relatives, it being the custom in La Mancha for wives to take their husbands' surnames.

"Do not be in such a hurry to know all this, Juana," he said. "It is enough that I am telling you the truth. Sew up your mouth, then; for all I will say, in passing, is that there is nothing in the world that is more pleasant than being a respected man, squire to a knight-errant who goes in search of adventures. It is true that most of the adventures you meet with do not come out the way you'd like them to, for ninety-nine out of a hundred will prove to be all twisted and crosswise. I know that from experience, for I've come out of some of them blanketed and out of others beaten to a pulp. But, all the same, it's a fine thing to go along waiting for what will happen next, crossing mountains, making your way through woods, climbing over cliffs, visiting castles, and putting up at inns free of charge, and the devil take the maravedi that is to pay."

Such was the conversation that took place between Sancho Panza and Juana Panza, his wife, as Don Quixote's housekeeper and niece were taking him in, stripping him, and stretching him out on his old-time bed. He gazed at them blankly, being unable to make out where he was. The curate charged the niece to take great care to see that her uncle was comfortable and to keep close watch over him so that he would not slip away from them another time. He then told them of what it had been necessary to do in order to get him home, at which they once more screamed to Heaven and began cursing the books of chivalry all over again, praying God to plunge the authors of such lying nonsense into the center of the bottomless pit. In short, they scarcely knew what to do, for they were very much afraid that their master and uncle would give them the slip once more, the moment he was a little better, and it turned out just the way they feared it might.

* * *

From Part II

[Prologue]

To the Reader

God bless me, gentle or, it may be, plebeian reader, how eagerly you must be awaiting this prologue, thinking to find in it vengeful scoldings and vituperations directed against the author of the second Don Quixote—I mean the one who, so it is said, was begotten in Tordesillas and born in Tarragona.[1] The truth is, however, that I am not going to be able to satisfy you in this regard; for granting that injuries are capable of awakening wrath in the humblest of bosoms, my own must be an exception to the rule. You would, perhaps, have me call him an ass, a crackbrain, and an upstart, but it is not my intention so to chastise him for his sin. Let him eat it with his bread and have done with it.

What I cannot but resent is the fact that he describes me as being old and one-handed, as if it were in my power to make time stand still for me, or as if I had lost my hand in some tavern instead of upon the greatest occasion that the past or present has ever known or the future may ever hope to see.[2] If my wounds are not resplendent in the eyes of the chance beholder, they are at least highly thought of by those who know where they were received. The soldier who lies dead in battle has a more impressive mien than the one who by flight attains his liberty. So strongly do I feel about this that even if it were possible to work a miracle in my case, I still would rather have taken part in that prodigious battle than be today free of my wounds without having been there. The scars that the soldier has to show on face and breast are stars that guide others to the Heaven of honor, inspiring them with a longing for well-merited praise. What is more, it may be noted that one does not write with gray hairs but with his understanding, which usually grows better with the years.

I likewise resent his calling me envious; and as though I were some ignorant person, he goes on to explain to me what is meant by envy; when the truth of the matter is that of the two kinds, I am acquainted only with that which is holy, noble, and right-intentioned.[3] And this being so, as indeed it is, it is not likely that I should attack any priest, above all, one that is a familiar of the Holy Office.[4] If he made this statement, as it appears that he did, on behalf of a certain person, then he is utterly mistaken; for the person in question is one whose genius I hold in veneration and whose works I admire, as well as his constant industry and powers of application. But when all is said, I wish to thank this gentlemanly author for observing that my *Novels*[5] are more satirical than exemplary, while admitting at the same time that they are good; for they could not be good unless they had in them a little of everything.

1. A continuation of *Don Quixote* was published by a writer who gave himself the name of Avellaneda and claimed to come from Tordesillas. The mood of the second prologue is grim in comparison to the optimistic and witty prologue to Part I.
2. Cervantes received three gunshot wounds in the Battle of Lepanto (1571); one of them cost him the use of his left hand.

3. *Jealousy* and *zealousness* are etymologically related.
4. An allusion to the Spanish playwright Lope de Vega (1562–1635), who had been made a priest and appointed an official of the Spanish Inquisition. Avellaneda accused Cervantes of envying Lope's enormous popularity.
5. *Exemplary Novels* (1613).

You will likely tell me that I am being too restrained and overmodest, but it is my belief that affliction is not to be heaped upon the afflicted, and this gentleman must be suffering greatly, seeing that he does not dare to come out into the open and show himself by the light of day, but must conceal his name and dissemble his place of origin, as if he had been guilty of some treason or act of lese majesty. If you by chance should come to know him, tell him on my behalf that I do not hold it against him; for I know what temptations the devil has to offer, one of the greatest of which consists in putting it into a man's head that he can write a book and have it printed and thereby achieve as much fame as he does money and acquire as much money as he does fame; in confirmation of which I would have you, in your own witty and charming manner, tell him this tale.

There was in Seville a certain madman whose madness assumed one of the drollest forms that ever was seen in this world. Taking a hollow reed sharpened at one end, he would catch a dog in the street or somewhere else; and, holding one of the animal's legs with his foot and raising the other with his hand, he would fix his reed as best he could in a certain part, after which he would blow the dog up, round as a ball. When he had it in this condition he would give it a couple of slaps on the belly and let it go, remarking to the bystanders, of whom there were always plenty, "Do your Worships think, then, that it is so easy a thing to inflate a dog?" So you might ask, "Does your Grace think that it is so easy a thing to write a book?" And if this story does not set well with him, here is another one, dear reader, that you may tell him. This one, also, is about a madman and a dog.

The madman in this instance lived in Cordova. He was in the habit of carrying on his head a marble slab or stone of considerable weight, and when he met some stray cur he would go up alongside it and drop the weight full upon it, and the dog in a rage, barking and howling, would then scurry off down three whole streets without stopping. Now, it happened that among the dogs that he treated in this fashion was one belonging to a capmaker, who was very fond of the beast. Going up to it as usual, the madman let the stone fall on its head, whereupon the animal set up a great yowling, and its owner, hearing its moans and seeing what had been done to it, promptly snatched up a measuring rod and fell upon the dog's assailant, flaying him until there was not a sound bone left in the fellow's body; and with each blow that he gave him he cried, "You dog! You thief! Treat my greyhound like that, would you? You brute, couldn't you see it was a greyhound?" And repeating the word "greyhound" over and over, he sent the madman away beaten to a pulp.

Profiting by the lesson that had been taught him, the fellow disappeared and was not seen in public for more than a month, at the end of which time he returned, up to his old tricks and with a heavier stone than ever on his head. He would go up to a dog and stare at it, long and hard, and without daring to drop his stone, would say, "This is a greyhound; beware." And so with all the dogs that he encountered: whether they were mastiffs or curs, he would assert that they were greyhounds and let them go unharmed.

The same thing possibly may happen to our historian; it may be that he will not again venture to let fall the weight of his wit in the form of books which, being bad ones, are harder than rocks.

As for the threat he has made to the effect that through his book he will deprive me of the profits on my own,[6] you may tell him that I do not give a rap.

---

6. Avellaneda asserted that his second part would earn the profits Cervantes might have expected from a continuation of his own.

Quoting from the famous interlude, *La Perendenga*,[7] I will say to him in reply, "Long live my master, the Four-and-twenty,[8] and Christ be with us all." Long live the great Count of Lemos, whose Christian spirit and well-known liberality have kept me on my feet despite all the blows an unkind fate has dealt me. Long life to his Eminence of Toledo, the supremely charitable Don Bernardo de Sandoval y Rojas.[9] Even though there were no printing presses in all the world, or such as there are should print more books directed against me than there are letters in the verses of *Mingo Revulgo*,[1] what would it matter to me? These two princes, without any cringing flattery or adulation on my part but solely out of their own goodness of heart, have taken it upon themselves to grant me their favor and protection, in which respect I consider myself richer and more fortunate than if by ordinary means I had attained the peak of prosperity. The poor man may keep his honor, but not the vicious one. Poverty may cast a cloud over nobility but cannot wholly obscure it. Virtue of itself gives off a certain light, even though it be through the chinks and crevices and despite the obstacles of adversity, and so comes to be esteemed and as a consequence favored by high and noble minds.

Tell him no more than this, nor do I have anything more to say to you, except to ask you to bear in mind that this *Second Part of Don Quixote*, which I herewith present to you, is cut from the same cloth and by the same craftsman as Part I. In this book I give you Don Quixote continued and, finally, dead and buried, in order that no one may dare testify any further concerning him, for there has been quite enough evidence as it is. It is sufficient that a reputable individual should have chronicled these ingenious acts of madness once and for all without going into the matter again; for an abundance even of good things causes them to be little esteemed, while scarcity may lend a certain worth to those that are bad.

I almost forgot to tell you that you may look forward to the Persiles on which I am now putting the finishing touches, as well as Part Second of the *Galatea*.[2]

[*"Put into a Book"*]

CHAPTER III

Of the laughable conversation that took place between
Don Quixote, Sancho Panza, and the bachelor Sansón Carrasco.

Don Quixote remained in a thoughtful mood as he waited for the bachelor Carrasco,[3] from whom he hoped to hear the news as to how he had been put into a book, as Sancho had said. He could not bring himself to believe that any such

---

7. No interlude by this name has survived.
8. Municipal authorities of Seville, Cordova, and Granada.
9. Archbishop of Toledo, uncle of the duke of Lerma, and patron of Cervantes.
1. Long verse satire, well known in Cervantes' time; it is alluded to again in Part II, chapter LXXIII (see p. 507).
2. *The Trials of Persiles and Sigismunda* was published in 1617, two years after Part II of *Don Quixote*. A second part of *The Galatea*

was never published.
3. I.e., the bachelor of arts Sansón Carrasco, an important new character who appears at the beginning of Part II and will play a considerable role in the story with his attempts at "curing" Don Quixote. In the preceding chapter he has been telling Sancho about a book relating the adventures of Don Quixote and his squire, by which the two have been made famous; the book is, of course, *Don Quixote*, Part I.

history existed, since the blood of the enemies he had slain was not yet dry on the blade of his sword; and here they were trying to tell him that his high deeds of chivalry were already circulating in printed form. But, for that matter, he imagined that some sage, either friend or enemy, must have seen to the printing of them through the art of magic. If the chronicler was a friend, he must have undertaken the task in order to magnify and exalt Don Quixote's exploits above the most notable ones achieved by knights-errant of old. If an enemy, his purpose would have been to make them out as nothing at all, by debasing them below the meanest acts ever recorded of any mean squire. The only thing was, the knight reflected, the exploits of squires never were set down in writing. If it was true that such a history existed, being about a knight-errant, then it must be eloquent and lofty in tone, a splendid and distinguished piece of work and veracious in its details.

This consoled him somewhat, although he was a bit put out at the thought that the author was a Moor, if the appellation "Cid" was to be taken as an indication,[4] and from the Moors you could never hope for any word of truth, seeing that they are all of them cheats, forgers, and schemers. He feared lest his love should not have been treated with becoming modesty but rather in a way that would reflect upon the virtue of his lady Dulcinea del Toboso. He hoped that his fidelity had been made clear, and the respect he had always shown her, and that something had been said as to how he had spurned queens, empresses, and damsels of every rank while keeping a rein upon those impulses that are natural to a man. He was still wrapped up in these and many other similar thoughts when Sancho returned with Carrasco.

Don Quixote received the bachelor very amiably. The latter, although his name was Sansón, or Samson, was not very big so far as bodily size went, but he was a great joker, with a sallow complexion and a ready wit. He was going on twenty-four and had a round face, a snub nose, and a large mouth, all of which showed him to be of a mischievous disposition and fond of jests and witticisms. This became apparent when, as soon as he saw Don Quixote, he fell upon his knees and addressed the knight as follows:

"O mighty Don Quixote de la Mancha, give me your hands; for by the habit of St. Peter that I wear[5]—though I have received but the first four orders—your Grace is one of the most famous knights-errant that ever have been or ever will be anywhere on this earth. Blessings upon Cid Hamete Benengeli who wrote down the history of your great achievements, and upon that curious-minded one who was at pains to have it translated from the Arabic into our Castilian vulgate for the universal entertainment of the people."

Don Quixote bade him rise. "Is it true, then," he asked, "that there is a book about me and that it was some Moorish sage who composed it?"

"By way of showing you how true it is," replied Sansón, "I may tell you that it is my belief that there are in existence today more than twelve thousand copies of that history. If you do not believe me, you have but to make inquiries in Portugal, Barcelona, and Valencia, where editions have been brought out, and there is even a report to the effect that one edition was printed at Antwerp. In short, I feel certain that there will soon not be a nation that does not know it or a language into which it has not been translated."

4. The allusion is to Cid Hamete Benengeli (see p. 395, n. 5). The word *cid* is of Arabic derivation.

5. The dress of one of the minor clerical orders.

"One of the things," remarked Don Quixote, "that should give most satisfaction to a virtuous and eminent man is to see his good name spread abroad during his own lifetime, by means of the printing press, through translations into the languages of the various peoples. I have said 'good name,' for if he has any other kind, his fate is worse than death."

"If it is a matter of good name and good reputation," said the bachelor, "your Grace bears off the palm from all the knights-errant in the world; for the Moor in his tongue and the Christian in his have most vividly depicted your Grace's gallantry, your courage in facing dangers, your patience in adversity and suffering, whether the suffering be due to wounds or to misfortunes of another sort, and your virtue and continence in love, in connection with that platonic relationship that exists between your Grace and my lady Doña Dulcinea del Toboso."

At this point Sancho spoke up. "Never in my life," he said, "have I heard my lady Dulcinea called 'Doña,' but only 'la Señora Dulcinea del Toboso'; so on that point, already, the history is wrong."

"That is not important," said Carrasco.

"No, certainly not," Don Quixote agreed. "But tell me, Señor Bachelor, what adventures of mine as set down in this book have made the deepest impression?"

"As to that," the bachelor answered, "opinions differ, for it is a matter of individual taste. There are some who are very fond of the adventure of the windmills—those windmills which to your Grace appeared to be so many Briareuses and giants. Others like the episode at the fulling mill. One relishes the story of the two armies which took on the appearance of droves of sheep, while another fancies the tale of the dead man whom they were taking to Segovia for burial. One will assert that the freeing of the galley slaves is the best of all, and yet another will maintain that nothing can come up to the Benedictine giants and the encounter with the valiant Biscayan."

Again Sancho interrupted him. "Tell me, Señor Bachelor," he said, "does the book say anything about the adventure with the Yanguesans, that time our good Rocinante took it into his head to go looking for tidbits in the sea?"

"The sage," replied Sansón, "has left nothing in the inkwell. He has told everything and to the point, even to the capers which the worthy Sancho cut as they tossed him in the blanket."

"I cut no capers in the blanket," objected Sancho, "but I did in the air, and more than I liked."

"I imagine," said Don Quixote, "that there is no history in the world, dealing with humankind, that does not have its ups and downs, and this is particularly true of those that have to do with deeds of chivalry, for they can never be filled with happy incidents alone."

"Nevertheless," the bachelor went on, "there are some who have read the book who say that they would have been glad if the authors had forgotten a few of the innumerable cudgelings which Señor Don Quixote received in the course of his various encounters."

"But that is where the truth of the story comes in," Sancho protested.

"For all of that," observed Don Quixote, "they might well have said nothing about them; for there is no need of recording those events that do not alter the veracity of the chronicle, when they tend only to lessen the reader's respect for the hero. You may be sure that Aeneas was not as pious as Vergil would have us believe, nor was Ulysses as wise as Homer depicts him."

"That is true enough," replied Sansón, "but it is one thing to write as a poet and another as a historian. The former may narrate or sing of things not as they were but as they should have been; the latter must describe them not as they should have been but as they were, without adding to or detracting from the truth in any degree whatsoever."

"Well," said Sancho, "if this Moorish gentleman is bent upon telling the truth, I have no doubt that among my master's thrashings my own will be found; for they never took the measure of his Grace's shoulders without measuring my whole body. But I don't wonder at that; for as my master himself says, when there's an ache in the head the members have to share it."

"You are a sly fox, Sancho," said Don Quixote. "My word, but you can remember things well enough when you choose to do so!"

"Even if I wanted to forget the whacks they gave me," Sancho answered him, "the welts on my ribs wouldn't let me, for they are still fresh."

"Be quiet, Sancho," his master admonished him, "and do not interrupt the bachelor. I beg him to go on and tell me what is said of me in this book."

"And what it says about me, too," put in Sancho, "for I have heard that I am one of the main presonages in it—"

"*Personages*, not *presonages*, Sancho my friend," said Sansón.

"So we have another one who catches you up on everything you say," was Sancho's retort. "If we go on at this rate, we'll never be through in a lifetime."

"May God put a curse on *my* life," the bachelor told him, "if you are not the second most important person in the story; and there are some who would rather listen to you talk than to anyone else in the book. It is true, there are those who say that you are too gullible in believing it to be the truth that you could become the governor of that island that was offered you by Señor Don Quixote, here present."

"There is still sun on the top of the wall," said Don Quixote, "and when Sancho is a little older, with the experience that the years bring, he will be wiser and better fitted to be a governor than he is at the present time."

"By God, master," said Sancho, "the island that I couldn't govern right now I'd never be able to govern if I lived to be as old as Methuselah.[6] The trouble is, I don't know where that island we are talking about is located; it is not due to any lack of noddle on my part."

"Leave it to God, Sancho," was Don Quixote's advice, "and everything will come out all right, perhaps even better than you think; for not a leaf on the tree stirs except by His will."

"Yes," said Sansón, "if it be God's will, Sancho will not lack a thousand islands to govern, not to speak of one island alone."

"I have seen governors around here," said Sancho, "that are not to be compared to the sole of my shoe, and yet they call them 'your Lordship' and serve them on silver plate."

"Those are not the same kind of governors," Sansón informed him. "Their task is a good deal easier. The ones that govern islands must at least know grammar."

6. In the Bible's Book of Genesis, a man who lived 969 years.

"I could make out well enough with the *gram*," replied Sancho, "but with the *mar* I want nothing to do, for I don't understand it at all. But leaving this business of the governorship in God's hands—for He will send me wherever I can best serve Him—I will tell you, Señor Bachelor Sansón Carrasco, that I am very much pleased that the author of the history should have spoken of me in such a way as does not offend me; for, upon the word of a faithful squire, if he had said anything about me that was not becoming to an old Christian, the deaf would have heard of it."

"That would be to work miracles," said Sansón.

"Miracles or no miracles," was the answer, "let everyone take care as to what he says or writes about people and not be setting down the first thing that pops into his head."

"One of the faults that is found with the book," continued the bachelor, "is that the author has inserted in it a story entitled *The One Who Was Too Curious for His Own Good*. It is not that the story in itself is a bad one or badly written; it is simply that it is out of place there, having nothing to do with the story of his Grace, Señor Don Quixote."[7]

"I will bet you," said Sancho, "that the son of a dog has mixed the cabbages with the baskets."[8]

"And I will say right now," declared Don Quixote, "that the author of this book was not a sage but some ignorant prattler who at haphazard and without any method set about the writing of it, being content to let things turn out as they might. In the same manner, Orbaneja,[9] the painter of Ubeda, when asked what he was painting would reply, 'Whatever it turns out to be.' Sometimes it would be a cock, in which case he would have to write alongside it, in Gothic letters, 'This is a cock.' And so it must be with my story, which will need a commentary to make it understandable."

"No," replied Sansón, "that it will not; for it is so clearly written that none can fail to understand it. Little children leaf through it, young people read it, adults appreciate it, and the aged sing its praises. In short, it is so thumbed and read and so well known to persons of every walk in life that no sooner do folks see some skinny nag than they at once cry, 'There goes Rocinante!' Those that like it best of all are the pages; for there is no lord's antechamber where a *Don Quixote* is not to be found. If one lays it down, another will pick it up; one will pounce upon it, and another will beg for it. It affords the pleasantest and least harmful reading of any book that has been published up to now. In the whole of it there is not to be found an indecent word or a thought that is other than Catholic."

"To write in any other manner," observed Don Quixote, "would be to write lies and not the truth. Those historians who make use of falsehoods ought to be burned like the makers of counterfeit money. I do not know what could have led the author to introduce stories and episodes that are foreign to the subject matter when he had so much to write about in describing my adventures. He must, undoubtedly, have been inspired by the old saying, 'With straw or with hay . . .'[1] For, in truth, all he had to do was to record my thoughts, my

---

7. The story, a tragic tale about a jealousy-ridden husband, occupies several chapters of Part I. Here, as elsewhere in this chapter, Cervantes echoes criticism currently aimed at his book.

8. I.e., has jumbled together things of differ-ent kinds.

9. This painter, possibly Cervantes' invention, has never been identified.

1. The proverb concludes either "the mattress is filled" or "I fill my belly."

sighs, my tears, my lofty purposes, and my undertakings, and he would have had a volume bigger or at least as big as that which the works of El Tostado[2] would make. To sum the matter up, Señor Bachelor, it is my opinion that, in composing histories or books of any sort, a great deal of judgment and ripe understanding is called for. To say and write witty and amusing things is the mark of great genius. The cleverest character in a comedy is the clown, since he who would make himself out to be a simpleton cannot be one. History is a near-sacred thing, for it must be true, and where the truth is, there is God. And yet there are those who compose books and toss them out into the world as if they were no more than fritters."

"There is no book so bad," opined the bachelor, "that there is not some good in it."

"Doubtless that is so," replied Don Quixote, "but it very often happens that those who have won in advance a great and well-deserved reputation for their writings, lose it in whole or in part when they give their works to the printer."

"The reason for it," said Sansón, "is that, printed works being read at leisure, their faults are the more readily apparent, and the greater the reputation of the author the more closely are they scrutinized. Men famous for their genius, great poets, illustrious historians, are almost always envied by those who take a special delight in criticizing the writings of others without having produced anything of their own."

"That is not to be wondered at," said Don Quixote, "for there are many theologians who are not good enough for the pulpit but who are very good indeed when it comes to detecting the faults or excesses of those who preach."

"All of this is very true, Señor Don Quixote," replied Carrasco, "but, all the same, I could wish that these self-appointed censors were a bit more forbearing and less hypercritical; I wish they would pay a little less attention to the spots on the bright sun of the work that occasions their fault-finding. For if *aliquando bonus dormitat Homerus*,[3] let them consider how much of his time he spent awake, shedding the light of his genius with a minimum of shade. It well may be that what to them seems a flaw is but one of those moles which sometimes add to the beauty of a face. In any event, I insist that he who has a book printed runs a very great risk, inasmuch as it is an utter impossibility to write it in such a manner that it will please all who read it."

"This book about me must have pleased very few," remarked Don Quixote.

"Quite the contrary," said Sansón, "for just as *stultorum infinitus est mumerus*,[4] so the number of those who have enjoyed this history is likewise infinite. Some, to be sure, have complained of the author's forgetfulness, seeing that he neglected to make it plain who the thief was who stole Sancho's gray;[5] for it is not stated there, but merely implied, that the ass was stolen; and, a little further on, we find the knight mounted on the same beast, although it has not made its reappearance in the story. They also say that the author forgot to tell us what Sancho did with those hundred crowns that he found in the valise on the Sierra Morena, as nothing more is said of them and there are

2. Alonso de Madrigal (c. 1400–1455), bishop of Ávila, a prolific author of devotional works.
3. Good Homer sometimes nods too (Latin)—

Horace, *Art of Poetry*, l. 359.
4. Infinite is the number of fools (Latin).
5. In Part I, chapter 23.

many who would like to know how he disposed of the money or how he spent it. This is one of the serious omissons to be found in the work."

To this Sancho replied, "I, Señor Sansón, do not feel like giving any account or accounting just now; for I feel a little weak in my stomach, and if I don't do something about it by taking a few swigs of the old stuff, I'll be sitting on St. Lucy's thorn.[6] I have some of it at home, and my old woman is waiting for me. After I've had my dinner, I'll come back and answer any questions your Grace or anybody else wants to ask me, whether it's about the loss of the ass or the spending of the hundred crowns."

And without waiting for a reply or saying another word, he went on home. Don Quixote urged the bachelor to stay and take potluck with him, and Sansón accepted the invitation and remained. In addition to the knight's ordinary fare, they had a couple of pigeons, and at table their talk was of chivalry and feats of arms. Carrasco was careful to humor his host, and when the meal was over they took their siesta.

[A Victorious Duel]

CHAPTER XII

Of the strange adventure that befell the valiant Don Quixote with the fearless Knight of the Mirrors.[7]

The night following the encounter with Death was spent by Don Quixote and his squire beneath some tall and shady trees,[8] the knight having been persuaded to eat a little from the stock of provisions carried by the gray.

"Sir," said Sancho, in the course of their repast, "how foolish I'd have been if I had chosen the spoils from your Grace's first adventure rather than the foals from the three mares.[9] Truly, truly, a sparrow in the hand is worth more than a vulture on the wing."[1]

"And yet, Sancho," replied Don Quixote, "if you had but let me attack them as I wished to do, you would at least have had as spoils the Empress's gold crown and Cupid's painted wings;[2] for I should have taken them whether or no and placed them in your hands."

"The crowns and scepters of stage emperors," remarked Sancho, "were never known to be of pure gold; they are always of tinsel or tinplate."

6. I.e., I shall be weak and exhausted (proverbial).
7. Until he earns this title (in chapter 15), he will be referred to as the Knight of the Wood.
8. Don Quixote and his squire are now in the woody region around El Toboso, Dulcinea's hometown. Sancho has been sent to look for his knight's lady and has saved the day by pretending to see the beautiful damsel in a "village wench, and not a pretty one at that, for she was round-faced and snub-nosed." But by his imaginative lie he has succeeded, as he had planned, in setting in motion Don Quixote's belief in spells and enchantments: enemy

magicians, envious of him, have hidden his lady's splendor only from his sight. While the knight was still under the shock of this experience, farther along their way he and his squire have met a group of itinerant players dressed in their proper costumes for a religious play, *The Parliament of Death.*
9. Don Quixote has promised them to Sancho as a reward for bringing news of Dulcinea.
1. I.e., a bird in the hand is worth two in the bush.
2. The Empress and Cupid are characters in *The Parliament of Death.*

"That is the truth," said Don Quixote, "for it is only right that the accessories of a drama should be fictitious and not real, like the play itself. Speaking of that, Sancho, I would have you look kindly upon the art of the theater and, as a consequence, upon those who write the pieces and perform in them, for they all render a service of great value to the State by holding up a mirror for us at each step that we take, wherein we may observe, vividly depicted, all the varied aspects of human life; and I may add that there is nothing that shows us more clearly, by similitude, what we are and what we ought to be than do plays and players.

"Tell me, have you not seen some comedy in which kings, emperors, pontiffs, knights, ladies, and numerous other characters are introduced? One plays the ruffian, another the cheat, this one a merchant and that one a soldier, while yet another is the fool who is not so foolish as he appears, and still another the one of whom love has made a fool. Yet when the play is over and they have taken off their players' garments, all the actors are once more equal."

"Yes," replied Sancho, "I have seen all that."

"Well," continued Don Quixote, "the same thing happens in the comedy that we call life, where some play the part of emperors, others that of pontiffs—in short, all the characters that a drama may have—but when it is all over, that is to say, when life is done, death takes from each the garb that differentiates him, and all at last are equal in the grave."

"It is a fine comparison," Sancho admitted, "though not so new but that I have heard it many times before. It reminds me of that other one, about the game of chess. So long as the game lasts, each piece has its special qualities, but when it is over they are all mixed and jumbled together and put into a bag, which is to the chess pieces what the grave is to life."

"Every day, Sancho," said Don Quixote, "you are becoming less stupid and more sensible."

"It must be that some of your Grace's good sense is sticking to me," was Sancho's answer. "I am like a piece of land that of itself is dry and barren, but if you scatter manure over it and cultivate it, it will bear good fruit. By this I mean to say that your Grace's conversation is the manure that has been cast upon the barren land of my dry wit; the time that I spend in your service, associating with you, does the cultivating; and as a result of it all, I hope to bring forth blessed fruits by not departing, slipping, or sliding, from those paths of good breeding which your Grace has marked out for me in my parched understanding."

Don Quixote had to laugh at this affected speech of Sancho's, but he could not help perceiving that what the squire had said about his improvement was true enough; for every now and then the servant would speak in a manner that astonished his master. It must be admitted, however, that most of the time when he tried to use fine language, he would tumble from the mountain of his simple-mindedness into the abyss of his ignorance. It was when he was quoting old saws and sayings, whether or not they had anything to do with the subject under discussion, that he was at his best, displaying upon such occasions a prodigious memory, as will already have been seen and noted in the course of this history.

With such talk as this they spent a good part of the night. Then Sancho felt a desire to draw down the curtains of his eyes, as he was in the habit of saying when he wished to sleep, and, unsaddling his mount, he turned him loose to graze at will on the abundant grass. If he did not remove Rocinante's saddle, this was due to his master's express command; for when they had taken the field and were not sleeping under a roof, the hack was under no circumstances to be stripped. This was in accordance with an old and established custom which knights-errant faithfully observed: the bridle and saddlebow might be removed, but beware of touching the saddle itself! Guided by this precept, Sancho now gave Rocinante the same freedom that the ass enjoyed.

The close friendship that existed between the two animals was a most unusual one, so remarkable indeed that it has become a tradition handed down from father to son, and the author of this veracious chronicle even wrote a number of special chapters on the subject, although, in order to preserve the decency and decorum that are fitting in so heroic an account, he chose to omit them in the final version. But he forgets himself once in a while and goes on to tell us how the two beasts when they were together would hasten to scratch each other, and how, when they were tired and their bellies were full, Rocinante would lay his long neck over that of the ass—it extended more than half a yard on the other side—and the pair would then stand there gazing pensively at the ground for as much as three whole days at a time, or at least until someone came for them or hunger compelled them to seek nourishment.

I may tell you that I have heard it said that the author of this history, in one of his writings, has compared the friendship of Rocinante and the gray to that of Nisus and Euryalus and that of Pylades and Orestes;[3] and if this be true, it shows for the edification of all what great friends these two peace-loving animals were, and should be enough to make men ashamed, who are so inept at preserving friendship with one another. For this reason it has been said:

> There is no friend for friend,
> Reeds to lances turn . . . [4]

And there was the other poet who sang:

> Between friend and friend the bug . . . [5]

Let no one think that the author has gone out of his way in comparing the friendship of animals with that of men; for human beings have received valuable lessons from the beasts and have learned many important things from them. From the stork they have learned the use of clysters; the dog has taught them the salutary effects of vomiting as well as a lesson in gratitude; the cranes have taught them vigilance, the ants foresight, the elephants modesty, and the horse loyalty.[6]

Sancho had at last fallen asleep at the foot of a cork tree, while Don Quixote was slumbering beneath a sturdy oak. Very little time had passed when the knight was awakened by a noise behind him, and, starting up, he began looking about him and listening to see if he could make out where it came from. Then he caught sight of two men on horseback, one of whom, slipping down from the saddle, said to the other, "Dismount, my friend, and unbridle the horses; for there seems to be plenty of grass around here for them and sufficient silence and solitude for my amorous thoughts."

Saying this, he stretched himself out on the ground, and as he flung himself down the armor that he wore made such a noise that Don Quixote knew at once,

3. Famous examples of friendship in Virgil's *Aeneid* and in Greek tradition and drama.
4. From a popular ballad.
5. The Spanish expression "a bug in the eye"

implies keeping a watchful eye on somebody.
6. All folkloristic beliefs about the virtues of animals. "Clysters": enemas.

for a certainty, that he must be a knight-errant. Going over to Sancho, who was still sleeping, he shook him by the arm and with no little effort managed to get him awake.

"Brother Sancho," he said to him in a low voice, "we have an adventure on our hands."

"God give us a good one," said Sancho. "And where, my master, may her Ladyship, Mistress Adventure, be?"

"Where, Sancho?" replied Don Quixote. "Turn your eyes and look, and you will see stretched out over there a knight-errant who, so far as I can make out, is not any too happy; for I saw him fling himself from his horse to the ground with a certain show of despondency, and as he fell his armor rattled."

"Well," said Sancho, "and how does your Grace make this out to be an adventure?"

"I would not say," the knight answered him, "that this is an adventure in itself, but rather the beginning of one, for that is the way they start. But listen; he seems to be tuning a lute or guitar, and from the way he is spitting and clearing his throat he must be getting ready to sing something."

"Faith, so he is," said Sancho. "He must be some lovesick knight."

"There are no knights-errant that are not lovesick," Don Quixote informed him. "Let us listen to him, and the thread of his song will lead us to the yarn-ball of his thoughts; for out of the abundance of the heart the mouth speaketh."

Sancho would have liked to reply to his master, but the voice of the Knight of the Wood, which was neither very good nor very bad, kept him from it; and as the two of them listened attentively, they heard the following:

SONNET

Show me, O lady, the pattern of thy will,
That mine may take that very form and shape;
For my will in thine own I fain would drape,
Each slightest wish of thine I would fulfill.
If thou wouldst have me silence this dread ill
Of which I'm dying now, prepare the crape!
Or if I must another manner ape,
Then let Love's self display his rhyming skill.
Of opposites I am made, that's manifest:
In part soft wax, in part hard-diamond fire;
Yet to Love's laws my heart I do adjust,
And, hard or soft, I offer thee this breast:
Print or engrave there what thou may'st desire,
And I'll preserve it in eternal trust.

With an *Ay!* that appeared to be wrung from the very depths of his heart, the Knight of the Wood brought his song to a close, and then after a brief pause began speaking in a grief-stricken voice that was piteous to hear.

"O most beautiful and most ungrateful woman in all the world!" he cried, "how is it possible, O most serene Casildea de Vandalia,[7] for you to permit this captive knight of yours to waste away and perish in constant wanderings, amid

---

7. The Knight of the Wood's counterpart to Don Quixote's Dulcinea del Toboso.

rude toils and bitter hardships? Is it not enough that I have compelled all the knights of Navarre, all those of León, all the Tartessians and Castilians, and, finally, all those of La Mancha, to confess that there is no beauty anywhere that can rival yours?"

"That is not so!" cried Don Quixote at this point. "I am of La Mancha, and I have never confessed, I never could nor would confess a thing so prejudicial to the beauty of my lady. The knight whom you see there, Sancho, is raving; but let us listen and perhaps he will tell us more."

"That he will," replied Sancho, "for at the rate he is carrying on, he is good for a month at a stretch."

This did not prove to be the case, however; for when the Knight of the Wood heard voices near him, he cut short his lamentations and rose to his feet.

"Who goes there?" he called in a loud but courteous tone. "What kind of people are you? Are you, perchance, numbered among the happy or among the afflicted?"

"Among the afflicted," was Don Quixote's response.

"Then come to me," said the one of the Wood, "and, in doing so, know that you come to sorrow's self and the very essence of affliction."

Upon receiving so gentle and courteous an answer, Don Quixote and Sancho as well went over to him, whereupon the sorrowing one took the Manchegan's arm.

"Sit down here, Sir Knight," he continued, "for in order to know that you are one of those who follow the profession of knight-errantry, it is enough for me to have found you in this place where solitude and serenity keep you company, such a spot being the natural bed and proper dwelling of wandering men of arms."

"A knight I am," replied Don Quixote, "and of the profession that you mention; and though sorrows, troubles, and misfortunes have made my heart their abode, this does not mean that compassion for the woes of others has been banished from it. From your song a while ago I gather that your misfortunes are due to love—the love you bear that ungrateful fair one whom you named in your lamentations."

As they conversed in this manner, they sat together upon the hard earth, very peaceably and companionably, as if at daybreak they were not going to break each other's heads.

"Sir Knight," inquired the one of the Wood, "are you by any chance in love?"

"By mischance I am," said Don Quixote, "although the ills that come from well-placed affection should be looked upon as favors rather than as misfortunes."

"That is the truth," the Knight of the Wood agreed, "if it were not that the loved one's scorn disturbs our reason and understanding; for when it is excessive scorn appears as vengeance."

"I was never scorned by my lady," said Don Quixote.

"No, certainly not," said Sancho, who was standing near by, "for my lady is gentle as a ewe lamb and soft as butter."

"Is he your squire?" asked the one of the Wood.

"He is," replied Don Quixote.

"I never saw a squire," said the one of the Wood, "who dared to speak while his master was talking. At least, there is mine over there; he is as big as your father, and it cannot be proved that he has ever opened his lips while I was conversing."

"Well, upon my word," said Sancho, "I have spoken, and I will speak in front of any other as good—but never mind; it only makes it worse to stir it."

The Knight of the Wood's squire now seized Sancho's arm. "Come along," he said, "let the two of us go where we can talk all we like, squire fashion, and leave these gentlemen our masters to come to lance blows as they tell each other the story of their loves; for you may rest assured, daybreak will find them still at it."

"Let us, by all means," said Sancho, "and I will tell your Grace who I am, so that you may be able to see for yourself whether or not I am to be numbered among the dozen most talkative squires."

With this, the pair went off to one side, and there then took place between them a conversation that was as droll as the one between their masters was solemn.

CHAPTER XIII

In which is continued the adventure of the Knight of the Wood, together with the shrewd, highly original, and amicable conversation that took place between the two squires.

The knights and the squires had now separated, the latter to tell their life stories, the former to talk of their loves; but the history first relates the conversation of the servants and then goes on to report that of the masters. We are told that, after they had gone some little distance from where the others were, the one who served the Knight of the Wood began speaking to Sancho as follows:

"It is a hard life that we lead and live, *Señor mio*, those of us who are squires to knights-errant. It is certainly true that we eat our bread in the sweat of our faces, which is one of the curses that God put upon our first parents."[8]

"It might also be said," added Sancho, "that we eat it in the chill of our bodies, for who endures more heat and cold than we wretched ones who wait upon these wandering men of arms? It would not be so bad if we did eat once in a while, for troubles are less where there is bread; but as it is, we sometimes go for a day or two without breaking our fast, unless we feed on the wind that blows."

"But all this," said the other, "may very well be put up with, by reason of the hope we have of being rewarded; for if a knight is not too unlucky, his squire after a little while will find himself the governor of some fine island or prosperous earldom."

"I," replied Sancho, "have told my master that I would be satisfied with the governorship of an island, and he is so noble and so generous that he has promised it to me on many different occasions."

"In return for my services," said the Squire of the Wood, "I'd be content with a canonry. My master has already appointed me to one—and what a canonry!"

"Then he must be a churchly knight," said Sancho, "and in a position to grant favors of that sort to his faithful squire; but mine is a layman, pure and simple, although, as I recall, certain shrewd and, as I see it, scheming persons

---

8. Cf. Genesis 3.19: "In the sweat of thy face shalt thou eat bread, till thou return unto the ground."

did advise him to try to become an archbishop. However, he did not want to be anything but an emperor. And there I was, all the time trembling for fear he would take it into his head to enter the Church, since I was not educated enough to hold any benefices. For I may as well tell your Grace that, though I look like a man, I am no more than a beast where holy orders are concerned."

"That is where you are making a mistake," the Squire of the Wood assured him. "Not all island governments are desirable. Some of them are misshapen bits of land, some are poor, others are gloomy, and, in short, the best of them lays a heavy burden of care and trouble upon the shoulders of the unfortunate one to whose lot it falls. It would be far better if we who follow this cursed trade were to go back to our homes and there engage in pleasanter occupations, such as hunting or fishing, for example; for where is there in this world a squire so poor that he does not have a hack, a couple of greyhounds, and a fishing rod to provide him with sport in his own village?"

"I don't lack any of those," replied Sancho. "It is true, I have no hack, but I do have an ass that is worth twice as much as my master's horse. God send me a bad Easter, and let it be the next one that comes, if I would make a trade, even though he gave me four fanegas[9] of barley to boot. Your Grace will laugh at the price I put on my gray—for that is the color of the beast. As to greyhounds, I shan't want for them, as there are plenty and to spare in my village. And, anyway, there is more pleasure in hunting when someone else pays for it."

"Really and truly, Sir Squire," said the one of the Wood, "I have made up my mind and resolved to have no more to do with the mad whims of these knights; I intend to retire to my village and bring up my little ones—I have three of them, and they are like oriental pearls."

"I have two of them," said Sancho, "that might be presented to the Pope in person, especially one of my girls that I am bringing up to be a countess, God willing, in spite of what her mother says."

"And how old is this young lady that is destined to be a countess?"

"Fifteen," replied Sancho, "or a couple of years more or less. But she is tall as a lance, fresh as an April morning, and strong as a porter."

"Those," remarked the one of the Wood, "are qualifications that fit her to be not merely a countess but a nymph of the verdant wildwood. O whore's daughter of a whore! What strength the she-rogue must have!"

Sancho was a bit put out by this. "She is not a whore," he said, "nor was her mother before her, nor will either of them ever be, please God, so long as I live. And you might speak more courteously. For one who has been brought up among knights-errant, who are the soul of courtesy, those words are not very becoming."

"Oh, how little your Grace knows about compliments, Sir Squire!" the one of the Wood exclaimed. "Are you not aware that when some knight gives a good lance thrust to the bull in the plaza, or when a person does anything remarkably well, it is the custom for the crowd to cry out, 'Well done, whoreson rascal!' and that what appears to be vituperation in such a case is in reality high praise? Sir, I would bid you disown those sons or daughters who do nothing to cause such praise to be bestowed upon their parents."

9. One fanega is about 1.6 bushels, or 56 liters.

"I would indeed disown them if they didn't," replied Sancho, "and so your Grace may go ahead and call me, my children, and my wife all the whores in the world if you like, for everything that they say and do deserves the very highest praise. And in order that I may see them all again, I pray God to deliver me from mortal sin, or, what amounts to the same thing, from this dangerous calling of squire, seeing that I have fallen into it a second time, decoyed and deceived by a purse of a hundred ducats that I found one day in the heart of the Sierra Morena.[1] The devil is always holding up a bag full of doubloons in front of my eyes, here, there—no, not here, but there—everywhere, until it seems to me at every step I take that I am touching it with my hand, hugging it, carrying it off home with me, investing it, drawing an income from it, and living on it like a prince. And while I am thinking such thoughts, all the hardships I have to put up with serving this crackbrained master of mine, who is more of a madman than a knight, seem to me light and easy to bear."

"That," observed the Squire of the Wood, "is why it is they say that avarice bursts the bag. But, speaking of madmen, there is no greater one in all this world than my master; for he is one of those of whom it is said, 'The cares of others kill the ass.' Because another knight has lost his senses, he has to play mad too[2] and go hunting for that which, when he finds it, may fly up in his snout."

"Is he in love, maybe?"

"Yes, with a certain Casildea de Vandalia, the rawest[3] and best-roasted lady to be found anywhere on earth; but her rawness is not the foot he limps on, for he has other and greater schemes rumbling in his bowels, as you will hear tell before many hours have gone by."

"There is no road so smooth," said Sancho, "that it does not have some hole or rut to make you stumble. In other houses they cook horse beans, in mine they boil them by the kettleful.[4] Madness has more companions and attendants than good sense does. But if it is true what they say, that company in trouble brings relief, I may take comfort from your Grace, since you serve a master as foolish as my own."

"Foolish but brave," the one of the Wood corrected him, "and more of a rogue than anything else."

"That is not true of my master," replied Sancho. "I can assure you there is nothing of the rogue about him; he is as open and aboveboard as a wine pitcher and would not harm anyone but does good to all. There is no malice in his makeup, and a child could make him believe it was night at midday. For that very reason I love him with all my heart and cannot bring myself to leave him, no matter how many foolish things he does."

"But, nevertheless, good sir and brother," said the Squire of the Wood, "with the blind leading the blind, both are in danger of falling into the pit. It would be better for us to get out of all this as quickly as we can and return to our old haunts; for those that go seeking adventures do not always find good ones."

Sancho kept clearing his throat from time to time, and his saliva seemed rather viscous and dry; seeing which, the woodland squire said to him, "It looks

1. When Don Quixote retired there in Part I, chapter 23.
2. In the Sierra Morena, Don Quixote had decided to imitate Amadis de Gaula and Ariosto's Roland "by playing the part of a desperate and raving madman" as a consequence of love.
3. The Spanish has a pun on *crudo*, meaning both "raw" and "cruel."
4. Meaning that his misfortunes always come in large quantities.

to me as if we have been talking so much that our tongues are cleaving to our palates, but I have a loosener over there, hanging from the bow of my saddle, and a pretty good one it is." With this, he got up and went over to his horse and came back a moment later with a big flask of wine and a meat pie half a yard in diameter. This is no exaggeration, for the pasty in question was made of a hutch-rabbit of such a size that Sancho took it to be a goat, or at the very least a kid.

"And are you in the habit of carrying this with you, Señor?" he asked.

"What do you think?" replied the other. "Am I by any chance one of your wool-and-water[5] squires? I carry better rations on the flanks of my horse than a general does when he takes the field."

Sancho ate without any urging, gulping down mouthfuls that were like the knots on a tether, as they sat there in the dark.

"You are a squire of the right sort," he said, "loyal and true, and you live in grand style as shown by this feast, which I would almost say was produced by magic. You are not like me, poor wretch, who have in my saddlebags only a morsel of cheese so hard you could crack a giant's skull with it, three or four dozen carob beans, and a few nuts. For this I have my master to thank, who believes in observing the rule that knights-errant should nourish and sustain themselves on nothing but dried fruits and the herbs of the field."

"Upon my word, brother," said the other squire, "my stomach was not made for thistles, wild pears, and woodland herbs. Let our masters observe those knightly laws and traditions and eat what their rules prescribe; I carry a hamper of food and a flask on my saddlebow, whether they like it or not. And speaking of that flask, how I love it! There is scarcely a minute in the day that I'm not hugging and kissing it, over and over again."

As he said this, he placed the wine bag in Sancho's hands, who put it to his mouth, threw his head back, and sat there gazing up at the stars for a quarter of an hour. Then, when he had finished drinking, he let his head loll on one side and heaved a deep sigh.

"The whoreson rascal!" he exclaimed, "that's a fine vintage for you!"

"There!" cried the Squire of the Wood, as he heard the epithet Sancho had used, "do you see how you have praised this wine by calling it 'whoreson'?"

"I grant you," replied Sancho, "that it is no insult to call anyone a son of a whore so long as you really do mean to praise him. But tell me, sir, in the name of what you love most, is this the wine of Ciudad Real?"[6]

"What a winetaster you are! It comes from nowhere else, and it's a few years old, at that."

"Leave it to me," said Sancho, "and never fear, I'll show you how much I know about it. Would you believe me, Sir Squire, I have such a great natural instinct in this matter of wines that I have but to smell a vintage and I will tell you the country where it was grown, from what kind of grapes, what it tastes like, and how good it is, and everything that has to do with it. There is nothing so unusual about this, however, seeing that on my father's side were two of the best winetasters La Mancha has known in many a year, in proof of which, listen to the story of what happened to them.

5. I.e., lowly or paltry.
6. The main town in La Mancha and the center of a wine-producing region.

"The two were given a sample of wine from a certain vat and asked to state its condition and quality and determine whether it was good or bad. One of them tasted it with the tip of his tongue while the other merely brought it up to his nose. The first man said that it tasted of iron, the second that it smelled of Cordovan leather. The owner insisted that the vat was clean and that there could be nothing in the wine to give it a flavor of leather or of iron, but, nevertheless, the two famous wine-tasters stood their ground. Time went by, and when they came to clean out the vat they found in it a small key attached to a leather strap. And so your Grace may see for yourself whether or not one who comes of that kind of stock has a right to give his opinion in such cases."

"And for that very reason," said the Squire of the Wood, "I maintain that we ought to stop going about in search of adventures. Seeing that we have loaves, let us not go looking for cakes, but return to our cottages, for God will find us there if He so wills."

"I mean to stay with my master," Sancho replied, "until he reaches Saragossa, but after that we will come to an understanding."

The short of the matter is, the two worthy squires talked so much and drank so much that sleep had to tie their tongues and moderate their thirst, since to quench the latter was impossible. Clinging to the wine flask, which was almost empty by now, and with half-chewed morsels of food in their mouths, they both slept peacefully; and we shall leave them there as we go on to relate what took place between the Knight of the Wood and the Knight of the Mournful Countenance.

CHAPTER XIV

Wherein is continued the adventure of the Knight of the Wood.

In the course of the long conversation that took place between Don Quixote and the Knight of the Wood, the history informs us that the latter addressed the following remarks to the Manchegan:

"In short, Sir Knight, I would have you know that my destiny, or, more properly speaking, my own free choice, has led me to fall in love with the peerless Casildea de Vandalia. I call her peerless for the reason that she has no equal as regards either her bodily proportions or her very great beauty. This Casildea, then, of whom I am telling you, repaid my worthy affections and honorable intentions by forcing me, as Hercules[7] was forced by his stepmother, to incur many and diverse perils; and each time as I overcame one of them she would promise me that with the next one I should have that which I desired; but instead my labors have continued, forming a chain whose links I am no longer able to count, nor can I say which will be the last one, that shall mark the beginning of the realization of my hopes.

"One time she sent me forth to challenge that famous giantess of Seville, known as La Giralda,[8] who is as strong and brave as if made of brass, and who without moving from the spot where she stands is the most changeable and fickle woman in the world. I came, I saw, I conquered her. I made her stand still

7. In Greek mythology, the hero son of Zeus and Alcmena; he was persecuted by Zeus's wife, Hera.
8. Actually the bell tower of the cathedral of Seville, originally built as a minaret.

and point in one direction only, and for more than a week nothing but north winds blew. Then, there was that other time when Casildea sent me to lift those ancient stones, the mighty Bulls of Guisando,[9] an enterprise that had better have been entrusted to porters than to knights. On another occasion she commanded me to hurl myself down into the Cabra chasm[1]—an unheard-of and terribly dangerous undertaking—and bring her back a detailed account of what lay concealed in that deep and gloomy pit. I rendered La Giralda motionless, I lifted the Bulls of Guisando, and I threw myself into the abyss and brought to light what was hidden in its depths; yet my hopes are dead—how dead!—while her commands and her scorn are as lively as can be.

"Finally, she commanded me to ride through all the provinces of Spain and compel all the knights-errant whom I met with to confess that she is the most beautiful woman now living and that I am the most enamored man of arms that is to be found anywhere in the world. In fulfillment of this behest I have already traveled over the greater part of these realms and have vanquished many knights who have dared to contradict me. But the one whom I am proudest to have overcome in single combat is that famous gentleman, Don Quixote de la Mancha; for I made him confess that my Casildea is more beautiful than his Dulcinea, and by achieving such a conquest I reckon that I have conquered all the others on the face of the earth, seeing that this same Don Quixote had himself routed them. Accordingly, when I vanquished him, his fame, glory, and honor passed over and were transferred to my person.

> The brighter is the conquered one's lost crown,
> The greater is the conqueror's renown.[2]

Thus, the innumerable exploits of the said Don Quixote are now set down to my account and are indeed my own."

Don Quixote was astounded as he listened to the Knight of the Wood, and was about to tell him any number of times that he lied; the words were on the tip of his tongue, but he held them back as best he could, thinking that he would bring the other to confess with his own lips that what he had said was a lie. And so it was quite calmly that he now replied to him.

"Sir Knight," he began, "as to the assertion that your Grace has conquered most of the knights-errant in Spain and even in all the world, I have nothing to say, but that you have vanquished Don Quixote de la Mancha, I am inclined to doubt. It may be that it was someone else who resembled him, although there are very few that do."

"What do you mean?" replied the one of the Wood. "I swear by the heavens above that I did fight with Don Quixote and that I overcame him and forced him to yield. He is a tall man, with a dried-up face, long, lean legs, graying hair, an eagle-like nose somewhat hooked, and a big, black, drooping mustache. He takes the field under the name of the Knight of the Mournful Countenance, he has for squire a peasant named Sancho Panza, and he rides a famous steed called Rocinante. Lastly, the lady of his heart is a certain Dulcinea del Toboso, once upon a time known as Aldonza Lorenzo, just as my own lady, whose name

9. Statues representing animals and supposedly marking a place where Caesar defeated Pompey.
1. Possibly an ancient mine in the Sierra de Cabra near Cordova.
2. From Alonso de Ercilla y Zúñiga's *Araucana*, a poem about the Spanish struggle against the Araucanian Indians of Chile.

is Casildea and who is an Andalusian by birth, is called by me Casildea de Vandalia. If all this is not sufficient to show that I speak the truth, here is my sword
which shall make incredulity itself believe."

"Calm yourself, Sir Knight," replied Don Quixote, "and listen to what I have
to say to you. You must know that this Don Quixote of whom you speak is the
best friend that I have in the world, so great a friend that I may say that I feel
toward him as I do toward my own self; and from all that you have told me, the
very definite and accurate details that you have given me, I cannot doubt that
he is the one whom you have conquered. On the other hand, the sight of my
eyes and the touch of my hands assure me that he could not possibly be the one,
unless some enchanter who is his enemy—for he has many, and one in particular who delights in persecuting him—may have assumed the knight's form and
then permitted himself to be routed, by way of defrauding Don Quixote of the
fame which his high deeds of chivalry have earned for him throughout the known
world. To show you how true this may be, I will inform you that not more than a
couple of days ago those same enemy magicians transformed the figure and person of the beauteous Dulcinea del Toboso into a low and mean village lass, and
it is possible that they have done something of the same sort to the knight who is
her lover. And if all this does not suffice to convince you of the truth of what I
say, here is Don Quixote himself who will maintain it by force of arms, on foot or
on horseback, or in any way you like."

Saying this, he rose and laid hold of his sword, and waited to see what the
Knight of the Wood's decision would be. That worthy now replied in a voice as
calm as the one Don Quixote had used.

"Pledges," he said, "do not distress one who is sure of his ability to pay. He who
was able to overcome you when you were transformed, Señor Don Quixote, may
hope to bring you to your knees when you are your own proper self. But inasmuch as it is not fitting that knights should perform their feats of arms in the
darkness, like ruffians and highway-men, let us wait until it is day in order that
the sun may behold what we do. And the condition governing our encounter
shall be that the one who is vanquished must submit to the will of his conqueror
and perform all those things that are commanded of him, provided they are such
as are in keeping with the state of knighthood."

"With that condition and understanding," said Don Quixote, "I shall be satisfied."

With this, they went off to where their squires were, only to find them
snoring away as hard as when sleep had first overtaken them. Awakening the
pair, they ordered them to look to the horses; for as soon as the sun was up
the two knights meant to stage an arduous and bloody single-handed combat.
At this news Sancho was astonished and terrified, since, as a result of what
the other squire had told him of the Knight of the Wood's prowess, he was
led to fear for his master's safety. Nevertheless, he and his friend now went
to seek the mounts without saying a word, and they found the animals all
together, for by this time the two horses and the ass had smelled one another
out. On the way the Squire of the Wood turned to Sancho and addressed him
as follows:

"I must inform you, brother, that it is the custom of the fighters of Andalusia, when they are godfathers in any combat, not to remain idly by, with folded
hands, while their godsons fight it out. I tell you this by way of warning you

that while our masters are settling matters, we, too, shall have to come to blows and hack each other to bits."

"That custom, Sir Squire," replied Sancho, "may be all very well among the fighters and ruffians that you mention, but with the squires of knights-errant it is not to be thought of. At least, I have never heard my master speak of any such custom, and he knows all the laws of chivalry by heart. But granting that it is true and that there is a law which states in so many words that squires must fight while their masters do, I have no intention of obeying it but rather will pay whatever penalty is laid on peaceable-minded ones like myself, for I am sure it cannot be more than a couple of pounds of wax,[3] and that would be less expensive than the lint which it would take to heal my head—I can already see it split in two. What's more, it's out of the question for me to fight since I have no sword nor did I ever in my life carry one."

"That," said the one of the Wood, "is something that is easily remedied. I have here two linen bags of the same size. You take one and I'll take the other and we will fight that way, on equal terms."

"So be it, by all means," said Sancho, "for that will simply knock the dust out of us without wounding us."

"But that's not the way it's to be," said the other squire. "Inside the bags, to keep the wind from blowing them away, we will put a half-dozen nice smooth pebbles of the same weight, and so we'll be able to give each other a good pounding without doing ourselves any real harm or damage."

"Body of my father!" cried Sancho, "just look, will you, at the marten and sable and wads of carded cotton that he's stuffing into those bags so that we won't get our heads cracked or our bones crushed to a pulp. But I am telling you, *Señor mio*, that even though you fill them with silken pellets, I don't mean to fight. Let our masters fight and make the best of it, but as for us, let us drink and live; for time will see to ending our lives without any help on our part by way of bringing them to a close before they have reached their proper season and fall from ripeness."

"Nevertheless," replied the Squire of the Wood, "fight we must, if only for half an hour."

"No," Sancho insisted, "that I will not do. I will not be so impolite or so ungrateful as to pick any quarrel however slight with one whose food and drink I've shared. And, moreover, who in the devil could bring himself to fight in cold blood, when he's not angry or vexed in any way?"

"I can take care of that, right enough," said the one of the Wood. "Before we begin, I will come up to your Grace as nicely as you please and give you three or four punches that will stretch you out at my feet; and that will surely be enough to awaken your anger, even though it's sleeping sounder than a dormouse."

"And I," said Sancho, "have another idea that's every bit as good as yours. I will take a big club, and before your Grace has had a chance to awaken my anger I will put yours to sleep with such mighty whacks that if it wakes at all it will be in the other world; for it is known there that I am not the man to let my face be mussed by anyone, and let each look out for the arrow.[4] But the best thing to do

---

3. In some confraternities, penalties for being absent were paid in wax, presumably to make church candles.

4. A proverbial expression from archery: let each one take care of his or her own arrow. Other obviously proverbial expressions follow, as is typical of Sancho's speech.

would be to leave each one's anger to its slumbers, for no one knows the heart of any other, he who comes for wool may go back shorn, and God bless peace and curse all strife. If a hunted cat when surrounded and cornered turns into a lion, God knows what I who am a man might not become. And so from this time forth I am warning you, Sir Squire, that all the harm and damage that may result from our quarrel will be upon your head."

"Very well," the one of the Wood replied, "God will send the dawn and we shall make out somehow."

At that moment gay-colored birds of all sorts began warbling in the trees and with their merry and varied songs appeared to be greeting and welcoming the fresh-dawning day, which already at the gates and on the balconies of the east was revealing its beautiful face as it shook out from its hair an infinite number of liquid pearls. Bathed in this gentle moisture, the grass seemed to shed a pearly spray, the willows distilled a savory manna, the fountains laughed, the brooks murmured, the woods were glad, and the meadows put on their finest raiment. The first thing that Sancho Panza beheld, as soon as it was light enough to tell one object from another, was the Squire of the Wood's nose, which was so big as to cast into the shade all the rest of his body. In addition to being of enormous size, it is said to have been hooked in the middle and all covered with warts of a mulberry hue, like eggplant; it hung down for a couple of inches below his mouth, and the size, color, warts, and shape of this organ gave his face so ugly an appearance that Sancho began trembling hand and foot like a child with convulsions and made up his mind then and there that he would take a couple of hundred punches before he would let his anger be awakened to the point where he would fight with this monster.

Don Quixote in the meanwhile was surveying his opponent, who had already adjusted and closed his helmet so that it was impossible to make out what he looked like. It was apparent, however, that he was not very tall and was stockily built. Over his armor he wore a coat of some kind or other made of what appeared to be the finest cloth of gold, all bespangled with glittering mirrors that resembled little moons and that gave him a most gallant and festive air, while above his helmet were a large number of waving plumes, green, white, and yellow in color. His lance, which was leaning against a tree, was very long and stout and had a steel point of more than a palm in length. Don Quixote took all this in, and from what he observed concluded that his opponent must be of tremendous strength, but he was not for this reason filled with fear as Sancho Panza was. Rather, he proceeded to address the Knight of the Mirrors, quite boldly and in a highbred manner.

"Sir Knight," he said, "if in your eagerness to fight you have not lost your courtesy, I would beg you to be so good as to raise your visor a little in order that I may see if your face is as handsome as your trappings."

"Whether you come out of this emprise the victor or the vanquished, Sir Knight," he of the Mirrors replied, "there will be ample time and opportunity for you to have a sight of me. If I do not now gratify your desire, it is because it seems to me that I should be doing a very great wrong to the beauteous Casildea de Vandalia by wasting the time it would take me to raise my visor before having forced you to confess that I am right in my contention, with which you are well acquainted."

"Well, then," said Don Quixote, "while we are mounting our steeds you might at least inform me if I am that knight of La Mancha whom you say you conquered."

"To that our[5] answer," said he of the Mirrors, "is that you are as like the knight I overcame as one egg is like another; but since you assert that you are persecuted by enchanters, I should not venture to state positively that you are the one in question."

"All of which," said Don Quixote, "is sufficient to convince me that you are laboring under a misapprehension; but in order to relieve you of it once and for all, let them bring our steeds, and in less time than you would spend in lifting your visor, if God, my lady, and my arm give me strength, I will see your face and you shall see that I am not the vanquished knight you take me to be."

With this, they cut short their conversation and mounted, and, turning Rocinante around, Don Quixote began measuring off the proper length of field for a run against his opponent as he of the Mirrors did the same. But the Knight of La Mancha had not gone twenty paces when he heard his adversary calling to him, whereupon each of them turned halfway and he of the Mirrors spoke.

"I must remind you, Sir Knight," he said, "of the condition under which we fight, which is that the vanquished, as I have said before, shall place himself wholly at the disposition of the victor."

"I am aware of that," replied Don Quixote, "not forgetting the provision that the behest laid upon the vanquished shall not exceed the bounds of chivalry."

"Agreed," said the Knight of the Mirrors.

At that moment Don Quixote caught sight of the other squire's weird nose and was as greatly astonished by it as Sancho had been. Indeed, he took the fellow for some monster, or some new kind of human being wholly unlike those that people this world. As he saw his master riding away down the field preparatory to the tilt, Sancho was alarmed; for he did not like to be left alone with the big-nosed individual, fearing that one powerful swipe of that protuberance against his own nose would end the battle so far as he was concerned and he would be lying stretched out on the ground, from fear if not from the force of the blow.

He accordingly ran after the knight, clinging to one of Rocinante's stirrup straps, and when he thought it was time for Don Quixote to whirl about and bear down upon his opponent, he called to him and said, "*Señor mio*, I beg your Grace, before you turn for the charge, to help me up into that cork tree yonder where I can watch the encounter which your Grace is going to have with this knight better than I can from the ground and in a way that is much more to my liking."

"I rather think, Sancho," said Don Quixote, "that what you wish to do is to mount a platform where you can see the bulls without any danger to yourself."

"The truth of the matter is," Sancho admitted, "the monstrous nose on that squire has given me such a fright that I don't dare stay near him."

"It is indeed of such a sort," his master assured him, "that if I were not the person I am, I myself should be frightened. And so, come, I will help you up."

While Don Quixote tarried to see Sancho ensconced in the cork tree, the Knight of the Mirrors measured as much ground as seemed to him necessary and then, assuming that his adversary had done the same, without waiting for sound of trumpet or any other signal, he wheeled his horse, which was no swifter nor any more impressive-looking than Rocinante, and bore down upon

---

5. Note the dignified, "majestic" plural form.

his enemy at a mild trot; but when he saw that the Manchegan was busy helping his squire, he reined in his mount and came to a stop midway in his course,
for which his horse was extremely grateful, being no longer able to stir a single
step. To Don Quixote, on the other hand, it seemed as if his enemy was flying,
and digging his spurs with all his might into Rocinante's lean flanks he caused
that animal to run a bit for the first and only time, according to the history, for
on all other occasions a simple trot had represented his utmost speed. And so
it was that, with an unheard-of fury, the Knight of the Mournful Countenance came down upon the Knight of the Mirrors as the latter sat there sinking his spurs all the way up to the buttons without being able to persuade his
horse to budge a single inch from the spot where he had come to a sudden
standstill.

It was at this fortunate moment, while his adversary was in such a predicament, that Don Quixote fell upon him, quite unmindful of the fact that the
other knight was having trouble with his mount and either was unable or did
not have time to put his lance at rest. The upshot of it was, he encountered
him with such force that, much against his will, the Knight of the Mirrors went
rolling over his horse's flanks and tumbled to the ground, where as a result of
his terrific fall he lay as if dead, without moving hand or foot.

No sooner did Sancho perceive what had happened than he slipped down
from the cork tree and ran up as fast as he could to where his master was. Dismounting from Rocinante, Don Quixote now stood over the Knight of the Mirrors, and undoing the helmet straps to see if the man was dead, or to give him
air in case he was alive, he beheld—who can say what he beheld without creating astonishment, wonder, and amazement in those who hear the tale? The
history tells us that it was the very countenance, form, aspect, physiognomy,
effigy, and image of the bachelor Sansón Carrasco!

"Come, Sancho," he cried in a loud voice, "and see what is to be seen but is
not to be believed. Hasten, my son, and learn what magic can do and how great
is the power of wizards and enchanters."

Sancho came, and the moment his eyes fell on the bachelor Carrasco's face
he began crossing and blessing himself a countless number of times. Meanwhile, the overthrown knight gave no signs of life.

"If you ask me, master," said Sancho, "I would say that the best thing for your
Grace to do is to run his sword down the mouth of this one who appears to be
the bachelor Carrasco; maybe by so doing you would be killing one of your
enemies, the enchanters."

"That is not a bad idea," replied Don Quixote, "for the fewer enemies the
better." And, drawing his sword, he was about to act upon Sancho's advice and
counsel when the Knight of the Mirrors' squire came up to them, now minus
the nose which had made him so ugly.

"Look well what you are doing, Don Quixote!" he cried. "The one who lies
there at your feet is your Grace's friend, the bachelor Sansón Carrasco, and
I am his squire."

"And where is your nose?" inquired Sancho, who was surprised to see him
without that deformity.

"Here in my pocket," was the reply. And, thrusting his hand into his coat, he
drew out a nose of varnished pasteboard of the make that has been described.
Studying him more and more closely, Sancho finally exclaimed, in a voice that

was filled with amazement, "Holy Mary preserve me! And is this not my neighbor and crony, Tomé Cecial?"

"That is who I am!" replied the de-nosed squire, "your good friend Tomé Cecial, Sancho Panza. I will tell you presently of the means and snares and falsehoods that brought me here. But, for the present, I beg and entreat your master not to lay hands on, mistreat, wound, or slay the Knight of the Mirrors whom he now has at his feet; for without any doubt it is the rash and ill-advised bachelor Sansón Carrasco, our fellow villager."

The Knight of the Mirrors now recovered consciousness, and, seeing this, Don Quixote at once placed the naked point of his sword above the face of the vanquished one.

"Dead you are, knight," he said, "unless you confess that the peerless Dulcinea del Toboso is more beautiful than your Casildea de Vandalia. And what is more, you will have to promise that, should you survive this encounter and the fall you have had, you will go to the city of El Toboso and present yourself to her in my behalf, that she may do with you as she may see fit. And in case she leaves you free to follow your own will, you are to return to seek me out— the trail of my exploits will serve as a guide to bring you wherever I may be— and tell me all that has taken place between you and her. These conditions are in conformity with those that we arranged before our combat and they do not go beyond the bounds of knight-errantry."

"I confess," said the fallen knight, "that the tattered and filthy shoe of the lady Dulcinea del Toboso is of greater worth than the badly combed if clean beard of Casildea, and I promise to go to her presence and return to yours and to give you a complete and detailed account concerning anything you may wish to know."

"Another thing," added Don Quixote, "that you will have to confess and believe is that the knight you conquered was not and could not have been Don Quixote de la Mancha, but was some other that resembled him, just as I am convinced that you, though you appear to be the bachelor Sansón Carrasco, are another person in his form and likeness who has been put here by my enemies to induce me to restrain and moderate the impetuosity of my wrath and make a gentle use of my glorious victory."

"I confess, think, and feel as you feel, think, and believe," replied the lamed knight. "Permit me to rise, I beg of you, if the jolt I received in my fall will let me do so, for I am in very bad shape."

Don Quixote and Tomé Cecial the squire now helped him to his feet. As for Sancho, he could not take his eyes off Tomé but kept asking him one question after another, and although the answers he received afforded clear enough proof that the man was really his fellow townsman, the fear that had been aroused in him by his master's words—about the enchanters' having transformed the Knight of the Mirrors into the bachelor Sansón Carrasco—prevented him from believing the truth that was apparent to his eyes. The short of it is, both master and servant were left with this delusion as the other ill-errant knight and his squire, in no pleasant state of mind, took their departure with the object of looking for some village where they might be able to apply poultices and splints to the bachelor's battered ribs.

Don Quixote and Sancho then resumed their journey along the road to Saragossa, and here for the time being the history leaves them in order to give an account of who the Knight of the Mirrors and his long-nosed squire really were.

CHAPTER XV

Wherein is told and revealed who the Knight of the Mirrors and his squire were.

Don Quixote went off very happy, self-satisfied, and vainglorious at having achieved a victory over so valiant a knight as he imagined the one of the Mirrors to be, from whose knightly word he hoped to learn whether or not the spell which had been put upon his lady was still in effect; for, unless he chose to forfeit his honor, the vanquished contender must of necessity return and give an account of what had happened in the course of his interview with her. But Don Quixote was of one mind, the Knight of the Mirrors of another, for, as has been stated, the latter's only thought at the moment was to find some village where plasters were available.

The history goes on to state that when the bachelor Sansón Carrasco advised Don Quixote to resume his feats of chivalry, after having desisted from them for a while, this action was taken as the result of a conference which he had held with the curate and the barber as to the means to be adopted in persuading the knight to remain quietly at home and cease agitating himself over his unfortunate adventures. It had been Carrasco's suggestion, to which they had unanimously agreed, that they let Don Quixote sally forth, since it appeared to be impossible to prevent his doing so, and that Sansón should then take to the road as a knight-errant and pick a quarrel and do battle with him. There would be no difficulty about finding a pretext, and then the bachelor knight would overcome him (which was looked upon as easy of accomplishment), having first entered into a pact to the effect that the vanquished should remain at the mercy and bidding of his conqueror. The behest in this case was to be that the fallen one should return to his village and home and not leave it for the space of two years or until further orders were given him, it being a certainty that, once having been overcome, Don Quixote would fulfill the agreement, in order not to contravene or fail to obey the laws of chivalry. And it was possible that in the course of his seclusion he would forget his fancies, or they would at least have an opportunity to seek some suitable cure for his madness.

Sansón agreed to undertake this, and Tomé Cecial, Sancho's friend and neighbor, a merry but featherbrained chap, offered to go along as squire. Sansón then proceeded to arm himself in the manner that has been described, while Tomé disguised his nose with the aforementioned mask so that his crony would not recognize him when they met. Thus equipped, they followed the same route as Don Quixote and had almost caught up with him by the time he had the adventure with the Cart of Death. They finally overtook him in the wood, where those events occurred with which the attentive reader is already familiar; and if it had not been for the knight's extraordinary fancies, which led him to believe that the bachelor was not the bachelor, the said bachelor might have been prevented from ever attaining his degree of licentiate, as a result of having found no nests where he thought to find birds.

Seeing how ill they had succeeded in their undertaking and what an end they had reached, Tomé Cecial now addressed his master.

"Surely, Señor Sansón Carrasco," he said, "we have had our deserts. It is easy enough to plan and embark upon an enterprise, but most of the time it's hard to get out of it. Don Quixote is a madman and we are sane, yet he goes away sound and laughing while your Grace is left here, battered and sorrowful. I wish you would tell me now who is the crazier: the one who is so because he cannot help it, or he who turns crazy of his own free will?"

"The difference between the two," replied Sansón, "lies in this: that the one who cannot help being crazy will be so always, whereas the one who is a madman by choice can leave off being one whenever he so desires."

"Well," said Tomé Cecial, "since that is the way it is, and since I chose to be crazy when I became your Grace's squire, by the same reasoning I now choose to stop being insane and to return to my home."

"That is your affair," said Sansón, "but to imagine that I am going back before I have given Don Quixote a good thrashing is senseless; and what will urge me on now is not any desire to see him recover his wits, but rather a thirst for vengeance; for with the terrible pain that I have in my ribs, you can't expect me to feel very charitable."

Conversing in this manner they kept on until they reached a village where it was their luck to find a bonesetter to take care of poor Sansón. Tomé Cecial then left him and returned home, while the bachelor meditated plans for revenge. The history has more to say of him in due time, but for the present it goes on to make merry with Don Quixote.

CHAPTER XVI

Of what happened to Don Quixote upon his meeting with a prudent gentleman of La Mancha.

With that feeling of happiness and vainglorious self-satisfaction that has been mentioned, Don Quixote continued on his way, imagining himself to be, as a result of the victory he had just achieved, the most valiant knight-errant of the age. Whatever adventures might befall him from then on he regarded as already accomplished and brought to a fortunate conclusion. He thought little now of enchanters and enchantments and was unmindful of the innumerable beatings he had received in the course of his knightly wanderings, of the volley of pebbles that had knocked out half his teeth, of the ungratefulness of the galley slaves and the audacity of the Yanguesans whose poles had fallen upon his body like rain. In short, he told himself, if he could but find the means, manner, or way of freeing his lady Dulcinea of the spell that had been put upon her, he would not envy the greatest good fortune that the most fortunate of knights-errant in ages past had ever by any possibility attained.

He was still wholly wrapped up in these thoughts when Sancho spoke to him.

"Isn't it strange, sir, that I can still see in front of my eyes the huge and monstrous nose of my old crony, Tomé Cecial?"

"And do you by any chance believe, Sancho, that the Knight of the Mirrors was the bachelor Sansón Carrasco and that his squire was your friend Tomé?"

"I don't know what to say to that," replied Sancho. "All I know is that the things he told me about my home, my wife and young ones, could not have come from anybody else; and the face, too, once you took the nose away, was the same as Tomé Cecial's, which I have seen many times in our village, right next door to my own house, and the tone of voice was the same also."

"Let us reason the matter out, Sancho," said Don Quixote. "Look at it this way: how can it be thought that the bachelor Sansón Carrasco would come as a knight-errant, equipped with offensive and defensive armor, to contend with me? Am I, perchance, his enemy? Have I given him any occasion to cherish a grudge against me? Am I a rival of his? Or can it be jealousy of the fame I have acquired that has led him to take up the profession of arms?"

"Well, then, sir," Sancho answered him, "how are we to explain the fact that the knight was so like the bachelor and his squire like my friend? And if this was a magic spell, as your Grace has said, was there no other pair in the world whose likeness they might have taken?"

"It is all a scheme and a plot," replied Don Quixote, "on the part of those wicked magicians who are persecuting me and who, foreseeing that I would be the victor in the combat, saw to it that the conquered knight should display the face of my friend the bachelor, so that the affection which I bear him would come between my fallen enemy and the edge of my sword and might of my arm, to temper the righteous indignation of my heart. In that way, he who had sought by falsehood and deceits to take my life, would be left to go on living. As proof of all this, Sancho, experience, which neither lies nor deceives, has already taught you how easy it is for enchanters to change one countenance into another, making the beautiful ugly and the ugly beautiful. It was not two days ago that you beheld the peerless Dulcinea's beauty and elegance in its entirety and natural form, while I saw only the repulsive features of a low and ignorant peasant girl with cataracts over her eyes and a foul smell in her mouth. And if the perverse enchanter was bold enough to effect so vile a transformation as this, there is certainly no cause for wonderment at what he has done in the case of Sansón Carrasco and your friend, all by way of snatching my glorious victory out of my hands. But in spite of it all, I find consolation in the fact that, whatever the shape he may have chosen to assume, I have laid my enemy low."

"God knows what the truth of it all may be," was Sancho's comment. Knowing as he did that Dulcinea's transformation had been due to his own scheming and plotting, he was not taken in by his master's delusions. He was at a loss for a reply, however, lest he say something that would reveal his own trickery.

As they were carrying on this conversation, they were overtaken by a man who, following the same road, was coming along behind them. He was mounted on a handsome flea-bitten mare and wore a hooded great-coat of fine green cloth trimmed in tawny velvet and a cap of the same material, while the trappings of his steed, which was accoutered for the field, were green and mulberry in hue, his saddle being of the *jineta*[6] mode. From his broad green and gold shoulder strap there dangled a Moorish cutlass, and his half-boots were of the same make as the baldric. His spurs were not gilded but were covered with highly polished green lacquer, so that, harmonizing as they did with the rest of his apparel, they seemed more appropriate than if they had been of purest gold. As he came up, he greeted the pair courteously and, spurring his mare, was about to ride on past when Don Quixote called to him.

"Gallant sir," he said, "if your Grace is going our way and is not in a hurry, it would be a favor to us if we might travel together."

---

6. I.e., it has a high pommel and short stirrups.

"The truth is," replied the stranger, "I should not have ridden past you if I had not been afraid that the company of my mare would excite your horse."

"In that case, sir," Sancho spoke up, "you may as well rein in, for this horse of ours is the most virtuous and well mannered of any that there is. Never on such an occasion has he done anything that was not right—the only time he did misbehave, my master and I suffered for it aplenty. And so, I say again, your Grace may slow up if you like; for even if you offered him your mare on a couple of platters, he'd never try to mount her."

With this, the other traveler drew rein, being greatly astonished at Don Quixote's face and figure. For the knight was now riding along without his helmet, which was carried by Sancho like a piece of luggage on the back of his gray, in front of the packsaddle. If the green-clad gentleman stared hard at his newfound companion, the latter returned his gaze with an even greater intensity. He impressed Don Quixote as being a man of good judgment, around fifty years of age, with hair that was slightly graying and an aquiline nose, while the expression of his countenance was half humorous, half serious. In short, both his person and his accouterments indicated that he was an individual of some worth.

As for the man in green's impression of Don Quixote de la Mancha, he was thinking that he had never before seen any human being that resembled this one. He could not but marvel at the knight's long neck, his tall frame, and the leanness and the sallowness of his face, as well as his armor and his grave bearing, the whole constituting a sight such as had not been seen for many a day in those parts. Don Quixote in turn was quite conscious of the attentiveness with which the traveler was studying him and could tell from the man's astonished look how curious he was; and so, being very courteous and fond of pleasing everyone, he proceeded to anticipate any questions that might be asked him.

"I am aware," he said, "that my appearance must strike your Grace as being very strange and out of the ordinary, and for that reason I am not surprised at your wonderment. But your Grace will cease to wonder when I tell you, as I am telling you now, that I am a knight, one of those

> *Of whom it is folks say,*
> *They to adventures go.*[7]

I have left my native heath, mortgaged my estate, given up my comfortable life, and cast myself into fortune's arms for her to do with me what she will. It has been my desire to revive a knight-errantry that is now dead, and for some time past, stumbling here and falling there, now throwing myself down headlong and then rising up once more, I have been able in good part to carry out my design by succoring widows, protecting damsels, and aiding the fallen, the orphans, and the young, all of which is the proper and natural duty of knights-errant. As a result, owing to my many valiant and Christian exploits, I have been deemed worthy of visiting in printed form nearly all the nations of the world. Thirty thousand copies of my history have been published, and, unless Heaven forbid, they will print thirty million of them.

"In short, to put it all into a few words, or even one, I will tell you that I am Don Quixote de la Mancha, otherwise known as the Knight of the Mournful

---

7. These two verses, which recall medieval popular romance ballads, appear in a Spanish translation of Petrarch's allegorical poem, the *Triumphs*, although they are not in the original.

Countenance. Granted that self-praise is degrading, there still are times when I must praise myself, that is to say, when there is no one else present to speak in my behalf. And so, good sir, neither this steed nor this lance nor this buckler nor this squire of mine, nor all the armor that I wear and arms I carry, nor the sallowness of my complexion, nor my leanness and gauntness, should any longer astonish you, now that you know who I am and what the profession is that I follow."

Having thus spoken, Don Quixote fell silent, and the man in green was so slow in replying that it seemed as if he was at a loss for words. Finally, however, after a considerable while, he brought himself to the point of speaking.

"You were correct, Sir Knight," he said, "about my astonishment and my curiosity, but you have not succeeded in removing the wonderment that the sight of you has aroused in me. You say that, knowing who you are, I should not wonder any more, but such is not the case, for I am now more amazed than ever. How can it be that there are knights-errant in the world today and that histories of them are actually printed? I find it hard to convince myself that at the present time there is anyone on earth who goes about aiding widows, protecting damsels, defending the honor of wives, and succoring orphans, and I should never have believed it had I not beheld your Grace with my own eyes. Thank Heaven for that book that your Grace tells me has been published concerning your true and exalted deeds of chivalry, as it should cast into oblivion all the innumerable stories of fictitious knights-errant with which the world is filled, greatly to the detriment of good morals and the prejudice and discredit of legitimate histories."

"As to whether the stories of knights-errant are fictitious or not," observed Don Quixote, "there is much that remains to be said."

"Why," replied the gentleman in green, "is there anyone who can doubt that such tales are false?"

"I doubt it," was the knight's answer, "but let the matter rest there. If our journey lasts long enough, I trust with God's help to be able to show your Grace that you are wrong in going along with those who hold it to be a certainty that they are not true."

From this last remark the traveler was led to suspect that Don Quixote must be some kind of crackbrain, and he was waiting for him to confirm the impression by further observations of the same sort; but before they could get off on another subject, the knight, seeing that he had given an account of his own station in life, turned to the stranger and politely inquired who his companion might be.

"I, Sir Knight of the Mournful Countenance," replied the one in the green-colored greatcoat, "am a gentleman, and a native of the village where, please God, we are going to dine today. I am more than moderately rich, and my name is Don Diego de Miranda. I spend my life with my wife and children and with my friends. My occupations are hunting and fishing, though I keep neither falcon nor hounds but only a tame partridge[8] and a bold ferret or two. I am the owner of about six dozen books, some of them in Spanish, others in Latin, including both histories and devotional works. As for books of chivalry, they have not as yet crossed the threshold of my door. My own preference is for profane[9] rather than devotional writings, such as afford an innocent amusement, charming us by

8. Used as a decoy.   9. I.e., secular, nonreligious.

their style and arousing and holding our interest by their inventiveness, although I must say there are very few of that sort to be found in Spain.

"Sometimes," the man in green continued, "I dine with my friends and neighbors, and I often invite them to my house. My meals are wholesome and well prepared and there is always plenty to eat. I do not care for gossip, nor will I permit it in my presence. I am not lynx-eyed and do not pry into the lives and doings of others. I hear mass every day and share my substance with the poor, but make no parade of my good works lest hypocrisy and vainglory, those enemies that so imperceptibly take possession of the most modest heart, should find their way into mine. I try to make peace between those who are at strife. I am the devoted servant of Our Lady,[1] and my trust is in the infinite mercy of God Our Savior."

Sancho had listened most attentively to the gentleman's account of his mode of life, and inasmuch as it seemed to him that this was a good and holy way to live and that the one who followed such a pattern ought to be able to work miracles, he now jumped down from his gray's back and, running over to seize the stranger's right stirrup, began kissing the feet of the man in green with a show of devotion that bordered on tears.

"Why are you doing that, brother?" the gentleman asked him. "What is the meaning of these kisses?"

"Let me kiss your feet," Sancho insisted, "for if I am not mistaken, your Grace is the first saint riding *jineta* fashion that I have seen in all the days of my life."

"I am not a saint," the gentleman assured him, "but a great sinner. It is you, brother, who are the saint; for you must be a good man, judging by the simplicity of heart that you show."

Sancho then went back to his packsaddle, having evoked a laugh from the depths of his master's melancholy and given Don Diego fresh cause for astonishment.

Don Quixote thereupon inquired of the newcomer how many children he had, remarking as he did so that the ancient philosophers, who were without a true knowledge of God, believed that mankind's greatest good lay in the gifts of nature, in those of fortune, and in having many friends and many and worthy sons.

"I, Señor Don Quixote," replied the gentleman, "have a son without whom I should, perhaps, be happier than I am. It is not that he is bad, but rather that he is not as good as I should like him to be. He is eighteen years old, and for six of those years he has been at Salamanca studying the Greek and Latin languages. When I desired him to pass on to other branches of learning, I found him so immersed in the science of Poetry (if it can be called such) that it was not possible to interest him in the Law, which I wanted him to study, nor in Theology, the queen of them all. My wish was that he might be an honor to his family; for in this age in which we are living our monarchs are in the habit of highly rewarding those forms of learning that are good and virtuous, since learning without virtue is like pearls on a dunghill. But he spends the whole day trying to decide whether such and such a verse of Homer's *Iliad* is well conceived or not, whether or not Martial is immodest in a certain epigram, whether certain lines of Vergil are to

---

1. The Virgin Mary, mother of Jesus.

be understood in this way or in that. In short, he spends all his time with the books written by those poets whom I have mentioned and with those of Horace, Persius, Juvenal, and Tibullus. As for our own moderns, he sets little store by them, and yet, for all his disdain of Spanish poetry, he is at this moment racking his brains in an effort to compose a gloss on a quatrain that was sent him from Salamanca and which, I fancy, is for some literary tournament."

To all this Don Quixote made the following answer:

"Children, sir, are out of their parents' bowels and so are to be loved whether they be good or bad, just as we love those that gave us life. It is for parents to bring up their offspring, from the time they are infants, in the paths of virtue, good breeding, proper conduct, and Christian morality, in order that, when they are grown, they may be a staff to the old age of the ones that bore them and an honor to their own posterity. As to compelling them to study a particular branch of learning, I am not so sure as to that, though there may be no harm in trying to persuade them to do so. But where there is no need to study *pane lucrando*[2]— where Heaven has provided them with parents that can supply their daily bread—I should be in favor of permitting them to follow that course to which they are most inclined; and although poetry may be more pleasurable than useful, it is not one of those pursuits that bring dishonor upon those who engage in them.

"Poetry in my opinion, my dear sir," he went on, "is a young and tender maid of surpassing beauty, who has many other damsels (that is to say, the other disciplines) whose duty it is to bedeck, embellish, and adorn her. She may call upon all of them for service, and all of them in turn depend upon her nod. She is not one to be rudely handled, nor dragged through the streets, nor exposed at street corners, in the market place, or in the private nooks of palaces. She is fashioned through an alchemy of such power that he who knows how to make use of it will be able to convert her into the purest gold of inestimable price. Possessing her, he must keep her within bounds and not permit her to run wild in bawdy satires or soulless sonnets. She is not to be put up for sale in any manner, unless it be in the form of heroic poems, pity-inspiring tragedies, or pleasing and ingenious comedies. Let mountebanks keep hands off her, and the ignorant mob as well, which is incapable of recognizing or appreciating the treasures that are locked within her. And do not think, sir, that I apply that term 'mob' solely to plebeians and those of low estate; for anyone who is ignorant, whether he be lord or prince, may, and should, be included in the vulgar herd.

"But," Don Quixote continued, "he who possesses the gift of poetry and who makes the use of it that I have indicated, shall become famous and his name shall be honored among all the civilized nations of the world. You have stated, sir, that your son does not greatly care for poetry written in our Spanish tongue, and in that I am inclined to think he is somewhat mistaken. My reason for saying so is this: the great Homer did not write in Latin, for the reason that he was a Greek, and Vergil did not write in Greek since he was a Latin. In a word, all the poets of antiquity wrote in the language which they had imbibed with their mother's milk and did not go searching after foreign ones to express their loftiest conceptions. This being so, it would be well if the same custom were to be adopted by all nations, the German poet being no longer looked down upon

2. Earning one's bread (Latin).

because he writes in German, nor the Castilian or the Basque for employing his native speech.

"As for your son, I fancy, sir, that his quarrel is not so much with Spanish poetry as with those poets who have no other tongue or discipline at their command such as would help to awaken their natural gift; and yet, here, too, he may be wrong. There is an opinion, and a true one, to the effect that 'the poet is born,' that is to say, it is as a poet that he comes forth from his mother's womb, and with the propensity that has been bestowed upon him by Heaven, without study or artifice, he produces those compositions that attest the truth of the line: '*Est deus in nobis*,' etc.[3] I further maintain that the born poet who is aided by art will have a great advantage over the one who by art alone would become a poet, the reason being that art does not go beyond, but merely perfects, nature; and so it is that, by combining nature with art and art with nature, the finished poet is produced.

"In conclusion, then, my dear sir, my advice to you would be to let your son go where his star beckons him; for being a good student as he must be, and having already successfully mounted the first step on the stairway of learning, which is that of languages, he will be able to continue of his own accord to the very peak of humane letters, an accomplishment that is altogether becoming in a gentleman, one that adorns, honors, and distinguishes him as much as the miter does the bishop or his flowing robe the learned jurisconsult. Your Grace well may reprove your son, should he compose satires that reflect upon the honor of other persons; in that case, punish him and tear them up. But should he compose discourses in the manner of Horace, in which he reprehends vice in general as that poet so elegantly does, then praise him by all means; for it is permitted the poet to write verses in which he inveighs against envy and the other vices as well, and to lash out at the vicious without, however, designating any particular individual. On the other hand, there are poets who for the sake of uttering something malicious would run the risk of being banished to the shores of Pontus.[4]

"If the poet be chaste where his own manners are concerned, he will likewise be modest in his verses, for the pen is the tongue of the mind, and whatever thoughts are engendered there are bound to appear in his writings. When kings and princes behold the marvelous art of poetry as practiced by prudent, virtuous, and serious-minded subjects of their realm, they honor, esteem, and reward those persons and crown them with the leaves of the tree that is never struck by lightning[5]—as if to show that those who are crowned and adorned with such wreaths are not to be assailed by anyone."

The gentleman in the green-colored greatcoat was vastly astonished by this speech of Don Quixote's and was rapidly altering the opinion he had previously held, to the effect that his companion was but a crackbrain. In the middle of the long discourse, which was not greatly to his liking, Sancho had left the highway to go seek a little milk from some shepherds who were draining the udders of their ewes near by. Extremely well pleased with the knight's sound sense and excellent reasoning, the gentleman was about to resume the conversation when,

---

3. There is a god in us (Latin); Ovid's *Fasti* 6.5.
4. As the poet Ovid was by the Roman emperor Augustus in 8 C.E.
5. An ancient folk belief about the laurel.

raising his head, Don Quixote caught sight of a cart flying royal flags that was coming toward them down the road and, thinking it must be a fresh adventure, began calling to Sancho in a loud voice to bring him his helmet. Whereupon Sancho hastily left the shepherds and spurred his gray until he was once more alongside his master, who was now about to encounter a dreadful and bewildering ordeal.

[*"For I Well Know the Meaning of Valor"*]

CHAPTER XVII

Wherein Don Quixote's unimaginable courage reaches its highest point, together with the adventure of the lions and its happy ending.

The history relates that, when Don Quixote called to Sancho to bring him his helmet, the squire was busy buying some curds from the shepherds and, flustered by his master's great haste, did not know what to do with them or how to carry them. Having already paid for the curds, he did not care to lose them, and so he decided to put them into the headpiece, and, acting upon this happy inspiration, he returned to see what was wanted of him.

"Give me that helmet," said the knight; "for either I know little about adventures or here is one where I am going to need my armor."

Upon hearing this, the gentleman in the green-colored greatcoat looked around in all directions but could see nothing except the cart that was approaching them, decked out with two or three flags which indicated that the vehicle in question must be conveying his Majesty's property. He remarked as much to Don Quixote, but the latter paid no attention, for he was always convinced that whatever happened to him meant adventures and more adventures.

"Forewarned is forearmed," he said. "I lose nothing by being prepared, knowing as I do that I have enemies both visible and invisible and cannot tell when or where or in what form they will attack me."

Turning to Sancho, he asked for his helmet again, and as there was no time to shake out the curds, the squire had to hand it to him as it was. Don Quixote took it and, without noticing what was in it, hastily clapped it on his head; and forthwith, as a result of the pressure on the curds, the whey began running down all over his face and beard, at which he was very much startled.

"What is this, Sancho?" he cried. "I think my head must be softening or my brains melting, or else I am sweating from head to foot. If sweat it be, I assure you it is not from fear, though I can well believe that the adventure which now awaits me is a terrible one indeed. Give me something with which to wipe my face, if you have anything, for this perspiration is so abundant that it blinds me."

Sancho said nothing but gave him a cloth and at the same time gave thanks to God that his master had not discovered what the trouble was. Don Quixote wiped his face and then took off his helmet to see what it was that made his head feel so cool. Catching sight of that watery white mass, he lifted it to his nose and smelled it.

"By the life of my lady Dulcinea del Toboso!" he exclaimed. "Those are curds that you have put there, you treacherous, brazen, ill-mannered squire!"

To this Sancho replied, very calmly and with a straight face, "If they are curds, give them to me, your Grace, so that I can eat them. But no, let the devil eat them, for he must be the one who did it. Do you think I would be so bold as to soil your Grace's helmet? Upon my word, master, by the understanding that God has given me, I, too, must have enchanters who are persecuting me as your Grace's creature and one of his members, and they are the ones who put that filthy mess there to make you lose your patience and your temper and cause you to whack my ribs as you are in the habit of doing. Well, this time, I must say, they have missed the mark; for I trust my master's good sense to tell him that I have neither curds nor milk nor anything of the kind, and if I did have, I'd put it in my stomach and not in that helmet."

"That may very well be," said Don Quixote.

Don Diego was observing all this and was more astonished than ever, especially when, after he had wiped his head, face, beard, and helmet, Don Quixote once more donned the piece of armor and, settling himself in the stirrups, proceeded to adjust his sword and fix his lance.

"Come what may, here I stand, ready to take on Satan himself in person!" shouted the knight.

The cart with the flags had come up to them by this time, accompanied only by a driver riding one of the mules and a man seated up in front.

"Where are you going, brothers?" Don Quixote called out as he placed himself in the path of the cart. "What conveyance is this, what do you carry in it, and what is the meaning of those flags?"

"The cart is mine," replied the driver, "and in it are two fierce lions in cages which the governor of Oran is sending to court as a present for his Majesty. The flags are those of our lord the King, as a sign that his property goes here."

"And are the lions large?" inquired Don Quixote.

It was the man sitting at the door of the cage who answered him. "The largest," he said, "that ever were sent from Africa to Spain. I am the lionkeeper and I have brought back others, but never any like these. They are male and female. The male is in this first cage, the female in the one behind. They are hungry right now, for they have had nothing to eat today; and so we'd be obliged if your Grace would get out of the way, for we must hasten on to the place where we are to feed them."

"Lion whelps against me?" said Don Quixote with a slight smile. "Lion whelps against me? And at such an hour? Then, by God, those gentlemen who sent them shall see whether I am the man to be frightened by lions. Get down, my good fellow, and since you are the lionkeeper, open the cages and turn those beasts out for me; and in the middle of this plain I will teach them who Don Quixote de la Mancha is, notwithstanding and in spite of the enchanters who are responsible for their being here."

"So," said the gentleman to himself as he heard this, "our worthy knight has revealed himself. It must indeed be true that the curds have softened his skull and mellowed his brains."

At this point Sancho approached him. "For God's sake, sir," he said, "do something to keep my master from fighting those lions. For if he does, they're going to tear us all to bits."

"Is your master, then, so insane," the gentleman asked, "that you fear and believe he means to tackle those fierce animals?"

"It is not that he is insane," replied Sancho, "but, rather, foolhardy."

"Very well," said the gentleman, "I will put a stop to it." And going up to Don Quixote, who was still urging the lionkeeper to open the cages, he said, "Sir Knight, knights-errant should undertake only those adventures that afford some hope of a successful outcome, not those that are utterly hopeless to begin with; for valor when it turns to temerity has in it more of madness than of bravery. Moreover, these lions have no thought of attacking your Grace but are a present to his Majesty, and it would not be well to detain them or interfere with their journey."

"My dear sir," answered Don Quixote, "you had best go mind your tame partridge and that bold ferret of yours and let each one attend to his own business. This is my affair, and I know whether these gentlemen, the lions, have come to attack me or not." He then turned to the lionkeeper. "I swear, Sir Rascal, if you do not open those cages at once, I'll pin you to the cart with this lance!"

Perceiving how determined the armed phantom was, the driver now spoke up. "Good sir," he said, "will your Grace please be so kind as to let me unhitch the mules and take them to a safe place before you turn those lions loose? For if they kill them for me, I am ruined for life, since the mules and cart are all the property I own."

"O man of little faith!" said Don Quixote. "Get down and unhitch your mules if you like, but you will soon see that it was quite unnecessary and that you might have spared yourself the trouble."

The driver did so, in great haste, as the lionkeeper began shouting, "I want you all to witness that I am being compelled against my will to open the cages and turn the lions out, and I further warn this gentleman that he will be responsible for all the harm and damage the beasts may do, plus my wages and my fees. You other gentlemen take cover before I open the doors; I am sure they will not do any harm to me."

Once more Don Diego sought to persuade his companion not to commit such an act of madness, as it was tempting God to undertake anything so foolish as that; but Don Quixote's only answer was that he knew what he was doing. And when the gentleman in green insisted that he was sure the knight was laboring under a delusion and ought to consider the matter well, the latter cut him short.

"Well, then, sir," he said, "if your Grace does not care to be a spectator at what you believe is going to turn out to be a tragedy, all you have to do is to spur your flea-bitten mare and seek safety."

Hearing this, Sancho with tears in his eyes again begged him to give up the undertaking, in comparison with which the adventure of the windmills and the dreadful one at the fulling mills—indeed, all the exploits his master had ever in the course of his life undertaken—were but bread and cakes.

"Look, sir," Sancho went on, "there is no enchantment here nor anything of the sort. Through the bars and chinks of that cage I have seen a real lion's claw, and judging by the size of it, the lion that it belongs to is bigger than a mountain."

"Fear, at any rate," said Don Quixote, "will make him look bigger to you than half the world. Retire, Sancho, and leave me, and if I die here, you know our ancient pact: you are to repair to Dulcinea—I say no more."

To this he added other remarks that took away any hope they had that he might not go through with his insane plan. The gentleman in the green-colored greatcoat was of a mind to resist him but saw that he was no match for the knight in the matter of arms. Then, too, it did not seem to him the part of wisdom to fight it out with a madman; for Don Quixote now impressed him as being quite mad in every way. Accordingly, while the knight was repeating his threats to the lionkeeper, Don Diego spurred his mare, Sancho his gray, and the driver his mules, all of them seeking to put as great a distance as possible between themselves and the cart before the lions broke loose.

Sancho already was bewailing his master's death, which he was convinced was bound to come from the lions' claws, and at the same time he cursed his fate and called it an unlucky hour in which he had taken it into his head to serve such a one. But despite his tears and lamentations, he did not leave off thrashing his gray in an effort to leave the cart behind them. When the lionkeeper saw that those who had fled were a good distance away, he once more entreated and warned Don Quixote as he had warned and entreated him before, but the answer he received was that he might save his breath as it would do him no good and he had best hurry and obey. In the space of time that it took the keeper to open the first cage, Don Quixote considered the question as to whether it would be well to give battle on foot or on horseback. He finally decided that he would do better on foot, as he feared that Rocinante would become frightened at sight of the lions; and so, leaping down from his horse, he fixed his lance, braced his buckler, and drew his sword, and then advanced with marvelous daring and great resoluteness until he stood directly in front of the cart, meanwhile commending himself to God with all his heart and then to his lady Dulcinea.

Upon reaching this point, the reader should know, the author of our veracious history indulges in the following exclamatory passage:

"O great-souled Don Quixote de la Mancha, thou whose courage is beyond all praise, mirror wherein all the valiant of the world may behold themselves, a new and second Don Manuel de León,[6] once the glory and the honor of Spanish knighthood! With what words shall I relate thy terrifying exploit, how render it credible to the ages that are to come? What eulogies do not belong to thee of right, even though they consist of hyperbole piled upon hyperbole? On foot and singlehanded, intrepid and with greathearted valor, armed but with a sword, and not one of the keen-edged Little Dog make,[7] and with a shield that was not of gleaming and polished steel, thou didst stand and wait for the two fiercest lions that ever the African forests bred! Thy deeds shall be thy praise, O valorous Manchegan; I leave them to speak for thee, since words fail me with which to extol them."

Here the author leaves off his exclamations and resumes the thread of the story.

Seeing Don Quixote posed there before him and perceiving that, unless he wished to incur the bold knight's indignation there was nothing for him to do but release the male lion, the keeper now opened the first cage, and it could be seen at once how extraordinarily big and horribly ugly the beast was. The first thing the recumbent animal did was to turn round, put out a claw, and stretch himself all over. Then he opened his mouth and yawned very slowly, after

---

6. Don Manuel Ponce de León, a paragon of gallantry and knightly courtesy, from the time of Ferdinand and Isabella.

7. The trademark of a famous armorer of Toledo and Saragossa.

which he put out a tongue that was nearly two palms in length and with it licked the dust out of his eyes and washed his face. Having done this, he stuck his head outside the cage and gazed about him in all directions. His eyes were now like live coals and his appearance and demeanor were such as to strike terror in temerity itself. But Don Quixote merely stared at him attentively, waiting for him to descend from the cart so that they could come to grips, for the knight was determined to hack the brute to pieces, such was the extent of his unheard-of madness.

The lion, however, proved to be courteous rather than arrogant and was in no mood for childish bravado. After having gazed first in one direction and then in another, as has been said, he turned his back and presented his hind parts to Don Quixote and then very calmly and peaceably lay down and stretched himself out once more in his cage. At this, Don Quixote ordered the keeper to stir him up with a stick in order to irritate him and drive him out.

"That I will not do," the keeper replied, "for if I stir him, I will be the first one he will tear to bits. Be satisfied with what you have already accomplished, Sir Knight, which leaves nothing more to be said on the score of valor, and do not go tempting your fortune a second time. The door was open and the lion could have gone out if he had chosen; since he has not done so up to now, that means he will stay where he is all day long. Your Grace's stoutheartedness has been well established; for no brave fighter, as I see it, is obliged to do more than challenge his enemy and wait for him in the field; his adversary, if he does not come, is the one who is disgraced and the one who awaits him gains the crown of victory."

"That is the truth," said Don Quixote. "Shut the door, my friend, and bear me witness as best you can with regard to what you have seen me do here. I would have you certify: that you opened the door for the lion, that I waited for him and he did not come out, that I continued to wait and still he stayed there, and finally went back and lay down. I am under no further obligation. Away with enchantments, and God uphold the right, the truth, and true chivalry! So close the door, as I have told you, while I signal to the fugitives in order that they who were not present may hear of this exploit from your lips."

The keeper did as he was commanded, and Don Quixote, taking the cloth with which he had dried his face after the rain of curds, fastened it to the point of his lance and began summoning the runaways, who, all in a body with the gentleman in green bringing up the rear were still fleeing and turning around to look back at every step. Sancho was the first to see the white cloth.

"May they slay me," he said, "if my master hasn't conquered those fierce beasts, for he's calling to us."

They all stopped and made sure that the one who was doing the signaling was indeed Don Quixote, and then, losing some of their fear, they little by little made their way back to a point where they could distinctly hear what the knight was saying. At last they returned to the cart, and as they drew near Don Quixote spoke to the driver.

"You may come back, brother, hitch your mules, and continue your journey. And you, Sancho, may give each of them two gold crowns to recompense them for the delay they have suffered on my account."

"That I will, right enough," said Sancho. "But what has become of the lions? Are they dead or alive?"

The keeper thereupon, in leisurely fashion and in full detail, proceeded to tell them how the encounter had ended, taking pains to stress to the best of his ability the valor displayed by Don Quixote, at sight of whom the lion had been so cowed that he was unwilling to leave his cage, though the door had been left open quite a while. The fellow went on to state that the knight had wanted him to stir the lion up and force him out, but had finally been convinced that this would be tempting God and so, much to his displeasure and against his will, had permitted the door to be closed.

"What do you think of that, Sancho?" asked Don Quixote. "Are there any spells that can withstand true gallantry? The enchanters may take my luck away, but to deprive me of my strength and courage is an impossibility."

Sancho then bestowed the crowns, the driver hitched his mules, and the lionkeeper kissed Don Quixote's hands for the favor received, promising that, when he reached the court, he would relate this brave exploit to the king himself.

"In that case," replied Don Quixote, "if his Majesty by any chance should inquire who it was that performed it, you are to say that it was the Knight of the Lions; for that is the name by which I wish to be known from now on, thus changing, exchanging, altering, and converting the one I have previously borne, that of Knight of the Mournful Countenance; in which respect I am but following the old custom of knights-errant, who changed their names whenever they liked or found it convenient to do so."

With this, the cart continued on its way, and Don Quixote, Sancho, and the gentleman in the green-colored greatcoat likewise resumed their journey. During all this time Don Diego de Miranda had not uttered a word but was wholly taken up with observing what Don Quixote did and listening to what he had to say. The knight impressed him as being a crazy sane man and an insane one on the verge of sanity. The gentleman did not happen to be familiar with the first part of our history, but if he had read it he would have ceased to wonder at such talk and conduct, for he would then have known what kind of madness this was. Remaining as he did in ignorance of his companion's malady, he took him now for a sensible individual and now for a madman, since what Don Quixote said was coherent, elegantly phrased, and to the point, whereas his actions were nonsensical, foolhardy, and downright silly. What greater madness could there be, Don Diego asked himself, than to don a helmet filled with curds and then persuade oneself that enchanters were softening one's cranium? What could be more rashly absurd than to wish to fight lions by sheer strength alone? He was roused from these thoughts, this inward soliloquy, by the sound of Don Quixote's voice.

"Undoubtedly, Señor Don Diego de Miranda, your Grace must take me for a fool and a madman, am I not right? And it would be small wonder if such were the case, seeing that my deeds give evidence of nothing else. But, nevertheless, I would advise your Grace that I am neither so mad nor so lacking in wit as I must appear to you to be. A gaily caparisoned knight giving a fortunate lance thrust to a fierce bull in the middle of a great square makes a pleasing appearance in the eyes of his king. The same is true of a knight clad in shining armor as he paces the lists in front of the ladies in some joyous tournament. It is true of all those knights who, by means of military exercises or what appear to be such, divert and entertain and, if one may say so, honor the courts of princes. But the best showing of all is made by a knight-errant who, traversing deserts and solitudes, crossroads, forests, and mountains, goes seeking dangerous adventures with the intention of bringing them to a happy and successful conclusion, and solely for the purpose of winning a glorious and enduring renown.

"More impressive, I repeat, is the knight-errant succoring a widow in some unpopulated place than a courtly man of arms making love to a damsel in the city. All knights have their special callings: let the courtier wait upon the ladies and lend luster by his liveries to his sovereign's palace; let him nourish impoverished gentlemen with the splendid fare of his table; let him give tourneys and show himself truly great, generous, and magnificent and a good Christian above all, thus fulfilling his particular obligations. But the knight-errant's case is different.

"Let the latter seek out the nooks and corners of the world; let him enter into the most intricate of labyrinths; let him attempt the impossible at every step; let him endure on desolate highlands the burning rays of the midsummer sun and in winter the harsh inclemencies of wind and frost; let no lions inspire him with fear, no monsters frighten him, no dragons terrify him, for to seek them out, attack them, and conquer them all is his chief and legitimate occupation. Accordingly, I whose lot it is to be numbered among the knights-errant cannot fail to attempt anything that appears to me to fall within the scope of my duties, just as I attacked those lions a while ago even though I knew it to be an exceedingly rash thing to do, for that was a matter that directly concerned me.

"For I well know the meaning of valor: namely, a virtue that lies between the two extremes of cowardice on the one hand and temerity on the other. It is, nonetheless, better for the brave man to carry his bravery to the point of rashness than for him to sink into cowardice. Even as it is easier for the prodigal to become a generous man than it is for the miser, so is it easier for the foolhardy to become truly brave than it is for the coward to attain valor. And in this matter of adventures, you may believe me, Señor Don Diego, it is better to lose by a card too many than a card too few, and 'Such and such a knight is temerarious and overbold' sounds better to the ear than 'That knight is timid and a coward.'"

"I must assure you, Señor Don Quixote," replied Don Diego, "that everything your Grace has said and done will stand the test of reason; and it is my opinion that if the laws and ordinances of knight-errantry were to be lost, they would be found again in your Grace's bosom, which is their depository and storehouse. But it is growing late; let us hasten to my village and my home, where your Grace shall rest from your recent exertions; for if the body is not tired the spirit may be, and that sometimes results in bodily fatigue."

"I accept your offer as a great favor and an honor, Señor Don Diego," was the knight's reply. And, by spurring their mounts more than they had up to then, they arrived at the village around two in the afternoon and came to the house that was occupied by Don Diego, whom Don Quixote had dubbed the Knight of the Green-colored Greatcoat.

[Last Duel]

CHAPTER LXIV

Which treats of the adventure that caused Don Quixote the most sorrow of all those that have thus far befallen him.[8]

* * *

One morning, as Don Quixote went for a ride along the beach, clad in full armor—for, as he was fond of saying, that was his only ornament, his only rest the fight and, accordingly, he was never without it for a moment—he saw approaching him a horseman similarly arrayed from head to foot and with a brightly shining moon blazoned upon his shield.

As soon as he had come within earshot the stranger cried out to Don Quixote in a loud voice, "O illustrious knight, the never to be sufficiently praised Don Quixote de la Mancha, I am the Knight of the White Moon, whose incomparable exploits you will perhaps recall. I come to contend with you and try the might of my arm, with the purpose of having you acknowledge and confess that my lady, whoever she may be, is beyond comparison more beautiful than your own Dulcinea del Toboso. If you will admit the truth of this fully and freely, you will escape death and I shall be spared the trouble of inflicting it upon you. On the other hand, if you choose to fight and I should overcome you, I ask no other satisfaction than that, laying down your arms and seeking no further adventures, you retire to your own village for the space of a year, during which time you are not to lay hand to sword but are to dwell peacefully and tranquilly, enjoying a beneficial rest that shall redound to the betterment of your worldly fortunes and the salvation of your soul. But if you are the victor, then my head shall be at your disposal, my arms and steed shall be the spoils, and the fame of my exploits shall go to increase your own renown. Consider well which is the better course and let me have your answer at once, for today is all the time I have for the dispatching of this business."

Don Quixote was amazed at the knight's arrogance as well as at the nature of the challenge, but it was with a calm and stern demeanor that he replied to him.

"Knight of the White Moon," he said, "of whose exploits up to now I have never heard, I will venture to take an oath that you have not once laid eyes upon the illustrious Dulcinea; for I am quite certain that if you had beheld her you would not be staking your all upon such an issue, since the sight of her would have convinced you that there never has been, and never can be, any beauty to compare with hers. I do not say that you lie, I simply say that you are mistaken; and so I accept your challenge with the conditions you have laid down, and at once, before this day you have fixed upon shall have ended. The only exception I make is with regard to the fame of your deeds being added to my renown, since I do not know what the character of your exploits has been and am quite content

---

8. Don Quixote and Sancho, after a great many encounters and experiences (of which the most prominent have been Don Quixote's descent into the cave of Montesinos and their residence at the castle of the playful ducal couple who give Sancho the "governorship of an island" for ten days), are now in Barcelona. Famous as they are, they meet the viceroy and the nobles; their host is Don Antonio Moreno, "a gentleman of wealth and discernment who was fond of amusing himself in an innocent and kindly way."

with my own, such as they are. Take, then, whichever side of the field you like, and I will take up my position, and may St. Peter bless what God may give."

Now, as it happened, the Knight of the White Moon was seen by some of the townspeople, who informed the viceroy that he was there, talking to Don Quixote de la Mancha. Believing this to be a new adventure arranged by Don Antonio Moreno or some other gentleman of the place, the viceroy at once hastened down to the beach, accompanied by a large retinue, including Don Antonio, and they arrived just as Don Quixote was wheeling Rocinante to measure off the necessary stretch of field. When the viceroy perceived that they were about to engage in combat, he at once interposed and inquired of them what it was that impelled them thus to do battle all of a sudden.

The Knight of the White Moon replied that it was a matter of beauty and precedence and briefly repeated what he had said to Don Quixote, explaining the terms to which both parties had agreed. The viceroy then went up to Don Antonio and asked him if he knew any such knight as this or if it was some joke that they were playing, but the answer that he received left him more puzzled than ever; for Don Antonio did not know who the knight was, nor could he say as to whether this was a real encounter or not. The viceroy, accordingly, was doubtful about letting them proceed, but inasmuch as he could not bring himself to believe that it was anything more than a jest, he withdrew to one side, saying, "Sir Knights, if there is nothing for it but to confess or die, and if Señor Don Quixote's mind is made up and your Grace, the Knight of the White Moon, is even more firmly resolved, then fall to it in the name of God and may He bestow the victory."

The Knight of the White Moon thanked the viceroy most courteously and in well-chosen words for the permission which had been granted them, and Don Quixote did the same, whereupon the latter, commending himself with all his heart to Heaven and to his lady Dulcinea, as was his custom at the beginning of a fray, fell back a little farther down the field as he saw his adversary doing the same. And then, without blare of trumpet or other warlike instrument to give them the signal for the attack, both at the same instant wheeled their steeds about and returned for the charge. Being mounted upon the swifter horse, the Knight of the White Moon met Don Quixote two-thirds of the way and with such tremendous force that, without touching his opponent with his lance (which, it seemed, he deliberately held aloft) he brought both Rocinante and his rider to the ground in an exceedingly perilous fall. At once the victor leaped down and placed his lance at Don Quixote's visor.

"You are vanquished, O knight! Nay, more, you are dead unless you make confession in accordance with the conditions governing our encounter."

Stunned and battered, Don Quixote did not so much as raise his visor but in a faint, wan voice, as if speaking from the grave, he said, "Dulcinea del Toboso is the most beautiful woman in the world and I the most unhappy knight upon the face of this earth. It is not right that my weakness should serve to defraud the truth. Drive home your lance, O knight, and take my life since you already have deprived me of my honor."

"That I most certainly shall not do," said the one of the White Moon. "Let the fame of my lady Dulcinea del Toboso's beauty live on undiminished. As for me, I shall be content if the great Don Quixote will retire to his village for a year or until such a time as I may specify, as was agreed upon between us before joining battle."

The viceroy, Don Antonio, and all the many others who were present heard this, and they also heard Don Quixote's response, which was to the effect that, seeing nothing was asked of him that was prejudicial to Dulcinea, he would fulfill all the other conditions like a true and punctilious knight. The one of the White Moon thereupon turned and with a bow to the viceroy rode back to the city at a mild canter. The viceroy promptly dispatched Don Antonio to follow him and make every effort to find out who he was; and, in the meanwhile, they lifted Don Quixote up and uncovered his face, which held no sign of color and was bathed in perspiration. Rocinante, however, was in so sorry a state that he was unable to stir for the present.

Brokenhearted over the turn that events had taken, Sancho did not know what to say or do. It seemed to him that all this was something that was happening in a dream and that everything was the result of magic. He saw his master surrender, heard him consent not to take up arms again for a year to come as the light of his glorious exploits faded into darkness. At the same time his own hopes, based upon the fresh promises that had been made him, were whirled away like smoke before the wind. He feared that Rocinante was maimed for life, his master's bones permanently dislocated—it would have been a bit of luck if his madness also had been jolted out of him.[9]

Finally, in a hand litter which the viceroy had them bring, they bore the knight back to town. The viceroy himself then returned, for he was very anxious to ascertain who the Knight of the White Moon was who had left Don Quixote in so lamentable a condition.

From CHAPTER LXV

Wherein is revealed who the Knight of the White Moon was,
with the freeing of Don Gregorio and other events.

The Knight of the White Moon was followed not only by Don Antonio Moreno, but by a throng of small boys as well, who kept after him until the doors of one of the city's hostelries had closed behind him. A squire came out to meet him and remove his armor, for which purpose the victor proceeded to shut himself up in a lower room, in the company of Don Antonio, who had also entered the inn and whose bread would not bake until he had learned the knight's identity. Perceiving that the gentleman had no intention of leaving him, he of the White Moon then spoke.

"Sir," he said, "I am well aware that you have come to find out who I am; and, seeing that there is no denying you the information that you seek, while my servant here is removing my armor I will tell you the exact truth of the matter. I would have you know, sir, that I am the bachelor Sansón Carrasco from the same village as Don Quixote de la Mancha, whose madness and absurdities inspire pity in all of us who know him and in none more than me. And so, being convinced that his salvation lay in his returning home for a period of rest in his own house, I formed a plan for bringing him back.

"It was three months ago that I took to the road as a knight-errant, calling myself the Knight of the Mirrors, with the object of fighting and overcoming him without doing him any harm, intending first to lay down the condition that

9. The original Spanish has an untranslatable pun on *deslocado*, which means "out of joint" ("dislocated") and also "cured of madness" (from *loco*, "mad").

the vanquished was to yield to the victor's will. What I meant to ask of him—for I looked upon him as conquered from the start—was that he should return to his village and not leave it for a whole year, in the course of which time he might be cured. Fate, however, ordained things otherwise; for he was the one who conquered me and overthrew me from my horse, and thus my plan came to naught. He continued on his wanderings, and I went home, defeated, humiliated, and bruised from my fall, which was quite a dangerous one. But I did not for this reason give up the idea of hunting him up once more and vanquishing him as you have seen me do today.

"Since he is the soul of honor when it comes to observing the ordinances of knight-errantry, there is not the slightest doubt that he will keep the promise he has given me and fulfill his obligations. And that, sir, is all that I need to tell you concerning what has happened. I beg you not to disclose my secret or reveal my identity to Don Quixote, in order that my well-intentioned scheme may be carried out and a man of excellent judgment be brought back to his senses—for a sensible man he would be, once rid of the follies of chivalry."

"My dear sir," exclaimed Don Antonio, "may God forgive you for the wrong you have done the world by seeking to deprive it of its most charming madman! Do you not see that the benefit accomplished by restoring Don Quixote to his senses can never equal the pleasure which others derive from his vagaries? But it is my opinion that all the trouble to which the Señor Bachelor has put himself will not suffice to cure a man who is so hopelessly insane; and if it were not uncharitable, I would say let Don Quixote never be cured, since with his return to health we lose not only his own drolleries but also those of his squire, Sancho Panza, for either of the two is capable of turning melancholy itself into joy and merriment. Nevertheless, I will keep silent and tell him nothing, that I may see whether or not I am right in my suspicion that Señor Carrasco's efforts will prove to have been of no avail."

The bachelor replied that, all in all, things looked very favorable and he hoped for a fortunate outcome. With this, he took his leave of Don Antonio, after offering to render him any service that he could; and, having had his armor tied up and placed upon a mule's back, he rode out of the city that same day on the same horse on which he had gone into battle, returning to his native province without anything happening to him that is worthy of being set down in this veracious chronicle.

* * *

[Homecoming and Death]

CHAPTER LXXIII

Of the omens that Don Quixote encountered upon entering
his village, with other incidents that embellish and lend credence
to this great history.

As they entered the village, Cid Hamete informs us, Don Quixote caught sight of two lads on the communal threshing floor who were engaged in a dispute.

"Don't let it worry you, Periquillo," one of them was saying to the other; "you'll never lay eyes on it again as long as you live."

Hearing this, Don Quixote turned to Sancho. "Did you mark what that boy said, my friend?" he asked. " 'You'll never lay eyes on it[1] again . . .' "

"Well," replied Sancho, "what difference does it make what he said?"

"What difference?" said Don Quixote. "Don't you see that, applied to the one I love, it means I shall never again see Dulcinea."

Sancho was about to answer him when his attention was distracted by a hare that came flying across the fields pursued by a large number of hunters with their greyhounds. The frightened animal took refuge by huddling down beneath the donkey, whereupon Sancho reached out his hand and caught it and presented it to his master.

"Malum signum, malum signum,"[2] the knight was muttering to himself. "A hare flees, the hounds pursue it, Dulcinea appears not."

"It is very strange to hear your Grace talk like that," said Sancho. "Let us suppose that this hare *is* Dulcinea del Toboso and the hounds pursuing it are those wicked enchanters that transformed her into a peasant lass; she flees, I catch her and turn her over to your Grace, you hold her in your arms and caress her. Is that a bad sign? What ill omen can you find in it?"

The two lads who had been quarreling now came up to have a look at the hare, and Sancho asked them what their dispute was about. To this the one who had uttered the words "You'll never lay eyes on it again as long as you live," replied that he had taken a cricket cage from the other boy and had no intention of returning it ever. Sancho then brought out from his pocket four cuartos and gave them to the lad in exchange for the cage, which he placed in Don Quixote's hands.

"There, master," he said, "these omens are broken and destroyed, and to my way of thinking, even though I may be a dunce, they have no more to do with what is going to happen to us than the clouds of yesteryear. If I am not mistaken, I have heard our curate say that sensible persons of the Christian faith should pay no heed to such foolish things, and you yourself in the past have given me to understand that all those Christians who are guided by omens are fools. But there is no need to waste a lot of words on the subject; come, let us go on and enter our village."

The hunters at this point came up and asked for the hare, and Don Quixote gave it to them. Continuing on their way, the returning pair encountered the curate and the bachelor Carrasco, who were strolling in a small meadow on the outskirts of the town as they read their breviaries. And here it should be mentioned that Sancho Panza, by way of sumpter cloth, had thrown over his gray and the bundle of armor it bore the flame-covered buckram robe in which they had dressed the squire at the duke's castle, on the night that witnessed Altisidora's[3] resurrection; and he had also fitted the miter over the donkey's head, the result being the weirdest transformation and the most bizarrely appareled ass that ever were seen in this world. The curate and the bachelor recognized

1. The pronoun *it* is the same as *her* in the Spanish, because the boy's reference is to a cricket cage, which is a feminine noun. (In Spanish, all nouns are either masculine or feminine.) Hence Don Quixote's inference that the boys are discussing Dulcinea.
2. An ill omen (Latin)—that is, meeting a

hare is considered a bad sign.
3. A girl in the duke's castle, where Don Quixote and Sancho were guests for a time. She dramatically pretended to be in love with Don Quixote. "Sumpter cloth": decorative or protective covering for a pack animal.

the pair at once and came forward to receive them with open arms. Don Quixote dismounted and gave them both a warm embrace; meanwhile, the small boys (boys are like lynxes in that nothing escapes them), having spied the ass's miter, ran up for a closer view.

"Come, lads," they cried, "and see Sancho Panza's ass trigged out finer than Mingo,[4] and Don Quixote's beast is skinnier than ever!"

Finally, surrounded by the urchins and accompanied by the curate and the bachelor, they entered the village and made their way to Don Quixote's house, where they found the housekeeper and the niece standing in the doorway, for the news of their return had preceded them. Teresa Panza, Sancho's wife, had also heard of it, and, half naked and disheveled, dragging her daughter Sanchica by the hand, she hastened to greet her husband and was disappointed when she saw him, for he did not look to her as well fitted out as a governor ought to be.

"How does it come, my husband," she said, "that you return like this, tramping and footsore? You look more like a vagabond than you do like a governor."

"Be quiet, Teresa,"[5] Sancho admonished her, "for very often there are stakes where there is no bacon. Come on home with me and you will hear marvels. I am bringing money with me, which is the thing that matters, money earned by my own efforts and without harm to anyone."

"You just bring along the money, my good husband," said Teresa, "and whether you got it here or there, or by whatever means, you will not be introducing any new custom into the world."

Sanchica then embraced her father and asked him if he had brought her anything, for she had been looking forward to his coming as to the showers in May. And so, with his wife holding him by the hand while his daughter kept one arm about his waist and at the same time led the gray, Sancho went home, leaving Don Quixote under his own roof in the company of niece and housekeeper, the curate and the barber.

Without regard to time or season, the knight at once drew his guests to one side and in a few words informed them of how he had been overcome in battle and had given his promise not to leave his village for a year, a promise that he meant to observe most scrupulously, without violating it in the slightest degree, as every knight-errant was obliged to do by the laws of chivalry. He accordingly meant to spend that year as a shepherd,[6] he said, amid the solitude of the fields, where he might give free rein to his amorous fancies as he practiced the virtues of the pastoral life; and he further begged them, if they were not too greatly occupied and more urgent matters did not prevent their doing so, to consent to be his companions. He would purchase a flock sufficiently large to justify their calling themselves shepherds; and, moreover, he would have them know, the most important thing of all had been taken care of, for he had hit upon names that would suit them marvelously well. When the curate asked him what these names were, Don Quixote replied that he himself would be known as "the

---

4. The allusion is to the opening lines of *Mingo Revulgo* (15th century), a satire: "Hey! Mingo Revulgo, hey! What have you done with your blue cloth doublet? Do you not wear it on Sundays?"

5. Sancho's wife, here referred to as Teresa, is earlier named Juana.

6. Because the knight-errant's life has been forbidden him by his defeat, Don Quixote for a time plans to live according to another and no less "literary" code, that of the pastoral. The following paragraphs, especially through the bachelor Carrasco, refer humorously to some of the conventions of pastoral literature.

shepherd Quixotiz," the bachelor as "the shepherd Carrascón," the curate as "the shepherd Curiambro," and Sancho Panza as "the shepherd Pancino."

Both his listeners were dismayed at the new form which his madness had assumed. However, in order that he might not go faring forth from the village on another of his expeditions (for they hoped that in the course of the year he would be cured), they decided to fall in with his new plan and approve it as being a wise one, and they even agreed to be his companions in the calling he proposed to adopt.

"What's more," remarked Sansón Carrasco, "I am a very famous poet, as everyone knows, and at every turn I will be composing pastoral or courtly verses or whatever may come to mind, by way of a diversion for us as we wander in those lonely places; but what is most necessary of all, my dear sirs, is that each one of us should choose the name of the shepherd lass to whom he means to dedicate his songs, so that we may not leave a tree, however hard its bark may be, where their names are not inscribed and engraved as is the custom with lovelorn shepherds."

"That is exactly what we should do," replied Don Quixote, "although, for my part, I am relieved of the necessity of looking for an imaginary shepherdess, seeing that I have the peerless Dulcinea del Toboso, glory of these brookside regions, adornment of these meadows, beauty's mainstay, cream of the Graces—in short, one to whom all praise is well becoming however hyperbolical it may be."

"That is right," said the curate, "but we will seek out some shepherd maids that are easily handled, who if they do not square with us will fit in the corners."

"And," added Sansón Carrasco, "if we run out of names we will give them those that we find printed in books the world over: such as Fílida, Amarilis, Diana, Flérida, Galatea, and Belisarda; for since these are for sale in the market place, we can buy them and make them our own. If my lady, or, rather, my shepherdess, should by chance be called Ana, I will celebrate her charms under the name of Anarda; if she is Francisca, she will become Francenia; if Lucía, Luscinda; for it all amounts to the same thing. And Sancho Panza, if he enters this confraternity, may compose verses to his wife, Teresa Panza, under the name of Teresaina."

Don Quixote had to laugh at this, and the curate then went on to heap extravagant praise upon him for his noble resolution which did him so much credit, and once again he offered to keep the knight company whenever he could spare the time from the duties of his office. With this, they took their leave of him, advising and beseeching him to take care of his health and to eat plentifully of the proper food.

As fate would have it, the niece and the housekeeper had overheard the conversation of the three men, and as soon as the visitors had left they both descended upon Don Quixote.

"What is the meaning of this, my uncle? Here we were thinking your Grace had come home to lead a quiet and respectable life, and do you mean to tell us you are going to get yourself involved in fresh complications—

> Young shepherd, thou who comest here,
> Young shepherd, thou who goest there . . . [7]

7. From a pastoral ballad.

For, to tell the truth, the barley is too hard now to make shepherds' pipes of it."[8]

"And how," said the housekeeper, "is your Grace going to stand the midday heat in summer, the winter cold, the howling of the wolves out there in the fields? You certainly cannot endure it. That is an occupation for robust men, cut out and bred for such a calling almost from their swaddling clothes. Setting one evil over against another, it is better to be a knight-errant than a shepherd. Look, sir, take my advice, for I am not stuffed with bread and wine when I give it to you but am fasting and am going on fifty years of age: stay at home, attend to your affairs, go often to confession, be charitable to the poor, and let it be upon my soul if any harm comes to you as a result of it."

"Be quiet, daughters," said Don Quixote. "I know very well what I must do. Take me up to bed, for I do not feel very well; and you may be sure of one thing: whether I am a knight-errant now or a shepherd to be, I never will fail to look after your needs as you will see when the time comes."

And good daughters that they unquestionably were, the housekeeper and the niece helped him up to bed, where they gave him something to eat and made him as comfortable as they could.

From CHAPTER LXXIV

Of how Don Quixote fell sick, of the will that he made, and of the manner of his death.

Inasmuch as nothing that is human is eternal but is ever declining from its beginning to its close, this being especially true of the lives of men, and since Don Quixote was not endowed by Heaven with the privilege of staying the downward course of things, his own end came when he was least expecting it. Whether it was owing to melancholy occasioned by the defeat he had suffered, or was, simply, the will of Heaven which had so ordained it, he was taken with a fever that kept him in bed for a week, during which time his friends, the curate, the bachelor, and the barber, visited him frequently, while Sancho Panza, his faithful squire, never left his bedside.

Believing that the knight's condition was due to sorrow over his downfall and disappointment at not having been able to accomplish the disenchantment and liberation of Dulcinea, Sancho and the others endeavored to cheer him up in every possible way. The bachelor urged him to take heart and get up from bed that he might begin his pastoral life, adding that he himself had already composed an eclogue that would cast in the shade all that Sannazaro[9] had ever written, and had purchased with his own money from a herdsman of Quintanar two fine dogs to guard the flock, one of them named Barcino and the other Butrón. All this, however, did not serve to relieve Don Quixote's sadness; whereupon his friends called in the doctor, who took his pulse and was not very well satisfied with it. In any case, the physician told them, they should attend to the health of his soul as that of his body was in grave danger.

Don Quixote received this news calmly enough, but not so his housekeeper, niece, and squire, who began weeping bitterly, as if he were already lying dead

---

8. A proverb.
9. Jacopo Sannazaro (1456–1530), Italian poet

whose *Arcadia* is one of the milestones in the pastoral tradition.

in front of them. It was the doctor's opinion that melancholy and depression were putting an end to his patient's life. The knight then requested them to leave him alone as he wished to sleep a little, and they complied. He slept for more than six hours at a stretch, as the saying is, and so soundly that the housekeeper and niece thought he would never wake.

At last he did, however, and at once cried out in a loud voice, "Blessed be Almighty God who has given me so many blessings! Truly His mercy is boundless and is not limited or restrained by the sins of men."

The niece listened carefully to what her uncle said, and it seemed to her that he was speaking more rationally than was his wont, at least during his illness.

"Sir," she said to him, "what does your Grace mean? Has something occurred that we know nothing about? What is this talk of mercy and sins?"

"The mercy that I speak of," replied Don Quixote, "is that which God is showing me at this moment—in spite of my sins, as I have said. My mind now is clear, unencumbered by those misty shadows of ignorance that were cast over it by my bitter and continual reading of those hateful books of chivalry. I see through all the nonsense and fraud contained in them, and my only regret is that my disillusionment has come so late, leaving me no time to make any sort of amends by reading those that are the light of the soul. I find myself, niece, at the point of death, and I would die in such a way as not to leave the impression of a life so bad that I shall be remembered as a madman; for even though I have been one, I do not wish to confirm it on my deathbed. And so, my dear, call in my good friends: the curate, the bachelor Sansón Carrasco, and Master Nicholas the barber; for I want to confess my sins and make my last will and testament."

The niece, however, was relieved of this errand, for the three of them came in just then.

"I have good news for you, kind sirs," said Don Quixote the moment he saw them. "I am no longer Don Quixote de la Mancha but Alonso Quijano, whose mode of life won for him the name of 'Good.' I am the enemy of Amadis of Gaul and all his innumerable progeny; for those profane stories dealing with knight-errantry are odious to me, and I realize how foolish I was and the danger I courted in reading them; but I am in my right senses now and I abominate them."

Hearing this, they all three were convinced that some new kind of madness must have laid hold of him.

"Why, Señor Don Quixote!" exclaimed Sansón. "What makes you talk like that, just when we have received news that my lady Dulcinea is disenchanted? And just when we are on the verge of becoming shepherds so that we may spend the rest of our lives in singing like a lot of princes, why does your Grace choose to turn hermit? Say no more, in Heaven's name, but be sensible and forget these idle tales."

"Tales of that kind," said Don Quixote, "have been the truth for me in the past, and to my detriment, but with Heaven's aid I trust to turn them to my profit now that I am dying. For I feel, gentlemen, that death is very near; so, leave all jesting aside and bring me a confessor for my sins and a notary to draw up my will. In such straits as these a man cannot trifle with his soul. Accordingly, while the Señor Curate is hearing my confession, let the notary be summoned."

Amazed at his words, they gazed at one another in some perplexity, yet they could not but believe him. One of the signs that led them to think he was dying was this quick return from madness to sanity and all the additional things he had to say, so well reasoned and well put and so becoming in a Christian that none of them could any longer doubt that he was in full possession of his faculties. Sending the others out of the room, the curate stayed behind to confess him, and before long the bachelor returned with the notary and Sancho Panza, who had been informed of his master's condition, and who, finding the housekeeper and the niece in tears, began weeping with them. When the confession was over, the curate came out.

"It is true enough," he said, "that Alonso Quijano the Good is dying, and it is also true that he is a sane man. It would be well for us to go in now while he makes his will."

At this news the housekeeper, niece, and the good squire Sancho Panza were so overcome with emotion that the tears burst forth from their eyes and their bosoms heaved with sobs; for, as has been stated more than once, whether Don Quixote was plain Alonso Quijano the Good or Don Quixote de la Mancha, he was always of a kindly and pleasant disposition and for this reason was beloved not only by the members of his household but by all who knew him.

The notary had entered along with the others, and as soon as the preamble had been attended to and the dying man had commended his soul to his Maker with all those Christian formalities that are called for in such a case, they came to the matter of bequests, with Don Quixote dictating as follows:

"ITEM. With regard to Sancho Panza, whom, in my madness, I appointed to be my squire, and who has in his possession a certain sum of money belonging to me: inasmuch as there has been a standing account between us, of debits and credits, it is my will that he shall not be asked to give any accounting whatsoever of this sum, but if any be left over after he has had payment for what I owe him, the balance, which will amount to very little, shall be his, and much good may it do him. If when I was mad I was responsible for his being given the governorship of an island, now that I am of sound mind I would present him with a kingdom if it were in my power, for his simplicity of mind and loyal conduct merit no less."

At this point he turned to Sancho. "Forgive me, my friend," he said, "for having caused you to appear as mad as I by leading you to fall into the same error, that of believing that there are still knights-errant in the world."

"Ah, master," cried Sancho through his tears, "don't die, your Grace, but take my advice and go on living for many years to come; for the greatest madness that a man can be guilty of in this life is to die without good reason, without anyone's killing him, slain only by the hands of melancholy. Look you, don't be lazy but get up from this bed and let us go out into the fields clad as shepherds as we agreed to do. Who knows but behind some bush we may come upon the lady Dulcinea, as disenchanted as you could wish. If it is because of worry over your defeat that you are dying, put the blame on me by saying that the reason for your being overthrown was that I had not properly fastened Rocinante's girth. For the matter of that, your Grace knows from reading your books of chivalry that it is a common thing for certain knights to overthrow others, and he who is vanquished today will be the victor tomorrow."

"That is right," said Sansón, "the worthy Sancho speaks the truth."

"Not so fast, gentlemen," said Don Quixote. "In last year's nests there are no birds this year. I was mad and now I am sane; I was Don Quixote de la Mancha, and now I am, as I have said, Alonso Quijano the Good. May my repentance and the truth I now speak restore to me the place I once held in your esteem. And now, let the notary proceed:

"ITEM. I bequeath my entire estate, without reservation, to my niece Antonia Quijana, here present, after the necessary deductions shall have been made from the most available portion of it to satisfy the bequests that I have stipulated. The first payment shall be to my housekeeper for the wages due her, with twenty ducats over to buy her a dress. And I hereby appoint the Señor Curate and the Señor Bachelor Sansón Carrasco to be my executors.

"ITEM. It is my will that if my niece Antonia Quijana should see fit to marry, it shall be to a man who does not know what books of chivalry are; and if it shall be established that he is acquainted with such books and my niece still insists on marrying him, then she shall lose all that I have bequeathed her and my executors shall apply her portion to works of charity as they may see fit.

"ITEM. I entreat the aforementioned gentlemen, my executors, if by good fortune they should come to know the author who is said to have composed a history now going the rounds under the title of *Second Part of the Exploits of Don Quixote de la Mancha*, to beg his forgiveness in my behalf, as earnestly as they can, since it was I who unthinkingly led him to set down so many and such great absurdities as are to be found in it; for I leave this life with a feeling of remorse at having provided him with the occasion for putting them into writing."

The will ended here, and Don Quixote, stretching himself at length in the bed, fainted away. They all were alarmed at this and hastened to aid him. The same thing happened very frequently in the course of the three days of life that remained to him after he had made his will. The household was in a state of excitement, but with it all the niece continued to eat her meals, the housekeeper had her drink, and Sancho Panza was in good spirits; for this business of inheriting property effaces or mitigates the sorrow which the heir ought to feel and causes him to forget.

Death came at last for Don Quixote, after he had received all the sacraments and once more, with many forceful arguments, had expressed his abomination of books of chivalry. The notary who was present remarked that in none of those books had he read of any knight-errant dying in his own bed so peacefully and in so Christian a manner. And thus, amid the tears and lamentations of those present, he gave up the ghost; that is to say, he died. Perceiving that their friend was no more, the curate asked the notary to be a witness to the fact that Alonso Quijano the Good, commonly known as Don Quixote, was truly dead, this being necessary in order that some author other than Cid Hamete Benengeli might not have the opportunity of falsely resurrecting him and writing endless histories of his exploits.

Such was the end of the Ingenious Gentleman of La Mancha, whose birthplace Cid Hamete was unwilling to designate exactly in order that all the towns and villages of La Mancha might contend among themselves for the right to adopt him and claim him as their own, just as the seven cities of Greece did in the case of Homer. The lamentations of Sancho and those of Don Quixote's niece and his housekeeper, as well as the original epitaphs that were composed for his tomb, will not be recorded here, but mention may be made of the verses by Sansón Carrasco:

> *Here lies a gentleman bold*
> *Who was so very brave*
> *He went to lengths untold,*
> *And on the brink of the grave*
> *Death had on him no hold.*
> *By the world he set small store—*
> *He frightened it to the core—*
> *Yet somehow, by Fate's plan,*
> *Though he'd lived a crazy man,*
> *When he died he was sane once more.*

* * *

POPOL VUH
transcribed 1554–58

A compendium of stories cherished by the ancient, the colonial, and even the modern Quiché Maya people of Guatemala, the sixteenth-century Popol Vuh has been compared to the **Odyssey** of the Greeks and the **Mahābhārata** of India. Woven together, its stories form an epic narrative that leads from the creation of the world and of humankind to the time of the text's writing, amid the violence of the Spanish Conquest. Inevitably, following the conquest of Mexico in 1521, Spanish imperialism cast its eye toward Guatemala, and in 1524, after a brief struggle, Quiché fell to Spanish and Mexican troops under the command of Pedro de Alvarado (called "the sun" by native people). By the 1530s, Quiché scribes, presumably including the Popol Vuh author, were being trained to use alphabetic writing. The book thus represents the cultural and intellectual mix born of the encounter: it is written in the Quiché language but in the Roman alphabet, and translates into book form what may have been an earlier text. In the narrative itself the anonymous author hints at the existence of a certain "council book" (*popol vuh*), presumably a pre-Columbian screen-fold that served him as a source. The Maya were the only civilization in the New World to have developed a full writing system, based on an elaborate system of glyphs.

The sixteenth-century Quiché were well acquainted with "council books," some dating from the classic period of Maya culture (100–900 C.E.), which saw the rise of such imposing centers as Tikal, Copán, and Palenque. By the time of European contact those important sites, abandoned in the mysterious collapse of Maya civilization ca. C.E. 900, lay in ruins. But Maya learning survived in southern Guatemala among the Quiché and their neighbors, and in the northern part of the Yucatán peninsula. Mayanists conclude that although the Popol Vuh is not an actual transcription of ancient screen-folds, it no doubt borrows from them.

The modern text survives thanks to a copy made by a Dominican friar in the early eighteenth century, but it may have lost accompanying illustrations or hieroglyphs, which were standard for Mayan writings.

Stylistically, the text is fascinated by numbers, as evidenced in the pairing, tripling, and quadrupling of phrases. Major characters and deities also are paired, occasionally tripled, with a strong suggestion that they are the same. The work has a repeating structure, fitted to a traditional pattern of four successive worlds, or creations: the first three are said to have ended in failure; our own is the fourth. Yet against the background of this formal pattern, the hero-gods appear as lighthearted boys, even as tricksters. Their adventures, which are sometimes quite bawdy, have a playful, anecdotal quality.

As the author plainly states in the preamble that begins part 1, "We shall write about this now amid the preaching of God, in Christendom now." Admittedly, then, the Popol Vuh is written after the conquest, but the question of how much of it was influenced by Christian missionaries is not easy to settle. Most critics have assumed that the account of the Earth's creation that immediately follows the preamble owes something to the **Book of Genesis**. If so, the material has been thoroughly assimilated to the Maya pantheon and to the Native American concept of primordial water. The text may be as easily compared to Aztec accounts of creation, in which the gods deliberate, then place the Earth on the surface of a preexisting sea, as to Genesis.

Part 1 continues with a description of the first three efforts at creating humans, in line with a widespread pattern shared by Aztec and other Mesoamerican traditions. As part 1 ends, the narrative moves on to the exploits of the divine heroes Hunahpu and Xbalanque. The work of these two heroes may be said to prepare the world for society and for the wellbeing of individuals within society when they bring low the overproud Seven Macaw, while part 3, the most celebrated portion of the Popol Vuh, confronts the scourge of death.

In the cycle of tales that comprises part 3, Hunahpu and Xbalanque vanquish the lords of the Maya underworld, called Xibalba (a term of obscure etymology, provisionally translated "place of fright"). This material is quintessentially Mayan: scenes from the story are preserved on painted vases of the classic period, recovered by archaeologists from Maya burial chambers. The story told here must have aided the Maya in their journey through the realms of death somewhat as the *Book of the Dead* comforted the ancient Egyptians. Parts 4 and 5 complete the vast epic, relating the connected stories of the origin of humans, the discovery of corn, the birth of the sun, and the history of the Quiché tribes and their royal lineages down to the time of the Spanish Conquest and, subsequently, to the 1550s.

Old as the stories are, they are also new. Narratives of the origin and destruction of early humans can still be heard in traditional Maya storytelling sessions. The tale of the discovery of corn continues to be widely told; and the exploits of the trickster Zipacna and the hero twins also persist in shorter versions. Beyond the native community, knowledge of the Popol Vuh among Central Americans is not only widespread but taken for granted. For the Salvadoran novelist Manlio Argueta (*Cuzcatlán*, 1986) the story of the origin of humans from corn as told in the Popol Vuh is a reminder, in Argueta's words, that "the species will not perish." The theme appears also in the 1949 novel *Men of Maize* by the Guatemalan Nobel laureate Miguel Angel Asturias, inspired by the same source.

In the translation printed here, wherever the text solidifies into a string of three or more couplets, the passage is set apart as though it were a poem. This is a device of the translator. It is not meant to imply that the lines were chanted but rather to show off the more pronounced moments of formalism in a prose that borders on oratory.

From Popol Vuh[1]

FROM PART I

[Prologue, Creation]

THIS IS THE BEGINNING OF THE ANCIENT WORD, here in this place called Quiché. Here we shall inscribe, we shall implant the Ancient Word, the potential and source for everything done in the citadel of Quiché, in the nation of Quiché people.

And here we shall take up the demonstration, revelation, and account of how things were put in shadow and brought to light by

> the Maker, Modeler,
> named Bearer, Begetter,
> Hunahpu Possum, Hunahpu Coyote,
> Great White Peccary,
> Sovereign Plumed Serpent,
> Heart of the Lake, Heart of the Sea,
> plate shaper,
> bowl shaper,[2] as they are called,
> also named, also described as
> the midwife, matchmaker
> named Xpiyacoc, Xmucane,
> defender, protector,[3]
> twice a midwife, twice a matchmaker,

as is said in the words of Quiché. They accounted for everything—and did it, too—as enlightened beings, in enlightened words. We shall write about this now amid the preaching of God, in Christendom now. We shall bring it out because there is no longer

> a place to see it, a Council Book,
> a place to see "The Light That Came from
>   Beside the Sea,"
> the account of "Our Place in the Shadows,"
> a place to see "The Dawn of Life,"

as it is called. There is the original book and ancient writing, but the one who reads and assesses it has a hidden identity.[4] It takes a long performance and account to complete the lighting of all the sky-earth:

> the fourfold siding, fourfold cornering,
> measuring, fourfold staking,
> halving the cord, stretching the cord
> in the sky, on the earth,

1. Translated by Dennis Tedlock.
2. All thirteen names refer to the Creator or to a company of creators, a designation applicable clearly to the first four names and *Sovereign Plumed Serpent*. *Heart of the Lake* and *Heart of the Sea* also apply, since the creators will later be described as "in the water," and somewhat obscurely, so does the last pair of names (*plate* and *bowl* may be read as "earth" and "sky," respectively). *Hunahpu Pos-*

sum, Hunahpu Coyote, Great White Peccary, and *Coati* refer specifically to the grandparents of the gods, usually called Xpiyacoc and Xmucane.
3. Four names for Xpiyacoc and Xmucane.
4. The hieroglyphic source (*Council Book*) was suppressed by missionaries; it was said to have been brought to Quiché in ancient times from the far side of a lagoon (*Sea*). The reader hides his identity to avoid the missionaries.

the four sides, the four corners,[5]
by the Maker, Modeler,
mother-father of life, of humankind,
giver of breath, giver of heart,
bearer, upbringer in the light that lasts
of those born in the light, begotten in the light;
worrier, knower of everything, whatever there is:
sky-earth, lake-sea.

THIS IS THE ACCOUNT, here it is:

Now it still ripples, now it still murmurs, ripples, it still sighs, still hums, and it is empty under the sky.

Here follow the first words, the first eloquence:

There is not yet one person, one animal, bird, fish, crab, tree, rock, hollow, canyon, meadow, forest. Only the sky alone is there; the face of the earth is not clear. Only the sea alone is pooled under all the sky; there is nothing whatever gathered together. It is at rest; not a single thing stirs. It is held back, kept at rest under the sky.

Whatever there is that might be is simply not there: only the pooled water, only the calm sea, only it alone is pooled.

Whatever might be is simply not there: only murmurs, ripples, in the dark, in the night. Only the Maker, Modeler alone, Sovereign Plumed Serpent, the Bearers, Begetters are in the water, a glittering light. They are there, they are enclosed in quetzal feathers, in blue-green.

Thus the name, "Plumed Serpent." They are great knowers, great thinkers in their very being.

And of course there is the sky, and there is also the Heart of Sky. This is the name of the god, as it is spoken.

And then came his word, he came here to the Sovereign Plumed Serpent, here in the blackness, in the early dawn. He spoke with the Sovereign Plumed Serpent, and they talked, then they thought, then they worried. They agreed with each other, they joined their words, their thoughts. Then it was clear, then they reached accord in the light, and then humanity was clear, when they conceived the growth, the generation of trees, of bushes, and the growth of life, of humankind, in the blackness, in the early dawn, all because of the Heart of Sky, named Hurricane. Thunderbolt Hurricane comes first, the second is Newborn Thunderbolt, and the third is Sudden Thunderbolt.[6]

So there were three of them, as Heart of Sky, who came to the Sovereign Plumed Serpent, when the dawn of life was conceived:

"How should the sowing be, and the dawning? Who is to be the provider, nurturer?"[7]

"Let it be this way, think about it: this water should be removed, emptied out for the formation of the earth's own plate and platform, then should come the sowing, the dawning of the sky-earth. But there will be no high days and no bright praise for our work, our design, until the rise of the human work, the human design," they said.

5. As though a farmer were measuring and staking a cornfield.
6. Alternate names for Heart of Sky, the deity who cooperates with Sovereign Plumed Serpent. The triple naming adapts the Christian trinity to native theology, perhaps more in the spirit of defiant preemption than of conciliation.
7. That is, humanity, which alone is capable of *nurturing* the gods with sacrifices.

And then the earth arose because of them, it was simply their word that brought it forth. For the forming of the earth they said "Earth." It arose suddenly, just like a cloud, like a mist, now forming, unfolding. Then the mountains were separated from the water, all at once the great mountains came forth. By their genius alone, by their cutting edge[8] alone they carried out the conception of the mountain-plain, whose face grew instant groves of cypress and pine.

And the Plumed Serpent was pleased with this:

"It was good that you came, Heart of Sky, Hurricane, and Newborn Thunderbolt, Sudden Thunderbolt. Our work, our design will turn out well," they said.

And the earth was formed first, the mountain-plain. The channels of water were separated; their branches wound their ways among the mountains. The waters were divided when the great mountains appeared.

Such was the formation of the earth when it was brought forth by the Heart of Sky, Heart of Earth, as they are called, since they were the first to think of it. The sky was set apart, and the earth was set apart in the midst of the waters.

Such was their plan when they thought, when they worried about the completion of their work.[9]

FROM PART 2

[The Twins Defeat Seven Macaw]

HERE IS THE BEGINNING OF THE DEFEAT AND DESTRUCTION OF THE DAY OF SEVEN MACAW by the two boys, the first named Hunahpu and the second named Xbalanque.[1] Being gods, the two of them saw evil in his attempt at self-magnification before the Heart of Sky.

* * *

This is the great tree of Seven Macaw, a nance,[2] and this is the food of Seven Macaw. In order to eat the fruit of the nance he goes up the tree every day. Since Hunahpu and Xbalanque have seen where he feeds, they are now hiding beneath the tree of Seven Macaw, they are keeping quiet here, the two boys are in the leaves of the tree.

And when Seven Macaw arrived, perching over his meal, the nance, it was then that he was shot by Hunahpu. The blowgun shot went right to his jaw, breaking his mouth. Then he went up over the tree and fell flat on the ground. Suddenly Hunahpu appeared, running. He set out to grab him, but actually it was the arm of Hunahpu that was seized by Seven Macaw. He yanked it straight back, he bent it back at the shoulder. Then Seven Macaw tore it right out of Hunahpu. Even so, the boys did well: the first round was not their defeat by Seven Macaw.

And when Seven Macaw had taken the arm of Hunahpu, he went home. Holding his jaw very carefully, he arrived:

8. ...Refers to the cutting of flesh with a knife....In the present context, it implies that "the mountains were separated from the water" through an act resembling the extraction of the heart (or other organs) from a sacrifice [translator's note].

9. That is, the creation of humans; an account of the first three, unsuccessful, attempts at creating humans occupies the remainder of part 1.

1. First mention of the twin hero gods (their origin is recounted in part 3). Here they confront the false god Seven Macaw, who has arisen during the time of primordial darkness, boasting, "My eyes are of metal; my teeth just glitter with jewels, and turquoise as well.... I am like the sun and the moon." Note that all the characters in parts 1, 2, and 3 are supernatural; humans are not created until part 4.

2. A pickle tree (*Byrsonima crassifolia*).

"What have you got there?" said Chimalmat, the wife of Seven Macaw.

"What is it but those two tricksters! They've shot me, they've dislocated my jaw.[3] All my teeth are just loose, now they ache. But once what I've got is over the fire—hanging there, dangling over the fire—then they can just come and get it. They're real tricksters!" said Seven Macaw, then he hung up the arm of Hunahpu.

Meanwhile Hunahpu and Xbalanque were thinking. And then they invoked a grandfather, a truly white-haired grandfather, and a grandmother, a truly humble grandmother—just bent-over, elderly people. Great White Peccary is the name of the grandfather, and Great White Coati is the name of the grandmother.[4] The boys said to the grandmother and grandfather:

"Please travel with us when we go to get our arm from Seven Macaw; we'll just follow right behind you. You'll tell him:

'Do forgive us our grandchildren, who travel with us. Their mother and father are dead, and so they follow along there, behind us. Perhaps we should give them away, since all we do is pull worms out of teeth.' So we'll seem like children to Seven Macaw, even though *we're* giving *you* the instructions," the two boys told them.

"Very well," they replied.

After that they approached the place where Seven Macaw was in front of his home. When the grandmother and grandfather passed by, the two boys were romping along behind them. When they passed below the lord's house, Seven Macaw was yelling his mouth off because of his teeth. And when Seven Macaw saw the grandfather and grandmother traveling with them:

"Where are you headed, our grandfather?" said the lord.

"We're just making our living, your lordship," they replied.

"Why are you working for a living? Aren't those your children traveling with you?"

"No, they're not, your lordship. They're our grandchildren, our descendants, but it is nevertheless *we* who take pity on *them*. The bit of food they get is the portion we give them, your lordship," replied the grandmother and grandfather. Since the lord is getting done in by the pain in his teeth, it is only with great effort that he speaks again:

"I implore you, please take pity on me! What sweets can you make, what poisons[5] can you cure?" said the lord.

"We just pull the worms out of teeth, and we just cure eyes. We just set bones, your lordship," they replied.

"Very well, please cure my teeth. They really ache, every day. It's insufferable! I get no sleep because of them—and my eyes. They just shot me, those two tricksters! Ever since it started I haven't eaten because of it. Therefore take pity on me! Perhaps it's because my teeth are loose now."

"Very well, your lordship. It's a worm, gnawing at the bone.[6] It's merely a matter of putting in a replacement and taking the teeth out, sir."

"But perhaps it's not good for my teeth to come out—since I am, after all, a lord. My finery is in my teeth—and my eyes."

"But then we'll put in a replacement. Ground bone will be put back in." And this is the "ground bone": it's only white corn.

---

3. This is the origin of the way a macaw's beak looks, with a huge upper mandible and a small, retreating lower one [translator's note].

4. Animal names of the divine grandparents, Xpiyacoc and Xmucane, who are also the twins' genealogical grandparents.

5. Play on words as *qui* is translated as both "sweet" and "poison."

6. The present-day Quiché retain the notion that a toothache is caused by a worm gnawing at the bone [translator's note].

"Very well. Yank them out! Give me some help here!" he replied.

And when the teeth of Seven Macaw came out, it was only white corn that went in as a replacement for his teeth—just a coating shining white, that corn in his mouth. His face fell at once, he no longer looked like a lord. The last of his teeth came out, the jewels that had stood out blue from his mouth.

And when the eyes of Seven Macaw were cured, he was plucked around the eyes, the last of his metal came off.[7] Still he felt no pain; he just looked on while the last of his greatness left him. It was just as Hunahpu and Xbalanque had intended.

And when Seven Macaw died, Hunahpu got back his arm. And Chimalmat, the wife of Seven Macaw, also died.

Such was the loss of the riches of Seven Macaw: only the doctors got the jewels and gems that had made him arrogant, here on the face of the earth. The genius of the grandmother, the genius of the grandfather did its work when they took back their arm: it was implanted and the break got well again. Just as they had wished the death of Seven Macaw, so they brought it about. They had seen evil in his self-magnification.

After this the two boys went on again. What they did was simply the word of the Heart of Sky.

FROM PART 3
[Victory over the Underworld]

AND NOW WE SHALL NAME THE NAME OF THE FATHER OF HUNAHPU AND XBAL-ANQUE. Let's drink to him, and let's just drink to the telling and accounting of the begetting of Hunahpu and Xbalanque. We shall tell just half of it, just a part of the account of their father. Here follows the account.

These are the names: One Hunahpu and Seven Hunahpu,[8] as they are called.

* * *

AND ONE AND SEVEN HUNAHPU WENT INSIDE DARK HOUSE.[9]

And then their torch was brought, only one torch, already lit, sent by One and Seven Death, along with a cigar for each of them, also already lit, sent by the lords. When these were brought to One and Seven Hunahpu they were cowering, here in the dark. When the bearer of their torch and cigars arrived, the torch was bright as it entered; their torch and both of their cigars were burning. The bearer spoke:

"'They must be sure to return them in the morning—not finished, but just as they look now. They must return them intact,' the lords say to you," they were told, and they were defeated. They finished the torch and they finished the cigars that had been brought to them.

And Xibalba is packed with tests, heaps and piles of tests.

This is the first one: the Dark House, with darkness alone inside.

---

7. This is clearly meant to be the origin of the large white and completely featherless eye patches and very small eyes of the scarlet macaw [translator's note].

8. Twin sons of Xpiyacoc and Xmucane; the elder of these twins, One Hunahpu, will become the father of Hunahpu and Xbalanque. "As for Seven Hunahpu," according to the text, "he has no wife. He's just a partner and just secondary; he just remains a boy."

9. The first of the "test" houses in Xibalba (the underworld) to which One and Seven Hunahpu, avid ballplayers, have been lured by the underworld lords, One and Seven Death; the lords have promised them a challenging ball game. The Mesoamerican ball game, remotely comparable to both basketball and soccer, was played on a rectangular court, using a ball of native rubber.

And the second is named Rattling House, heavy with cold inside, whistling with drafts, clattering with hail. A deep chill comes inside here.

And the third is named Jaguar House, with jaguars alone inside, jostling one another, crowding together, with gnashing teeth. They're scratching around; these jaguars are shut inside the house.

Bat House is the name of the fourth test, with bats alone inside the house, squeaking, shrieking, darting through the house. The bats are shut inside; they can't get out.

And the fifth is named Razor House, with blades alone inside. The blades are moving back and forth, ripping, slashing through the house.

These are the first tests of Xibalba, but One and Seven Hunahpu never entered into them, except for the one named earlier, the specified test house.

And when One and Seven Hunahpu went back before One and Seven Death, they were asked:

"Where are my cigars? What of my torch? They were brought to you last night!"

"We finished them, your lordship."

"Very well. This very day, your day is finished, you will die, you will disappear, and we shall break you off. Here you will hide your faces: you are to be sacrificed!" said One and Seven Death.

And then they were sacrificed and buried. They were buried at the Place of Ball Game Sacrifice,[1] as it is called. The head of One Hunahpu was cut off; only his body was buried with his younger brother.

"Put his head in the fork of the tree that stands by the road," said One and Seven Death.

And when his head was put in the fork of the tree, the tree bore fruit. It would not have had any fruit, had not the head of One Hunahpu been put in the fork of the tree.

This is the calabash tree, as we call it today, or "the skull of One Hunahpu," as it is said.

And then One and Seven Death were amazed at the fruit of the tree. The fruit grows out everywhere, and it isn't clear where the head of One Hunahpu is; now it looks just the way the calabashes look. All the Xibalbans see this, when they come to look.

The state of the tree loomed large in their thoughts, because it came about at the same time the head of One Hunahpu was put in the fork. The Xibalbans said among themselves:

"No one is to pick the fruit, nor is anyone to go beneath the tree," they said. They restricted themselves; all of Xibalba held back.

It isn't clear which is the head of One Hunahpu; now it's exactly the same as the fruit of the tree. Calabash came to be its name, and much was said about it. A maiden heard about it, and here we shall tell of her arrival.

AND HERE IS THE ACCOUNT OF A MAIDEN, the daughter of a lord named Blood Gatherer.[2]

And this is when a maiden heard of it, the daughter of a lord. Blood Gatherer is the name of her father, and Blood Moon is the name of the maiden.

---

1. Probably not a place name, but rather a name for the altar where losing ball players were sacrificed [translator's note].

2. Fourth-ranking lord of Xibalba, whose commission is to draw blood from people.

And when he heard the account of the fruit of the tree, her father retold it. And she was amazed at the account:

"I'm not acquainted with that tree they talk about. '"Its fruit is truly sweet!" they say,' I hear," she said.

Next, she went all alone and arrived where the tree stood. It stood at the Place of Ball Game Sacrifice:

"What? Well! What's the fruit of this tree? Shouldn't this tree bear something sweet? They shouldn't die, they shouldn't be wasted. Should I pick one?" said the maiden.

And then the bone spoke; it was here in the fork of the tree:

"Why do you want a mere bone, a round thing in the branches of a tree?" said the head of One Hunahpu when it spoke to the maiden. "You don't want it," she was told.

"I do want it," said the maiden.

"Very well. Stretch out your right hand here, so I can see it," said the bone.

"Yes," said the maiden. She stretched out her right hand, up there in front of the bone.

And then the bone spit out its saliva, which landed squarely in the hand of the maiden.

And then she looked in her hand, she inspected it right away, but the bone's saliva wasn't in her hand.

"It is just a sign I have given you, my saliva, my spittle. This, my head, has nothing on it—just bone, nothing of meat. It's just the same with the head of a great lord: it's just the flesh that makes his face look good. And when he dies, people get frightened by his bones. After that, his son is like his saliva, his spittle, in his being, whether it be the son of a lord or the son of a craftsman, an orator. The father does not disappear, but goes on being fulfilled. Neither dimmed nor destroyed is the face of a lord, a warrior, craftsman, orator. Rather, he will leave his daughters and sons. So it is that I have done likewise through you. Now go up there on the face of the earth; you will not die. Keep the word. So be it," said the head of One and Seven Hunahpu—they were of one mind when they did it.

This was the word Hurricane, Newborn Thunderbolt, Sudden Thunderbolt had given them. In the same way, by the time the maiden returned to her home, she had been given many instructions. Right away something was generated in her belly, from the saliva alone, and this was the generation of Hunahpu and Xbalanque.

And when the maiden got home and six months had passed, she was found out by her father. Blood Gatherer is the name of her father.

* * *

AND THEY CAME TO THE LORDS.[3] Feigning great humility, they bowed their heads all the way to the ground when they arrived. They brought themselves low, doubled over, flattened out, down to the rags, to the tatters. They really looked like vagabonds when they arrived.

3. Forced to flee the underworld the maiden (Blood Moon) finds refuge on earth with Xmucane. There she gives birth to the twins, who, like their father and uncle, become ballplayers and are enticed to the underworld. Surviving the Dark House and other tests, they disguise themselves as vagabonds and earn a reputation as clever entertainers among the denizens of Xibalba; as such they are summoned to entertain the high lords.

So then they were asked what their mountain[4] and tribe were, and they were also asked about their mother and father:

"Where do you come from?" they were asked.

"We've never known, lord. We don't know the identity of our mother and father. We must've been small when they died," was all they said. They didn't give any names.

"Very well. Please entertain us, then. What do you want us to give you in payment?" they were asked.

"Well, we don't want anything. To tell the truth, we're afraid," they told the lord.

"Don't be afraid. Don't be ashamed. Just dance this way: first you'll dance to sacrifice yourselves, you'll set fire to my house after that, you'll act out all the things you know. We want to be entertained. This is our heart's desire, the reason you had to be sent for, dear vagabonds. We'll give you payment," they were told.

So then they began their songs and dances, and then all the Xibalbans arrived, the spectators crowded the floor, and they danced everything: they danced the Weasel, they danced the Poorwill,[5] they danced the Armadillo. Then the lord said to them:

"Sacrifice my dog, then bring him back to life again," they were told.

"Yes," they said.

> When they sacrificed the dog
> he then came back to life.
> And that dog was really happy
> when he came back to life.
> Back and forth he wagged his tail
> when he came back to life.

And the lord said to them:

"Well, you have yet to set my home on fire," they were told next, so then they set fire to the home of the lord. The house was packed with all the lords, but they were not burned. They quickly fixed it back again, lest the house of One Death be consumed all at once, and all the lords were amazed, and they went on dancing this way. They were overjoyed.

And then they were asked by the lord:

"You have yet to kill a person! Make a sacrifice without death!" they were told.

"Very well," they said.

And then they took hold of a human sacrifice.

And they held up a human heart on high.

And they showed its roundness to the lords.

And now One and Seven Death admired it, and now that person was brought right back to life. His heart was overjoyed when he came back to life, and the lords were amazed:

"Sacrifice yet again, even do it to yourselves! Let's see it! At heart, that's the dance we really want from you," the lords said now.

"Very well, lord," they replied, and then they sacrificed themselves.

AND THIS IS THE SACRIFICE OF HUNAHPU BY XBALANQUE. One by one his legs, his arms were spread wide. His head came off, rolled far away outside. His heart, dug out, was smothered in a leaf,[6] and all the Xibalbans went crazy at the sight.

---

4. A metonym for almost any settlement, but especially a fortified town or citadel, located on a defensible elevation [translator's note].

5. The goatsucker. The dances apparently were imitations of these animals and birds.

6. As a tamale is wrapped. In the typical Mesoamerican heart sacrifice, the victim's arms and legs were stretched wide and the heart was excised and offered to a deity.

So now, only one of them was dancing there: Xbalanque.

"Get up!" he said, and Hunahpu came back to life. The two of them were overjoyed at this—and likewise the lords rejoiced, as if they were doing it themselves. One and Seven Death were as glad at heart as if they themselves were actually doing the dance.

And then the hearts of the lords were filled with longing, with yearning for the dance of little Hunahpu and Xbalanque, so then came these words from One and Seven Death:

"Do it to us! Sacrifice us!" they said. "Sacrifice both of us!" said One and Seven Death to Hunahpu and Xbalanque.

"Very well. You ought to come back to life. What is death to you?[7] And aren't we making you happy, along with the vassals of your domain?" they told the lords.

And this one was the first to be sacrificed: the lord at the very top, the one whose name is One Death, the ruler of Xibalba.

And with One Death dead, the next to be taken was Seven Death. They did not come back to life.

And then the Xibalbans were getting up to leave, those who had seen the lords die. They underwent heart sacrifice there, and the heart sacrifice was performed on the two lords only for the purpose of destroying them.

As soon as they had killed the one lord without bringing him back to life, the other lord had been meek and tearful before the dancers. He didn't consent, he didn't accept it:

"Take pity on me!" he said when he realized. All their vassals took the road to the great canyon, in one single mass they filled up the deep abyss. So they piled up there and gathered together, countless ants, tumbling down into the canyon, as if they were being herded there. And when they arrived, they all bent low in surrender, they arrived meek and tearful.

Such was the defeat of the rulers of Xibalba. The boys accomplished it only through wonders, only through self-transformation.

*　*　*

Such was the beginning of their disappearance and the denial of their worship.

> Their ancient day was not a great one,
> these ancient people only wanted conflict,
> their ancient names are not really divine,
> but fearful is the ancient evil of their faces.
>
> They are makers of enemies, users of owls,[8]
> they are inciters to wrongs and violence,
> they are masters of hidden intentions as well,
> they are black and white,[9]
> masters of stupidity, masters of perplexity,

as it is said. By putting on appearances they cause dismay.

Such was the loss of their greatness and brilliance. Their domain did not return to greatness. This was accomplished by little Hunahpu and Xbalanque.

---

7. Evident sarcasm.
8. The lords had used owls as messengers to

lure the ballplayers to Xibalba.
9. Contradictory, duplicitous.

[Origin of Humanity, First Dawn]

AND HERE IS THE BEGINNING OF THE CONCEPTION OF HUMANS, and of the search for the ingredients of the human body. So they spoke, the Bearer, Begetter, the Makers, Modelers named Sovereign Plumed Serpent:

"The dawn has approached, preparations have been made, and morning has come for the provider, nurturer, born in the light, begotten in the light. Morning has come for humankind, for the people of the face of the earth," they said. It all came together as they went on thinking in the darkness, in the night, as they searched and they sifted, they thought and they wondered.

And here their thoughts came out in clear light. They sought and discovered what was needed for human flesh. It was only a short while before the sun, moon, and stars were to appear above the Makers and Modelers. Split Place, Bitter Water Place is the name: the yellow corn, white corn came from there.

And these are the names of the animals who brought the food: fox, coyote, parrot, crow. There were four animals who brought the news of the ears of yellow corn and white corn. They were coming from over there at Split Place, they showed the way to the split.[1]

And this was when they found the staple foods.

And these were the ingredients for the flesh of the human work, the human design, and the water was for the blood. It became human blood, and corn was also used by the Bearer, Begetter.

And so they were happy over the provisions of the good mountain, filled with sweet things, thick with yellow corn, white corn, and thick with pataxte and cacao, countless zapotes, anonas, jocotes, nances, matasanos,[2] sweets—the rich foods filling up the citadel named Split Place, Bitter Water Place. All the edible fruits were there: small staples, great staples, small plants, great plants. The way was shown by the animals.

And then the yellow corn and white corn were ground, and Xmucane did the grinding nine times. Corn was used, along with the water she rinsed her hands with, for the creation of grease; it became human fat when it was worked by the Bearer, Begetter, Sovereign Plumed Serpent, as they are called.

After that, they put it into words:

> the making, the modeling of our first mother-father,
> with yellow corn, white corn alone for the flesh,
> food alone for the human legs and arms,
> for our first fathers, the four human works.

It was staples alone that made up their flesh.

THESE ARE THE NAMES OF THE FIRST PEOPLE WHO WERE MADE AND MODELED.

This is the first person: Jaguar Quitze.
And now the second: Jaguar Night.

---

1. In the widespread Mesoamerican story of the discovery of corn, one or more animals reveal that corn and other foods are hidden within a rock or a mountain, accessible through a cleft; in some versions the mountain is split apart by lightning.
2. Quincelike fruits of the tree *Casimiroa edu-lis*. Pataxte (*Theobroma bicolor*) is a species of cacao that is inferior to cacao proper (*T. cacao*). Zapotes are fruits of the sapota tree (*Lucuma mammosa*). Anonas are custard apples (genus *Anona*). Jocotes are yellow plumlike fruits of the tree *Spondias purpurea*.

And now the third: Not Right Now.
And the fourth: Dark Jaguar.[3]

And these are the names of our first mother-fathers.[4] They were simply made and modeled, it is said; they had no mother and no father. We have named the men by themselves. No woman gave birth to them, nor were they begotten by the builder, sculptor, Bearer, Begetter. By sacrifice alone, by genius alone they were made, they were modeled by the Maker, Modeler, Bearer, Begetter, Sovereign Plumed Serpent. And when they came to fruition, they came out human:

> They talked and they made words.
> They looked and they listened.
> They walked, they worked.

They were good people, handsome, with looks of the male kind. Thoughts came into existence and they gazed; their vision came all at once. Perfectly they saw, perfectly they knew everything under the sky, whenever they looked. The moment they turned around and looked around in the sky, on the earth, everything was seen without any obstruction. They didn't have to walk around before they could see what was under the sky; they just stayed where they were.

As they looked, their knowledge became intense. Their sight passed through trees, through rocks, through lakes, through seas, through mountains, through plains. Jaguar Quitze, Jaguar Night, Not Right Now, and Dark Jaguar were truly gifted people.

And then they were asked by the builder and mason:

"What do you know about your being? Don't you look, don't you listen? Isn't your speech good, and your walk? So you must look, to see out under the sky. Don't you see the mountain-plain clearly? So try it," they were told.

And then they saw everything under the sky perfectly. After that, they thanked the Maker, Modeler:

> "Truly now,
> double thanks, triple thanks
> that we've been formed, we've been given
> our mouths, our faces,
> we speak, we listen,
> we wonder, we move,
> our knowledge is good, we've understood
> what is far and near,
> and we've seen what is great and small
> under the sky, on the earth.
> Thanks to you we've been formed,
> we've come to be made and modeled,
> our grandmother, our grandfather,"

they said when they gave thanks for having been made and modeled. They understood everything perfectly, they sighted the four sides, the four corners in the sky, on the earth, and this didn't sound good to the builder and sculptor:

"What our works and designs have said is no good:

'We have understood everything, great and small,' they say." And so the Bearer, Begetter took back their knowledge:

"What should we do with them now? Their vision should at least reach nearby, they should see at least a small part of the face of the earth, but what

---

3. The four original Quiché males.
4. That is, parents, although only the first three

founded lineages; Dark Jaguar had no son.

they're saying isn't good. Aren't they merely 'works' and 'designs' in their very names? Yet they'll become as great as gods, unless they procreate, proliferate at the sowing, the dawning, unless they increase."

"Let it be this way: now we'll take them apart just a little, that's what we need. What we've found out isn't good. Their deeds would become equal to ours, just because their knowledge reaches so far. They see everything," so said

> the Heart of Sky, Hurricane,
> Newborn Thunderbolt, Sudden Thunderbolt,
> Sovereign Plumed Serpent,
> Bearer, Begetter,
> Xpiyacoc, Xmucane,
> Maker, Modeler,

as they are called. And when they changed the nature of their works, their designs, it was enough that the eyes be marred by the Heart of Sky. They were blinded as the face of a mirror is breathed upon. Their vision flickered. Now it was only from close up that they could see what was there with any clarity.

And such was the loss of the means of understanding, along with the means of knowing everything, by the four humans. The root was implanted.

And such was the making, modeling of our first grandfather, our father, by the Heart of Sky, Heart of Earth.

AND THEN THEIR WIVES AND WOMEN CAME INTO BEING. Again, the same gods thought of it. It was as if they were asleep when they received them, truly beautiful women were there with Jaguar Quitze, Jaguar Night, Not Right Now, and Dark Jaguar. With their women there they really came alive. Right away they were happy at heart again, because of their wives.

Red Sea Turtle is the name of the wife of Jaguar Quitze.

Prawn House is the name of the wife of Jaguar Night.

Water Hummingbird is the name of the wife of Not Right Now.

Macaw House is the name of the wife of Dark Jaguar.

So these are the names of their wives, who became ladies of rank, giving birth to the people of the tribes, small and great.

* * *

AND HERE IS THE DAWNING AND SHOWING OF THE SUN, MOON, AND STARS. And Jaguar Quitze, Jaguar Night, Not Right Now, and Dark Jaguar were overjoyed when they saw the sun carrier.[5] It came up first. It looked brilliant when it came up, since it was ahead of the sun.

After that they unwrapped their copal[6] incense, which came from the east, and there was triumph in their hearts when they unwrapped it. They gave their heartfelt thanks with three kinds at once:

Mixtam Copal is the name of the copal brought by Jaguar Quitze.

Cauiztan Copal, next, is the name of the copal brought by Jaguar Night.

Godly Copal, as the next one is called, was brought by Not Right Now.

The three of them had their copal, and this is what they burned as they incensed the direction of the rising sun. They were crying sweetly as they shook their burning copal,[7] the precious copal.

---

5. The morning star.
6. Resin used as incense.
7. Note that the Mesoamerican pottery cen-

ser must be shaken or swayed back and forth to keep the incense burning.

After that they cried because they had yet to see and yet to witness the birth of the sun.

And then, when the sun came up, the animals, small and great, were happy. They all came up from the rivers and canyons; they waited on all the mountain peaks. Together they looked toward the place where the sun came out.

So then the puma and jaguar cried out, but the first to cry out was a bird, the parrot by name. All the animals were truly happy. The eagle, the white vulture, small birds, great birds spread their wings, and the penitents and sacrificers knelt down.

FROM PART 5

[Prayer for Future Generations]

AND THIS IS THE CRY OF THEIR HEARTS, HERE IT IS:

> "Wait! On this blessed day,
> thou Hurricane, thou Heart of the Sky-Earth,
> thou giver of ripeness and freshness,
> and thou giver of daughters and sons,
> spread thy stain, spill thy drops
> of green and yellow;[8]
> give life and beginning
> to those I bear and beget,
> that they might multiply and grow,
> nurturing and providing for thee,
> calling to thee along the roads and paths,
> on rivers, in canyons,
> beneath the trees and bushes;
> give them their daughters and sons.
>
> "May there be no blame, obstacle, want or misery;
> let no deceiver come behind or before them,
> may they neither be snared nor wounded,
> nor seduced, nor burned,
> nor diverted below the road nor above it;
> may they neither fall over backward nor stumble;
> keep them on the Green Road, the Green Path.
>
> "May there be no blame or barrier for them
> through any secrets or sorcery of thine;
> may thy nurturers and providers be good
> before thy mouth and thy face,
> thou, Heart of Sky; thou, Heart of Earth;
> thou, Bundle of Flames;[9]
> and thou, Tohil, Auilix, Hacauitz,[1]
> under the sky, on the earth,
> the four sides, the four corners;
> may there be only light, only continuity within,
> before thy mouth and thy face, thou god."

8. The imagery, denoting human offspring, alludes to semen and plant growth.
9. A sacred relic left to the Quiché lords by Jaguar Quitze; like the sacred bundles of the North American peoples, a cloth-wrapped ark with mysterious contents [translator's note].
1. Patron deities of the Quiché lineages.

s.catherina
Ins

THE ENCOUNTER OF EUROPE
AND THE NEW WORLD

As it dawned on Europeans that Christopher Columbus's voyages had led him not to the East Indies but to a continent previously unknown to them, the enormity of Columbus's "discovery" shattered the certainties of the medieval world, introducing a new era of extensive exploration around the globe and increased skepticism about received knowledge. Both the "brave new world" (in William Shakespeare's phrase) and its inhabitants produced in the Europeans a sense that reality had been decisively altered and could never revert to older, familiar ways. Europe, with its traditions rooted in the medieval and ancient eras, seemed almost magically transformed into the Old World by its encounter with the New World. Columbus's initial forays into the Caribbean were soon followed by multiple expeditions to present-day Brazil, Central America, Mexico, and Peru, as the European presence gradually spread over the American continent. Portuguese, Dutch, French, and English explorers all set sail in an attempt to emulate the Spanish conquests and establish colonial outposts.

Wonder at radically different cultures and landscapes permeates the early Spanish and Portuguese accounts of the New World. The Europeans idealize the native peoples for their artlessness and generosity, while keeping a sharp eye on the commercial and extractive possibili-

A 1592 engraving by Theodore de Bry that depicts the encounter between the Spanish and native people at the Río de San Francisco in Brazil, 1549.

ties that such innocence enables. "Of anything they have, if it be asked for, they never say no," Columbus exclaims, yet he also reveals that he has taken some Indians "by force" to train them as interpreters, while leaving a group of his men behind in a well-armed fort. Columbus reads his surroundings largely by denying all evidence of culture: a cursory glance tells him that the Indians have no clothing, no religion, no guile, even as he confesses that he can barely communicate with them.

The contradictions in Columbus's letter to Ferdinand and Isabella regarding his first voyage are magnified in later texts that relate the conquest of the powerful Aztec Empire for Spain by Hernán Cortés, as wonder gives way to military calculation. The conquest of Mexico forever changed the stakes of New World exploration, as other European nations were forced to grapple with the enormous power and riches that it granted Spain. The immediate consequence of the fall of Tenochtitlán (now Mexico City) was the dismantling of the Aztec Empire, which had stretched from the Gulf Coast to the Pacific and from what is now the state of San Luis Potosí in central Mexico eastward to just within the present boundary of Guatemala. In due course, Tenochtitlán became the base from which Spain launched further conquests, ultimately reaching to the upper Rio Grande Valley and deep into Central America. Cortés's example inspired a generation of opportunistic intruders, notably Francisco Pizarro, whose conquest of the Inca Empire of Peru was completed in 1533. Explora-

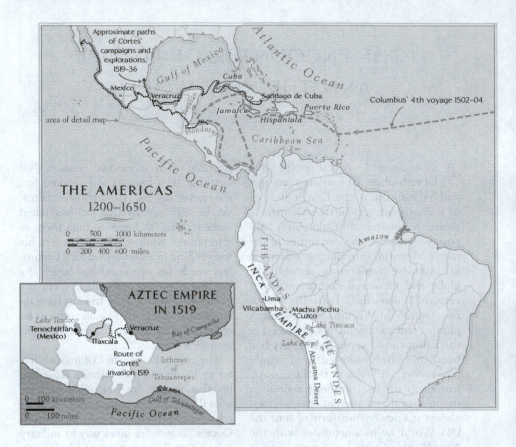

THE AMERICAS
1200–1650

AZTEC EMPIRE
IN 1519

tion by other European nations, including Britain and Portugal, had begun even before Cortés, and within a hundred years of the initial contact, European outposts would be implanted all along the eastern rim of the Americas.

With Spain's huge empire came administrative and moral dilemmas. Spain established vice-royalties in Mexico (1535) and Peru (1542) that ruled over impossibly large territories. As Indian labor proved insufficient for the colonists' needs, Spain and other nations began importing enslaved Africans into the New World. The conquest remained a work in progress, as Spaniards were forced to confront native hierarchies that complicated any possible allegiance to Spain, religious beliefs that seemed quite capable of surviving the forcible teaching of Christianity, and a bewildering admix-

ture of populations. All these made the conquest a long and complex process.

While Spain's European rivals eagerly circulated reports of Spanish cruelty and greed (a war of words known as the "black legend"), the Spaniards themselves embarked on a vigorous internal debate about the legitimacy of the conquest and the status of their indigenous subjects. The most famous advocate for the Indians was the Spanish friar **Bartolomé de las Casas**, who loudly denounced Spanish excesses in an effort to reform the colonial administration. Las Casas persuaded the Spanish Crown to pass laws protecting the Indians, but exploitation of the native population in mines and other forms of forced labor was intractable.

Devastating to native people and permanently disruptive to long-established cultures, the conquests nevertheless prepared the way for exchange. Wheat, livestock, horses, and firearms entered the so-called New World. From the Americas came tomatoes, chocolate, chilies, avocados (the names are all from Nahuatl, the language of the Aztecs: *tomatl, xocolatl, chilli, ahuacatl*), not to mention tobacco, corn, potatoes, and the near-legendary gold and silver that heated the economy of Europe through the sixteenth century.

There were intellectual exchanges as well. In Aztec territory Spaniards, especially members of the clergy, learned Nahuatl, while native people became proficient in Spanish. Founded in 1536, the Royal College of Santa Cruz in the borough of Tlatelolco (part of Mexico City) taught young Aztec men to read and write Spanish and Nahuatl and sometimes even Latin. This Franciscan-run academy proved to be the principal training ground for what in retrospect would be recognized as the great era of Nahuatl letters, extending to about 1650. During this period **Aesop's Fables**, the "Life of Saint Francis," portions of the **Bible**, and writings by **St. Augustine**, Calderón de la Barca, **Lope de Vega**, and other authors were translated into Nahuatl and recorded in the alphabetic script used by Europeans (the Aztecs had used a pictographic and ideographic recording system rather than a standardized written language). At the same time, the Spaniards published grammars of many of the native languages that they encountered, as part of their efforts to convert indigenous peoples to Christianity.

During these years, works of Aztec poetry and history were recorded for posterity and, in some cases, translated into Spanish. Among the most noteworthy is the massive **Florentine Codex** (including traditional narratives, oratory, and the history of the Spanish Conquest). Because of censorship and fear of encouraging native religion,

however, none of these works, whether in the native language or in translation, was published in its own time. Instead, they were prepared in manuscript and stored in libraries on both sides of the Atlantic. In some cases missionary-scholars served as the recorders, writing from the dictation of a knowledgeable elder. In other cases native scribes actually wrote from live recitals or transcribed old pictorial books. These often magnificent volumes were bark-paper screen-folds that opened to form a lengthy streamer, crowded with illustrations typically read from right to left. Although the pictures contained a few phonetic features, they were essentially mnemonic, intended to call forth a text that had been learned orally.

As the Europeans solidified control over the New World, the texts that they encountered and in some cases helped produce—the **Popol Vuh**, the **Huarochiri Manuscript**, the *Florentine Codex*—made it clear that this world was new only to Europeans and that it had its own origin myths and revered ancients. These texts make the point that New World cultures had carefully charted their own histories, political organization, and belief systems, however much Columbus idealized their material and religious innocence. The European project of collecting and preserving information about the cultures the Europeans encountered, in a kind of early ethnography, contrasts markedly with the violence and rapacity of the conquest.

The conquest also produced indigenous responses, as *mestizo* (born of a Spaniard and an Indian) and Indian writers struggled to present their view of their societies and of the cataclysmic disruption of the conquest. Authors such as **Inca Garcilaso de la Vega** and **Guaman Poma** wrote extensive histories, using their knowledge of their homelands to correct and augment Spanish accounts and offering in the process advice to Spanish rulers on how better to administer the colonies by incorporating native expertise. Written decades after the conquest, these accounts chart the cultural and political negotiation that came of the encounter, and the urgent claims by both indigenous and mestizo voices to participate in the debates.

THE HUAROCHIRÍ MANUSCRIPT
compiled ca. 1598

At the turn of the seventeenth century, sixty years after the Spanish conquest of Peru, the anonymous indigenous author of this text was charged by a Spanish friar, Francisco de Avila, with documenting non-Christian religious practices, presumably in order to put an end to the beliefs that challenged Spanish efforts at Christianization. Despite this mandate, the text manages to demonstrate that prehispanic religion had its own logic and complexity. Although the manuscript is written mostly in Quechua, its frequent Christian and biblical references make it clear that no "pure" indigenous voice can exist by this late point, and that even accounts of the prehispanic past are colored by the tremendous rupture of the conquest.

The Andean religious imaginary described here is populated by *huacas*—deities who inhabit the landscape in very concrete terms, as sacred objects and places. The first selection describes an ancient time before the appearance of Paria Caca, the most important deity in the text, who is associated with an imposing mountain. A second excerpt relates the prophecy of the Spaniards' arrival and the end of the cult of Paria Caca, events that had occurred in the author's own lifetime. A final section ties the power of the *huacas* to the Incas' own conquest of the region, long before the arrival of the Spaniards, and depicts the uneven power struggles between rulers and deities.

From The Huarochirí Manuscript[1]

[Preface]

If the ancestors of the people called Indians[2] had known writing in earlier times, then the lives they lived would not have faded from view until now.

As the mighty past of the Spanish Vira Cochas[3] is visible until now, so, too, would theirs be.

But since things are as they are, and since nothing has been written until now,

I set forth here the lives of the ancestors of the Huaro Cheri people, who all descend from one forefather:

---

1. Translated by Frank Salomon and George L. Urioste.
2. The original uses the term *indio* here, which flattens the distinctions among the

many peoples described in the text.
3. In colonial as in modern Quechua, the name of this principal deity is often used to refer to the Spanish.

What faith[4] they held, how they live up until now, those things and more;

Village by village it will be written down: how they lived from their dawning age onward.

CHAPTER I

How the Idols of Old Were, and How They Warred among Themselves, and How the Natives Existed at That Time

In very ancient times, there were *huacas* named Yana Namca and Tuta Ñamca.

Later on another *huaca* named Huallallo Caruincho defeated them.

After he defeated them, he ordered the people to bear two children and no more.

He would eat one of them himself.

The parents would raise the other, whichever one was loved best.

Although people did die in those times, they came back to life on the fifth day exactly.

And as for their foodstuffs, they ripened exactly five days after being planted.

These villages and all the others like them were full of Yunca.[5]

When a great number of people had filled the land, they lived really miserably, scratching and digging the rock faces and ledges to make terraced fields.

These fields, some small, others large, are still visible today on all the rocky heights.

And all the birds of that age were perfectly beautiful, parrots and toucans all yellow and red.

Later, at the time when another *huaca* named Paria Caca[6] appeared, these beings and all their works were cast out to the hot Anti lands[7] by Paria Caca's actions.

Further on we'll speak of Paria Caca's emergence and of his victories.

Also, as we know, there was another *huaca* named Cuni Raya.[8]

Regarding him, we're not sure whether he existed before Paria Caca or maybe after him.

However, Cuni Raya's essential nature almost matches Vira Cocha's.[9] For when people worshiped this *huaca*, they would invoke him, saying,

"Cuni Raya Vira Cocha,

You who animate mankind,
Who charge the world with being,
All things are yours!
Yours the fields and yours the people."

---

4. The original uses the Spanish term *fe*, for non-Christian religious practice, making the indigenous cults analogous to the true faith, and therefore subject to greater penalties from colonial religious authorities than mere "superstition."
5. The warm regions of the Pacific coast of Peru, their flora and fauna, and the peoples who lived there.
6. A sacred mountain, Paria Caca is the dominant deity in the manuscript.
7. The eastern slopes of the Andes and western fringes of Amazonia.
8. A coastal water deity, creator of irrigation.
9. A tricksterlike deity associated with the transformation of landforms.

And so, long ago, when beginning anything difficult, the ancients, even though they couldn't see Vira Cocha, used to throw coca leaves to the ground,[1] talk to him, and worship him before all others, saying,

> "Help me remember how,
> Help me work it out,
> Cuni Raya Vira Cocha!"

And the master weaver would worship and call on him whenever it was hard for him to weave.

For that reason, we'll write first about this *huaca* and about his life, and later on about Paria Caca.

* * *

CHAPTER 18

We already mentioned that the Inca revered Paria Caca and acted as *huacsa*.[2]

It's said that he, the Inca himself, decreed, "Let thirty men from the Upper Yauyos and the Lower Yauyos serve Paria Caca according to the full and waning lunar cycles."

In obedience to that command, thirty men served him in shifts of fifteen days, offering him food and feeding him.

One day they sacrificed one of his llamas, a llama named Yauri Huanaca.

When those thirty people examined the heart and entrails of the llama, one of the thirty, a fellow called Quita Pariasca the Mountain Man, spoke up and said, "Alas, brothers, the world is not good! In coming times our father Paria Caca will be abandoned."

"No," the others retorted, "you're talking nonsense!"

"It's a good augury!"

"What do you know?"

One of them called out, "Hey, Quita Pariasca! What makes you think that? In these llama innards our father Paria Caca is foretelling something wonderful!"

But at the time he said that, the mountaineer hadn't even approached the llama to inspect its innards. He had prophesied so just by watching from afar.[3]

The mountaineer spoke out and rebuked them: "It's Paria Caca himself who says it, brothers."

Then they derided Quita Pariasca with spiteful words:

"That smelly mountain man, what could he know?"

"Our father Paria Caca has subjects as far away as the limits of the land called Chinchay Suyo.[4] Could such a power ever fall desolate?"

"What does a guy like that know?"

They talked in great anger.

---

1. Either as a sacrifice or for purposes of divination.
2. A priestlike figure responsible for ritual dances.
3. The "mountain man" seems to see easily what the other soothsayers cannot even divine, a possible reflection on the failure to foresee the disastrous Spanish invasion.
4. The northern quarter of the Inca state included parts of Peru, Ecuador, and Colombia.

But just a very few days after the day when he'd said these things, they heard someone say, "Vira Cochas[5] have appeared in Caxa Marca!"

A certain man who was also from Checa, named Tama Lliuya Casa Lliuya, a member of the Caca Sica *ayllu*[6] is known to have dwelt as one of Paria Caca's retainers.

At that time, they say, there were thirty priests at Paria Caca and this Casa Lliuya Tama Lliuya was the eldest of them all.

When the Vira Cochas, the Spaniards, arrived there, they kept asking insistently, "What about this *huaca*'s silver and garments?"

But the thirty refused to reveal anything.

Because they did, the Spanish Vira Cochas got furious, and, ordering some straw piled up, they burned Casa Lliuya.

When half the straw had burned, the wind began to blow it away.

And so although this man suffered horribly, he did survive.

But by that time the others had handed the clothing and the rest of the things over to the Spaniards.

It was then that all the men said, "Very truly indeed were we warned by this mountain man Quita Pariasca!"

"Brothers, let's go away, let's disband."

"The world is no longer good," they said. And so they dispersed, each going back to his own village.

When the burned man from Checa healed up, he arrived at a village called Limca in the territory of the Quinti, carrying along a child of Paria Caca named Maca Uisa.

We'll describe these things in the next chapter.

* * *

CHAPTER 23

We Shall Write Here about the Inca's Summons to All the Huacas. We Shall Also Speak Here of Maca Uisa's Victory

When Tupay Ynga Yupanqui was king, they say, he first conquered all the provinces and then happily rested for many years.

But then enemy rebellions arose from some provinces: those called Alancu Marca, Calanco Marca, and Chaque Marca.

These peoples didn't want to be peoples of the Inca.

The Inca mobilized many thousands of men and battled them for a period of about twelve years.

They exterminated all the people he sent, and so the Inca, grieving deeply, said, "What'll become of us?" He became very downhearted.

5. I.e., the Spaniards. Cajamarca, as it is spelled today, is the place where the Incas first encountered the troops of Francisco Pizarro, in 1532, and where the Inca Atahualpa was taken prisoner by the Spaniards.
6. An Inca social and political unit, a kind of extended family around which life was organized.

One day he thought to himself, "Why do I serve all these *huacas* with my gold and my silver, with my clothing and my food, with everything I have? Enough! I'll call them to help me against my enemies."

He summoned them: "From every single village, let all those who have received gold and silver come here!"

The *huacas* responded, "Yes!" and went to him. Even Pacha Camac went, riding in a litter, and so did the local *huacas* from the whole of Tauantin Suyo all in their own litters.

When all the village *huacas* had arrived at Aucay Pata,[7] Paria Caca hadn't yet arrived. He was still grumbling, "Should I go or not?"

Finally Paria Caca sent his child Maca Uisa, saying, "Go and find out about it."

Maca Uisa arrived and sat at the end of the gathering on his litter called *chicsi rampa*.

Then the Inca began to speak: "Fathers, *huacas* and *villcas*,[8] you already know how wholeheartedly I serve you with my gold and my silver. Since I do so, being at your service as I am, won't you come to my aid now that I'm losing so many thousands of my people? It's for this reason that I've had you called together."

But after he said this not a single one spoke up. Instead they sat there mute.

The Inca then said, "Yao! Speak up! Shall the people you've made and fostered perish in this way, savaging one another? If you refuse to help me, I'll have all of you burned immediately!

"Why should I serve you and adorn you with my gold, with my silver, with basketfuls of my food and drinks, with my llamas and everything else I have? Now that you've heard the greatness of my grief, won't you come to my aid? If you do refuse, you'll burn immediately!"

Then Pacha Camac spoke up: "Inca, Mid-Day Sun! As for me, I didn't reply because I am a power who would shake you and the whole world around you. It wouldn't be those enemies alone whom I would destroy, but you as well. And the entire world would end with you. That's why I've sat silent."

As the other *huacas* sat mute, Maca Uisa then spoke up: "Inca, Mid-Day Sun! I'll go there. You must remain right here, instructing your people and making plans. I'll go and subdue them for you, right away, once and for all!"

While Maca Uisa spoke, a bright greenish-blue color blew from his mouth like smoke.

At that very moment he put on his golden panpipe (his flute was likewise of gold) and he wrapped the *chumprucu* around his head. His *pusuca*[9] was of gold, too, and as for his tunic, it was black.

For Maca Uisa's journey the Inca gave him a litter, called the *chicsi rampa*, made for the travels of an Inca in person.

7. A plaza in the heart of Cuzco, the Inca's capital.
8. Sacred ones.

9. Possibly a lower-body garment. "*Chumprucu*": turbanlike garment.

The people called Calla Uaya were chosen by the Inca because they were all very strong.

These people could carry him, in a few days, a journey of many days.

They were the ones who carried Maca Uisa and bore his litter to the battle-front.

As soon as they brought him up a hill, Maca Uisa, child of Paria Caca, began to rain upon them, gently at first.

The natives of that country said, "What could this mean?" and began to ready themselves.

When they did so, Maca Uisa reduced all those villages to eroded chasms by flashing lightning and pouring down more rain, and washing them away in a mudslide. Striking with lightning bolts, he exterminated the great *curacas*[1] and all the other strong-men. Only a few of the common people were spared. If he had wanted to, he could have exterminated them all. When he had overpowered them completely, he drove some of the people back to Cuzco.

From that time onward, the Inca revered Paria Caca even more, and gave him fifty of his retainers.

The Inca said, "Father Maca Uisa, what shall I give you? Ask me for anything you want. I will not stint."

"I don't want anything," Maca Uisa replied, "except that you should serve as *huacsa* the way our children from the Yauyo do."

The Inca was deeply afraid when he said this, and answered, "Very well then, father!" He was willing to offer Maca Uisa anything at all, for he thought to himself, "He could destroy me, too!"

The Inca then said, "Father, eat!" and had some food served to him, but Maca Uisa replied with a demand:

"I am not in the habit of eating stuff like this. Bring me some thorny oyster shells!"

As soon as the Inca gave him thorny oyster shells, Maca Uisa ate them all at once, making them crunch with a "Cap cap" sound.

Since Maca Uisa didn't want anything else to eat, the Inca ordered some of his Inca ladies of the nobility assigned to him; but he didn't agree to that either.

So Maca Uisa went back home to inform his father Paria Caca.

From then on, and for a long time afterward, the Inca acted as *huacsa* in Xauxa and danced ceremonially, holding Maca Uisa in great honor.

They gathered in Cuzco at Aucay Pata square as we mentioned, the *huacas*, all of them.

Among these *huacas* seated there, as we said before, it was Siua Caña Villca Coto who was the most beautiful of all. None of the other *huacas* could match this one in beauty.

This much we know about them.

---

1. Officials, magistrates.

CHRISTOPHER COLUMBUS

Born in Italy, most likely in Genoa, Columbus (1450–1506) became a sailor on the Mediterranean and the Atlantic oceans, eventually establishing himself also as a navigator and mapmaker. While most thinkers of his day agreed that the Earth was spherical, there was considerable disagreement over its size and the habitability of its various zones. Convinced that he was led by Providence, Columbus persuaded the Spanish King Ferdinand and Queen Isabella to fund an expedition in 1492 that he hoped would find a shorter route to the East Indies and its lucrative spice trade by sailing west. In this sense, the discovery of the New World was an accident, and Columbus continued to believe for some time that he had reached Asia, hence the pervasive misnomer "Indians" that he uses for the peoples he encounters. In Hispaniola (present-day Haiti and the Dominican Republic), he found what seemed to him an earthly paradise, filled with an inexhaustible variety of flowers and fruits, and gentle natives who, in his telling, denied him nothing.

Columbus's letter about his first voyage is a public version of the more sensitive information that he sent his patrons, and emphasizes the potential utility of the islands as a source of gold and other commodities. Columbus also envisions the island's population as future converts, introducing the theme of evangelization that was to be an important justification for the conquest, or as docile laborers. Although it idealizes the islands, the letter also reveals the difficulties that attended the encounter, and the threat of violence that overshadows the idyll. Excited at the promise of gold on the next island beyond the horizon, he disregards both the actual scarcity of treasure and the Indians' urgent insistence that he move on to search elsewhere.

Later voyages were to prove far less idyllic: Columbus returned to Hispaniola to find the fort he had left there destroyed and his men lost, and a great deal more hostility from the Indians who had suffered their depredations. In Spain, meanwhile, he faced strong opposition to his demands for reward and recognition, and increasing skepticism as gold remained elusive in the Caribbean. For the Taínos, the native inhabitants of the Caribbean islands, the contact with Europeans proved fatal: through a combination of war, smallpox, and the violent exploitation of their labor by the Spanish, their population was decimated by the mid-sixteenth century. Although Columbus's early accounts cannot envision such dire outcomes, the tremendous destruction wrought on this population has tainted the legacy of his voyages over the centuries.

Letter Concerning the First Voyage[1]

Sir: As I know that you will have pleasure from the great victory which our Lord hath given me in my voyage, I write you this, by which you shall know that in thirty-three days I passed over to the Indies with the fleet which the most illustrious King and Queen, our Lords, gave me; where I found very many islands peopled

1. Translated by Sir Clements R. Markham.

with inhabitants beyond number. And, of them all, I have taken possession for their Highnesses, with proclamation and the royal standard displayed; and I was not gainsaid. To the first which I found, I gave the name Sant Salvador, in commemoration of His High Majesty, who marvellously hath given all this: the Indians call it Guanaham. The second I named the Island of Santa Maria de Concepcion, the third Ferrandina, the fourth, Fair Island, the fifth La Isla Juana; and so for each one a new name. When I reached Juana, I followed its coast westwardly, and found it so large that I thought it might be mainland, the province of Cathay. And as I did not thus find any towns and villages on the sea-coast, save small hamlets with the people whereof I could not get speech, because they all fled away forthwith, I went on further in the same direction, thinking I should not miss of great cities or towns. And at the end of many leagues, seeing that there was no change, and that the coast was bearing me northwards, whereunto my desire was contrary, since the winter was already confronting us, I formed the purpose of making from thence to the South, and as the wind also blew against me, I determined not to wait for other weather and turned back as far as a port agreed upon; from which I sent two men into the country to learn if there were a king, or any great cities. They traveled for three days, and found innumerable small villages and a numberless population, but nought of ruling authority; wherefore they returned. I understood sufficiently from other Indians whom I had already taken, that this land, in its continuousness, was an island; and so I followed its coast eastwardly for a hundred and seven leagues as far as where it terminated; from which headland I saw another island to the east, eighteen leagues distant from this, to which I at once gave the name La Española. And I proceeded thither, and followed the northern coast, as with La Juana, eastwardly for a hundred and eighty-eight great leagues in a direct easterly course, as with La Juana. The which, and all the others, are most fertile to an excessive degree, and this extremely so. In it, there are many havens on the sea-coast, incomparable with any others that I know in Christendom, and plenty of rivers so good and great that it is a marvel. The lands thereof are high, and in it are very many ranges of hills, and most lofty mountains incomparably beyond the island of Tenerife, all most beautiful in a thousand shapes, and all accessible, and full of trees of a thousand kinds, so lofty that they seem to reach the sky. And I am assured that they never lose their foliage; as may be imagined, since I saw them as green and as beautiful as they are in Spain during May. And some of them were in flower, some in fruit, some in another stage according to their kind. And the nightingale was singing, and other birds of a thousand sorts, in the month of November, there where I was going. There are palm-trees of six or eight species, wondrous to see for their beautiful variety; but so are the other trees, and fruits, and plants therein. There are wonderful pine-groves, and very large plains of verdure, and there is honey, and many kinds of birds, and many various fruits. In the earth there are many mines of metals; and there is a population of incalculable number. Española is a marvel; the mountains and hills, and plains, and fields, and the soil, so beautiful and rich for planting and sowing, for breeding cattle of all sorts, for building of towns and villages. There could be no believing, without seeing, such harbors as are here, as well as the many and great rivers, and excellent waters, most of which contain gold. In the trees and fruits and plants, there are great diversities from those of Juana. In this, there are many spiceries, and great mines of gold and other metals. The people of this island, and of all the others that I have found and seen, or not seen, all go naked, men and women, just as their mothers bring them forth; although some women cover a single place with the leaf of a plant, or a cotton something which they make for that purpose. They have no iron or steel, nor any weapons; nor are they fit thereunto; not because they be not a well-formed people and of fair stature, but that they are most wondrously timorous. They have no other weapons than the stems of reeds in their seeding state, on the end of which they fix little sharpened stakes. Even these, they dare not use; for many times has it happened that I sent two or three men ashore to some village to parley, and countless numbers of them sallied forth, but as soon as they saw those approach, they fled away in such wise that even a father would not wait for his son. And this was not because any hurt had ever been done to any of them:—on the contrary, at every headland where I have gone and been able to hold speech with them, I gave them of everything which I had, as well cloth as many other things, without accepting aught therefore;—but such they are, incurably timid. It is true that since they have become more assured, and are losing that terror, they are artless and generous with what they have, to such a degree as no one would believe but him who had seen it. Of anything they have, if it be asked for, they never say no, but do rather invite the person to accept it, and show as much lovingness as though they would give their hearts. And whether it be a thing of value, or one of little worth, they are straightway content with whatsoever trifle of whatsoever kind may be given them in return for it. I forbade that anything so worthless as fragments of broken platters, and pieces of broken glass, and strap buckles, should be given them; although when they were able to get such things, they seemed to think they had the best jewel in the world, for it was the hap of a sailor to get, in exchange for a strap, gold to the weight of two and a half castellanos, and others much more for other things of far less value; while for new blancas they gave everything they had, even though it were [the worth of] two or three gold castellanos, or one or two arrobas of spun cotton. They took even pieces of broken barrel-hoops, and gave whatever they had, like senseless brutes; insomuch that it seemed to me bad. I forbade it, and I gave gratuitously a thousand useful things that I carried, in order that they may conceive affection, and furthermore may become Christians; for they are inclined to the love and service of their Highnesses and of all the Castilian nation, and they strive to combine in giving us things which they have in abundance, and of which we are in need. And they knew no sect, nor idolatry; save that they all believe that power and goodness are in the sky, and they believed very firmly that I, with these ships and crews, came from the sky; and in such opinion, they received me at every place where I landed, after they had lost their terror. And this comes not because they are ignorant: on the contrary, they are men of very subtle wit, who navigate all those seas, and who give a marvelously good account of everything, but because they never saw men wearing clothes nor the like of our ships. And as soon as I arrived in the Indies, in the first island that I found, I took some of them by force, to the intent that they should learn [our speech] and give me information of what there was in those parts. And so it was, that very soon they understood [us] and we them, what by speech or what by signs; and those [Indians] have been of much service. To this day I carry them [with me] who are still of the opinion that I come from Heaven [as appears] from much conversation which they have had with me. And they were the first to proclaim it wherever I arrived; and the others went running from house to house and to the neighboring villages, with loud cries of "Come! come to see the people from Heaven!" Then, as soon as their minds were reassured about us, every one came, men as well as women, so that there remained none behind, big or little; and they all brought something to eat and drink, which they gave with wondrous lovingness. They have in all the islands very many *canoas*, after the manner of rowing-galleys, some larger, some smaller; and a good many are larger than a galley of eighteen benches. They are not so wide, because they are made of a single log of timber, but a galley could not keep up with them in rowing, for their motion is a thing beyond belief. And with these, they navigate through all those islands, which are numberless, and ply their traffic. I have seen some of those *canoas* with seventy and eighty men in them, each one with his oar. In all those islands, I saw not much diversity in the looks of the people, nor in their manners and language; but they all understand each other, which is a thing of singular advantage for what I hope their Highnesses will decide upon for converting them to our holy faith, unto which they are well disposed. I have already told how I had gone a hundred and seven leagues, in a straight line from West to East, along the sea-coast of the Island of Juana; according to which itinerary, I can declare that that island is larger than England and Scotland combined; as, over and above those hundred and seven leagues, there remain for me, on the western side, two provinces whereto I did not go—one of which they call Avan, where the people are born with tails—which provinces cannot be less in length than fifty or sixty leagues, according to what may be understood from the Indians with me, who know all the islands. This other, Española, has a greater circumference than the whole of Spain from Col[ibre in Catal]unya, by the sea-coast, as far as Fuente Ravia in Biscay; since, along one of its four sides, I went for a hundred and eighty-eight great leagues in a straight line from west to east. This is [a land] to be desired,—and once seen, never to be relinquished—in which (although, indeed, I have taken possession of them all for their Highnesses, and all are more richly endowed than I have skill and power to say, and I hold them all in the name of their Highnesses who can dispose thereof as much and as completely as of the kingdoms of Castile) in this Española, in the place most suitable and best for its proximity to the gold mines, and for traffic with the mainland both on this side and with that over there belonging to the Great Can, where there will be great commerce and profit, I took possession of a large town which I named the city of Navidad. And I have made fortification there, and a fort (which by this time will have been completely finished) and I have left therein men enough for such a purpose, with arms and artillery, and provisions for more than a year, and a boat, and a [man who is] master of all seacraft for making others; and great friendship with the king of that land, to such a degree that he prided himself on calling and holding me as his brother. And even though his mind might change towards attacking those men, neither he nor his people know what arms are, and go naked. As I have already said, they are the most timorous creatures there are in the world, so that the men who remain there are alone sufficient to destroy all that land, and the island is without personal danger for them if they know how to behave themselves. It seems to me that in all those islands, the men are all content with a single wife; and to their chief or king they give as many as twenty. The women, it appears to me, do more work than the men. Nor have I been able to learn whether they held personal property, for it seemed to me that whatever one had, they all took share of, especially of eatable things. Down to the present, I have not found in those islands any monstrous men, as many expected, but on the contrary all the people are very comely; nor are they black like those in Guinea, but have flowing hair; and they are not begotten where there is an excessive violence of the rays of the sun. It is true that the sun is there very strong, although it is twenty-six degrees distant from the equinoctial line. In those islands, where there are lofty mountains, the cold was very keen there, this winter; but they endure it by being accustomed thereto, and by the help of the meats which they eat with many and inordinately hot spices. Thus I have not found, nor had any information of monsters, except of an island which is here the second in the approach to the Indies, which is inhabited by a people whom, in all the islands, they regard as very ferocious, who eat human flesh. These have many canoes with which they run through all the islands of India, and plunder and take as much as they can. They are no more ill-shaped than the others, but have the custom of wearing their hair long, like women; and they use bows and arrows of the same reed stems, with a point of wood at the top, for lack of iron which they have not. Among those other tribes who are excessively cowardly, these are ferocious; but I hold them as nothing more than the others. These are they who have to do with the women of Matinino—which is the first island that is encountered in the passage from Spain to the Indies—in which there are no men. Those women practise no female usages, but have bows and arrows of reed such as above mentioned; and they arm and cover themselves with plates of copper of which they have much. In another island, which they assure me is larger than Española, the people have no hair. In this there is incalculable gold; and concerning these and the rest I bring Indians with me as witnesses. And in conclusion, to speak only of what has been done in this voyage, which has been so hastily performed, their Highnesses may see that I shall give them as much gold as they may need, with very little aid which their Highnesses will give me; spices and cotton at once, as much as their Highnesses will order to be shipped, and as much as they shall order to be shipped of mastic,—which till now has never been found except in Greece, in the island of Xio, and the Seignory sells it for what it likes; and aloe-wood as much as they shall order to be shipped; and slaves as many as they shall order to be shipped,—and these shall be from idolators. And I believe that I have discovered rhubarb and cinnamon, and I shall find that the men whom I am leaving there will have discovered a thousand other things of value; as I made no delay at any point, so long as the wind gave me an opportunity of sailing, except only in the town of Navidad till I had left things safely arranged and well established. And in truth I should have done much more if the ships had served me as well as might reasonably have been expected. This is enough; and [thanks to] Eternal God our Lord who gives to all those who walk His way, victory over things which seem impossible; and this was signally one such, for although men have talked or written of those lands, it was all by conjecture, without confirmation from eyesight, amounting only to this much that the hearers for the most part listened and judged that there was more fable in it than anything actual, however trifling. Since thus our Redeemer has given to our most illustrious King and Queen, and to their famous kingdoms, this victory in so high a matter, Christendom should have rejoicing therein and make great festivals, and give solemn thanks to the Holy Trinity for the great exaltation they shall have by the conversion of so many peoples to our holy faith; and next for the temporal benefit which will bring hither refreshment and profit, not only to Spain, but to all Christians. This briefly, in accordance with the facts. Dated, on the caravel, off the Canary Islands, the 15 February of the year 1493.

At your command,

THE ADMIRAL.

PERO VAZ DE CAMINHA

Vaz de Caminha (ca. 1468–ca. 1520) was a captain on the first Portuguese expedition to reach present-day Brazil, and his account is the first report of its land and people, a vibrant description of an almost unimaginably verdant landscape. Vaz de Caminha provides far more detail on the first encounter with the indigenous population than **Columbus** does in his report, turning from idealization to derision and back again. He praises the Indians' innocence, yet reads their inevitable suspicion of the newcomers as a sign that they are too primitive, too much like animals, to engage with them. The brief convivial interlude in which Indians and Portuguese share a dance ends abruptly when the Indians flee, Vaz de Caminha tells us, "like sparrows at a feeding-place." This ambivalence about how to categorize the Indians would haunt the Iberian colonizers, as scholars, churchmen, and government officials debated the extent of their humanity and their capacity for reason, which had serious implications for the legitimacy of the conquest and the exploitation of indigenous labor. Although Vaz de Caminha's vision of Europeans intermingled with the indigenous population has often been romanticized as an early harbinger of a Brazilian meltingpot, or as a sign that the Portuguese Empire was less violent than the Spanish, his letter reveals much of the same ambivalence and calculation as Columbus's account, even as it observes the New World from a less distanced perspective.

From Letter to King Manuel[1]

* * *

And afterwards the captain moved up along the river, which flows continuously even with the shore, and there an old man was waiting who carried in his hand the oar of an *almadia*.[2] When the captain reached him he spoke in our presence, without any one understanding him, nor did he understand us with reference to the things he was asked about, particularly gold, for we wished to know whether they had any in this land. This old man had his lip so bored that a large thumb could be thrust through the hole, and in the opening he carried a worthless green stone which closed it on the outside. And the captain made him take it out; and I do not know what devil spoke to him, but he went with it to put it in the captain's mouth. We laughed a little at this and then the captain got angry and left him; and one of our men gave him an old hat for the stone, not because it was worth anything but to show. And afterwards the captain got it, I believe to send it with the other things to Your Highness. We went along there looking at the river, which has much and very good water. Along it are many palms, not very high, in which there are many good sprouts. We gathered and ate many of them. Then the captain turned towards the mouth of the river where we had disembarked, and on the other side of the river were many of

---

1. Translated by William Brooks Greenlee.　　2. A bark canoe.

them, dancing and diverting themselves before one another, without taking each other by the hand, and they did it well. Then Diogo Dias, who was revenue officer of Sacavem,[3] crossed the river. He is an agreeable and pleasure-loving man, and he took with him one of our bagpipe players and his bagpipe, and began to dance among them, taking them by the hands, and they were delighted and laughed and accompanied him very well to the sound of the pipe. After they had danced he went along the level ground, making many light turns and a remarkable leap which astonished them, and they laughed and enjoyed themselves greatly. And although he reassured and flattered them a great deal with this, they soon became skittish like wild animals and went away upstream. And then the captain crossed over the river with all of us, and we went along the shore, the boats going along close to land, and we came to a large lake of sweet water which is near the seashore, because all that shore is marshy above and the water flows out in many places. And after we had crossed the river some seven or eight of the natives joined our sailors who were retiring to the boats. And they took from there a shark which Bartolomeu Dias killed and brought to them and threw on the shore. It suffices to say that up to this time, although they were somewhat tamed, a moment afterwards they became frightened like sparrows at a feeding-place. And no one dared to speak strongly to them for fear they might be more frightened; and everything was done to their liking in order to tame them thoroughly. To the old man with whom the captain spoke he gave a red cap; and in spite of all the talking that he did with him, and the cap which he gave him, as soon as he left and began to cross the river, he immediately became more cautious and would not return again to this side of it. The other two whom the captain had on the ships, and to whom he gave what has already been mentioned, did not appear again, from which I infer that they are bestial people and of very little knowledge; and for this reason they are so timid. Yet withal they are well cared for and very clean, and in this it seems to me that they are rather like birds or wild animals, to which the air gives better feathers and better hair than to tame ones. And their bodies are so clean and so fat and so beautiful that they could not be more so; and this causes me to presume that they have no houses or dwellings in which to gather, and the air in which they are brought up makes them so. Nor indeed have we up to this time seen any houses or anything which looks like them. The captain ordered the convict Affonso Ribeiro[4] to go with them again, which he did. And he went there a good distance, and in the afternoon he returned, for they had made him come and were not willing to keep him there; and they had given him bows and arrows and had not taken from him anything which was his. On the contrary, he said, one of them had taken from him some yellow beads which he was wearing and fled with them; and he complained and the others at once went after him and returned to give them back to him. And then they ordered him to go back. He said that he had not seen there among them anything but some thatched huts of green branches, and made very large, like those of Entre Doiro e Minho.[5] And thus we returned to the ships to sleep when it was already almost night.

---

3. City northeast of Lisbon, in Portugal. "Diogo Dias": brother of Bartolomeu Dias, and commander of one of the caravels on the expedition.

4. A young convict who was a servant on the expedition.

5. Northernmost province of Portugal and Caminha's homeland.

HERNÁN CORTÉS

The heroism and brutality of conquest are the main themes in the life of Hernán Cortés (1485–1547). As he encountered in the Aztec Empire the untold riches that had eluded Christopher Columbus in the Caribbean, Cortés was forced to negotiate a formidable and sophisticated enemy that he barely understood. Yet he proved remarkably astute at harnessing local discontent with Aztec rule, establishing alliances with native peoples who also served as interpreters and spies. Despite the evasiveness of the Aztec ruler Moctezuma, Cortés and his men took him prisoner, and he died while in their custody. After many setbacks and the destruction of Tenochtitlán, chief city of the Aztecs, Cortés succeeded in his conquest—an astonishing achievement given the slender resources with which he faced the massive and well-organized Aztec Empire.

Cortés had disobeyed his superiors' explicit orders in pressing on to the land he would name New Spain. His letters to the Spanish ruler Charles V must therefore make the case that his spectacular achievements far outweighed his transgressions. Cortés foregrounds his heroic role as wise military leader, conveying the magnificence of the defeated empire while carefully justifying his own violent acts. "The manner of living among the people is very similar to that in Spain," he states, recognizing the sophistication of Aztec civilization even as he destroys it. Religion plays an important role in Cortés's effort to justify his military actions and the authority he had already claimed for himself in Mexico. Emphasizing his own efforts to convert the Aztecs to Christianity, he suggests to both Moctezuma and to Charles V that the Aztecs met their downfall because they refused to give up their devotion to their local gods. In Cortés's account, certain religious and sexual practices (human sacrifice and sodomy) of the Aztecs become mandates for the conquest. Finally, the Aztecs' belief that the Spanish conquerors were ancestral gods returning to claim their vassals is ably harnessed by Cortés: although he neither accepts nor denies the identification, it serves him as proof of Aztec idolatry and as sanction for the Spanish conquest of Mexico.

From The Second Letter[1]

On the following day I set out again and after half a mile entered upon a causeway which crosses the middle of the lake arriving finally at the great city of Tenochtitlán[2] which is situated at its center. This causeway was as broad as two lances and very stoutly made such that eight horsemen could ride along it abreast, and in these two leagues either on the one hand or the other we met with three cities all containing very fine buildings and towers, especially the houses of the chief men and the mosques and little temples in which they keep

1. Translated by J. Bayard Morris.
2. The capital of the Aztec Empire, site of present-day Mexico City.

their idols. In these towns there is quite a brisk trade in salt which they make from the water of the lake and what is cast up on the land that borders it; this they cook in a certain manner and make the salt into cakes which they sell to the inhabitants and neighboring tribes. I accordingly proceeded along this causeway and half a league from the city of Tenochtitlán itself, at the point where another causeway from the mainland joins it, I came upon an extremely powerful fort with two towers, surrounded by a six foot wall with a battlement running round the whole of the side abutting on the two causeways, and having two gates and no more for going in and out. Here nearly a thousand of the chief citizens came out to greet me, all dressed alike and, as their custom is, very richly; on coming to speak with me each performed a ceremony very common among them, to wit, placing his hand on the ground and then kissing it, so that for nearly an hour I stood while they performed this ceremony. Now quite close to the city there is a wooden bridge some ten paces broad, which cuts the causeway and under which the water can flow freely, for its level in the two parts of the lake is constantly changing: moreover it serves as a fortification to the city, for they can remove certain very long and heavy beams which form the bridge whenever they so desire; and there are many such bridges throughout the city as your Majesty will see from that which I shall presently relate.

When we had passed this bridge Moctezuma himself came out to meet us with some two hundred nobles, all barefoot and dressed in some kind of uniform also very rich, in fact more so than the others. They came forward in two long lines keeping close to the walls of the street, which is very broad and fine and so straight that one can see from one end of it to the other, though it is some two-thirds of a league in length and lined on both sides with very beautiful, large houses, both private dwellings and temples. Moctezuma himself was borne along in the middle of the street with two lords one on his right hand and one on his left. * * * All three were dressed in similar fashion except that Moctezuma wore shoes whereas the others were barefoot. The two lords bore him along each by an arm, and as he drew near I dismounted and advanced alone to embrace, but the two lords prevented me from touching him, and they themselves made me the same obeisance as did their comrades, kissing the earth. * * * After he had spoken to me all the other lords who were in the two long lines came up likewise in order one after the other, and then re-formed in line again. And while speaking to Moctezuma I took off a necklace of pearls which I was wearing and threw it round his neck; whereupon having proceeded some little way up the street a servant of his came back to me with two necklaces wrapped up in a napkin, made from the shells of sea snails, which are much prized by them; and from each necklace hung eight prawns fashioned very beautifully in gold some six inches in length. The messenger who brought them put them round my neck and we then continued up the street in the manner described until we came to a large and very handsome house which Moctezuma had prepared for our lodging. There he took me by the hand and led me to a large room opposite the patio by which we had entered, and seating me on a daïs very richly worked, for it was intended for royal use, he bade me await him there, and took his departure. After a short time, when all my company had found lodging, he returned with many various ornaments of gold, silver and featherwork, and some five or six thousand cotton clothes, richly dyed and embroidered in various ways, and having made me a present of them he seated himself on another low bench which was placed next to mine, and addressed me in this manner:

"Long time have we been informed by the writings of our ancestors that neither myself nor any of those who inhabit this land are natives of it, but rather strangers who have come to it from foreign parts. We likewise know that from those parts our nation was led by a certain lord (to whom all were subject), and who then went back to his native land, where he remained so long delaying his return that at his coming those whom he had left had married the women of the land and had many children by them and had built themselves cities in which they lived, so that they would in no wise return to their own land nor acknowledge him as lord; upon which he left them. And we have always believed that among his descendants one would surely come to subject this land and us as rightful vassals. Now seeing the regions from which you say you come, which is from where the sun rises, and the news you tell of this great king and ruler who sent you hither, we believe and hold it certain that he is our natural lord: especially in that you say he has long had knowledge of us. Wherefore be certain that we will obey you and hold you as lord in place of that great lord of whom you speak, in which service there shall be neither slackness nor deceit: and throughout all the land, that is to say all that I rule, you may command anything you desire, and it shall be obeyed and done, and all that we have is at your will and pleasure. And since you are in your own land and house, rejoice and take your leisure from the fatigues of your journey and the battles you have fought; for I am well informed of all those that you have been forced to engage in on your way here from Potonchan, as also that the natives of Cempoal and Tlascala have told you many evil things of me; but believe no more than what you see with your own eyes, and especially not words from the lips of those who are my enemies, who were formerly my vassals and on your coming rebelled against me and said these things in order to find favor with you: I am aware, moreover, that they have told you that the walls of my houses were of gold as was the matting on my floors and other household articles, even that I was a god and claimed to be so, and other like matters. As for the houses, you see that they are of wood, stones and earth." Upon this he lifted his clothes showing me his body, and said: "and you see that I am of flesh and blood like yourself and everyone else, mortal and tangible."

Grasping with his hands his arms and other parts of his body, he continued: "You see plainly how they have lied. True I have a few articles of gold which have remained to me from my forefathers, and all that I have is yours at any time that you may desire it. I am now going to my palace where I live. Here you will be provided with all things necessary for you and your men, and let nothing be done amiss seeing that you are in your own house and land."

I replied to all that he said, satisfying him in those things which seemed expedient, especially in having him believe that your Majesty was he whom they had long expected, and with that he bade farewell. On his departure we were very well regaled with great store of chickens, bread, fruit, and other necessities, particularly household ones. And in this wise I continued six days very well provided with all that was necessary and visited by many of the principal men of the city.

I have already related, most catholic Lord, how at the time when I departed from the town of Vera Cruz in search of this ruler Moctezuma, I left in it a hundred and fifty men to finish the fortress which I had already begun: like-wise how that I had left many neighboring towns and strongholds under the dominion of your royal Majesty, and the natives very peaceably disposed and loyal subjects of your Majesty. Being in the city of Cholula I received letters from the officer whom I left in Vera Cruz, by which I learnt that Qualpopoca, the native ruler of Almería, had sent in messengers to say that he desired to become a vassal of your Majesty, the reason for his delay being that enemy country lay between him and Vera Cruz and he had been chary of passing through it, but that if four Spaniards would return to his land, the enemies through whose country they would have to pass would refrain from molesting them and he would come forthwith to make his submission. The officer, think-ing the message to have been sent in good faith, for many others had done the same, sent four Spaniards as requested. But Qualpopoca having once received them into his house ordered them to be killed . . . and two of them thus died.

* * *

Having passed six days, then, in the great city of Tenochtitlán, invincible Prince, and having seen something of its marvels, though little in comparison with what there was to be seen and examined, I considered it essential both from my observation of the city and the rest of the land that its ruler should be in my power and no longer entirely free; to the end that he might in nowise change his will and intent to serve your Majesty, more especially as we Span-iards are somewhat intolerant and stiff-necked, and should he get across with us he would be powerful enough to do us great damage, even to blot out all memory of us in the land; and in the second place, could I once get him in my power all the other provinces subject to him would come more promptly to the knowledge and service of your Majesty, as indeed afterward happened. I decided to capture him and place him in the lodging where I was, which was extremely strong.

* * *

But before beginning to relate the wonders of this city and people, their rights and government, I should perhaps for a better understanding say something of the state of Mexico itself which contains this city and the others of which I have spoken, and is the principal seat of Moctezuma. The province is roughly circular in shape and entirely surrounded by very lofty and rocky mountains, the level part in the middle being some seventy leagues[3] in circumference and containing two lakes which occupy it almost entirely, for canoes travel over fifty leagues in making a circuit of them. One of the lakes is of fresh water, the other and larger one of salt. A narrow but very lofty range of mountains cuts across the valley and divides the lakes almost completely save for the western end where they are joined by a narrow strait no wider than a sling's throw which runs between the mountains. Commerce is carried on between the two lakes and the cities on their banks by means of canoes, so that land traffic is avoided. Moreover, since the salt lake rises and falls with the tide sea water pours from it at high tide into the fresh water lake with the rapidity of a moun-tain torrent, and likewise at low tide flows back from the fresh to the salt.

---

3. Cortés's estimations of distance are approximate; a Spanish league is about three to four miles.

The great city of Tenochtitlán is built in the midst of this salt lake, and it is two leagues from the heart of the city to any point on the mainland. Four causeways lead to it, all made by hand and some twelve feet wide. The city itself is as large as Seville or Córdova. The principal streets are very broad and straight, the majority of them being of beaten earth, but a few and at least half the smaller thoroughfares are waterways along which they pass in their canoes. Moreover, even the principal streets have openings at regular distances so that the water can freely pass from one to another, and these openings which are very broad are spanned by great bridges of huge beams, very stoutly put together, so firm indeed that over many of them ten horsemen can ride at once. Seeing that if the natives intended any treachery against us they would have every opportunity from the way in which the city is built, for by removing the bridges from the entrances and exits they could leave us to die of hunger with no possibility of getting to the mainland, I immediately set to work as soon as we entered the city on the building of four brigs, and in a short space of time had them finished, so that we could ship three hundred men and the horses to the mainland whenever we so desired.

The city has many open squares in which markets are continuously held and the general business of buying and selling proceeds. One square in particular is twice as big as that of Salamanca and completely surrounded by arcades where there are daily more than sixty thousand folk buying and selling. Every kind of merchandise such as may be met with in every land is for sale there, whether of food and victuals, or ornaments of gold and silver, or lead, brass, copper, tin, precious stones, bones, shells, snails and feathers; limestone for building is likewise sold there, stone both rough and polished, bricks burnt and unburnt, wood of all kinds and in all stages of preparation. There is a street of game where they sell all manner of birds that are to be found in their country, including hens, partridges, quails, wild duck, fly-catchers, widgeon, turtle doves, pigeons, little birds in round nests made of grass, parrots, owls, eagles, vulcans, sparrow-hawks and kestrels; and of some of these birds of prey they sell the skins complete with feathers, head, bill and claws. They also sell rabbits, hares, deer and small dogs which they breed especially for eating. There is a street of herb-sellers where there are all manner of roots and medicinal plants that are found in the land. There are houses as it were of apothecaries where they sell medicines made from these herbs, both for drinking and for use as ointments and salves. There are barbers' shops where you may have your hair washed and cut. There are other shops where you may obtain food and drink. There are street porters such as we have in Spain to carry packages. There is a great quantity of wood, charcoal, braziers made of clay and mats of all sorts, some for beds and others more finely woven for seats, still others for furnishing halls and private apartments. All kinds of vegetables may be found there, in particular onions, leeks, garlic, cresses, watercress, borage, sorrel, artichokes, and golden thistles. There are many different sorts of fruits including cherries and plums very similar to those found in Spain. They sell honey obtained from bees, as also the honeycomb and that obtained from maize plants which are as sweet as sugar canes; they also obtain honey from plants which are known both here and in other parts as *maguey*,[4] which is preferable to grape juice; from

4. Mexican aloe.

maguey in addition they make both sugar and a kind of wine, which are sold in their markets. All kinds of cotton thread in various colors may be bought in skeins, very much in the same way as in the great silk exchange of Granada, except that the quantities are far less. They have colors for painting of as good quality as any in Spain, and of as pure shades as may be found anywhere. There are leathers of deer both skinned and in their natural state, and either bleached or dyed in various colors. A great deal of chinaware is sold of very good quality and including earthen jars of all sizes for holding liquids, pitchers, pots, tiles and an infinite variety of earthenware all made of very special clay and almost all decorated and painted in some way. Maize is sold both as grain and in the form of bread and is vastly superior both in the size of the ear and in taste to that of all the other islands or the mainland. Pasties made from game and fish pies may be seen on sale, and there are large quantities of fresh and salt water fish both in their natural state and cooked ready for eating. Eggs from fowls, geese and all the other birds I have described may be had, and likewise omelettes ready made. There is nothing to be found in all the land which is not sold in these markets, for over and above what I have mentioned there are so many and such various other things that on account of their very number and the fact that I do not know their names, I cannot now detail them. Each kind of merchandise is sold in its own particular street and no other kind may be sold there: this rule is very well enforced. All is sold by number and measure, but up till now no weighing by balance has been observed. A very fine building in the great square serves as a kind of audience chamber where ten or a dozen persons are always seated, as judges, who deliberate on all cases arising in the market and pass sentence on evildoers. In the square itself there are officials who continually walk among the people inspecting goods exposed for sale and the measures by which they are sold, and on certain occasions I have seen them destroy measures which were false.

There are a very large number of mosques or dwelling places for their idols throughout the various districts of this great city, all fine buildings, in the chief of which their priests live continuously, so that in addition to the actual temples containing idols there are sumptuous lodgings. These pagan priests are all dressed in black and go habitually with their hair uncut; they do not even comb it from the day they enter the order to that on which they leave. Chief men's sons, both nobles and distinguished citizens, enter these orders at the age of six or seven and only leave when they are of an age to marry, and this occurs more frequently to the first-born who will inherit their fathers' estates than to others. They are denied all access to women, and no woman is ever allowed to enter one of the religious houses. Certain foods they abstain from and more so at certain periods of the year than at others. Among these temples there is one chief one in particular whose size and magnificence no human tongue could describe. For it is so big that within the lofty wall which entirely circles it one could set a town of fifteen thousand inhabitants.

Immediately inside this wall and throughout its entire length are some admirable buildings containing large halls and corridors where the priests who live in this temple are housed. There are forty towers at the least, all of stout construction and very lofty, the largest of which has fifty steps leading up to its base: this chief one is indeed higher than the great church of Seville. The workmanship both in wood and stone could not be bettered anywhere, for all the stonework within the actual temples where they keep their idols is cut into ornamental borders of flowers, birds, fishes and the like, or trelliswork, and the woodwork is likewise all in relief highly decorated with monsters of very various device. The towers all serve as burying places for their nobles, and the little temples which they contain are all dedicated to a different idol to whom they pay their devotions.

There are three large halls in the great mosque where the principal idols are to be found, all of immense size and height and richly decorated with sculptured figures both in wood and stone, and within these halls are other smaller temples branching off from them and entered by doors so small that no daylight ever reaches them. Certain of the priests but not all are permitted to enter, and within are the great heads and figures of idols, although as I have said there are also many outside. The greatest of these idols and those in which they placed most faith and trust I ordered to be dragged from their places and flung down the stairs, which done I had the temples which they occupy cleansed for they were full of the blood of human victims who had been sacrificed, and placed in them the image of Our Lady and other saints, all of which made no small impression upon Moctezuma and the inhabitants. They at first remonstrated with me, for should it be known, they said, by the people of the country they would rise against me, believing as they did that to these idols were due all temporal goods, and that should they allow them to be ill used they would be wroth against them and would give them nothing, denying them the fruits of the earth, and thus the people would die of starvation. I instructed them by my interpreters how mistaken they were in putting their trust in idols made by their own hands from unclean things, and that they must know that there was but one God, Lord of all, Who created the sky, the earth and all things, Who made both them and ourselves, Who was without beginning and immortal, Whom alone they had to adore and to believe in, and not in any created thing whatsoever: I told them moreover all things else that I knew of touching this matter in order to lead them from their idolatry and bring them to the knowledge of Our Lord: and all, especially Moctezuma, replied that they had already told me that they were not natives of this land but had come to it long time since, and that therefore they were well prepared to believe that they had erred somewhat from the true faith during the long time since they had left their native land, and I as more lately come would know more surely the things that it was right for them to hold and believe than they themselves: and that hence if I would instruct them they would do whatever I declared to be best. Upon this Moctezuma and many of the chief men of the city went with me to remove the idols, cleanse the chapels, and place images of the saints therein, and all with cheerful faces. I forbade them moreover to make human sacrifice to the idols as was their wont, because besides being an abomination in the sight of God it is prohibited by your Majesty's laws which declare that he who kills shall be killed. From this time henceforth they departed from it, and during the whole time that I was in the city not a single living soul was known to be killed and sacrificed.

* * *

Finally, to avoid prolixity in telling all the wonders of this city, I will simply say that the manner of living among the people is very similar to that in Spain, and considering that this is a barbarous nation shut off from a knowledge of the true God or communication with enlightened nations, one may well marvel at the orderliness and good government which is everywhere maintained.

* * *

On the day of Saint John after having heard mass I entered the city about midday, seeing few people about, and certain doors at the crossroads and turnings taken down, which appeared to be a bad sign, although I considered that it was done out of fright for what had already occurred and that my entrance would serve to calm them. I went straight to the fortress and the great temple next to it in which my men had taken up their quarters, and where they received us with such joy as if we had given them back their lives which they counted already lost: and so we remained there very much at ease throughout the rest of that day and night, thinking that all disturbance had settled down. Next day after hearing mass I despatched a messenger to Vera Cruz giving them the good news that I had entered the city to find the Christians alive and the city now quiet. But in half an hour he returned all covered with bruises and wounds, crying that the whole populace of the city was advancing in war dress and all the bridges were raised. And immediately behind him came a multitude of people from all parts so that the streets and house-roofs were black with natives; all of whom came on with the most frightful yells and shouts it is possible to imagine.

The stones from their slings came down on us within the fortress as if they were raining from the sky; the arrows and darts fell so thickly that the walls and courtyards were full of them and one could hardly move without treading on them. I made sallies in one or two parts and they fought against us with tremendous fury; one of my officers led two hundred men out by another door and before he could retire they had killed four of them and wounded both him and many others. I myself and many of my men were also wounded. We killed but few of them for they were waiting for us on the other side of the bridges, and did us much damage from the flat housetops with stones: some of these flat roofs we gained possession of and burnt the houses. But there were so many and so strongly fortified, being held by such numbers of natives and all so well provided with stones and other missiles, that we were not numerous enough to take all of them nor to hold what we had taken, for they could attack us at their pleasure.

The fight went on so fiercely in the fortress itself that they succeeded in setting fire to it in many parts, and actually burnt a large portion, without our being able to stop the flames until at last we broke down a stretch of wall and thus prevented it from spreading further. Indeed, had it not been for the strong guard I placed there of musketeers, crossbowmen and guns they would have entered under our eyes without our being able to stop them. We continued thus fighting all day until night was well come, though even then the yelling and commotion did not cease. During the night I ordered the doorways which had suffered by the fire to be repaired and all other places of the fortress which seemed to me weak. I decided upon the squads that were to defend the various parts of the fortress on the morrow and also the one that was to sally out with me to attack the Indians outside: I also ordered the wounded to be looked to, who numbered more than eighty.

As soon as it was day the enemy began to attack us with greater fury even than the day before: they came on in such numbers that the gunners had no need to take aim but simply poured their shot into the mass. Yet in spite of the damage done by the guns, for there were three arquebuses[5] without counting muskets and crossbows, they made so little impression that their effect could hardly be perceived, for wherever a shot carried away ten or a dozen men, the gap closed up with others so that it seemed as if no damage had been done. Upon this, leaving such suitable guard as I could in the fortress I sallied out and got possession of a few houses, killing many of those who were defending them: but their numbers were so great that although we had done still greater damage it would have had but slight effect. Moreover, whereas we had to continue fighting all the day they could fight for several hours and then give way to others, for their forces were amply sufficient. They again wounded as many as fifty to seventy Spaniards that day, although no one was killed, and so we fought on till nightfall when we had to retire worn out to the fortress.

Seeing then the great damage that our enemies did us, and that they could wound and kill us almost unhurt themselves, we spent the whole of that night and next day in making three wooden engines, each one of which would protect twenty men when they had got inside it: the engines were covered with boards to protect the men from the stones which were thrown from the house-tops; and those chosen to go inside were crossbowmen and musketeers together with others provided with pickaxes, hoes and iron bars to burrow under the houses and tear down the barricades which they had erected in the streets. All the while these wooden affairs were being made fighting did not cease for a moment, in such wise that as we prepared to make a sally[6] out of the fortress they attempted to force an entrance, and it was as much as we could do to resist them. Moctezuma, who was still a prisoner together with his son and many other nobles who had been taken on our first entering the city, requested to be taken out on to the flat roof of the fortress, where he would speak to the leaders of the people and make them stop fighting. I ordered him to be brought forth and as he mounted a breast-work that extended beyond the fortress, wishing to speak to the people who were fighting there, a stone from one of their slings struck him on the head so severely that he died three days later: when this happened I ordered two of the other Indian prisoners to take out his dead body on their shields to the people, and I know not what became of it; save only this that the fighting did not cease but rather increased in intensity every day.

The day that Moctezuma was wounded they called out to me from the place where he had been struck down saying that some of the native captains wished to speak to me; and thither I went and spent much time talking with them, begging them to cease fighting against me, for they had no reason to do so, and should consider that I had always treated them very well. They replied that I should depart and abandon their land when they would immediately stop fighting; but otherwise they were of a mind to kill us, or die themselves to a man. This they said, as it appeared, in order to persuade me to leave the fortress, when they would fall upon us at their pleasure between the bridges as we left

5. A heavy but portable gun of the 15th century.

6. A rush made by the defense on an attacking army.

the city. I replied that they were not to think that I besought them for peace because I feared them in any way, but because I was grieved at the damage I was doing them and should have to do them, and in order not to destroy so fine a city: to which they still replied that they would not cease fighting until I should leave the city.

* * *

They forced their way almost to the inner towers and succeeded in taking the temple, the chief tower of which was quickly filled with as many as five hundred Indians, all seemingly of high rank. Forthwith they proceeded to carry up large stores of bread, water and other food, together with plentiful supplies of stones. Most of them, moreover, were armed with long lances with heads of flint broader but no whit less sharp than our own; and from their position they did great damage to my men within the fortress for they were very close. The Spaniards two or three times attacked this tower and attempted to mount it, but as it was very tall and steep, having more than a hundred steps, and those above were well provided with stones and arms and moreover protected to a certain extent since we had been unable to take the neighboring roofs, they were forced to descend every time they attempted, and suffered many casualties; whereupon the natives in other parts of the city were so encouraged as to rush on the fortress without any signs of fear. Seeing that if our enemies were allowed to hold the tower they would not only do us much damage but would encourage the rest, I sallied out from the fortress, though disabled in the left hand from a wound received in the first day's fighting. Tying my shield on to my arm, however, I made for the tower followed by certain others and we surrounded it entirely at its base; this was done with no great difficulty, although not without danger, since my men had to deal with the enemy who were rushing up on all sides to support their comrades. I myself with a few behind me began to mount the staircase of the tower. And although they defended themselves very furiously, so much so that three or four Spaniards were knocked spinning downstairs, nevertheless with the help of God and our Gracious Mother, to whose honor the building had been dedicated and crowned with her statue, we finally got up the tower, and fought with them on top so fiercely that they were forced to leap down on to certain flat roofs, between which and the tower there was a gap of about a yard. There were about three or four of these all about eighteen feet below the top of the tower. Some fell right to the ground and were either broken by the fall or dispatched by the Spaniards who were below. Those who escaped on to the flat roofs continued to fight with extreme bravery so that it was more than three hours before we finished with them, and then there was not a man left alive. And your Majesty may well believe that had not God broken their ranks twenty of them might have stopped a thousand men from mounting the tower. Nevertheless those who died fought very valiantly. When it was all over I set fire to this tower and the other towers of the temple, having already abandoned them and removed all the images of the saints which we had placed there.

They lost somewhat of their pride on our taking this stronghold from them; so much so that on all sides their attack slackened, on which I returned to the housetop and spoke to the captains with whom I had already held speech and who were somewhat dismayed by what they had seen. On their approach I bade them note that they could not help themselves, that each day we should do them great hurt and kill many of them; already we were burning and destroying their city and would have to continue so to do until nothing of it or of them remained. To which they replied that they plainly perceived this but were determined to die to a man, if need be, to finish with us. And they bade me observe that the streets, squares and rooftops were all packed full of people, and that they had reckoned that if twenty-five thousand of them were to die for every one of us yet we should perish sooner, for we were few and they were many; and they gave me to know that all the bridges in the streets had been removed, as was indeed the case excepting a single one. We had therefore no way of escape except by water. Moreover, they knew well that we had but slight store of food and drinking water so that we could not hold out long without dying of hunger, even if they should not kill us themselves. And in truth they were perfectly right: for had we no other foes than hunger and general shortness of provisions, we were like to die in a short time. Many other arguments were put forward each supporting his own position.

After nightfall I went out with a few Spaniards and taking them off their guard succeeded in capturing a whole street in which we burnt more than three hundred houses. So soon as the natives had rushed there I returned by another street where I likewise set fire to many houses, especially to certain ones with low flat roofs lying close to the fortress from which they had inflicted great damage upon us. What was done that night inspired them with great terror. * * *

THE FLORENTINE CODEX

Compiled over three decades (1547–79), the encyclopedic *Florentine Codex* represents the joint effort of the Franciscan missionary-ethnographer Bernardino de Sahagún and the knowledgeable Aztec elders and scribes who labored with him to produce a permanent record of Aztec culture. There had never been a document quite like this, and there have been few since. In view of its linguistic precision, its scope, and its objectivity, it can be considered the first work of modern anthropology. The name *Florentine Codex* is merely a latter-day scholar's designation for the most finished version of a corpus properly known as *General History of the Things of New Spain*. Several versions of the *History* have survived. But the manuscript now at the Laurentian Library in Florence, although it lacks some texts preserved in the so-called Madrid codices, is the copy that best deserves to be called complete.

Written in paired columns, with Nahuatl on the left and a Spanish paraphrase on the right, the Codex's twelve books begin with descriptions of the preconquest gods and ceremonies, followed by detailed expositions of native astronomy, botany, zoology, commerce, industry, medicine, time counting, prophecy, and other topics. The final book is devoted to a native history of the Spanish Conquest.

The excerpt reproduced here relates the initial Aztec encounter with the Spaniards: messengers relay the news of the strangers' extraordinary appearance and weapons to Moctezuma, as terror takes hold of the land. It shows **Cortés** taking advantage of native alliances and enmities, while the Indians also arguably take advantage of him, as when the Tlaxcallans use the Spaniards to destroy their enemies, the Cholulans, in an infamous massacre in a temple courtyard. The eventual meeting between Moctezuma and Cortés is described in all its magnificence, with the emperor receiving the conqueror as the embodiment of the prophecy that gods would return from the east. The text recognizes the important role played by the female interpreter Malintzin (known as Doña Marina or La Malinche to the Spaniards), who advised and guided Cortés.

From The Florentine Codex[1]

BOOK 12, THE CONQUEST OF MEXICO

What the messengers who had gone to see the boats told Moctezuma.

And when this was done, they thereupon reported to Moctezuma; so they told him how they had gone marveling, and they showed him what [the Spaniards'] food was like.

And when he had so heard what the messengers reported, he was terrified, he was astounded. And much did he marvel at their food.

Especially did it cause him to faint away when he heard how the gun, at [the Spaniards'] command, discharged [the shot]; how it resounded as if it thundered when it went off. It indeed bereft one of strength; it shut off one's ears. And when it discharged, something like a round pebble came forth from within. Fire went showering forth; sparks went blazing forth. And its smoke smelled very foul; it had a fetid odor which verily wounded the head. And when [the shot] struck a mountain, it was as if it were destroyed, dissolved. And a tree was pulverized; it was as if it vanished; it was as if someone blew it away.

All iron was their war array. In iron they clothed themselves. With iron they covered their heads. Iron were their swords. Iron were their crossbows. Iron were their shields. Iron were their lances.

And those which bore them upon their backs, their deer, were as tall as roof terraces.

And their bodies were everywhere covered; only their faces appeared. They were very white; they had chalky faces; they had yellow hair, though the hair of some was black. Long were their beards; they also were yellow. They were yellow-bearded. [The Negroes' hair] was kinky, it was curly.

And their food was like fasting food—very large, white; not heavy like [tortillas]; like maize stalks, good-tasting as if of maize stalk flour; a little sweet, a little honeyed. It was honeyed to eat; it was sweet to eat.

And their dogs were very large. They had ears folded over; great dragging jowls. They had fiery eyes—blazing eyes; they had yellow eyes—fiery yellow

1. Translated by Arthur J. O. Anderson and Charles E. Dibble.

eyes. They had thin flanks—flanks with ribs showing. They had gaunt stomachs. They were very tall. They were nervous; they went about panting, with tongues hanging. They were spotted like ocelots; they were varicolored.

And when Moctezuma so heard, he was much terrified. It was as if he fainted away. His heart saddened; his heart failed him.

* * *

How Moctezuma wept, and [how] the Mexicans wept, when they knew that the Spaniards were very powerful.

And Moctezuma loudly expressed his distress. He felt distress, he was terrified, he was astounded; he expressed his distress because of the city.

And indeed everyone was greatly terrified. There were terror, astonishment, expressions of distress, feelings of distress. There were consultations. There were formations of groups; there were assemblies of people. There was weeping—there was much weeping, there was weeping for others. There was only the hanging of heads, there was dejection. There were tearful greetings, there were tearful greetings given others. There was the encouragement of others; there was mutual encouragement. There was the smoothing of the hair; the hair of small boys was smoothed. Their fathers said: "Alas, O my beloved sons! How can what is about to come to pass have befallen you?" And their mothers said: "My beloved sons, how will you marvel at what is about to befall you?"

And it was told, declared, shown, announced, made known to Moctezuma, it was fixed in his heart, that a woman from among us people here brought them here; she interpreted for them. Her name was Marina.[2] Her home was Teticpac. There on the coast they had first come to take her.

And then at that time [this] began—that no more was there the placing of themselves at [the Spaniards'] feet. The emissaries, those who had interceded for them for everything, everywhere, that they might need, just went, turning their backs.

And at just this same time [the Spaniards] came enquiring about Moctezuma: "What sort [of man is he]? Is he perchance a youth? Is he perchance mature? Is he perchance already old? Is he perchance already advanced in years? Is he perchance an able old man? Is he perchance already an aged man? Is he perchance already white-headed?" And they answered the gods, the Spaniards: "He is a mature man, not fat but rather slender; thin—rather thin."

And when Moctezuma had thus heard that he was much enquired about, that he was much sought, [that] the gods wished to look upon his face, it was as if his heart was afflicted; he was afflicted. He would flee; he wished to flee; he needed to flee; he would take himself hence. He would hide himself; he needed to hide himself; he would hide himself—he wished to take refuge from the gods. And he was determining for himself in secret, he determined for himself in secret; he was imagining to himself, he imagined to himself; he was inventing, he invented; he thus was consulting within his heart, he consulted within his heart; he was saying to himself, he secretly said to himself that he would somewhere enter a cave. And of those whom he much unburdened himself to, confided in, held especially easy conversation with, some told what they knew; they said: "[Some] know where Mictlan is, and Tonatiuh ichan, and

2. The Spanish name for Malintzin.

Tlalocan, and Cincalco,[3] that one may be benefited. [Determine] in what place indeed is thy need."

And indeed he wished, he desired [to go] there to Cincalco. So was it well known; it was so rumored.

But this he could not do. He could not hide. He could not take refuge. No longer had he strength; no longer was there any use; no longer had he energy. No longer were verified, no longer could be accomplished the words of the soothsayers by which they had changed his mind, had misled him, had troubled him. Thus they were taking vengeance upon him when they were feigning to be wise in knowing [the way] there [to places] named.

[Moctezuma] only awaited [the Spaniards]; he made himself resolute; he put forth great effort; he quieted, he controlled his heart; he submitted himself entirely to whatsoever he was to see, at which he was to marvel.

* * *

How the Spaniards arrived in Tlaxcalla.

[The Tlaxcallans] went guiding them. They accompanied them there; they guided them there in order to go to leave them, to quarter them, in their palaces. They made very much of them. They gave them whatsoever they required; they attended to them. And then they gave them their maidens.

Then [the Spaniards] asked them: "Where is Mexico? What manner of place is it? Is it yet distant?"

[The Tlaxcallans] answered them: "It is by no means distant now; it may be reached in perhaps but three days. It is a very good place. And [the Mexicans] are very strong, very brave. They are conquerors; they go everywhere."

And the Tlaxcallans had formerly been at enmity with the Cholulans. There was regarding with rage, there was regarding with hatred; there was detesting. They were disgusted; they could have nothing to do with them. Wherefore they incited [the Spaniards] against them, so that they might harm them.

They said to them: "They are very wicked. They are our foes. The Cholulan is as strong as the Mexican. He is the Mexican's friend."

When the Spaniards had so heard, they then went to Cholula. The Tlaxcallans and the Cempoallans accompanied them. They went arrayed for war. When they went arriving, thereupon there was calling out, there was shouting [that] all the noblemen, the lords, those who led one, the brave warriors and the commoners should come. There was crowding into the temple courtyard. And when all had come together, then [the Spaniards and their allies] closed off each of the entrances—as many places as there was entrance.

There was thereupon the stabbing, the slaying, the beating of the people. The Cholulan had suspected nothing; neither with arrows nor with shields had he contended against the Spaniards. Just so were they treacherously slain, deceitfully slain, unknowingly slain. For in truth the Tlaxcallans had incited [the Spaniards] against them.[4]

And of all which had come to pass, they gave, told, related all the account to Moctezuma. And all the messengers who arrived here all departed; they just

3. Lands to the north, east, south, and west, respectively.
4. The Tlaxcallans, like the neighboring Cempoallans, were indigenous groups that allied with the Spaniards against the Aztecs, and used them in their own rivalries with other groups, in this case the Cholulans.

went fleeing. No longer did there remain listening anyone to hear the news which was to be heard. And indeed everyone among the commoners went about overwrought; often they rose in revolt. It was just as if the earth moved; just as if the earth rebelled; just as if all revolved before one's eyes. There was terror.

And when there had been death in Cholula,[5] then [the Spaniards] started forth in order already to come to Mexico. They came grouped, they came assembled, they came raising dust. Their iron lances, their halberds seemed to glisten, and their iron swords were wavy, like a water [course]. Their cuirasses, their helmets seemed to resound. And some came all in iron; they came turned into iron; they came gleaming. Hence they went causing great astonishment; hence they went causing great fear; hence they were regarded with fear; hence they were dreaded.

And their dogs came leading; they came preceding them. They kept coming at their head; they remained coming at their head. They came panting; their foam came dripping [from their mouths].

* * *

How Moctezuma sent emissaries to the Spaniards.

And Moctezuma thereupon sent [and] charged the noblemen, whom Tziuacpo-pocatzin led, and many others besides of his officials, to go to meet [Cortés] between Popocatepetl and Iztac tepetl, there in Quauhtechcac.[6] They gave them golden banners, precious feather streamers, and golden necklaces.

And when they had given them these, they appeared to smile; they were greatly contented, gladdened. As if they were monkeys they seized upon the gold. It was as if there their hearts were satisfied, brightened, calmed. For in truth they thirsted mightily for gold; they stuffed themselves with it; they starved for it; they lusted for it like pigs.

And they went about lifting on high the golden banners; they went moving them back and forth; they went taking them to themselves. It was as if they babbled. What they said was gibberish.

* * *

How Moctezuma went peacefully to meet the Spaniards.

And when this had happened, when [the Spaniards] had come to reach Xoloco,[7] when already matters were at this conclusion, had come to this point, there-upon Moctezuma arrayed himself, attired himself, in order to meet them, and also a number of great lords [and] princes, his ruling men, his noblemen [arrayed themselves]. Thereupon they went to meet them. In gourd supports they set out precious flowers—helianthus, talauma,[8] in the midst of which went standing popcorn flowers, yellow tobacco flowers, cacao blossoms, wreaths for the head, garlands of flowers. And they bore golden necklaces, necklaces with pendants, plaited neck bands.

---

5. The massacre at Cholula was one of the key events in the conquest of Mexico, and one of the most violent.

6. A nearby town. "Popocatepetl and Iztac tepetl": two peaks southeast of Tenochtitlán.

7. A locality on the outskirts of Tenochtitlán, to the south.

8. Mexican magnolia, a flower reserved for the nobility.

And already Moctezuma met them there in Uitzillan.[9] Thereupon he gave gifts to the commandant, the commander of soldiers; he gave him flowers, he bejeweled him with necklaces, he hung garlands about him, he covered him with flowers, he wreathed his head with flowers. Thereupon he had the golden necklaces laid before him—all the kinds of gifts of greeting, with which the meeting was concluded. On some he hung necklaces.

Then [Cortés] said to Moctezuma: "Is this not thou? Art thou not he? Art thou Moctezuma?"

Moctezuma replied: "Indeed yes; I am he."

Thereupon he arose; he arose to meet him face to face. He inclined his body deeply. He drew him close. He arose firmly.

Thus he besought him: he said to him: "O our lord, thou hast suffered fatigue, thou hast endured weariness. Thou hast come to arrive on earth. Thou hast come to govern thy city of Mexico; thou hast come to descend upon thy mat, upon thy seat, which for a moment I have watched for thee, which I have guarded for thee. For thy governors are departed—the rulers Itzcoatl, Moctezuma the Elder, Axayacatl, Tizoc, Auitzotl, who yet a very short time ago had come to stand guard for thee, who had come to govern the city of Mexico. Under their protection thy common folk came. Do they yet perchance know it in their absence? O that one of them might witness, might marvel at what to me now hath befallen, at what I see quite in the absence of our lords. I by no means merely dream, I do not merely see in a dream, I do not see in my sleep; I do not merely dream that I see thee, that I look into thy face. I have been afflicted for some time. I have gazed at the unknown place whence thou hast come—from among the clouds, from among the mists. And so this. The rulers departed maintaining that thou wouldst come to visit thy city, that thou wouldst come to descend upon thy mat, upon thy seat. And now it hath been fulfilled; thou hast come; thou hast endured fatigue, thou hast endured weariness. Peace be with thee. Rest thyself. Visit thy palace. Rest thy body. May peace be with our lords."

And when Moctezuma's address which he directed to the Marquis was ended, Marina then interpreted it, she translated it to him. And when the Marquis had heard Moctezuma's words, he spoke to Marina; he spoke to them in a barbarous tongue; he said in his barbarous tongue:

"Let Moctezuma put his heart at ease; let him not be frightened. We love him much. Now our hearts are indeed satisfied, for we know him, we hear him. For a long time we have wished to see him, to look upon his face. And this we have seen. Already we have come to his home in Mexico. At his leisure he will hear our words."

Thereupon [the Spaniards] grasped [Moctezuma] by the hand. Already they went leading him by it. They caressed him with their hands to make their love known to him.

And the Spaniards looked at him; they each looked at him thoroughly. They were continually active on their feet; they continually mounted, they continually dismounted in order to look at him.

And the rulers who had gone with him were, first, Cacamatzin, ruler of Texcoco; second, Tetlepanquetzatzin, ruler of Tlacopan; third, the *tlacochcalcatl*[1] Itzquauhtzin, ruler of Tlatilulco; fourth, Topantemoctzin, Moctezuma's

9. Cortés describes this as a large and beautiful building.

1. High general.

storekeeper in Tlatilulco. These went. And still other noblemen of Tenochtitlan were Atlixcatzin, the *tlacateccatl*; Tepeuatzin, the *tlacochcalcatl*; Quetzalaztatzin, the *tiçociauacatl*;[2] Totomotzin, Ecatenpatiltzin, Quappiatzin. When Moctezuma was made captive, they not only hid themselves, took refuge, [but] they abandoned him in anger.

> *How the Spaniards took Moctezuma with them when they went*
> *to enter the great palace, and what there happened.*

And when they had gone to arrive in the palace, when they had gone to enter it, at once they firmly seized Moctezuma. They continually kept him closely under observation; they never let him from their sight. With him was Itzquauhtzin. But the others just came forth [unimpeded].

And when this had come to pass, then each of the guns shot off. As if in confusion there was going off to one side, there was scattering from one's sight, a jumping in all directions. It was as if one had lost one's breath; it was as if for the time there was stupefaction, as if one were affected by mushrooms, as if something unknown were shown one. Fear prevailed. It was as if everyone had swallowed his heart. Even before it had grown dark, there was terror, there was astonishment, there was apprehension, there was a stunning of the people.

And when it dawned, thereupon were proclaimed all the things which [the Spaniards] required: white tortillas, roasted turkey hens, eggs, fresh water, wood, firewood, charcoal, earthen bowls, polished vessels, water jars, large water pitchers, cooking vessels, all manner of clay articles. This had Moctezuma indeed commanded.

But when he summoned forth the noblemen, no longer did they obey him. They only grew angry. No longer did they come to him, no longer did they go to him. No longer was he heeded. But nevertheless he was not therefore neglected; he was given all that he required—food, drink, and water [and] fodder for the deer.

And when [the Spaniards] were well settled, they thereupon inquired of Moctezuma as to all the city's treasure—the devices, the shields. Much did they importune him; with great zeal they sought gold. And Moctezuma thereupon went leading the Spaniards. They went surrounding him, scattered about him; he went among them, he went in their lead; they went each holding him, each grasping him. And when they reached the storehouse, a place called Teocalco, thereupon were brought forth all the brilliant things; the quetzal feather head fan, the devices, the shields, the golden discs, the devils' necklaces, the golden nose crescents, the golden leg bands, the golden arm bands, the golden forehead bands.

Thereupon was detached the gold which was on the shields and which was on all the devices. And as all the gold was detached, at once they ignited, set fire to, applied fire to all the various precious things [which remained]. They all burned. And the gold the Spaniards formed into separate bars. And the green stone, as much as they saw to be good they took. But the rest of the green stone the Tlaxcallans just stole. And the Spaniards walked everywhere; they went everywhere taking to pieces the hiding places, storehouses, storage places. They took all, all that they saw which they saw to be good.

---

2. A great lord. "*Tlacateccatl*": general.

BARTOLOMÉ DE LAS CASAS

A Spanish priest and colonist, Bartolomé de las Casas (1484–1566) experienced first-hand the brutality of Spain's conquest of the New World and became a passionate and energetic defender of the rights of native populations. Although Las Casas had participated in the conquests of Hispaniola and Cuba, the violence he witnessed spurred him to spiritual conversion (he became the first priest ordained in the New World) and political activism. He used the resources of law, the Church, and the press to sway the Spanish Crown and public sentiment; most effective were his published accounts of the practices—including slavery, torture, and mass murder—used by the colonists to subjugate the Indians, including the explosive *Short Account of the Destruction of the Indies* (1552) from which this excerpt is taken. He worked especially hard to reform the *encomienda*, a system designed to offer legal protection, religious instruction, and a small wage to Indians placed in the care of a Spaniard, but which quickly devolved into highly abusive forced labor. Las Casas believed that the Indians should be brought to Christianity, yet he advocated a system of peaceable conversion that respected their humanity.

Las Casas's writings circulated widely through Europe—and especially the Protestant states—because they provided powerful anti-Spanish propaganda, yet none of Spain's imperial rivals underwent the same internal debates and political tussles over the legitimacy of the conquest. Although the conquest was almost unimaginably violent, it is highly debatable whether Spain was more cruel than other European nations in their own encounters with native populations. What is undeniable is that figures such as Las Casas forced Spain into a uniquely serious and consequential debate about whether the conquest was permissible.

From A Short Account of the Destruction of the Indies[1]

PROLOGUE

of Bishop Brother Bartolomé de las Casas, or Casaus, to the most high and most mighty Prince of Spain, our Lord the Prince Philip

Most high and most mighty Lord:

As Divine Providence has ordained that the world shall, for the benefit and proper government of the human race, be divided into kingdoms and peoples and that these shall be ruled by kings, who are (as Homer has it) fathers and shepherds to their people and are, accordingly, the noblest and most virtuous of beings, there is no doubt, nor could there in all reason be any such doubt, but that these kings entertain nothing save that which is morally unimpeachable. It

---

1. Translated by Nigel Griffin.

follows that if the commonwealth suffers from some defect, or shortcoming, or evil, the reason can only be that the ruler is unaware of it; once the matter is brought to his notice, he will work with the utmost diligence to set matters right and will not rest content until the evil has been eradicated. This would appear to be the sense of the words of Solomon in the Bible: "A king that sitteth in the throne of judgment scattereth away all evil with his eyes."[2] For, granted the innate and natural virtue of the ruler, it follows that the simple knowledge that something is wrong in his kingdom is quite sufficient to ensure that he will see that it is corrected, for he will not tolerate any such evil for a moment longer than it takes him to right it.

Contemplating, therefore (most mighty Lord), as a man with more than fifty years' experience of seeing at first hand the evil and the harm, the losses and diminutions suffered by those great kingdoms, each so vast and so wonderful that it would be more appropriate to refer to them as the New World of the Americas—kingdoms granted and entrusted by God and His Church to the Spanish Crown so that they might be properly ruled and governed, converted to the Faith, and tenderly nurtured to full material and spiritual prosperity[3]— I am persuaded that, if Your Highness had been informed of even a few of the excesses which this New World has witnessed, all of them surpassing anything that men hitherto have imagined even in their wildest dreams, Your Highness would not have delayed for even one moment before entreating His Majesty to prevent any repetition of the atrocities which go under the name of "conquests," excesses which, if no move is made to stop them, will be committed time and again, and which (given that the indigenous peoples of the region are naturally so gentle, so peace-loving, so humble and so docile) are of themselves iniquitous, tyrannical, contrary to natural, canon, and civil law, and are deemed wicked and are condemned and proscribed by all such legal codes. I therefore concluded that it would constitute a criminal neglect of my duty to remain silent about the enormous loss of life as well as the infinite number of human souls despatched to Hell in the course of such "conquests," and so resolved to publish an account of a few such outrages (and they can be only a few out of the countless number of such incidents that I could relate) in order to make that account the more accessible to Your Highness.

* * *

[PREFACE]

The Americas were discovered in 1492, and the first Christian settlements established by the Spanish the following year. It is accordingly forty-nine years now since Spaniards began arriving in numbers in this part of the world. They first settled the large and fertile island of Hispaniola,[4] which boasts six hundred leagues of coastline and is surrounded by a great many other large islands, all of them, as I saw for myself, with as high a native population as anywhere on earth. Of the coast of the mainland, which, at its nearest point, is a little

2. Proverbs 20.8.
3. Pope Alexander VI granted sovereignty over the Americas to Ferdinand and Isabella in 1493 and required the Spanish kings to convert the natives to Christianity.
4. Present-day Haiti and the Dominican Republic.

over two hundred and fifty leagues from Hispaniola, more than ten thousand leagues had been explored by 1541, and more are being discovered every day. This coastline, too, was swarming with people and it would seem, if we are to judge by those areas so far explored, that the Almighty selected this part of the world as home to the greater part of the human race.

God made all the peoples of this area, many and varied as they are, as open and as innocent as can be imagined. The simplest people in the world— unassuming, long-suffering, unassertive, and submissive—they are without malice or guile, and are utterly faithful and obedient both to their own native lords and to the Spaniards in whose service they now find themselves. Never quarrelsome or belligerent or boisterous, they harbor no grudges and do not seek to settle old scores; indeed, the notions of revenge, rancor, and hatred are quite foreign to them. At the same time, they are among the least robust of human beings: their delicate constitutions make them unable to withstand hard work or suffering and render them liable to succumb to almost any ill- ness, no matter how mild. Even the common people are no tougher than princes or than other Europeans born with a silver spoon in their mouths and who spend their lives shielded from the rigors of the outside world. They are also among the poorest people on the face of the earth; they own next to noth- ing and have no urge to acquire material possessions. As a result they are nei- ther ambitious nor greedy, and are totally uninterested in worldly power. Their diet is every bit as poor and as monotonous, in quantity and in kind, as that enjoyed by the Desert Fathers. Most of them go naked, save for a loincloth to cover their modesty; at best they may wrap themselves in a piece of cotton material a yard or two square. Most sleep on matting, although a few possess a kind of hanging net, known in the language of Hispaniola as a hammock. They are innocent and pure in mind and have a lively intelligence, all of which makes them particularly receptive to learning and understanding the truths of our Catholic faith and to being instructed in virtue; indeed, God has invested them with fewer impediments in this regard than any other people on earth. Once they begin to learn of the Christian faith they become so keen to know more, to receive the Sacraments, and to worship God, that the missionaries who instruct them do truly have to be men of exceptional patience and forbear- ance; and over the years I have time and again met Spanish laymen who have been so struck by the natural goodness that shines through these people that they frequently can be heard to exclaim: "These would be the most blessed people on earth if only they were given the chance to convert to Christianity."

It was upon these gentle lambs, imbued by the Creator with all the qualities we have mentioned, that from the very first day they clapped eyes on them the Spanish fell like ravening wolves upon the fold, or like tigers and savage lions who have not eaten meat for days. The pattern established at the outset has remained unchanged to this day, and the Spaniards still do nothing save tear the natives to shreds, murder them and inflict upon them untold misery, suffer- ing and distress, tormenting, harrying and persecuting them mercilessly. * * *

* * *

The reason the Christians have murdered on such a vast scale and killed any- one and everyone in their way is purely and simply greed. They have set out to line their pockets with gold and to amass private fortunes as quickly as possible so that they can then assume a status quite at odds with that into which they were born. Their insatiable greed and overweening ambition know no bounds; the land is fertile and rich, the inhabitants simple, forbearing, and submissive. The Spaniards have shown not the slightest consideration for these people, treating them (and I speak from first-hand experience, having been there from the outset) not as brute animals—indeed, I would to God they had done and had shown them the consideration they afford their animals—so much as piles of dung in the middle of the road. They have had as little concern for their souls as for their bodies, all the millions that have perished having gone to their deaths with no knowledge of God and without the benefit of the Sacraments. One fact in all this is widely known and beyond dispute, for even the tyrannical murderers themselves acknowledge the truth of it: the indigenous peoples never did the Europeans any harm whatever; on the contrary, they believed them to have descended from the heavens, at least until they or their fellow-citizens had tasted, at the hands of these oppressors, a diet of robbery, murder, violence, and all other manner of trials and tribulations.

HISPANIOLA

As we have said, the island of Hispaniola was the first to witness the arrival of Europeans and the first to suffer the wholesale slaughter of its people and the devastation and depopulation of the land. It all began with the Europeans taking native women and children both as servants and to satisfy their own base appetites; then, not content with what the local people offered them of their own free will (and all offered as much as they could spare), they started taking for themselves the food the natives contrived to produce by the sweat of their brows, which was in all honesty little enough. Since what a European will consume in a single day normally supports three native households of ten persons each for a whole month, and since the newcomers began to subject the locals to other vexations, assaults, and iniquities, the people began to realize that these men could not, in truth, have descended from the heavens. Some of them started to conceal what food they had, others decided to send their women and children into hiding, and yet others took to the hills to get away from the brutal and ruthless cruelty that was being inflicted on them. The Christians punched them, boxed their ears and flogged them in order to track down the local leaders, and the whole shameful process came to a head when one of the European commanders raped the wife of the paramount chief of the entire island. It was then that the locals began to think up ways of driving the Europeans out of their lands and to take up arms against them. Their weapons, however, were flimsy and ineffective both in attack and in defence (and, indeed, war in the Americas is no more deadly than our jousting, or than many European children's games) and, with their horses and swords and lances, the Spaniards easily fended them off, killing them and committing all kind of atrocities against them.

They forced their way into native settlements, slaughtering everyone they found there, including small children, old men, pregnant women, and even women who had just given birth. They hacked them to pieces, slicing open their bellies with their swords as though they were so many sheep herded into a pen. They even laid wagers on whether they could manage to slice a man in two at a stroke, or cut an individual's head from his body, or disembowel him with a single blow of their axes. They grabbed suckling infants by the feet and, ripping them from their mothers' breasts, dashed them head-long against the rocks. Others, laughing and joking all the while, threw them over their shoulders into a river, shouting: "Wriggle, you little perisher." They slaughtered anyone and everyone in their path, on occasion running through a mother and her baby with a single thrust of their swords. They spared no one, erecting especially wide gibbets on which they could string their victims up with their feet just off the ground and then burn them alive thirteen at a time, in honor of our Savior and the twelve Apostles, or tie dry straw to their bodies and set fire to it. Some they chose to keep alive and simply cut their wrists, leaving their hands dangling, saying to them: "Take this letter"—meaning that their sorry condition would act as a warning to those hiding in the hills. The way they normally dealt with the native leaders and nobles was to tie them to a kind of griddle consisting of sticks resting on pitchforks driven into the ground and then grill them over a slow fire, with the result that they howled in agony and despair as they died a lingering death.

* * *

After the fighting was over and all the men had been killed, the surviving natives—usually, that is, the young boys, the women, and the children—were shared out between the victors. One got thirty, another forty, a third as many as a hundred or even twice that number; everything depended on how far one was in the good books of the despot who went by the title of governor. The pretext under which the victims were parceled out in this way was that their new masters would then be in a position to teach them the truths of the Christian faith; and thus it came about that a host of cruel, grasping and wicked men, almost all of them pig-ignorant, were put in charge of these poor souls. And they discharged this duty by sending the men down the mines, where working conditions were appalling, to dig for gold, and putting the women to labor in the fields and on their master's estates, to till the soil and raise the crops, properly a task only for the toughest and strongest of men. Both women and men were given only wild grasses to eat and other unnutritious foodstuffs. The mothers of young children promptly saw their milk dry up and their babies die; and, with the women and the men separated and never seeing each other, no new children were born. The men died down the mines from overwork and starvation, and the same was true of the women who perished out on the estates. The islanders, previously so numerous, began to die out as would any nation subjected to such appalling treatment. For example, they were made to carry burdens of three and four *arrobas*[5] for distances of up to a hundred or even two hundred leagues, and were forced to carry their Christian masters in hammocks, which are like nets slung from the shoulders of the bearers. In short, they were treated as beasts of burden and developed huge sores on their shoulders and backs as happens with animals made to carry excessive loads. And this is not to mention the floggings, beatings, thrashings, punches, curses and countless other vexations and cruelties to which they were routinely subjected and to which no chronicle could ever do justice nor any reader respond save with horror and disbelief.

5. A unit of weight about 25 pounds.

It is of note that all these island territories began to go to the dogs once news arrived of the death of our most gracious Queen Isabella, who departed this life in 1504. Up to then, only a small number of provinces had been destroyed through unjust military action, not the whole area, and news of even this partial destruction had by and large been kept from the queen, because, she—may her soul rest in peace—took a close personal interest in the physical and spiritual welfare of the native peoples, as those of us who lived through those years and saw examples of it with our own eyes can attest. There is one other general rule in all this, and it is that, wherever the Spaniards set foot, right throughout the Americas, they subjected the native inhabitants to the cruelties of which we have spoken, killing these poor and innocent people, tyrannizing them, and oppressing them in the most abominable fashion. The longer they spent in the region the more ingenious were the torments, each crueler than the last, that they inflicted on their victims, as God finally abandoned them and left them to plummet headlong into a life of full-time crime and wickedness.

JEAN DE LÉRY

Jean de Léry's *History of a Voyage to the Land of Brazil*, his account of a year among the Tupinamba Indians, is a marvel of early modern ethnography, with unprecedented detail presented in a remarkably sympathetic tone. Léry's life (1534–1613) was shaped by the violent conflicts over religion that swept across Europe and divided France, and his narrative connects the experience of the New World with the upheavals of the Reformation. In 1554, Léry sailed on the first Protestant mission to the New World, landing where Rio de Janeiro stands today. Both the French and the Portuguese, who had established an earlier claim to Brazil, interacted with the Tupinamba Indians of the coast, but the French seem to have maintained friendlier relations with them as traders and guests. Some even moved into their villages and adopted their ways, becoming invaluable liaisons for the missionaries.

Upon his return to France, Léry found a nation torn apart by religious differences. Partly because of the violence of the times, his account of Brazil was not written until years later, after he had experienced the persecution of Huguenots amid scenes of unimaginable cruelty. The violence that Léry witnessed among his compatriots profoundly marked his sense of what constituted savagery and civilization, and gave his subsequent description of the Tupinamba a strikingly detached, even-handed tone. Léry watches closely, reports in detail, yet recognizes the limits of his own knowledge. He acknowledges his interpreter—perhaps one of the Frenchmen who had gone to live with the Tupinamba—and shows the reader how experience changes his initial impressions. This constant recalibration, as Léry keeps himself and his reader from jumping to conclusions, makes *History of a*

Voyage a fascinating example of the skeptical relativism that reaches its greatest incarnation in **Montaigne's** *Essays*. Montaigne's famous "**Of Cannibals**" was based in part on his reading of Léry.

From History of a Voyage to the Land of Brazil[1]

Law and Civil Order among the Savages

As for the civil order of our savages, it is an incredible thing—a thing that cannot be said without shame to those who have both divine and human laws—how a people guided solely by their nature, even corrupted as it is, can live and deal with each other in such peace and tranquillity. (I mean, however, each nation within itself, or among allied nations: as for enemies, you have seen in another chapter how harshly they are treated.) Nevertheless, if it happens that some of them quarrel (which occurs so rarely that during almost a year I was with them I only saw them fight with each other twice), by no means do the others try to separate them or make peace; on the contrary, even when the adversaries are on the point of putting each others' eyes out, they let them go ahead without saying a word to prevent them. However, if anyone is wounded by his neighbor, and if he who struck the blow is apprehended, he will receive a similar blow in the same part of his body by the kinsmen of the one injured. If the wounds of the latter prove to be mortal, or if he is killed on the spot, the relatives of the dead man will take the life of the killer in the same way. In short, it is a life for a life, an eye for an eye, a tooth for a tooth, and so forth; but as I have said, this is very rarely seen among them.

The real property of this people consists of houses and of many more excellent pieces of land than they need for their subsistence. In a given village of five or six hundred people, while several families may live in the same house, nevertheless each has its own place, and the husband keeps his wife and children separate; however, there is nothing to keep you from seeing down the full length of these buildings, which are usually more than sixty feet long.

It is a curious fact worth noting that the Brazilians, who usually stay only five or six months in a place, carry with them the big pieces of wood and tall *pindo* plants, with which their houses are made and covered; thus they often move their very villages from place to place. These, however, still retain their former names, so that we have sometimes found villages at a quarter- or half-league's distance from the location where we had visited them before. Their dwellings being so easily transported, you can imagine that they have no great palaces (such as those attributed to the Peruvian Indians, whose wooden houses are so well built that there are rooms one hundred fifty feet long and eighty feet wide); and no one of the Tupinamba nation ever begins a dwelling or any other building that he will not see built and rebuilt twenty times in his life, if he lives to the age of manhood. If you ask them why they move their

1. Translated by Janet Whatley.

household so often, they simply answer that the change of air keeps them healthier, and that if they did other than what their grandfathers did, they would die immediately.

* * *

Although the Tupinamba receive very humanely the friendly strangers who go to visit them, nevertheless the Frenchmen and others from over here who do not understand their language find themselves at first marvelously disconcerted in their midst. The first time that I myself frequented them was three weeks after we arrived at Villegagnon's island,[2] when an interpreter took me along to four or five villages on the mainland. The first one—called *Yabouraci* in the native language and "Pepin" by the French (because of a ship that loaded there once, whose master had that name)—was only two leagues from our fort. When we arrived there, I immediately found myself surrounded by savages, who were asking me "*Marapé-derere, marapé derere?*" meaning "What is your name? What is your name?" (which at that time I understood no better than High German). One of them took my hat, which he put on his head; another my sword and my belt, which he put around his naked body; yet another my tunic, which he donned. Deafening me with their yells, they ran through the village with my clothing. Not only did I think that I had lost everything, but I didn't know what would become of me. As experience has shown me several times since, that was only from ignorance of their way of doing things; for they do the same thing to everyone who visits them, and especially those they haven't seen before. After they have played around a little with one's belongings, they carry them all back and return them to their owners.

The interpreter had warned me that they wanted above all to know my name; but if I had said to them Pierre, Guillaume, or Jean, they would have been able neither to retain it nor to pronounce it (in fact, instead of saying "Jean," they would say "Nian"). So I had to accommodate by naming something that was known to them. Since by a lucky chance my surname, "Léry," means "oyster" in their language, I told them that my name was "*Léry-oussou*," that is, a big oyster. This pleased them greatly; with their "*Teh!*" of admiration, they began to laugh, and said, "That is a fine name; we have not yet seen any *Mair* (that is, a Frenchman) of that name." And indeed, I can say with assurance that never did Circe metamorphose a man into such a fine oyster, nor into one who could converse so well with Ulysses, as since then I have been able to do with our savages.[3]

One must note that their memory is so good that as soon as someone has told them his name, if they were to go a hundred years (so to speak) without seeing him, they will never forget it. Presently I will tell about the other ceremonies they observe when they receive friends who go to see them.

But for the moment I will continue to recount some of the noteworthy things that happened to me during my first journey among the Tupinamba. That same day the interpreter and I were going on to spend the night in another village called *Euramiri* (the French call it "Goset," because of an interpreter of that

---

2. An island in the mouth of Guanabara Bay, in what is today Rio de Janeiro, Brazil, named after the French explorer who led Léry's expedition.

3. In the *Odyssey*, the sorceress Circe transformed Odysseus's men into animals. "Ulysses": the Latin name for Odysseus.

name who stayed there). Arriving at sunset, we found the savages dancing and finishing up the *caouin* of a prisoner whom they had killed only six hours earlier, the pieces of whom we saw on the *boucan*.[4] Do not ask whether, with this beginning, I was astonished to see such a tragedy; however, as you will hear, that was nothing compared to the fright that I had soon after.

We had entered one of the village houses, where each of us sat, according to custom, in a cotton bed hung in the air. After the women had wept (in a manner that I will describe in a moment) and the old man, the master of the house, had made his speech of welcome, the interpreter—who was not new to the customs of the savages, and who, moreover, liked to drink and *caouiner*[5] as much as they did—without saying a single word to me, nor warning me of anything, went over to the big crowd of dancers and left me there with some of the savages. So after eating a little root flour and other food they had offered us, I, weary and asking only for rest, lay down in the cotton bed I had been sitting on.

Not only was I kept awake by the noise that the savages made, dancing and whistling all night while eating their prisoner; but, what is more, one of them approached me with the victim's foot in hand, cooked and *boucané*, asking me (as I learned later, for I didn't understand at the time) if I wanted to eat some of it. His countenance filled me with such terror that you need hardly ask if I lost all desire to sleep. Indeed, I thought that by brandishing the human flesh he was eating, he was threatening me and wanted to make me understand that I was about to be similarly dealt with. As one doubt begets another, I suspected straight away that the interpreter, deliberately betraying me, had abandoned me and delivered me into the hands of these barbarians. If I had seen some exit through which to flee, I would not have hesitated. But seeing myself surrounded on all sides by those whose intentions I failed to understand (for as you will hear, they had not the slightest thought of doing me harm), I firmly expected shortly to be eaten, and all that night I called on God in my heart. I will leave it to those who understand what I am saying, and who put themselves in my place, to consider whether that night seemed long.

At daybreak my interpreter (who had been off carousing with those rascals of savages all night long in other village houses) came to find me. Seeing me, as he said, not only ashen-faced and haggard but also feverish, he asked me whether I was sick, or if I hadn't rested well. Distraught, I answered wrathfully that they had well and truly kept me from sleeping, and that he was a scoundrel to have left me among these people whom I couldn't understand at all; still as anxious as ever, I urged that we get ourselves out of there with all possible speed. Thereupon he told me that I should have no fear, and that it wasn't us they were after. When he recounted the whole business to the savages—who, rejoicing at my coming, and thinking to show me affection, had not budged from my side all night—they said that they had sensed that I had been somewhat frightened of them, for which they were very sorry. My one consolation was the hoot of laughter they sent up—for they are great jokers—at having (without meaning to) given me such a scare.

* * *

4. A grill. Léry explains elsewhere that *cauin* is an alcoholic drink brewed from a grain called *avati*, here by extension a feast.
5. To carouse.

Now to return to the treatment the savages offer visitors. After the guests have drunk and eaten, in the way I have described, and rested or slept in their houses, if they are courteous, they ordinarily present knives to men, or scissors, or tweezers for plucking out beards; to the women, combs and mirrors; and to the little boys, fishhooks. If beyond that there are dealings about food supplies or other things that they have, you ask what they want for it, and upon giving them whatever is agreed upon, you can carry it off and go on your way.

Since, as I have said elsewhere, there are no horses, donkeys, or other beasts of burden in their country, they simply travel on their own two feet. If the foreign visitors are weary, they have only to present a knife or some other object to the savages; the latter, prompt as they are to please their friends, will offer to carry them. In fact, while I was over there, there were those who put us on their shoulders, with their heads between our thighs and our legs hanging against their bellies, and carried us that way more than a league without resting. Sometimes, to give them some relief, we told them to stop; laughing at us, they would say in their language: "What? Do you think we are women, or so slack and weak of heart that we might faint under the burden?" "I would carry you a whole day without stopping for rest," said one of them who had me around his neck. We, for our part, would roar with laughter at these two-footed mounts, applauding them and cheering them on, and saying, "Well then! Let's keep going!"

As for their natural fellow-feeling, every day they distribute and present each to each the venison, fish, fruit, and the other good things of their country, and not only would a savage die of shame (so to speak) if he saw his neighbor lacking what he has in his power to give, but also, as I have experienced it, they practice the same liberality toward foreigners who are their allies. As an example of this I will recount the time when, as I mentioned in Chapter X, two Frenchmen and I had lost our way in the woods—when we thought we were going to be eaten by a huge and terrifying lizard—, and moreover, during the space of two days and a night that we were lost, suffered greatly from hunger. When we finally found ourselves in a village called *Pauo*, where we had been on other occasions, we could not have received a better welcome than we had from the savages of that place. To begin with, when they heard us recount the troubles we had endured, and the danger we had been in—not only of being devoured by cruel beasts, but also of being seized and eaten by the Margaia, our enemy and theirs, whose land we had unintentionally approached—and when they saw the state we were in, all scratched up by the thorns that we had gone through in the wilderness, they took such pity on us that I can't help saying that the hypocritical welcomes of those over here who use only slippery speech for consolation of the afflicted is a far cry from the humanity of these people, whom nonetheless we call "barbarians."

* * *

INCA GARCILASO DE LA VEGA

Born in the city of Cuzco, in present-day Peru, to a prominent Spanish conquistador and an Inca princess, the young *mestizo* Gómez Suárez de Figueroa (1539–1616) traveled to Spain as a young man. Fashioning himself as a man of letters, he took on a new name that combined his indigenous expertise on the New World with the authority of Spanish literary forebears (his distant relative **Garcilaso de la Vega** was the Petrarchan poet whose sonnets appear in this anthology), hence the *Inca Garcilaso*. His most famous work, the *Royal Commentaries of the Incas* (1609) describes their world before the arrival of the Spaniards, including the expansion of the Inca Empire, while the *General History of Peru* (published posthumously in 1617) narrates the Spanish conquest of Peru and its aftermath. By the time Garcilaso

wrote these massive works, the Spaniards had written countless histories of the conquest. Acutely aware of the prejudice and even surprise with which European readers might respond to a *mestizo* writer going over the same ground, Garcilaso astutely establishes his own authority, explaining with a mixture of tact and pride how his intimate knowledge of Inca culture allows him to correct the misunderstandings that plague Spanish accounts. The very name Peru, he explains, comes from one such misunderstanding. Garcilaso admires the Inca Empire, comparing it both to Rome and to the Spaniards, thus suggesting that the problem is not so much empire itself but its misman-agement. He takes pride in his *mestizo* identity, and describes the tremendous mixing of peoples that ensued from the New World encounter.

From Royal Commentaries of the Incas and General History of Peru[1]

Preface

Though there have been learned Spaniards who have written accounts of the states of the New World, such as those of Mexico and Peru and the other king-doms of the heathens, they have not described these realms so fully as they might have done. This I have remarked particularly in what I have seen written about Peru, concerning which, as a native of the city of Cuzco, which was for-merly the Rome of that empire[2] I have fuller and more accurate information than that provided by previous writers. It is true that these have dealt with many of the very remarkable achievements of that empire, but they have set them down so briefly that, owing to the manner in which they are told, I am scarcely able to understand even such matters as are well known to me. For this reason, impelled by my natural love for my native country, I have

---

1. Translated by Harold V. Livermore.　　2. I.e., the capital city of the Inca Empire.

undertaken the task of writing these *Commentaries*, in which everything in the Peruvian empire before the arrival of the Spaniards is clearly and distinctly set down, from the rites of their vain religion to the government of their kings in time of peace and war, and all else that can be told of these Indians, from the highest affairs of the royal crown to the humblest duties of its vassals. I write only of the empire of the Incas, and do not deal with other monarchies, about which I can claim no similar knowledge. In the course of my history I shall affirm its truthfulness and shall set down no important circumstances without quoting the authority of Spanish historians who may have touched upon it in part or as a whole. For my purpose is not to gainsay them, but to furnish a commentary and gloss, and to interpret many Indian expressions which they, as strangers to that tongue, have rendered inappropriately. This will be fully seen in the course of my history, which I commend to the piety of those who may peruse it, with no other interest than to be of service to Christendom and to inspire gratitude to Our Lord Jesus Christ and the Virgin Mary His mother, by whose merits and intercession the Eternal Majesty has deigned to draw so many great peoples out of the pit of idolatry and bring them into the bosom of His Roman Catholic Church, our mother and lady. I trust that it will be received in the same spirit as I offer it, for this is the return my intention deserves, even though the work may not. I am still writing two other books about the events that took place in my land among the Spaniards, down to the year 1560 when I left it. I hope to see them finished, and to make the same offering of them as I do of these. Our Lord, etc.

Notes on the General Language of the Indians of Peru

For the better understanding of what, with divine aid, we shall write in this history, it will be well to give some notes on the general language of the Indians of Peru, many words of which we shall quote. The first is that there are three different ways of pronouncing some of the syllables. They are quite different from the pronunciation in Spanish, and the differences of pronunciation give different meanings to the same word. Certain syllables are pronounced on the lips, others on the palate, and others in the lower part of the throat, as we shall show later by examples as they occur. To accentuate the words it must be noticed that the stress almost always falls on the penultimate syllable, rarely on the antepenultimate, and never at all on the last syllable. This does not contradict those who say that words of barbarous languages should be stressed on the last syllable: they say this because they do not know the language. It is also to be noted that in the general language of Cuzco (of which it is my purpose to speak, rather than of the local pronunciations of each province, which are innumerable), the following letters are lacking: *b, d, f, g, jota.* There is no single *l*, only double *ll*; on the other hand, there is no double *rr* at the beginning of words or in the middle: it is always pronounced single. There is no *x*; so that in all six letters of the Spanish ABC's are missing, and we might say eight if we include single *l* and double *rr*. The Spaniards add these letters to the detriment and corruption of the language; and as the Indians do not have them, they usually mispronounce Spanish words where they occur. To avoid further corruption, I may be permitted, since I am an Indian, to write like an Indian in this history, using the letters that should be used in these words. Let none who read take exception to this novelty in opposition to the incorrect usage that is usually adopted: they should rather be glad to be able to read the words written correctly and with purity. As I have to quote much from Spanish historians in support of what I say, I shall copy their words as they write them with their corruptions; and I must warn the reader that it does not seem to me inconsistent to write the letters I have mentioned which do not appear in the Indian language, since I only do so to quote faithfully what the Spanish author has written.

It is also noteworthy that there is no plural number in the general language, though there are particles that indicate plurality. The singular is used for both numbers. If I put any Indian word in the plural, it will be a Spanish corruption used to keep the agreement of words, for it would sound wrong to write Indian words in the singular and Spanish adjectives or relatives in the plural. In many other respects the language differs from Castilian, Italian, and Latin. These points will be noted by learned mestizos and creoles, since the language is their own. For my part, it is sufficient that I point out for them from Spain the principles of their language, so that they may maintain its purity, for it is certainly a great pity that so elegant a language should be lost or spoilt, especially as the fathers of the Holy Society of Jesus,[3] as well as those of other orders, have worked a great deal at it so as to speak it well, and have greatly benefited the instruction of the Indians by their good example, which is what matters most.

* * *

CHAPTER 4

The derivation of the name Peru.

As we have to deal with Peru, we may properly say here how this name was derived, since the Indians do not have it in their language. In 1513 Vasco Núñez de Balboa, a gentleman born at Jerez de Badajoz, discovered the Southern Sea,[4] and was the first Spaniard to set eyes upon it. He was granted by the Catholic monarchs the title of *adelantado*[5] of this sea with the right to conquer and govern any kingdoms he might discover on its shores, and in the few years he had to live after receiving this honor—until his own father-in-law, Governor Pedro Arias de Ávila, instead of rewarding him with the many favors his deeds had merited, had him beheaded—this knight strove to discover and know what was the land running from Panama southwards and what it was called. For this purpose he had three or four ships built, which he sent one by one at various seasons of the year to reconnoiter that coast while he made the necessary preparations for its discovery and conquest. These ships made as many investigations as they could and returned with report of many lands on those shores.

One ship went further than the rest and passed the equinoctial line southwards; and not far beyond it, while hugging the shore—which was the method of navigation then employed on this voyage—sighted an Indian fishing at the mouth of one of the numerous rivers that flow from that land into the sea. The Spaniards on the ship landed four of their number who were good swimmers

---

3. In order more effectively to Christianize the indigenous population, the Jesuits learned native languages.

4. The Pacific Ocean.

5. Military title granted to Spanish conquerors.

and runners as quickly as possible some distance from where the Indian was, so that he should not escape by land or water. Having taken this precaution, they passed before the Indian in the ship so that he fixed his gaze on it, unmindful of the trap that had been prepared for him. Seeing on the sea so strange a sight as a ship with all sail set, something never before seen on that shore, he was lost in amazement and stood astonished and bewildered, wondering what the thing he beheld on the sea before him could be. He was so distracted and absorbed in this thought that those who were to capture him had seized him before he perceived their approach, and so they took him on board with general rejoicings and celebrations.

Having petted him to help him overcome his fear at the sight of their beards and unaccustomed clothes, the Spaniards asked him by signs and words what land it was and what it was called. The Indian understood that they were asking him something from the gestures and grimaces they were making with hands and face, as if they were addressing a dumb man, but he did not understand what they were asking, so he told them what he thought they wanted to know. Thus fearing they might do him harm, he quickly replied by giving his own name, saying, "*Berú*," and adding another, "*pelú*." He meant: "If you're asking my name, I'm called *Berú*, and if you're asking where I was, I was in the river." The word *pelú* is a noun in the language of that province and means "a river" in general, as we shall see from a reliable author. To a like question the Indian in our history of Florida[6] answered by giving the name of his master saying, "*Breços*" and "*Bredos*" (Book VI, ch. xv, where I inserted this passage referring to that incident: I now remove it to put it in its proper place). The Christians understood what they wanted to understand, supposing the Indian had understood them and had replied as pat as if they had been conversing in Spanish; and from that time, which was 1515 or 1516, they called that rich and great empire *Peru*, corrupting both words, as the Spaniards corrupt almost all the words they take from the Indian language of that land. Thus if they took the Indian's name, *Berú*, they altered the *B* to a *P*, and if they took the word *pelú*, "a river," they altered the *l* to an *r*, and in one way or another they turned it into *Peru*. Others, more modern, and priding themselves on their refinement, alter two letters and write *Pirú* in their histories. The older historians such as Pedro de Cieza de León and the treasurer Agustín de Zárate, and Francisco López de Gómara, and Diego Fernández de Palencia, and also the Reverend Father Jerónimo Román, though more modern, all write *Peru* and not *Pirú*. And as the place where this happened chanced to be in the confines of the land the Inca kings had conquered and subjected to their rule, they called everything from there onwards *Peru*, that is from the district of Quito to the Charcas,[7] or the main part over which they reigned. The region is over seven hundred leagues in length, though their empire reached as far as Chile, which is five hundred leagues beyond and is another most rich and fertile kingdom.

6. Garcilaso had published *La Florida del Inca*, an account of Hernando de Soto's expedition to Florida, in 1605.

7. Quito is in what is now Ecuador, Charcas (today Sucre), in Bolivia.

CHAPTER II

The fruit of larger [plants and] trees.

There is another excellent fruit which the Spaniards call cucumbers, because they rather resemble these in shape, though not in taste or in their wholesomeness for those suffering from fever or in the ease with which they are digested: in these ways they are rather the opposite of the Spanish cucumber. I do not recall the Indian name, though I have often racked my brain for days on end, and when I reproved memory for failing to retain so many words in our language it offered as an apology the word *cácham*, for cucumber. I do not know if my memory, relying on my inability easily to rectify its mistakes because of the distance that separates me from my own people, is indeed deceiving me: my relatives, the Indians and mestizos of Cuzco and the whole of Peru, shall be the judges of this piece of ignorance on my part and doubtless of many others in my work. I hope they will forgive me, for I am all theirs and have only undertaken a task so out of proportion with my feeble strength as this book, and without any hope of reward from anyone, in order to serve them. The cucumbers are of three sizes: the smallest are heart-shaped and are the best. They grow in small clumps. Another fruit called *chili* reached Cuzco in 1557. It has an excellent taste and is a great delicacy. It grows on a low plant which almost rests on the ground. It has berries like the arbutus, and is of the same size, though instead of being round it is rather elongated in the shape of a heart.

* * *

Another fruit is what the Spaniards call *piña* because in appearance and shape it resembles a Spanish pinecone, though there is no other connection between the two plants. The Peruvian *piña*, when the rind is removed with a knife, reveals a very tasty white pulp, all of which can be eaten. It has a faintly acid taste which makes it even more palatable. In size they are twice as big as pine cones. There is also in the Antis[8] another fruit which the Spaniards call *manjar blanco*,[9] since when cleft in two it resembles two bowls of *manjar blanco* in color and flavor. It has inside black pips like small almonds, which are not edible. In size the fruit is like a small melon. It has a hard rind like a dry calabash and almost as thick. Inside the much-esteemed pulp is found. It is sweet but with a slight bitter tang which makes it luscious.

Many other fruits grow wild in the Antis, such as what the Spaniards call "almonds" and "walnuts" because of some slight resemblance with those of Spain. For the first Spaniards who went to the Indies had a mania for applying the names for Spanish fruits to American fruits with very little likeness and no real connection. Indeed when compared the fruits are seen to differ in far more respects than they resemble one another, and some are even the opposite, not only in taste but in their properties, as are these walnuts and almonds, which are of little importance and which we shall dismiss together with other fruits and vegetables of the Antis to turn to others of greater worth and note.

8. Andes.

9. A dessert made of milk and almonds.

CHAPTER 31
New names for various racial groups.

We were forgetting the best imports into the Indies, namely the Spaniards, and the Negroes who have since been taken there as slaves, for they were previously unknown in my country. These two races have mingled [with the Indians] in various ways to form others which are distinguished by the use of different names. Although I spoke a little about this in the *History of Florida*, I have decided to repeat it here, as being the proper place. Thus any Spanish man or woman who arrives from Spain is called a Spaniard or Castilian, the two words being quite interchangeable in Peru; and I have used them indifferently in this history and in the *Florida*. The children of Spaniards by Spanish women born there are called *criollos* or *criollas*, implying that they were born in the Indies. The name was invented by the Negroes, as its use shows. They use it to mean a Negro born in the Indies, and they devised it to distinguish those who come from this side and were born in Guinea from those born in the New World, since the former are held in greater honor and considered to be of higher rank because they were born in their own country, while their children were born in a strange land. The parents take offence if they are called *criollos*. The Spaniards have copied them by introducing this word to describe those born in the New World, and in this way both Spaniards and Guinea Negroes are called *criollos* if they are born in the New World. The Negro who arrives there from the Old World is called Negro or Guineo. The child of a Negro by an Indian woman or of an Indian and a Negro woman is called *mulato* or *mulata*. Their children are called *cholos*, a word from the Windward Islands: it means a dog, but is not used for a thoroughbred dog, but only for a mongrel cur: the Spaniards use the word in a pejorative and vituperative sense. The children of Spaniards by Indians are called mestizos, meaning that we are a mixture of the two races. The word was applied by the first Spaniards who had children by Indian women, and because it was used by our fathers, as well as on account of its meaning, I call myself by it in public and am proud of it, though in the Indies, if a person is told: "You're a mestizo," or "He's a mestizo," it is taken as an insult. This is the reason why they have adopted with such enthusiasm the name *montañés* which some potentate applied to them, among other slights and insults, instead of the word mestizo. They do not stop to consider that, although in Spain the word *montañés* is an honorable appellation, on account of the privileges that have been bestowed on the natives of the Asturian and Basque mountains,[1] if it is applied to anyone who is not from these parts, it assumes a pejorative sense derived from its original meaning "something from the mountains." This is brought out by our great master Antonio de Lebrija,[2] to whom all good Latinists in Spain today are indebted, in his vocabulary. In the general language of Peru the word for a mountaineer is *sacharuna*, properly "savage," and whoever applied the word *montañés* was privately calling them savages: those of my own generation, not understanding

---

1. People from these regions claimed that their Christianity went back further than anyone else's in Spain, as they had not been conquered in the Muslim invasions.

2. Antonio de Lebrija (or Nebrija) (1441–1552), Spanish humanist who in 1492 produced the first European grammar for a modern language, the *Gramática de la lengua castellana*.

this malicious implication, took pride in the insulting epithet, when they should rather have avoided and abominated it, using the name our fathers bestowed on us rather than accepting new-fangled indignities.

The children of a Spaniard and a mestizo, or vice versa, are called *cuatralvos*, meaning they have one part of Indian blood and three of Spanish. The children of a mestizo and an Indian, or vice versa, are called *tresalvos*, meaning that they have three parts of Indian blood and one of Spanish. All these names, and others which we omit to avoid tedium, have been devised in Peru to describe the racial groups that have come into existence since the arrival of the Spaniards, and we can therefore say that they were brought in together with the other things not previously found in Peru. With this we return to the Inca kings, the children of the great Huaina Cápac,[3] who are calling us to relate great events that occurred in their time.

---

3. Inca ruler who died in 1525, shortly before the arrival of the Spaniards.

GUAMAN POMA DE AYALA

Poma (ca. 1535–ca. 1616) was an indigenous Peruvian born soon after Francisco Pizarro conquered Peru. Educated and converted to Christianity by the Spaniards, Poma was an *indio ladino*, or Spanish-speaking Indian. He also spoke at least two indigenous languages: *quechua* and *aymara*, and had apparently traveled widely across Peru. In the early years of the seventeenth century, Poma wrote an impassioned nine-hundred-page letter to the king of Spain, now known as *The First New Chronicle and Good Government*, to alert him to the abuses he saw in the colonial administration around him, complete with recommendations for improvement. Almost four hundred illustrations accompany the text, registering an indigenous perspective and eloquently making visible Poma's case to the king. The *New Chronicle* relates

Peruvian history from a new perspective, while *Good Government* lays out the author's recommendations, including the wishful suggestion that an indigenous viceroy—Poma generously volunteers his son—should rule Peru for the king of Spain.

Poma's massive letter apparently never reached its destination, and was instead collected in a Danish archive as proof of Spanish excesses in the New World. It was not until 1908 that it was rediscovered and its immense importance as *auto-ethnography* (a description of a culture by one of its own members) recognized. Poma provides a wealth of information on colonial Peru, yet his text is much more a polemic than a description. He strongly condemns *mestizaje*—unions between Spaniards and Indians—claiming that it will gradually lead to the disappearance of his besieged culture. In a vividly imagined chapter toward the end of the text, Poma pictures himself in direct conversation with the king, forcefully addressing his recommendations to the one man who he imagined could right the wrongs committed in Peru. Like many other mestizo and native writers, Guaman Poma was a colonial subject who acknowledged Spanish rule, as long as it preserved the status of the local elite as mediators.

From The First New Chronicle and Good Government[1]

[Letter to the King]

* * *

You must consider the great majesty of the Inca Topa Inca Yupanqui, king of Peru, and of Wayna Capac Inca.[2] For, having read in all the histories and chronicles of the world of all the kings, princes, and emperors of the world—the Christians, the Great Turk, the king of China, the emperors of Rome and all of Christendom, and of the Jews, and the kings of Guinea—I have found none with such great majesty. [All the others] were lesser; none have ever had such great majesty or been such great kings with such high crowns as my grandfather,[3] the king Topa Inca Yupanqui, and Wayna Capac—the Incas, whose majesty was extremely great.

Consider: if any king were to see another king or great lord, he would immediately kill him or have him killed, and then would dethrone him and rule alone. Yet the Inca kept four kings, for the four parts of this kingdom.[4] The greatest of them was the capac apo[5] himself; he made Waman Chawa of the Allauca Wanoco–Yaro Willca lineage his second-in-command and viceroy. Once he had given them the crown, his sons and grandsons never took it away from them; such was the case with my most honorable great-grandfather. Likewise, the three princes were crowned to accompany and increase the grandeur of His Royal Majesty the Inca, who ordered that he be crowned with the crown of his ancestors. In this way, the Inca king gave himself authority and rose up higher, and because of the majesty of the Inca, no one could talk to him nor communicate with him nor laugh with him, nor could he feast with gentlemen nor with commoners, nor could he ever cry; rather, His Majesty the Inca was always contented. He would eat and drink and offer toasts, [but he did not] toast the common people; instead, he honored the kings who were his ancestors. With this, he expanded his city and his kingdom, and his majesty was greater and greater.

Secondly: no king in any city, town, or countryside, had a throne in the public square like the Inca's.

1. Translated by David Frye.
2. Topa Inca Yupanqui ruled 1471–93, father of Wayna Capac. Wayna Capac (alternate spelling for Huayna [Hvaina] Capac) died in 1525, shortly before the arrival of the Spaniards.
3. Guaman Poma's forebear Waman Chaua, of the Yarovilca culture, served as a governor for the Incas, and his mother may have been a descendant of Topa Inca Yupanqui.
4. The Incas referred to their empire as Tawantinsuyu, or "the four regions." It had four provincial governments with strong rulers.
5. Ruler.

Thirdly: throughout the kingdom he kept all the roads clean, divided into day's travels, with inns all set up so that they even had dispensaries, and measured league by league and marked along the way.

Fourth: he ate shellfish that were brought to him live from a thousand leagues away, *mullo* from the city of Tumi.[6]

Fifth: he kept the chiefs of the naked *Chuncho* Indians, who eat human flesh, for the memory and the greatness of the world.

Consider the greatness of the Inca king, who, though he was barbarian, was descended in the woman's line from the lady Mama Waco, the *Coya* or queen, [a line] that had governed this kingdom for fifteen hundred years.

Thus, considering that my grandfather, for the greatness of the world, had been the monarch of all the people created by God in the four parts of the world, the monarch should be the king Don Philip III, may God prolong his life, to provide for the government of the world and the defense of our holy Catholic faith in the service of God.

[To serve as his] first [viceroy], I offer one of my sons, a prince of this kingdom, a grandson and great-grandson of Topa Inca Yupanqui, the tenth king, a great wise man who established laws; he should keep the prince in his court for the memory and greatness of the world.

The second [viceroy should be] a prince of the black king of Guinea.

The third [viceroy should be a prince] of the king of the Christians of Rome or some other kingdom of the world.

The fourth [viceroy should be] the king of the Moors of the Great Turk.

All four shall be crowned, with their scepters and fleece. In the center of these four parts of the world shall be the majesty and monarch of the world, king Don Philip, may God save his high crown. He represents the monarch of the world, and the four kings mentioned represent his lower, equal crowns. Whenever His Majesty, the monarch, goes out on foot, they should all go out on foot; whenever he goes on horseback, they should go on horseback with their mantels: on his right hand, the Christian king; behind him, the Moorish king; on his left hand, the king of the Indies; behind him, the black king of Guinea. In this way, he will represent the monarch of the world, for no king nor emperor could equal this monarch; for the king is the king of his jurisdiction, and the emperor is the emperor of his jurisdiction, but the monarch has no jurisdiction: he holds under his hand the worlds of these crowned kings. They should be salaried employees of his court, for the greatness of the universal world of all nations and kinds of people: the Indians, blacks, Christian Spaniards, Turks, Jews, and Moors of the world. A consideration for the greatness of His Majesty the king.

* * *

His Majesty Questions, the Author Replies

* * *

His Royal Catholic Majesty questions the author Ayala to learn everything there is to know about the kingdom of the Indies of Peru, for good government and justice, for remedying troubles and misfortunes, for the poor Indians of

---

6. The city of Tumi (Tumibamba, now Cuenca, in Ecuador), is nearly one thousand miles from Cuzco. "*Mullo*": mullu, a thorny oyster, a luxury food.

the kingdom to multiply, and for the reform and good example of the Spaniards, *corregidores*, justices, *doctrina* padres, *encomenderos*, noble *caciques*,[7] and petty authorities.

Hearing His Majesty's questions, the author replies and speaks with His Majesty, saying:

"Your Royal Catholic Majesty, you should listen closely to me. When I have finished, please ask me questions. I am delighted to give you my report on everything in the kingdom, for the memory of the world and Your Majesty's greatness."

Your Royal Catholic Majesty, I will communicate with Your Majesty regarding the service of God our Lord and regarding the service to your royal crown and the increase and welfare of the Indians of this kingdom, because some people report lies to you, others report the truth, and others give their reports in order to get Your Majesty to grant them a position as bishop, dean, canon, president, *Audiencia*[8] judge, or some other rank and post.

I, as the grandson of the king of Peru, would like to serve Your Majesty; to meet with you face to face; to speak and communicate about these things in your presence. But I cannot travel so far, being eighty years old and infirm. I hope you will be pleased with my thirty years of working in poverty, leaving my house, children, and estates to serve Your Majesty. Therefore, we will meet through writing and sending letters. So, Your Majesty, please ask me questions, and I will reply to them in this way.

His Majesty asks: "Don Felipe, author Ayala, tell me how the Indians of this kingdom had multiplied even before there was an Inca."

I say to Your Majesty that, in those times, there were a king and nobles. [The people] peacefully served the king, mining gold and silver, serving in fields and pastures, and upholding fortresses. Even a little pueblo had many women; the smallest one would have a thousand soldiers. Others had fifty thousand to a hundred thousand. Therefore, they had warfare and fortresses among them.

"Tell me, Don Felipe Ayala, about those times: how could there have been so many Indians in the time of the Incas?"

I say to Your Majesty that, in those times, the Inca alone was king, though there were also dukes, counts, marquises, and great noble lords. But they lived under the laws and commandments of the Incas, and, because they had a king, they peacefully served in this kingdom; they multiplied, and had estates, plenty to eat, and their own children and wives.

"Tell me, author, why do the Indians not multiply now? Why are they becoming poor?"

I will say to Your Majesty, first, that they do not multiply because all the best women and maidens are taken by the *doctrina* padres, *encomenderos*, *corregidores*, Spaniards, stewards, deputies, and officers, and their servants. That is why there are so many little mestizos and mestizas in this kingdom. They claim that the women have lovers as a pretext for taking them and their estates from the poor. Because of all these things, all these offenses and harms, the Indians

---

7. Indian chiefs. "*Corregidores*": local Spanish administrators. "*Doctrina* padres": catechizing priests. "*Encomenderos*": Spaniards granted Indians as laborers, ostensibly in exchange for their Christianization.

8. Local Spanish administrative and legislative institution.

hang themselves, as the *Changas* did in Andahuayllas—that was a small mountain range, once filled with Indian men and women; they preferred to die once and for all rather than face all the harm that was being done to them.

"Tell me, author, how will the people multiply?"

I say to Your Majesty, just as I have written: the padres, priests, *encomenderos*, *corregidores*, other Spaniards, and noble *caciques* should live as Christians, as Your Majesty has ordained, and not go beyond that. They should let [the people] enjoy their wives and estates, and should leave their maidens alone. There should not be so many kings and justices over the people, and they should let the people multiply, or else be severely punished and removed from their offices and benefices.

"Tell me, author, how will the Indians become rich?"

Your Majesty should know that they should keep community estates (which they call *sapsi*), with fields planted with corn, wheat, potatoes, peppers, *macno*, cotton, and grapes, [as well as] textile workshops, dyeworks, coca fields, and fruit orchards. The maidens and widows should spin and weave—ten women working on one piece of cloth. On one portion of the community land (*sapsi*), they should keep Castilian cattle. Each Indian man and woman should have a piece of an estate from their community land (*sapsi*).

Overseeing this, in every province there should be an administrator with a salary set at one seventh [of the income from the community lands]—one main overseer for each province. Whenever there is need, Your Majesty would be able to borrow money and take your royal fifth from the commoners.

With this, the Indians of this kingdom will become rich people; God and Your Majesty's royal crown will be served in this kingdom; and the Indians will increase in this kingdom.

"Tell me, author: how can the absent Indians in that kingdom be gathered in?"

I say to Your Majesty that, in every province, these Indian men, women, and children should be gathered into some old pueblo, for they are lost. Give them cropland and bounded pastures, so that they may serve God and Your Majesty. Let them be called your royal crown Indians, and let them pay taxes and tribute, and hold no other office. Their administrator, the noble *cacique*, should be subject to you. No one but the administrator should take a salary from what they pay, in keeping with the Indians' wishes; the rest [of their taxes] should be applied to the service of your royal crown. In this way, [the absent Indians] will be gathered in throughout the kingdom. It should be the administrator's office to gather them.

Your Royal Catholic Majesty. As you must know, the dozen learned men and the four notaries of the world[9] set forth, in their council, an order and a law for the world: that there should be no slaves or tribute for priests, and that no tribute should be paid to priests or to any other such person in the world. Therefore, the *doctrina* padres and priests may not take a salary from the tribute; instead, they must make their living by working at the altar. A priest can make two thousand pesos a year, or one thousand pesos at the very least, from celebrating Mass, offerings, and prayers for the dead, and from gifts, Christmas

---

9. I.e., the twelve apostles and the four evangelists of the New Testament.

bonuses, and alms. That would easily provide a man with plenty to be able to dress and eat. But collecting tribute, and calling himself "proprietor," IS NULL AND VOID by the laws of God and the holy Church. He should live from the tithes and the first-fruits paid by the Spanish.

* * *

"Tell me, author, how will it be possible for the Indians of that kingdom not to die, become ill from quicksilver poisoning, or suffer hard labor?"

Regarding this, I say to Your Majesty: first, they are greatly harmed by the mine owners and the justices who enter with them. They hang them by their feet, and they whip them while they are hanging with their shameful parts exposed. They force them to work day and night and do not pay them. When they do pay them, they give them only half their wages and steal the other half. They send them out to the low plains, where they die. Of every eleven Indians, only one gets out alive.

What they should do is draw lots. One province should be given six months to rest while the next province comes in.

Also, Your Majesty should order that a grant be given to any Indian, black, or Spaniard who discovers how to cure quicksilver poisoning and heal the ill; let him be paid. In this way, the poor Indians will multiply and will not begrudge the labor.

"Tell me, author, how will the hidden mines of that kingdom be discovered?"

I say to Your Majesty that, as soon as mines are discovered—mines of gold, silver, quicksilver, lead, tin, copper, dyes—as soon as they are discovered, the Spaniards immediately meddle, take them over, and mistreat the Indians. That is why the Indians do not want to report to the mines. If Your Majesty would arrange to grant the mining rights to the discoverer, all the good mines would be discovered, the kingdom would become very rich, and Your Majesty would be very rich—richer than all other kings. Your Majesty will be the greatest monarch in the world; if you carry out what is started here, Your Majesty will be very rich, as will your royal crown. Because of all this, you may enjoy the kingship over all the world, in service to God and your royal crown.

Your Royal Catholic Majesty, I tell you that in this kingdom the Indians are coming to an end, and they will come utterly to an end. Twenty years from now, there will be no Indians in this kingdom to serve your royal crown and defend our holy Catholic faith. Without the Indians, Your Majesty is worth nothing, because, remember, Castile is Castile because of the Indians. His Serenity the emperor-king (may God keep him in heaven) was powerful because of the Indians of this kingdom.[1] Your Majesty's father was also a monarch of great power and renowned strength because of the Indians of this kingdom.[2] The same is true of Your Majesty.

Your Majesty should consider the idea of losing so valuable a kingdom, one which has been so valuable—losing it and seeing the end of all the Indians, for they are already being depopulated. Where there were once a thousand souls, now there are not even one hundred, and all of them are old men and women who can no longer multiply. Even if there are a few unmarried men, they marry old women who cannot give birth. Besides this, they are oppressed with great troubles,

---

1. Holy Roman Emperor Charles V (Charles I of Spain).

2. Philip II, father of Philip III, whom Poma imagines himself addressing.

disturbed, and robbed. Even their daughters, sons, and married women are being stolen. And there is no remedy, because everyone has joined together—the judges, *corregidores*, deputies, *encomenderos*, stewards, other Spaniards and mestizos, inspectors of the Holy Mother Church, vicars, priests. All work together against the poor; all have joined hands to favor the Spanish Dons and the lady Doñas.[3] They take advantage of all the poor; not only that, but they enter into their possessions, estates, lands, pastures, and houses, by force and against their will.

Writing this is enough to make one cry. None of them report these things to Your Majesty. I will say the truth regarding the value, price, benefits, income, and services that the Indians have had and should have, and which they are losing and will lose throughout the kingdom. Your Majesty should know that you are being served by the Indians when, every six months—twice a year—they pay silver, corn, wheat, clothes, chickens, pullets, local cattle, and other products. In addition, they serve in the mines, the plazas, and the *tambos* [royal inns]. They also fix the bridges in your kingdom, and clean the roads and byways. It is from them that the royal fifth,[4] the tithe, the personal tax, and the excise tax are paid, because Your Majesty does not get as much benefit at all from the mestizos, mulattos, or even the Spaniards. Therefore, I place their worth at a very estimable value.

Take care that this kingdom should not lose these Indians, because, if a Spaniard steals and keeps four Indian women to give birth to his little mestizos, he will refuse to recognize them before the bribed judges; nor is there any point, because [Spaniards] have so many [mestizo children] and so many women. This is, first, because the Spaniards look for women in their houses and scattered settlements. They do not leave them alone, day or night. If the women's fathers and mothers defend them, they are mistreated. The Spaniards go to seek them out where they hold their fiestas. They do not allow them to get married or to lead a married life with their husbands. Married Indian women do not have children by their husbands; instead, they give birth to little mestizo children, and then refuse to recognize them. The mestizo children wander around dressed like poor Indians. The whole kingdom is like this.

As soon as an Indian woman appears who has given birth by a poor Indian man, everyone comes down on her right away—the inspector, the vicar, the priest, the *corregidor*, the deputy, the *encomendero*. They punish her, fine her, and banish her to the house of some lady or to the padre's kitchen. There they fornicate with her right away, and she soon gives birth to a mestizo. No one is upset about this. Thus, they prefer to have her living in sin and giving birth to mestizos.

Then they go out to search for more Indian women, since they look on them so favorably, as I have said. When one gives birth to an Indian man's son, they are all thrown into an uproar—it seems like the sky is falling. They punish the mothers and fathers in the public stocks, and they shear the mother's hair. Telling these stories and writing them is an endless task.

"Tell me, author Ayala. You have told me many rueful stories and described how the Indians are coming to an end: they are suffering troubles and cannot multiply because people come in and steal their wives, daughters, and their property in houses and land, utterly skinning them. I do not send my judges to

3. *Don* and *Doña* are male and female honorifics in Spanish.
4. The royal fifth was the tax levied by the Crown on all mineral wealth from the New World.

do harm and damage and to rob, but rather to honor the nobles, *caciques*, petty authorities, and the poor Indians, that they might increase and multiply in the service of God and the defense of the holy Catholic faith and in service of my royal crown. Tell me now, author Ayala, how can these things be remedied?"

I say to Your Majesty that all the Spaniards should live like Christians. They should endeavor to marry ladies of equal station, and should leave the poor Indian women to multiply. They should leave their property—their lands and houses—alone; they should return those that they have entered by force, and should pay for the use that they have enjoyed of them. The penalties for these things should be enforced.

Next, whoever deflowers a virgin Indian, makes a married Indian woman give birth, or forces her to fornicate, should be banished for six years to the galleys or to Chile, and all his possessions should be taken as a fine for your royal treasuries and to pay the Indian woman and court expenses. If the judge does not execute this sentence, he deserves the same punishment. All these things should be carried out, and no justice should be against the poor Indians. Those who are not justices—the *doctrina* padres, *encomenderos*, and other Spaniards—should not pretend to be justices. Whoever does so should be well punished, fined, and banished from among the Indians of this kingdom. In this way, the Indians will multiply.

Your Royal Catholic Majesty, about the community lands (*sapsi*) of the Indians and the churches, religious brotherhoods, and hospitals: so that these may multiply and increase in this kingdom, it would be beneficial that [the Indians] be asked to give an accounting to [me, as] the second-in-command of the Inca and Your Majesty in this kingdom. They should come give [me] an accounting every sixth month of the year, paying me a salary of one-seventh throughout the kingdom, so that I will be able to send myself to the service of God and your royal crown, should the need arise, and collect the royal fifth. In this, I will serve God, Your Majesty, the well-being of the Indians of this kingdom, and the increase of wealth.

Your Royal Catholic Majesty should request that each noble *cacique*, second-in-command, and petty authority in this kingdom come here to receive their testimonies, so that I may give testimony of what they each deserve; for, as the second-in-command of the Inca and of Your Majesty, I know all about them, their ways and manners. I and my descendents must give these testimonies to you, according to the law, signed in my name in perpetuity. In this way, no one will make himself a *curaca*[5] by force, or take the title of Don or Doña in this kingdom, or wear Spaniards' clothes. They will have to be well-proven, loyal, and Christian, eager to serve God and Your Majesty; and they will favor the poor. Only then will Your Majesty give them titles, throughout the kingdom.

* * *

"Well, tell me, author: since you are the grandson of Topa Inca Yupanqui, the tenth former king, and you are the son of his second-in-command and viceroy, how is it that you do not favor them in my name and stand up for them?"

That is indeed why I stand up for them, Your Royal Catholic Majesty, as a prince of the Indians of this kingdom. I have suffered such poverty, and I have labored for thirty years in the service of God and Your Majesty. I defend the

5. Magistrate.

kingdom, and that is why I am writing this history—to be a memorial, to be placed in the archive, so that justice may be seen.

It would be very beneficial for Your Majesty to send a general inspector to punish the prelates, and, if necessary, to banish them to the court in Spain, for these reasons. The inspector should stay in the city of Los Reyes de Lima and be sent out from there to inspect every city in its jurisdiction.

If Your Majesty does not agree with this idea, then please communicate with His Holiness, so that he might send us his second-in-command, a cardinal who would rank higher than all the priests and prelates, and who could punish or banish anyone who needs punishment—prelates, cathedral chapters, clerics, friars, monasteries, everything relating to the Holy Mother Church. He should also come with a special charge to help the nobles and other poor Indians of this kingdom. Then the Indians will multiply and be tranquil, and will rally to the service of God and Your Majesty in this kingdom.

LOPE DE VEGA

1562–1635

The foremost dramatist of the Spanish golden age, Lope Félix de Vega Carpio achieved enormous popularity and admiration in his lifetime. His contemporary, **Miguel de Cervantes**, called him a "monster of nature" for his outsize talent. By his own reckoning, Lope produced some 1,500 plays, of which 425 have survived. An accomplished poet who moved easily between low and high culture, Lope insisted that the theater must cater to the pleasure of the people, and in this, he led by example. Many of the thousands of characters he created were based on favorite types he frequently recycled, yet they never failed to appeal to his appreciative audience. Lope's successful formula of three-act plays with comic or serious subplots dominated Spanish drama well into the eighteenth century.

LIFE AND TIMES

Born in the bustling new Spanish capital, Madrid, to a family of modest means, Lope de Vega led a tumultuous early life as a soldier and poet. His prodigious talent was recognized early on, and, after a Jesuit education, he was sent to university by the Bishop of Ávila. Soon famous for his romantic entanglements, however, Lope did not attempt to enter the priesthood. Instead, he enlisted in the army and eventually returned to Madrid to attempt his career as a playwright in its newly built playhouses. When a long-term affair with the actress Elena Osorio ended in her rejecting him for another suitor, Lope took his revenge with his pen, in satirical writings about her and her family. This outburst led to his trial for libel and eight years of exile from Castile, which he spent writing in the city of Valencia before making his way once again to Madrid. Eventually married twice, Lope had at least sixteen children (six in wedlock) and innumerable affairs chronicled in his passionate verse. Nonetheless, religious faith played a serious role in his private and public lives: Lope finally took holy orders in 1614, was elected a judge by the Spanish Inquisition, and served as an official censor. A series of personal tragedies late in his life, including the death of his son at sea, reinforced his religious fervor. Lope's enormous output reflects his various passions: as a dramatist he wrote comedies and also brilliant sacred plays, while as a poet he produced both religious and love poetry, much of it among the finest examples of the period.

Lope's efforts to link his plays to the idea of Spain as a nation are, perhaps, the clearest evidence of a consistent theme in his drama. He believed that plays should deal with historically important issues, such as "the events, wars, peace, counsels, fortune, change, prosperity, the decline of kingdoms and epochs of great empires and monarchies," as he puts it in his play *The Bell of Aragon*. Although many of his plays are far more lighthearted than this list would suggest, a significant subset concerns questions of political authority and representation.

Lope's Spain was undergoing a great transformation: a number of small medieval realms became a modern dynastic state when Isabel of Castile married Ferdinand of Aragon in 1469, uniting the two crowns. The central political problem of early-modern Spain, as for many emerging European nations, was how to organize a strong centralized monarchy that would triumph over feudal lords while avoiding the excesses of absolutism. The new political reality destabilized the traditional balance of power among lords, their king, and their vassals, pitting older arrangements against the necessities of the new state. These political quandaries were hardly abstract questions: they governed the everyday realities of taxation, political representation, and social hierarchies. As Spain took on its foes abroad and at home in countless expensive wars, the issue of how much a ruler could extract from

his subjects became particularly pressing. Lope had a special talent for translating these problems into powerful dramatic terms, pitting poor villagers against abusive lords, with the wise monarchs as their judges and saviors. One play is tellingly titled *The Best Judge, the King*.

FUENTEOVEJUNA

In *Fuenteovejuna* (1614), Lope explores the problem of political authority in a specific historical context: the civil war fought in Spain in the 1470s between the supporters of the new Queen Isabel of Castile and Juana, the dispossessed heir to the throne. Such tumultuous times required towns and nobles to give their allegiance to one leader or the other, and provided the perfect backdrop for Lope to explore questions of loyalty and obedience. While the villagers of Fuenteovejuna are trying to decide how much fealty they owe a governor who abuses them, the Comendador (Commander) and his superior, the young Maestre (Master) of the military Order of Calatrava, must decide whether to support Isabel and her husband Ferdinand. Plot and subplot work together to bring to the stage pressing debates over dominion by consent, divine right, and force.

Lope did not invent the subject of *Fuenteovejuna*: he drew on historical events that took place in the small pastoral village of that name in the province of Córdoba. His principal source records that the Commander "committed great injuries and dishonors to the people of the village, taking their daughters and wives by force, and robbing their households to maintain his soldiers." At last the villagers, calling out "long live Kings Ferdinand and Isabel, and death to traitors and bad Christians," rebelled, killing him along with fourteen of his men. The rebels were promptly arrested, and tortured to identify the ringleaders. Had a single villager collapsed under torture and identified the ringleaders in order to save his or her own skin, the events at Fuenteovejuna would be chronicled as a lurid and bloody uprising during a period of widespread upheaval in Spanish history. But since each was willing to die for the others, they left a memorable and even proverbial example of resistance and solidarity.

Lope's *Fuenteovejuna* is a comedy ending in a jubilant affirmation of community and social order. Along the way, it makes daring forays into questions about law and government. The play hews quite closely to the historical record, with an important exception: Lope invents the Commander's most glaring transgression, and portrays in individualized detail the human costs of his highhandedness. Throughout, the playwright shows considerable sympathy for his peasants, who are goaded into their seditious frenzy. Left to their own devices, the villagers are law abiding and peaceable: even their names—Frondoso ("Leafy") and Laurencia ("Laurel")—associate them with a pastoral nature, as they celebrate the loves of young couples. The villagers speak in a simple, everyday language full of lively humor; although they are not idealized, they are very appealing characters. Lope's unforgiving spotlight shines instead on the Commander's abuses, and his violent disregard for consent, the key term in all social contracts. What compels Lope's imagination is the villagers' redemptive commitment to their community. The playwright uses the historical events of Fuenteovejuna to raise fundamental questions of political philosophy: Does authority come from above (God) or below (the people)? Is government based on a social contract? Do laborers have the right to dignity? Are the people, if governed cruelly, entitled to revoke their consent or even to resist by violence? Lope, who was no political radical, suggests that government without popular consent and mutual respect is morally bankrupt.

The rapacious and arrogant style of dominion exemplified by Lope's Guzmán contrasts with the military and judicial policies of the so-called Catholic kings, Isabel and Ferdinand, whom Lope celebrates as prudent, just, and respectful of law. Guzmán violates the reciprocal obligations governing the relationship of the good ruler and his subjects: he contemptuously rejects the suggestion that he owes anything to the villagers, and it is in the role of bad counselor that he coerces the powerful but impressionable Master of Calatrava. The Catholic kings, on the other hand, exemplify the magnanimous and prudential nature of good monarchs.

The Commander's abuses habitually force peasants—otherwise typical comic characters—to think strenuously about the nature of social contracts. They conclude that those who govern owe a debt to those who serve and that communal bonds are formed by love: the willingness to enter into a social relationship and to treat the interests of others as one's own. This is the lesson that gives the villagers the courage to protect their community despite torture. In Lope's play, love is both the mainstay of comedy and the harmonizing principle of government: in matters of the heart and of law, the subject must have the right to consent.

Eventually deemed "the first proletarian drama," *Fuenteovejuna* became increasingly popular from the nineteenth century on, as critics and audiences warmed to its revolutionary portrayal of resistance. Politically trenchant yet full of humor and pastoral idealism, the play transcends its immediate historical context to serve as a lasting meditation on the power of community.

Fuenteovejuna[1]

CHARACTERS:

FERNÁN GÓMEZ DE GUZMÁN,
  Commander of the Order of
  Calatrava
FLORES
ORTUÑO } his retainers
RODRIGO TÉLLEZ GIRÓN, Master of
  the Order of Calatrava
LAURENCIA
PASCUALA
JACINTA
FRONDOSO } villagers
MENGO
BARRILDO
ESTEBAN
ALONSO } village magistrates

CUADRADO, village alderman
JUAN ROJO, village councilman
QUEEN ISABEL OF CASTILE
KING FERDINAND OF ARAGON
DON MANRIQUE, a courtier, Master of
  the Order of Santiago
A JUDGE
LEONELO, a University of Salamanca
  graduate
CIMBRANOS, a soldier
A BOY
ALDERMEN from Ciudad Real,
  SOLDIERS, VILLAGERS, MUSICIANS
    The action takes place in 1476.

Act I

[A Room in the Palace of Rodrigo Téllez Girón, Master of the Order of Calatrava]

   (*Enter the* COMMANDER, *Fernán Gómez de Guzmán, with his retainers*
   FLORES *and* ORTUÑO.)

COMMANDER The Master[2] knows I mark my time
  Awaiting him.
FLORES   Indeed, he does.
ORTUÑO He's more mature, sir, than he was.
COMMANDER Enough to be aware that I'm
  Still Fernán Gómez de Guzmán?   5
FLORES He's just a boy. Don't take this wrong.
COMMANDER He has to have known all along
  The title that's conferred upon
  Me is Commander of the Ranks.
ORTUÑO His counselors undoubtedly   10
  Incline him toward discourtesy.
COMMANDER This stance will win him little thanks,
  For courtesy unlocks the gate
  Behind which man's goodwill resides
  As surely as offense betides   15
  An enmity fomenting hate.
ORTUÑO If only men so keen to slight
  Knew how they were abhorred by all—
  Not least by sycophants who fall

---

1. Translated by G. J. Racz.
2. Leader of the Order of Calatrava, a Spanish military and religious order founded by

Cistercian monks in the 12th century to defend against Moorish attacks.

To kiss their feet and praise their might—   20
They'd much prefer to die before
Insulting anyone again.

FLORES   Mistreatment from unmannered men
Is harsh and something to deplore,
Yet while discourtesy between   25
Two equals is a foolish game,
When men aren't peers, it's not the same
But vile, tyrannical and mean.
No sense to take offense, my lord.
He's still a boy and ignorant of   30
The need for your auspicious love.

COMMANDER   The obligation that the sword
He girded on when first this Cross
Of Calatrava graced his chest
Bids courtesy be shown all, lest   35
Our noble Order suffer loss.

FLORES   We'll know soon if his heart's been set
Against your person or your cause.

ORTUÑO   Leave now if all this gives you pause.

COMMANDER   I'll take the stripling's measure yet.   40

(Enter the MASTER of Calatrava, Rodrigo Téllez Girón,
with retinue.)

MASTER   Dear Fernán Gómez de Guzmán!
I've just been told that you were come
And rue this inattention from
My heart's own core.

COMMANDER   I looked upon
The matter ill, with wounded pride,   45
As I'd thought my affection for
You and my standing would ensure
More noble treatment by your side,
We two of Calatrava, you
The Master, I Commander, though   50
Your humble servant, well you know.

MASTER   I only was alerted to
Your presence here at this late hour,
Fernán, and join you now in fond
Embrace.

COMMANDER   You honor well our bond   55
As I've done all that's in my power—
Nay, risked my life—to ease affairs
For you, petitioning the pope[3]

3. Pope Pius II (1405–1464), elected to the papacy in 1458. Before his death he issued a papal bull granting Master Pedro Girón's request that he be allowed to relinquish his post and appoint his illegitimate son, Rodrigo, to the position of Master. Pius's successor, Paul II, reaffirmed Pius's decree (see line 80, below) and in 1466 the eight-year-old Rodrigo was appointed Master and his uncle, Don Juan Pacheco, coadjutor (see lines 81–83). In 1474 (not long before the action of the play unfolds), Rodrigo attained his majority and was able to assume full command of the Order of Calatrava.

To disregard your youth.
MASTER   I hope
That, by this holy sign each wears   60
Upon his chest, as I repay
Your kindness with respect, you'll own
Such honor as my sire had known.
COMMANDER   I'm satisfied with what you say.
MASTER   What news have you about the war?   65
COMMANDER   Attend these words and soon you'll learn
How duty makes this your concern.
MASTER   It's this report I've waited for.
COMMANDER   Rodrigo Téllez Girón, this
Illustrious station you've attained   70
Derives from the profound esteem
Your sire claimed for your family name.[4]
When he relinquished, eight years past,
The rank of Master to his son,
Commanders joined with kings to pledge   75
The cross should pass to one so young
While further confirmation came
From papal bulls that blessed soul
His Holiness Pope Pius wrote,
Which Paul[5] did follow with his own.   80
Your uncle, Juan Pacheco,[6] then
The Master of Santiago, was
Appointed your coadjutor
And, when he died, we placed our trust
In your ability to lead   85
Our Order at your tender age.
Upholding past allegiances
Is vital in the present case
To honor these progenitors,
So know your kin, since Henry's[7] death,   90
Support Alfonso,[8] Portugal's
Good king, who has inherited
Castile, your blood contend, because
His queen, they vow, was Henry's child.
Prince Ferdinand of Aragon[9]   95
Disputes this claim, and through his wife

---

4. The historical father of Rodrigo Téllez-Girón,
Pedro Girón, relinquished leadership of the
Order of Calatrava in order to marry the Infanta
Isabel, sister of King Henry IV of Castile, but
died before their marriage could take place.
5. Pope Paul II (1417–1471), elected pope in
1464.
6. Marquis of Villena (see line 125), first
duke of Escalona and leader of the chivalric
Order of Santiago.

7. King Henry IV of Castile (1420–1474, r.
1454–74).
8. King Alfonso V of Portugal (1432–1481,
r.1438–81), who married King Henry's daughter
Juana in 1475 (see lines 94, 101).
9. The future King Ferdinand II of Aragón
(1452–1516, r. 1479–1516) and King Ferdinand V of Castile (r. 1474–1516); he claimed
the Castilian throne through his marriage to Isabel and was known as "Ferdinand the Catholic."

And Henry's sister, Isabel,[1]
Asserts his title to the throne
Against your family's cause. In short,
Yours see no treachery imposed   100
By Juana's[2] just succession here.
Your cousin keeps her under guard
Until the day when she will reign.
I come, then, with this counsel: charge
Your Knights of Calatrava in   105
Almagro here to mount their steeds
And capture Ciudad Real,[3]
Which straddles the frontier between
Castile and Andalusia, thus
Strategically commanding both.   110
You'd hardly need a host of men
To have it fall to your control;
Their only soldiers left there are
Its landowners and citizens
Who still defend Queen Isabel   115
And follow Ferdinand as king.
How grand, Rodrigo, to avail
Yourself of such a siege and prove
Those wrong who think these shoulders far
Too slight to bear the cross you do!   120
Your gallant ancestors, the Counts
Of Urueña,[4] beckon from
Their eminence in proud display
Of all the laurels they have won;
The Marquis of Villena,[5] too,   125
And countless other captains, ones
So noble that the wings of Fame
Could scarcely bear them higher up!
Come, bare the whiteness of your sword
And stain its blade in fierce assaults   130
With blood red as our Order's sign
So that you may be rightly called
By all men Master of that Cross
You wear upon your chest! If white
It stays, that title stays unearned.   135
Yes, both the weapon at your side

---

1. Queen Isabel (sometimes Isabella) of Castile (1451–1504, r. 1474–1504), half sister of King Henry IV. Following her marriage to Ferdinand of Aragón in 1469, Pope Alexander VI named them the "Catholic Monarchs."
2. King Henry IV's only child (1462–1504); because of the alleged infidelity of her mother, Princess Joana of Portugal, Juana was considered illegitimate by many, and upon her father's death the crown of Castile passed not to Juana but to her aunt, Isabel of Castile,

sparking the War of the Castilian Succession (the backdrop of *Fuenteovejuna*).
3. A city in south-central Spain whose name means "Royal City." "Almagro": a town near Ciudad Real and the seat of the Order of Calatrava.
4. Among these ancestors was Alfonso Téllez-Girón, the father of Juan Pacheco and grandfather of Rodrigo.
5. That is, Juan Pacheco (see line 81 and note above).

And that dear cross must shine blood-red.
Thus you, magnificent Girón,
Shall be at last enshrined the first
Among your line and most extolled!   140
MASTER   Fernán Gómez, it's my intent
To side with blood in a dispute
Whose rightness seems beyond refute,
So rest assured of this event.
If Ciudad Real, then, must   145
Be leveled by my hands, I'll burn
Its walls with lightning speed and turn
The city into ash and dust.
The friend or stranger who insists
That with my uncle died my youth   150
Could not be farther from the truth:
The spirit of my years persists.
I'll bare this still-white blade and lead
My forces by its dazzling light   155
Till, like these crosses, it shines bright
With blood the reddened wounded bleed.
Do any soldiers now subsist
Among your village retinue?
COMMANDER   They're loyal servitors, though few,   160
But should you summon them to list
With you, they'll fight like lions, for
In Fuenteovejuna all
The townsfolk heed the humble call
Of agriculture, not of war,   165
And farm to reap their daily fare.
MASTER   You've quarters near?
COMMANDER   It pleased the crown
To grant me land once in that town
So, mid these perils, I dwell there.
MASTER   I'll need a tally of our strength.
COMMANDER   No vassal there shall stay behind!   170
MASTER   This day you'll see me ride, and find
My couching lance atilt full length!

(*Exit* COMMANDER *and* MASTER.)

[The Town Square in Fuenteovejuna]

(*Enter the village women* PASCUALA *and* LAURENCIA.)

LAURENCIA   I'd hoped that he was gone for good!
PASCUALA   To tell the truth, I really thought
The news of his return here ought   175
To have perturbed you . . . and still would!
LAURENCIA   I wish to God, I swear to you,
That we had seen the last of him!
PASCUALA   Laurencia, I've known girls as prim
And tough as you—nay, more so—who,   180

Beneath the guise of harsh facades,
Have hearts as soft as cooking lard.
LAURENCIA   You couldn't find an oak as hard
And dry as I am toward these clods!
PASCUALA   Go on, now! You don't mean to say   185
You'd never drink to quench your thirst?
LAURENCIA   I do, though I won't be the first
To have to protest in this way.
Besides, how would it profit me
To yield to all Fernán's false woo?   190
I couldn't marry him.
PASCUALA   That's true.
LAURENCIA   I can't abide his infamy!
So many girls were gullible
In trusting the Commander's plights
And now live days that rue those nights.   195
PASCUALA   Still, it would be a miracle
If you don't wind up in his grasp.
LAURENCIA   Pascuala, one full month's gone by
Since you first saw this scapegrace try
In vain to land me in his clasp.   200
His pander, Flores, and that knave,
Ortuño, came by with a hat,
A jerkin and a choker that
Their master had assumed I'd crave.
They started off regaling me   205
With vows his lovelorn heart declared,
Which left me all a little scared,
Though just as disinclined to see
Myself his latest vanquished maid.
PASCUALA   Where did they speak to you?
LAURENCIA   Down by   210
The brook six days ago, as I
Recall.
PASCUALA   Laurencia, I'm afraid
They'll end up getting what they wish.
LAURENCIA   From me?
PASCUALA   No, from the priest—yes, you!
LAURENCIA   The meat on this young chick he'd woo   215
Is still too tough to grace his dish.
I mean, good lord, Pascuala! Look:
You know how much I'd rather take
A slice of ham when I awake
And place it on the fire to cook;   220
Then eat it with a hunk of bread
I baked and kneaded by myself
With wine pinched off my mother's shelf
From jugs that tightly store her red;
And how much happier I'd be   225

At noon to watch beef frolicking
With heads of cabbage, rollicking
In frothy pots of harmony!
Or, when I come home peeved and tired,
To marry eggplant in full bloom   230
With bacon—there's no rasher groom!—
For just the pick-me-up required.
Then later, for some toothsome snacks
To hold me till our supper's served,
I'd pick grapes off my vines, preserved   235
By God alone from hail attacks.
For dinner, I would eat the lot
Of spicy peppered meat in oil,
Then go to bed content with toil
And give thanks with a "lead us not   240
Into temptation"[6] of sheer praise.
But you know how men are: until
They get their way in love, what skill
They use in finding crafty ways
To make us, in the end, forlorn!   245
When, worn down, we give up the fight,
They take their pleasure in the night
And leave us wretched on the morn.

PASCUALA   You're right, Laurencia! It's no joke!
Once men are sated, they grow rude   250
And show us more ingratitude
Than sparrows do to villagefolk.
In winter, when the weather keeps
Our snowy fields devoid of crops,
These birds swoop down from off the tops   255
Of houses, all sweet coos and cheeps,
But indoors, head straight for the room
Where they can feed upon our crumbs.
Then, once the warm spring weather comes
And sparrows see the fields in bloom,   260
We hear the last of all their coos.
Forgetting our benevolence
And cutting off their blandishments,
They chirp accusingly: "Jews? Jews?"[7]
Yes, men are like that, too. As long   265
As they desire us, we're their soul,
Their heart, their everything, their whole
Life's being, and can do no wrong,
But once the fire of passion's spent,

6. From the Lord's Prayer: see Matthew 6.13;
Luke 11.4.
7. Intolerance for all non-Christian religions
increased during the Reconquest of territories
from Muslim forces, and Jews who did not
convert to Catholicism were expelled from
Spain in 1492.

They start to treat us worse than Jews   270
And what were once seductive coos
Now chastise us for our consent.

LAURENCIA   You can't trust any of their kind.

PASCUALA   Laurencia, sweetheart, I'm with you!

(*Enter the villagers* MENGO, BARRILDO, *and* FRONDOSO.)

FRONDOSO   Barrildo, argue till you're blue,   275
You'll never change old Mengo's mind!

BARRILDO   Now, here's a person who could bring
An end to this discussion, men.

MENGO   Let's all be in agreement, then,
Before you ask her anything: 280
If she concurs that I'm correct,
You promise that you won't forget
To hand me over what we've bet?

BARRILDO   That's fine with me. I don't object,
But what do we net if you lose?   285

MENGO   My boxwood rebec,[8] which I hold
More precious than a granary's gold,
If I may be allowed to choose.

BARRILDO   That's good enough.

FRONDOSO   Then, let's not wile.
God keep you, lovely ladies both.   290

LAURENCIA   Frondoso, "ladies"? By my oath!

FRONDOSO   Just keeping with the latest style:
These days, a college boy goes by
"Professor," "one-eyed" means you're blind,
The cross-eyed "squint," lame are "inclined,"   295
And now a spendthrift's a "good guy."
The dumbest person is called "bright,"
The none-too-brave are "placable";
No one has thick lips—lips are "full"—
And beady eyes are "piercing," right?   300
The nitpicker is "thorough," while
The meddler is "engaged." In speech,
A windbag is "well-spoken," each
Annoying bore said to "beguile."
Thus, cowards are "dispirited"   305
And blowhards "full of fight." With twits,
The useful catchword "fellows" fits
While loons are "uninhibited."
The cheerless are alone "discreet";
"Authority" falls to the bald.   310
If silliness is "charm," who called
"Well-grounded" someone with big feet?

---

8. A bowed string instrument of medieval origin, played while held against the arm or under the chin like a violin.

A "chest cold" means the pox in code;
The haughty now are "self-possessed";
The shrewd are "sly," but here's the best: 315
The humpback "shoulders quite a load"!
So maybe now you'll comprehend
Just how you're "ladies," and although
I've more examples, I'll forego
Reciting all of them on end. 320

LAURENCIA   Well, that may pass for courtesy,
Frondoso, with the city folk,
But I've heard other people cloak
Their thoughts in language that strikes me
As far more coarse in every phrase 325
They use and every cutting word.

FRONDOSO   Give us a taste of what you've heard.

LAURENCIA   It's just the opposite of praise:
You're "tiresome" if you're serious
And "brazen" if you look well heeled. 330
You're "somber" if you're even-keeled
And "spiteful" if you're virtuous.
Give counsel and you "interfere";
You "lavish" when you freely give.
Love justice and you're "punitive," 335
Show mercy and be "inaustere."
The steadfast now are "dull as sin,"
Politeness is "sheer flattery,"
Sweet charity, "hypocrisy,"
And Christian faith "the sure way in." 340
"Dumb luck" is hard-won merit's name
While truth-telling is "recklessness."
Forbearance is deemed "cowardice"
And misadventure now means "blame."
A decent woman's called a "ponce," 345
A proper, lovely girl is "plain,"
A chaste . . . Why should I wrack my brain
More? Let this serve as my response.

MENGO   The devil! That was quite a list!

BARRILDO   She's not a half-bad orator! 350

MENGO   I bet the priest who christened her
Laid on the salt, fist after fist![9]

LAURENCIA   What quarrel is it brings you here,
If I have heard you right, today?

FRONDOSO   Just listen, on your soul.

LAURENCIA   Tell, pray. 355

FRONDOSO   Laurencia, lend me but your ear.

---

9. Prior to the Second Vatican Council (1962–65), Roman Catholic baptisms often included the placing of a small amount of salt on a baby's lips as a symbol of purification and wisdom.

LAURENCIA   I'll give it to you out and out,
  A special present, not a loan.
FRONDOSO   I trust your judgment as my own.
LAURENCIA   So, what's this famous bet about?   360
FRONDOSO   Barrildo casts his lot with me.
LAURENCIA   And Mengo?
BARRILDO   He insists upon
  Denying a phenomenon
  That's clearly real.
MENGO   It cannot be;
  Experience refutes its name.   365
LAURENCIA   Which is . . . ?
BARRILLDO   That love does not exist.[1]
LAURENCIA   Love's vital and would sure be missed.
BARRILDO   Yes, vital; it's a silly claim.
  This world has a most pressing need
  For love, or life would fade away.   370
MENGO   Philosophy's not my forte
  And now I wish that I could read,
  But here goes: if the elements[2]—
  Earth, water, fire and air—all live
  In endless discord and then give   375
  Our very bodies sustenance—
  Their melancholy and, let's see,
  Blood, choler . . . phlegm[3]—I've proved my point.
BARRILDO   This world is nowhere out of joint,
  Dear Mengo; all is harmony[4]   380
  For harmony is love distilled
  And love, pure concert from above.
MENGO   I don't dispute that natural love
  Abides on earth, as God has willed.
  Love does exist, but of the sort   385
  That rules relations in advance—
  Compulsory ties, not bonds of chance—
  Among all beings these realms support.
  And never once have I denied
  That each man's humor finds some fit   390

---

1. The following is a comic pastiche of tenets of classical philosophy.
2. I.e., the four elements that make up all matter (earth, air, fire, and water); this theory of matter, still current during the Renaissance, was first propounded by the Greek philosopher Empedocles (c. 493—ca. 433 B.C.E.)
3. According to the humoral theory of psychology and physiology, elaborated by the Greek physician Galen (129–ca. 199 C.E.) and dominant for centuries, imbalances between the four humors, or bodily fluids, determined health and personality. An excess of black bile (a cold, dry substance in the body corresponding to the earth) made people melancholic, while blood and air were associated with the sanguine; yellow bile and fire, with the choleric; and phlegm and water, with the phlegmatic.
4. I.e., the harmony produced by a balance in bodily systems; "pure concert from above" (line 382) also suggests the harmony produced by the music of the spheres, a concept generally credited to the Greek mathematician and philosopher Pythagoras (6th century B.C.E.) but taken up more literally in the Middle Ages.

With love that corresponds to it
To keep his being unified.
If someone tries to punch my face,
I block the impact with my arm
And when I'm facing bodily harm,   395
My feet run to a safer place.
My lids and lashes likewise move
To counter danger to my eye
And all from natural love, I vie.

PASCUALA   What point is it you seek to prove?   400
MENGO   I mean that we should be agreed
That only self-love rules the day.
PASCUALA   That's not true, Mengo, if I may,
For isn't there a vital need
A man experiences when   405
He loves a woman, or a brute
Its mate?
MENGO   Yes, but without dispute,
It's self-love and not true love, then.
Now, what is love?
PASCUALA   It's a desire
For beauty.[5]
MENGO   And why does love pursue   410
Said beauty, in your humble view?
PASCUALA   For pleasure.
MENGO   Right! May I inquire,
Then, whether this enjoyment might
Serve love itself?
PASCUALA   I'm sure that's so.
MENGO   So, self-love, then, will make love go   415
And seek what causes it delight?
PASCUALA   Why, yes.
MENGO   Then, as I'm claiming, there
Can be no love but of the kind
That everybody seeks to find
By courting pleasure everywhere.   420
BARRILDO   I seem to have some memory of
A sermon I heard by and by
Regarding Plato,[6] some Greek guy
Who taught humanity to love,
Although the love he felt was aimed   425
At virtue and his loved one's soul.
PASCUALA   This line of thought has, on the whole,
Both stumped great intellects and shamed
Top scholars in our 'cademies

5. A position drawn from Plato's *Symposium* (c. 384 B.C.E.). See below line 423 and note.
6. Greek philosopher (c. 427–c. 347 B.C.E.), whose themes were much debated in the 15th century by Neoplatonists.

Who fry their brains debating it.   430
LAURENCIA   She's right; don't fly into a snit
  By arguing for such fallacies.
  Go thank your stars for leaving you
  Without love, Mengo, in this sphere.
MENGO   Don't you love?
LAURENCIA   Just my honor here.   435
FRONDOSO   I hope God makes you jealous, too.
BARRILDO   So, who's the winner?
PASCUALA   You can take
  That question to the sacristan.
  If he won't tell you, the priest can
  And that should settle what's at stake.   440
  As I've not much experience
  And our Laurencia loves not well,
  I wonder how we'll ever tell?
FRONDOSO   To suffer such indifference!

    (*Enter* FLORES.)

FLORES   God keep you, good folk! As you were.   445
PASCUALA   So the retainer's sent to talk
  For the Commander.
LAURENCIA   Chicken hawk!
  What brings you here today, fine sir?
FLORES   You see this uniform, don't you?
LAURENCIA   So then, Fernán is coming back?   450
FLORES   The battle's won, though our attack
  Entailed the loss of not a few
  Brave men and blood of good allies.
FRONDOSO   Do tell us how the fighting raged.
FLORES   Who better to, since war was waged   455
  Before these witnesses, my eyes?
  To undertake this swift campaign
  Against a city by the name
  Of Ciudad Real, our most
  Courageous, noble Master raised   460
  An army of two thousand men—
  All loyal vassals—with whom rode
  Three hundred more of mounted troops
  Comprised of friars and laymen both
  For anyone who wears this Cross   465
  Must rally to its battle cry,
  Including priests, especially when
  The foes are Moors,[7] you read me right?
  Thus did the gallant youth ride forth
  Bedecked in an embroidered coat   470

7. North African Muslims who conquered Spain and Portugal in 711 and ruled for centuries
over much of the Iberian Peninsula (see below, line 500 and note).

Of green with golden monograms.
His glistening brassards[8] alone
Shone through the openings in his sleeves
Held fast by hooks with golden braids.
A sturdy charger rode he, bred   475
In our fair South and dapple-gray,
Which drank from the Guadalquivir[9]
And grazed upon the fertile spots
Nearby. Its tailpiece was adorned
With buckskin straps, its curled forelock   480
In pure-white bows resembling cloth
That expert weavers deftly wove
To match the patches on its hide,
Or "flies on snow," as they are known.
Your liege lord, Fernán Gómez, rode   485
Beside him on a honeyed steed
That bore some white upon its nose,
Accenting its black mane and feet.
Atop a Turkish coat of mail
His armor breast- and back-plate shone   490
Both bordered with an orange trim
Relucent with pearls set in gold.
And from his burnished helmet waved
A crown of plumes that seemed to stretch
In orange-blossom whiteness down   495
To meet his orange vestment's edge.
A red and white brace held his lance
In readiness, although this bore
More likeness to a huge ash tree
To petrify Granada's[1] Moors.   500
And so the city took up arms
In affirmation of the stance
That it obeyed the rightful crown
And would defend its king and lands.
The Master mounted an attack   505
And, after fierce resistance there,
Decreed that all who'd wagged their tongues
Against his honor be prepared
To die beheaded for their crime,
While those who rallied round the flag   510
Among the simple city folk
Were flogged in public, bound and gagged.
There in the city he abides,
As well loved as he is well feared;

8. Armor for protecting the arm, usually from
elbow to shoulder.
9. A river that passes through the southern
Spanish cities of Córdoba and Seville.

1. A city in southern Spain; the site of the
Alhambra, the palace of the Moorish kings, it
was the Moors' last stronghold, from which
they were expelled in 1492.

A man who battles, castigates 515
And crushes foes, still raw in years,
The town believes will come to be
The scourge of Africa someday,
Subjecting blue and crescent moons[2]
To that Red Cross his garb displays. 520
So many gifts has he bestowed
On our Commander and on all,
It seems that he's despoiling not
The city, but his private vaults.
But listen! Hear the music play? 525
Come welcome your great hero home,
For no wreath suits a victor like
The good will shown him by his own.

(Enter the COMMANDER and ORTUÑO, MUSICIANS, Village Magistrates
ESTEBAN and ALONSO, and Village Councilman JUAN ROJO.)

MUSICIANS   (Singing) All hail, victorious
Commander! Thy bold deeds be praised! 530
For thou hast slain our foes
And left their rebel cities razed!
Long life to thy Guzmáns
And to our Master's proud Giróns!
In times of peace thy speech 535
Is couched in calm and measured tones
Though thou wouldst battle Moors
Courageous as an oak is strong.
From Ciudad Real
To Fuenteovejuna throng 540
Thy still triumphant troops
And here thy lofty pennants wave!
Fernán Gómez, God grant
A thousand years to one so brave!

COMMANDER   Kind villagers, I thank you for this true 545
Outpouring of affection I've been shown.

ALONSO   'Tis but a fraction of our love for you
And scarce reflects the sentiments you're known
To merit.

ESTEBAN   Fuenteovejuna deems
Your presence here an honor, and our own 550
Town council begs you to accept what seems
No doubt a paltry offering conveyed
By cart to one the village so esteems
And tendered in goodwill mid poles arrayed
With ribbons, though the gifts themselves be small. 555
To start, glazed earthenware our potters made.
Next, an entire stock of geese—see all

2. Islamic insignia.

Their heads protruding through the mesh to voice
Praise for your valor with their cackling call!
Ten salted hogs, each specimen more choice, 560
Jerked beef, rich delicacies, and pork hides
Which, more than perfumed gloves, make men rejoice.
A hundred capons and plump hens, the brides
Of future widowed roosters of the same
Sort dotting these lush fields, are yours besides. 565
You'll not fetch arms or horses for your fame,
Nor trappings here embroidered with pure gold
Unless you take for gold the love you claim.
And having said "pure," may I be so bold
As to suggest these wineskins bear such wine 570
That poor bare soldiers scarce would mind the cold
As they patrolled outdoors if they could line
Their stomachs with this, steelier than steel,
For wine can cause the dullest blades to shine.
I'll skip the savories and the cheese you'll feel 575
Most tempted by, except to say it's right
That we should pay you tribute for our weal
And wish your household hearty appetite.

COMMANDER   For this, much thanks, good councilmen.
  You may retire with all my best. 580

ALONSO   We bid you, sir, enjoy some rest
  And welcome you back home again.
  This sedge and bulrush at your door,
  A touch of grace our town unfurls,
  Might well have been oriental pearls— 585
  Though surely you deserve far more—
  Had we but means to furnish these.

COMMANDER   Kind folk, I doubt not what you say.
  May God be with you.

ESTEBAN   Singers, play
  Our song of triumph once more, please. 590

MUSICIANS   (*Singing.*) *All hail, victorious*
Commander! Thy bold deeds be praised!
For thou hast slain our foes
And left their rebel cities razed!

(*Exit* MUSICIANS. *The* COMMANDER *turns toward his residence but
stops at the entrance to speak with* LAURENCIA *and* PASCUALA.)

COMMANDER   Abide a while, the two of you. 595
LAURENCIA   What can we do for you, good sir?
COMMANDER   Why, just the other day you were
  Aloof toward me, is that not true?
LAURENCIA   It's you he's coming to harass.
PASCUALA   Oh God, no! Let it not be that! 600
COMMANDER   I'm talking both to you, wildcat,
  And to this other lovely lass,

For aren't you mine?

PASCUALA   Good sir, no doubt,
But hardly for such things as these.

COMMANDER   Just come inside and be at ease.   605
You see my servants are about.

LAURENCIA   Well, had the magistrates come, too—
For one's my father, you may know—
It might have seemed correct to go.

COMMANDER   You, Flores!

FLORES   Sir!

COMMANDER   Can it be true   610
That they refuse what I implore?

FLORES   He said, go in!

LAURENCIA   Stop grabbing, man!

FLORES   You're being foolish.

PASCUALA   While you plan
To lock us in and bolt the door?

FLORES   He only thought you'd like to see   615
The spoils he gathered in this batch.

(*The* COMMANDER *turns to enter his dwelling.*)

COMMANDER   (*Aside to Ortuño.*) If they do enter, draw the latch.

LAURENCIA   I told you, Flores, leave us be!

ORTUÑO   You mean the two of you are not
More booty?

PASCUALA   Let it rest awhile   620
And get out of my way or I'll . . .

FLORES   Enough, for now. You see they're hot.

LAURENCIA   How much more tribute would it take
To make him happy with these meats?

ORTUÑO   Your meats would be the sweeter treats.   625

LAURENCIA   I hope they make his belly ache!

(*Exit* LAURENCIA *and* PASCUALA.)

FLORES   He'll give us both an earful when
We dare return without the girls
And curse us like a pair of churls
While we take his abuse again.   630

ORTUÑO   Well, masters sometimes grow annoyed.
To prosper in the servant class,
You have to let their foul moods pass:
Be patient or be unemployed.

(*Exit* FLORES *and* ORTUÑO.)

[A Room in the Palace of the Catholic Kings]

(*Enter King* FERDINAND, *Queen* ISABEL, *the courtier Don* MANRIQUE,
and retinue.)

ISABEL   You would do well to heed the threat   635
Alfonso's army now presents.
His Portuguese have pitched their tents

In nearby fields and must be met
With troops who'll counter this deceit
By striking ere these foes attack   640
For if our men don't drive them back
Our side will suffer sure defeat.
FERDINAND   Navarre and Aragon[3] both aid
Our righteous cause and shall until
We steel our forces in Castile   645
And see their re-formation made,
A measure which should guarantee
Our triumph in an allied thrust.
ISABEL   Your Royal Majesty, we must
Be certain of this victory.   650
MANRIQUE   Your Highness, there are aldermen
From Ciudad Real here who
Request an audience with you.
FERDINAND   Brave Don Manrique, show them in.

(*Enter two* ALDERMEN *from Ciudad Real.*)

1ST ALDERMAN   Great Ferdinand, most Catholic king,   655
Whom Heaven's sent with grace to reign
Through all Castile and Aragon,
Our noble succor and true aid,
On Ciudad Real's behalf
We've come to sue for royal help   660
In true humility before
Your valiant and all-powerful self.
We'd held our own selves fortunate
To be the subjects of this crown
Till adverse fortune intervened   665
And turned our destinies around.
Rodrigo Téllez Girón, sire,
Famed bearer of his family name
Whose courage on the battlefield
And strength belie his tender age,   670
Of Calatrava Master, has
Assailed our city to expand
The Order's power and estate,
His lands erstwhile by royal grant.
We bravely readied our defense   675
In hopes resistance would rebuff
His forces, but our streams ran red,
Discolored with the fallen's blood.
In short, he took the city but
He never could have had Fernán   680
Gómez withheld his counsel, troops,

3. Provinces of northern Spain. Following the events depicted in this play, Ferdinand succeeded his father as king of Aragón in 1479; in 1511 he conquered the southern half of the kingdom of Navarre, uniting it with Spain.

And guidance in this treacherous plot.
He bides still in our captured town,
His vassals and sad subjects we
Who suffer this loss with regret   685
And hope it soon be remedied.

FERDINAND   And where is Fernán Gómez now?

1ST ALDERMAN   In Fuenteovejuna, sire,
The village where he makes his home
And where his seat of power resides,   690
The cruel Commander acts unchecked,
More freely than we care to state,
And keeps his vassals there as far
From happiness as they can stay.

FERDINAND   Have you no captain in your ranks?   695

2ND ALDERMAN   It's sure we haven't anymore,
As every nobleman they seized
Was wounded or has faced the sword.

ISABEL   This matter begs a quick display
Of strength, for cautious remedy   700
Would only make this enemy
The bolder given our delay.
Thus Portugal might view this stall
A chance occasion fortune yields,
Thrust through Extremadura's[4] fields   705
And so bring grievous harm to all.

FERDINAND   Manrique, take two companies
Of soldiers to their bivouac
And launch a merciless attack
To quell such excesses as these.   710
The Count of Cabra, widely famed
For bravery and a Córdoba,[5]
Will ride with you, and never a
More valiant soldier has Spain claimed!
This seems the most expedient   715
Proceeding we can now effect.

MANRIQUE   Your judgment, sire, is most correct
And this dispatch most provident.
As long as life runs through my veins,
I'll see them all put in their place.   720

ISABEL   I'm confident success shall grace
Our cause with such men at the reins.

    (*Exit all.*)

---

4. A province of southwest Spain bordering Portugal.

5. Diego Fernandez de Córdoba (b. 1438), count of Cabra and marshal of Baena.

[An Open Field in Fuenteovejuna]

(*Enter* LAURENCIA *and* FRONDOSO.)

LAURENCIA   I had to leave the wash half wet,
   Frondoso, just to keep the town
   From gossiping. The brook's no place   725
   For men to gallivant around.
   The villagers are whispering
   About how you persist. They know
   I've caught your eye as you have mine
   And keep their eyes now on us both.   730
   As you're the type of brazen swain
   To strut throughout the village clad
   In elegant attire that costs
   Far more than any other lad's,
   There's not a girl or guy about   735
   These woodlands, meadows, groves, and brush
   Who isn't saying to himself
   That we two are already one.
   They all await that blessed day
   When Juan Chamorro, sacristan,   740
   Will leave the church's organ long
   Enough to carry out our banns,
   Though they'd be better off by far
   To see their granaries duly stuffed
   With heaps of autumn's golden wheat   745
   And have their wine jars filled with must.
   The rumors that the villagers
   Keep spreading here have caused me pique
   But aren't so irritating as
   To have deprived me of dear sleep.   750
FRONDOSO   Your harsh disdain so flusters me,
   Laurencia, that I fear each time
   I see your face or hear your voice
   I place existence on the line!
   For if you know my sole desire   755
   Is that we marry, why repay
   These good intentions with such scorn?
LAURENCIA   I know but one way to behave.
FRONDOSO   How can it be you feel no pain
   To see me in the grip of grief   760
   When, at the merest thought of you,
   I lose desire for food and sleep?
   How can that sweet, angelic face
   Bring such hardheartedness with it?
   But, Lord, how rabidly I rave!   765
LAURENCIA   Then you must seek a curative.
FRONDOSO   The cure I seek resides in you
   So we can be like turtledoves

That perch together rubbing beaks
And coo contentedly in love— 770
I mean, provided that the church . . .

LAURENCIA   Go ask my uncle from your heart,
The good Juan Rojo. Though I feel
No passion yet, I sense a spark.

FRONDOSO   Oh, no! Look over there—it's him! 775

LAURENCIA   He must be hunting deer nearby.
Quick, run and hide within these woods!

FRONDOSO   It's jealousy I need to hide!

(*Enter the* COMMANDER.)

COMMANDER   I can't say it displeases me
To set out for a fearsome buck 780
And come upon a lovely doe.

LAURENCIA   I left my pile of wash half done
For this brief respite from my chores
But now, I fear, the brook awaits
So, by your leave, I'll go now, sir. 785

COMMANDER   The brusqueness in your cruel disdain,
Laurencia, is a sharp affront
To all the grace and comely looks
The heavens have bestowed on you
And makes you seem unnatural. 790
You've managed in the past to flee
The loving of my arms' embrace
But now this field, our silent friend,
Has pledged to keep our secret safe.
Come, there's no need for diffidence 795
Or any reason to avert
Your gaze from me, your rightful lord,
As if I were some peasant churl.
Did not Pedro Redondo's wife
Sebastiana gladly yield, 800
And young Martín del Pozo's, too,
Although the latter's wedding seal
Had scarcely dried, our happy tryst
But two days after she was wed?

LAURENCIA   These women, sir, could by that time 805
Claim much experience with men
As that same road you took to them
Had been well traveled for some years
By all the lads with whom they'd lain.
God keep you as you hunt your deer; 810
Were you not costumed with that cross,
I'd take you for the devil's spawn
To hound me so relentlessly.

COMMANDER   What haughty insolence you flaunt!
I'll lay my crossbow on the ground 815

And use these hands to put an end
To all your mincing ways.
LAURENCIA   How now?
You don't mean you'd be capable . . .

  (*Enter* FRONDOSO, *who picks up the crossbow.*)

COMMANDER (*Not noticing* FRONDOSO.) Don't try to fight me off.
FRONDOSO (*Aside.*)   I pick 820
His weapon up, but hope to God
I'll have no cause for using it.
COMMANDER Relent already!
LAURENCIA   Heavens, help
A girl in need!
COMMANDER We're all alone.
There's no need now to be afraid.
FRONDOSO Commander, you've a generous soul 825
So leave her be or rest assured
I'll make a bull's-eye of your chest
Though, even in my rage, that cross
Elicits my profound respect.
COMMANDER Vile dog!
FRONDOSO   I see no dogs round here. 830
Quick, run, Laurencia!
LAURENCIA   Careful now,
Frondoso!
FRONDOSO Off with you, I said!

  (*Exit* LAURENCIA.)

COMMANDER The fool who'd lay his own sword down
Deserves the trouble he incurs.
I feared my prey would hear its clap 835
So I pursued the hunt ungirt.
FRONDOSO By God, don't make me loose the catch
Or you'll be pierced like game, my lord.
COMMANDER She's gone! Come, give the crossbow up,
You thieving, treacherous, peasant rogue! 840
Just give it here, I said!
FRONDOSO   For what,
So you could take my life with it?
Remember, sir, that love is deaf
And, from that day it reigns supreme,
Will not be swayed by argument. 845
COMMANDER Am I to turn my back upon
A village churl? Shoot! Shoot, you knave,
But be prepared to stand on guard,
For as a nobleman I break
Chivalric code to challenge you. 850
FRONDOSO No need, sir, for I'm satisfied
With my low station here on earth

But, as I must protect my life,
I'll take this crossbow as I flee.

COMMANDER   He plays a rash and perilous game   855
But I shall have my vengeance for
This crime of standing in my way!
Why didn't I just attack the clod?
The heavens see how I've been shamed!

Act II

[The Town Square in Fuenteovejuna]

(Enter ESTEBAN *and Village Alderman* CUADRADO.*)*

ESTEBAN   We've still abundant stocks of wheat reserved   860
But really mustn't raid our granaries more.
These recent forecasts have us all unnerved
And I believe our strength lies in this store
Though some don't see what good these stocks have served.

CUADRADO   I've always been of one mind on this score;   865
Abundance means there's governance in peace.

ESTEBAN   We'll tell Fernán Gómez, then, this must cease.
These fool astrologers do irritate!
Though ignorant of the future, they've a hoard
Of unconvincing prattles that relate   870
Grave secrets vital only to the Lord.
They think they're theologians and conflate
Before and after into one accord:
Ask any one about the present, though,
And you'll soon learn how little any know!   875
What, do they own the clouds that dot the air
Or the trajectory of the heavens' light?
How can they see what's happening up there
To give us all an endless case of fright?
They tell us when to plant our crops and where—   880
Wheat there, now greens, your barley to the right,
Here mustard, pumpkins, now cucumber beds—
I swear to God that they're the pumpkin heads!
First, they predict a herd of cows will die
And die they do—in Transylvania![6]   885
They forecast that our wine yield won't be high
But see beer flowing in Westphalia.[7]
The cherry frost in Gascony[8] they spy
And hordes of tigers in Hyrcania.[9]
Plant what we will, though, blessed by them or cursed,   890
The year still ends December thirty-first.

6. A region of present-day Romania, invoked here as a place remote from Spain.
7. A western region of present-day Germany.
8. A region of southwest France.
9. An area of ancient Persia (present-day northern Iran), associated in classical and later literature with tigers.

(Enter the university graduate LEONELO *and* BARRILDO.*)*

LEONELO   Looks like the gossip corner's doing well;
　The tardy pupil can't be teacher's pet!
BARRILDO   Was Salamanca[1] grand?
LEONELO　　　　　　　　　　　　　I've much to tell.
BARRILDO   You'll be Law's second Bartolus.[2]
LEONELO　　　　　　　　　　　　　　Not yet.　　　　　895
　A barber, maybe. What I'd dwell
　Upon is doctrine for the jurist set.
BARRILDO   I'm sure you studied with the utmost care.
LEONELO   I tried to gain important knowledge there.
BARRILDO   So many volumes are in print today　　　　　900
　The multitudes imagine they are wise.
LEONELO   Yet they know less, it saddens me to say,
　For so much wisdom's hard to summarize
　And all their vain attempts to find a way
　Just make the letters swim before their eyes.　　　　　905
　The more a person reads the printed word
　The more the letters on the page look blurred.
　I don't doubt that the art of print has saved
　The best cuts from this cloth of rhetoric
　By salvaging sage works from Time's depraved　　　　　910
　Consignment of all earthly things to quick
　Oblivion; this the printing press has staved.
　To Gutenberg[3] we owe this curious trick,
　A German from the town of Mainz whose fame
　Is more than any Fame herself can claim.　　　　　915
　Some writers who were once deemed erudite,
　Though, lost their erudition on the page
　While dumber men who never learned to write
　Have published using names of men more sage.
　Still others have penned treatises so trite　　　　　920
　That, overcome by jealousy and rage,
　They've signed their rivals' names to these poor works
　To make their readers think these authors jerks!
BARRILDO   They couldn't do such things!
LEONELO　　　　　　　　　　　　　It's natural
　For fools to reap revenge on real success.　　　　　925
BARRILDO   Still, Leonelo, print is notable.
LEONELO   We've lived for centuries without the press
　And I don't see these modern times more full

---

1. A city in western Spain where the country's oldest university was founded in 1134 and chartered in 1218.
2. Bartolus of Saxoferrato (1313–1357), Ital-ian jurist, author of influential doctrines based on Roman civil law.
3. Johannes Gutenberg (c. 1400–1468), inventor of the movable-type printing press.

Of Saint Augustines or Jeromes,[4] do you?

BARRILDO   Let's sit a while before you start to stew.   930

(*Enter* JUAN ROJO *and a* VILLAGER.)

JUAN ROJO   If what we've seen is true, you couldn't raise
A dowry out of what four farms would yield.
Now anyone who'd know the truth can gaze
Upon our town's disruption unconcealed.

VILLAGER   Peace, friend. What news of the Commander's days?   935

JUAN ROJO   He cornered poor Laurencia in a field!

VILLAGER   That lecherous animal! I'd love to see
The villain hanging from that olive tree!

(*Enter the* COMMANDER *with* ORTUÑO *and* FLORES.)

COMMANDER   God keep you, townsfolk, in His grace.

CUADRADO   My lord.

COMMANDER   Good villagers, at ease   940
Now, as you were.

ESTEBAN   Your lordship, please
Be seated in your wonted place.
We'll stand, as this suits everyone.

COMMANDER   I'll order you to sit down, then.

ESTEBAN   You honor us as only men   945
Of honor can, as men who've none
Can scarcely proffer what they've not.

COMMANDER   Come, sit. I'd like us to confer.

ESTEBAN   Have you received the greyhound, sir?

COMMANDER   The dog continues to besot   950
My valets, magistrate, and stuns
The servants with its noble speed.

ESTEBAN   A fine example of its breed!
Good lord, that noble creature runs
As fast as any suspect or   955
Delinquent that the law pursues.

COMMANDER   Well, given but the choice, I'd choose
To have you point the dog straight for
A certain frisky little hare
Too swift for any but this hound.   960

ESTEBAN   I will, but where might she be found?

COMMANDER   I'm speaking of your daughter there.

ESTEBAN   My daughter?

COMMANDER   Yes.

ESTEBAN   How could she be
A consort suitable for you?

COMMANDER   Do give her a good talking to.   965

---

4. Two revered church fathers: Saint Augustine (354–430), bishop of Hippo and author of many commentaries and the *Confessions*; Saint Jerome (c. 347–419 or 420), author of ecclesiastical histories, exegeses, and a Latin version of the Bible (the Vulgate).

ESTEBAN   Why, pray?

COMMANDER   She's set on vexing me.
A lady here in town you'd call
Distinguished noted my designs
And, at the first sign of my signs,
Succumbed.

ESTEBAN   Then she disgraced us all.   970
If you don't mind me saying, sir,
Your language ought to be less free.

COMMANDER   The rustic speaks so loftily!
Ah, Flores! Have this villager
Read one of Aristotle's tomes,   975
The *Politics*.[5]

ESTEBAN   We of the land
Are glad to live by your command
And seek but honor for our homes
As Fuenteovejuna, too,
Can boast distinguished residents.   980

LEONELO   (*Aside.*) To hear that villain's insolence!

COMMANDER   Has what I said offended you
Or any gathered here today?

CUADRADO   Commander, this is most unjust.
You're wrong to say such things and must   985
Not stain our honor in this way.

COMMANDER   Your what? Who do you think you are,
The Friars of Calatrava, then?

CUADRADO   No doubt that Order numbers men
Who wear the cross with bloodlines far   990
Less pure than simple townsfolk own.

COMMANDER   So should our lines mix, theirs would be
Forever fouled?

CUADRADO   Iniquity
Defiles, not cleanses—that's well known.

COMMANDER   Whatever reasoning you seek,   995
Your women should be honored so.

ESTEBAN   Such words do shame us all, and no
One thinks you'd do the deeds you speak.

COMMANDER   These peasants can be tiresome!
In cities they know how to treat   1000
A man of qualities and meet
His every wish when he is come.
There, husbands deem it flattery
When other men pursue their wives.

ESTEBAN   You say this so we'll all live lives   1005
Of equal moral laxity.
God still inhabits cities, though,
Where vengeance is more swift and clean.

5. A treatise on the city-state by the Greek philosopher (384–322 B.C.E.)

COMMANDER   That's it! Be on your way!

ESTEBAN   You mean

You wish the two of us to go?   1010

COMMANDER   No, I don't want to see a soul!

Now clear the square and don't come back!

ESTEBAN   We're leaving then.

COMMANDER   Not in a pack!

FLORES   Sir, please, a little self-control.

COMMANDER   They'll plot against me left alone,   1015

Each boor a co-conspirator.

ORTUÑO   Have patience with these rustics, sir.

COMMANDER   I marvel at how much I've shown.

Now head off home, the lot of you—

I won't have anything amiss.   1020

LEONELO   *(Aside.)* Just heavens, will you suffer this?

ESTEBAN   It's time that I returned home, too.

(Exit the Villagers.)

COMMANDER   Men, don't you find these clods absurd?

ORTUÑO   They know you scarcely deign to mask

Your condescension when they ask   1025

That their petitioning be heard.

COMMANDER   So now they think us peers of sorts?

FLORES   Who equals whom does not pertain.

COMMANDER   How does that crossbow thief remain

At large, unsentenced by our courts?   1030

FLORES   I thought I'd spied him lingering near

Laurencia's doorstep late last night,

Though now I know I wasn't right:

I slit some knave's throat ear to ear

When I mistook his cloak to be   1035

Frondoso's in the eventide.

COMMANDER   I can't imagine where he'd hide.

FLORES   Oh, he'll turn up eventually.

COMMANDER   Would anyone who tried to kill

A man like me remain close by?   1040

FLORES   The heedless bird will blithely fly

Into a snare lured by a trill,

The foolish fish swim toward the hook.

COMMANDER   To think a clod, a boy at best,

Could point a crossbow at the chest   1045

Of this brave captain, whose sword shook

Granada and Córdoba both!

It's at an end, this world we knew!

FLORES   He acted as love bid him to.

You're still alive, so by my oath,   1050

I think you're in the peasant's debt.

COMMANDER   I swear, Ortuño, had I not

Disguised my feelings toward this lot,

Two hours would not have passed by yet
And I'd have run the whole town through.   1055
Until I judge the time is right,
I'll keep the reins on vengeance tight
And then do what I need to do.
What says Pascuala?

FLORES   She replied
That any day now she's to wed.

COMMANDER   If she'd still care to lend her bed . . .   1060

FLORES   She's sending you where they'll provide
Your lordship with such things for cash.

COMMANDER   What says Olalla, then?

ORTUÑO   The girl's
A lively one.

COMMANDER   Her quips are pearls.   1065
To wit?

ORTUÑO   She and her husband clash
Of late because, she'd have you know,
He's jealous of the notes I bring
And mad that you'd go visiting
His wife with manservants in tow.   1070
Just wait until he drops his guard
And you'll be first inside again!

COMMANDER   This knight is glad upon it, then.
The peasant watches her but hard.

ORTUÑO   It's true, though his attention strays.   1075

COMMANDER   And sweet Inés?

FLORES   Who?

COMMANDER   Anton's bit.

FLORES   Her offer stands most definite
And ought to liven up your days.
We spoke in the corral outside—
Go round the back and in that door.   1080

COMMANDER   Loose women I've a soft spot for
But less so once I'm satisfied.
Ah, Flores, if they only were
Aware of what their charms are worth!

FLORES   As letdowns go, there's none on earth   1085
Like plain capitulation, sir.
A woman's quick surrender blights
The pleasure men anticipate,
Though certain girls corroborate
A wise philosopher[6] who writes   1090
That females crave male company
As form desires material shape,
Which shouldn't leave your mouths agape

---

6. That is, Aristotle, who expresses this idea (in less sexualized terms) in his *Physics* and *On the Generation of Animals.*

For this is but reality.

COMMANDER   A man whom ardor's heat lays waste   1095
Is glad to have his pleasure sealed
By lady friends who readily yield,
Though he disdain them for this haste.
The surest course for love to run
Once all delight has been bestowed   1100
Is down oblivion's well-worn road
Of favors far too easily won.

(*Enter* CIMBRANOS, *a soldier.*)

CIMBRANOS   Is the Commander hereabouts?

ORTUÑO   What, don't you see him standing there?

CIMBRANOS   Oh, brave Fernán Gómez! Throw off   1105
Your hunter's cap and be prepared
To strap your battle helmet on!
Replace your cloak with armor now!
The Master of Santiago and
The Count of Cabra's troops surround   1110
Young Don Rodrigo Girón in
Support of the Castilian queen
At Ciudad Real. Good sir,
I'm certain you can plainly see
That all the blood your Order's lost   1115
Will be for naught should they succeed.
Our forces can already glimpse
The figures on their coats of arms:
Castile's two castles paired with lions
By Aragon's heraldic bars.[7]   1120
So while the King of Portugal
Would like to honor staunch Girón,
The youth would do well just to reach
Almagro and be safely home.
Quick, saddle up your charger, sir;   1125
They'll head back to Castile as soon
As you ride boldly into sight.

COMMANDER   Be still while I think what to do.
Ortuño, have the trumpet sound
So all may hear it from the square.   1130
How many soldiers have I here?

ORTUÑO   Some fifty horsemen stand prepared.

COMMANDER   Inform them that we sally forth.

CIMBRANOS   If we don't start out now, good sirs,
Then Ciudad Real will fall.   1135

COMMANDER   Fear not, we shan't let this occur.

(*Exit all.*)

---

7. The symbols of two formerly autonomous kingdoms joined by the marriage of Isabel of Castile and Ferdinand of Aragón.

[An Open Field in Fuenteovejuna]

(*Enter* MENGO, LAURENCIA, *and* PASCUALA, *fleeing.*)

PASCUALA   Oh, please don't leave us here alone!

MENGO   How can these fields inspire such dread?

LAURENCIA   I think it's best for us to head
  To town now, Mengo, on our own— 1140
  Just women, unaccompanied—
  In case we should cross paths with him.

MENGO   He couldn't make our lives more grim
  Were he the very demon's seed!

LAURENCIA   He's sure to hound us till we're his. 1145

MENGO   Oh, lightning bolts, cast down your fires
  And purify these mad desires!

LAURENCIA   A bloody beast is what he is,
  Our arsenic and pestilence
  In town.

MENGO   Laurencia, I've been told 1150
  That poor Frondoso grew so bold
  In championing your innocence
  He aimed at the Commander's chest.

LAURENCIA   You know how much I've hated men
  But, Mengo, I confess since then 1155
  I've realized he's not like the rest.
  How valiant Frondoso was!
  I fear this bravery might mean
  His death.

MENGO   He never can be seen
  In town, whatever else he does. 1160

LAURENCIA   I love the man, although it's plain
  That I, too, know that he must flee.
  Still, he responds to such a plea
  With raging anger and disdain
  While our Commander wastes no breath 1165
  Affirming he'll hang upside down.

PASCUALA   I hope he chokes and spares our town.

MENGO   I'd rather see him stoned to death.
  Sweet heavens, if I only knew
  Some way to use my sling, I vouch 1170
  Just stretching back this leather pouch
  Would good as crack his skull in two!
  You wouldn't find depravity
  Like his in Rome's own Sabalus.[8]

LAURENCIA   You mean Heliogabalus,[9] 1175
  Whose reign surpassed indecency.

8. A chieftain in North Africa (1st century
C.E.) who unsuccessfully revolted against
Roman rule.
9. The Roman emperor Elagabalus (r. 218–
22), whose reign was marked by sexual
decadence, cruelty, and his devotion to a non-
Roman god.

MENGO   Sir Gawain's[1] misdeeds were no worse.
　　Though history's outside my ken,
　　Our own Commander's crueler than
　　This legendary rogue of verse.   1180
　　Has nature spawned another fiend
　　Of Fernán Gómez's brute ilk?
PASCUALA   It had to be off tigress milk
　　That such a furious man was weaned.

　　　　(Enter JACINTA, *a village woman.)*

JACINTA   For God's sake, if you hold our oath   1185
　　Of friendship dear, just help me hide!
LAURENCIA   Jacinta, you look petrified!
PASCUALA   You may rely upon us both.
JACINTA   The vile Commander's men head towards
　　Old Ciudad Real, a place   1190
　　Where, armed with their innate disgrace
　　Far more than with ennobled swords,
　　They'd take me to him as he bade.
LAURENCIA   God free you from the wrongs they'd do,
　　But if he'd be so free with you,   1195
　　How cruelly would he treat this maid?

　　　　(Exit LAURENCIA.)

PASCUALA   A man might help you to escape;
　　I can't defend you in distress.

　　　　(Exit PASCUALA.)

MENGO   I'll have to act like one, I guess,
　　As I'm a man in name and shape.   1200
　　Come by my side and never fear.
JACINTA   But have you arms?
MENGO   The oldest known
　　To man.
JACINTA   A sling without a stone?
MENGO   Jacinta, there are stones right here.

　　　　(Enter FLORES *and* ORTUÑO.)

FLORES   Thought you could run away, did you?   1205
JACINTA   Now I'm as good as dead!
MENGO   Good sirs,
　　How can these honest villagers . . .
ORTUÑO   So, mustering up the derring-do
　　To champion a lady's cause?
MENGO   I'd first defend her with my pleas,   1210

---

1. One of the legendary Knights of the Round Table (and King Arthur's nephew); he is generally
presented in English versions of the tales as heroic, courtly, and brave, but in some French works
he is cruel and treacherous.

As I'm male kin, but failing these,
Would look to force and nature's laws.
FLORES   Enough, now. Run the beggar through.
MENGO   Compel me to unsling my sling
And you will rue the day I fling   1215
A volley of these rocks at you.

(*Enter the* COMMANDER *and* CIMBRANOS.)

COMMANDER   A person of my rank alight
To settle such a petty case?
FLORES   The rabble in this horrid place,
Which you could purge by every right   1220
For giving you no end of grief,
Now brandish arms against our own.
MENGO   Good sir, if you cannot condone
Such conduct, as is my belief,
Then punish these vile soldiers who'd   1225
Abduct this woman in your name.
Her husband's and her parents' fame
Bespeaks the highest rectitude.
Now, by your leave, I'll take the girl
Back home where all her family wait.   1230
COMMANDER   My leave, you want? Retaliate,
Men, by my leave, against the churl.
Come, drop the sling.
MENGO   My lord, they bade . . .
COMMANDER   Peace! Flores and Ortuño, bind
His hands. Cimbranos, help in kind.   1235
MENGO   You'd act thus, called to virtue's aid?
COMMANDER   What do the townsfolk think of me
In Fuenteovejuna, cur?
MENGO   How has our village or I, sir,
Offended you so grievously?   1240
FLORES   Are we to kill him, then?
COMMANDER   Why draw
Your swords to sully steel you'd grace
With honor in a better place?
ORTUÑO   What are your orders?
COMMANDER   Whip him raw.
There, lash the peasant to that oak   1245
And, when his back is bared, go seize
Your horse's reins . . .
MENGO   Have mercy, please,
Sir! Mercy! You are gentlefolk.
COMMANDER   . . . And flog this man relentlessly
Until the studs fly off the straps.   1250
MENGO   Do heaven's righteous laws collapse
To grant these deeds impunity?

(*Exit* FLORES, ORTUÑO, CIMBRANOS, *and* MENGO.)

COMMANDER   You, girl, what are you running for?
   You find a clod that tills the earth
   More pleasing than a man of worth?   1255
JACINTA   Is this the way you would restore
   Lost honor when it was your plan
   To have me carried off by force?
COMMANDER   So, I desired you?
JACINTA   Of course,
   Because my father is a man   1260
   Well spoken of, though not your peer
   In birth, with manners gentler still
   Than any you possess.
COMMANDER   This shrill
   Effrontery will not, I fear,
   Assuage my wrath or aid your plight.   1265
   Now, come along at once.
JACINTA   With you?
COMMANDER   Correct.
JACINTA   Pay heed to what you do.
COMMANDER   I'll heed your detriment, all right.
   Who needs you? Why should I deprive
   The troops of coveted supplies?   1270
JACINTA   Not all the force beneath the skies
   Could make me suffer this alive!
COMMANDER   Come on now, strumpet, move along.
JACINTA   Have mercy!
COMMANDER   Mercy won't exist.
JACINTA   Then I've no choice but to enlist   1275
   The heavens to redress this wrong.

   (*The* COMMANDER *exits as soldiers carry* JACINTA *off.*
   Enter LAURENCIA *and* FRONDOSO.)

LAURENCIA   How can you show your face around
   Here unafraid?
FRONDOSO   I thought that some
   Such recklessness would make you come
   To see the troth to which we're bound.   1280
   I watched the dread Commander part
   While hiding in the hills above
   And, seeing you deserve my love,
   Lost all the fear that plagued my heart.
   I hope he goes far off to thrive!   1285
   Good riddance, too!
LAURENCIA   Don't waste your breath.
   Besides, the more men wish your death,
   The longer you'll remain alive.
FRONDOSO   If that's so, then long life to him,
   For both sides profit by this quirk: 1290

I live while our best wishes work
Against him in the interim!
Laurencia, is there any place
For me in your affections, dear?
I need to know if my sincere   1295
Devotion's found its port of grace.
I mean, the village speaks as one
By now, considering us a pair,
And it astounds the townsfolk there
To see our coupling left undone.   1300
So put aside these harsh extremes
And tell me if there is or not.

LAURENCIA   I swear to both you and that lot
That all will soon be as it seems.

FRONDOSO   For this great mercy, let me kiss   1305
Your lovely feet, my future wife!
You've granted me a second life,
I must confess, in saying this.

LAURENCIA   Enough with blandishments! We mince
Words when it's evident to us   1310
That you have only to discuss
The matter with my father since
He comes now with my uncle, see?
Frondoso, don't lose faith, for I'm
To be your wedded wife in time—   1315
That much is sure.

FRONDOSO   God bolster me!

(They hide. Enter ESTEBAN, ALONSO, *and* JUAN ROJO.*)*

ALONSO   So, in the end, the townsfolk rose
In vocal protest on the square,
And rightly so, for they'll not bear
More crimes from him resembling those.   1320
The scale of his intemperance
These days can scarcely fail to stun
While poor Jacinta's now the one
Who suffers his incontinence.

JUAN ROJO   All Spain will soon be governed by   1325
The Catholic Kings, whose well-earned fame
For piety bestows their name,
Which they do both exemplify.
Soon, too, brave Santiago will
Reach Ciudad Real's razed lands   1330
And win it back from Girón's hands
By marshaling his general's skill.
I'm sorry for Jacinta, though,
A stalwart lass in every way.

ALONSO   They whipped old Mengo's hide, you say?   1335

JUAN ROJO   No ink or flannel that I know

Of ever looked more black or blue.
ALONSO   Enough! You know my blood begins
    To boil just picturing the sins
    That make his reputation true.   1340
    Why should I carry this baton
    Of office if it serves no use?
JUAN ROJO   His men inflicted the abuse,
    So why should you feel woebegone?
ALONSO   Well, what about the time they found   1345
    Redondo's wife in this deep glen,
    Left raped by the Commander's men,
    Among whom she'd been passed around
    Detestably when he did cease
    To take by force what she'd deny?   1350
JUAN ROJO   I hear someone! Who's there?
FRONDOSO   Just I,
    Who look for leave to speak my piece.
JUAN ROJO   Frondoso, as my house is yours,
    Speak freely if you feel the need.
    You owe life to your sire's seed   1355
    But I'm owed what your grace ensures.
    You're like a son to me; I reared
    You with much love.
FRONDOSO   Then, sir, I seek—
    Based on this love of which you speak—
    A gracious favor volunteered.   1360
    You know who fathered this proud son.
ESTEBAN   Were you aggrieved by that crazed beast
    Fernán Gómez?
FRONDOSO   To say the least.
ESTEBAN   I thought as much—another one.
FRONDOSO   This pledge of love that you confide   1365
    Now moves me likewise to profess
    I love Laurencia and express
    My wish here that she be my bride.
    This tongue deserves a reprimand
    For hastiness, which you'll excuse,   1370
    As usually another sues
    The sire for his daughter's hand.
ESTEBAN   Your swift return here is a boon,
    Frondoso, and prolongs my years.
    Dispelling what my heart most fears,   1375
    Your coming is most opportune
    And so I thank the skies above
    That you've emerged to cleanse my name
    And thank your passion just the same
    For showing purity in love.   1380
    It's only right that your good sire
    Should learn at once what you've proposed.

For my part, I am well disposed
To help you realize this desire.
I would consider myself blessed   1385
If this sweet union came to pass.

JUAN ROJO   Well, first we'd better ask the lass
To verify she's acquiesced.

ESTEBAN   You needn't go through all that fuss;
In this case nothing is untoward: 1390
The two were firmly of accord
Before he pled his case to us.
We may as well, then, at our ease,
Discuss the dowry that is due.
The sum I gladly offer you   1395
Was saved up in *maravedís*.[2]

FRONDOSO   If I decline, don't feel forlorn;
What I don't need can pass unwept.

JUAN ROJO   You should be thankful he'll accept
The girl as bare as she was born.   1400

ESTEBAN   That may be, but in any case,
I'll ask the maid if she approves.

FRONDOSO   Good thinking, as it ill behooves
Your pressing what she won't embrace.

ESTEBAN   Sweet child! Laurencia!

LAURENCIA   Father dear.   1405

ESTEBAN   I'm sure she will, though you decide.
You see how promptly she replied?
My child, Laurencia! Only sheer
Love urges me to ask today—
Come closer, girl—would you commend   1410
Frondoso marrying your friend,
Good Gila? He's some fiancé,
The most upstanding of our men,
Proud Fuenteovejuna's son.

LAURENCIA   What? Gila wed . . . ?

ESTEBAN   If any one   1415
Among our maids deserves him, then . . .

LAURENCIA   I do commend their union, yes.

ESTEBAN   Yes—though she's ugly, which makes some
Believe Frondoso should become
Your husband. That we all could bless.   1420

LAURENCIA   Oh, father! Still inclined to jest
And gibe at your advanced age, too!

ESTEBAN   You love him, child?

LAURENCIA   He knows I do
And, though his love's likewise professed,
Unpleasant actualities . . .   1425

ESTEBAN   Should I inform him you consent?

2. Relatively low-value Spanish coins.

LAURENCIA   Yes, bring him news of my intent.
ESTEBAN   So then it's I who hold the keys?
   Well, said and done! Let's all away
   To seek our good friend in the square.   1430
JUAN ROJO   Let's go.
ESTEBAN   My lad, as for a fair
   Amount in dowry, would you say
   Four thousand might work like a charm?
   I've that much in *maravedís*.
FRONDOSO   How can you speak of such things? Please,   1435
   You do my honor grievous harm.
ESTEBAN   Come now, son, you'll feel otherwise
   Within a day for, by my word,
   A dowry that's left unconferred
   Goes wanting in some other guise.   1440

   (*All exit except* FRONDOSO *and* LAURENCIA.)

LAURENCIA   Frondoso, are you happy, dear?
FRONDOSO   Just happy? I'm so overjoyed,
   The state I'm in leaves me devoid
   Of all my senses when you're near!
   The smiles to which my heart is prone   1445
   Pour out in gladness from my eyes
   To think, Laurencia, my sweet prize,
   That I can claim you as my own.

   (*Exit* FRONDOSO *and* LAURENCIA. *Enter the* MASTER, *the* COMMANDER,
   FLORES, *and* ORTUÑO.)

COMMANDER   Sir, flee! We can't do more to hold our ground!
MASTER   The weakness of these city walls before   1450
   Their army's forces brought about our fall.
COMMANDER   The blood it's cost them, and the countless lives!
MASTER   They failed to seize our standard, though, to count
   The Calatravan colors mid their spoils,
   Though it had brought great honor to their toils.   1455
COMMANDER   Your stratagems are at an end, Girón.
MASTER   What can I do if turns of fate from night
   To morn appear to be blind Fortune's will?
VOICES   (*Within.*) A victory for the monarchs of Castile!
MASTER   Our foes now crown the battlements with lights,   1460
   Emblazoning the windows in the towers
   Above with standards marking victory.
COMMANDER   And well they might, for all the blood it's cost.
   Their joy seems tragic given what they've lost.
MASTER   I'll set back out for Calatrava, then.   1465
COMMANDER   And I to Fuenteovejuna while
   You ponder whether to support your kin
   Or pledge allegiance to the Catholic king.
MASTER   I'll write when I'm resolved of my intent.

COMMANDER   Here Time itself will be your guide.

MASTER   Ah, youth!   1470
    May your deceptions keep me not from Truth!

[ESTEBAN's House]

(The wedding is in progress. Enter MUSICIANS, MENGO, FRONDOSO,
LAURENCIA, PASCUALA, BARRILDO, ESTEBAN, ALONSO, *and* JUAN ROJO.*)*

MUSICIANS   *Oh, many happy years*
    To you, sweet bride and groom!
    Oh, many happy years!

MENGO   You dashed that off in seconds flat,   1475
    Now didn't you? It's not much good.

BARRILDO   What? You don't mean to say you could
    Compose a better song than that?

FRONDOSO   He's more familiar with the lash
    Than with the melodies of verse.   1480

MENGO   Don't shrink, but some have suffered worse.
    One man that blackguard didn't thrash
    Was taken to the vale one day . . .

BARRILDO   Stop, Mengo, please! Be merciful!
    That homicidal animal   1485
    Dishonors all who pass his way.

MENGO   A hundred soldiers—not one less—
    Administered my pummeling.
    I'd nothing on me but my sling
    And never suffered such duress.   1490
    But, as I was just saying, a
    Fine man whose name I won't evoke,
    Esteemed by all the village folk,
    Was given quite the enema
    Of ink and pebbles all in one.   1495
    Who'd stand for vileness of that sort?

BARRILDO   The savage looked on it as sport.

MENGO   Well, enemas are far from fun
    And, while they are salubrious,
    I'd rather that my death come fast.   1500

FRONDOSO   So, may we hear now at long last
    The ditty you've composed for us?

MENGO   *Oh, many happy years to you,*
    Dear newlyweds! God's grace decree
    That envy and vile jealousy
    Should never come between you two!   1505
    And when your years on earth are through,
    Depart this life from satiety!
    Oh, many happy years!

FRONDOSO   A curse upon the rhyming hack   1510
    Who dashed off such a poor refrain!

BARRILDO   It did sound hasty.

MENGO   Let me deign

To say a word about this pack:
You know how fritter-makers throw
Their bits of batter in the oil   1515
And add more as they watch it boil
Until the kettle's filled with dough?
How some look swollen when they're turned,
Misshapen and a sorry sight,
Some lumpy on the left or right,   1520
Some nicely fried but others burned?
That's what I've come to understand
A poet does to draft a strain,
Material sprung from his brain
Like dough he forms with pen in hand.   1525
Then, whoosh! He plops the poetry
On sheets—the role the kettle plays—
Assuming that a honey glaze
Will mute the public's mockery.
Though once the audience takes a look,   1530
There's scarce a buyer to be found
Because the only one around
Who'll eat that rubbish is the cook!

BARRILDO   I think we've heard enough of this;
It's time the lovers made a speech.   1535

LAURENCIA   Give us your hand, sir, we beseech.

JUAN ROJO   Sweet child, my hand you wish to kiss?
First ask your father for this grace
On both yours and Frondoso's part.

ESTEBAN   I pray God sees it in His heart   1540
To fold them in His fond embrace
And bless the new life they've begun.

FRONDOSO   May you both bless us all life long.

JUAN ROJO   We shall. Come, lads, let's have a song
For now these two are joined as one!   1545

MUSICIANS   *The maid with flowing tresses roamed*
Through Fuenteovejuna's vale
And all the while, unknown to her,
A Knight of Calatrava trailed.
She hid within the leafy wood,   1550
Pretending she had spied him not
And, by turns bashful and abashed,
Concealed herself amid the copse.
"Why do you steal away, fair lass?"
He asked the maiden in the grove,   1555
"You know full well my lynx-eyed love
Has penetrated walls of stone."
The knight approached the maiden who,
Abashed and quite disquieted,
Began to fashion jealousies   1560
From boughs entangled overhead.

But just as anyone who loves
Will think it insignificant
To cross the mountains and the seas,
The knight asked his fair maid again: 1565
"Why do you steal away, fair lass,
My lovely maiden in the grove?
You know full well my lynx-eyed love
Has penetrated walls of stone."

(*Enter the* COMMANDER, FLORES, ORTUÑO, *and* CIMBRANOS.)

COMMANDER   Don't stop the feast on my account. 1570
Calm now, no need to be distraught.
JUAN ROJO   We recognize you're in command,
But this, sir, is no game you halt.
Sit here if you would stay. What cause
Is there for such warlike array? 1575
Had you some triumph? But, why ask?
FRONDOSO   Stars, I'm a dead man! Send me aid!
LAURENCIA   Frondoso, flee while you've the chance!
COMMANDER   Not this time. Bind the peasant tight.
JUAN ROJO   Resign yourself to prison, son. 1580
FRONDOSO   I'll never leave the place alive!
JUAN ROJO   Why? What is your offense?
COMMANDER   I'm not
The sort to kill without due cause
For, if I were, this cur who stands
Before us would by now have lost 1585
His life, run through here by my guard.
Confine him to a prison cell
Until his father should pronounce
The punishment his crime compels.
PASCUALA   Please, sir, not on his wedding day. 1590
COMMANDER   Why should these nuptials change my mind?
Are there no other men in town?
PASCUALA   You're able to forgive his crime;
You have that power.
COMMANDER   Were I the one
Aggrieved, Pascuala, then I could. 1595
But Master Téllez Girón was
Insulted by this criminal,
His Order and his honor both,
And it's imperative that all
Bear witness to this punishment 1600
In case some other foe feels called
To raise a standard versus his.
You may have heard one afternoon
He aimed a crossbow at the chest—
My vassals, such a loyal group!— 1605
Of your esteemed commander here.

ESTEBAN   Sir, if a father-in-law may
　　Defend a deed of his new son,
　　It isn't hard to contemplate
　　How someone so in love as he   1610
　　Might well have rankled with chagrin
　　If it is certain you conspired
　　To take his wife away from him.
　　What swain would not have done the same?
COMMANDER   You're talking nonsense, magistrate.   1615
ESTEBAN   I speak for your own virtue, sir.
COMMANDER   I'm innocent of all you claim;
　　She wasn't yet his wife back then.
ESTEBAN   You're guilty, sir. I'll say no more
　　But rest assured the king and queen   1620
　　Who rule Castile will issue forth
　　New orders for disorder's end.
　　They'd be remiss, though now at rest
　　From war, to suffer that their towns
　　And far-flung villages let men   1625
　　As powerful and cruel as you
　　Display a cross so grandiose.
　　This sign is but for noble breasts
　　So let it grace the monarch's robes
　　And not the cloaks of lesser men.   1630
COMMANDER   You, there! Relieve him of the staff.
ESTEBAN   Obedient, I surrender it.
COMMANDER   (Striking Esteban.)   I'll use it on you as I'd lash
　　An untamed and unruly horse.
ESTEBAN   As you're my lord, I must submit.   1635
PASCUALA   You'd cudgel an old man like that?
LAURENCIA   He thrashes him because he is
　　My sire. Avenge yourself on me!
COMMANDER   You, take her to the prison grounds
　　And station ten guards at her cell.   1640

　　　(The COMMANDER exits with his men.)

ESTEBAN   Sweet heavens, send your justice down!

　　　(Exit ESTEBAN.)

PASCUALA   The wedding has become a wake!

　　　(Exit PASCUALA.)

BARRILDO   Who'll speak? Are there no men around?
MENGO   I took my licks, thanks much! The welts
　　Are red as cardinals[3] on my back   1645

---

3. Newly invested cardinals of the Catholic
Church are given a scarlet cap, and other scar-
let vestments further signify their rank. In
Spanish, cardenal also means "bruise."

So save yourselves that trip to Rome!
Let someone else provoke his wrath.
JUAN ROJO   We'll speak to him as one.
MENGO   Perhaps,
  Though now we'd best let silence reign;
  Don't you recall they whipped my cheeks   1650
  Till they were pink as salmon steaks?

Act III

[The council chamber in Fuenteovejuna]

(*Enter* ESTEBAN, ALONSO, *and* BARRILDO.)

ESTEBAN   What's keeping them?
BARRILDO   They know full well we wait.
ESTEBAN   Assembling here grows riskier by the hour.
BARRILDO   Most everyone's heard why we congregate.
ESTEBAN   With poor Frondoso captive in the tower   1655
  And my Laurencia under such duress,
  If God does not do all within His power . . .

(*Enter* JUAN ROJO *and* CUADRADO.)

JUAN ROJO   Why raise your voice, Esteban, when our chief
  Aid must be stealth if we're to have success?
ESTEBAN   It's shocking I'm not louder, to be brief.   1660

(*Enter* MENGO.)

MENGO   I'll slip into the meeting hall as well.
ESTEBAN   An old man whose gray hairs are bathed in grief
  Asks you, good villagers, how best the bell
  For our dear town's lost honor might be tolled
  Now that she's been so ravished and abused.   1665
  And how, if these be honors, can we hold
  Such rites? Is there a single man left here
  Whom that barbarian has not unsoulled?
  Why don't you answer? Is it, as I fear,
  That you've all had your honor basely used?   1670
  Then, make your firm commiseration clear
  For, if this common loss can't be excused,
  What stays your hand? Or have these blows been slight?
JUAN ROJO   The world knows none more wretched and diffused
  Though news now reaching us appears more bright: 1675
  The Catholic kings, who brought peace to Castile,
  Will stop soon in Córdoba, where we might
  Dispatch two aldermen who'll sue until
  They're pledged redress, bowed at their royal feet.
BARRILDO   Before the monarchs do come, though, we will   1680
  Still need to find a remedy to meet
  This enemy in that our king, who smote

So many foes, has others yet to beat.

CUADRADO If anyone here asks me for my vote,
I vote that we forsake this baneful town.   1685

JUAN ROJO We haven't time; besides, they might take note.

MENGO If the Commander hears the noise, he'll frown
So on this council, he might kill us all.

CUADRADO Our tree of patience has come crashing down,
Our ship of fear floats lost beneath this pall.   1690
For such an upright man, who leads this land,
To watch his daughter dragged away in thrall
To brutes, and have the staff of his command
So splintered on his head, I ask of you,
What slave endures more from his master's hand?   1695

JUAN ROJO What is it you would have our village do?

CUADRADO Die, die or put those tyrants to the sword.
We've many villagers, while they are few.

BARRILDO Rise up in arms against our rightful lord?

ESTEBAN The king's our only lord by heaven's laws,   1700
Not that barbaric and inhuman horde.
If God assists us in our righteous cause,
What have we all to lose?

MENGO   Take care, good sirs,
Rash actions such as these should give us pause.
I speak for all the simple villagers   1705
Who bear the brunt of this vile injury
And fear still more harm from these tormentors.

JUAN ROJO We suffer this misfortune equally;
Why should we wait until our lives are lost?
They burn our homes and vineyards down with glee;   1710
Revenge upon such tyrants bears no cost!

(Enter LAURENCIA, disheveled.)

LAURENCIA You let me pass, for I've a right
To enter where the men confer.
A woman may not have a vote
But she can make her voice be heard.   1715
Don't you know me?

ESTEBAN   Good God, are you
My daughter?

JUAN ROJO   You don't recognize
Your own Laurencia?

LAURENCIA   I'm afraid
I must appear a dreadful sight
For you to doubt it's I you see.   1720

ESTEBAN My child!

LAURENCIA   Don't dare call me your child
Again.

ESTEBAN   Why not, my dearest heart,
Why not?

LAURENCIA   I've reasons of all kinds,
 But let the first among them be
 Allowing tyrants, unavenged,   1725
 To snatch me from my family's grasp
 Without you seeking due revenge.
 I'm not Frondoso's wife yet, so
 You cannot claim reprisal's weight
 Devolves upon a husband's lot   1730
 When such revenge is yours to take.
 Until the wedding night has passed,
 Our codes prescribe that you'd assume
 This obligation stands among
 A father's duties, not a groom's.   1735
 For even if I buy a jewel,
 Until it isn't brought to me,
 It's not my place to fret about
 Who's guarding it or who's a thief.
 You watched Fernán Gómez abduct   1740
 A maid and didn't lift a hand
 Like coward shepherds who allow
 The wolf to carry off the lamb.
 How many daggers at my heart
 And lewd advances I endured!   1745
 How many threats and foul misdeeds
 From one who'd be my paramour
 And yearned to see my chastity
 Surrendered to his appetites!
 Look at my hair for evidence   1750
 Of how I fought him through the night
 And see the blood spilt by his blows.
 Have you no honor left as men?
 Have I no kinsmen here, no sire?
 How has my sorry plight not left   1755
 Your likes contorted with the pain
 Of seeing me so cruelly pained?
 You're lambs, the sheep from which our town's
 Old sheep well takes its timid name![4]
 Give me your weapons, then, if you'd 1760
 Stand useless there like stones, bronze shards
 Or jasper blocks. Brute tigers! No,
 Not tigers. While these creatures are
 Unfeeling, they hunt down and kill
 The beasts that rob them of their cubs. 1765
 Not even waves can harbor those
 That venture to attack their young.
 You cowards were born craven hares,

4. *Fuente ovejuna*, "fount (or well) of sheep" (Spanish).

Not Spaniards but barbarians,
Frail chickens—hens!—whose women are   1770
Abandoned to their captors' whims!
Wear distaffs[5] on your belts, not swords!
Why even gird those rapiers on?
By God above, I'll see to it
That only womenfolk respond   1775
To tyrants who'd leave honor stained
By seeking their perfidious blood!
They'll just throw stones at you and laugh,
You spinning women! Sissies! What
Men, cowardly as little girls!   1780
Perhaps, tomorrow you can use
Our headdresses and petticoats
Or make your faces up with rouge!
That cruel Commander, meanwhile, plans
To hang Frondoso for his crime   1785
From high upon a battlement
In secret and without a trial.
He'll do the same to all of us,
You half-men, which is why I yearn
For that day when our town, bereft   1790
Of every woman, will revert
To that illustrious Golden Age
Of Amazons[6] who made men quake.

ESTEBAN   Brave child, I cannot count myself
Among those you would designate   1795
With such dishonorable terms.
I'll go myself now, even if
The whole world stands against my cause.

JUAN ROJO   I, too, however daunted with
The power of this enemy.   1800

CUADRADO   We'll die together, then.

BARRILDO   A rag
Tied to a stick is flag enough.
Now let those monsters breathe their last!

JUAN ROJO   What order should we recognize?

MENGO   Kill all of them disorderly!   1805
The village must be of one mind
And all the villagers agreed
The tyrant and his men must die.

ESTEBAN   Then grab your cudgels and your bows,
Your pikes and swords and lances, too!   1810

MENGO   Long live the Catholic kings, our sole
True lords!

---

5. Staffs used in spinning to hold flax or wool, and a traditional symbol of women's work and of women in general.

6. In classical mythology, a fierce race of women warriors.

ALL   Long may they live and reign!

MENGO   And death to tyrant traitors! Death!

ALL   Yes, traitorous tyrants, you must die!

(*The men exit.*)

LAURENCIA (*To the village women.*)   The heavens echo your behest,   1815
So forward, women of the town!
March on if you would set about
Regaining your lost honor! March!

(*Enter* PASCUALA, JACINTA, *and other village women.*)

PASCUALA   What's happening? We heard these shouts.

LAURENCIA   Girls, can't you see the town is off   1820
To kill Fernán Gómez today?
The merest boys have joined the men
To send that devil to his grave.
But why should they alone enjoy
The honor stemming from this feat?   1825
As women we have suffered most
The outrage from his foul misdeeds.

JACINTA   What is it you would have us do?

LAURENCIA   Let's all of us form ordered ranks
And undertake an act so bold   1830
We'll leave the wondering world aghast.
Jacinta, for your suffering,
I name you corporal; you're in charge
Of this brave women's squadron here.

JACINTA   Yet you've endured much worse by far.   1835

LAURENCIA   Pascuala, standard-bearer, right?

PASCUALA   I'll look around here for a pole
So we can hoist a flag on it.
You'll see I'm worthy of the post!

LAURENCIA   We haven't time for that right now   1840
Since fortune presses us to fight
But let us use our headdresses
As pennants we can wave on high.

PASCUALA   We'll have to name a captain, though.

LAURENCIA   Not true.

PASCUALA   How so?

LAURENCIA   Because who needs   1845
A Cid or Rodomonte[7] when
It's I who'll lead with gallantry?

7. Both great fighters. Rodomonte, a major character in Ludovico Ariosto's Italian romance *Orlando Furioso* (1516, 1532), is a fearsome and boastful leader of the Moors; El Cid ("the Lord" in Arabic) is Rodrigo (or Ruy) Díaz de Vivar (c. 1043–1099), a Spanish military leader who is the hero of the 12th-century Castilian epic *The Poem of My Cid*.

[A Room in the Commander's Residence]

(*Enter* FRONDOSO *with his hands bound,* FLORES, ORTUÑO, CIMBRANOS, *and the* COMMANDER.)

COMMANDER   Now take the extra rope you used to bind
  His hands and hang him so he's punished more.
FRONDOSO   You're leaving a black legacy behind.   1850
COMMANDER   This battlement should serve us on that score.
FRONDOSO   But sir, it never even crossed my mind
  To seek your death!
FLORES   What's all the ruckus for?

(*Loud noise is heard offstage.*)

COMMANDER   What ruckus?
FLORES   Would the peasants in this town
  Obstruct our justice?
ORTUÑO   Sir, the doors are down!   1855

(*The noise grows louder.*)

COMMANDER   How dare they when they know this is the seat
  Of our command?
FLORES   Together they rebel!
JUAN ROJO   (*Offstage*) Now burn and raze the place! We'll not retreat!
ORTUÑO   These popular revolts are hard to quell.
COMMANDER   They rise against their lord?
FLORES   The peasants beat   1860
  Your doors down, sir, from grudges that impel
  Their fury on.
COMMANDER   Come, set the prisoner free.
  Frondoso, calm the magistrate for me.
FRONDOSO   Yes, sir. It's love that made their passion wake.

(*He exits.*)

MENGO (*Offstage*)   May Ferdinand and Isabel prevail!   1865
  But death to traitors!
FLORES   Sir, for your own sake
  I urge you, flee!
COMMANDER   It's futile to assail
  A garrison one cannot hope to take.
  They'll soon turn back.
FLORES   Those wronged on such a scale   1870
  Aren't likely to retreat until blood flows
  And they've exacted vengeance on their foes.
COMMANDER   We'll make a stand here in this room and fight,
  This door as good as any gate, I gauge.
FRONDOSO (*Offstage*)   On, Fuenteovejuna!
COMMANDER   Hey, they've quite
  A leader there! I say we meet their rage.   1875
FLORES   It's your rage, sir, not theirs that gives me fright.

ESTEBAN   The tyrant and accomplices, I wage.
  Fight, Fuenteovejuna! Tyrants, fall!

    (*Enter all.*)

COMMANDER   Wait, men!
ALL   No, vengeance cannot wait at all!
COMMANDER   Then tell me where I've erred. Upon the crown   1880
  And as a knight, I'll make it up to you.
ALL   Long live King Ferdinand! Onward, town!
  Die, wicked Christians and false traitors, too!
COMMANDER   I'm speaking to you and you shout me down?
  I am your rightful lord!
ALL   Our sole true lords   1885
  Remain the Catholic kings!
COMMANDER   Men, wait. Stand by!
ALL   On, Fuenteovejuna! Now you die!

    (*The* COMMANDER *and his men flee, pursued by the men of Fuenteove-*
    juna. Enter the village women, armed.)

LAURENCIA   Let's stop a bit and reconnoiter here,
  Not women but brave soldiers in my ken!
PASCUALA   For vengefulness, a woman has no peer.   1890
  We'll spill his blood right here! If not now, when?
JACINTA   Yes, let's impale his body on a spear.
PASCUALA   We're all agreed. Come on, let's do it then!
ESTEBAN   (*Offstage*) Now die, Commander traitor!
COMMANDER   Here's my death!
  I beg Your mercy, Lord, with my last breath.   1895
BARRILDO   (*Offstage*) There's Flores!
MENGO   That's the rogue so quick to dole
  My lashes out. Lay into him and how!
FRONDOSO   (*Offstage*) I'll be avenged when I tear out his soul!
LAURENCIA   We need no leave to enter.
PASCUALA   Steady now.
  We'll guard the door.
BARRILDO (*Offstage*)   I've lost all self-control   1900
  So, tears, my lordships, we can disallow.
LAURENCIA   I'm going in, Pascuala, for my sword
  Must stay unsheathed until my name's restored.

    (*She exits.*)

BARRILDO (*Offstage*)   Look, there's Ortuño!
FRONDOSO (*Offstage*)   Slash his ugly face!

    (FLORES *enters, fleeing, with* MENGO *in pursuit.*)

FLORES   Have mercy, Mengo, please! I'm not to blame!   1905
MENGO   If being his pimp could not secure our case,
  Your flogging me would fault you all the same.
PASCUALA   Come, hand him to us women. Where's the race,

Man? Stop your pointless running.
MENGO   Sure, I'm game.
   This sounds like punishment enough to me.   1910
PASCUALA   You'll be avenged.
MENGO   That's all I want to see.
JACINTA   Die!
FLORES   Being killed by women isn't just.
JACINTA   Seems quite a turn of fate.
PASCUALA   What tears are these?
JACINTA   Perverse procurer for your master's lust!
PASCUALA   Oh, die now, traitor!
FLORES   Mercy, ladies, please!   1915

   (*Enter* ORTUÑO, *fleeing from* LAURENCIA.)

ORTUÑO   Look here, I'm not . . .
LAURENCIA   I know you well, I trust!
   Come, let the blood of these vile dogs appease
   Your swords!
PASCUALA   Oh, let me meet death slaughtering!
ALL   On, Fuenteovejuna! Thrive, dear king!

      (*Exit all.*)

   [A Room in the Palace of the Catholic Kings]

   (*Enter King* FERDINAND, *Queen* ISABEL, *and Don* MANRIQUE.)

MANRIQUE   Our plan of action worked so well   1920
   That all objectives were attained
   And we were met with no sustained
   Resistance as the city fell.
   The opposition, sire, was light
   But, had their side presented more   1925
   To counteract our force at war,
   It surely would have proven slight.
   The Count of Cabra stays behind
   To guard the city from attack
   In case their army doubles back   1930
   To mount a second thrust in kind.
FERDINAND   We deem it wise that he remain
   To muster and command our troops,
   Ensuring that our force regroups
   And curbing passage through the plain.   1935
   It ought to be impossible
   For any harm to blight us, then,
   Although Alfonso gathers men
   To join his force in Portugal.
   It's fitting that the city should   1940
   Be left in such reliable hands
   For, where our able Count commands,
   All marvel at his hardihood.

In this way, he can turn aside
The danger threatening our realm,   1945
A loyal guardian at the helm
Who'll keep our kingdom fortified.

    (*Enter* FLORES, *wounded.*)

FLORES   King Ferdinand, good Catholic sire,
To whom the heavens did concede
The crown of proud Castile in light   1950
Of all your noble qualities,
Attend to this account of acts
Unmatched in cruelty by men
Throughout this world, from where the sun
First rises bright to where it sets.   1955

FERDINAND   Come, steady now, man!

FLORES   Sovereign king,
The wounds you see would not consent
To my delaying this report
For this life surely nears its end.
In Fuenteovejuna, sire,   1960
That farming town from which I've fled,
The people with inclement breast
Have put their rightful lord to death.
Fernán Gómez lies murdered there,
A victim of the grievances   1965
Those traitorous vassals claimed to bear,
For those aggrieved scarce need pretext.
Thus, dubbing him tyrannical
By full consensus, these vile plebs
Became emboldened over time   1970
To carry out this treachery.
They stormed through the Commander's home
And, though he was a nobleman,
Did not provide him with the chance
To quit these debts and make amends.   1975
Not only were his pleas ignored
But, spurred by their impulsiveness,
The villagers left him with wounds
That rent the cross worn on his chest
Then hurled him out a window down   1980
Into a furious waiting horde
Of women, who proceeded to
Impale him on their pikes and swords.
They dragged his body to a house
And, each displaying greater rage,   1985
Began to pluck his hair and beard
While cruelly slicing up his face.
So outsized did their fury seem
And fierce their mounting hate appear,

The largest pieces left intact   1990
On the Commander were his ears!
Expunging, next, his coat of arms,
They shouted that they wished, instead,
To march beneath your own because
The former caused them great offense.   1995
Then, lastly, they ransacked his home
As if it were some enemy's
And happily among themselves
Divided up his property.
All this I saw with my two eyes   2000
For, infelicitously, fate
Would not consent that I should die
While lying in my hiding-place,
My wounds fresh, waiting out the day
In hope the dark of night would come   2005
So I could steal away unseen
And tell you what the town had done.
You're merciful and just, good sire,
So see these wanton criminals
Are punished by your code of law   2010
For acts so reprehensible.
Oh, hear his spilt blood crying out
And make them pay harsh recompense!

FERDINAND   Brave fellow, you may rest assured
They won't escape our punishment.   2015
So grievous are these late events
We find ourselves bereft of words
And therefore deem it best a judge
Should verify such deeds occurred
To castigate the culpable   2020
And make examples of their breed.
A captain shall escort him hence
To warrant his security.
Malfeasance such as this deserves
Exemplary punition soon.   2025
But now, look to this soldier here
And be attentive to his wounds.

     (Exit all.)

[The Town Square in Fuenteovejuna]

(Enter the villagers, with the head of Fernán Gómez on a lance.)

MUSICIANS   *Oh, many happy years*
   To you, good Catholic kings,
   And death to tyrants all!   2030
BARRILDO   Frondoso, let's hear your song now.
FRONDOSO   Here goes, however freshly penned.
   Let quibblers with my meter mend
   The verse the best way they know how.

Long live our lovely Isabel   2035
And Ferdinand of Aragon,
Whose union is a paragon
And who, though two, are one as well!
Saint Michael[8] *take you both to dwell*
In Heaven when you hear God's call.   2040
Long life to you, we wish,
But death to tyrants all!

LAURENCIA   Your turn, Barrildo.

BARRILDO   Here goes mine.
  I put a lot of thought in it.

PASCUALA   Recite the poem as you see fit   2045
  And it should come out sounding fine.

BARRILDO   *Oh, many happy years to you,*
Famed monarchs, fresh from victory!
From this day forward you shall be
Our lords, who bring us luck anew!   2050
May evil dwarves and giants, too,
Succumb before your battle call
And death to tyrants all!

MUSICIANS   *Oh, many happy years*
To you, good Catholic kings,   2055
And death to tyrants all!

LAURENCIA   Now Mengo sing.

FRONDOSO   Let's hear your stuff.

MENGO   I dabble, so I'll take a whack.

PASCUALA   Those hash marks on your belly's back
  Are witness you've had whacks enough!   2060

MENGO   *'Twas on a lovely Sunday morn*
When I, on orders of this here,
Was whipped until my aching rear
Writhed frightfully, its soft skin torn,
I bearing what hence won't be borne.   2065
Long live our Christian monarchers
And death to all these tyranters!

MUSICIANS   *Oh, many happy years!*

ESTEBAN   Remove his noggin from that lance.

MENGO   His face has all a hanged man's charms.   2070

    (*Enter* JUAN ROJO, *bearing an escutcheon with the*
    royal coat of arms.)

CUADRADO   Look here, the royal coat of arms.

ESTEBAN   Let our whole village cast a glance.

JUAN ROJO   Where should its splendidness be hung?

CUADRADO   Right here, upon our own town hall.

ESTEBAN   Shine on, brave shield!

BARRILDO   Bring joy to all!   2075

---

8. The archangel who, in Christian tradition, guides the souls of the faithful to heaven.

FRONDOSO   The warm sun rising here among
　　These symbols hails a bright new day.
ESTEBAN   Long live León! Castile, live on,
　　And prosper, bars of Aragon,[9]
　　But death to tyrants and their sway!   2080
　　Dear Fuenteovejuna, heed
　　The sage advice of this old man
　　For none who've marked my counsel can
　　Affirm I've ventured to mislead.
　　It won't be long before the crown   2085
　　Sends someone to investigate
　　The goings-on round here of late
　　And, with the king lodged near our town,
　　We ought devise, while there's still time,
　　Some story no one can dismiss.   2090
FRONDOSO   Your thoughts?
ESTEBAN   Claim unto death that this
　　Was Fuenteovejuna's crime
　　So none be taken off to die.
FRONDOSO   By us, then, all must be agreed:
　　It's Fuenteovejuna's deed.   2095
ESTEBAN   Is this how we will answer?
ALL   Aye!
ESTEBAN   Why don't I act like I've the task
　　Of the investigator now
　　So I might best instruct you how
　　To face the questions he will ask?   2100
　　Here, let's have Mengo be the first
　　Upon the rack.
MENGO   You couldn't choose
　　A frailer guy?
ESTEBAN   I'll only use
　　You to rehearse.
MENGO   Then, do your worst!
ESTEBAN   Who killed the town's Commander, you?   2105
MENGO   All Fuenteovejuna, sir!
ESTEBAN   Don't make me torture you, vile cur!
MENGO   Kill me and it would still be true!
ESTEBAN   Confess, thief!
MENGO   I do as I'm told.
ESTEBAN   So?
MENGO   Fuenteovejuna! There!   2110
ESTEBAN   Pull tight.
MENGO   It's nothing I can't bear.
ESTEBAN   We'll foul up any trial they hold!

　　　　(*Enter* CUADRADO.)

9. I.e., heraldic bars (see line 1120 and note). "León": a province of northwestern Spain.

CUADRADO   What are you doing, dallying here?
FRONDOSO   Cuadrado, what's so troublesome?
CUADRADO   The crown's investigator's come.   2115
ESTEBAN   Hide quickly while the coast is clear!
CUADRADO   A captain also guards the man.
ESTEBAN   The Devil watch his back this day!
   We all know what we have to say.
CUADRADO   They're seizing everyone they can   2120
   As hardly any soul has hid.
ESTEBAN   There's no need fear should make us weak.
   You, who killed the Commander? Speak!
MENGO   Who? Fuenteovejuna did!

     (Exit all.)

[A Room in the Mansion of the Master of Calatrava]

(Enter the MASTER of Calatrava and a SOLDIER.)

MASTER   This murderous deed's left me distraught.   2125
   That such should be his last reward!
   I ought to put you to the sword
   As payment for the news you've brought.
SOLDIER   I'm just a message-bearer, sir,
   And didn't meant to cause you ire.   2130
MASTER   To have a town turned mob conspire
   And wrong me thus may not occur.
   I'll take five hundred men with me
   And raze the village to the ground.
   The lawless names of those still found   2135
   There will be struck from memory.
SOLDIER   You might well calm such fury down
   As they're now subjects of the king
   And surely not for anything
   Would one wish to enrage the crown.   2140
MASTER   But they fall under my command
   So whence their fealty to Castile?
SOLDIER   These grievances our own courts will
   Consider when the time's at hand.
MASTER   Now when did any such assize   2145
   Remove possessions from the throne?
   They are our sovereign lords, I own,
   A truth I duly recognize.
   We're all the monarch's vassals now
   And, given this, I'll check my ire   2150
   Although an audience with my sire
   Might serve my case best and allow
   A youthful aspect to excuse
   Whatever grave offense I've done.
   My tender age may well be one   2155
   Defense this loyal heart can use.

I'll go to see the king in shame,
Compelled by honor to proceed
With fortitude in pressing need
To clear my honorable name.   2160

    (They exit.)

                   [The Town Square in Fuenteovejuna]

    (Enter LAURENCIA, *alone.)*

LAURENCIA   True love's concern for its beloved's good
Becomes thereafter love's appended pain
For fear harm may befall love is a bane
That brings concern as all new worries would.
Though watchful thought decrease this likelihood,   2165
The mind, perturbed, will readily show strain
As love's well-being, stolen, roils the brain,
A torment nowise easily withstood.
I do adore my husband and this dire
Occasion will condemn me to duress   2170
Should fortune fail to favor him on high.
His happiness is all that I desire;
When he is present, sure is my distress,
When he is absent, just as sure I die.

    (Enter FRONDOSO.*)*

FRONDOSO   Laurencia, love!
LAURENCIA   Sweet husband, here?   2175
This move displays a steely nerve!
FRONDOSO   Does such solicitude deserve
This cold reception from you, dear?
LAURENCIA   I beg you, darling mine, beware,
For here you'll meet a ghastly end.   2180
FRONDOSO   Laurencia, may the skies forfend
That my well-being should cause you care.
LAURENCIA   Aren't you afraid to view the throes
Your townsmen face in their ordeal
Or the investigator's zeal   2185
In hastening to inflict their woes?
Stay out of harm's way while you can
And flee before they capture you.
FRONDOSO   What? How could you expect me to
Do deeds unworthy of a man?   2190
Would it be proper to betray
The others in this circumstance
Or not see you when I've the chance?
Don't order me to go away.
What reason would there be for me   2195
To save myself, untouched and whole,
But not acknowledge my own soul
When facing such calamity?

(Cries are heard offstage.)

If I can trust my ears, it seems
The noise I'm hearing are the cries   2200
Some tortured wretch hurls toward the skies.
Come listen closely to his screams.

(The JUDGE is heard interrogating villagers offstage.)

JUDGE   The truth and you'll be freed, kind gent.

FRONDOSO   They torture an old man to make
   Him speak.

LAURENCIA   He's too strong-willed to break.   2205

ESTEBAN   Pray, loose the ropes a bit.

JUDGE   Relent.
   Now say, who killed Fernán, good man?

ESTEBAN   Give Fuenteovejuna blame.

LAURENCIA   Brave father, may God praise your name!

FRONDOSO   What courage!

JUDGE   Grab that boy there. Wretch!   2210
   Lay on! Still tighter! Cur! Yes, I'm
   Convinced you know. Who did this crime?
   No answer? Stretch him, drunkard, stretch!

BOY   Sir, Fuenteovejuna did!

JUDGE   Dumb clods, by all the king commands,   2215
   I'll strangle you with my own hands!
   Who murdered the Commander, kid?

FRONDOSO   To think a tender lad could face
   Such torment and resist so long!

LAURENCIA   Brave villagers!

FRONDOSO   Yes, brave and strong!   2220

JUDGE   You, seize that woman there and place
   Her body next upon the rack.
   Now it will be the maiden's turn.

LAURENCIA   His anger's causing him to burn.

JUDGE   You'll tell me or I'll kill the pack   2225
   Of you right here if he's not caught.
   Which one's the guilty villager?

PASCUALA   It's Fuenteovejuna, sir!

JUDGE   Still tighter!

FRONDOSO   This is all for naught.

LAURENCIA   Pascuala hasn't said a thing.   2230

FRONDOSO   The children, either. What's to fear?

JUDGE   Have you bewitched the townsfolk here?
   Pull!

PASCUALA   Heaven ease my suffering!

JUDGE   What are you, deaf? I told you, pull!

PASCUALA   Still Fuenteovejuna, yes!   2235

JUDGE   That fat oaf clad in tattered dress
   Is next, the one whose paunch looks full.

LAURENCIA   Poor Mengo! Who else could it be?

FRONDOSO Though no one's broken yet, he might.
MENGO Ow, ow!
JUDGE   Just slowly stretch him tight.   2240
MENGO Ow!
JUDGE   This should jog your memory.
MENGO Ow, ow!
JUDGE   Come, bumpkin, out with it:
   Who laid the town's Commander low?
MENGO Please stop! I'll tell you all I know!
JUDGE You, let up on the ropes a bit.   2245
FRONDOSO He's breaking.
JUDGE   Use your back until
   The lever halts.
MENGO   I'll tell you when
   You stop!
JUDGE   All right, who slew him, then?
MENGO Old Fuenteovejunaville!   2250
JUDGE I've never seen such villainy!
   They make a mockery of pain!
   The one I thought could least refrain
   From talking held up valiantly.
   I'm weary. Come, let us depart.
FRONDOSO Good Mengo, may God keep you near!   2255
   Your courage has dispelled the fear
   I felt for us both in my heart.

   (*Enter* MENGO, BARRILDO, *and* CUADRADO.)

BARRILDO Three cheers there, Mengo!
CUADRADO   Yes, my word!
BARRILDO And one cheer more!
FRONDOSO   That was some feat!
MENGO Ooh!
BARRILDO   Here, friend, have a bit to eat   2260
   And drink.
MENGO   What is it?
BARRILDO   Lemon curd.
MENGO Ooh!
FRONDOSO   There you go, man, drain the cup!
BARRILDO I knew you could.
FRONDOSO He's swilling, so it must be good.
LAURENCIA More food here while he's drinking up.   2265
MENGO Ooh, ooh!
BARRILDO   This round is my treat, too.
LAURENCIA He's stately as he knocks them back.
FRONDOSO It's easy once you're off the rack.
BARRILDO More?
MENGO   Ooh! As long as it's on you . . .
FRONDOSO Drink up, old friend. Lord knows you've grounds.   2270
LAURENCIA This makes one quaff per turn, all told.

FRONDOSO   Bring him some clothes, he must be cold.

BARRILDO   More still?

MENGO   Uh, maybe three more rounds.
    Ooh, ooh!

FRONDOSO   Yooh . . . want the wine you've earned?

BARRILDO   Yooh dooh? Here's more to slake your thirst.   2275
    Home brew should fill resisters first.
    What's wrong?

MENGO   I think this wine has turned.
    Let's go before I catch a chill.

FRONDOSO   This jug, you'll see, holds better wine,
    But who killed the Commander, swine?   2280

MENGO   Old Fuenteovejunaville!

        (*Exit all except* FRONDOSO *and* LAURENCIA.)

FRONDOSO   He's honored by our show of love
    But could you please inform me, wife,
    Who took the town Commander's life?

LAURENCIA   Who? Fuenteovejuna, dove.   2285

FRONDOSO   Who killed him?

LAURENCIA   Stop, you're scaring me!
    Sure, Fuenteovejuna, churl!

FRONDOSO   And how did I slay you, sweet girl?

LAURENCIA   By loving me so tenderly.

        (*Exit* FRONDOSO *and* LAURENCIA.)

        [The Queen's Chamber]

      (*Enter* FERDINAND *and* ISABEL.)

ISABEL   Your presence here is a surprise,   2290
    My lord. Good fortune smiles on me.

FERDINAND   You are a glorious sight to see,
    My queen, a comfort to these eyes.
    We make for Portugal and seize
    This chance to stop en route and rest.   2295

ISABEL   Your Majesty knows when it's best
    To change his course and take his ease.

FERDINAND   How did you leave our dear Castile?

ISABEL   In peace, sire, quiet and serene.

FERDINAND   We wonder not when such a queen   2300
    Imparts tranquility at will.

      (*Enter Don* MANRIQUE.)

MANRIQUE   Sire, Calatrava is now just
    Arrived and seeks an audience
    With you in humble reverence
    To pledge his troth and ask your trust.   2305

ISABEL   It's been my hope to meet the lad.

MANRIQUE   My lady, though he may look young,

I promise you he ranks among
The finest soldiers we have had.

(The MASTER *of Calatrava enters as Don* MANRIQUE *exits.)*

MASTER   I'm Rodrigo Téllez Girón,   2310
Your servant, sire, and Master of
The Calatravan ranks whose love
Entreats forgiveness from the throne.
I here confess I've been deceived
Into transgressing noble laws   2315
Established by Castile because
Of faulty counsel I'd received
From cruel Fernán, who led me down
A road of false self-interest, true
But faithless. As you now construe,   2320
I beg forgiveness of the crown
And, should Your Highness grant to me
This mercy, which I scarce deserve,
I promise this day forth to serve
The royal cause stoutheartedly   2325
In, say, your long campaign, my lord,
Against Granada, where you ride
And where you will observe with pride
The valor latent in my sword
Whose unsheathed steel will bravely vie   2330
With foes who'll suffer crushing loss
So I might drape my Order's cross
O'er Moorish battlements on high.
For this, I'll send five hundred men
To fight beside your own troops now   2335
And hereby give my solemn vow,
Sire, never to displease again.
FERDINAND   Rise, Master, off this bended knee,
For we two hold your presence dear
And you are always welcome here.   2340
MASTER   These favors are grief's remedy.
ISABEL   Your words are equally as fine
As your brave feats and gallant air.
MASTER   You are, dear queen, an Esther fair
And you a Xerxes,[1] sire, divine!   2345

(Enter Don MANRIQUE.*)*

MANRIQUE   Your Majesty, the judge is back
From Fuenteovejuna, whence
He comes with news of the events
There that occasioned the attack.

---

1. The Greek name of the king of Persia (r. 486–465 B.C.E.) whom the Bible calls Ahasueros. The Book of Esther recounts how he made Esther his queen, not knowing that she was Jewish, and how she prevented a massacre of her people.

FERDINAND   You judge the rogues who cut him down.   2350

MASTER   I'd show them, were you not here, sire,
   What doom awaits those who conspire
   To kill Commanders of the crown.

FERDINAND   Their punishment rests with the throne.

ISABEL   I do confess, I'd love to see   2355
   My lord wield this authority
   Should it please God this power be shown.

(Enter the JUDGE.)

JUDGE   I rode, sire, with due diligence
   To Fuenteovejuna where,
   Attending to my charge with care,   2360
   I acted with expedience,
   Investigating how this crime
   Was carried out before I'd come
   But bear no signed confession from
   A soul there after all this time.   2365
   The townsfolk spoke as one with stout
   Conviction for their common good
   And when I'd ask "Who did this?" would
   Shout "Fuenteovejuna" out!
   Three hundred villagers there swore   2370
   That they knew nothing through their pain
   And I despair we'll ever gain
   More information on that score.
   We even lashed lads ten years old
   Upon the rack who held their peace   2375
   Despite our promises to cease
   And other such things they were told.
   In short, I've started so to frown
   On finding someone to condemn
   That either you must pardon them   2380
   Or else eradicate the town.
   To back these findings I've made known,
   All journeyed hence to make their case
   And tell you more of this disgrace.

FERDINAND   Then let them come before the throne.   2385

(Enter ESTEBAN, ALONSO, FRONDOSO, LAURENCIA, *the village women,
and as many other villagers as are needed.)*

LAURENCIA   Are those the monarchs over there?

FRONDOSO   Castile's own might, however far.

LAURENCIA   My God, what handsome beings they are!
   Saint Anthony[2] exalt the pair!

ISABEL   Are these the murderers you mean?   2390

ESTEBAN   Amassed before you at a stroke

---

2. Saint Anthony of Padua (1195–1231), a Franciscan missionary who was born in Lisbon.

Stand Fuenteovejuna's folk
Who humbly wish to serve their queen.
It was the tyranny and cursed
Insistence on purveying dread   2395
Of that Commander who's now dead—
But not before he'd done his worst—
That was behind our vengeful role.
He had our scant possessions seized
And raped our women when he pleased,   2400
All mercy alien to his soul.

FRONDOSO   So much so that when finally
This lovely lass the heavens sent
To make my heart on earth content
And me as happy as can be   2405
Agreed to take me as her spouse,
He acted as if he'd been wived
And, when our wedding night arrived,
Had her abducted to his house!
Were that pure girl not prone to fend   2410
Off the advances he'd begun,
I think it's clear to everyone
Her virtue would have met its end.

MENGO   Is it not time I said a word?
If, by your leave, I may say so,   2415
You'll all be scandalized to know
How bruised I was by what occurred
For rushing straight to the defense
Of one of our poor village girls
As she was being snatched by churls   2420
To undergo some vile offense.
My sorry derriere still aches
From that perverted Nero's[3] lash
And darn it if they didn't thrash
My backside pink as salmon steaks!   2425
Three men administered the belts
So utterly unsparingly
That I'm convinced you still can see
The stripes they left beneath the welts.
All told, the ointment and the salve   2430
Concocted from the myrtle shrub
Which I use as a soothing rub
Are worth more than the farm I have!

ESTEBAN   In short, sire, we do gladly serve
As humble vassals of the crown   2435
And have long since hung in our town
Your coat of arms, which all observe.
We ask, my lord, that you respond

3. A Roman emperor (r. 54–68 C.E.) notorious for his cruelty and dissolution.

With clement mercy in this case.
To recompense this act of grace,
We pledge our innocence as bond.   2440
FERDINAND   As it appears that at no time
There'll be confessions signed in ink,
Though murder is most foul, we think
To grant forgiveness for this crime.   2445
It's well the village should repair
To the protection of Castile
And may depend on us until
We send a new Commander there.
FRONDOSO   This speech, Your Majesty, commends   2450
The measure of your providence
So with these words, wise audience,
Here *Fuenteovejuna* ends.

WILLIAM SHAKESPEARE
1564–1616

Hamlet portrays the doubts and fears of a conflicted prince whose dead father places on him the most burdensome of obligations: to avenge the king's murder by none other than his brother, Hamlet's uncle Claudius, who has married the recently widowed queen, Gertrude. Hamlet's personal tragedy is also that of Denmark, a state left rudderless by the domestic and familial conflicts of the play. Rich though it may be in plot, the most striking thing about *Hamlet* is its representation of the main character's interiority. Balancing the public and the private, Shakespeare gives the audience intimate access to the prince's mind, by transforming his thoughts into powerful dialogue and unprecedented soliloquies. Using older dramatic forms such as revenge tragedy, Shakespeare forged an entirely new type of play that depicts the inner doubts and hesitations of his quintessential protagonist.

LIFE AND TIMES

William Shakespeare was born in the rural community of Stratford-upon-Avon in Warwickshire. His father, John Shakespeare, was a glover and, when William was born, prominent in the town's government. Little is known of Shakespeare's early life, although it is likely that he received an education at the good local grammar school. He married Anne Hathaway, about seven years his senior, when he was eighteen. The couple had three children, Susanna (1583) and the twins Judith and Hamnet (1585).

Shakespeare lived in a period of great nationalist fervor. Under Queen Elizabeth I (1533–1603, ruled 1558–1603), a successful and much beloved ruler, England solidified its sense of itself as a small but heroic Protestant nation valiantly resisting the encroachment of Spain and other enemies. In 1587, fearing a Catholic conspiracy, Elizabeth put to death her cousin, Mary Queen of Scots, who had sought refuge in England in 1568. Even after a powerful storm scattered the Spanish Armada, the fleet sent to invade England in 1588, the nation continued to fear Spanish invasion and Catholic plots against Elizabeth. The sense of a state under siege in *Hamlet* would thus have echoed powerfully for the English, just as they would have recognized the public tragedy of a nation undone by its rulers' outsized appetites for power. The play's reliance on the truth spoken by a ghost trapped in Purgatory—Catholic notions rejected by Protestantism— is also striking in a period that saw both the strong official repudiation of Catholicism and an enduring popular attachment to its rituals.

After a youth spent in the provinces, by 1592 Shakespeare had made his way to the burgeoning city of London. There he rapidly became the "greatest shake-scene" around, in the irritated words of a rival who envied Shakespeare's ability to impress audiences despite his lack of a university education. Shakespeare soon became a shareholder in a prominent players' company that claimed the Lord Chamberlain as patron and the tragic actor Richard Burbage and the comedian Will Kempe as members. Shakespeare's company originally performed at the theatre, north of the city of London, where its actor-owner, James Burbage, faced steady opposition from puritanical city officials who sought to close the theaters, which they considered to be hotbeds of immorality. Burbage conceived of a means to escape civic legislation against theatrical performances, and secretly moved the boards of his playhouse across the river Thames to the south bank; with these planks he constructed the Globe, the theater most often associated with Shakespeare's name.

The Globe was open to all social classes: anyone who wished could enter the theater by paying a penny, and at the cost of another, get a bench, cushion, and protection (in the boxes) from inclement weather. This mixing of social classes in his audience was echoed in Shakespeare's plays: rather than submitting to the stricter forms of classical drama, Shakespeare mixed comic routines with tragic soliloquies, the speech of common soldiers and bawds with the elegant language of the court. The Globe used almost no scenery and few stage props, so Shakespeare had to evoke the scene through language and deploy stage props sparingly. Only the costumes were lavish and constituted one of the most valuable possessions of the company. Shakespeare knew the theater inside out and his plays used its resources to the fullest, including sudden entrances and concealed eavesdroppers, brutal swordfights and touching love scenes, and witty asides and striking double entendres.

Although he began his career as a player, Shakespeare found his calling as a playwright and his fortune as a shareholder in his company. His financial successes enabled him to purchase the title of gentleman for his father, a purchase that made Shakespeare himself officially a "gentleman born," and a fine house in Stratford to which he eventually retired. Despite the unparalleled success of his plays, Shakespeare seems to have valued them only in performance, and never sought to have them printed. Early versions of the plays were often published in unauthorized versions, in some cases on the basis of actors' recollections of their lines. After Shakespeare's death in 1616, his friends published most of his plays in the collection we know as the "First Folio" (1623), the basis for most later editions.

HAMLET

Shakespeare's plays constitute the most important body of dramatic work in the modern world, and no character in literature is more familiar to audiences around the globe than Hamlet. Beyond the impact of the protagonist, *Hamlet* has commanded a leading place in our literary heritage for juxtaposing political obligation and human limitations, idealized virtue and actual experience. Though it is a drama about characters of superior station and the conflicts and problems associated with men and women of high degree, it reveals these problems in a particular family, but presents the domestic conflict within the larger world of politics— like the plays of antiquity that deal with the Theban myth, such as *Oedipus* or *Antigone*. Shakespeare underscores the humanity and frailty of rulers, providing a window into their interiority, whether it be the portrayal of a villainous king in *Richard III* or of a frail and diminished one in *King Lear*. The vulnerability of Hamlet, the disproportion between the heroism demanded of him and the response he can muster, and his acute awareness of how he fails all make him a singularly compelling figure. Leavened with odd moments of black humor, the portrayal of Hamlet's exquisitely self-conscious dilemma amid the increasingly dangerous and opaque machinations of his uncle's court is gripping and casts doubt on dynastic rule itself.

Based on a medieval Scandinavian legend, Shakespeare's play brings the figure of the hero who feigns madness much closer to his own time. In spite of the Danish locale and the relatively remote period of the action, the setting of *Hamlet* is plainly a Renaissance court. There is a ruler holding power, and much of the action is related to questions concerning the nature of that power—the way in which he had acquired it and the ways in which it can be preserved. Around the king are several courtiers, among whom Hamlet, the heir apparent, is only the most prominent. The sense of outside dangers and internal disruption everywhere frames the personal story of Hamlet, of his revenge, and of Claudius's crime. These individual stories are signs of a general societal breakdown. The play charts a kingdom and a society going to pieces, and the realization by its most privileged subjects that it has already crumbled. Lurking behind it all is a sense of the vanity of those forms of human endeavor and power of which the kingdom and the court are symbols.

The tone Shakespeare wants to establish is evident from the opening scenes: the night air is full of premonitions; sentinels turn their eyes toward the threatening outside world; meanwhile, the Ghost has already made his appearance, a sinister omen. The kingdom is presented in terms that are an almost point-by-point reversal of the ideal. Claudius, whether we believe the Ghost's indictment or not (Hamlet does not necessarily, and some of his famous indecision has been attributed to his seeking evidence of the Ghost's truthfulness before acting), has by marrying the queen committed an act that by Elizabethan standards is incestuous. There is an overwhelming sense of disintegration in the body of the state, evident in the first court assembly and in all subsequent ones. Instead of supporting the throne, the two most promising courtiers, Hamlet and Laertes, are restless presences, contemplating departure from a troubled scene.

Decadent and overwrought, the court is marked by semblance instead of substance. Thus Polonius, who after

Hamlet is the major figure in the king's retinue, is presented satirically in his empty formalities and conventional behavior. Often, as with the minor figure of Osric, manners are replaced by mannerisms. Courtly life as depicted in the play suggests always the hollow, the fractured, and the crooked. The traditional forms and institutions of gentle living and all the pomp and solemnity of the court are marred by corruption and distortion. Courtship and love are reduced to Hamlet's mockery of Ophelia, and all but undone by the punning undercurrents of bawdiness. In the famous play-within-the-play, the theater, a traditional institution of court life, is used by the hero as a device to expose the king's crime. There are elements of macabre caricature in Shakespeare's treatment of the solemn theme of death, as in the black comedy of Polonius's death, or the clownish talk of the gravediggers. Finally, the arms tournament, the typical occasion for the display of courtiers' gallantry in front of their king, is here turned by the scheming of the king himself into an almost farcical scene of carnage.

This sense of corruption and decadence dominates the temper of the play and situates Hamlet, his indecision, and his sense of vanity and disenchantment with the world in which he must live. In Hamlet the relationship between thought and deed, intent and realization, is confused, while all around him the norms and institutions that regulate a well-ordered court have been replaced by duplicity and dissimulation. He and the king are "mighty opposites," and it can be argued that against Hamlet's indecision and negativism the king presents a more positive scheme of action, at least in the purely Machiavellian sense, at the level of practical power politics. On various occasions the king shows a high and competent conception of his office: a culminating instance is the courageous and cunning way in which he confronts and handles

Laertes' wrath. Since his life is obviously threatened by Hamlet (who was seeking to kill him when by mistake he killed Polonius instead), one might argue that the king acts within a legitimate pattern of politics in wanting to have Hamlet liquidated. Yet this argument cannot be carried so far as to demonstrate that he represents a fully positive attitude toward life and the world, even in the strictly amoral terms of political technique. For in fact his action is corroded by the vexations of his own conscience. Despite his energy and his extrovert qualities, he too becomes part of the negative picture of disruption and lacks concentration of purpose. The images of decay and putrescence that characterize his court extend to his own speech: his "offense," in his own words, "smells to heaven."

Hamlet as a Renaissance tragedy presents a world particularly "out of joint," a world that, having long ago lost the sense of a grand timeless design that was so important in medieval times (to Hamlet the thought of the afterlife is even more puzzling and dark than that of this life), looks with an even greater sense of disenchantment at the temporal world symbolized by the kingdom and the court. They could have given individual action a purposeful meaning. Yet now their order has been destroyed, and ideals that once had power and freshness have lost their vigor under the impact of satiety, doubt, and melancholy.

Because communal values are so degraded, it is natural to ask in the end whether some alternative attempt at a settlement could be imagined, with Hamlet—like other Renaissance heroes—adopting an individual code of conduct, however extravagant. On the whole, Hamlet seems too steeped in his own hopelessness and in the courtly mechanism to which he inevitably belongs to be able to find personal intellectual and moral compromise or his own version of escape. Still, the tone of his brooding and often moralizing speech, his melancholy and dissatisfaction, his very desire for revenge imply a nostalgia for a world—associated with his father—of loyal allegiances and ideals of honor. Yet in *Hamlet* the political world turns out to offer no protection for the values—friendship, loyalty, and honesty—that Hamlet himself most cherishes. This is perhaps the reason why Hamlet has struck many later readers as a representative modern, someone forced to make his way in a world no longer ordered by traditional institutions.

The influence of Shakespeare's plays on the course of English literature is matched only by the King James translation of the Bible. In his time,

Shakespeare garnered the interest of two British monarchs (Elizabeth I and James I), the love of popular audiences, and the respect of such tough critics as the poet and playwright Ben Jonson, who saw him as "the Soule of the Age" yet recognized that he was "Not of an age, but for all time!" *Hamlet* has always been one of Shakespeare's best loved and most widely produced plays. A tantalizing window into an inscrutable interiority, the play has fascinated thinkers and writers from Sigmund Freud, who offered it as an example of the Oedipal complex, to Tom Stoppard, who portrayed the absurdity of the minor characters with great humor in his *Rosencrantz and Guildenstern Are Dead* (1966).

Hamlet, Prince of Denmark

CHARACTERS

CLAUDIUS, *king of Denmark*
HAMLET, *son to the late, and nephew to the present king*
POLONIUS, *lord chamberlain*
HORATIO, *friend to Hamlet*
LAERTES, *son of Polonius*
PRIEST
MARCELLUS, } *officers*
BERNARDO,
FRANCISCO, *a soldier*
REYNALDO, *servant to Polonius*
PLAYERS
TWO CLOWNS, *grave-diggers*
FORTINBRAS, *prince of Norway*
CAPTAIN

VOLTIMAND,
CORNELIUS,
ROSENCRANTZ,
GUILDENSTERN, } *courtiers*
OSRIC,
GENTLEMAN,
ENGLISH AMBASSADORS
GERTRUDE, *queen of Denmark, and mother to Hamlet*
OPHELIA, *daughter of Polonius*
LORDS, LADIES, OFFICERS, SOLDIERS, SAILORS, MESSENGERS, *and* OTHER ATTENDANTS
GHOST OF HAMLET'S FATHER

[SCENE: *Denmark.*]

Act 1

SCENE I

[SCENE: *Elsinore. A platform before the castle.*]

[FRANCISCO *at his post. Enter to him* BERNARDO.]

BERNARDO Who's there?
FRANCISCO Nay, answer me: stand, and unfold yourself.

BERNARDO   Long live the king!

FRANCISCO   Bernardo?

BERNARDO   He.

FRANCISCO   You come most carefully upon your hour.   5

BERNARDO   'Tis now struck twelve; get thee to bed, Francisco.

FRANCISCO   For this relief much thanks: 'tis bitter cold,
  And I am sick at heart.

BERNARDO   Have you had quiet guard?

FRANCISCO   Not a mouse stirring.   10

BERNARDO   Well, good night.
  If you do meet Horatio and Marcellus,
  The rivals¹ of my watch, bid them make haste.

FRANCISCO   I think I hear them. Stand, ho! Who is there?
      [*Enter* HORATIO *and* MARCELLUS.]

HORATIO   Friends to this ground.

MARCELLUS   And liegemen to the Dane.²   15

FRANCISCO   Give you good night.

MARCELLUS   O, farewell, honest soldier:
  Who hath relieved you?

FRANCISCO   Bernardo hath my place.
  Give you good night.
      [*Exit.*]

MARCELLUS   Holla! Bernardo!

BERNARDO   Say,
  What, is Horatio there?

HORATIO   A piece of him.

BERNARDO   Welcome, Horatio; welcome, good Marcellus.   20

MARCELLUS   What, has this thing appeared again to-night?

BERNARDO   I have seen nothing.

MARCELLUS   Horatio says 'tis but our fantasy,
  And will not let belief take hold of him
  Touching this dreaded sight, twice seen of us: 25
  Therefore I have entreated him along
  With us to watch the minutes of this night,
  That if again this apparition come,
  He may approve our eyes³ and speak to it.

HORATIO   Tush, tush, 'twill not appear.

BERNARDO   Sit down a while;   30
  And let us once again assail your ears,
  That are so fortified against our story,
  What we have two nights seen.

HORATIO   Well, sit we down,
  And let us hear Bernardo speak of this.

BERNARDO   Last night of all,   35
  When yond same star that's westward from the pole
  Had made his course to illume that part of heaven

1. Partners.   3. Confirm what we saw.
2. The king of Denmark.

Where now it burns, Marcellus and myself,
The bell then beating one,—
　　　[*Enter* GHOST.]

MARCELLUS　　Peace, break thee off; look, where it comes again!　　　40
BERNARDO　　In the same figure, like the king that's dead.
MARCELLUS　　Thou art a scholar; speak to it, Horatio.
BERNARDO　　Looks it not like the king? mark it, Horatio.
HORATIO　　Most like it: it harrows me with fear and wonder.
BERNARDO　　It would be spoke to.
MARCELLUS　　　　　　　　　　　　　Question it, Horatio.　　　45
HORATIO　　What art thou, that usurp'st this time of night,
　Together with that fair and warlike form
　In which the majesty of buried Denmark
　Did sometimes[4] march? by heaven I charge thee, speak!
MARCELLUS　　It is offended.
BERNARDO　　　　　　　　　　See, it stalks away!　　　50
HORATIO　　Stay! speak, speak! I charge thee, speak!
　　　[*Exit* GHOST.]
MARCELLUS　　'Tis gone, and will not answer.
BERNARDO　　How now, Horatio! you tremble and look pale:
　Is not this something more than fantasy?
　What think you on't?　　　55
HORATIO　　Before my God, I might not this believe
　Without the sensible and true avouch
　Of mine own eyes.
MARCELLUS　　　　　　　Is it not like the king?
HORATIO　　As thou art to thyself:
　Such was the very armor he had on　　　60
　When he the ambitious Norway[5] combated;
　So frown'd he once, when, in an angry parle,
　He smote the sledded[6] Polacks on the ice.
　'Tis strange.
MARCELLUS　　Thus twice before, and jump[7] at this dead hour,　　　65
　With martial stalk hath he gone by our watch.
HORATIO　　In what particular thought to work I know not;
　But, in the gross and scope of my opinion,[8]
　This bodes some strange eruption to our state.
MARCELLUS　　Good now, sit down, and tell me, he that knows,　　　70
　Why this same strict and most observant watch
　So nightly toils the subject[9] of the land,
　And why such daily cast of brazen cannon,
　And foreign mart for implements of war;
　Why such impress of shipwrights, whose sore task　　　75
　Does not divide the Sunday from the week;

4. Formerly, "Denmark": the king of Denmark.
5. The king of Norway (the elder Fortinbras).
6. They travel in sledges. "Parle": parley.
7. Just.

8. Taking a general view.
9. The people.
1. Ship carpenters. "Mart": trading. "Impress": pressing into service.

What might be toward,[2] that this sweaty haste
Doth make the night joint-laborer with the day:
Who is't that can inform me?

HORATIO   That can I;
  At least the whisper goes so. Our last king,   80
  Whose image even but now appear'd to us,
  Was, as you know, by Fortinbras of Norway,
  Thereto pricked on by a most emulate pride,
  Dared to the combat; in which our valiant Hamlet—
  For so this side of our known world esteem'd him—   85
  Did slay this Fortinbras; who by a seal'd compact
  Well ratified by law and heraldry,[3]
  Did forfeit, with his life, all those his lands
  Which he stood seized of, to the conqueror:
  Against the which, a moiety competent   90
  Was gagèd[4] by our king; which had returned
  To the inheritance of Fortinbras,
  Had he been vanquisher; as, by the same covenant
  And carriage[5] of the article design'd,
  His fell to Hamlet. Now, sir, young Fortinbras,   95
  Of unimprovèd metal hot and full,
  Hath in the skirts[6] of Norway here and there
  Shark'd up a list of lawless resolutes,
  For food and diet, to some enterprise
  That hath a stomach in't:[7] which is no other—   100
  As it doth well appear unto our state—
  But to recover of us, by strong hand
  And terms compulsatory, those foresaid lands
  So by his father lost: and this, I take it,
  Is the main motive of our preparations,   105
  The source of this our watch and the chief head
  Of this post-haste and romage[8] in the land.

BERNARDO   I think it be no other but e'en so:
  Well may it sort,[9] that this portentous figure
  Comes armèd through our watch, so like the king   110
  That was and is the question of these wars.

HORATIO   A mote it is to trouble the mind's eye.
  In the most high and palmy state of Rome,
  A little ere the mightiest Julius fell,
  The graves stood tenantless, and the sheeted dead   115
  Did squeak and gibber in the Roman streets:
  As stars with trains of fire and dews of blood,
  Disasters in the sun; and the moist star,

2. Impending.
3. Duly ratified and proclaimed through heralds.
4. Pledged. "Seized": possessed. "Moiety competent": equal share.
5. Purport.

6. Outskirts, border regions. "Unimprovèd": untested.
7. Calls for courage.
8. Bustle. "Head": origin, cause.
9. Fit with the other signs of war.

Upon whose influence Neptune's empire stands,[1]
Was sick almost to doomsday with eclipse: 120
And even the like precurse[2] of fierce events,
As harbingers preceding still the fates
And prologue to the omen coming on,
Have heaven and earth together demonstrated
Unto our climatures[3] and countrymen.   125
      [*Re-enter* GHOST.]
But soft, behold! lo, where it comes again!
I'll cross it, though it blast me. Stay, illusion!
If thou hast any sound, or use of voice,
Speak to me:
If there be any good thing to be done,   130
That may to thee do ease and grace to me,
Speak to me:
If thou art privy to thy country's fate,
Which, happily, foreknowing may avoid,
O, speak!   135
Or if thou hast uphoarded in thy life
Extorted treasure in the womb of earth,
For which, they say, you spirits oft walk in death,
Speak of it: stay, and speak! [*The cock crows.*] Stop it, Marcellus.
MARCELLUS   Shall I strike at it with my partisan?   140
HORATIO   Do, if it will not stand.
BERNARDO   'Tis here!
HORATIO   'Tis here!
      [*Exit* GHOST.]
MARCELLUS   'Tis gone!
We do it wrong, being so majestical,
To offer it the show of violence;
For it is, as the air, invulnerable,
And our vain blows malicious mockery.   145
BERNARDO   It was about to speak, when the cock crew.
HORATIO   And then it started like a guilty thing
Upon a fearful summons. I have heard
The cock, that is the trumpet to the morn,
Doth with his lofty and shrill-sounding throat   150
Awake the god of day, and at his warning,
Whether in sea or fire, in earth or air,
The extravagant[4] and erring spirit hies
To his confine: and of the truth herein
This present object made probation.[5]   155
MARCELLUS   It faded on the crowing of the cock.
Some say that ever 'gainst[6] that season comes

1. The moon (*moist star*) regulates the sea's
tides. "Disasters": ill omens.
2. Foreboding.
3. Regions.

4. Wandering out of its confines.
5. Gave proof.
6. Just before.

Wherein our Saviour's birth is celebrated,
The bird of dawning singeth all night long: 160
And then, they say, no spirit dare stir abroad,
The nights are wholesome, then no planets strike,
No fairy takes nor witch hath power to charm,
So hallowed and so gracious[7] is the time.
HORATIO   So have I heard and do in part believe it. 165
But look, the morn, in russet mantle clad,
Walks o'er the dew of yon high eastward hill:
Break we our watch up; and by my advice,
Let us impart what we have seen to-night
Unto young Hamlet; for, upon my life, 170
This spirit, dumb to us, will speak to him:
Do you consent we shall acquaint him with it,
As needful in our loves, fitting our duty?
MARCELLUS   Let's do't, I pray; and I this morning know
Where we shall find him most conveniently. 175
        [*Exeunt.*]

SCENE 2

[SCENE: *A room of state in the castle.*]

> [*Flourish. Enter the* KING, QUEEN, HAMLET, POLONIUS, LAERTES,
> VOLTIMAND, CORNELIUS, LORDS, *and* ATTENDANTS.]

KING   Though yet of Hamlet our dear brother's death
The memory be green, and that it us befitted
To bear our hearts in grief and our whole kingdom
To be contracted in one brow of woe,
Yet so far hath discretion[8] fought with nature 5
That we with wisest sorrow think on him,
Together with remembrance of ourselves.
Therefore our sometime sister, now our queen,
The imperial jointress to this warlike state,
Have we, as 'twere with a defeated joy,— 10
With an auspicious and a dropping eye,
With mirth in funeral and with dirge in marriage,
In equal scale weighing delight and dole,—
Taken to wife: nor have we herein barr'd[9]
Your better wisdoms, which have freely gone 15
With this affair along. For all, our thanks.
Now follows, that[1] you know, young Fortinbras,
Holding a weak supposal of our worth,
Or thinking by our late dear brother's death
Our state to be disjoint and out of frame, 20
Colleaguèd with this dream[2] of his advantage,

---

7. Full of blessing. "Strike": exercise evil
influence (compare *moonstruck*). "Fairy takes":
bewitches.
8. Restraint (on grief).

9. Ignored. "Dole": grief.
1. What.
2. Combined with this fantastic notion.

He hath not failed to pester us with message,
Importing the surrender of those lands
Lost by his father, with all bonds of law,
To our most valiant brother. So much for him   25
Now for ourself, and for this time of meeting:
Thus much the business is: we have here writ
To Norway, uncle of young Fortinbras,—
Who, impotent and bed-rid, scarcely hears
Of this his nephew's purpose,—to suppress   30
His further gait herein; in that the levies,
The lists and full proportions,[3] are all made
Out of his subject: and we here dispatch
You, good Cornelius, and you, Voltimand,
For bearers of this greeting to old Norway,   35
Giving to you no further personal power
To business with the king more than the scope
Of these delated[4] articles allow.
Farewell, and let your haste commend your duty.

CORNELIUS ⎫
VOLTIMAND ⎭   In that and all things will we show our duty.   40

KING   We doubt it nothing: heartily farewell.
          [*Exeunt* VOLTIMAND *and* CORNELIUS.]
And now, Laertes, what's the news with you?
You told us of some suit; what is't, Laertes?
You cannot speak of reason to the Dane,
And lose your voice: what wouldst thou beg, Laertes,   45
That shall not be my offer, not thy asking?
The head is not more native to[5] the heart,
The hand more instrumental to the mouth,
Than is the throne of Denmark to thy father.
What wouldst thou have, Laertes?

LAERTES   My dread lord,   50
Your leave and favor to return to France,
From whence though willingly I came to Denmark,
To show my duty in your coronation,
Yet now, I must confess, that duty done,
My thoughts and wishes bend again toward France   55
And bow them to your gracious leave and pardon.

KING   Have you your father's leave? What says Polonius?

POLONIUS   He hath, my lord, wrung from me my slow leave
By laborsome petition, and at last
Upon his will I sealed my hard consent: 60
I do beseech you, give him leave to go.

KING   Take thy fair hour, Laertes; time be thine,
And thy best graces spend it at thy will!
But now, my cousin Hamlet, and my son,—

3. Amounts of forces and supplies. "Gait":   4. Detailed.
proceeding.   5. Naturally bound to.

HAMLET [*Aside*.]   A little more than kin, and less than kind.   65
KING   How is it that the clouds still hang on you?
HAMLET   Not so, my lord; I am too much i' the sun.[6]
QUEEN   Good Hamlet, cast thy nighted color off,
   And let thine eye look like a friend on Denmark.
   Do not for ever with thy vailèd[7] lids   70
   Seek for thy noble father in the dust:
   Thou know'st 'tis common; all that lives must die,
   Passing through nature to eternity.
HAMLET   Aye, madam, it is common.
QUEEN   If it be,
   Why seems it so particular with thee?   75
HAMLET   Seems, madam! nay, it is; I know not "seems."
   'Tis not alone my inky cloak, good mother,
   Nor customary suits of solemn black,
   Nor windy suspiration of forced breath,
   No, nor the fruitful river in the eye,   80
   Nor the dejected havior of the visage,
   Together with all forms, moods, shapes of grief,
   That can denote me truly: these indeed seem,
   For they are actions that a man might play:
   But I have that within which passeth show;   85
   These but the trappings and the suits of woe.
KING   'Tis sweet and cómmendàble in your nature, Hamlet,
   To give these mourning duties to your father:
   But, you must know, your father lost a father,
   That father lost, lost his, and the survivor bound   90
   In filial obligation for some term
   To do obsequious[8] sorrow: but to persevere
   In obstinate condolement is a course
   Of impious stubbornness; 'tis unmanly grief:
   It shows a will most incorrect[9] to heaven,   95
   A heart unfortified, a mind impatient,
   An understanding simple and unschool'd:
   For what we know must be and is as common
   As any the most vulgar thing to sense,
   Why should we in our peevish opposition   100
   Take it to heart? Fie! 'tis a fault to heaven,
   A fault against the dead, a fault to nature,
   To reason most absurd, whose common theme
   Is death of fathers, and who still hath cried,
   From the first corse till he that died to-day,   105
   "This must be so." We pray you, throw to earth
   This unprevailing[1] woe, and think of us

---

6. The cue to Hamlet's irony is given by the
King's "my cousin . . . my son" (line 64). Hamlet is punning on *son*.
7. Downcast.

8. Dutiful, especially concerning funeral rites
(obsequies).
9. Not subdued.
1. Useless.

As of a father: for let the world take note,
You are the most immediate to our throne,
And with no less nobility of love   110
Than that which dearest father bears his son
Do I impart toward you. For your intent
In going back to school in Wittenberg,
It is most retrograde[2] to our desire:
And we beseech you, bend you to remain   115
Here in the cheer and comfort of our eye,
Our chiefest courtier, cousin and our son.

QUEEN   Let not thy mother lose her prayers, Hamlet:
    I pray thee, stay with us; go not to Wittenberg.

HAMLET   I shall in all my best obey you, madam.   120

KING   Why, 'tis a loving and a fair reply:
    Be as ourself in Denmark. Madam, come;
    This gentle and unforced accord of Hamlet
    Sits smiling to my heart: in grace whereof,
    No jocund health that Denmark drinks to-day,   125
    But the great cannon to the clouds shall tell,
    And the king's rouse the heaven shall bruit[3] again,
    Re-speaking earthly thunder. Come away.
        [*Flourish. Exeunt all but* HAMLET.]

HAMLET   O, that this too too sullied flesh would melt,
    Thaw and resolve itself into a dew!   130
    Or that the Everlasting had not fixed
    His canon[4] 'gainst self-slaughter! O God! God!
    How weary, stale, flat and unprofitable
    Seem to me all the uses of this world!
    Fie on't! ah fie! 'tis an unweeded garden,   135
    That grows to seed; things rank and gross in nature
    Possess it merely. That it should come to this!
    But two months dead! nay, not so much, not two:
    So excellent a king; that was, to this,
    Hyperion to a satyr: so loving to my mother,   140
    That he might not beteem[5] the winds of heaven
    Visit her face too roughly. Heaven and earth!
    Must I remember? why, she would hang on him,
    As if increase of appetite had grown
    By what it fed on: and yet, within a month—   145
    Let me not think on't—Frailty, thy name is woman!—
    A little month, or ere those shoes were old
    With which she followed my poor father's body,
    Like Niobe,[6] all tears:—why she, even she,—

2. Opposed. "Wittenberg": the seat of a university; at the peak of fame in Shakespeare's time because of its connection with Martin Luther.
3. Proclaim, echo. "Rouse": carousal, revel.
4. Law.
5. Allow. "Hyperion": the sun god.

6. A proud mother who boasted of having more children than Leto; her seven sons and seven daughters were slain by Apollo and Artemis, children of Leto. The grieving Niobe was changed by Zeus into a continually weeping stone.

O God! a beast that wants discourse[7] of reason 150
Would have mourned longer,—married with my uncle,
My father's brother, but no more like my father
Than I to Hercules: within a month;
Ere yet the salt of most unrighteous tears
Had left the flushing in her gallèd[8] eyes, 155
She married. O, most wicked speed, to post
With such dexterity to incestuous sheets![9]
It is not, nor it cannot come to good:
But break, my heart, for I must hold my tongue!

    [*Enter* HORATIO, MARCELLUS, *and* BERNARDO.]

HORATIO   Hail to your lordship!

HAMLET   I am glad to see you well: 160
  Horatio,—or I do forget myself.

HORATIO   The same, my lord, and your poor servant ever.

HAMLET   Sir, my good friend; I'll change[1] that name with you:
  And what make you from Wittenberg, Horatio?
  Marcellus? 165

MARCELLUS   My good lord?

HAMLET   I am very glad to see you. [*To* BERNARDO.] Good even, sir.
  But what, in faith, make you from Wittenberg?

HORATIO   A truant disposition, good my lord.

HAMLET   I would not hear your enemy say so, 170
  Nor shall you do my ear that violence,
  To make it truster of your own report
  Against yourself: I know you are no truant.
  But what is your affair in Elsinore?
  We'll teach you to drink deep ere you depart. 175

HORATIO   My lord, I came to see your father's funeral.

HAMLET   I pray thee, do not mock me, fellow-student;
  I think it was to see my mother's wedding.

HORATIO   Indeed, my lord, it followed hard upon.

HAMLET   Thrift, thrift, Horatio! the funeral baked-meats 180
  Did coldly furnish forth the marriage tables.
  Would I had met my dearest[2] foe in heaven
  Or ever I had seen that day, Horatio!
  My father!—methinks I see my father.

HORATIO   O where, my lord?

HAMLET   In my mind's eye, Horatio. 185

HORATIO   I saw him once; he was a goodly king.

HAMLET   He was a man, take him for all in all,
  I shall not look upon his like again.

HORATIO   My lord, I think I saw him yesternight.

HAMLET   Saw? who? 190

---

7. Lacks the faculty.
8. Inflamed.
9. According to principles that Hamlet accepts,

marrying one's brother's widow is incest.
1. Exchange.
2. Bitterest.

HORATIO   My lord, the king your father.

HAMLET   The king my father!

HORATIO   Season your admiration[3] for a while
  With an attent ear, till I may deliver,
  Upon the witness of these gentlemen,
  This marvel to you.

HAMLET   For God's love, let me hear.   195

HORATIO   Two nights together had these gentlemen,
  Marcellus and Bernardo, on their watch,
  In the dead vast and middle of the night,
  Been thus encountered. A figure like your father,
  Armed at point exactly, cap-a-pe,[4]   200
  Appears before them, and with solemn march
  Goes slow and stately by them: thrice he walked
  By their oppressed and fear-surprisèd eyes,
  Within his truncheon's length; whilst they, distilled
  Almost to jelly with the act of fear,   205
  Stand dumb, and speak not to him. This to me
  In dreadful secrecy impart they did;
  And I with them the third night kept the watch:
  Where, as they had delivered, both in time,
  Form of the thing, each word made true and good,   210
  The apparition comes: I knew your father;
  These hands were not more like.

HAMLET   But where was this?

MARCELLUS   My lord, upon the platform where we watched.

HAMLET   Did you not speak to it?

HORATIO   My lord, I did.
  But answer made it none: yet once methought   215
  It lifted up its head and did address
  Itself to motion, like as it would speak:
  But even then the morning cock crew loud,
  And at the sound it shrunk in haste away
  And vanished from our sight.

HAMLET   'Tis very strange.   220

HORATIO   As I do live, my honored lord, 'tis true,
  And we did think it writ down in our duty
  To let you know of it.

HAMLET   Indeed, indeed, sirs, but this troubles me.
  Hold you the watch to-night?

MARCELLUS }
BERNARDO   }   We do, my lord.   225

HAMLET   Armed, say you?

MARCELLUS }
BERNARDO   }   Armed, my lord.

---

3. Restrain your astonishment.   4. From head to foot. "At point": completely.

HAMLET   From top to toe?

MARCELLUS }

BERNARDO }   My lord, from head to foot.

HAMLET   Then saw you not his face?

HORATIO   O, yes, my lord; he wore his beaver⁵ up.

HAMLET   What, looked he frowningly?   230

HORATIO   A countenance more in sorrow than in anger.

HAMLET   Pale, or red?

HORATIO   Nay, very pale.

HAMLET   And fixed his eyes upon you?

HORATIO   Most constantly.

HAMLET   I would I had been there.

HORATIO   It would have much amazed you.   235

HAMLET   Very like, very like. Stayed it long?

HORATIO   While one with moderate haste might tell⁶ a hundred.

MARCELLUS }

BERNARDO } Longer, longer.

HORATIO   Not when I saw't.

HAMLET   His beard was grizzled?⁷ no?

HORATIO   It was, as I have seen it in his life,   240

    A sable silvered.⁸

HAMLET   I will watch to-night;

    Perchance 'twill walk again.

HORATIO   I warrant it will.

HAMLET   If it assume my noble father's person,

    I'll speak to it, though hell itself should gape

    And bid me hold my peace. I pray you all,   245

    If you have hitherto concealed this sight,

    Let it be tenable in your silence still,⁹

    And whatsoever else shall hap to-night,

    Give it an understanding, but no tongue:

    I will requite your loves. So fare you well: 250

    Upon the platform, 'twixt eleven and twelve,

    I'll visit you.

ALL   Our duty to your honor.

HAMLET   Your loves, as mine to you: farewell.

        [*Exeunt all but* HAMLET.]

    My father's spirit in arms! all is not well;

    I doubt¹ some foul play: would the night were come!   255

    Till then sit still, my soul: foul deeds will rise,

    Though all the earth o'erwhelm them, to men's eyes.

        [*Exit.*]

---

5. Visor.   8. Black and white.
6. Count.   9. Consider it still a secret.
7. Gray.   1. Suspect.

SCENE 3

[SCENE: *A room in Polonius's house.*]

[*Enter* LAERTES *and* OPHELIA.]

LAERTES   My necessaries are embarked: farewell:
  And, sister, as the winds give benefit
  And convoy[2] is assistant, do not sleep,
  But let me hear from you.
OPHELIA   Do you doubt that?
LAERTES   For Hamlet, and the trifling of his favor,   5
  Hold it a fashion, and a toy in blood,
  A violet in the youth of primy nature,
  Forward,[3] not permanent, sweet, not lasting,
  The perfume and suppliance of a minute;
  No more.   10
OPHELIA   No more but so?
LAERTES   Think it no more:
  For nature crescent does not grow alone
  In thews and bulk; but, as this temple[4] waxes,
  The inward service of the mind and soul   15
  Grows wide withal. Perhaps he loves you now;
  And now no soil nor cautel[5] doth besmirch
  The virtue of his will: but you must fear,
  His greatness weighed,[6] his will is not his own;
  For he himself is subject to his birth: 20
  He may not, as unvalued persons do,
  Carve for himself, for on his choice depends
  The safety and health of this whole state,
  And therefore must his choice be circumscribed
  Unto the voice and yielding[7] of that body   25
  Whereof he is the head. Then if he says he loves you,
  It fits your wisdom so far to believe it
  As he in his particular act and place
  May give his saying deed; which is no further
  Than the main voice of Denmark goes withal.[8]   30
  Then weigh what loss your honor may sustain,
  If with too credent ear you list his songs,
  Or lose your heart, or your chaste treasure open
  To his unmastered importunity.
  Fear it, Ophelia, fear it, my dear sister,   35
  And keep you in the rear of your affection,
  Out of the shot and danger of desire.
  The chariest maid is prodigal enough

2. Conveyance, means of transport.
3. Early. "Fashion": passing mood. "Primy": early, young.
4. The body. "Crescent": growing.
5. No foul or deceitful thoughts.
6. When you consider his rank. "Will": desire.
7. Assent.
8. Goes along with, agrees. "Main": powerful.

If she unmask her beauty to the moon:
Virtue itself 'scapes not calumnious strokes: 40
The canker galls the infants of the spring
Too oft before their buttons be disclosed,
And in the morn and liquid dew of youth
Contagious blastments[9] are most imminent.
Be wary then; best safety lies in fear: 45
Youth to itself[1] rebels, though none else near.

OPHELIA   I shall the effect of this good lesson keep,
As watchman to my heart. But, good my brother,
Do not, as some ungracious pastors do,
Show me the steep and thorny way to heaven,   50
Whilst, like a puffed and reckless libertine,
Himself the primrose path of dalliance treads
And recks not his own rede.[2]

LAERTES   O, fear me not.
I stay too long; but here my father comes.
    [Enter POLONIUS.]
A double blessing is a double grace;   55
Occasion smiles upon a second leave.

POLONIUS   Yet here, Laertes! Aboard, aboard, for shame!
The wind sits in the shoulder of your sail,
And you are stayed for. There; my blessing with thee!
And these few precepts in thy memory   60
See thou character.[3] Give thy thoughts no tongue,
Nor any unproportioned[4] thought his act.
Be thou familiar, but by no means vulgar.
Those friends thou hast, and their adoption tried,
Grapple them to thy soul with hoops of steel,   65
But do not dull thy palm[5] with entertainment
Of each new-hatched unfledged comrade. Beware
Of entrance to a quarrel; but being in,
Bear't, that the opposèd may beware of thee.
Give every man thy ear, but few thy voice: 70
Take each man's censure,[6] but reserve thy judgment.
Costly thy habit as thy purse can buy,
But not expressed in fancy; rich, not gaudy:
For the apparel oft proclaims the man;
And they in France of the best rank and station   75
Are of a most select and generous chief[7] in that.
Neither a borrower nor a lender be:
For loan oft loses both itself and friend,
And borrowing dulls the edge of husbandry.[8]
This above all: to thine own self be true,   80

9. Blights.
1. Against its better self.
2. Does not follow his own advice.
3. Engrave in your memory.
4. Unsuitable.

5. Make the palm of your hand callous (by the indiscriminate shaking of hands).
6. Opinion.
7. Preeminence.
8. Thriftiness.

And it must follow, as the night the day,
Thou canst not then be false to any man.
Farewell: my blessing season[9] this in thee!

LAERTES   Most humbly do I take my leave, my lord.

POLONIUS   The time invites you; go, your servants tend.[1]   85

LAERTES   Farewell, Ophelia, and remember well
What I have said to you.

OPHELIA   'Tis in my memory locked,
And you yourself shall keep the key of it.

LAERTES   Farewell.
        [Exit.]

POLONIUS   What is't, Ophelia, he hath said to you?

OPHELIA   So please you, something touching the Lord Hamlet.   90

POLONIUS   Marry, well bethought:
'Tis told me, he hath very oft of late
Given private time to you, and you yourself
Have of your audience been most free and bounteous:
If it be so—as so 'tis put on me,   95
And that in way of caution—I must tell you,
You do not understand yourself so clearly
As it behoves my daughter and your honor.
What is between you? give me up the truth.

OPHELIA   He hath, my lord, of late made many tenders   100
Of his affection to me.

POLONIUS   Affection! pooh! you speak like a green girl,
Unsifted[2] in such perilous circumstance.
Do you believe his tenders, as you call them?

OPHELIA   I do not know, my lord, what I should think.   105

POLONIUS   Marry, I'll teach you: think yourself a baby,
That you have ta'en these tenders for true pay,
Which are not sterling. Tender[3] yourself more dearly;
Or—not to crack the wind of the poor phrase,
Running it thus—you'll tender me a fool.[4]   110

OPHELIA   My lord, he hath importuned me with love
In honorable fashion.

POLONIUS   Aye, fashion you may call it; go to, go to.

OPHELIA   And hath given countenance[5] to his speech, my lord,
With almost all the holy vows of heaven.   115

POLONIUS   Aye, springes to catch woodcocks. I do know,
When the blood burns, how prodigal the soul
Lends the tongue vows: these blazes, daughter,
Giving more light than heat, extinct in both,
Even in their promise, as it is a-making,   120
You must not take for fire. From this time
Be something scanter of your maiden presence;

9. Ripen.
1. Wait.
2. Untested.
3. Regard.

4. You'll furnish me with a fool (a foolish daughter).
5. Authority.

Set your entreatments[6] at a higher rate
Than a command to parley. For Lord Hamlet,
Believe so much in him, that he is young,   125
And with a larger tether may he walk
Than may be given you: in few, Ophelia,
Do not believe his vows; for they are brokers,
Not of that dye which their investments[7] show,
But mere implorators of unholy suits,   130
Breathing like sanctified and pious bawds,
The better to beguile. This is for all:
I would not, in plain terms, from this time forth,
Have you so slander any moment[8] leisure,
As to give words or talk with the Lord Hamlet.   135
Look to't, I charge you: come your ways.
OPHELIA   I shall obey, my lord.
    [*Exeunt.*]

SCENE 4

[SCENE: *The platform.*]

    [*Enter* HAMLET, HORATIO, *and* MARCELLUS.]
HAMLET   The air bites shrewdly; it is very cold.
HORATIO   It is a nipping and an eager[9] air.
HAMLET   What hour now?
HORATIO   I think it lacks of twelve.
MARCELLUS   No, it is struck.
HORATIO   Indeed? I heard it not: it then draws near the season   5
    Wherein the spirit held his wont to walk.
    [*A flourish of trumpets, and ordnance shot off within.*]
    What doth this mean, my lord?
HAMLET   The king doth wake to-night, and takes his rouse,
    Keeps wassail, and the swaggering up-spring reels;
    And as he drains his draughts of Rhenish[1] down,   10
    The kettle-drum and trumpet thus bray out
    The triumph of his pledge.[2]
HORATIO   Is it a custom?
HAMLET   Aye, marry, is't:
    But to my mind, though I am native here
    And to the manner born, it is a custom   15
    More honored[3] in the breach than the observance.
    This heavy-headed revel east and west
    Makes us traduced and taxed of other nations:
    They clepe us drunkards, and with swinish phrase
    Soil our addition;[4] and indeed it takes   20

---

6. Conversation, company.
7. Clothes. "Brokers": procurers, panders.
8. Use badly any momentary.
9. Sharp.

1. Rhine wine. "Up-spring reels": wild dances.
2. In downing the cup in one draught.
3. Honorable.
4. Reputation. "Taxed": blamed. "Clepe": call.

From our achievements, though performed at height,[5]
The pith and marrow of our attribute.[6]
So, oft it chances in particular men,
That for some vicious mole of nature in them,
As, in their birth,—wherein they are not guilty, 25
Since nature cannot choose his origin,—
By the o'ergrowth of some complexion,[7]
Oft breaking down the pales and forts of reason,
Or by some habit that too much o'er-leavens[8]
The form of plausive[9] manners, that these men,— 30
Carrying, I say, the stamp of one defect,
Being nature's livery, or fortune's star,—
Their virtues else[1]—be they as pure as grace,
As infinite as man may undergo—
Shall in the general censure take corruption 35
From that particular fault: the dram of evil
Doth all the noble substance often dout
To his own scandal.[2]
     [*Enter* GHOST.]

HORATIO   Look, my lord it comes!
HAMLET   Angels and ministers of grace defend us!
   Be thou a spirit of health or goblin damned, 40
   Bring with thee airs from heaven or blasts from hell,
   Be thy intents wicked or charitable,
   Thou comest in such a questionable shape
   That I will speak to thee: I'll call thee Hamlet,
   King, father, royal Dane: O, answer me! 45
   Let me not burst in ignorance; but tell
   Why thy canónized bones, hearsèd in death,
   Have burst their cerements; why the sepulchre,
   Wherein we saw thee quietly inurned,
   Hath oped his ponderous and marble jaws, 50
   To cast thee up again. What may this mean,
   That thou, dead corse, again, in complete steel,
   Revisit'st thus the glimpses of the moon,
   Making night hideous; and we fools of nature
   So horridly to shake our disposition 55
   With thoughts beyond the reaches of our souls?
   Say, why is this? Wherefore? what should we do?
     [GHOST *beckons* HAMLET.]
HORATIO   It beckons you to go away with it,
   As if it some impartment did desire
   To you alone. 60
MARCELLUS   Look, with what courteous action
   It waves you to a more removèd ground:

---

5. Done in the best possible manner.
6. Reputation.
7. Excess in one side of their temperament.
8. Modifies, as yeast changes dough.

9. Agreeable.
1. The rest of their qualities.
2. To its own harm. "Dout": extinguish, nullify.

But do not go with it.

HORATIO   No, by no means.

HAMLET   It will not speak; then I will follow it.

HORATIO   Do not, my lord.

HAMLET   Why, what should be the fear?   65
I do not set my life at a pin's fee;
And for my soul, what can it do to that,
Being a thing immortal as itself?
It waves me forth again: I'll follow it.

HORATIO   What if it tempt you toward the flood, my lord,   70
Or to the dreadful summit of the cliff
That beetles o'er[3] his base into the sea,
And there assume some other horrible form,
Which might deprive your sovereignty of reason
And draw you into madness? think of it: 75
The very place puts toys[4] of desperation,
Without more motive, into every brain
That looks so many fathoms to the sea
And hears it roar beneath.

HAMLET   It waves me still.
Go on; I'll follow thee.   80

MARCELLUS   You shall not go, my lord.

HAMLET   Hold off your hands.

HORATIO   Be ruled; you shall not go.

HAMLET   My fate cries out,
And makes each petty artery in this body
As hardy as the Nemean lion's nerve.[5]
Still am I called, unhand me, gentlemen;   85
By heaven, I'll make a ghost of him that lets[6] me:
I say, away! Go on; I'll follow thee.
        [Exeunt GHOST and HAMLET.]

HORATIO   He waxes desperate with imagination.

MARCELLUS   Let's follow; 'tis not fit thus to obey him.

HORATIO   Have after. To what issue will this come?   90

MARCELLUS   Something is rotten in the state of Denmark.

HORATIO   Heaven will direct it.

MARCELLUS   Nay, let's follow him.
        [Exeunt.]

SCENE 5

[SCENE: Another part of the platform.]

        [Enter GHOST and HAMLET.]

HAMLET   Whither wilt thou lead me? speak; I'll go no further.

GHOST   Mark me.

HAMLET   I will.

---

3. Juts over.
4. Fancies.
5. Sinew, muscle. "Nemean lion": slain by

Hercules as one of his twelve labors.
6. Hinders.

GHOST   My hour is almost come,
When I to sulphurous and tormenting flames[7]
Must render up myself.
HAMLET   Alas, poor ghost!
GHOST   Pity me not, but lend thy serious hearing   5
To what I shall unfold.
HAMLET   Speak; I am bound to hear.
GHOST   So art thou to revenge, when thou shalt hear.
HAMLET   What?
GHOST   I am thy father's spirit;
Doomed for a certain term to walk the night,   10
And for the day confined to fast in fires,
Till the foul crimes done in my days of nature
Are burnt and purged away. But that I am forbid
To tell the secrets of my prison-house,
I could a tale unfold whose lightest word   15
Would harrow up thy soul, freeze thy young blood,
Make thy two eyes, like stars, start from their spheres,[8]
Thy knotted and combinèd locks to part
And each particular hair to stand on end,
Like quills upon the fretful porpentine: 20
But this eternal blazon[9] must not be
To ears of flesh and blood. List, list, O, list!
If thou didst ever thy dear father love—
HAMLET   O God!
GHOST   Revenge his foul and most unnatural murder.   25
HAMLET   Murder!
GHOST   Murder most foul, as in the best it is,
But this most foul, strange, and unnatural.
HAMLET   Haste me to know't, that I, with wings as swift
As meditation or the thoughts of love,   30
May sweep to my revenge.
GHOST   I find thee apt;
And duller shouldst thou be than the fat weed
That roots itself in ease on Lethe[1] wharf,
Wouldst thou not stir in this. Now, Hamlet, hear:
'Tis given out that, sleeping in my orchard,   35
A serpent stung me; so the whole ear of Denmark
Is by a forgèd process of my death
Rankly abused: but know, thou noble youth,
The serpent that did sting thy father's life
Now wears his crown.
HAMLET   O my prophetic soul!   40
My uncle!

---

7. Of purgatory.
8. Transparent revolving shells in each of which, according to Ptolemaic astronomy, a planet or other heavenly body was placed.

9. Publication of the secrets of the other world (of eternity). "Porpentine": porcupine.
1. The river of forgetfulness in Hades.

GHOST   Aye, that incestuous, that adulterate beast,
With witchcraft of his wit, with traitorous gifts,—
O wicked wit and gifts, that have the power
So to seduce!—won to his shameful lust   45
The will of my most seeming-virtuous queen:
O Hamlet, what a falling-off was there!
From me, whose love was of that dignity
That it went hand in hand even with the vow
I made to her in marriage; and to decline   50
Upon a wretch, whose natural gifts were poor
To those of mine!
But virtue, as it never will be moved,
Though lewdness court it in a shape of heaven,[2]
So lust, though to a radiant angel linked,   55
Will sate itself in a celestial bed
And prey on garbage.
But, soft! methinks I scent the morning air;
Brief let me be. Sleeping within my orchard,
My custom always of the afternoon.   60
Upon my secure hour thy uncle stole,
With juice of cursed hebenon[3] in a vial,
And in the porches of my ears did pour
The leperous distilment; whose effect
Holds such an enmity with blood of man   65
That swift as quicksilver it courses through
The natural gates and alleys of the body;
And with a sudden vigor it doth posset
And curd, like eager[4] droppings into milk,
The thin and wholesome blood: so did it mine;   70
And a most instant tetter barked about,[5]
Most lazar-like,[6] with vile and loathsome crust,
All my smooth body.
Thus was I, sleeping, by a brother's hand
Of life, of crown, of queen, at once dispatched: 75
Cut off even in the blossoms of my sin,
Unhouseled, disappointed, unaneled;[7]
No reckoning made, but sent to my account
With all my imperfections on my head:
O, horrible! O, horrible! most horrible!   80
If thou hast nature in thee, bear it not;
Let not the royal bed of Denmark be
A couch for luxury and damned incest.
But, howsoever thou pursuest this act,
Taint not thy mind, nor let thy soul contrive   85

2. A heavenly, angelic form.
3. Henbane, a poisonous herb.
4. Sour. "Posset": coagulate.
5. The skin immediately became thick like
the bark of a tree.

6. Leper-like (from the beggar Lazarus, "full
of sores," in Luke 16.20).
7. Without sacrament, unprepared, without
extreme unction.

Against thy mother aught: leave her to heaven,
And to those thorns that in her bosom lodge,
To prick and sting her. Fare thee well at once!
The glow-worm shows the matin to be near,
And 'gins to pale his uneffectual fire: 90
Adieu, adieu, adieu! remember me.
     [*Exit.*]
HAMLET   O all you host of heaven! O earth! what else?
And shall I couple hell? O, fie! Hold, hold, my heart;
And you, my sinews, grow not instant old,
But bear me stiffly up. Remember thee!   95
Aye, thou poor ghost, while memory holds a seat
In this distracted globe. Remember thee!
Yea, from the table[8] of my memory
I'll wipe away all trivial fond records,
All saws of books, all forms, all pressures past,   100
That youth and observation copied there:
And thy commandment all alone shall live
Within the book and volume of my brain,
Unmixed with baser matter: yes, by heaven!
O most pernicious woman!   105
O villain, villain, smiling, damnèd villain!
My tables,—meet it is I set it down,
That one may smile, and smile, and be a villain;
At least I'm sure it may be so in Denmark.
     [*Writing.*]
So, uncle, there you are. Now to my word;   110
It is "Adieu, adieu! remember me."
I have sworn't.

HORATIO   } [*Within.*] My lord, my lord!
MARCELLUS

     [*Enter* HORATIO *and* MARCELLUS.]

MARCELLUS   Lord Hamlet!
HORATIO   Heaven
                                  secure him!

HAMLET   So be it!
MARCELLUS   Illo,[9] ho, ho, my lord!   115
HAMLET   Hillo, ho, ho, boy! come, bird, come.
MARCELLUS   How is't, my noble lord?
HORATIO   What news, my lord?
HAMLET   O, wonderful!
HORATIO   Good my lord, tell it.
HAMLET   No; you will reveal it.
HORATIO   Not I, my lord, by heaven.

8. Writing tablet; used in the same sense in   9. A falconer's call.
line 107. "Globe": head.

MARCELLUS   Nor I, my lord.   120

HAMLET   How say you, then; would heart of man once think it?
  But you'll be secret?

HORATIO }
MARCELLUS }   Aye, by, heaven, my lord.

HAMLET   There's ne'er a villain dwelling in all Denmark
  But he's an arrant knave.

HORATIO   There needs no ghost, my lord, come from the grave   125
  To tell us this.

HAMLET   Why, right; you are i' the right;
  And so, without more circumstance[1] at all,
  I hold it fit that we shake hands and part:
  You, as your business and desire shall point you;
  For every man hath business and desire,   130
  Such as it is; and for my own poor part,
  Look you, I'll go pray.

HORATIO   These are but wild and whirling words, my lord.

HAMLET   I'm sorry they offend you, heartily;
  Yes, faith, heartily.

HORATIO   There's no offense, my lord.   135

HAMLET   Yes, by Saint Patrick, but there is, Horatio,
  And much offense too. Touching this vision here,
  It is an honest[2] ghost, that let me tell you:
  For your desire to know what is between us,
  O'ermaster't as you may. And now, good friends,   140
  As you are friends, scholars and soldiers,
  Give me one poor request.

HORATIO   What is't, my lord? we will.

HAMLET   Never make known what you have seen tonight.

MARCELLUS }
HORATIO }   My lord, we will not.

HAMLET   Nay, but swear't.

HORATIO   In faith,
  My lord, not I.

MARCELLUS   Nor I, my lord, in faith.   145

HAMLET   Upon my sword.

MARCELLUS   We have sworn, my lord, already.

HAMLET   Indeed, upon my sword, indeed.

GHOST [Beneath.]   Swear.

HAMLET   Ah, ha, boy! say'st thou so? art thou there, true-penny?[3]
  Come on: you hear this fellow in the cellarage:
  Consent to swear.

HORATIO   Propose the oath, my lord.   150

1. Ceremony.   3. Honest fellow.
2. Genuine.

HAMLET   Never to speak of this that you have seen,
  Swear by my sword.
GHOST [*Beneath.*]   Swear.
HAMLET   Hic et ubique?[4] then we'll shift our ground.
  Come hither, gentlemen,   155
  And lay your hands again upon my sword:
  Never to speak of this that you have heard,
  Swear by my sword.
GHOST [*Beneath.*]   Swear.
HAMLET   Well said, old mole! canst work i' the earth so fast?   160
  A worthy pioner![5] Once more remove, good friends.
HORATIO   O day and night, but this is wondrous strange!
HAMLET   And therefore as a stranger give it welcome.
  There are more things in heaven and earth, Horatio,
  Than are dreamt of in your philosophy.   165
  But come;
  Here, as before, never, so help you mercy,
  How strange or odd soe'er I bear myself,
  As I perchance hereafter shall think meet
  To put an antic[6] disposition on,   170
  That you, at such times seeing me, never shall,
  With arms encumbered[7] thus, or this head-shake,
  Or by pronouncing of some doubtful phrase,
  As "Well, well, we know," or "We could, an if we would,"
  Or "If we list to speak," or "There be, an if they might,"   175
  Or such ambiguous giving out, to note
  That you know aught of me: this not to do,
  So grace and mercy at your most need help you,
  Swear.
GHOST [*Beneath.*]   Swear.   180
HAMLET   Rest, rest, perturbèd spirit!
      [*They swear.*]
  So, gentlemen,
  With all my love I do commend[8] me to you:
  And what so poor a man as Hamlet is
  May do, to express his love and friending to you,   185
  God willing, shall not lack. Let us go in together;
  And still your fingers on your lips, I pray,
  The time is out of joint: O cursèd spite,
  That ever I was born to set it right!
  Nay, come, let's go together.   190
      [*Exeunt.*]

4. Here and everywhere (Latin).   7. Folded.
5. Miner.   8. Entrust.
6. Odd, fantastic.

Act 2

SCENE I

[SCENE: *A room in Polonius's house.*]

[*Enter* POLONIUS *and* REYNALDO.]

POLONIUS   Give him this money and these notes, Reynaldo.

REYNALDO   I will, my lord.

POLONIUS   You shall do marvelous wisely, good Reynaldo,
Before you visit him, to make inquire
Of his behavior.

REYNALDO   My lord, I did intend it.   5

POLONIUS   Marry, well said, very well said. Look you, sir,
Inquire me first what Danskers are in Paris,
And how, and who, what means, and where they keep,[9]
What company, at what expense, and finding
By this encompassment[1] and drift of question   10
That they do know my son, come you more nearer
Than your particular demands will touch it:
Take you, as 'twere, some distant knowledge of him,
As thus, "I know his father and his friends,
And in part him": do you mark this, Reynaldo?   15

REYNALDO   Aye, very well, my lord.

POLONIUS   "And in part him; but," you may say, "not well:
But if 't be he I mean, he's very wild,
Addicted so and so"; and there put on him
What forgeries you please; marry, none so rank   20
As may dishonor him; take heed of that;
But, sir, such wanton, wild and usual slips
As are companions noted and most known
To youth and liberty.

REYNALDO   As gaming, my lord.

POLONIUS   Aye, or drinking, fencing, swearing, quarreling,   25
Drabbing:[2] you may go so far.

REYNALDO   My lord, that would dishonor him.

POLONIUS   Faith, no; as you may season it in the charge.[3]
You must not put another scandal on him,
That he is open to incontinency;   30
That's not my meaning: but breathe his faults so quaintly[4]
That they may seem the taints of liberty,
The flash and outbreak of a fiery mind,
A savageness in unreclaimèd blood,
Of general assault.[5]

REYNALDO   But, my good lord,—   35

---

9. Dwell. "Danskers": Danes.
1. Roundabout way.
2. Whoring.
3. Qualify it in making the accusation.

4. Delicately, skillfully. "Incontinency": extreme
sensuality.
5. Assailing all. "Unreclaimèd": untamed.

POLONIUS   Wherefore should you do this?

REYNALDO   Aye, my lord,
   I would know that.

POLONIUS   Marry, sir, here's my drift,
   And I believe it is a fetch of warrant:[6]
   You laying these slight sullies on my son,
   As 'twere a thing a little soiled i' the working,   40
   Mark you,
   Your party in converse, him you would sound,
   Having ever seen in the prenominate[7] crimes
   The youth you breathe of guilty, be assured
   He closes with you in this consequence;[8]   45
   "Good sir," or so, or "friend," or "gentleman,"
   According to the phrase or the addition[9]
   Of man and country.

REYNALDO   Very good, my lord.

POLONIUS   And then, sir, does he this—he does—what was I about to
   say? By the mass, I was about to say something: where did I leave?   50

REYNALDO   At "closes in the consequence," at "friend or so," and
   "gentleman."

POLONIUS   At "closes in the consequence," aye, marry;
   He closes with you thus: "I know the gentleman;
   I saw him yesterday, or t' other day,   55
   Or then, or then, with such, or such, and, as you say,
   There was a' gaming, there o'ertook in 's rouse,[1]
   There falling out at tennis": or perchance,
   "I saw him enter such a house of sale,"
   Videlicet,[2] a brothel, or so forth.   60
   See you now;
   Your bait of falsehood takes this carp of truth:
   And thus do we of wisdom and of reach,[3]
   With windlasses and with assays of bias,[4]
   By indirections find directions out: 65
   So, by my former lecture and advice,
   Shall you my son. You have me, have you not?

REYNALDO   My lord, I have.

POLONIUS   God be wi' ye; fare ye well.

REYNALDO   Good my lord!

POLONIUS   Observe his inclination in yourself.[5]   70

REYNALDO   I shall, my lord.

POLONIUS   And let him ply his music.

REYNALDO   Well, my lord.

---

6. Allowable stratagem.
7. Aforementioned. "Having ever": if he has
ever.
8. You may be sure he will agree in this
conclusion.
9. Title.
1. Intoxicated in his reveling.

2. Namely.
3. Wise and far-sighted.
4. Sending the ball indirectly (in bowling),
devious attacks. "Windlasses": winding ways,
round-about courses.
5. Ways of procedure by yourself.

POLONIUS Farewell!
    [*Exit* REYNALDO.—*Enter* OPHELIA.]
  How now, Ophelia! what's the matter?
OPHELIA O, my lord, I have been so affrighted!   75
POLONIUS With what, i' the name of God?
OPHELIA My lord, as I was sewing in my closet,
  Lord Hamlet, with his doublet[6] all unbraced,
  No hat upon his head, his stockings fouled,
  Ungartered and down-gyvèd[7] to his ankle;   80
  Pale as his shirt, his knees knocking each other,
  And with a look so piteous in purport
  As if he had been loosèd out of hell
  To speak of horrors, he comes before me.
POLONIUS Mad for thy love?
OPHELIA   My lord, I do not know,   85
  But truly I do fear it.
POLONIUS   What said he?
OPHELIA He took me by the wrist and held me hard;
  Then goes he to the length of all his arm,
  And with his other hand thus o'er his brow,
  He falls to such perusal of my face   90
  As he would draw it. Long stayed he so;
  At last, a little shaking of mine arm,
  And thrice his head thus waving up and down,
  He raised a sigh so piteous and profound
  As it did seem to shatter all his bulk   95
  And end his being: that done, he lets me go:
  And with his head over his shoulder turned,
  He seemed to find his way without his eyes;
  For out o' doors he went without their help,
  And to the last bended their light on me.   100
POLONIUS Come, go with me: I will go seek the king.
  This is the very ecstasy of love;
  Whose violent property fordoes itself[8]
  And leads the will to desperate undertakings
  As oft as any passion under heaven   105
  That does afflict our natures. I am sorry.
  What, have you given him any hard words of late?
OPHELIA No, my good lord, but, as you did command,
  I did repel his letters and denied
  His access to me.
POLONIUS   That hath made him mad.   110
  I am sorry that with better heed and judgment
  I had not quoted him: I fear'd he did but trifle
  And meant to wreck thee; but beshrew my jealousy![9]

6. Jacket. "Closet": private room.
7. Pulled down like fetters on a prisoner's leg.
8. Which, when violent, destroys itself. "Ecstasy":

madness.
9. Curse my suspicion. "Quoted": noted.

By heaven, it is as proper to our age
To cast beyond ourselves[1] in our opinions   115
As it is common for the younger sort
To lack discretion. Come, go we to the king:
This must be known; which, being kept close, might move
More grief to hide than hate to utter love.[2]
Come.   120

        [*Exeunt.*]

SCENE 2

[SCENE: *A room in the castle.*]

    [*Flourish. Enter* KING, QUEEN, ROSENCRANTZ, GUILDENSTERN, *and*
    ATTENDANTS.]

KING   Welcome, dear Rosencrantz and Guildenstern!
  Moreover that we much did long to see you,
  The need we have to use you did provoke
  Our hasty sending. Something have you heard
  Of Hamlet's transformation; so call it,   5
  Sith[3] nor the exterior nor the inward man
  Resembles that it was. What it should be,
  More than his father's death, that thus hath put him
  So much from the understanding of himself,
  I cannot dream of: I entreat you both,   10
  That, being of so young days brought up with him
  And sith so neighbored to his youth and behavior,
  That you vouchsafe your rest[4] here in our court
  Some little time: so by your companies
  To draw him on to pleasures, and to gather   15
  So much as from occasion you may glean,
  Whether aught to us unknown afflicts him thus,
  That opened[5] lies within our remedy.
QUEEN   Good gentlemen, he hath much talked of you,
  And sure I am two men there are not living   20
  To whom he more adheres.[6] If it will please you
  To show us so much gentry[7] and good will
  As to expend your time with us awhile
  For the supply and profit of our hope,
  Your visitation shall receive such thanks   25
  As fits a king's remembrance.
ROSENCRANTZ   Both your majesties
  Might, by the sovereign power you have of us,
  Put your dread pleasures more into[8] command

---

1. Overshoot, go too far.
2. If Hamlet's love is revealed. "To hide": if
kept hidden.
3. Since.
4. Consent to stay.

5. Once revealed.
6. Is more attached.
7. Courtesy.
8. Give your sovereign wishes the form of.

Than to entreaty.
GUILDENSTERN   But we both obey,
And here give up ourselves, in the full bent[9]   30
To lay our service freely at your feet,
To be commanded.
KING   Thanks, Rosencrantz and gentle Guildenstern.
QUEEN   Thanks, Guildenstern and gentle Rosencrantz:
And I beseech you instantly to visit   35
My too much changéd son. Go, some of you,
And bring these gentlemen where Hamlet is.
GUILDENSTERN   Heavens make our presence and our practices
Pleasant and helpful to him!
QUEEN   Aye, amen!
        [*Exeunt* ROSENCRANTZ, GUILDENSTERN, *and some* ATTENDANTS.—*Enter*
        POLONIUS.]
POLONIUS   The ambassadors from Norway, my good lord,   40
Are joyfully returned.
KING   Thou still[1] hast been the father of good news.
POLONIUS   Have I, my lord? I assure my good liege,
I hold my duty as I hold my soul,
Both to my God and to my gracious king: 45
And I do think, or else this brain of mine
Hunts not the trail of policy so sure
As it hath used to do, that I have found
The very cause of Hamlet's lunacy.
KING   O, speak of that; that do I long to hear.   50
POLONIUS   Give first admittance to the ambassadors;
My news shall be the fruit to that great feast.
KING   Thyself do grace[2] to them, and bring them in.
        [*Exit* POLONIUS.]
He tells me, my dear Gertrude, he hath found
The head and source of all your son's distemper.   55
QUEEN   I doubt it is no other but the main;
His father's death and our o'erhasty marriage.
KING   Well, we shall sift him.
        [*Re-enter* POLONIUS, *with* VOLTIMAND *and* CORNELIUS.]
                                Welcome, my good friends!
Say, Voltimand, what from our brother Norway?
VOLTIMAND   Most fair return of greetings and desires.   60
Upon our first,[3] he sent out to suppress
His nephew's levies, which to him appeared
To be a preparation 'gainst the Polack,
But better looked into, he truly found
It was against your highness: whereat grieved,   65
That so his sickness, age and impotence

9. Bent (as a bow) to the limit.   2. Honor. "Fruit": dessert.
1. Always.   3. As soon as we made the request.

Was falsely borne in hand,[4] sends out arrests
On Fortinbras; which he, in brief, obeys,
Receives rebuke from Norway, and in fine[5]
Makes vow before his uncle never more   70
To give the assay[6] of arms against your majesty.
Whereon old Norway, overcome with joy,
Gives him three thousand crowns in annual fee
And his commission to employ those soldiers,
So levied as before, against the Polack: 75
With an entreaty, herein further shown,
     [*Giving a paper.*]
That it might please you to give quiet pass
Through your dominions for this enterprise,
On such regards of safety and allowance
As therein are set down.
KING   It likes us well,   80
And at our more considered time we'll read,
Answer, and think upon this business.
Meantime we thank you for your well-took labor:
Go to your rest; at night we'll feast together:
Most welcome home!
     [*Exeunt* VOLTIMAND *and* CORNELIUS.]
POLONIUS   This business is well ended.   85
My liege, and madam, to expostulate
What majesty should be, what duty is,
Why day is day, night night, and time is time,
Were nothing but to waste night, day and time.
Therefore, since brevity is the soul of wit   90
And tediousness the limbs and outward flourishes,
I will be brief. Your noble son is mad:
Mad call I it; for, to define true madness,
What is 't but to be nothing else but mad?
But let that go.
QUEEN   More matter, with less art.   95
POLONIUS   Madam, I swear I use no art at all.
That he is mad, 'tis true: 'tis true 'tis pity,
And pity 'tis 'tis true: a foolish figure;[7]
But farewell it, for I will use no art.
Mad let us grant him then: and now remains   100
That we find out the cause of this effect,
Or rather say, the cause of this defect,
For this effect defective comes by cause:
Thus it remains and the remainder thus.
Perpend.[8]   105
I have a daughter,—have while she is mine,—

4. Deceived, deluded.   7. Of speech.
5. Finally.   8. Consider.
6. Test.

Who in her duty and obedience, mark,
Hath given me this: now gather and surmise.
[*Reads.*] "To the celestial, and my soul's idol, the most beautified
Ophelia,"—That's an ill phrase, a vile phrase; "beautified" is a vile   110
phrase; but you shall hear. Thus:
      [*Reads.*] "In her excellent white bosom, these," &c.

QUEEN   Came this from Hamlet to her?

POLONIUS   Good madam, stay awhile; I will be faithful.
        [*Reads.*]   "Doubt thou the stars are fire;   115
               Doubt that the sun doth move;
               Doubt truth to be a liar;
               But never doubt I love.
"O dear Ophelia, I am ill at these numbers;[9] I have not art to reckon
my groans: but that I love thee best, O most best, believe it. Adieu.   120
        "Thine evermore, most dear lady, whilst this
             machine is to him,[1] HAMLET."
This in obedience hath my daughter shown me;
And more above,[2] hath his solicitings,
As they fell out by time, by means and place,   125
All given to mine ear.

KING   But how hath she
Received his love?

POLONIUS   What do you think of me?

KING   As of a man faithful and honorable.

POLONIUS   I would fain prove so. But what might you think,
When I had seen this hot love on the wing,—   130
As I perceived it, I must tell you that,
Before my daughter told me,—what might you,
Or my dear majesty your queen here, think,
If I had played the desk or table-book,[3]
Or given my heart a winking,[4] mute and dumb,   135
Or looked upon this love with idle sight;
What might you think? No, I went round[5] to work,
And my young mistress thus I did bespeak:
"Lord Hamlet is a prince, out of thy star;[6]
This must not be:" and then I prescripts gave her,   140
That she should lock herself from his resort,
Admit no messengers, receive no tokens.
Which done, she took the fruits of my advice;
And he repulsed, a short tale to make,
Fell into a sadness, then into a fast,   145
Thence to a watch, thence into a weakness,
Thence to a lightness,[7] and by this declension
Into the madness wherein now he raves

---

9. Verses.
1. Body is attached.
2. Moreover.
3. If I had acted as a desk or notebook (in keeping the matter secret).

4. Shut my heart's eye.
5. Straight.
6. Sphere.
7. Light-headedness. "Watch": insomnia.

And all we mourn for.

KING   Do you think this?

QUEEN   It may be, very like.   150

POLONIUS   Hath there been such a time, I'd fain know that,
    That I have positively said "'tis so,"
    When it proved otherwise?

KING   Not that I know.

POLONIUS [*Pointing to his head and shoulder.*]   Take this, from this,
    if this be otherwise: 155
    If circumstances lead me, I will find
    Where truth is hid, though it were hid indeed
    Within the center.[8]

KING   How may we try it further?

POLONIUS   You know, sometimes he walks for hours together
    Here in the lobby.

QUEEN   So he does, indeed.   160

POLONIUS   At such a time I'll loose my daughter to him:
    Be you and I behind an arras then;
    Mark the encounter: if he love her not,
    And be not from his reason fall'n thereon,[9]
    Let me be no assistant for a state,   165
    But keep a farm and carters.

KING   We will try it.

QUEEN   But look where sadly the poor wretch comes reading.

POLONIUS   Away, I do beseech you, both away:
    I'll board him presently.[1]

      [*Exeunt* KING, QUEEN, *and* ATTENDANTS.—*Enter* HAMLET, *reading.*]

    O, give me leave: how does my good Lord Hamlet?   170

HAMLET   Well, God-a-mercy.

POLONIUS   Do you know me, my lord?

HAMLET   Excellent well; you are a fishmonger.[2]

POLONIUS   Not I, my lord.

HAMLET   Then I would you were so honest a man.   175

POLONIUS: Honest, my lord!

HAMLET   Aye, sir; to be honest, as this world goes, is to be one man
    picked out of ten thousand.

POLONIUS   That's very true, my lord.

HAMLET   For if the sun breed maggots in a dead dog, being a good   180
    kissing carrion[3]—Have you a daughter?

POLONIUS   I have, my lord.

HAMLET   Let her not walk i' the sun: conception is a blessing; but as
    your daughter may conceive,—friend, look to 't.

POLONIUS [*Aside.*]   How say you by that? Still harping on my daughter: 185
    yet he knew me not at first; he said I was a fishmonger: he is far
    gone: and truly in my youth I suffered much extremity for love; very

---

8. Of the earth.
9. For that reason.
1. Approach him at once.

2. Fish seller but also slang for procurer.
3. Good bit of flesh for kissing.

near this. I'll speak to him again.—What do you read, my lord?

HAMLET Words, words, words.

POLONIUS What is the matter,[4] my lord? 190

HAMLET Between who?

POLONIUS I mean, the matter that you read, my lord.

HAMLET Slanders, sir: for the satirical rogue says here that old men have gray beards, that their faces are wrinkled, their eyes purging thick amber and plum-tree gum, and that they have a plentiful lack 195
of wit, together with most weak hams: all which, sir, though I most powerfully and potently believe, yet I hold it not honesty to have it thus set down; for yourself, sir, shall grow old as I am, if like a crab you could go backward.

POLONIUS [Aside.] Though this be madness, yet there is method in 200
't.—Will you walk out of the air, my lord?

HAMLET Into my grave.

POLONIUS Indeed, that's out of the air.

[Aside.]

How pregnant sometimes his replies are! a happiness[5] that often madness hits on, which reason and sanity could not so prosperously 205
be delivered of. I will leave him, and suddenly contrive the means of meeting between him and my daughter.—My honorable lord, I will most humbly take my leave of you.

HAMLET You cannot, sir, take from me any thing that I will more willingly part withal: except my life, except my life, except my life. 210

POLONIUS Fare you well, my lord.

HAMLET These tedious old fools.

[Re-enter ROSENCRANTZ and GUILDENSTERN.]

POLONIUS You go to seek the Lord Hamlet; there he is.

ROSENCRANTZ [To POLONIUS.] God save you, sir!

[Exit POLONIUS.]

GUILDENSTERN My honored lord! 215

ROSENCRANTZ My most dear lord!

HAMLET My excellent good friends! How dost thou, Guildenstern? Ah, Rosencrantz! Good lads, how do you both?

ROSENCRANTZ As the indifferent[6] children of the earth.

GUILDENSTERN Happy, in that we are not over-happy; 220
On Fortune's cap we are not the very button.[7]

HAMLET Nor the soles of her shoe?

ROSENCRANTZ Neither, my lord.

HAMLET Then you live about her waist, or in the middle of her favors? 225

GUILDENSTERN Faith, her privates[8] we.

HAMLET In the secret parts of Fortune? O, most true; she is a strumpet. What's the news?

---

4. The subject matter of the book. Hamlet responds as if he referred to the subject of a quarrel.
5. Aptness of expression.

6. Average.
7. Top.
8. Ordinary men (with obvious play on the sexual term *private parts*).

ROSENCRANTZ   None, my lord, but that the world's grown honest.

HAMLET   Then is doomsday near: but your news is not true. Let 230
me question more in particular: what have you, my good friends,
deserved at the hands of Fortune, that she sends you to prison
hither?

GUILDENSTERN   Prison, my lord!

HAMLET   Denmark's a prison. 235

ROSENCRANTZ   Then is the world one.

HAMLET   A goodly one; in which there are many confines, wards[9] and
dungeons, Denmark being one o' the worst.

ROSENCRANTZ   We think not so, my lord.

HAMLET   Why, then, 'tis none to you; for there is nothing either good 240
or bad, but thinking makes it so: to me it is a prison.

ROSENCRANTZ   Why, then your ambition makes it one; 'tis too narrow
for your mind.

HAMLET   O God, I could be bounded in a nut-shell and count myself
a king of infinite space, were it not that I have bad dreams. 245

GUILDENSTERN   Which dreams indeed are ambition; for the very substance of the ambitious is merely the shadow of a dream.

HAMLET   A dream itself is but a shadow.

ROSENCRANTZ   Truly, and I hold ambition of so airy and light a quality
that it is but a shadow's shadow. 250

HAMLET   Then are our beggars bodies, and our monarchs and outstretched heroes the beggars' shadows. Shall we to the court? for,
by my fay, I cannot reason.

ROSENCRANTZ
GUILDENSTERN } We'll wait upon you.

HAMLET   No such matter: I will not sort you[1] with the rest of my 255
servants; for, to speak to you like an honest man, I am most dreadfully
attended. But, in the beaten way of friendship, what make you at
Elsinore?

ROSENCRANTZ   To visit you, my lord; no other occasion.

HAMLET   Beggar that I am, I am even poor in thanks; but I thank you: 260
and sure, dear friends, my thanks are too dear a halfpenny.[2] Were
you not sent for? Is it your own inclining? Is it a free visitation?
Come, deal justly[3] with me: come, come; nay, speak.

GUILDENSTERN   What should we say, my lord?

HAMLET   Why, any thing, but to the purpose. You were sent for; and 265
there is a kind of confession in your looks, which your modesties
have not craft enough to color: I know the good king and queen
have sent for you.

ROSENCRANTZ   To what end, my lord?

HAMLET   That you must teach me. But let me conjure you, by the 270
rights of our fellowship, by the consonancy of our youth, by the
obligation of our ever-preserved love, and by what more dear

9. Cells. "Confines": places of confinement.   2. If priced at a halfpenny.
1. Put you together.   3. Honestly.

a better proposer[4] could charge you withal, be even and direct with me, whether you were sent for, or no.

ROSENCRANTZ [*Aside to* GUILDENSTERN.] What say you? 275

HAMLET [*Aside.*] Nay then, I have an eye of[5] you.—If you love me, hold not off.

GUILDENSTERN My lord, we were sent for.

HAMLET I will tell you why; so shall my anticipation prevent your discovery,[6] and your secrecy to the king and queen moult no feather. 280 I have of late—but wherefore I know not—lost all my mirth, forgone all custom of exercises; and indeed it goes so heavily with my disposition that this goodly frame, the earth, seems to me a sterile promontory; this most excellent canopy, the air, look you, this brave o'erhanging firmament, this majestical roof fretted[7] with golden fire, 285 why, it appears no other thing to me than a foul and pestilent congregation of vapors. What a piece of work is a man! how noble in reason! how infinite in faculty! in form and moving how express[8] and admirable! in action how like an angel! in apprehension how like a god! the beauty of the world! the paragon of animals! And yet, to me, 290 what is this quintessence of dust? man delights not me; no, nor woman an neither, though by your smiling you seem to say so.

ROSENCRANTZ My lord, there was no such stuff in my thoughts.

HAMLET Why did you laugh then, when I said "man delights not me"?

ROSENCRANTZ To think, my lord, if you delight not in man, what 295 lenten entertainment the players shall receive from you: we coted[9] them on the way; and hither are they coming, to offer you service.

HAMLET He that plays the king shall be welcome; his majesty shall have tribute of me; the adventurous knight shall use his foil and target; the lover shall not sigh gratis; the humorous[1] man shall end 300 his part in peace; the clown shall make those laugh whose lungs are tickle o' the sere,[2] and the lady shall say her mind freely, or the blank verse shall halt for 't. What players are they?

ROSENCRANTZ Even those you were wont to take such delight in, the tragedians of the city. 305

HAMLET How chances it they travel? their residence, both in reputation and profit, was better both ways.

ROSENCRANTZ I think their inhibition comes by means of the late innovation.[3]

HAMLET Do they hold the same estimation they did when I was in the 310 city? are they so followed?

ROSENCRANTZ No, indeed, are they not.

HAMLET How comes it? do they grow rusty?

ROSENCRANTZ Nay, their endeavor keeps in the wonted pace: but

---

4. Speaker.
5. On.
6. Precede your disclosure.
7. Adorned.
8. Precise.
9. Overtook.

1. Eccentric, whimsical.
2. Ready to shoot off at a touch.
3. The introduction of the children (line 315), as Rosencrantz explains in his subsequent replies to Hamlet. "Inhibition": prohibition.

there is, sir, an eyrie of children, little eyases,[4] that cry out on the   315
top of question[5] and are most tyrannically clapped for 't: these are
now the fashion, and so berattle[6] the common stages—so they call
them—that many wearing rapiers are afraid of goose-quills,[7] and
dare scarce come thither.

HAMLET   What, are they children? who maintains 'em? how are they   320
escoted? Will they pursue the quality[8] no longer than they can sing?
will they not say afterwards, if they should grow themselves to
common players—as it is most like, if their means are no better,—
their writers do them wrong, to make them exclaim against their
own succession?[9]   325

ROSENCRANTZ   Faith, there has been much to-do on both sides, and
the nation holds it no sin to tarre[1] them to controversy: there was
for a while no money bid for argument unless the poet and the player
went to cuffs in the question.[2]

HAMLET   Is 't possible?   330

GUILDENSTERN   O, there has been much throwing about of brains.

HAMLET   Do the boys carry it away?[3]

ROSENCRANTZ   Aye, that they do, my lord; Hercules and his load too.[4]

HAMLET   It is not very strange; for my uncle is king of Denmark,
and those that would make mows[5] at him while my father lived, give   335
twenty, forty, fifty, a hundred ducats a-piece, for his picture in little.
'Sblood, there is something in this more than natural, if philosophy
could find it out.

   [*Flourish of trumpets within.*]

GUILDENSTERN   There are the players.

HAMLET   Gentlemen, you are welcome to Elsinore. Your hands, come   340
then: the appurtenance of welcome is fashion and ceremony: let me
comply with you in this garb, lest my extent[6] to the players, which,
I tell you, must show fairly outwards, should more appear like
entertainment[7] than yours. You are welcome: but my uncle-father
and aunt-mother are deceived.   345

GUILDENSTERN   In what, my dear lord?

HAMLET   I am but mad north-north-west: when the wind is southerly
I know a hawk from a handsaw.[8]

   [*Re-enter POLONIUS.*]

POLONIUS   Well be with you, gentlemen!

HAMLET   Hark you, Guildenstern; and you too: at each ear a hearer: 350

---

4. Nestling hawks. "Eyrie": nest.
5. Above others on matter of dispute.
6. Berate.
7. Gentlemen are afraid of pens (that is, of poets satirizing the "common stages").
8. Profession of acting. "Escoted": financially supported.
9. Recite satiric pieces against what they are themselves likely to become, common players.
1. Incite.
2. No offer to buy a plot for a play if it did not

contain a quarrel between poet and player on that subject.
3. Win out.
4. The sign in front of the Globe Theater showed Hercules bearing the world on his shoulders.
5. Faces, grimaces.
6. Welcoming behavior. "Garb": style.
7. Welcome.
8. A hawk from a heron as well as a kind of ax from a handsaw.

that great baby you see there is not yet out of his swaddling clouts.[9]

ROSENCRANTZ   Happily he's the second time come to them; for they
say an old man is twice a child.

HAMLET   I will prophesy he comes to tell me of the players; mark it.
You say right, sir: o' Monday morning; 'twas so, indeed.[1]   355

POLONIUS   My lord, I have news to tell you.

HAMLET   My lord, I have news to tell you. When Roscius[2] was an actor
in Rome,—

POLONIUS   The actors are come hither, my lord.

HAMLET   Buz, buz![3]   360

POLONIUS   Upon my honor,—

HAMLET   Then came each actor on his ass,—

POLONIUS   The best actors in the world, either for tragedy, comedy,
history,   pastoral,   pastoral-comical,   historical-pastoral,   tragical-
historical, tragical-comical-historical-pastoral, scene individable,   365
or poem unlimited:[4] Seneca cannot be too heavy, nor Plautus too
light. For the law of writ and the liberty,[5] these are the only men.

HAMLET   O Jephthah,[6] judge of Israel, what a treasure hadst thou!

POLONIUS   What a treasure had he, my lord?

HAMLET   Why,   370
   "One fair daughter, and no more,
      The which he lovèd passing well."[7]

POLONIUS [Aside.]   Still on my daughter.

HAMLET   Am I not i' the right, old Jephthah?

POLONIUS   If you call me Jephthah, my lord, I have a daughter that I   375
love passing well.

HAMLET   Nay, that follows not.

POLONIUS   What follows, then, my lord?

HAMLET   Why,
   "As by lot, God wot."
and then you know,   380
   "It came to pass, as most like it was,"—
the first row of the pious chanson will show you more; for look, where
my abridgment[8] comes.

   [Enter four or five PLAYERS.]

You are welcome, masters; welcome, all. I am glad to see thee well.
Welcome, good friends. O, my old friend! Why thy face is valanced[9]   385
since I saw thee last; comest thou to beard me in Denmark? What,
my young lady and mistress! By'r lady, your ladyship is nearer to

9. Clothes.
1. Hamlet, for Polonius's sake, pretends he is
deep in talk with Rosencrantz.
2. A famous Roman comic actor (ca. 126–
62 B.C.E.).
3. An expression used to stop the teller of a
stale story.
4. For plays governed and those not governed
by classical rules.
5. Possibly, for both written and extempo-

rized plays. Seneca (after 4 B.C.E.–65 C.E.) was
a Roman who wrote tragedies. Plautus (c.
254–184 B.C.E.) was a Roman who wrote comedies.
6. Who was compelled to sacrifice a dearly
beloved daughter (Judges II).
7. From an old ballad about Jephthah.
8. That is, the players interrupting him. "Row":
stanza. "Chanson": song.
9. Draped (with a beard).

heaven than when I saw you last, by the altitude of a chopine. Pray
God, your voice, like a piece of uncurrent gold, be not cracked within
the ring.[1] Masters, you are all welcome. We'll e'en to 't like French   390
falconers, fly at any thing we see: we'll have a speech straight: come,
give us a taste of your quality; come, a passionate speech.

FIRST PLAYER   What speech, my good lord?

HAMLET   I heard thee speak me a speech once, but it was never acted;
or, if it was, not above once; for the play, I remember, pleased not   395
the million; 'twas caviare to the general:[2] but it was—as I received
it, and others, whose judgments in such matters cried in the top of
mine[3]—an excellent play, well digested in the scenes, set down with
as much modesty as cunning. I remember, one said there were no
sallets in the lines to make the matter savory, nor no matter in the   400
phrase that might indict the author of affection;[4] but called it an
honest method, as wholesome as sweet, and by very much more
handsome than fine.[5] One speech in it I chiefly loved: 'twas Æneas'
tale to Dido; and thereabout of it especially, where he speaks of
Priam's slaughter:[6] it live in your memory, begin at this line; let me   405
see, let me see;
"The rugged Pyrrhus, like th' Hyrcanian beast,"[7]—
It is not so: it begins with "Pyrrhus."
"The rugged Pyrrhus, he whose sable arms,
Black as his purpose, did the night resemble   410
When he lay couchèd in the ominous horse,[8]
Hath now this dread and black complexion smeared
With heraldry more dismal: head to foot
Now is he total gules; horridly tricked[9]
With the blood of fathers, mothers, daughters, sons,   415
Baked and impasted with the parching streets,
That lend a tyrannous[1] and a damnèd light
To their lord's murder: roasted in wrath and fire,
And thus o'er-sizèd[2] with coagulate gore,
With eyes like carbuncles, the hellish Pyrrhus   420
Old grandsire Priam seeks."
So, proceed you.

POLONIUS   'Fore God, my lord, well spoken, with good accent and
good discretion.

FIRST PLAYER   'Anon he finds him   425
Striking too short at Greeks; his antique sword,
Rebellious to his arm, lies where it falls,

---

1. A pun on the *ring* of the voice and the *ring*
around the king's head on a coin. "Chopine":
a thick-soled shoe. "Uncurrent": unfit for
currency.
2. A delicacy wasted on the general public.
3. Were louder (more authoritative than) mine.
4. Affectation. "Sallets": salads (that is, relish,
spicy passages).
5. More elegant than showy.

6. The story of the fall of Troy, told by Aeneas
to Queen Dido. Priam was the king of Troy.
7. Tiger. "Pyrrhus": Achilles' son (also called
Neoptolemus).
8. The wooden horse in which Greek warriors
were smuggled into Troy.
9. Adorned. "Gules": heraldic term for red.
1. Savage.
2. Glued over.

Repugnant to command: unequal matched,
Pyrrhus at Priam drives; in rage strikes wide;
But with the whiff and wind of his fell sword   430
The unnervèd father falls. Then senseless Ilium,[3]
Seeming to feel this blow, with flaming top
Stoops to his base, and with a hideous crash
Takes prisoner Pyrrhus's ear: for, lo! his sword,
Which was declining on the milky[4] head   435
Of reverend Priam seemed i' the air to stick:
So, as a painted tyrant, Pyrrhus stood,
And like a neutral to his will and matter,
Did nothing.
But as we often see, against some storm,   440
A silence in the heavens, the rack[5] stand still,
The bold winds speechless and the orb below
As hush as death, anon the dreadful thunder
Doth rend the region, so after Pyrrhus's pause
Aroused vengeance sets him new a-work;   445
And never did the Cyclops'[6] hammers fall
On Mars's armor, forged for proof[7] eterne,
With less remorse than Pyrrhus's bleeding sword
Now falls on Priam.
Out, thou strumpet, Fortune! All you gods,   450
In general synod take away her power,
Break all the spokes and fellies from her wheel,
And bowl the round nave[8] down the hill of heaven
As low as to the fiends!

POLONIUS   This is too long.   455

HAMLET   It shall to the barber's, with your beard. Prithee, say on: he's
for a jig[9] or a tale of bawdry, or he sleeps: say on: come to Hecuba.

FIRST PLAYER   "But who, O, who had seen the mobled[1] queen—"

HAMLET   "The mobled queen?"

POLONIUS   That's good; "mobled queen" is good.   460

FIRST PLAYER   "Run barefoot up and down, threatening the flames
With bisson rheum; a clout[2] upon that head
Where late the diadem stood; and for a robe,
About her lank and all o'er-teemèd loins,[3]
A blanket, in the alarm of fear caught up: 465
Who this had seen, with tongue in venom steeped
'Gainst Fortune's state[4] would treason have pronounced:
But if the gods themselves did see her then,
When she saw Pyrrhus make malicious sport

---

3. Troy's citadel.
4. White-haired.
5. Clouds. "Against": just before.
6. The gigantic workmen of Hephaestus (Vulcan), god of blacksmiths and fire.
7. Protection.
8. Hub. "Fellies": rims.

9. Ludicrous sung dialogue, short farce.
1. Muffled.
2. Cloth. "Bisson rheum": blinding moisture, tears.
3. Worn out by childbearing.
4. Government.

In mincing with his sword her husband's limbs,   470
The instant burst of clamor that she made,
Unless things mortal move them[5] not at all,
Would have made milch the burning eyes of heaven[6]
And passion in the gods."

POLONIUS   Look, whether he has not turned his color and has tears in   475
's eyes. Prithee, no more.

HAMLET   'Tis well; I'll have thee speak out the rest of this soon. Good
my lord, will you see the players well bestowed?[7] Do you hear, let
them be well used, for they are the abstracts and brief chronicles
of the time: after your death you were better have a bad epitaph than   480
their ill report while you live.

POLONIUS   My lord, I will use them according to their desert.

HAMLET   God's bodykins,[8] man, much better: use every man after his
desert, and who shall 'scape whipping? Use them after your own
honor and dignity: the less they deserve, the more merit is in your   485
bounty. Take them in.

POLONIUS   Come, sirs.

HAMLET   Follow him, friends: we'll hear a play to-morrow. [*Exit*
POLONIUS *with all the* PLAYERS *but the first.*] Dost thou hear me, old
friend; can you play the Murder of Gonzago?   490

FIRST PLAYER   Aye, my lord.

HAMLET   We'll ha 't to-morrow night. You could, for a need, study a
speech of some dozen or sixteen lines, which I would set down and
insert in 't, could you not?

FIRST PLAYER   Aye, my lord.   495

HAMLET   Very well. Follow that lord; and look you mock him not.
[*Exit* FIRST PLAYER.] My good friends, I'll leave you till night: you are
welcome to Elsinore.

ROSENCRANTZ   Good my lord!

HAMLET   Aye, so, God be wi' ye! [*Exeunt* ROSENCRANTZ *and* GUIL-   500
DENSTERN.] Now I am alone.
O, what a rogue and peasant slave am I!
Is it not monstrous that this player here,
But in a fiction, in a dream of passion,
Could force his soul so to his own conceit   505
That from her[9] working all his visage wanned;
Tears in his eyes, distraction in 's aspect,
A broken voice, and his whole function[1] suiting
With forms to his conceit? and all for nothing!
For Hecuba![2]   510
What's Hecuba to him, or he to Hecuba,
That he should weep for her? What would he do,

---

5. The gods.
6. The stars. "Milch": moist (milk-giving).
7. Taken care of, lodged.
8. By God's little body.

9. His soul's.
1. Bodily action.
2. Queen of Troy, Priam's wife. "Conceit": imagination, conception of the role played.

Had he the motive and the cue for passion
That I have? He would drown the stage with tears
And cleave the general air with horrid speech, 515
Make mad the guilty and appal the free,
Confound the ignorant, and amaze indeed
The very faculties of eyes and ears.
Yet I,
A dull and muddy-mettled rascal, peak,[3] 520
Like John-a-dreams, unpregnant of my cause,[4]
And can say nothing; no, not for a king,
Upon whose property and most dear life
A damn'd defeat was made. Am I a coward?
Who calls me villain? breaks my pate across? 525
Plucks off my beard, and blows it in my face?
Tweaks me by the nose? gives me the lie i' the throat,
As deep as to the lungs? who does me this?
Ha!
'Swounds, I should take it: for it cannot be 530
But I am pigeon-livered and lack gall
To make oppression bitter, or ere this
I should have fatted all the region kites[5]
With this slave's offal: bloody, bawdy villain!
Remorseless, treacherous, lecherous, kindless[6] villain! 535
O, vengeance!
Why, what an ass am I! This is most brave,
That I, the son of a dear father murdered,
Prompted to my revenge by heaven and hell,
Must, like a whore, unpack my heart with words, 540
And fall a-cursing, like a very drab,
A scullion!
Fie upon 't! About,[7] my brain! Hum, I have heard
That guilty creatures, sitting at a play,
Have by the very cunning of the scene 545
Been struck so to the soul that presently
They have proclaimed their malefactions;
For murder, though it have no tongue, will speak
With most miraculous organ. I'll have these players
Play something like the murder of my father 550
Before mine uncle: I'll observe his looks;
I'll tent him to the quick: if he but blench,[8]
I know my course. The spirit that I have seen
May be the devil; and the devil hath power

3. Mope. "Muddy mettled": of poor metal (spirit, temper), dull-spirited.
4. Not really conscious of my cause, unquickened by it. "John-a-dreams": a dreamy, absentminded character.
5. Kites (hawks) of the air.
6. Unnatural.
7. To work!
8. Flinch. "Tent": probe.

To assume a pleasing shape; yea, and perhaps   555
Out of my weakness and my melancholy,
As he is very potent with such spirits,
Abuses me to damn me. I'll have grounds
More relative⁹ than this. The play's the thing
Wherein I'll catch the conscience of the king.   560
    [*Exit.*]

Act 3

SCENE I

[SCENE: *A room in the castle.*]

    [*Enter* KING, QUEEN, POLONIUS, OPHELIA, ROSENCRANTZ, *and*
    GUILDENSTERN.]

KING   And can you, by no drift of circumstance,¹
  Get from him why he puts on this confusion,
  Grating so harshly all his days of quiet
  With turbulent and dangerous lunacy?

ROSENCRANTZ   He does confess he feels himself distracted,   5
  But from what cause he will by no means speak.

GUILDENSTERN   Nor do we find him forward to be sounded;
  But, with a crafty madness, keeps aloof,
  When we would bring him on to some confession
  Of his true state.

QUEEN   Did he receive you well?   10

ROSENCRANTZ   Most like a gentleman.

GUILDENSTERN   But with much forcing of his disposition.

ROSENCRANTZ   Niggard of question, but of our demands
  Most free in his reply.

QUEEN   Did you assay² him
  To any pastime?   15

ROSENCRANTZ   Madam, it so fell out that certain players
  We o'er-raught³ on the way: of these we told him,
  And there did seem in him a kind of joy
  To hear of it: they are about the court,
  And, as I think, they have already order   20
  This night to play before him.

POLONIUS   'Tis most true:
  And he beseeched me to entreat your majesties
  To hear and see the matter.

KING   With all my heart; and it doth much content me
  To hear him so inclined.   25
  Good gentlemen, give him a further edge,⁴
  And drive his purpose on to these delights.

---

9. Relevant.
1. Turn of talk, or roundabout way.
2. Try to attract him.

3. Overtook.
4. Incitement.

ROSENCRANTZ   We shall, my lord.
    [*Exeunt* ROSENCRANTZ *and* GUILDENSTERN.]
KING   Sweet Gertrude, leave us too;
  For we have closely[5] sent for Hamlet hither,
  That he, as 'twere by accident, may here   30
  Affront Ophelia:
  Her father and myself, lawful espials,
  Will so bestow[6] ourselves that, seeing unseen,
  We may of their encounter frankly judge,
  And gather by him, as he is behaved,   35
  If't be the affliction of his love or no
  That thus he suffers for.
QUEEN   I shall obey you:
  And for your part, Ophelia, I do wish
  That your good beauties be the happy cause
  Of Hamlet's wildness: so shall I hope your virtues   40
  Will bring him to his wonted way again,
  To both your honors.
OPHELIA   Madam, I wish it may.
    [*Exit* QUEEN.]
POLONIUS   Ophelia, walk you here. Gracious, so please you,
  We will bestow ourselves. [*To* OPHELIA.] Read on this book;
  That show of such an exercise may color[7]   45
  Your loneliness. We are oft to blame in this,—
  'Tis too much proved—that with devotion's visage
  And pious action we do sugar o'er
  The devil himself.
KING [*Aside*.]   O, 'tis too true!
  How smart a lash that speech doth give my conscience!   50
  The harlot's cheek, beautied with plastering art,
  Is not more ugly to the thing that helps it
  Than is my deed to my most painted word:
  O heavy burthen!
POLONIUS   I hear him coming: let's withdraw, my lord.   55
    [*Exeunt* KING *and* POLONIUS.—*Enter* HAMLET.]
HAMLET   To be, or not to be: that is the question:
  Whether 'tis nobler in the mind to suffer
  The slings and arrows of outrageous fortune,
  Or to take arms against a sea of troubles,
  And by opposing end them. To die: to sleep;   60
  No more; and by a sleep to say we end
  The heart-ache, and the thousand natural shocks
  That flesh is heir to, 'tis a consummation[8]
  Devoutly to be wished. To die, to sleep;
  To sleep: perchance to dream: aye, there's the rub;[9]   65

---

5. Privately.
6. Place. "Affront": confront. "Espials": spies.
7. Excuse.

8. Final settlement.
9. The impediment (a bowling term).

For in that sleep of death what dreams may come,
When we have shuffled off this mortal coil,[1]
Must give us pause: there's the respect
That makes calamity of so long life;[2]
For who would bear the whips and scorns of time,   70
The oppressor's wrong, the proud man's contumely,
The pangs of despisèd love, the law's delay,
The insolence of office, and the spurns
That patient merit of the unworthy takes,
When he himself might his quietus make   75
With a bare bodkin? who would fardels[3] bear,
To grunt and sweat under a weary life,
But that the dread of something after death,
The undiscovered country from whose bourn[4]
No traveler returns, puzzles the will,   80
And makes us rather bear those ills we have
Than fly to others that we know not of?
Thus conscience does make cowards of us all,
And thus the native hue of resolution
Is sicklied o'er with the pale cast of thought,   85
And enterprises of great pitch[5] and moment
With this regard their currents turn awry
And lose the name of action. Soft you now!
The fair Ophelia! Nymph, in thy orisons[6]
Be all my sins remembered.

OPHELIA   Good my lord,   90
How does your honor for this many a day?

HAMLET   I humbly thank you: well, well, well.

OPHELIA   My lord, I have remembrances of yours,
That I have longed to re-deliver;
I pray you, now receive them.

HAMLET   No, not I;   95
I never gave you aught.

OPHELIA   My honored lord, you know right well you did;
And with them words of so sweet breath composed
As made the things more rich: their perfume lost,
Take these again; for to the noble mind   100
Rich gifts wax poor when givers prove unkind.
There, my lord.

HAMLET   Ha, ha! are you honest?

OPHELIA   My lord?

HAMLET   Are you fair?   105

OPHELIA   What means your lordship?

HAMLET   That if you be honest and fair, your honesty should admit
no discourse to your beauty.

---

1. Have rid ourselves of the turmoil of mortal life.
2. So long-lived. "Respect": consideration.
3. Burdens. "Bodkin": poniard, dagger.
4. Boundary.
5. Height.
6. Prayers.

OPHELIA   Could beauty, my lord, have better commerce[7] than with
honesty?   110

HAMLET   Aye, truly; for the power of beauty will sooner transform
honesty from what it is to a bawd than the force of honesty can
translate beauty into his[8] likeness: this was sometime a paradox,
but now the time gives it proof.[9] I did love you once.

OPHELIA   Indeed, my lord, you made me believe so.   115

HAMLET   You should not have believed me; for virtue cannot so
inoculate our old stock, but we shall relish[1] of it: I loved you not.

OPHELIA   I was the more deceived.

HAMLET   Get thee to a nunnery: why wouldst thou be a breeder of
sinners? I am myself indifferent honest; but yet I could accuse me   120
of such things that it were better my mother had not borne me:
I am very proud, revengeful, ambitious; with more offenses at my
beck than I have thoughts to put them in, imagination to give them
shape or time to act them in. What should such fellows as I do
crawling between heaven and earth! We are arrant knaves all; believe   125
none of us. Go thy ways to a nunnery. Where's your father?

OPHELIA   At home, my lord.

HAMLET   Let the doors be shut upon him, that he may play the fool
no where but in 's own house. Farewell.

OPHELIA   O, help him, you sweet heavens!   130

HAMLET   If thou dost marry, I'll give thee this plague for thy dowry:
be thou as chaste as ice, as pure as snow, thou shalt not escape
calumny. Get thee to a nunnery, go: farewell. Or, if thou wilt needs
marry, marry a fool; for wise men know well enough what monsters[2]
you make of them. To a nunnery, go; and quickly too. Farewell.   135

OPHELIA   O heavenly powers, restore him!

HAMLET   I have heard of your paintings too, well enough; God hath
given you one face, and you make yourselves another: you jig, you
amble, and you lisp, and nick-name God's creatures, and make your
wantonness your ignorance.[3] Go to, I'll no more on 't; it hath made   140
me mad. I say, we will have no more marriages: those that are
married already, all but one, shall live; the rest shall keep as they are.
To a nunnery, go.
        [*Exit.*]

OPHELIA   O, what a noble mind is here o'erthrown!
The courtier's, soldier's, scholar's, eye, tongue, sword: 145
The expectancy and rose of the fair state,
The glass of fashion and the mould of form.[4]
The observed of all observers, quite, quite down!
And I, of ladies most deject and wretched,
That sucked the honey of his music vows,   150

---

7. Intercourse.
8. Its.
9. In his mother's adultery.
1. Retain the flavor of. "Inoculate": graft itself
onto.
2. Cuckolds bear imaginary horns and "a

horned man's a monster" (*Othello* 4.1).
3. Misname (out of affectation) the most natural things, and pretend that this is due to
ignorance instead of affectation.
4. The mirror of fashion and the model of
behavior.

Now see that noble and most sovereign reason,
Like sweet bells jangled, out of tune and harsh;
That unmatched form and feature of blown⁵ youth
Blasted with ecstasy: O, woe is me,
To have seen what I have seen, see what I see!   155
                   [*Re-enter* KING *and* POLONIUS.]
KING   Love! his affections do not that way tend;
   Nor what he spake, though it lacked form a little,
   Was not like madness. There's something in his soul
   O'er which his melancholy sits on brood,
   And I do doubt⁶ the hatch and the disclose   160
   Will be some danger: which for to prevent,
   I have in quick determination
   Thus set it down:—he shall with speed to England,
   For the demand of our neglected tribute:
   Haply the seas and countries different   165
   With variable objects shall expel
   This something-settled matter in his heart,
   Whereon his brains still beating puts him thus
   From fashion of himself.⁷ What think you on 't?
POLONIUS   It shall do well: but yet do I believe   170
   The origin and commencement of his grief
   Sprung from neglected love. How now, Ophelia!
   You need not tell us what Lord Hamlet said;
   We heard it all. My lord, do as you please;
   But, if you hold it fit, after the play,   175
   Let his queen mother all alone entreat him
   To show his grief: let her be round⁸ with him;
   And I'll be placed, so please you, in the ear
   Of all their conference. If she find him not,
   To England send him, or confine him where   180
   Your wisdom best shall think.
KING   It shall be so:
   Madness in great ones must not unwatched go.
          [*Exeunt.*]

                          SCENE 2

[SCENE: *A hall in the castle.*]

          [*Enter* HAMLET *and* PLAYERS.]
HAMLET   Speak the speech, I pray you, as I pronounced it to you,
   trippingly on the tongue: but if you mouth it, as many of your players
   do, I had as lief the town-crier spoke my lines. Nor do not saw
   the air too much with your hand, thus; but use all gently: for in the
   very torrent, tempest, and, as I may say, whirlwind of your passion,   5

---

5. In full bloom.   7. Makes him behave unusually.
6. Fear.   8. Direct.

you must acquire and beget a temperance that may give it smoothness. O, it offends me to the soul to hear a robustious periwig-pated fellow tear a passion to tatters, to very rags, to split the ears of the groundlings,[9] who, for the most part, are capable of nothing but inexplicable dumb-shows and noise: I would have such a fellow whipped for o'er doing Termagant;[1] it out-herods Herod: pray you, avoid it.

FIRST PLAYER   I warrant your honor.

HAMLET   Be not too tame neither, but let your own discretion be your tutor: suit the action to the word, the word to the action; with this special observance, that you o'erstep not the modesty[2] of nature: for anything so overdone is from the purpose of playing, whose end, both at the first and now, was and is, to hold, as 'twere, the mirror up to nature; to show virtue her own feature, scorn her own image, and the very age and body of the time his form and pressure.[3] Now this overdone or come tardy off, though it make the unskillful laugh, cannot but make the judicious grieve; the censure of the which one must in your allowance o'erweigh a whole theater of others. O, there be players that I have seen play, and heard others praise, and that highly, not to speak it profanely,[4] that neither having the accent of Christians nor the gait of Christian, pagan, nor man, have so strutted and bellowed, that I have thought some of nature's journeymen had made men, and not made them well, they imitated humanity so abominably.

FIRST PLAYER   I hope we have reformed that indifferently[5] with us, sir.

HAMLET   O, reform it altogether. And let those that play your clowns speak no more than is set down for them: for there be of them that will themselves laugh, to set on some quantity of barren[6] spectators to laugh too, though in the mean time some necessary question of the play be then to be considered: that's villainous, and shows a most pitiful ambition in the fool that uses it. Go, make you ready.

[*Exeunt* PLAYERS. —*Enter* POLONIUS, ROSENCRANTZ, *and* GUILDENSTERN.]

How now, my lord! will the king hear this piece of work?

POLONIUS   And the queen too, and that presently.

HAMLET   Bid the players make haste.

[*Exit* POLONIUS.]

Will you two help to hasten them?

ROSENCRANTZ
GUILDENSTERN   } We will, my lord.

[*Exeunt* ROSENCRANTZ *and* GUILDENSTERN.]

HAMLET   What ho! Horatio!

[*Enter* HORATIO.]

HORATIO   Here, sweet lord, at your service.

---

9. Spectators in the pit, where admission was cheapest.
1. God of the Muslims in old romances and morality plays; he was portrayed as being noisy and excitable.
2. Moderation.

3. Impress, shape. "Feature": form. "His": its.
4. Hamlet apologizes for the profane implication that there could be men not of God's making.
5. Pretty well.
6. Silly.

HAMLET   Horatio, thou art e'en as just a man
   As e'er my conversation coped withal.[7]   45

HORATIO   O, my dear lord,—

HAMLET   Nay, do not think I flatter;
   For what advancement may I hope from thee,
   That no revenue hast but thy good spirits,
   To feed and clothe thee? Why should the poor be flattered?
   No, let the candied tongue lick absurd pomp,   50
   And crook the pregnant hinges of the knee
   Where thrift may follow fawning.[8] Dost thou hear?
   Since my dear soul was mistress of her choice,
   And could of men distinguish, her election
   Hath sealed thee for herself: for thou hast been   55
   As one, in suffering all, that suffers nothing;
   A man that fortune's buffets and rewards
   Hast ta'en with equal thanks: and blest are those
   Whose blood and judgment[9] are so well commingled
   That they are not a pipe for fortune's finger   60
   To sound what stop she please.[1] Give me that man
   That is not passion's slave, and I will wear him
   In my heart's core, ay, in my heart of heart,
   As I do thee. Something too much of this.
   There is a play to-night before the king;   65
   One scene of it comes near the circumstance
   Which I have told thee of my father's death:
   I prithee, when thou sees that act a-foot,
   Even with the very comment of thy soul[2]
   Observe my uncle: if his occulted guilt   70
   Do not itself unkennel in one speech
   It is a damned ghost that we have seen,
   And my imaginations are as foul
   As Vulcan's stithy.[3] Give him heedful note;
   For I mine eyes will rivet to his face,   75
   And after we will both our judgments join
   In censure of his seeming.[4]

HORATIO   Well, my lord:
   If he steal aught the whilst this play is playing,
   And 'scape detecting, I will pay the theft.

HAMLET   They are coming to the play: I must be idle:[5]   80
   Get you a place.
      [*Danish march. A flourish. Enter* KING, QUEEN, POLONIUS, OPHELIA,
      ROSENCRANTZ, GUILDENSTERN, *and other* LORDS *attendant, with the*
      GUARD *carrying torches.*]

---

7. As I ever associated with.
8. Material profit may be derived from cringing. "Pregnant hinges": supple joints.
9. Passion and reason.
1. For Fortune to put her finger on any wind-

hole of the pipe she wants.
2. With all your powers of observation.
3. Smithy.
4. To judge his behavior.
5. Crazy.

KING   How fares our cousin Hamlet?

HAMLET   Excellent, i' faith; of the chameleon's dish: I eat the air,[6]
promise-crammed: you cannot feed capons so.

KING   I have nothing with this answer, Hamlet; these words are not   85
mine.[7]

HAMLET   No, nor mine now. [*To* POLONIUS.] My lord, you played once
i' the university, you say?

POLONIUS   That did I, my lord, and was accounted a good actor.

HAMLET   What did you enact?   90

POLONIUS   I did enact Julius Caesar: I was killed i' the Capitol; Brutus
killed me.

HAMLET   It was a brute part of him to kill so capital a calf there. Be
the players ready?

ROSENCRANTZ   Aye, my lord: they stay upon your patience.   95

QUEEN   Come hither, my dear Hamlet, sit by me.

HAMLET   No, good mother, here's metal more attractive.

POLONIUS   [*To the* KING.]   O, ho! do you mark that?

HAMLET   Lady, shall I lie in your lap? [*Lying down at* OPHELIA's *feet.*]

OPHELIA   No, my lord.   100

HAMLET   I mean, my head upon your lap?

OPHELIA   Aye, my lord.

HAMLET   Do you think I meant country matters?

OPHELIA   I think nothing, my lord.

HAMLET   That's a fair thought to lie between maids' legs.   105

OPHELIA   What is, my lord?

HAMLET   Nothing.[8]

OPHELIA   You are merry, my lord.

HAMLET   Who, I?

OPHELIA   Aye, my lord.   110

HAMLET   O God, your only jig-maker.[9] What should a man do but be
merry? for, look you, how cheerfully my mother looks, and my father
died within 's two hours.

OPHELIA   Nay, 'tis twice two months, my lord.

HAMLET   So long? Nay then, let the devil wear black, for I'll have a   115
suit of sables.[1] O heavens! die two months ago, and not forgotten
yet? Then there's hope a great man's memory may outlive his life
half a year: but, by 'r lady, he must build churches then; or else shall
he suffer not thinking on, with the hobby-horse,[2] whose epitaph is,
"For, O, for, O, the hobby-horse is forgot."   120

[*Hautboys play. The dumb-show enters. —Enter a King and a Queen very
lovingly; the Queen embracing him and he her. She kneels, and makes
show of protestation unto him. He takes her up, and declines his head upon
her neck; lays him down upon a bank of flowers: she, seeing him asleep,*

---

6. The chameleon was supposed to feed on
air.
7. Have nothing to do with my question.
8. A sexual pun: no thing.
9. Maker of comic songs.

1. Hamlet notes sarcastically the lack of
mourning for his father in the fancy dress of
court and king.
2. A figure in the old May Day games and
Morris dances.

leaves him. Anon comes in a fellow, takes off his crown, kisses it, and pours poison in the King's ears, and exits. The Queen returns; finds the King dead, and makes passionate action. The Poisoner, with some two or three Mutes comes in again, seeming to lament with her. The dead body is carried away. The Poisoner woos the Queen with gifts: she seems loath and unwilling awhile, but in the end accepts his love. —Exeunt.]

OPHELIA What means this, my lord?

HAMLET Marry, this is miching mallecho;[3] it means mischief.

OPHELIA Belike this show imports the argument of the play.

      [Enter PROLOGUE.*]*

HAMLET We shall know by this fellow: the players cannot keep counsel;[4] they'll tell all.   125

OPHELIA Will he tell us what this show meant?

HAMLET Aye, or any show that you'll show him: be not you ashamed to show, he'll not shame to tell you what it means.

OPHELIA You are naught,[5] you are naught: I'll mark the play.

PROLOGUE For us, and for our tragedy,   130
      Here stooping to your clemency,
      We beg your hearing patiently.

HAMLET Is this a prologue, or the posy[6] of a ring?

OPHELIA 'Tis brief, my lord.

HAMLET As woman's love.   135

      [Enter two PLAYERS, KING *and* QUEEN.*]*

PLAYER KING Full thirty times hath Phœbus's cart[7] gone round
  Neptune's salt wash and Tellus's orbed ground,
  And thirty dozen moons with borrowed sheen
  About the world have times twelve thirties been,
  Since love our hearts and Hymen did our hands   140
  Unite commutual in most sacred bands.

PLAYER QUEEN So many journeys may the sun and moon
  Make us again count o'er ere love be done!
  But, woe is me, you are so sick of late,
  So far from cheer and from your former state,   145
  That I distrust you.[8] Yet, though I distrust,
  Discomfort you, my lord, it nothing must:
  For women's fear and love holds quantity,[9]
  In neither aught, or in extremity.
  Now, what my love is, proof hath made you know,   150
  And as my love is sized, my fear is so:
  Where love is great, the littlest doubts are fear,
  Where little fears grow great, great love grows there.

PLAYER KING Faith, I must leave thee, love, and shortly too;
  My operant powers their functions leave[1] to do: 155
  And thou shalt live in this fair world behind,

---

3. Sneaking misdeed.
4. A secret.
5. Naughty, improper.
6. Motto, inscription.

7. The chariot of the sun.
8. I am worried about you.
9. Maintain mutual balance.
1. Cease.

Honored, beloved; and haply one as kind
For husband shalt thou—
PLAYER QUEEN   O, confound the rest!
  Such love must needs be treason in my breast:
  In second husband let me be accurst!   160
  None wed the second but who killed the first.
HAMLET [*Aside.*]   Wormwood, wormwood.
PLAYER QUEEN   The instances that second marriage move
  Are base respects of thrift,[2] but none of love:
  A second time I kill my husband dead,   165
  When second husband kisses me in bed.
PLAYER KING   I do believe you think what now you speak,
  But what we do determine oft we break.
  Purpose is but the slave to memory,
  Of violent birth but poor validity: 170
  Which now, like fruit unripe, sticks on the tree,
  But fall unshaken when they mellow be.
  Most necessary 'tis that we forget
  To pay ourselves what to ourselves is debt:
  What to ourselves in passion we propose,   175
  The passion ending, both the purpose lose.
  The violence of either grief or joy
  Their own enactures[3] with themselves destroy:
  Where joy most revels, grief doth most lament;
  Grief joys, joy grieves, on slender accident.   180
  This world is not for aye, nor 'tis not strange
  That even our loves should with our fortunes change,
  For 'tis a question left us yet to prove,
  Whether love lead fortune or else fortune love.
  The great man down, you mark his favorite flies;   185
  The poor advanced makes friends of enemies:
  And hitherto doth love on fortune tend;
  For who not needs shall never lack a friend,
  And who in want a hollow friend doth try
  Directly seasons[4] him his enemy.   190
  But, orderly to end where I begun,
  Our wills and fates do so contrary run,
  That our devices still are overthrown,
  Our thoughts are ours, their ends none of our own:
  So think thou wilt no second husband wed,   195
  But die thy thoughts when thy first lord is dead.
PLAYER QUEEN   Nor earth to me give food nor heaven light!
  Sport and repose lock from me day and night!
  To desperation turn my trust and hope!
  An anchor's cheer in prison be my scope!   200
  Each opposite, that blanks[5] the face of joy,

2. Considerations of material profit. "Instan-   4. Matures.
ces": motives.   5. Makes pale. "Anchor's cheer": hermit's, or
3. Their own fulfillment in action.   anchorite's, fare.

Meet what I would have well and it destroy!
Both here and hence pursue me lasting strife,
If, once a widow, ever I be wife!

HAMLET   If she should break it now!   205

PLAYER KING   'Tis deeply sworn. Sweet, leave me here a while;
My spirits grow dull, and fain I would beguile
The tedious day with sleep.
        [*Sleeps.*]

PLAYER QUEEN   Sleep rock thy brain;
And never come mischance between us twain!
        [*Exit.*]

HAMLET   Madam, how like you this play?   210

QUEEN   The lady doth protest[6] too much, methinks.

HAMLET   O, but she'll keep her word.

KING   Have you heard the argument?[7] Is there no offense in 't?

HAMLET   No, no, they do but jest, poison in jest; no offense i' the
world.   215

KING   What do you call the play?

HAMLET   The Mouse-Trap. Marry, how? Tropically.[8] This play is the
image of a murder done in Vienna: Gonzago is the duke's name; his
wife, Baptista: you shall see anon; 'tis a knavish piece of work; but
what o' that? your majesty, and we that have free souls, it touches   220
us not: let the galled jade wince, our withers are unwrung.[9]
        [*Enter* LUCIANUS.]
This is one Lucianus, nephew to the king.

OPHELIA   You are as good as a chorus, my lord.

HAMLET   I could interpret[1] between you and your love, if I could see
the puppets dallying.   225

OPHELIA   You are keen,[2] my lord, you are keen.

HAMLET   It would cost you a groaning to take off my edge.

OPHELIA   Still better and worse.

HAMLET   So you must take[3] your husbands. Begin, murderer; pox,
leave thy damnable faces, and begin. Come: the croaking raven doth   230
bellow for revenge.

LUCIANUS   Thoughts black, hands apt, drugs fit, and time agreeing;
Confederate season, else no creature seeing;
Thou mixture rank, of midnight weeds collected,
With Hecate's ban[4] thrice blasted, thrice infected,   235
Thy natural magic and dire property,
On wholesome life usurp immediately.
        [*Pours the poison into the sleeper's ear.*]

HAMLET   He poisons him i' the garden for his estate. His name's

---

6. Promise.
7. Plot of the play in outline.
8. By a trope, figuratively.
9. Not wrenched. "Galled jade": injured horse.
"Withers": the area between a horse's shoulders.
1. Act as interpreter (regular feature in puppet shows).

2. Bitter, but Hamlet chooses to take the word sexually.
3. That is, for better or for worse, as in the marriage service—but in fact you "mis-take," deceive them.
4. Goddess of witchcraft's curse. "Confederate": favorable.

Gonzago: the story is extant, and written in very choice Italian: you
shall see anon how the murderer gets the love of Gonzago's wife.   240

OPHELIA   The king rises.

HAMLET   What, frighted with false fire![5]

QUEEN   How fares my lord?

POLONIUS   Give o'er the play.

KING   Give me some light. Away!   245

POLONIUS   Lights, lights, lights!

[*Exeunt all but* HAMLET *and* HORATIO.]

HAMLET   Why, let the stricken deer go weep,
         The hart ungallèd play;
      For some must watch, while some must sleep:
         Thus runs the world away.   250

Would not this, sir, and a forest of feathers—if the rest of my fortunes
turn Turk with me—with two Provincial roses on my razed shoes,
get me a fellowship in a cry[6] of players, sir?

HORATIO   Half a share.

HAMLET   A whole one, I.   255
      For thou dost know, O Damon dear,
         This realm dismantled was
      Of Jove himself; and now reigns here
         A very, very—pajock.

HORATIO   You might have rhymed.[7]   260

HAMLET   O good Horatio, I'll take the ghost's word for a thousand
pound. Didst perceive?

HORATIO   Very well, my lord.

HAMLET   Upon the talk of the poisoning?

HORATIO   I did very well note him.   265

HAMLET   Ah, ha! Come, some music! come, the recorders!
      For if the king like not the comedy,
         Why then, belike, he likes it not, perdy.[8]
      Come, some music!

[*Re-enter* ROSENCRANTZ *and* GUILDENSTERN.]

GUILDENSTERN   Good my lord, vouchsafe me a word with you.   270

HAMLET   Sir, a whole history.

GUILDENSTERN   The king, sir—

HAMLET   Aye, sir, what of him?

GUILDENSTERN   Is in his retirement marvelous distempered.

HAMLET   With drink, sir?   275

GUILDENSTERN   No, my lord, rather with choler.[9]

HAMLET   Your wisdom should show itself more richer to signify this to
the doctor; for, for me to put him to his purgation would perhaps
plunge him into far more choler.

GUILDENSTERN   Good my lord, put your discourse into some frame,   280
and start not so wildly from my affair.

---

5. Blank shot.
6. Company; a term generally used with
hounds. "Turk with": betray. "Razed shoes":
sometimes worn by actors.

7. *Ass* would have rhymed. "Pajock": peacock.
8. By God (*per Dieu*).
9. Bile, anger.

HAMLET   I am tame, sir: pronounce.

GUILDENSTERN   The queen, your mother, in most great affliction of
spirit, hath sent me to you.

HAMLET   You are welcome. 285

GUILDENSTERN   Nay, good my lord, this courtesy is not of the right
breed. If it shall please you to make me a wholesome[1] answer, I will
do your mother's commandment: if not, your pardon and my return
shall be the end of my business.

HAMLET   Sir, I cannot. 290

GUILDENSTERN   What, my lord?

HAMLET   Make you a wholesome answer; my wit's diseased: but, sir,
such answer as I can make, you shall command; or rather, as you
say, my mother: therefore no more, but to the matter: my mother,
you say,— 295

ROSENCRANTZ   Then thus she says; your behavior hath struck her into
amazement and admiration.[2]

HAMLET   O wonderful son, that can so astonish a mother! But is there
no sequel at the heels of this mother's admiration? Impart.

ROSENCRANTZ   She desires to speak with you in her closet, ere you go 300
to bed.

HAMLET   We shall obey, were she ten times our mother. Have you any
further trade with us?

ROSENCRANTZ   My lord, you once did love me.

HAMLET   So I do still, by these pickers and stealers.[3] 305

ROSENCRANTZ   Good my lord, what is your cause of distemper? you do
surely bar the door upon your own liberty, if you deny your griefs to
your friend.

HAMLET   Sir, I lack advancement.[4]

ROSENCRANTZ   How can that be, when you have the voice of the king 310
himself for your succession in Denmark?

HAMLET   Aye, sir, but "while the grass grows,"[5]—the proverb is
something musty.

[Re-enter PLAYERS with recorders.]

O, the recorders! let me see one. To withdraw with you:—why
do you go about to recover the wind of me, as if you would drive 315
me into a toil?[6]

GUILDENSTERN   O, my lord, if my duty be too bold, my love is too
unmannerly.

HAMLET   I do not well understand that. Will you play upon this pipe?

GUILDENSTERN   My lord, I cannot. 320

HAMLET   I pray you.

GUILDENSTERN   Believe me, I cannot.

HAMLET   I do beseech you.

---

1. Sensible.
2. Confusion and surprise.
3. The hands.
4. Hamlet pretends that the cause of his "distemper" is frustrated ambition.

5. The proverb ends: "oft starves the silly steed."
6. Snare. "Withdraw": retire, talk in private. "Recover the wind of": get to the windward.

GUILDENSTERN   I know no touch of it, my lord.

HAMLET   It is as easy as lying: govern these ventages[7] with your fingers   325
and thumb, give it breath with your mouth, and it will discourse most
eloquent music. Look you, these are the stops.

GUILDENSTERN   But these cannot I command to any utterance of
harmony; I have not the skill.

HAMLET   Why, look you now, how unworthy a thing you make of me!   330
You would play upon me; you would seem to know my stops; you
would pluck out the heart of my mystery; you would sound me from
my lowest note to the top of my compass: and there is much music,
excellent voice, in this little organ; yet cannot you make it speak.
'Sblood, do you think I am easier to be played on than a pipe? Call   335
me what instrument you will, though you can fret[8] me, yet you cannot
play upon me.

    [*Re-enter* POLONIUS.]

God bless you, sir!

POLONIUS   My lord, the queen would speak with you, and presently.

HAMLET   Do you see yonder cloud that's almost in shape of a camel?   340

POLONIUS   By the mass, and 'tis like a camel, indeed.

HAMLET   Methinks it is like a weasel.

POLONIUS   It is backed like a weasel.

HAMLET   Or like a whale?

POLONIUS   Very like a whale.   345

HAMLET   Then I will come to my mother by and by. They fool me to
the top of my bent. I will come by and by.

POLONIUS   I will say so.

    [*Exit* POLONIUS.]

HAMLET   "By and by" is easily said. Leave me, friends.

    [*Exeunt all but* HAMLET.]

'Tis now the very witching time of night,   350
When churchyards yawn, and hell itself breathes out
Contagion to this world: now could I drink hot blood,
And do such bitter business as the day
Would quake to look on. Soft! now to my mother.
O heart, lose not thy nature; let not ever   355
The soul of Nero[9] enter this firm bosom:
Let me be cruel, not unnatural:
I will speak daggers to her, but use none;
My tongue and soul in this be hypocrites;
How in my words soever she be shent,   360
To give them seals[1] never, my soul, consent!

    [*Exit.*]

---

7. Windholes.
8. Vex, with a pun on *frets*, the ridges placed
across the finger board of a guitar to regulate
the fingering.

9. A Roman emperor (37–68 C.E.) who murdered his mother.
1. Ratify them by action. "Shent": reproached.

SCENE 3

[SCENE: *A room in the castle.*]

[*Enter* KING, ROSENCRANTZ, *and* GUILDENSTERN.]

KING   I like him not, nor stands it safe with us
To let his madness range. Therefore prepare you;
I your commission will forthwith dispatch,
And he to England shall along with you:
The terms of our estate[2] may not endure   5
Hazard so near us as doth hourly grow
Out of his lunacies.

GUILDENSTERN   We will ourselves provide:
Most holy and religious fear it is
To keep those many many bodies safe
That live and feed upon your majesty.   10

ROSENCRANTZ   The single and peculiar[3] life is bound
With all the strength and armor of the mind
To keep itself from noyance; but much more
That spirit upon whose weal depends and rests
The lives of many. The cease[4] of majesty   15
Dies not alone, but like a gulf doth draw
What 's near it with it; it is a massy wheel,
Fixed on the summit of the highest mount,
To whose huge spokes ten thousand lesser things
Are mortised[5] and adjoined; which, when it falls,   20
Each small annexment, petty consequence,
Attends the boisterous ruin. Never alone
Did the king sigh, but with a general groan.

KING   Arm you, I pray you, to this speedy voyage,
For we will fetters put about this fear,   25
Which now goes too free-footed.

ROSENCRANTZ
                    } We will haste us.
GUILDENSTERN

[*Exeunt* ROSENCRANTZ *and* GUILDENSTERN.—*Enter* POLONIUS.]

POLONIUS   My lord, he's going to his mother's closet:
Behind the arras I'll convey myself,
To hear the process: I'll warrant she'll tax him home:[6]   30
And, as you said, and wisely was it said
'Tis meet that some more audience than a mother,
Since nature makes them partial, should o'erhear
The speech, of vantage.[7] Fare you well, my liege:
I'll call upon you ere you go to bed,   35
And tell you what I know.

KING   Thanks, dear my lord.

[*Exit* POLONIUS.]

O, my offense is rank, it smells to heaven;

---

2. My position as king.
3. Individual.
4. Decease, extinction.

5. Fastened.
6. Take him to task thoroughly.
7. From a vantage point.

It hath the primal eldest curse[8] upon 't,
A brother's murder. Pray can I not,
Though inclination be as sharp as will: 40
My stronger guilt defeats my strong intent,
And like a man to double business bound,
I stand in pause where I shall first begin,
And both neglect. What if this cursed hand
Were thicker than itself with brother's blood,   45
Is there not rain enough in the sweet heavens
To wash it white as snow? Whereto serves mercy
But to confront the visage of offense?[9]
And what's in prayer but this twofold force,
To be forestalled ere we come to fall,   50
Or pardoned being down? Then I'll look up;
My fault is past. But O, what form of prayer
Can serve my turn? "Forgive me my foul murder?"
That cannot be, since I am still possessed
Of those effects for which I did the murder,   55
My crown, mine own ambition and my queen.
May one be pardoned and retain the offense?[1]
In the corrupted currents of this world
Offense's gilded hand may shove by justice,
And oft 'tis seen the wicked prize itself   60
Buys out the law:[2] but 'tis not so above;
There is no shuffling, there the action lies
In his[3] true nature, and we ourselves compelled
Even to the teeth and forehead of our faults
To give in evidence. What then? what rests?[4]   65
Try what repentance can: what can it not?
Yet what can it when one can not repent?
O wretched state! O bosom black as death!
O limèd soul, that struggling to be free
Art more engaged! Help, angels! make assay![5]   70
Bow, stubborn knees, and, heart with strings of steel,
Be soft as sinews of the new-born babe!
All may be well.
      [*Retires and kneels.—Enter* HAMLET.]
HAMLET   Now might I do it pat,[6] now he is praying
And now I'll do 't: and so he goes to heaven: 75
And so am I revenged. That would be scanned:[7]
A villain kills my father; and for that,
I, his sole son, do this same villain send
To heaven.

---

8. The curse of Cain.
9. Guilt.
1. The things obtained through the offense.
2. The wealth unduly acquired is used for bribery.
3. Its.

4. What remains?
5. Make the attempt! "Limèd": caught as with birdlime.
6. Conveniently.
7. Would have to be considered carefully.

O, this is hire and salary, not revenge.   80
He took my father grossly, full of bread,
With all his crimes broad blown, as flush as May;
And how his audit[8] stands who knows save heaven?
But in our circumstance and course of thought,
'Tis heavy with him: and am I then revenged,   85
To take him in the purging of his soul,
When he is fit and seasoned[9] for his passage?
No.
Up, sword, and know thou a more horrid hent:[1]
When he is drunk asleep, or in his rage,   90
Or, in the incestuous pleasure of his bed;
At game, a-swearing, or about some act
That has no relish of salvation in 't;
Then trip him, that his heels may kick at heaven
And that his soul may be as damned and black   95
As hell, whereto it goes. My mother stays:
This physic but prolongs thy sickly days.
    [Exit.]
KING [Rising.]   My words fly up, my thoughts remain below:
Words without thoughts never to heaven go.
    [Exit.]

SCENE 4

[SCENE: The Queen's closet.]

[Enter QUEEN and POLONIUS.]
POLONIUS   He will come straight. Look you lay home to him:
  Tell him his pranks have been too broad[2] to bear with,
  And that your grace hath screen'd and stood between
  Much heat and him. I'll sconce me even here.
  Pray you, be round[3] with him.
HAMLET [Within.]   Mother, mother, mother!   5
QUEEN   I'll warrant you; fear me not. Withdraw,
  I hear him coming.
    [POLONIUS hides behind the arras.—Enter HAMLET.]
HAMLET   Now, mother, what's the matter?
QUEEN   Hamlet, thou hast thy father much offended.
HAMLET   Mother, you have my father much offended.   10
QUEEN   Come, come, you answer with an idle tongue.
HAMLET   Go, go, you question with a wicked tongue.
QUEEN   Why, how now, Hamlet!
HAMLET   What's the matter now?
QUEEN   Have you forgot me?
HAMLET   No, by the rood,[4] not so:
  You are the queen, your husband's brother's wife;   15

8. Account. "Broad blown": in full bloom.   lesson.
9. Ripe, ready.   3. Straightforward.
1. Grip.   4. Cross.
2. Unrestrained. "Lay home": give him a stern

And—would it were not so!—you are my mother.

QUEEN   Nay, then, I'll set those to you that can speak.

HAMLET   Come, come, and sit you down; you shall not budge:
You go not till I set you up a glass[5]
Where you may see the inmost part of you.   20

QUEEN   What wilt thou do? thou wilt not murder me?
Help, help, ho!

POLONIUS [Behind.]   What, ho! help, help, help!

HAMLET [Drawing.]   How now! a rat? Dead, for a ducat, dead!
   [Makes a pass through the arras.]

POLONIUS [Behind.]   O, I am slain!
   [Falls and dies.]

QUEEN   O me, what hast thou done?   25

HAMLET   Nay, I know not: is it the king?

QUEEN   O, what a rash and bloody deed is this!

HAMLET   A bloody deed! almost as bad, good mother,
As kill a king, and marry with his brother.

QUEEN   As kill a king!

HAMLET   Aye, lady, 'twas my word.   30
   [Lifts up the arras and discovers POLONIUS.]
Thou wretched, rash, intruding fool, farewell!
I took thee for thy better: take thy fortune;
Thou find'st to be too busy[6] is some danger.
Leave wringing of your hands: peace! sit you down,
And let me wring your heart: for so I shall,   35
If it be made of penetrable stuff;
If damned custom have not brassed it so,
That it be proof and bulwark against sense.[7]

QUEEN   What have I done, that thou darest wag thy tongue
In noise so rude against me?

HAMLET   Such an act   40
That blurs the grace and blush of modesty,
Calls virtue hypocrite, takes off the rose
From the fair forehead of an innocent love,
And sets a blister there; makes marriage vows
As false as dicers' oaths: O, such a deed   45
As from the body of contraction[8] plucks
The very soul, and sweet religion makes
A rhapsody of words: heaven's face doth glow;[9]
Yea, this solidity and compound mass,
With tristful visage, as against the doom,[1]   50
Is thought-sick at the act.

QUEEN   Aye me, what act,
That roars so loud and thunders in the index?[2]

HAMLET   Look here, upon this picture, and on this,
The counterfeit presentment[3] of two brothers.   55

5. Mirror.
6. Too much of a busybody.
7. Feeling.
8. Duty to the marriage contract.

9. Blush with shame.
1. Doomsday. "Tristful": sad.
2. Prologue, table of contents.
3. Portrait.

See what a grace was seated on this brow;
Hyperion's curls, the front of Jove himself,
An eye like Mars, to threaten and command;
A station[4] like the herald Mercury
New-lighted on a heaven-kissing hill;   60
A combination and a form indeed,
Where every god did seem to set his seal
To give the world assurance of a man:
This was your husband. Look you now, what follows:
Here is your husband; like a mildewed ear,[5]   65
Blasting his wholesome brother. Have you eyes?
Could you on this fair mountain leave to feed,
And batten[6] on this moor? Ha! have you eyes?
You cannot call it love, for at your age
The hey-day in the blood is tame, it's humble,   70
And waits upon[7] the judgment: and what judgment
Would step from this to this? Sense sure you have,
Else could you not have motion: but sure that sense
Is apoplexed: for madness would not err,
Nor sense to ecstasy was ne'er so thralled   75
But it reserved some quantity of choice,
To serve in such a difference. What devil was 't
That thus hath cozened you at hoodman-blind?[8]
Eyes without feeling, feeling without sight,
Ears without hands or eyes, smelling sans[9] all,   80
Or but a sickly part of one true sense
Could not so mope.[1]
O shame! where is thy blush? Rebellious hell,
If thou canst mutine in a matron's bones,
To flaming youth let virtue be as wax   85
And melt in her own fire: proclaim no shame
When the compulsive ardor gives the charge,[2]
Since frost itself as actively doth burn,
And reason panders[3] will.
QUEEN   O Hamlet, speak no more:
Thou turn'st mine eyes into my very soul,   90
And there I see such black and grained spots
As will not leave their tinct.[4]
HAMLET   Nay, but to live
In the rank sweat of an enseamèd[5] bed,
Stew'd in corruption, honeying and making love
Over the nasty sty,—
QUEEN   O, speak to me no more;   95
These words like daggers enter in my ears;

4. Posture.
5. Of corn.
6. Gorge, fatten. "Leave": cease.
7. Is subordinated to.
8. Blindman's buff. "Cozened": tricked.
9. Without.

1. Be stupid.
2. Attack.
3. Becomes subservient to.
4. Lose their color. "Grained": dyed in.
5. Greasy.

No more, sweet Hamlet!

HAMLET   A murderer and a villain;
    A slave that is not twentieth part the tithe[6]
    Of your precédent lord; a vice of kings;
    A cutpurse[7] of the empire and the rule,   100
    That from a shelf the precious diadem stole
    And put it in his pocket!

QUEEN   No more!

HAMLET   A king of shreds and patches—
    [*Enter* GHOST.]
    Save me, and hover o'er me with your wings,
    You heavenly guards! What would your gracious figure?   105

QUEEN   Alas, he's mad!

HAMLET   Do you not come your tardy son to chide,
    That, lapsed in time and passion, lets go by
    The important acting of your dread command?
    O, say!

GHOST   Do not forget: this visitation   110
    Is but to whet thy almost blunted purpose.
    But look, amazement on thy mother sits:
    O, step between her and her fighting soul:
    Conceit[8] in weakest bodies strongest works:
    Speak to her, Hamlet.

HAMLET   How is it with you, lady?   115

QUEEN   Alas, how is 't with you,
    That you do bend your eye on vacancy
    And with the incorporal air do hold discourse?
    Forth at your eyes your spirits wildly peep;
    And, as the sleeping soldiers in the alarm,   120
    Your bedded hairs, like life in excrements,[9]
    Start up and stand on end. O gentle son,
    Upon the heat and flame of thy distemper
    Sprinkle cool patience. Whereon do you look?

HAMLET   On him, on him! Look you how pale he glares!   125
    His form and cause conjoined, preaching to stones,
    Would make them capable.[1] Do not look upon me,
    Lest with this piteous action you convert
    My stern effects:[2] then what I have to do
    Will want true color; tears perchance for[3] blood.   130

QUEEN   To whom do you speak this?

HAMLET   Do you see nothing there?

QUEEN   Nothing at all; yet all that is I see.

HAMLET   Nor did you nothing hear?

QUEEN   No, nothing but ourselves.

HAMLET   Why, look you there! look, how it steals away!

---

6. Tenth.
7. Pickpocket. "Vice": clown, from the custom in the old morality plays of having a buffoon take the part of Vice or of a particular vice.

8. Imagination.
9. Outgrowths. "Alarm": call to arms.
1. Of feeling.
2. You make me change my purpose.
3. Instead of.

My father, in his habit as he lived!   135
Look, where he goes, even now, out at the portal!
    [*Exit* GHOST.]
QUEEN   This is the very coinage of your brain:
This bodiless creation ecstasy
Is very cunning in.
HAMLET   Ecstasy!
My pulse, as yours, doth temperately keep time,   140
And makes as healthful music: it is not madness
That I have uttered: bring me to the test,
And I the matter will re-word, which madness
Would gambol from. Mother, for love of grace,
Lay not that flattering unction to your soul,   145
That not your trespass but my madness speaks:
It will but skin and film the ulcerous place,
Whiles rank corruption, mining all within,
Infects unseen. Confess yourself to heaven;
Repent what's past, avoid what is to come,   150
And do not spread the compost on the weeds,
To make them ranker. Forgive me this my virtue,
For in the fatness of these pursy[4] times
Virtue itself of vice must pardon beg.
Yea, curb[5] and woo for leave to do him good.   155
QUEEN   O Hamlet, thou hast cleft my heart in twain.
HAMLET   O, throw away the worser part of it,
And live the purer with the other half.
Good night: but go not to my uncle's bed;
Assume a virtue, if you have it not.   160
That monster, custom, who all sense doth eat,
Of habits devil, is angel yet in this,
That to the use of actions fair and good
He likewise gives a frock or livery,
That aptly is put on.[6] Refrain to-night,   165
And that shall lend a kind of easiness
To the next abstinence; the next more easy;
For use almost can change the stamp[7] of nature,
And either curb the devil, or throw him out
With wondrous potency. Once more, good night: 170
And when you are desirous to be blest,
I'll blessing beg of you. For this same lord,
    [*Pointing to* POLONIUS.]
I do repent: but heaven hath pleased it so,
To punish me with this, and this with me,
That I must be their scourge and minister.   175
I will bestow[8] him, and will answer well
The death I gave him. So, again, good night.

---

4. Swollen from pampering.
5. Bow.
6. I.e., habit, although like a devil in establishing evil ways in us, is like an angel in doing the same for virtues. "Aptly": easily.
7. Cast, form. "Use": habit.
8. Stow away. "Minister": agent of punishment.

I must be cruel, only to be kind:
Thus bad begins, and worse remains behind.
One word more, good lady.

QUEEN   What shall I do?   180

HAMLET   Not this, by no means, that I bid you do:
Let the bloat[9] king tempt you again to bed;
Pinch wanton on your cheek, call you his mouse;
And let him, for a pair of reechy[1] kisses,
Or paddling in your neck with his damned fingers,   185
Make you to ravel all this matter out,
That I essentially am not in madness,
But mad in craft.[2] 'Twere good you let him know;
For who, that's but a queen, fair, sober, wise,
Would from a paddock, from a bat, a gib,   190
Such dear concernings[3] hide? who would do so?
No, in despite of sense and secrecy,
Unpeg the basket on the house's top,
Let the birds fly, and like the famous ape,[4]
To try conclusions, in the basket creep   195
And break your own neck down.

QUEEN   Be thou assured, if words be made of breath
And breath of life, I have no life to breathe
What thou hast said to me.

HAMLET   I must to England; you know that?

QUEEN   Alack,   200
I had forgot: 'tis so concluded on.

HAMLET   There's letters sealed: and my two schoolfellows,
Whom I will trust as I will adders fanged,
They bear the mandate; they must sweep my way,
And marshal me to knavery. Let it work;   205
For 'tis the sport to have the enginer
Hoist with his own petar:[5] and 't shall go hard
But I will delve one yard below their mines,
And blow them at the moon: I, 'tis most sweet
When in one line two crafts directly meet.   210
This man shall set me packing:
I'll lug the guts into the neighbor room.
Mother, good night. Indeed this councillor
Is now most still, most secret and most grave,[6]
Who was in life a foolish prating knave.   215
Come, sir, to draw toward an end with you.
Good night, mother.

       [*Exeunt severally*; HAMLET *dragging in* POLONIUS.]

---

9. Bloated with drink.
1. Fetid.
2. Simulation.
3. Matters with which one is closely concerned. "Paddock": toad. "Gib": tomcat.
4. The ape in the unidentified animal fable to which Hamlet alludes; apparently the animal

saw birds fly out of a basket and drew the conclusion that by placing himself in a basket he could fly, too.
5. Petard, a variety of bomb. "Marshal": lead. "Enginer": military engineer. "Hoist": blow up.
6. Hamlet is punning on the word.

Act 4

SCENE I

[SCENE: *A room in the castle.*]

      [*Enter* KING, QUEEN, ROSENCRANTZ, *and* GUILDENSTERN.]

KING   There's matter in these sighs, these profound heaves:
You must translate: 'tis fit we understand them.
Where is your son?

QUEEN   Bestow this place on us[7] a little while.

      [*Exeunt* ROSENCRANTZ *and* GUILDENSTERN.]

Ah, mine own lord, what have I seen to-night!   5

KING   What, Gertrude? How does Hamlet?

QUEEN   Mad as the sea and wind, when both contend
Which is the mightier: in his lawless fit,
Behind the arras hearing something stir,
Whips out his rapier, cries "A rat, a rat!"   10
And in this brainish apprehension[8] kills
The unseen good old man.

KING   O heavy deed!
It had been so with us, had we been there:
His liberty is full of threats to all,
To you yourself, to us, to every one.   15
Alas, how shall this bloody deed be answered?
It will be laid to us, whose providence
Should have kept short,[9] restrained and out of haunt,
This mad young man: but so much was our love,
We would not understand what was most fit,   20
But, like the owner of a foul disease,
To keep it from divulging, let it feed
Even on the pith of life. Where is he gone?

QUEEN   To draw apart the body he hath killed:
O'er whom his very madness, like some ore   25
Among a mineral[1] of metals base,
Shows itself pure; he weeps for what is done.

KING   O Gertrude, come away!
The sun no sooner shall the mountains touch,
But we will ship him hence: and this vile deed   30
We must, with all our majesty and skill,
Both countenance[2] and excuse. Ho, Guildenstern!

      [*Re-enter* ROSENCRANTZ *and* GUILDENSTERN.]

Friends both, go join you with some further aid:
Hamlet in madness hath Polonius slain,
And from his mother's closet hath he dragged him: 35
Go seek him out; speak fair, and bring the body
Into the chapel. I pray you, haste in this.

      [*Exeunt* ROSENCRANTZ *and* GUILDENSTERN.]

---

7. Leave us alone.
8. Imaginary notion.
9. Under close watch.

1. Mine. "Ore": gold.
2. Recognize.

Come, Gertrude, we'll call up our wisest friends;
And let them know, both what we mean to do,
And what's untimely done. . . .[3]   40
Whose whisper o'er the world's diameter
As level as the cannon to his blank[4]
Transports his poisoned shot, may miss our name
And hit the woundless air. O, come away!
My soul is full of discord and dismay.   45

[*Exeunt.*]

SCENE 2

[SCENE: *Another room in the castle.*]

[*Enter* HAMLET.]

HAMLET   Safely stowed.

ROSENCRANTZ ⎫
              ⎬   [*Within.*] Hamlet! Lord Hamlet!
GUILDENSTERN ⎭

HAMLET   But soft, what noise? who calls on Hamlet?
O, here they come.

[*Enter* ROSENCRANTZ *and* GUILDENSTERN.]

ROSENCRANTZ   What have you done, my lord, with the dead body?   5

HAMLET   Compounded[5] it with dust, whereto 'tis kin.

ROSENCRANTZ   Tell us where 'tis, that we may take it thence
And bear it to the chapel.

HAMLET   Do not believe it.

ROSENCRANTZ   Believe what?   10

HAMLET   That I can keep your counsel and not mine own. Besides, to
be demanded of a sponge! what replication[6] should be made by the
son of a king?

ROSENCRANTZ   Take you me for a sponge, my lord?

HAMLET   Aye, sir; that soaks up the king's countenance,[7] his rewards,   15
his authorities. But such officers do the king best service in the end:
he keeps them, like an ape, in the corner of his jaw; first mouthed,
to be last swallowed: when he needs what you have gleaned, it is but
squeezing you, and sponge, you shall be dry again.

ROSENCRANTZ   I understand you not, my lord.   20

HAMLET   I am glad of it: a knavish speech sleeps in a foolish ear.

ROSENCRANTZ   My lord, you must tell us where the body is, and go
with us to the king.

HAMLET   The body is with the king, but the king is not with the body.
The king is a thing—   25

GUILDENSTERN   A thing, my lord?

HAMLET   Of nothing: bring me to him. Hide fox, and all after.[8]

[*Exeunt.*]

---

3. This gap in the text has been guessingly filled
in with "So envious slander."
4. His target.
5. Mixed.

6. Formal reply. "Demanded": questioned by.
7. Favor.
8. A children's game.

SCENE 3

[SCENE: *Another room in the castle.*]

[*Enter* KING, *attended.*]

KING I have sent to seek him, and to find the body.
How dangerous is it that this man goes loose!
Yet must not we put the strong law on him:
He's loved of the distracted multitude,
Who like not in their judgment, but their eyes;   5
And where 'tis so, the offender's scourge is weighed,
But never the offense. To bear⁹ all smooth and even,
This sudden sending away must seem
Deliberate pause: diseases desperate grown
By desperate appliance¹ are relieved,   10
Or not at all.
      [*Enter* ROSENCRANTZ.]
            How now! what hath befall'n?

ROSENCRANTZ Where the dead body is bestowed, my lord,
We cannot get from him.

KING   But where is he?

ROSENCRANTZ Without, my lord; guarded, to know your pleasure.

KING Bring him before us.   15

ROSENCRANTZ Ho, Guildenstern! bring in my lord.

      [*Enter* HAMLET *and* GUILDENSTERN.]

KING Now, Hamlet, where's Polonius?

HAMLET At supper.

KING At supper! where?

HAMLET Not where he eats, but where he is eaten: a certain convocation   20
of public worms are e'en at him. Your worm is your only emperor for
diet:² we fat all creatures else to fat us, and we fat ourselves for
maggots: your fat king and your lean beggar is but variable service,³
two dishes, but to one table: that's the end.

KING Alas, alas!   25

HAMLET A man may fish with the worm that hath eat of a king, and
eat of the fish that hath fed of that worm.

KING What dost thou mean by this?

HAMLET Nothing but to show you how a king may go a progress⁴
through the guts of a beggar.   30

KING Where is Polonius?

HAMLET In heaven; send thither to see: if your messenger find him
not there, seek him i' the other place yourself. But indeed, if you
find him not within this month, you shall nose⁵ him as you go up
the stairs into the lobby.   35

KING [*To some* ATTENDANTS.] Go seek him there.

HAMLET He will stay till you come.

9. Conduct. "Scourge": punishment.
1. Treatment. "Deliberate pause": the result
of careful argument.
2. Possibly a punning reference to the Diet

(assembly) of the Holy Roman Empire at Worms.
3. That is, the service varies, not the food.
4. Royal state journey.
5. Smell.

[*Exeunt* ATTENDANTS.]

KING Hamlet, this deed, for thine especial safety,
  Which we do tender,[6] as we dearly grieve
  For that which thou hast done, must send thee hence   40
  With fiery quickness: therefore prepare thyself;
  The bark is ready and the wind at help,
  The associates tend, and every thing is bent
  For England.
HAMLET   For England?
KING   Aye, Hamlet.
HAMLET   Good.
KING So is it, if thou knew'st our purposes.   45
HAMLET I see a cherub that sees them. But, come; for England!
  Farewell, dear mother.
KING Thy loving father, Hamlet.
HAMLET My mother: father and mother is man and wife; man and
  wife is one flesh, and so, my mother. Come, for England!   50
       [*Exit.*]
KING Follow him at foot;[7] tempt him with speed aboard;
  Delay it not; I'll have him hence to-night:
  Away! for every thing is sealed and done
  That else leans on[8] the affair: pray you, make haste.
       [*Exeunt* ROSENCRANTZ *and* GUILDENSTERN.]
  And, England,[9] if my love thou hold'st at aught—   55
  As my great power thereof may give thee sense,
  Since yet thy cicatrice looks raw and red
  After the Danish sword, and thy free awe
  Pays homage to us—thou mayst not coldly set[1]
  Our sovereign process; which imports at full,   60
  By letters conjuring[2] to that effect,
  The present death of Hamlet. Do it, England;
  For like the hectic[3] in my blood he rages,
  And thou must cure me; till I know 'tis done,
  Howe'er my haps, my joys were ne'er begun.   65
       [*Exit.*]

SCENE 4

[SCENE: *A plain in Denmark.*]

       [*Enter* FORTINBRAS, *a* CAPTAIN *and* SOLDIERS, *marching.*]
FORTINBRAS Go, captain, from me greet the Danish king;
  Tell him that by his license Fortinbras
  Craves the conveyance[4] of a promised march
  Over his kingdom. You know the rendezvous.
  If that his majesty would aught with us,   5

6. Care for.
7. At his heels.
8. Pertains to.
9. The king of England.

1. Regard with indifference.
2. Enjoining.
3. Fever.
4. Convoy.

We shall express our duty in his eye;[5]
And let him know so.
CAPTAIN   I will do 't, my lord.
FORTINBRAS   Go softly on.

> [*Exeunt* FORTINBRAS *and* SOLDIERS.—*Enter* HAMLET, ROSENCRANTZ,
> GUILDENSTERN, *and others.*]

HAMLET   Good sir, whose powers[6] are these?
CAPTAIN   They are of Norway, sir.   10
HAMLET   How purposed, sir, I pray you?
CAPTAIN   Against some part of Poland.
HAMLET   Who commands them, sir?
CAPTAIN   The nephew to Old Norway, Fortinbras.
HAMLET   Goes it against the main[7] of Poland, sir,   15
Or for some frontier?
CAPTAIN   Truly to speak, and with no addition,
We go to gain a little patch of ground
That hath in it no profit but the name.
To pay five ducats, five, I would not farm it;   20
Nor will it yield to Norway or the Pole
A ranker rate, should it be sold in fee.[8]
HAMLET   Why, then the Polack never will defend it.
CAPTAIN   Yes, it is already garrisoned.
HAMLET   Two thousand souls and twenty thousand ducats   25
Will not debate the question of this straw!
This is the imposthume[9] of much wealth and peace,
That inward breaks, and shows no cause without
Why the man dies. I humbly thank you, sir.
CAPTAIN   God be wi' you, sir.
> [*Exit.*]
ROSENCRANTZ   Will 't please you go, my lord?   30
HAMLET   I'll be with you straight. Go a little before.
> [*Exeunt all but* HAMLET.]
How all occasions do inform against[1] me,
And spur my dull revenge! What is a man,
If his chief good and market[2] of his time
Be but to sleep and feed? a beast, no more.   35
Sure, he that made us with such large discourse,[3]
Looking before and after, gave us not
That capability and god-like reason
To fust[4] in us unused. Now, whether it be
Bestial oblivion, or some craven scruple   40
Of thinking too precisely on the event,[5]—
A thought which, quartered, hath but one part wisdom
And ever three parts coward,—I do not know
Why yet I live to say "this thing's to do,"

---

5. Presence.
6. Armed forces.
7. The whole of.
8. For absolute possession. "Ranker": higher.
9. Ulcer.

1. Denounce.
2. Payment for, reward.
3. Reasoning power.
4. Become moldy, taste of the cask.
5. Outcome.

Sith I have cause, and will, and strength, and means,   45
To do 't. Examples gross as earth exhort me:
Witness this army, of such mass and charge,[6]
Led by a delicate and tender prince,
Whose spirit with divine ambition puffed
Makes mouths[7] at the invisible event,   50
Exposing what is mortal and unsure
To all that fortune, death, and danger dare,
Even for an egg-shell. Rightly to be great
Is not to stir without great argument,
But greatly to find quarrel in a straw   55
When honor's at the stake. How stand I then,
That have a father killed, a mother stained,
Excitements of my reason and my blood,
And let all sleep, while to my shame I see
The imminent death of twenty thousand men,   60
That for a fantasy and trick[8] of fame
Go to their graves like beds, fight for a plot
Whereon the numbers cannot try the cause,[9]
Which is not tomb enough and continent[1]
To hide the slain? O, from this time forth,   65
My thoughts be bloody, or be nothing worth!
    [*Exit.*]

SCENE 5

[SCENE: *Elsinore. A room in the castle.*]

    [*Enter* QUEEN, HORATIO, *and a* GENTLEMAN.]
QUEEN   I will not speak with her.
GENTLEMAN   She is importunate, indeed distract:
  Her mood will needs be pitied.
QUEEN   What would she have?
GENTLEMAN   She speaks much of her father, says she hears
  There's tricks i' the world, and hems and beats her heart,   5
  Spurns enviously at straws;[2] speaks things in doubt,
  That carry but half sense: her speech is nothing,
  Yet the unshapèd use of it doth move
  The hearers to collection; they aim[3] at it,
  And botch[4] the words up fit to their own thoughts;   10
  Which, as her winks and nods and gestures yield them,
  Indeed would make one think there might be thought,
  Though nothing sure, yet much unhappily.
HORATIO   'Twere good she were spoken with, for she may strew
  Dangerous conjectures in ill-breeding minds.[5]   15

6. Cost.
7. Laughs at.
8. Trifle.
9. So small that it cannot hold the men who
fight for it.
1. Container.

2. Gets angry at trifles.
3. Guess. "Collection": gathering up her words
and trying to make sense of them.
4. Patch.
5. Minds breeding evil thoughts.

QUEEN   Let her come in.
        [*Exit* GENTLEMAN.]
    [*Aside.*] To my sick soul, as sin's true nature is,
    Each toy seems prologue to some great amiss:
    So full of artless jealousy[6] is guilt,
    It spills itself in fearing to be spilt.   20
        [*Re-enter* GENTLEMAN, *with* OPHELIA.]
OPHELIA   Where is the beauteous majesty of Denmark?
QUEEN   How now, Ophelia!
OPHELIA [*Sings.*]   How should I your true love know
              From another one?
              By his cockle hat and staff   25
              And his sandal shoon.[7]

QUEEN   Alas, sweet lady, what imports this song?
OPHELIA   Say you? nay, pray you, mark.
    [*Sings.*]   He is dead and gone, lady,
            He is dead and gone;
            At his head a grass-green turf,   30
            At his heels a stone.
    Oh, oh!
QUEEN   Nay, but Ophelia,—
OPHELIA   Pray you, mark.
    [*Sings.*]   White his shroud as the mountain snow,—   35
        [*Enter* KING.]
QUEEN   Alas, look here, my lord.
OPHELIA [*Sings.*]   Larded[8] with sweet flowers;
              Which bewept to the grave did—not—go
              With true-love showers.
KING   How do you, pretty lady?   40
OPHELIA   Well, God 'ild[9] you! They say the owl was a baker's daughter.
    Lord, we know what we are, but know not what we may be.[1] God be
    at your table!
KING   Conceit upon her father.
OPHELIA   Pray you, let's have no words of this; but when they ask you   45
    what it means, say you this:
    [*Sings.*]   To-morrow is Saint Valentine's day
            All in the morning betime,
            And I a maid at your window,
              To be your Valentine.   50
            Then up he rose, and donned his clothes,
              And dupped[2] the chamber-door;
            Let in the maid, that out a maid
              Never departed more.

---

6. Uncontrolled suspicion. "Toy": trifle.
"Amiss": misfortune.
7. Shoes. These are all typical signs of pilgrims traveling to places of devotion.
8. Garnished.

9. Yield—that is, repay.
1. An allusion to a folk tale about a baker's daughter changed into an owl for having shown no charity to those in need.
2. Opened.

KING   Pretty Ophelia!   55
OPHELIA   Indeed, la, without an oath, I'll make an end on 't:

  [*Sings.*] By Gis[3] and by Saint Charity,
        Alack, and fie for shame!
     Young men will do 't, if they come to 't;
        By Cock,[4] they are to blame.   60
     Quoth she, before you tumbled me,
        You promised me to wed.

He answers:

     So would I ha' done, by yonder sun,
        An thou hadst not come to my bed.   65
KING   How long hath she been thus?
OPHELIA   I hope all will be well. We must be patient: but I cannot
choose but weep, to think they should lay him i' the cold ground.
My brother shall know of it: and so I thank you for your good counsel.
Come, my coach! Good night, ladies; good night, sweet ladies; good   70
night, good night.
    [*Exit.*]
KING   Follow her close; give her good watch, I pray you.
    [*Exit* HORATIO.]
O, this is the poison of deep grief; it springs
All from her father's death. O Gertrude, Gertrude,
When sorrows come, they come not single spies,   75
But in battalions! First, her father slain:
Next, your son gone; and he most violent author
Of his own just remove: the people muddied,[5]
Thick and unwholesome in their thoughts and whispers,
For good Polonius' death; and we have done but greenly   80
In hugger-mugger[6] to inter him: poor Ophelia
Divided from herself and her fair judgment,
Without the which we are pictures, or mere beasts:
Last, and as much containing as all these,
Her brother is in secret come from France,   85
Feeds on his wonder,[7] keeps himself in clouds,
And wants not buzzers[8] to infect his ear
With pestilent speeches of his father's death;
Wherein necessity, of matter beggared,[9]
Will nothing stick our person to arraign[1]   90
In ear and ear. O my dear Gertrude, this,
Like to a murdering-piece,[2] in many places
Gives me superfluous death.

---

3. By Jesus.
4. Corruption of *God*, but with a sexual undermeaning.
5. Confused, their thoughts made turbid (as water by mud).
6. Hasty secrecy. "Greenly": foolishly.
7. Broods, keeps wondering.

8. Lacks not tale-bearers.
9. The necessity to build up a story without the materials for doing so.
1. Will not hesitate to accuse me.
2. A variety of cannon that scattered its shot in many directions.

[*A noise within.*]

QUEEN   Alack, what noise is this?

KING   Where are my Switzers?[3] Let them guard the door.

      [*Enter another* GENTLEMAN.]

    What is the matter?

GENTLEMAN   Save yourself, my lord: 95
    The ocean, overpeering of his list,[4]
    Eats not the flats with more impetuous haste
    Than young Laertes, in a riotous head,[5]
    O'erbears your officers. The rabble call him lord;
    And, as the world were now but to begin,   100
    Antiquity forgot, custom not known,
    The ratifiers and props of every word,
    They cry "Choose we; Laertes shall be king!"
    Caps, hands and tongues applaud it to the clouds,
    "Laertes shall be king, Laertes king!"   105

QUEEN   How cheerfully on the false trail they cry!
    O, this is counter,[6] you false Danish dogs!

      [*Noise within.*]

KING   The doors are broke.

      [*Enter* LAERTES, *armed;* DANES *following.*]

LAERTES   Where is this king? Sirs, stand you all without.

DANES   No, let's come in.

LAERTES   I pray you, give me leave.   110

DANES   We will, we will.

      [*They retire without the door.*]

LAERTES   I thank you: keep the door. O thou vile king,
    Give me my father!

QUEEN   Calmly, good Laertes.

LAERTES   That drop of blood that's calm proclaims me bastard;
    Cries cuckold to my father; brands the harlot   115
    Even here, between the chaste unsmirchèd brows
    Of my true mother.

KING   What is the cause, Laertes,
    That thy rebellion looks so giant-like?
    Let him go, Gertrude; do not fear[7] our person
    There's such divinity doth hedge a king,   120
    That treason can but peep to what it would,[8]
    Acts little of his[9] will. Tell me, Laertes,
    Why thou art thus incensed: let him go, Gertrude
    Speak, man.

LAERTES   Where is my father?

KING   Dead.

QUEEN   But not by him.   125

KING   Let him demand his fill.

3. Swiss guards.
4. Overflowing above the high-water mark.
5. Group of rebels.
6. Following the scent in the wrong direction.
7. Fear for.
8. Look from a distance at what it desires.
9. Its.

LAERTES   How came he dead? I'll not be juggled with
    To hell, allegiance! vows, to the blackest devil!
    Conscience and grace, to the profoundest pit
    I dare damnation: to this point I stand,   130
    That both the worlds I give to negligence,[1]
    Let come what comes; only I'll be revenged
    Most thoroughly for my father.
KING   Who shall stay you?
LAERTES   My will, not all the world
    And for my means, I'll husband them so well,   135
    They shall go far with little.
KING   Good Laertes,
    If you desire to know the certainty
    Of your dear father's death, is 't writ in your revenge
    That, swoopstake,[2] you will draw both friend and foe,
    Winner and loser?   140
LAERTES   None but his enemies.
KING   Will you know them then?
LAERTES   To his good friends thus wide I'll ope my arms;
    And, like the kind life-rendering pelican,[3]
    Repast them with my blood.
KING   Why, now you speak
    Like a good child and a true gentleman.   145
    That I am guiltless of your father's death,
    And am most sensibly in grief for it,
    It shall as level to your judgment pierce
    As day does to your eye.
DANES [Within.]   Let her come in.
LAERTES   How now! what noise is that?   150
    [Re-enter OPHELIA.]
    O heat, dry up my brains! tears seven times salt,
    Burn out the sense and virtue[4] of mine eye!
    By heaven, thy madness shall be paid with weight,
    Till our scale turn the beam. O rose of May!
    Dear maid, kind sister, sweet Ophelia!   155
    O heavens! is 't possible a young maid's wits
    Should be as mortal as an old man's life?
    Nature is fine in love, and where 'tis fine
    It sends some precious instance[5] of itself
    After the thing it loves.   160
OPHELIA [Sings.]   They bore him barefaced on the bier
                Hey non nonny, nonny, hey nonny
                And in his grave rained many a tear,—
    Fare you well, my dove!

---

1. I don't care what may happen to me in either this world or the next.
2. Without making any distinction, as the winner takes the whole stake in a card game.

3. In myth, the pelican is supposed to feed its young with its own blood.
4. Power, faculty.
5. Sample, token. "Fine": refined.

LAERTES Hadst thou thy wits, and didst persuade revenge, 165
It could not move thus.

OPHELIA [*Sings.*] You must sing down a-down,
                              An you call him a-down-a.
O, how the wheel becomes it! It is the false steward,[6] that stole his
master's daughter. 170

LAERTES This nothing's more than matter.[7]

OPHELIA There's rosemary, that's for remembrance: pray you, love,
remember: and there is pansies, that's for thoughts.

LAERTES A document[8] in madness; thoughts and remembrance fitted.

OPHELIA There's fennel for you, and columbines: there's rue for you: 175
and here's some for me: we may call it herbs of grace o' Sundays: O,
you must wear your rue with a difference. There's a daisy: I would
give you some violets,[9] but they withered all when my father died:
they say he made a good end,—

[*Sings.*] For bonnie sweet Robin is all my joy. 180

LAERTES Thought and affliction, passion, hell itself,
She turns to favor[1] and to prettiness.

OPHELIA [*Sings.*] And will he not come again?
                              And will he not come again?
                                    No, no, he is dead, 185
                                    Go to thy death-bed,
                              He never will come again.
                              His beard was as white as snow,
                              All flaxen was his poll
                                    He is gone, he is gone, 190
                                    And we cast away moan
                              God ha' mercy on his soul!
And of all Christian souls, I pray God. God be wi' you.
    [*Exit.*]

LAERTES Do you see this, O God?

KING Laertes, I must commune with your grief, 195
Or you deny me right. Go but apart,
Make choice of whom your wisest friends you will.
And they shall hear and judge 'twixt you and me:
If by direct or by collateral hand
They find us touched,[2] we will our kingdom give, 200
Our crown, our life, and all that we call ours,
To you in satisfaction; but if not,
Be you content to lend your patience to us,
And we shall jointly labor with your soul
To give it due content.

---

6. An allusion (probably to a lost ballad) further expressing Ophelia's preoccupation with betrayal, lost love, and death. "How the wheel becomes it": that is, how well the refrain fits.
7. This nonsense is more indicative than sane speech.
8. Lesson. Traditionally, flowers and herbs have symbolic meanings. Here rosemary is the

symbol for remembrance and pansies symbolize thoughts.
9. Violets symbolize faithfulness. Fennel stands for flattery, columbines for cuckoldom, and rue for sorrow and repentance (compare the verb *rue*).
1. Charm.
2. Involved (in the murder). "Collateral": indirect.

LAERTES   Let this be so;   205
His means of death, his obscure funeral,
No trophy, sword, nor hatchment[3] o'er his bones,
No noble rite nor formal ostentation,
Cry to be heard, as 'twere from heaven to earth,
That I must call 't in question.
KING   So you shall;   210
And where the offense is let the great axe fall.
I pray you, go with me.
        [Exeunt.]

SCENE 6

[SCENE: *Another room in the castle.*]

        [*Enter* HORATIO *and a* SERVANT.]
HORATIO   What are they that would speak with me?
SERVANT   Sea-faring men, sir: they say they have letters for you.
HORATIO   Let them come in.
        [*Exit* SERVANT.]
I do not know from what part of the world
I should be greeted, if not from Lord Hamlet.   5
        [*Enter* SAILORS.]
FIRST SAILOR   God bless you, sir.
HORATIO   Let him bless thee too.
FIRST SAILOR   He shall, sir, an 't please him.
There's a letter for you, sir; it comes from the ambassador that was
bound for England; if your name be Horatio, as I am let to know   10
it is.
HORATIO [*Reads.*]   "Horatio, when thou shalt have overlooked[4] this,
give these fellows some means to the king: they have letters for him.
Ere we were two days old at sea, a pirate of very warlike appointment
gave us chase. Finding ourselves too slow of sail, we put on a compelled   15
valor, and in the grapple I boarded them: on the instant they
got clear of our ship; so I alone became their prisoner. They have
dealt with me like thieves of mercy:[5] but they knew what they did;
I am to do a good turn for them. Let the king have the letters I have
sent; and repair thou to me with as much speed as thou wouldst fly   20
death. I have words to speak in thine ear will make thee dumb; yet
are they much too light for the bore[6] of the matter. These good
fellows will bring thee where I am. Rosencrantz and Guildenstern
hold their course for England: of them I have much to tell thee.
Farewell.   25
        "He that thou knowest thine, HAMLET."
Come, I will make you way for these your letters;
And do 't the speedier, that you may direct me
To him from whom you brought them.
        [*Exeunt.*]

3. Coat of arms.   5. Merciful.
4. Read over.   6. Caliber, that is, importance.

SCENE 7

[SCENE: *Another room in the castle.*]

        [*Enter* KING *and* LAERTES.]

KING   Now must your conscience my acquittance seal,
And you must put me in your heart for friend,
Sith you have heard, and with a knowing ear,
That he which hath your noble father slain
Pursued my life.
LAERTES   It well appears: but tell me   5
Why you proceeded not against these feats,
So crimeful and so capital in nature,
As by your safety, wisdom, all things else,
You mainly[7] were stirred up.
KING   O, for two special reasons,
Which may to you perhaps seem much unsinewed,[8]   10
But yet to me they're strong. The queen his mother
Lives almost by his looks; and for myself—
My virtue or my plague, be it either which—
She's so conjunctive[9] to my life and soul,
That, as the star moves not but in his sphere,   15
I could not but by her. The other motive,
Why to a public count I might not go,
Is the great love the general gender[1] bear him;
Who, dipping all his faults in their affection,
Would, like the spring that turneth wood to stone,   20
Convert his gyves[2] to graces; so that my arrows,
Too slightly timber'd for so loud a wind,
Would have reverted to my bow again
And not where I had aim'd them.
LAERTES   And so have I a noble father lost;   25
A sister driven into desperate terms,
Whose worth, if praises may go back again,
Stood challenger on mount of[3] all the age
For her perfections: but my revenge will come.
KING   Break not your sleeps for that: you must not think   30
That we are made of stuff so flat and dull
That we can let our beard be shook with danger
And think it pastime. You shortly shall hear more:
I loved your father, and we love ourself;
And that, I hope, will teach you to imagine—   35
        [*Enter a* MESSENGER, *with letters.*]
How now! what news?
MESSENGER   Letters, my lord, from Hamlet:
This to your majesty; this to the queen.
KING   From Hamlet! who brought them?

---

7. Powerfully.
8. Weak.
9. Closely joined.

1. Common people. "Count": accounting, trial.
2. Leg irons (shames).
3. Above. "Go back": to what she was before her madness.

MESSENGER   Sailors, my lord, they say; I saw them not:
They were given me by Claudio; he received them   40
Of him that brought them.
KING   Laertes, you shall hear them.
Leave us.
        [Exit MESSENGER.]
[Reads.] "High and mighty, you shall know I am set naked on your
kingdom. To-morrow shall I beg leave to see your kingly eyes: when
I shall, first asking your pardon thereunto, recount the occasion of   45
my sudden and more strange return.   HAMLET.
What should this mean? Are all the rest come back?
Or is it some abuse, and no such thing?[4]
LAERTES   Know you the hand?
KING   'Tis Hamlet's character.[5] "Naked!"   50
And in a postscript here, he says "alone."
Can you advise me?
LAERTES   I'm lost in it, my lord. But let him come;
It warms the very sickness in my heart,
That I shall live and tell him to his teeth,   55
"Thus diddest thou."
KING   If it be so, Laertes,—
As how should it be so? how otherwise?—
Will you be ruled by me?
LAERTES   Aye, my lord;
So you will not o'errule me to a peace.
KING   To thine own peace. If he be now returned,   60
As checking[6] at his voyage, and that he means
No more to undertake it, I will work him
To an exploit now ripe in my device,
Under the which he shall not choose but fall:
And for his death no wind of blame shall breathe;   65
But even his mother shall uncharge the practice,[7]
call it accident.
LAERTES   My lord, I will be ruled;
The rather, if you could devise it so
That I might be the organ.[8]
KING   It falls right.
You have been talked of since your travel much,   70
And that in Hamlet's hearing, for a quality
Wherein, they say, you shine; your sum of parts[9]
Did not together pluck such envy from him,
As did that one, and that in my regard
Of the unworthiest siege.[1]
LAERTES   What part is that, my lord?   75
KING   A very riband in the cap of youth,

---

4. A delusion, not a reality.
5. Handwriting.
6. Changing the course of, refusing to
continue.

7. Not recognize it as a plot.
8. Instrument.
9. The sum of your gifts.
1. Seat, that is, rank.

Yet needful too; for youth no less becomes[2]
The light and careless livery that it wears
Than settled age his sables and his weeds,[3]
Importing health and graveness. Two months since   80
Here was a gentleman of Normandy:—
I've seen myself, and served against, the French,
And they can well on horseback: but this gallant
Had witchcraft in 't; he grew unto his seat,
And to such wondrous doing brought his horse   85
As had he been incorpsed and demi-natured[4]
With the brave beast: so far he topped my thought
That I, in forgery of shapes and tricks,[5]
Come short of what he did.

LAERTES   A Norman was 't?
KING   A Norman.   90
LAERTES   Upon my life, Lamord.
KING   The very same.
LAERTES   I know him well: he is the brooch[6] indeed
  And gem of all the nation.
KING   He made confession of you,
  And gave you such a masterly report,   95
  For art and exercise in your defense,[7]
  And for your rapier most especial,
  That he cried out, 'twould be a sight indeed
  If one could match you: the scrimers[8] of their nation,
  He swore, had neither motion, guard, nor eye,   100
  If you opposed them. Sir, this report of his
  Did Hamlet so envenom with his envy
  That he could nothing do but wish and beg
  Your sudden coming o'er, to play with him.
  Now, out of this—
LAERTES   What out of this, my lord?   105
KING   Laertes, was your father dear to you?
  Or are you like the painting of a sorrow,
  A face without a heart?
LAERTES   Why ask you this?
KING   Not that I think you did not love your father,
  But that I know love is begun by time,   110
  And that I see, in passages of proof,[9]
  Time qualifies[1] the spark and fire of it.
  There lives within the very flame of love
  A kind of wick or snuff[2] that will abate it;

2. Is the appropriate age for. "Riband": ribbon, ornament.
3. Furs (also meaning "blacks," dark colors) and robes.
4. Incorporated and split his nature in two.
5. In imagining methods and skills of horsemanship.

6. Ornament.
7. Report of your mastery in the theory and practice of fencing.
8. Fencers.
9. Instances that prove it.
1. Weakens.
2. Charred part of the wick.

And nothing is at a like goodness still, 115
For goodness, growing to a plurisy,[3]
Dies in his own too much: that we would do
We should do when we would; for this "would" changes
And hath abatements and delays as many
As there are tongues, are hands, are accidents, 120
And then this "should" is like a spendthrift sigh,
That hurts by easing.[4] But, to the quick o' the ulcer:
Hamlet comes back: what would you undertake,
To show yourself your father's son in deed
More than in words?

LAERTES   To cut his throat i' the church. 125

KING   No place indeed should murder sanctuarize;
Revenge should have no bounds. But, good Laertes,
Will you do this, keep close within your chamber.
Hamlet returned shall know you are come home:
We'll put on[5] those shall praise your excellence 130
And set a double varnish on the fame
The Frenchman gave you; bring you in fine together
And wager on your heads: he, being remiss,[6]
Most generous and free from all contriving,
Will not peruse[7] the foils, so that with ease, 135
Or with a little shuffling, you may choose
A sword unbated, and in a pass of practice[8]
Requite him for your father.

LAERTES   I will do 't;
And for that purpose I'll anoint my sword.
I bought an unction of a mountebank,[9] 140
So mortal that but dip a knife in it,
Where it draws blood no cataplasm so rare,
Collected from all simples[1] that have virtue
Under the moon, can save the thing from death
That is but scratched withal: I'll touch my point 145
With this contagion, that, if I gall[2] him slightly,
It may be death.

KING   Let's further think of this;
Weigh what convenience both of time and means
May fit us to our shape: if this should fail,
And that our drift look through[3] our bad performance, 150
'Twere better not assayed: therefore this project
Should have a back or second, that might hold
If this did blast in proof.[4] Soft! let me see:

---

3. Excess. "Still": constantly.
4. A sigh that gives relief but is harmful
(according to an old notion that it draws
blood from the heart).
5. Instigate.
6. Careless. "In fine": finally.
7. Examine closely.
8. Treacherous thrust. "Unbated": not blunted

(as a rapier for exercise ordinarily would be).
9. Ointment of a peddler of quack medicines.
1. Healing herbs. "Cataplasm": plaster.
2. Scratch.
3. Our design should show through. "Shape":
plan.
4. Burst (like a new firearm) once it is put to
the test.

We'll make a solemn wager on your cunnings:
I ha 't: 155
When in your motion you are hot and dry—
As make your bouts more violent to that end—
And that he calls for drink, I'll have prepared him
A chalice for the nonce;[5] whereon but sipping,
If he by chance escape your venomed stuck,[6]   160
Our purpose may hold there. But stay, what noise?
        [*Enter* QUEEN.]
How now, sweet queen!
QUEEN   One woe doth tread upon another's heel,
    So fast they follow: your sister's drowned, Laertes.
LAERTES   Drowned! O, where?   165
QUEEN   There is a willow grows aslant[7] a brook,
    That shows his hoar leaves in the glassy stream;
    There with fantastic garlands did she come
    Of crow-flowers, nettles, daisies, and long purples,
    That liberal shepherds give a grosser name,   170
    But our cold maids do dead men's fingers call them:
    There, on the pendent boughs her coronet weeds
    Clambering to hang, an envious sliver[8] broke;
    When down her weedy trophies and herself
    Fell in the weeping brook. Her clothes spread wide,   175
    And mermaid-like a while they bore her up:
    Which time she chanted snatches of old tunes,
    As one incapable of[9] her own distress,
    Or like a creature native and indued[1]
    Unto that element: but long it could not be   180
    Till that her garments, heavy with their drink,
    Pulled the poor wretch from her melodious lay
    To muddy death.
LAERTES   Alas, then she is drowned!
QUEEN   Drowned, drowned.
LAERTES   Too much of water hast thou, poor Ophelia,   185
    And therefore I forbid my tears: but yet
    It is our trick;[2] nature her custom holds,
    Let shame say what it will: when these are gone,
    The woman[3] will be out. Adieu, my lord:
    I have a speech of fire that fain would blaze,   190
    But that this folly douts[4] it.
        [*Exit.*]
KING   Let's follow, Gertrude:
    How much I had to do to calm his rage!
    Now fear I this will give it start again;

5. For that particular occasion.
6. Thrust.
7. Across.
8. Malicious bough.
9. Insensitive to.

1. Adapted, in harmony with.
2. Peculiar trait.
3. The softer qualities, the woman in me.
4. Extinguishes.

Therefore let's follow.
    [*Exeunt.*]

Act 5

SCENE I

[SCENE: *A churchyard.*]

    [*Enter two* CLOWNS, *with spades, etc.*]

FIRST CLOWN   Is she to be buried in Christian burial that willfully seeks her own salvation?

SECOND CLOWN   I tell thee she is; and therefore make her grave straight: the crowner[5] hath sat on her, and finds it Christian burial.

FIRST CLOWN   How can that be, unless she drowned herself in her own defense?   5

SECOND CLOWN   Why, 'tis found so.

FIRST CLOWN   It must be "se offendendo";[6] it cannot be else. For here lies the point: if I drown myself wittingly, it argues an act: and an act hath three branches; it is, to act, to do, to perform: argal,[7] she   10 drowned herself wittingly.

SECOND CLOWN   Nay, but hear you, goodman delver.

FIRST CLOWN   Give me leave. Here lies the water; good: here stands the man; good: if the man go to this water and drown himself, it is, will he, nill he,[8] he goes; mark you that; but if the water come to   15 him and drown him, he drowns not himself: argal, he that is not guilty of his own death shortens not his own life.

SECOND CLOWN   But is this law?

FIRST CLOWN   Aye, marry, is 't; crowner's quest[9] law.

SECOND CLOWN   Will you ha' the truth on 't? If this had not been a   20 gentlewoman, she should have been buried out o' Christian burial.

FIRST CLOWN   Why, there thou say'st: and the more pity that great folk should have countenance[1] in this world to drown or hang themselves, more than their even[2] Christian. Come, my spade. There is no ancient gentlemen but gardeners, ditchers and gravemakers: they hold   25 up Adam's profession.

SECOND CLOWN   Was he a gentleman?

FIRST CLOWN   A' was the first that ever bore arms.

SECOND CLOWN   Why, he had none.

FIRST CLOWN   What, art a heathen? How dost thou understand the   30 Scripture? The Scripture says Adam digged: could he dig without arms? I'll put another question to thee: if thou answerest me not to the purpose, confess thyself—

SECOND CLOWN   Go to.

FIRST CLOWN   What is he that builds stronger than either the mason,   35 the shipwright, or the carpenter?

---

5. Coroner. "Straight": right away.
6. The Clown's blunder for *se defendendo*: "in self-defense" (Latin).
7. Blunder for *ergo*: "therefore" (Latin).

8. Willy-nilly.
9. Inquest.
1. Sanction.
2. Fellow.

SECOND CLOWN   The gallows-maker; for that frame outlives a thousand
tenants.

FIRST CLOWN   I like thy wit well, in good faith: the gallows does well;
but how does it well? it does well to those that do ill: now, thou dost
ill to say the gallows is built stronger than the church: argal, the
gallows may do well to thee. To 't again, come.

SECOND CLOWN   "Who builds stronger than a mason, a shipwright, or
a carpenter?"

FIRST CLOWN   Aye, tell me that, and unyoke.[3]

SECOND CLOWN   Marry, now I can tell.

FIRST CLOWN   To 't.

SECOND CLOWN   Mass, I cannot tell.

[*Enter* HAMLET *and* HORATIO, *afar off.*]

FIRST CLOWN   Cudgel thy brains no more about it, for your dull ass
will not mend his pace with beating, and when you are asked this
question next, say "a grave-maker": the houses that he makes last till
doomsday. Go, get thee to Yaughan; fetch me a stoup[4] of liquor.

[*Exit* SECOND CLOWN.—FIRST CLOWN *digs and sings.*]

In youth, when I did love, did love,
    Methought it was very sweet,
To contract, O, the time, for-a my behove,
    O, methought, there-a was nothing-a meet.[5]

HAMLET   Has this fellow no feeling of his business that he sings at
grave-making?

HORATIO   Custom hath made it in him a property of easiness.[6]

HAMLET   'Tis e'en so: the hand of little employment hath the daintier[7]
sense.

FIRST CLOWN [*Sings.*]   But age, with his stealing steps,
            Hath clowed me in his clutch,
        And hath shipped me intil[8] the land,
            As if I had never been such.

[*Throws up a skull.*]

HAMLET   That skull had a tongue in it, and could sing once: how the
knave jowls it to the ground, as if it were Cain's jaw-bone, that did
the first murder! It might be the pate of a politician,[9] which this ass
now o'er-reaches;[1] one that would circumvent God, might it not?

HORATIO   It might, my lord.

HAMLET   Or of a courtier, which could say, "Good morrow, sweet lord!
How dost thou, sweet lord?" This might be my lord such-a-one, that
praised my lord such-a-one's horse, when he meant to beg it; might
it not?

HORATIO   Aye, my lord.

HAMLET   Why, e'en so: and now my Lady Worm's; chapless, and
knocked about the mazzard[2] with a sexton's spade: here's fine revolution,

3. Call it a day.
4. Mug. "Yaughan": apparently a tavern keeper's name.
5. Fitting. "Contract": shorten. "Behove": profit.
6. Has made it a matter of indifference to him.
7. Finer sensitivity. "Of little employment":
that does little labor.
8. Into.
9. In a pejorative sense. "Jowls": knocks. "First murder": possibly an allusion to the legend that Cain slew Abel with an ass's jawbone.
1. Outwits.
2. Pate. "Chapless": the lower jawbone missing.

an we had the trick to see 't. Did these bones cost no more
the breeding, but to play at loggats[3] with 'em? mine ache to think
on 't.   80

FIRST CLOWN [Sings.]   A pick-axe, and a spade, a spade,
                    For a shrouding sheet:
             O, a pit of clay for to be made
                 For such a guest is meet.
   [Throws up another skull.]

HAMLET   There's another: why may not that be the skull of a lawyer?   85
Where be his quiddities now, his quillets, his cases, his tenures,[4] and
his tricks? why does he suffer this rude knave now to knock him
about the sconce with a dirty shovel, and will not tell him of his
action of battery?[5] Hum! This fellow might be in 's time a great buyer
of land, with his statutes, his recognizances,[6] his fines, his double   90
vouchers, his recoveries: is this the fine[7] of his fines and the recovery
of his recoveries, to have his fine pate full of fine dirt? will his vouchers
vouch him no more of his purchases, and double ones too, than the
length and breadth of a pair of indentures? The very conveyances[8] of
his lands will hardly lie in this box; and must the inheritor himself   95
have no more, ha?

HORATIO   Not a jot more, my lord.

HAMLET   Is not parchment made of sheep-skins?

HORATIO   Aye, my lord, and of calf-skins too.

HAMLET   They are sheep and calves which seek out assurance[9] in that.   100
I will speak to this fellow. Whose grave's this, sirrah?

FIRST CLOWN   Mine, sir.
   [Sings.]   O, a pit of clay for to be made
             For such a guest is meet.

HAMLET   I think it be thine indeed, for thou liest in 't.   105

FIRST CLOWN   You lie out on 't, sir, and therefore 'tis not yours: for my
part, I do not lie in 't, and yet it is mine.

HAMLET   Thou dost lie in 't, to be in 't and say it is thine: 'tis for the dead,
not for the quick;[1] therefore thou liest.

FIRST CLOWN   'Tis a quick lie, sir; 'twill away again, from me to you.   110

HAMLET   What man dost thou dig it for?

FIRST CLOWN   For no man, sir.

HAMLET   What woman then?

FIRST CLOWN   For none neither.

HAMLET   Who is to be buried in 't?   115

FIRST CLOWN   One that was a woman, sir; but, rest her soul, she's dead.

HAMLET   How absolute the knave is! we must speak by the card,[2] or
equivocation will undo us. By the Lord, Horatio, these three years I

3. A game resembling bowls. "Trick": faculty.
4. Real estate holdings. "Quiddities": subtle
definitions. "Quillets": quibbles.
5. Assault. "Sconce": head.
6. Varieties of bonds. This passage contains
legal terms relating to the transfer of estates.
7. End. Hamlet is punning on the legal and
nonlegal meanings of the word.
8. Deeds. "Indentures": contracts drawn in

duplicate on the same piece of parchment; the
two copies were separated by an indented line.
9. Security; another pun, because the word is
also a legal term.
1. Living.
2. By the chart, that is, exactness. "Absolute":
positive.

have taken note of it; the age is grown so picked[3] that the toe of the peasant comes so near the heel of the courtier, he galls his kibe.[4] How long hast thou been a grave-maker?

FIRST CLOWN   Of all the days i' the year, I came to 't that day that our last King Hamlet o'ercame Fortinbras.

HAMLET   How long is that since?

FIRST CLOWN   Cannot you tell that? every fool can tell that: it was that very day that young Hamlet was born: he that is mad, and sent into England.

HAMLET   Aye, marry, why was he sent into England?

FIRST CLOWN   Why, because a' was mad; a' shall recover his wits there: or, if a' do not, 'tis no great matter there.

HAMLET   Why?

FIRST CLOWN   'Twill not be seen in him there; there the men are as mad as he.

HAMLET   How came he mad?

FIRST CLOWN   Very strangely, they say.

HAMLET   How "strangely?"

FIRST CLOWN   Faith, e'en with losing his wits.

HAMLET   Upon what ground?

FIRST CLOWN   Why, here in Denmark: I have been sexton here, man and boy, thirty years.

HAMLET   How long will a man lie i' the earth ere he rot?

FIRST CLOWN   I' faith, if a' be not rotten before a' die—as we have many pocky corses now-a-days, that will scarce hold the laying in[5]— a' will last you some eight year or nine year: a tanner will last you nine year.

HAMLET   Why he more than another?

FIRST CLOWN   Why, sir, his hide is so tanned with his trade that a' will keep out water a great while; and your water is a sore decayer of your whoreson dead body. Here's a skull now: this skull has lain in the earth three and twenty years.

HAMLET   Whose was it?

FIRST CLOWN   A whoreson mad fellow's it was: whose do you think it was?

HAMLET   Nay, I know not.

FIRST CLOWN   A pestilence on him for a mad rogue! a' poured a flagon of Rhenish on my head once. This same skull, sir, was Yorick's skull, the king's jester.

HAMLET   This?

FIRST CLOWN   E'en that.

HAMLET   Let me see. [*Takes the skull.*] Alas, poor Yorick! I knew him, Horatio: a fellow of infinite jest, of most excellent fancy: he hath borne me on his back a thousand times; and now how abhorred in my imagination it is! my gorge rises at it. Here hung those lips that I have kissed I know not how oft. Where be your gibes now? your gambols? your songs? your flashes of merriment, that were wont to

120

125

130

135

140

145

150

155

160

165

---

3. Choice, fastidious.
4. Hurts the chilblain on the courtier's heel.

5. Hold together till they are buried. "Pocky": with marks of disease (from "pox").

set the table on a roar? Not one now, to mock your own grinning?
quite chop-fallen?[6] Now get you to my lady's chamber, and tell her,
let her paint an inch thick, to this favor[7] she must come; make her
laugh at that. Prithee, Horatio, tell me one thing.

HORATIO   What's that, my lord?   170
HAMLET   Dost thou think Alexander looked o' this fashion i' the earth?
HORATIO   E'en so.
HAMLET   And smelt so? pah!
        [*Puts down the skull.*]
HORATIO   E'en so, my lord.
HAMLET   To what base uses we may return, Horatio! Why may not imagi-   175
nation trace the noble dust of Alexander, till he find it stopping a bung-
hole?
HORATIO   'Twere to consider too curiously, to consider so.
HAMLET   No, faith, not a jot; but to follow him thither with modesty
enough[8] and likelihood to lead it: as thus: Alexander died, Alexander   180
was buried, Alexander returneth into dust; the dust is earth; of earth
we make loam; and why of that loam, whereto he was converted, might
they not stop a beer-barrel?
        Imperious Caesar, dead and turned to clay,
        Might stop a hole to keep the wind away: 185
        O, that that earth, which kept the world in awe,
        Should patch a wall to expel the winter's flaw!
    But soft! but soft! aside: here comes the king.
        [*Enter* PRIESTS *etc., in procession; the Corpse of* OPHELIA, LAERTES
        and MOURNERS *following;* KING, QUEEN, *their trains, etc.*]
    The queen, the courtiers: who is this they follow?
    And with such maimèd rites?[9] This doth betoken   190
    The corse they follow did with desperate hand
    Fordo its own life: 'twas of some estate.[1]
    Couch we awhile, and mark.
        [*Retiring with* HORATIO.]
LAERTES   What ceremony else?
HAMLET   That is Laertes, a very noble youth: mark.   195
LAERTES   What ceremony else?
FIRST PRIEST   Her obsequies have been as far enlarged
    As we have warranty: her death was doubtful;
    And, but that great command o'ersways the order[2]
    She should in ground unsanctified have lodged   200
    Till the last trumpet; for[3] charitable prayers,
    Shards, flints and pebbles should be thrown on her:
    Yet here she is allowed her virgin crants,
    Her maiden strewments and the bringing home[4]
    Of bell and burial.   205

6. The lower jaw fallen down, hence dejected.
7. Appearance.
8. Without exaggeration.
9. Incomplete, mutilated ritual.
1. Rank. "Fordo": destroy.
2. The king's command prevails against ordi-

nary rules. "Doubtful": of uncertain cause
(that is, accident or suicide).
3. Instead of.
4. Laying to rest. "Crants": garlands. "Strew-
ments": strews the grave with flowers.

LAERTES   Must there no more be done?

FIRST PRIEST   No more be done:
We should profane the service of the dead
To sing a requiem and such rest to her
As to peace-parted souls.

LAERTES   Lay her i' the earth:
And from her fair and unpolluted flesh   210
May violets spring! I tell thee, churlish priest,
A ministering angel shall my sister be,
When thou liest howling.

HAMLET   What, the fair Ophelia!

QUEEN [*Scattering flowers.*]   Sweets to the sweet: farewell!
I hoped thou shouldst have been my Hamlet's wife;   215
I thought thy bride-bed to have decked, sweet maid,
And not have strewed thy grave.

LAERTES   O, treble woe
Fall ten times treble on that cursed head
Whose wicked deed thy most ingenious sense
Deprived thee of! Hold off the earth a while,   220
Till I have caught her once more in mine arms.
        [*Leaps into the grave.*]
Now pile your dust upon the quick and dead,
Till of this flat a mountain you have made
To o'ertop old Pelion[5] or the skyish head
Of blue Olympus.

HAMLET [*Advancing.*]   What is he whose grief   225
Bears such an emphasis? whose phrase of sorrow
Conjures the wandering stars and makes them stand
Like wonder-wounded hearers? This is I,
Hamlet the Dane.
        [*Leaps into the grave.*]

LAERTES   The devil take thy soul!
        [*Grappling with him.*]

HAMLET   Thou pray'st not well.   230
I prithee, take thy fingers from my throat;
For, though I am not splenitive[6] and rash,
Yet have I in me something dangerous,
Which let thy wisdom fear. Hold off thy hand.

KING   Pluck them asunder.

QUEEN   Hamlet, Hamlet!

ALL   Gentlemen,—   235

HORATIO   Good my lord, be quiet.
        [*The* ATTENDANTS *part them, and they come out of the grave.*]

HAMLET   Why, I will fight with him upon this theme
Until my eyelids will no longer wag.

QUEEN   O my son, what theme?

5. The mountain on which the Aloadae, two   Olympus.
rebellious giants in Greek mythology, piled   6. Easily moved to anger.
up Mount Ossa in their attempt to reach

HAMLET   I loved Ophelia: forty thousand brothers   240
    Could not, with all their quantity of love,
    Make up my sum. What wilt thou do for her?
KING   O, he is mad, Laertes.
QUEEN   For love of God, forbear him.
HAMLET   'Swounds, show me what thou 'lt do: 245
    Woo't weep? woo't fight? woo't fast? woo't tear thyself?
    Woo't drink up eisel?[7] eat a crocodile?
    I'll do't. Dost thou come here to whine?
    To outface me with leaping in her grave?
    Be buried quick with her, and so will I: 250
    And, if thou prate of mountains, let them throw
    Millions of acres on us, till our ground,
    Singeing his pate against the burning zone,
    Make Ossa like a wart! Nay, an thou 'lt mouth,
    I'll rant as well as thou.
QUEEN   This is mere madness: 255
    And thus a while the fit will work on him;
    Anon, as patient as the female dove
    When that her golden couplets are disclosed,[8]
    His silence will sit drooping.
HAMLET   Hear you, sir;
    What is the reason that you use me thus?   260
    I loved you ever: but it is no matter;
    Let Hercules himself do what he may,
    The cat will mew, and dog will have his day.
        [*Exit.*]
KING   I pray thee, good Horatio, wait upon him.
        [*Exit* HORATIO.]
    [*To* LAERTES.] Strengthen your patience in our last night's speech;   265
    We'll put the matter to the present push.[9]
    Good Gertrude, set some watch over your son.
    This grave shall have a living monument:
    An hour of quiet shortly shall we see;
    Till then, in patience our proceeding be.   270
        [*Exeunt.*]

SCENE 2

[SCENE: *A hall in the castle.*]

    [*Enter* HAMLET *and* HORATIO.]
HAMLET   So much for this, sir: now shall you see the other;
    You do remember all the circumstance?
HORATIO   Remember it, my lord?

---

7. Vinegar (the bitter drink given to Christ).   8. Twins are hatched.
"Woo't": wilt thou.   9. We'll push the matter on immediately.

HAMLET   Sir, in my heart there was a kind of fighting,
   That would not let me sleep: methought I lay   5
   Worse than the mutines in the bilboes.[1] Rashly,
   And praised be rashness for it, let us know,
   Our indiscretion sometime serves us well
   When our deep plots do pall;[2] and that should learn us
   There's a divinity that shapes our ends,   10
   Rough-hew them how we will.
HORATIO   That is most certain.
HAMLET   Up from my cabin,
   My sea-gown scarfed about me, in the dark
   Groped I to find out them; had my desire,
   Fingered their packet, and in fine withdrew   15
   To mine own room again; making so bold,
   My fears forgetting manners, to unseal
   Their grand commission; where I found, Horatio,—
   O royal knavery!—an exact command,
   Larded with many several sorts of reasons,   20
   Importing[3] Denmark's health and England's too,
   With, ho! such bugs and goblins in my life,
   That, on the supervise, no leisure bated,[4]
   No, not to stay the grinding of the axe,
   My head should be struck off.
HORATIO   Is't possible?   25
HAMLET   Here's the commission: read it at more leisure.
   But wilt thou hear now how I did proceed?
HORATIO   I beseech you.
HAMLET   Being thus be-netted round with villainies,—
   Ere I could make a prologue to my brains,   30
   They had begun the play,—I sat me down;
   Devised a new commission; wrote it fair:
   I once did hold it, as our statists[5] do,
   A baseness to write fair, and labored much
   How to forget that learning; but, sir, now   35
   It did me yeoman's service:[6] wilt thou know
   The effect of what I wrote?
HORATIO   Aye, good my lord.
HAMLET   An earnest conjuration from the king,
   As England was his faithful tributary,
   As love between them like the palm might flourish,
   As peace should still her wheaten garland wear   40
   And stand a comma[7] 'tween their amities,

---

1. Mutineers in iron fetters.
2. Become useless.
3. Concerning.
4. As soon as the message was read, with no time subtracted for leisure. "Bugs": imaginary

horrors to be expected if I lived.
5. Statesmen.
6. Excellent service.
7. Connecting element.

And many such-like "As"es of great charge,[8]
That, on the view and knowing of these contents,
Without debatement further, more or less,   45
He should the bearers put to sudden death,
Not shriving-time[9] allowed.
HORATIO   How was this sealed?
HAMLET   Why, even in that was heaven ordinant.[1]
I had my father's signet in my purse,
Which was the model of that Danish seal;   50
Folded the writ up in the form of the other;
Subscribed it; gave 't the impression;[2] placed it safely,
The changeling never known. Now, the next day
Was our sea-fight; and what to this was sequent
Thou know'st already.   55
HORATIO   So Guildenstern and Rosencrantz go to 't.
HAMLET   Why, man, they did make love to this employment;
They are not near my conscience; their defeat
Does by their own insinuation[3] grow:
'Tis dangerous when the baser nature comes   60
Between the pass and fell[4]-incensèd points
Of mighty opposites.
HORATIO   Why, what a king is this!
HAMLET   Does it not, think'st thee, stand me now upon[5]—
He that hath killed my king, and whored my mother;
Popped in between the election and my hopes;   65
Thrown out his angle for my proper life,[6]
And with such cozenage—is't not perfect conscience,
To quit[7] him with this arm? and is't not to be damned,
To let this canker of our nature come
In further evil?   70
HORATIO   It must be shortly known to him from England
What is the issue of the business there.
HAMLET   It will be short: the interim is mine;
And a man's life's no more than to say "One."
But I am very sorry, good Horatio,   75
That to Laertes I forgot myself;
For, by the image of my cause, I see
The portraiture of his: I'll court his favors:
But, sure, the bravery[8] of his grief did put me

8. "'As'es": a pun on *as* and *ass*, which extends to "of great charge," signifying both "moral weight" and "ass's burden."
9. Time for confession and absolution.
1. Ordaining.
2. Of the seal.
3. Meddling. "Defeat": destruction.

4. Fiercely. "Baser": lower in rank than the king and Prince Hamlet. "Pass": thrust.
5. Is it not my duty now?
6. An angling line for my own life.
7. Pay back.
8. Ostentation, bravado.

Into a towering passion.

HORATIO   Peace! who comes here?   80

    [*Enter* OSRIC.]

OSRIC   Your lordship is right welcome back to Denmark.

HAMLET   I humbly thank you, sir. Dost know this waterfly?

HORATIO   No, my good lord.

HAMLET   Thy state is the more gracious, for 'tis a vice to know him. He
hath much land, and fertile: let a beast be lord of beasts, and his crib   85
shall stand at the king's mess: 'tis a chough,[9] but, as I say, spacious in
the possession of dirt.

OSRIC   Sweet lord, if your lordship were at leisure, I should impart a thing
to you from his majesty.

HAMLET   I will receive it, sir, with all diligence of spirit. Put your bonnet   90
to his right use; 'tis for the head.

OSRIC   I thank your lordship, it is very hot.

HAMLET   No, believe me, 'tis very cold; the wind is northerly.

OSRIC   It is indifferent[1] cold, my lord, indeed.

HAMLET   But yet methinks it is very sultry and hot, or my complexion—   95

OSRIC   Exceedingly, my lord; it is very sultry, as 'twere,—I cannot tell
how. But, my lord, his majesty bade me signify to you that he has laid
a great wager on your head: sir, this is the matter—

HAMLET   I beseech you, remember—

    [HAMLET *moves him to put on his hat.*]

OSRIC   Nay, good my lord; for mine ease, in good faith. Sir, here is newly   100
come to court Laertes; believe me, an absolute gentleman, full of most
excellent differences, of very soft society and great showing:[2] indeed,
to speak feelingly of him, he is the card or calendar of gentry,[3] for
you shall find in him the continent of what part[4] a gentleman would
see.   105

HAMLET   Sir, his definement suffers no perdition in you; though, I
know, to divide him inventorially would dizzy the arithmetic[5] of memory, and yet but yaw neither, in respect of his quick sail.[6] But in the
verity of extolment, I take him to be a soul of great article, and his
infusion[7] of such dearth and rareness, as, to make true diction of him,   110
his semblable is his mirror, and who else would trace him, his umbrage,[8]
nothing more.

OSRIC   Your lordship speaks most infallibly of him.

HAMLET   The concernancy, sir? why do we wrap the gentleman[9] in our
more rawer breath?   115

---

9. Jackdaw. "Mess": table.
1. Fairly.
2. Agreeable company, handsome in appearance. "Differences": distinctions.
3. Chart and model of gentlemanly manners.
4. Whatever quality. "Continent": container.
5. Arithmetical power. "Definement": definition. "Perdition": loss. "Inventorially": make
an inventory of his virtues.

6. And yet would only be able to steer unsteadily
(unable to catch up with the *sail* of Laertes's
virtues).
7. The virtues infused into him. "Verify of
extolments": to prize Laertes truthfully. "Article": importance.
8. Keep pace with him, his shadow.
9. Laertes. "Concernancy": meaning.

OSRIC Sir?

HORATIO Is 't not possible to understand in another tongue?[1] You will do 't, sir, really.

HAMLET What imports the nomination of this gentleman?

OSRIC Of Laertes?   120

HORATIO His purse is empty already; all's golden words are spent.

HAMLET Of him, sir.

OSRIC I know you are not ignorant—

HAMLET I would you did, sir; yet, in faith, if you did, it would not much approve me.[2] Well, sir?   125

OSRIC You are not ignorant of what excellence Laertes is—

HAMLET I dare not confess that, lest I should compare with him in excellence; but, to know a man well, were to know himself.[3]

OSRIC I mean, sir, for his weapon; but in the imputation laid on him by them, in his meed he's unfellowed.[4]   130

HAMLET What's his weapon?

OSRIC Rapier and dagger.

HAMLET That's two of his weapons: but, well.

OSRIC The king, sir, hath wagered with him six Barbary horses: against the which he has imponed, as I take it, six French rapiers and poniards,   135
with their assigns,[5] as girdle, hanger, and so: three of the carriages, in faith, are very dear to fancy, very responsive[6] to the hilts, most delicate carriages, and of very liberal conceit.[7]

HAMLET What call you the carriages?

HORATIO I knew you must be edified by the margent[8] ere you had   140
done.

OSRIC The carriages, sir, are the hangers.

HAMLET The phrase would be more germane to the matter if we could carry a cannon by our sides:[9] I would it might be hangers till then. But, on: six Barbary horses against six French swords, their assigns,   145
and three liberal-conceited carriages; that's the French bet against the Danish. Why is this "imponed," as you call it?

OSRIC The king, sir, hath laid, sir, that in a dozen passes between yourself and him, he shall not exceed you three hits: he hath laid on twelve for nine; and it would come to immediate trial, if your lordship   150
would vouchsafe the answer.[1]

HAMLET How if I answer "no"?

---

1. In a less affected jargon or in the same jargon when spoken by another (that is, Hamlet's) tongue.
2. Be to my credit.
3. To know others one has to know oneself.
4. In the reputation given him by his weapons, his merit is unparalleled.
5. Appendages. "Imponed": wagered.
6. Closely matched. "Carriages": ornamented straps by which the rapiers hung from the belt. "Very dear to fancy": agreeable to the taste.
7. Elegant design.
8. Instructed by the marginal note.
9. Hamlet is playfully criticizing Osric's affected application of the term *carriage*, more properly used to mean "gun carriage."
1. The terms of this wager have never been satisfactorily clarified.

OSRIC   I mean, my lord, the opposition of your person in trial.

HAMLET   Sir, I will walk here in the hall: if it please his majesty, it is the breathing time[2] of day with me; let the foils be brought, the gentleman willing, and the king hold his purpose, I will win for him an I can; if not, I will gain nothing but my shame and the odd hits.   155

OSRIC   Shall I redeliver you e'en so?[3]

HAMLET   To this effect, sir, after what flourish your nature will.

OSRIC   I commend my duty to your lordship.   160

HAMLET   Yours, yours. [*Exit* OSRIC] He does well to commend it himself; there are no tongues else for's turn.

HORATIO   This lapwing[4] runs away with the shell on his head.

HAMLET   He did comply with his dug before he sucked it. Thus has he— and many more of the same breed that I know the drossy[5] age dotes   165 on—only got the tune of the time and outward habit of encounter; a kind of yesty[6] collection, which carries them through and through the most fond and winnowed opinions;[7] and do but blow them to their trial, the bubbles are out.

[*Enter a* LORD.]

LORD   My lord, his majesty commended him[8] to you by young Osric,   170 who brings back to him, that you attend him in the hall: he sends to know if your pleasure hold to play with Laertes, or that you will take longer time.

HAMLET   I am constant to my purposes; they follow the king's pleasure: if his fitness speaks, mine is ready; now or whensoever, provided I be   175 so able as now.

LORD   The king and queen and all are coming down.

HAMLET   In happy time.

LORD   The queen desires you to use some gentle entertainment[9] to Laertes before you fall to play.   180

HAMLET   She well instructs me.

[*Exit* LORD.]

HORATIO   You will lose this wager, my lord.

HAMLET   I do not think so; since he went into France, I have been in continual practice; I shall win at the odds. But thou wouldst not think how ill all's here about my heart: but it is no matter.   185

HORATIO   Nay, good my lord,—

HAMLET   It is but foolery; but it is such a kind of gaingiving[1] as would perhaps trouble a woman.

HORATIO   If your mind dislike anything, obey it. I will forestall their repair[2] hither, and say you are not fit.   190

2. Time for exercise.
3. Is that the reply you want me to carry back?
4. A bird supposedly able to run as soon as it is out of its shell.
5. Degenerate. "Comply": use ceremony.
6. Frothy.

7. Makes them pass the test of the most refined judgment.
8. Sent his regards.
9. Kind word of greeting.
1. Misgiving.
2. Coming.

HAMLET   Not a whit; we defy augury: there is special providence in the
    fall of a sparrow. If it be now, 'tis not to come; if it be not to come, it
    will be now; if it be not now, yet it will come: the readiness is all; since
    no man has aught of what he leaves, what is't to leave betimes?[3]
    Let be.   195

[*Enter* KING, QUEEN, LAERTES, *and* LORDS, OSRIC *and other* ATTENDANTS
    with foils and gauntlets; a table and flagons of wine on it.]
KING   Come, Hamlet, come, and take this hand from me.

[*The* KING *puts* LAERTES's *hand into* HAMLET's.]
HAMLET   Give me your pardon, sir: I've done you wrong;
    But pardon't, as you are a gentleman.
    This presence[4] knows,
    And you must needs have heard, how I am punished   200
    With sore distraction. What I have done,
    That might your nature, honor and exception[5]
    Roughly awake, I here proclaim was madness.
    Was't Hamlet wronged Laertes? Never Hamlet:
    If Hamlet from himself be ta'en away,   205
    And when he's not himself does wrong Laertes,
    Then Hamlet does it not, Hamlet denies it.
    Who does it then? His madness: if't be so,
    Hamlet is of the faction that is wronged;
    His madness is poor Hamlet's enemy.   210
    Sir, in this audience,
    Let my disclaiming from a purposed evil
    Free me so far in your most generous thoughts,
    That I have shot mine arrow o'er the house,
    And hurt my brother.
LAERTES   I am satisfied in nature,   215
    Whose motive, in this case, should stir me most
    To my revenge: but in my terms of honor[6]
    I stand aloof, and will no reconcilement,
    Till by some elder masters of known honor
    I have a voice and precedent of peace,   220
    To keep my name ungored.[7] But till that time
    I do receive your offered love like love
    And will not wrong it.
HAMLET   I embrace it freely,
    And will this brother's wager frankly play.
    Give us the foils. Come on.
LAERTES   Come, one for me.   225

---

3. What is wrong with dying early (leaving
betimes), because man knows nothing of life
(*what he leaves*)?
4. Audience.
5. Objection.

6. "Nature" is Laertes' natural feeling toward
his father. "Honor" is the code of honor with its
conventional rules.
7. Unwounded. "A voice and": an opinion
based on.

HAMLET   I'll be your foil,[8] Laertes: in mine ignorance
  Your skill shall, like a star i' the darkest night,
  Stick fiery off[9] indeed.
LAERTES   You mock me, sir.
HAMLET   No, by this hand.
KING   Give them the foils, young Osric. Cousin Hamlet,   230
  You know the wager?
HAMLET   Very well, my lord;
  Your grace has laid the odds o' the weaker side.
KING   I do not fear it; I have seen you both:
  But since he is bettered, we have therefore odds.
LAERTES   This is too heavy; let me see another.   235
HAMLET   This likes me well. These foils have all a length?
      [*They prepare to play.*]
OSRIC   Aye, my good lord.
KING   Set me the stoups[1] of wine upon that table.
  If Hamlet give the first or second hit,
  Or quit in answer of the third exchange,[2]   240
  Let all the battlements their ordnance fire;
  The king shall drink to Hamlet's better breath;
  And in the cup an union[3] shall he throw,
  Richer than that which four successive kings
  In Denmark's crown have worn. Give me the cups;   245
  And let the kettle[4] to the trumpet speak,
  The trumpet to the cannoneer without,
  The cannons to the heavens, the heaven to earth,
  "Now the king drinks to Hamlet." Come, begin;
  And you, the judges, bear a wary eye.   250
HAMLET   Come on, sir.
LAERTES   Come, my lord.
      [*They play.*]
HAMLET   One.
LAERTES   No.
HAMLET   Judgment.
OSRIC   A hit, a very palpable hit.
LAERTES   Well; again.
KING   Stay; give me drink. Hamlet, this pearl is thine;
  Here's to thy health.
      [*Trumpets sound, and cannon shot off within.*]
                          Give him the cup.
HAMLET   I'll play this bout first; set it by awhile.   255
  Come. [*They play.*] Another hit; what say you?
LAERTES   A touch, a touch, I do confess.

8. A pun, because "foil" means both "rapier"
and "a thing that sets off another to advantage" (as gold leaf under a jewel).
9. Stand out brilliantly.
1. Cups.

2. Requite, or repay (by scoring a hit) on the
third bout.
3. A large pearl.
4. Kettledrum.

KING Our son shall win.

QUEEN   He's fat and scant of breath.
  Here, Hamlet, take my napkin,[5] rub thy brows:
  The queen carouses to thy fortune, Hamlet.   260

HAMLET Good madam!

KING   Gertrude, do not drink.

QUEEN I will, my lord; I pray you, pardon me.

KING [*Aside*.] It is the poisoned cup; it is too late.

QUEEN Come, let me wipe thy face.

LAERTES My lord, I'll hit him now.

KING   I do not think't.   265

LAERTES [*Aside*.] And yet it is almost against my conscience.

HAMLET Come, for the third, Laertes: you but dally;
  I pray you, pass with your best violence;
  I am afeard you make a wanton[6] of me.

LAERTES Say you so? come on.
    [*They play.*]

OSRIC   Nothing, neither way.   270

LAERTES Have at you now!
    [LAERTES *wounds* HAMLET; *then, in scuffling, they change rapiers, and* HAMLET
    wounds LAERTES.]

KING   Part them; they are incensed.

HAMLET Nay, come, again.
    [*The* QUEEN *falls.*]

OSRIC   Look to the queen there, ho!

HORATIO They bleed on both sides. How is it, my lord?

OSRIC How is't, Laertes?

LAERTES Why, as a woodcock to mine own springe,[7] Osric;   275
  I am justly killed with mine own treachery.

HAMLET How does the queen?

KING She swounds to see them bleed.

QUEEN No, no, the drink, the drink,—O my dear Hamlet,—
  The drink, the drink! I am poisoned.   280
    [*Dies.*]

HAMLET O villainy! Ho! let the door be locked:
  Treachery! seek it out.
    [LAERTES *falls.*]

LAERTES It is here, Hamlet: Hamlet, thou art slain;
  No medicine in the world can do thee good,
  In thee there is not half an hour of life;   285
  The treacherous instrument is in thy hand,
  Unbated and envenomed: the foul practice[8]
  Hath turned itself on me; lo, here I lie,
  Never to rise again: thy mother's poisoned:
  I can no more: the king, the king's to blame.   290

---

5. Handkerchief. "Fat": sweaty, or soft, because
out of training.
6. Weakling, spoiled child.

7. Snare.
8. Plot.

HAMLET   The point envenomed too!
  Then, venom, to thy work.
     [*Stabs the* KING.]
ALL   Treason! treason!
KING   O, yet defend me, friends; I am but hurt.
HAMLET   Here, thou incestuous, murderous, damnèd Dane,   295
  Drink off this potion: is thy union here?
  Follow my mother.
     [KING *dies.*]
LAERTES   He is justly served;
  It is a poison tempered[9] by himself.
  Exchange forgiveness with me, noble Hamlet:
  Mine and my father's death come not upon thee,   300
  Nor thine on me!
     [*Dies.*]
HAMLET   Heaven make thee free of it! I follow thee.
  I am dead, Horatio. Wretched queen, adieu!
  You that look pale and tremble at this chance,
  That are but mutes or audience to this act,   305
  Had I but time—as this fell sergeant, death,
  Is strict in his arrest—O, I could tell you—
  But let it be. Horatio, I am dead;
  Thou livest; report me and my cause aright
  To the unsatisfied.
HORATIO   Never believe it: 310
  I am more an antique Roman than a Dane:
  Here's yet some liquor left.
HAMLET   As thou'rt a man,
  Give me the cup: let go; by heaven, I'll have 't.
  O good Horatio, what a wounded name,
  Things standing thus unknown, shall live behind me!   315
  If thou didst ever hold me in thy heart,
  Absent thee from felicity a while,
  And in this harsh world draw thy breath in pain,
  To tell my story.
     [*March afar off, and shot within.*]
           What warlike noise is this?
OSRIC   Young Fortinbras, with conquest come from Poland,   320
  To the ambassadors of England gives
  This warlike volley.
HAMLET   O, I die, Horatio;
  The potent poison quite o'er-crows[1] my spirit:
  I cannot live to hear the news from England;
  But I do prophesy the election lights   325
  On Fortinbras: he has my dying voice;
  So tell him, with the occurrents, more and less,

---

9. Compounded.   1. Overcomes.

Which have solicited.[2] The rest is silence.
    [*Dies.*]
HORATIO   Now cracks a noble heart. Good night sweet prince,
And flights of angels sing thee to thy rest;   330
    [*March within.*]
Why does the drum come hither?
    [*Enter* FORTINBRAS, *and the* ENGLISH AMBASSADORS, *with drum, colors, and*
    ATTENDANTS.]
FORTINBRAS   Where is this sight?
HORATIO   What is it you would see?
If aught of woe or wonder, cease your search.
FORTINBRAS   This quarry cries on havoc.[3] O proud death,
What feast is toward[4] in thine eternal cell,   335
That thou so many princes at a shot
So bloodily hast struck?
FIRST AMBASSADOR   The sight is dismal;
And our affairs from England come too late:
The ears are senseless that should give us hearing,
To tell him his commandment is fulfilled,   340
That Rosencrantz and Guildenstern are dead:
Where should we have our thanks?
HORATIO   Not from his mouth
Had it the ability of life to thank you:
He never gave commandment for their death.
But since, so jump upon[5] this bloody question,   345
You from the Polack wars, and you from England
Are here arrived, give order that these bodies
High on a stage be placèd to the view;
And let me speak to the yet unknowing world
How these things came about; so shall you hear   350
Of carnal, bloody and unnatural acts,
Of accidental judgments, casual slaughters,
Of deaths put on[6] by cunning and forced cause,
And, in this upshot, purposes mistook
Fall'n on the inventors' heads: all this can I   355
Truly deliver.
FORTINBRAS   Let us haste to hear it,
And call the noblest to the audience.
For me, with sorrow I embrace my fortune:
I have some rights of memory in this kingdom,
Which now to claim my vantage[7] doth invite me.   360
HORATIO   Of that I shall have also cause to speak,

---

2. Which have brought all this about. "Occurrents": occurrences.
3. This heap of corpses proclaims a carnage.
4. Imminent.

5. So immediately on.
6. Prompted. "Casual": chance.
7. Advantageous position, opportunity. "Have some rights of memory": am still remembered.

And from his mouth whose voice will draw on more:[8]
But let this same be presently performed,
Even while men's minds are wild; lest more mischance
On[9] plots and errors happen.
FORTINBRAS   Let four captains   365
Bear Hamlet, like a soldier, to the stage;
For he was likely, had he been put on,[1]
To have proved most royal: and, for his passage,[2]
The soldiers' music and the rites of war
Speak loudly for him.   370
Take up the bodies: such a sight as this
Becomes the field, but here shows much amiss.
Go, bid the soldiers shoot.
        [A *dead march. Exeunt, bearing off the bodies: after which a peal
        of ordnance is shot off.*]

8. More voices.   1. Tried (as a king).
9. Following on.   2. Death.

GOD, CHURCH, and SELF

Over the course of the sixteenth century, the lands formerly known as "Christendom" underwent profound religious transformations that would forever fracture the Catholic Church. The Protestant Reformation, as the reform movements are collectively known, drastically changed the European political landscape, contributing to the development of nation-states and in many cases new national churches that no longer recognized the authority of the Pope.

Led by Desiderius Erasmus, humanists proposed reforms from within the Church, targeting the rigidity of Church institutions and the corruption and venality of its hierarchy, and in doing so, they laid the groundwork for the Reformation. They stressed the importance of personal devotion over public ritual, and of the original text of the Bible over its interpretation or commentary. In the religious realm, the humanist admonition to go to the sources ("*Ad fontem!*") meant that the individual reader of the Bible was granted as much insight and authority as his or her priest. In the face of the threat of Protestantism, simply reading the Bible in the local language, or circulating a translation, was soon considered proof of heresy.

This 16th-century engraving by Lucas Cranach the Elder depicts the Protestant dispensation of two types of communion to congregants, a practice that stood in sharp contrast to the Catholic Church's more restrictive policies regarding the sacrament of communion.

The Reformation began in earnest in 1517, when the German monk and theologian **Martin Luther** (1483–1546) nailed onto the door of a church in Wittenberg his Ninety-Five Theses, a detailed protest against the Church's sale of indulgences to the faithful. An indulgence promised a reduction in the time one's soul would spend in Purgatory expiating one's sins. Functioning as "get-out-of-jail-free" cards for the sinner, indulgences proved an easy target for reformists. The Church had long sold indulgences as a way to raise funds, but the crass marketing involved in using them to build St. Peter's Basilica in Rome finally led Luther to protest what seemed like the buying and selling of salvation.

Luther went much further with his program than did Erasmus and his followers, however, because he challenged the Church hierarchy and urged a definitive break with Rome. His revolutionary propositions included clerical marriage (for which he himself set the example, by marrying a nun); the translation of the Bible into local languages (his celebrated version of the New Testament in German was published in 1522, and the complete Bible in 1534); and the denial of salvation through good works. Only grace (*sola fide*), Luther argued, could save the sinner, so that the entire Church apparatus of rewards and punishments was irrelevant. Not surprisingly, Luther was excommunicated in 1521, ending any possibility that his reforms could operate from within the Catholic Church, even as his writing circulated widely across Europe. Included below is a section of Luther's letter **"To the Christian Nobility,"** in which he exhorts his readers to question the authority of the Pope, denouncing error and instead standing up for "the whole community" as interpreters of the Bible.

As Protestantism spread throughout Europe, rulers found themselves required to choose sides, and religion became intertwined as never before with national identity. When Henry VIII of England broke with Rome and established the Church of England with himself as its head, his actions had profound implications not just for religious practice in England but also for its development as a nation-state. Conversely, in Spain Philip II took on the role of "Defender of the Faith," making the containment of Protestantism one of his main foreign policy goals.

In response to the tremendous upheavals unleashed by the Protestant reform movements, the Catholic Church convened the Council of Trent (1545–63) to denounce what it considered Protestant heresies and offer its own prescriptions for reform. This retrenchment and increased policing of conformity to Catholic tenets is known as the Counter-Reformation, a religious and cultural movement that affected writers and artists all over Catholic Europe.

The Counter-Reformation was not merely repressive, however: it also channeled some of the reformist fervor of Protestantism within Catholicism. Reformers stressed the importance of restoring religious orders to their original purpose and fostered a personalized, intimate relationship with the divinity. Some of the most important reformers within the Church in this period were women, as in the case of the hugely successful and charismatic **Teresa of Ávila** (1515–1582), whose vision for the formation of a reformed convent appears below. Teresa's influential autobiography, *The Book of Her Life*, relates her intensely personal

relation to God, even as she finds her place within the Church.

At the same time, exceptional women remained outspoken critics of Church abuses, especially those that concerned their own sex. An aristocratic woman consigned to a convent against her will at a young age, **Arcangela Tarabotti** (1604–1652), voices a passionate complaint against a system that disregarded the will of the woman in such an important matter as religious enclosure. Tarabotti's *Paternal Tyranny* indicts her society—even after the Counter-Reformation reforms—for putting convenience and tradition ahead of the will of the individual, and for replacing monastic ideals with a hypocritical sham.

With its focus on the speaker's inward thoughts, lyric poetry was particularly well suited to exploring the effects of the Reformation and Counter-Reformation on the Renaissance subject. The Catholic emphasis on devotional intimacy found its most sublime literary expression in the poetry of the Spanish mystics, which mobilizes all the resources of the Petrarchan tradition to explore the soul's desire for Christ. The poetry of St. Teresa, **San Juan de la Cruz**, and Luis de León uses very simple language in an attempt to describe ineffable searching and spiritual longing. These men and women were all born into families of *conversos* (Jews forced to convert to Christianity but nonetheless stigmatized by their forebears' religion), and their mysticism channels into the Counter-Reformation much older traditions of contemplation and communion with the divine.

The poems of **John Donne** (1572–1631), a poet and preacher born into a Catholic family who eventually joined the Church of England, offer a much more intellectualized, though similarly urgent, invocation of the divine. Central to his poetry is the conviction that little can be taken for granted: who we are and what the nature of our relationship to the divinity might be are under constant review. In his finely wrought language of extended metaphors and paradoxes, Donne cries out to his God for attention. In a world marked by religious upheaval and new uncertainties, the poetry of John Donne calls for a skeptical focus on the place of humankind in a mysterious universe and, simultaneously, an act of faith.

Although Catholics deplored the profound division in their Church occasioned by the Protestant "schism," the Reformation invigorated thought and letters across Christendom, as writers struggled with conceiving a more immediate and vibrant relationship to their God. Just as Renaissance humanism's challenge to medieval canons of learning led to a huge flourishing of intellectual activity, the negotiation of God, church, and self in a time of reformation produced powerful statements of devotion and of criticism.

MARTIN LUTHER

The German priest and theologian Martin Luther (1483–1546) was arguably the main figure behind the Protestant Reformation, and was swiftly excommunicated for his positions in 1521. His program of reform was truly radical: he questioned the authority of the Pope and the entire Church hierarchy, arguing that every baptized Christian was part of the priesthood and that everyone should personally read the Bible in everyday language, a case he makes in his letter "To the Christian Nobility," excerpted below. Luther believed that only faith could achieve salvation, and that no number of good works (and much less the indulgences that the Church sold for money) could buy God's grace. His own marriage to the former nun Katharina von Bora in 1525 was a resounding statement against clerical celibacy. In his later years, Luther became more and more embittered by the resistance to his ideas, and his writing became increasingly strident, particularly in his positions toward the Jews.

From To the Christian Nobility[1]

* * *

The Romanists[2] want to be the only masters of Holy Scripture, although they never learn a thing from the Bible all their life long. They assume the sole authority for themselves, and, quite unashamed, they play about with words before our very eyes, trying to persuade us that the pope cannot err in matters of faith,[3] regardless of whether he is righteous or wicked. Yet they cannot point

1. Translated by Charles M. Jacobs.
2. Those who follow Rome, i.e., the Pope.

3. The doctrine of papal infallibility held that the Pope, when speaking as pope, could not err.

to a single letter.[4] This is why so many heretical and un-Christian, even unnatural, ordinances stand in the canon law. But there is no need to talk about these ordinances at present. Since these Romanists think the Holy Spirit never leaves them, no matter how ignorant and wicked they are, they become bold and decree only what they want. And if what they claim were true, why have Holy Scripture at all? Of what use is Scripture? Let us burn the Scripture and be satisfied with the unlearned gentlemen at Rome who possess the Holy Spirit! And yet the Holy Spirit can be possessed only by pious hearts. If I had not read the words with my own eyes, I would not have believed it possible for the devil to have made such stupid claims at Rome, and to have won supporters for them.

But so as not to fight them with mere words, we will quote the Scriptures. St. Paul says in I Corinthians 14 [:30], "If something better is revealed to anyone, though he is already sitting and listening to another in God's word, then the one who is speaking shall hold his peace and give place." What would be the point of this commandment if we were compelled to believe only the man who does the talking, or the man who is at the top? Even Christ said in John 6 [:45] that all Christians shall be taught by God. If it were to happen that the pope and his cohorts were wicked and not true Christians, were not taught by God and were without understanding, and at the same time some obscure person had a right understanding, why should the people not follow the obscure man? Has the pope not erred many times? Who would help Christendom when the pope erred if we did not have somebody we could trust more than him, somebody who had the Scriptures on his side?

Therefore, their claim that only the pope may interpret Scripture is an outrageous fancied fable. They cannot produce a single letter [of Scripture] to maintain that the interpretation of Scripture or the confirmation of its interpretation belongs to the pope alone. They themselves have usurped this power. And although they allege that this power was given to St. Peter when the keys were given him, it is clear enough that the keys were not given to Peter alone but to the whole community.[5] Further, the keys were not ordained for doctrine or government, but only for the binding or loosing of sin. Whatever else or whatever more they arrogate to themselves on the basis of the keys is a mere fabrication. But Christ's words to Peter, "I have prayed for you that your faith fail not" [Luke 22:32], cannot be applied to the pope, since the majority of the popes have been without faith, as they must themselves confess. Besides, it is not only for Peter that Christ prayed, but also for all apostles and Christians, as he says in John 17 [:9, 20], "Father, I pray for those whom thou hast given me, and not for these only, but for all who believe on me through their word." Is that not clear enough?

Just think of it! The Romanists must admit that there are among us good Christians who have the true faith, spirit, understanding, word, and mind of Christ. Why, then, should we reject the word and understanding of good Christians and follow the pope, who has neither faith nor the Spirit? To follow

---

4. I.e., a single passage in the Bible to support their claim.

5. In Christian tradition, the keys of heaven, which Peter received from Jesus, represented papal authority.

the pope would be to deny the whole faith as well as the Christian church. Again, if the article, "I believe in one holy Christian church," is correct, then the pope cannot be the only one who is right. Otherwise, we would have to confess, "I believe in the pope at Rome." This would reduce the Christian church to one man, and be nothing else than a devilish and hellish error.

Besides, if we are all priests, as was said above, and all have one faith, one gospel, one sacrament,[6] why should we not also have the power to test and judge what is right or wrong in matters of faith? What becomes of Paul's words in I Corinthians 2 [:15], "A spiritual man judges all things, yet he is judged by no one"? And II Corinthians 4 [:13], "We all have one spirit of faith"? Why, then, should not we perceive what is consistent with faith and what is not, just as well as an unbelieving pope does?

We ought to become bold and free on the authority of all these texts, and many others. We ought not to allow the Spirit of freedom (as Paul calls him [II Cor. 3:17]) to be frightened off by the fabrications of the popes, but we ought to march boldly forward and test all that they do, or leave undone, by our believing understanding of the Scriptures. We must compel the Romanists to follow not their own interpretation but the better one. Long ago Abraham had to listen to Sarah, although she was in more complete subjection to him than we are to anyone on earth [Gen. 21:12]. And Balaam's ass was wiser than the prophet himself [Num. 22:21–35]. If God spoke then through an ass against a prophet, why should he not be able even now to speak through a righteous man against the pope? Similarly, St. Paul rebukes St. Peter as a man in error in Galatians 2 [:11–12]. Therefore, it is the duty of every Christian to espouse the cause of the faith, to understand and defend it, and to denounce every error.

* * *

6. I.e., baptism.

TERESA OF ÁVILA

A tireless reformer who worked within the Catholic Church in Spain, Teresa (1515–1582) was born into a family of Jewish origins. As she narrates in *The Book of Her Life*, she had been a highly imaginative girl who loved stories of knights and saints. Teresa entered the convent at a young age. Frequently ill, she experienced in her youth a series of powerful mystical visions of Jesus Christ. The desire to find a practical outlet for her intense spirituality eventually led her to found a reformed convent, the Order of the Discalced (barefoot) Carmelites. Teresa describes a richly spiritual interiority, achieved through mental prayer and the pursuit of a mystical communion with God.

From The Book of Her Life[1]

CHAPTER I

[*Her Childhood*]

* * *

We were in all three sisters and nine brothers. All resembled their parents in being virtuous, through the goodness of God, with the exception of myself—although I was the most loved of my father. And it seemed he was right—before I began to offend God. For I am ashamed when I recall the good inclinations the Lord gave me and how poorly I knew how to profit by them.

My brothers and sisters did not in any way hold me back from the service of God. I had one brother about my age. We used to get together to read the lives of the saints. (He was the one I liked most, although I had great love for them all and they for me.) When I considered the martyrdoms the saints suffered for God, it seemed to me that the price they paid for going to enjoy God was very cheap, and I greatly desired to die in the same way. I did not want this on account of the love I felt for God but to get to enjoy very quickly the wonderful things I read there were in heaven. And my brother and I discussed together the means we should take to achieve this. We agreed to go off to the land of the Moors[2] and beg them, out of love of God, to cut off our heads there. It seemed to me the Lord had given us courage at so tender an age, but we couldn't discover any means. Having parents seemed to us the greatest obstacle. We were terrified in what we read about the suffering and the glory that was to last forever. We spent a lot of time talking about this and took delight in often repeating: forever and ever and ever. As I said this over and over, the Lord was pleased to impress upon me in childhood the way of truth.

When I saw it was impossible to go where I would be killed for God, we made plans to be hermits. And in a garden that we had in our house, we tried as we could to make hermitages piling up some little stones which afterward would quickly fall down again. And so in nothing could we find a remedy for our desire. It gives me devotion now to see how God gave me so early what I lost through my own fault.

I gave what alms I could, but that was little. I sought out solitude to pray my devotions, and they were many, especially the rosary, to which my mother was very devoted; and she made us devoted to it too. When I played with other girls I enjoyed it when we pretended we were nuns in a monastery, and it seemed to me that I desired to be one, although not as much as I desired the other things I mentioned.

I remember that when my mother died I was twelve years old or a little less. When I began to understand what I had lost, I went, afflicted, before an image of our Lady and besought her with many tears to be my mother. It seems to me that although I did this in simplicity it helped me. For I have found favor with this sovereign Virgin in everything I have asked of her, and in the end she has

---

1. Translated by Kieran Kavanaugh and Otilio Rodriguez.
2. North Africa. After defeating the "Moors" (Muslims) in Granada in 1492, Spain continued its territorial expansion into North Africa.

drawn me to herself. It wearies me now to see and think that I was not constant in the good desires I had in my childhood.

O my Lord, since it seems You have determined to save me, I beseech Your Majesty that it may be so. And since You have granted me as many favors as You have, don't You think it would be good (not for my gain but for Your honor) if the inn where You have so continually to dwell were not to get so dirty? It wearies me, Lord, even to say this, for I know that the whole fault was mine. It doesn't seem to me that there was anything more for You to do in order that from this age I would be all Yours. If I start to complain about my parents, I am not able to do so, for I saw nothing but good in them and solicitude for my own good.

As I grew older, when I began to know of the natural attractive qualities the Lord had bestowed on me (which others said were many), instead of thanking Him for them, I began to make use of them all to offend Him, as I shall now tell.

CHAPTER 32

[A Vision of Hell, and a New Monastery]

Discusses how the Lord desired to put her spirit in a place in hell she had deserved because of her sins. Gives a brief account of what was shown her there. Begins to deal with the way in which the monastery of St. Joseph, where she now is, was founded.

A long time after the Lord had already granted me many of the favors I've mentioned and other very lofty ones, while I was in prayer one day, I suddenly found that, without knowing how, I had seemingly been put in hell. I understood that the Lord wanted me to see the place the devils had prepared there for me and which I merited because of my sins. This experience took place within the shortest space of time, but even were I to live for many years I think it would be impossible for me to forget it. The entrance it seems to me was similar to a very long and narrow alleyway, like an oven, low and dark and confined; the floor seemed to me to consist of dirty, muddy water emitting a foul stench and swarming with putrid vermin. At the end of the alleyway a hole that looked like a small cupboard was hollowed out in the wall; there I found I was placed in a cramped condition. All of this was delightful to see in comparison with what I felt there. What I have described can hardly be exaggerated.

What I felt, it seems to me, cannot even begin to be exaggerated; nor can it be understood. I experienced a fire in the soul that I don't know how I could describe. The bodily pains were so unbearable that though I had suffered excruciating ones in this life and according to what doctors say, the worst that can be suffered on earth (for all my nerves were shrunken when I was paralyzed, plus many other sufferings of many kinds that I endured, and even some, as I said, caused by the devil), these were all nothing in comparison with the ones I experienced there. I saw furthermore that they would go on without end and without ever ceasing. This, however, was nothing next to the soul's agonizing: a constriction, a suffocation, an affliction so keenly felt and with such a despairing and tormenting unhappiness that I don't know how to word it strongly enough. To say the experience is as though the soul were continually being wrested from the body would be insufficient, for it would make you think somebody else is taking away the life, whereas here it is the soul itself that tears itself in pieces. The fact is that I don't know how to give a sufficiently powerful description of that interior fire and that despair, coming in addition to such extreme torments and pains. I didn't see who inflicted them on me, but, as it seemed to me, I felt myself burning and crumbling; and I repeat the worst was that interior fire and despair.

Being in such an unwholesome place, so unable to hope for any consolation, I found it impossible either to sit down or to lie down, nor was there any room, even though they put me in this kind of hole made in the wall. Those walls, which were terrifying to see, closed in on themselves and suffocated everything. There was no light, but all was enveloped in the blackest darkness. I don't understand how this could be, that everything painful to see was visible.

The Lord didn't want me to see any more of hell at that time. Afterward I saw another vision of frightful things, the punishment of some vices. With respect to the sight they seemed much more frightening, but since I didn't feel the pain, they didn't cause me so much fear. For in the former vision the Lord wanted me actually to feel those spiritual torments and afflictions, as though the body were suffering. I don't know how such an experience was possible, but I well understood that it was a great favor and that the Lord desired me to see with my own eyes the place His mercy had freed me from. It amounts to nothing to hear these pains spoken of, nor have I at other times thought about different torments (although not many, since my soul did not fare well with such fearful thoughts; that is, that devils tear off the flesh with pincers, or other various tortures I've read about) that are anything in comparison to this pain; it is something different. In sum, as a resemblance to the reality, being burned here on earth is very little when compared to being burned by the fire that is there.

I was left terrified, and still am now in writing about this almost six years later, and it seems to me that on account of the fear my natural heat fails me right here and now. Thus I recall no time of trial or suffering in which it doesn't seem to me that everything that can be suffered here on earth is nothing; so I think in a way we complain without reason. Hence I repeat that this experience was one of the greatest favors the Lord granted me because it helped me very much to lose fear of the tribulations and contradictions of this life as well as to grow strong enough to suffer them and give thanks to the Lord who freed me, as it now appears to me, from such everlasting and terrible evils.

Since that time, as I say, everything seems to me easy when compared to undergoing for a moment what I suffered there in hell. I marvel how after having often read books in which the pains of hell were somewhat explained I didn't fear them or take them for what they were. Where was I? How could I find relaxation in anything when I was causing myself to go to such an evil place? May You be blessed, my God, forever! How obvious it is that You loved me much more than I did myself! How many times, my Lord, have You freed me from so dark a prison, and how often have I put myself in it again against Your will!

* * *

I was thinking about what I could do for God, and I thought that the first thing was to follow the call to the religious life, which His Majesty had given me, by keeping my rule as perfectly as I could. Even though there were many servants of God in the house where I was, and He was very well served in it, the nuns because of great necessity often went out to places where they could stay—with the decorum proper to religious. Also, the rule was not kept in its prime rigor, but was observed the way it was in the whole order, that is, according to the bull of mitigation.[3] There were also other disadvantages; it seemed to me the monastery had a lot of comfort since it was a large and pleasant one. But this disadvantage of going out, even though I was one who did so a great deal, was now a serious one for me because some persons to whom the superiors couldn't say "no" liked to have me in their company; and when urged, the superiors ordered me to go. So, by reason of their commands I wasn't able to remain in the monastery much. The devil must have helped partly to keep me from staying home; for since I was sharing with some of the nuns what those with whom I was consulting were teaching me, much good was being done.

It happened once while I was with someone that she mentioned to me and to the others in the group that if we couldn't be nuns like the discalced,[4] it would still be possible to found a monastery. Since I was having these desires, I began to discuss the matter with that lady companion of mine, the widow I mentioned, who had the same desires. She began to draw up plans to provide the new house with income. Now I see that there was little chance these plans would succeed, but our desire made us think they would. Yet since, on the other hand, I was so perfectly content in the house in which I was because it was very much to my liking and the cell in which I lived was just what I wanted, I was still delaying. Nevertheless, we agreed to pray fervently to God over the matter.

One day after Communion, His Majesty earnestly commanded me to strive for this new monastery with all my powers, and He made great promises that it would be founded and that He would be highly served in it. He said it should be called St. Joseph and that this saint would keep watch over us at one door, and our Lady at the other, that Christ would remain with us, and that it would be a star shining with great splendor. He said that even though religious orders were mitigated[5] one shouldn't think He was little served in them; He asked what would become of the world if it were not for religious and said that I should tell my confessor what He commanded, that He was asking him not to go against this or hinder me from doing it.

* * *

---

3. Pope Eugenius IV had moderated the order's 13th-century rule of strict poverty, chastity, and obedience in a Bull of Mitigation in 1432. The modified rule did not require that nuns renounce their worldly possessions upon entering the convent.
4. A religious order that, striving for simplicity, went barefoot or wore sandals.
5. Moderated.

SAN JUAN DE LA CRUZ

Born in humble circumstances as Juan de Yepes, the mystic and reformer best known in English as St. John of the Cross (1542–1591) was a close associate of **Teresa of Ávila**. He worked with her to reform the Carmelite religious order, to which he belonged. At Salamanca, Juan had studied with the great, controversial scholar and poet Luis de León, who had produced a daring translation of the Song of Songs into Spanish. Juan was persecuted by opponents of religious reform within his order, and wrote some of his work while imprisoned under harsh conditions. His poems conjure a world in which there is nothing but the soul and her (the soul is typically described as female in this poetry) longing for Christ, a longing virtually erotic in its force. Figured as the lover, the soul embarks on an intense, erotically charged journey from her "dark night" (the title of one of the poems below) to the perfect union with Christ, her beloved. The transcendent imagery of the poetry contrasts with the simplicity of Juan's language and form, creating a powerful lyricism. The intimacy of the lyric "I"'s connection to the divine makes these poems a burning record of intense emotion.

Song II: The Dark Night[1]

Songs
Of the soul that rejoices at having reached
the high state of perfection, which
is union with God, by means of the path
of spiritual denial of the self

On a dark night, deep and black,
when I, on fire with the passions of love
—what great good fortune was mine!—
slipped out, hidden, unseen,
when my sleeping house was silent and still;   5

and protected in the dark,
concealed by the quiet, secret staircase
—what great good fortune was mine!—
in the ebon dark, well-hidden
when my sleeping house was silent and still;   10

and on that fortunate night,
in secret, when no one's eyes could see me,

---

1. Translated by Edith Grossman.

I saw nothing around me
and had no light or guide
but the one that was blazing in my heart.   15

This was the fire that led me,
more clear and certain than the light of noon,
to where he waited for me
—I knew who he was, oh I knew—
there where no one was seen, no one appeared.   20

O dark night who guided me!
O night, kinder by far than any dawn!
O night, you who have joined
lover with beloved,
beloved into lover here transformed!   25

On my flowering bosom,
meant only for him, kept for him alone,
he rested his head to sleep,
and I with love caressed him,
and the swaying cedars sent a breeze for him.   30

The wind from the battlements
when I loosed his hair and smoothed it, unbound,
with serene and tranquil hand,
struck my neck, pierced and wounded it,
dimming and suspending all my senses.   35

I stayed there, self forgotten,
lowered my face, leaning over my lover,
all things ceased, self abandoned,
abandoning all my care
that lies, forgotten, there among the lilies.   40

Song III: Flame of Living Love[1]

Songs
Of the soul in the intimate communion
* of its union with God's love*

O flame of living love
that wounds with such tenderness
the deep, the deepest center of my soul,
now that you have come to me,
conclude, if you so wish,   5
and rend the fabric of this sweet encounter.

Oh, so gentle the searing!
Oh, so delicate the wound!

---

1. Translated by Edith Grossman.

Oh, sweet the hand, oh, soft so soft the blow
that tastes of life eternal   10
and pays each and every debt!
By killing, you have changed death into life.

O burning lamps of fire
in whose brilliant, searing light
the inmost caves and caverns of our senses,   15
which once were dark and blind,
now offer their heat and light
and give an unknown joy to their beloved!

How peaceful and how loving
you waken on my bosom   20
where you alone do dwell so secretly;
and with your perfumed breath,
so filled with good and glory,
how delicately you show your love to me.

ARCANGELA TARABOTTI

Born Elena Cassandra, the writer and polemicist Arcangela Tarabotti (1604–1652) was a forceful proto-feminist voice and a passionate foe of forcing women into convents. From behind the walls of the Benedictine convent of Sant' Anna in Venice, Tarabotti devoted much of her literary life to speaking out against the enclosure of women and girls with no religious vocation. She debated some of the major literary voices of seventeenth-century Venice, defending her sex against charges of vanity and frivolity and the more serious accusation that women lacked souls. Tarabotti's six surviving works demonstrate a sharp wit, a deep engagement with her literary milieu, and a keen grasp of the political underpinnings of coercing women into convents. Today, Tarabotti is considered a fundamental figure in the evolution of feminist discourse in early modern Italy.

From Paternal Tyranny[1]

BOOK ONE

The Crime of Enforced Enclosure

Men's depravity could not have devised a more heinous crime than the wanton defiance of God's inviolable decrees. Yet day in and day out, men never cease defying them by deeds dictated by self-interest.

Among their blameworthy excesses, pride of place must go to enclosing innocent women within convent walls under apparently holy (but really wicked) pretexts. Men dare to endanger free will, bestowed on men and women alike by the Divine Majesty; they force women to dwell in life-long prisons, although guilty of no fault other than being born the weaker sex—and consequently more deserving of compassion, assistance, and support, rather than being locked up forever in dungeons.

* * *

Merits of a Freely Chosen Religious Life

* * * I would be willing to pour out blood as well as ink if it meant that cloistered nuns led a holy life, following the rules of their orders to the letter, for the honor and glory of the Catholic faith. I bear a holy envy of the religious life of true nuns, called by the Holy Spirit to follow their vocations: giving good example and performing holy deeds for the glory of God in the highest, their own salvation, and the encouragement of devout souls desirous of walking along the path of perfect virtue. These nuns deserve to enjoy the virginal crown in Heaven. Saints Euphrosina and Teresa of Avila[2] were like that; the former dedicated herself to God as a young girl against her parents' wishes, and the latter made such progress in the religious life that she left volumes of writings in which even the learned are amazed to read by what means the Redeemer led her to perfect holiness—not to mention innumerable hordes of virgins whose praises I would like to sing in lofty style and with sublime conceits, since I revere them with all my heart. Our age is not worthy of such exemplars; nor can I speak about them. I can only relate what I have heard or read, since even when it comes to the modern condition of religious forced to take vows, I am only able to have an imperfect and shadowy knowledge, as I myself am a layperson.[3]

It nevertheless pains me not to have at least eloquent speech and learning, as I might perhaps be able to restrain fathers or other men convinced of such wicked barbarity. I might exhort religious superiors as well to inquire more diligently whether the vocations of young girls are dictated by a heavenly spirit or rather a kind of human spirit deserving the title of infernal. Dear, immortal God, of how many, many evils are cruel spirits the source! What kinds of woe do they invent for wretched unwilling nuns! I can describe their state only by means of a comparison so repulsive it causes everyone who has colluded in this crime in any way to shudder.

---

1. Translated by Letizia Panizza.
2. See p. 757. "Euphrosina": a virgin who entered a male monastery to escape her parents' persecution.

3. Tarabotti writes from the convent but considers herself an observer or reporter rather than a nun.

Convents Are a Living Hell for Those without Vocation

The place where these unfortunate women dwell—I refer always to unwilling nuns—can be likened to an inferno. The word is dreadful to hear, but a true comparison. Only Hell itself bears a likeness to the suffering of these enforced slaves of Christ. Over the gate of Hell, Dante says, are inscribed the words

Abandon every hope, who enter here.[4]

The same could be inscribed over the portals of convents. Indeed, at such sorrowful entrances, one could intone mournfully with a voice like a dying swan, "The sorrows of death surrounded me . . . the sorrows of Hell encompassed me" (Ps 17:5–6). In this life, all adversity can be mitigated by hope, which provides relief even when in vain. But if "Hope that is deferred afflicteth the soul" (Prv 13:12), what can be said of an anguish that torments with the thought of eternal pain? This is an incomparable, if not incomprehensible torment. In like fashion, these enforced nuns experience a short Hell in this life as a prelude to the eternal Hell they are doomed to endure on account of your cruelty.

We read in Genesis how Cain and Abel, the first two sons of Adam and Eve, both offered sacrifice to the Lord, different in kind and in intention. Cain offered the most contemptible things he possessed, a sign and proof of his heart's meanness and wickedness, intent solely on material gain. Abel, on the other hand, a biblical type of the innocent, gladly sacrificed the fattest, unblemished lambs of his herd to the Lord with sincere heart and thus symbolized the sacrifice of Christ on the cross. The Divine Majesty looked upon Abel's offerings with benign compassion: "And the Lord had respect to Abel and to his offerings. / But to Cain and his offerings he had no respect" (Gn 4:4–5). Whereupon, enraged with envy, Cain drew his innocent brother to a secreted place away from the parental eye and brutally murdered him.

For his purity and innocence, Abel was a figure of Christ Our Lord; Cain, perpetrator of fratricide, was in my opinion a perfect example of those followers of Lucifer I speak of. In imitation of the traitor of traitors, they seek out the most maimed creatures within their own households and consecrate these to the Lord, divine maledictions slipping their minds: "Cursed is the deceitful man that hath in his flock a male, and making a vow offereth in sacrifice that which is feeble to the Lord" (Mal 1:14). They do not offer as brides of Jesus their most beautiful and virtuous daughters, but the most repulsive and deformed: lame, hunchbacked, crippled, or simple-minded. They are blamed for whatever natural defect they are born with and condemned to lifelong prison.

* * *

My final point: if murderous Cain slew the living flesh of his own innocent brother because he contradicted and opposed Cain's impious counsel about there being no justice and no judge, no reward for the just in another world, and no punishment for the wicked,[5] male relatives are not so very different. They too seek to satisfy their every craving and show by their deeds that they believe that after death there is no pleasure and that the Lord does not see them. If they were not heretics, would they put to death—I don't say an inno-

---

4. *Inferno* 3.9.
5. Genesis 4.1–17. The biblical account does not mention Abel opposing Cain on these grounds.

cent brother—but their own long-suffering daughters and sisters, who will end their days feeling smothered, overwhelmed by despair at not finding some spiritual escape from the intricate labyrinth enclosing them. Oh, what dire happenings will befall these women!

Fathers Should Make Allowance for Individual Talents and Desires

God did not grant one and the same will, one and the same desire, one and the same motivation to each and every woman; although He Himself is unchangeable and everlasting in Himself, He nevertheless takes pleasure in creation's variety. The dispositions of those sinning are diverse; and if the great fabric of the world, created with such design and skill by the Eternal Artificer, did not abound in almost infinite variety, if everything were instead similar to everything else, it would not prove so delightful to the observer.

* * *

Why, then, do you defy the works of the Most Just One by decreeing that many women should live all together, alike in dress, dwelling place, food, and conduct, when the Lord of Lords makes it a miracle of His infinite wisdom for all things He created to be different? Why do you want to bend to your whim contrasting wills created so by nature? It is nothing less than wanting to change and correct the deeds of a Creator who cannot err. For each young girl inclined to lead a secluded life, a thousand others will shun it. If a young girl is pleased to consecrate her life to God in a cloister, is granted supernatural grace, and is attracted by the Holy Spirit's promptings, then do not fail to attend to her desire by giving her your blessing. Do not dissuade her from her good thoughts, for you would be guilty of sin; and whatever is against one's conscience is sin. If, on the other hand, her inclination runs contrary to this life and she wants to live with modest means in the world, do not force her into the cloister, for I assure you that the eternal abyss awaits you as punishment.

* * *

Ponder my words, judicious Reader, for I have undertaken to describe only in part the sacrilege of these inhumane men who mass together wealth, titles, and prestige for their male offspring (who then go on to dissipate the wealth, despise the titles, and sully the prestige with their dissolute life, vices, and degradation), but who cast away as wretches their own flesh and blood that happens to be born female. I believe it was said of them in prophecy, "[Jerusalem's] filthiness is on her feet, and she hath not remembered her end" (Lam 1:9). This passage undoubtedly refers to the souls of men who never think about their mortality, but walk along the filthy road of sin, which leads to perdition. Their conduct leads one to believe that they truly imagine that happiness lasts forever in this temporary, precarious life; they wake up to their wretchedness too late, since "the thoughts of men . . . are vain" (Ps 93:11). Their chimerical hopes often delude them, as when, overtaken by divine justice (it cannot err!), they remain deprived of the sons meant to bring them glory and from whom they hoped for immortality in further progeny. The fathers themselves die of grief in ignominy, only to be shut up forever within a narrow tomb—a fitting punishment for having shut up their own daughters within four walls.

JOHN DONNE

John Donne (1572–1631) was born into a Catholic family in Protestant England, which prevented him from taking a university degree despite years of study. Yet his great intellectual talents led him to an important position as secretary to Sir Thomas Egerton, who presided over the House of Lords. Donne destroyed his own prospects by secretly marrying Anne More, Lady Egerton's niece, and the couple spent many years in great financial hardship, with an ever larger family to support. Donne eventually converted to the Church of England, which made his advancement much easier, and followed a Church career as an alternative to public service. Most famous in our time for the finely wrought wit of his erotic poetry, Donne brought to his pastoral charge as priest and dean of St. Paul's Cathedral the same passion and intelligence that seduced readers of his verse. His *Holy Sonnets*, two of which are reproduced here, were probably written during the period 1609–10, when he wrestled with his religious allegiance amid great financial penury. In "Oh my black soul," he despairs of the possibility of grace, while "I am a little world" contrasts the confident new geographical discoveries with the poet's own inability to transcend sin without God's forceful intervention. "Batter my heart," he pleads, for only such divine force can overcome his conflicted resistance. Donne's religious poetry displays the same talent for the precise conceit, the unexpected metaphor, and the powerful turn of phrase as his love poetry, as he examines humankind's connection with a God too inattentive to compel faith in any satisfying fashion.

HOLY SONNETS

4

Oh my black soul, now thou art summoned
By sickness, Death's herald and champion,
Thou'rt like a pilgrim, which abroad hath done
Treason, and dar'st not turn to whence he's fled,
Or like a thief, which till death's doom be read,   5
Wisheth himself deliver'd from prison,
But damn'd and haled[1] to execution,
Wisheth that still he might be imprisoned.
Yet grace, if thou repent, thou canst not lack,
But who shall give thee that grace to begin?[2]   10

---

1. Hauled.
2. The Reformation included heated debates over whether divine grace predates human actions, and the extent to which humanity's free will can change it.

Oh, make thyself with holy mourning black,
And red with blushing, as thou art with sin,
Or wash thee in Christ's blood, which hath this might,
That being red, it dyes red souls to white.

5

I am a little world made cunningly
Of elements, and an angelic sprite,
But black sin hath betray'd to endless night
My world's both parts, and, oh, both parts must die.
You which beyond that heaven which was most high   5
Have found new spheres, and of new lands can write,[3]
Pour new seas in mine eyes, that so I might
Drown my world with my weeping earnestly,
Or wash it if it must be drown'd no more.[4]
But oh, it must be burnt, alas![5] The fire   10
Of lust and envy have burnt it heretofore
And made it fouler; let their flames retire,
And burn me, Oh Lord, with a fiery zeal
Of Thee and Thy house, which doth in eating heal.[6]

14

Batter my heart, three-person'd God;[7] for you
As yet but knock, breathe, shine, and seek to mend,
That I may rise, and stand; o'erthrow me, and bend
Your force, to break, blow, burn, and make me new.
I, like an usurp'd town, to another due,   5
Labor to admit you, but oh, to no end.
Reason, your viceroy in me, me should defend,
But is captived, and proves weak or untrue.
Yet dearly I love you, and would be loved fain,[8]
But am betroth'd unto your enemy.   10
Divorce me, untie, or break that knot again,
Take me to you, imprison me, for I,
Except you enthrall me, never shall be free,
Nor ever chaste, except you ravish me.

3. Astronomers who made new observations, and explorers who described their discoveries.
4. God made a covenant with Noah never again to destroy the earth by flood (Genesis 9. 11–17).
5. According to 2 Peter 3.10, the world will be consumed by fire.
6. Psalm 69.9: "For the zeal of thine house hath eaten me up."
7. The three persons of the Trinity: Father, Son, and Holy Spirit.
8. Eagerly.

JOHN MILTON
1608–1674

A passionate advocate of political liberty during the heady years of the English Civil War (1642–51), John Milton is best known to us for his epic retelling of Adam and Eve's fall from Paradise. Milton's strong beliefs in the pursuit of knowledge and the wisdom of experience make his version of the Fall a profound exploration of human possibility, in which the adventurer Satan is often the most compelling character. Milton's reliance on the classical tradition as he tells a central Christian story makes his poem a grand compendium of Renaissance inquiry and knowledge.

LIFE AND TIMES

Milton's life divides into three stages: a period of long study, which culminated in the great pastoral elegy *Lycidas* (1637) and his travels on the Continent (1638–39), during which he met important literary figures in addition to the astronomer Galileo; his long involvement in doctrinal and political controversy and his service as secretary to Oliver Cromwell's Council of State (1640–60); and, after the restoration of the English monarchy and his banishment from politics, the more solitary and disillusioned years in which Milton (totally blind since 1651) produced his major poetic works, *Paradise Lost* (1667), *Paradise Regained* (1671), and *Samson Agonistes* (1671).

Born in London, Milton received an excellent education at St. Paul's in London and Christ's College, Cambridge, where he prepared for a career in the ministry. Due to his growing dissatisfaction with the Church of England, however, he did not take orders. Instead, he lived reclusively at his father's estate at Horton, near Windsor, where he continued his studies and followed his dream curriculum of science and the new discoveries, mathematics, Greek and Latin authors, music, the systematic research of world history, and volumes upon volumes of poetry. In his view, his intensive studies were preparing him for the poet's role as moral leader: whoever hopes to write well, he wrote in an autobiographical sketch, "ought himself to be a true poem, that is, a composition and pattern of the best and honorablest things; not presuming to sing high praises of heroic men or famous Cities, unless he have in himself the experience and the practice of all that is praiseworthy."

Politics and not poems were on Milton's mind, however, when he returned from his travels in Italy. Political trouble was brewing at home: tensions between King Charles I (r. 1625–49) and his Parliament over the limits of royal power tried the patience of the Puritans, who agitated for religious freedom. The Puritans' fight for tolerance became part of a larger struggle to limit the king's powers and restore the role of Parliament as a check on royal power. By 1642, the differences between Charles and the parliamentary party had led to outright war. The triumph of the rebellious Parliament culminated in the unprecedented execution of Charles I in 1649 for his abuses of power. Amid huge social, political, and religious unrest, the Puritan Oliver Cromwell (1599–1658) became Lord Protector of the Commonwealth (1653–58), in an autocratic regime widely perceived to replicate many of the abuses it was designed to correct.

During this turbulent period, Milton wrote pamphlets that he hoped would inspire debate, even while he served the Puritan regime. Some of his political arguments shaped the concepts of religious, civil, and domestic liberties that he explores in *Paradise Lost* (1667). His most notable tract, *Areopagitica* (1644), opposed censorship of the press and took to task the parliamentary government for trying to restrict the opposition: Parliament was historically bound to defend the liberties of the people, and Milton could not stand by while this principle was violated. Throughout his public career he forcefully insisted on popular liberty from arbitrary rule, going so far as to defend, in print, the execution of his king. How could he justify regicide? Law, he felt, should arise from the reasoning conscience of the individual Christian; to deprive individuals of the free exercise of their reason called for violent resistance.

His most notorious prose writings, however, were inspired by his first, failed marriage and earned him the epithet "the Divorcer": at thirty-two he married the seventeen-year-old Mary Powell, who left him after six weeks. Milton complained bitterly of the English law that permitted divorce only to those who had not consummated their marriages and protested that the law left unhappy couples to "grind in the mill of an undelighted and servile copulation." Without depth of conversation, he argued, men and women were not joined in a genuine marriage. God, he claimed, meant spouses to be spiritual helpmeets and partners in "civil fellowship." In *Paradise Lost*, where Adam and Eve make love without shame and converse with delight, he illustrates his ideal of marriage. Conversation and the "sweet intercourse / Of looks and smiles" turn out to be the essential ingredients of a successful marriage. Eventually, Milton reconciled with Mary Powell, and, after her death, was married two more times.

After Cromwell's death in 1658, the English soon became disillusioned with the Puritan regime, and in 1660 Charles II (1630–1685) returned from his exile in the Spanish Netherlands for a peaceful restoration of the Stuart dynasty. Milton was imprisoned and fined for his service to the Commonwealth. He began his work on *Paradise Lost* after his banishment from public life: Restoration England had "fallen on evil days," and to his mind no longer had political glory to celebrate. For his greatest poem, Milton thus turned away from the Renaissance epic's preoccupation with the birth of a nation, in the tradition of **Virgil's** *Aeneid*, and chose instead a biblical, cosmic theme.

PARADISE LOST

Renaissance epic poets, like Christian humanists, struggled in varying degrees with their mixed allegiances to secular knowledge and to religious faith. Throughout his work, Milton draws liberally from the classical tradition and from Puritan Christianity, although the two are often in tension. This conflict comes to a head in *Paradise Lost*, where Milton tackles the story of Genesis with the toolkit of a classical epic poet. Milton tells a highly individual version of "man's first disobedience": the story of Adam and Eve breaking God's prohibition and eating from the tree of knowledge offers an opportunity to set forth and examine his own ideas about liberty, knowledge, doubt, sexuality, and marriage.

Milton's chief source for *Paradise Lost* is the biblical account of Creation, Eden, the Fall, and the expulsion of Adam and Eve from Paradise. From the first three chapters of Genesis, he forged twelve books of epic verse, which he fleshed out with his vast knowledge of the classics, history, theology, and science. Milton's subject, he insists, is more heroic than his epic precedents: "Not less but more heroic than the wrath / Of stern Achilles" or the "rage / of Turnus," that Aeneas must defeat in order to found Rome. It is also, he claims, historical, as opposed to those romance tales that feature merely "*fabled* knights / In battles *feigned*." While epic poets usually claim continuity with earlier examples of the genre, Milton insists that his own poem disrupts the tradition. *Paradise Lost* alone, he implies, is genuinely concerned with historical origins and is wholly original as creative verse. The poem also breaks with established form: instead of the rhyming couplets and stanzas of the epic tradition, Milton gives us long rolling sentences in unrhymed verse (iambic pentameter)—a formal departure that shocked his readers but was quickly adopted by other poets tackling weighty subjects.

Even more bewildering than its new form was the poem's truly cosmic scope, summoning for the reader the vast spaces of Heaven, Hell, and Paradise. *Paradise Lost* opens with a council of devils, intent on revenge for their own fall from Heaven. Satan suggests corrupting Man as a fitting reprisal, and undertakes the epic voyage from Hell to Paradise. In these first books, especially, Satan is a complex and dramatic figure, whose resistance against God's tyranny makes him disturbingly sympathetic. The Romantic poet William Blake (1757–1827) claimed that Milton was "of the Devil's party without knowing it," and many readers have found in Satan the epic hero of the poem. But Adam and Eve attain their own tragic condition, as they come to terms with what they have lost and gained through their fall.

The status of knowledge is a central problem in *Paradise Lost*. In *Areopagitica*, Milton had argued that virtue is meaningful only when it is gained and tested by experience. Goodness based on mere ignorance of evil, for him, seems inferior to the reasoned choice of the good over a known and alluring evil. Milton speculated that the Fall caused a change in the way that human beings gained knowledge. In Eden humanity knew only good; after the Fall, humanity knew good by distinguishing it from evil. "What wisdom can there be to choose, what continence to forbear without the knowledge of evil?" he asked. "I cannot praise a fugitive and cloistered virtue, unexercised and unbreathed, that never sallies out and sees her adversary."

This is the position that the more cautious Milton of *Paradise Lost* places in the mouth of his "Adventurous" Eve just before the Fall. Eve, always more independent than Adam, wants to work alone in another part of the Garden, and when she suspects that her husband mistrusts her ability to withstand the temptations of Satan by herself, she grows adamant about facing a trial, should Satan come her way: "what is Faith, Love, Virtue unassay'd / Alone, without exterior help sustain'd?" Like the younger and rasher Milton, she considers such virtue "but a name"; she rejects the idea that her obedience has any significance if it is maintained only by "exterior help." If she is to enjoy a reputation for virtue, she wants it to arise from a personal history of her experiences and trials.

Adam, by contrast, seems both curious and anxious about his relationship to knowledge. In his conversations with God and with the angel Raphael, he reveals how inquisitive he is about himself, Eve, the world around him, and above all, the mysterious heavens. When Raphael warns him that "Heav'n is for thee too high / To know what passes there; be lowly wise; / Think only what concerns thee and thy being; / Dream not of other Worlds," Adam declares himself "cleared of doubt." He assures the angel (or himself) that it is better to refrain from unbounded curiosity or restless thoughts, only to be chastened by experience. Although the difference between receiving a warning and learning from experience is great, Adam takes a very conservative attitude toward the pursuit of knowledge, as summed up in the caution to "be lowly wise": don't analyze or use empirical observation to make inquiries that can lead only to hypothesis and speculation.

Adam's caution casts Eve's independence in a different light. In the classical tradition, beautiful temptresses (like **Homer's** Circe and Ariosto's Alcina) waylay epic heroes who are otherwise constant and honorable. To a limited extent, this model of heroic manhood threatened by female corruption applies to *Paradise Lost*. Yet Milton also complicates the traditional scapegoating of Eve by making her a complex character, with her own motivations. More important, for Milton, the "kindly rupture" of sex-

ual experience relates to the acquisition of knowledge and therefore can never be considered purely negative.

Milton's achievements in *Paradise Lost* include his powerful rendering of human spiritual need and its relationship to marital life. His poem is "adventurous" in its explorations of the rational, sexual, and emotional factors that lead his Adam and Eve to fall, although it is also uncompromising about the fatal error of the Fall. Milton committed himself intellectually to questioning the received wisdom of the classics and the Church in order to discover truths verifiable by experience. In the story of Genesis he discovers questions central both to the Renaissance and to the Reformation: how do we know things? to what extent should "external help" such as warnings govern us? how much more rewarding—and dangerous—is the wisdom of experience? can we learn from vicarious experiences, such as sympathy and interpretation (a possibility that enlarges the moral role of art)? John Milton, who wished to break the bonds constraining the intellectual and imaginative possibilities of his readers, bestowed on them the burden of interpreting art and life on their own: Milton works to make the reading of *Paradise Lost* a simultaneously demanding and highly personal experience.

Paradise Lost

FROM BOOK I

The Argument[1]

This first book proposes, first in brief, the whole subject, man's disobedience, and the loss thereupon of Paradise wherein he was placed: then touches the prime cause of his fall, the Serpent, or rather Satan in the Serpent; who revolting from God, and drawing to his side many legions of angels, was by the command of God driven out of Heaven with all his crew into the great deep. Which action passed over, the poem hastes into the midst of things,[2] presenting Satan with his angels now fallen into Hell, described here, not in the center[3] (for Heaven and Earth may be supposed as yet not made, certainly not yet accursed) but in a place of utter darkness, fitliest called Chaos: here Satan with his angels lying on the burning lake, thunderstruck and astonished, after a certain space recovers, as from confusion, calls up him who next in order and dignity lay by him; they confer of their miserable fall. Satan awakens all his legions, who lay till then in the same manner confounded; they rise, their numbers, array of battle, their chief leaders named, according to the idols known afterwards in Canaan and the countries adjoining. To these Satan directs his speech, comforts them with hope yet of regaining Heaven, but tells them lastly of a new world and new kind of creature to be created, according to an ancient prophecy or report in Heaven; for that angels were long before this visible creation, was the opinion of many ancient Fathers.[4] To find out the truth of this prophecy, and what to determine[5] thereon he refers to a full council. What his associates thence attempt. Pandemonium the palace of Satan rises, suddenly built out of the deep: the infernal peers there sit in council.

[*"This Great Argument"*]

Of man's first disobedience, and the fruit[6]
Of that forbidden tree, whose mortal taste[7]
Brought death into the world, and all our woe,
With loss of Eden, till one greater Man[8]
Restore us, and regain the blissful seat,   5
Sing Heav'nly Muse,[9] that on the secret top

---

1. *Paradise Lost* appeared originally without any sort of prose aid to the reader, but the printer asked Milton for some "Arguments," or summary explanations of the action in the various books, and these were prefixed to later issues of the poem.
2. According to Horace, the epic poet should begin, *"in medias res."*
3. I.e., of the earth.
4. Church Fathers, the Christian writers of the first century.
5. I.e., what action to take.
6. The apple itself, and also the consequences of Adam and Eve's disobedience.
7. The tasting of which brought mortality into the world.
8. Christ.
9. The opening invocation to the muse who will inspire (*sing to*) the poet is a regular feature of epic poems. Milton's heavenly muse elsewhere in the poem (7.1) is given the name of the mythological Urania; in another passage (9.21) she is given the adjective *celestial*. Both words—of Greek and Latin derivation, respectively—mean "heavenly." Clearly and typically, in Milton's heavenly muse pagan elements and images are adopted and given new substance within the framework of Judeo-Christian culture and beliefs.

Of Oreb, or of Sinai, didst inspire
That shepherd, who first taught the chosen seed,[1]
In the beginning how the Heavens and earth
Rose out of Chaos: or if Sion hill   10
Delight thee more, and Siloa's brook that flowed
Fast by the oracle of God,[2] I thence
Invoke thy aid to my adventurous song,
That with no middle flight intends to soar
Above th' Aonian mount,[3] while it pursues   15
Things unattempted yet in prose or rhyme.
And chiefly thou O Spirit,[4] that dost prefer
Before all temples th' upright heart and pure,
Instruct me,[5] for thou know'st; thou from the first
Wast present, and, with mighty wings outspread,   20
Dove-like sat'st brooding[6] on the vast abyss,
And mad'st it pregnant: what in me is dark
Illumine, what is, low raise and support;
That, to the height of this great argument,[7]
I may assert Eternal Providence,   25
And justify the ways of God[8] to men.

[Satan on the Fiery Lake]

Say first, for Heav'n hides nothing from thy view
Nor the deep tract of Hell, say first what cause[9]
Moved our grand parents in that happy state,
Favored of Heav'n so highly, to fall off   30
From their Creator, and transgress his will
For one restraint, lords of the world besides?
Who first seduced them to that foul revolt?
Th' infernal Serpent; he it was, whose guile
Stirred up with envy and revenge, deceived   35
The mother of mankind, what time his pride

1. The Hebrew people. Oreb and Sinai designate the mountain where God spoke to Moses (*that shepherd*), who in Genesis taught the Hebrew people the story of the Creation.
2. The Temple. The biblical localities suggested here as haunts for Milton's muse are emblematic of his certainty about the higher nature of his theme compared with the epic subjects of pagan antiquity. The fact that *Siloa's brook* is flowing by the Temple suggests the holy nature of Milton's subject. "Adventurous" (line 13): perilous, as the poet is daring something new (see line 16).
3. Helicon, the Greek mountain that was the seat of the Nine Muses. The spring Aganippe, which gives poetic power, and an altar of Zeus were part of that landscape (compare the location of Siloa's brook, lines 11–12).
4. Described in Milton's Latin treatise on

Christian doctrine as "that impulse or voice of God by which the prophets were inspired," the *Spirit* is a further source of inspiration over and above the heavenly muse.
5. The poet asks not for song but for knowledge (*instruct me*) and identifies the Spirit with the Spirit of God that "moved upon the face of the waters" (Genesis 1.2).
6. As a bird hatching eggs. The image is pursued in line 22 with *pregnant*. "Dove-like": the traditional figuration of the Holy Spirit (for example, Luke 3.22: "the Holy Ghost descended in a bodily shape like a dove").
7. Subject, theme. "Assert" (line 25): champion, vindicate.
8. Demonstrate the justice of the course of God's providence.
9. An opening question like this is an epic convention.

Had cast him out from Heav'n, with all his host
Of rebel angels, by whose aid aspiring
To set himself in glory above his peers,
He trusted to have equaled the Most High,   40
If he opposed; and with ambitious aim
Against the throne and monarchy of God
Raised impious war in Heav'n and battle proud
With vain attempt. Him the Almighty Power
Hurled headlong flaming from th' ethereal sky   45
With hideous ruin and combustion down
To bottomless perdition, there to dwell
In adamantine chains and penal fire,
Who durst defy th' Omnipotent to arms.
Nine times the space that measures day and night   50
To mortal men, he with his horrid crew
Lay vanquished, rolling in the fiery gulf
Confounded though immortal: but his doom
Reserved him to more wrath; for now the thought
Both of lost happiness and lasting pain   55
Torments him; round he throws his baleful eyes
That witnessed huge affliction and dismay
Mixed with obdúrate pride and steadfast hate:
At once as far as angels ken[1] he views
The dismal situation waste and wild,   60
A dungeon horrible, on all sides round
As one great furnace flamed, yet from those flames
No light, but rather darkness visible
Served only to discover sights of woe,
Regions of sorrow, doleful shades, where peace   65
And rest can never dwell, hope never comes
That comes to all; but torture without end
Still urges, and a fiery deluge, fed
With ever-burning sulphur unconsumed:
Such place Eternal Justice had prepared   70
For those rebellious, here their prison ordained
In utter darkness, and their portion set
As far removed from God and light of Heav'n
As from the center thrice to th' utmost pole.[2]
O how unlike the place from whence they fell!   75
There the companions of his fall, o'erwhelmed
With floods and whirlwinds of tempestuous fire,
He soon discerns, and welt'ring by his side
One next himself in power, and next in crime,
Long after known in Palestine, and named   80
Beëlzebub.[3] To whom th' Arch-Enemy,
And thence in Heav'n called Satan,[4] with bold words

1. Range of sight.
2. According to the Ptolemaic conception of
the universe, the earth is the center of the cos-
mos of ten concentric spheres; the fall from
Heaven to Hell is thrice as far as the distance

from the center (earth) to the outermost sphere.
3. A Phoenician deity, or Baal, he is called
the prince of devils in Matthew 12.24.
4. In Hebrew the name means "adversary."

Breaking the horrid silence thus began.
   "If thou beest he; but O how fall'n! how changed
From him, who in the happy realms of light   85
Clothed with transcendent brightness didst outshine
Myriads though bright: if he whom mutual league,
United thoughts and counsels, equal hope
And hazard in the glorious enterprise,
Joined with me once, now misery hath joined   90
In equal ruin: into what pit thou seest
From what height fall'n, so much the stronger proved
He with his thunder: and till then who knew
The force of those dire arms? Yet not for those,
Nor what the potent victor in his rage   95
Can else inflict, do I repent or change,
Though changed in outward luster, that fixed mind
And high disdain, from sense of injured merit,
That with the mightiest raised me to contend,
And to the fierce contention brought along   100
Innumerable force of Spirits armed
That durst dislike his reign, and me preferring,
His utmost power with adverse power opposed
In dubious battle on the plains of Heav'n,
And shook his throne. What though the field be lost?   105
All is not lost; the unconquerable will,
And study of revenge, immortal hate,
And courage never to submit or yield:
And what is else not to be overcome?
That glory never shall his wrath or might   110
Extort from me. To bow and sue for grace
With suppliant knee, and deify his power
Who from the terror of this arm so late
Doubted his empire, that were low indeed,
That were an ignominy and shame beneath   115
This downfall; since by fate the strength of gods
And this empyreal[5] substance cannot fail,
Since through experience of this great event
In arms not worse, in foresight much advanced,
We may with more succesful hope resolve   120
To wage by force or guile eternal war
Irreconcilable, to our grand foe,
Who now triúmphs, and in th' excess of joy
Sole reigning holds the tyranny of Heav'n."
   So spake th' apostate angel, though in pain,   125
Vaunting aloud, but racked with deep despair:
And him thus answered soon his bold compeer.
   "O Prince, O Chief of many thronéd Powers,
That led th' embattled Seraphim[6] to war
Under thy conduct, and in dreadful deeds   130

---

5. Divine element.
6. One of nine orders of angels, including the

cherubim, thrones, dominions, virtues, powers,
principalities, archangels, and angels.

Fearless, endangered Heav'ns perpetual King;
And put to proof his high supremacy,
Whether upheld by strength, or chance, or fate;
Too well I see and rue the dire event,
That with sad overthrow and foul defeat   135
Hath lost us Heav'n, and all this mighty host
In horrible destruction laid thus low,
As far as gods and heav'nly essences
Can perish: for the mind and spirit remains
Invincible, and vigor soon returns,   140
Though all our glory extinct, and happy state
Here swallowed up in endless misery.
But what if he our conqueror (whom I now
Of force believe almighty, since no less
Than such could have o'erpow'red such force as ours)   145
Have left us this our spirit and strength entire
Strongly to suffer and support our pains,
That we may so suffice his vengeful ire,
Or do him mightier service as his thralls
By right of war, whate'er his business be   150
Here in the heart of Hell to work in fire,
Or do his errands in the gloomy deep;
What can it then avail though yet we feel
Strength undiminished, or eternal being
To undergo eternal punishment?"   155
Whereto with speedy words th' Arch-Fiend replied.
   "Fall'n Cherub, to be weak is miserable
Doing or suffering: but of this be sure,
To do aught good never will be our task,
But ever to do ill our sole delight,   160
As being the contrary to his high will
Whom we resist. If then his providence
Out of our evil seek to bring forth good,
Our labor must be to pervert that end,
And out of good still to find means of evil;   165
Which ofttimes may succeed, so as perhaps
Shall grieve him, if I fail not, and disturb
His inmost counsels from their destined aim.
But see the angry victor hath recalled
His ministers of vengeance and pursuit   170
Back to the gates of Heav'n: the sulphurous hail
Shot after us in storm, o'erblown hath laid
The fiery surge, that from the precipice
Of Heav'n received us falling, and the thunder,
Winged with red lightning and impetuous rage,   175
Perhaps hath spent his shafts, and ceases now
To bellow through the vast and boundless deep.
Let us not slip th' occasion, whether scorn,
Or satiate fury yield it from our foe.
Seest thou yon dreary plain, forlorn and wild,   180
The seat of desolation, void of light,

Save what the glimmering of these livid flames
Casts pale and dreadful? Thither let us tend
From off the tossing of these fiery waves,
There rest, if any rest can harbor there, 185
And reassembling our afflicted powers,[7]
Consult how we may henceforth most offend
Our enemy, our own loss how repair,
How overcome this dire calamity,
What reinforcement we may gain from hope, 190
If not what resolution from despair."

[*Satan summons his army of fallen angels, who rise from the Fiery lake to attend their commander.*]

       * * * he above the rest
In shape and gesture proudly eminent 590
Stood like a tow'r; his form had yet not lost
All her[8] original brightness, nor appeared
Less than Archangel ruined, and th' excess
Of glory obscured: as when the sun new-ris'n
Looks through the horizontal misty air 595
Shorn of his beams, or from behind the moon
In dim eclipse disastrous twilight sheds
On half the nations, and with fear of change
Perplexes monarchs. Darkened so, yet shone
Above them all th' Archangel: but his face 600
Deep scars of thunder had intrenched, and care
Sat on his faded cheek, but under brows
Of dauntless courage, and considerate pride
Waiting revenge: cruel his eye, but cast
Signs of remorse and passion to behold 605
The fellows of his crime, the followers rather
(Far other once beheld in bliss) condemned
For ever now to have their lot in pain,
Millions of Spirits for his fault amerced[9]
Of Heav'n, and from eternal splendors flung 610
For his revolt, yet faithful how they stood,
Their glory withered: as when Heaven's fire
Hath scathed the forest oaks, or mountain pines,
With singèd top their stately growth though bare
Stands on the blasted heath. He now prepared 615
To speak; whereat their doubled ranks they bend
From wing to wing, and half enclose him round
With all his peers: attention held them mute.
Thrice he essayed, and thrice, in spite of scorn,
Tears such as angels weep burst forth: at last 620
Words interwove with sighs found out their way.

7. Military forces.   9. Deprived.
8. "Forma" in Latin is feminine.

"O myriads of immortal Spirits, O Powers
Matchless, but with th' Almighty, and that strife
Was not inglorious, though th' event[1] was dire,
As this place testifies, and this dire change   625
Hateful to utter: but what power of mind
Foreseeing or presaging, from the depth
Of knowledge past or present, could have feared,
How such united force of gods, how such
As stood like these, could ever know repulse?   630
For who can yet believe, though after loss,
That all these puissant[2] legions, whose exile
Hath emptied Heav'n, shall fail to reascend
Self-raised, and repossess their native seat?
For me, be witness all the host of Heav'n,   635
If counsels different, or danger shunned
By me, have lost our hopes. But he who reigns
Monarch in Heav'n, till then as one secure
Sat on his throne, upheld by old repute,
Consent or custom, and his regal state   640
Put forth at full, but still his strength concealed,
Which tempted our attempt, and wrought our fall.
Henceforth his might we know, and know our own
So as not either to provoke, or dread
New war, provoked; our better part remains   645
To work in close design, by fraud or guile
What force effected not: that he no less
At length from us may find, who overcomes
By force, hath overcome but half his foe.
Space may produce new worlds; whereof so rife[3]   650
There went a fame[4] in Heav'n that he ere long
Intended to create, and therein plant
A generation, whom his choice regard
Should favor equal to the sons of Heaven:
Thither, if but to pry, shall be perhaps   655
Our first eruption, thither or elsewhere:
For this infernal pit shall never hold
Celestial Spirits in bondage, not th' abyss
Long under darkness cover. But these thoughts
Full counsel must mature: peace is despaired,   660
For who can think submission? War then, war
Open or understood must be resolved."
    He spake: and to confirm his words, out flew
Millions of flaming swords, drawn from the thighs
Of mighty Cherubim; the sudden blaze   665
Far round illumined Hell: highly they raged
Against the Highest, and fierce with grasp'ed arms
Clashed on their sounding shields the din of war,
Hurling defiance toward the vault of Heav'n.

1. Outcome.   3. Common.
2. Powerful.   4. Rumor.

FROM BOOK 2

The Argument

The consultation begun, Satan debates whether another battle be to be hazarded for the recovery of heaven: some advise it, others dissuade: a third proposal is preferred, mentioned before by Satan, to search the truth of that prophecy or tradition in heaven concerning another world, and another kind of creature equal or not much inferior to themselves, about this time to be created: their doubt who shall be sent on this difficult search: Satan their chief undertakes alone the voyage, is honored and applauded. The council thus ended, the rest betake them several ways and to several employments, as their inclinations lead them, to entertain the time till Satan returns. He passes on his journey to hell gates, finds them shut, and who sat there to guard them, by whom at length they are opened, and discover to him the great gulf between hell and heaven; with what difficulty he passes through, directed by Chaos, the power of that place, to the sight of this new world which he sought.

[The Devil's Consult]

High on a throne of royal state, which far
Outshone the wealth of Ormus and of Ind,[5]
Or where the gorgeous East with richest hand
Show'rs on her kings barbaric pearl and gold,
Satan exalted sat, by merit raised   5
To that bad eminence; and from despair
Thus high uplifted beyond hope, aspires
Beyond thus high, insatiate to pursue
Vain war with Heav'n, and by success untaught
His proud imaginations[6] thus displayed.   10
    "Powers and Dominions, deities of Heaven,
For since no deep within her gulf can hold
Immortal vigor, though oppressed and fall'n,
I give not Heav'n for lost. From this descent
Celestial Virtues rising, will appear   15
More glorious and more dread than from no fall,
And trust themselves to fear no second fate.
Me though just right, and the fixed laws of Heav'n
Did first create your leader, next, free choice,
With what besides, in counsel or in fight,   20
Hath been achieved of merit, yet this loss
Thus far at least recovered, hath much more
Established in a safe unenvied throne
Yielded with full consent. The happier state
In Heaven, which follows dignity, might draw   25
Envy from each inferior; but who here
Will envy whom the highest place exposes
Foremost to stand against the Thunderer's aim

---

5. India. "Ormus": an island in the Persian
Gulf, modern Hormuz, famous for pearls.

6. Plans or schemes.

Your bulwark, and condemns to greatest share
Of endless pain? Where there is then no good 30
For which to strive, no strife can grow up there
From faction; for none sure will claim in Hell
Precédence, none, whose portion is so small
Of present pain, that with ambitious mind
Will covet more. With this advantage then 35
To union, and firm faith, and firm accord,
More than can be in Heav'n, we now return
To claim our just inheritance of old,
Surer to prosper than prosperity
Could have assured us; and by what best way, 40
Whether of open war or covert guile,
We now debate; who can advise, may speak."
    He ceas'd, and next him Moloch, sceptered king
Stood up, the strongest and the fiercest Spirit
That fought in Heav'n; now fiercer by despair: 45
His trust was with th' Eternal to be deemed
Equal in strength, and rather than be less
Cared not to be at all; with that care lost
Went all his fear: of God, or Hell, or worse
He recked[7] not, and these words thereafter spake. 50
    "My sentence[8] is for open war: of wiles,
More unexpert, I boast not: them let those
Contrive who need, or when they need, not now.
For while they sit contriving, shall the rest,
Millions that stand in arms, and longing wait 55
The signal to ascend, sit lingering here
Heav'n's fugitives, and for their dwelling-place
Accept this dark opprobrious den of shame,
The prison of his tyranny who reigns
By our delay? No, let us rather choose 60
Armed with Hell flames and fury all at once
O'er Heav'n's high tow'rs to force resistless way,
Turning our tortures into horrid[9] arms
Against the Torturer; when to meet the noise
Of his almighty engine[1] he shall hear 65
Infernal thunder, and for lightning see
Black fire and horror shot with equal rage
Among his angels; and his throne itself
Mixed with Tartarean[2] sulfur, and strange fire,
His own invented torments. But perhaps 70
The way seems difficult and steep to scale
With upright wing against a higher foe.
Let such bethink them, if the sleepy drench
Of that forgetful lake benumb not still,
That in our proper motion we ascend 75

7. Cared.
8. Judgment.
9. Bristling, terrible.

1. The thunderbolt.
2. "Tartarus" is a classical name for Hell.

Up to our native seat: descent and fall
To us is adverse. Who but felt of late
When the fierce foe hung on our broken rear
Insulting, and pursued us through the deep,
With what compulsion and laborious flight   80
We sunk thus low? Th' ascent is easy then;
Th' event is feared; should we again provoke
Our stronger, some worse way his wrath may find
To our destruction: if there be in Hell
Fear to be worse destroyed: what can be worse   85
Than to dwell here, driven out from bliss, condemned
In this abhorrèd deep to utter woe;
Where pain of unextinguishable fire
Must exercise us without hope of end
The vassals of his anger, when the scourge   90
Inexorably, and the torturing hour
Calls us to penance? More destroyed than thus
We should be quite abolished and expire.
What fear we then? What[3] doubt we to incense
His utmost ire? which to the heighth enraged,   95
Will either quite consume us, and reduce
To nothing this essential,[4] happier far
Than miserable to have eternal being:
Or if our substance be indeed divine,
And cannot cease to be, we are at worst   100
On this side nothing;[5] and by proof we feel
Our power sufficient to disturb his Heav'n,
And with perpetual inroads to alarm,
Though inaccessible, his fatal[6] throne:
Which if not victory is yet revenge."   105
   He ended frowning, and his look, denounced
Desperate revenge, and battle dangerous
To less than gods. On th' other side up rose
Belial, in act more graceful and humane;
A fairer person lost not Heav'n; he seemed   110
For dignity composed and high exploit:
But all was false and hollow; though his tongue
Dropped manna, and could make the worse appear
The better reason, to perplex and dash
Maturest counsels: for his thoughts were low;   115
To vice industrious, but to nobler deeds
Timorous and slothful: yet he pleased the ear,
And with persuasive accent thus began.
   "I should be much for open war, O Peers,
As not behind in hate; if what was urged   120
Main reason to persuade immediate war,
Did not dissuade me most, and seem to cast

---

3. Why.
4. Essence.
5. I.e., we are already experiencing the worst

possible form of existence.
6. Established by Fate, deadly to challenge.

Ominous conjecture on the whole success:
When he who most excels in fact of arms,
In what he counsels and in what excels   125
Mistrustful, grounds his courage on despair
And utter dissolution, as the scope
Of all his aim, after some dire revenge.
First, what revenge? The tow'rs of Heav'n are filled
With armèd watch, that render all access   130
Impregnable; oft on the bordering deep
Encamp their legions, or with óbscure wing
Scout far and wide into the realm of Night,
Scorning surprise. Or could we break our way
By force, and at our heels all Hell should rise   135
With blackest insurrection, to confound
Heav'n's purest light, yet our great enemy
All incorruptible would on his throne
Sit unpolluted, and th' ethereal mold[7]
Incapable of stain would soon expel   140
Her mischief, and purge off the baser fire
Victorious. Thus repulsed, our final hope
Is flat despair: we must exasperate
Th' almighty victor to spend all his rage,
And that must end us, that must be our cure,   145
To be no more; sad cure; for who would lose,
Though full of pain, this intellectual being,
Those thoughts that wander through eternity,
To perish rather, swallowed up and lost
In the wide womb of uncreated night,   150
Devoid of sense and motion? And who knows,
Let this be good, whether our angry foe
Can give it, or will ever? How he can
Is doubtful; that he never will is sure.
Will he, so wise, let loose at once his ire,   155
Belike[8] through impotence, or unaware,
To give his enemies their wish, and end
Them in his anger, whom his anger saves
To punish endless? 'Wherefore cease we then?'
Say they who counsel war, 'We are decreed,   160
Reserved and destined to eternal woe;
Whatever doing, what can we suffer more,
What can we suffer worse?' Is this then worst,
Thus sitting, thus consulting, thus in arms?
What when we fled amain, pursued and strook[9]   165
With Heav'n's afflicting thunder, and besought
The deep to shelter us? This Hell then seemed
A refuge from those wounds. Or when we lay
Chained on the burning lake? That sure was worse.
What if the breath that kindled those grim fires   170

7. "Ether" is the purest of the elements.   9. Struck.
8. Perhaps.

Awaked should blow them into sevenfold rage
And plunge us in the flames? Or from above
Should intermitted vengeance[1] arm again
His red right hand to plague us? What if all
Her[2] stores were opened, and this firmament   175
Of Hell should spout her cataracts of fire,
Impendent[3] horrors, threat'ning hideous fall
One day upon our heads; while we perhaps
Designing or exhorting glorious war,
Caught in a fiery tempest shall be hurled   180
Each on his rock transfixed, the sport and prey
Of racking whirlwinds, or for ever sunk
Under yon boiling ocean, wrapped in chains;
There to converse with everlasting groans,
Unrespited, unpitied, unreprieved,   185
Ages of hopeless end; this would be worse.
War therefore, open or concealed, alike
My voice dissuades; for what can force or guile[4]
With him, or who deceive his mind, whose eye
Views all things at one view? He from Heav'n's high   190
All these our motions[5] vain, sees and derides;
Not more almighty to resist our might
Than wise to frustrate all our plots and wiles.
Shall we then live thus vile, the race of Heav'n
Thus trampled, thus expelled to suffer here   195
Chains and these torments? Better these than worse
By my advice; since fate inevitable
Subdues us, and omnipotent decree,
The victor's will. To suffer, as to do,
Our strength is equal, nor the law unjust   200
That so ordains: this was at first resolved,
If we were wise, against so great a foe
Contending, and so doubtful what might fall.
I laugh, when those who at the spear are bold
And vent'rous, if that fail them, shrink and fear   205
What yet they know must follow, to endure
Exile, or ignominy, or bonds, or pain,
The sentence of their conqueror: This is now
Our doom; which if we can sustain and bear,
Our Súpreme Foe in time may much remit   210
His anger, and perhaps thus far removed
Not mind us not offending, satisfied
With what is punished; whence these raging fires
Will slacken, if his breath stir not their flames.
Our purer essence then will overcome   215
Their noxious vapor, or inured not feel,
Or changed at length, and to the place conformed

---

1. Revenge temporarily suspended.
2. Hell's.
3. Looming, overhanging.

4. The verb "achieve" is understood.
5. Proposals.

In temper and in nature, will receive
Familiar the fierce heat, and void of pain;
This horror will grow mild, this darkness light,   220
Besides what hope the never-ending flight
Of future days may bring, what chance, what change
Worth waiting, since our present lot appears
For happy though but ill, for ill not worst,[6]
If we procure not to ourselves more woe."   225
    Thus Belial, with words clothed in reason's garb,
Counseled ignoble ease and peaceful sloth,
Not peace: and after him thus Mammon spake.
    "Either to disenthrone the King of Heav'n
We war, if war be best, or to regain   230
Our own right lost: him to unthrone we then
May hope when everlasting fate shall yield
To fickle chance, and Chaos judge the strife:
The former vain to hope argues as vain
The latter: for what place can be for us   235
Within Heav'n's bound, unless Heav'n's Lord supreme
We overpower? Suppose he should relent
And publish grace to all, on promise made
Of new subjection; with what eyes could we
Stand in his presence humble, and receive   240
Strict laws imposed, to celebrate his throne
With warbled hymns, and to his Godhead sing
Forced hallelujahs; while he lordly sits
Our envied Sovran,[7] and his altar breathes
Ambrosial[8] odors and ambrosial flowers,   245
Our servile offerings. This must be our task
In Heav'n, this our delight; how wearisome
Eternity so spent in worship paid
To whom we hate. Let us not then pursue
By force impossible, by leave obtained   250
Unácceptable, though in Heav'n, our state
Of splendid vassalage,[9] but rather seek
Our own good from ourselves, and from our own
Live to ourselves, though in this vast recess,
Free, and to none accountable, preferring   255
Hard liberty before the easy yoke
Of servile pomp. Our greatness will appear
Then most conspicuous, when great things of small,
Useful of hurtful, prosperous of adverse
We can create, and in what place soe'er   260
Thrive under evil, and work ease out of pain
Through labor and endurance. This deep world
Of darkness do we dread? How oft amidst

6. I.e., although happiness is not possible, our state could be worse.
7. Sovereign, lord.
8. Divinely aromatic.
9. Servitude.

Thick clouds and dark doth Heav'n's all-ruling Sire
Choose to reside, his glory unobscured, 265
And with the majesty of darkness round
Covers his throne; from whence deep thunders roar
Must'ring their rage, and Heav'n resembles Hell?
As he our darkness, cannot we his light
Imitate when we please? This desert soil 270
Wants[1] not her hidden luster, gems and gold;
Nor want we skill or art, from whence to raise
Magnificence; and what can Heav'n show more?
Our torments also may in length of time
Become our elements, these piercing fires 275
As soft as now severe, our temper[2] changed
Into their temper; which must needs remove
The sensible of pain.[3] All things invite
To peaceful counsels, and the settled state
Of order, how in safety best we may 280
Compose our present evils, with regard
Of what we are and where, dismissing quite
All thoughts of war: ye have what I advise."
　　He scarce had finished, when such murmur filled
Th' assembly, as when hollow rocks retain 285
The sound of blust'ring winds, which all night long
Had roused the sea, now with hoarse cadence lull
Seafaring men o'erwatched, whose bark by chance
Or pinnace anchors in a craggy bay
After the tempest: such applause was heard 290
As Mammon ended, and his sentence pleased,
Advising peace: for such another field
They dreaded worse than Hell: so much the fear
Of thunder and the sword of Michaël[4]
Wrought still within them; and no less desire 295
To found this nether empire, which might rise
By policy, and long process of time,
In emulation opposite to Heav'n.
Which then Beëlzebub perceived, than whom,
Satan except, none higher sat, with grave 300
Aspect he rose, and in his rising seemed
A pillar of state; deep on his front engraven
Deliberation sat and public care;
And princely counsel in his face yet shone,
Majestic though in ruin: sage he stood 305
With Atlantean[5] shoulders fit to bear
The weight of mightiest monarchies; his look
Drew audience and attention still as night
Or summer's noontide air, while thus he spake.

1. Lacks.
2. Constitution.
3. Pain felt by the senses.
4. The warrior angel, chief of the angelic armies.
5. Atlas, the Titan who held up the heavens on his shoulders.

"Thrones and imperial Powers, offspring of Heav'n   310
Ethereal Virtues; or these titles[6] now
Must we renounce, and changing style be called
Princes of Hell? for so the popular vote
Inclines, here to continue, and build up here
A growing empire. Doubtless! while we dream,   315
And know not that the King of Heav'n hath doomed
This place our dungeon, not our safe retreat
Beyond his potent arm, to live exempt
From Heav'n's high jurisdiction, in new league
Banded against his throne, but to remain   320
In strictest bondage, though thus far removed,
Under th' inevitable curb, reserved
His captive multitude: for he, be sure,
In height or depth, still first and last will reign
Sole King, and of his kingdom lose no part   325
By our revolt, but over Hell extend
His empire, and with iron scepter rule
Us here, as with his golden those in Heav'n.
What sit we then projecting peace and war?
War hath determined us, and foiled with loss   330
Irreparable; terms of peace yet none
Vouchsafed or sought; for what peace will be giv'n
To us enslaved, but custody severe,
And stripes, and arbitrary punishment
Inflicted? And what peace can we return,   335
But, to our power,[7] hostility and hate,
Untamed reluctance,[8] and revenge though slow,
Yet ever plotting how the conqueror least
May reap his conquest, and may least rejoice
In doing what we most in suffering feel?   340
Nor will occasion want, nor shall we need
With dangerous expedition to invade
Heav'n, whose high walls fear no assault or siege,
Or ambush from the deep. What if we find
Some easier enterprise? There is a place   345
(If ancient and prophetic fame in Heav'n
Err not) another world, the happy seat
Of some new race called Man, about this time
To be created like to us, though less
In power and excellence, but favored more   350
Of him who rules above; so was his will
Pronounced among the gods, and by an oath,
That shook Heav'n's whole circumference, confirmed.
Thither let us bend all our thoughts, to learn
What creatures there inhabit, of what mold,   355
Or substance, how endued, and what their power,
And where their weakness, how attempted best,

6. The official titles of angelic orders.   8. Resistance.
7. I.e., to the best of our ability.

By force or subtlety. Though Heav'n be shut,
And Heav'n's high arbitrator sit secure
In his own strength, this place may lie exposed,   360
The utmost border of his kingdom, left
To their defense who hold it:[9] here perhaps
Some advantageous act may be achieved
By sudden onset, either with Hell fire
To waste his whole creation, or possess   365
All as our own, and drive as we were driven,
The puny habitants, or if not drive,
Seduce them to our party, that their God
May prove their foe, and with repenting hand
Abolish his own works. This would surpass   370
Common revenge, and interrupt his joy
In our confusion, and our joy upraise
In his disturbance; when his darling sons
Hurled headlong to partake with us, shall curse
Their frail original,[1] and faded bliss,   375
Faded so soon. Advise[2] if this be worth
Attempting, or to sit in darkness here
Hatching vain empires." Thus Beëlzebub
Pleaded his devilish counsel, first devised
By Satan, and in part proposed: for whence,   380
But from the author of all ill could spring
So deep a malice, to confound the race
Of mankind in one root,[3] and earth with Hell
To mingle and involve, done all to spite
The great Creator? But their spite still serves   385
His glory to augment. The bold design
Pleased highly those infernal States, and joy
Sparkled in all their eyes; with full assent
They vote: whereat his speech he thus renews.
    "Well have ye judged, well ended long debate,   390
Synod of gods, and like to what ye are,
Great things resolved, which from the lowest deep
Will once more lift us up, in spite of fate,
Nearer our ancient seat; perhaps in view
Of those bright confines, whence with neighboring arms   395
And opportune excursion we may chance
Re-enter Heav'n; or else in some mild zone
Dwell not unvisited of Heav'n's fair light
Secure, and at the bright'ning orient beam
Purge off this gloom; the soft delicious air,   400
To heal the scar of these corrosive fires
Shall breathe her balm. But first whom shall we send
In search of this new world, whom shall we find
Sufficient? Who shall tempt with wand'ring feet

9. To be defended by the occupants.
1. Original or first parent.
2. Consider.

3. Adam, the first man, is the "root" of the human race.

The dark unbottomed infinite abyss 405
And through the palpable obscure[4] find out
His uncouth[5] way, or spread his aery flight
Upborne with indefatigable wings
Over the vast abrupt,[6] ere he arrive
The happy isle? what strength, what art can then 410
Suffice, or what evasion bear him safe
Through the strict senteries[7] and stations thick
Of angels watching round? Here he had need
All circumspection, and we now no less
Choice in our suffrage; for on whom we send, 415
The weight of all and our last hope relies."
　　This said, he sat; and expectation held
His look suspense, awaiting who appeared
To second, or oppose, or undertake
The perilous attempt: but all sat mute, 420
Pondering the danger with deep thoughts; and each
In other's count'nance read his own dismay
Astonished. None among the choice and prime
Of those Heav'n-warring champions could be found
So hardy as to proffer or accept 425
Alone the dreadful voyage; till at last
Satan, whom now transcendent glory raised
Above his fellows, with monarchal pride
Conscious of highest worth, unmoved thus spake.
　　"O progeny of Heav'n, empyreal Thrones, 430
With reason hath deep silence and demur[8]
Seized us, though undismayed: long is the way
And hard, that out of Hell leads up to light;
Our prison strong, this huge convex of fire,
Outrageous to devour, immures us round 435
Ninefold[9] and gates of burning adamant
Barred over us prohibit all egress.
These passed, if any pass, the void profound
Of unessential Night receives him next
Wide gaping, and with utter loss of being 440
Threatens him, plunged in that abortive gulf.
If thence he scape into whatever world,
Or unknown region, what remains him less
Than unknown dangers and as hard escape?
But I should ill become this throne, O Peers, 445
And this imperial sovranty, adorned
With splendor, armed with power, if aught proposed
And judged of public moment, in the shape
Of difficulty or danger could deter
Me from attempting. Wherefore do I assume 450
These royalties, and not refuse to reign,

---

4. Darkness so heavy it oppresses the senses.　　7. Sentries.
5. Unfamiliar.　　8. Hesitation.
6. Chaos.　　9. Hell's walls have nine thicknesses.

Refusing to accept as great a share
Of hazard as of honor, due alike
To him who reigns, and so much to him due
Of hazard more, as he above the rest   455
High honored sits? Go therefore mighty Powers,
Terror of Heav'n, though fall'n; intend[1] at home,
While here shall be our home, what best may ease
The present misery, and render Hell
More tolerable; if there be cure or charm   460
To respite or deceive, or slack the pain
Of this ill mansion: intermit no watch
Against a wakeful foe, while I abroad
Through all the coasts of dark destruction seek
Deliverance for us all: this enterprise   465
None shall partake with me." Thus saying rose
The monarch, and prevented all reply,
Prudent, lest from his resolution raised
Others among the chief might offer now
(Certain to be refused) what erst they feared;   470
And so refused might in opinion stand
His rivals, winning cheap the high repute
Which he through hazard huge must earn. But they
Dreaded not more th' adventure than his voice
Forbidding; and at once with him they rose;   475
Their rising all at once was as the sound
Of thunder heard remote. Towards him they bend
With awful reverence prone; and as a god
Extol him equal to the Highest in Heav'n:
Nor failed they to express how much they praised,   480
That for the general safety he despised
His own: for neither do the Spirits damned
Lose all their virtue; lest bad men should boast
Their specious deeds on earth, which glory excites,
Or close ambition varnished o'er with zeal.   485
    Thus they their doubtful consultations dark
Ended rejoicing in their matchless chief:
As when from mountain tops the dusky clouds
Ascending, while the north wind sleeps, o'erspread
Heav'n's cheerful face, the louring element   490
Scowls o'er the darkened landscape snow, or show'r;
If chance the radiant sun with farewell sweet
Extend his evening beam, the fields revive,
The birds their notes renew, and bleating herds
Attest their joy, that hill and valley rings.   495
O shame to men! Devil with devil damned
Firm concord holds, men only disagree
Of creatures rational, though under hope
Of heavenly grace: and God proclaiming peace,
Yet live in hatred, enmity, and strife   500

1. Consider.

Among themselves, and levy cruel wars,
Wasting the earth, each other to destroy:
As if (which might induce us to accord)
Man had not hellish foes enow besides,
That day and night for his destruction wait.   505

[*Satan leaves Hell to find and destroy Eden.*]

* * *

FROM BOOK 4

The Argument

Satan now in prospect of Eden, and nigh the place where he must now attempt the bold enterprise which he undertook alone against God and man, falls into many doubts with himself, and many passions, fear, envy, and despair; but at length confirms himself in evil, journeys on to Paradise, whose outward prospect and situation is described, overleaps the bounds, sits in the shape of a cormorant on the Tree of Life, as highest in the Garden to look about him. The Garden described; Satan's first sight of Adam and Eve; his wonder at their excellent form and happy state, but with resolution to work their fall; overhears their discourse, thence gathers that the Tree of Knowledge was forbidden them to eat of, under penalty of death; and thereon intends to found his temptation, by seducing them to transgress: then leaves them a while, to know further of their state by some other means. Meanwhile Uriel descending on a sunbeam warns Gabriel, who had in charge the gate of Paradise, that some evil Spirit had escaped the deep, and passed at noon by his sphere in the shape of a good angel down to Paradise, discovered after by his furious gestures in the mount. Gabriel promises to find him ere morning. Night coming on, Adam and Eve discourse of going to their rest: their bower described; their evening worship. Gabriel drawing forth his bands of nightwatch to walk the round of Paradise, appoints two strong angels to Adam's bower, lest the evil Spirit should be there doing some harm to Adam or Eve sleeping; there they find him at the ear of Eve, tempting her in a dream, and bring him, though unwilling, to Gabriel; by whom questioned, he scornfully answers, prepares resistance, but hindered by a sign from heaven, flies out of Paradise.

[*Satan's Entry into Paradise; Adam and Eve in Their Bower*]

O for that warning voice which he[2] who saw
Th' Apocalypse heard cry in Heaven aloud,
Then when the dragon, put to second rout,
Came furious down to be revenged on men,
Woe to the inhabitants on Earth! that now,   5
While time was, our first parents had been warned
The coming of their secret foe, and scaped,
Haply so scaped, his mortal snare! For now

2. St. John, author of Revelation.

Satan, now first inflamed with rage, came down,
The tempter ere th' accuser of mankind, 10
To wreak on innocent frail man his loss
Of that first battle, and his flight to Hell.
Yet not rejoicing in his speed though bold
Far off and fearless, nor with cause to boast,
Begins his dire attempt; which nigh the birth 15
Now rolling, boils in his tumultuous breast,
And like a devilish engine[3] back recoils
Upon himself. Horror and doubt distract
His troubled thoughts, and from the bottom stir
The Hell within him; for within him Hell 20
He brings, and round about him, nor from Hell
One step no more than from himself can fly
By change of place. Now conscience wakes despair
That slumbered, wakes the bitter memory
Of what he was, what is, and what must be 25
Worse; of worse deeds worse sufferings must ensue.
Sometimes towards Eden, which now in his view
Lay pleasant, his grieved look he fixes sad;
Sometimes towards heaven and the full-blazing sun,
Which now sat high in his meridian tower; 30
Then, much revolving, thus in sighs began:
  "O thou that with surpassing glory crowned
Look'st from thy sole dominion like the god
Of this new world—at whose sight all the stars
Hide their diminished heads—to thee I call, 35
But with no friendly voice, and add thy name,
O sun, to tell thee how I hate thy beams,
That bring to my remembrance from what state
I fell, how glorious once above thy sphere,
Till pride and worse ambition threw me down, 40
Warring in Heaven against Heaven's matchless King!
Ah, wherefore? He deserved no such return
From me, whom he created what I was
In that bright eminence, and with his good
Upbraided none; nor was his service hard. 45
What could be less than to afford him praise,
The easiest recompense, and pay him thanks,
How due! Yet all his good proved ill in me,
And wrought but malice. Lifted up so high,
I'sdained[4] subjection, and thought one step higher 50
Would set me highest, and in a moment quit
The debt immense of endless gratitude,
So burdensome, still paying, still to owe,
Forgetful what from him I still received;
And understood not that a grateful mind 55
By owing owes not, but still pays, at once
Indebted and discharged—what burden then?

3. A cannon.   4. Disdained.

O had his powerful destiny ordained
Me some inferior angel, I had stood
Then happy; no unbounded hope had raised   60
Ambition. Yet why not? Some other power
As great might have aspired, and me, though mean,
Drawn to his part. But other powers as great
Fell not, but stand unshaken, from within
Or from without to all temptations armed!   65
Hadst thou the same free will and power to stand?
Thou hadst. Whom hast thou then, or what, to accuse,
But Heaven's free love dealt equally to all?
Be then his love accursed, since, love or hate,
To me alike it deals eternal woe.   70
Nay, cursed be thou; since against his thy will
Chose freely what it now so justly rues.
Me miserable! which way shall I fly
Infinite wrath and infinite despair?
Which way I fly is Hell; myself am Hell;   75
And in the lowest deep a lower deep
Still threatening to devour me opens wide,
To which the Hell I suffer seems a Heaven.
O then at last relent! Is there no place
Left for repentance, none for pardon left?   80
None left but by submission; and that word
Disdain forbids me, and my dread of shame
Among the spirits beneath, whom I seduced
With other promises and other vaunts
Than to submit, boasting I could subdue   85
Th' omnipotent. Ay me! they little know
How dearly I abide that boast so vain,
Under what torments inwardly I groan.
While they adore me on the throne of Hell,
With diadem and scepter high advanced,   90
The lower still I fall, only supreme
In misery: such joy ambition finds!
But say I could repent and could obtain
By act of grace my former state, how soon
Would height recall high thoughts, how soon unsay   95
What feigned submission swore! Ease would recant
Vows made in pain, as violent and void.
For never can true reconcilement grow
Where wounds of deadly hate have pierced so deep;
Which would but lead me to a worse relapse   100
And heavier fall: so should I purchase dear
Short intermission, bought with double smart.
This knows my punisher; therefore as far
From granting he, as I from begging, peace.
All hope excluded thus, behold, instead   105
Of us outcast, exiled, his new delight,
Mankind created, and for him this world!

So farewell hope, and with hope farewell fear,
Farewell remorse! All good to me is lost;
Evil, be thou my good: by thee at least   110
Divided empire with Heaven's king I hold,
By thee, and more than half perhaps will reign;
As man ere long, and this new world, shall know."
　　Thus while he spake, each passion dimmed his face,
Thrice changed with pale—ire, envy, and despair;   115
Which marred his borrowed visage, and betrayed
Him counterfeit, if any eye beheld:
For heavenly minds from such distempers foul
Are ever clear. Whereof he soon aware
Each perturbation smoothed with outward calm,   120
Artificer of fraud; and was the first
That practiced falsehood under saintly show,
Deep malice to conceal, couched with revenge:
Yet not enough had practiced to deceive
Uriel,[5] once warned; whose eye pursued him down   125
The way he went, and on th' Assyrian mount[6]
Saw him disfigured, more than could befall
Spirit of happy sort: his gestures fierce
He marked and mad demeanor, then alone,
As he supposed, all unobserved, unseen.   130
　　So on he fares, and to the border comes
Of Eden, where delicious Paradise,
Now nearer, crowns with her enclosure green
As with a rural mound the champaign head
Of a steep wilderness, whose hairy sides   135
With thicket overgrown, grotesque and wild,
Access denied; and overhead up grew
Insuperable height of loftiest shade,
Cedar, and pine, and fir, and branching palm,
A sylvan scene, and as the ranks ascend   140
Shade above shade, a woody theater
Of stateliest view. Yet higher than their tops
The verdurous wall of Paradise up sprung;
Which to our general sire gave prospect large
Into his nether empire neighboring round.   145
And higher than that wall a circling row
Of goodliest trees loaden with fairest fruit,
Blossoms and fruits at once of golden hue,
Appeared, with gay enameled colors mixed;
On which the sun more glad impressed his beams   150
Than in fair evening cloud, or humid bow,
When God hath showered the earth: so lovely seemed
That landscape. And of pure now purer air
Meets his approach, and to the heart inspires

5. An angel set to guard Eden from Satan's assault.

6. Niphates, a mountain on the border of Armenia and Assyria.

Vernal delight and joy, able to drive[7]   155
All sadness but despair. Now gentle gales,
Fanning their odoriferous wings, dispense
Native perfumes, and whisper whence they stole
Those balmy spoils. As when to them who sail
Beyond the Cape of Hope, and now are past   160
Mozambic, off at sea northeast winds blow
Sabean[8] odors from the spicy shore
Of Araby the Blest, with such delay
Well pleased they slack their course, and many a league
Cheered with the grateful smell old Ocean smiles;   165
So entertained those odorous sweets the fiend
Who came their bane, though with them better pleased
Than Asmodëus[9] with the fishy fume
That drove him, though enamored, from the spouse
Of Tobit's son,[1] and with a vengeance sent   170
From Media post to Egypt, there fast bound.
    Now to th' ascent of that steep savage hill
Satan had journeyed on, pensive and slow;
But further way found none; so thick entwined,
As one continued brake, the undergrowth   175
Of shrubs and tangling bushes had perplexed
All path of man or beast that passed that way.
One gate there only was, and that looked east
On th' other side; which when th' arch-felon saw,
Due entrance he disdained, and in contempt   180
At one slight bound high overleaped all bound
Of hill or highest wall, and sheer within
Lights on his feet. As when a prowling wolf,
Whom hunger drives to seek new haunt for prey,
Watching where shepherds pen their flocks at eve   185
In hurdled cotes amid the field secure,
Leaps o'er the fence with ease into the fold;
Or as a thief, bent to unhoard the cash
Of some rich burgher, whose substantial doors,
Cross-barred and bolted fast, fear no assault,   190
In at the window climbs, or o'er the tiles;
So clomb this first grand thief into God's fold:
So since into his church lewd hirelings climb.
Thence up he flew, and on the Tree of Life,
The middle tree and highest there that grew,   195
Sat like a cormorant; yet not true life
Thereby regained, but sat devising death
To them who lived; nor on the virtue thought
Of that life-giving plant, but only used

---

7. Drive out.
8. Sheba of the Bible. Mozambique was an important Portuguese province in the trade route. Milton joins biblical, classical, and modern sources to describe the exotic pleasures of Eden.
9. Demon lover of Sara in the Apocryphal Book of Tobit.
1. Tobias.

For prospect, what, well used, had been the pledge   200
Of immortality. So little knows
Any, but God alone, to value right
The good before him, but perverts best things
To worst abuse, or to their meanest use.
    Beneath him with new wonder now he views   205
To all delight of human sense exposed
In narrow room Nature's whole wealth; yea more,
A Heaven on Earth; for blissful Paradise
Of God the garden was, by him in the east
Of Eden planted. Eden stretched her line   210
From Auran eastward to the royal towers
Of great Seleucia, built by Grecian kings,
Or where the sons of Eden long before
Dwelt in Telassar.[2] In this pleasant soil
His far more pleasant garden God ordained.   215
Out of the fertile ground he caused to grow
All trees of noblest kind for sight, smell, taste;
And all amid them stood the Tree of Life,
High eminent, blooming ambrosial fruit
Of vegetable gold; and next to life,   220
Our death, the Tree of Knowledge, grew fast by—
Knowledge of good bought dear by knowing ill.
Southward through Eden went a river large,
Nor changed his course, but through the shaggy hill
Passed underneath engulfed; for God had thrown   225
That mountain, as his garden-mold, high raised
Upon the rapid current, which, through veins
Of porous earth with kindly thirst up drawn,
Rose a fresh fountain, and with many a rill
Watered the garden; thence united fell   230
Down the steep glade, and met the nether flood,
Which from his darksome passage now appears,
And now, divided into four main streams,
Runs diverse, wandering many a famous realm
And country, whereof here needs no account;   235
But rather to tell how, if art could tell,
How from that sapphire fount the crispèd brooks,
Rolling on orient pearl and sands of gold,
With mazy error under pendant shades
Ran nectar, visiting each plant, and fed   240
Flowers worthy of Paradise; which not nice art
In beds and curious knots, but Nature boon
Poured forth profuse on hill and dale and plain,
Both where the morning sun first warmly smote
The open field, and where the unpierced shade   245
Embrowned the noontide bowers. Thus was this place,
A happy rural seat of various view:
Groves whose rich trees wept odorous gums and balm;

2. City in Eden.

Others whose fruit, burnished with golden rind,
Hung amiable—Hesperian fables[3] true,   250
If true, here only—and of delicious taste.
Betwixt them lawns, or level downs, and flocks
Grazing the tender herb, were interposed,
Or palmy hillock; or the flowery lap
Of some irriguous valley spread her store,   255
Flowers of all hue, and without thorn the rose.
Another side, umbrageous grots and caves
Of cool recess, o'er which the mantling vine
Lays forth her purple grape, and gently creeps
Luxuriant; meanwhile murmuring waters fall   260
Down the slope hills dispersed, or in a lake,
That to the fringèd bank with myrtle crowned
Her crystal mirror holds, unite their streams.
The birds their choir apply; airs, vernal airs,
Breathing the smell of field and grove, attune   265
The trembling leaves, while universal Pan,[4]
Knit with the Graces and the Hours in dance,
Led on th' eternal spring. Not that fair field
Of Enna, where Proserpin gathering flowers,
Herself a fairer flower, by gloomy Dis   270
Was gathered, which cost Ceres all that pain
To seek her through the world;[5] nor that sweet grove
Of Daphne, by Orontes and th' inspired
Castalian spring,[6] might with this Paradise
Of Eden strive; nor that Nyseian isle,   275
Girt with the river Triton, where old Cham,
Whom Gentiles Ammon call and Libyan Jove,
Hid Amalthea and her florid son
Young Bacchus from his stepdame Rhea's eye;[7]
Nor where Abassin kings their issue guard,   280
Mount Amara (though this by some supposed
True Paradise), under the Ethiop line[8]
By Nilus's head, enclosed with shining rock,
A whole day's journey high, but wide remote
From this Assyrian[9] garden, where the fiend   285

---

3. In Ovid's *Metamorphoses* 10, a dragon guarded the golden apples on the islands known as the Hesperides.
4. A pastoral god whose name Renaissance mythographers took from the Greek *pas* or *pan*, meaning "all" (or "universal").
5. In Ovid's *Fasti* 4, Dis, the god of the underworld, abducts Proserpine, daughter of Ceres (the goddess of the Earth's natural fecundity). Because she eats seven seeds of a pomegranate in the underworld, Proserpine must remain there seven months of each year, during which time Ceres mourns and blights the Earth.

6. The groves of Daphne by the river Orontes in Syria had a temple to Apollo and a spring named after the Castalian spring of Parnassus.
7. Ammon, king of Libya, had an affair with the nymph Amalthea, who bore the god Bacchus; Ammon hid the child from his jealous wife, Rhea, on the island of Nysa. Ammon was identified with the Libyan Jove and with Ham, or Cham, son of Noah.
8. I.e., on the equator in Abyssinia.
9. The garden was near the Euphrates in Assyria.

Saw undelighted all delight, all kind
Of living creatures, new to sight and strange.
Two of far nobler shape, erect and tall,
Godlike erect, with native honor clad
In naked majesty, seemed lords of all, 290
And worthy seemed; for in their looks divine
The image of their glorious Maker shone,
Truth, wisdom, sanctitude severe and pure—
Severe, but in true filial freedom placed,
Whence true authority in men; though both 295
Not equal, as their sex not equal seemed;[1]
For contemplation he and valor formed,
For softness she and sweet attractive grace;
He for God only, she for God in him.[2]
His fair large front and eye sublime declared 300
Absolute rule;[3] and hyacinthine locks
Round from his parted forelock manly hung
Clustering, but not beneath his shoulders broad:
She, as a veil down to the slender waist,
Her unadornèd golden tresses wore 305
Disheveled, but in wanton ringlets waved
As the vine curls her tendrils, which implied
Subjection,[4] but required with gentle sway,
And by her yielded, by him best received,
Yielded with coy submission, modest pride, 310
And sweet, reluctant, amorous delay.
Nor those mysterious parts were then concealed;
Then was not guilty shame. Dishonest shame
Of Nature's works, honor dishonorable,
Sin-bred, how have ye troubled all mankind 315
With shows instead, mere shows of seeming pure,
And banished from man's life his happiest life,
Simplicity and spotless innocence!
So passed they naked on, nor shunned the sight
Of God or angel, for they thought no ill; 320
So hand in hand they passed, the loveliest pair
That ever since in love's embraces met:
Adam the goodliest man of men since born
His sons; the fairest of her daughters Eve.
Under a tuft of shade that on a green 325
Stood whispering soft, by a fresh fountain-side,
They sat them down; and after no more toil

---

1. Milton includes both biblical accounts of creation, beginning with Genesis 1.27: "So God created man in his own image, in the image of God created he him; male and female created he them." He next uses the account of creating Eve from Adam's rib.
2. "The head of every man is Christ; and the head of the woman is the man" (1 Corinthians 11.3).
3. Adam's body "declares" the political theory associated with monarchical absolutism.
4. Eve's body "implies" the subjection that fulfills Adam's "Absolute rule," but negotiates the distribution of "Authority in men." In *Tetrachordon*, Milton writes of the "golden dependence of [male] headship and [female] subjection" in marriage.

Of their sweet gardening labor than sufficed
To recommend cool Zephyr,[5] and made ease
More easy, wholesome thirst and appetite   330
More grateful, to their supper fruits they fell,
Nectarine fruits which the compliant boughs
Yielded them, sidelong as they sat recline
On the soft downy bank damasked[6] with flowers.
The savory pulp they chew, and in the rind   335
Still as they thirsted scoop the brimming stream;
Nor gentle purpose, nor endearing smiles
Wanted, nor youthful dalliance, as beseems
Fair couple linked in happy nuptial league,
Alone as they. About them frisking played   340
All beasts of th' earth, since wild, and of all chase
In wood or wilderness, forest or den.
Sporting the lion ramped, and in his paw
Dandled the kid; bears, tigers, ounces, pards,[7]
Gamboled before them; th' unwieldy elephant   345
To make them mirth used all his might, and wreathed
His lithe proboscis;[8] close the serpent sly,
Insinuating, wove with Gordian twine
His braided train, and of his fatal guile
Gave proof unheeded. Others on the grass   350
Couched, and now filled with pasture gazing sat,
Or bedward ruminating; for the sun,
Declined, was hasting now with prone career
To th' ocean isles, and in th' ascending scale
Of heaven the stars that usher evening rose: 355
When Satan, still in gaze as first he stood,
Scarce thus at length failed speech recovered sad:
  "O Hell! what do mine eyes with grief behold?
Into our room of bliss thus high advanced
Creatures of other mold, Earth-born perhaps,   360
Not spirits, yet to heavenly spirits bright
Little inferior; whom my thoughts pursue
With wonder, and could love; so lively shines
In them divine resemblance, and such grace
The hand that formed them on their shape hath poured.   365
Ah! gentle pair, ye little think how nigh
Your change approaches, when all these delights
Will vanish, and deliver ye to woe,
More woe, the more your taste is now of joy:
Happy, but for so happy ill secured   370
Long to continue, and this high seat, your Heaven,
Ill fenced for Heaven to keep out such a foe
As now is entered; yet no purposed foe
To you, whom I could pity thus forlorn,
Though I unpitied. League with you I seek,   375

5. West wind.   7. Lynxes and leopards.
6. Richly patterned.   8. Trunk.

And mutual amity so strait, so close,
That I with you must dwell, or you with me,
Henceforth. My dwelling, haply, may not please,
Like this fair Paradise, your sense; yet such
Accept your Maker's work; he gave it me,   380
Which I as freely give. Hell shall unfold,
To entertain you two, her widest gates,
And send forth all her kings; there will be room,
Not like these narrow limits, to receive
Your numerous offspring; if no better place,   385
Thank him who puts me, loath, to this revenge
On you, who wrong me not, for him who wronged.
And should I at your harmless innocence
Melt, as I do, yet public reason just—
Honor and empire with revenge enlarged   390
By conquering this new world—compels me now
To do what else, though damned, I should abhor."
    So spake the fiend, and with necessity,
The tyrant's plea, excused his devilish deeds.
Then from his lofty stand on that high tree   395
Down he alights among the sportful herd
Of those four-footed kinds, himself now one,
Now other, as their shape served best his end
Nearer to view his prey, and unespied
To mark what of their state he more might learn   400
By word or action marked. About them round
A lion now he stalks with fiery glare;
Then as a tiger, who by chance hath spied
In some purlieu⁹ two gentle fawns at play,
Straight couches close; then, rising, changes oft   405
His couchant¹ watch, as one who chose his ground,
Whence rushing he might surest seize them both
Gripped in each paw; when Adam first of men
To first of women Eve thus moving speech,
Turned him all ear to hear new utterance flow.   410
    "Sole partner and sole part of all these joys,
Dearer thyself than all; needs must the power
That made us, and for us this ample world,
Be infinitely good, and of his good
As liberal and free as infinite,   415
That raised us from the dust and placed us here
In all this happiness, who at his hand
Have nothing merited, nor can perform
Aught of which he hath need; he who requires
From us no other service than to keep   420
This one, this easy charge, of all the trees
In Paradise that bear delicious fruit
So various, not to taste that only Tree

9. Region on the outskirts of a given area.
1. From heraldry: lying down with the head raised.

Of Knowledge, planted by the Tree of Life,
So near grows death to life, whate'er death is, 425
Some dreadful thing, no doubt; for well thou know'st
God hath pronounced it death to taste that tree,
The only sign of our obedience left
Among so many signs of power and rule
Conferred upon us, and dominion given 430
Over all other creatures that possess
Earth, air, and sea. Then let us not think hard
One easy prohibition, who enjoy
Free leave so large to all things else, and choice
Unlimited of manifold delights; 435
But let us ever praise him, and extol
His bounty, following our delightful task
To prune these growing plants and tend these flowers,
Which were it toilsome, yet with thee were sweet."
    To whom thus Eve replied: "O thou for whom 440
And from whom I was formed flesh of thy flesh,
And without whom am to no end, my guide
And head, what thou hast said is just and right.
For we to him indeed all praises owe
And daily thanks, I chiefly who enjoy 445
So far the happier lot, enjoying thee
Preeminent by so much odds, while thou
Like consort to thyself canst nowhere find.
That day I oft remember, when from sleep
I first awaked, and found myself reposed 450
Under a shade on flowers, much wondering where
And what I was, whence thither brought, and how.
Not distant far from thence a murmuring sound
Of waters issued from a cave and spread
Into a liquid plain, then stood unmoved, 455
Pure as th' expanse of heaven; I thither went
With unexperienced thought, and laid me down
On the green bank, to look into the clear
Smooth lake that to me seemed another sky.
As I bent down to look, just opposite, 460
A shape within the wat'ry gleam appeared,
Bending to look on me. I started back,
It started back; but pleased I soon returned,
Pleased it returned as soon with answering looks
Of sympathy and love. There I had fixed 465
Mine eyes till now, and pined with vain desire,[2]
Had not a voice thus warned me: 'What thou seest,
What there thou seest, fair creature, is thyself;
With thee it came and goes. But follow me,
And I will bring thee where no shadow stays 470

2. Like Ovid's Narcissus in *Metamorphoses* 3.339–510, Eve falls in love with her image; unlike
Narcissus, she is led by God's voice to Adam, whose image she is.

Thy coming, and thy soft embraces, he
Whose image thou art, him thou shalt enjoy
Inseparably thine, to him shalt bear
Multitudes like thyself, and thence be called
Mother of human race,'³ What could I do   475
But follow straight, invisibly thus led?
Till I espied thee, fair indeed and tall
Under a platan, yet methought⁴ less fair,
Less winning soft, less amiably mild
Than that smooth wat'ry image. Back I turned;   480
Thou following cried'st aloud, 'Return, fair Eve,
Whom fli'st thou? whom thou fli'st, of him thou art,
His flesh, his bone; to give thee being I lent
Out of my side to thee, nearest my heart,
Substantial life, to have thee by my side   485
Henceforth an individual solace dear.
Part of my soul I seek thee, and thee claim
My other half.' With that, thy gentle hand
Seized mine, I yielded, and from that time see
How beauty is excelled by manly grace   490
And wisdom, which alone is truly fair."
    So spake our general mother, and with eyes
Of conjugal attraction unreproved
And meek surrender, half embracing leaned
On our first father; half her swelling breast   495
Naked met his under the flowing gold
Of her loose tresses hid. He in delight
Both of her beauty and submissive charms
Smiled with superior love, as Jupiter
On Juno smiles,⁵ when he impregns the clouds   500
That shed May flowers, and pressed her matron lip
With kisses pure. Aside the Devil turned
For envy, yet with jealous leer malign
Eyed them askance, and to himself thus plained:
    "Sight hateful, sight tormenting! thus these two   505
Imparadised in one another's arms,
The happier Eden, shall enjoy their fill
Of bliss on bliss, while I to Hell am thrust,
Where neither joy nor love, but fierce desire,
Among our other torments not the least,   510
Still unfulfilled with pain of longing pines.
Yet let me not forget what I have gained
From their own mouths: all is not theirs, it seems.
One fatal tree there stands, of knowledge called,
Forbidden them to taste. Knowledge forbidden?   515

3. Eve means "Mother of all things living" (11.159).
4. It seemed to me. "Platan": a plane tree.
5. In Greco-Roman mythology, Jupiter is king of the gods and Juno is his sister and wife. The marital hierarchies of the pagan gods and of the human couple differ. While Jupiter reigns (and rains) supreme, Adam and Eve enjoy "give and take." Adam smiles *with superior love*, yet Eve is physically "on top."

Suspicious, reasonless. Why should their lord
Envy them that? Can it be sin to know,
Can it be death? and do they only stand
By ignorance, is that their happy state,
The proof of their obedience and their faith?   520
O fair foundation laid whereon to build
Their ruin! Hence I will excite their minds
With more desire to know, and to reject
Envious commands, invented with design
To keep them low whom knowledge might exalt   525
Equal with gods. Aspiring to be such,
They taste and die; what likelier can ensue?
But first with narrow search I must walk round
This garden, and no corner leave unspied;
A chance but chance may lead where I may meet   530
Some wandering spirit of Heaven, by fountain side
Or in thick shade retired, from him to draw
What further would be learnt. Live while ye may,
Yet happy pair; enjoy, till I return,
Short pleasures, for long woes are to succeed."   535

* * *

FROM BOOK 8

The Argument

Adam inquires concerning celestial motions, is doubtfully answered, and
exhorted to search rather things more worthy of knowledge: Adam assents, and
still desirous to detain Raphael, relates to him what he remembered since his
own creation, his placing in Paradise, his talk with God concerning solitude
and fit society, his first meeting and nuptials with Eve, his discourse with the
angel thereupon; who after admonitions repeated departs.

[*Adam Describes His Own Creation and That of Eve;*
The Angel Repeats His Warning and Departs]

* * *

"Solicit not thy thoughts with matters hid,[6]
Leave them to God above, him serve and fear;
Of other creatures, as him pleases best,
Wherever placed, let him dispose: joy thou   170
In what he gives thee, this Paradise
And thy fair Eve; heaven is for thee too high
To know what passes there; be lowly wise:
Think only what concerns thee and thy being;
Dream not of other worlds, what creatures there   175
Live, in what state, condition or degree,
Contented that thus far hath been revealed

6. In conversation with the angel Raphael, Adam has asked questions about astronomy and
expressed uncertainty about divine intention.

Not of earth only but of highest heaven."
    To whom thus Adam cleared of doubt, replied.
"How fully hast thou satisfied me, pure   180
Intelligence of heaven, angel serene,
And freed from intricacies, taught to live,
The easiest way, nor with perplexing thoughts
To interrupt the sweet of life, from which
God hath bid dwell far off all anxious cares,   185
And not molest us, unless we ourselves
Seek them with wandering thoughts, and notions vain.
But apt the mind or fancy is to rove
Unchecked, and of her roving is no end;
Till warned, or by experience taught, she learn,   190
That not to know at large of things remote
From use, obscure and subtle, but to know
That which before us lies in daily life,
Is the prime wisdom, what is more is fume,
Or emptiness, or find impertinence,   195
And renders us in things that most concern
Unpracticed, unprepared, and still to seek.
Therefore from this high pitch let us descend
A lower flight, and speak of things at hand
Useful, whence haply mention may arise   200
Of something not unseasonable to ask
By sufferance, and they wonted favor deigned.
Thee I have heard relating what was done
Ere my remembrance: now hear me relate
My story, which perhaps thou hast not heard;   205
And Day is yet not spent; till then thou seest
How subtly to detain thee I devise,
Inviting thee to hear while I relate,
Fond, were it not in hope of thy reply:
For while I sit with thee, I seem in heaven,   210
And sweeter thy discourse is to my ear
Then fruits of palm-tree pleasantest to thirst
And hunger both, from labor, at the hour
Of sweet repast; they satiate, and soon fill,
Though pleasant, but thy words with grace divine   215
Imbued, bring to their sweetness no satiety."
    To whom thus Raphael answered heavenly meek.
"Nor are thy lips ungraceful, sire of men,
Nor tongue ineloquent; for God on thee
Abundantly his gifts hath also poured   220
Inward and outward both, his image fair:
Speaking or mute all comeliness and grace
Attends thee, and each word, each motion forms.
Nor less think we in heaven of thee on earth
Than of our fellow servant, and inquire   225
Gladly into the ways of God with man:
For God we see hath honored thee, and set
On man his equal love: say therefore on;

For I that day was absent, as befell,
Bound on a voyage uncouth and obscure, 230
Far on excursion toward the gates of hell;[7]
Squared in full legion (such command we had)
To see that none thence issued forth a spy,
Or enemy, while God was in his work,
Lest he incensed at such eruption bold, 235
Destruction with creation might have mixed.
Nor that they durst without his leave attempt,
But us he sends upon his high behests
For state, as sovereign king, and to inure
Our prompt obedience. Fast we found, fast shut 240
The dismal gates, and barricadoed strong;
But long ere our approaching heard within
Noise, other then the sound of dance or song,
Torment, and loud lament, and furious rage.
Glad we returned up to the coasts of light 245
Ere Sabbath evening: so we had in charge.
But thy relation now; for I attend,
Pleased with thy words no less than thou with mine."
    So spake the godlike power, and thus our sire:
"For man to tell how human life began 250
Is hard; for who himself beginning knew?
Desire with thee still longer to converse
Induced me. As new waked from soundest sleep,
Soft on the flowery herb I found me laid
In balmy sweat, which with his beams the sun 255
Soon dried, and on the reeking[8] moisture fed.
Straight toward heaven my wondering eyes I turned,
And gazed a while the ample sky, till raised
By quick instinctive motion up I sprung
As thitherward endeavoring, and upright 260
Stood on my feet; about me round I saw
Hill, dale, and shady woods, and sunny plains
And liquid lapse of murmuring streams; by these,
Creatures that lived and moved, and walked or flew,
Birds on the branches warbling. All things smiled; 265
With fragrance and with joy my heart o'erflowed.
Myself I then perused, and limb by limb
Surveyed, and sometimes went and sometimes ran
With supple joints as lively vigor led:
But who I was, or where, or from what cause, 270
Knew not. To speak I tried, and forthwith spake,
My tongue obeyed, and readily could name
Whate'er I saw. 'Thou sun,' said I, 'fair light,
And thou enlightened earth, so fresh and gay,
Ye hills and dales, ye rivers, woods, and plains, 275
And ye that live and move, fair creatures, tell,
Tell, if ye saw, how came I thus, how here?

---

7. God sent Raphael to watch the gates of hell and prevent Satan from disturbing Him during the Creation of the world. 8. Steaming.

Not of myself; by some great maker, then,
In goodness and in power preëminent.
Tell me how may I know him, how adore,   280
From whom I have that thus I move and live,
And feel that I am happier than I know.'
    "While thus I called, and strayed I knew not whither
From where I first drew air and first beheld
This happy light, when answer none returned,   285
On a green shady bank profuse of flowers
Pensive I sat me down; there gentle sleep
First found me and with soft oppression seized
My drowsèd sense—untroubled, though I thought
I then was passing to my former state   290
Insensible, and forthwith to dissolve;
When suddenly stood at my head a dream,
Whose inward apparition gently moved
My fancy to believe I yet had being
And lived. One came, methought, of shape divine,   295
And said, 'Thy mansion wants thee, Adam, rise,
First man, of men innumerable ordained
First father; called by thee I come thy guide
To the garden of bliss, thy seat prepared.'
So saying, by the hand he took me raised,   300
And over fields and waters, as in air
Smooth sliding without step, last led me up
A woody mountain whose high top was plain,
A circuit wide, enclosed, with goodliest trees
Planted, with walks and bowers, that what I saw   305
Of earth before scarce pleasant seemed. Each tree
Loaden with fairest fruit that hung to the eye
Tempting, stirred in me sudden appetite
To pluck and eat; whereat I waked, and found
Before mine eyes all real, as the dream   310
Had lively shadowed. Here had new begun
My wandering, had not he who was my guide
Up hither, from among the trees appeared,
Presence divine. Rejoicing, but with awe,
In adoration at his feet I fell   315
Submiss: he reared me, and, 'Whom thou soughtest I am,'
Said mildly, 'author[9] of all this thou seest
Above or round about thee or beneath.
This Paradise I give thee, count it thine
To till and keep, and of the fruit to eat.   320
Of every tree that in the garden grows
Eat freely with glad heart; fear here no dearth.
But of the tree whose operation brings
Knowledge of good and ill, which I have set
The pledge of thy obedience and thy faith   325
Amid the garden by the Tree of Life,
Remember what I warn thee, shun to taste

9. Creator, augmenter.

And shun the bitter consequence: for know
The day thou eat'st thereof, my sole command
Transgressed, inevitably thou shalt die,   330
From that day mortal, and this happy state
Shalt lose, expelled from hence into a world
Of woe and sorrow.' Sternly he pronounced
The rigid interdiction, which resounds
Yet dreadful in mine ear, though in my choice   335
Not to incur; but soon his clear aspèct
Returned, and gracious purpose thus renewed:
'Not only these fair bounds, but all the Earth
To thee and to thy race I give; as lords
Possess it, and all things that therein live,   340
Or live in sea or air, beast, fish, and fowl.
In sign whereof each bird and beast behold
After their kinds; I bring them to receive
From thee their names, and pay thee fealty
With low subjection; understand the same   345
Of fish within their watery residence,
Not hither summoned, since they cannot change
Their element to draw the thinner air.'
As thus he spake, each bird and beast behold
Approaching two and two, these cowering low   350
With blandishment, each bird stooped on his wing.
I named them as they passed, and understood
Their nature, with such knowledge God endued
My sudden apprehension. But in these
I found not what methought I wanted[1] still,   355
And to the heavenly vision thus presumed:
    "'O by what name, for thou above all these,
Above mankind, or aught than mankind higher,
Surpassest far my naming, how may I
Adore thee, author of this universe   360
And all this good to man, for whose well-being
So amply and with hands so liberal
Thou hast provided all things? But with me
I see not who partakes. In solitude
What happiness? Who can enjoy alone,   365
Or all enjoying, what contentment find?'
Thus I presumptuous; and the vision bright,
As with'a smile more brightened, thus replied:
    "'What callest thou solitude? Is not the earth
With various living creatures, and the air,   370
Replenished, and all these at thy command
To come and play before thee? Knowest thou not
Their language and their ways? They also know
And reason not contemptibly; with these
Find pastime and bear rule; thy realm is large.'   375
So spake the universal Lord, and seemed
So ordering. I with leave of speech implored

---

1. Desired, lacked.

And humble deprecation, thus replied:
"'Let not my words offend thee, heavenly power,
My maker; be propitious while I speak.   380
Hast thou not made me here thy substitute,
And these inferior far beneath me set?
Among unequals what society
Can sort, what harmony or true delight?
Which must be mutual, in proportion due   385
Given and received. But in disparity,
The one intense, the other still remiss,
Cannot well suit with either, but soon prove
Tedious alike. Of fellowship I speak
Such as I seek, fit to participate   390
All rational delight, wherein the brute
Cannot be human consort. They rejoice
Each with their kind, lion with lioness,
So fitly them in pairs thou hast combined:
Much less can bird with beast, or fish with fowl   395
So well converse, nor with the ox the ape;
Worse then can man with beast, and least of all.'
    "Whereto the Almighty answered, not displeased:
'A nice and subtle happiness I see
Thou to thyself proposest, in the choice   400
Of thy associates, Adam, and wilt taste
No pleasure, though in pleasure, solitary.
What thinkest thou then of me and this my state?
Seem I to thee sufficiently possessed
Of happiness or not? who am alone   405
From all eternity, for none I know
Second to me or like, equal much less.
How have I then with whom to hold converse
Save with the creatures which I made, and those
To me inferior, infinite descents   410
Beneath what other creatures are to thee?'
    "He ceased, I lowly answered: 'To attain
The height and depth of thy eternal ways
All human thoughts come short, supreme of things.
Thou in thyself art perfect, and in thee   415
Is no deficience found; not so is man,
But in degree, the cause of his desire
By conversation with his like to help
Or solace his defects. No need that thou
Shouldst propagate, already infinite,   420
And through all number absolute, though one.
But man by number is to manifest
His single imperfection, and beget
Like of his like, his image multiplied,
In unity defective, which requires   425
Collateral² love and dearest amity.
Thou in thy secrecy although alone,

---

2. Equal, with a pun on Latin *latus, lateris,* the "side" from which Eve will be formed.

Best with thyself accompanied, seekest not
Social communication; yet, so pleased,
Canst raise thy creature to what height thou wilt   430
Of union or communion, deified;
I by conversing cannot these erect
From prone, nor in their ways complacence find.'
Thus I emboldened spake, and freedom used
Permissive, and acceptance found, which gained   435
This answer from the gracious voice divine:
    "'Thus far to try thee, Adam, I was pleased,
And find thee knowing, not of beasts alone
Which thou hast rightly named, but of thyself,
Expressing well the spirit within thee free,   440
My image, not imparted to the brute,
Whose fellowship, therefore unmeet for thee,
Good reason was thou freely shouldst dislike;
And be so minded still. I, ere thou spak'st,
Knew it not good for man to be alone,   445
And no such company as then thou sawest
Intended thee, for trial only brought,
To see how thou couldst judge of fit and meet.
What next I bring shall please thee, be assured:
Thy likeness, thy fit help, thy other self,   450
Thy wish exactly to thy heart's desire.'
    "He ended, or I heard no more, for now,
My earthly by his heavenly overpowered
Which it had long stood under, strained to the height
In that celestial colloquy sublime,   455
As with an object that excels the sense
Dazzled and spent, sunk down and sought repair
Of sleep, which instantly fell on me, called
By nature as in aid, and closed mine eyes.
Mine eyes he closed, but open left the cell   460
Of fancy,³ my internal sight, by which
Abstract as in a trance methought I saw,
Though sleeping, where I lay, and saw the shape
Still glorious before whom awake I stood;
Who stooping opened my left side, and took   465
From thence a rib, with cordial⁴ spirits warm
And life-blood streaming fresh. Wide was the wound,
But suddenly with flesh filled up and healed.
The rib he formed and fashioned with his hands;
Under his forming hands a creature grew,   470
Manlike, but different sex, so lovely fair
That what seemed fair in all the world seemed now
Mean, or in her summed up, in her contained,
And in her looks, which from that time infused
Sweetness into my heart, unfelt before,   475
And into all things from her air inspired
The spirit of love and amorous delight.

3. Imagination.
4. From the Latin *cors, cordis* relating to the heart.

She disappeared, and left me dark; I waked
To find her or forever to deplore
Her loss, and other pleasures all abjure;   480
When out of hope, behold her, not far off,
Such as I saw her in my dream, adorned
With what all Earth or Heaven could bestow
To make her amiable. On she came,
Led by her heavenly maker, though unseen,   485
And guided by his voice, nor uninformed
Of nuptial sanctity and marriage rites.
Grace was in all her steps, heaven in her eye,
In every gesture dignity and love.
I overjoyed could not forbear aloud: 490
    "'This turn hath made amends; thou hast fulfilled
Thy words, Creator bounteous and benign,
Giver of all things fair, but fairest this
Of all thy gifts; nor enviest. I now see
Bone of my bone, flesh of my flesh, my self   495
Before me; woman is her name, of man
Extracted; for this cause he shall forego
Father and mother, and to his wife adhere,
And they shall be one flesh, one heart, one soul.'
    "She heard me thus, and though divinely brought,   500
Yet innocence and virgin modesty,
Her virtue and the conscience of her worth
That would be wooed and not unsought be won,
Not obvious, not obtrusive, but retired,
The more desirable—or, to say all,   505
Nature herself, though pure of sinful thought,
Wrought in her so that, seeing me, she turned.
I followed her; she what was honor knew,
And with obsequious⁵ majesty approved
My pleaded reason. To the nuptial bower   510
I led her blushing like the morn. All heaven
And happy constellations on that hour
Shed their selectest influence; the earth
Gave sign of gratulation,⁶ and each hill;
Joyous the birds; fresh gales and gentle airs   515
Whispered it to the woods, and from their wings
Flung rose, flung odors from the spicy shrub,
Disporting, till the amorous bird of night
Sung spousal, and bid haste the evening star
On his hill-top, to light the bridal lamp.   520
    "Thus have I told thee all my state, and brought
My story to the sum of earthly bliss
Which I enjoy, and must confess to find
In all things else delight indeed, but such
As, used or not, works in the mind no change,   525
Nor vehement⁷ desire—these delicacies
I mean of taste, sight, smell, herbs, fruits, and flowers,

5. Obedient ("following," literally), displaying
the essential virtue of the wife.
6. Congratulation.
7. Overpowering, distracting.

Walks and the melody of birds. But here,
Far otherwise, transported I behold,
Transported touch; here passion first I felt, 530
Commotion strange, in all enjoyments else
Superior and unmoved, here only weak
Against the charm of beauty's powerful glance.
Or nature failed in me and left some part
Not proof enough such object to sustain, 535
Or from my side subducting[8] took perhaps
More than enough; at least on her bestowed
Too much of ornament, in outward show
Elaborate, of inward less exact.
For well I understand in the prime end 540
Of nature her th' inferior, in the mind
And inward faculties which most excel,
In outward also her resembling less
His image who made both, and less expressing
The character of that dominion given 545
O'er other creatures. Yet when I approach
Her loveliness, so absolute she seems
And in herself complete, so well to know
Her own, that what she wills to do or say
Seems wisest, virtuousest, discreetest, best. 550
All higher knowledge in her presence falls
Degraded; wisdom in discourse with her
Loses discountenanced, and like folly shows;
Authority and reason on her wait
As one intended first, not after made 555
Occasionally;[9] and to consùmmate all,
Greatness of mind and nobleness their seat
Build in her loveliest, and create an awe
About her as a guard angelic placed."
　　To whom the Angel with contracted brow: 560
"Accuse not nature, she hath done her part;
Do thou but thine, and be not diffident
Of wisdom; she deserts thee not if thou
Dismiss not her when most thou need'st her nigh
By àttributing overmuch to things 565
Less excellent, as thou thyself perceiv'st.
For what admir'st thou, what transports thee so?
An outside? Fair no doubt, and worthy well
Thy cherishing, thy honoring, and thy love;
Not thy subjection. Weigh her with thyself, 570
Then value. Ofttimes nothing profits more
Then self-esteem, grounded on just and right
Well managed. Of that skill the more thou know'st,
The more she will acknowledge thee her head,
And to realities yield all her shows— 575
Made so adorn for thy delight the more,

8. Taking away.
9. For a particular purpose or occasion, i.e., Adam's request for a companion.

So aweful[1] that with honor thou may'st love
Thy mate, who sees when thou art seen least wise.
But if the sense of touch whereby mankind
Is propagated seem such dear delight   580
Beyond all other, think the same vouchsafed
To cattle and each beast; which would not be
To them made common and divulged if aught
Therein enjoyed were worthy to subdue
The soul of man, or passion in him move.   585
What higher in her society thou find'st
Attractive, human, rational—love still;
In loving thou dost well, in passion not,
Wherein true love consists not. Love refines
The thoughts, and heart enlarges, hath his seat   590
In reason, and is judicious, is the scale
By which to heavenly love thou may'st ascend,
Not sunk in carnal pleasure, for which cause
Among the beasts no mate for thee was found."
　　To whom thus half abashed Adam replied: 595
"Neither her outside formed so fair, nor aught
In procreation common to all kinds
(Though higher of the genial[2] bed by far
And with mysterious reverence I deem)
So much delights me as those graceful acts,   600
Those thousand decencies that daily flow
From all her words and actions, mixed with love
And sweet compliance, which declare unfeigned
Union of mind, or in us both one soul,
Harmony to behold in wedded pair   605
More grateful than harmonious sound to the ear.
Yet these subject not; I to thee disclose
What inward thence I feel, not therefore foiled,
Who meet with various objects from the sense
Variously representing; yet still free   610
Approve the best, and follow what I approve.
　　"To love thou balm'st me not, for love thou say'st
Leads up to Heaven, is both the way and guide;
Bear with me then, if lawful what I ask:
Love not the heavenly spirits, and how their love   615
Express they, by looks only, or do they mix
Irradiance, virtual or immediate touch?"
　　To whom the Angel with a smile that glowed
Celestial rosy red, love's proper hue,
Answered: "Let it suffice thee that thou know'st   620
Us happy, and without love no happiness.
Whatever pure thou in the body enjoy'st
(And pure thou wert created), we enjoy
In eminence, and obstacle find none
Of membrane, joint, or limb, exclusive bars.   625
Easier than air with air, if spirits embrace,

1. Awe-inspiring.　　　　　　　　　　2. Procreative.

Total they mix, union of pure with pure
Desiring; nor restrained conveyance need
As flesh to mix with flesh, or soul with soul.
But I can now no more; the parting sun   630
Beyond the earth's green cape and verdant isles
Hesperian sets, my signal to depart.
Be strong, live happy, and love, but first of all
His whom to love is to obey, and keep
His great command; take heed lest passion sway   635
Thy judgment to do aught which else free will
Would not admit; thine and of all thy sons
The weal or woe in thee is placed: beware.
I in thy persevering shall rejoice,
And all the blest. Stand fast; to stand or fall   640
Free in thine own arbitrement³ it lies.
Perfect within, no outward aid require;
And all temptation to transgress repel."
    So saying, he arose; whom Adam thus
Followed with benediction: "Since to part,   645
Go, heavenly guest, ethereal messenger,
Sent from whose sovereign goodness I adore.
Gentle to me and affable⁴ hath been
Thy condescension, and shall be honored ever
With grateful memory. Thou to mankind   650
Be good and friendly still, and oft return."
    So parted they, the Angel up to Heaven
From the thick shade, and Adam to his bower.

BOOK 9

The Argument

Satan, having compassed the Earth, with meditated guile returns as a mist by night into Paradise; enters into the serpent sleeping. Adam and Eve in the morning go forth to their labors, which Eve proposes to divide in several places, each laboring apart: Adam consents not, alleging the danger lest that enemy of whom they were forewarned should attempt her found alone. Eve, loath to be thought not circumspect or firm enough, urges her going apart, the rather desirous to make trial of her strength; Adam at last yields. The serpent finds her alone: his subtle approach, first gazing, then speaking, with much flattery extolling Eve above all other creatures. Eve, wondering to hear the serpent speak, asks how he attained to human speech and such understanding not till now; the serpent answers that by tasting of a certain tree in the garden he attained both to speech and reason, till then void of both. Eve requires him to bring her to that tree, and finds it to be the Tree of Knowledge forbidden: the serpent, now grown bolder, with many wiles and arguments induces her at length to eat. She, pleased with the taste, deliberates a while whether to impart thereof to Adam or not; at last brings him of the fruit; relates what persuaded her to eat thereof. Adam, at first amazed, but perceiving her lost, resolves, through vehemence of love, to perish with her, and, extenuating the trespass,

---

3. Judgment.   4. Easy to converse with.

eats also of the fruit. The effects thereof in them both; they seek to cover their nakedness; then fall to variance and accusation of one another.

[Temptation and Fall]

No more of talk where God or angel guest[5]
With man, as with his friend, familiar used
To sit indulgent, and with him partake
Rural repast, permitting him the while
Venial[6] discourse unblamed. I now must change   5
Those notes to tragic; foul distrust, and breach
Disloyal, on the part of man, revolt
And disobedience; on the part of Heaven,
Now alienated, distance and distaste,
Anger and just rebuke, and judgment given,   10
That brought into this world a world of woe,
Sin and her shadow Death, and Misery,
Death's harbinger. Sad task! yet argument
Not less but more heroic than the wrath
Of stern Achilles on his foe pursued   15
Thrice fugitive about Troy wall;[7] or rage
Of Turnus for Lavinia disespoused;[8]
Or Neptune's ire, or Juno's, that so long
Perplexed the Greek, and Cytherea's son:[9]
If answerable style I can obtain   20
Of my celestial Patroness,[1] who deigns
Her nightly visitation unimplored,
And dictates to me slumbering, or inspires
Easy my unpremeditated[2] verse,
Since first this subject for heroic song   25
Pleased me,[3] long choosing and beginning late,
Not sedulous by nature to indite
War, hitherto the only argument
Heroic deemed, chief mastery to dissect[4]
With long and tedious havoc fabled knights   30
In battles feigned (the better fortitude
Of patience and heroic martyrdom

5. Raphael, the "affable archangel," who in preceding books (5–8) has sat with Adam sharing "rural repast" and discoursing on such highly relevant matters as Lucifer's fall, the Creation, the structure of the universe. To him, Adam has told of the warning he has received from God not to touch the Tree of Knowledge.
6. Unblemished.
7. At the end of the *Iliad* Achilles, whose *wrath* is the subject announced in the first line of the epic, will chase his enemy, the Trojan Hector, three times around the walls of Troy before killing him.
8. In Virgil's *Aeneid*, Lavinia, fated to be Aeneas's wife, had earlier been promised to King Turnus.
9. In the *Odyssey* Neptune (Poseidon) is the god hostile to Odysseus (*the Greek*). In the *Aeneid* the hero is persecuted by the wrath of the goddess Juno, who had quarreled with Aeneas's mother, Cytherea (Venus).
1. Urania, originally the Muse of astronomy. To Milton she is the source of *celestial* inspiration. "Answerable": suitable.
2. In other passages of the poem, Milton refers to inspiration coming to him at night or at early dawn, with spontaneous (*unpremeditated*) ease.
3. The choice of his present heroic theme had occurred early, as had the rejection of the kind of subject matter described in the following lines.
4. To analyze but also to cut up; a possible allusion to the abundance of bloody battle wounds described in classical epics.

Unsung), or to describe races and games,[5]
Or tilting furniture, emblazoned shields,
Impresses quaint, caparisons and steeds,   35
Bases[6] and tinsel trappings, gorgeous knights
At joust and tournament; then marshaled feast
Served up in hall with sewers and seneschals:[7]
The skill of artifice or office mean;
Not that which justly gives heroic name   40
To person or to poem. Me,[8] of these
Nor skilled nor studious, higher argument
Remains, sufficient of itself to raise
That name, unless an age too late, or cold
Climate, or years, damp my intended wing[9]   45
Depressed; and much they may if all be mine,
Not hers who brings it nightly to my ear.
    The sun was sunk, and after him the star
Of Hesperus, whose office is to bring
Twilight upon the Earth, short arbiter   50
'Twixt day and night, and now from end to end
Night's hemisphere had veiled the horizon round,
When Satan, who late fled before the threats
Of Gabriel out of Eden,[1] now improved
In meditated fraud and malice, bent   55
On man's destruction, mauger[2] what might hap
Of heavier on himself, fearless returned.
By night he fled, and at midnight returned
From compassing the Earth—cautious of day
Since Uriel, regent of the sun, descried   60
His entrance, and forewarned the Cherubim[3]
That kept their watch. Thence, full of anguish, driven,
The space of seven continued nights he rode
With darkness; thrice the equinoctial line
He circled, four times crossed the car of Night   65
From pole to pole, traversing each colure;[4]
On the eighth returned, and on the coast averse[5]
From entrance or cherubic watch by stealth
Found unsuspected way. There was a place
(Now not, though sin, not time, first wrought the change)   70
Where Tigris, at the foot of Paradise,[6]

5. There are long descriptions of games in the *Iliad* (23) and in the *Aeneid* (10).
6. Skirtlike housing for warhorses. "Tilting furniture": the paraphernalia of arms tournaments. "Impresses": fancy emblems on shields.
7. Attendants at meals and stewards in noble households.
8. To me.
9. The notion that nordic climates *damp* (benumb) human wit was accepted by Milton and is as old as Aristotle. "That name": that of epic poet. "An age too late": a time no longer fit for epic poetry.
1. As described in the conclusion of book 4.

2. In spite of.
3. Gabriel's troops. Uriel (whose name means "fire of God") is, according to Milton, *regent of the sun* and heat. In book 4, he warns Gabriel and his troops against Satan entering Eden.
4. A celestial circle that crosses the poles. Satan manages always to stay on the dark side of the Earth by circling it three times along the equator (*the equinoctial line*) and twice on each of the two colures.
5. The side opposite the gate guarded by Gabriel.
6. Cf. Genesis 2.10: "And a river went out of Eden to water the garden."

Into a gulf shot under ground, till part
Rose up a fountain by the Tree of Life.
In with the river sunk, and with it rose,
Satan, involved in rising mist; then sought   75
Where to lie hid. Sea he had searched and land
From Eden over Pontus, and the pool
Maeotis, up beyond the river Ob;[7]
Downward as far antarctic; and, in length,
West from Orontes to the ocean barred   80
At Darien,[8] thence to the land where flows
Ganges and Indus.[9] Thus the orb he roamed
With narrow search, and with inspection deep
Considered every creature, which of all
Most opportune might serve his wiles, and found   85
The serpent subtlest beast of all the field.[1]
Him, after long debate, irresolute
Of thoughts revolved, his final sentence chose
Fit vessel, fittest imp[2] of fraud, in whom
To enter, and his dark suggestions hide   90
From sharpest sight; for in the wily snake
Whatever sleights none would suspicious mark,
As from his wit and native subtlety
Proceeding, which, in other beasts observed,
Doubt[3] might beget of diabolic power   95
Active within beyond the sense of brute.
Thus he resolved, but first from inward grief
His bursting passion into plaints thus poured:
   "O Earth, how like to Heaven, if not preferred
More justly, seat worthier of Gods, as built   100
With second thought, reforming what was old!
For what God, after better, worse would build?
Terrestrial Heaven, danced round by other Heavens,
That shine, yet bear their bright officious[4] lamps,
Light above light, for thee alone, as seems,   105
In thee concent'ring all their precious beams
Of sacred influence! As God in Heaven
Is center, yet extends to all, so thou
Cent'ring receiv'st from all those orbs; in thee,
Not in themselves, all their known virtue appears,   110
Productive in herb, plant, and nobler birth
Of creatures animate with gradual life
Of growth, sense, reason, all summed up in man.[5]
With what delight could I have walked thee round,
If I could joy in aught; sweet interchange   115
Of hill and valley, rivers, woods, and plains,

7. Siberian river flowing into the Arctic Ocean. "Pontus": the Black Sea. "Maeotis": the Sea of Azov.
8. The Isthmus of Panama. "Orontes": a river in Syria.
9. Rivers in India.
1. Cf. Genesis 3.1: "Now the serpent was more subtil than any beast of the field."

2. Offspring, with a devilish connotation. "Sentence": decision.
3. Suspicion.
4. Performing their function.
5. What Adam called (5.509) "the scale of Nature" ascends from the vegetable order (pure growth), to the animal (sensation), to the human (the two plus reason).

Now land, now sea, and shores with forest crowned,
Rocks, dens, and caves! But I in none of these
Find place or refuge; and the more I see
Pleasures about me, so much more I feel   120
Torment within me, as from the hateful siege[6]
Of contraries; all good to me becomes
Bane,[7] and in Heaven much worse would be my state.
But neither here seek I, no, nor in Heaven,
To dwell, unless by mastering Heaven's Supreme;   125
Nor hope to be myself less miserable
By what I seek, but others to make such
As I, though thereby worse to me redound.
For only in destroying I find ease
To my relentless thoughts, and him[8] destroyed,   130
Or won to what may work his utter loss,
For whom all this was made, all this[9] will soon
Follow, as to him linked in weal or woe:
In woe then, that destruction wide may range!
To me shall be the glory sole among   135
The infernal Powers, in one day to have marred
What he, Almighty styled, six nights and days
Continued making, and who knows how long
Before had been contriving? though perhaps
Not longer than since I in one night freed   140
From servitude in glorious well-nigh half
Th' angelic name,[1] and thinner left the throng
Of his adorers. He, to be avenged,
And to repair his numbers thus impaired,
Whether such virtue,[2] spent of old, now failed   145
More angels to create (if they at least
Are his created),[3] or to spite us more,
Determined to advance into our room
A creature formed of earth, and him endow,
Exalted from so base original,   150
With heavenly spoils, our spoils. What he decreed
He effected; man he made, and for him built
Magnificent this World, and Earth his seat,
Him lord pronounced, and, O indignity!
Subjected to his service angel-wings   155
And flaming ministers, to watch and tend
Their earthy charge. Of these the vigilance
I dread, and to elude, thus wrapt in mist
Of midnight vapor, glide obscure, and pry
In every bush and brake, where hap may find   160
The serpent sleeping, in whose mazy folds
To hide me, and the dark intent I bring.

6. Seat, place.
7. Poison.
8. Man.
9. All of created nature.
1. Family, clan.

2. Power, force.
3. Inciting the angels to rebellion, Satan pretended that they were not God's creation, but "self-begot" (5.860).

O foul descent! that I, who erst contended
With Gods to sit the highest, am now constrained
Into a beast, and, mixed with bestial slime,   165
This essence[4] to incarnate and imbrute,
That to the height of deity aspired!
But what will not ambition and revenge
Descend to? Who aspires must down as low
As high he soared, obnoxious,[5] first or last,   170
To basest things. Revenge, at first though sweet,
Bitter ere long back on itself recoils.
Let it; I reck not, so it light well aimed,
Since higher[6] I fall short, on him who next
Provokes my envy, this new favorite   175
Of Heaven, this man of clay, son of despite,
Whom, us the more to spite, his Maker raised
From dust: spite then with spite is best repaid."
　　So saying, through each thicket, dank or dry,
Like a black mist low-creeping, he held on   180
His midnight search, where soonest he might find
The serpent. Him fast sleeping soon he found,
In labyrinth of many a round self-rolled,
His head the midst, well stored with subtle wiles:
Not yet in horrid shade or dismal den,   185
Nor nocent[7] yet, but on the grassy herb,
Fearless, unfeared, he slept. In at his mouth
The devil entered, and his brutal sense,
In heart or head, possessing soon inspired
With act intelligential; but his sleep   190
Disturbed not, waiting close[8] th' approach of morn.
　　Now, when as sacred light began to dawn
In Eden on the humid flowers, that breathed
Their morning incense, when all things that breathe
From th' Earth's great altar send up silent praise   195
To the Creator, and his nostrils fill
With grateful smell, forth came the human pair,
And joined their vocal worship to the choir
Of creatures wanting[9] voice; that done, partake
The season, prime for sweetest scents and airs;   200
Then còmmune how that day they best may ply
Their growing work; for much their work outgrew
The hands' dispatch of two gardening so wide:
And Eve first to her husband thus began:
　　"Adam, well may we labor still[1] to dress   205
This garden, still to tend plant, herb, and flower,
Our pleasant task enjoined; but, till more hands
Aid us, the work under our labor grows,

---

4. The supernatural substance of which he considers himself to be made.
5. Exposed to.
6. Against God. "I reck not": I don't mind.
7. Harmful.

8. Hidden. "Act intelligential": intellectual activity.
9. Lacking.
1. Constantly.

Luxurious by restraint: what we by day
Lop overgrown, or prune, or prop, or bind,   210
One night or two with wanton growth derides,
Tending to wild. Thou, therefore, now advise,
Or hear what to my mind first thoughts present.
Let us divide our labors; thou where choice
Leads thee, or where most needs, whether to wind   215
The woodbine round this arbor, or direct
The clasping ivy where to climb; while I
In yonder spring[2] of roses intermixed
With myrtle find what to redress till noon.
For, while so near each other thus all day   220
Our task we choose, what wonder if so near
Looks intervene and smiles, or objects new
Casual discourse draw on, which intermits
Our day's work, brought to little, though begun
Early, and th' hour of supper comes unearned!"   225
To whom mild answer Adam thus returned:
"Sole Eve, associate sole, to me beyond
Compare above all living creatures dear!
Well hast thou motioned,[3] well thy thoughts employed
How we might best fulfil the work which here   230
God hath assigned us, nor of me shalt pass
Unpraised; for nothing lovelier can be found
In woman than to study household good,
And good works in her husband to promote.
Yet not so strictly hath our Lord imposed   235
Labor as to debar us when we need
Refreshment, whether food or talk between,
Food of the mind, or this sweet intercourse
Of looks and smiles; for smiles from reason flow,
To brute denied, and are of love the food,   240
Love, not the lowest end[4] of human life.
For not to irksome toil, but to delight,
He made us, and delight to reason joined.
These paths and bowers doubt not but our joint hands
Will keep from wilderness[5] with ease, as wide   245
As we need walk, till younger hands ere long
Assist us. But, if much converse perhaps
Thee satiate, to short absence I could yield;
For solitude sometimes is best society,
And short retirement urges sweet return.   250
But other doubt possesses me, lest harm
Befall thee, severed from me; for thou know'st
What hath been warned us, what malicious foe,
Envying our happiness, and of his own
Despairing, seeks to work us woe and shame   255
By sly assault, and somewhere nigh at hand
Watches, no doubt, with greedy hope to find

2. Thicket, grove.   4. Object.
3. Suggested.   5. Wildness.

His wish and best advantage, us asunder,
Hopeless to circumvent us joined, where each
To other speedy aid might lend at need. 260
Whether his first design be to withdraw
Our fealty from God, or to disturb
Conjugal love, than which perhaps no bliss
Enjoyed by us excites his envy more;
Or this, or worse,[6] leave not the faithful side 265
That gave thee being, still shades thee and protects.
The wife, where danger or dishonor lurks,
Safest and seemliest by her husband stays,
Who guards her, or with her the worst endures."
    To whom the virgin[7] majesty of Eve, 270
As one who loves, and some unkindness meets,
With sweet austere composure thus replied:
    "Offspring of Heaven and Earth, and all Earth's lord!
That such an enemy we have, who seeks
Our ruin, both by thee informed I learn, 275
And from the parting angel[8] overheard,
As in a shady nook I stood behind,
Just then returned at shut of evening flowers.
But that thou shouldst my firmness therefore doubt
To God or thee, because we have a foe 280
May tempt it, I expected not to hear.
His violence thou fear'st not, being such
As we, not capable of death or pain,
Can either not receive, or can repel.
His fraud is, then, thy fear; which plain infers 285
Thy equal fear that my firm faith and love
Can by his fraud be shaken or seduced:
Thoughts, which how found they harbor in thy breast,
Adam, misthought of her to thee so dear?"[9]
    To whom, with healing words, Adam replied: 290
"Daughter of God and man, immortal Eve,
For such thou art, from sin and blame entire,[1]
Not diffident of thee do I dissuade
Thy absence from my sight, but to avoid
Th' attempt itself, intended by our foe. 295
For he who tempts, though in vain, at least asperses[2]
The tempted with dishonor foul, supposed
Not incorruptible of faith,[3] not proof
Against temptation. Thou thyself with scorn
And anger wouldst resent the offered wrong, 300
Though ineffectual found; misdeem not, then,
If such affront I labor to avert
From thee alone, which on us both at once
The enemy, though bold, will hardly dare;

6. Whether his design be this or something
even worse.
7. Pure, sinless.
8. Raphael.

9. A misjudgment (*misthought*) of me.
1. Intact.
2. Literally, sprinkles.
3. Faithfulness, loyalty.

Or, daring, first on me th' assault shall light. 305
Nor thou his malice and false guile contemn—
Subtle he needs must be who could seduce
Angels—nor think superfluous others' aid.
I from the influence of thy looks receive
Access in every virtue;[4] in thy sight 310
More wise, more watchful, stronger, if need were
Of outward strength; while shame, thou looking on,
Shame to be overcome or overreached,[5]
Would utmost vigor raise, and raised unite.
Why shouldst not thou like sense[6] within thee feel 315
When I am present, and thy trial choose
With me, best witness of thy virtue tried?"
    So spake domestic Adam in his care
And matrimonial love; but Eve, who thought
Less[7] àttributed to her faith sincere, 320
Thus her reply with accent sweet renewed:
    "If this be our condition, thus to dwell
In narrow circuit straitened by a foe,
Subtle or violent, we not endued[8]
Single with like defence wherever met, 325
How are we happy, still in fear of harm?
But harm precedes not sin: only our foe
Tempting affronts us with his foul esteem
Of our integrity: his foul esteem
Sticks no dishonor on our front,[9] but turns 330
Foul on himself; then wherefore shunned or feared
By us, who rather double honor gain
From his surmise proved false, find peace within,
Favor from Heaven, our witness, from th' event?
And what is faith, love, virtue, unassayed 335
Alone, without exterior help sustained?[1]
Let us not then suspect our happy state
Left so imperfect by the Maker wise
As not secure to single or combined.
Frail is our happiness, if this be so; 340
And Eden were no Eden, thus exposed."
    To whom thus Adam fervently replied:
"O woman, best are all things as the will
Of God ordained them; his creating hand
Nothing imperfect or deficient left 345
Of all that he created, much less man,
Or aught that might his happy state secure,
Secure from outward force. Within himself
The danger lies, yet lies within his power;
Against his will he can receive no harm. 350
But God left free the will; for what obeys

4. Increased strength.
5. Outdone.
6. Sensation.
7. Less than she deserves.

8. Endowed. "Straitened": confined.
9. Brow.
1. Without being put to test by outside forces.

Reason is free; and reason he made right,
But bid her well beware, and still erect,[2]
Lest, by some fair appearing good surprised,
She dictate false, and misinform the will   355
To do what God expressly hath forbid.
Not then mistrust, but tender love, enjoins
That I should mind[3] thee oft; and mind thou me.
Firm we subsist, yet possible to swerve,
Since reason not impossibly may meet   360
Some specious object by the foe suborned,[4]
And fall into deception unaware,
Not keeping strictest watch, as she was warned.
Seek not temptation, then, which to avoid
Were better, and most likely if from me   365
Thou sever not: trial will come unsought.
Wouldst thou approve[5] thy constancy, approve
First thy obedience; th' other who can know,
Not seeing thee attempted, who attest?
But if thou think trial unsought may find   370
Us both securer[6] than thus warned thou seem'st,
Go; for thy stay, not free, absents thee more.
Go in thy native innocence; rely
On what thou hast of virtue; summon all;
For God towards thee hath done his part: do thine." 375
  So spake the patriarch of mankind; but Eve
Persisted; yet submiss,[7] though last, replied:
  "With thy permission, then, and thus forewarned,
Chiefly by what thy own last reasoning words
Touched only, that our trial, when least sought,   380
May find us both perhaps far less prepared,
The willinger I go, nor much expect
A foe so proud will first the weaker seek;
So bent, the more shall shame him his repulse."
Thus saying, from her husband's hand her hand   385
Soft she withdrew, and like a wood nymph light,
Oread or dryad, or of Delia's train,[8]
Betook her to the groves, but Delia's self
In gait surpassed and goddesslike deport,
Though not as she with bow and quiver armed,   390
But with such gardening tools as art yet rude,
Guiltless of fire[9] had formed, or angels brought.
To Pales, or Pomona, thus adorned,
Likest she seemed, Pomona when she fled

2. On the alert against temptation, because God
has "created Man free and able enough to have
withstood his Tempter" (3, "The Argument").
3. Remind.
4. Procured for treacherous purposes.
5. Give proof, test.
6. Less careful, less alert to danger.
7. Submissive. Eve's submissiveness, however,
is qualified by Adam's reluctant tone as he
agrees to let her go and by the fact that it is she
who speaks the final words of their dialogue.
8. Delia (born on the island of Delos) is the
goddess Diana (Artemis), the huntress, with
her train of nymphs. In Greek mythology the
oreads were mountain nymphs and the dryads
were wood nymphs.
9. The ability to produce fire will become necessary only after the Fall (cf. 10.1070–82).

Vertumnus, or to Ceres in her prime, 395
Yet virgin of Proserpina from Jove.[1]
Her long with ardent look his eye pursued
Delighted, but desiring more her stay.
Oft he to her his charge of quick return
Repeated; she to him as oft engaged 400
To be returned by noon amid the bower,
And all things in best order to invite
Noontide repast, or afternoon's repose.
O much deceived, much failing, hapless Eve,
Of[2] thy presumed return! Event perverse! 405
Thou never from that hour in Paradise
Found'st either sweet repast, or sound repose;
Such ambush hid among sweet flowers and shades
Waited with hellish rancor imminent[3]
To intercept thy way, or send thee back 410
Despoiled of innocence, of faith, of bliss.
For now, and since first break of dawn, the fiend,
Mere serpent in appearance, forth was come,
And on his quest, where likeliest he might find
The only two of mankind, but in them 415
The whole included race, his purposed prey.
In bower and field he sought, where any tuft
Of grove or garden-plot more[4] pleasant lay,
Their tendance[5] or plantation for delight;
By fountain or by shady rivulet 420
He sought them both, but wished his hap might find
Eve separate; he wished, but not with hope
Of what so seldom chanced; when to his wish,
Beyond his hope, Eve separate he spies,
Veiled in a cloud of fragrance, where she stood, 425
Half spied, so thick the roses bushing round
About her glowed, oft stooping to support
Each flower of slender stalk, whose head though gay
Carnation, purple, azure, or specked with gold,
Hung drooping unsustained, them she upstays 430
Gently with myrtle band, mindless the while
Herself, though fairest unsupported flower,
From her best prop so far, and storm so nigh.
Nearer he drew, and many a walk traversed
Of stateliest covert, cedar, pine, or palm; 435
Then voluble and bold, now hid, now seen
Among thick-woven arborets and flowers
Embordered on each bank, the hand[6] of Eve:

---

1. In practical-minded Roman mythology, Pales and Pomona are deities who preside over flocks and fruit, respectively. Ceres is the goddess of agriculture in general. Both Pomona and Ceres are presented here in virginal youth: Pomona fleeing from her suitor Vertumnus (another agriculture deity), and Ceres before the time when Jove (Jupiter) made her the mother of Proserpina.
2. About.
3. Ominously ready.
4. Particularly.
5. A spot that they tended.
6. Handiwork. "Voluble": rolling. "Arborets": shrubs. "Embordered on each bank": bordering a walk.

Spot more delicious than those gardens feigned[7]
Or of revived Adonis, or renowned   440
Alcinous, host of old Laertes's son,[8]
Or that, not mystic, where the sapient king
Held dalliance with his fair Egyptian spouse.[9]
Much he the place admired, the person more.
As one who long in populous city pent,   445
Where houses thick and sewers annoy[1] the air,
Forth issuing on a summer's morn to breathe
Among the pleasant villages and farms
Adjoined, from each thing met conceives delight,
The smell of grain, or tedded[2] grass, or kine,   450
Or dairy, each rural sight, each rural sound:
If chance with nymphlike step fair virgin pass,
What pleasing seemed, for her[3] now pleases more,
She most, and in her look sums[4] all delight.
Such pleasure took the serpent to behold   455
This flowery plat,[5] the sweet recess of Eve
Thus early, thus alone; her heavenly form
Angelic, but more soft, and feminine,
Her graceful innocence, her every air
Of gesture or least action overawed   460
His malice, and with rapine[6] sweet bereaved
His fierceness of the fierce intent it brought:
That space the evil one abstracted[7] stood
From his own evil, and for the time remained
Stupidly good, of enmity disarmed,   465
Of guile, of hate, of envy, of revenge.
But the hot Hell that always in him burns,
Though in mid Heaven, soon ended his delight,
And tortures him now more, the more he sees
Of pleasure not for him ordained: then soon   470
Fierce hate he recollects, and all his thoughts
Of mischief, gratulating,[8] thus excites:
    "Thoughts, whither have ye led me? with what sweet
Compulsion thus transported to forget
What hither brought us? hate, not love, nor hope   475
Of Paradise for Hell, hope here to taste
Of pleasure, but all pleasure to destroy,
Save what[9] is in destroying; other joy
To me is lost. Then let me not let pass

---

7. Imagined by the poets (cf. 9.31).
8. Odysseus. Alcinous was the king of the Phaeacians. His perpetually flowering garden is described in the *Odyssey* (7). "Of revived Adonis": the mythical garden where Aphrodite (Venus) nursed her lover Adonis, wounded by a boar. The most famous description of the garden, certainly known to Milton, is in Spenser's *Faerie Queene* 3.
9. Pharaoh's daughter (see 1 Kings 3.1). "Not mystic": not mythical like the previous "feigned" gardens of pagan antiquity. "Sapient

king": Solomon.
1. Make noisome, pollute.
2. Spread out for drying.
3. Because of her. "If chance": if it should happen that.
4. Rounds out and brings to perfection.
5. Plot.
6. Theft.
7. Drawn off, separated.
8. Rejoicing.
9. Whatever pleasure.

Occasion which now smiles; behold alone 480
The woman, opportune to all attempts,[1]
Her husband, for I view far round, not nigh,
Whose higher intellectual more I shun,
And strength, of courage haughty, and of limb
Heroic built, though of terrestrial mold.[2] 485
Foe not informidable, exempt from wound,
I not; so much hath Hell debased, and pain
Enfeebled me, to what I was in Heaven.
She fair, divinely fair, fit love for gods,
Not terrible, though terror be in love 490
And beauty, not approached by stronger hate,[3]
Hate stronger, under show of love well feigned,
The way which to her ruin now I tend."
    So spake the enemy of mankind, enclosed
In serpent, inmate bad, and toward Eve 495
Addressed his way, not with indented wave,[4]
Prone on the ground, as since, but on his rear,
Circular base of rising folds, that towered
Fold above fold a surging maze; his head
Crested aloft, and carbuncle[5] his eyes; 500
With burnished neck of verdant gold, erect
Amidst his circling spires, that on the grass
Floated redundant.[6] Pleasing was his shape,
And lovely; never since of serpent kind
Lovelier, not those that in Illyria changed 505
Hermione and Cadmus,[7] or the god
In Epidaurus,[8] nor to which transformed
Ammonian Jove, or Capitoline was seen,
He with Olympias, this with her who bore
Scipio, the height of Rome.[9] With tract oblique 510
At first, as one who sought access, but feared
To interrupt, sidelong he works his way.
As when a ship by skillful steersman wrought
Nigh river's mouth or foreland, where the wind
Veers oft, as oft so steers, and shifts her sail: 515
So varied he, and of his tortuous train
Curled many a wanton wreath in sight of Eve,

1. In the appropriate situation for Satan's attempts on her.
2. Formed of earth.
3. If not approached, and counteracted, by hate.
4. Zigzagging.
5. Fiery red.
6. In great abundance. "Spires": coils, loops.
7. Those that Hermione and Cadmus were turned into. Cadmus, the founder of Thebes, and his wife Hermione (Harmonia), according to their story as told by Ovid (*Metamorphoses* 4.562–602), were transformed into snakes when they retired to Illyria after much family tragedy.

8. The place in Greece where Aesculapius, the god of medicine, had his major temple and appeared to worshipers in the form of an erect, flashy-eyed serpent (Ovid's *Metamorphoses* 15.622–744).
9. According to hero-deifying legends, Jove, in his personification as Jupiter Ammon (a mingling of Greco-Roman and Egyptian cults), loved Princess Olympias and became the father of Alexander the Great. As the Capitoline Jupiter (worshiped in the major Roman temple on the Capitol), he fathered Scipio, the supreme hero (*the height*) of Rome's African wars. In both cases, the father god appeared in the form of a snake.

To lure her eye: she busied heard the sound
Of rustling leaves, but minded not, as used
To such disport before her through the field,   520
From every beast, more duteous at her call,
Than at Circean call the herd disguised.[1]
He bolder now, uncalled before her stood:
But as in gaze admiring; oft he bowed
His turret[2] crest, and sleek enameled neck,   525
Fawning, and licked the ground whereon she trod.
His gentle dumb expression turned at length
The eye of Eve to mark his play: he, glad
Of her attention gained, with serpent tongue
Organic, or impulse of vocal air,[3]   530
His fraudulent temptation thus began.
    "Wonder not, sovereign mistress, if perhaps
Thou canst, who art sole wonder; much less arm
Thy looks, the heaven of mildness, with disdain,
Displeased that I approach thee thus, and gaze   535
Insatiate, I thus single, nor have feared
Thy awful brow, more awful thus retired.
Fairest resemblance of thy Maker fair,
Thee all things living gaze on, all things thine
By gift, and thy celestial beauty adore   540
With ravishment beheld, there best beheld
Where universally admired: but here
In this enclosure wild, these beasts among,
Beholders rude, and shallow[4] to discern
Half what in thee is fair, one man except,   545
Who sees thee? (and what is one?) who shouldst be seen
A goddess among gods, adored and served
By angels numberless, thy daily train."
    So glozed the tempter, and his proem[5] tuned;
Into the heart of Eve his words made way,   550
Though at the voice much marveling: at length,
Not unamazed, she thus in answer spake.
    "What may this mean? Language of man pronounced
By tongue of brute, and human sense expressed?
The first at least of these I thought denied   555
To beasts, whom God on their creation-day
Created mute to all articulate sound;
The latter I demur, for in their looks
Much reason,[6] and in their actions oft appears.
Thee, serpent, subtlest beast of all the field   560

1. The enchantress Circe, in the *Odyssey* (10), is surrounded by subjected beasts and transforms some of the hero's companions into swine.
2. Towering.
3. Producing a voice either by using his serpent's (*organic*) tongue or by some more direct impulse on the air.
4. Mentally inadequate.
5. Preamble, introduction. "Glozed": flattered.
6. Eve, well acquainted with animals, which are *duteous at her call* (line 521), questions the notion (*I demur*) that they are wholly deprived of *human sense and reason*.

I knew, but not with human voice endued:
Redouble then this miracle, and say,
How cam'st thou speakable of mute,[7] and how
To me so friendly grown above the rest
Of brutal kind, that daily are in sight?   565
Say, for such wonder claims attention due."
   To whom the guileful tempter thus replied:
"Empress of this fair world, resplendent Eve!
Easy to me it is to tell thee all
What thou command'st and right thou shouldst be obeyed: 570
I was at first as other beasts that graze
The trodden herb, of abject thoughts and low,
As was my food, nor aught but food discerned
Or sex, and apprehended nothing high:
Till on a day, roving the field, I chanced   575
A goodly tree far distant to behold
Loaden with fruit of fairest colors mixed,
Ruddy and gold; I nearer drew to gaze;
When from the boughs a savory odor blown,
Grateful to appetite, more pleased my sense   580
Than smell of sweetest fennel, or the teats
Of ewe or goat dropping with milk[8] at even,
Unsucked of lamb or kid, that tend their play.
To satisfy the sharp desire I had
Of tasting those fair apples, I resolved   585
Not to defer: hunger and thirst at once,
Powerful persuaders, quickened at the scent
Of that alluring fruit, urged me so keen.
About the mossy trunk I wound me soon,
For, high from ground, the branches would require   590
Thy utmost reach, or Adam's: round the tree
All other beasts that saw, with like desire
Longing and envying stood, but could not reach.
Amid the tree now got, where plenty hung
Tempting so nigh, to pluck and eat my fill   595
I spared not; for such pleasure till that hour
At feed or fountain never had I found.
Sated at length, ere long I might perceive
Strange alteration in me, to degree
Of reason[9] in my inward powers, and speech   600
Wanted not long, though to this shape retained.[1]
Thenceforth to speculations high or deep
I turned my thoughts, and with capacious mind
Considered all things visible in Heaven,
Or Earth, or middle, all things fair and good: 605

7. How did you acquire speech after being
dumb?
8. According to old folklore, snakes were fond
of fennel, which was supposed to sharpen
their eyesight, and of goat's milk.

9. To the point of acquiring the faculty of
reason.
1. Restrained, kept to his outward appearance. "Wanted not long": the faculty of speech
soon followed.

But all that fair[2] and good in thy divine
Semblance, and in thy beauty's heavenly ray
United I beheld: no fair to thine
Equivalent or second, which compelled
Me thus, though importune perhaps, to come   610
And gaze, and worship thee of right declared
Sovereign of creatures, universal dame."[3]
　　So talked the spirited[4] sly snake: and Eve
Yet more amazed, unwary thus replied:
　　"Serpent, thy overpraising leaves in doubt   615
The virtue of that fruit, in thee first proved.
But say, where grows the tree, from hence how far?
For many are the trees of God that grow
In Paradise, and various, yet unknown
To us; in such abundance lies our choice,   620
As leaves a greater store of fruit untouched,
Still hanging incorruptible, till men
Grow up to their provision, and more hands
Help to disburden Nature of her bearth."[5]
　　To whom the wily adder, blithe and glad: 625
"Empress, the way is ready, and not long,
Beyond a row of myrtles, on a flat,
Fast by a fountain, one small thicket past
Of blowing[6] myrrh and balm: if thou accept
My conduct, I can bring thee thither soon."   630
　　"Lead then," said Eve. He leading swiftly rolled
In tangles, and made intricate seem straight,
To mischief swift. Hope elevates, and joy
Brightens his crest; as when a wandering fire
Compact of unctuous vapor,[7] which the night   635
Condenses, and the cold environs round,
Kindled through agitation to a flame
(Which oft, they say, some evil spirit attends),
Hovering and blazing with delusive light,
Misleads th' amazed night-wanderer from his way   640
To bogs and mires, and oft through pond or pool,
There swallowed up and lost, from succor far:
So glistered the dire snake, and into fraud
Led Eve our credulous mother, to the tree
Of prohibition,[8] root of all our woe: 645
Which when she saw, thus to her guide she spake:
　　"Serpent, we might have spared our coming hither,
Fruitless to me, though fruit be here to excess,
The credit of whose virtue rest with thee;[9]

---

2. Fairness, beauty. "Middle": the air.
3. Mistress of this world.
4. Possessed by an evil spirit.
5. Products.
6. Blossoming.
7. Composed of greasy vapor. "Wandering

fire": will-o'-the-wisp, a light attributed to marsh gas.
8. The forbidden Tree of Knowledge.
9. Because the forbidden tree is as good as fruitless to Eve, the only proof of its power (*virtue*) will remain with the Serpent.

Wondrous indeed, if cause of such effects!   650
But of this tree we may not taste nor touch:
God so commanded, and left that command
Sole daughter of his voice; the rest,[1] we live
Law to ourselves; our reason is our law."
    To whom the tempter guilefully replied: 655
"Indeed? Hath God then said that of the fruit
Of all these garden trees ye shall not eat,
Yet lords declared of all in Earth or air?"
To whom thus Eve, yet sinless: "Of the fruit
Of each tree in the garden we may eat,   660
But of the fruit of this fair tree amidst
The garden, God hath said, 'Ye shall not eat
Thereof, nor shall yet touch it, lest ye die.'"
    She scarce had said, though brief, when now more bold,
The tempter, but with show of zeal and love   665
To man, and indignation at his wrong,
New part puts on, and as to passion moved,
Fluctuates disturbed, yet comely, and in act
Raised,[2] as of some great matter to begin.
As when of old some orator renowned   670
In Athens or free Rome, where eloquence
Flourished, since mute, to some great cause addressed,
Stood in himself collected, while each part,[3]
Motion, each act, won audience ere the tongue,
Sometimes in height began, as no delay   675
Of preface brooking,[4] through his zeal of right.
So standing, moving, or to height upgrown
The tempter all impassioned thus began:
    "O sacred, wise, and wisdom-giving plant,
Mother of science![5] now I feel thy power   680
Within me clear, not only to discern
Things in their causes, but to trace the ways
Of highest agents, deemed however wise.
Queen of this universe! do not believe
Those rigid threats of death. Ye shall not die;   685
How should ye? By the fruit? it gives you life
To[6] knowledge; by the Threatener? look on me,
Me who have touched and tasted, yet both live,
And life more perfect have attained than Fate
Meant me, by venturing higher than my lot.   690
Shall that be shut to man, which to the beast
Is open? Or will God incense his ire
For such a petty trespass, and not praise

---

1. For the rest. "Sole daughter of his voice": translation from the Hebrew of God's command, described as "one easy prohibition" (4.433).
2. Assuming the orator's posture. "New part": new role, as of an actor in drama. "Fluctuates": undulates his body.
3. Of the body.
4. Plunging into the middle of the subject (*in medias res*), without any preamble.
5. Knowledge.
6. As well as.

Rather your dauntless virtue, whom the pain
Of death denounced, whatever thing death be,   695
Deterred not from achieving what might lead
To happier life, knowledge of good and evil?
Of good, how just! Of evil, if what is evil
Be real, why not known, since easier shunned?
God therefore cannot hurt ye, and be just;   700
Not just, not God; not feared then, nor obeyed:
Your fear itself of death removes the fear.[7]
Why then was this forbid? Why but to awe,
Why but to keep ye low and ignorant,
His worshipers? He knows that in the day   705
Ye eat thereof, your eyes that seem so clear,
Yet are but dim, shall perfectly be then
Opened and cleared, and ye shall be as gods,
Knowing both good and evil, as they know.
That ye should be as gods, since I as man,   710
Internal man,[8] is but proportion meet,
I, of brute, human; ye, of human, gods.
So ye shall die perhaps, by putting off
Human, to put on gods:[9] death to be wished,
Though threatened, which no worse than this can bring.   715
And what are gods that man may not become
As they, participating godlike food?
The gods are first, and that advantage use
On our belief, that all from them proceeds.
I question it; for this fair Earth I see,   720
Warmed by the sun, producing every kind,
Them nothing: If they[1] all things, who enclosed
Knowledge of good and evil in this tree,
That whoso eats thereof forthwith attains
Wisdom without their leave? And wherein lies   725
Th' offense, that man should thus attain to know?
What can your knowledge hurt him, or this tree
Impart against his will if all be his?
Or is it envy, and can envy dwell
In heavenly breasts? These, these, and many more   730
Causes import[2] your need of this fair fruit.
Goddess humane, reach then, and freely taste!"
　　He ended, and his words, replete with guile,
Into her heart too easy entrance won:
Fixed on the fruit she gazed, which to behold   735
Might tempt alone, and in her ears the sound
Yet rung of his persuasive words, impregned[3]

---

7. The Serpent's captious argument is that
God is by definition just, but because a death-
giving God would not be just, he would not be
God; consequently, he would not have to be
feared and obeyed.
8. The Serpent has acquired human faculties

although his outer form has remained
unchanged (compare *inward*, line 600).
9. Divinity. "Human": humanity.
1. If they produced.
2. Imply, indicate.
3. Impregnated, filled.

With reason, to her seeming, and with truth;
Meanwhile the hour of noon drew on, and waked
An eager appetite, raised by the smell   740
So savory of that fruit, which with desire,
Inclinable[4] now grown to touch or taste,
Solicited her longing eye; yet first
Pausing a while, thus to herself she mused:
　　"Great are thy virtues, doubtless, best of fruits,   745
Though kept from man, and worthy to be admired,
Whose taste, too long forborne, at first assay
Gave elocution to the mute, and taught
The tongue not made for speech to speak thy praise:
Thy praise he also who forbids they use,   750
Conceals not from us, naming thee the Tree
Of Knowledge, knowledge both of good and evil;
Forbids us then to taste; but his forbidding
Commends thee more, while it infers[5] the good
By thee communicated, and our want: 755
For good unknown, sure is not had, or had
And yet unknown, is as not had at all.
In plain[6] then, what forbids he but to know?
Forbids us good, forbids us to be wise!
Such prohibitions bind not.[7] But if Death   760
Bind us with after-bands, what profits then
Our inward freedom?[8] In the day we eat
Of this fair fruit, our doom is, we shall die.
How dies the serpent? He hath eaten and lives,
And knows, and speaks, and reasons, and discerns,   765
Irrational till then. For us alone
Was death invented? Or to us denied
This intellectual food, for beasts reserved?
For beasts it seems: yet that one beast which first
Hath tasted, envies not, but brings with joy   770
The good befallen him, author unsuspect,[9]
Friendly to man, far from deceit or guile.
What fear I then, rather what know to fear
Under this ignorance of good and evil,[1]
Of God or death, of law or penalty?   775
Here grows the cure of all, this fruit divine,
Fair to the eye, inviting to the taste,
Of virtue[2] to make wise: what hinders then
To reach, and feed at once both body and mind?"

4. Favorably disposed.
5. Implies.
6. In plain words.
7. Eve, who has learned from the Serpent the art of sophistical argument, claims that God himself, by naming the tree, has indicated the *good* in it, but a *good unknown* is as nothing. Besides, forbidding the experience of the Tree of Knowledge is forbidding humanity *to be*

wise; hence the prohibition is not binding.
8. Death would constitute a later bond (*after-bands*), after God has granted free will (*inward freedom*).
9. An unsuspectable authority on the subject.
1. Having no knowledge of good and evil, Eve doesn't know what is to be feared.
2. With the power.

So saying, her rash hand in evil hour,   780
Forth reaching to the fruit, she plucked, she eat.[3]
Earth felt the wound, and Nature from her seat
Sighing through all her works gave signs[4] of woe,
That all was lost. Back to the thicket slunk
The guilty serpent, and well might, for Eve   785
Intent now wholly on her taste, naught else
Regarded; such delight till then, as seemed,
In fruit she never tasted, whether true
Or fancied so, through expectation high
Of knowledge; nor was godhead from her thought.[5]   790
Greedily she engorged without restraint,
And knew not eating[6] death: satiate at length,
And heightened as with wine, jocund and boon,[7]
Thus to herself she pleasingly began:
    "O sovereign, virtuous, precious of all trees   795
In Paradise! of operation blest
To sapience, hitherto obscured, infamed,[8]
And thy fair fruit let hang, as to no end
Created; but henceforth my early care,
Not without song each morning, and due praise   800
Shall tend thee, and the fertile burden ease
Of thy full branches offered free to all;
Till dieted by thee I grow mature
In knowledge, as the gods who all things know;
Though others envy what they cannot give: 805
For had the gift been theirs, it had not here
Thus grown.[9] Experience, next to thee I owe,
Best guide; not following thee I had remained
In ignorance; thou open'st Wisdom's way,
And giv'st access, though secret she retire.   810
And I perhaps am secret; Heaven is high,
High and remote to see from thence distinct
Each thing on Earth; and other care perhaps
May have diverted from continual watch
Our great Forbidder, safe[1] with all his spies   815
About him. But to Adam in what sort[2]
Shall I appear? Shall I to him make known
As yet my change, and give him to partake
Full happiness with me, or rather not,
But keep the odds[3] of knowledge in my power   820
Without copartner? so to add what wants
In female sex, the more to draw his love,
And render me more equal, and perhaps,

---

3. Ate.
4. Omens, metaphorically given as—and punning with—the sighs of Nature; forebodings of disaster.
5. She thought of acquiring divinity.
6. That she was eating.
7. Cheerful.

8. Made famous. "Blest to sapience": endowed with the power to give wisdom.
9. Eve has adopted the Serpent's argument (cf. lines 720–30).
1. Not dangerous.
2. Manner.
3. Advantage.

A thing not undesirable, sometime
Superior: for, inferior, who is free? 825
This may be well: but what if God have seen
And death ensue? Then I shall be no more,
And Adam, wedded to another Eve,
Shall live with her enjoying, I extinct;
A death to think. Confirmed then I resolve, 830
Adam shall share with me in bliss or woe:
So dear I love him, that with him all deaths
I could endure, without him live no life."[4]
    So saying, from the tree her step she turned,
But first low reverence done, as to the power 835
That dwelt within, whose presence had infused
Into the plant sciential[5] sap, derived
From nectar, drink of gods. Adam the while
Waiting desirous her return, had wove
Of choicest flowers a garland to adorn 840
Her tresses, and her rural labors crown,
As reapers oft are wont their harvest queen.
Great joy he promised to his thoughts, and new
Solace in her return, so long delayed:
Yet oft his heart, divine of[6] something ill, 845
Misgave him; he the faltering measure[7] felt;
And forth to meet her went, the way she took
That morn when first they parted. By the Tree
Of Knowledge he must pass; there he her met,
Scarce from the tree returning; in her hand 850
A bough of fairest fruit that downy smiled,
New gathered, and ambrosial smell diffused.
To him she hastened, in her face excuse
Came prologue, and apology to prompt,[8]
Which with bland words at will she thus addressed: 855
    "Hast thou not wondered, Adam, at my stay?
Thee I have missed, and thought it long, deprived
Thy presence, agony of love till now
Not felt, nor shall be twice; for never more
Mean I to try, what rash untried I sought, 860
The pain of absence from thy sight. But strange
Hath been the cause, and wonderful to hear:
This tree is not as we are told, a tree

4. In these crucial lines Eve's thoughts are shown moving through three stages: first, the idea of not sharing her knowledge with Adam, so as to enhance her own power, with the gratuitous notion that lesser power brings no freedom at all; then jealously at the thought of her own possible death and Adam *wedded to another Eve*; finally, with an opportune resurgence of *love*, the resolve to be with Adam *in bliss or woe*, i.e., to make him her partner in sin. Thus the passage is centrally representative of Milton's characterization of Eve in her relation to Adam and possibly of some of the poet's own conceptions of women in general (cf. lines 377–84, 869–85, and 1155–61).

5. Infusing knowledge.

6. Divining, foreseeing.

7. Irregularity of heartbeats.

8. A pleading expression on her face came as an introduction (the *prologue* to a play) to prepare for (*prompt*) the formal *apology*.

Of danger tasted,[9] nor to evil unknown
Opening the way, but of divine effect   865
To open eyes, and make them gods who taste;
And hath been tasted such.[1] The serpent wise,
Or not restrained as we, or not obeying,
Hath eaten of the fruit, and is become,
Not dead, as we are threatened, but thenceforth   870
Endued with human voice and human sense,
Reasoning to admiration,[2] and with me
Persuasively hath so prevailed, that I
Have also tasted, and have also found
Th' effects to correspond, opener mine eyes,   875
Dim erst, dilated spirits, ampler heart,
And growing up to godhead; which for thee
Chiefly I sought, without thee can despise.
For bliss, as thou hast part, to me is bliss,
Tedious, unshared with thee, and odious soon.   880
Thou therefore also taste, that equal lot
May join us, equal joy, as equal love;
Lest, thou not tasting, different degree[3]
Disjoin us, and I then too late renounce
Deity for thee, when Fate will not permit."[4]   885
     Thus Eve with countenance blithe her story told;
But in her cheek distemper[5] flushing glowed.
On th' other side, Adam, soon as he heard
The fatal trespass done by Eve, amazed,
Astonied stood and blank, while horror chill   890
Ran through his veins, and all his joints relaxed;[6]
From his slack hand the garland wreathed for Eve
Down dropped, and all the faded roses shed.
Speechless he stood and pale, till thus at length
First to himself he inward silence broke: 895
     "O fairest of creation, last and best
Of all God's works, creature in whom excelled
Whatever can to sight or thought be formed,
Holy, divine, good, amiable, or sweet!
How art thou lost, how on a sudden lost,   900
Defaced, deflowered, and now to death devote?[7]
Rather how hast thou yielded to transgress
The strict forbiddance, how to violate
The sacred fruit forbidden! Some cursèd fraud
Of enemy hath beguiled thee, yet unknown,[8]   905
And me with thee hath ruined, for with thee
Certain my resolution is to die.
How can I live without thee, how forgo

---

9. When tasted.
1. Has been proved by tasting.
2. Admirably.
3. A difference in rank between us.
4. Cf. lines 825–33.

5. Disharmony in the body's humors, disease.
6. Slackened. "Astonied": stunned.
7. Doomed.
8. Unknown enemy.

Thy sweet converse and love so dearly joined,
To live again in these wild woods forlorn?   910
Should God create another Eve, and I
Another rib afford, yet loss of thee
Would never from my heart; no, no! I feel
The link of nature draw me: flesh of flesh,
Bone of my bone thou art, and from thy state   915
Mine never shall be parted, bliss or woe."
   So having said, as one from sad dismay
Recomforted, and after thoughts disturbed
Submitting to what seemed remediless,
Thus in calm mood his words to Eve he turned: 920
   "Bold deed thou hast presumed, adventurous Eve
And peril great provoked, who thus hath dared
Had it been only coveting to eye
That sacred fruit, sacred to abstinence,
Much more to taste it, under ban to touch.   925
But past who can recall, or done undo?
Not God omnipotent, nor Fate! Yet so
Perhaps thou shalt not die, perhaps the fact
Is not so heinous now, foretasted fruit,
Profaned first by the serpent, by him first   930
Made common and unhallowed ere our taste,
Nor yet on him found deadly; he yet lives,
Lives, as thou saidst, and gains to live as man
Higher degree of life: inducement strong
To us, as likely, tasting, to attain   935
Proportional[9] ascent, which cannot be
But to be gods, or angels, demigods.
Nor can I think that God, Creator wise,
Though threatening, will in earnest so destroy
Us his prime creatures, dignified so high,   940
Set over all his works, which in our fall,
For us created, needs with us must fail,
Dependent made; so God shall uncreate,
Be frustrate, do, undo, and labor lose;
Not well conceived of God,[1] who, though his power   945
Creation could repeat, yet would be loath
Us to abolish, lest the adversary
Triùmph and say: 'Fickle their state whom God
Most favors; who can please him long? Me first
He ruined, now mankind; whom will he next?'   950
Matter of scorn, not to be given the foe.
However, I with thee have fixed my lot.
Certain[2] to undergo like doom: if death
Consort with thee, death is to me as life;
So forcible within my heart I feel   955
The bond of nature draw me to my own,

---

9. Proportionate to our human status (compare the Serpent's argument, lines 710–12).

1. That would be a wrong conception of God.
2. Resolved.

My own in thee, for what thou art is mine;
Our state cannot be severed; we are one,
One flesh; to lose thee were to lose myself."
    So Adam, and thus Eve to him replied:
"O glorious trial of exceeding love, 960
Illustrious evidence, example high!
Engaging me to emulate; but short
Of thy perfection, how shall I attain,
Adam? from whose dear side I boast me sprung,
And gladly of our union hear thee speak, 965
One heart, one soul in both; whereof good proof
This day affords, declaring thee resolved,
Rather than death or aught than death more dread
Shall separate us, linked in love so dear,
To undergo with me one guilt, one crime, 970
If any be, of tasting this fair fruit;
Whose virtue (for of good still good proceeds,
Direct, or by occasion)[3] hath presented
This happy trial of thy love, which else
So eminently never had been known. 975
Were it[4] I thought death menaced would ensue
This my attempt, I would sustain alone
The worst, and not persuade thee, rather die
Deserted, than oblige[5] thee with a fact
Pernicious to thy peace, chiefly assured 980
Remarkably so late of thy so true,
So faithful love unequaled; but I feel
Far otherwise th' event,[6] not death, but life
Augmented, opened eyes, new hopes, new joys,
Taste so divine, that what of sweet before 985
Hath touched my sense, flat seems to this, and harsh.
On my experience, Adam, freely taste,
And fear of death deliver to the winds."
    So saying, she embraced him, and for joy
Tenderly wept, much won that he his love 990
Had so ennobled, as of choice to incur
Divine displeasure for her sake, or death.
In recompense (for such compliance bad
Such recompense best merits), from the bough
She gave him of that fair enticing fruit 995
With liberal hand; he scrupled not to eat,
Against his better knowledge, not deceived,[7]
But fondly overcome with female charm.
Earth trembled from her entrails, as again
In pangs, and Nature gave a second groan. 1000
Sky lowered, and muttering thunder, some sad drops

3. Indirectly.
4. If.
5. Involve Adam in her guilty action.
6. The eventual consequence of her trans-

gression.
7. Adam, unlike Eve, acts in full consciousness, not having been *deceived* by the Serpent.

Wept at completing of the mortal sin
Original; while Adam took no thought,
Eating his fill, nor Eve to iterate
Her former trespass feared, the more to soothe   1005
Him with her loved society; that now
As with new wine intoxicated both,
They swim in mirth, and fancy that they feel
Divinity within them breeding wings
Wherewith to scorn the Earth. But that false fruit   1010
Far other operation first displayed,
Carnal desire inflaming; he on Eve
Began to cast lascivious eyes, she him
As wantonly repaid; in lust they burn,
Till Adam thus 'gan Eve to dalliance move: 1015
    "Eve, now I see thou art exact of taste,
And elegant, of sapience[8] no small part,
Since to each meaning savor we apply,
And palate call judicious. I the praise
Yield thee, so well this day thou hast purveyed.   1020
Much pleasure we have lost, while we abstained
From this delightful fruit, nor known till now
True relish, tasting; if such pleasure be
In things to us forbidden, it might be wished,
For[9] this one tree had been forbidden ten.   1025
But come; so well refreshed, now let us play,
As meet is, after such delicious fare;
For never did thy beauty, since the day
I saw thee first and wedded thee, adorned
With all perfections, so enflame my sense   1030
With ardor to enjoy thee, fairer now
Than ever, bounty of this virtuous[1] tree."
    So said he, and forbore not glance or toy
Of[2] amorous intent, well understood
Of Eve, whose eye darted contagious fire.   1035
Her hand he seized, and to a shady bank,
Thick overhead with verdant roof embowered
He led her, nothing loath; flowers were the couch,
Pansies, and violets, and asphodel,
And hyacinth, Earth's freshest, softest lap.   1040
There they their fill of love and love's disport
Took largely, of their mutual guilt the seal,
The solace of their sin, till dewy sleep
Oppressed them, wearied with their amorous play.
    Soon as the force of that fallacious fruit,   1045
That with exhilarating vapor bland
About their spirits had played, and inmost powers

8. In both meanings—"wisdom" and "taste."
Both *sapience* and *savor* (line 1018) are from
the Latin *sapere*. "Elegant": choosy, refined.
9. Instead of.

1. Endowed with special power (compare
lines 649 and 778).
2. With. "Toy": toying, playing.

Made err, was now exhaled, and grosser sleep
Bred of unkindly fumes,[3] with conscious dreams
Encumbered, now had left them, up they rose   1050
As from unrest, and each the other viewing,
Soon found their eyes how opened, and their minds
How darkened. Innocence, that as a veil
Had shadowed them from knowing ill, was gone;
Just confidence, and native righteousness,   1055
And honor from about them, naked left
To guilty Shame; he covered, but his robe
Uncovered more. So rose the Danite[4] strong,
Hercùlean Samson, from the harlot-lap
Of Philìstean Dàlilàh, and waked   1060
Shorn of his strength;[5] they destitute and bare
Of all their virtue. Silent, and in face
Confounded, long they sat, as strucken mute;
Till Adam, though not less than Eve abashed,
At length gave utterance to these words constrained: 1065
      "O Eve, in evil hour thou didst give ear
To that false worm,[6] of whomsoever taught
To counterfeit man's voice, true in our fall,
False in our promised rising; since our eyes
Opened we find indeed, and find we know   1070
Both good and evil, good lost, and evil got:
Bad fruit of knowledge, if this be to know,
Which leaves us naked thus, of honor void,
Of innocence, of faith, of purity,
Our wonted ornaments now soiled and stained,   1075
And in our faces evident the signs
Of foul concupiscence; whence evil store,
Even shame, the last[7] of evils; of the first
Be sure then. How shall I behold the face
Henceforth of God or angel, erst with joy   1080
And rapture so oft beheld? Those heavenly shapes
Will dazzle now this earthly[8] with their blaze
Insufferably bright. O might I here
In solitude live savage, in some glade
Obscured, where highest woods, impenetrable   1085
To star or sunlight, spread their umbrage broad,
And brown[9] as evening! Cover me, ye pines,
Ye cedars, with innumerable boughs
Hide me, where I may never see them[1] more!
But let us now, as in[2] bad plight, devise   1090
What best may for the present serve to hide
The parts of each from other, that seem most

---

3. Unnatural exhalations.
4. Of the tribe of Dan. Shame (personified) covered them, but his cover (robe) only made them aware of their nakedness (uncovered more).
5. See Judges 16.4–20.
6. I.e., the Serpent, now disparaged.

7. Extreme, ultimate. "Evil store": an abundance of evils.
8. Adam's now earthly nature and sense.
9. Dark.
1. The heavenly shapes (line 1081).
2. As we are in.

To shame obnoxious,[3] and unseemliest seen;
Some tree whose broad smooth leaves together sewed,
And girded on our loins, may cover round   1095
Those middle parts, that this newcomer, Shame,
There sit not, and reproach us as unclean."
    So counseled he, and both together went
Into the thickest wood; there soon they chose
The figtree, not that kind for fruit renowned   1100
But such as at this day, to Indians known,
In Malabar or Deccan[4] spreads her arms
Branching so broad and long, that in the ground
The bended twigs take root, and daughters grow
About the mother tree, a pillared shade   1105
High overarched, and echoing walks between;
There oft the Indian herdsman, shunning heat,
Shelters in cool, and tends his pasturing herds
At loopholes cut through thickest shade. Those leaves
They gathered, broad as Amazonian targe,[5]   1110
And with what skill they had, together sewed,
To gird their waist; vain covering, if to hide
Their guilt and dreaded shame! O how unlike
To that first naked glory! Such of late
Columbus found th' American, so girt   1115
With feathered cincture,[6] naked else and wild
Among the trees on isles and woody shores.
Thus fenced, and, as they thought, their shame in part
Covered, but not at rest or ease of mind,
They sat them down to weep; nor only tears   1120
Rained at their eyes, but high winds worse within
Began to rise, high passions, anger, hate,
Mistrust, suspicion, discord, and shook sore
Their inward state of mind, calm region once
And full of peace, now tossed and turbulent: 1125
For Understanding ruled not, and the Will
Heard not her lore, both in subjection now
To sensual Appetite, who, from beneath
Usurping over sovereign Reason, claimed
Superior sway.[7] From thus distempered breast,   1130
Adam, estranged in look and altered style,
Speech intermitted thus to Eve renewed:
    "Would thou hadst hearkened to my words, and stayed
With me, as I besought thee, when that strange
Desire of wandering, this unhappy morn,   1135

3. Exposed to.
4. In southern India. "Figtree": identified as the banyan or Indian fig tree, also classified in botany as *Ficus religiosa*.
5. Shield. The Amazons were women warriors in Greco-Roman myth (and in Virgil's *Aeneid*). Actually the tree's leaf is small; Milton's inaccurate notion comes from contemporary

sources and goes back to antiquity.
6. Belt.
7. The victory of *Sensual Appetite* over *Reason* (cf. line 113 and p. 817, n. 5) and over humankind's free will (compare lines 351 ff.)—humanity's distinguishing traits—summarizes the history of the Fall.

I know not whence possessed thee! we had then
Remained still happy, not as now, despoiled
Of all our good, shamed, naked, miserable.
Let none henceforth seek needless cause to approve
The faith they owe;[8] when earnestly they seek   1140
Such proof, conclude, they then begin to fail."
   To whom, soon moved with touch of blame, thus Eve:
"What words have passed thy lips, Adam severe?
Imput'st thou that to my default, or will
Of wandering, as thou call'st it, which who knows   1145
But might as ill have happened, thou being by,
Or to thyself perhaps? Hadst thou been there,
Or here th' attempt, thou couldst not have discerned
Fraud in the serpent, speaking as he spake;
No ground of enmity between us known,   1150
Why he should mean me ill, or seek to harm?
Was I to have never parted from thy side?
As good have grown there still a lifeless rib.
Being as I am, why didst not thou, the head,
Command me absolutely not to go,   1155
Going into such danger, as thou saidst?
Too facile then, thou didst not much gainsay,
Nay, didst permit, approve, and fair dismiss.
Hadst thou been firm and fixed in thy dissent,
Neither had I transgressed, nor thou with me."[9]   1160
   To whom, then first incensed, Adam replied:
"Is this the love, is this the recompense
Of mine to thee, ingrateful Eve, expressed[1]
Immutable when thou were lost, not I,
Who might have lived and joyed immortal bliss,   1165
Yet willingly chose rather death with thee?
And am I now upbraided as the cause
Of thy transgressing? not enough severe,
It seems, in thy restraint![2] What could I more?
I warned thee, I admonished thee, foretold   1170
The danger, and the lurking enemy
That lay in wait; beyond this had been force,
And force upon free will hath here no place.
But confidence then bore thee on, secure
Either to meet no danger, or to find   1175
Matter of glorious trial and perhaps
I also erred in overmuch admiring
What seemed in thee so perfect, that I thought
No evil durst attempt thee! but I rue
That error now, which is become my crime,   1180

8. Own. "Approve": prove by testing.
9. The notion of man's authority over
woman—recognized by Milton's Eve (e.g., in
4.442–43: "my guide / and head") and echoing
St. Paul (1 Corinthians 11.3: "the head of the

woman is the man") is here used by her to
make Adam her equal in guilt, accusing him of
indulgence in letting her go (*too facile*).
1. Demonstrated, proved.
2. In restraining Eve.

And thou th' accuser. Thus it shall befall
Him who, to worth in women overtrusting,
Lets her will rule; restraint she will not brook,[3]
And, left to herself, if evil thence ensue,
She first his weak indulgence will accuse."   1185
      Thus they in mutual accusation spent
The fruitless hours, but neither self-condemning;
And of their vain contést appeared no end.

FROM BOOK 10

The Argument

Man's transgression known, the guardian Angels forsake Paradise, and return
up to Heaven to approve their vigilance, and are approved; God declaring that
the entrance of Satan could not be by them prevented. He sends his Son to
judge the transgressors; who descends, and gives sentence accordingly; then,
in pity, clothes them both, and reascends. Sin and Death, sitting till then at the
gates of Hell, by wondrous sympathy feeling the success of Satan in this new
World, and the sin by Man there committed, resolve to sit no longer confined
in Hell, but to follow Satan, their sire, up to the place of Man: to make the way
easier from Hell to this World to and fro, they pave a broad highway or bridge
over Chaos, according to the track that Satan first made; then, preparing for
Earth, they meet him, proud of his success, returning to Hell; their mutual
gratulation. Satan arrives at Pandemonium; in full assembly relates, with
boasting, his success against Man; instead of applause is entertained with a
general hiss by all his audience, transformed, with himself also, suddenly into
Serpents, according to his doom given in Paradise; then, deluded with a show
of the Forbidden Tree springing up before them, they, greedily reaching to take
of the fruit, chew dust and bitter ashes. The proceedings of Sin and Death:
God foretells the final victory of his Son over them, and the renewing of all
things; but, for the present, commands his Angels to make several alterations
in the Heavens and Elements. Adam, more and more perceiving his fallen condition, heavily bewails,[4] rejects the condolement of Eve; she persists, and at
length appeases him: then, to evade the curse likely to fall on their offspring,
proposes to Adam violent ways; which he approves not, but, conceiving better
hope, puts her in mind of the late promise made them, that her seed should be
revenged on the Serpent, and exhorts her, with him, to seek peace of the
offended Deity by repentance and supplication.

[Acceptance, Reconciliation, Hope]

                    * * * Thus began
Outrage from lifeless things; but Discord first,
Daughter of Sin, among th' irrational
Death introduced through fierce antipathy:[5]

---

3. Put up with.
4. The selection printed here starts toward
the end of Adam's long lamentation.
5. I.e., Discord introduced death to the irratio-

nal (beasts) through antipathy; Milton paves the
way for the role of sympathy in reconciling
Adam to Eve.

Beast now with beast 'gan war, and fowl with fowl,   710
And fish with fish: to graze the herb all leaving,
Devoured each other; nor stood much in awe
Of man, but fled him, or with countenance grim
Glared on him passing. These were from without
The growing miseries, which Adam saw   715
Already in part, though hid in gloomiest shade,
To sorrow abandoned, but worse felt within,
And in a troubled sea of passion tossed,
Thus to disburden sought with sad complaint:
    "O miserable of happy! Is this the end   720
Of this new glorious world, and me so late
The glory of that glory? who now, become
Accursed of blessèd, hide me from the face
Of God, whom to behold was then my height
Of happiness! Yet well, if here would end   725
The misery; I deserved it, and would bear
My own deservings; but this will not serve.
All that I eat or drink, or shall beget,
Is propagated curse.[6] O voice, once heard
Delightfully, 'Increase and multiply,'   730
Now death to hear! for what can I increase
Or multiply, but curses on my head?
Who of all ages to succeed, but, feeling
The evil on him brought by me, will curse
My head: 'Ill fare our ancestor impure!   735
For this we may thank Adam!' but his thanks
Shall be the execration;[7] so besides
Mine own that bide upon me, all from me
Shall with a fierce reflux on me redound,
On me, as on their natural center, light   740
Heavy, though in their place. O fleeting joys
Of Paradise, dear bought with lasting woes!
Did I request thee, Maker, from my clay
To mold me man? Did I solicit thee
From darkness to promote me, or here place   745
In this delicious garden? As my will
Concurred not to my being, it were but right
And equal to reduce me to my dust,
Desirous to resign and render back
All I received, unable to perform   750
Thy terms too hard, by which I was to hold
The good I sought not. To the loss of that,
Sufficient penalty, why hast thou added
The sense of endless woes? Inexplicable
Thy justice seems; yet to say truth, too late   755
I thus contèst; then should have been refused

---

6. Eating, drinking, and procreating all increase   7. I.e., posterity's curses on Adam.
or extend God's curse.

Those terms whatever, when they were proposed.
Thou didst accept them; wilt thou enjoy the good,
Then cavil[8] the conditions? And though God
Made thee without thy leave, what if thy son   760
Prove disobedient, and reproved, retort,
'Wherefore didst thou beget me? I sought it not.'
Wouldst thou admit for his contempt of thee
That proud excuse? Yet him not thy election,
But natural necessity begot.   765
God made thee of choice his own, and of his own
To serve him; thy reward was of his grace;
Thy punishment then justly is at his will.
Be it so, for I submit; his doom is fair,[9]
That dust I am and shall to dust return.   770
O welcome hour whenever! Why delays
His hand to execute what his decree
Fixed on this day? Why do I overlive?
Why am I mocked with death, and lengthened out
To deathless pain? How gladly would I meet   775
Mortality, my sentence, and be earth
Insensible! how glad would lay me down
As in my mother's lap![1] here I should rest
And sleep secure; his dreadful voice no more
Would thunder in my ears; no fear of worse   780
To me and to my offspring would torment me
With cruel expectation. Yet one doubt
Pursues me still, lest all I cannot die;
Lest that pure breath of life, the spirit of man
Which God inspired, cannot together perish   785
With this corporeal clod; then, in the grave,
Or in some other dismal place, who knows
But I shall die a living death? O thought
Horrid, if true![2] Yet why? It was but breath
Of life that sinned; what dies but what had life   790
And sin? the body properly hath neither.
All of me then shall die: let this appease
The doubt, since human reach no further knows.
For though the Lord of all be infinite,
Is his wrath also? Be it, man is not so,   795
But mortal doomed. How can he exercise
Wrath without end on man whom death must end?
Can he make deathless death? That were to make
Strange contradiction, which to God himself

Impossible is held, as argument 800
Of weakness, not of power.[3] Will he draw out,
For anger's sake, finite to infinite
In punished man, to satisfy his rigor
Satisfied never? That were to extend
His sentence beyond dust and Nature's law; 805
By which all causes else according still
To the reception of their matter act,
Not to th' extent of their own sphere.[4] But say
That death be not one stroke, as I supposed,
Bereaving sense, but endless misery 810
From this day onward, which I feel begun
Both in me and without[5] me, and so last
To perpetuity—Ay me! that fear
Comes thundering back with dreadful revolution
On my defenseless head! Both death and I 815
Am found eternal, and incorporate both:[6]
Nor I on my part single; in me all
Posterity stands cursed. Fair patrimony
That I must leave ye, sons! O, were I able
To waste it all myself, and leave ye none! 820
So disinherited, how would ye bless
Me, now your curse! Ah, why should all mankind
For one man's fault thus guiltless be condemned,
If guiltless? But from me what can proceed,
But all corrupt, both mind and will depraved, 825
Not to do only, but to will the same
With me? How can they then acquitted stand
In sight of God?[7] Him, after all disputes,
Forced I absolve. All my evasions vain
And reasonings, though through mazes, lead me still 830
But to my own conviction: first and last
On me, me only, as the source and spring
Of all corruption, all the blame lights due;
So might the wrath! Fond[8] wish! Couldst thou support
That burden, heavier than the earth to bear; 835
Than all the world much heavier, though divided

3. Adam corrects himself, arguing (as Milton did in his theological writings) that because only the spirit (*breath of life*, line 784) sinned it shall die with the body (and, implicitly, await resurrection). Otherwise, according to the same theological line of thinking, there would be *strange contradiction*, an inadmissible sign of weakness in God.
4. Once body and spirit die, further punishment is impossible. According to *Nature's law* the power of all agents, God excepted (*all causes else*), cannot be exercised to its utmost (the *extent of their own sphere*) but is limited by the capacity for *reception* that the object of that power possesses.
5. Outside. "Bereaving sense": removing all sensory powers.
6. The use of *am*, the singular form, stresses Adam's concentration on himself and on the fact that he and death are now united in one body (*incorporate*).
7. Inheriting Adam's original sin, his descendants, like him (*with me*), are going to act sinfully by their own free will.
8. Foolish.

With that bad woman? Thus, what thou desir'st,
And what thou fear'st, alike destroys all hope[9]
Of refuge, and concludes thee miserable
Beyond all past example[1] and future;   840
To Satan only like, both crime and doom.[2]
O Conscience! into what abyss of fears
And horrors hast thou driven me; out of which
I find no way, from deep to deeper plunged!"
    Thus Adam to himself lamented loud   845
Through the still night, not now, as ere man fell,
Wholesome and cool and mild, but with black air
Accompanied, with damps and dreadful gloom;
Which to his evil conscience represented
All things with double terror. On the ground   850
Outstretched he lay, on the cold ground, and oft
Cursed his creation; Death as oft accused
Of tardy execution, since denounced
The day of his offense. "Why comes not Death,"
Said he, "with one thrice-àcceptàble stroke   855
To end me? Shall Truth fail to keep her word,
Justice divine not hasten to be just?
But Death comes not at call; Justice divine
Mends not her slowest pace for prayers or cries.
O woods, O fountains, hillocks, dales, and bowers!   860
With other echo late I taught your shades
To answer, and resound far other song."
Whom thus afflicted when sad Eve beheld,
Desolate where she sat, approaching nigh,
Soft words to his fierce passion she essayed;   865
But her with stern regard he thus repelled:
    "Out of my sight, thou serpent! that name best
Befits thee, with him leagued, thyself as false
And hateful: nothing wants, but that thy shape,
Like his, and color serpentine, may show   870
Thy inward fraud, to warn all creatures from thee
Henceforth; lest that too heavenly form, pretended[3]
To hellish falsehood, snare them. But for thee
I had persisted happy, had not thy pride
And wandering vanity, when least was safe,   875
Rejected my forewarning, and disdained
Not to be trusted, longing to be seen
Though by the devil himself, him overweening
To overreach,[4] but, with the serpent meeting,
Fooled and beguiled; by him thou, I by thee,   880

9. Actually, by his desperate self-accusation and by wanting to assume, alone, the burden of guilt, Adam is shown to be already on the way to full repentance and to his own regeneration.
1. That of the fallen angels. "Concludes thee": demonstrates that you are.

2. The comparison is clearly invalid, Adam's remorse and repentant despair being opposite to Satan's choice, as seen, for example, in 4.109–10: "Farewell remorse! All good to me is lost; / Evil, be thou my good."
3. Put up as a screen.
4. Overestimating your power to outwit him.

To trust thee from my side, imagined wise,
Constant, mature, proof against all assaults;
And understood not all was but a show
Rather than solid virtue, all but a rib
Crooked by nature—bent, as now appears,   885
More to the part sinìster—from me drawn;
Well if thrown out, as supernumerary
To my just number found!⁵ Oh, why did God,
Creator wise, that peopled highest Heaven
With spirits masculine, create at last   890
This novelty on earth, this fair defect
Of nature, and not fill the world at once
With men, as angels, without feminine;
Or find some other way to generate
Mankind?⁶ This mischief had not then befallen,   895
And more that shall befall—innumerable
Disturbances on earth through female snares,
And strait conjunction with this sex. For either
He never shall find out fit mate, but such
As some misfortune brings him, or mistake;   900
Or whom he wishes most shall seldom gain,
Through her perverseness, but shall see her gained
By a far worse, or, if she love, withheld
By parents, or his happiest choice too late
Shall meet, already linked and wedlock-bound   905
To a fell⁷ adversary, his hate or shame:
Which infinite calamity shall cause
To human life, and household peace confound."
    He added not, and from her turned; but Eve,
Not so repulsed, with tears that ceased not flowing,   910
And tresses all disordered, at his feet
Fell humble, and, embracing them, besought
His peace, and thus proceeded in her plaint:
    "Forsake me not thus, Adam! witness Heaven
What love sincere and reverence in my heart   915
I bear thee, and unweeting have offended,
Unhappily deceived! Thy suppliant⁸
I beg, and clasp thy knees; bereave me not,
Whereon I live, thy gentle looks, thy aid,
Thy counsel in this uttermost distress,   920
My only strength and stay: forlorn of thee,
Whither shall I betake me, where subsist?
While yet we live, scarce one short hour perhaps,
Between us two let there be peace; both joining,
As joined in injuries, one enmity   925

---

5. Folklore has it that the rib from which Eve was created was an extra rib on Adam's left (Latin: *sinister*) side. Note double meaning of *sinister*.

6. Adam's frenzied speech belongs to a tradition of misogynistic rhetoric that goes back to antiquity. These lines, in particular, seem to echo Euripides' *Hippolytus*, lines 617–20 (Euripides was one of Milton's favorite writers).

7. Fierce, bitter. "Already linked": i.e., when he is already linked.

8. As thy suppliant. "Unweeting": unknowingly.

Against a foe by doom express assigned us,
That cruel serpent. On me exercise not
Thy hatred for this misery befallen;
On me already lost, me than thyself
More miserable. Both have sinned, but thou   930
Against God only; I against God and thee,
And to the place of judgment will return,
There with my cries importune Heaven, that all
The sentence, from thy head removed, may light
On me, sole cause to thee of all this woe,   935
Me, me only, just object of his ire."
    She ended weeping; and her lowly plight,
Immovable[9] till peace obtained from fault
Acknowledged and deplored, in Adam wrought
Commiseration. Soon his heart relented   940
Towards her, his life so late and sole delight,
Now at his feet submissive in distress,
Creature so fair his reconcilement seeking,
His counsel, whom she had displeased, his aid;
As one disarmed, his anger all he lost,   945
And thus with peaceful words upraised her soon:
    "Unwary, and too desirous, as before,
So now, of what thou know'st not,[1] who desir'st
The punishment all on thyself! Alas!
Bear thine own first, ill able to sustain   950
His full wrath, whose thou feel'st as yet least part,[2]
And my displeasure bear'st so ill. If prayers
Could alter high decrees, I to that place
Would speed before thee, and be louder heard,
That on my head all might be visited,   955
Thy frailty and infirmer sex forgiven,
To me committed, and by me exposed.[3]
But rise; let us no more contend, nor blame
Each other, blamed enough elsewhere,[4] but strive
In offices of love, how we may lighten   960
Each other's burden in our share of woe;
Since this day's death denounced, if aught I see,
Will prove no sudden, but a slow-paced evil,
A long day's dying to augment our pain,
And to our seed (O hapless seed!) derived."[5]   965
    To whom thus Eve, recovering heart, replied:—
"Adam, by sad experiment I know

9. Modifies both Eve in her lowly posture of
repentance and Adam in his first reluctance to
forgive.
1. Once more Eve is *too desirous* of the
unknown, but her situation and her tone are
now totally different—as are those of Adam,
whose counsel and *aid* she has sought.
2. Eve would not be able to bear the weight of
God's full wrath, of which she has until now

experienced only the smallest part.
3. In the present atmosphere of reconciliation,
Adam seems to accept Eve's earlier charge (see
p. 841, n. 9); now he blames himself for having
exposed her to temptation.
4. I.e., at the place of judgment (see also lines
932, 953, and 1098–99).
5. Transmitted.

How little weight my words with thee can find,
Found so erroneous, thence by just event
Found so unfortunate. Nevertheless,   970
Restored by thee, vile as I am, to place
Of new acceptance, hopeful to regain
Thy love, the sole contentment of my heart,
Living or dying from thee I will not hide
What thoughts in my unquiet breast are risen,   975
Tending to some relief of our extremes,
Or end, though sharp and sad, yet tolerable,
As in our evils,[6] and of easier choice.
If care of our descent[7] perplex us most,
Which must be born to certain woe, devoured   980
By Death at last (and miserable it is
To be to others cause of misery,
Our own begotten, and of our loins to bring
Into this cursed world a woeful race,
That, after wretched life, must be at last   985
Food for so foul a monster), in thy power
It lies, yet ere conception, to prevent
The race unblest, to being yet unbegot.[8]
Childless thou art; childless remain. So Death
Shall be deceived his glut,[9] and with us two   990
Be forced to satisfy his ravenous maw.
But, if thou judge it hard and difficult,
Conversing, looking, loving, to abstain
From love's due rites, nuptial embraces sweet,
And with desire to languish without hope   995
Before the present object[1] languishing
With like desire—which would be misery
And torment less than none of what we dread—
Then, both our selves and seed at once to free
From what we fear for both, let us make short;   1000
Let us seek Death, or, he not found, supply
With our own hands his office on ourselves.
Why stand we longer shivering under fears
That show no end but death, and have the power,
Of many ways to die the shortest choosing   1005
Destruction with destruction to destroy?"[2]
    She ended here, or vehement despair
Broke off the rest; so much of death her thoughts
Had entertained as dyed her cheeks with pale.
But Adam, with such counsel nothing swayed,   1010
To better hopes his more attentive mind
Laboring had raised, and thus to Eve replied:—

6. We being in such evils.
7. Descendants, lineage.
8. To forestall, by abstinence, the birth of descendants.
9. Shall be cheated of its fill.

1. Eve herself, object of Adam's love, and now in his presence.
2. Destroy destruction (Death's power to destroy future mankind) by destroying ourselves now.

"Eve, thy contempt of life and pleasure seems
To argue in thee something more sublime
And excellent than what thy mind contemns: 1015
But self-destruction therefore sought refutes
That excellence thought in thee, and implies
Not thy contempt, but anguish and regret
For loss of life and pleasure overloved.[3]
Or, if thou covet death, as utmost end   1020
Of misery, so thinking to evade
The penalty pronounced, doubt not but God
Hath wiselier armed his vengeful ire than so
To be forestalled. Much more I fear lest death
So snatched will not exempt us from the pain   1025
We are by doom to pay; rather such acts
Of contumacy will provoke the Highest
To make death in us live. Then let us seek
Some safer resolution—which methinks
I have in view, calling to mind with heed   1030
Part of our sentence,[4] that thy seed shall bruise
The Serpent's head. Piteous amends! unless
Be meant whom I conjecture,[5] our grand foe,
Satan, who in the Serpent hath contrived
Against us this deceit. To crush his head   1035
Would be revenge indeed—which will be lost
By death brought on ourselves, or childless days
Resolved as thou proposest; so our foe
Shall scape his punishment ordained, and we
Instead shall double ours upon our heads.   1040
No more be mentioned, then, of violence
Against ourselves, and wilful barrenness
That cuts us off from hope, and savors only
Rancor and pride, impatience and despite,
Reluctance[6] against God and his just yoke   1045
Laid on our necks. Remember with what mild
And gracious temper he both heard and judged,
Without wrath or reviling. We expected
Immediate dissolution, which we thought
Was meant by death that day; when, lo! to thee   1050
Pains only in child-bearing were foretold,
And bringing forth, soon recompensed with joy,

---

3. The suicide project excludes (*refutes*) the idea that Eve be contemptuous of life and pleasure in view of *something more sublime*; it rather implies *anguish and regret* at the thought of losing those goods.
4. Earlier in this book (the Argument and lines 163–208) the Lord gives sentence on the Serpent and the transgressors. The references here are to that passage, which is quite literally based on Genesis 30 (esp. lines 179–81; "Between thee and the Woman I will put /

Enmity, and between thine and her seed; / Her seed shall bruise thy head, thou bruise his heel").
5. The notion that Satan spoke through the Serpent was not at first given to humanity (lines 170–71: "Concerned not Man.... / Nor altered his offense"). Adam is late in coming to that conclusion (*I conjecture*), and on it he bases the following eloquent argument in favor of survival, hope, procreation, and activity.
6. Resistance, opposition.

Fruit of thy womb. On me the curse aslope
Glanced on the ground.[7] With labor I must earn
My bread; what harm: Idleness had been worse; 1055
My labor will sustain me; and, lest cold
Or heat should injure us, his timely care
Hath, unbesought, provided, and his hands
Clothed us unworthy, pitying while he judged.
How much more, if we pray him, will his ear 1060
Be open, and his heart to pity incline,
And teach us further by what means to shun
The inclement seasons, rain, ice, hail, and snow!
Which now the sky, with various face, begins
To show us in this mountain,[8] while the winds 1065
Blow moist and keen, shattering the graceful locks
Of these fair spreading trees; which bids us seek
Some better shroud, some better warmth to cherish
Our limbs benumbed—ere this diurnal star
Leave cold the night, how we his gathered beams 1070
Reflected may with matter sere foment,[9]
Or by collision of two bodies grind
The air attrite to fire;[1] as late the clouds,
Justling, or pushed with winds, rude in their shock,
Tine the slant lightning, whose thwart[2] flame, driven down, 1075
Kindles the gummy bark of fir or pine,
And sends a comfortable heat from far,
Which might supply the Sun. Such fire to use,
And what may else be remedy or cure
To evils which our own misdeeds have wrought, 1080
He will instruct us praying,[3] and of grace
Beseeching him; so as we need not fear
To pass commodiously this life, sustained
By him with many comforts, till we end
In dust, our final rest and native home. 1085

7. The curse descending (*aslope*) on Adam took an oblique course (*glanced*) toward the ground. Thus Adam is not only accepting the Lord's sentence (in lines 201–02 and 205; "Curs'd is the ground for thy sake; thou in sorrow / Shalt eat thereof all the days of thy life; /... In the sweat of thy face thou shalt eat bread") but turning it into a project for an active life after the Fall.

8. In his description of *delicious Paradise* (4.132–58), Milton situates it on a high plateau at the top of a "steep wilderness" that denies access to the "enclosure green" and its "Insuperable height of loftiest shade, / Cedar, and pine, and fir, and branching palm, / A sylvan scene, and as the ranks ascend / Shade above shade, a woody theater / Of stateliest view" where "gentle gales /... dispense / Native perfumes, and whisper whence they

stole / Those balmy spoils." That stately and blissful order is now disrupted, and after the radical alterations in the heavens and in the elements that God has commanded, Adam is preparing to cope with the hardships and challenges of his mortal state in a time-conditioned universe of seasonal changes, dawns and sunset, heat and ice, and shattering winds.

9. Heat, warm. "Diurnal star": day star, the sun. "How": seek how.

1. The implied belief is that rubbing two *bodies* (as two flints) against each other, the air thus ground down by the attrition (*attrite*) turns into fire.

2. Passing across the sky. "Tine": kindle; that fire was produced by lightning is one of the ancient theories about its origin on earth.

3. If we pray to him.

What better can we do, than to the place
Repairing where he judged us, prostrate fall
Before him reverent, and there confess
Humbly our faults, and pardon beg, with tears
Watering the ground, and with our sighs the air   1090
Frequenting,[4] sent from hearts contrite, in sign
Of sorrow unfeigned and humiliation meek?
Undoubtedly he will relent, and turn
From his displeasure, in whose look serene,
When angry most he seemed and most severe,   1095
What else but favor, grace, and mercy shone?"
　　So spake our Father penitent; nor Eve
Felt less remorse. They, forthwith to the place
Repairing where he judged them, prostrate fell
Before him reverent, and both confessed   1100
Humbly their faults, and pardon begged, with tears
Watering the ground, and with their sighs the air
Frequenting, sent from hearts contrite, in sign
Of sorrow unfeigned and humiliation meek.

FROM BOOK 12

[*After God's acceptance of the transgressors' prayers and the decree that "they must no longer abide in Paradise" (11, "The Argument"), Michael the archangel, with a band of cherubim, has been sent "to dispossess them." After Eve's lamentation and his own pleading, Adam has submitted; Michael has led him up to a high hill where, in a mixture of prophecy and instruction, he has set "before him in vision" the future of humankind, from Cain and Abel through Noah (11) and the prophets, thus coming "by degrees to explain who that Seed of Woman shall be which was promised Adam and Eve in the Fall: his incarnation, death, resurrection, and ascension; the state of the Church till his second coming" (12, "The Argument"). Toward the close of his speech, Michael has recommended the exercise of the basic Christian virtues, culminating in love, "By name to come called Charity, the soul / Of all the rest: then will thou not be loath / To leave this Paradise, but shalt possess / A Paradise within thee, happier far" (12.584–87). Michael has just ended his long speech.*]

["The World Was All before Them"]

* * *

He ended, and they both descend the hill.
Descended, Adam to the bower where Eve
Lay sleeping[5] ran before, but found her waked;
And thus with words not sad she him received:

4. Filling.
5. Michael has just said to Adam (lines 594–97): "Go, waken Eve; / Her also I with

gentle dreams have calmed, / Portending good, and all her spirits composed / To meek submission."

"Whence thou return'st and whither went'st, I know;   610
For God is also in sleep, and dreams[6] advise,
Which he hath sent propitious, some great good
Presaging, since, with sorrow and heart's distress
Wearied, I fell asleep. But now lead on;
In me is no delay; with thee to go   615
Is to stay here; without thee here to stay
Is to go hence unwilling; thou to me
Art all things under Heaven, all places thou,
Who for my willful crime art banished hence.
This further consolation yet secure   620
I carry hence: though all by me is lost,
Such favor I unworthy am vouchsafed,
By me the Promised Seed shall all restore."
    So spake our mother Eve; and Adam heard
Well pleased, but answered not; for now too nigh   625
Th' archangel stood, and from the other hill[7]
To their fixed station, all in bright array,
The cherubim descended; on the ground
Gliding meteorous, as evening mist
Risen from a river o'er the marish[8] glides,   630
And gathers ground fast at the laborer's heel
Homeward returning. High in front advanced,[9]
The brandished sword of God before them blazed,
Fierce as a comet; which with torrid heat,
And vapor as the Libyan air adust,[1]   635
Began to parch that temperate clime; whereat
In either hand the hastening angel caught
Our lingering parents, and to th' eastern gate[2]
Led them direct, and down the cliff as fast
To the subjected[3] plain; then disappeared.   640
They, looking back, all th' eastern side beheld
Of Paradise, so late their happy seat,
Waved over by that flaming brand,[4] the gate
With dreadful faces thronged and fiery arms.
Some natural tears they dropped, but wiped them soon;   645
The world was all before them, where to choose
Their place of rest,[5] and Providence their guide.
They, hand in hand, with wandering steps and slow,
Through Eden took their solitary way.

6. The fact that Adam was granted a vision and Eve a dream may symbolize a difference in the mode of perception between man and woman; at any rate, both are God's revelations.

7. The hill that Michael had pointed out to Adam in lines 590–93: "and, see! the guards, / By me encamped on yonder hill, expect / Their motion, at whose front a flaming sword, / In signal of remove, waves fiercely round."

8. Marsh.

9. Raised high, carried like a banner.

1. Burned up, as the air of the Sahara Desert in Libya.

2. *The eastern gate* of Eden, guarded by Gabriel, was described earlier (4.543–47): "It was a rock / Of alabaster, piled up to the clouds, / Conspicuous far, winding with one ascent / Accessible from earth, one entrance high; / The rest was craggy cliff."

3. Lying below.

4. Here meaning sword, but also conveying the image of burning (*flaming*). "Seat": abode.

5. Not, of course, a place of repose, but their new, earthly abode.

Selected Bibliographies

I. Encounters with Islam

The most comprehensive reference for the Ottoman Empire for years to come will be *The Cambridge History of Turkey*, which includes contributions on all aspects of land, state, society, and culture: *Volume 1, Byzantium to Turkey, 1071–1453*, ed. by Kate Fleet, appeared in 2009; *Volume 3, The Later Ottoman Empire, 1603–1839*, ed. by Suraiya Faroqhi, in 2006. *Volume 2, The Ottoman Empire as a World Power, 1453–1603*, ed. by Faroqhi and Fleet, is due to appear in 2011. Faroqhi's *Subjects of the Sultans* (2000) is a very readable overview of Ottoman cultural history. Fleet and Ebru Boyar give a vivid picture of life in Istanbul, the center of the Ottoman universe: *A Social History of Ottoman Istanbul* (2010). The most original, and most engaging, work on Ottoman literature in society is Walter Andrews and Mehmed Kalpakli, *The Age of Beloveds: Love and the Beloved in Early-Modern Ottoman and European Culture and Society* (2005).

David Conrad's *Empires of Medieval West Africa* (rev. ed. 2010) provides a broad introduction to West Africa, as does Nehemia Levtzion's *Ancient Ghana and Mali* (1980). Levtzion and J. F. P. Hopkins's *Corpus of Early Arabic Sources for West African History* (1981) is an excellent source book for the study of the region. For the history of Islam in West Africa, consult Levtzion and R. L. Pouwels's *The History of Islam in Africa* (2000) and Levtzion and Jay Spaulding's *Medieval West Africa: Views from Arab Scholars and Merchants* (2003).

Stanley Wolpert's *A New History of India* (2008) places Islam's multifaceted impact on South Asia in its historical and political contexts; Ira M. Lapidus's *A History of Islamic Societies* (1988) analyzes that impact in a global and comparative perspective. Richard M. Eaton's *The Rise of Islam and the Bengal Frontier, 1204–1760* (1993), though more specialized, provides an excellent historical, social, and political account of the arrival and spread of Islam in India. On many specific aspects of Muslim India, see David Waines's *An Introduction to Islam* (1995); and on the transformation of Indian literature under Muslim influence, see Vinay Dharwadker's *Kabir: The Weaver's Songs* (2003). Excellent essays by many scholars on the Delhi Sultanate and the Mughal Empire are included in Irfan Habib's *Medieval India* (1992) and *Akbar and His India* (1997); and in Muzaffar Alam and Sanjay Subrahmanyam's *The Mughal State, 1526–1750* (1998).

The Abencerraje
Maria Soledad Carrasco-Urgoiti's *The Moorish Novel: "El Abencerraje" and Pérez de Hita* (1976) offers an approachable introduction to the genre. Barbara Fuchs, Larissa Brewer-García, and Aaron Ilika's translation includes an extensive introduction and contemporary legal documents, polemics, and ballads that situate *The Abencerraje* in its historical and intellectual context. In "Power, Discourse, and Metaphor in the Abencerraje" (*MLN* 99.2 [March 1984]: 195–213), Israel Burshatin challenges maurophile readings of the novella, while Laura Bass's "Homosocial Bonds and Desire in *The Abencerraje*" (*Revista Canadiense de Estudios Hispánicos* 24.3 [Spring

2000]: 453–71) offers a gender-studies perspective.

The Book of Dede Korkut

Michael Meeker, "The Dede Korkut Ethic" *International Journal of Middle East Studies* 243 (1992): 395–417 gives a detailed analysis of the tale of Goggle-Eye, and a helpful summary of the discussion of origins; his suggestion of a continuing relevance of the tales differs from the arguments presented above. Karl Reichl has devoted numerous books to epic literatures. His *Turkic Oral Epic Poetry* (1992), is the essential introduction to the topic, and a useful survey of existing texts and traditions. In *Singing the past: Turkic and Medieval heroic poetry* (2000), he compares structure and performance of Turkic and medieval English and German epics. İlhan Başgöz, *Hikāye: Turkish folk romance as performance art* (2008), is the sum of a lifetime of studying Turkish folk narratives and the problems of oral performance.

Evliya Çelebi

No complete English translation of the *Book of Travels* has been undertaken; a rich array of the most colorful passages is found in *An Ottoman Traveller. Selections from the* Book of Travels *of Evliya Çelebi*, trans. and ed. by Robert Dankoff & Sooyong Kim (2010). Dankoff's *Evliya Çelebi—An Ottoman Mentality* 2nd ed. (2006) is the best introduction to the person and work of Evliya. Dankoff's *The Intimate Life of an Ottoman Statesman: Melek Ahmed Pasha (1588–1662): As Portrayed In Evliya Çelebi's Book of Travels (Seyahat-name)* (1991) offers further details of the lives of Evliya and his most important patron. Both works translate extensively from the *Book of Travels*. The background of the Vienna episode is studied in Karl Teply's *Türkische Sagen und Legenden um die Kaiserstadt Wien* (1980).

Indian Poetry after Islam

A. K. Ramanujan's *Speaking of Siva* (1973) offers the best English translations of the Virasaiva poets in Kannada, including Basavanna and Mahadeviyakka, as well as an excellent introduction to the *bhakti* movement, especially in southern India. The most reliable and poetic translations of a representative selection of Kabir's poetry, accompanied by an extensive commentary on the Hindi and northern Indian *bhakti* traditions, are available in Vinay Dharwadker's *Kabir: The Weaver's Songs* (2003). John Stratton Hawley and Mark Juergensmeyer's *Songs of the Saints of India* (1988) provides basic selections of poems and introductions to several northern Indian *bhakti* figures, including Kabir and Mirabai; Hawley's *Three Bhakti Voices; Mirabai, Surdas, and Kabir in Their Time and Ours* (2005) contains more recent translations and scholarly accounts of the poets. Vinay Dharwadker's "Poems of Tukaram," in Donald Lopez's *Religions of India in Practice* (1996) offers a handy overview of the poet's life and work. Christian Noetzke, *Religion and Public Memory: A Cultural History of Saint Namdev in India* (2008), provides a wider perspective on *bhakti* in Marathi literature and culture.

Sunjata

Musical performances involving the singing of stories and praises about Sunjata are called *Sunjata fasa*, and the prose narrative in its many versions is known as *Manden maana*, or *Manden tariku*. The version excerpted here was collected and translated by David C. Conrad; his *Sunjata* (2004) offers a detailed introduction. Conrad's *Epic Ancestors of the Sunjata Era: Oral Tradition from the Maninka of Guinea* collects seven variants of the Sunjata epic. Laye Camara's *The Guardian of the Word* (1984) is a prose variant in novel form, based on the narrative by Babu Condé of Fadama, Guinea, recorded in 1963. But it was another prose variant, Djibril Tamsir Niane's *Sundiata: An Epic of Old Mali* (1965) that first drew worldwide attention to this epic. The three versions edited by Gordon Innes in *Sunjata* (1974) were narrated in the Mandinka dialect of the Gambia, and the one published by John Johnson in 1986 as *Son-Jara* third edition (2003) represents the Kita region of Mali. Eric Charry's *Mande Music* (2000) describes the musical instruments involved in performing the epic, while Stephen Belcher, *Epic Traditions of Africa* (1999), and Marloes Janson, *The Best Hand is the Hand that Always Gives: Griottes and their Profession in Eastern Gambia* (2002), provide broad context and analytical insight.

II. Europe and the New World

Eugene Rice with Anthony Grafton, *The Foundations of Early Modern Europe*, second edition (1994), is the finest introduction to the contexts in which Renaissance or early modern literature was produced. William Bouwsma, *A Usable Past: Essays in European Cultural History* (1990), especially the chapter "Anxiety and the Formation of Early Modern Culture," also offers illuminating perspectives on the intellectual character of the period. Constance Jordan, *Renaissance Feminism: Literary Texts and Political Models* (1990), is a recommended study of the place of women in history and political thought. William Kerrigan and Gordon Braden, *The Idea of the Renaissance* (1989), offers a helpful and direct analysis of the critical construction of the Renaissance as a concept. Harry Berger Jr., *Second World and Green World: Studies in Renaissance Fiction-Making* (1988), especially the title essay, is a dense but recommended study of the aims of fiction making. Stephen Greenblatt, *Renaissance Self-Fashioning* (1980), describes the construction of identity in the period. J. H. Elliott's *The Old World and the New: 1492–1650* (1992) and *Imperial Spain: 1492–1716*, second edition (2002) provide good introductions.

Ludovico Ariosto
Important studies of Ariosto include Patricia Parker, *Inescapable Romance* (1970) and A. Bartlett Giamatti, *The Earthly Paradise and the Renaissance Epic* (1966). A more specialized study can be found in Elizabeth J. Bellamy, *Translations of Power* (1992). Other useful readings are Albert Ascoli, *Ariosto's Bitter Harmony* (1987) and Sergio Zatti, *The Quest for Epic: From Ariosto to Tasso* (2006).

Miguel de Cervantes
William Byron, *Cervantes: A Biography* (1978), is thorough. Ruth El Saffar, ed., *Critical Essays on Cervantes* (1986), and Anne Cruz and Carroll Johnson, eds., *Cervantes and his Postmodern Constituencies* (1998) offer interesting essays by eminent scholars. Vladimir Nabokov, *Lectures on Don Quixote* (1983), presents an elegant engagement with Cervantes' fiction. More technical studies include Carroll Johnson, *Cervantes and the Material World* (2000) and David Quint, *Cervantes' Novel of Modern Times: A New Reading of* Don Quixote (2003).

Lope de Vega
Walter Cohen, *Drama of a Nation: Public Theater and Renaissance England and Spain* (1985); Robert L. Fiore, *Drama and Ethos: Natural-Law Ethics in Spanish Golden Age Theater* (1975); and Melveena McKendrick, *Theatre in Spain, 1490–1700* (1989), present useful and illuminating studies of Lope de Vega's work and its relation to Spanish theater in general. Richard Helgerson, *Adulterous Alliances* (2000), considers the political implications of the play. J. H. Elliott's *Imperial Spain 1469–1716* (1963), is an indispensable study of Spanish history and politics.

Niccolò Machiavelli
Peter E. Bondanella focuses on the literary aspects of Machiavelli's works in *Machiavelli and the Art of Renaissance History* (1973). Sebastian de Grazia, *Machiavelli in Hell* (1989), on politics in *The Prince,* contains indexes and a bibliography. J. R. Hale's biography, *Machiavelli and Renaissance Italy* (1972), places Machiavelli in a historical perspective. A political analysis is provided by Anthony Parel in *The Political Calculus: Essays on Machiavelli's Political Philosophy* (1972). Roberto Ridolfi, *The Life of Niccolò Machiavelli* (1963), is still considered the best and most accurate biography. Silvia Ruffo-Fiore, *Niccolò Machiavelli* (1982), is a useful comprehensive guide for the beginning student. Victoria Kahn, *Machiavellian Rhetoric: From the Counter-Reformation to Milton* (1994), and Wayne A. Rebhorn, *Foxes and Lions: Machiavelli's Confidence Men* (1988), are recommended.

Marguerite de Navarre
P. A. Chilton's justly praised translation of the *Heptameron* (1984) has an excellent introduction. John D. Lyons and Mary B. McKinley, eds., *Critical Tales: New Studies of the Heptameron and Early Modern Culture* (1993), con-

tains useful essays on the *Heptameron*. B. J. Davis, *The Storytellers in Marguerite de Navarre's Heptameron* (1978), presents detailed discussions of the narrators. Timothy Hampton, *Literature and Nation in the Sixteenth Century: Inventing Renaissance France* (2001) offers a historical reading of story 10. Samuel Putnam, *Marguerite de Navarre* (1935), is an informative and readable biography. Barbara M. Stephenson, *The Power and Patronage of Marguerite de Navarre* (2004), uses Marguerite's letters to trace her involvement in politics and in religious reform.

John Milton
The standard biography is William Riley Parker, *Milton: A Biography*, 2 vols. (1981). Annabel Patterson, ed., *John Milton* (1992), and David Quint, *Epic and Empire: Politics and Generic Form from Virgil to Milton* (1993), offer useful recent studies of Milton. Rewarding essays can also be found in *Remembering Milton: Essays on the Texts and Traditions* (1987), ed. Mary Nyquist and Margaret W. Ferguson. Barbara Kiefer Lewalski, *Paradise Lost and the Rhetoric of Literary Forms* (1985), offers a lucid and comprehensive study of Milton's uses of literary genre. Patricia Parker discusses Milton's suggestive linkage of doubt, the romance form, and Eve in a chapter of *Inescapable Romance* (1975). Stanley Fish directs attention to the role of readers' responses in determining or creating meaning in *Surprised by Sin: The Reader in Paradise Lost* (1967). A. Bartlett Giamatti, *The Earthly Paradise and the Renaissance Epic* (1966), analyzes the "coalescence of classical and Christian material" in the poem. Robert Crosman, *Reading Paradise Lost* (1980), is a helpful introduction for first-time readers of Milton's poem.

Michel de Montaigne
Hugo Friedrich, *Montaigne* (1991), is a careful historical study of the author. David Quint, *Montaigne and the Quality of Mercy* (1998) analyzes the political and ethical goals of the *Essays*. Judith Shklar, *Ordinary Vices* (1984), and Edwin Duval, "Lessons of the New World: Design and Meaning in Montaigne's 'Des Cannibales' (I:31) and 'Des coches' (III:6)," in *Montaigne: Essays in Reading*, ed. Gerard Defaux, *Yale French Studies* 64 (1983): 95–112, provide excellent studies of Montaigne that include, but are not limited to, his New World contexts. Marcel Tetel, *Montaigne,* updated edition

(1990), and Richard Sayce, *The Essays of Montaigne: A Critical Exploration* (1972), are excellent introductions designed for the general reader.

Sir Thomas More
The Life of Sir Thomas More (1557?), by his son-in-law, William Roper, is the earliest and most intimate biography of More, reprinted in a modern edition. Louis L. Martz, *Thomas More: The Search for the Inner Man* (1992) analyzes More's writings as well as the Holbein portraits of More and his family. Northrop Frye's classic essay, "Varieties of Literary Utopias" (1965), surveys the genre More inaugurated. Dominic Baker-Smith, *More's Utopia* (2000) is a good introduction to the text and its critical reception.

Petrarch and the Love Lyric
Ernest Hatch Wilkins' biography, *Life of Petrarch* (1961), is informative, but tends to take Petrarch's autobiographical writings at face value. Giuseppe Mazzotta, *The Worlds of Petrarch* (1993), is an encyclopedic introduction to Petrarch's work and times. Victoria Kirkham and Armando Maggi have compiled the useful *Petrarch: A Critical Guide to the Complete Works* (2009). Robert Durling's introduction to *Petrarch's Lyric Poems* (1976) provides a rich overview of his poetry. Diana Vickers, "Diana Described: Scattered Woman and Scattered Rhyme," *Writing and Sexual Difference*, ed. Elizabeth Abel (1982), is the central feminist reading of Petrarch's lyric. In *Unrequited Conquests* (2000), Roland Greene reads Petrarchism in relation to early modern imperialism.

Popol Vuh
Dennis Tedlock's translation, satisfyingly annotated, is published as *Popol Vuh: The Mayan Book of the Dawn of Life* (1985; revised 1996). The text in this volume is from the 1996 edition. Older translations with useful introductions are Adrián Recinos, Delia Goetz, and Sylvanus Morley, *Popol Vuh: The Sacred Book of the Ancient Quiché Maya* (1950); and Munro S. Edmonson. *The Book of Counsel: The Popol Vuh of the Quiché Maya of Guatemala* (1971). Edmonson's is the only Quiché-English edition. Essays on the Popol Vuh and related topics are in Tedlock's *The Spoken Word and the Work of Interpretation* (1983).

William Shakespeare

Recent biographies placing Shakespeare in his social and intellectual context include Stephen Greenblatt, *Will in the World: How Shakespeare Became Shakespeare* (2004) and Jonathan Bate, *Soul of the Age: A Biography of the Mind of William Shakespeare* (2009). Marjorie Garber, *Shakespeare After All* (2005), provides a lively introduction, with individual essays on all the plays. Paul Arthur Cantor, *Shakespeare, "Hamlet"* (1989), is an in-depth study of the tragedy. Valuable studies are to be found in Harry Levin, *The Question of "Hamlet"* (1959) and Margreta de Grazia, *"Hamlet" without Hamlet* (2007).

Timeline

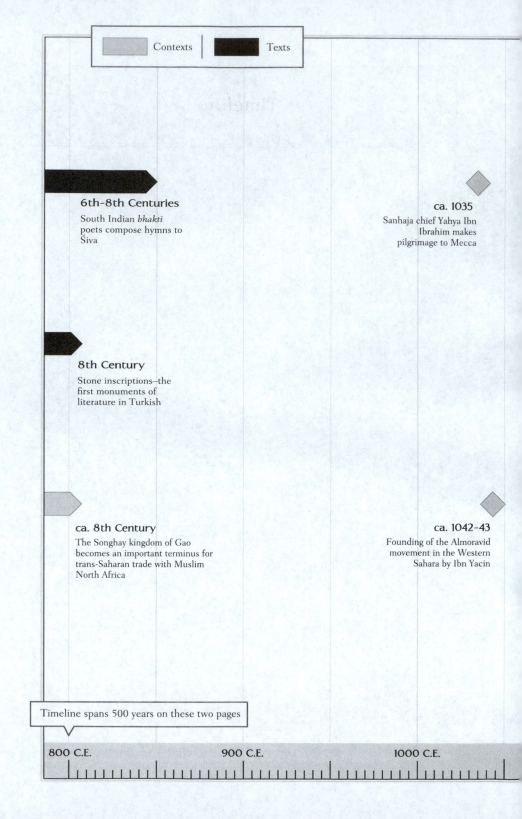

Contexts | Texts

6th–8th Centuries

South Indian *bhakti* poets compose hymns to Śiva

8th Century

Stone inscriptions–the first monuments of literature in Turkish

ca. 8th Century

The Songhay kingdom of Gao becomes an important terminus for trans-Saharan trade with Muslim North Africa

ca. 1035

Sanhaja chief Yahya Ibn Ibrahim makes pilgrimage to Mecca

ca. 1042–43

Founding of the Almoravid movement in the Western Sahara by Ibn Yacin

Timeline spans 500 years on these two pages

800 C.E.   900 C.E.   1000 C.E.

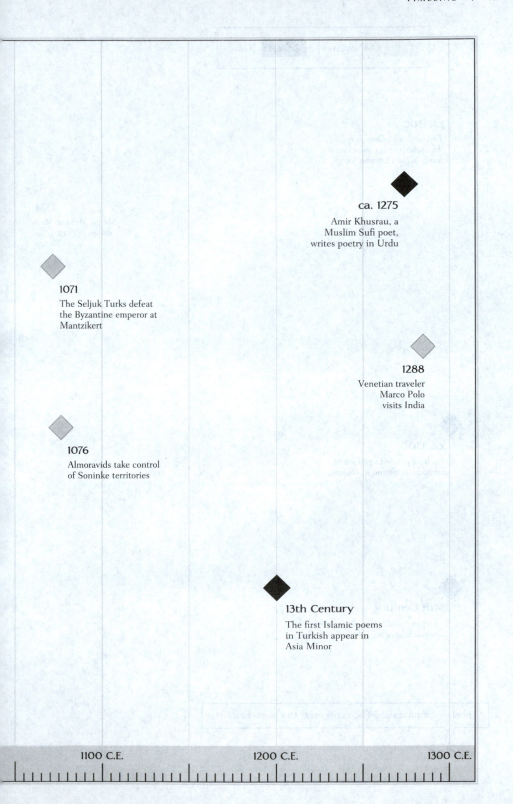

ca. 1275

Amir Khusrau, a
Muslim Sufi poet,
writes poetry in Urdu

1071

The Seljuk Turks defeat
the Byzantine emperor at
Mantzikert

1288

Venetian traveler
Marco Polo
visits India

1076

Almoravids take control
of Soninke territories

13th Century

The first Islamic poems
in Turkish appear in
Asia Minor

1100 C.E.   1200 C.E.   1300 C.E.

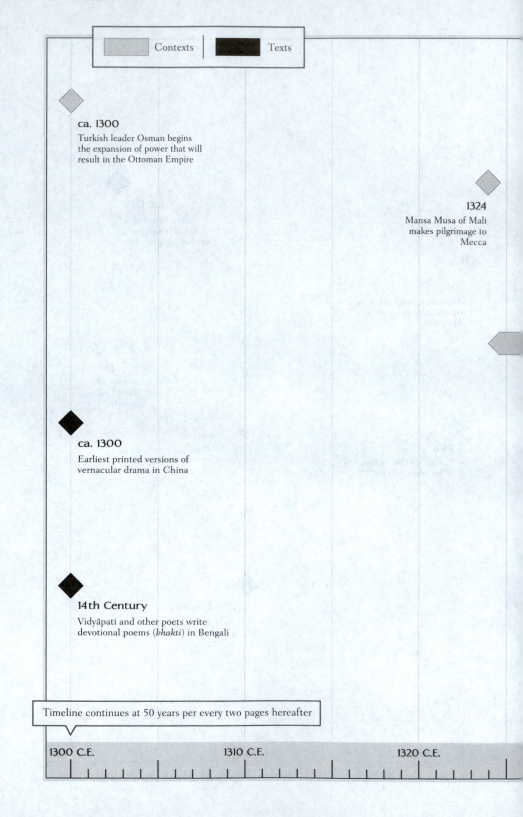

Contexts | Texts

ca. 1300
Turkish leader Osman begins
the expansion of power that will
result in the Ottoman Empire

1324
Mansa Musa of Mali
makes pilgrimage to
Mecca

ca. 1300
Earliest printed versions of
vernacular drama in China

14th Century
Vidyāpati and other poets write
devotional poems (*bhakti*) in Bengali

Timeline continues at 50 years per every two pages hereafter

1300 C.E.   1310 C.E.   1320 C.E.

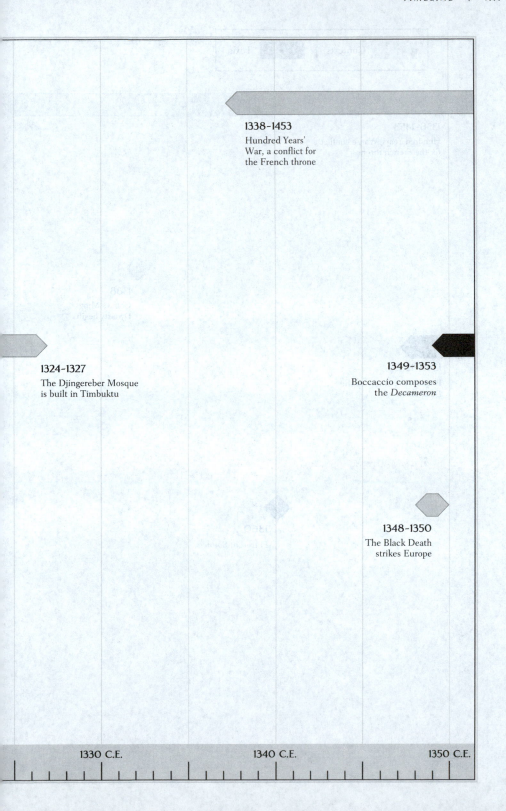

1338–1453
Hundred Years'
War, a conflict for
the French throne

1324–1327
The Djingereber Mosque
is built in Timbuktu

1349–1353
Boccaccio composes
the *Decameron*

1348–1350
The Black Death
strikes Europe

1330 C.E.   1340 C.E.   1350 C.E.

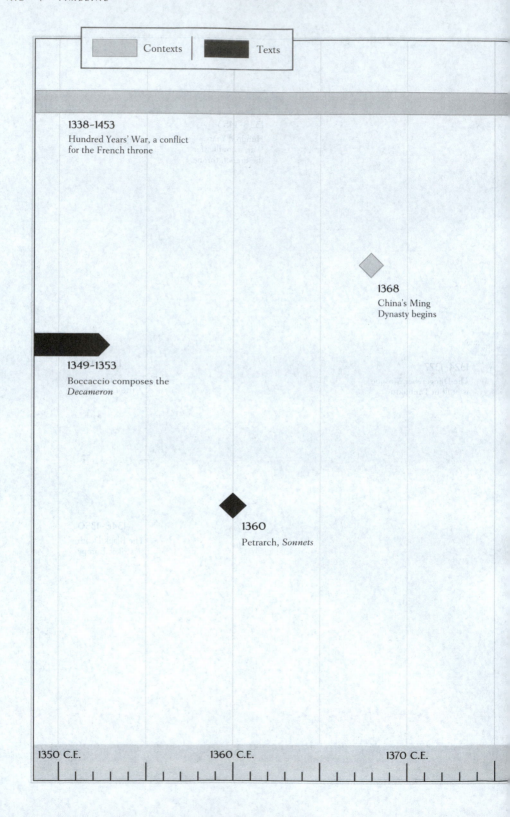

Contexts | Texts

1338–1453
Hundred Years' War, a conflict
for the French throne

1368
China's Ming
Dynasty begins

1349–1353
Boccaccio composes the
Decameron

1360
Petrarch, *Sonnets*

1350 C.E.   1360 C.E.   1370 C.E.

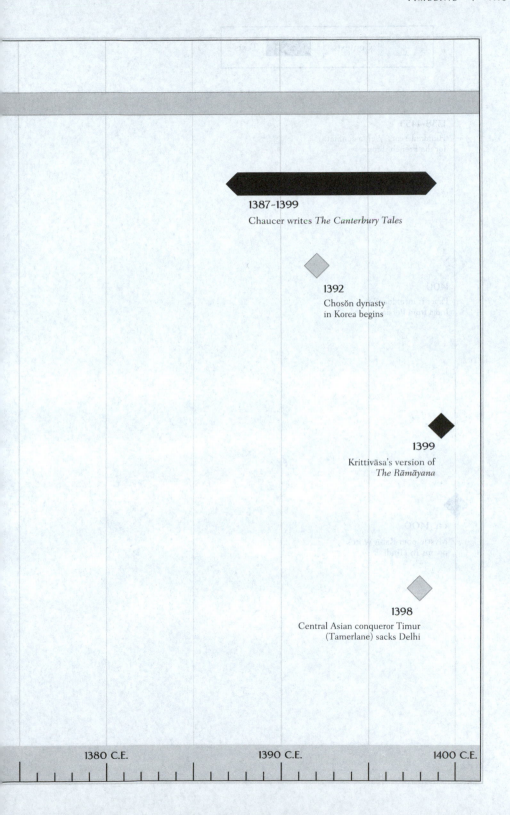

1387–1399

Chaucer writes *The Canterbury Tales*

1392

Chosŏn dynasty
in Korea begins

1399

Krittivāsa's version of
The Rāmāyana

1398

Central Asian conqueror Timur
(Tamerlane) sacks Delhi

1380 C.E.   1390 C.E.   1400 C.E.

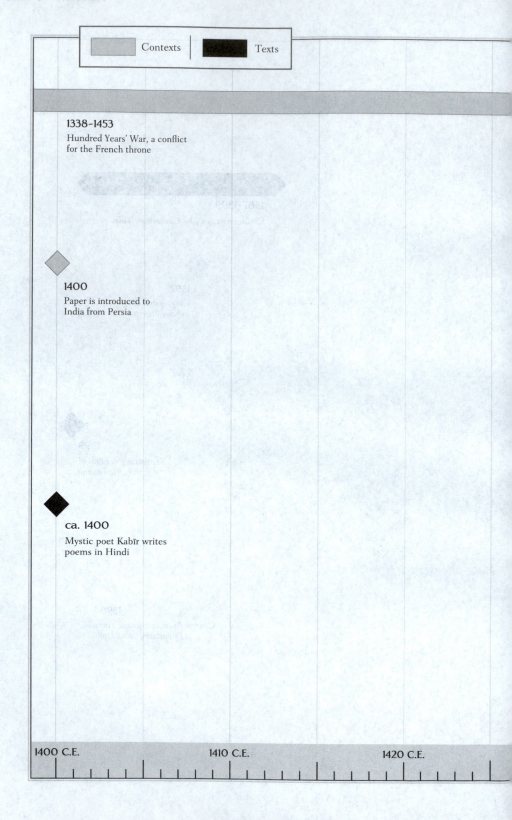

Contexts | Texts

1338–1453
Hundred Years' War, a conflict
for the French throne

1400
Paper is introduced to
India from Persia

ca. 1400
Mystic poet Kabīr writes
poems in Hindi

1400 C.E.   1410 C.E.   1420 C.E.

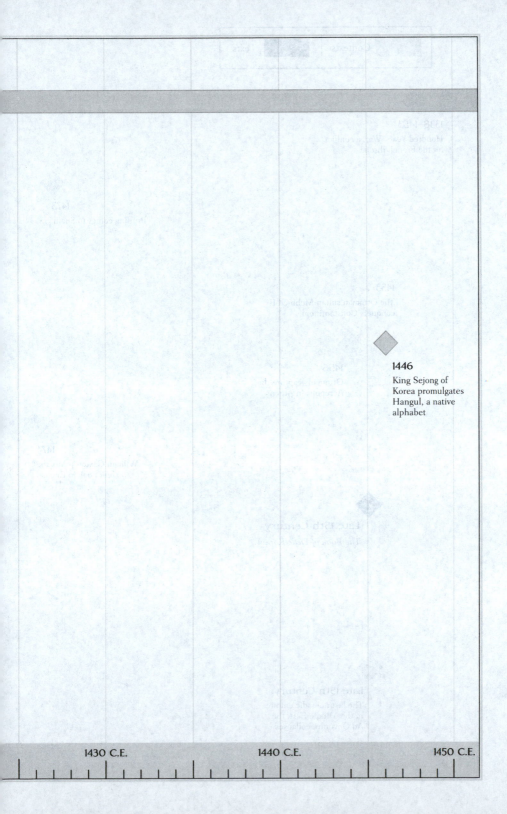

1446
King Sejong of
Korea promulgates
Hangul, a native
alphabet

1430 C.E.   1440 C.E.   1450 C.E.

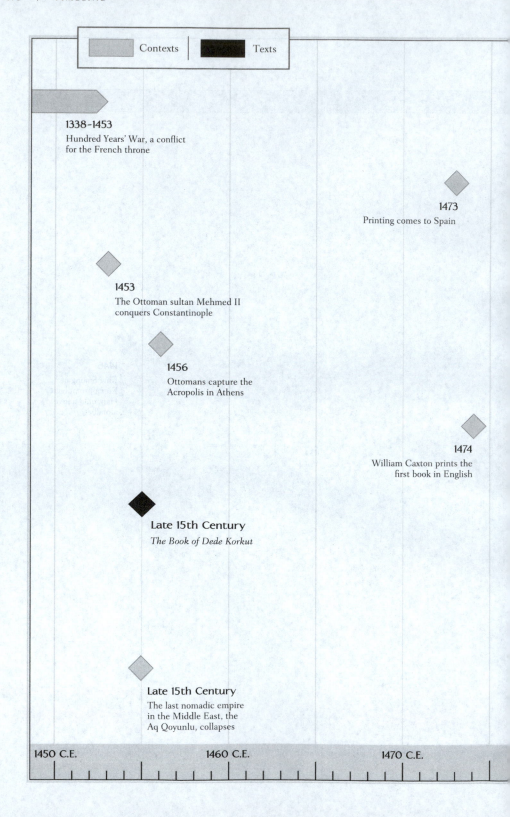

Contexts   Texts

1338–1453
Hundred Years' War, a conflict
for the French throne

1473
Printing comes to Spain

1453
The Ottoman sultan Mehmed II
conquers Constantinople

1456
Ottomans capture the
Acropolis in Athens

1474
William Caxton prints the
first book in English

Late 15th Century
The Book of Dede Korkut

Late 15th Century
The last nomadic empire
in the Middle East, the
Aq Qoyunlu, collapses

1450 C.E.   1460 C.E.   1470 C.E.

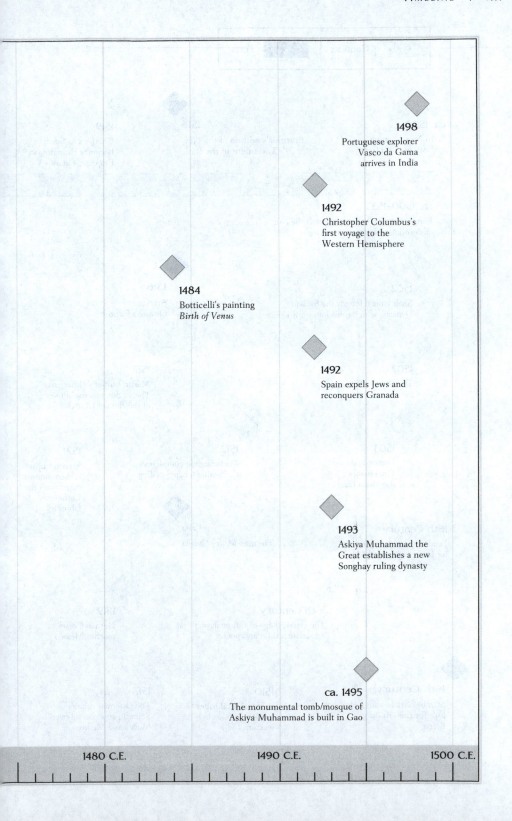

1498
Portuguese explorer
Vasco da Gama
arrives in India

1492
Christopher Columbus's
first voyage to the
Western Hemisphere

1484
Botticelli's painting
Birth of Venus

1492
Spain expels Jews and
reconquers Granada

1493
Askiya Muhammad the
Great establishes a new
Songhay ruling dynasty

ca. 1495
The monumental tomb/mosque of
Askiya Muhammad is built in Gao

1480 C.E.   1490 C.E.   1500 C.E.

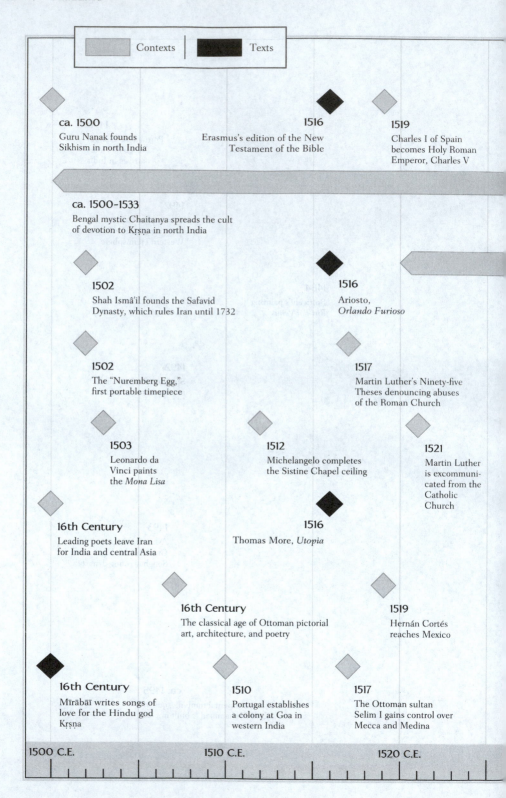

Contexts   Texts

ca. 1500
Guru Nanak founds
Sikhism in north India

1516
Erasmus's edition of the New
Testament of the Bible

1519
Charles I of Spain
becomes Holy Roman
Emperor, Charles V

ca. 1500–1533
Bengal mystic Chaitanya spreads the cult
of devotion to Kṛṣṇa in north India

1502
Shah Ismâ'il founds the Safavid
Dynasty, which rules Iran until 1732

1516
Ariosto,
Orlando Furioso

1502
The "Nuremberg Egg,"
first portable timepiece

1517
Martin Luther's Ninety-five
Theses denouncing abuses
of the Roman Church

1503
Leonardo da
Vinci paints
the *Mona Lisa*

1512
Michelangelo completes
the Sistine Chapel ceiling

1521
Martin Luther
is excommuni-
cated from the
Catholic
Church

16th Century
Leading poets leave Iran
for India and central Asia

1516
Thomas More, *Utopia*

16th Century
The classical age of Ottoman pictorial
art, architecture, and poetry

1519
Hernán Cortés
reaches Mexico

16th Century
Mīrābāī writes songs of
love for the Hindu god
Kṛṣṇa

1510
Portugal establishes
a colony at Goa in
western India

1517
The Ottoman sultan
Selim I gains control over
Mecca and Medina

1500 C.E.   1510 C.E.   1520 C.E.

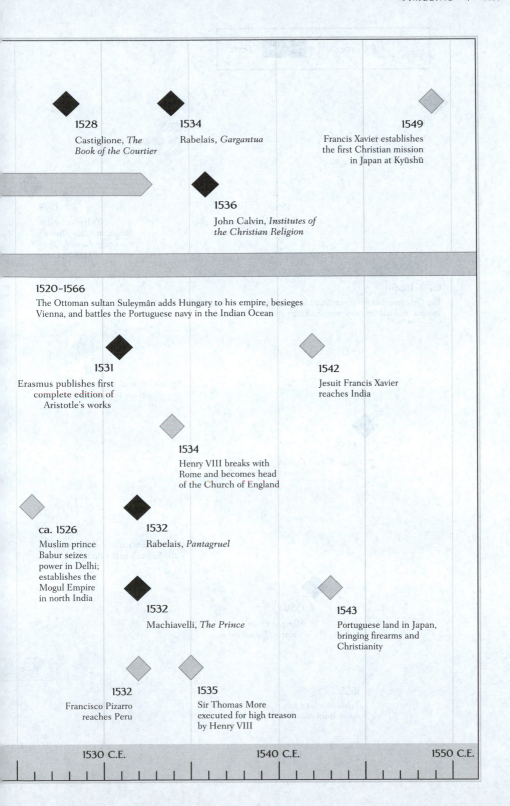

1528

Castiglione, *The Book of the Courtier*

1534

Rabelais, *Gargantua*

1549

Francis Xavier establishes the first Christian mission in Japan at Kyūshū

1536

John Calvin, *Institutes of the Christian Religion*

1520–1566

The Ottoman sultan Suleymân adds Hungary to his empire, besieges Vienna, and battles the Portuguese navy in the Indian Ocean

1531

Erasmus publishes first complete edition of Aristotle's works

1542

Jesuit Francis Xavier reaches India

1534

Henry VIII breaks with Rome and becomes head of the Church of England

ca. 1526

Muslim prince Babur seizes power in Delhi; establishes the Mogul Empire in north India

1532

Rabelais, *Pantagruel*

1532

Machiavelli, *The Prince*

1543

Portuguese land in Japan, bringing firearms and Christianity

1532

Francisco Pizarro reaches Peru

1535

Sir Thomas More executed for high treason by Henry VIII

1530 C.E.   1540 C.E.   1550 C.E.

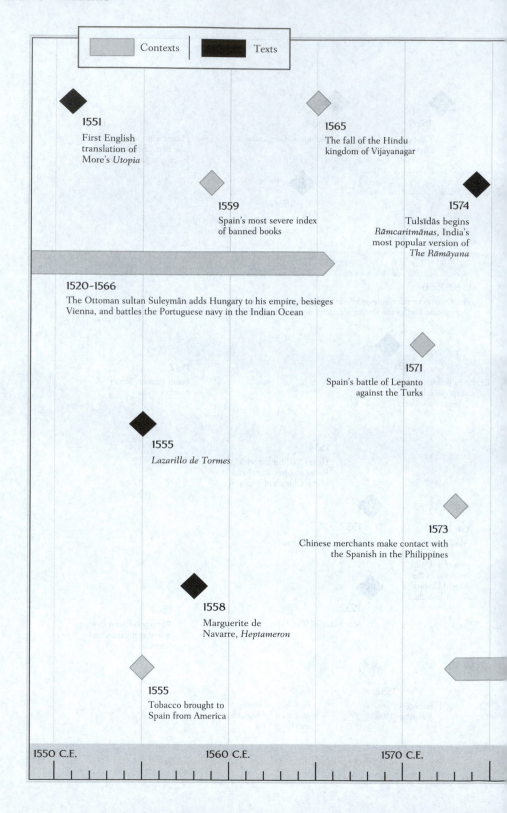

Contexts | Texts

1551

First English
translation of
More's *Utopia*

1565

The fall of the Hindu
kingdom of Vijayanagar

1559

Spain's most severe index
of banned books

1574

Tulsīdās begins
Rāmcaritmānas, India's
most popular version of
The Rāmāyana

1520-1566

The Ottoman sultan Suleymân adds Hungary to his empire, besieges
Vienna, and battles the Portuguese navy in the Indian Ocean

1571

Spain's battle of Lepanto
against the Turks

1555

Lazarillo de Tormes

1573

Chinese merchants make contact with
the Spanish in the Philippines

1558

Marguerite de
Navarre, *Heptameron*

1555

Tobacco brought to
Spain from America

1550 C.E.   1560 C.E.   1570 C.E.

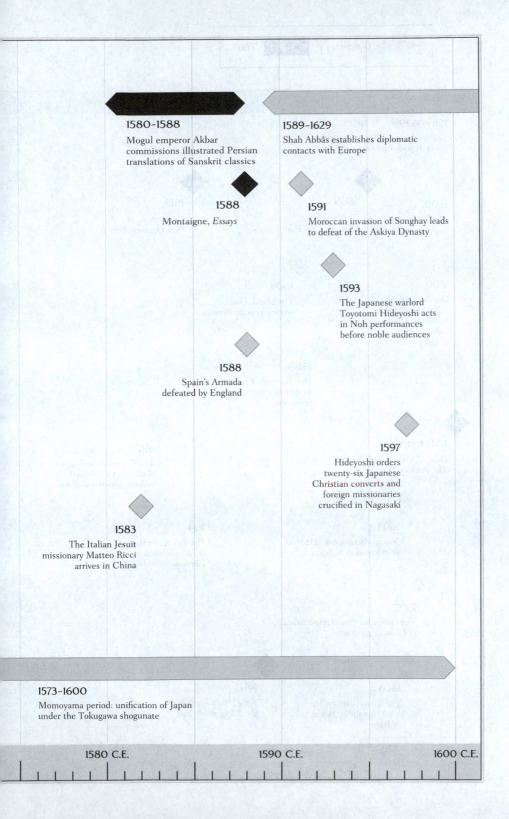

1580-1588

Mogul emperor Akbar commissions illustrated Persian translations of Sanskrit classics

1589-1629

Shah Abbâs establishes diplomatic contacts with Europe

1588

Montaigne, *Essays*

1591

Moroccan invasion of Songhay leads to defeat of the Askiya Dynasty

1593

The Japanese warlord Toyotomi Hideyoshi acts in Noh performances before noble audiences

1588

Spain's Armada defeated by England

1597

Hideyoshi orders twenty-six Japanese Christian converts and foreign missionaries crucified in Nagasaki

1583

The Italian Jesuit missionary Matteo Ricci arrives in China

1573-1600

Momoyama period: unification of Japan under the Tokugawa shogunate

1580 C.E.   1590 C.E.   1600 C.E.

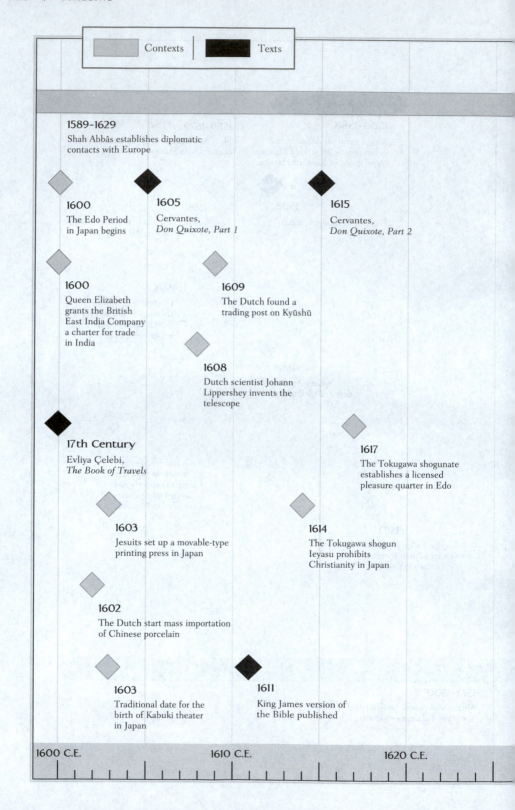

| Contexts | Texts |

1589–1629
Shah Abbâs establishes diplomatic
contacts with Europe

1600
The Edo Period
in Japan begins

1605
Cervantes,
Don Quixote, Part 1

1615
Cervantes,
Don Quixote, Part 2

1600
Queen Elizabeth
grants the British
East India Company
a charter for trade
in India

1609
The Dutch found a
trading post on Kyūshū

1608
Dutch scientist Johann
Lippershey invents the
telescope

17th Century
Evliya Çelebi,
The Book of Travels

1617
The Tokugawa shogunate
establishes a licensed
pleasure quarter in Edo

1603
Jesuits set up a movable-type
printing press in Japan

1614
The Tokugawa shogun
Ieyasu prohibits
Christianity in Japan

1602
The Dutch start mass importation
of Chinese porcelain

1603
Traditional date for the
birth of Kabuki theater
in Japan

1611
King James version of
the Bible published

1600 C.E.   1610 C.E.   1620 C.E.

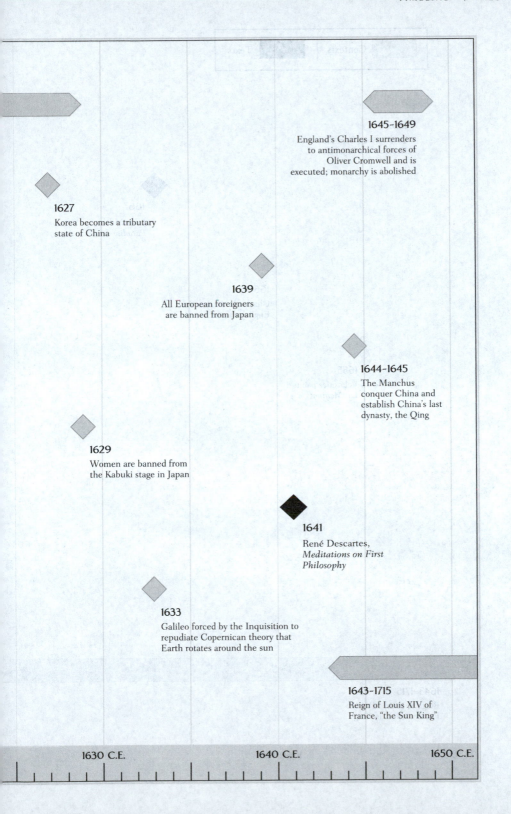

1645–1649
England's Charles I surrenders
to antimonarchical forces of
Oliver Cromwell and is
executed; monarchy is abolished

1627
Korea becomes a tributary
state of China

1639
All European foreigners
are banned from Japan

1644–1645
The Manchus
conquer China and
establish China's last
dynasty, the Qing

1629
Women are banned from
the Kabuki stage in Japan

1641
René Descartes,
*Meditations on First
Philosophy*

1633
Galileo forced by the Inquisition to
repudiate Copernican theory that
Earth rotates around the sun

1643–1715
Reign of Louis XIV of
France, "the Sun King"

1630 C.E.   1640 C.E.   1650 C.E.

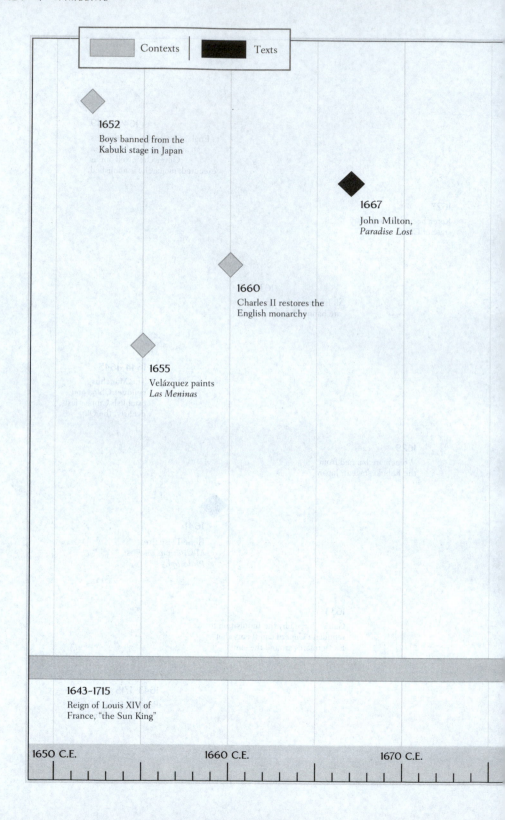

Contexts   Texts

1652
Boys banned from the
Kabuki stage in Japan

1667
John Milton,
Paradise Lost

1660
Charles II restores the
English monarchy

1655
Velázquez paints
Las Meninas

1643–1715
Reign of Louis XIV of
France, "the Sun King"

1650 C.E.   1660 C.E.   1670 C.E.

1683
The second unsuccessful siege
of Vienna marks the limits of
Ottoman power in Europe

1699
Kong Shangren,
The Peach Blossom Fan

1680 C.E.   1690 C.E.   1700 C.E.

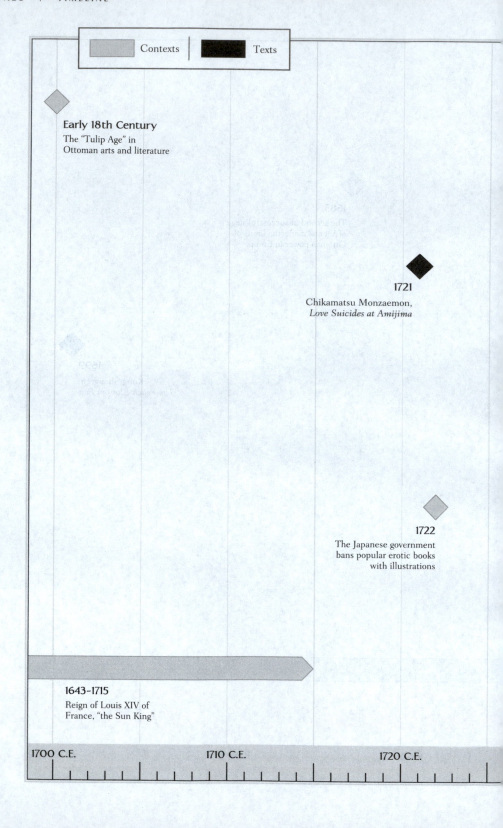

Contexts | Texts

Early 18th Century
The "Tulip Age" in
Ottoman arts and literature

1721
Chikamatsu Monzaemon,
Love Suicides at Amijima

1722
The Japanese government
bans popular erotic books
with illustrations

1643–1715
Reign of Louis XIV of
France, "the Sun King"

1700 C.E.   1710 C.E.   1720 C.E.

1726
Nader Shah, founder of
the Afshar dynasty, defeats
the Safavids in Persia

1729
Nader Shah sacks Delhi,
further weakening the
Mughals

1729
Arabic books set from
movable type are printed
in the Ottoman Empire

1730 C.E.   1740 C.E.   1750 C.E.

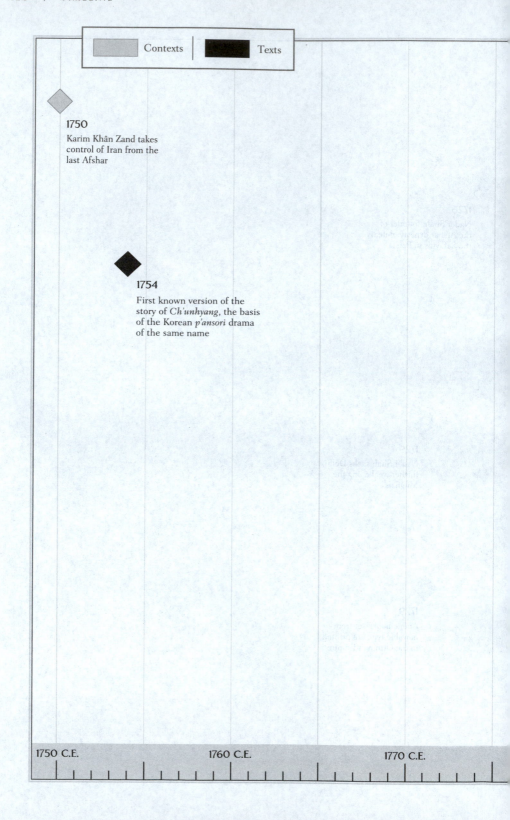

Contexts | Texts

1750
Karim Khân Zand takes
control of Iran from the
last Afshar

1754
First known version of the
story of *Ch'unhyang*, the basis
of the Korean *p'ansori* drama
of the same name

1750 C.E. · · · · · · · · · 1760 C.E. · · · · · · · · · 1770 C.E. · · · · · · · ·

1798
Napoleon Bonaparte
invades Egypt

1779–1924
The Qajars gradually take
control of Iran from the Zands

1780 C.E.   1790 C.E.   1800 C.E.

Permissions Acknowledgments

The Abencerraje: Excerpts from THE ABENCERRAJE and OZMIN AND DARAJA: TWO SIX-TEENTH CENTURY NOVELLAS FROM SPAIN, ed. and trans. by Barbara Fuchs, Larissa Brewer-Garcia, and Aaron J. Ilika, pp. 27–46. Copyright © 2014 by the University of Pennsylvania Press. Reprinted by permission of the University of Pennsylvania Press.

Ludovico Ariosto: From ORLANDO FURIOSO, trans. by Guido Waldman (1983). By permission of Oxford University Press.

Basavaṇṇā: From SPEAKING OF SIVA, trans. with an introduction by A. K. Ramanujan (Penguin Classics, 1973). Copyright © 1973 by A. K. Ramanujan. Reproduced by permission of Penguin Books Ltd.

The Book of Dede Korkut: From THE BOOK OF DEDE KORKUT, trans. with an introduction and notes by Geoffrey Lewis (Penguin Books, 1974). Introduction, translation, and notes copyright © 1974 Geoffrey Lewis. Reproduced by permission of Penguin Books Ltd.

Miguel de Cervantes: Excerpts from DON QUIXOTE: Two Volumes in One, trans. by Samuel Put-nam, translation copyright 1949 by The Viking Press, Inc. Used by permission of Viking Books, an imprint of Penguin Publishing Group, a division of Random House LLC. All rights reserved. Any third party use of this material, outside of this publication, is prohibited. Interested parties must apply directly to Penguin Random House LLC for permission.

Hernán Cortés: From HERNANDO CORTES: FIVE LETTERS 1519–1526, trans. by J. Bayard Morris. Copyright © 1969, 1991. All rights reserved. Used by permission of W. W. Norton & Company, Inc.

Joachim du Bellay: From "The Antiquities of Rome" Sonnets 3, 5, 13, 15 from THE REGRETS, ed. and trans. by Richard Helgerson, pp. 251, 252, 260, 263. Copyright © 2006 University of Pennsyl-vania Press. Reprinted with permission of the University of Pennsylvania Press.

The Florentine Codex: From Book 12 "The Conquest of Mexico" from FLORENTINE CODEX: GENERAL HISTORY OF THE THINGS OF NEW SPAIN, ed. and trans. by Arthur J. O. Ander-son and Charles E. Dibble. Used by permission of the University of Utah Press.

Veronica Franco: Capitolo 13, "A Challenge to a Lover Who Has Offended Her" from POEMS AND SELECTED LETTERS, trans. by Ann Rosalind Jones and Margaret F. Rosenthal. Copyright © 1998 by the University of Chicago. Reprinted by permission of the University of Chicago Press.

Garcilaso de la Vega: Sonnets from THE GOLDEN AGE: POEMS OF THE SPANISH RENAIS-SANCE, trans. by Edith Grossman. Copyright © 2006 by Edith Grossman. Used by permission of W. W. Norton & Company, Inc.

Inca Garcilaso de la Vega: From ROYAL COMMENTARIES OF THE INCAS AND GENERAL HISTORY OF PERU, PART ONE, trans. by Harold V. Livermore. Copyright © 1966 by the Uni-versity of Texas Press. Reprinted by permission of the University of Texas Press.

The Huarochirí Manuscript: From THE HUAROCHIRÍ MANUSCRIPT: A TESTAMENT OF ANCIENT AND COLONIAL ANDEAN RELIGION, trans. and ed. by Frank Salomon and George L. Urioste. Copyright © 1991 by the University of Texas Press. By permission of the Uni-versity of Texas Press.

San Juan de la Cruz: From THE GOLDEN AGE: POEMS OF THE SPANISH RENAISSANCE, trans. by Edith Grossman. Copyright © 2006 by Edith Grossman. Used by permission of W. W. Norton & Company, Inc.

Kabir: Poems from KABIR: THE WEAVER'S SONGS trans. by Vinay Dharwadker are reprinted by permission of Penguin Group (India).

Louise Labé: Sonnets from COMPLETE POETRY AND PROSE, trans. Annie Finch, ed. by Deborah Lesko Baker. Copyright © 2006 The University of Chicago. Reprinted by permission of the Univer-sity of Chicago Press.

Bartolomé de las Casas: From A SHORT ACCOUNT OF THE DESTRUCTION OF THE INDIES, ed. and trans. by Nigel Griffin, introduction by Anthony Pagden (Penguin Classics, 1992). The Translation and Notes copyright © 1992 Nigel Griffin. Introduction copyright © 1992 Anthony Pagden. Reproduced by permission of Penguin Books Ltd.

Jean de Léry: From HISTORY OF A VOYAGE TO THE LAND OF BRAZIL, trans. by Janet Whatley. Copyright © 1990 by the Regents of the University of California. Printed by permission of the University of California Press.

COLOR INSERT

Index